THE FAMILY OF STORIES

AN ANTHOLOGY OF CHILDREN'S LITERATURE

Anita Moss / Jon C. Stott

Holt, Rinehart and Winston, Inc.
Fort Worth • Chicago • San Francisco
Philadelphia • Montreal • Toronto • London
Sydney

Requests for permission to make copies of any part of
the work should be mailed to: Permissions Department,
Holt, Rinehart and Winston, Inc., 8th Floor, Orlando,
Florida 32887.

Canadian Cataloguing in Publication Data

Main entry under title:
The Family of stories

Includes bibliographies.
ISBN 0-03-921832-5

1. Children's stories.   2. Children's literature –
History and criticism.   I. Moss, Anita. II. Stott,
Jon C.

PZ5.F35 1986   808.8'99282   C85-099182-X

Publisher: Anthony Luengo
Managing Editor: Mary Lynn Mulroney
Cover Design: Michael Van Elsen
Interior Design: Blair Kerrigan
Typesetting and Assembly:
    Compeer Typographic Services, Ltd.

Printed in the United States of America

7 8   039   12 11 10 9

For Rod — A.M.
For Carol, Pat, and Art — J.C.S.

Contents

General Introduction

All themes and characters and stories that you encounter in literature belong to one big interlocking family. . . . You keep associating your literary experiences together: you're always being reminded of some other story you read or movie you saw or character that impressed you.

This statement made by literary critic Northrop Frye in *The Educated Imagination* underlies the selection and organization of children's stories in this text. Although stories may remind readers of reality, that is, of experiences they have undergone or heard of, stories resemble each other more than they resemble life. Authors often imitate others' stories, or, in a more general sense, they imitate their conventions and patterns. There are many ways in which stories resemble or relate to each other, many ways in which they can be considered members of "The Family of Stories."

One fundamental characteristic of stories is their careful selection and order of details. Unlike life, where events happen in what often appears to be a random fashion, a story includes only those characters, actions, and settings which are important to the story. These elements contribute to plot, characterization, mood and theme; moreover, they are arranged in a pattern or structure which introduces, develops, and resolves the central problem or conflict of the story. While life abounds with problems and conflicts, it is also filled with routine, mundane matters, and conflicts are sometimes never resolved. Conflict, however, is central to a story. It could be said that conflict determines the selection and order of the details in a story.

There are, of course, many ways to categorize the conflict structures of stories. In Children's Literature, one useful method orders stories according to their journey patterns. In nearly all children's stories, characters make physical journeys, journeys that conclude either in a new setting (linear), or at the point of departure (circular). By grouping these stories according to their journey patterns, readers are in a position to discover some fundamental relationships between these tales. For both the linear and circular forms, a number of questions should be asked. What is the nature of the place of departure and the quality of life of the central character or characters? In linear journeys such as "Beauty and the Beast" or "Inchelina," do the central characters wish to reach their destinations? How do they overcome obstacles on the way, and how have their characters developed? In circular journeys such as "Hansel and Gretel," the reader should investigate the reasons for the protagonists' return, changes in the relationship between the characters and their places of origin, and the reasons for those changes. By placing stories within the broad categories of linear and circular journeys, readers will be equipped with a fundamental tool for discerning patterns within "The Family of Stories." In addition, the experience gained by reading stories within this framework should serve as a guide for further reading outside of it.

Another method of organization is by genre. The term "genre" is difficult to define, for it has been used in a variety of ways by a great number of literary critics. In its most general sense, genre refers to literary works grouped together because they share a number of characteristics such as types of characters and actions, style of language, and overall form or structure. Traditional stories, those orginally transmitted orally from generation to generation, have often been divided into the three genres: folktale, hero tale, and myth. Those stories grouped in each of these categories share many characteristics (dealt with fully in the introductions to the first three sections). The stories of modern writers consciously employing the characteristics of these genres have been called literary folktales, literary hero tales, and literary myths.

Other large generic categories have also been employed by critics. Those works which do not include magical forces or supernatural beings, and those which present characters in a world operating according to the laws of nature and science, have been classified as "realism." Those which suspend these laws, or present characters and events influenced by, or using magical or supernatural powers, have often been categorized as "fantasy." Obviously, individual stories can exist in more than one genre, since each genre exists within a system defined by a general set of characteristics.

The above genre classifications are quite broad. Often genres are more narrowly defined, consisting of stories which embody limited characteristics. For example, traditional stories have often been grouped as tale types in which similar characters are engaged in similar actions. For instance, there are the "dragon slayer" stories of Western Europe; dragons were huge, clever, evil, and almost invulnerable creatures defeated by apparently weak, but brave and clever human beings. Modern fantasies are often categorized by such subject matter or character types as "Dream Journeys," "Time Travel," "Animated Toys," and "Talking Animals."

Given the variety of genre classification systems, the value of categorizing the selections in "The Family of Stories" as they relate to the traditional genres enables the reader to understand individual stories more fully. By noticing how stories make use of genre characteristics, readers are in possession of a framework that will assist them in approaching specific works.

In addition to the organizing principle of conflict, the larger patterns of linear and circular journeys, and the various genre classification systems, there is a more basic unifying principle. Joseph Campbell indicates this principle in the title of his book *The Hero With a Thousand Faces*. While each story may appear unique on the surface, each is concerned with a fundamental subject: the quest of human beings to discover their identities and their places within their societies, to discover who they are and where they belong. This quest he calls the monomyth. Northrop Frye in *The Educated Imagination* also suggests that literature forms one story: "This story of the loss and regaining of identity, I think, is the framework of all literature. Inside it comes the story of the hero with a thousand faces ... whose adventures, death, disappearance, and marriage or resurrection are the focal points of what later become romance and tragedy and satire and comedy and fiction."

For Frye, these stories can be roughly grouped into the four categories listed above (although there are, he admits, many overlaps). The *romance* is concerned with the hero's birth, education, and initiation. It involves a quest with a series of tests and is "nearest ... to the wish-fulfillment dream." *Tragedy* deals with the finite condition of human beings. While human aspiration is limitless, the power to achieve goals is limited. Tragedy may thus end in the death and destruction of the hero. *Irony* (and the closely related form, satire) emphasizes the contrast between the ideal and the actual. In some ironic stories the expectations of the characters are reversed. *Comedy* focuses on the notion of rebirth and renewal after the obstacles to happiness and the threats to a secure social order have been overcome.

Applying Frye's categories to selections in *The Family of Stories*, Wilder's "The Wolf-Pack" and Andersen's "Inchelina" could be called romance. In the former, Pa resembles the hero of the romance as he ventures from the shelter of the little house, confronts the wolf-pack, and returns home to protect his family; in the latter, the tiny heroine goes on a quest to discover her identity and place of belonging. The heroine of Andersen's "The Little Match Girl" is tragic. Irony can be seen in the reversal of characters' expectations in Potter's *The Tale of Peter Rabbit* and John Neihardt's "Chased by a Cow." The comic emphasis on rebirth and renewal are found in Beaumont's "Beauty and the Beast" and McCloskey's "Nothing New Under the Sun (Hardly)."

Both Campbell and Frye emphasize that no matter what kind of story we read, real or fantastic, contemporary or historical, containing apparently normal characters or supernatural ones, the story is understood because the characters, settings, and actions embody universal elements of human nature.

In *The Family of Stories*, an attempt has been made to group selections in a manner that reveals the many ways in which these selections resemble each other. The first three sections present stories that illustrate the characteristics of the three main traditional genres: folktales, hero tales, and myths. The folktales chosen illustrate major character types, settings, and actions as they are found in a variety of cultures from around the world. They have also been identified as linear and circular journeys to illustrate the basic patterns of those important structures. Hero tales have been chosen to illustrate the basic episodes in the life of the hero as outlined by Joseph Campbell in *The Hero With a Thousand Faces*. Individual myths have been ordered to illustrate the ways that specific myths relate to the overall structure of mythology, here called "cosmic history." The next three sections, on literary folktales, hero tales, and myths, show how children's writers of the last two centuries have consciously adapted the characteristics of the traditional genres when creating their own stories. The diversity of children's stories over the last century requires, in the seventh section, the organizing principle of the first section. Stories are grouped as either linear or circular journeys. By comparing journey patterns and motifs that are found in both folktales and modern stories, readers will acquire a better understanding of the underlying similarities between members in "The Family of Stories," and the various ways these are expressed in different genres.

Introductions to the first six sections outline the basic characteristics of the genres, indicate how stories within each genre have been adapted for children, and indicate ways in which these stories can be presented to children. Headnotes for each selection draw attention to important aspects of the stories and relate them to stories found both within that section and in other sections. Annotated bibliographies at the end of each section indicate other related stories.

For reasons of space and cost it has not been possible to include novels and picture books in our selections. However, two appendices have been included in an attempt to overcome these omissions. The first appendix provides an introduction to the nature and history of the picture book and presents detailed analyses of a number of individual picture books which have received wide critical acclaim. The second appendix performs a similar function for novels. In both appendices, individual works are related to selections found in this anthology. Both the section introductions and the discussions of specific titles are intended to assist the reader in relating novels and picture books to selections in the anthology and to general patterns in "The Family of Stories."

The third appendix is designed for those readers planning to be school teachers or librarians. Drawing on the experiences of the editors in elementary and high schools, and in their work with teachers and librarians, this appendix suggests methods for helping children become alert and responsive readers, and suggests strategies for developing literature curriculums in the schools.

A fourth appendix consists of an annotated bibliography of secondary materials which will be useful for those students who wish to engage in further study in the field of Children's Literature.

One final point should be made. Although this anthology emphasizes the structural and generic similarities of stories, and specifically links stories in headnotes, the concept of "The Family of Stories" should be considered as a guide to reading. Classification and categorization are means, not ends. The relationships between stories and between them and their general story patterns, are merely frameworks. The experience of reading a story should be a unique one. Not only is each reader an individual, but each story presents a unique vision within its general story pattern. The goal of *The Family of Stories* is to assist adult readers to become more familiar with the general nature of stories and how they work, to understand and enjoy individual stories more fully, and, most important, to increase children's love of reading so that it may last a lifetime.

The editors wish to acknowledge gratefully the patience, energy, and expertise provided by Tony Luengo and Brian Henderson of Holt, Rinehart, and Winston, and to thank the following people from whose detailed comments many valuable insights were gained; Phyllis Bixler (Kansas State University), David Jenkinson (University of Manitoba), John Cech (University of Florida), JoAnna Dutka (University of Toronto), Pose Lamb (Purdue University), Frank Zidonis (Ohio State University), Yvonne Miller (Norfolk State University), Hugh Agee (University of Georgia), Perry Nodelman (University of Winnipeg). *The Family of Stories* has been greatly improved through their input; its limitations remain our own.

Anita Moss,
University of North Carolina, Charlotte
Jon C. Stott,
University of Alberta

Folktales

Folktales

An Introduction

In *The Folktale*, Stith Thompson notes that the oral tale "is the most universal of all narrative forms."[1] Folktales, frequently referred to as fairy tales, have been found all over the world and have presumably existed since the earliest periods of human history. They are easily recognized: short, highly stylized stories, they contain stock characters, events, and settings. Folktales are also embodiments of beliefs of specific cultures. For example, over three hundred versions of the Cinderella story have been discovered from China to the southwestern United States. The human emotions portrayed are similar in nearly all of the versions; however, the individual manifestations of these emotions reflect the customs and beliefs of the group telling the story.

The universality and cultural specificity of folktales can in part be accounted for by the fact that they are anonymous creations; they are tales of the folk rather than products of an individual storyteller. Thus, they reflect general emotions and cultural beliefs rather than personal points of view. Passed orally from generation to generation by skilled and unskilled narrators, folktales, while keeping their basic form and content, have been modified by changing social and religious conditions, and differing attitudes of tellers toward their audiences.

Two key terms in studying folktales are *motif* and *tale type*. Thompson defines the *motif* as the "smallest element in a tale having the power to exist in tradition."[2] One finds certain characters, types, actions, objects, and settings appearing in a large number of tales. In his monumental six-volume *Motif-Index of Folk-Literature* Thompson lists thousands of recurrent elements, many of which are found in the selections in this anthology. A brief list of motifs and the tales including them will illustrate their uses and natures. Characters can be fitted into such general categories as youngest siblings ("Oochigeas and the Invisible Boy"), wicked stepmothers ("Hansel and Gretel"), or people forced to assume animal forms ("East o' the Sun and West o' the Moon"). Characters may, without hope for reward, perform kind deeds ("New Year's Hats for the Statues"), may gain power over another by discovering that person's name ("Rumpelstiltzkin"), or may misuse magic wishes granted to them ("The Fisherman and His Wife"). Each motif has potential for adding significance to the story of which it is a part: the youngest sibling has far more obstacles to overcome before finding fulfillment; wicked stepmothers are often threats to family unity and particularly to the security of small children. By giving aid without promise of reward, characters reveal their fundamental kindness and generosity; the misuse of magic wishes demonstrates that the individual probably never possessed qualities of character requisite to deserve the wishes, and suggests the futility of misdirected human desires. The prevalence of motifs argues for their considerable effectiveness in advancing plot and developing characterization and theme.

Thompson defines a *tale type* as "a traditional tale that has an independent existence."[3] That is, although superficial aspects of characterization, setting, and action may vary, the basic elements and structure of the tale can be found intact in many different versions. Among the many well-known tale types listed by Thompson are the boy who steals the giant's treasure ("Jack and the Beanstalk"), speaking first ("Get Up and Bar the Door"), and the maiden in the tower ("Rapunzel"). Of course, the Cinderella story is, as we have seen, one of the most widely distributed of all tale types. Thompson also lists more general tale types such as cumulative tales ("Henny Penny"), numbskull stories ("Mayor Gimpel's Golden Shoes"), and tales of the stupid ogre ("Jack in the Giants' Newground"). As was the case with motifs, the widespread existence of these and other tale types may be a result of their effectiveness as interesting, entertaining story structures. The impact may range from the humor of a husband and wife's foolish, stubborn quarrel, to the romantic fulfillment experienced by Cinderella when her true goodness and beauty are rewarded with marriage to the prince.

In addition to recognizable and frequently used motifs and tale types, folktales also possess recognizable stylistic patterns. Retold over generations, they have acquired, particularly in the hands of skillful narrators, several verbal formulas. This is most evident in European tales, which often begin with a phrase such as "once upon a time" and, when there is a marriage at the conclusion, end with the words "they lived happily ever after." Within stories, certain phrases are often repeated at key points, as is seen in such stories as "The Story of the Three Little Pigs" and "East o' the Sun and West o' the Moon." Many of the trickster stories of the North American Plains Indians begin with a variant of the phrase "Trickster was going along." Not only do these stylistic devices help to give shape or pattern to the stories, but they also serve as techniques to assist in memorization of tales.

The implicit significance of the content of folktales is often reinforced by the stylistic devices. The stock "once upon a time" opening of European tales not only helps a fantastic tale achieve credibility by removing it from familiar times and places, but also emphasizes the universality of the themes present: the conflicts are not local but of all times and for all places. If the central characters live "happily ever after," it is because they have developed as human beings to such a degree that they deserve the happiness they receive. Repetition is also significant; it helps to show that, as events become increasingly difficult, a continuing personal development is necessary for ongoing success and achievement. Such meaningful repetition is found in "The Story of the Three Little Pigs."

Psychologists and critics have noted that, although folktales generally contain *imaginary* characters and situations, they symbolize basic human concerns. They are, as European scholar Max Luthi suggested in *Once Upon a Time: On the Nature of Fairy Tales*, "a poetic vision of man and his relationship to the world."[4] Each story presents the central characters with the opportunity to achieve fulfillment, both personally and in relation to their social and natural environments. The characters presented are types rather than individuals. They embody basic aspects of human nature and experience essential human dilemmas. In the tales most often read to children today, the main characters are frequently children, vulnerable beings in a world of adults and threatening natural and supernatural forces. Orphans and youngest siblings are especially important characters because they are most vulnerable and, if victorious at a tale's conclusion, appear to overcome even greater obstacles. In order to survive and triumph, they must face severe tests, engage in great struggles, and make wise choices. Often they take on royal roles, for as Luthi has noted, "to be a king [or queen] is an image for complete self-realization."[5] Thus, while readers or listeners cannot all become kings or queens, they can, like the characters in the stories, work to achieve as complete a self-realization as possible.

In the search for self-fulfillment, the central character is generally alone; responsibility for achieving one's destiny rests with the individual. Usually the character makes a dangerous physical journey leaving a home which, for various reasons, is no longer secure. The geography is generally austere: dark, threatening forests and violent weather abound helping to symbolize the unknown and perilous aspects of the quest. The negative characters encountered — witches, giants, dragons, and malicious, hypocritical human beings are most common in European stories — symbolize the evils that must be overcome. The heroes often have helpers such as fairy godmothers or talking animals, or they possess magic objects. But these are only effective when the characters realize their inner potential. The heroes must develop and/or exhibit such positive virtues as courage, cleverness, and kindness if the external aid received is to be beneficial, and if they are to pass successfully their progressively more difficult tasks. Not all folktale characters develop these qualities, and as a result, they receive appropriate punishments. In many African and North American trickster tales, the protagonist, because of his mischievousness, does not receive the rewards he expects. Cleverness, because it is selfishly motivated, backfires. At times, indeed, the trickster's deviousness seems to have no motivating force other than pure evil.

While they embody universal processes of individual growth, folktales also reflect elements of the specific cultures in which they are told, as noted before. Their supernatural characters are those found in the superstitions of the various cultures: malicious dragons in Northern Europe, Baba Yaga in Russia, trolls in Norway, the Little People in England, shape-shifting animals in North America, and Jizo in Japan. These beings have very definite characteristics which were well-known to original listeners, and are thus part of the implicit meaning of the stories in which they appear. For example, in hearing "New Year's Hats for the Statues," original Japanese audiences would have immediately recognized that the jizo were patrons of travelers and, accordingly, could have predicted that the old man's beneficent actions toward them might lead to reward. The Baba Yaga, because of her cannibalistic nature, would be seen as a formidable opponent for the young heroine of "Vasilisa the Beautiful." That the Three Billy-Goats Gruff could easily outwit the troll would not be surprising to a Norwegian audience which would be well aware of the characteristic stupidity of those ogres. Modern readers who are aware of these specific connotations will be able to appreciate individual stories more fully.

Folktales embody elements of the lifestyles of various cultures. The dangers of hunting, which dominated Arctic life, are constantly present in Inuit stories. The economic emphasis in the legend of Dick Whittington reflects the upward mobility found in England during the periods of mercantile and industrial expansion. In the United States, the African slaves survived through disguise and wit, and they transferred these qualities to one of their favorite folktale heroes, Br'er Rabbit.

Over the last two centuries, several theories have been advanced to explain the origins of folktales. The German scholars Jacob and Wilhelm Grimm, two of the earliest collectors of folktales, believed that such stories were the fragmentary pieces of earlier myths which had broken up over the centuries and had lost their specific religious content. "Little Red-Cap," they traced back to a solar myth; after being devoured by the wolf, the heroine is later rescued, representing the setting and rising of the sun. During the nineteenth century, several scholars, influenced by the prevailing theories of the origins of language, argued that all folktales originated in India — the "Cradle of Civilization" — and gradually spread throughout the world. This single place of origin explained for some the existence of similar motifs and tale types in different locations. In contrast to this theory, referred to as monogenesis, Andrew Lang and other folklorists in the late nineteenth and early twentieth centuries argued that the similarities arose because there were a limited number of basic situations and emotional reponses common to all people. He advanced the theory of polygenesis: similar stories found in widely separated areas had developed independently of each other. Twentieth-century psychologist Carl Jung suggested that the tales originated in archetypes or fundamental images found within the unconscious minds of everyone; that is, since all people are similar psychologically, they produce similar stories.

Regardless of the nature of their origins, it *is* known that many stories have traveled from one culture to another. For example, it is believed that the Grimm Brothers' version of "Little Red-Cap" is derived from Perrault's "Little Red Riding Hood," which slowly traveled across Europe, gradually altering in shape. Many well-known European stories were brought across the Atlantic with the explorers, traders, and colonizers, and were adapted to specific local conditions. In the following selections, the reader will notice, for example, the influence of "Cinderella" on "Oochigeas and the Invisible Boy" and of "Jack the Giant Killer" on "Jack in the Giants' Newground." North American tales also traveled widely. The trickster Coyote appears in Blackfoot tales as the Old Man (Nape). The tale of "The Blind Boy and the Loon" is found among the Inuit across the Canadian and Alaskan Arctic and is also found among the Native Indians of the Northern Pacific coast.

Over the centuries, storytellers have been adapting these oral stories to their own purposes. In Homer's *Odyssey*, for example, the hero's exploits among beings such as the Cyclops are believed to have derived from earlier folktales. In the fourteenth century, the English poet Geoffrey Chaucer used many well-known fables and folktales in his *Canterbury Tales*. However, it was not until 1697, when Frenchman Charles Perrault published *Histoires ou Contes du Temps passé, avec des Moralités*, a collection of eleven retold tales, that folktales came to the attention of a large, international reading public. Containing such now well-known stories as "Sleeping Beauty," "Cinderella," "Puss in Boots," and "Little Red Riding Hood," the work was published in English in 1729, and fostered a vogue for writing folk-like stories which lasted throughout the eighteenth century. Perrault drew on a variety of sources, many of them being earlier collections of oral stories. However, he adapted them freely so that they reflected in both style and content the grace and elegance of the late seventeenth-century French court. The results were highly polished pieces of literature, often witty and satiric. However, these were not original stories, because they contained the basic motifs, structures, and details of the oral tales from which they were derived.

In the late eighteenth century, an academic interest in traditional literature developed, and in 1812, Jacob and Wilhelm Grimm published *Kinder und Hausmärchen (Nursery and Household Tales)*, a book of folktales collected from friends, relations, neighbors, and nearby peasants. Although the brothers, particularly Wilhelm, often edited the materials, they were not attempting to adapt the stories for children. Like many scholars of their era, they were motivated by a sense of nationalism and hoped that the preservation of one aspect of traditional culture would help to foster pride in the Germanic past. Moreover, they were influenced by currents of European Romanticism, which emphasized the value of the unsophisticated literature of the folk.

These stories were quickly seized upon by publishers interested in selling books to the rapidly increasing juvenile market. In 1869, English author John Ruskin noted about the Grimms' tales: "[Children] will find in the apparently vain and fitful courses of any tradition of old time, honestly delivered to them, a teaching for which no other can be substituted, and of which the power cannot be measured; animating for them the material world with inextinguishable fire, fortifying them against the glacial cold of selfish science, and preparing them submissively, and with no bitterness of astonishment, to behold in later years the mystery of the fates that happen alike to the evil and the good."

Since the nineteenth century, the practice of recording and studying folktales has developed into a science. The detailed collections of Norwegians Peter Asbjørnsen and Jorgen Møe, Englishman Joseph Jacobs, American Richard Chase, and Canadian Marius Barbeau have provided the basis for hundreds of adaptations for children. Many of the Native Indian and Inuit tales compiled by Franz Boas have also been adapted.

Because the writing, publishing, and selection of children's stories have generally been in the hands of adults, folktales have frequently been adapted to fit adult ideas of what constitutes acceptable material for young readers. Critic Jack Zipes remarked in *Breaking the Magic Spell* [6] that many of the best-known stories have been watered down and rendered innocuous over the last century and a half because in their original forms they presented messages threatening to the dominant class.

As early as 1803, Mrs. Trimmer, reviewing children's books in *The Guardian of Education* wrote: ''Though we well remember the interest with which, in our childish days, when books of amusement for children were scarce, we read, or listened to the history of *Little Red Riding Hood*, and *Blue Beard*, &c., we do not wish to have such sensations awakened in the hearts of our grandchildren, by the same means; for the terrible images, which tales of this nature represent to the imagination, usually make deep impressions, and injure the tender minds of children, by exciting unreasonable and groundless fears.''[7]

Mrs. Trimmer was raising an objection to folktales that is raised to this day: the inclusion in these stories of very violent incidents. Many adaptors, in order to make these stories acceptable to young readers, have bowdlerized them. That is, they have deleted or changed parts of stories they have found objectionable or have added elements which rendered them acceptable. Some versions of ''The Story of the Three Little Pigs'' have been changed so that the first two pigs do not die, but rush to safety in their brother's brick home. The wolf is not boiled alive and eaten, but flees from the area in terror, never to be seen again.

Folktales are indeed filled with violence, though not with the type children see regularly on television programs. The violence of folktales has purpose; it is ''literary violence.'' It has been included to meet the needs of a specific story, and exaggerated though it often is, it is not intended to represent aspects of the real world. In ''The Three Billy-Goats Gruff'' the troll, who is considered a wicked creature in most Scandinavian tales, would have eaten any or all of the goats, and thus his death on the horns of the largest goat is fitting. In a world in which survival depends on cleverness, two of the three little pigs do not act thoughtfully and meet swift ends. In the Inuit story ''The Blind Boy and the Loon,'' the mother has violated accepted cultural norms by refusing to render the products of the hunt and by blinding her son. Revenge in Inuit stories was an accepted subject, and that visited on this woman is totally justified in the context of the tale.

Adaptors have also made drastic changes in the folktales of so-called primitive cultures. Cultural and religious beliefs, because they are so different from those of the dominant Anglo-European culture, have at times been viewed as foolish superstition, the products of unenlightened, primitive minds. Characters have been presented according to European standards, with only their physical appearances and geographical surroundings relating them to their own cultures.

Similarly, folktales from earlier historical periods have been adapted. Often they have been modernized so that, even if physical aspects of twentieth-century life are not introduced, characters act too much in accordance with twentieth-century notions of conduct and psychology. While these stories must be accessible to young contemporary readers, such adaptations hinder their awareness of the fact that in other times different attitudes about basic human concerns were held.

A fairly recent criticism of many traditional stories states that female characters are often relegated to inferior roles. It should be noted, however, that all cultures have specifically defined sex roles, and readers of folktales should be aware of how the stories reflect these roles. Moreover, one should be mindful of the fact that the concept of sexual equality has only recently acquired widespread acceptance. It is true that a majority of folktales present male characters in heroic roles, but there are many stories which present equally heroic female characters. Molly Whuppie, Kate Crackernuts, Gretel, and Vasilisa are European characters who are equally as heroic as men. In fact, Gretel, rather than Hansel, provides the leadership which allows the children to return home. The central figures in "The Magic Orange Tree," "The Little Guava," and "The Ghost Owl" are significant non-European heroines. In "A Legend of Knockmany" Oonagh is far more clever and courageous than her husband. Thus, while adult selectors of folktales can easily discover examples of sexual stereotyping, they can, with careful searching, find many stories which provide excellent examples of female heroes.

These remarks are not intended to suggest that all children's adaptations are debased, simplistic versions of the original materials. In fact some of the finest children's authors and illustrators have created excellent versions of folktales. Among them are Walter Crane, Leslie Brooke, Walter de la Mare, and Wanda Gàg in earlier years. More recently, Paul Galdone, Marcia Brown, Gerald McDermott, Tomie de Paola, Christie Harris, and Alison Lurie have been credited with outstanding work. However, in choosing a children's version of a folktale, the selector should ascertain how closely it resembles the original version and, particularly in the case of stories dealing with ethnic minorities, how accurate it is in its reflection of the culture in question.

Whenever possible, the adult reader should compare the specific adaptation with the source the adaptor has used. In the case of a Grimm or Perrault folktale, this means consulting a reliable, unabridged translation. In the case of stories based on less accessible tales, the reader should discover as much as possible about the cultural beliefs and customs of the peoples who originally created the stories, and the nature and extent of the adaptor's departure from these.

As with the folktales themselves, the illustrations which accompany them are components of no small importance. In fact, picture books are now the major vehicle through which young readers are introduced to most traditional tales. All of the major European folktales have been illustrated many times; lesser-known

European stories, as well as others from around the world, have also appeared in picture-book form. The range of quality in such books is great: on one hand there are the mass produced volumes with lifeless, inferior illustrations; on the other, there are books in which the pictures are works of art themselves. In addition to pictures of high artistic quality, an illustrated version of a folktale should accurately reflect the text and add further dimensions of meaning to it. Nuances of character, implications of actions, and suggestions of atmosphere can be communicated by the design, details, and coloring of individual pictures and by the interrelationships between pictures. They should also capture the period of the stories as well as accurately reflect the physical and non-physical aspects of the people who originally created them.

Since folktales entered the mainstream of printed children's literature in the nineteenth century, there has been a great deal of discussion concerning their value to young readers. They have always been regarded as extremely entertaining stories, as excellent means of enhancing children's sense of wonder and delight, and as we have seen, they have been considered useful vehicles for inculcating the moral beliefs of a specific culture. Others have emphasized their psychological and educational values.

Drawing on the similarities between traditional stories and dreams, and noting their relationship to the rituals and religious ceremonies which gave order and security to "primitive" cultures, many modern researchers have emphasized the psychological value of folktales. Max Luthi has noted that the ordered, stylized quality of these stories creates a sense of security within the reader or listener. In *Touch Magic: Fantasy, Faerie and Folklore in the Literature of Childhood*, Jane Yolen has called folktales, "the perfect guidebook to the human psyche.[8] In *The Uses of Enchantment*, the eminent child psychologist Bruno Bettelheim has written: "By dealing with universal problems, particularly those which occupy a child's mind, these stories speak to his budding ego and encourage its development, while at the same time relieving preconscious and unconscious pressures."[9]

In the formal education of children, folktales have specific value. They are, as we have seen, cultural artifacts and, as many educators have stated, the best way to understand a culture fully is to read the stories it creates. Folktales, as Jane Yolen has noted, "provide a way of looking at another culture from the inside out."[10]

Perhaps more important, a reading of folktales provides the foundation for a thorough literary training. Folktales have been called paradigmatic; that is, they embody in very clear fashion, the basic elements and structures of the story. In reading or hearing them, children become familiar with fundamental story patterns, conflicts, character types, settings, and actions. They are, it might be said, acquiring the vocabulary and grammar of stories, the details and structural patterns which will enable them later to read more complex works with greater understanding and, hence, enjoyment. Because the characters, actions, and settings, which are so concretely presented, implicitly convey the meanings of the stories, folktales can provide an introduction to symbolic meaning, an understanding of which is crucial to the comprehension of most literature.

In folktales, conflicts are quickly introduced: generally within the first two paragraphs the opposing characters and/or forces are presented. None of the material which follows is extraneous. Characters who advance the action represent basic aspects of human nature (often in opposition of each other): the good and the evil, the wise and the foolish, the selfish and the selfless, the strong and the weak, the inexperienced and the experienced, the honest and the deceitful, the brave and the cowardly. Actions occur which reveal these basic characteristics and the conflicts between them: children are abandoned or cruelly treated, stronger characters seek to destroy weaker ones, weaker characters are placed in situations where their courage and cleverness must be exercised, characters are given opportunities to develop morally or psychologically as they face a series of increasingly difficult tests.

Folktales should form a central part of children's literary experience from kindergarten onward. Simple cumulative stories like ''The Gingerbread Boy'' and ''Henny Penny'' provide examples of tales in which characters' actions lead to disastrous consequences. In the middle elementary grades, tales from a variety of cultures can be introduced and compared to each other. Child heroes like Jack, or Hansel and Gretel can be studied at this time as well. Native trickster tales can be used to reinforce concepts of irony. In the upper elementary grades the characteristics of folktales as a genre can be examined and more sophisticated tales such as ''East o' the Sun and West o' the Moon'' presented. Folktales should at first be related to other types of stories—rather than treated in isolation—enabling children to become aware of interrelationships within ''The Family of Stories.'' For example, ''Henny Penny'' can be compared to Pat Hutchins' *Rosie's Walk*. Although both deal with conflicts between a predatory fox and an apparently helpless hen, the outcome is different in each story. Robert Browning's ''The Pied Piper of Hamelin'' is similar in plot to Robert McCloskey's ''Nothing New Under the Sun (Hardly).'' In each the children follow a mysterious musician, but in the latter story, the children are not passive victims. At all grade levels, students can compare different illustrators' depictions of specific scenes or characters from a folktale and can discuss why they think certain illustrations are more effective than others.

In the selections which follow, and in their order, these educational aspects have been kept clearly in mind. The stories, containing many motifs and reflecting a variety of tale types, cultures, and retellers, have been categorized according to two basic narrative patterns: linear and circular journeys. Within each section, the stories have been arranged so that the reader can see both their similarities and their relation within "The Family of Stories."

In both linear and circular journeys, the central character, as stated previously, is displaced from the home environment, either voluntarily or involuntarily. The chief reasons for this displacement are often poverty or parental rejection or both. In either case, as many psychologists have noted, the displacement may be seen as the first step toward achieving maturity. In the linear journey, the hero overcomes inner doubts, natural objects, and human and supernatural adversaries to reach a new, happier, and more fulfilling home. In the circular journey, although similar obstacles are overcome, the point of departure is also the destination. However, because of their experiences, the central figures return home able to assume more self-fulfilling roles within the family structure. Circular journeys resemble the initiation rites practiced in many "primitive" societies. Alone, the individual must develop the skills and inner resources necessary for him to return a functioning member of society.

In many cases, the object of the linear journey is simply survival. The Three Billy-Goats Gruff must successfully cross a bridge to reach their food supply; Little Guava and her brother have been abandoned by their parents and are about to be sold by a witch. The slaves who fly to Africa and the girl who cultivates the magic orange tree escape from intolerable situations. For Dick Whittington and the Japanese boy who draws cats, the goal is success. Success is coupled with marriage to royalty in "The Daughter of the Dragon King," "Molly Whuppie," "East o' the Sun and West o' the Moon," and several versions of the Cinderella story. Completion of the process of maturation is the focus of such stories as "Rapunzel," "La Belle au Bois Dormant," and "Snow-White and the Seven Dwarfs." Whatever the object, each story is structured around a journey from one setting to another.

Many of the characters who undertake circular journeys are children. Little Red-Cap, the Native girl stolen by the owls, Goldilocks, and Hansel and Gretel are placed in alien and generally threatening situations. In these situations they are given the opportunity to learn. After her escape from the wolf, Red-Cap learns not to trust strangers; the Native girl returns home because she pays attention to the advice of animal helpers; Goldilocks (we presume) discovers the dangers of invading private property; and Gretel effects the rescue of her brother because she clearly perceives the dangers of the witch. Several circular journeys involve tricksters who willingly leave home on quests and return successful and often wealthy. The two Jacks and Tricksy Rabbit are among these. Husbands and wives are also involved in circular journeys: Finn McCool and Jacques the Wood-cutter end their journeys with domestic peace and tranquility.

Several of the linear and circular journeys conclude ironically. Often, protagonists do not reach their destinations. When they do, the results are not those expected. Two of the three little pigs build their own homes but do not survive in them; Little Red Riding Hood does not return home from her grand-mother's house; Coyote does not enjoy the wonderful feast he anticipated; the girl who doesn't return from the village festival in time loses her turkeys; the fisherman and his wife end up back in their lowly hut instead of in a magnificent palace. In these stories, the ironic results are generally the consequences of character failings or weaknesses.

Finally, it should be worth noting that while a folktale reflects the characteris-tics of the genre, contains fundamental story elements, and embodies universal human qualities, each is a unique story. Although readers should recognize the ways in which each tale is related to "The Family of Stories," they should also be able to see how each is individual, with its own distinctive qualities.

Notes

1 Stith Thompson, *The Folktale* (Berkeley: Univer-sity of California Press, 1977), p. vii.

2 Thompson, p. 415.

3 Thompson, p. 415.

4 Max Luthi, *Once Upon a Time: On the Nature of Fairy Tales* (Bloomington: Indiana University Press, 1976). p. 143.

5 Luthi, p. 139.

6 Jack Zipes, *Breaking the Magic Spell: Radical Theo-ries of Folk and Fairy Tales* (London: Heinemann, 1979), *passim*.

7 Nicholas Tucker, ed., *Suitable for Children? Con-troversies in Children's Literature* (London: Sussex Uni-versity Press, 1976), p. 38.

8 Jane Yolen, *Touch Magic: Fantasy, Faerie and Folk-lore in the Literature of Childhood* (New York: Philomel, 1981), p. 50.

9 Bruno Bettelheim, *The Uses of Enchantment: the Meaning and Importance of Fairy Tales* (New York: Ran-dom House, 1977), p. 6.

10 Yolen, p. 16.

Linear Journeys

"The Three Billy-Goats Gruff," from East o'
the Sun and West o' the Moon, *by George
Webbe Dasent (Edinburgh: David Douglas,
1888).*

*One of the most popular of folktales, this
Norwegian story presents a very basic conflict:
life against death. In their linear journey, the
goats move from the possiblity of starvation
or annihilation to a secure life. Through their
cleverness they outwit the typically evil, greedy
and stupid troll, whose violent death is a just
conclusion to his life. His character and fate
can be compared to those of the trolls in J. R.
R. Tolkien's* The Hobbit. *As in many European
folktales, the three-fold repetition is not merely
stylistic: it advances conflict and helps to
reveal character.*

The Three Billy-Goats Gruff

Once on a time there were three Billy-goats,
who were to go up to the hill-side to make
themselves fat, and the name of all three was
"Gruff."

On the way up was a bridge over a burn
they had to cross; and under the bridge lived a
great ugly Troll, with eyes as big as saucers,
and a nose as long as a poker.

So first of all came the youngest billy-goat
Gruff to cross the bridge.

"Trip, trap! trip, trap!" went the bridge.

"WHO'S THAT tripping over my bridge?"
roared the Troll.

"Oh, it is only I, the tiniest billy-goat Gruff;
and I'm going up to the hill-side to make myself
fat," said the billy-goat, with such a small voice.

"Now I'm coming to gobble you up," said
the Troll.

"Oh no! pray don't take me. I'm too little,
that I am," said the billy-goat; "wait a bit till
the second billy-goat Gruff comes, he's much
bigger."

"Well, be off with you;" said the Troll.

A little while after came the second billy-
goat Gruff to cross the bridge.

"TRIP, TRAP! TRIP, TRAP! TRIP, TRAP!" went the
bridge.

"WHO'S THAT tripping over my bridge?"
roared the Troll.

Illustration by Paul Galdone, from *The Three Billy Goats Gruff*. Copyright © 1973 by Paul Galdone. Reprinted by permission of Ticknor and Fields/Clarion Books, a Houghton Mifflin Company.

"Oh, it's the second billy-goat Gruff, and I'm going up to the hill-side to make myself fat," said the billy-goat, who hadn't such a small voice.

"Now I'm coming to gobble you up," said the Troll.

"Oh no! don't take me, wait a little till the big billy-goat Gruff comes, he's much bigger."

"Very well! be off with you," said the Troll.

But just then came the big billy-goat Gruff.

"TRIP, TRAP! TRIP, TRAP! TRIP, TRAP!" went the bridge, for the billy-goat was so heavy that the bridge creaked and groaned under him.

"WHO'S THAT tramping over my bridge?" roared the Troll.

"IT'S I! THE BIG BILLY-GOAT GRUFF," said the billy-goat, who had an ugly hoarse voice of his own.

"Now I'm coming to gobble you up," roared the Troll.

"Well, come along! I've got two spears,
And I'll poke your eyeballs out at your ears;
I've got besides two curling-stones,
And I'll crush you to bits, body and bones."

That was what the big billy-goat said; and so he flew at the Troll, and poked his eyes out with his horns, and crushed him to bits, body and bones, and tossed him out into the burn, and after that went up to the hill-side. There the billy-goats got so fat they were scarce able to walk home again; and if the fat hasn't fallen off them, why, they're still fat; and so —

"Snip, snap, snout.
This tale's told out."

"The Little Guava," from Folktales of Mexico, *translated and edited by Americo Paredes (Chicago: University of Chicago Press, 1970).*

Many Mexican folktales derive from European sources which have been imposed upon Mexican Indian material and presented as historical fact. A large part of Mexican folklore is presented in the form of legends, songs, and religious narrative. Even so, the wonder tale — probably the result of an amalgam of European and Indian sources — has also held its own through the centuries since the Spaniards conquered Mexico.

"The Little Guava," strongly reminiscent of the Grimms' "Hansel and Gretel," features several typical folk motifs: children abandoned in the forest at the behest of an evil stepmother; children wandering into the false home of an evil old woman; children saving themselves by trickery; and the beneficent effect of a dream. One unusual feature of "The Little Guava" is that the sister is clearly dominant. Unlike some versions of this well-known tale type, this version features a linear rather than a circular structure, and the brother and sister are separated in the end.

The Little Guava

These were two children, brother and sister, who had no mother; but they did have a stepmother. She was tired of the children, and one day she said to her husband, "See what you can do with your children, because I'm tired of them."

Next day at dawn the father said to the children, "Get ready, children; we are going out to chop wood." And the children got ready and went with their father. When they got to a mountain, he said to them, "Wait for me here, my dear children, and stay together. I'm going to see if I can find some wood around here." And he went away.

The children waited many hours; night came, and since the father did not return, the girl says to the boy, "Little brother, our father has left us here to get lost."

"Why, little sister?"

"Because it is already dark, and he hasn't come."

Then the boy said, "Little sister, let's go back the way he brought us here. I picked a guava and threw the peelings all along the way."

"Well, I put ashes in my coat and scattered them all along the way too."

"Well, let's see if we can find the house," the boy said. "We'll find it, little brother, because our house will be where the ashes and the guava peelings stop."

And they did just that. They walked and walked until they got to their house. Then the girl said, "Now let's climb into the attic so father won't see us."

It was very late at night when the father came back, and he asked for supper. When his wife took it to him, he said just before taking the first bite, "At this hour I used to have supper with my children."

When they heard this, the children answered, "Dear father, here we are."

"Children, how did you find the house?" The children told what they had done, and the father sent them to bed.

The stepmother said, "Well, your children have returned. You must choose between them and me."

The father said, "Tomorrow I'll take them out again."

Next morning he told them, "Children, get ready, because this time we are going for wood. I didn't get any last night." They went, and he took them to the mountain again and said the same words, "Wait here and stay close together."

Night came, and the father did not return. The girl said, "Little brother, now we really are lost."

"Why, little sister?"

"Because father hasn't come back, and it's already dark. Look, little brother, let's find some beehives. You crawl into one and I into another, and we'll spend the night so the wild beasts won't eat us, because there are a lot of them here." The brother, who was the smaller, did what he was told. They found some beehives and spent the night in them.

When it was morning, they took a road and walked a long while on it until they saw a little house, just a little hut. Soon they saw a little old woman who was making pancakes. The girl said, "Look, little brother. You are smaller, so creep up and when you see the little old woman put the pancakes in her little basket, creep up very carefully, take them out, and bring them here."

They did just that, and they divided the little pancakes between them. But the boy did it so many times that the old woman saw him and said, "No wonder I never finish cooking them, if you are eating them."

Then the girl came out and said, "Ma'am, we have been traveling for a long time; we have had no supper or breakfast."

"And why have you traveled for so long without eating?"

"Because our father abandoned us on the mountain," said the girl.

Very well, come in and I'll give you something to eat." And so she did; she would feed them, sometimes good food and sometimes bad food. One night when the children were in their little room, a lady appeared to them and said, "Tomorrow I will prepare a little rat's tail for you and bring it to you."

The next day she appeared again and gave them the rat's tail, saying, "When someone comes and asks you to show your finger, show them the rat's tail."

Meanwhile the old woman of the house had called some hog buyers and offered them two very fat ones. But they wanted to see them first. They went and told the children to stick a finger through a crack, but they showed the little rat's tail instead. The buyers said, "How can we buy those hogs when they are so lean? Let them get fat, and we'll come back."

The old woman said, "I don't know why those hogs haven't fattened up. I feed them a lot. But anyway, come back in a few days."

So then she gave them a lot more to eat so they would get fat, but one night the lady appeared to them again and told them, "Tomorrow I will bring you a gift."

Next morning she came with a little jackass for the boy and a little jenny for the girl. Since the old woman wasn't up yet, she took them out to the plain and told them, "Each of you mount his donkey, and one of you go left, and the other one go right."

Now my tale is done, and yours has not begun.

———

"People Who Could Fly," from Black Folktales, *by Julius Lester, illustrated by Tom Feelings (New York: Richard W. Baron, 1969).*

"People Who Could Fly" was a popular tale among Afro-Americans living throughout the coast regions of Georgia and South Carolina. A linear journey in structure, the tale expresses poignant wish-fulfillment, stresses the magical power of words uttered by the prophet-like witch doctor, and no doubt served to sustain American slaves in their misery. The plight of slaves abducted from their homeland is also the subject of Paula Fox's novel The Slave Dancer.

People Who Could Fly

It happened long, long ago, when black people were taken from their homes in Africa and forced to come here to work as slaves. They were put onto ships, and many died during the long voyage across the Atlantic Ocean. Those that survived stepped off the boats into a land they had never seen, a land they never knew existed, and they were put into the fields to work.

Many refused, and they were killed. Others would work, but when the white man's whip lashed their backs to make them work harder, they would turn and fight. And some

of them killed the white men with the whips. Others were killed by the white men. Some would run away and try to go back home, back to Africa where there were no white people, where they worked their own land for the good of each other, not for the good of white men. Some of those who tried to go back to Africa would walk until they came to the ocean, and then they would walk into the water, and no one knows if they did walk to Africa through the water or if they drowned. It didn't matter. At least they were no longer slaves.

Now when the white man forced Africans onto the slave-ships, he did not know, nor did he care, if he took the village musicians, artists, or witch doctors. As long as they were black and looked strong, he wanted them — men, women, and children. Thus, he did not know that sometimes there would be a witch doctor among those he had captured. If he had known, and had also known that the witch doctor was the medium of the gods, he would have thought twice. But he did not care. These black men and black women were not people to him. He looked at them and counted each one as so much money for his pocket.

It was to a plantation in South Carolina that one boatload of Africans was brought. Among them was the son of a witch doctor who had not completed by many months studying the secrets of the gods from his father. This young man carried with him the secrets and powers of generations of Africa.

One day, one hot day when the sun singed the very hair on the head, they were working in the fields. They had been in the fields since before the sun rose, and, as it made its journey to the highest part of the sky, the very air seemed to be on fire. A young woman, her body curved with the child that grew deep inside her, fainted.

Before her body struck the ground, the white man with the whip was riding toward her on his horse. He threw water in her face. "Get back to work, you lazy nigger! There ain't going to be no sitting down on the job as long as I'm here." He cracked the whip against her back and, screaming, she staggered to her feet.

All work had stopped as the Africans watched, saying nothing.

"If you niggers don't want a taste of the same, you'd better get to work!"

They lowered their heads and went back to work. The young witch doctor worked his way slowly toward the young mother-to-be, but before he could reach her, she collapsed again, and the white man with the whip was upon her, lashing her until her body was raised from the ground by the sheer violence of her sobs. The young witch doctor worked his way to her side and whispered something in her ear. She, in turn, whispered to the person beside her. He told the next person, and on around the field it went. They did it so quickly and quietly that the white man with the whip noticed nothing.

A few moments later, someone else in the field fainted, and, as the white man with the whip rode toward him, the young witch doctor shouted, "Now!" He uttered a strange word, and the person who had fainted rose from the ground, and moving his arms like wings, he flew into the sky and out of sight.

The man with the whip looked around at the Africans, but they only stared into the distance, tiny smiles softening their lips. "Who did that? Who was that who yelled out?" No one said anything. "Well, just let me get my hands on him."

Not too many minutes had passed before the young woman fainted once again. The man was almost upon her when the young witch doctor shouted, "Now!" and uttered a strange word. She, too, rose from the ground and, waving her arms like wings, she flew into the distance and out of sight.

This time the man with the whip knew who was responsible, and as he pulled back his arm to lash the young witch doctor, the young man yelled, "Now! Now! Everyone!" He uttered the strange word, and all of the Africans dropped their hoes, stretched out their arms, and flew away, back to their home, back to Africa.

That was long ago, and no one now remembers what word it was that the young witch doctor knew that could make people fly. But who knows? Maybe one morning someone will awake with a strange word on his tongue and, uttering it, we will all stretch out our arms and take to the air, leaving these blood-drenched fields of our misery behind.

"The Magic Orange Tree," from The Magic Orange Tree and Other Haitian Folktales, *collected and edited by Diane Wolkstein, Illustrated by Elsa Henriquez (New York: Knopf, 1978).*

Diane Wolkstein writes that a Haitian storyteller calls out, "Cric?" when he or she wants to tell a story. If the audience wishes to hear the tale, they answer, "Crac!" In the countryside outside the capital city of Port-au-Prince, the Haitian people still practice the art of storytelling as a communal activity in which the audience (composed of both adults and children) participates. This feature is present in "The Magic Orange Tree," which includes several songs and choruses which are also sung by the members of the audience. Wolkstein explains that "The Magic Orange Tree" may be based upon a common Haitian practice: "When a child is born in the countryside, the umbilical cord may be saved and dried and planted in the earth, with a pit from a fruit tree placed on top of the cord. The tree that grows then belongs to the child." This tale depicts the innocent young girl who suffers from the aggressions of an evil stepmother. The girl must rely upon nature and upon her own efforts to survive and to prosper.

The motif of a magic tree springing from the grave of the child's dead mother is also seen in the Grimm Brothers' version of "Cinderella."

The Magic Orange Tree
Cric? Crac!

There was once a girl whose mother died when she was born. Her father waited for some time to remarry, but when he did, he married a woman who was both mean and cruel. She was so mean there were some days she would not give the girl anything at all to eat. The girl was often hungry.

One day the girl came from school and saw on the table three round ripe oranges. *Hmmmm.* They smelled good. The girl looked around her. No one was there. She took one orange, peeled it, and ate it. *Hmmmm-mmm.* It was good. She took a second orange and ate it. She ate the third orange. Oh-oh, she was happy. But soon her step-mother came home.

"Who has taken the oranges I left on the table?" she said. "Whoever has done so had better say their prayers now, for they will not be able to say them later."

The girl was so frightened she ran from the house. She ran through the woods until she came to her own mother's grave. All night she cried and prayed to her mother to help her. Finally she fell asleep.

Illustration by Elsa Hendriguez from *The Magic Orange Tree and Other Haitian Folktales* collected by Diane Wolkstein. Copyright © 1978 by Alfred A. Knopf Publishers. Reprinted by permission of the publisher.

In the morning the sun woke her, and as she rose to her feet something dropped from her skirt onto the ground. What was it? It was an orange pit. And the moment it entered the earth a green leaf sprouted from it. The girl watched, amazed. She knelt down and sang:

Orange tree,
Grow and grow and grow.

Orange tree, orange tree.
Grow and grow and grow,
Orange tree.
Stepmother is not real mother,
Orange tree.

The orange tree grew. It grew to the size of the girl. The girl sang:

Orange tree,
Branch and branch and branch.
Orange tree, orange tree,
Branch and branch and branch,
Orange tree.
Stepmother is not real mother,
Orange tree.

And many twisting, turning, curving branches appeared on the tree. Then the girl sang:

Orange tree,
Flower and flower and flower.
Orange tree, orange tree,
Flower and flower and flower,
Orange tree.
Stepmother is not real mother,
Orange tree.

Beautiful white blossoms covered the tree. After a time they began to fade, and small green buds appeared where the flowers had been. The girl sang:

Orange tree,
Ripen and ripen and ripen.
Orange tree, orange tree,
Ripen and ripen and ripen,
Orange tree.
Stepmother is not real mother.
Orange tree.

The oranges ripened, and the whole tree was filled with golden oranges. The girl was so delighted she danced around and around the tree, singing:

Orange tree,
Grow and grow and grow.
Orange tree, orange tree,
Grow and grow and grow.
Orange tree.
Stepmother is not real mother,
Orange tree.

But then when she looked, she saw the orange tree had grown up to the sky, far beyond her reach. What was she to do? Oh she was a clever girl. She sang:

> Orange tree,
> Lower and lower and lower.
> Orange tree, orange tree,
> Lower and lower and lower,
> Orange tree.
> Stepmother is not real mother,
> Orange tree.

When the orange tree came down to her height, she filled her arms with oranges and returned home.

The moment the stepmother saw the gold oranges in the girl's arms, she seized them and began to eat them. Soon she had finished them all.

"Tell me, my sweet," she said to the girl, "where have you found such delicious oranges?"

The girl hesitated. She did not want to tell. The stepmother seized the girl's wrist and began to twist it.

"Tell me!" she ordered.

The girl led her stepmother through the woods to the orange tree. You remember the girl was very clever? Well, as soon as the girl came to the tree, she sang:

> Orange tree,
> Grow and grow and grow.
> Orange tree, orange tree,
> Grow and grow and grow.
> Orange tree.
> Stepmother is not real mother,
> Orange tree.

And the orange tree grew up to the sky. What was the stepmother to do then? She began to plead and beg.

"Please," she said. "You shall be my own dear child. You may always have as much as you want to eat. Tell the tree to come down and *you* shall pick the oranges for me." So the girl quietly sang:

> Orange tree,
> Lower and lower and lower.
> Orange tree, orange tree,

> Lower and lower and lower,
> Orange tree.
> Stepmother is not real mother,
> Orange tree.

The tree began to lower. When it came to the height of the stepmother, she leapt on it and began to climb so quickly you might have thought she was the daughter of an ape. And as she climbed from branch to branch, she ate every orange. The girl saw that there would soon be no oranges left. What would happen to her then? The girl sang:

> Orange tree,
> Grow and grow and grow.
> Orange tree, orange tree,
> Grow and grow and grow,
> Orange tree.
> Stepmother is not real mother,
> Orange tree.

The orange tree grew and grew and grew and grew "Help!" cried the stepmother as she rose into the sky. "H-E-E-lp . . . ."

The girl cried: *Break!* Orange tree, *Break!*

The orange tree broke into a thousand pieces . . . and the stepmother as well.

Then the girl searched among the branches until she found . . . a tiny orange pit. She carefully planted it in the earth. Softly she sang:

> Orange tree,
> Grow and grow and grow.
> Orange tree, orange tree,
> Grow and grow and grow,
> Orange tree.
> Stepmother is not real mother,
> Orange tree.

The orange tree grew to the height of the girl. She picked some oranges and took them to market to sell. They were so sweet the people bought all her oranges.

Every Saturday she is at the marketplace selling her oranges. Last Saturday, I went to see her and asked her if she would give me a free orange. "What?" she cried. "After all I've been through!" And she gave me such a kick in the pants that that's how I got here today, to tell you the story — "The Magic Orange Tree."

"The Story of the Three Little Pigs," from English Folk and Fairy Tales, *collected by Joseph Jacobs (New York: Putnam's [1890]).*

Although very simple in its plot line, this English folktale is a classic example of the importance of three-fold repetition. It is used to differentiate the characters of the three pigs and to indicate the third pig's increasing cleverness as he leaves the brick house in search of food. The wolf, having failed through the use of force, tries to deceive the third pig, but is outwitted. A symbol of death, as wolves often are in European tales, he precipitates his own end when, enraged, he unthinkingly climbs down the chimney.

The Story of the Three Little Pigs

Once upon a time when pigs spoke rhyme
And monkeys chewed tobacco,
And hens took snuff to make them tough,
And ducks went quack, quack, quack, O!

There was an old sow with three little pigs, and as she had not enough to keep them, she sent them out to seek their fortune. The first that went off met a man with a bundle of straw, and said to him:

"Please, man, give me that straw to build me a house."

Which the man did, and the little pig built a house with it. Presently came along a wolf, and knocked at the door, and said:

"Little pig, little pig, let me come in."

To which the pig answered:

"No, no, by the hair of my chiny chin chin."

The wolf then answered to that:

"Then I'll huff, and I'll puff, and I'll blow your house in."

So he huffed, and he puffed, and he blew his house in, and ate up the little pig.

The second little pig met a man with a bundle of furze and said:

"Please, man, give me that furze to build a house.

Which the man did, and the pig built his house. Then along came the wolf, and said:

"Little pig, little pig, let me come in."

"No, no, by the hair of my chiny chin chin."

"Then I'll puff, and I'll huff, and I'll blow your house in."

So he huffed, and he puffed, and he puffed, and he huffed, and at last he blew the house down, and he ate up the little pig.

The third little pig met a man with a load of bricks, and said:

"Please, man, give me those bricks to build a house with."

Illustration by L. Leslie Brooke, "The Story of the Three Little Pigs" from *The Golden Goose Book.* Copyright © 1976. Reprinted by permission of Frederick Warne Publishers, London.

So the man gave him the bricks, and he built his house with them. So the wolf came, as he did to the other little pigs, and said:

"Little pig, little pig, let me come in."

"No, no, by the hair on my chiny chin chin."

"Then I'll huff, and I'll puff, and I'll blow your house in."

Well, he huffed, and he puffed, and he huffed and he puffed, and he puffed and huffed; but he could *not* get the house down. When he found that he could not, with all his huffing and puffing, blow the house down, he said:

"Little pig, I know where there is a nice field of turnips."

"Where?" said the little pig.

"Oh, in Mr. Smith's Home-field, and if you will be ready to-morrow morning I will call for you, and we will go together, and get some for dinner."

"Very well," said the little pig, "I will be ready. What time do you mean to go?"

"Oh, at six o'clock."

Well, the little pig got up at five, and got the turnips before the wolf came (which he did about six), who said:

"Little pig, are you ready?"

The little pig said: "Ready! I have been and come back again, and got a nice potful for dinner."

The wolf felt very angry at this, but thought that he would be up to the little pig somehow or other, so he said:

"Little pig, I know where there is a nice appletree."

"Where?" said the pig.

"Down at Merry-garden," replied the wolf, "and if you will not deceive me I will come for you at five o'clock to-morrow and get some apples."

Well, the little pig bustled up the next morning at four o'clock, and went off for the apples, hoping to get back before the wolf came; but he had further to go, and had to climb the tree, so that just as he was coming down from it, he saw the wolf coming, which, as you may suppose, frightened him very much. When the wolf came up he said:

"Little pig, what! are you here before me? Are they nice apples?"

"Yes, very," said the little pig. "I will throw you down one."

And he threw it so far, that, while the wolf was gone to pick it up, the little pig jumped down and ran home. The next day the wolf came again, and said to the little pig:

"Little pig, there is a fair at Shanklin this afternoon, will you go?"

"Oh yes," said the pig, "I will go; what time shall you be ready?"

"At three," said the wolf. So the little pig went off before the time as usual, and got to the fair, and bought a butter-churn, which he was going home with, when he saw the wolf coming. Then he could not tell what to do. So

he got into the churn to hide, and by so doing turned it round, and it rolled down the hill with the pig in it, which frightened the wolf so much, that he ran home without going to the fair. He went to the little pig's house, and told him how frightened he had been by a great round thing which came down the hill past him. Then the little pig said:

"Hah, I frightened you, then. I had been to the fair and bought a butter-churn, and when I saw you, I got into it, and rolled down the hill."

Then the wolf was very angry indeed, and declared he *would* eat up the little pig, and that he would get down the chimney after him. When the little pig saw what he was about, he hung on the pot full of water, and made up a blazing fire, and, just as the wolf was coming down, took off the cover, and in fell the wolf; so the little pig put on the cover again in an instant, boiled him up, and ate him for supper, and lived happy ever afterwards.

———

"Henny Penny," from Chimney Corner Stories, *by Veronica S. Hutchinson (New York: Minton, Balch & Co., 1925).*

In this well-known British cumulative tale, the ironic ending of the linear journey results from the foolishness of the hen. In some adaptations, the hen discovers at the last moment the wicked intentions of the sly fox and escapes to her home. Such a circular pattern seems to have been created by adaptors who consider the violence of the earlier version too great for young readers. In its portrayal of the consequences of actions undertaken without sufficient knowledge, this story is similar to the African tale Why Mosquitoes Buzz in People's Ears, *retold by Verna Aardema (not included in this anthology).*

Henny Penny

One day Henny Penny was picking up corn in the farm-yard, when an acorn fell out of a tree and struck her on the head. "Goodness gracious me!" said Henny Penny, "the sky is falling. I must go and tell the King."

Illustration by Leonard B. Lubin from *Henny Penny* by Veronica S. Hutchinson. Copyright ©
1976. Reprinted by permission of Little, Brown and Co.

So she went along and she went along and she went along until she met Cocky Locky.

"Where are you going, Henny Penny?" asked Cocky Locky.

"Oh," said Henny Penny, "the sky is falling and I am going to tell the King."

"May I go with you, Henny Penny?" asked Cocky Locky.

"Certainly," said Henny Penny.

So Henny Penny and Cocky Locky went to tell the King that the sky was falling. They went along and they went along and they went along, until they met Ducky Daddles.

"Where are you going, Henny Penny and Cocky Locky?" asked Ducky Daddles.

"Oh, we are going to tell the King that the sky is falling," said Henny Penny and Cocky Locky.

"May I go with you?" asked Ducky Daddles.

"Certainly," said Henny Penny and Cocky Locky.

So Henny Penny, Cocky, Locky, and Ducky Daddles went to tell the King that the sky was falling. They went along and they went along and they went along until they met Goosey Poosey.

"Where are you going, Henny Penny, Cocky Locky, and Ducky Daddles?" asked Goosey Poosey.

"Oh, we are going to tell the King the sky is falling," said Henny Penny, Cocky Locky, and Ducky Daddles.

"May I go with you?" asked Goosey Poosey.

"Certainly," said Henny Penny, Cocky Locky, and Ducky Daddles.

So Henny Penny, Cocky Locky, Ducky Daddles and Goosey Poosey went to tell the King that the sky was falling. They went along and they went along and they went along until they met Turkey Lurkey.

"Where are you going, Henny Penny and Cocky Locky, Ducky Daddles, and Goosey Poosey?" asked Turkey Lurkey.

"Oh, we are going to tell the King the sky is falling," said Henny Penny, Cocky Locky, Ducky Daddles, and Goosey Poosey.

"May I go with you?" asked Turkey Lurkey.

"Certainly," said Henny Penny, Cocky Locky, Ducky Daddles, and Goosey Poosey.

So Henny Penny, Cocky Locky, Ducky Daddles, Goosey Poosey, and Turkey Lurkey went on to tell the King the sky was falling. They went along and they went along and they went along until they met Foxy Woxy.

"Where are you going, Henny Penny, Cocky Locky, Ducky Daddles, Goosey Poosey, and Turkey Lurkey?" asked Foxy Woxy.

"Oh, we are going to tell the King the sky is falling," said Henny Penny, Cocky Locky, Ducky Daddles, Goosey Poosey, and Turkey Lurkey.

Oh, but that is not the way to the King, Henny Penny, Cocky Locky, Ducky Daddles, Goosey Poosey, and Turkey Lurkey," said Foxy Woxy, "come with me and I will show you a short way to the King's Palace."

"Certainly," said Henny Penny, Cocky Locky, Ducky Daddles, Goosey Poosey, and Turkey Lurkey.

They went along and they went along and they went along until they reached Foxy Woxy's Cave. In they went, and they never came out again.

To this day the King has never been told that the sky was falling.

"Little Red Riding Hood," from The Fairy Tales of Charles Perrault, *translated by Angela Carter (London: Gollancz, 1977).*

Perrault's version of this story, which predates the Grimm Brothers' version by more than a century, emphasizes its moral very powerfully: grave dangers await the naive and innocent. Psychological critics, in addition to "discovering" implicit sexual messages, have suggested that the heroine is a victim of excessive adoration and her own willingness to be led astray. The irony of this story arises when a short circular journey becomes a devastatingly linear one! As is the case in "The Story of the Three Little Pigs," the wolf easily devours the unwary victim. Laura Ingalls Wilder draws from the fear of wolves evoked in traditional tales such as this one to help create the mood of her story "The Wolf-Pack." Jean Craighead George, in her novel Julie of the Wolves, *presents an opposing view to those above.*

Little Red Riding Hood

Once upon a time, deep in the heart of the country, there lived a pretty little girl whose mother adored her, and her grandmother adored her even more. This good woman made her a red hood like the ones that fine ladies wear when they go riding. The hood suited the child so much that soon everybody was calling her Little Red Riding Hood.

One day, her mother baked some cakes on the griddle and said to Little Red Riding Hood:

"Your granny is sick; you must go and visit her. Take her one of these cakes and a little pot of butter."

Little Red Riding Hood went off to the next village to visit her grandmother. As she walked through the wood, she met a wolf, who wanted to eat her but did not dare to because there were woodcutters working nearby. He asked where she was going. The poor child did not know how dangerous it is to chatter away to wolves and replied innocently:

"I'm going to visit my grandmother to take her this cake and this little pot of butter from my mother."

"Does your grandmother live far away?" asked the wolf.

"Oh yes," said Little Red Riding Hood. "She lives beyond the mill you can see over there, in the first house you come to in the village."

"Well, I shall go and visit her, too," said the wolf. "I will take *this* road and you shall take *that* road and let's see who can get there first."

The wolf ran off by the shortest path and Red Riding Hood went off the longest way and she made it still longer because she dawdled along, gathering nuts and chasing butterflies and picking bunches of wayside flowers.

The wolf soon arrived at Grandmother's house. He knocked on the door, rat tat tat.

"Who's there?"

"Your grand-daughter, Little Red Riding Hood," said the wolf, disguising his voice. "I've brought you a cake baked on the griddle and a little pot of butter from my mother."

Grandmother was lying in bed because she was poorly. She called out:

"Lift up the latch and walk in!"

The wolf lifted the latch and opened the door. He had not eaten for three days. He threw himself on the good woman and gobbled her up. Then he closed the door behind him and lay down in Grandmother's bed to wait for Little Red Riding Hood. At last she came knocking on the door, rat tat tat.

"Who's there?"

Little Red Riding Hood heard the hoarse voice of the wolf and thought that her grandmother must have caught a cold. She answered:

"It's your grand-daughter, Little Red Riding Hood. I've brought you a cake baked on the griddle and a little pot of butter from my mother."

The wolf disguised his voice and said:

"Lift up the latch and walk in."

Little Red Riding Hood lifted the latch and opened the door.

When the wolf saw her come in, he hid himself under the bedclothes and said to her:

"Put the cake and the butter down on the bread-bin and come and lie down with me."

Little Red Riding Hood took off her clothes and went to lie down in the bed. She was surprised to see how odd her grandmother looked. She said to her:

"Grandmother, what big arms you have!"

"All the better to hold you with, my dear."

"Grandmother, what big legs you have!"

"All the better to run with, my dear."

"Grandmother, what big ears you have!"

"All the better to hear with, my dear."

"Grandmother, what big eyes you have!"

"All the better to see with, my dear!"

"Grandmother, what big teeth you have!"

"All the better to eat you up!"

At that, the wicked wolf threw himself upon Little Red Riding Hood and gobbled her up, too.

MORAL

Children, especially pretty, nicely brought-up young ladies, ought never to talk to strangers; if they are foolish enough to do so, they should not be surprised if some greedy wolf consumes them, elegant red riding hoods and all.

Now, there are real wolves, with hairy pelts and enormous teeth; but also wolves who seem perfectly charming, sweet-natured and obliging, who pursue young girls in the street and pay them the most flattering attentions.

Unfortunately, these smooth-tongued, smooth-pelted wolves are the most dangerous beasts of all.

Illustration by Raymond Briggs, "Little Red Riding Hood" from *The Fairy Tale Treasury,* selected by Virginia Haviland. Copyright © 1972 by Raymond Briggs.

"From Tiger to Anansi," from Anansi the Spider Man: Jamaican Folktales, *told by Philip M. Sherlock, illustrated by Marcia Brown (New York: Crowell, 1954).*

Rooted in the folklore of West Africa, the Anansi stories of Jamaica are the most popular folktales in the West Indies. When Anansi's life goes smoothly, he is a man. When danger comes, he transforms himself into a spider. Perhaps Anansi is best-known as the wily trickster. In "From Tiger to Anansi" we see this dimension of Anansi's character when he tricks Tiger into relinquishing his stories. Like Jack and the Biblical David in their contests against giants, Anansi completes his quest by using his wits to compensate for his diminutive size. In A Story, a Story *(not in this anthology), Gail Haley presents another version of how stories came into Anansi's possession.*

From Tiger to Anansi

Once upon a time and a long long time ago the Tiger was king of the forest.

At evening when all the animals sat together in a circle and talked and laughed together, Snake would ask,

"Who is the strongest of us all?"

"Tiger is strongest," cried the dog. "When Tiger whispers the trees listen. When Tiger is angry and cries out, the trees tremble."

"And who is the weakest of all?" asked Snake.

"Anansi," shouted the dog, and they all laughed together. Anansi the spider is weakest of all. When he whispers no one listens. When he shouts everyone laughs."

Now one day the weakest and strongest came face to face, Anansi and Tiger. They met in a clearing of the forest. The frogs hiding under the cool leaves saw them. The bright green parrots in the branches heard them.

When they met, Anansi bowed so low that his forehead touched the ground. Tiger did not greet him. Tiger just looked at Anansi.

"Good morning, Tiger," cried Anansi. "I have a favor to ask."

"And what is it, Anansi?" said Tiger.

"Tiger, we all know that you are strongest of us all. This is why we give your name to many things. We have Tiger lilies, and Tiger stories and Tiger moths and Tiger this and Tiger that. Everyone knows that I am weakest of all. This is why nothing bears my name. Tiger, let something be called after the weakest one so that men may know my name too."

"Well," said Tiger, without so much as a glance toward Anansi, "what would you like to bear your name?"

"The stories," cried Anansi. "The stories that we tell in the forest at evening time when the sun goes down, the stories about Br'er Snake and Br'er Tacumah, Br'er Cow and Br'er Bird and all of us."

Now Tiger liked these stories and he meant to keep them as Tiger stories. He thought to himself, How stupid, how weak this Anansi is. I will play a trick on him so that all the animals will laugh at him. Tiger moved his tail slowly from side to side and said, "Very good, Anansi, very good. I will let the stories be named after you, if you do what I ask."

"Tiger, I will do what you ask"

"Yes, I am sure you will, I am sure you will," said Tiger, moving his tail slowly from side to side. "It is a little thing that I ask. Bring me Mr. Snake alive. Do you know Snake who lives down by the river, Mr. Anansi? Bring him to me alive and you can have the stories."

Tiger stopped speaking. He did not move his tail. He looked at Anansi and waited for him to speak. All the animals in the forest waited. Mr. Frog beneath the cool leaves, Mr. Parrot up in the tree, all watched Anansi. They were all ready to laugh at him.

"Tiger, I will do what you ask," said Anansi. At these words a great wave of laughter burst from the forest. The frogs and parrots laughed. Tiger laughed loudest of all, for how could feeble Anansi catch Snake alive?

Anansi went away. He heard the forest laughing at him from every side.

That was on Monday morning. Anansi sat before his house and thought of plan after plan. At last he hit upon one that could not fail. He would build a Calaban.

On Tuesday morning Anansi built a Calaban. He took a strong vine and made a noose. He hid the vine in the grass. Inside the noose he set some of the berries that Snake loved best. Then he waited. Soon Snake came up the path. He saw the berries and went toward them. He lay across the vine and ate the berries. Anansi pulled at the vine to tighten the noose, but Snake's body was too heavy. Anansi saw that the Calaban had failed.

Illustration by Marcia Brown, ''From Tiger to Anansi'' from *Anansi the Spider Man: Jamaican Folktales,* by Philip M. Sherlock. Copyright © 1954 by Marcia Brown.

Wednesday came. Anansi made a deep hole in the ground. He made the sides slippery with grease. In the bottom he put some of the bananas that Snake loved. Then he hid in the bush beside the road and waited.

Snake came crawling down the path toward the river. He was hungry and thirsty. He saw the bananas at the bottom of the hole. He saw that the sides of the hole were slippery. First he wrapped his tail tightly around the trunk of a tree, then he reached down into the hole and ate the bananas. When he was finished he pulled himself up by his tail and crawled away. Anansi had lost his bananas and he had lost Snake, too.

Thursday morning came. Anansi made a Fly Up. Inside the trap he put an egg. Snake came down the path. He was happy this morning,

so happy that he lifted his head and a third of his long body from the ground. He just lowered his head, took up the egg in his mouth, and never even touched the trap. The Fly Up could not catch Snake.

What was Anansi to do? Friday morning came. He sat and thought all day. It was no use.

Now it was Saturday morning. This was the last day. Anansi went for a walk down by the river. He passed by the hole where Snake lived. There was Snake, his body hidden in the hole, his head resting on the ground at the entrance to the hole. It was early morning. Snake was watching the sun rise above the mountains.

"Good morning, Anansi," said Snake.

"Good morning, Snake," said Anansi.

Anansi, I am very angry with you. You have been trying to catch me all week. You set a Fly Up to catch me. The day before you made a Slippery Hole for me. The day before that you made a Calaban. I have a good mind to kill you, Anansi."

"Ah, you are too clever, Snake," said Anansi. "You are much too clever. Yes, what you say is so. I tried to catch you, but I failed. Now I can never prove that you are the longest animal in the world, longer even than the bamboo tree."

"Of course I am the longest of all animals," cried Snake. "I am much longer than the bamboo tree."

"What, longer than the bamboo tree across there?" asked Anansi.

"Of course I am," said Snake. "Look and see." Snake came out of the hole and stretched himself out at full length.

"Yes, you are very, very long," said Anansi, "but the bamboo tree is very long, too. Now that I look at you and at the bamboo tree I must say that the bamboo tree seems longer. But it's hard to say because it is farther away."

"Well, bring it nearer," cried Snake. "Cut it down and put it beside me. You will soon see that I am much longer."

Anansi ran to the bamboo tree and cut it down. He placed it on the ground and cut off all its branches. Bush, bush, bush, bush! There it was, long and straight as a flagstaff.

"Now put it beside me," said Snake.

Anansi put the long bamboo tree down on

the ground beside Snake. Then he said:

"Snake, when I go up to see where your head is, you will crawl up. When I go down to see where your tail is, you will crawl down. In that way you will always seem to be longer than the bamboo tree, which really is longer than you are."

"Tie my tail, then!" said Snake. "Tie my tail! I know that I am longer than the bamboo, whatever you say."

Anansi tied Snake's tail to the end of the bamboo. Then he ran up to the other end.

"Stretch, Snake, stretch, and we will see who is longer."

A crowd of animals were gathering round. Here was something better than a race. "Stretch, Snake, stretch," they called.

Snake stretched as hard as he could. Anansi tied him around his middle so that he should not slip back. Now one more try. Snake knew that if he stretched hard enough he would prove to be longer than the bamboo.

Anansi ran up to him. "Rest yourself for a little, Snake, and then stretch again. If you can stretch another six inches you will be longer than the bamboo. Try your hardest. Stretch so that you even have to shut your eyes. Ready?"

"Yes," said Snake. Then Snake made a mighty effort. He stretched so hard that he had to squeeze his eyes shut. "Hooray!" cried the animals. "You are winning, Snake. Just two inches more."

And at that moment Anansi tied Snake's head to the bamboo. There he was. At last he had caught Snake, all by himself.

The animals fell silent. Yes, there Snake was, all tied up, ready to be taken to Tiger. And feeble Anansi had done this. They could laugh at him no more.

And never again did Tiger dare to call these stories by his name. They were Anansi stories forever after, from that day to this.

"The History of Whittington," from The Blue Fairy Book, *edited by Andrew Lang (London: Longmans, Green, 1899).*

This story, unlike most folktales, contains no magical elements and recounts the life of an actual person from the Middle Ages. However, as in many folktales, this story portrays a poor orphan earning wealth, love, and power through perseverance. The story was very popular in England during the eighteenth and nineteenth centuries because it emphasized the values of work, charity, and respect for money earned. Folktales about the acquisition of wealth must have influenced the Bastable children in E. Nesbit's story "Digging for Treasure."

The History of Whittington

Dick Whittington was a very little boy when his father and mother died; so little indeed, that he never knew them, nor the place where he was born. He strolled about the country as ragged as a colt, till he met with a waggoner who was going to London, and who gave him leave to walk all the way by the side of his waggon without paying anything for his passage. This pleased little Whittington very much, as he wanted to see London sadly, for he had heard that the streets were paved with gold, and he was willing to get a bushel of it; but how great was his disappointment, poor boy! when he saw the streets covered with dirt instead of gold, and found himself in a strange place, without a friend, without food, and without money.

Though the waggoner was so charitable as to let him walk up by the side of the waggon for nothing, he took care not to know him when he came to town, and the poor boy was, in a little time, so cold and so hungry that he wished himself in a good kitchen and by a warm fire in the country.

In this distress he asked charity of several people, and one of them bid him 'Go to work for an idle rogue.' 'That I will,' says Whittington, 'with all my heart; I will work for you if you will let me.'

The man, who thought this savoured of wit and impertinence (though the poor lad intended only to show his readiness to work), gave him a blow with a stick which broke his head so that the blood ran down. In this situation, and fainting for want of food, he laid himself down at the door of one Mr. Fitzwarren, a merchant, where the cook saw him, and, being an ill-natured hussey, ordered him to go about his business or she would scald him. At this time Mr. Fitzwarren came from the Exchange, and began also to scold at the poor boy, bidding him to go to work.

Illustrations by Marcia Brown from *Dick Whittington and His Cat*. Copyright © 1950 by Marcia Brown; copyright renewed © 1978 by Marcia Brown. Reprinted with the permission of Charles Scribner's Sons.

Whittington answered that he should be glad to work if anybody would employ him, and that he should be able if he could get some victuals to eat, for he had had nothing for three days, and he was a poor country boy, and knew nobody, and nobody would employ him.

He then endeavoured to get up, but he was so very weak that he fell down again, which excited so much compassion in the merchant that he ordered the servants to take him in and give him some meat and drink, and let him help the cook to do any dirty work that she had to set him about. People are too apt to reproach those who beg with being idle, but give themselves no concern to put them in the way of getting business to do, or considering whether

they are able to do it, which is not charity.

But we return to Whittington, who would have lived happy in this worthy family had he not been bumped about by the cross cook, who must be always roasting or basting, and when the spit was idle employed her hands upon poor Whittington! At last Miss Alice, his master's daughter, was informed of it, and then she took compassion on the poor boy, and made the servants treat him kindly.

Besides the crossness of the cook, Whittington had another difficulty to get over before he could be happy. He had, by order of his master, a flock-bed placed for him in a garret, where there was a number of rats and mice that often ran over the poor boy's nose and disturbed him in his sleep. After some time, however, a gentleman who came to his master's house gave Whittington a penny for brushing his shoes. This he put into his pocket, being determined to lay it out to the best advantage; and the next day, seeing a woman in the street with a cat under her arm, he ran up to know the price of it. The woman (as the cat was a good mouser) asked a deal of money for it, but on Whittington's telling her he had but a penny in the world, and that he wanted a cat sadly, she let him have it.

This cat Whittington concealed in the garret, for fear she should be beat about by his mortal enemy the cook, and here she soon killed or frightened away the rats and mice, so that the poor boy could now sleep as sound as a top.

Soon after this merchant, who had a ship ready to sail, called for his servants, as his custom was, in order that each of them might venture something to try their luck; and whatever they sent was to pay neither freight nor custom, for he thought justly that God Almighty would bless him the more for his readiness to let the poor partake of his fortune.

All the servants appeared but poor Whittington, who, having neither money nor goods, could not think of sending anything to try his luck; but his good friend Miss Alice, thinking his poverty kept him away, ordered him to be called.

She then offered to lay down something for him, but the merchant told his daughter that

Illustrations by Marcia Brown from *Dick Whittington and His Cat*. Copyright © 1950 by Marcia Brown; copyright renewed © 1978 by Marcia Brown. Reprinted with the permission of Charles Scribner's Sons.

would not do, it must be something of his own. Upon which poor Whittington said he had nothing but a cat which he bought for a penny that was given him. 'Fetch thy cat, boy,' said the merchant, 'and send her.' Whittington brought poor puss and delivered her to the captain, with tears in his eyes, for he said he should now be disturbed by the rats and mice as much as ever. All the company laughed at the adventure but Miss Alice, who pitied the poor boy, and gave him something to buy another cat.

While puss was beating the billows at sea, poor Whittington was severely beaten at home by his tyrannical mistress the cook, who used him so cruelly, and made such game of him for sending his cat to sea, that at last the poor boy determined to run away from his place, and, having packed up the few things he had, he set out very early in the morning on All-Hallows day. He travelled as far as Holloway, and there sat down on a stone to consider what course he should take; but while he was thus ruminating, Bow bells, of which there were only six, began to ring; and he thought their sounds addressed him in this manner:

Turn again, Whittington,
Thrice Lord Mayor of London.'

'Lord Mayor of London!' said he to himself; 'what would not one endure to be Lord Mayor of London, and ride in such a fine coach? Well, I'll go back again, and bear all the pummelling and ill-usage of Cicely rather than miss the opportunity of being Lord Mayor!' So home he went, and happily got into the house and about his business before Mrs. Cicely made her appearance.

We must now follow Miss Puss to the coast of Africa. How perilous are voyages at sea, how uncertain the winds and the waves, and how many accidents attend a naval life!

The ship which had the cat on board was long beaten at sea, and at last, by contrary winds, driven on a part of the coast of Barbary which was inhabited by Moors unknown to the English. These people received our countrymen with civility, and therefore the captain, in order to trade with them, showed them the patterns of the goods he had on board, and sent some of them to the King of the country, who was so well pleased that he sent for the captain and the factor to his palace, which was about a mile from the sea. Here they were placed, according to the custom of the country, on rich carpets, flowered with gold and silver; and the King and Queen being seated at the upper end of the room, dinner was brought in, which consisted of many dishes; but no sooner were the dishes put down but an amazing number of rats and mice came from all quarters, and devoured all the meat in an instant.

The factor, in surprise, turned round to the nobles and asked if these vermin were not offensive. 'Oh! yes,' said they, 'very offensive; and the King would give half his treasure to be freed of them, for they not only destroy his dinner, as you see, but they assault him in his chamber, and even in bed, so that he is obliged to be watched while he is sleeping, for fear of them.'

The factor jumped for joy; he remembered poor Whittington and his cat, and told the King he had a creature on board the ship that would despatch all these vermin immediately. The King's heart heaved so high at the joy which this news gave him that his turban dropped off his head. 'Bring this creature to me,' said he; 'vermin are dreadful in a court, and if she will perform what you say I will load your ship with gold and jewels in exchange for her.' The factor, who knew his business, took this opportunity to set forth the merits of Miss Puss. He told his Majesty that it would be inconvenient to part with her, as, when she was gone, the rats and mice might destroy the goods in the ship — but to oblige his Majesty he would fetch her. 'Run, run,' said the Queen' 'I am impatient to see the dear creature.'

Away flew the factor, while another dinner was providing, and returned with the cat just as the rats and mice were devouring that also. He immediately put down Miss Puss, who killed a great number of them.

The King rejoiced greatly to see his old enemies destroyed by so small a creature, and the Queen was highly pleased, and desired the cat might be brought near that she might look at her. Upon which the factor called 'Pussy, pussy, pussy!' and she came to him. He then presented her to the Queen, who started back, and was afraid to touch a creature who had made such a havoc among the rats and mice; however, when the factor stroked the cat and called 'Pussy, pussy!' the Queen also touched her and cried 'Putty, putty!' for she had not learned English.

He then put her down on the Queen's lap, where she, purring, played with her Majesty's hand, and then sang herself to sleep.

The King having seen the exploits of Miss Puss, and being informed that her kittens would stock the whole country, bargained with the captain and factor for the whole ship's cargo, and then gave them ten times as much for the cat as all the rest amounted to. On which, taking leave of their Majesties and other great personages at court, they sailed with a fair wind for England, whither we must now attend them.

The morn had scarcely dawned when Mr. Fitzwarren arose to count over the cash and settle the business for that day. He had just entered the counting-house, and seated himself at the desk, when somebody came, tap, tap, at the door. 'Who's there?' said Mr. Fitzwarren. 'A friend,' answered the other. 'What friend can come at this unseasonable time?' 'A real friend is never unseasonable,' answered the other. 'I come to bring you good news of your ship *Unicorn*.' The merchant bustled up in such a hurry that he forgot his gout; instantly opened the door, and who should be seen waiting but the captain and factor, with a cabinet of jewels, and a bill of lading, for which the merchant lifted up his eyes and thanked heaven for sending him such a prosperous voyage. Then they told him the adventures of the cat, and showed him the cabinet of jewels which they had brought for Mr. Whittington. Upon which he cried out with great earnestness, but in the most poetical manner:

'Go send him in, and tell him of his fame,
And call him Mr. Whittington by name.'

It is not our business to animadvert upon these lines; we are not critics, but historians. It is sufficient for us that they are the words of Mr. Fitzwarren; and though it is beside our purpose, and perhaps not in our power to prove him a good poet, we shall soon convince the reader that he was a good man, which was a much better character; for when some who were present told him that this treasure was too much for such a poor boy as Whittington, he said; 'God forbid that I should deprive him of a penny; it is his own, and he shall have it to a farthing.' He then ordered Mr. Whittington in, who was at this time cleaning the kitchen and would have excused himself from going into the counting-house, saying the room was swept and his shoes were dirty and full of hob-nails. The merchant, however, made him come in, and ordered a chair to be set for him. Upon which, thinking they intended to make sport of him, as had been too often the case in the kitchen, he besought his master not to mock a poor simple fellow who intended them no harm, but let him go about his business. The merchant, taking him by the hand, said: 'In-deed, Mr. Whittington, I am in earnest with you, and sent for you to congratulate you on your great success. Your cat has procured you more money than I am worth in the world, and may you long enjoy it and be happy!'

At length, being shown the treasure, and convinced by them that all of it belonged to him, he fell upon his knees and thanked the Almighty for his providential care of such a poor and miserable creature. He then laid all the treasure at his master's feet, who refused to take any part of it, but told him he heartily rejoiced at his prosperity, and hoped the wealth he had acquired would be a comfort to him, and would make him happy. He then applied to his mistress, and to his good friend Miss Alice, who refused to take any part of the money, but told him she heartily rejoiced at his good success, and wished him all imaginable felicity. He then gratified the captain, factor, and the ship's crew for the care they had taken of his cargo. He likewise distributed presents to all the servants in the house, not forgetting even his old enemy the cook, though she little de-served it.

After this Mr. Fitzwarren advised Mr. Whittington to send for the necessary people and dress himself like a gentleman, and made him the offer of his house to live in till he could provide himself with a better.

Now it came to pass when Mr. Whittington's face was washed, his hair curled, and he dressed in a rich suit of clothes, that he turned out a genteel young fellow; and, as wealth contributes much to give a man confi-dence, he in a little time dropped the sheepish behaviour which was principally occasioned

by a depression of spirits, and soon grew a sprightly and good companion, insomuch that Miss Alice, who had formerly pitied him, now fell in love with him.

When her father perceived they had this good liking for each other he proposed a match between them, to which both parties cheer-fully consented, and the Lord Mayor, Court of Aldermen, Sheriffs, the Company of Stationers, the Royal Academy of Arts, and a number of eminent merchants attended the ceremony, and were elegantly treated at an entertainment made for that purpose.

History further relates that they lived very happily, had several children, and died at a good old age. Mr. Whittington served Sheriff of London and was three times Lord Mayor. In the last year of his mayoralty he entertained King Henry V. and his Queen, after his con-quest of France, upon which occasion the King, in consideration of Whittington's merit, said: 'Never had prince such a subject;' which being told to Whittington at the table, he replied: 'Never had subject such a king.' His Majesty, out of respect to his good character, conferred the honour of knighthood on him soon after.

Sir Richard many years before his death constantly fed a great number of poor citizens, built a church and a college to it, with a yearly allowance for poor scholars, and near it erected a hospital.

He also built Newgate for criminals, and gave liberally to St. Bartholomew's Hospital and other public charities.

___

"The Boy Who Drew Cats," from Japanese Fairy Tales. *Retold by Lafcadio Hearn and others (New York: Liveright, 1953).*

This Japanese folktale bears many simi-larities to the story of Dick Whittington. Pov-erty forces the boy into the world where cats assist him. However, this boy's cats are not real, but creatures of his imagination; the story thus suggests the power and value of artistic creativity. Ironically, the boy's talent had at first seemed a detriment as he had been dismissed from one temple because of his doo-dling. Unlike the hero of Dennis Lee's poem

"Nicholas Knock," the boy in this tale achieves fulfillment through the exercise of his imagination.

The Boy Who Drew Cats

A long, long time ago, in a small country-village in Japan, there lived a poor farmer and his wife, who were very good people. They had a number of children, and found it very hard to feed them all. The elder son was strong enough when only fourteen years old to help his father; and the little girls learned to help their mother almost as soon as they could walk.

But the youngest child, a little boy, did not seem to be fit for hard work. He was very clever, — cleverer than all his brothers and sisters; but he was quite weak and small, and people said he could never grow very big. So his parents thought it would be better for him to become a priest than to become a farmer. They took him with them to the village-temple one day, and asked the good old priest who lived there, if he would have their little boy for his acolyte, and teach him all that a priest ought to know.

The old man spoke kindly to the lad, and asked him some hard questions. So clever were the answers that the priest agreed to take the little fellow into the temple as an acolyte, and to educate him for the priesthood.

The boy learned quickly what the old priest taught him, and was very obedient in most things. But he had one fault. He liked to draw cats during study-hours, and to draw cats even where cats ought not to have been drawn at all.

Whenever he found himself alone, he drew cats. He drew them on the margins of the priest's books, and on all the screens of the temple, and on the walls, and on the pillars. Several times the priest told him this was not right; but he did not stop drawing cats. He drew them because he could not really help it. He had what is called "the genius of an *artist*," and just for that reason he was not quite fit to be an acolyte; — a good acolyte should study books.

One day after he had drawn some very clever pictures of cats upon a paper screen, the old priest said to him severely: "My boy, you must go away from this temple at once. You will never make a good priest, but perhaps you will become a great artist. Now let me give you a last piece of advice, and be sure you never forget it. *Avoid large places at night; — keep to small!*"

The boy did not know what the priest meant by saying, "*Avoid large places; — keep to small.*" He thought and thought, while he was tying up his little bundle of clothes to go away; but he could not understand those words, and he was afraid to speak to the priest any more, except to say good-by.

He left the temple very sorrowfully, and began to wonder what he should do. If he went straight home he felt sure his father would punish him for having been disobedient to the priest: so he was afraid to go home. All at once he remembered that at the next village, twelve miles away, there was a very big temple. He had heard there were several priests at that temple; and he made up his mind to go to them and ask them to take him for their acolyte.

Now that big temple was closed up but the boy did not know this fact. The reason it had been closed up was that a goblin had frightened the priests away, and had taken possession of the place. Some brave warriors had afterward gone to the temple at night to kill the goblin; but they had never been seen alive again. Nobody had ever told these things to the boy; — so he walked all the way to the village hoping to be kindly treated by the priests.

When he got to the village it was already dark, and all the people were in bed; but he saw the big temple on a hill at the other end of the principal street, and he saw there was a light in the temple. People who tell the story say the goblin used to make the light, in order to tempt lonely travelers to ask for shelter. The boy went at once to the temple, and knocked. There was no sound inside. He knocked and knocked again; but still nobody came. At last he pushed gently at the door, and was quite glad to find that it had not been fastened. So he went in, and saw a lamp burning, — but no priest.

He thought some priest would be sure to come very soon, and he sat down and waited. Then he noticed that everything in the temple was gray with dust, and thickly spun over with cobwebs. So he thought to himself that the priests would certainly like to have an acolyte, to keep the place clean. He wondered why they had allowed everything to get so dusty. What most pleased him, however, were some big white screens, good to paint cats upon. Though he was tired, he looked at once for a writing-box, and found one, and ground some ink, and began to paint cats.

He painted a great many cats upon the screens; and then he began to feel very, very sleepy. He was just on the point of lying down to sleep beside one of the screens, when he suddenly remembered the words, *"Avoid large places; — keep to small!"*

The temple was very large; he was all alone; and as he thought of these words, — though he could not quite understand them — he began to feel for the first time a little afraid; and he resolved to look for a *small place* in which to sleep. He found a little cabinet, with a sliding door, and went into it, and shut himself up. Then he lay down and fell fast asleep.

Very late in the night he was awakened by a most terrible noise, — a noise of fighting and screaming. It was so dreadful that he was afraid even to look through a chink of the little cabinet: he lay very still, holding his breath for fright.

The light that had been in the temple went out; but the awful sounds continued, and became more awful, and all the temple shook. After a long time silence came; but the boy was still afraid to move. He did not move until the light of the morning sun shone into the cabinet through the chinks of the little door.

Then he got out of his hiding-place very cautiously, and looked about. The first thing he saw was that all the floor of the temple was covered with blood. And then he saw, lying dead in the middle of it, an enormous, monstrous rat, — a goblin-rat, — bigger than a cow!

But who or what could have killed it? There was no man or other creature to be seen. Suddenly the boy observed that the mouths of all the cats he had drawn the night before, were red and wet with blood. Then he knew that the goblin had been killed by the cats which he had drawn. And then also, for the first time,

he understood why the wise old priest had said to him, *"Avoid large places at night; — keep to small."*

Afterward that boy became a very famous artist. Some of the cats which he drew are still shown to travelers in Japan.

——

"The Half-Chick," from The Green Fairy Book. *Edited by Andrew Lang (London: Longmans, Green, and Co., 1892).*

Unlike such an improbable hero as Hans Christian Andersen's Ugly Duckling (who reaches self-fulfillment), the central figure of this Spanish linear journey reaches an ironic end as a result of his disobedience, unkindness, and egotism. In addition to being a parable about the evils of these unredeeming qualities, the tale also exists as a pourquoi story explaining the origin of a weather-cock whose unhappy situation atop a Madrid church serves as a warning to others with similar faults.

The Half-Chick

Once upon a time there was a handsome black Spanish hen, who had a large brood of chickens. They were all fine, plump little birds, except the youngest, who was quite unlike his brothers and sisters. Indeed, he was such a strange, queer-looking creature, that when he first chipped his shell his mother could scarcely believe her eyes, he was so different from the twelve other fluffy, downy, soft little chicks who nestled under her wings. This one looked just as if he had been cut in two. He had only one leg, and one wing, and one eye, and he had half a head and half a beak. His mother shook her head sadly as she looked at him and said:

'My youngest born is only a half-chick. He can never grow up a tall handsome cock like his brothers. They will go out into the world and rule over poultry yards of their own; but this poor little fellow will always have to stay at home with his mother.' And she called him Medio Pollito, which is Spanish for half-chick.

Now though Medio Pollito was such an odd, helpless-looking little thing, his mother soon found that he was not at all willing to remain under her wing and protection. Indeed, in character he was as unlike his brothers and sisters as he was in appearance. They were good, obedient chickens, and when the old hen chicked after them, they chirped and ran back to her side. But Medio Pollito had a roving spirit in spite of his one leg, and when his mother called to him to return to the coop, he pretended that he could not hear, because he had only one ear.

When she took the whole family out for a walk in the fields, Medio Pollito would hop away by himself, and hide among the Indian corn. Many an anxious minute his brothers and sisters had looking for him, while his mother ran to and fro cackling in fear and dismay.

As he grew older he became more self-willed and disobedient, and his manner to his mother was often very rude, and his temper to the other chickens very disagreeable.

One day he had been out for a longer expedition than usual in the fields. On his return he strutted up to his mother with the peculiar little hop and kick which was his way of walking, and cocking his one eye at her in a very bold way he said:

'Mother I am tired of this life in a dull farm-yard, with nothing but a dreary maize field to look at. I'm off to Madrid to see the King.'

'To Madrid, Medio Pollito!' exclaimed his mother; 'why, you silly chick, it would be a long journey for a grown-up cock, and a poor little thing like you would be tired out before you had gone half the distance. No, no, stay at home with your mother, and some day, when you are bigger, we will go a little journey together.'

But Medio Pollito had made up his mind, and he would not listen to his mother's advice, nor to the prayers and entreaties of his brothers and sisters.

'What is the use of our all crowding each other up in this poky little place?' he said. 'When I have a fine courtyard of my own at the King's palace, I shall perhaps ask some of you to come and pay me a short visit,' and scarcely waiting to say good-bye to his family, away he stumped down the high road that led to Madrid.

'Be sure that you are kind and civil to everyone you meet,' called his mother, running after him; but he was in such a hurry to be off, that he did not wait to answer her, or even to look back.

A little later in the day, as he was taking a short cut through a field, he passed a stream. Now the stream was all choked up, and overgrown with weeds and water-plants, so that its waters could not flow freely.

'Oh! Medio Pollito,' it cried, as the half-chick hopped along its banks, 'do come and help me by clearing away these weeds.'

'Help you, indeed!' exclaimed Medio Pollito, tossing his head, and shaking the few feathers in his tail. 'Do you think I have nothing to do but to waste my time on such trifles? Help yourself, and don't trouble busy travellers. I am off to Madrid to see the King,' and hoppity-kick, hoppity-kick, away stumped Medio Pollito.

A little later he came to a fire that had been left by some gipsies in a wood. It was burning very low, and would soon be out.

'Oh! Medio Pollito,' cried the fire, in a weak, wavering voice as the half-chick approached, 'in a few minutes I shall go quite out, unless you put some sticks and dry leaves upon me. Do help me, or I shall die!'

'Help you, indeed! answered Medio Pollito. 'I have other things to do. Gather sticks for yourself, and don't trouble me. I am off to Madrid to see the King,' and hoppity-kick, hoppity-kick, away stumped Medio Pollito.

The next morning, as he was getting near Madrid, he passed a large chestnut tree, in whose branches the wind was caught and entangled. 'Oh! Medio Pollito,' called the wind, 'do hop up here, and help me to get free of these branches. I cannot come away, and it is so uncomfortable.'

'It is your own fault for going there,' answered Medio Pollito. 'I can't waste all my morning stopping here to help you. Just shake yourself off, and don't hinder me, for I am off to Madrid to see the King,' and hoppity-kick, hoppity-kick, away stumped Medio Pollito in great glee, for the towers and roofs of Madrid were now in sight. When he entered the town he saw before him a great splendid house, with soldiers standing before the gates. This he knew must be the King's palace, and he determined to hop up to the front gate and wait there until the King came out. But as he was hopping past one of the back windows the King's cook saw him:

'Here is the very thing I want,' he exclaimed, 'for the King has just sent a message to say that he must have chicken broth for his dinner,' and opening the window he stretched out his arm, caught Medio Pollito, and popped him into the broth-pot that was standing near the fire. Oh! how wet and clammy the water felt as it went over Medio Pollito's head, making his feathers cling to his side.

'Water, water!' he cried in his despair, 'do have pity upon me and do not wet me like this.'

'Ah! Medio Pollito,' replied the water, 'you would not help me when I was a little stream away on the fields, now you must be punished.'

Then the fire began to burn and scald Medio Pollito, and he danced and hopped from one side of the pot to the other, trying to get away from the heat, and crying out in pain:

'Fire, fire! do not scorch me like this; you can't think how it hurts.'

'Ah! Medio Pollito,' answered the fire, 'you would not help me when I was dying away in the wood. You are being punished.'

At last, just when the pain was so great that Medio Pollito thought he must die, the cook lifted up the lid of the pot to see if the broth was ready for the King's dinner.

'Look here!' he cried in horror, 'this chicken is quite useless. It is burnt to a cinder. I can't send it up to the royal table;' and opening the window he threw Medio Pollito out into the street. But the wind caught him up, and whirled him through the air so quickly that Medio Pollito could scarcely breathe, and his heart beat against his side till he thought it would break.

'Oh, wind!' at last he gasped out, 'if you hurry me along like this you will kill me. Do let me rest a moment, or ——' but he was so breathless that he could not finish his sentence.

'Ah! Medio Pollito,' replied the wind, 'when I was caught in the branches of the chestnut tree you would not help me; now you are punished.' And he swirled Medio Pollito over the roofs of the houses till they reached the highest church in the town, and there he left him fastened to the top of the steeple.

And there stands Medio Pollito to this day. And if you go to Madrid, and walk through the streets till you come to the highest church, you will see Medio Pollito perched on his one leg on the steeple, with his one wing drooping at his side, and gazing sadly out of his one eye over the town.

——

"Coyote Loses His Dinner," from Coyote Tales. *Adapted by Hettie Jones, illustrated by Louis Mofsie (New York: Holt, Rinehart, and Winston, 1974).*

Coyote, the major trickster-hero of the Plains Indians, has a dual nature. At times he is the helper, using his wits to aid people; at others, he is filled with mischief, causing discomfort to others in his selfish quest for food. In the latter case, his plans often go wrong and he becomes victim, as does Anansi in many African tales. "Roadrunner" cartoons emphasize this aspect of his life. The following tale begins, as do most of the Coyote tales, with the central figure trotting across the plains by himself. In his greed, he violates the Native belief that one should kill no more than one needs. Adventures similar to those of Coyote happen to such other North American tricksters as Old Man (Nape), Raven, Wisakijak, and Sayanday.

Coyote Loses His Dinner

Coyote was so hungry he could hardly walk. He dragged himself up the steep hill he had decided to climb and looked down from the top. A large flock of geese was feeding at the edge of a lake below.

"What luck!" Coyote sat down to rest and planned how he would trick them. "First I'll pretend to be in mourning." Taking his knife, he scratched himself in various places and cut off his hair. Then he picked up a large stick, and leaning heavily on it, made his way slowly down the hill.

To the geese he appeared to be someone bent over with sorrow. As he drew near they noticed he was crying. "What's the matter?"

one asked. Soon all the others stopped eating and came to investigate.

Coyote sat down in the grass. "My brother has been killed," he answered between sobs. "I am out to revenge his death, and I don't care if I get killed myself." He wailed mightily, making as much noise as possible. "Last night, I dreamed that by the shore of a big lake I would find my brothers the geese. And I dreamed——" he raised his voice to a shout, "that they would join my war party."

The geese began to honk excitedly, for they were not often included in such an effort. When their chief came forward to ask if all this were true, Coyote repeated his story.

"But I want only the biggest and fattest of your tribe to come," he added slyly. "I don't want any weak geese fighting on my side."

"That is agreed," said the chief. "I will even accompany you myself."

"Good," said Coyote. "Before we start, though, we should hold a dance here. I'll show you how."

Since the geese were extremely curious, Coyote could do exactly as he pleased with them. In the outermost circle he placed those with the fattest breasts. Inside in the next ring he put the next best, and so on, until four circles were formed. Then he warned them: "This dance has a special rule which you must not break, or we won't be able to perform it. Will you obey?"

"Of course," said the silly geese.

"Well then, while I am singing, you must dance with your eyes closed. If you open your eyes for any reason, they will turn red."

The geese closed their eyes. Coyote beat his drum and began singing:

> *Dance with your eyes closed*
> *No red eye, shall we spy,*
> *Dance with your eyes closed.*

The geese danced on with their eyes closed. It was quite a sight. As they danced, Coyote walked around chanting, "Dance with your eyes closed," killing each goose in the first circle by wringing its neck. "No red eye, shall we spy," Coyote sang as he killed all the geese in the second circle. On and on he chanted, until

soon all the geese in the third circle were dead. "No red eye, shall we . . ."

Suddenly one of the dancers in the last circle stumbled on a stone and accidentally opened his eyes. Seeing his dead brothers, he ran for the lake, screaming to those who were left, "Run! Run for your lives! Coyote is killing us all!"

The geese fled, honking fearfully and flapping their wings until they were well out over the lake where Coyote couldn't reach them. But Coyote didn't care. "Don't worry," he called, "I don't want any more of you — I've got enough here!" He set to work tying up his prey, feeling very pleased with himself.

With the geese slung over his shoulder, Coyote walked along looking for a good place to have his feast. He was delighted to find a pleasant clearing full of soft, thick grass where he built a fire. He put some of the geese up on spits; the rest he covered with hot ashes. Soon a delicious aroma filled the clearing. Coyote, his mouth watering, lay down to rest until the food was ready.

He definitely wasn't planning to have company for dinner. But the good smell wafted through the woods like an invitation, and soon Fox arrived at the edge of the woods and stood peeking through the trees. Knowing how tricky Coyote was and seeing the geese, she decided it would be fun to outtrick Coyote. First she bandaged one of her legs, making it look horribly swollen. Then she waited until the geese were done and hobbled into the clearing, leaning on a stick and looking as miserable as she dared.

Coyote jumped in alarm, but noticing Fox's injured leg he said kindly, "Come here, my poor little sister."

Fox dragged herself to the fire and lay down panting. She gazed hungrily at the geese. Coyote, seeing her hungry glances, covered his food with leaves. Then he tried to change the subject. "Little sister, how did you hurt your leg?" he asked.

"I fell jumping over some rocks when I was out looking for food," answered Fox, tears gathering in her eyes.

Though Coyote felt sorry for her, he never gave up a good meal easily. "If you really want

Illustration by Louis Mosfie, "Coyote Loses His Dinner" from *Coyote Tales*, adapted by hettie Jones. Copyright © 1974. Reprinted by permission of Holt, Rinehart and Winston, New York.

my geese, little sister," he said slyly, "why don't we race for them? Once around the lake — whoever wins gets the geese."

"But my leg," Fox whined pitifully. "I couldn't possibly run. I'm not even sure I can get up!"

Now that was a different problem to consider. Coyote knew he had to get Fox out of the clearing — why, he wouldn't be able to eat a bite with her sitting there watching him! "I'll tie a big stone to my foot and then we'll be even," he offered.

"I think even a stone-tied leg can beat this bad one of mine," sighed Fox, "but that is very generous of you. I'll run then, even though my leg hurts." Grasping the stick, she pulled herself to her feet and managed a few limping steps.

"What a race this is going to be," Coyote thought, observing Fox's condition. "Poor little sister doesn't look able to run past the next tree." As he looked for and found a suitable stone, he felt rather sorry for her. And so he told Fox she could have a head start.

Leaving Coyote to tie on the stone, Fox went limping away slowly. As soon as she was hidden by the woods, she tore off the bandage and raced away. Keeping to the woods, she ran all around the lake back to the clearing.

Ah, how delicious those geese were! She ate all of them down to the bone. "Mmmm, that Coyote's a fine cook — I must remember to tell him," Fox laughed. "But not right now," she added, hearing a noise not too far away. "Right now I'd better get out of here!" Hastily she covered over all the bones with leaves and hid.

Moments later Coyote crashed into the clearing. With a sigh of relief he threw himself down in the soft grass, untied the stone and irritably tossed it into the bushes. "It's terrible," he said, rubbing his ankle. "I had to go through all this just to eat my own dinner, and now I'm almost too tired . . . . But I may as well get started" — he reached under the leaves — "or that Fox will be back limping around and looking pitiful, trying to . . . " His voice trailed off as he gazed at the bone he had pulled out. He stared at it as though it were something difficult to recognize. "Oh," he said finally, "a bone." And then, "Someone must have eaten one of my geese." He threw the bone over his shoulder and, reaching in again, grabbed another. "More bones!" He jumped up and frantically dug through the leaves.

"All bones!" He kicked at them. "Nothing but bones! All my geese . . . that Fox . . . I've been tricked!" In a fury Coyote ran howling through the woods down to the lake, calling for Fox to appear and swearing to do away with her.

On the opposite side stood Fox, grinning and patting her full stomach. "Coyote!" She waved and bounded down to the shore with no trace of a limp. "Thanks for dinner, little brother! It was delicious. You're a fine cook!"

"Come back here, Fox ... you ... youoooo ..." Coyote's voice rose in a howl.

"You think you can fool everyone, but this time I fooled you, *little brother*," Fox teased.

"No one can fool me and get away with it," Coyote cried.

"But I did!" Fox shouted triumphantly as she disappeared through the trees. "And one day you may even be fooled again!"

"Never!" yelled Coyote. "No one will ever fool me again!"

And still hungry, he went along.

―――――

"The Pied Piper of Hamelin," from The Complete Poetical Works of Browning, *by Robert Browning (Boston: Houghton, Mifflin, 1895).*

This version of "The Pied Piper," by nineteenth century English poet Robert Browning, illustrates the consequences of breaking a trust. In their smugness and greed, the members of the town council underestimate the magical powers of the unassuming musician they employ. As is often the case in folktales, children are the innocent victims of the failings of adults; in this instance they make an ironic linear journey. Other stories which deal with plagues of rats are "The History of Whittington" and Gail Haley's award winning picture book The Post Office Cat. *Robert McCloskey has created deliberate parallels to this story in "Nothing New Under the Sun (Hardly)."*

The Pied Piper of Hamelin

I

Hamelin Town's in Brunswick,
By famous Hanover city;
The river Weser, deep and wide,
Washes its wall on the southern side;
A pleasanter spot you never spied;
But, when begins my ditty,
Almost five hundred years ago,
To see the townsfolk suffer so
    From vermin, was a pity.

II

Rats!
They fought the dogs and killed the cats,
    And bit the babies in the cradles,
And ate the cheeses out of the vats,
    And licked the soup from the cooks' own
      ladles,
Split open the kegs of salted sprats,
Made nests inside men's Sunday hats,
And even spoiled the women's chats
    By drowning their speaking
    With shrieking and squeaking
In fifty different sharps and flats.

III

At last the people in a body
    To the Town Hall came flocking:
" 'T is clear," cried they, "our Mayor's a noddy;
    And as for our Corporation — shocking
To think we buy gowns lined with ermine
For dolts that can't or won't determine
What's best to rid us of our vermin!
You hope, because you're old and obese,
To find in the furry civic robe ease?
Rouse up, sirs! Give your brains a racking
To find the remedy we're lacking,
Or, sure as fate, we'll send you packing!"
At this the Mayor and Corporation
Quaked with a mighty consternation.

IV

An hour they sat in council;
    At length the Mayor broke silence:
    "For a guilder I'd my ermine gown sell,
    I wish I were a mile hence!
It's easy to bid one rack one's brain —
I'm sure my poor head aches again,
I've scratched it so, and all in vain.

Oh for a trap, a trap, a trap!"
Just as he said this, what should hap
At the chamber-door but a gentle tap?
"Bless us," cried the Mayor, "what's that?"
(With the Corporation as he sat,
Looking little though wondrous fat;
Nor brighter was his eye, nor moister
Than a too-long-opened oyster,
Save when at noon his paunch grew mutinous
For a plate of turtle green and glutinous)
"Only a scraping of shoes on the mat?
Anything like the sound of a rat
Makes my heart go pit-a-pat!"

V

"Come in!" — the Mayor cried, looking
    bigger:
And in did come the strangest figure!
His queer long coat from heel to head
Was half of yellow and half of red,
And he himself was tall and thin,
With sharp blue eyes, each like a pin,
And light loose hair, yet swarthy skin,
No tuft on cheek nor beard on chin,
But lips where smiles went out and in;
There was no guessing his kith and kin:
And nobody could enough admire
The tall man and his quaint attire.
Quoth one: "It's as my great-grandsire,
Starting up at the Trump of Doom's tone,
Had walked this way from his painted
tombstone!"

VI

He advanced to the council-table:
And, "Please your honors," said he, "I'm
    able,
By means of a secret charm, to draw
All creatures living beneath the sun,
That creep or swim or fly or run,
After me so as you never saw!
And I chiefly use my charm
On creatures that do people harm,
The mole and toad and newt and viper;
And people call me the Pied Piper.
(And here they noticed round his neck
A scarf of red and yellow stripe,
To match with his coat of the self-same cheque;

And at the scarf's end hung a pipe;
And his fingers, they noticed, were ever
straying
As if impatient to be playing
Upon this pipe, as low it dangled
Over his vesture so old-fangled.)
"Yet," said he, "poor piper as I am,
In Tartary I freed the Cham,
Last June, from his huge swarms of gnats;
I eased in Asia the Nizam
Of a monstrous brood of vampire-bats:
And as for what your brain bewilders,
If I can rid your town of rats
Will you give me a thousand guilders?"
"One? fifty thousand!" — was the exclamation
Of the astonished Mayor and Corporation.

VII

Into the street the Piper stept,
    Smiling first a little smile,
As if he knew what magic slept
    In his quiet pipe the while;
Then, like a musical adept,
To blow the pipe his lips he wrinkled,
And green and blue his sharp eyes twinkled,
Like a candle-flame where salt is sprinkled;
And ere three shrill notes the pipe uttered,
You heard as if an army muttered;
And the muttering grew to a grumbling;
And the grumbling grew to a mighty rumbling;
And out of the houses the rats came tumbling.
Great rats, small rats, lean rats, brawny rats,
Brown rats, black rats, gray rats, tawny rats,
Grave old plodders, gay young friskers,
    Fathers, mothers, uncles, cousins,
Cocking tails and pricking whiskers,
    Families by tens and dozens,
Brothers, sisters, husbands, wives —
Followed the Piper for their lives.
From street to street he piped advancing,
And step for step they followed dancing,
Until they came to the river Weser,
Wherein all plunged and perished!
— Save one who, stout as Julius Caesar,
Swam across and lived to carry
(As he, the manuscript he cherished)
To Rat-land home his commentary:
Which was, "At the first shrill notes of the pipe,
I heard a sound as of scraping tripe,

And putting apples, wondrous ripe,
Into a cider-press's gripe:
And a moving away of pickle-tub-boards,
And a leaving ajar of conserve-cupboards,
And a drawing the corks of train-oil-flasks,
And a breaking the hoops of butter-casks:
And it seemed as if a voice
(Sweeter far than by harp or by psaltery
Is breathed) called out, 'Oh rats, rejoice!
The world is grown to one vast drysaltery!
So munch on, crunch on, take your nuncheon,
Breakfast, supper, dinner, luncheon!'
And just as a bulky sugar-puncheon,
All ready staved, like a great sun shone
Glorious scarce an inch before me,
Just as methought it said, 'Come, bore me!'
—I found the Weser rolling o'er me.''

VIII

You should have heard the Hamelin people
Ringing the bells till they rocked the steeple.
"Go," cried the Mayor, "and get long poles,
Poke out the nests and block up the holes!
Consult with carpenters and builders,
And leave in our town not even a trace
Of the rats!" — when suddenly, up the face
Of the Piper perked in the market-place,
With a, "First, if you please, my thousand
        guilders!"

IX

A thousand guilders! The Mayor looked blue;
So did the Corporation too.
For council dinners made rare havoc
With Claret, Moselle, Vin-de-Grave, Hock;
And half the money would replenish
Their cellar's biggest butt with Rhenish.
To pay this sum to a wandering fellow
With a gypsy coat of red and yellow!
"Beside," quoth the Mayor with a knowing
        wink,
"Our business was done at the river's brink;
We saw with our eyes the vermin sink,
And what's dead can't come to life, I think.
So, friend, we're not the folks to shrink
From the duty of giving you something for
        drink,

And a matter of money to put in your poke;
But as for the guilders, what we spoke
Of them, as you very well know, was in joke.
Beside, our losses have made us thrifty.
A thousand guilders! Come, take fifty!"

X

The Piper's face fell, and he cried,
"No trifling! I can't wait, beside!
I've promised to visit by dinner time
Bagdat, and accept the prime
Of the Head-Cook's pottage, all he's rich in,
For having left, in the Caliph's kitchen,
Of a nest of scorpions no survivor:
With him I proved no bargain-driver,
With you, don't think I'll bate a stiver!
And folks who put me in a passion
May find me pipe after another fashion."

XI

"How?" cried the Mayor, "d'ye think I brook
Being worse treated than a Cook?
Insulted by a lazy ribald
With idle pipe and vesture piebald?
You threaten us, fellow? Do your worst,
Blow your pipe there till you burst!"

XII

Once more he stept into the street,
        And to his lips again
Laid his long pipe of smooth straight cane;
        And ere he blew three notes (such sweet
Soft notes as yet musician's cunning
        Never gave the enraptured air)
There was a rustling that seemed like a bustling
Of merry crowds justling at pitching and hus-
        tling;
Small feet were pattering, wooden shoes clat-
        tering,
Little hands clapping and little tongues chat-
        tering,
And, like fowls in a farm-yard when barley is
        scattering,
Out came the children running.
All the little boys and girls,
With rosy cheeks and flaxen curls,
And sparkling eyes and teeth like pearls,

Tripping and skipping, ran merrily after
The wonderful music with shouting and laugh-
        ter.

XIII

The Mayor was dumb, and the Council stood
As if they were changed into blocks of wood,
Unable to move a step, or cry
To the children merrily skippping by,
— Could only follow with the eye
That joyous crowd at the Piper's back.
But how the Mayor was on the rack,
And the wretched Council's bosoms beat,
As the Piper turned from the High Street
To where the Weser rolled its waters
Right in the way of their sons and daughters!
However, he turned from South to West,
And to Koppelberg Hill his steps addressed,
And after him the children pressed;
Great was the joy in every breast.
"He never can cross that mighty top!
He's forced to let the piping drop,
And we shall see our children stop!"
When, lo, as they reached the mountain-side,
A wondrous portal opened wide,
As if a cavern was suddenly hollowed;
And the Piper advanced and the children fol-
        lowed,
And when all were in to the very last,
The door in the mountain-side shut fast.
Did I say, all? No! One was lame,
And could not dance the whole of the way;
And in after years, if you would blame
His sadness, he was used to say, —
"It's dull in our town since my playmates left!
I can't forget that I'm bereft
Of all the pleasant sights they see,
Which the Piper also promised me.
For he led us, he said, to a joyous land,
Joining the town and just at hand,
Where waters gushed and fruit-trees grew
And flowers put forth a fairer hue,
And everything was strange and new,
The sparrows were brighter than peacocks
        here,
And their dogs outran our fallow deer,
And honey-bees had lost their stings,
And horses were born with eagles' wings:
And just as I became assured

My lame foot would be speedily cured,
The music stopped and I stood still,
And found myself outside the hill,
Left alone against my will,
To go now limping as before,
And never hear of that country more!"

XIV

Alas, alas for Hamelin!
    There came into many a burgher's pate
    A text which says that heaven's gate
    Opes to the rich at as easy rate
As the needle's eye takes a camel in!
The Mayor sent East, West, North and South,
To offer the Piper, by word of mouth,
    Wherever it was men's lot to find him,
Silver and gold to his heart's content,
If he'd only return the way he went,
    And bring the children behind him.
But when they saw 't was a lost endeavor,
And Piper and dancers were gone forever,
They made a decree that lawyers never
    Should think their records dated duly
If, after the day of the month and year,
These words did not as well appear,
"And so long after what happened here
    On the Twenty-second of July,
Thirteen hundred and seventy-six:"
And the better in memory to fix
The place of the children's last retreat,
They called it, the Pied Piper's Street —
Where any one playing on pipe or tabor
Was sure for the future to lose his labor.
Nor suffered they hostelry or tavern
    To shock with mirth a street so solemn;
But opposite the place of the cavern
    They wrote the story on a column,
And on the great church-window painted
The same, to make the world acquainted
How their children were stolen away,
And there it stands to this very day.
And I must not omit to say
That in Transylvania there's a tribe
Of alien people who ascribe
The outlandish ways and dress
On which their neighbors lay such stress,
To their fathers and mothers having risen
Out of some subterraneous prison

Into which they were trepanned
Long time ago in a mighty band
Out of Hamelin town in Brunswick land,
But how or why, they don't understand.

XV

So, Willy, let me and you be wipers
Of scores out with all men — especially pipers!
And, whether they pipe us free from rats or
    from mice,
If we've promised them aught, let us keep our
    promise!

―――――

"Mayor Gimpel's Golden Shoes," from More
Wise Men of Helm and Their Merry Tales.
*Edited by Hannah Goodman (New York:
Berhrman House, 1965).*

*Yiddish people delight in the stories of
Helm, the legendary valley of simpletons.
These droll stories full of pranks, wit, and
proverbs most often leave issues to be settled
by the reader. The humorously curious intel-
lects of Helm inquire: "What kind of order
is that in the world? Why does God send snow
and frost upon the world in the winter time,
which is a hard time for people as it is?
Couldn't He send the frost and snow in summer time when it's hot? I say it's unjust."*

*"Mayor Gimpel's Golden Shoes" epito-
mizes the ingenuity of the characters who
populate Yiddish folktales. Mayor Gimpel's
absurd quest for respect reveals in him the
comic archetype of the Fool or Simpleton. The
tone of this comic tale, in which a child is superior to foolish and pretentious adults, is
similar to that of Hans Christian Andersen's
"The Emperor's New Clothes," and Astrid
Lindgren's "Pippi Goes to the Circus."*

Mayor Gimpel's Golden Shoes

The railroad brought a restlessness to Helm.
It started with Gimpel, who was not only the
richest man in Helm, but a descendant of its
first settler. He was a Helmite: the son, the
grandson, and the great, great grandson of a
Helmite! Besides all that, or because of it, he
had been mayor for fifteen years.

He called a Town Meeting and laid a griev-
ance before the open assembly.

"I have been mayor of our city for fifteen
years. When we have a Town Meeting I sit at
the head of the table, so everybody knows I'm
mayor and pays me the proper respect. But
when I walk in the street, I'm dressed like anybody else and nobody recognizes me. No one
gives me the honor due me, not even the children. At the railroad station every official wears
a uniform to show his rank. Even the lowliest
has a cockade on his hat. But look at me! Do I
have anything to signify my station and importance? I demand a uniform fitting to my high
office!"

Everybody agreed that Gimpel was right.
But what insignia should he be given? They discussed and argued, they reasoned and debated,
and came to no conclusion. They couldn't
imitate the uniforms of the Gentile officials.
Isn't it written, "Neither shall ye walk in their
statutes?" And what uniforms are there besides
those of the Gentile officials?

After discussing this for seven nights, it was
decided to turn the question over to a committee of three: Shloime the Scientist, Pinya
the Philosopher, and Berel the Beadle. They
were given seven weeks to study the matter
and bring in a report.

At the end of seven weeks, a Town Meeting was called and Shloime read the committee's recommendation.

"We have thought over the problem carefully. We can't recommend a fine satin *kaftan*
for the mayor, for this is the garment which
distinguishes the Rabbi of the town. We don't
want people to confuse the two. The Rabbi is
honored for his Torah, for his learning, and
Gimpel demands *kovod*, honor for his wealth
and station. These are different kinds of honor.

"Neither can we recommend a fine fur hat
with twelve tails, for that is the distinction of
a Chasidic Rabbi — the badge of Holiness. We
don't want anyone to confuse the mayor with
the Chasidic Rabbi. The Rabbi is of holy stock,
but Gimpel is only rich and famous. Therefore,
we recommend a pair of golden shoes for our

mayor. When he wears them, everybody will know that he is Gimpel, different from everybody else, the mayor of the town, to whom respect is due."

The people acclaimed the recommendation.

In two weeks, the shoes were ready. Gimpel the Mayor put them on and went for a stroll. That self-same evening he called a Town Meeting.

"I don't want to belittle, God forbid, the labor and the merit of the distinguished committee," he announced. "They meant well. The idea would probably work in Warsaw, where the streets are paved and washed every day. But here, in Helm! Our city is at the foot of the mountain. The streets are muddy in the spring and autumn, dusty in the summer, and wet with snow in the winter. I took a short stroll today. Before I had gone twenty steps, the shoes became muddy! Even the goldsmith would not have known that I wore his golden shoes. Therefore, no one recognized me and no one paid me honor. In the summer the shoes will get dusty; in the autumn they will be muddy, and in the winter they will be covered with snow. So what good do they do me?"

Shloime the Scientist was calm. "This is easily remedied. We'll order a of pair of leather overshoes. You'll wear them over the golden shoes, to protect them from becoming muddy."

"An excellent idea!" the whole of Helm cried. "Excellent!" repeated the elders seated about the table.

No sooner said than done! Gimpel put leather overshoes on the golden shoes and strolled in the muddy streets of Helm. The same day he called a Town Meeting.

"Now, what's the trouble?" wondered the burghers of Helm.

Well, there was trouble, indeed!

"True, my dear Helmites, the overshoes did protect the golden shoes from mud," Gimpel complained. "But they also covered their glitter, so that no one recognized me or paid me honor."

This was a knotty problem. The Helmites sat in council for seven days and seven nights. Finally, they hit upon an idea. The shoemaker would make holes in the overshoes so that the gold would show through, and everybody would know who the wearer was.

But it didn't work again! A Town Meeting had to be called the same day that Gimpel ventured out with the perforated overshoes. He explained, "True, when I put on the overshoes with the little round holes at home, the gold shone and glistened very impressively. But no sooner did I go out to the street . . . well, nothing prevented the mud from going through the holes! No one saw the gold. No one knew that I was Gimpel the Mayor, and nobody paid me any honor."

Now the Helmites began to think in earnest. This required real thought. After seven days and nights, a solution was offered by Reuben the Water-Carrier, the rising star of Helm.

"Let's stuff the holes in the overshoes with straw. That will prevent the mud from getting on the shoes."

"It's an idea," they all agreed. "But it has a big defect. The straw will also cover the glitter of the gold." Reuben argued that this might be so, but everybody who saw the overshoes with holes stuffed with straw would suspect that there was something behind the overshoes.

The Helmites thought differently. People might take Gimpel for a common pauper who wore shoes with holes stuffed with straw to keep his feet dry. Then Abba, the Mayor's grandson, came up with a brilliant idea.

"My grandfather, the mayor, should go back to his ordinary leather shoes and, over them, the overshoes with the holes stuffed with straw. But, so that people won't mistake him for a pauper, he should also wear the golden shoes—not on his feet, but on his hands—the left shoe on his left hand and the right shoe on his right hand. The golden shoes will never get dirty. People will see the shining gold and will know that he's Gimpel, the mayor of the town, and they'll give him his due honor."

If you ever go to Helm, and see a man walking in torn shoes, the holes stuffed with straw, you might suspect that he is the mayor of the town who neglected to put the golden shoes on his hands. He left them at home, where his wife guards them.

"The Daughter of the Dragon King," from Tales of a Chinese Grandmother, *by Frances Carpenter. Illustrated by Malthe Hasselriis (New York: Doubleday, 1937).*

This story, which begins as an ironic circular journey — the hero returns home having failed his examinations — ends as a linear journey with the boy turned into a dragon. Unlike European tales, in which dragons are evil characters, Oriental stories treat them as forces of good. The framework of this adaptation of the folktale is important: by telling the story to her grandchildren, the old lady is providing both cultural background and moral instruction. Maria Campbell, in her literary myth Little Badger and the Fire Spirit, *makes similar use of the storyteller framework.*

The Daughter of the Dragon King

"How was it with Scholar Shih in the hall of learning today, Ah Shung?" asked Grandmother Ling one winter afternoon as she sat with her grandchildren gathered about her.

"It was good, Lao Lao," the boy answered. "Scholar Shih was graciously pleased with me. With my back turned so that I could not get help from his face, I could repeat without stopping four whole pages of the sayings of our wise teacher, Confucius. I have brought you some of the words I made with my writing brush."

The boy unrolled a strip of thin paper upon which he had painted a column of large word symbols, one below the other. Each stroke and dot was carefully done. Yu Lang looked at them admiringly. The little girl thought her brother's words looked as beautiful as the writing in the scroll poems that hung on the walls of the family hall. Indeed, all the younger children looked up to Ah Shung because he was learning to read and to write.

"You have done well, Little Bear," Grandmother Ling said, nodding her head in approval. "Your words are well made." The old woman was a beautiful writer herself. When she wrote she took as great care with each brush stroke as when she painted delicate

pictures on strips of thin silk. Much pleased with her grandson, she rose from her chair and crossed the room to a red lacquer cabinet. From one of its many small drawers she took out a folded piece of soft yellow silk.

"This is for the young scholar, a reward for good work," she said, and she put the silk into the boy's hands. The other children gathered about him as he unfolded it. It was a triangle of yellow with a gorgeous green dragon twisting its snaky body about on it and trying to grasp a pearl with its curving claws.

"Our flag!" Ah Shung exclaimed in delight. "I shall hang it over our brick bed, Yu Lang. It will be good to have this dragon there to protect us from the bad spirits."

These Chinese children loved dragons. They believed that these fairy-tale creatures really lived down under the waters, back in the mountains, and up in the sky. Just because they had never met a live dragon did not prove to Ah Shung and Yu Lang that they did not exist. They had seen dragons embroidered on satins and silks. Dragons were carved on the tables and chairs in the Hall of the Ancestors, and even on the bed frame in the Old Old One's room. Dragons on pictures, dragons painted on china, and dragons in their grandmother's stories made these flying serpents real to them.

Ah Shung and Yu Lang knew that dragons fighting in the sky made the thunder and shook the rain out of the clouds. Dragons brought good luck and kept unfriendly spirits away. The Emperor himself had chosen the dragon as his own special sign. The dragon was the national animal of all the land, and no one in the Flowery Kingdom doubted its goodness or power.

"Tell us a story about a dragon, Lao Lao," Yu Lang asked her grandmother, as Ah Shung laid his dragon flag across the side of a small table where everyone could admire it.

"Let me think," the old woman said, smiling. "Well then, I will tell you the tale of the Dragon King's daughter and how she rewarded the youth named Liu Ye.

"In a certain part of our land there was long, long ago a family named Liu. Their son, Liu Ye, had studied and studied to prepare for the examinations that were held every year by order of the Emperor. He hoped, when he had passed them, to receive a government position that would bring him much money.

"But, my children, in spite of the days and nights which poor Liu Ye spent in the examination cell, he did not pass. Take warning from him, Ah Shung! When you go to take the examinations yourself, be sure that you have studied enough and that you know your books by heart. This young man turned his face sadly toward home, and as he walked over the land he came upon a young woman who was tending her goats on the banks of the River Ching.

"Now this young woman was poorly dressed, but her face was as fair as a plum blossom in spring, and her body was as slender as a willow branch. Liu Ye was so struck by her beauty that he halted to speak to her.

"'Good maiden,' he said, bowing politely, 'who may you be, and where do you come from?'

Illustration by Malthe Hasselriis, "The Daughter of the Dragon King" from *Tales of A Chinese Grandmother* by Frances Carpenter. Copyright © 1937 by Malthe Hasselriis. Reprinted by permission of Doubleday Co.

"'O Excellent Sir,' the young woman replied, 'I am the youngest daughter of the Dragon King who lives in the Lake of Tung Ting. Not long ago my father gave me in marriage to the son of the dragon who lives in this river. His servants were jealous when I entered his palace. They told lies about me and my husband believed them. He put me outside his courts. I am now forced to earn my rice by tending the goats of the farmers in yonder village.' Tears rolled down the pale cheeks of the fair young woman, and the heart of Liu Ye was touched by her misery.

"'What can I do to help you, O Daughter of the Dragon King?' he asked.

"'Should you be going in the direction of the Lake of Tung Ting, you could indeed be of use to me, O Noble Young Man,' the weeping girl said.

"'My home lies in that direction. You have but to command me,' Liu Ye replied with a bow.

"'I would ever be grateful if you would deliver this letter to my father,' the young woman said. 'On the northern bank of the Lake of Tung Ting there stands a giant orange tree. Strike it thrice with your belt and there will come a messenger to guide you to the Dragon King's palace.'

"Liu Ye took the letter. As soon as he had returned to his home, he set forth across the fields until he came to the orange tree of which the young woman had told him. He unfastened his belt, and three times he lashed the trunk of the orange tree. At once there rose from the lake a young man dressed in armor and carrying a shining sword in his hand.

"'Who struck yonder orange tree? Was it you, young man?' he said to Liu Ye.

"'It was I,' Liu replied, 'I bear a message for the Dragon King who lives in the Lake of Tung Ting. I would go to his palace.'

"The young man in armor thrust his sword into the lake. The waters parted and he led Liu Ye safely to the palace of the Dragon King. What splendid sights the young man saw there! The Dragon King's palace was made of bright-colored stones, so clear that one could see through them almost as easily as through a hole in a window paper. Liu was led through one crystal door after another. He passed heaps of opals and pearls and he saw precious stones of beautiful colors.

"At last in one splendid courtyard he came upon the great Dragon King himself. He had the form of a man, dressed in robes of bright purple, and in his hand gleamed a piece of the purest green jade-stone.

"'I come from your daughter, O Dragon

King,' Liu Ye said, kowtowing before him. 'I live in the neighboring kingdom of Wu. I have spent years in study, and I was returning from the Examination Halls, where, alas, I failed to pass. As I was walking along I saw your fair daughter, tending her goats upon the banks of the River Ching. Her clothes were in tatters. Her shoes were worn through. She seemed so very sad that my heart wept at the sight. She gave me this letter to deliver to your majesty.'

When the Dragon King read the pitiful letter from his beloved daughter, the tears flowed from his eyes. His attendants who stood near him began to weep and to wail.

"'Stop that noise!' cried the Dragon King. 'Stop it at once! Chien Tang will hear.'

"'Who is Chien Tang?' asked Liu Ye.

"'He is my elder brother,' the Dragon King answered. 'He is the dragon who once lived in the River Chien Tang. Now he is the king of all river dragons.'

"'But why do you fear lest Chien Tang should hear the news I have brought you?'

"'Ai, Chien Tang has a temper, a terrible temper,' the Dragon King said, shaking his head. 'Once, in years gone by, he flew into a rage and ordered his river dragons to send water flowing out over their banks. The flood he caused then covered the land with water deep as the ocean, and it lasted nine years.'

"The Dragon King had scarcely uttered the last word when there arose a clattering sound. A red dragon so large that it darkened the sky flew through the air. Its scales were red gold, its mane shone like fire, and its eyes flashed like lightning. Quicker than I can tell you, the giant red dragon disappeared into the clouds.

"The Dragon King barely had time to tell Liu Ye that the giant red dragon was his brother, Chien Tang, before the shining beast appeared once again. A lovely young woman rode on his back as he flew down from the heavens.

"'It is the young woman who tended the goats!' Liu exclaimed in surprise.

"'It is my dear youngest daughter,' the Dragon King cried.

"'Ai, I found her in a sad plight,' the Red dragon said, 'but I have punished her wicked husband. I have carried him off to my own kingdom. He will cause her sorrow no more.'

"'The beautiful daughter of the Dragon King was so grateful to Liu Ye that she persuaded her father to offer her hand to him in marriage. But the young man was troubled. 'They have just killed her first husband,' he said to himself, 'I had best go on my way.' And so he refused.

"'I only wished to reward you, O Excellent Youth,' the Dragon King's daughter said as she bade Liu Ye good-by. 'But perhaps the lucky hour has not yet arrived. We shall wait a while.'

"The youth went to his home. In time his family arranged a marriage for him with a daughter of the Chang family. But scarcely had they eaten the wedding rice when the bride died. Liu Ye's second marriage with a daughter of a family named Han was no more successful, for again the bride flew away to the Shadowy World.

"'The gods do not smile upon me,' Liu Ye said to his mother. 'I shall go to another city to live. Perhaps there I shall find better luck.'

"But in the strange city the young man was lonely. 'I will take another wife,' he decided, and he went to seek a go-between to arrange matters for him.

"'I know of a beautiful young widow,' the go-between said. 'Her husband has died, and since she is so young her mother is anxious that she should marry again.'

"Well, it all ended in Liu Ye's marrying the young widow. For more than a year they lived happily together, and when the gods sent them a son, the woman said to her husband, 'This blessing from heaven binds us together forever. Now I can tell you that I am the daughter of the Dragon King of Lake Tung Ting, the woman you saved from her misery on the banks of the River Ching. I made a vow I would reward you. I wished to marry you then, but you refused. My father forced me to wed the son of a silk merchant, but I never stopped wishing that the day might come when I should be your wife.'

"The story goes that Liu Ye and the Dragon King's daughter went to live in a splendid palace in the Lake of Tung Ting and that in time the fortunate youth became a dragon himself. In the books his name is written as 'Golden Dragon Great Prince.'"

―――

"Molly Whuppie," from English Folk and Fairy Tales. *Collected by Joseph Jacobs (New York: Putnam's, [1890]).*

Often called the female counterpart to Jack, the Giant Killer, Molly Whuppie, the heroine of this British folktale, saves her siblings, as does Gretel in "Hansel and Gretel" and the title heroine of "The Little Guava." Having done so, Molly then enables the three sisters to complete their linear journeys by marrying the princes. This she does by robbing the giant three times. It is important to notice that Molly does not kill the giant or use physical force of any kind; she uses her quick wits to force the ogre to do violence to his own family.

Molly Whuppie

Once upon a time there was a man and a wife who had too many children, and they could not get meat for them, so they took the three youngest and left them in a wood. They travelled and travelled and could see never a house. It began to be dark, and they were hungry. At last they saw a light and made for it; it turned out to be a house. They knocked at the door, and a woman came to it, who said: "What do you want?" They said: "Please let us in and give us something to eat." The woman said: "I can't do that, as my man is a giant, and he would kill you if he comes home." They begged hard. "Let us stop for a little while," said they, "and we will go away before he comes." So she took them in, and set them down before the fire, and gave them milk and bread; but just as they had begun to eat, a great knock came to the door, and a dreadful voice said:

"Fee, fie, fo fum,
I smell the blood of some earthly one. Who have you there, wife?" "Eh," said the wife, "it's three poor lassies cold and hungry, and they will go away. Ye won't touch 'em, man." He said nothing, but ate up a big supper, and ordered them to stay all night. Now he had three lassies of his own, and they were to sleep in the same bed with the three strangers. The youngest of the three strange lassies was called Molly Whuppie, and she was very

clever. She noticed that before they went to bed the giant put straw ropes round her neck and her sisters', and round his own lassies' necks, he put gold chains. So Molly took care and did not fall asleep, but waited till she was sure every one was sleeping sound. Then she slipped out of the bed, and took the straw ropes off her own and her sisters' necks, and took the gold chains off the giant's lassies. She then put the straw ropes on the giant's lassies and the gold on herself and her sisters, and lay down. And in the middle of the night up rose the giant, armed with a great club, and felt for the necks with the straw. It was dark. He took his own lassies out of bed on to the floor, and battered them until they were dead, and then lay down again, thinking he had managed finely. Molly thought it time she and her sisters were off and away, so she wakened them and told them to be quiet, and they slipped out of the house. They all got out safe, and they ran and ran, and never stopped until morning, when they saw a grand house before them. It turned out to be a king's house: so Molly went in, and told her story to the king. He said: "Well, Molly, you are a clever girl, and you have managed well; but, if you would manage better, and go back and steal the giant's sword that hangs on the back of his bed, I would give your eldest sister my eldest son to marry." Molly said she would try. So she went back, and managed to slip into the giant's house, and crept in below the bed. The giant came home and ate up a great supper, and went to bed. Molly waited until he was snoring, and she crept out, and reached over the giant and got down the sword; but just as she got it out over the bed it gave a rattle, and up jumped the giant, and Molly ran out at the door and the sword with her; and she ran, and he ran, till they came to the "Bridge of one hair;" and she got over, but he couldn't, and he says, "Woe worth ye, Molly Whuppie! never ye come again." And she says: "Twice yet, carle," quoth she, "I'll come to Spain." so Molly took the sword to the king, and her sister was married to his son.

Well, the king he says: "Ye've managed well, Molly; but if ye would manage better, and steal the purse that lies below the giant's pillow, I would marry your second sister to my second son." And Molly said she would try. So she set out for the giant's house, and slipped in, and hid again below the bed, and waited till the giant had eaten his supper, and was snoring sound asleep. She slipped out and slipped her hand below the pillow, and got out the purse; but just as she was going out the giant wakened, and ran after her; and she ran, and he ran, till they came to the "Bridge of one hair," and she got over, but he couldn't, and he said, "Woe worth ye, Molly Whuppie! never you come again." "Once yet, carle," quoth she, "I'll come to Spain." So Molly took the purse to the king, and her second sister was married to the king's second son.

After that the king says to Molly: "Molly, you are a clever girl, but if you would do better yet, and steal the giant's ring that he wears on his finger, I will give you my youngest son for yourself." Molly said she would try. So back she goes to the giant's house, and hides herself below the bed. The giant wasn't long ere he came home, and, after he had eaten a great big supper, he went to bed, and shortly was snoring loud. Molly crept out and reached over the bed, and got hold of the giant's hand, and she pulled and she pulled until she got off the ring; but just as she got it off the giant got up, and gripped her by the hand and he says, "Now I have caught you, Molly Whuppie, and, if I had done as much ill to you as ye have done to me, what would ye do to me?"

Molly says: "I would put you into a sack, and I'd put the cat inside wi' you, and the dog aside you, and a needle and thread and a shears, and I'd hang you up upon the wall, and I'd go to the wood, and choose the thickest stick I could get, and I would come home, and take you down, and bang you till you were dead."

"Well, Molly," says the giant, "I'll just do that to you."

So he gets a sack, and puts Molly into it, and the cat and the dog beside her, and a needle and thread and shears, and hangs her up upon the wall, and goes to the wood to choose a stick.

Molly she sings out: "Oh, if ye saw what I see."

"Oh," says the giant's wife, "what do ye see, Molly?"

But Molly never said a word but, "Oh, if ye saw what I see!"

The giant's wife begged that Molly would take her up into the sack till she would see what Molly saw. So Molly took the shears and cut a hole in the sack, and took out the needle and thread with her, and jumped down and helped the giant's wife up into the sack, and sewed up the hole.

The giant's wife saw nothing, and began to ask to get down again; but Molly never minded, but hid herself at the back of the door. Home came the giant, and a great big tree in his hand, and he took down the sack, and began to batter it. His wife cried, "It's me, man"; but the dog barked and the cat mewed, and he did not know his wife's voice. But Molly came out from the back of the door, and the giant saw her and he ran after her; and he ran, and she ran, till they came to the "Bridge of one hair," and she got over but he couldn't; and he said, "Woe worth you, Molly Whuppie! never you come again." "Never more, carle," quoth she, "will I come again to Spain."

So Molly took the ring to the king, and she was married to his youngest son, and she never saw the giant again.

"East o' the Sun and West o' the Moon," from East o' the Sun and West o' the Moon, *by George Webbe Dasent (Edinburgh: David Douglas, 1888).*

This folktale about the faithless maiden who must undertake an arduous journey to prove her worth reflects the harsh landscape of northern Europe. As in many Norwegian folktales two elements stand out quite sharply: the journey is a very involved one with many stages; the major evil characters are trolls — in the end, the power of love causes them to burst.

This story is similar to the Greek myth "Cupid and Psyche" in its treatment of the faithless spouse, and to the literary folktales "Beauty and the Beast" and "The White Cat" in its portrayal of enchanted lovers.

East o' the Sun and West o' the Moon

Once on a time there was a poor husbandman who had so many children that he hadn't much of either food or clothing to give them. Pretty children they all were, but the prettiest was the youngest daughter, who was so lovely there was no end to her loveliness.

So one day, 'twas on a Thursday evening late at the fall of the year, the weather was so wild and rough outside, and it was so cruelly dark, and rain fell and wind blew, till the walls of the cottage shook again. There they all sat round the fire busy with this thing and that. But just then, all at once something gave three taps on the window-pane. Then the father went out to see what was the matter; and, when he got out of doors, what should he see but a great big White Bear.

"Good evening to you," said the White Bear.

"The same to you," said the man.

"Will you give me your youngest daughter? If you will, I'll make you as rich as you are now poor," said the Bear.

Well, the man would not be at all sorry to be so rich; but still he thought he must have a bit of a talk with his daughter first; so he went in and told them how there was a great White bear waiting outside, who had given his word to make them so rich if he could only have the youngest daughter.

The lassie said "No" outright. Nothing could get her to say anything else; so the man went out and settled it with the White Bear, that he should come again the next Thursday evening and get an answer. Meantime he talked his daughter over, and kept telling her of all the riches they would get, and how well off she would be herself; and so at last she thought better of it, and washed and mended her rags, made herself as smart as she could, and was ready to start. I can't say her packing gave her much trouble.

Next Thursday evening came the White Bear to fetch her, and she got upon his back with her bundle, and off they went. So, when they had gone a bit of the way, the White Bear said —

"Are you afraid?"

"No!" she wasn't.

"Well! mind and hold tight by my shaggy coat, and then there's nothing to fear," said the Bear.

So she rode a long, long way, till they came to a great steep hill. There, on the face of it, the White Bear gave a knock, and a door opened, and they came into a castle, where there were many rooms all lit up; rooms gleaming with silver and gold; and there too was a table ready laid, and it was all as grand as grand could be. Then the White Bear gave her a silver bell; and when she wanted anything, she was only to ring it, and she would get it at once.

Well, after she had eaten and drunk, and evening wore on, she got sleepy after her journey, and thought she would like to go to bed, so she rang the bell; and she had scarce taken hold of it before she came into a chamber, where there was a bed made, as fair and white as any one would wish to sleep in, with silken pillows and curtains, and gold fringe. All that was in the room was gold or silver; but when she had gone to bed, and put out the light, a man came and laid himself alongside her. That was the White Bear, who threw off his beast shape at night; but she never saw him, for he always came after she had put out the light, and before the day dawned he was up and off again. So things went on happily for a while, but at last she began to get silent and sorrowful; for there she went about all day alone, and she longed to go home to see her father and mother, and brothers and sisters. So one day, when the White Bear asked what it was that she lacked, she said it was so dull and lonely there, and how she longed to go home to see her father and mother, and brothers and sisters, and that was why she was so sad and sorrowful, because she couldn't get to them.

"Well, well!" said the Bear, "perhaps there's a cure for all this; but you must promise me one thing, not to talk alone with your mother, but only when the rest are by to hear; for she'll take you by the hand and try to lead you into a room alone to talk; but you must mind and not do that, else you'll bring bad luck on both of us."

So one Sunday the White Bear came and said now they could set off to see her father and mother. Well, off they started, she sitting on his back; and they went far and long. At last they came to a grand house, and there her brothers and sisters were running about out of doors at play, and everything was so pretty, 'twas a joy to see.

"This is where you father and mother live now," said the White Bear; "but don't forget what I told you, else you'll make us both unlucky."

"No! bless her, she'd not forget;" and when she had reached the house, the White Bear turned right about and left her.

Then when she went in to see her father and mother, there was such joy, there was no end to it. None of them thought they could thank her enough for all she had done for them. Now, they had everything they wished, as good as good could be, and they all wanted to know how she got on where she lived.

Well, she said, it was very good to live where she did; she had all she wished. What she said beside I don't know; but I don't think any of them had the right end of the stick, or that they got much out of her. But so in the afternoon, after they had done dinner, all happened as the White Bear had said. Her mother wanted to talk with her alone in her bed-room; but she minded what the White Bear had said, and wouldn't go up stairs.

"Oh, what we have to talk about will keep," she said, and put her mother off. But somehow or other, her mother got round her at last, and she had to tell her the whole story. So she said, how every night, when she had gone to bed, a man came and lay down beside her as soon as she had put out the light, and how she never saw him, because he was always up and away before the morning dawned; and how she went about woeful and sorrowing, for she thought she should so like to see him, and how all day long she walked about there alone, and how dull and dreary, and lonesome it was.

"My!" said her mother; "it may well be a Troll you slept with! But now I'll teach you a lesson how to set eyes on him. I'll give you a bit of candle, which you can carry home in your bosom; just light that while he is asleep, but take care not to drop the tallow on him."

Yes! she took the candle, and hid it in her bosom, and as night drew on, the White Bear came and fetched her away.

But when they had gone a bit of the way, the White Bear asked if all hadn't happened as he had said.

"Well, she couldn't say it hadn't."

"Now, mind," said he, "if you have listened to your mother's advice, you have brought bad luck on us both, and then, all that has passed between us will be as nothing."

"No," she said, she hadn't listened to her mother's advice.

So when she reached home, and had gone to bed, it was the old story over again. There came a man and lay down beside her; but at dead of night, when she heard he slept, she got up and struck a light, lit the candle, and let the light shine on him, and so she saw that he was the loveliest Prince one ever set eyes on, and she fell so deep in love with him on the spot, that she thought she couldn't live if she didn't give him a kiss there and then. And so she did, but as she kissed him, she dropped three hot drops of tallow on his shirt, and he woke up.

"What have you done?" he cried; "now you have made us both unlucky, for had you held out only this one year, I had been freed. For I have a stepmother who has bewitched me, so that I am a White Bear by day, and a Man by night. But now all ties are snapt between us; now I must set off from you to her. She lives in a castle which stands EAST O' THE SUN AND WEST O' THE MOON, and there, too, is a Princess, with a nose three ells long, and she's the wife I must have now."

She wept and took it ill, but there was no help for it; go he must.

Then she asked if she mightn't go with him. No, she mightn't.

"Tell me the way, then," she said, "and I'll search you out; *that* surely I may get leave to do."

"Yes, she might do that," he said; but there was no way to that place. It lay EAST O' THE SUN AND WEST O' THE MOON, and thither she'd never find her way.

So next morning, when she woke up, both Prince and the castle were gone, and then she lay on a little green patch, in the midst of the gloomy thick wood, and by her side lay the same bundle of rags she had brought with her from her old home.

So when she had rubbed the sleep out of her eyes, and wept till she was tired, she set out on her way, and walked many, many days, till she came to a lofty crag. Under it sat an old hag, and played with a gold apple which she tossed about. Her the lassie asked if she knew the way to the Prince, who lived with his step-mother in the castle that lay EAST O' THE SUN AND WEST O' THE MOON, and who was to marry the Princess with a nose three ells long.

"How did you come to know about him?" asked the old hag; "but maybe you are the lassie who ought to have had him?"

Yes, she was.

"So, so; it's you, is it?" said the old hag. "Well, all I know about him is, that he lives in the castle that lies EAST O' THE SUN AND WEST O' THE MOON, and thither you'll come, late or never; but still you may have the loan of my horse, and on him you can ride to my next neighbour. Maybe she'll be able to tell you; and when you get there, just give the horse a switch under the left ear, and beg him to be off home; and, stay, this gold apple you may take with you."

So she got upon the horse, and rode a long long time, till she came to another crag, under which sat another old hag, with a gold carding-comb. Her the lassie asked if she knew the way to the castle that lay EAST O' THE SUN AND WEST O' THE MOON, and she answered, like the first old hag, that she knew nothing about it, except it was east o' the sun and west o' the moon.

"And thither you'll come, late or never; but you shall have the loan of my horse to my next neighbour; maybe she'll tell you all about it; and when you get there, just switch the horse under the left ear, and beg him to be off home."

And this old hag gave her the golden carding-comb; it might be she'd find some use for it, she said. So the lassie got up on the horse, and rode a far far way, and a weary time; and so at last she came to another great crag, un-

der which sat another old hag, spinning with a golden spinning-wheel. Her, too, she asked if she knew the way to the Prince, and where the castle was that lay EAST O' THE SUN AND WEST O' THE MOON. So it was the same thing over again.

"Maybe it's you who ought to have had the Prince?" said the old hag.

Yes, it was.

But she, too, didn't know the way a bit better than the other two. "East o' the sun and west o' the moon it was," she knew — that was all.

"And thither you'll come, late or never; but I'll lend you my horse, and then I think you'd best ride to the East Wind and ask him; maybe he knows those parts, and can blow you thither. But when you get to him, you need only give the horse a switch under the left ear, and he'll trot home of himself."

And so, too, she gave her the gold spinning-wheel. "Maybe you'll find a use for it," said the old hag.

Then on she rode many many days, a weary time, before she got to the East Wind's house, but at last she did reach it, and then she asked the East Wind if he could tell her the way to the Prince who dwelt east o' the sun and west o' the moon. Yes, the East Wind had often heard tell of it, the Prince and the castle, but he couldn't tell the way, for he had never blown so far.

"But, if you will, I'll go with you to my brother the West Wind, maybe he knows, for he's much stronger. So, if you will just get on my back, I'll carry you thither."

Yes, she got on his back, and I should just think they went briskly along.

So when they got there, they went into the West Wind's house, and the East Wind said the lassie he had brought was the one who ought to have had the Prince who lived in the castle EAST O' THE SUN AND WEST O' THE MOON; and so she had set out to seek him, and how he had come with her, and would be glad to know if the West Wind knew how to get to the castle.

"Nay," said the West Wind, "so far I've never blown; but if you will, I'll go with you to our brother the South Wind, for he's much stronger than either of us, and he has flapped his wings far and wide. Maybe he'll tell you. You can get on my back, and I'll carry you to him.''

Yes! she got on his back, and so they travelled to the South Wind, and weren't so very long on the way, I should think.

When they got there, the West Wind asked him if he could tell her the way to the castle that lay EAST O' THE SUN AND WEST O' THE MOON, for it was she who ought to have had the Prince who lived there.

"You don't say so! That's she, is it?" said the South Wind.

"Well, I have blustered about in most places in my time, but so far have I never blown; but if you will, I'll take you to my brother the North Wind; he is the oldest and strongest of the whole lot of us, and if he don't know where it is , you'll never find any one in the world to tell you. You can get on my back, and I'll carry you thither.''

Yes! she got on his back, and away he went from his house at a fine rate. And this time, too, she wasn't long on her way.

So when they got to the North Wind's house, he was so wild and cross, cold puffs came from him a long way off.

"BLAST YOU BOTH, WHAT DO YOU WANT?" he roared out to them ever so far off, so that it struck them with an icy shiver.

"Well," said the South Wind, "you needn't be so foul-mouthed, for here I am, your brother, the South Wind, and here is the lassie who ought to have had the Prince who dwells in the castle that lies EAST O' THE SUN AND WEST O' THE MOON, and now she wants to ask you if you ever were there, and can tell her the way, for she would be so glad to find him again.''

"YES, I KNOW WELL ENOUGH WHERE IT IS," said the North Wind; "once in my life I blew an aspen-leaf thither, but I was so tired I couldn't blow a puff for ever so many days after. But if you really wish to go thither, and aren't afraid to come along with me, I'll take you on my back and see if I can blow you thither.''

Yes! with all her heart; she must and would get thither if it were possible in any way; and as for fear, however madly he went, she wouldn't be at all afraid.

"Very well, then," said the North Wind, "but you must sleep here to-night, for we must have the whole day before us, if we're to get thither at all.''

Early next morning the North Wind woke her, and puffed himself up, and blew himself out, and made himself so stout and big, 'twas gruesome to look at him; and so off they went high up through the air, as if they would never stop till they got to the world's end.

Down here below there was such a storm; it threw down long tracts of wood and many houses, and when it swept over the great sea, ships foundered by hundreds.

So they tore on and on, — no one can believe how far they went, — and all the while they still went over the sea, and the North Wind got more and more weary, and so out of breath he could scarce bring out a puff, and his wings drooped and drooped, till at last he sunk so low that the crests of the waves dashed over his heels.

"Are you afraid?" said the North Wind.

"No!" she wasn't.

But they weren't very far from land; and the North Wind had still so much strength left in him that he managed to throw her up on the shore under the windows of the castle which lay EAST O' THE SUN AND WEST O' THE MOON; but then he was so weak and worn out, he had to stay there and rest many days before he could get home again.

Next morning the lassie sat down under the castle window, and began to play with the gold apple; and the first person she saw was the Long-nose who was to have the Prince.

"What do you want for your gold apple, you lassie?" said the Long-nose, and threw up the window.

"It's not for sale, for gold or money," said the lassie.

"If it's not for sale for gold or money, what is it that you will sell it for? You may name your own price," said the Princess.

"Well! if I may get to the Prince, who lives here, and be with him to-night, you shall have it," said the lassie whom the North Wind had brought.

Yes! she might; that could be done. So the Princess got the gold apple; but when the lassie came up to the Prince's bed-room at night he was fast asleep; she called him and shook him, and between whiles she wept sore; but all she could do she couldn't wake him up. Next morning as soon as day broke, came the Princess with the long nose, and drove her out again.

So in the day-time she sat down under the castle windows and began to card with her golden carding-comb, and the same thing happened. The Princess asked what she wanted for it; and she said it wasn't for sale for gold or money, but if she might get leave to go up to the Prince and be with him that night, the Princess should have it. But when she went up she found him fast asleep again, and all she called, and all she shook, and wept, and prayed, she couldn't get life into him; and as soon as the first gray peep of day came, then came the Princess with the long nose, and chased her out again.

So in the day-time the lassie sat down outside under the castle window, and began to spin with her golden spinning-wheel, and that, too, the Princess with the long nose wanted to have. So she threw up the window and asked what she wanted for it. The lassie said, as she had said twice before, it wasn't for sale for gold or money; but if she might go up to the Prince who was there, and be with him alone that night, she might have it.

Yes! she might do that and welcome. But now you must know there were some Christian folk who had been carried off thither, and as they sat in their room, which was next the Prince, they had heard how a woman had been in there, and wept and prayed, and called to him two nights running, and they told that to the Prince.

That evening, when the Princess came with her sleepy drink, the Prince made as if he drank, but threw it over his shoulder, for he could guess it was a sleepy drink. So, when the lassie came in, she found the Prince wide awake; and then she told him the whole story how she had come thither.

"Ah," said the Prince, "you've just come in the very nick of time, for to-morrow is to be our wedding-day; but now I won't have the Long-nose, and you are the only woman in the world who can set me free. I'll say I want to see what my wife is fit for, and beg her to wash the shirt which has the three spots of tallow on it; she'll say yes, for she doesn't know 'tis you who put them there; but that's a work only for Christian folk, and not for such a pack of Trolls, and so I'll say that I won't have any other for my bride than the woman who can wash them out, and ask you to do it."

So there was great joy and love between them all that night. But next day, when the wedding was to be, the Prince said —

"First of all, I'd like to see what my bride is fit for."

"Yes!" said the step-mother, with all her heart.

"Well," said the Prince, "I've got a fine shirt which I'd like for my wedding skirt, but some how or other it has got three spots of tallow on it, which I must have washed out; and I have sworn never to take any other bride than the woman who's able to do that. If she can't, she's not worth having."

Well, that was no great thing they said, so they agreed, and she with the long nose began to wash away as hard as she could, but the more she rubbed and scrubbed, the bigger the spots grew.

"Ah!" said the old hag, her mother, "you can't wash; let me try."

But she hadn't long taken the shirt in hand, before it got far worse than ever, and with all her rubbing, and wringing, and scrubbing, the spots grew bigger and blacker, and the darker and uglier was the shirt.

Then all the other Trolls began to wash, but the longer it lasted, the blacker and uglier the shirt grew, till at last it was as black all over as if it had been up the chimney.

"Ah!" said the Prince, "you're none of you worth a straw: you can't wash. Why there, outside, sits a beggar lassie, I'll be bound she knows how to wash better than the whole lot of you. COME IN LASSIE!" he shouted.

Well, in she came.

"Can you wash this shirt clean, lassie, you?" said he.

"I don't know," she said, "but I think I can."

And almost before she had taken it and

dipped it in the water, it was as white as driven snow, and whiter still.

"Yes; you are the lassie for me," said the Prince.

At that the old hag flew into such a rage, she burst on the spot, and the Princess with the long nose after her, and the whole pack of Trolls after her, — at least I've never heard a word about them since.

As for the Prince and Princess, they set free all the poor Christian folk who had been carried off and shut up there; and they took with them all the silver and gold, and flitted away as far as they could from the castle that lay EAST O' THE SUN AND WEST O' THE MOON.

"The Poor Woodcutter," from Folktales of Mexico. *Translated and edited by Americo Paredes (Chicago: University of Chicago Press, 1970).*

The Mexican wonder tale "The Poor Woodcutter" is clearly derived from European sources and displays several typical folk motifs: the presence of tests, the transformation of animals into humans, and the presence of a magical object. This linear tale contains a humorous, ironic twist: the poor woodcutter first receives a gift from the king — a magical mirror — and then uses that gift to pass the king's tests and marry his daughter. In Aztec mythology, the serpent was a positive figure symbolizing the culture hero Quatzalcoatl.

The Poor Woodcutter

Here is another tale. Anacia Ventura was the boy's name. He was an orphan. He went into the forest to chop wood.

One day he heard the cry of an animal. It was crying and crying out there in the forest. He thought, "What could be wrong with the animal? I'm going to see what's the matter with it."

And he went. When he got there, he saw that a serpent had caught a deer. It was the deer that kept crying out. So then he came close.

He saw the serpent had seven heads. It was trying to bite the deer, but it could not manage to kill the deer, because its mouths were too small.

Then Anacia said: "Poor little animal! How can you get anything to eat like that? I'm going to help you."

So then he killed the deer and cut it up in nice little pieces. Piece by little piece, he fed it into each little mouth, until the deer was all gone. Nothing was left but a pile of bones and the head.

Then the serpent said: "Thank you very much for feeding me. Now come with me. I'm going to take you to my father's house."

So they went. She took him where her father was. But she changed shape. She no longer was a serpent but a very beautiful woman. When they got to the house, she said to her father, "Father, I've brought a boy here with me. He helped me very much. I wanted to eat a deer very much. I caught it, but I couldn't kill it. He killed it for me and fed it to me very nicely. I'm full now."

"How good, daughter. Now, what are we going to do with him? Let's give him livestock."

"No, father."

"Then we'll give him money."

"No, father."

"Then, what are we going to give him?"

"Father, give him what you have in your pocket."

"No, daughter. What would I do then?"

"That is what you are going to give him, father. You can get another one for yourself."

So he took a little round mirror from his pocket. And he said, "This is going to be useful to you. Just handle it like this. Move it around like this. [Informant gestures: right to left and left to right at shoulder height and very close to the body.] Then you command, 'Bring me money, bring me food,' or anything else. 'Do this.' That is what you will say."

"Very well, señor." And Anacia went home. He stopped working. All he had to do was move the mirror like this and command. "Bring me food, bring me money."

One day he said to his mother, "Mother, I want to marry the king's daughter."

"You do, my son?"

"Yes, mother. I want you to go to the king with a marriage offer."

"Very well, my son." And she went to where the king was.

"Lord king, here I am. My son wants to marry your daughter."

"He does?"

"Yes, lord king."

"Well, all right. I have heard he's very clever. Let's see. Let him come and work for a while. Then he can marry my daughter."

Then the woman went home and told her son. So Anacia went to work at the king's house. The first task the king gave him, he gave him full sacks, all mixed up, of beans, corn, and pumpkin seeds. Three, four sacks he gave him, and he said, "You are going to put all of this, each in its own sack. You will work one night. Tomorrow you must have for me each of these sacks, beans and corn and pumpkin seeds." And he gave him plenty of candles, so he could work all night.

So then, when the king was gone, Anacia took out his mirror. He commanded, "Sort all of this out, pile by pile." The ants were the ones who helped him. They made separate piles of beans, corn, and pumpkin seeds. The work took only an hour. Then he lay down to sleep.

Next day, the king came. "Wake up! Get up! Have you done your work?"

"Yes, there it is, sack by sack."

"Well, you are really clever. Today you are going out to clear some ground for planting. You will work for three days. I want to plant three, four hundred pounds of grain. Let's see how much grain I will plant."

He worked just one day. The king planted four hundred pounds of grain.

Then the king said, "Now we'll see whether you really are clever. You are going to sleep with my daughter. And by about midnight, she must bear a child."

"All right," said Anacia, and the king went away.

Then Anacia thought, "Who can help me now!" He took out his mirror, and he called the *tsox*, that bird that brings the babies. About four in the morning, the *tsox* brought the babies. There they were, crying, and the king woke up. And there you have the king, taking

care of the babies and changing their diapers.

Next day he said, "Truly you are very clever! You are going to marry my daughter right now!"

"Rumpelstiltzkin," from The Blue Fairy Book. *Edited by Andrew Lang (London: Longmans, Green, 1889).*

A bargain with the devil or other evil, magical characters is a standard folklore motif. In this story, unlike many others, the heroine is motivated by her desperate situation, for she is a victim of her father's pride and the king's greed. The tale also reflects the belief that in possessing a person's secret name, the individual has power over that person. This belief is also seen in such modern novels as Scott O'Dell's Island of the Blue Dolphins *and Ursula LeGuin's* A Wizard of Earthsea. *As in "Molly Whuppie," "East o' the Sun and West o' the Moon," and "The Poor Woodcutter," the protagonist ends up marrying royalty; the marriage in this story, however, does not bring immediate happiness.*

Rumpelstiltzkin

There was once upon a time a poor miller who had a very beautiful daughter. Now it happened one day that he had an audience with the King, and in order to appear a person of some importance he told him that he had a daughter who could spin straw into gold. 'Now that's a talent worth having,' said the King to the miller; 'if your daughter is as clever as you say, bring her to my palace to-morrow, and I'll put her to the test.' When the girl was brought to him he led her into a room full of straw, gave her a spinning-wheel and spindle, and said: 'Now set to work and spin all night till early dawn, and if by that time you haven't spun the straw into gold you shall die.' Then he closed the door behind him and left her alone inside.

So the poor miller's daughter sat down, and didn't know what in the world she was to do. She hadn't the least idea of how to spin straw into gold, and became at last so miserable that she began to cry. Suddenly the door opened, and in stepped a tiny little man and said: 'Good-evening, Miss Miller-maid; why are you crying so bitterly?' 'Oh!' answered the girl, 'I have to spin straw into gold, and haven't a notion how it's done.' 'What will you give me if I spin it for you?' asked the manikin. 'My necklace,' replied the girl. The little man took the necklace, sat himself down at the wheel, and whir, whir, whir, the wheel went round three times, and the bobbin was full. Then he put on another, and whir, whir, whir, the wheel went round three times, and the second too was full;

Illustration by Henry Ford and G.P. Jacomb Hood, "Rumpelstiltzkin" from *The Blue Fairy Book* by Andrew Lang. Copyright © 1889 by Henry Ford. Reprinted by permission of the Longman's Group Ltd.

and so it went on till the morning, when all the straw was spun away, and all the bobbins were full of gold. As soon as the sun rose the King came, and when he perceived the gold he was astonished and delighted, but his heart only lusted more than ever after the precious metal. He had the miller's daughter put into another room full of straw, much bigger than the first, and bade her, if she valued her life,

spin it all into gold before the following morning. The girl didn't know what to do, and began to cry; then the door opened as before, and the tiny little man appeared and said: 'What'll you give me if I spin the straw into gold for you?' 'The ring from my finger,' answered the girl. The manikin took the ring, and whir! round went the spinning-wheel again, and when morning broke he had spun all the straw into glittering gold. The King was pleased beyond measure at the sight, but his greed for gold was still not satisfied, and he had the miller's daughter brought into a yet bigger room full of straw, and said: 'You must spin all this away in the night; but if you succeed this time you shall become my wife.' 'She's only a miller's daughter, it's true,' he thought; 'but I couldn't find a richer wife if I were to search the whole world over.' When the girl was alone the little man appeared for the third time, and said: ''What'll you give me if I spin the straw for you once again?' 'I've nothing more to give,' answered the girl. 'Then promise me when you are Queen to give me your first child.' 'Who knows what mayn't happen before that?' thought the miller's daughter; and besides, she saw no other way out of it, so she promised the manikin what he demanded, and he set to work once more and spun the straw into gold. When the King came in the morning, and found everything as he had desired, he straightway made her his wife, and the miller's daughter became a queen.

When a year had passed a beautiful son was born to her, and she thought no more of the little man, till all of a sudden one day he stepped into her room and said: 'Now give me what you promised.' The Queen was in a great state, and offered the little man all the riches in her kingdom if he would only leave her the child. But the manikin said: 'No, a living creature is dearer to me than all the treasures in the world.' Then the Queen began to cry and sob so bitterly that the little man was sorry for her, and said: 'I'll give you three days to guess my name, and if you find it out in that time you may keep your child.'

Then the Queen pondered the whole night over all the names she had ever heard, and sent a messenger to scour the land, and to pick up far and near any names he should come across. When the little man arrived on the following day she began with Kasper, Melchior, Belshazzar, and all the other names she knew, in a string, but at each one the manikin called out: 'That's not my name.' The next day she sent to inquire the names of all the people in the neighbourhood, and had a long list of the most uncommon and extraordinary for the little man when he made his appearance. 'Is your name, perhaps, Sheepshanks, Cruickshanks, Spindleshanks?' but he always replied: 'That's not my name.' On the third day the messenger returned and announced: 'I have not been able to find any new names, but as I came upon a high hill round the corner of the wood, where the foxes and hares bid each other good night, I saw a little house, and in front of the house burned a fire, and round the fire sprang the most grotesque little man, hopping on one leg and crying:

> To-morrow I brew, to-day I bake,
> And then the child away I'll take;
> For little deems my royal dame
> That Rumpelstiltzkin is my name!

You may imagine the Queen's delight at hearing the name, and when the little man stepped in shortly afterwards and asked: 'Now, my lady Queen, what's my name?' she asked first: 'Is your name Conrad?' 'No' 'Is your name Harry?' 'No' 'Is your name, perhaps, Rumpelstiltzkin?' 'Some demon has told you that, some demon has told you that,' screamed the little man, and in his rage drove his right foot so far into the ground that it sank in up to his waist; then in a passion he seized the left foot with both hands and tore himself in two.

"Cinderella," by Charles Perrault, from Tales from Times Past. *Edited by Bryan Holme (New York: Viking-Studio, 1977), and "Cinderella," by the Brothers Grimm, from* The Complete Grimm's Fairy Tales *(New York: Pantheon, 1944).*

The story of the rejected girl who wins the prince has been found all over the world. Of the over three hundred versions which have been found, the best-known are the French adaptation by Charles Perrault and the German one by the Brothers Grimm. Although both end with the marriage of Cinderella to the prince, and although both use the slipper as a symbol of the girl's unique and exquisite goodness and beauty, each differs considerably from the other. Perrault's Cinderella is a far more patient girl, aided by a fairy godmother; the Grimms' heroine is far more active and must overcome greater difficulties, one of the most significant of which is her father's attempt to deny her. Perrault's style captures the grandeur of the late seventeeth century French court; the Grimms' version employs far less embellishment; perhaps this is a reflection of their version's German peasant origins. In both, however, the emphasis is not on Cinderella's earning the right to her final happiness; her goodness is present from the beginning and is made manifest in spite of the attempts of others to conceal it.

Cinderella

There was once an honest gentleman who took for his second wife a lady, the proudest and most disagreeable in the whole country. She had two daughters exactly like herself in all things. He also had one little girl, who resembled her dead mother, the best woman in all the world. Scarcely had the second marriage taken place than the stepmother became jealous of the good qualities of the little girl, who was so great a contrast to her own two daughters. She gave her all the menial occupations of the house — compelled her to wash the floors and staircases, to dust the bedrooms, and clean the grates; and while her sisters occupied carpeted chambers hung with mirrors, where they could see themselves from head to foot, this poor little damsel was sent to sleep in an attic, on an old straw mattress, with only one chair and not a looking-glass in the room.

She suffered all in silence, not daring to complain to her father, who was entirely ruled by his new wife. When her daily work was done, she sat down in the chimney-corner among the ashes; from which the two sisters gave her the nickname of Cinderella. But Cinderella, however shabbily clad, was handsomer than they were with all their fine clothes.

It happened that the King's son gave a series of balls, to which were invited all the rank and fashion of the city, and among the rest the two elder sisters. They were very proud and happy, and occupied their whole time in deciding what they should wear: a source of new trouble to Cinderella, whose duty it was to get up their fine linen and laces, and who never could please them however much she tried. They talked of nothing but their clothes.

"I," said the elder, "shall wear my velvet gown and my trimmings of English lace."

"And I," added the younger, "will have but my ordinary silk petticoat, but I shall adorn it with an upper skirt of flowered brocade, and shall put on my diamond tiara, which is a great deal finer than anything of yours."

Here the elder sister grew angry, and the dispute began to run so high that Cinderella, who was known to have excellent taste, was called upon to decide between them. She gave them the best advice she could, and gently and submissively offered to dress them herself, and especially to arrange their hair — an accomplishment in which she excelled many a noted coiffeur. The important evening came, and she exercised all her skill to adorn the two young ladies.

While she was combing out the elder's hair, this ill-natured girl said sharply, "Cinderella, do you not wish you were going to the ball?"

"Ah, madam" (they obliged her always to say "madam"), "you are only mocking me; it is not my fortune to have any such pleasure."

"You are right: people would only laugh to see a little cinder-wench at a ball."

Any other than Cinderella would have dressed the hair all awry; but she was good, and dressed it perfectly even and smooth, and as prettily as she could.

The sisters had scarcely eaten for two days, and had broken a dozen stay-laces a day in trying to make themselves slender; but to-night they broke a dozen more, and lost their tem-

pers over and over again before they had completed their toilet. When at last the happy moment arrived, Cinderella followed them to the coach; after it had whirled them away, she sat down by the kitchen fire and cried.

Immediately her Godmother, who was a Fairy, appeared beside her.

"What are you crying for, my little maid?"

"Oh, I wish — I wish —" Her sobs stopped her.

"You wish to go to the ball; isn't it so?"

Cinderella nodded.

"Well, then, be a good girl, and you shall go. First run into the garden and fetch me the largest pumpkin you can find."

Cinderella did not comprehend what this had to do with her going to the ball, but being obedient and obliging she went. Her Godmother took the pumpkin, and having scooped out all its inside, struck it with her wand; it became a splendid gilt coach, lined with rose-coloured satin.

"Now fetch me the mouse-trap out of the pantry, my dear."

Cinderella brought it; it contained six of the fattest, sleekest mice. The Fairy lifted up the wire door, and as each mouse ran out she struck it and changed it into a beautiful black horse.

"But what shall I do for your coachman, Cinderella?"

Cinderella suggested that she had seen a large black rat in the rat-trap, and he might serve for want of better.

"You are right; go and look again for him."

He was found, and the Fairy made him into a most respectable coachman, with the finest coat imaginable. She afterwards took six lizards from behind the pumpkin frame, and changed them into six footmen, all in splendid livery, who immediately jumped up behind the carriage, as if they had been footmen all their days.

"Well, Cinderella, now you can go to the ball."

"What, in these clothes?" said Cinderella piteously, looking down on her ragged frock.

Her Godmother laughed, and touched her also with the wand; at which her wretched thread-bare jacket became stiff with gold and sparkling with jewels, and her ragged frock lengthened into a gown of sweeping satin, from underneath which peeped out her little feet, no longer bare, but covered with silk stockings and the prettiest glass slippers in the world.

"Now, Cinderella, depart; remember, if you stay one instant after midnight, your carriage will become a pumpkin, your coachman a rat, your horses mice, and your footmen lizards; while you yourself will be the little cinder-wench you were an hour ago."

Cinderella promised without fear, her heart was so full of joy.

Arrived at the palace, the King's son, whom some one, probably the Fairy, had told to await the coming of an uninvited Princess whom nobody knew, was standing at the entrance, ready to receive her. He offered her his hand, and led her with the utmost courtesy through the assembled guests, who stood aside to let her pass, whispering to one another, "Oh, how beautiful she is!" It might have turned the head of any one but poor Cinderella, who was so used to be despised that she took it all as if it were something happening in a dream.

Her triumph was complete; even the old King said to the Queen that never since Her Majesty's young days had he seen so charming and elegant a person. All the Court ladies scanned her eagerly, clothes and all, determining to have theirs made next day of exactly the same pattern. The King's son himself led her out to dance, and she danced so gracefully that he admired her more and more. Indeed, at supper, which was fortunately early, his admiration quite took away his appetite. As for Cinderella herself, with an involuntary shyness she sought out her sisters, placed herself beside them, and offered them all sorts of civil attentions, which, coming as they supposed from a stranger, and so magnificent a lady, almost overwhelmed them with delight.

While she was talking with them, she heard the clock strike a quarter to twelve; and making a courteous adieu to the royal family, she re-entered her carriage, escorted tenderly by the King's son, and arrived in safety at her own door. There she found her Godmother, who smiled approval, and of whom she begged permission to go to a second ball, the follow-

ing night, to which the Queen had earnestly invited her.

While she was talking, the two sisters were heard knocking at the gate, and the Fairy God-Mother vanished, leaving Cinderella sitting in the chimney-corner, rubbing her eyes and pretending to be very sleepy.

"Ah," cried the eldest sister maliciously, "it has been the most delightful ball; and there was present the most beautiful Princess I ever saw, who was so exceedingly polite to us both."

"Was she?" said Cinderella indifferently. "And who might she be?"

"Nobody knows, though everybody would give their eyes to know, especially the King's son."

"Indeed!" replied Cinderella, a little more interested. "I should like to see her. Miss Javotte" — that was the elder sister's name — "will you not let me go to-morrow, and lend me your yellow gown that you wear on Sundays?"

"What, lend my yellow gown to a cinder-wench! I am not so mad as that." At which refusal Cinderella did not complain, for if her sister really had lent her the gown, she would have been considerably embarrassed.

The next night came, and the two young ladies, richly dressed in different toilets, went to the ball. Cinderella, more splendidly attired and beautiful than ever, followed them shortly after. "Now remember twelve o'clock," was her Godmother's parting speech, and she thought she certainly should. But the Prince's attentions to her were greater even than during the first evening, and in the delight of listening to his pleasant conversation, time slipped by unperceived. While she was sitting beside him in a lovely alcove, and looking at the moon from under a bower of orange blossoms, she heard a clock strike the first stroke of twelve. She started up, and fled away as lightly as a deer.

Amazed, the Prince followed, but could not catch her. Indeed he missed his lovely Princess altogether, and only saw running out of the palace doors a little dirty lass whom he had never beheld before, and of whom he certainly would never have taken the least notice. Cinderella

Illustration by Sheilah Beckett, from *Cinderella,* adapted by John Fowles. Copyright © 1974 by Sheilah Beckett. Reprinted by permission of Little, Brown and Co.

arrived home breathless and weary, ragged and cold, without carriage, or footman, or coachman — the only remnant of her past magnificence being one of her little glass slippers; the other she had dropped in the ballroom as she ran away.

When the two sisters returned, they were full of this strange adventure: how the beautiful lady had appeared at the ball more beautiful than ever, and enchanted every one who looked at her; and how, as the clock was striking twelve, she had suddenly risen up and fled through the ballroom, disappearing no one knew how or where, and dropping one of her glass slippers behind her in her flight; how the King's son had remained inconsolable until he chanced to pick up the little glass slipper, which he carried away in his pocket, and was seen to take it out continually and look at it affectionately, with the air of a man very much in love; in fact, from his behaviour during the remainder of the evening, all the court and royal family were convinced that he had become desperately enamoured of the wearer of the little glass slipper.

Cinderella listened in silence, turning her face to the kitchen fire, and perhaps it was that which made her look so rosy; but nobody ever noticed or admired her at home, so it did not signify, and next morning she went to her weary work again just as before.

A few days after, the whole city was attracted by the sight of a herald going round with a little glass slipper in his hand, publishing, with a flourish of trumpets, that the King's son ordered this to be fitted on the foot of every lady in the kingdom, and that he wished to marry the lady whom it fitted best, or to whom it and the fellow-slipper belonged. Princesses, duchesses, countesses, and simple gentlewomen all tried it on, but being a Fairy slipper it fitted nobody; and besides, nobody could produce its fellow-slipper, which lay all the time safely in the pocket of Cinderella's old linsey gown.

At last the herald came to the house of the two sisters, and though they well knew neither of themselves was the beautiful lady, they made every attempt to get their clumsy feet into the glass slipper, but in vain.

"Let me try it on," said Cinderella from the chimney-corner.

"What, you?" cried the others, bursting into shouts of laughter; but Cinderella only smiled, and held out her hand.

Her sisters could not prevent her, since the command was that every young maiden in the city should try on the slipper, in order that no chance might be left untried, for the prince was nearly breaking his heart; and his father and mother were afraid that, though a Prince, he would actually die for love of the beautiful unknown lady.

So the herald bade Cinderella sit down on a three-legged stool in the kitchen, and himself put the slipper on her pretty little foot, which it fitted exactly. She then drew from her pocket the fellow slipper, which she also put on, and stood up — for with the touch of the magic shoes all her dress was changed likewise — no longer the poor despised cinder-wench, but the beautiful lady whom the King's son loved.

Her sisters recognized her at once. Filled with astonishment, mingled with no little alarm, they threw themselves at her feet, begging her pardon for all their former unkindness. She raised and embraced them; told them she forgave them with all her heart, and only hoped they would love her always. Then she departed with the herald to the King's palace, and told her whole story to His Majesty and the royal family, who were not in the least surprised, for everybody believed in Fairies, and everybody longed to have a Fairy Godmother.

For the young Prince, he found her more lovely and lovable than ever, and insisted upon marrying her immediately. Cinderella never went home again, but she sent for her two sisters to the palace, and with the consent of all parties married them shortly afterwards to two rich gentlemen *of the Court*.

Cinderella

The wife of a rich man fell sick, and as she felt that her end was drawing near, she called her only daughter to her bedside and said: "Dear child, be good and pious, and then the good God will always protect you, and I will look down on you from heaven and be near you." Thereupon she closed her eyes and departed. Every day the maiden went out to her mother's grave and wept, and she remained pious and good. When winter came the snow spread a white sheet over the grave, and by the time the spring sun had drawn it off again, the man had taken another wife.

The woman had brought with her into the house two daughters, who were beautiful and fair of face, but vile and black of heart. Now began a bad time for the poor step-child. "Is the stupid goose to sit in the parlor with us?" they said. "He who wants to eat bread must earn it; out with the kitchen-wench." They took her pretty clothes away from her, put an old grey bedgown on her, and gave her wooden shoes. "Just look at the proud princess, how decked out she is!" they cried, and laughed, and led her into the kitchen. There she had to do hard work from morning till night, get up before daybreak, carry water, light fires, cook and wash. Besides this, the sisters did her every imaginable injury—they mocked her and emptied her peas and lentils into the ashes, so that she was forced to sit and pick them out again. In the evening when she had worked till she was weary she had no bed to go to, but had to sleep by the hearth in the cinders. And as on that account she always looked dusty and dirty, they called her Cinderella.

It happened that the father was once going to the fair, and he asked his two step-daughters what he should bring back for them. "Beautiful dresses," said one, "pearls and jewels," said the second. "And you, Cinderella," said he, "what will you have?" "Father, break off for me the first branch which knocks against your hat on your way home". So he bought beautiful dresses, pearls and jewels for his two step-daughters, and on his way home, as he was riding through a green thicket, a hazel twig brushed against him and knocked off his hat.

Then he broke off the branch and took it with him. When he reached home he gave his step-daughters the things which they had wished for, and to Cinderella he gave the branch from the hazel-bush. Cinderella thanked him, went to her mother's grave and planted the branch on it, and wept so much that the tears fell down on it and watered it. And it grew and became a handsome tree. Thrice a day Cinderella went and sat beneath it, and wept and prayed, and a little white bird always came on the tree, and if Cinderella expressed a wish, the bird threw down to her what she had wished for.

It happened, however, that the King gave orders for a festival which was to last three days, and to which all the beautiful young girls in the country were invited, in order that his son might choose himself a bride. When the two step-sisters heard that they too were to appear among the number, they were delighted, called Cinderella and said: "Comb our hair for us, brush our shoes and fasten our buckles, for we are going to the wedding at the King's palace." Cinderella obeyed, but wept, because she too would have liked to go with them to the dance, and begged her step-mother to allow her to do so. "You go, Cinderella!" said she; "covered in dust and dirt as you are, and would go to the festival? You have no clothes and shoes, and yet would dance!" As, however, Cinderella went on asking, the step-mother said at last: "I have emptied a dish of lentils into the ashes for you, if you have picked them out again in two hours, you shall go with us." The maiden went through the back-door into the garden, and called: "You tame pigeons, you turtle-doves, and all you birds beneath the sky, come and help me to pick

The good into the pot,
The bad into the crop."

Then two white pigeons came in by the kitchen-window, and afterwards the turtle-doves, and at last all the birds beneath the sky, came whirring and crowding in, and alighted amongst the ashes. And the pigeons nodded with their heads and began pick, pick, pick, pick, and the rest began also pick, pick, pick,

pick, and gathered all the good grains into the dish. Hardly had one hour passed before they had finished, and all flew out again. Then the girl took the dish to her step-mother, and was glad, and believed that now she would be allowed to go with them to the festival. But the step-mother said: "No, Cinderella, you have no clothes and you can not dance; you would only be laughed at." And as Cinderella wept at this, the step-mother said: "If you can pick two dishes of lentils out of the ashes for me in one hour, you shall go with us." And she thought to herself: "That she most certainly cannot do again." When the step-mother had emptied the two dishes of lentils amongst the ashes, the maiden went through the back-door into the garden and cried: "You tame pigeons, you turtle-doves, and all you birds beneath the sky, come and help me to pick

> The good into the pot,
> The bad into the crop."

Then two white pigeons came in by the kitchen-window, and afterwards the turtle-doves, and at length all the birds beneath the sky, came whirring and crowding in, and alighted amongst the ashes. And the doves nodded with their heads and began pick, pick, pick, pick, and the others began also pick, pick, pick, pick, and gathered all the good seeds into the dishes, and before half an hour was over they had already finished, and all flew out again. Then the maiden carried the dishes to the step-mother and was delighted, and believed that she might now go with them to the wedding. But the step-mother said: "All this will not help; you cannot go with us, for you have no clothes and can not dance; we should be ashamed of you!" On this she turned her back on Cinderella, and hurried away with her two proud daughters.

As no one was now at home, Cinderella when to her mother's grave beneath the hazel-tree, and cried:

> "Shiver and quiver, little tree,
> Silver and gold throw down over me."

Then the bird threw a gold and silver dress down to her, and slippers embroidered with silk and silver. She put on the dress with all speed, and went to the wedding. Her step-sisters and the step-mother however did not know her, and thought she must be a foreign princess, for she looked so beautiful in the golden dress. They never once thought of Cinderella, and believed that she was sitting at home in the dirt, picking lentils out of the ashes. The prince approached her, took her by the hand and danced with her. He would dance with no other maiden, and never let loose of her hand, and if any one else came to invite her, he said: "This is my partner."

She danced till it was evening, and then she wanted to go home. But the King's son said: "I will go with you and bear you company," for he wished to see to whom the beautiful maiden belonged. She escaped from him, however, and sprang into the pigeon-house. The King's son waited until her father came, and then he told him that the unknown maiden had leapt into the pigeon-house. The old man thought: "Can it be Cinderella?" and they had to bring him an axe and a pickaxe that he might hew the pigeon-house to pieces, but no one was inside it. And when they got home Cinderella lay in her dirty clothes among the ashes, and a dim little oil-lamp was burning on the mantle-piece, for Cinderella had jumped quickly down from the back of the pigeon-house and had run to the little hazel-tree, and there she had taken off her beautiful clothes and laid them on the grave, and the bird had taken them away again, and then she had seated herself in the kitchen amongst the ashes in her grey grown.

Next day when the festival began afresh, and her parents and the the step-sisters had gone once more, Cinderella went to the hazel-tree and said:

> "Shiver and quiver, my little tree,
> Silver and gold throw down over me."

Then the bird threw down a much more beautiful dress than on the preceding day. And when Cinderella appeared at the wedding in this dress, every one was astonished at her beauty. The King's son had waited until she came, and instantly took her by the hand and danced with no one but her. When others came and invited her, he said: "This is my partner."

Illustration by Nonny Hogrogian in *Cinderella* retold from The Brothers Grimm. Copyright © 1981 by Nonny Hogrogian Kheridan. By permission of Greenwillow Books (A Division of William Morrow and Company).

When evening came she wished to leave, and the King's son followed her and wanted to see into which house she went. But she sprang away from him, and into the garden behind the house. Therein stood a beautiful tree on which hung the most magnificent pears. She clambered so nimbly between the branches like a squirrel that the King's son did not know where she was gone. He waited until her father came, and said to him: "The unknown maiden has escaped from me, and I believe she has climbed up the pear-tree." The father thought: "Can it be Cinderella?" and had an axe brought and cut the tree down, but no one was on it. And when they got into the kitchen, Cinderella lay there among the ashes, as usual, for she had jumped down on the other side of the tree, had taken the beautiful dress to the bird on the little hazel-tree, and put on her grey gown.

On the third day, when the parents and sisters had gone away, Cinderella went once more to her mother's grave and said to the little tree:

> "Shiver and quiver, my little tree,
> Silver and gold throw down over me."

And now the bird threw down to her a dress which was more splendid and magnificent than any she had yet had, and the slippers were golden. And when she went to the festival in the dress, no one knew how to speak for astonishment. The King's son danced with her only, and if any one invited her to dance, he said: "This is my partner."

When evening came, Cinderella wished to leave, and the King's son was anxious to go with her, but she escaped from him so quickly that he could not follow her. The King's son, however, had employed a ruse, and had caused the whole staircase to be smeared with pitch, and there, when she ran down, had the maiden's left slipper remained stuck. The King's son picked it up, and it was small and dainty, and all golden. Next morning, he went with it to the father, and said to him: "No one shall be my wife but she whose foot this golden slipper fits." Then were the two sisters glad, for they had pretty feet. The eldest went with the shoe into her room and wanted to try it on, and her mother stood by. But she could not get her big toe into it, and the shoe was too small for her. Then her mother gave her a knife and said: "Cut the toe off; when you are Queen you will have no more need to go on foot." The maiden cut the toe off, forced the foot into the shoe, swallowed the pain, and went out to the King's son. Then he took her on his horse as his bride and rode away with her. They were obliged, however, to pass the grave, and there, on the hazel-tree, sat the two pigeons and cried:

> "Turn and peep, turn and peep,
> There's blood within the shoe,
> The shoe it is too small for her,
> The true bride waits for you."

Then he looked at her foot and saw how the blood was trickling from it. He turned his horse round and took the false bride home again, and said she was not the true one, and that the other sister was to put the shoe on. Then this one went into her chamber and got her toes safely into the shoe, but her heel was too large. So her mother gave her a knife and said: "Cut a bit off your heel; when you are Queen you will have no more need to go on foot." The maiden cut a bit off her heel, forced her foot into the shoe, swallowed the pain, and went out to the King's son. He took her on his horse as his bride, and rode away with her, but when they passed by the hazel-tree, the two little pigeons sat on it and cried:

> "Turn and peep, turn and peep,
> There's blood within the shoe,
> The shoe it is too small for her,
> The true bride waits for you."

He looked down at her foot and saw how the blood was running out of her shoe, and how it had stained her white stocking quite red. Then he turned his horse and took the false bride home again. "This also is not the right one," said he, "have you no other daughter?" "No," said the man, "there is still a little stunted kitchen-wench which my late wife left behind her, but she cannot possibly be the bride." The King's son said he was to send her up to him; but the mother answered: "Oh no, she is much too dirty, she cannot show herself!" But he absolutely insisted on it, and Cinderella had to be called. She first washed her hands and face clean, and then went and bowed down before the King's son, who gave her the golden shoe. Then she seated herself on a stool, drew her foot out of the heavy wooden shoe, and put it into the slipper, which fitted like a glove. And when she rose up and the King's son looked at her face he recognized the beautiful maiden who had danced with him and cried: "That is the true bride!" The step-mother and the two sisters were horrified and became pale with rage; he, however, took Cinderella on his horse and rode away with her. As they passed by the hazel-tree, the two white doves cried:

> "Turn and peep, turn and peep,
> No blood is in the shoe,
> The shoe is not too small for her,
> The true bride rides with you,"

and when they had cried that, the two came flying down and placed themselves on Cinderella's shoulders, one on the right, the other on the left, and remained sitting there.

When the wedding with the King's son was to be celebrated, the two false sisters came and wanted to get into favor with Cinderella and share her good fortune. When the betrothed couple went to church, the elder was at the right side and the younger at the left, and the pigeons pecked out one eye from each of them. Afterwards as they came back, the elder was at the left, and the younger at the right, and then the pigeons pecked out the other eye from each. And thus, for their wickedness and falsehood, they were punished with blindness all their days.

Illustration by Alan Suddon from *Cinderella*, Copyright © 1969. Reprinted by permission of Oberon Press.

"Vasilisa the Beautiful," from Vasilisa the Beautiful: Russian Fairy Tales. *Edited and translated by Irina Zhelezova (Moscow: Progress Publishers, 1966).*

In this Russian folktale are found two common motifs: ill-treatment by stepsisters and confrontation with a witch in a perilous forest. Vasilisa first completes a circular journey, escaping from Baba-Yaga, a cannibalistic witch found in many Russian tales; she then completes a linear journey, marrying the Tsarevich. She succeeds through the aid of her magical doll and through her goodness, courage, and kindness. Vengeance is swift as the cruel step-sisters and mother are destroyed by the same light that they had selfishly demanded Vasilisa procure.

Vasilisa the Beautiful

Long, long ago, in a certain tsardom there lived an old man and an old woman and their daughter Vasilisa. They had only a small hut for a home, but their life was a peaceful and happy one.

However, even the brightest of skies may become overcast, and misfortune stepped over their threshold at last. The old woman fell gravely ill and, feeling that her end was near, she called Vasilisa to her bedside, gave her a little doll, and said:

"Do as I tell you, my child. Take good care of this little doll and never show it to anyone. If ever anything bad happens to you, give the doll something to eat and ask its advice. It will help you out in all your troubles."

And, giving Vasilisa a last, parting kiss, the old woman died.

The old man sorrowed and grieved for a time, and then he married again. He had thought to give Vasilisa a second mother, but he gave her a cruel stepmother instead.

The stepmother had two daughters of her own, two of the most spiteful, mean and hard to please young women that ever lived. The stepmother loved them dearly and was always kissing and coddling them, but she nagged at Vasilisa and never let her have a moment's peace. Vasilisa felt very unhappy, for her stepmother and stepsisters kept chiding and scolding her and making her work beyond her strength. They hoped that she would grow thin and haggard with too much work and that her face would turn dark and ugly in the wind and sun. All day long they were at her, one or the other of them, shouting:

"Come, Vasilisa! Where are you, Vasilisa? Fetch the wood, don't be slow! Start a fire, mix the dough! Wash the plates, milk the cow! Scrub the floor, hurry now! Work away and don't take all day!"

Vasilisa did all she was told to do, she waited on everyone and always got her chores done on time. And with every day that passed she grew more and more beautiful. Such was her beauty as could not be pictured and could not be told, but was a true wonder and joy to behold. And it was her little doll that helped Vasilisa in everything.

Early in the morning Vasilisa would milk the cow and then, locking herself in in the pantry, she would give some milk to the doll and say:

"Come, little doll, drink your milk, my dear, and I'll pour out all my troubles in your ear, your ear!"

And the doll would drink the milk and comfort Vasilisa and do all her work for her. Vasilisa would sit in the shade twining flowers into her braid and, before she knew it, the vegetable beds were weeded, the water brought in, the fire lighted and the cabbage watered. The doll showed her a herb to be used against sun-burn, and Vasilisa used it and became more beautiful than ever.

One day, late in the fall, the old man set out from home and was not expected back for some time.

The stepmother and the three sisters were left alone. They sat in the hut and it was dark outside and raining and the wind was howling. The hut stood at the edge of a dense forest and in the forest there lived Baba-Yaga, a cunning witch and sly, who gobbled people up in the wink of an eye.

Now to each of the three sisters the stepmother gave some work to do: the first she set to weaving lace, the second to knitting stockings, and Vasilisa to spinning yarn. Then, putting out all the lights in the house except for a single splinter of birch that burnt in the corner where the three sisters were working, she went to bed.

The splinter crackled and snapped for a time, and then went out.

"What are we to do?" cried the stepmother's two daughters. "It is dark in the hut, and we must work. One of us will have to go to Baba-Yaga's house to ask for a light."

"I'm not going," said the elder of the two. "I am making lace, and my needle is bright enough for *me* to see by."

"I'm not going, either," said the second. "I am knitting stockings, and my two needles are bright enough for *me* to see by."

Then, both of them shouting: "Vasilisa is the one, she must go for the light! Go to Baba-Yaga's house this minute, Vasilisa!" they pushed Vasilisa out of the hut.

The blackness of night was about her, and the dense forest, and the wild wind. Vasilisa was frightened, she burst into tears and she took out her little doll from her pocket.

"O my dear little doll," she said between sobs, "they are sending me to Baba-Yaga's house for a light, and Baba-Yaga gobbles people up, bones and all."

"Never you mind," the doll replied, "you'll be all right. Nothing bad can happen to you while I'm with you."

"Thank you for comforting me, little doll," said Vasilisa, and she set off on her way.

About her the forest rose like a wall and, in the sky above, there was no sign of the bright crescent moon and not a star shone.

Vasilisa walked along trembling and holding the little doll close.

All of a sudden whom should she see but a man on horseback galloping past. He was clad all in white, his horse was white and the horses's harness was of silver and gleamed white in the darkness.

It was dawning now, and Vasilisa trudged on, stumbling and stubbing her toes against tree roots and stumps. Drops of dew glistened on her long plait of hair and her hands were cold and numb.

Suddenly another horseman came gallop

ing by. He was dressed in red, his horse was red and the horse's harness was red too.

The sun rose, it kissed Vasilisa and warmed her and dried the dew on her hair.

Vasilisa never stopped but walked on for a whole day, and it was getting on toward evening when she came out on to a small glade.

She looked, and she saw a hut standing there. The fence round the hut was made of human bones and crowned with human skulls. The gate was no gate but the bones of men's legs, the bolts were no bolts but the bones of men's arms, and the lock was no lock but a set of sharp teeth.

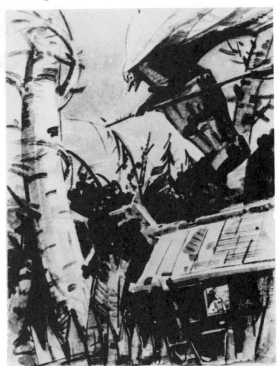

"Vasilisa the Beautiful" from *Vasilisa the Beautiful: Russian Fairy Tales,* by Irina Zholeznova, Moscow: Progress Press, 1966.

Valilisa was horrified and stood stock-still. Suddenly a horseman came riding up. He was dressed in black, his horse was black and the horse's harness was black too. The horseman galloped up to the gate and vanished as if into thin air.

Night descended, and lo! the eyes of the

skulls crowning the fence began to glow, and it became as light as if it was day.

Vasilisa shook with fear. She could not move her feet which seemed to have frozen to the spot and refused to carry her away from this terrible place.

All of a sudden, she felt the earth trembling and rocking beneath her, and there was Baba-Yaga flying up in a mortar, swinging her pestle like a whip and sweeping the tracks away with a broom. She flew up to the gate and, sniffing the air, cried:

"I smell Russian flesh! Who is here?"

Vasilisa came up to Baba-Yaga, bowed low to her and said very humbly:

"It is I, Vasilisa, Grandma. My stepsisters sent me to you to ask for a light."

"Oh, it's you, is it?" Baba-Yaga replied. "Your stepmother is a kinswoman of mine. Very well, then, stay with me for a while and work, and then we'll see what is to be seen."

And she shouted at the top of her voice:

"Come unlocked, my bolts so strong! Open up, my gate so wide!"

The gate swung open, Baba-Yaga rode in in her mortar and Vasilisa walked in behind her.

Now at the gate there grew a birch-tree and it made as if to lash Vasilisa with its branches.

"Do not touch the maid, birch-tree, it was I who brought her," said Baba-Yaga.

They came to the house, and at the door there lay a dog and it made as if to bite Vasilisa.

"Do not touch the maid, it was I who brought her," said Baba-Yaga.

They came inside and in the passage an old grumbler-rumbler of a cat met them and made as if to scratch Vasilisa.

"Do not touch the maid, you old grumbler-rumbler of a cat, it was I who brought her," said Baba-Yaga.

"You see, Vasilisa," she added, turning to her, "it is not easy to run away from me. My cat will scratch you, my dog will bite you, my birch-tree will lash you, and put out your eyes, and my gate will not open to let you out."

Baba-Yaga came into her room, and she stretched out on a bench.

"Come, black-browed maid, give us something to eat," she cried.

And the black-browed maid ran in and be-

gan to feed Baba-Yaga. She brought her a pot of *borshch* and half a cow, ten jugs of milk and a roasted sow, twenty chickens and forty geese, two whole pies and an extra piece, cider and mead and home-brewed ale, beer by the barrel and *kvass* by the pail.

Baba-Yaga ate and drank up everything, but she only gave Vasilisa a chunk of bread.

"And now, Vasilisa," said she, "take this sack of millet and pick it over seed by seed. And mind that you take out all the black bits, for if you don't I shall eat you up."

And Baba-Yaga closed her eyes and began to snore.

Vasilisa took the piece of bread, put it before her little doll and said:

"Come, little doll, eat this bread, my dear, and I'll pour out all my troubles in your ear, you ear! Baba-Yaga has given me a hard task to do, and she threatens to eat me up if I do not do it."

Said the doll in reply:

"Do not grieve and do not weep, but close your eyes and go to sleep. For morning is wiser than evening."

And the moment Vasilisa was asleep, the doll called out in a loud voice:

"Tomtits, pigeons, sparrows, hear me,
There is work to do, I fear me.
On your help, my feathered friends,
Vasilisa's life depends.
Come in answer to my call,
You are needed, one and all."

And the birds came flying from all sides, flocks and flocks of them, more than eye could see or tongue could tell. They began to chirp and to coo, to set up a great to-do, and to pick over the millet seed by seed very quickly indeed. Into the sack the good seeds went, and the black went into the crop, and before they knew it the night was spent, and the sack was filled to the top.

They had only just finished when the white horseman galloped past the gate on his white horse. Day was dawning.

Baba-Yaga woke up and asked:

"Have you done what I told you to do, Vasilisa?"

"Yes, it's all done, Grandma."

Baba-Yaga was very angry, but there was

nothing more to be said.

"Humph," she snorted, "I am off to hunt and you take that sack yonder, it's filled with peas and poppy seeds, pick out the peas from the seeds and put them in two separate heaps. And mind, now, if you do not do it, I shall eat you up."

Baba-Yaga went out into the yard and whistled, and the mortar and pestle swept up to her.

The red horseman galloped past, and the sun rose.

Baba-Yaga got into the mortar and rode out of the yard, swinging her pestle like a whip and whisking the tracks away with a broom.

Vasilisa took a crust of bread, fed her little doll and said:

"Do take pity on me, little doll, my dear, and help me out."

And the doll called out in ringing tones:

"Come to me, o mice of the house, the barn and the field, for there is work to be done!"

And the mice came running, swarms and swarms of them, more than eye could see or tongue could tell, and before the hour was up the work was all done.

It was getting on toward evening, and the black-browed maid set the table and began to wait for Baba-Yaga's return.

The black horseman galloped past the gate, night fell, and the eyes of the skulls crowning the fence began to glow. And now the trees groaned and crackled, the leaves rustled, and Baba-Yaga, the cunning witch and sly, who gobbled people up in the wink of an eye, came riding home.

"Have you done what I told you to do, Vasilisa?" she asked.

"Yes, it's all done, Grandma."

Baba-Yaga was very angry, but what could she say!

"Well, then, go to bed. I am going to turn in myself in a minute."

Vasilisa went behind the stove, and she heard Baba-Yaga say:

"Light the stove, black-browed maid, and make the fire hot. When I wake up, I shall roast Vasilisa."

And Baba-Yaga lay down on a bench, placed her chin on a shelf, covered herself with her foot and began to snore so loudly that the whole forest trembled and shook.

Vasilisa burst into tears and, taking out her doll, put a crust of bread before it.

"Come, little doll, have some bread, my dear, and I'll pour out all my troubles in your ear, your ear. For Baba-Yaga wants to roast me and to eat me up," said she.

And the doll told her what she must do to get out of trouble without more ado.

Vasilisa rushed to the black-browed maid and bowed low to her.

"Please, black-browed maid, help me!" she cried. "When you are lighting the stove, pour water over the wood so it does not burn the way it should. Here is my silken kerchief for you to reward you for your trouble."

Said the black-browed maid in reply:

"Very well, my dear, I shall help you. I shall take a long time heating the stove, and I shall tickle Baba-Yaga's heels and scratch them too so she may sleep very soundly the whole night through. And you run away, Vasilisa!"

"But won't the three horsemen catch me and bring me back?"

"Oh, no," replied the black-browed maid. "The white horseman is the bright day, the red horseman is the golden sun, and the black horseman is the black night, and they will not touch you."

Vasilisa ran out into the passage, and Grumbler-Rumbler the Cat rushed at her and was about to scratch her. But she threw him a pie, and he did not touch her.

Vasilisa ran down from the porch, and the dog darted out and was about to bite her. But she threw him a piece of bread, and the dog let her go.

Vasilisa started running out of the yard, and the birch-tree tried to lash her and to put out her eyes. But she tied it with a ribbon, and the birch-tree let her pass.

The gate was about to shut before her, but Vasilisa greased its hinges, and it swung open.

Vasilisa ran into the dark forest, and just then the black horseman galloped by and it became pitch black all around. How was she to go back home without a light? What would she say? Why, her stepmother would do her to death.

So she asked her little doll to help her and

did what the doll told her to do.

She took one of the skulls from the fence and, mounting it on a stick, set off across the forest. Its eyes glowed, and by their light the dark night was as bright as day.

As for Baba-Yaga, she woke up and stretched and, seeing that Vasilisa was gone, rushed out into the passage.

"Did you scratch Vasilisa as she ran past, Grumbler-Rumbler?" she demanded.

And the cat replied:

"No, I let her pass, for she gave me a pie. I served you for ten years, Baba-Yaga, but you never gave me so much as a crust of bread."

Baba-Yaga rushed out into the yard.

"Did you bite Vasilisa, my faithful dog?" she demanded.

Said the dog in reply:

"No, I let her pass, for she gave me some bread. I served you for ever so many years, but you never gave me so much as a bone."

"Birch-tree, birch-tree!" Baba-Yaga roared. "Did you put out Vasilisa's eyes for her?"

Said the birch-tree in reply:

"No, I let her pass, for she bound my branches with a ribbon. I have been growing here for ten years, and you never even tied them with a string."

Baba-Yaga ran to the gate.

"Gate, gate!" she cried. "Did you shut before her that Vasilisa might not pass?"

Said the gate in reply:

"No, I let her pass, for she greased my hinges. I served you for ever so long, but you never even put water on them."

Baba-Yaga flew into a temper. She began to beat the dog and thrash the cat, to break down the gate and to chop down the birch-tree, and she was so tired by then that she forgot all about Vasilisa.

Vasilisa ran home, and she saw that there was no light on in the house. Her stepsisters rushed out and began to chide and scold her.

"What took you so long fetching the light?" they demanded. "We cannot seem to keep one on in the house at all. We have tried to strike a light again and again but to no avail, and the one we got from the neighbours went out the moment it was brought in. Perhaps yours will keep burning."

They brought the skull into the hut, and its eyes fixed themselves on the stepmother and her two daughters and burnt them like fire. The stepmother and her daughters tried to hide but, run where they would, the eyes followed them and never let them out of their sight.

By morning they were burnt to a cinder, all three, and only Vasilisa remained unharmed.

She buried the skull outside the hut, and a bush of red roses grew up on the spot.

After that, not liking to stay in the hut any longer, Vasilisa went into the town and made her home in the house of an old woman.

One day she said to the old woman:

"I am bored sitting around doing nothing, Grandma. Buy me some flax, the best you can find."

The old woman bought her some flax, and Vasilisa set to spinning yarn. She worked quickly and well, the spinning-wheel humming and the golden thread coming out as even and thin as a hair. She began to weave cloth, and it turned out so fine that it could be passed through the eye of a needle, like a thread. She bleached the cloth, and it came out whiter than snow.

The old woman looked at the cloth and gasped.

"No, my child, such cloth is only fit for a Tsarevich to wear. I had better take it to the palace."

She took the cloth to the palace, and when the Tsarevich saw it, he was filled with wonder.

"How much do you want for it?" he asked.

"This cloth is too fine to be sold, I have brought it to you for a present."

The Tsarevich thanked the old woman, showered her with gifts and sent her home.

But he could not find anyone to make him a shirt out of the cloth, for the workmanship had to be as fine as the fabric. So he sent for the old woman again and said:

"You wove this fine cloth, so you must know how to make a shirt out of it."

"It was not I that spun the yarn or wove the cloth, Tsarevich, but a maid named Vasilisa."

"Well, then, let her make me a shirt."

The old woman went home, and she told Vasilisa all about it.

Vasilisa made two shirts, embroidered them with silken threads, studded them with large, round pearls and, giving them to the old woman to take to the palace, sat down at the window with a piece of embroidery.

By and by whom should she see but one of the Tsar's servants come running toward her.

"The Tsarevich bids you come to the palace," said the servant.

Vasilisa went to the palace and, seeing her, the Tsarevich was smitten with her beauty.

"I cannot bear to let you go away again, you shall be my wife," said he.

He took both her milk-white hands in his and he placed her in the seat beside his own.

And so Vasilisa and the Tsarevich were married, and, when Vasilisa's father returned afterwards, he made his home in the palace with them.

Vasilisa took the old woman to live with her too, and, as for her little doll, she always carried it about with her in her pocket.

And thus are they living to this day, waiting for us to come for a stay.

"Tattercoats," from English Fairy Tales. *Retold by Flora Annie Steel, illustrated by Arthur Rackham (New York: Macmillan, 1918).*

This English tale has been compared to the Cinderella story in its treatment of the rejected child, the magic transformation of her clothing, and her marriage to a prince. However, there are two significant differences: Firstly, she is loved by the prince before the ball; travelling incognito, he sees her and loves her in spite of her poverty-stricken appearance. Secondly, her grandfather has rejected her because her birth has caused the death of his favorite daughter. He is strikingly portrayed at the opening and closing of the tale as an individual who cannot accept the fact that death is a natural aspect of life.

Tattercoats

In a great Palace by the sea there once dwelt a very rich old lord, who had neither wife nor children living, only one little granddaughter, whose face he had never seen in all her life. He hated her bitterly. because at her birth his favourite daughter died; and when the old nurse brought him the baby he swore that it might live or die as it liked, but he would never look on its face as long as it lived.

So he turned his back, and sat by his window looking out over the sea, and weeping great tears for his lost daughter, till his white hair and beard grew down over his shoulders and twined round his chair and crept into the chinks of the floor, and his tears, dropping on to the window-ledge, wore a channel through the stone, and ran away in a little river to the great sea. Meanwhile, his granddaughter grew up with no one to care for her, or clothe her; only the old nurse, when no one was by, would sometimes give her a dish of scraps from the kitchen, or a torn petticoat from the rag-bag; while the other servants of the palace would drive her from the house with blows and mocking words, calling her "Tattercoats," and pointing to her bare feet and shoulders, till she ran away, crying, to hide among the bushes.

So she grew up, with little to eat or to wear, spending her days out of doors, her only companion a crippled gooseherd, who fed his flock of geese on the common. And this gooseherd was a queer, merry little chap, and when she was hungry, or cold, or tired, he would play to her so gaily on his little pipe, that she forgot all her troubles, and would fall to dancing with his flock of noisy geese for partners.

Now one day people told each other that the King was travelling through the land, and was to give a great ball to all the lords and ladies of the country in the town near by, and that the Prince, his only son, was to choose a wife from amongst the maidens in the company. In due time one of the royal invitations to the ball was brought to the Palace by the sea, and the servants carried it up to the old lord, who still sat by his window, wrapped in his long white hair and weeping into the little river that was fed by his tears.

But when he heard the King's command, he dried his eyes and bade them bring shears to cut him loose, for his hair had bound him a fast prisoner, and he could not move. And then he sent them for rich clothes, and jewels, which he put on; and he ordered them to saddle the white horse, with gold and silk, that he might ride to meet the King; but he quite forgot he had a granddaughter to take to the ball.

Meanwhile Tattercoats sat by the kitchen-door weeping, because she could not go to see the grand doings. And when the old nurse heard her crying she went to the Lord of the Palace, and begged him to take his granddaughter with him to the King's ball.

But he only frowned and told her to be silent; while the servants laughed and said, "Tattercoats is happy in her rags, playing with the gooseherd! Let her be — it is all she is fit for."

A second, and then a third time, the old nurse begged him to let the girl go with him, but she was answered only by black looks and fierce words, till she was driven from the room by the jeering servants, with blows and mocking words.

Weeping over her ill-success, the old nurse went to look for Tattercoats; but the girl had been turned from the door by the cook, and had run away to tell her friend the gooseherd how unhappy she was because she could not go to the King's ball.

Now when the gooseherd had listened to her story, he bade her cheer up, and proposed that they should go together into the town to see the King, and all the fine things; and when she looked sorrowfully down at her rags and bare feet he played a note or two upon his pipe, so gay and merry, that she forgot all about her tears and her troubles, and before she well knew, the gooseherd had taken her by the hand, and she and he, and the geese before them, were dancing down the road towards the town.

"Even cripples can dance when they choose," said the gooseherd.

Before they had gone very far a handsome young man, splendidly dressed, riding up, stopped to ask the way to the castle where the King was staying, and when he found that they too were going thither, he got off his horse and walked beside them along the road.

"You seem merry folk," he said, "and will be good company."

"Good company, indeed," said the goose-

herd, and played a new tune that was not a dance.

It was a curious tune, and it made the strange young man stare and stare and stare at Tattercoats till he couldn't see her rags — till he couldn't, to tell the truth, see anything but her beautiful face.

Then he said, "You are the most beautiful maiden in the world. Will you marry me?"

Then the gooseherd smiled to himself, and played sweeter than ever.

But Tattercoats laughed. "Not I," said she; "you would be finely put to shame, and so would I be, if you took a goose-girl for your wife! Go and ask one of the great ladies you will see to-night at the King's ball, and do not flout poor Tattercoats."

But the more she refused him the sweeter the pipe played, and the deeper the young man fell in love; till at last he begged her to come that night at twelve to the King's ball, just as she was, with the gooseherd and his geese, in her torn petticoat and bare feet, and see if he wouldn't dance with her before the King and the lords and ladies, and present her to them all, as his dear and honoured bride.

Now at first Tattercoats said she would not; but the gooseherd said, "Take fortune when it comes, little one."

So when night came, and the hall in the castle was full of light and music, and the lords and ladies were dancing before the King, just as the clock struck twelve, Tattercoats and the gooseherd, followed by his flock of noisy geese, hissing and swaying their heads, entered at the great doors, and walked straight up the ball-room, while on either side the ladies whispered, the lords laughed, and the King seated at the far end stared in amazement.

But as they came in front of the throne Tattercoats' lover rose from beside the King, and came to meet her. Taking her by the hand, he kissed her thrice before them all, and turned to the King.

"Father!" he said — for it was the Prince himself — "I have made my choice, and here is my bride, the loveliest girl in all the land, and the sweetest as well!"

Before he finished speaking, the gooseherd had put his pipe to his lips and played a few notes that sounded like a bird singing far off in the woods; and as he played Tattercoats' rags were changed to shining robes sewn with glittering jewels, a golden crown lay upon her golden hair, and the flock of geese behind her became a crowd of dainty pages, bearing her long train.

And as the King rose to greet her as his daughter the trumpets sounded loudly in honour of the new Princess, and the people outside in the street said to each other:

"Ah! now the Prince has chosen for his wife the loveliest girl in all the land!"

But the gooseherd was never seen again, and no one knew what became of him; while the old lord went home once more to his Palace by the sea, for he could not stay at Court, when he had sworn never to look on his granddaughter's face.

So there he still sits by his window, — if you could only see him, as you may some day — weeping more bitterly than ever. And his white hair has bound him to the stones, and the river of his tears runs away to the great sea.

"Oochigeas and the Invisible Boy," from Glooscap and His Magic: Legends of the Wabanaki Indians, *by Kay Hill. Illustrations by Robert Frankenberg (Toronto: McClelland and Stewart, 1963).*

Often called the "Indian Cinderella," this East Coast Indian story may reflect the influence of European stories brought to North America in the eighteenth and early nineteenth centuries. However, it also embodies the cultural values of the Wabanaki people. Marriage was important because of the division of labor among these people: males hunted to provide the raw materials necessary for life, while females prepared these by cooking and making clothing. Glooscap, the demi-god, is a helper who enables people to realize their inner potentials, the most important of which is courage. His role is similar to that of fairy godmothers in many European tales.

Oochigeas and the Invisible Boy

There was once a Malicete Indian village on the edge of a lake in the land of the Wabanaki, and in this village lived three sisters. The two older girls, Oona and Abit, were handsome and proud, but the youngest, whom they called Oochigeas, was timid and plain. She suffered much from the selfishness of her sisters, but bore all their ill-treatment without complaint.

Because these girls had no parents, they were given meat by the tribe's hunters in return for making pottery. Through much practice, they had become the best makers of pots in the village. And this is how they made them. First Oona, the eldest, wove a basket from ash splints, then Abit lined it with wet clay. Finally, it was given to the youngest girl to harden in the fire. As the clay slowly baked, the wind blew the fire into Oochigeas' face, and in time her hair was singed close to her head and her face covered with burns. And that is why her sisters mocked her with the name Oochigeas, which means "little scarred one."

Now Glooscap the Great Chief knew all his People. He saw the misery of Oochigeas and pitied her, and he scowled at the cruelty of her sisters — yet he did nothing. And this was something that Marten, his servant, could not understand.

"My elder brother," said Marten, "though she is plain, her heart is kind. Can you not help her?"

"We will see," said the Great Chief with a wise nod. "Oochigeas must help herself first. Kindness is a great virtue, but courage is the first rule of my People."

Now on the far side of the lake, remote from the village, there lived an Indian youth called Team, who had the wonderful power of making himself invisible. To all save his sister he was as the rustle of a leaf in the forest, a sigh of wind in the treetops, or a breath of air in the heavens. His name meant "moose" and the moose was his *teomul*, or charm, that gave him his power. Having this magical power, Team needed no bow and arrow. He could walk straight up to game, without being seen or heard, and slay it with his bare hands.

One day, Team's sister appeared in the village.

"My brother is tired of living alone," she said to the people. "Team will marry the first girl who is able to see him."

Now, though no person had seen Team, or knew if he was tall or short, fat or thin, plain or handsome, yet they knew of his magic power and his great success in hunting. To the Indians, who live by hunting, a brave who can keep meat in his lodge all the time is admired above all others. He is a kind of prince. It is no wonder that every maiden in the village yearned to become the bride of the Invisible Boy.

All the unmarried maidens were eager to try their fortune and, one after another, each made a visit to the lodge across the lake. And, one after another, each came back disappointed. At last, all had made the attempt except the three sisters.

"Now it is my turn," said Oona. "I'm sure *I* shall be able to see him."

"You indeed!" sniffed Abit. "I'm as likely to see him as you are. Why should you go first?"

"I am the eldest!"

"Team is sure to want a younger woman!"

The two sisters glared at each other.

"You needn't think I shall let you go alone," declared Oona angrily.

"Then we'll go together," said Abit. And so they did.

Dressing themselves in their finest robes, they set off for the lodge across the lake. Team's sister received them kindly and took them to the wigwam to rest after their journey. Then, when it was time for her brother's return, she led them to the shore.

"Do you see my brother?" she asked.

The two girls gazed eagerly out over the lake. They saw a canoe approaching, but though it moved swiftly through the water, it appeared to be empty! No paddle could be seen, for whatever Team held or wore became also invisible.

Abit thought to herself that she would pretend to see him, and Team's sister would never know the difference.

"I see him!" she cried.

And Oona, not to be outdone, echoed, "Yes! I see him too!"

Team's sister knew that at least one of the girls lied, for only one maiden would be allowed to see her brother and that would be his future bride.

"Of what is his shoulder strap made?" she asked.

The two girls thought for a moment. They knew that, generally, Indians used rawhide or withe for their shoulder straps.

"A strip of rawhide," guessed Abit.

"No — withe!" cried Oona.

Then Team's sister knew that neither had seen her brother and she resolved to punish them for their dishonesty.

"Very well," she said quietly. "Come to the wigwam and help me prepare my brother's supper."

The two girls were anxious to know which of them had given the correct answer, so they followed Team's sister and helped her prepare the meal. Each hoped that she alone would see Team when he came. When all was ready, the sister of Team warned the girls not to sit in her brother's place but to remain on her side of the fire. Then, looking up, she greeted her brother — but the girls could see no one.

"Take my brother's load of meat," she told Abit, who looked around her in dismay. As long as the meat was on Team's shoulder, it could not be seen. Suddenly, a great load of venison dropped from nowhere on Abit's toes. Abit screamed and ran from the lodge in pain and fright. Now Team's sister told Oona to remove her brother's wet moccasins and put them to dry. Of course Oona could not do so. A pair of wet moccasins came suddenly sailing through the air and slapped her across the face. Then Oona too ran away, crying with mortification.

"My bride is a long time coming," sighed Team. "And those were very fine looking girls."

"Patience, my brother. You must have one who is brave and truthful, as well as lovely, and such a one has not come yet."

Abit and Oona returned home to vent their rage and spite on poor Oochigeas. To escape their cruelty, she fled to the woods and there, in a secluded spot, relieved her heart with tears. But when there were no tears left, and her spirit had been calmed by the peace of the forest, Oochigeas began to think. Now that her sisters had failed, she was the only maid left in the village who had not tried to see the Invisible Boy. Yet, if her fine sisters had failed, what chance had she, poor and plain as she was? A great hunter like Team would not wish a scar-faced girl like Oochigeas for a bride. All the same, hope stirred in her breast. Her heart began to beat fast at the thought of going to Team's lodge. She had no fine clothes to wear. Her sisters might try to stop her. The people would laugh. It would take courage —

Her mind was made up!

Oochigeas gathered sheets of birchbark and cut out a gown and cap and leggings, and sewed them together with grass. The clothing was stiff and awkward, and it crackled when she walked, but it covered her. Then she went home and found a pair of Oona's discarded moccasins. They were huge on her small feet and she had to tie them on by winding the strings around her ankles. She was truly an odd-looking sight, and her two sisters stared at her in amazement.

"Where are you going in that ridiculous outfit?" Oona asked.

"I am going to Team's lodge," answered Oochigeas.

"What! You foolish girl! Come back!"

"Oh, let her go," said Abit. "Let the people see her and she'll come back soon enough, in tears."

Oochigeas' way lay through the village, and the men and boys shouted and jeered at her.

"Shame, shame!"

"Ugly creature!"

"See how her burned hair sticks out from her cap!"

"Why does she wear birchbark instead of skins?"

"Come back, Oochigeas. Where do you think you're going? To see Team?" And they laughed so hard they rolled on the ground.

But, though her heart burned with shame, Oochigeas pretended not to hear, and walked on with her head high, until she was out of their sight. Then she hurried through the woods and around the edge of the lake, trying not to think of the ordeal ahead. Doubtless Team's sister would laugh at her too. Still she went on, and came at last to the lodge and saw Team's sister at the door.

"I have come," gasped Oochigeas before the other could speak, "I have come — to see Team — if I can." And she looked pleadingly at Team's sister.

"Come in and rest," said the sister of Team gently, and Oochigeas nearly wept at the unexpected kindness, but she managed to retain her dignity as they waited in silence for the sun to go down. Then Team's sister led her to the lake.

"Do you see my brother?"

Oochigeas looked and saw a canoe, empty. She heard the dip of a paddle and the swish of the water at the bow, but though she gazed with all her might, she saw no one. She whispered with a sinking heart, "No, I cannot see him."

"Look again," urged Team's sister, out of pity, and because the girl had so far been truthful. Oochigeas gazed once more at the canoe, and suddenly gave a gasp.

'Oh! Yes! Now I see him!"

"If you see him," said Team's sister quickly, "of what is his shoulder strap made?"

"Why it is made of a rainbow," marveled Oochigeas, and Team's sister knew her brother had found his bride. She led the girl back to the wigwam and stripped off her ugly clothes, bathed her, and dressed her in a doeskin, then gave her a comb to tidy her hair.

"Alas," thought Oochigeas, "I have so little hair to comb," but as she drew the comb against her head, she found to her amazement that her hair had grown suddenly long and thick. Moreover, the scars had gone from her face. She was beautiful!

Then the handsome Team came, laughing, and crying out, "At last I've found you, my lovely bride." And he led her to the wife's place in the wigwam. And from that day on, Oochigeas and Team, and Team's sister, lived out their days in peace and happiness.

Far away on Blomidon, Glooscap looked at Marten with a wise smile. He had known all along, you see, that Oochigeas had courage under her gentleness — and a brave spirit makes all things possible.

And so it happened. Kespeadooksit.

"The Girl Who Took Care of the Turkeys," *from* Finding the Center; Narrative Poetry of the Zuni Indians. *Translated by Dennis Tedlock (Lincoln: University of Nebraska Press, 1978).*

Although this story bears resemblance to "Cinderella," it illustrates another theme, that "just because there's a dance it doesn't relieve you of any responsibilities." The girl is punished because she has broken a promise to other beings who depended on her. In his translation, Tedlock has attempted to recapture the oral delivery of the Zuni people. Different sizes of type represent different levels of voice volume. Short pauses should be taken at the end of each line, longer ones for a single line gap in the text, and the longest pause for larger gaps. Notice that the number 4, sacred for most Native Peoples, is used, not the number 3, as is common in European stories.

The Girl Who Took Care of the Turkeys

Illustration by Harry P. Mera from "The Girl Who Took Care of Turkeys" from *Finding the Center,* by Dennis Tedlock. Copyright © 1978 by Harry P. Mera.

Son'ahchi.
(*audience*) Ee — — so.
There were villagers at the Middle Place

and
a girl
had her home

there
at Wind Place
where she kept a flock of turkeys.
At the Middle Place they were having a Yaaya Dance.
They were having a Yaaya Dance, and
during the first day
this girl
wasn't
drawn to the dance.
She stayed
with her turkeys
taking care of them.
That's the way
she lived:

it seems
she didn't go to the dance on the FIRST day, that day
she fed her turkeys, that's the way
they lived
and so
the dance went on
and she could hear the drum.
When she spoke to her turkeys about this, they said
"If you went
it wouldn't turn out well: who would take care of us?"
      that's what her turkeys told her.
She listened to them and they slept through the night.
Then it was the second day
of the dance
and night came.
That night
with the Yaaya Dance half over
she spoke to her big tom turkey:

"My father-child, if they're going to do it again tomorrow why can't I go?" she said. "Well if you went, it wouldn't turn out well."
That's what he told her. "Well then
I mustn't go."
That's what the girl said, and they slept through the night.
They slept through the night, and the next day
was a nice warm day, and
again she heard the drum over there.
Then she
went around feeding her turkeys, and

when it was the middle of the day, she asked
  again, right at noon.
(tight) "If you
went, it wouldn't turn out well.
There's no point in going:
let the dance be, you don't need to go, and our
lives depend on your thoughtfulness," that's
  what the turkeys told her.
"Well then, that's the way it will be," she said,
  and
she listened to them.
But around sunset the drum could be heard,
  and she was getting more anxious to go.
She went up on her roof and
  she could see the crowd of people.
It was the third day of the dance.
That night she asked the same one she'd asked
  before
and he told her, "Well, if you
must go

then you must dress well.
YOU
must go around
just four times:
you must THINK OF US," that's what he told
  her.
"You must think of us, for if
you stay all afternoon, until sunset
then it won't turn out well for you," he told
  her. "Well
well, I'll certainly do as you say: why should I
  stay there for a long time?
They get started early and I'll
do as you say," that's what she told her
her
tom turkey.
"Let's get some rest," they said, and they went
to sleep,
    but the girl JUST COULDN'T GET TO
    SLEEP.
So
she got up and built a fire in the fireplace
  then
she made some yucca suds.
She washed her body all over and then went
  back to bed
but she couldn't sleep, she
was so anxious, she was
EXCITED
about going to the dance, she was so excited.
  She passed the night.

THE NEXT DAY
the sun was shining, and
she went among her turkeys and spread their
  feed.
When she had fed them she said, "My
fathers, my children, I'm
going
to the Middle Place.
I'm going to the dance," she said. "Be on your
  way, but think of us.
Well
they'll start when you get to those
tall weeds, so
you'll get to the dance in plenty of time," that's
  what
her children told her. "Then that's the way it
  will be," she
  said, and she LEFT. *(pained)* It was getting
  so hot.
It was so hot when
she entered the village.
They noticed her then.
They noticed her when she came up.
She went to where
Rat Place is today, and
when she entered the plaza, the dance direc-
  tors noticed her.
Then they asked her to dance.
She went down and danced, and she didn't
didn't think about her children.
Finally it was midday, and when midday came
she was just dancing awa — —y until
it was late, the time when the shadows are very
  long.
The turkeys said, "Tisshomahha! our mother,
  our child
doesn't know what's right."
"Well then, I must GO
and I'll just warn her and come right back
and whether she hears me or not, we'll
LEAVE

before she gets here," that's what the tom turkey said, and
he flew away.
He flew along until he came to

where they were dancing, and there

he glided down to the Priest Kiva and perched
on the top crosspiece of the ladder, then he
sang:

KYANA
    A
     A
      A
       A
        A TOK TOK KYANA
                 A
                  A
                   A
                    A
                     A TOK TOK

   LI   LI   LI
YEE-E-E-E HU HU HU TOK TOK TOK TOK

THE ONE WHO WAS DANCING HEARD HIM.
     PAA_____
   LHA
   HE FLEW BACK to the place
where they were penned, and
the girl ran all the way back.
When she got to the place where they were
penned, they
    sang again, they sang and FLEW AWAY,
    GOING ON
until they came to what is now Turkey Tracks,
   and they glided down there.
When they glided down they stood there and
made their
    tracks.
WHEN SHE CAME NEAR they all went away
and she couldn't catch up with them.
Long ago, this was lived. That's why there's a
   place called Turkey Tracks. Lee — sem-
konikya.

"Kate Crackernuts," from Clever Gretchen
and Other Forgotten Folktales, *retold by
Alison Lurie. Illustrated by Margot Tomes
(New York: Crowell, 1980).*

   *In many linear journeys, the protagonist
begins in a position of wealth and security,
loses it, and at the end, because of the character's deeds, achieves greater fulfillment. Kate,
one of two step-sisters in this story, is unusual
in that she does not behave vindictively toward her sibling, but opposes her own mother
to rescue the girl. Like other female heroes such
as Molly Whuppie, she couples cleverness with
courage to achieve her goals.*

Kate Crackernuts

Once upon a time there was a king and a queen,
such as there have been in many lands. The king
had a daughter, and the queen had one also.
And though they were no kin, yet the two girls
loved each other better than sisters. But the
queen was jealous because the king's daughter
Anne was prettier than her own daughter Kate.
She wished to find some way to spoil Ann's
beauty; so she went to consult the henwife,
who was a witch.

   "Aye, I can help you," said the henwife.
"Send her to me in the morning; but make sure
she does not eat anything before she comes."
And she put her big black pot on the fire, and
boiled a sheep's hide and bones in it, with other
nasty things.

   Early in the morning the queen told Ann
to go to the henwife and fetch some eggs. But
as she left the house, Ann took up a crust of
bread to eat on the way. When she asked for
the eggs, the witch said to her, "Lift the lid off
that pot, and you will find what you need." So
the king's daughter lifted the lid; but nothing
came out of the pot except an evil smell. "Go
back to your mother, and tell her to keep her
pantry door better locked," said the henwife.

   When the queen heard this message, she
knew that Ann must have had something to eat.
So she locked her pantry, and next morning
sent the girl off again. But as Ann went through
the garden she saw the gardener picking vegetables. Being a friendly girl, she stopped to
speak with him, and he gave her a handful of
peas to eat. And when she got to the henwife's
house, everything happened just as before.

   On the third morning the queen went down
to the gate with Ann, so as to be certain she
would eat nothing on her way to the witch.
And this time, when Ann lifted the lid of the
pot, off jumped her own pretty head, and on
jumped a sheep's head in its place.

   When the queen looked out her window
and saw Ann coming back with her sheep's
head, she laughed out loud with satisfaction.
"Look at your sister," she said to her own
daughter Kate. "Now you are the prettiest by
far."

   "That pleases me not," said Kate. And she

would say no more to her mother, but wrapped a fine linen cloth around her sister's head, and took her by the hand, and they went out into the world together to seek their fortunes.

They walked on far, and further than I can tell, eating the berries that grew by the roadside, and the nuts that Kate gathered in her apron and cracked as they went along. At last they came to a tall castle. Kate knocked at the castle door, and begged a night's lodging for herself and her sister.

Now the king and queen of that place had two sons, and the elder of them was ill with a strange wasting illness. Though he ate heartily, and slept late, yet every morning he was more thin and pale than the evening before. The king had offered a peck of gold to anyone who would sit up with his son for three nights and find out what ailed him. Many had tried, but all had failed. But Kate was a clever girl and a brave girl, and she offered to sit up with the prince. She did not go boldly into his room as the others had, but arranged to have her self hidden there in the evening, and watched to see what would happen.

Till midnight all was quiet. As twelve o'clock struck, however, the sick prince rose, dressed himself, and went downstairs. He walked as if in a dream, and did not seem to notice Kate following after him. He went to the stables, saddled his horse, called his hound, and mounted. Kate leapt up behind him, but he paid her no heed. Away went the horse with the prince and Kate through the greenwood, where the nuts were ripe. As they passed under the trees, Kate picked the nuts and filled her apron with them, for she did not know when they might come back again.

They rode on and on, till they came to a green hill. There the prince drew rein and spoke for the first time, saying, "Open, open, green hill, and let in the young prince with his horse and his hound."

And Kate added, "And his lady behind him."

Then the hill opened, and they passed into a great hall filled with bright light that seemed to come from nowhere, and a strange music playing. Kate slipped down off the horse, and hid herself behind the door. At once the prince was surrounded by fairy ladies who led him off to the dance. All night he danced without stopping, first with one and then with another, and though he looked weary and worn they would not let him leave off.

At last the cock crew, and the prince made haste to mount his horse. Kate jumped up behind, and they rode home, where the prince lay down to sleep paler and more ill than before.

The next night when the clock struck twelve the same thing happened; and again Kate rode through the forest behind the prince into the green hill. This time she did not watch the dancing, but crept near to where some of the fairy people were sitting together and a fairy baby was playing with a wand.

"What news in the world above?" said one.

"No news," said the other, "but that a sad lady with a sheep's head has come to lodge in the castle."

"Is that so?" said the first, laughing. "If only she knew that three strokes of that wand would make her as fair as she ever was."

Kate heard this, and thought that she must have the wand. She took some nuts and rolled them toward the baby from behind the door, till the baby ran after the nuts and let the wand fall, and Kate snatched it up and put it in her apron. At cockcrow she rode home as before, and the prince lay down to sleep, looking weary and ill unto death. Kate ran to her room and tapped her sister Ann three times with the wand; and the sheep's head jumped off and Ann had her own pretty head again. Then Ann dressed herself and went into the great hall of the castle where all welcomed her, and the king's younger son thought that he had never seen anyone sweeter and prettier in his life.

On the third night, Kate watched the sick prince again, and rode behind him to the green hill. Again she hid behind the door and listened to the talk of the fairy people. This time the little child was playing with a yellow bird.

"What news in the world above?" said one fairy to the other.

"No news, but that the king and queen are at their wits' end to know what ails their eldest son."

"Is that so?" said the first fairy, laughing.

"If only they knew that three bites of that birdie would free him from the spell and make him as well as ever he was."

Kate heard this, and thought that she must have the yellow birdie. So she rolled nuts to the baby until he ran after them and dropped the birdie, and she caught it up and put it in her apron.

At cockcrow they set off for home again, and as soon as they got there Kate plucked and cooked the yellow birdie and took it to the prince. He was lying in bed more dead than alive after his night's dancing; but when he smelled the dish, he opened his eyes and said, "Oh, I wish I had a bite of that birdie!" So Kate gave him a bite, and he rose up on his elbow.

By and by he cried out again, "Oh, if only I had another bite of that birdie!" Kate gave him another bite, and the prince sat up on his bed and looked about him. Then he said again, "Oh, if only I had a third bite of that birdie!" Kate gave him a third bite, and he got out of bed, well and strong again. He dressed himself and sat down by the fire, and Kate told him all that had passed. They stayed there till it was full morning, and the people of the castle came in and found them cracking nuts together.

So Kate married the king's eldest son, and Ann married his brother, and they lived happily together ever after.

"Rapunzel," from The Complete Grimm's Fairy Tales *(New York: Pantheon, 1944).*

The early part of this German tale contains two widespread motifs: the arrival of a long-awaited child who, while growing up, will have a difficult life; and the parents' promise, in desperation, to give up their first born. Although the circumstances of Rapunzel's early life are beyond her control, she does influence the events of her life with the prince. In fact, this phase of the story has often been interpreted psychologically. As she matures, the girl is seen as coming to understand the true value of adult love.

Rapunzel

There were once a man and a woman who had long in vain wished for a child. At length the woman hoped that God was about to grant her desire. These people had a little window at the back of their house from which a splendid garden could be seen, which was full of the most beautiful flowers and herbs. It was, however, surrounded by a high wall, and no one dared to go into it because it belonged to an enchantress, who had great power and was dreaded by all the world. One day the woman was standing by this window and looking down into the garden, when she saw a bed which was planted with the most beautiful rampion (rapunzel), and it looked so fresh and green that she longed for it, and had the greatest desire to eat some. This desire increased every day, and as she knew that she could not get any of it, she quite pined away, and began to look pale and miserable. Then her husband was alarmed, and asked: "What ails you, dear wife?" "Ah," she replied, "if I can't eat some of the rampion, which is in the garden behind our house, I shall die." The man, who loved her, thought: "Sooner than let your wife die, bring her some of the rampion yourself, let it cost what it will." At twilight, he clambered down over the wall into the garden of the enchantress, hastily clutched a handful of rampion, and took it to his wife. She at once made herself a salad of it, and ate it greedily. It tasted so good to her — so very good, that the next day she longed for it three times as much as before. If he was to have any rest, her husband must once more descend into the garden. In the gloom of evening, therefore, he let himself down again; but when he had clambered down the wall he was terribly afraid, for he saw the enchantress standing before him. "How can you dare," said she with angry look, "descend into my garden and steal my rampion like a thief? You shall suffer for it!" "Ah," answered he, "let mercy take the place of justice, I only made up my mind to do it out of necessity. My wife saw your rampion from the window, and felt such a longing for it that she would have died if she had not got some to eat." Then the enchantress allowed her anger to be softened, and said to him: "If the case be as you say, I will allow you to take away with you as much rampion as you will, only I make one condition, you must give me the child which your wife will bring into the world; it shall be well treated, and I will care for it like a mother." The man in his terror consented to everything, and when the woman was brought to bed, the enchantress appeared at once, gave the child the name of Rapunzel, and took it away with her.

Rapunzel grew into the most beautiful child under the sun. When she was twelve years old, the enchantress shut her into a tower, which lay in a forest, and had neither stairs nor door, but quite at the top was a little window. When the enchantress wanted to go in, she placed herself beneath it and cried:

> "Rapunzel, Rapunzel,
> Let down your hair to me."

Rapunzel had magnificent long hair, fine as spun gold, and when she heard the voice of the enchantress she unfastened her braided tresses, wound them round one of the hooks of the window above, and then the hair fell twenty ells down, and the enchantress climbed up by it.

After a year or two, it came to pass that the King's son rode through the forest and passed by the tower. Then he heard a song, which was so charming that he stood still and listened. This was Rapunzel, who in her solitude passed her time in letting her sweet voice resound. The King's son wanted to climb up to her, and looked for the door of the tower, but none was to be found. He rode home, but the singing had so deeply touched his heart, that every day he went out into the forest and listened to it. Once when he was thus standing behind a tree, he saw that an enchantress came there, and he heard how she cried:

> "Rapunzel, Rapunzel,
> Let down your hair."

Then Rapunzel let down the braids of her hair, and the enchantress climbed up to her. "If that is the ladder by which one mounts, I too will

try my fortune," said he, and the next day when it began to grow dark, he went to the tower and cried:

> "Rapunzel, Rapunzel,
> Let down your hair."

Immediately the hair fell down and the King's son climbed up.

At first Rapunzel was terribly frightened when a man, such as her eyes had never yet beheld, came to her; but the King's son began to talk to her quite like a friend, and told her that his heart had been so stirred that it had let him have no rest, and he had been forced to see her. Then Rapunzel lost her fear, and when he asked her if she would take him for her husband, and she saw that he was young and handsome, she thought: "He will love me more than old Dame Gothel does"; and she said yes, and laid her hand in his. She said: "I will willingly go away with you, but I do not know how to get down. Bring with you a skein of silk every time that you come, and I will weave a ladder with it, and when that is ready I will descend, and you will take me on your horse." They agreed that until that time he should come to her every evening, for the old woman came by day. The enchantress remarked nothing of this, until once Rapunzel said to her: "Tell me, Dame Gothel, how it happens that you are so much heavier for me to draw up than the young King's son — he is with me in a moment." "Ah! you wicked child," cried the enchantress. "What do I hear you say! I thought I had separated you from all the world, and yet you have deceived me!" In her anger she clutched Rapunzel's beautiful tresses, wrapped them twice round her left hand, seized a pair of scissors with the right, and snip, snap, they were cut off, and the lovely braids lay on the ground. And she was so pitiless that she took poor Rapunzel into a desert where she had to live in great grief and misery.

On the same day that she cast out Rapunzel, however, the enchantress fastened the braids of hair, which she had cut off, to the hook of the window, and when the King's son came and cried:

> "Rapunzel, Rapunzel,
> Let down your hair,"

she let the hair down. The King's son ascended, but instead of finding his dearest Rapunzel, he found the enchantress, who gazed at him with wicked and venomous looks. "Aha!" she cried mockingly, "you would fetch your dearest, but the beautiful bird sits no longer singing in the nest; the cat has got it, and will scratch out your eyes as well. Rapunzel is lost to you; you will never see her again." The King's son was beside himself with pain, and in his despair he leapt down from the tower. He escaped with his life, but the thorns into which he fell pierced his eyes. Then he wandered quite blind about the forest, ate nothing but roots and berries, and did naught but lament and weep over

the loss of his dearest wife. Thus he roamed about in misery for some years, and at length came to the desert where Rapunzel, with the twins to which she had given birth, a boy and a girl, lived in wretchedness. He heard a voice, and it seemed so familiar to him that he went towards it, and when he approached, Rapunzel knew him and fell on his neck and wept. Two of her tears wetted his eyes and they grew clear again, and he could see with them as before. He led her to his kingdom where he was joyfully received, and they lived for a long time afterwards, happy and contented.

"La Belle au Bois Dormant," from About Sleeping Beauty, *by P.L. Travers. Illustrated by Charles Keeping (New York: McGraw-Hill, 1975), and "Little Briar-Rose," from* The Complete Grimm's Fairy Tales *(New York: Pantheon, 1944).*

Like "Rapunzel," the story of the Sleeping Beauty contains the motif of the long-awaited child. It can also be interpreted as a study of the maturation process. The princess's sleep has been interpreted as a period of self-contemplation necessary before the arrival at mature adulthood symbolized by the awak-

ening kiss of the prince. The girl's parents, by ordering the destruction of all spindles, have foolishly attempted to stop the inevitable growth process. The Brothers Grimm's version ends with the marriage, while Perrault's includes a narration of the princess's troubled married life. Perrault places greater emphasis on the prince's character. At first, he is immature, hiding his marriage from his ogre mother; later he fails in his responsibilities as a father and husband by departing for the wars. Only at the conclusion does he accept his commitments.

La Belle
au Bois Dormant
(The Beauty Sleeping in the Wood)

Once upon a time there were a king and a queen who were very unhappy because they had no children. They were more unhappy than words can tell. They went to all the watering places in the world. They tried everything — prayers, pilgrimages, vows to saints — but it made no difference. At last, however, the Queen conceived and gave birth to a daughter. A splendid christening was arranged. All the fairies who could be found in the country — there were seven of them — were invited to be godmothers, so that, if each of them brought a gift

(as was the custom of the fairies in those days), the little Princess would be endowed with every quality imaginable.

When the christening was over, the whole company went back to the King's palace, where a great banquet had been prepared for the fairies. A magnificent place was laid for each of them, with a solid gold case containing a knife, a fork, and a spoon of finest gold inset with diamonds and rubies. But just as they were all sitting down, who should come in but an old fairy who had not been invited because she had remained shut up in a tower for fifty years or more and everyone had believed her to be dead or under a spell.

The King ordered a place to be laid for her, but it was impossible to give her a gold case like the others because only seven had been made, for the seven known fairies. The old fairy took this as a slight and muttered threats under her breath. One of the younger fairies, who was sitting next to her, heard this muttering and guessed that she might give the Princess some harmful gift. So, the moment the meal was finished, she went and hid behind the tapestry. In that way she would be the last to speak and could make up, as far as lay in her power, for any harm that the old fairy might do.

Meanwhile, the fairies began to present their gifts to the Princess. The youngest gave her the gift of perfect beauty; the next promised that she should be marvellously witty and gay; the third that she should be exquisitely graceful in all her movements; the fourth, that she should dance beautifully; the fifth that she should sing like a nightingale; and the sixth that she should play all kinds of instruments to perfection. When the turn of the old fairy came, she said, trembling more with anger than with age, that the Princess would run a spindle into her hand and would die in consequence.

When they heard her make this terrible gift a shudder ran through the whole company, and none could restrain their tears. But at that moment the young fairy came out from behind the tapestry and said:

"Set your minds at rest, King and Queen,

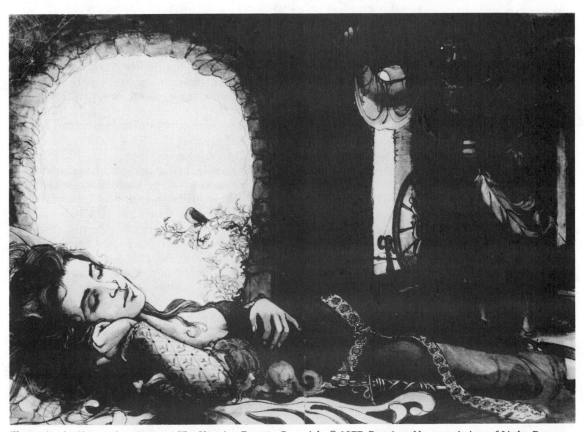

Illustration by Trina Schart Hyman, *The Sleeping Beauty.* Copyright © 1977. Reprinted by permission of Little, Brown and Co.

your daughter shall not die from this cause. It is true that I have not the power to undo entirely what my senior has done. The Princess *will* run a spindle into her hand. But, instead of dying, she will simply fall into a deep sleep which will last a hundred years, at the end of which the son of a king will come to wake her.''

Hoping to avoid the disaster predicted by the old fairy, the King immediately issued a proclamation forbidding all his subjects to spin with spindles, or to have spindles in their homes, on pain of death.

Fifteen or sixteen years later, when the King and Queen were away at one of their country houses, it happened that the young Princess was playing about in the castle. Running from room to room, she reached the top of a big tower and came to a little attic where a dear old woman was sitting by herself spinning. This old woman had not heard of the King's proclamation forbidding the use of spindles.

''What is that you are doing?'' asked the Princess.

''Spinning, my dear,'' said the old woman, who did not know who she was.

''How pretty it is,'' said the Princess. ''How do you do it? Give it to me and let me try.''

No sooner had she taken it up than—since she was hasty and rather careless and, besides, the fairies had so ordained it—she ran the spindle into her hand and immediately fainted away.

The old woman was greatly upset and called for help. People came running from all over the palace. They poured water on the Princess's face, unlaced her dress, chafed her hands and rubbed her forehead with essence of rosemary, but nothing would bring her back to life.

Then the King, who had returned to the palace and came up to see what the noise was about, remembered the fairy's prophecy. Realising that this had to happen, since the fairies had said so, he had the Princess carried to the finest room in the palace and placed on a bed embroidered in gold and silver. She looked like an angel — she was so beautiful. Her swoon had not drained the colour from her face; her cheeks were still rosy, her lips like coral. Her eyes were closed, but she could be heard breathing gently, which showed that she was not dead.

The King gave orders that she was to be left to sleep there quietly until the day came when she was to awake. The good fairy who had saved her life by dooming her to sleep for a hundred years was in the Kingdom of Mataquin, twelve thousand leagues away, at the time of the accident. But the news was brought to her instantly by a little dwarf with seven-league boots (that is, boots which covered seven leagues at a single stride). The fairy set off immediately in a carriage of fire drawn by dragons, and was there within the hour. The King came out to hand her down from her carriage. She approved everything that he had done. But, as she was extremely farsighted, she reflected that, when the Princess eventually awoke, she would feel most uncomfortable to be all alone in that old castle. So this is what she did.

She touched with her wand everything in the castle, except the King and Queen; governesses, maids-of-honour, chambermaids, gentlemen-in-waiting, officers of the household, stewards, cooks, scullions, potboys, guards, doorkeepers, pages, footmen. She also touched all the horses in the stables, with the grooms, the big watchdogs, and little Puff, the Princess's puppy, who was lying beside her on the bed. No sooner had she touched them than they all fell asleep, to wake only when their mistress did, ready to serve her when she needed them. Even the roasting-spits which were turning before the fire crammed with partridges and pheasants went to sleep, and the fire also. All this was performed in a twinkling, for the fairies always did their work fast.

The King and Queen, having kissed their dear child without her waking, left the castle and gave orders that no one was to go near it. These orders were not necessary for within a quarter of an hour there grew up all around such a number of big and little trees, brambles, and tangled thorns, that neither man nor beast could have passed through. Nothing but the tops of the towers could be seen and then only from a considerable distance. It was obvious that the fairy had worked another of her magic spells to guard the Princess from prying eyes while she slept.

At the end of a hundred years, the son of the King who was then reigning and who belonged to a different family from the sleeping Princess, was out hunting in that neighbourhood and inquired what were the towers which he could see above the trees of a thick wood.

His followers gave him different answers according to the versions they had heard. Some said that it was an old castle haunted by spirits; others that it was the place where all the witches of the region held their sabbath. The most widespread belief was that it was the home of an ogre who carried off all the children he could catch to eat them there undisturbed, since he alone had the power of passing through the wood.

The Prince did not know what to believe, when an old peasant came forward and said: "Your Highness, more than fifty years ago I heard my father say that there was a most beautiful princess in that castle. He said that she was to sleep for a hundred years and that she would be awakened by a king's son, for whom she was intended."

These words acted on the young Prince like a spur. He felt certain that this was an exploit which he could accomplish and, fired by love and the desire for glory, he determined to put the story to the test there and then. As he entered the wood, all the big trees, the brambles and the thorn bushes bent aside of their own accord to let him pass. He advanced towards the castle, which he could see at the far end of a long avenue. He was a little surprised to find that none of his men had been able to follow him, since the trees had sprung back as soon as he had passed through. But that did not deter him from going on. A prince is always brave when he is young and in love. He reached the great forecourt, where everything that met his eyes might well have stricken him with fear. There was a dreadful silence. The image of death was everywhere. The place was full of the prostrate bodies of men and animals, all apparently dead. But the Prince soon saw, by the red noses and ruddy cheeks of the doorkeepers, that they were only asleep; and their glasses, which still contained a few drops of

wine, showed plainly enough that they had fallen asleep while drinking.

He went on into a big courtyard paved with marble, up a staircase and into the guardroom, where the guards were drawn up in two lines with their harquebusses on their shoulders, snoring away loudly. He passed through several rooms filled with ladies and gentlemen who were all asleep, some on their feet, others seated. At last he came to a room with golden panelling and saw on a bed, whose curtains were drawn aside, the loveliest sight he had ever seen; a princess of about fifteen or sixteen, whose radiant beauty seemed to glow with a kind of heavenly light. Trembling and wondering, he drew near and knelt down before her.

Then, as the spell had come to its end, the Princess awoke and, looking at him more tenderly than would seem proper for a first glance, "Is it you, my Prince?" she said. "You have been a long time coming."

Delighted by these words, and still more so by the tone in which they were uttered, the Prince hardly knew how to express his joy and gratitude. He swore that he loved her better than life itself. His speech was halting, but it pleased her all the more; for the less ready the tongue, the stronger the love. He was more confused than she was and it was scarcely surprising. She had had time to think out what she would say to him, for it seems very probable (though the story does not say so) that the good fairy had arranged for her long sleep to be filled with pleasant dreams. In short, they went on talking to each other for four hours, and still had not said half the things they wanted to say.

Meanwhile, the whole palace had awakened with the Princess. Each had gone about his duties and, since they were not all in love, they were dying of hunger. The lady-in-waiting, as famished as the others, grew impatient and loudly announced that dinner was ready. The Prince helped the Princess to get up. She was fully dressed in sumptuous clothes, and the Prince took good care not to tell her that she was turned out just like my grandmother, even to the high starched collar. She was no less beautiful for that.

They passed into a hall of mirrors, and there they supped, attended by the officers of the Princess's household. Violins and oboes played old but delightful airs, which had not been heard for nearly a hundred years. And after supper, without wasting time, the chaplain married them in the palace chapel and the lady-in-waiting drew the bed-curtains round them. They slept little. The Princess hardly needed to and the Prince had to leave her early in the morning to get back to the town, where his father would be growing anxious about him.

The Prince told him that he had lost his way while out hunting in the forest and had spent the night in a charcoal-burner's hut, where he had supped on black bread and cheese. The King was an easygoing man and believed him. But his mother was not entirely convinced and noticing that he went out hunting nearly every day and always had an excuse ready when he did not come home at night, she felt certain that he was engaged in some love affair. For he lived with the Princess for more than two years and they had two children. The first, a daughter, was called Dawn and the second, a son, was called Day because he looked even more beautiful than his sister.

Several times the Queen tried to make her son confide in her by saying to him that it was natural to take one's pleasures in life, but he never dared reveal his secret to her. Although he loved her, he feared her because she came of a family of ogres, and the King had only married her for the sake of her wealth. It was even whispered that she had ogreish appetites herself and that when she saw little children about she had the greatest difficulty in restraining herself from pouncing on them. That was why the Prince would not confide in her.

But when the King died, as he did after two years, and the Prince became the master, he announced his marriage publicly and went with great ceremony to fetch his wife, the Queen, from the castle. She was given a royal welcome when she drove into the capital seated between her two children.

Some time after that, the King went to war against his neighbour, the Emperor Cantalabutto. He left the kingdom in charge of the Queen Mother, bidding her to take the great-est care of his wife and children. He was to be away at the war for the whole summer. As soon as he had gone, the Queen Mother sent her daughter-in-law and the children to a country house in the woods where she would be able to satisfy her horrible appetites more easily. She herself followed them a few days later, and one evening she said to her steward: "I wish to have little Dawn for my dinner tomorrow."

"But Your Majesty — " said the steward.

"It is my wish," said the Queen (and her voice was the voice of an ogress who is craving for human flesh) "and I wish to have her served with mustard-and-onion sauce."

The miserable steward, realising that it was useless to trifle with an ogress, took his largest knife and went up to little Dawn's room. She was then four years old and she came skipping and laughing to fling her arms round his neck and asked him for sweets. Tears came into his eyes and the knife fell from his hand. He went out to the farmyard and killed a young lamb which he cooked with such a delicious sauce that his mistress declared she had never eaten anything so good. At the same time he took away little Dawn and gave her to his wife to hide in the cottage they had at the bottom of the farmyard.

A week later the wicked Queen said to the steward:

"I wish to have little Day for my supper."

He made no reply, having decided to trick her in the same way as before. He went to fetch little Day and found him with a tiny foil in his hand, fencing with a pet monkey, though he was only three. He carried him down to his wife, to be hidden with little Dawn, and served instead a very tender young kid which the orgress found excellent.

So far, things had gone very well. But one evening the wicked Queen said to the steward: "I wish to have the Queen, served with the same sauce as her children."

When he heard this, the poor steward despaired of tricking her again. The young Queen was over twenty, without counting the hundred years during which she had been asleep. Her skin was a little tough, although it was smooth and white. Where would he find a skin as tough as that among the farmyard animals?

Since his own life was at stake, he made up his mind to cut the Queen's throat and went up to her room intending to act quickly. Working himself into a fury, he burst into the room, knife in hand. But he did not want to take her unawares, so he told her with great respect of the order he had received from the Queen Mother.

"Do your duty, then," she said, baring her throat to the knife. "Carry out the order you have been given. I shall see my children again, my poor children whom I loved so dearly!" For she believed them to be dead, since they had been taken away without a word of explanation.

"No, no, Your Majesty," replied the unhappy steward, completely won over, "you shall not die and you shall still see your dear children. But you shall see them in my house, where I have hidden them. And I will trick the Queen again, by giving her a young doe to eat in place of you."

He took her quickly to his house and, leaving her there to embrace her children, he set about preparing a doe which the Queen Mother ate for supper with as much relish as if it had been the young Queen herself. She was well pleased with her cruelty and she intended to tell the King, when he came back, that ravening wolves had devoured his wife and his two children.

One evening when she was prowling as usual about the yards and courtyards of the castle to see if she could smell out some young human flesh, she heard the voice of little Day in a ground-floor room. He was crying because he had been naughty and his mother was threatening to have him whipped. She also heard little Dawn, who was begging for her brother to be let off.

The ogress recognised the voices of the Queen and her children and was furious to find that she had been tricked. The next morning she called in a voice of thunder for a huge vat to be placed in the middle of the courtyard and filled with toads, vipers, adders, and other poisonous reptiles. Into this were to be cast the Queen and her children, with the steward, his wife, and his servant, who had all been led out on her order with their hands tied behind their backs.

They were standing there and the executioners were preparing to cast them into the vat when the King, who was not expected back so soon, came riding into the courtyard. He had been travelling posthaste and, filled with amazement, he demanded to know the meaning of this horrible sight. No one dared to enlighten him, but the ogress, furious at the turn things had taken, flung herself headlong into the vat and was devoured in an instant by the foul creatures which she had placed there. The King could not help feeling sorry, for she was his mother. But he soon consoled himself with his beautiful wife and his children.

Little Briar-Rose

A long time ago there were a King and Queen who said every day: "Ah, if only we had a child!" but they never had one. But it happened that once when the Queen was bathing, a frog crept out of the water on to the land, and said to her: "Your wish shall be fulfilled; before a year has gone by, you shall have a daughter."

What the frog had said came true, and the Queen had a little girl who was so pretty that the King could not contain himself for joy, and ordered a great feast. He invited not only his kindred, friends and acquaintances, but also the Wise Women, in order that they might be kind and well-disposed towards the child. There were thirteen of them in his kingdom, but, as he had only twelve golden plates for them to eat out of, one of them had to be left at home.

The feast was held with all manner of splendor, and when it came to an end the Wise Women bestowed their magic gifts upon the baby: one gave virtue, another beauty, a third riches, and so on with everything in the world that one can wish for.

When eleven of them had made their promises, suddenly the thirteenth came in. She wished to avenge herself for not having been invited, and without greeting, or even looking at anyone, she cried with a loud voice: "The King's daughter shall in her fifteenth year prick herself with a spindle, and fall down dead."

And, without saying a word more, she turned round and left the room.

They were all shocked; but the twelfth, whose good wish still remained unspoken, came forward, and as she could not undo the evil sentence, but only soften it, she said: "It shall not be death, but a deep sleep of a hundred years, into which the princess shall fall."

The King, who would fain keep his dear child from the misfortune, gave orders that every spindle in the whole kingdom should be burnt. Meanwhile the gifts of the Wise Women were plenteously fulfilled on the young girl, for she was so beautiful, modest, good-natured, and wise, that everyone who saw her was bound to love her.

It happened that on the very day when she was fifteen years old, the King and Queen were not at home, and the maiden was left in the palace quite alone. So she went round into all sorts of places, looked into rooms and bed-chambers just as she liked, and at last came to an old tower. She climbed up the narrow winding-staircase, and reached a little door. A rusty key was in the lock, and when she turned it the door sprang open, and there in a little room sat an old woman with a spindle, busily spinning her flax.

"Good day, old mother," said the King's daughter; "what are you doing there?" "I am spinning," said the old woman, and nodded her head. "What sort of thing is that, that rattles round so merrily?" said the girl, and she took the spindle and wanted to spin too. But scarcely had she touched the spindle when the magic decree was fulfilled, and she pricked her finger with it.

And, in the very moment when she felt the prick, she fell down upon the bed that stood there, and lay in a deep sleep. And this sleep extended over the whole palace; the King and Queen who had just come home, and had entered the great hall, began to go to sleep, and the whole of the court with them. The horses, too, went to sleep in the stable, the dogs in the yard, the pigeons upon the roof, the flies on the wall; even the fire that was flaming on the hearth became quiet and slept, the roast meat left off frizzling, and the cook, who was just going to pull the hair of the scullery boy, be-cause he had forgotten something, let him go, and went to sleep. And the wind fell, and on the trees before the castle not a leaf moved again.

But round about the castle there began to grow a hedge of thorns, which every year became higher, and at last grew close up round the castle and all over it, so that there was nothing of it to be seen, not even the flag upon the roof. But the story of the beautiful sleeping "Briar-rose," for so the princess was named, went about the country, so that from time to time Kings' sons came and tried to get through the thorny hedge into the castle.

But they found it impossible, for the thorns held fast together, as if they had hands, and the youths were caught in them, could not get loose again, and died a miserable death.

After long, long years a King's son came again to that country, and heard an old man talking about the thorn-hedge, and that a castle was said to stand behind it in which a wonderfully beautiful princess, named Briar-rose, had been asleep for a hundred years; and that the King and Queen and the whole court were asleep likewise. He had heard, too, from his grandfather, that many kings' sons had already come, and had tried to get through the thorny hedge, but they had remained sticking fast in it, and had died a pitiful death. Then the youth said: "I am not afraid, I will go and see the beautiful Briar-rose." The good old man might dissuade him as he would, he did not listen to his words.

But by this time the hundred years had just passed, and the day had come when Briar-rose was to awake again. When the King's son came near to the thorn-hedge, it was nothing but large and beautiful flowers, which parted from each other of their own accord, and let him pass unhurt, then they closed again behind him like a hedge. In the castle yard he saw the horses and the spotted hounds lying asleep; on the roof sat the pigeons with their heads under their wings. And when he entered the house, the flies were asleep upon the wall, the cook in the kitchen was still holding out his hand to seize the boy, and the maid was sitting by the black hen which she was going to pluck.

He went on farther, and in the great hall he

saw the whole of the court lying asleep, and up by the throne lay the King and Queen.

Then he went on still farther, and all was so quiet that a breath could be heard, and at last he came to the tower, and opened the door into the little room where Briar-rose was sleeping. There she lay, so beautiful that he could not turn his eyes away; and he stooped down and gave her a kiss. But as soon as he kissed her, Briar-rose opened her eyes and awoke, and looked at him quite sweetly.

Then they went down together, and the King awoke, and the Queen, and the whole court, and looked at each other in great astonishment. And the horses in the courtyard stood up and shook themselves; the hounds jumped up and wagged their tails; the pigeons upon the roof pulled out their heads from under their wings, looked round, and flew into the open country; the flies on the wall crept again; the fire in the kitchen burned up and flickered and cooked the meat; the joint began to turn and sizzle again, and the cook gave the boy such a box on the ear that he screamed, and the maid finished plucking the fowl.

And then the marriage of the King's son with Briar-rose was celebrated with all splendor, and they lived contented to the end of their days.

"Snow-White and the Seven Dwarfs," from The Juniper Tree and Other Tales from Grimm. *Selected by Lore Segal and Maurice Sendak (New York: Farrar, Straus and Giroux, 1973).*

Like the three preceding folktales, this is a story of maturation. Snow-White's inability to resist the temptations of the disguised, wicked stepmother implies that she is not perfect herself, revealing vanity, and forgetting the strict warnings of the dwarfs. No one else can save her, and she, apparently, does not wish to save herself. Only the power of mature adult love can save her. The queen, who is so narcissistic that she cannot stand the threat of her stepdaughter's beauty, receives violent justice of a kind often found in the folktales collected by the Grimms.

Snow-White and the Seven Dwarfs

Once it was the middle of winter, and the snowflakes fell from the sky like feathers. At a window with a frame of ebony a queen sat and sewed. And as she sewed and looked out at the snow, she pricked her finger with the needle, and three drops of blood fell in the snow. And in the white snow the red looked so beautiful that she thought to herself: "If only I had a child as white as snow, as red as blood, and as black as the wood in the window frame!" And after a while she had a little daughter as white as snow, as red as blood, and with hair as black as ebony, and because of that she was called Snow-White. And when the child was born, the queen died.

After a year the king took himself another wife. She was a beautiful woman, but she was proud and haughty and could not bear that anyone should be more beautiful than she. She had a wonderful mirror, and when she stood in front of it and looked in it and said:

"Mirror, mirror on the wall,
Who is fairest of us all?"

then the mirror would answer:

"Queen, thou art the fairest of us all!"

Then she was satisfied, because she knew that the mirror spoke the truth.

But Snow-White kept growing, and kept

growing more beautiful, and when she was seven years old, she was as beautiful as the bright day, and more beautiful than the Queen herself. Once when she asked her mirror:

"Mirror, mirror on the wall,
    Who is fairest of us all?"

it answered:

"Queen, thou art the fairest in this hall,
    But Snow-White's fairer than us all."

Then the Queen was horrified, and grew yellow and green with envy. From that hour on, whenever she saw Snow-White the heart of her body would turn over, she hated the girl so. And envy and pride, like weeds, kept growing higher and higher in her heart, so that day and night she had no peace. Then she called a huntsman and said: "Take the child out into the forest, I don't want to lay eyes on her again. You kill her, and bring me her lung and liver as a token."

"Snow White and the Seven Dwarfs" from *The Juniper Tree and Other Tales from Grimm* tr. by Lore Segal and Randall Jarrell. Illustrated by Maurice Sendak. Copyright © 1973. Reprinted by permission of Farrar, Strauss, Giroux Publishers.

The hunter obeyed, and took her out, and when he had drawn his hunting knife and was about to pierce Snow-White's innocent heart, she began to weep and said: "Oh, dear huntsman, spare my life! I'll run off into the wild forest and never come home again." And because she was so beautiful, the huntsman pitied her and said: "Run away then, you poor child."

"Soon the wild beasts will have eaten you," he thought, and yet it was as if a stone had been lifted from his heart not to have to kill her. And as a young boar just then came running by, he killed it, cut out its lung and liver, and brought them to the Queen as a token. The cook had to cook them in salt, and the wicked woman ate them up and thought that she had eaten Snow-White's lung and liver.

Now the poor child was all, all alone in the great forest, and so terrified that she stared at all the leaves on the trees and didn't know what to do. She began to run, and ran over the sharp stones and through the thorns, and the wild beasts sprang past her, but they did her no harm. She ran on till her feet wouldn't go any farther, and when it was almost evening she saw a little house and went inside to rest. Inside the house everything was small, but cleaner and neater than words will say. In the middle there stood a little table with a white tablecloth, and on it were seven little plates, each plate with its own spoon, and besides that, seven little knives and forks and seven little mugs. Against the wall were seven little beds, all in a row, spread with snow-white sheets. Because she was so hungry and thirsty, Snow-White ate a little of the vegetables and bread from each of the little plates, and drank a drop of wine from each little mug, since she didn't want to take all of anybody's. After that, because she was so tired, she lay down in a bed, but not a one would fit; this one was too long, the other was too short, and so on, until finally the seventh was just right, and she lay down in it, said her prayers, and went to sleep.

As soon as it had got all dark, the owners of the house came back. These were seven dwarfs who dug and delved for ore in the mountains. They lighted their seven little candles, and as soon as it got light in their little house, they saw that someone had been inside, because everything wasn't the way they'd left it.

The first said: "Who's been sitting in my little chair?"

The second said: "Who's been eating out of my little plate?"

The third said: "Who's been taking some of my bread?"

The fourth said: "Who's been eating my vegetables?"

The fifth said: "Who's been using my little fork?"

The sixth said: "Who's been cutting with my little knife?"

The seventh said: "Who's been drinking out of my little mug?"

Then the first looked around and saw that his bed was a little mussed, so he said: "Who's been lying on my little bed?" The others came running and cried out: "Someone's been lying in mine too." But the seventh, when he looked in his bed, saw Snow-White, who was lying in it fast asleep.

He called the others, who came running up and shouted in astonishment, holding up their little candles so that the light shone on Snow-White. "Oh my goodness gracious! Oh my goodness gracious!" cried they, "how beautiful the child is!" And they were so happy that they didn't wake her, but let her go on sleeping in the little bed. The seventh dwarf, though, slept with the others, an hour with each, till the night was over.

When it was morning Snow-White awoke, and when she saw the seven dwarfs she was frightened. They were friendly, though, and asked: "What's your name?"

"I'm named Snow-White," she answered.

"How did you get to our house?" went on the dwarfs. Then she told them that her stepmother had tried to have her killed, but that the huntsman had spared her life, and that she'd run the whole day and at last had found their house.

The dwarfs said: "If you'll look after our house for us, cook, make the beds, wash, sew, and knit, and if you'll keep everything clean and neat, then you can stay with us, and you shall lack for nothing."

"Yes," said Snow-White, "with all my heart," and stayed with them. She kept their house in order: in the morning the dwarfs went to the mountains and looked for gold and ores, in the evening they came back, and then their food had to be ready for them. In the daytime the little girl was alone, so the good dwarfs warned her and said: "Watch out for your stepmother. Soon she'll know you're here; be sure not to let anybody inside."

But the Queen, since she thought she had eaten Snow-White's lung and liver, was sure that she was the fairest of all. But one day she stood before her mirror and said:

> "Mirror, mirror on the wall,
> Who is fairest of us all?"

Then the mirror answered:

> "Queen, thou art the fairest that I see
> But over the hills, where the seven dwarfs dwell,
> Snow-White is still alive and well,
> And there is none so fair as she."

This horrified her, because she knew that the mirror never told a lie; and she saw that the hunter had betrayed her, and that Snow-White was still alive. And she thought and thought about how to kill her, for as long as she wasn't the fairest in all the land, her envy gave her no rest. And when at last she thought of something, she painted her face and dressed herself like an old peddler woman, and nobody could have recognized her. In this disguise she went over the seven mountains to the seven dwarfs' house, knocked at the door, and called: "Lovely things for sale! Lovely things for sale!"

Snow-White looked out of the window and called: "Good day, dear lady, what have you to sell?"

"Good things, lovely things," she answered, "bodice laces of all colors," and she pulled out one that was woven of many-colored silk.

"It will be all right to let in the good old woman," thought Snow-White, unbolted the door, and bought herself some pretty laces.

"Child," said the old woman, "how it does become you! Come, I'll lace you up properly." Snow-White hadn't the least suspicion, and let the old woman lace her up with the new laces. But she laced so tight and laced so fast that it took Snow-White's breath away, and she fell down as if she were dead. "Now you're the most beautiful again," said the Queen to herself, and hurried away.

Not long after, at evening, the seven dwarfs came home, but how shocked they were to see their dear Snow-White lying on the ground; and she didn't move and she didn't stir, as if she were dead. They lifted her up, and when they saw how tightly she was laced, they cut the laces in two; then she began to breathe a little, and little by little returned to consciousness. When the dwarfs heard what had happened, they said: "The old peddler woman was no one else but that wicked Queen; be careful, don't ever let another soul inside when we're not with you."

But the wicked Queen, as soon as she'd got home, stood in front of the mirror and asked:

"Mirror, mirror on the wall,
Who is fairest of us all?"

It answered the same as ever:

"Queen, thou are the fairest that I see,
But over the hills, where the seven dwarfs
dwell,
Snow-White is still alive and well,
And there is none so fair as she."

When she heard this all the blood rushed to her heart, she was so horrified, for she saw plainly that Snow-White was alive again. "But now," said she, "I'll think of something that really will put an end to you," and with the help of witchcraft, which she understood, she made a poisoned comb. Then she dressed herself up and took the shape of another old woman. So she went over the seven mountains to the seven dwarfs' house, knocked on the door, and called: "Lovely things for sale! Lovely things for sale!"

Snow-White looked out and said: "You may as well go on, I'm not allowed to let anybody in."

"But surely you're allowed to look," said the old woman, and she took out the poisoned comb and held it up. It looked so nice to the child that she let herself be fooled, and opened the door. When they'd agreed on the price the old woman said: "Now, for once, I'll comb your hair properly." Poor Snow-White didn't suspect anything, and let the old woman do as she pleased. But hardly had she put the comb in Snow-White's hair than the poison in it began to work, and the girl fell down unconscious. "You paragon of beauty," cried the wicked woman, "now you're done for," and went away.

By good luck, though, it was almost evening, when the seven dwarfs came home. When they saw Snow-White lying on the ground as if she were dead, right away they suspected the stepmother and looked and found the poisoned comb. Hardly had they drawn it out than Snow-White returned to consciousness, and told them what had happened. Then they warned her all over again to stay in the house and open the door to no one.

At home the Queen stood in front of the mirror and said:

"Mirror, mirror on the wall,
Who is fairest of us all?"

It answered the same as ever:

"Queen, thou art the fairest that I see,
But over the hills, where the seven dwarfs
dwell,
Snow-White is still alive and well,
And there is none so fair as she."

When she heard the mirror say that, she shook with rage. "Snow-White shall die," cried she, "even if it costs me my own life!" Then she went to a very secret, lonely room that no one ever came to, and there she made a poisoned apple. On the outside it was beautiful, white with red cheeks, so that anyone who saw it wanted it; but whoever ate even the least bite of it would die. When the apple was ready she painted her face and disguised herself as a farmer's wife, and then went over the seven mountains to the seven dwarfs' house. She knocked, and Snow-White put her head out of the window and said: "I'm not allowed to let anybody in, the seven dwarfs told me not to."

"That's all right with me," answered the farmer's wife. "I'll get rid of my apples without any trouble. Here, I'll give you one."

"No," said Snow-White, "I'm afraid to take it."

"Are you afraid of poison?" said the old woman. "Look, I'll cut the apple in two halves; you eat the red cheek and I'll eat the white." But the apple was so cunningly made that only the red part was poisoned. Snow-White longed for the lovely apple, and when she saw that the old woman was eating it, she couldn't resist it any longer, put out her hand, and took the poisoned half. But hardly had she a bite of it in her mouth than she fell down on the ground dead. Then the Queen gave her a dreadful look, laughed aloud, and cried: "White as snow, red as blood, black as ebony! This time the dwarfs can't wake you!"

And when, at home, she asked the mirror:

"Mirror, mirror on the wall,
Who is fairest of us all?"

at last it answered:

"Queen, thou art the fairest of us all."

Then her envious heart had rest, as far as an envious heart can have rest.

When they came home at evening, the dwarfs found Snow-White lying on the ground. No breath came from her mouth, and she was dead. They lifted her up, looked to see if they could find anything poisonous, unlaced her, combed her hair, washed her with water and wine, but nothing helped; the dear child was dead and stayed dead. They laid her on a bier, and all seven of them sat down and wept for her, and wept for three whole days. Then they were going to bury her, but she still looked as fresh as though she were alive, and still had her beautiful red cheeks. They said: "We can't bury her in the black ground," and had made for her a coffin all of glass, into which one could see from every side, laid her in it, and wrote her name on it in golden letters, and that she was a king's daughter. Then they set the coffin out on the mountainside, and one of them always stayed by it and guarded it. And the animals, too, came and wept over Snow-White — first an owl, then a raven, and last of all a dove.

Now Snow-White lay in the coffin for a long, long time, and her body didn't decay. She

looked as if she were sleeping, for she was still as white as snow, as red as blood, and her hair was as black as ebony. But a king's son happened to come into the forest and went to the dwarfs' house to spend the night. He saw the coffin on the mountain, and the beautiful Snow-White inside, and read what was written on it in golden letters. Then he said to the dwarfs: "Let me have the coffin. I'll give you anything that you want for it."

But the dwarfs answered: "We wouldn't give it up for all the gold in the world."

Then he said: "Give it to me then, for I can't live without seeing Snow-White. I'll honor and prize her as my own beloved." When he spoke so, the good dwarfs took pity on him and gave him the coffin.

Now the king's son had his servants carry it away on their shoulders. They happened to stumble over a bush, and with the shock the poisoned piece of apple that Snow-White had bitten off came out of her throat. And in a little while she opened her eyes, lifted the lid of the coffin, sat up, and was alive again. "Oh, heavens, where am I?" cried she.

The king's son, full of joy, said: "You're with me," and told her what had happened, and said: "I love you more than anything in all the world. Come with me to my father's palace; you shall be my wife." And Snow-White loved him and went with him, and her wedding was celebrated with great pomp and splendor.

But Snow-White's wicked stepmother was invited to the feast. When she had put on her beautiful clothes, she stepped in front of the mirror and said:

"Mirror, mirror on the wall,
Who is fairest of us all?"

The mirror answered:

"Queen, thou art the fairest in this hall,
But the young queen's fairer than us all."

Then the wicked woman cursed and was so terrified and miserable, so completely miserable, that she didn't know what to do. At first she didn't want to go to the wedding at all, but it gave her no peace; she had to go and see the young queen. And as she went in she recognized Snow-White, and what with rage and terror, she stood there and couldn't move. But they had already put iron slippers over a fire of coals, and they brought them in with tongs and set them before her. Then she had to put on the red-hot slippers and dance till she dropped down dead.

"The Shrove Tuesday Visitor," from Canadian Wonder Tales*, by Cyrus Macmillan. Illustrated by George Sheringham (London: Bodley Head, 1918).*

This tale reflects the intense religious fabric of French Canadian society. On an ironic linear journey a young woman about to be happily married weakly yields to the temptations of the Devil. For her sins she must enter a convent and suffer an untimely death. The concluding lines place this story within the parameters of the pourquoi tale by explaining why the old custom of not dancing beyond midnight on Shrove Tuesday is still observed.

The Shrove Tuesday Visitor

In olden times in Canada, Shrove Tuesday, the day before the beginning of Lent, was more strictly observed than it is to-day. The night was always one of great merriment and feasting. Boys and girls of the villages and country places gathered there for the last time before the long period of quiet. They danced until midnight, but the youth or maiden who dared to dance after the hour of twelve was henceforth followed with little luck. This rule was not often broken, for when it was broken the Spirits of Evil always walked the earth and brought disaster to the youthful dancers.

In a remote village on the banks of a great river there dwelt in the seventeenth century a French peasant, a kind and devout old man. He had but one child, a daughter. She was a handsome girl, and naturally enough she had many suitors among the young men of the place. One of these she prized above all the others, and she had promised to become his wife. On the evening of the Shrove Tuesday before the date set for the wedding, as was the custom the young people of the village gathered at her home. It was a simple but joyous gathering, the last which the girl could attend before her marriage. Right merrily the dance went on, and all the guests were in high spirits. Soon after eleven o'clock a sleigh drawn by a great coal-black horse stopped at the door. It contained but one man. Without knocking at the door, the new-comer entered. The rooms were crowded, but the rumour soon spread whisperingly around that a new presence had appeared, and the simple villagers strove to get a look at the tall figure in fine clothes. The old man of the house received the stranger kindly and offered him the best he had in his home, for such was the custom in the old days. One thing the gathering particularly noted—the stranger kept his fur cap on his head, and he did not remove his gloves; but as the night was cold this caused but little wonder.

Illustration by Elizabeth Cleaver, "The Shrove Tuesday Visitor" from *Canadian Wonder Tales,* collected by Cyrus Macmillan. Copyright © 1974. Reprinted by permission of The Bodley Head.

After the silence caused by the stranger's entrance the music swelled, and again the dance went on. The new-comer chose the old man's daughter as his partner. He came to her and said, "My pretty lass, I hope you will dance with me to-night, and more than once, too." "Certainly," replied the girl, well pleased with the honour, and knowing that her friends would envy her. During the remainder of the evening the stranger never left her side, and dance after dance they had together. From a corner of the room the girl's lover watched the pair in silence and anger.

In a small room opening from that in which the dancers were gathered was an old and pious woman seated on a chest at the foot of a bed, praying fervently. She was the girl's aunt. In one hand she held her beads, with the other she beckoned to her niece to come to her.

"It is very wrong of you," she said, "to forsake your lover for this stranger; his manner is not pleasing to me. Each time I utter the name of the Saviour or the Virgin Mary as he passes the door, he turns from me with a look of anger." But the girl paid no heed to her aunt's advice.

At last it was midnight, and Lent had come. The old man gave the signal for the dance to cease. "Let us have one more dance," said the stranger. "Just one more," pleaded the girl; "my last dance before my marriage." And the old man wishing to please his only child, — for he loved her well, — consented, and although it was already Ash Wednesday the dance went on. The stranger again danced with the girl. "You have been mine all the evening," he whispered; "why should you not be mine for ever?" But the girl laughed at his question. "I am a strange fellow," said the stranger, "and when I will to do a thing it must be done. Only say yes, and nothing can ever separate us." The girl cast a glance towards her dejected lover in the corner of the room. "I understand," said the stranger. "I am too late; you love him."

"Yes," answered the girl, "I love him, or rather I did love him once," for the girl's head had been turned by the attentions of the stranger.

"That is well," said the stranger; "I will arrange all, and overcome all difficulties. Give me your hand to seal our plight."

She placed her hand in his, but at once she withdrew it with a low cry of pain. She had felt in her flesh the point of some sharp instrument as if the stranger held a knife in his hand. In great terror she fainted and was carried to a couch. At once the dance was stopped and the dancers gathered around her, wondering at the sudden happenings. At the same time two villagers came in and called the old man to the door to see a strange sight without. The deep snow for many yards around the stranger's horse and sleigh had melted in the hour since his arrival, and a large patch of bare ground was now showing. Terror soon spread among the guests; they spoke in whispers of fear, and shrank from the centre of the room to the walls as if eager to escape; but the old man begged them not to leave him. The stranger looked with a cold smile upon the dread of the company. He kept close to the couch where the girl was slowly coming back to life. He took from his pocket a beautiful necklace, and said to her, "Take off the glass beads you wear, and for my sake take this beautiful necklace." But to her glass beads was attached a little cross which she did not want to part with, and she refused to take his gift.

Meanwhile, in the home of the priest, some distance away, there was a strange happening. While he prayed for his flock the old priest had fallen asleep. He saw in his slumber a vision of the old man's home and what was happening there. He started quickly from his sleep and called his servant and told him to harness his horse at once, for not far away a soul was in danger of eternal death. He hurried to the old man's house. When he reached there, the stranger had already unfastened the beads from the girl's neck and was about to place his own necklace upon her and to seize her in his arms. But the old priest was too quick for him. He passed his sacred stole around the girl's neck and drew her towards him, and turning to the stranger he said, "What art thou, Evil One, doing among Christians?" At this remark terror was renewed among the guests; some fell to their knees in prayer; all were weeping, for they knew now that the stranger with the stately presence and the velvet clothes was the

Spirit of Evil and Death. And the stranger answered, "I do not know as Christians those who forget their faith by dancing on holy days. This fair girl has chosen to be mine. With the blood that flowed from her hand she sealed the compact which binds her to me for ever."

In answer, the old curé struck the stranger hard across the face with his stole, and repeated some Latin words which none of the guests understood. There was a great crash, as if it thundered, and in a moment amid the noise the stranger disappeared; with his horse and sleigh he had vanished as mysteriously and quickly as he had come.

The guests were long in recovering from their fear, and all night they prayed with the curé that their evil deeds might be forgiven. That she might be cleansed from her sins and that her promise to the stranger might be rightly broken, the girl entered a convent to pass the remainder of her life. A few years later she died. And since that day in her little village on the banks of the great river, the Shrove Tuesday dancers have always stopped their dance at midnight; for youths and maidens still keep in mind the strange dancer in the fine clothes who wooed the peasant's only daughter and almost carried her off.

Circular Journeys

"Little Red-Cap," from The Complete Grimm's Fairy Tales *(New York: Pantheon, 1944).*

Perhaps the most famous of all European cautionary tales, "Little Red-Cap" emphasizes the dangers that prey upon the innocent. The vulnerable heroine, never having been warned about wolves and never having encountered one, fails to recognize the threat the villain represents. Unlike Perrault's earlier version, which ends with the child being devoured, the Grimms' German version is a circular one—the girl returns home much wiser. Some scholars have suggested that this story is a debased solar myth: the red-clad heroine represents the sun which disappears nightly but is reborn each morning. As is so often the case in European tales, the forest is presented as a place of danger and terror.

Little Red-Cap

Once upon a time there was a dear little girl who was loved by every one who looked at her, but most of all by her grandmother, and there was nothing that she would not have given to the child. Once she gave her a little cap of red velvet, which suited her so well that she would never wear anything else; so she was always called 'Little Red-Cap.'

One day her mother said to her: "Come, Little Red-Cap, here is a piece of cake and a bottle of wine; take them to your grandmother, she is ill and weak, and they will do her good. Set out before it gets hot, and when you are going, walk nicely and quietly and do not run off the path, or you may fall and break the bottle, and then your grandmother will get nothing; and when you go into her room, don't forget to say, 'Good-morning,' and don't peep into every corner before you do it."

"I will take great care," said Little Red-Cap to her mother, and gave her hand on it.

The grandmother lived out in the wood, half a league from the village, and just as Little Red-Cap entered the wood, a wolf met her. Red-Cap did not know what a wicked creature he was, and was not at all afraid of him.

"Good-day, Little Red-Cap," said he.

"Thank you kindly, wolf."

"Whither away so early, Little Red-Cap?"

"To my grandmother's."

"What have you got in your apron?"

"Cake and wine; yesterday was baking-day, so poor sick grandmother is to have something good, to make her stronger."

"Where does your grandmother live, Little Red-Cap?"

"A good quarter of a league farther on in the wood; her house stands under the three large oak-trees, the nut-trees are just below; you surely must know it," replied Little Red-Cap.

The wolf thought to himself: "What a tender young creature! what a nice plump mouthful — she will be better to eat than the old woman. I must act craftily, so as to catch both." So he walked for a short time by the side of Little Red-Cap, and then he said: "See, Little Red-Cap, how pretty the flowers are about here — why do you not look around? I believe, too, that you do not hear how sweetly the little birds are singing; you walk gravely along as if you were going to school, while everything else out here in the wood is merry."

Little Red-Cap raised her eyes, and when she saw the sunbeams dancing here and there through the trees, and pretty flowers growing everywhere, she thought: "Suppose I take grandmother a fresh nosegay; that would please her too. It is so early in the day that I shall still get there in good time"; and so she ran from the path into the wood to look for flowers. And whenever she had picked one, she fancied that she saw a still prettier one farther on, and ran after it, and so got deeper and deeper into the wood.

Meanwhile the wolf ran straight to the grandmother's house and knocked at the door.

"Who is there?"

"Little Red-Cap," replied the wolf. "She is bringing cake and wine; open the door."

"Lift the latch," called out the grandmother, "I am too weak, and cannot get up."

The wolf lifted the latch, the door sprang open, and without saying a word he went straight to the grandmother's bed, and devoured her. Then he put on her clothes, dressed himself in her cap, laid himself in bed and drew the curtains.

Little Red-Cap, however, had been running about picking flowers, and when she had gathered so many that she could carry no more, she remembered her grandmother, and set out on the way to her.

She was surprised to find the cottage-door standing open, and when she went into the room, she had such a strange feeling that she said to herself: "Oh dear! how uneasy I feel to-day, and at other times I like being with grandmother so much. She called out: "Good morning," but received no answer; so she went to the bed and drew back the curtains. There lay her grandmother with her cap pulled far over her face, and looking very strange.

"Oh! grandmother," she said, "what big ears you have!"

"The better to hear you with, my child," was the reply.

"But, grandmother, what big eyes you have!" she said.

"The better to see you with, my dear."

"But, grandmother, what large hands you have!"

"The better to hug you with."

"Oh! but, grandmother, what a terrible big mouth you have!"

"The better to eat you with!"

And scarcely had the wolf said this, than with one bound he was out of bed and swallowed up Red-Cap.

When the wolf had appeased his appetite, he lay down again in the bed, fell asleep and began to snore very loud. The huntsman was just passing the house, and thought to himself: "How the old woman is snoring! I must just see if she wants anything." So he went into the room, and when he came to the bed, he saw that the wolf was lying in it. "Do I find you here, you old sinner!" said he. "I have long sought you!" Then just as he was going to fire at him, it occurred to him that the wolf might have devoured the grandmother, and that she might still be saved, so he did not fire, but took a pair of scissors, and began to cut open the stomach of the sleeping wolf. When he had made two snips, he saw the little Red-Cap shining, and then he made two snips more, and the little girl sprang out, crying: "Ah, how frightened I have been! How dark it was inside the wolf"; and after that the aged grandmother came out alive also, but scarcely able to breathe. Red-Cap, however, quickly fetched great stones with which they filled the wolf's belly, and when he awoke, he wanted to run away, but the stones were so heavy that he collapsed at once, and fell dead.

Then all three were delighted. The huntsman drew off the wolf's skin and went home with it; the grandmother ate the cake and drank the wine which Red-Cap had brought, and revived, but Red-Cap thought to herself: "As long as I live, I will never by myself leave the path, to run into the wood, when my mother has forbidden me to do so."

It is also related that once when Red-Cap was again taking cakes to the old grandmother, another wolf spoke to her, and tried to entice her from the path. Red-Cap, however, was on her guard, and went straight forward on her way, and told her grandmother that she had met the wolf, and that he had said "good-morning" to her, but with such a wicked look in his eyes, that if they had not been on the public road she was certain he would have eaten her up. "Well," said the grandmother, "we will shut the door, that he may not come in." Soon afterwards the wolf knocked, and cried: "Open the door, grandmother, I am little Red-Cap, and am bringing you some cakes." But they did not speak, or open the door, so the greybeard stole twice or thrice round the house, and at last jumped on the roof, intending to wait until Red-Cap went home in the evening, and then to steal her and devour her in the darkness. But the grandmother saw what was in his thoughts. In front of the house was a great stone trough, so she said to the child: "Take the pail, Red-Cap; I made some sausages yesterday, so carry the water in which I boiled them to the trough." Red-Cap carried until the great trough was quite full. Then the smell of the sausages reached the wolf, and he sniffed and peeped down, and at last stretched out his neck so far that he could no longer keep his footing and began to slip, and slipped down from the roof straight into the great trough, and was drowned. But Red-Cap went joyously

home, and no one ever did anything to harm her again.

"The Story of the Three Bears," from English Fairy Tales. *Told by Flora Annie Steel (London: Macmillan, 1918).*

In earlier versions of this well-known English folktale, an old woman or a fox entered the bears' house. However, regardless of species or age, the character was clearly presented as an unlawful intruder into private property. In the following retelling — the first to give the girl the name Goldilocks — the author makes the point abundantly clear, emphasizing in her language the goodness of the bears and the nastiness of the child, suggesting in the conclusion that the girl's punishment was completely deserved. Modern versions, many of which suggest that Goldilocks was merely lost, hungry, and tired, and which present the bears as threatening, distort the story's theme. In this version, both the bears and Goldilocks make ironic circular journeys: the former return from their walk to find their house invaded; the latter is awakened and leaves the house badly frightened. Goldilocks' confrontation with the three bears can be compared to the problems faced by Isabel in "The Adventures of Isabel."

The Story of the Three Bears

Once upon a time there were three Bears, who lived together in a house of their own, in a wood. One of them was a Little Wee Bear, and one was a Middle-sized Bear, and the other was a Great Big Bear. They had each a bowl for their porridge; a little bowl for the Little Wee Bear; and a middle-sized bowl for the Middle-sized Bear; and a great bowl for the Great Big Bear. And they had each a chair to sit in; a little chair for the Little Wee Bear; and a middle-sized chair for the Middle-sized Bear; and a great chair for the Great Big Bear. And they had each a bed to sleep in; a little bed for the Little Wee Bear; and a middle-sized bed for the Middle-sized Bear; and a great bed for the Great Big Bear.

One day, after they had made the porridge

Illustration by Lorinda Bryan Cauley from *Goldilocks and the Three Bears*. Copyright ©
1981 by Lorinda Bryan Cauley. Reprinted by permission of G.P. Putnam's Sons.

for their breakfast, and poured it into their porridge-bowls, they walked out into the wood while the porridge was cooling, that they might not burn their mouths by beginning too soon, for they were polite, well-brought-up Bears. And while they were away a little girl called Goldilocks, who lived at the other side of the wood and had been sent on an errand by her mother, passed by the house, and looked in at the window. And then she peeped in at the key-hole, for she was not at all a well-brought-up little girl. Then seeing nobody in the house she lifted the latch. The door was not fastened, because the Bears were good Bears, who did no-body any harm, and never suspected that any-body would harm them. So Goldilocks opened the door and went in; and well pleased was she when she saw the porridge on the table. If she had been a well-brought-up little girl she would have waited till the Bears came home, and then, perhaps, they would have asked her to breakfast; for they were good Bears — a little rough or so, as the manner of Bears is, but for all that very good-natured and hospitable. But

she was an impudent, rude little girl, and so she set about helping herself.

First she tasted the porridge of the Great Big Bear, and that was too hot for her. Next she tasted the porridge of the Middle-sized Bear, but that was too cold for her. And then she went to the porridge of the Little Wee Bear, and tasted it, and that was neither too hot nor too cold, but just right, and she liked it so well that she ate it all up, every bit!

Then Goldilocks, who was tired, for she had been catching butterflies instead of run-ning on her errand, sat down in the chair of the Great Big Bear, but that was too hard for her. And then she sat down in the chair of the Middle-sized Bear, and that was too soft for her. But when she sat down in the chair of the Lit-tle Wee Bear, that was neither too hard nor too soft, but just right. So she seated herself in it, and there she sat till the bottom of the chair came out, and down she came, plump upon the ground; and that made her very cross, for she was a bad-tempered little girl.

Now, being determined to rest, Goldilocks

went upstairs into the bedchamber in which the Three Bears slept. And first she lay down upon the bed of the Great Big Bear, but that was too high at the head for her. And next she lay down upon the bed of the Middle-sized Bear, and that was too high at the foot for her. And then she lay down upon the bed of the Little Wee Bear, and that was neither too high at the head nor at the foot, but just right. So she covered herself up comfortably, and lay there till she fell fast asleep.

By this time the Three Bears thought their porridge would be cool enough for them to eat it properly; so they came home to breakfast. Now careless Goldilocks had left the spoon of the Great Big Bear standing in his porridge.

"SOMEBODY HAS BEEN AT MY PORRIDGE!"

said the Great Big Bear in his great, rough, gruff voice.

Then the Middle-sized Bear looked at his porridge and saw the spoon was standing in it too.

"SOMEBODY HAS BEEN AT MY PORRIDGE!"

said the Middle-sized Bear in his middle-sized voice.

Then the Little Wee Bear looked at his, and there was the spoon in the porridge-bowl, but the porridge was all gone!

"SOMEBODY HAS BEEN AT MY PORRIDGE, AND HAS EATEN IT ALL UP!"

said the Little Wee Bear in his little wee voice.

Upon this the Three Bears, seeing that some one had entered their house, and eaten up the Little Wee Bear's breakfast, began to look about them. Now the careless Goldilocks had not put the hard cushion straight when she rose from the chair of the Great Big Bear.

"SOMEBODY HAS BEEN SITTING IN MY CHAIR!"

said the Great Big Bear in his great, rough, gruff voice.

And the careless Goldilocks had squatted down the soft cushion of the Middle-sized Bear.

"SOMEBODY HAS BEEN SITTING IN MY CHAIR!"

said the Middle-sized Bear in his middle-sized voice.

"SOMEBODY HAS BEEN SITTING IN MY CHAIR, AND HAS SAT THE BOTTOM THROUGH!"

said the Little Wee Bear in his little wee voice.

Then the Three Bears thought they had better make further search in case it was a burglar, so they went upstairs into their bedchamber. Now Goldilocks had pulled the pillow of the Great Big Bear out of its place.

"SOMEBODY HAS BEEN LYING IN MY BED!" said the Great Big Bear in his great, rough, gruff voice.

And Goldilocks had pulled the bolster of the Middle-sized Bear out of its place.

"SOMEBODY HAS BEEN LYING IN MY BED!" said the Middle-sized Bear in his middle-sized voice.

But when the Little Wee Bear came to look at his bed, there was the bolster in its place!

And the pillow was in its place upon the bolster!

And upon the pillow — ?

There was Goldilock's yellow head — which was not in its place, for she had no business there.

"SOMEBODY HAS BEEN LYING IN MY BED, — AND HERE SHE IS STILL!"

said the Little Wee Bear in his little wee voice.

Now Goldilocks had heard in her sleep the great, rough, gruff voice of the Great Big Bear; but she was so fast asleep that it was no more to her than the roaring of wind, or the rumbling of thunder. And she had heard the middle-sized voice of the Middle-sized Bear, but it was only as if she had heard some one speaking in a dream. But when she heard the little wee voice of the Little Wee Bear, it was so sharp, and so shrill, that it awakened her at once. Up she started, and when she saw the Three Bears on one side of the bed, she tumbled herself out at the other, and ran to the window. Now the window was open, because the Bears, like good, tidy Bears, as they were, always opened their bedchamber window when they got up in the morning. So naughty, frightened little Goldilocks jumped; and whether she broke her neck in the fall, or ran into the wood and was lost there, or found her way out of the wood and got whipped for being a bad girl and playing truant, no one can say. But the Three Bears never saw anything more of her.

"The Ghost Owl," from Plains Indian Mythology, *by Alice Marriott and Carol K. Rachlin (New York: Mentor, 1977).*

As is the case in "The Story of the Three Bears," the child in this Cheyenne Indian legend brings about her own problems. While dealing with the universal theme of separation and reunion, this story reflects many Native Indian and specifically Cheyenne characteristics: the four-fold repetition of incidents, the belief that owls are ghosts, and the origination of certain warrior societies. This legend provided the basic plot for Jamake Highwater's novel Legend Days.

The Ghost Owl

A little girl sat crying in her mother's lodge. She was angry because her mother wouldn't let her do what she wanted to do. It was night time, and her mother told her she couldn't go out of the lodge. Finally, the mother got so exasperated that she picked the little girl up and put her outside.

"Go on," the mother ordered. "The owls can have you if they want you."

It happened that there was an owl just outside the lodge, sitting in a tree, waiting for a mouse or a rabbit to come along. When he saw the little girl, he swooped down and picked her up in his claws and flew away with her. He carried her off to his lodge where his old grandfather lived.

"Here," the owl said, "this is something nice for you to have."

"Good," said the owl grandfather, and he clapped his wings together for pleasure. "You can sleep in that corner," he told the little girl, pointing with his lips to the women's place on the south side of the lodge, "and in the morning you can get busy and make yourself useful."

When the little girl woke up the next morning, the owl grandfather sent her out to get wood for a fire. "If you don't work, you can't eat," he said. "I can't stand daylight, so you'll have to do the outside work, except at night."

As the little girl went through the woods, picking up sticks and dry branches, a sparrow flew up to her. "You're gathering that for yourself," said the sparrow. "They're going to cook you and eat you." The child was frightened, and ran back to the owl's lodge, because it was the only place she knew to go.

"That isn't enough firewood," the grandfather said. "Go on. Go out and get a big pile. Nobody can cook with those little old sticks."

So the girl went out again, and this time a flycatcher flew up to her and warned her that she was going to be eaten. She ran back to the lodge and piled the wood on top of what she had already brought.

"That still isn't enough," scolded the old owl. "How am I going to get any dinner from that little heap?"

A third time the girl went out, and this time a red-winged blackbird warned her, "Don't do that. You're gathering it for yourself." And again she was frightened and ran back to the lodge.

"You'll never make a man a good wife," said the old owl, glaring at her. "Why, you can't even gather enough firewood to cook a meal."

Once again the girl set out to gather wood, and this time a red-tailed hawk flew up to her. "This is the last time," he said. "We have all tried to warn you. Now you must not go back."

"What shall I do?" the girl asked. "Where can I go to be safe?"

"Get on my back," the hawk said. "I will take you to a safe place on a high mountain, and I will tell you what to do when you get there."

So the girl put her hands on the hawk's shoulders, and he carried her away and away, up to the top of a high mountain, and on the way he told her what to do when they got there. The hawk landed right in front of a big rock on the mountain top.

"Now do just what I told you," he ordered.

The girl said to the rock, "My hawk grandfather, I have come to you for protection. My hawk father, I have come to you for protection. My hawk brother, I have come to you for protection. My hawk husband, I have come to you for protection."

Then she heard a voice say, "You will be safe here." The rock rolled aside, and there was a big cave. At first the girl was afraid to go in because she saw only the old hawk grandfather sitting there. "Come on, I won't hurt you," he reassured her, and she went in. Behind her the rock rolled back in its place.

When the old owl realized that the girl had escaped, he was very angry. "Those hawks must have played this trick on me," he said, "but I'll get her back. They can't keep her forever."

He started out for the mountain. Four times on the way he stopped; each time he hooted four times, and when he hooted the earth shook. The girl heard him coming and was terrified. The fourth time the owl hooted he was right outside the door.

"Bring out my meat," he howled. "If you don't, I'll come in and get it."

"Open the door just enough for him to get his head in," the hawk grandfather directed the girl.

She opened the door, and the owl thrust his head in. Then she slammed the rock back in place, and cut his head off so it rolled around on the floor.

"Roll the head out of the lodge with a stick," said the hawk grandfather. "Don't touch it, or any part of the body. Make a pile of dry wood and I will come out and help you."

They did so, and when the pile was big enough, the hawk grandfather set it on fire, and threw the head and the body on top of the flames. The body split open and all kinds of beads and pretty things came rolling out. The girl wanted to pick them up, but the hawk grandfather made her throw everything back in the fire with sticks for tongs.

Then they went back in the lodge, and the girl stayed with the hawks until she was grown up. She did a woman's work, and she became very beautiful. But she still missed her own people, and finally she told the hawks so.

'Well, you are old enough to take care of yourself now," the hawk grandfather said. "But you must do just exactly what I tell you if you are to get back safely."

"I will," the girl promised.

Then the grandfather made her a red-painted robe, and had her make a boy's moccasins and leggings. The grandfather made her a thunder bow with lightning designs on it, and he fastened buffalo bulls' tails to the heels of her moccasins to wipe out her tracks. Last he painted her face red, and tied the skin of a prairie owl on her forehead. She was dressed like one of the Backward-Talking Warriors, who were the greatest warriors of the Cheyennes, not like a girl.

When she was ready to leave, the grandfather gave her a live mink. "Keep this inside your robe," he instructed her. "Never let go of it. Then when you start out, pass by the first four villages you come to. On the evening of the fourth day you will come to your last great danger. An old woman will come out of her lodge and call to you and offer you food. Don't eat any of the first bowl; feed it to the mink. The second time she will give you buffalo meat and you will be safe to eat that. Be sure you keep the mink with you, but let it go when the old lady threatens you."

It all happened just that way. On the fourth evening the girl came to the old lady's lodge, and the woman came out and called to her, "Come in, my grandson. You must be tired and hungry."

So the girl went into the lodge, and the woman fixed her a bowl of brains cooked with mush, and gave her a horn spoon to eat it with. The girl pretended to eat, but instead she fed the mush to the mink.

"My, you are hungry, grandson," said the old woman. This time she gave her dried buffalo meat, and the girl ate it.

"Lie down and rest," said the old woman, and she took the bow with the lightning designs on it and hung it on the west side of the lodge. Then she spread out some hides in the man's place on the west side of the lodge and the girl lay down on them and pretended she went to sleep. She even snored a little. "I'll stay up a while and keep the fire going to warm you," said the old lady.

As soon as she thought the girl was asleep, the old woman sat down by the fire and began to scratch her leg. She scratched until the leg swelled up into a great club. Then the woman started for the girl to beat her to death, but the girl let the mink out of her robe. The mink ran across the floor and bit a big chunk out of the woman's leg.

"You've killed me!" she screamed, and fell down dead, while the mink ran away.

The next day the girl went on again, and that night she came to her own village. Everyone came running out to see who the handsome young man was. They all asked her questions, but she was ashamed to say she had been so naughty when she was little that her mother had given her to the owls. She hung her head and would not speak.

"Who are you? What tribe are you? Where have you come from?" all the people asked her.

At last she said, "I am the naughty girl whose mother threw her away, I have had a hard time and come through many dangers, but now I am back with my own people."

Then her mother came to her, weeping and crying to be forgiven. And some young men came to her, and asked if they could wear the same kind of clothes she had on. The girl thought a while and then she said, "Yes. But because I am a woman dressed like a man, you must always do some things backwards. If you are in battle, and someone tells you, 'Go forward,' then you can go back." And that is how the great soldier societies of the Cheyennes got started.

"Hansel and Gretel," from Tales From Grimm. *Translated and illustrated by Wanda Gág (New York: Coward, McCann, and Geoghegan, 1936).*

"Hansel and Gretel," the Grimm Brothers' classic tale of sibling loyalty, carefully delineates the character growth of the two children, especially Gretel. Early in the story, Hansel is the dominant character; however, his optimism is insufficient, so Gretel, like Molly Whuppie and the girl in "The Little Guava," demonstrates her cleverness and courage resulting in their release from the witch. As a child hero, Gretel succeeds against a superior adult foe where other children (the witch's earlier captives) have failed. In her retelling, Gág gives full descriptions of the forest, emphasizing its terrors for the lost children, and of the witch's cottage, indicating its deceptive ap-

pearance. The violence of the story has upset many adult readers. However, it should be noted that traditional belief held that witches could only be destroyed by fire. Moreover, the death of the witch is perfectly just considering that she murders children.

Hansel and Gretel

In a little hut near the edge of a deep, deep forest lived a poor woodchopper with his wife and his two children, Hansel and Gretel.

Times were hard. Work was scarce and the price of food was high. Many people were starving, and our poor woodchopper and his little brood fared as badly as all the rest.

One evening after they had gone to bed, the man said to his wife, "I don't know what will become of us. All the potatoes are gone, every head of cabbage is eaten, and there is only enough rye meal left for a few loaves of bread."

"You are right," said his wife, who was not the children's real mother, "and there is nothing for us to do but take Hansel and Gretel into the woods and let them shift for themselves."

She was a hard-hearted woman and did not much care what became of the children. But the father loved them dearly and said, "Wife, what are you saying? I would never have the heart to do such a thing!"

"Oh well then," snapped the stepmother, "if you won't listen to reason, we'll all have to starve." And she nagged and scolded until the poor man, not knowing what else to say, consented to do it. "May heaven keep them from harm," he sighed.

Hunger had kept the children awake that night, and, lying in their trundle-beds on the other side of the room, they had heard every word their parents had said. Gretel began to cry softly but her brother Hansel whispered, "Don't worry, little sister; I'll take care of you."

He waited until the father and mother were sleeping soundly. Then he put on his little jacket, unbarred the back door and slipped out. The moon was shining brightly, and the white pebbles which lay in front of the house glistened like silver coins. Hansel bent down and gathered as many of the shiny pebbles as his pockets would hold. Then he tiptoed back to bed and told Gretel he had thought of a very good plan for the morrow.

At break of day the mother came to wake the children. "Get up, you lazy things," she said, "we're off to the forest to gather wood. Here is a piece of bread for each of you. Don't eat it until noon; it's all you'll get today."

Gretel carried both pieces of bread in her apron because, of course, Hansel's pockets were so full of pebbles. They were soon on their way to the forest: the mother first with a jug of water, the father next with an ax over his shoulder, Gretel with the bread and Hansel bringing up the rear, his pockets bulging with pebbles. But Hansel walked very slowly. Often he would stand still and look back at the house.

"Come, come, Hansel!" said the father. "Why do you lag behind?"

"I'm looking at my little white kitten, papa. She's sitting on the roof and wants to say good-by."

"Fool!" said the mother. "That's not your kitten, That's only the morning sun shining on the chimney."

But Hansel lingered on and dropped the pebbles behind him, one at a time, all along the way.

It was a long walk, and Hansel and Gretel became very tired. At last the mother called a halt and said, "Sit down, children, and rest yourselves while we go off to gather some wood. If you feel sleepy you can take a little nap."

Hansel and Gretel sat down and munched their bread. They thought their father and mother were nearby, because they seemed to hear the sound of an ax. But what they heard was not an ax at all, only a dry branch which was bumping against a dead tree in the wind.

By and by the two little children became so drowsy they lay down on the moss and dropped off to sleep. When they awoke it was night and they were all alone.

"Oh Hansel, it's so dark! Now we'll never find our way home," said Gretel, and began to cry.

But Hansel said, "Don't cry, little sister. Just wait until the moon is out; I'll find the way home."

The moon did come out, full and round and bright, and it shone on the white pebbles which Hansel had strewn along the way. With the glistening pebbles to guide them, they found their way back easily enough.

Dawn was stealing over the mountains when they reached their home, and with happy faces they burst in at the door. When their mother saw them standing before her, she was taken aback. But then she said, "Why, you naughty children! Where have you been so long? I began to think you didn't want to come back home."

She wasn't much pleased but the father welcomed them joyfully. He had lain awake all night worrying over them.

Luckily, things now took a turn for the better, and for several weeks the woodchopper was able to earn enough money to keep his family from starving. But it did not last, and one evening the children, still awake in their trundle-beds, heard the mother say to the father: "I suppose you know there's only one loaf of bread left in the house, and after that's eaten, there's an end to the song. We must try once more to get rid of the children, and this time we'll take them still deeper into the woods, so our sly Hansel can't find his way back."

As before, the father tried to talk her out of it, but the hard-hearted stepmother wouldn't listen to him. He who says A must also say B, and because the father had given in the first time, he had to give in this time as well.

Hansel saw that he would have to get up and gather pebbles again, and as soon as his parents were asleep, he crept out of bed. But alas! the door was locked now and he had to go back to bed and think of a different plan.

The next day everything happened as it had the first time. Hansel and Gretel were each given a crust of bread and then they all went forth into the forest. Hansel brought up the rear as before, and kept straggling behind the rest.

"Come, come, Hansel!" said the father. "Why do you lag behind?"

"I see my pet dove, papa. It is sitting on the roof and wants to say good-by to me."

"Fool!" said the mother. "That's not your

Illustration by Wanda Gag, "Hansel and Gretel" from *Tales From Grimm*. Copyright © 1936 by Wanda Gág, copyright renewed © 1964 by Robert Janssen. Reprinted by permission of Coward, McCann and Geoghegan.

dove. That's only the morning sun shining on the chimney."

But Hansel kept on loitering because he was again busy making a trail to guide them back home. And what do you think he did this time? He had broken his bread-crust into tiny pieces and now he was carefully scattering the crumbs, one by one, behind him on the path.

They had to walk even farther than before, and again the parents went to gather wood, leaving Hansel and Gretel behind. At noon Gretel shared her bread with Hansel, and then they both fell asleep.

When they awoke, it was dark and they were all alone. This time Gretel did not cry because she knew Hansel had scattered crumbs to show them the way back. When the moon rose, Hansel took her hand and said, "Come, little sister, now it's time to go home."

But alas! when they looked for the crumbs they found none. Little twittering birds which fly about in the woods and glades, had eaten them all, all up.

The two unhappy children walked all that night and the next day too, but the more they looked for the way, the more they lost it. They found nothing to eat but a few sour berries; and at last, weak and hungry, they sank down on a cushion of moss and fell asleep.

It was now the third morning since they had left their home. They started to walk again, but they only got deeper and deeper into the wood.

They felt small and strange in the large, silent forest. The trees were so tall and the shade was so dense. Flowers could not grow in that dim, gloomy place — not even ferns. Only pale waxy mushrooms glowed faintly among the shadows, and weird lichens clung to the tree-trunks. Suddenly, into the vast green silence fell a ripple of sound so sweet, so gay, so silvery, that the children looked up in breathless wonder. A little white bird sat there in a tree; and when its beautiful song was ended, it spread its wings and fluttered away with anxious little chirps as though it wished to say, "Follow me! Follow me!"

Hansel and Gretel followed gladly enough, and all at once they found themselves in a fair flowery clearing, at the edge of which stood a tiny cottage.

The children stood hand in hand and gazed at it in wonder. "It's the loveliest house I ever saw," gasped Gretel, "and it looks good enough to eat."

They hurried on, and as they reached the little house, Hansel touched it and cried, "Gretel! It *is* good enough to eat."

And, if you can believe it, that's just what it was. Its walls were made of gingerbread, its roof was made of cake. It was trimmed with cookies and candy, and its window-panes were of pure transparent sugar. Nothing could have suited the children better and they began eating right away, they were so hungry! Hansel plucked a cookie from the roof and took a big bite out of it. Gretel munched big slabs of sugar-pane which she had broken from the window.

Suddenly a honeyed voice came floating from the house. It said:

Nibble, nibble, nottage,
Who's nibbling at my cottage?

To which the children said mischievously:

It's only a breeze,
Blowing down from the trees.

At this, the door burst open, and out slithered a bent old woman, waggling her head and leaning on a knotted stick. Hansel stopped munching his cookie and Gretel stopped crunching her sugar-pane. They were frightened—and no wonder! The Old One was far from beautiful. Her sharp nose bent down to meet her bristly chin. Her face, all folds and wrinkles, looked like an old shriveled pear; and she had only three teeth, two above and one below, all very long and yellow.

When the Old One saw that the children were turning to run away, she said in sugary tones, "Ei, ei! my little darlings, what has brought you here? Come right in and stay with me. I'll take good care of you."

She led them inside, and there in the middle of the room was a table neatly spread with toothsome dainties: milk, pancakes and honey, nuts, apples and pears.

While the children were eating their fill, the Old One made up two little beds which stood at one end of the room. She fluffed up the feather bed and puffed up the pillows, she turned back the lily-white linen, and then she said: "There, my little rabbits—a downy nest for each of you. Tumble in and slumber sweetly."

As soon as Hansel and Gretel were sound asleep, the Old One walked over and looked at them.

"Mm! Mm! Mm!" she said. "They're mine for certain!"

Now why should she do that? Well, I must tell you the real truth about the Old One. She wasn't as good and friendly as she pretended to be. She was a bad, bad witch who had built that sweet and sugary house on purpose to attract little children. Witches have ruby-red eyes and can hardly see at all, but oh! how they can smell with those long sharp noses of theirs! What they can smell is human beings; and that morning, as Hansel and Gretel were wandering around in the forest, the Old One knew it well enough. Sniff! sniff! sniff! went her nose—she had been sniffing and waiting for them all day.

The next morning while the two little innocents were still sleeping peacefully, the Old One looked greedily at their round arms and rosy cheeks. "Mm! Mm! Mm!" she mumbled. "Juicy morsels!"

She yanked Hansel out of bed, dragged him into the back yard, and locked him up in the goose-coop. Hansel screamed and cried but it did him no good.

Then the Old One went into the house, gave Gretel a rough shake and cried, "Up with you, lazy bones. Make haste and cook some food for your brother. He's out in the goose-coop and if we feed him well, ei! ei! what a tasty boy he'll make!"

When Gretel heard this she burst into tears, but the Old One gave her a cuff on the ears and said, "Stop howling, you fool. Pick up your legs and do as I tell you."

Each day Gretel had to cook big pots full of fattening food for Hansel, and each morning the Old One hobbled out to the goose-coop and cried, "Hansel, let me see your finger so I can tell how fat you're getting."

But Hansel never showed her his finger. He always poked out a dry old bone, and the Old One, because of her red eyes, never knew the difference. She thought it really was his finger, and wondered why it was that he did not, did not get fat.

When four weeks had passed and Hansel seemed to stay thin, the Old One became impatient and said to Gretel, "Hey there, girl! Heat up a big kettle of water. I'm tired of waiting and, be he fat or lean, I'm going to have Hansel for my supper tonight.''

Gretel cried and pleaded with her. But the Old One said, ''All that howling won't do you a bit or a whit of good. You might as well spare your breath.''

She built a roaring fire in the stove and said to Gretel, ''First we'll do some baking. I've mixed and kneaded the dough, and the loaves are all ready for the oven.'' Then she opened the oven door and added in a sweet voice, ''Do you think it's hot enough for the bread, Gretel dear? Just stick your head in the oven and see, there's a good girl!''

Gretel was about to obey, when a bird (the same white bird which had led them out of the forest) began to sing a song. It seemed to Gretel he was singing:

> Beware, beware,
> Don't look in there.

So Gretel didn't look into the oven. Instead she said to the Old One, ''Well, I really don't know how to go about it. Couldn't you first show me how?''

''Stupid!'' cried the Old One. ''It's easy enough. Just stick your head way in and give a good look around. See? Like this!''

As the Old One poked her horrid old head into the oven, Gretel gave her a push and a shove, closed the oven door, bolted it swiftly and ran away. The Old One called and cried, and frizzled and fried, but no one heard. That was the end of her, and who cares?

Gretel was already in the back yard. ''Hansel!'' she cried. ''We are free!'' She opened the door of the goose-coop and out popped Hansel. The children threw their arms about each other and hopped and skipped around wildly.

But now there came a soft whirr in the air. The children stopped dancing and looked up. The good white bird and many others — all the twittering birds from the fields and glades — were flying through the air and settling on the cake-roof of the gingerbread house.

On the roof was a nest full of pearls and sparkling gems. Each little forest-bird took out a pearl or a gem and carried it down to the children. Hansel held out his hands, and Gretel held up her apron to catch all these treasures,

while the little white bird sat on the roof and sang:

> Thank you for the crumbs of bread,
> Here are gems for you instead.

Now Hansel and Gretel understood that these were the very same birds who had eaten up their crumbs in the forest, and that this was how they wished to show their thanks.

As the birds fluttered away, Hansel said, ''And now, little sister, we must make haste and get out of this witchy wood. As for me, I got very homesick sitting in that goose-coop week after week.''

''And I,'' said Gretel. ''Yes, I've been homesick too. But, Hansel, here we are so far from home, and how can we ever find our way back?''

Ho, what luck! There was the little white bird fluttering ahead of them once more. It led them away and soon they were in a green meadow. In front of them lay a big, big pond. How to get over it! As Hansel and Gretel stood on the shore wondering what to do, a large swan came floating by, and the children said:

> Float, swan, float!
> Be our little boat.

The swan dipped its graceful head, raised it and dipped it again — that meant yes. When the swan had taken the children, one by one, to the other shore, they thanked it prettily and patted its long curved neck. Near the water's edge ran a neat little path. Hansel and Gretel followed it, and now the trees and the fields began to look familiar. Soon they saw their father's house gleaming through the trees and they ran home as fast as they could. The father, who had been grieving and looking for his lost children all this time, was sitting in front of the hearth gazing sadly into the fire. As the door burst open and his two little ones ran in with shouts and laughter, his eyes filled with tears of joy. He hugged them and kissed them, and all he could say was: ''My treasures, my little treasures!''

''Oh, as to treasures, papa,'' said Hansel, putting his hands into his pockets, ''we'll show you some! See, now we will never have to starve again.'' At this, Gretel poured a shower of jewels from her apron, while Hansel added handful after handful from his pockets.

And the hard-hearted stepmother, where was she? Well, I'll tell you. When Hansel and Gretel seemed to be gone for good, the woman saw that her husband could think of nothing but his lost children. This made her so angry that she packed up her things in a large red handkerchief and ran away. She never came back, and Hansel and Gretel and their good father lived happily ever after.

──────

"The Blind Boy and the Loon," from Tales from the Igloo. *Edited and translated by Father Maurice Metayer (Edmonton, Canada: Hurtig, 1972).*

This tale, which is also widely told among the West Coast Indians, reveals the importance of hunting among the Eskimo (Inuit) people. It was crucial that males hunt to provide the materials for food, clothing, and fuel, and that women prepare the animals caught. Both were arduous, time-consuming jobs requiring great skill, and both were necessary for survival. The deceit of the mother in this story places the lives of her family in jeopardy and, therefore, her violent death would be considered just by an Inuit audience. The loon is the boy's helper, which is appropriate, for this bird was often associated with shamans, the healers of the Inuit people.

The Blind Boy and the Loon

A woman lived with her son and daughter in a far away land. The son, although young in years, was already a skillful hunter and the four storage platforms built around the igloo were always filled with meat. His success at hunting was so great that the family never wanted for anything.

The young hunter's sister loved him dearly but his mother gradually grew tired of his hunting activities. Each time her son returned home with some game she would have to work hard at cleaning and skinning the animals and in preparing the meat for storage. As time went on the woman wished more and more to be able

to rest but as long as her son continued to hunt this was not possible. Eventually her weariness turned to hatred.

One day, while her son was sleeping, the woman took a piece of dirty blubber and rubbed it on his eyes, wishing as she did so that he would become blind. When the young man awoke his eyesight was gone. Try as he might he could see nothing but a dim whiteness.

From that day on increasing misery became the lot of the family. The son could do nothing but sit on his bed. His mother tried to provide food for the family by trapping foxes and hunting ptarmigan and ground squirrels. Yet when food was available the woman refused to give her son anything to eat or drink but the worst parts of the meat and some foul drinking water brought from the lake. Throughout the spring and summer the three people lived in this manner.

One day shortly after the arrival of winter, the young hunter heard steps on the snow. It was a polar bear trying to get into the igloo through the thin ice-window. Asking for his bow, he told his mother to aim the arrow while he pulled back the string. When all was in readiness the son let fly the arrow. Hearing the sound of the arrow as it thudded into the flesh of the bear, the son was confident that the kill had been made.

"I got him!" he cried.

"No," retorted his mother, "you merely struck an old piece of hide."

Shortly thereafter the smell of bear meat boiling in the cooking pot filled the igloo. The son said nothing but kept wondering why his mother had lied to him.

When the meat was cooked the woman fed her daughter and herself. To her son, she gave some old fox meat. It was only when she had left the igloo to get water from the lake that the young hunter was brought some bear meat by his sister.

Four long years went by while the son remained blind. Then one night, as the fluttering of wings and the cries of the birds announced the coming of spring, the son heard the call of the red-throated loon. As had been his habit during his blindness he began to crawl on his hands and knees to the lake

Illustration by Agnes Nanogak, "The Blind Boy and the Lion" from *Tales from the Igloo,*
tr. by Maurice Metayer. Copyright © 1972. Reprinted by permission of Hurtig Publishing.

where he knew the loon would be found.

When he arrived at the water's edge the bird came close to him and said, "Your mother made you blind by rubbing dirt into your eyes while you slept. If you wish, I can wash your eyes for you. Lie flat on my back and hold me by my neck. I shall carry you."

The son doubted that such a small bird would be able to perform such a feat, but the loon reassured him.

"Don't think those thoughts. Climb onto my back. I am going to dive with you into deep water. When you begin to lose your breath shake your body to signal me."

The young man did as he was told and down into the lake dove the loon with the hunter on his back. As they descended into the water the son could feel the body of the loon growing larger and larger and between his hands the neck seemed to be swelling. When he could hold his breath no longer he shook his body as he had been instructed and the loon brought him up to the surface.

"What can you see?" the loon asked.

"I can see nothing but a great light," replied the son.

"I shall take you down into the water once more," said the loon. "When you begin to choke, shake your body a little."

This time the dive lasted a long time but when they finally surfaced the young man could see clearly. He could distinguish the smallest rocks on the mountains far away. He described what he could see to the loon.

"My blindness is gone! My sight is sharper than before!"

"Your eyesight is too sharp for your own good," the loon told him. "Come down with me once more and your sight will be restored as it was before your blindness."

And it was so. When the young man came out of the water for the last time his eyesight was as it had been. Now the hunter could see the loon clearly and he realized that the bird was as large as a kayak.

When they had reached the lake shore the son asked the loon what he could give to him in return for his kindness.

The loon replied, "I do not want anything for myself other than a few fishes. Put some in the lake for me once in a while. This is the only food that I look for."

The son agreed and proceeded to return to his home. He was painfully surprised to see the wretched conditions in which he had been forced to live while he was blind. The skins he had used to sleep in were filthy with dirt and bugs. His drinking water and food were crawling with lice. Nevertheless he sat down in the corner and waited for his mother to awaken.

When his mother awoke the young hunter asked for food and drink. "I am hungry and thirsty. First bring me something to drink."

His mother did as she was told but the water she brought was so dirty that her son handed the cup back to her saying, "I will not touch such filth!"

"So you can see, my son," said the woman. She went then to fetch some clean food and water.

In time the young hunter was his old self again and was able to resume his successful hunting trips as before. A year went by during which time the storage platforms were once more filled with an abundance of game.

The following spring the hunter made ready to go whale hunting. He put a new skin cover on his whale boat, made lines, harpoons and spears. When the sea was free of ice he launched his boat and took his mother with him in search of whales.

"Mind the helm," he told her. "I shall look after the harpooning."

Here and there they saw a few whales blowing but the young hunter was waiting until they found a big one close to their boat. Eventually he called out to his mother who, not knowing what her son was about to do, came to assist him. He threw his harpoon, making certain that its head had caught in the flesh of the whale and then quickly tied the other end of the line to his mother's waist and threw her overboard.

Caught as she was the woman was dragged through the water, bobbing up and down in the waves. She cried out and reproached her son saying, "When you were young I gave you my breast to suckle. I fed you and kept you clean. And now you do this to me!"

Finally she disappeared from sight. For years to come hunters claimed that they saw her in the waves and heard her song of despair as it was carried far and wide by the winds.

"Jack and the Beanstalk," from English Folk and Fairy Tales. *Collected by Joseph Jacobs (New York: Putnam's, [1890]).*

This classic English folktale contains an outstanding example of the child-hero. Small, poor, and starving, Jack destroys the giant and steals his wealth, succeeding where other children have presumably failed, and taking action when his mother is paralyzed with fear. Each of Jack's three trips becomes progressively more dangerous, and in turn, he must be braver and trickier. The clever and optimistic Jack has been interpreted as symbolic of the child succeeding in the face of adult tyranny, of peasants surviving against tyrannical rulers, and of the English destroying mightier continental invaders. Jack is a member of the giant-killing tradition of stories which includes the Biblical David. The basic structure of the story is circular; the conflict is resolved when Jack brings security to his own home by returning with wealth, and finally, by killing the giant.

Jack and the Beanstalk

There was once upon a time a poor widow who had an only son named Jack, and a cow named Milky-white. And all they had to live on was the milk the cow gave every morning, which they carried to the market and sold. But one morning Milky-white gave no milk, and they didn't know what to do.

"What shall we do, what shall we do?" said the widow, wringing her hands.

"Cheer up, mother, I'll go and get work somewhere," said Jack.

"We've tried that before, and nobody would take you," said his mother; "we must sell Milky-white and with the money start shop, or something."

"All right, mother," says Jack; "it's market-day today, and I'll soon sell Milky-white, and then we'll see what we can do."

So he took the cow's halter in his hand, and off he started. He hadn't gone far when he met a funny looking old man, who said to him: "Good morning, Jack."

"Good morning to you," said Jack, and wondered how he knew his name.

"Well, Jack, and where are you off to?" said the man.

"I'm going to market to sell our cow here."

"Oh, you look the proper sort of chap to sell cows," said the man; "I wonder if you know how many beans make five."

"Two in each hand and one in your mouth," says Jack, as sharp as a needle.

"Right you are," says the man, "and here they are, the very beans themselves," he went on, pulling out of his pocket a number of strange-looking beans. "As you are so sharp," says he, "I don't mind doing a swap with you — your cow for these beans."

"Go along," says Jack; "wouldn't you like it?"

"Ah! you don't know what these beans are," said the man; "if you plant them overnight, by morning they grow right up to the sky."

"Really?" said Jack; "you don't say so."

"Yes, that is so, and if it doesn't turn out to be true you can have your cow back."

"Right," says Jack, and hands him over Milky-white's halter and pockets the beans.

Back goes Jack home, and as he hadn't gone very far it wasn't dusk by the time he got to his door.

"Back already, Jack?" said his mother; "I see you haven't got Milky-white, so you've sold her. How much did you get for her?"

"You'll never guess, mother," says Jack.

"No, you don't say so. Good boy! Five pounds, ten, fifteen, no, it can't be twenty."

"I told you you couldn't guess. What do you say to these beans; they're magical, plant them overnight and — "

"What!" says Jack's mother, "have you been such a fool, such a dolt, such an idiot, as to give away my Milky-white, the best milker in the parish, and prime beef to boot, for a set of paltry beans? Take that! Take that! Take that! And as for your precious beans here they go out of the window. And now off with you to bed. Not a sup shall you drink, and not a bit shall you swallow this very night."

So Jack went upstairs to his little room in the attic, and sad and sorry he was, to be sure,

as much for his mother's sake, as for the loss of his supper.

At last he dropped off to sleep.

When he woke up, the room looked so funny. The sun was shining into part of it, and yet all the rest was quite dark and shady. So Jack jumped up and dressed himself and went to the window. And what do you think he saw? Why, the beans his mother had thrown out of the window into the garden, had sprung up into a big beanstalk which went up and up and up till it reached the sky. So the man spoke truth after all.

The beanstalk grew up quite close past Jack's window, so all he had to do was to open it and give a jump on to the beanstalk which ran up just like a big ladder. So Jack climbed, and he climbed and he climbed and he climbed and he climbed and he climbed and he climbed till at last he reached the sky. And when he got there he found a long broad road going as straight as a dart. So he walked along and he walked along and he walked along till he came to a great big tall house, and on the doorstep there was a great big tall woman.

"Good morning, mum," says Jack, quite polite-like. "Could you be so kind as to give me some breakfast?" For he hadn't had anything to eat you know, the night before and was as hungry as a hunter.

"It's breakfast you want, is it?" says the great big tall woman, "it's breakfast you'll be if you don't move off from here. My man is an ogre and there's nothing he likes better than boys broiled on toast. You'd better be moving on or he'll soon be coming."

"Oh! please mum, do give me something to eat, mum. I've had nothing to eat since yesterday morning, really and truly, mum," says Jack. "I may as well be broiled as die of hunger."

Well, the ogre's wife was not half so bad after all. So she took Jack into the kitchen, and gave him a chunk of bread and cheese and a jug of milk. But Jack hadn't half finished these when thump! thump! thump! the whole house began to tremble with the noise of some one coming.

"Goodness gracious me! It's my old man," said the ogre's wife, "what on earth shall I do?

Come along quick and jump in here.'' And she bundled Jack into the oven just as the ogre came in.

He was a big one, to be sure. At his belt he had three calves strung up by the heels, and he unhooked them and threw them down on the table and said: ''Here, wife, broil me a couple of these for breakfast. Ah! what's this I smell?

> Fee-fi-fo-fum,
> I smell the blood of an Englishman,
> Be he alive, or be he dead
> I'll have his bones to grind my bread.''

''Nonsense, dear,'' said his wife, ''you're dreaming. Or perhaps you smell the scraps of that little boy you liked so much for yesterday's dinner. Here, you go and have a wash and tidy up, and by the time you come back your breakfast 'll be ready for you.''

So off the ogre went, and Jack was just going to jump out of the oven and run away when the woman told him not. ''Wait till he's asleep,'' says she; ''he always has a doze after breakfast.''

Well, the ogre had his breakfast, and after that he goes to a big chest and takes out of it a couple of bags of gold, and down he sits and counts till at last his head began to nod and he began to snore till the whole house shook again.

Then Jack crept out on tiptoe from his oven, and as he was passing the ogre he took one of the bags of gold under his arm, and off he pelters till he came to the beanstalk, and then he threw down the bag of gold, which of course fell into his mother's garden, and then he climbed down and climbed down till at last he got home and told his mother and showed her the gold and said: ''Well, mother, wasn't I right about the beans? They are really magical, you see.''

So they lived on the bag of gold for some time, but at last they came to the end of it, and Jack made up his mind to try his luck once more up at the top of the beanstalk. So one fine morning he rose up early, and got on to the beanstalk, and he climbed and he climbed and he climbed and he climbed and he climbed and he climbed till at last he came out on to the road again and up to the great big tall house he had been to before. There, sure enough, was the great big tall woman a-standing on the doorstep.

''Good morning, mum,'' says Jack, as bold as brass, ''could you be so good as to give me something to eat?''

''Go away, my boy,'' said the big tall woman, ''or else my man will eat you up for breakfast. But aren't you the youngster who came here once before? Do you know, that very day, my man missed one of his bags of gold.''

''That's strange mum,'' said Jack, ''I dare say I could tell you something about that, but I'm so hungry I can't speak till I've had something to eat.''

Well the big tall woman was so curious that she took him in and gave him something to eat. But he had scarcely begun munching it as slowly as he could when thump! thump! thump! they heard the giant's footstep, and his wife hid Jack away in the oven.

All happened as it did before. In came the ogre as he did before, said: ''Fee-fi-fo-fum,'' and had his breakfast of three broiled oxen. Then he said: ''Wife, bring me the hen that lays the golden eggs.'' So she brought it, and the ogre said: ''Lay,'' and it laid an egg all of gold. And then the ogre began to nod his head, and to snore till the house shook.

Then Jack crept out of the oven on tiptoe and caught hold of the golden hen, and was off before you could say ''Jack Robinson.'' But this time the hen gave a cackle which woke the ogre, and just as Jack got out of the house he heard him calling: ''Wife, wife, what have you done with my golden hen?''

And the wife said: ''Why, my dear?''

But that was all Jack heard, for he rushed off to the beanstalk and climbed down like a house on fire. And when he got home he showed his mother the wonderful hen, and said ''Lay'' to it; and it laid a golden egg every time he said ''Lay.''

Well, Jack was not content, and it wasn't very long before he determined to have another try at his luck up there at the top of the beanstalk. So one fine morning, he rose up early, and got on to the beanstalk, and he climbed and he climbed and he climbed and he climbed till he got to the top. But this time he knew better than to go straight to the ogre's house. And when he got near it, he waited behind a bush till he saw the ogre's wife come out with a pail to get some water, and then he crept into the house and got into the copper. He hadn't been there long when he heard thump! thump! thump! as before, and in came the ogre and his wife.

"Fee-fi-fo-fum, I smell the blood of an Englishman," cried out the ogre. "I smell him, wife, I smell him."

"Do you, my dearie?" says the ogre's wife. Then, if it's that little rogue that stole your gold and the hen that laid the golden eggs he's sure to have got into the oven." And they both rushed to the oven. But Jack wasn't there, luckily, and the ogre's wife said: "There you are again with your fee-fi-fo-fum. Why of course it's the boy you caught last night that I've just broiled for your breakfast. How forgetful I am, and how careless you are not to know the difference between live and dead after all these years."

So the ogre sat down to the breakfast and ate it, but every now and then he would mutter: "Well, I could have sworn — " and he'd get up and search the larder and the cupboards and everything, only, luckily, he didn't think of the copper.

After breakfast was over, the ogre called out: "Wife, wife, bring me my golden harp." So she brought it and put it on the table before him. Then he said: "Sing!" and the golden hearp sang most beautifully. And it went on singing till the ogre fell asleep, and commenced to snore like thunder.

Then Jack lifted up the copper-lid very quietly and got down like a mouse and crept on hands and knees till he came to the table, when up he crawled, caught hold of the golden harp and dashed with it towards the door. But the harp called out quite loud: "Master! Master!" and the ogre woke up just in time to see Jack running off with his harp.

Jack ran as fast as he could, and the ogre came rushing after, and would soon have caught him only Jack had a start and dodged him a bit and knew where he was going. When he got to the beanstalk the ogre was not more than twenty yards away when suddenly he saw Jack disappear like, and when he came to the end of the road he saw Jack underneath climbing down for dear life. Well, the ogre didn't like trusting himself to such a ladder, and he stood and waited, so Jack got another start. But just then the harp cried out: "Master! Master!" and the ogre swung himself down on to the beanstalk, which shook with his weight. Down climbs Jack, and after him climbed the ogre. By this time Jack had climbed down and climbed down and climbed down till he was very nearly home. So he called out: "Mother! Mother! bring me an axe, bring me an axe." And his mother came rushing out with the axe in her hand, but when she came to the beanstalk she stood stock still with fright for there she saw the ogre with his legs just through the clouds.

But Jack jumped down and got hold of the axe and gave a chop at the beanstalk which cut it half in two. The ogre felt the beanstalk shake and quiver so he stopped to see what was the matter. Then Jack gave another chop with the axe, and the beanstalk was cut in two and began to topple over. Then the ogre fell down and broke his crown, and the beanstalk came toppling after.

Then Jack showed his mother his golden harp, and what with showing that and selling the golden eggs Jack and his mother became very rich, and he married a great princess, and they lived happy ever after.

———

"Jack in the Giants' Newground," from The Jack Tales. *Edited by Richard Chase (Cambridge, Mass.: The Riverside Press, 1943).*

In his preface to The Jack Tales, *Richard Chase describes how he came to collect tales from Marshall Ward and his relatives who lived near Beech Mountain, North Carolina. One important function of such tales was to keep the children working at tedious tasks. Mrs. R.M. Ward explains: "We would all get down around a sheet full of dry beans and start in to shelling 'em. Mon-roe would tell the kids one of them tales and they'd work for life!"*

Chase explains how the Appalachian Jack

differs from his English forbear: "It is through this natural oral process that our Appalachian giant-killer has acquired the easy-going, unpretentious rural American manners that make him so different from his English cousin, the cocksure, dashing young hero of the 'fairy' tale." "Jack in the Giants' Newground" depicts this southern Appalachian hero at his giant-killing best. Featuring a circular structure, a quest, and a splendid reward for Jack's completed tasks, this tale reveals Jack's trickery and his amiable disposition.

Jack in the Giants' Newground

One time away back years ago there was a boy named Jack. He and his folks lived off in the mountains somewhere and they were awful poor, just didn't have a thing. Jack had two brothers, Will and Tom, and they are in some of the Jack Tales, but this one I'm fixin' to tell you now, there's mostly just Jack in it.

Jack was awful lazy sometimes, just wouldn't do ary lick of work. His mother and his daddy kept tryin' to get him to help, but they couldn't do a thing with him when he took a lazy spell.

Well, Jack decided one time he'd pull out from there and try his luck in some other section of the country. So his mother fixed him up a little snack of dinner, and he put on his old raggedy hat and lit out.

Jack walked on, walked on. He eat his snack 'fore he'd gone very far. Sun commenced to get awful hot. He traveled on, traveled on, till he was plumb out of the settle-ment what he knowed. Hit got to be about twelve, sun just a-beatin' down, and Jack started gettin' hungry again.

He came to a fine smooth road directly, decided he'd take that, see where it went, what kind of folks lived on it. He went on, went on, and pretty soon he came to a big fine stone house up above the road. Jack stopped. He never had seen such a big house as that before. Then he looked at the gate and saw it was made out of gold. Well, Jack 'lowed some well-doin' folks must live there, wondered whether or no they'd give him his dinner. Stepped back from the gate, hollered, "Hello!"

A man came to the door, says, "Hello, stranger. What'll ye have?"

"I'm a-looking' for a job of work."

"Don't know as I need to hire anybody right now. What's your name?"

"Name's Jack."

"Come on up, Jack, and sit a spell. Ain't it pretty hot walkin'?"

"Pretty hot," says Jack.

"Come on up on the porch and cool off. You're not in no hurry, are ye?"

Jack says, "Well, I'll stop a little while, I reckon."

Shoved back that gold gate and marched on in. The man reached in the door and pulled out a couple of chairs. Jack took one and they leaned back, commenced smokin'. Directly Jack says to that man, "What did you say your name was, mister?"

"Why, Jack, I'm the King."

"Well, now, King," says Jack, "hit looks like you'd be a-needin' somebody with all your land. I bet you got a heap of land to work."

"Are ye a hard worker, Jack?"

"Oh, I'm the workin'est one of all back home yonder."

"You a good hand to plow?"

"Yes sir!"

"Can ye clear newground?"

"Why, that's all I ever done back home."

"Can ye kill giants?"

"Huh?" says Jack, and he dropped his pipe. Picked it up, says, "Well, I reckon I could try."

The old King sort of looked at Jack and how little he was, says, "Well, now, Jack, I have got a little piece of newground I been tryin' for the longest to get cleared. The trouble is there's a gang of giants live over in the next holler, been disputin' with me about the claim. They kill ever' Englishman goes up there, kill 'em and eat 'em. I reckon I've done hired about a dozen men claimed to be giantkillers, but the giants killed them, ever' last one."

"Are these giants very big 'uns?" says Jack.

"Well, they're all about six times the size of a natural man, and there's five of 'em. The old man has got four heads and his old woman has got two. The oldest boy has got two heads, and there's a set of twins has got three heads a-piece."

Jack didn't say nothin', just kept studyin' about how hungry he was.

King says, "Think ye can clear that patch, Jack?"

"Why, sure!" says Jack. "All I can do is get killed, or kill them, one."

"All right, son. We'll make arrange-ments about the work after we eat. I expect my old woman's about got dinner ready now. Let's us go on in to the table."

"Thank ye, King," says Jack. "I hope it won't put ye out none."

"Why, no," says the King. "Hit ain't much, but you're welcome to what we got."

Well, Jack eat about all the dinner he could hold, but the King's old woman kept on pilin' up his plate till he was plumb foundered. His dish set there stacked up with chicken and cornbread and beans and greens and pie and cake, and the Queen had done poured him milk for the third time. The old King kept right on, and Jack didn't want them to think he couldn't eat as much as anybody else, so directly he reached down and took hold on the old leather apron he had on and doubled that up under his coat. Then he'd make like he was takin' a bite, but he'd slip it down in that leather apron. He poured about four glasses of milk down there, too. Had to fasten his belt down on it so's it 'uld hold.

Well, directly the King pushed his chair back, and then he and Jack went on out and sat down again, leaned back against the house and lit their pipes.

King says to Jack, says, "If you get that patch cleared, Jack, I'll pay ye a thousand dollars a-piece for ever' giant's head you bring down, and pay ye good wages for gettin' that patch cleared: ten cents a hour."

Jack said that suited him all right, and he got the King to point him out which ridge it was. Then Jack says to the King, "You say them giants live over in the other holler?"

King said they did.

Jack says, "Can they hear ye when ye start hackin'?"

"They sure can," says the King.

Jack didn't say nothin'.

The King says to him, "You don't feel un-easy now, do ye, Jack?"

"Why, no, bedads!" says Jack. "Why, I may be the very giant-killer you been lookin' for. I may not kill all of 'em today, but I'll try to get a start anyhow."

So the King told him maybe he'd better go on to work. Said for him to go on out past the woodpile and get him a axe, says, "You might get in a lick or two 'fore them giants come. You'll find a tree up there where them other men have knocked a couple of chips out'n. You can just start in on that same tree."

So Jack started on out to the woodpile. The King watched him, saw him lean over and pick up a little old Tommy hatchet, says, "Hey, Jack! You'll need the axe, won't ye?"

"Why, no," says Jack. "This here'll do me all right." He started on off, turned around, says, "I'll be back about time for supper."

The old King just grinned and let him go on.

When Jack fin'ly got up on that ridge, he was scared to death. He sat down on a log and studied awhile. He knowed if he started in cuttin', them giants would come up there; and he knowed if he didn't, the King 'uld know he hadn't done no work and he'd likely get fired and wouldn't get no supper. So Jack thought about it some more, then he picked out the tallest poplar he could see, and cloomb up in it, started in choppin' on the limbs way up at the very top . . .

Hack! Hack! Hack!

Heard a racket directly, sounded like a horse comin' up through the bresh. Jack looked down the holler, saw a man about thirty foot high comin' a-stompin' up the mountain, steppin' right over the laurel bushes and the rock-clifts. Jack was so scared he like to slipped his hold.

The old giant came on up, looked around till he fin'ly saw where Jack was settin', came over there under him, says, "Hello, stranger."

"Howdy do, daddy."

"What in the world you a doin' up there?"

"I'm a-clearin' newground for that man lives back down yonder."

"Clearin' land? Well, I never seen such a fool business, start in clearin' newground in the top of a tree! Ain't ye got no sense?"

"Why, that's allus the way we start in clearin' back home."

"What's your name, son?"

"My name's Jack."

"Well, you look-a-here, Jack. This patch of land is ours and we don't aim to have it cleared. We done told the King so."

"Oh, well, then," says Jack, "I didn't know that. If I'd 'a knowed that I'd 'a not started."

"Come on down, Jack. I'll take ye home for supper."

Didn't think Jack 'uld know what he meant. Jack hollered back, says, "All right, daddy. I'll be right down."

Jack cloomb down a ways, got on a limb right over the old giant's head, started in talkin' to him, says, "Daddy, they tell me giants are awful stout. Is that so?"

Illustration by Berkeley Williams Jr., "Jack in the Giant's Newground" from *The Jack Tales* by Richard Chase. Copyright © 1943 by Richard Chase. Copyright renewed © 1971 by Richard Chase. Reprinted by permission of Houghton Mifflin Company.

"Well, some, says the old giant. "I can carry a thousand men before me."

"Well, now, daddy, I bet I can do somethin' you can't do."

"What's that, Jack?"

"Squeeze milk out'n a flint rock."

"I don't believe ye."

"You throw me up a flint rock here and I'll show ye."

So while the old giant hunted him up a flint rock, Jack took his knife and punched a little hole in that old leather apron. The giant chunked the rock up to him and jack squeezed down on it, pushed up against his apron, and the milk commenced to dreen out . . .

Dreep, dreep, dreep.

"Do it again, Jack!"

So Jack pushed right hard that time, and hit just went like milkin' a cow.

The old giant hollered up to Jack, says, "Throw me down that rock."

He took the rock and squeezed and squeezed till fin'ly he got so mad he mashed down on it and they tell me he crumbled that flint rock plumb to powder.

Then Jack hollered down to him again, says, "I can do somethin' else you can't do."

"What's that, Jack?"

"I can cut myself wide open and sew it back up. And it won't hurt me none."

"Aw, shucks, Jack. I know you're lyin' now."

"You want to see me do it?"

"Go ahead."

Jack took his knife and ripped open that leather apron, took a piece of string he had, punched some holes, and sewed it back up, says, "See, daddy? I'm just as good as I ever was."

Well, the old giant just couldn't stand to let Jack out-do him, so he hollered up, says, "Hand here the knife, Jack."

Took Jack's knife and cut himself wide open, staggered around a little and fin'ly querled over on the ground dead. Well, Jack, he scaled down the tree and cut off the old giant's heads with that little Tommy hatchet, took 'em on back to the King's house.

II

The King paid Jack two thousand dollars like he said he would. Jack eat him a big supper and stayed the night. Next mornin', after he eat his breakfast, Jack told the King he reckoned he'd have to be a-gettin' on back home. Said his daddy would be a-needin' him settin' out tobacco.

But the King says, "Oh, no, Jack. Why, you're the best giant-killer I ever hired. There's some more of that giant gang yet, and I'd like awful well to get shet of the whole crowd of 'em."

Jack didn't want to do it. He figgered he'd done made him enough money to last him awhile, and he didn't want to get mixed up with them giants any more'n he could help. But the King kept on after him till Jack saw he couldn't get out of it very handy. So he went and got the Tommy hatchet, started on up to the newground again.

Jack hadn't hardly got up there that time 'fore he heard somethin' comin' up the holler stompin' and breakin' bresh, makin' the awfulest racket. He started to climb him a tree like he done before, but the racket was gettin' closer and closer, and Jack looked and saw it was them twin giants that had three heads a-piece. Jack looked up, saw them six heads a-comin' over the tree tops, says, "Law me! I can't stand that! I'll hide!"

He saw a big holler log down the hill a ways, grabbed him up a shirt-tail full of rocks and shot in that log like a ground squirrel. Hit was pretty big inside there. Jack could turn right around in it.

The old giants fin'ly got there. Jack heard one of 'em say to the other'n, "Law! Look a-yonder! Somebody's done killed brother."

"Law, yes! Now, who you reckon could a' done that? Why, he could 'a carried a thousand Englishmen before him, single-handed. I didn't hear no racket up here yesterday, did you?"

"Why, no, and the ground ain't trompled none, neither. Who in the world you reckon could 'a done it?"

Well, they mourned over him awhile, then they 'lowed they'd have to take him on down and fix up a buryin'. So they got hold on him,

one by the hands and the other by the feet, started on down.

"Poor brother!" says one of 'em. "If we knowed who it was killed him, we'd sure fix them!"

The other'n stopped all at once, says, "Hold on a minute. There ain't a stick of wood to the house. Mother sent us up here after wood; we sure better not forget that. We'll have to have plenty of wood too, settin' up with brother tonight."

'We better get about the handiest thing we can find," says the other'n. "Look yonder at that holler log. Suppose'n we take that down."

Well, they laid the old dead giant down across the top of that log and shouldered it up. Jack got shook around right considerable inside the log, but after he got settled again, he looked and saw the old giant in front had the log restin' right betwixt his shoulders. And directly Jack happened to recollect he had all them rocks. So after they'd done gone down the holler a little piece, Jack he picked him out a rock and cut-drive at the giant in front — fumped him right in the back of the head. Old giant stumbled, and stopped and hollered back at his brother, says, "You look-a-here! What you a-throwin' rocks at me for?"

"I never so throwed no rocks at you."

"You did so! You nearly knocked me down!"

"Why, I never done it!"

They argued awhile, fin'ly started on down again.

Jack waited a minute or two, then he cut loose with another good-sized rock. *Wham!*

"You con-founded thing! You've done hit me again!"

"I never done no such a thing!"

"You did too!"

"I never teched ye!"

"You're the very one. You needn't try to lie out of it neither. You can see as good as I can there ain't nobody else around here to throw no rocks. You just hit me one other time now, and I'll come back there and smack the fire out-a you!"

They jawed and cussed a right smart while till fin'ly they quit and got started on down again.

Well, this time Jack picked out the sharpest-edged rock he had, drew back and clipped him again right in the same place. *Pow*! The old giant in front hollered so loud you could 'a heard him five miles, throwed that log off'n his shoulder and just made for the other'n, says, "That makes three times you've done rocked me! And you'll just take a beatin' from me now or know I can't do it!"

Them twin giants started in to fightin' like horses kickin'. Beat any fightin' ever was seen: pinchin' and bitin' and kickin' and maulin' one another; made a noise like splittin' rails. They fit and scratched and scratched and fit till they couldn't stand up no more. Got to tumblin' around on the ground, knockin' down trees and a-kickin' up rocks and dirt. They were clinched so tight couldn't neither one break loose from the other'n, and directly they were so wore out they just lay there all tangled up in a pile, both of 'em pantin' for breath.

So when Jack saw there wasn't no danger in 'em, he crawled out from that log and chopped off their heads, put 'em in a sack and pulled on back to the King's house.

III

Well, the old King paid Jack six thousand dollars for that load of heads. Then Jack said he just had to get on in home. Said his folks would be uneasy about him, and besides that they couldn't get the work done up unless he was there.

But the King says to him, says, "Why, Jack, there ain't but two more of 'em now. You kill them for me and that'll wind 'em up. Then we won't have no trouble at all about that newground."

Jack said he'd see what he could do: went on back that same evenin'.

This time Jack didn't climb no tree or nothin'. Went to work makin' him a bresh pile, made all the racket he could. The old four-headed giant come a-tearin' up there in no time. Looked around, saw the other giants lyin' there dead, came over to where Jack was, says, "Hello, stranger."

"Hello, yourself."

"What's your name, buddy?"

"My name's Jack — Mister Jack."

"Well, Mister Jack, can you tell me how come all my boys layin' here dead?"

"Yes, bedads, I can tell ye," says Jack. "They came up here cussin' and 'busin' me, and I had to haul off and kill 'em. You just try and sass me ary bit now, and I'll kill you too!"

"Oh pray, Jack, don't do that! There's only me and the old woman left now, and she's got to have somebody to get in her stovewood and tote up water."

"You better be careful what ye say then. I ain't goin' to take nothin' off nobody."

"Well, now, I don't want to have no racket with ye at all, Mister Jack. You come on down and stay the night with us, help set up with our dead folks, and we'll get fixed to have a buryin' tomorrow."

"Well, I'll go," says Jack, "but you sure better watch out what you say."

"Oh, I'll not say nothin'," says the old giant. Says, "Law, Jack, you must be the awfulest man!"

So the old giant stuck the dead 'uns under his arms and he and Jack started on down. When they got close to the house, the giant stopped, says to Jack, "Now, Jack, you better wait till I go and tell the old lady you've come down for supper. She might cut a shine. She'll be mad enough already about her boys bein' killed."

He went on in and shut the door. Jack slipped up and laid his ear to the keyhole so's he could hear what they said. Heard him tell this old lady, says, "I've got Jack here, claims to be a giantkiller. I found the boys up yonder at the newground with their heads cut off, and this here Jack says he's the one done it."

The old woman just carried on. Fin'ly the old giant got her hushed, says, "He don't look to me like he's so stout as all that. We'll have to test him out a little, and see whe'er he's as bad as he claims he is."

Directly Jack heard him a-comin' to the door rattlin' buckets. So he stepped back from the house and made like he was just comin' up. The old giant came on out, says, "There ain't a bit of water up, Jack. The old woman wants you and me to tote her some from the creek."

Jack saw he had four piggins big as wash

tubs, had rope bails fixed on 'em, had 'em slung on one arm. So they went on down to the creek and the old giant set the piggins down. Stove his two in, got 'em full and started on back. Jack knowed he couldn't even tip one of them things over and hit empty. So he left his two piggins a-layin' there, waded out in the creek and started rollin' up his sleeves. The old giant stopped and looked back, saw Jack spit in his hands and start feelin' around under the water.

"What in the world ye fixin' to do, Jack?"

"Well, daddy," says Jack, "just as soon as I can find a place to ketch a hold, I'm a-goin' to take the creek back up there closer to the house where your old woman can get her water everwhen she wants it."

"Oh, no, Jack! Not take the creek back. Hit'll ruin my cornfield. And besides that, my old lady's gettin' sort-a shaky on her feet; she might fall in and get drownded."

"Well, then," says Jack, "I can't be a-wastin' my time takin' back them two little bitty bucketfulls. Why, I'd not want to be seen totin' such little buckets as them."

"Just leave 'em there, then, Jack. Come on, let's go back to the house. Mind, now, you come on here and leave the creek there where it's at."

When they got back, he told his old woman what Jack had said. Says, "Why, Law me! I had a time gettin' him to leave that creek alone."

He came on out again, told Jack supper wasn't ready yet, said for him to come on and they'd play pitch-crowbar till it was time to eat. They went on down to the level field, the old giant picked up a crowbar from the fence corner. Hit must 'a weighed about a thousand pounds. Says, "Now, Jack, we'll see who can pitch this crowbar the furthest. That's a game me and the boys used to play."

So he heaved it up, pitched it about a hundred yards, says, "You run get it now, Jack. See can you pitch it back here to where I'm at."

Jack ran to where it fell, reached down and took hold on it. Looked up 'way past the old giant, put his hand up to his mouth, hollers, "Hey, Uncle! Hey, Uncle!"

The old giant looked all around, says, "What you callin' me Uncle for?"

"I ain't callin' you. — Hey! *Uncle!*"

"Who are ye hollerin' at, Jack?"

"Why, I got a uncle over in Virginia," says Jack. "He's a blacksmith and this old crowbar would be the very thing for him to make up into horseshoes. Iron's mighty scarce over there. I thought I'd just pitch this out there to him. — Hey! UNCLE!"

"Oh, no, Jack. I need that crowbar. Pray don't pitch it over in Virginia."

"Well, now," says Jack, "I can't be bothered with pitchin' it back there just to where you are. If I can't pitch it where I want, I'll not pitch it at all."

"Leave it layin' then, Jack. Come on let's go back to the house. — You turn loose of my crowbar now."

They got back, the giant went in and told his old woman he couldn't find out nothin' about Jack. Said for her to test him awhile herself. Says, "I'll go after firewood. You see can't you get him in the oven against I get back, so's we can eat."

Went on out, says to Jack, "I got to go get a turn of wood, Jack. You can go on in the house and get ready for supper."

Jack went on in, looked around, didn't see a thing cookin', and there set a big old-fashioned clay oven with red-hot coals all across it, and the lid layin' to one side.

The old giant lady came at him, had a wash rag in one hand and a comb in the other'n, says, "Come here now, Jacky. Let me wash ye and comb ye for supper."

"You're no need to bother," says Jack. "I can wash."

"Aw, Jack. I allus did wash my own boys before supper. I just want to treat ye like one of my boys."

"Thank ye, m'am, but I gen'ally wash and comb myself."

"Aw, please, Jack. You let me wash ye a little now, and comb your head. Come on, Jacky, set up here on this shelf so's I won't have to stoop over."

Jack looked and saw that shelf was right on one side of the big dirt oven. He cloomb on up on the scaffle, rockled and reeled this-a-way and that-a-way. The old woman kept tryin' to get at him with the rag and comb, but Jack kept on teeterin' around till he slipped off on the wrong side. He cloomb back up and he'd rockle and reel some more. The old woman told him, says, "Sit straight now, Jack. Lean over this way a little. Sakes alive! Don't ye know how to sit up on a shelf?"

"I never tried sittin' on such a board before," says Jack. "I don't know how you mean."

"You get down from there a minute. I reckon I'll have to show ye."

She started to climb up there on the scaffle, says, "You put your shoulder under it, Jack. I'm mighty heavy and I'm liable to break it down."

Jack put his shoulder under the far end, and when the old woman went to turn around and sit, Jack shoved up right quick, fetched her spang in the oven. Grabbed him up a handspike and prized the lid on. Then he went and hid behind the door.

Old giant came in directly. Heard somethin' in the oven just a-crackin' and a-poppin'.

"Old woman!" Hey, old woman! Jack's a-burnin'."

When she didn't answer, the old giant fin'ly lifted the lid off and there was his old lady just about baked done, says, "Well, I'll be confounded! That's not Jack!"

Jack stepped out from behind the door, says, "No, hit sure ain't. And you better mind out or I'll put you in there too."

"Oh, pray, Jack, don't put me in there. You got us licked, Jack. I'm the only one left now, and I reckon I better just leave this country for good. Now, you help me get out of here, Jack, and I'll go off to some other place and I'll promise not to never come back here no more."

"I'd sure like to help ye, daddy, but I don't think we got time now. Hit's too late."

"Too late? Why, how come, Jack?"

"The King told me he was goin' to send a army of two thousand men down here to kill ye this very day. They ought to be here any minute now."

"Two thousand! That many will kill me sure. Law, what'll I do? Pray, Jack, hide me somewhere."

Jack saw a big chest there in the house, told the old giant to jump in that. Time he got in it and Jack fastened the lid down on him, Jack ran to the window and made-out like that army was a-comin' down the holler, says, "Yonder they come, daddy. Looks to me like about three thousand. I'll try to keep 'em off, though. You keep right still now and I'll do my best not to let 'em get ye."

Jack ran outside the house and commenced makin' a terrible racket, bangin' a stick on the walls, rattlin' the windows, shoutin' and a-hollerin', a-makin'-out like he was a whole army. Fin'ly he ran back in the house, knocked over the table and two or three chairs, says, "You quit that now and get on out of here! I done killed that old giant! No use in you a-breakin' up them chairs. He ain't here I tell ye!"

Then Jack 'uld tumble over some more chairs and throw the dishes around considerable, says, "You all leave them things alone now, 'fore I have to knock some of ye down."

Then he'd run by that chest and beat on it, says, "He ain't in there. You all leave that chest alone. He'd dead just like I told ye. Now you men march right on back to the King and tell him I done got shet of them giants and there ain't ary one left."

Well, Jack fin'ly made like he'd done run the army off. Let the old giant out the chest. He was just a-shakin', says, "Jack, I sure do thank ye for not lettin' all them men find out where I was at."

So Jack took the old giant on down to the depot, put him on a freight train, and they hauled him off to China.

The King paid Jack two thousand dollars for bakin' the old giant lady, but he said he couldn't allow him nothin' on the old giant because the trade they'd made was that Jack had to bring in the heads.

Jack didn't care none about that, 'cause his overhall pockets were just a-bulgin' with money when he got back home. He didn't have to clear that newground for the King, neither. He paid his two brothers, Will and Tom, to do it for him.

And the last time I went down to see Jack he was a-doin' real well.

―――

"Tricksy Rabbit," from Tales From the Story
Hat. *Retold by Verna Aardema (New York:
Coward-McCann, 1960).*

*The storyteller in West Africa wears a wide-
brimmed hat of guinea corn straw. Bits of
feathers, fur, and tiny wooden and ivory carv-
ings dangle from the brim of the story hat.
Whoever asks for a story may choose an object, and the storyteller begins the story it represents. Among the most famous of these West
African folktales are those about Anansi, who
later appears as Anansi or Nansii in the West
Indies, and Tricksy Rabbit, who came to the
United States as Brer Rabbit. "Tricksy Rabbit" is a very old story told by a man from the
Waganda Tribe to Henry M. Stanley in the late
1800s. The tale reveals the well-known dimensions of this famous trickster's personality: his
comic sense, his unerring instinct for survival
through wit and cunning, his capacity to
charm ladies, and his delight in his ability to
trick his adversaries. "Tricksy Rabbit" is a circular journey featuring a quest, along with
several memorable tricks. Tricksy Rabbit's gift
for outwitting much larger, stronger animals
no doubt accounts for the popularity the trickster rabbit has enjoyed among children.*

Tricksy Rabbit

In Uganda, deep in the heart of Africa, there
once lived a clever rabbit. He was so full of
fun and tricks that the forest folk called him
Tricksy Rabbit.

On the trail one day Tricksy met his friend
Elephant. The two stopped to chat. "I hear,"
said Tricksy, "that the Watusi herders are in
need of cloth. I would like to get a fine fat cow
for myself. This may be a wise time to go
trading."

"That is a fine idea!" said Elephant.

So the two prepared bales of cloth for the
journey. Tricksy gathered a rabbit-sized bundle, and Elephant an elephant-sized one.

They set out for the land of the Watusi in a
gay mood. Tricksy told one funny story after
another. He kept Elephant squealing with
laughter.

Presently they came to a river.

Elephant, who loved the water, waded
right in.

"Wait!" cried Tricksy. "You aren't going
to cross without me, I hope! Aren't we
partners?"

"Of course we're partners," said Elephant.
"But I didn't promise to carry you and your
pack. Step in! The water is hardly over my
feet."

"Over your feet is over my head," cried
Tricksy. "And you know I can't swim!"

"I can't help that," said Elephant. "If you
can't take care of yourself on the trail, then go
back home." And he splashed on across the
river.

"I'll get even with him for that!" muttered
Tricksy as he set about looking for a small log.
He found one nearby and, placing his bundle
on it, paddled across the river. He paddled so
fast to catch up with Elephant that he splashed
muddy water all over the cloth. Though he
wiped off the mud the best he could, the cloth
was ruined.

Tricksy soon overtook Elephant, and the
two reached the land of the Watusi with no
more trouble.

Elephant went straight to the men of the
tribe and told them he had come to trade his
cloth for cattle. He was so gruff about it that at
first the tall proud herders refused to deal with
him. At last they agreed to give him a knobby-
kneed little calf for his fine bale of cloth.

Tricksy went among the women. He
laughed and joked with them and told them
how pretty they were. They liked him so much
that when the subject of trade was brought up,
the wife of the chief was happy to give him
the finest cow in the herd for his muddy little
bundle of cloth.

As the traders set out for home, Elephant
said, "Now if we should meet any strangers,
you tell them that both animals belong to me.
If anyone were to guess that such a fine cow
belonged to a rabbit, it would be as good as
gone. You would never be able to defend it!"

"You're right!" said Tricksy. "I'm glad you
thought of that."

They hadn't gone far when they met some
people coming home from the market. The

strangers gathered around the cows to look them over.

"How beautiful the big one is," one man said.

"How fat!" said another.

"How sleek!" said a third.

Then a man approached Elephant. "The big cow is yours, I suppose. And does the little one belong to your small friend?" he asked.

Elephant coughed and tossed his head, preparing to boast that both belonged to him.

But Tricksy was too quick for him. "Ha!" he cried. "The *big* one is mine! Elephant and I went trading. I traded a small bundle of cloth for this fine cow. But all Elephant could get for his big bundle of cloth was that scabby little calf!"

The people had a good laugh over that!

The two went on. When they had gone a little way, Elephant said, "Tricksy, you shamed me in front of all those people! Next time let me do the talking."

"Those weren't the kind of people who would steal my cow anyway," said Tricksy.

Soon they met more people. They, too, stopped to look at the cattle. One man said, "That sleek fat cow couldn't be the mother of that rat-eaten calf, could she?"

Elephant opened his mouth to explain, but again Tricksy was too quick for him.

"No, no relation!" cried Tricksy. "You see, Elephant and I have been trading with the Watusi. And I, for a small bundle of muddy old cloth — "

Illustration by Elton Fax reprinted by permission of Coward-McCann from "Tricksy Rabbit" from *Tales from the Story Hat* by Verna Aardema, Copyright © 1960 by Coward-McCann Inc.

He never finished, for Elephant swung his trunk and sent him rolling.

The people scattered in a hurry.

Elephant said, "A fine partner you are! You can't keep a promise from here to a bend in the road. Take that cow of yours and go home by yourself!"

So at the first branching of the path, Rabbit separated from Elephant. From then on he knew he would never get his cow home safely unless he used his wits. He started to think.

Elephant hadn't gone far when he met a lion. "I happen to know," he told Lion, "that there's a rabbit with a bigger cow than this over on the next trail."

Soon he met a leopard, and then a hyena. He told them both the same thing. "One of the three will relieve him of that cow, for sure!" he chuckled.

Over on the next trail, the lion soon overtook Tricksy. "Rabbit!" he roared. "I could eat you in one bite! But go away fast — and I'll be satisfied with the cow!"

"Oh, Bwana Lion," cried Tricksy, "I'm sorry, but this cow isn't mine to give! She belongs to the Great Mugassa, the spirit of the forest. I'm only driving her for him to his feast. And, now I remember, Mugassa told me to invite you if I saw you!"

"Come now," said Lion, "are you trying to tell me that Mugassa has invited me to a feast?"

"Are you not the king of beasts?" asked Tricksy. "Surely he must plan to honor you! Anyway, come along and see!"

Lion fell into line behind Tricksy and the cow. They hadn't gone far when the leopard overtook them.

Leopard sidled up to Lion and said in a big whisper, "How about sharing the cow with me? You can *have* the rabbit!"

Tricksy overheard what Leopard said, and he broke in. "Bwana Leopard, you don't understand! This cow doesn't belong to either Lion or me. It belongs to Mugassa. We're just driving it to the feast for him. And, now I remember, I was told to invite you, too!"

"I'm invited, too," said Lion. "Mugassa is planning to honor me."

"Hmmm!" said Leopard. But he followed along behind the cow, the rabbit, and the lion.

Soon the hyena joined the procession in the same way.

A little farther on, a huge buffalo blocked the path. "Out of my way!" he bellowed.

"Oh, Bwana Buffalo," cried Tricksy, "I'm so glad you happened along! We're taking this cow to the feast of Mugassa, and I was told to invite you. I didn't know where to look for you. Now, here you are!"

"Are all of you going?" asked Buffalo.

"Yes," said Lion. "Mugassa is planning to honor *me*. Perhaps I shall be crowned!"

"Hmmm!" said Leopard.

Buffalo turned around and led the procession with Tricksy riding on his head to direct him.

Soon they arrived at Tricksy's compound. Two dogs who guarded the gate yapped wildly when they saw them. Tricksy quieted the dogs and sent one streaking off to his hut in the middle of the wide compound with a pretend message for Mugassa.

In a short time the dog came back with a pretend answer, which he whispered into Tricksy's ear.

Tricksy stood on a stump and spoke importantly. "Mugassa says that hyena is to butcher and cook the cow. Lion will carry water for the kettle. Buffalo will chop wood for the fire. Leopard will go to the banana grove yonder and watch for leaves to fall. We need fresh leaves for plates.

"Dogs will lay out mats inside the fence. Then, when the meat is cooked, all of us must help carry it in and spread it on the mats. When all is ready, Mugassa will come out and present each his portion.

"One warning — Mugassa says that if anyone steals so much as a bite, all of us will be punished!"

Tricksy gave Lion a pail with a hole in the bottom. He gave Buffalo an ax with a loose head. He told Leopard to catch the leaves with his eyelashes so as to keep them very clean. Then he climbed to the top of an anthill to watch and laugh.

The animals were so anxious to hurry the feast that Tricksy had many a chuckle over their foolish efforts.

Lion hurried back and forth from the river to the kettle with the leaky pail. Though he filled it to the top each time he dipped it into the river, there would be only a little water to pour into the kettle.

Every time Buffalo swung the ax he had to hunt for the head of it, for it always flew off into the bushes. At last he finished breaking up the wood with his feet.

Leopard fluttered his eyelashes at the long banana leaves, but not one came down.

Now, Hyena had never before in his life had a choice of meat. Always he had to eat what was left by other animals. This time he saw and smelled the choice parts. The liver smelled best to him. "I hope Mugassa gives me the liver!" he said. "But he won't. He'll think the rack of bones to clean is good enough for me — me, who did most of the work!"

Hyena lifted the liver out of the pot and hid it under a bush.

Tricksy saw him, but said nothing.

When the meat was done, all the animals helped carry it in and spread it on the mats laid out in Rabbit's compound. Then Tricksy began to check. "Four legs," he said, "back, sides, neck, tongue. . . . But where's the liver?"

Everyone began looking for the liver. "Someone has stolen the liver!" cried Tricksy.

"Here comes Mugassa!" cried one of the dogs. "Run! Run!"

The big animals stampeded through the gate. Tricksy slipped the bolt through the latch. Then he and his dogs rolled on the grass with laughter.

They were still laughing when Elephant poked his head over the gate. "I see you got home, Rabbit!" he called.

"Yes!" said Tricksy. "I got my cow home, too — and all cooked already!"

"What I should like to know," said Elephant, "is *how* you did it."

"With the help of Mugassa," laughed Tricksy.

"The Tar Baby Tricks Brer Rabbit," from The Days When the Animals Talked: Black American Folktales and How They Came to Be *by William J. Faulkner (Chicago: Follett, 1977).*

William J. Faulkner says that the folktales which he has recreated in The Days When the Animals Talked *were told to him by a former slave, Simon Brown, near Society Hill, South Carolina, when Faulkner was about ten years old. One of the pleasures of reading this volume, certainly, is the presence of the storyteller and the response of the child listener. Simon's repertoire of stories included a variety of animal, haunt, and preacher stories, conjure tales, master/slave anecdotes, tall tales, trickster tales, and other oral forms. The most exuberant character to emerge from this rich Afro-American tradition was, of course, the trickster, Brer Rabbit. As Simon Brown once said, "Brer Rabbit can't fight like a wildcat or climb a tree. But he's got big eyes that can see to the front and the sides and behind without turning his head. He's got long legs and a heap o'sense! To the slave, he's like a brother!"*

In Joel Chandler Harris's famous version of "The Tar Baby," dialect may present an obstacle to contemporary readers, though in Harris's rendition of the tale, one finds an excellent example of the "interrupted narrative," which engages the imagination and participation of the audience for completion. Simon Brown's version, "The Tar Baby Tricks Brer Rabbit," ends triumphantly as Brer Rabbit laughingly proclaims that the briar patch was indeed his birthplace.

The Tar Baby Tricks Brer Rabbit

The tar baby story is probably the most famous of all the Afro-American folktales. Simon Brown told me his version one day when he was scolding me for being lazy.

"Willie," he said, "you are so trifling that you're enough to aggravate the heart of a stone, let alone the heart of a man. Don't you know that everyone has to work for a living? If you don't believe in working, something's bound to happen to you like what happened to Brer Rabbit one day with Brer Wolf."

Of course, I wanted to know what trouble had caught up with Brer Rabbit. I knew that he was Simon's hero and most always came out ahead of any other creature down in the Deep Woods.

"Yes, Brer Rabbit is a very smart creature," said Simon. "But this time he got caught in serious trouble with Brer Wolf — all because he didn't want to work. It happened this way."

In olden times, Brer Rabbit and Brer Wolf lived close together, but they were a long way from any drinking water. They had to fetch their water from a stream down in the Deep Swamp. Finally Brer Wolf decided he was going to dig a well so he wouldn't have to tote his water up the hill. And one morning he spoke to Brer Rabbit about it.

"Let's go in together and dig us a well, Brer Rabbit. There's plenty of water under the ground, and we won't have to dig deep before we strike it nice and cold. We can put two buckets on the rope in the well, and we won't have to tote water from the stream down in the swamp anymore."

But Brer Rabbit said, "Man, the sun's too hot to dig a well. And besides, I don't need any well myself. I catch all my drinking water from the dew off the grass."

"All right, Brer Rabbit," said Brer Wolf. "I'm going to dig me a well anyway, and mind you, don't go fooling around it, drinking up my water."

"That's all right with me," answered Brer Rabbit. "I'm not going to fool around your well. I told you I get all my drinking water from the dew off the grass."

So Brer Wolf worked faithfully and dug a deep well and found nice cool water. He put a rope through the wheel over the well, and he tied two buckets to the rope so that he could draw up the water.

Now, Brer Rabbit had been watching Brer Wolf all this time. And when he thought Brer Wolf was home asleep, he slipped over to his well and drank all the water he wanted. But pretty soon Brer Wolf came out to draw some water from the well, and he found out somebody had been drinking it up. Brer Wolf started watching his well night and day, and though he watched and watched, the water continued to go down. This puzzled Brer Wolf and made him mad.

He was just about to give up when a big rain came and made a heap of mud around the well. In the mud the next morning, Brer Wolf saw Brer Rabbit's tracks. He knew then who had been stealing his water during the night, and he was mad as hops.

Brer Wolf studied and studied to find a way to catch Brer Rabbit. He scratched his head, and he pulled his chin whiskers until by and by he said, "I know what I'll do. I'll make me a tar baby, and I'll catch that good-for-nothing rabbit."

And so Brer Wolf worked and worked until he had made a pretty little girl out of tar. He dressed the tar baby in a calico apron and carried her up to the well, where he stood her up and fastened her to a post in the ground so that nobody could move her. Then Brer Wolf hid in the bushes and waited for Brer Rabbit to come for some water. But three days passed before Brer Rabbit visited the well again. On the fourth day, he came with a bucket in his hand.

When he saw the little girl, he stopped and looked at her. Then he said, "Hello. What's your name? What are you doing here, little girl?"

The little girl said nothing.

This made Brer Rabbit angry, and he shouted at her, "You no-mannered little snip, you! How come you don't speak to your elders?"

The little girl still said nothing.

"I know what to do with little children like you. I'll slap your face and teach you some manners if you don't speak to me," said Brer Rabbit.

Still the little girl said nothing.

And then Brer Rabbit lost his head and said, "Speak to me, I say. I'm going to slap you." With that, Brer Rabbit slapped the tar baby in the face, bam, and his right hand stuck.

"A-ha, you hold my hand, do you? Turn me loose, I say. Turn me loose. If you don't, I'm going to slap you with my left hand. And if I hit you with my left hand, I'll knock the daylights out of you."

But the little girl said nothing. So Brer Rabbit drew back his left hand and slapped the little girl in her face, bim, and his left hand stuck.

"Oh, I see. You're going to hold both my hands, are you? You better turn me loose. If you don't, I'm going to kick you. And if I kick you, it's going to be like thunder and lightning!'' With that, Brer Rabbit drew back his right foot and kicked the little girl in the shins with all his might, blap! Then his right foot stuck.

"Well, sir, isn't this something? You better turn my foot loose. If you don't, I've got another foot left, and I'm going to kick you with it, and you'll think a cyclone hit you.'' Then Brer Rabbit gave that little girl a powerful kick in the shins with his left foot, blip! With that, his left foot stuck, and there he hung off the ground, between the heavens and the earth. He was in an awful fix. But he still thought he could get loose.

So he said to the little girl, "You've got my feet and my hands all stuck up, but I've got one more weapon, and that's my head. If you don't turn me loose, I'm going to butt you! And if I butt you, I'll knock your brains out.'' Finally then, Brer Rabbit struck the little girl a powerful knock on the forehead with his head, and it stuck, and there he hung. Smart old Brer Rabbit, he couldn't move. He was held fast by the little tar baby.

Now, Brer Wolf was hiding under the bushes, watching all that was going on. And as soon as he was certain that Brer Rabbit was caught good by his little tar baby, he walked over to Brer Rabbit and said, "A-ha, you're the one who wouldn't dig a well. And you're the one who's going to catch his drinking water from the dew off the grass. A-ha, I caught the fellow who's been stealing my water. And he isn't anybody but you, Brer Rabbit. I'm going to fix you good.''

"No, sir, Brer Wolf, I haven't been bothering your water. I was just going over to Brer Bear's house, and I stopped by here long enough to speak to this little no-manners girl,'' said Brer Rabbit.

"Yes, you're the one,'' said Brer Wolf. "You're the very one who's been stealing my drinking water all this time. And I'm going to kill you.''

"Please, sir, Brer Wolf, don't kill me,'' begged Brer Rabbit. "I haven't done anything wrong.''

"Yes, I'm going to kill you, but I don't know how I'm going to do it yet,'' growled Brer Wolf. "Oh, I know what I'll do. I'll throw you in the fire and burn you up.''

"All right, Brer Wolf,'' said Brer Rabbit. "Throw me in the fire. That's a good way to die. That's the way my grandmother died, and she said it's a quick way to go. You can do anything with me, anything you want, but please, sir, don't throw me in the briar patch.''

"No, I'm not going to throw you in the fire, and I'm not going to throw you in the briar patch. I'm going to throw you down the well and drown you,'' said Brer Wolf.

"All right, Brer Wolf, throw me down the well,'' said Brer Rabbit. "That's an easy way to die, but I'm surely going to smell up your drinking water, sir.''

"No, I'm not going to drown you,'' said Brer Wolf. "Drowning is too good for you.'' Then Brer Wolf thought and thought and scratched his head and pulled his chin whiskers. Finally he said, "I know what I'm going to do with you. I'll throw you in the briar patch.''

"Oh, no, Brer Wolf,'' cried Brer Rabbit. "Please, sir, don't throw me in the briar patch. Those briars will tear up my hide, pull out my hair, and scratch out my eyes. That'll be an awful way to die, Brer Wolf. Please, sir, don't do that to me.''

"That's exactly what I'll do with you,'' said Brer Wolf all happy-like. Then he caught Brer Rabbit by his hind legs, whirled him around and around over his head, and threw him way over into the middle of the briar patch.

After a minute or two, Brer Rabbit stood up on his hind legs and laughed at Brer Wolf and said to him, "Thank you, Brer Wolf, thank you. This is the place where I was born. My grandmother and grandfather and all my family were born right here in the briar patch.''

And that's the end of the story.

───────

"The Fortune Hunt," from Tales of Land of
Death: Igbo Folktales. *Retold and illustrated
by Uche Okeke (Garden City, N.Y.: Doubleday, 1971).*

*"The Fortune Hunt," a Nigerian "Ita"
tale, as told by Nigerian storyteller Uche
Okeke, features several well-known folk motifs: the circular quest of three brothers, the
youngest of whom emerges as the virtuous
hero; the Wise Old Woman, who helps the
youngest brother after testing his virtue and
kindness; and the presence of the magical object, the agent of wishfulfillment. The tale reflects the agrarian culture of the people who
created it, and, appropriately, the boy shares
his fortune by making his people's land lush
and fertile.*

The Fortune Hunt

Three brothers left their home at the close of
the farming season to search for their fortune.
They all agreed to return at the early appearance of Alommuo, the festival moon, in time
for the beginning of the next farming year.

First they journeyed through a forest country and in time arrived at a crossroads. There,
they agreed to part. The eldest chose his way
first, and the youngest last.

As he went on, the youngest of the brothers helped both the old and the weak to carry
their loads. He played with children in some
places and began to feel that traveling was not
for him, for he became very homesick.

One day, he met an old woman who was
working very hard on her farm harvesting yams
and tying together yam stakes. As was his custom, he stopped to help her. They got on so
well that from that day on he lived with the
woman as son and mother.

Time moved on very fast with the happy
lot. At last the time arrived when the boy was
to rejoin his brothers at the crossroads to return home. The old woman was very sad to lose
her new-found son, but it was not her wish to
keep the young fellow from his parents. "Listen carefully, my child," she told the boy as
he was about to part from her. "Go outside this
house and look for two magic pots. When you

hear 'dum, dum, dum,' run inside the house
quickly, for it is the pot of suffering, leprosy,
small pox, and all types of diseases are in it.
When you hear 'chaka, chaka, chaka,' run out
and catch the pot. It is the pot of fortune, and
all the good things to know on earth are in it!
Break it when you return home, but take care
that it does not break on the way, my son."

By the time the boy arrived at their meeting point, his brothers and their twenty strong
carriers were already tired of waiting. They
were greatly disappointed with him, and made
fun of him and his old red earthen pot. The
two proudly showed off their great loads of
yam, goats, chickens, cowry and household
furniture. They even had three cows!

Back home, the story of the two brothers
spread very fast and all came to give thanks to
their guardian gods. The youngest of them was
not in the least worried by the open derisive
laughter with which he was always greeted.
"Beautiful red pot, isn't it!" they would laugh.
"He brought back his head, and that's what
counts! Ha! ha! ha!"

One day all were gathered and honor was
being done to the two successful brothers,
when the third brought out his pot and asked
to be heard. There were great roars of laughter. Suddenly, the boy broke the pot to pieces
on the ground, and the village was amazed at
the marvelous change which took place. The
land became very beautiful, and crops sprang
up everywhere. Even the livestock multiplied
quickly. The people all gathered around the
boy, showering him with praise and thanks,
and it was unanimously decided that indeed
the third boy had brought back the most wonderful thing of all.

───────

"A Legend of Knockmany," from Celtic Folk
and Fairy Tales, *by Eric and Nancy Protter
(New York: Duell, Sloan and Pearce, 1966).*

*Oonagh, in this Irish tale of role reversal,
uses her wits to save her husband by tricking
his greatest enemy, the giant Cuchulain. Like
Molly Whuppie, she uses the giant's gullibil-
ity to overcome him. Verbal and situational*

irony create the humor of this story. This legend can, in many ways, be compared to that of the tall tales about the American giant Paul Bunyan.

A Legend of Knockmany

What Irish man, woman, or child has not heard of the renowned Hibernian Hercules, the great and glorious Finn McCool? Not a one from Cape Clear to the Giant's Causeway, that's for sure. And, by the way, speaking of the Giant's Causeway brings one at once to the beginning of the story.

Well, it so happened that Finn and his men were all working at the Causeway in order to make a bridge across to Scotland, when Finn, who was very fond of his wife Oonagh, took it into his head to go home to visit her. Accordingly, he pulled up a fir tree with one hand and, after tearing off the roots and branches, made a walking stick of it, and set out on his way to Oonagh.

At that time, the McCool cottage was located on the very tip-top of Knockmany Hill, which faces a cousin of its own called Cullamore that rises up, half hill, half mountain, on the opposite side.

At that time, there lived another giant called Cuchulain. Some say he was Irish, and some say he was Scottish. No other giant of the day could stand before him, and such was his strength that, when he was angered, he could stamp his feet so hard that all the country round him shook and trembled. The fame and name of him went far and near, and neither man nor giant had any chance with him in a fight. With one blow of his fists he flattened a thunderbolt and kept it in his pocket, in the shape of a pancake, to show to his enemies when they were about to fight him. Barring Finn McCool, he had given every giant in Ireland a considerable beating.

He often swore that he would never rest, day or night, winter or summer, till he caught Finn and gave him the same treatment the others had received. The short and the long of it was that Finn heard Cuchulain was coming to the Causeway to have a trial of strength with him. And it so happened that that was exactly the time when Finn was seized with a sudden fit of affection for his wife and decided to visit her. Thus, he was off to Knockmany Hill to his dwelling, which was located in one of the windiest spots in all of Ireland.

"What can you mean, Mr. McCool," many of his compatriots had asked him, "by pitching your tent upon the top of Knockmany where you are never without a breeze day or night, winter or summer, and where there's the sorrow's own want of water?"

"Why," said Finn, "ever since I was the height of a round tower, I was known to be fond of having a good view of my own. And where the dickens, neighbors, could I find a better spot for a good view than the top of Knockmany? As for water, I'm sinking a pump, and, goodness knows, as soon as the Causeway's made, I intend to finish it."

Now, this was in fact nothing more than Finn's philosophy, for the real reason he pitched his house upon the top of Knockmany was so that he might be able to see the giant Cuchulain coming toward the place if he ever decided to pay him a visit. For this purpose there wasn't a neater or more convenient location in all the sweet and sagacious province of Ulster.

"God save all here!" said Finn good-humoredly as he put his honest face in his own door.

"Oh, Finn," said his wife. "Welcome home to your Oonagh, you darling bully." Here followed a loving kiss that is said to have made even the waters of the lake at the bottom of the hill roll and curl.

Finn spent two or three happy days with Oonagh and felt very comfortable, considering the dread he had of Cuchulain. However, after a couple of more days he acted funny and nervous, and after wheedling him and coaxing him, as wives are wont to do, Oonagh finally got Finn to tell her what the matter was.

"It's this Cuchulain," said he, "that's troubling me. When the fellow gets angry and begins to stamp, he'll shake a whole town to pieces. And it's well known that he can stop a thunderbolt, for he always carries one about him in the shape of a pancake, just to show anyone who might doubt him."

As he spoke, he clapped his thumb in his mouth, which he always did when he wanted to foretell the future or to know anything that had happened in his absence. His wife asked him why he did it.

"He's coming," said Finn. "I see him below Dungannon."

"Glory be to God, my dear!" exclaimed Oonagh. "Who's coming?"

"Why, that beast, Cuchulain," replied Finn, "and how I'll manage I don't know. If I run away, I'm disgraced. And I know that sooner or later I must meet him, for my thumb tells me so."

"When will he be here?" asked Oonagh.

"Tomorrow, about two o'clock," replied Finn with a groan.

"Well, my darling bully, don't be downcast," said Oonagh. "Depend on me, and maybe I'll get you out of this scrape in much better form than you could ever do yourself."

She then made a high smoke on the top of the hill, after which she put her finger in her mouth and gave three whistles. This was the signal by which Cuchulain knew that he was invited to Knockmany, for it was the way that long ago the Irish let stranger and travelers know that they were welcome to come and share whatever fare was available.

In the meantime, Finn was very melancholy and did not know what to do or how to act. Cuchulain was an ugly customer to have to meet up with, and the idea of the "pancake" flattened the very heart within him. What chance could he have — strong and brave though he was — with a man who could, when put in a temper, walk the country into earthquakes and knock thunderbolts into pancakes? Poor Finn was in a terrible state. He did not know which way to turn — right or left, backward or forward.

"Oonagh," said he at last, "can you do nothing for me? Where's all your invention? Am I to be crushed like a rabbit before your very eyes and have my name disgraced forever in the sight of all my tribe — and me the best man among them? How am I to fight this man-mountain? This huge cross between an earthquake and a thunderbolt? And with a pancake in his pocket?"

"Be easy, Finn," soothed Oonagh. "Troth, I'm ashamed of you. Keep your toe in your pump, will you? Talking of pancakes, perhaps we'll give him as good as any he brings with him, thunderbolt or other wise. If I don't treat him to as smart a feeding as he's got this many a day, never trust Oonagh again. Leave him to me, and do just as I bid you."

This relieved Finn very much, for after all, he had great confidence in his wife, knowing as he did that she had got him out of many a scrape before. Oonagh then drew nine woolen threads of different colors, which she always did to find out the best way of succeeding in anything of importance. She then braided them into three braids with three colors in each, putting one on her right arm, one round her heart, and the third round her right ankle, for then she knew that nothing she undertook could fail.

Having prepared herself, she sent round to the neighbors and borrowed one-and-twenty enormous iron griddles, which she took and kneaded into the hearts of one-and-twenty cakes of bread. These she baked on the fire in the usual way, setting them aside in the cupboard when they were done and in a special order. She then put down a large pot of new milk which she made into curds and whey. Having finished with these chores, she sat down quite contented and awaited Cuchulain's arrival about two o'clock the next day — the hour which Finn had predicted by sucking his thumb. Now, Finn's thumb was indeed a curious thing. Moreover, in this very thing he much resembled his great foe, Cuchulain, for it was well known that the huge strength Cuchulain possessed all lay in the middle finger of his right hand. And if by chance he happened to lose it, he would have no more special power, and for all his bulk he would have no more strength than any ordinary man.

At length, the next day, Cuchulain was seen coming across the valley, and Oonagh knew that it was time to begin operations. She immediately brought the cradle and made Finn lie down in it and cover himself up.

"You must pretend to be your own child," said she, "so just lie there snug and say nothing but be guided by me."

About two o'clock, Cuchulain arrived.

"God save all here!" said he. "Is this where the great Finn McCool lives?"

"Indeed it is, honest man," replied Oonagh. "God save you kindly. Won't you be sitting down?"

"Thank you, ma'am," says he, taking a chair. "You're Mrs. McCool, I suppose?"

"I am," said she, "and I have no reason, I hope, to be ashamed of my husband."

"No," said the other. "He has the name of being the strongest and bravest man in Ireland. But for all that, there's a man not far from you that's very desirous of challenging him. Is he at home?"

"Why, no," she replied, "and if ever a man left his house in a fury, he did. It appears that someone told him of a big basthoon of a giant called Cuchulain who was down at the Causeway looking for him. So he set out there to try to catch him. I hope, for the poor giant's sake, he won't meet with him, for if he does, Finn will make post of him at once."

"Well," said the other, "I am Cuchulain, and I have been seeking him these twelve months, but he always keeps clear of me. I will never rest night or day till I lay my hands on him."

At this Oonagh set up a loud laugh of great contempt and looked at Cuchulain as if he were only a mere handful of a man.

"Did you ever see Finn?" asked she, changing her manner all at once.

"How could I?" replied he. "He always took care to keep his distance."

"I thought so," said she. "I judged as much. If you take my advice, you poor-looking creature, you'll pray night and day that you may never see him, for I tell you it will be a black day when you do. But, in the meantime, you perceive that the wind's upon the door, and as Finn himself is not home, maybe you'd be civil enough to turn the house around, for it's always what Finn does when he's here."

This was a startler even to Cuchulain. But he got up, and after pulling the middle finger of his right hand until it cracked three times, he went outside and, getting his arms about the house, turned it around as she wished. When Finn saw this, he felt the sweat of fear oozing out through every pore of his skin. Oonagh, however, depending upon her woman's wit, felt not a bit daunted.

"Well, then," said she, "as you are so civil, maybe you'd do another obliging turn for us, as Finn's not here to do it himself. You see, after this long stretch of dry weather we've had, we feel very badly off for want of water. Now, Finn says there's a fine spring-well somewhere under the rocks below. It was his intention to pull them asunder. But having heard of you, he left the place in such a fury that he never got to doing it. Now, if you try to find the well, I'd indeed feel it a kindness."

She then brought Cuchulain down to see the place, which was, in fact, all one solid rock. After looking down at it for some time, he cracked his right middle finger nine times and, stooping down, tore a cleft about four hundred feet deep and a quarter of a mile in length — a spot which has since been christened by the name of Lumford's Glen.

"You'll come in now," said Oonagh, "and eat a bit of such humble fare as we can give you. Finn, even though you and he are enemies, would scorn not to treat you kindly in his own house. And, indeed, if I didn't do it in his absence, he would not be pleased with me."

Accordingly, she placed before him a half a dozen of the cakes she had made, together with a can or two of butter, a side of boiled bacon, and a stack of cabbage. She told him to help himself. Cuchulain put one of the cakes in his mouth to take a huge whack out of it when he made a thundering noise, something between a growl and a yell. "Blood and fury!" he shouted. "What's this! Here are two of my teeth out! What kind of bread is this you gave me?"

"What's the matter?" said Oonagh coolly.

"Matter!" shouted the other again. "Why, here are the two best teeth in my head gone."

"Why," said she, "that's Finn's bread, the only bread he ever eats when at home. But, indeed, I forgot to tell you that nobody can eat it but himself and that child in the cradle, there. I thought, however, that as you were reported to be rather a stout little fellow for your size, you might be able to manage it. Surely, I did not want to affront a man that thinks himself able to fight Finn. Here's another cake; maybe it's not so hard as that."

Cuchulain at the moment was not only hungry but ravenous. So, he eagerly made a fresh attack upon the second cake, and immediately another yell was heard twice as loud as the first. "Thunder and gibbets!" he roared. "Take your bread away, or I will not have a tooth in my head. There's another pair of them gone!"

"Well, honest man," replied Oonagh, "if you're not able to eat the bread, just say so quietly, and don't be waking the child in the cradle there. There, he's awake now."

Finn now howled so loudly that he startled the giant, who was more than a bit surprised to hear such a sound come from a baby.

"Mother," said Finn, "I'm hungry. Get me something to eat."

Oonagh went to the cradle and put into his hand a cake that had no iron griddle in the middle of it. Finn, whose appetite had been sharpened by smelling the food and seeing the eating going on, soon swallowed the cake. Cuchulain was thunderstruck and secretly thanked his stars that he had the good fortune to miss meeting Finn. "I'd have no chance with a man who can eat such bread as that and whose infant son can even munch on it," Cuchulain said to himself.

"I'd like to take a glimpse at the lad in the cradle," said he to Oonagh, "for I can tell you that a child who can manage that food is no joke to look at or to feed in a scarce summer."

"With all the veins in my heart," replied Oonagh. "Get up, my dear boy, and show this decent little man something that won't be unworthy of your father, Finn McCool."

Finn, who was dressed for the occasion as much like a child as possible, got up and said, "Are you strong?"

"Thunder and lightning!" exclaimed Cuchulain. "What a voice in so small a chap."

"Are you strong?" Finn asked again. "Are you able to squeeze water out of that white stone?" he asked, putting one into the giant's hand. The latter squeezed the stone but in vain.

"Ah, you're a poor creature!" said Finn. "You a giant! Give me the stone here, and when I've shown you what Finn's little son can do, you may then judge yourself of what the great

McCool is capable of doing."

Finn then took the stone and cleverly exchanged it for curds. He squeezed the curds until the whey, as clear as water, oozed in a little shower from his hand.

"I'll go in now to my cradle," he said, "for I scorn to waste my time with anyone that's not able to eat my daddy's bread or to squeeze water out of stone. Bedad, you'd better be off before he comes back, for if he catches you, it's pudding he'll make of you in two minutes."

Cuchulain, seeing what he had seen, was of the same opinion himself. His knees knocked together in terror of Finn's return, and he accordingly hastened to bid Oonagh farewell and to assure her that from that day on, he never wished to hear of, much less to see, her husband.

"I admit fairly, that I am not a match for him," said he, "strong as I am. Tell him I would avoid him as the plague and that I will make myself scarce in this part of the country."

In the meantime, Finn had crept back into his cradle. There he lay very quietly, his heart in his mouth with delight that Cuchulain was about to take his departure without having discovered the tricks that had been played on him.

"It's well for you," said Oonagh, "that he doesn't happen to be here, for it's nothing but hawk's meat he'd make of you."

"I know that," said Cuchulain, "but before I go, will you let me feel what kind of teeth Finn's lad has got that can eat griddle bread like this?"

"With all pleasure in life," said she, "only as they're far back in his head, you must put your finger a good way in."

Cuchulain was surprised to find such a powerful set of grinders in one so young. But he was still more surprised to find when he withdrew his hand from Finn's mouth, that he had left his middle finger—the very one upon which his whole strength depended—behind him. He gave a loud groan and fell down at once with terror and weakness. This was all Finn wanted. He now had his most powerful and bitterest enemy at his mercy. He started out of the cradle, and in a few minutes the great Cuchulain, who for so long a time had terrified Finn and his followers, lay a corpse on the floor.

Thus did Finn, through the wit, cunning, and invention of his wife Oonagh, overcome his enemy. It was the only way, for he could never have accomplished this task with force.

"New Year's Hats for the Statues," from The Sea of Gold and Other Tales from Japan. *Adapted by Yoshiko Uchida (New York: Scribner's, 1965).*

A hero's willingness to perform acts of kindness without thought of reward is a major motif of folktales. In this Japanese story, the poor, cold, old man selflessly shows consideration for the Jizo, the gods who aid children and other sufferers. As is often the case in Japanese folktales which conclude with the acquisition of wealth, the central characters return to their homes instead of moving to a new location. The final prosperity of the old couple can be contrasted to the situation of the fisherman and his wife in the Grimm Brothers' folktale. Moreover, the selflessness of the old man can be compared to the generosity of the hero in "The Fortune Hunt."

New Year's Hats for the Statues

Once a very kind old man and woman lived in a small house high in the hills of Japan. Although they were good people, they were very, very poor, for the old man made his living by weaving the reed hats that the farmers used to ward off the sun and rain, and even in a year's time, he could not sell very many.

One cold winter day as the year was drawing to an end, the old woman said to the old man, "Good husband, it will soon be New Year's Day, but we have nothing in the house to eat. How will we welcome the new year without even a pot of fresh rice?" A worried frown hovered over her face, and she sighed sadly as she looked into her empty cupboards.

But the old man patted her shoulders and said, "Now, now, don't you worry. I will make some reed hats and take them to the village to sell. Then with the money I earn I will buy some fish and rice for our New Year's feast."

On the day before New Year's, the old man set out for the village with five new red hats that he had made. It was bitterly cold, and from early morning, snow tumbled from the skies and blew in great drifts about their small house. The old man shivered in the wind, but he thought about the fresh warm rice and the fish turning crisp and brown over the charcoal, and he knew he must earn some money to buy them. He pulled his wool scarf tighter about his throat and plodded on slowly over the snow-covered roads.

When he got to the village, he trudged up and down its narrow streets calling, "Reed hats for sale! Reed hats for sale!" But everyone was too busy preparing for the new year to be bothered with reed hats. They scurried by him, going instead to the shops where they could buy sea bream and red beans and herring roe for their New Year's feasts. No one even bothered to look at the old man or his hats.

As the old man wandered about the village, the snow fell faster, and before long the sky began to grow dark. The old man knew it was useless to linger, and he sighed with longing as he passed the fish shop and saw the rows of fresh fish.

"If only I could bring home one small piece of fish for my wife," he thought glumly, but his pockets were even emptier than his stomach.

There was nothing to do but go home again with his five unsold hats. The old man headed wearily back toward his little house in the hills, bending his head against the biting cold of the wind. As he walked along, he came upon six stone statues of Jizo, the guardian god of children. They stood by the roadside covered with snow that had piled in small drifts on top of their heads and shoulders.

"*Mah, mah*, you are covered with snow," the old man said to the statues, and setting down his bundle, he stopped to brush the snow from the heads. As he was about to go on, a fine idea occurred to him.

"I am sorry these are only reed hats I could not sell," he apologized, "but at least they will keep the snow off your heads." And carefully he tied one on each of the Jizo statues.

"Now if I had one more there would be enough for each of them," he murmured as he looked at the row of statues. But the old man did not hesitate for long. Quickly he took the hat from his own head and tied it on the head of the sixth statue.

"There," he said looking pleased. "Now all of you are covered. Then, bowing in farewell, he told the statues that he must be going. "A happy new year to each of you," he called, and he hurried away content.

When he got home the old woman was waiting anxiously for him. "Did you sell your hats?" she asked. "Were you able to buy some rice and fish?"

The old man shook his head. "I couldn't sell a single hat," he explained, "but I did find a very good use for them." And he told her how he had put them on the Jizo statues that stood in the snow.

"Ah, that was a very kind thing to do," the old woman said. "I would have done exactly the same." And she did not complain at all that the old man had not brought home anything to eat. Instead she made some hot tea and added a precious piece of charcoal to the brazier so the old man could warm himself.

That night they went to bed early, for there was no more charcoal and the house had grown cold. Outside the wind continued to blow the snow in a white curtain that wrapped itself about the small house. The old man and woman huddled beneath their thick quilts and tried to keep warm.

"We are fortunate to have a roof over our heads on such a night," the old man said.

"Indeed we are," the old woman agreed, and before long they were both fast asleep.

About daybreak, when the sky was still a misty gray, the old man awakened for he heard voices outside.

"Listen," he whispered to the old woman.

"What is it? What is it?" the old woman asked.

Together they held their breath and listened. It sounded like a group of men pulling a very heavy load.

"*Yoi-sah! Hoi-sah! Yoi-sah! Hoi-sah!*" the

voices called and seemed to come closer and closer.

"Who could it be so early in the morning?" the old man wondered. Soon, they heard the men singing.

Where is the home of the kind old man,
The man who covered our heads?
Where is the home of the kind old man,
Who gave us his hats for our heads?"

The old man and woman hurried to the window to look out, and there in the snow they saw the six stone Jizo statues lumbering toward their house. They still wore the reed hats the old man had given them and each one was pulling a heavy sack.

"*Yoi-sah! Hoi-sah! Yoi-sah! Hoi-sah!*" they called as they drew nearer and nearer.

"They seem to be coming here!" the old man gasped in amazement. But the old woman was too surprised even to speak.

As they watched, each of the Jizo statues came up to their house and left his sack at the doorstep.

The old man hurried to open the door, and as he did, the six big sacks came tumbling inside. In the sacks the old man and woman found rice and wheat, fish and beans, wine and bean paste cakes, and all sorts of delicious things that they might want to eat.

"Why, there is enough here for a feast every day all during the year!" the old man cried excitedly.

"And we shall have the finest New Year's feast we have ever had in our lives," the old woman exclaimed.

"Ojizo Sama, thank you!" the old man shouted.

"Ojizo Sama, how can we thank you enough?" the old woman called out.

But the six stone statues were already moving slowly down the road, and as the old man and woman watched, they disappeared into the whiteness of the falling snow, leaving only their footprints to show that they had been there at all.

"Jacques the Woodcutter," from The Golden
Phoenix and Other Fairy Tales from Quebec,
*by Marius Barbeau. Retold by Michael
Hornyansky (Toronto: Oxford University
Press, 1958).*

*Like "A Legend of Knockmany," this French
Canadian tale deals with the re-establishment
of a secure household. The unmasking of the
faithless wife and the greedy prince may reflect the peasants' distrust of the powerful ruling classes. In retelling this story, which has
also been found in many European cultures,
the adaptors have omitted much of the cru-
dity of the oral version and have "aimed at
achieving in our own way a literary uplift-
ing similar to that of Grimm, Andersen, and
Perrault."*

Jacques the Woodcutter

This is the story of Jacques Cornaud, who lived
at the edge of a forest with his pretty wife
Finette.

Jacques was a woodcutter by trade. Each
morning he went off into the forest to cut
down trees and chop them into firewood. As
soon as he left the house, his wife Finette would
have a visitor — for she was not only pretty
and charming, but a fine cook besides. Not far
away lived a good-for-nothing Prince named
Bellay, who was extremely fond of eating.

Every day while Jacques was away working in the forest, the Prince would come to the
house and sit down to an enormous meal.
Finette didn't mind cooking for him. She had
no other company during the daytime, and besides, when the Prince had finished his meal
he always left a gold piece under the plate.

But Jacques the woodcutter was not so well
satisfied. At last he decided to speak to his wife
about it.

"Finette," he said, "I have nothing against
the Prince, and I don't mind his little visits to
our table. But does he have to come so often?"

Finette promised she would speak to the
Prince. Next morning Jacques went off to the
forest, and soon afterwards Prince Bellay
turned up as usual, with a smile on his lips and
a flower in his buttonhole.

"And what's on the menu today?" he asked,
patting his stomach.

"Savory dumplings," said Finette. "But I
have a message for you. My husband thinks you
come to the house too often."

Prince Bellay frowned (thinking was such
hard work that it always made him frown).
"Too often?" he repeated. "Well, you know,
he's right. I'm here every day. No wonder he's
annoyed! This will have to stop."

No more gold pieces, thought Finette. What
a pity, just when she was beginning to gather
together quite a tidy sum! She decided she
would try to change Prince Bellay's mind.

"No more onion soup," she said.

The Prince stared at her. "No more onion
soup?" he gasped. "Oh, I couldn't bear that.
Life without onion soup wouldn't be worth
living."

"And for next week," said Finette, "I had
planned a meal of roast pigeon. But now we'll
have to give up that idea."

"Roast pigeon!" exclaimed the Prince, licking his lips. "But couldn't I sneak in while he's
away in the forest without his knowing?"

"He might come back during the day," said
Finette. "Imagine how annoyed he would be
then."

"You're right," groaned the Prince. "We
must think of a plan to keep him away from
the house."

When his food was at stake the Prince could
think quite fast. After a moment he stopped
frowning and smiled.

"I have it!" he said. "This will keep him
away for at least two weeks, and by that time I
can think of something else. Now listen carefully."

And he told Finette his plan. Thinking of
the gold pieces, she listened carefully and
promised to do as he told her.

That evening, when she saw Jacques coming home from the forest with his axe on his
shoulder, she stuffed a handkerchief into her
cheek so that it would look swollen. Then she
lay down on her bed and began to moan.

"Oh Jacques, Jacques, I feel so awful!"

The woodcutter put down his axe and hurried to her bedside. "What is it? What's the
matter?"

"Toothache," moaned Finette. "The worst I've ever had. Ohhh—I've been in agony ever since you left this morning!"

Jacques reached for his coat. "I'll go and fetch the doctor at once."

Finette moaned harder than ever. "No, the doctor can't help me. There is only one thing that will cure this toothache, and that is water from the Fountain of Paris."

"But dear wife," said Jacques, "by the time I go to Paris and back you could be seven times dead with the pain."

"No, no," said Finette, "I'll wait for you. But you must hurry if you are to be back soon. I've made you a sandwich for the road. It's on the kitchen table."

Jacques was tired after a hard day in the woods, but he was so kind-hearted that he left at once and took the high road to Paris. No sooner had he gone than Finette got to work at the stove, and soon afterwards Prince Bellay was sitting down to a delicious supper of roast pigeon and artichokes with pepper sauce.

Meanwhile Jacques had gone only a little way when he met an old man with a big wicker basket on his back. It was the Peddler who often called at his home.

"Good evening, old friend," said the Peddler. "And pray, where are you going with such a sad face?"

"To Paris," said Jacques. "My wife Finette is dying of toothache, and I must bring her some water from the Fountain there."

The Peddler shut one eye and chuckled. "Tut, tut," he said. "Your wife no more has the toothache than I have."

"You don't know Finette," said Jacques indignantly. "If she says she has toothache, then she has. She isn't like other women."

The Peddler shut his other eye. "And she wants you to go all the way to Paris? Tell me, isn't there some reason why she'd like to have you out of the house?"

The woodcutter thought for a moment. "Well, there's that good-for-nothing Prince with the big appetite. But I can't believe she would send me all the way to Paris just for that."

"Well, old friend," said the Peddler, opening both his eyes, "never mind about the Foun-

Illustration by Arthur Price, "Jacques the Woodcutter" from *The Golden Phoenix and Other Fairy Tales from Quebec* by Marius Barbeau, retold by Michael Hornyansky. Copyright © 1958 by Oxford University Press, reprinted by permission.

tain of Paris. It just so happens that I have some of its water with me now, so I can save you the trip. Here, you're too tired to stand. Jump into my basket and I'll give you a ride back home."

So Jacques climbed into the Peddler's basket and rode back home. When they reached the cottage there was a fine smell of cooking in the air. The Peddler chuckled and knocked on the door.

"Who's there?" cried Finette.

"Only the Peddler and his basket, good lady. Will you open your door to a tired and hungry man?"

"The Peddler, at this time of night!" said Finette. "Is a woman never to have any peace?"

Then they heard Prince Bellay's voice from the dining table.

"Let him come in, good Finette. He's an old man, and tired. If you put him in the kitchen with his basket, he won't disturb us."

"All right," said Finette. She let in the Peddler and told him to sit down in the kitchen. The Peddler thanked her and put his basket next to the stove.

At the dining table the Prince was finishing his roast pigeon. Having eaten so well himself, he felt kindly to the rest of the world.

"Poor old fellow," he said. "He's probably come a long way with nothing to eat. Why don't we ask him in here to sup with us? These traveling men are always good company."

Finette was in good humor again. She invited the Peddler to come in and share their meal.

"Bless you, good lady," said the Peddler. "Never turn down an invitation, I always say. But you won't mind if I bring my basket along? It's my living, and I don't like to leave it behind."

"That great big basket in my dining-room?" said Finette. "What an idea!"

"Oh, let him bring it if he must," said the Prince kindly. "He can put it in the corner where it won't trouble anybody."

Finette thought of the gold piece under the plate and decided not to object. So the Peddler brought in his basket from the kitchen and put it in the corner behind his chair. He sat down to the table, smacking his lips, and soon made short work of the roast pigeon.

"Ah," he said when he had finished. "A fine meal, Hostess! With food like that, I'll wager you keep in good health."

"Indeed I do," said Finette. "I haven't had a day's illness in years."

At this there was a strange grumbling noise from the wicker basket in the corner. Finette turned pale, but the Peddler chuckled in his beard and told her not to be alarmed.

"It's the heat in here," he explained. "Bring an old wicker basket in out of the cold, and you'll hear it grunt and creak like a live thing."

Prince Bellay was feeling cheerful after his meal. "No speeches after dinner here, Master Peddler," he said. "Instead, let's have a jolly song or two."

"A fine plan!" said the Peddler. "Nothing would suit me better. But everyone in his place. You're a prince, and the chief guest here. It's proper that you should sing first."

The Prince was pleased, for he liked to think of himself as a gay fellow with a fine voice. He called for wine and sang a little verse that he had just made up:

"There is a good woman lives in a wood
(Savory dumplings and pigeon pie)
Who bakes and fries as a good wife should:
Savory dumplings and pigeon pie —
If Jacques won't eat them, why can't I?"

"Bless me, that was well sung," cried the Peddler, laughing and clapping his hands. "Why shouldn't you, indeed?"

The Prince beamed and called for more wine. "Now it's your turn," he said to Finette.

"No, no," said Finette. "Ask the Peddler. He's a traveling man, and he must know all kinds of songs."

The Peddler shook his head. "Everyone in his place," he said. "First the Hostess and afterwards the Peddler."

Finette gave in. And here is the song she sang:

"My husband has gone to Paris town
(Savory dumplings and pigeon pie)
So eat and drink till the moon goes down
(Savory dumplings and pigeon pie);
He won't be back till the snowflakes fly."

"Excellent, excellent!" laughed the Peddler. "Oh, my basket and I haven't had such a good time in a month of Sundays!"

"More wine," said the Prince. "And now, Master Peddler, will you warble us a tune in your turn?"

"Sir," said the Peddler, "since there is nobody left but myself and my basket, I am at your service."

And here is the song he sang:

"I met a man on the broad highway.
(We travel far, my basket and I.)
The man would go, but I made him stay
(We're full of surprises, my basket and I):
And where he is now, who can say?"

Finette didn't much like the sound of this song, especially when she heard another grunt from the corner where the basket stood. But Prince Bellay was too full of wine and good food to take notice. He clapped the Peddler on the back and shouted with laughter.

"I declare," said the Prince, "you talk about that old basket of yours as if it were alive! If it's as good as you say, why don't you tell it to sing the next song?"

The Peddler shut one eye and chuckled. "Bless me, why not?" he said. "It doesn't do much singing in the ordinary way — just creaks and groans — but I have a notion it will sing for you."

"We'll make sure of it," laughed the Prince. "Here, basket, have some wine."

And he poured a cup of wine over the basket.

"Enough!" said the Peddler. "Now, basket of mine, let's hear what kind of voice you have."

The basket creaked, and then in a muffled voice it began to sing. And this was its song:

"Good wife, your toothache's cured, I see.
(What was your medicine — pigeon pie?)
The Prince has dined; he'll pay the fee:
For savory dumplings and pigeon pie
The price is a beating. Fly, Prince, fly!"

And out of the basket sprang Jacques the woodcutter, shaking his fist. Never in your life did you see a Prince leave a house so fast. He didn't stop running till he was safe in his cas-

tle, with the door locked and barred. And he never went near Finette's table again.

As for Finette, she gave up her ideas of becoming rich. Nowadays Jacques Cornaud the woodcutter has onion soup whenever he wants it, and roast pigeon with artichokes on special days. Sometimes the Peddler calls on them, and he can be sure of a welcome and a fine dinner. While he is at the table his old wicker basket sits quietly in the corner. It creaks a little, but it doesn't say a word.

"Lord Randal," from English and Scottish Popular Ballads. *Student's Cambridge Edition (Boston: Houghton, Mifflin, 1904).*

Many traditional folktales were told in poetic form, as ballads. This British ballad has been traced back to the late seventeenth century. In this ironic circular journey, the son returns home to reveal both his condition and his feelings for the woman who has poisoned him. His grief and hatred are implicitly attributed to the betrayal of the love that he carried in his heart when he left home. The repetition of the last line of each stanza, a typical feature of ballads, emphasizes the deep sadness of the young man. Halfway through the poem the phrase, "I'm wearied wi huntin" changes to "I'm sick at the heart," an indication that his pain is less of his body than of his soul. This tragic love story can be compared to Alfred Noyes' "The Highway Man."

Lord Randal

'O WHERE ha you been, Lord Randal, my son?
And where ha you been, my handsome young man?'
'I ha been at the greenwood; mother, mak my bed soon,
For I'm wearied wi hunting, and fain wad lie down.'

'An wha met ye there, Lord Randal, my son?
An wha met you there, my handsome young man?'

'O I met wi my true-love; mother, mak my
   bed soon,
For I'm wearied wi huntin, an fain wad lie
   down.'
'And what did she give you, Lord Randal, my
   son?
And what did she give you, my handsome
   young man?'
'Eels fried in a pan; mother, mak my bed
   soon,
For I'm wearing wi huntin, and fain wad lie
   down.'
'And wha gat your leavins, Lord Randal, my
   son?
And wha gat your leavins, my handsome
   young man?'
'My hawks and my hounds; mother, mak my
   bed soon,
For I'm wearied wi hunting, and fain wad lie
   down.'
'And what becam of them, Lord Randal, my
   son?
And what becam of them, my handsome
   young man?'
'They stretched their legs out an died; mother,
   mak my bed soon,
For I'm wearied wi huntin, and fain wad lie
   down.'
'O I fear you are poisoned, Lord Randal, my
   son!
I fear you are poisoned, my handsome young
   man!'
'O yes, I am poisoned; mother, mak my bed
   soon,
For I'm sick at the heart, and I fain wad lie
   down.'
'What d'ye leave to your mother, Lord Randal,
   my son?
What d'ye leave to your mother, my handsome young man?'
'Four and twenty milk kye; mother, mak my
   bed soon,
For I'm sick at the heart, and I fain wad lie
   down.'
'What d'ye leave to your sister, Lord Randal,
   my son?
What d'ye leave to your sister, my handsome
   young man?'

'My gold and my silver; mother, mak my bed
   soon,
For I'm sick at the heart, an I fain wad lie
   down.'
'What d'ye leave to your brother, Lord Randal,
   my son?
What d'ye leave to your brother, my handsome
   young man?'
'My houses and my lands; mother, mak my
   bed soon,
For I'm sick at the heart, and I fain wad lie
   down.'
'What d'ye leave to your true-love, Lord Randal, my son?
What d'ye leave to your true-love, my handsome young man?'
'I leave her hell and fire; mother, mak my bed
   soon,
For I'm sick at the heart, and I fain wad lie
   down.'

———

"The Fisherman and His Wife," from The
Complete Grimm's Fairy Tales *(New York:
Pantheon, 1944).*

*An important motif of folklore is the mis-
use of magic, which can only help the individual achieve his ultimate desires if he has
the inner potential to employ magic wisely.
In her greed, pride, and ingratitude, the fisherman's wife embarks on a linear journey
only to end in the impoverished situation of
the story's opening. The tale of this couple is
in direct contrast to that of the old Japanese
man and lady in "New Year's Hats for the
Statues."*

The Fisherman and His Wife

There was once upon a time a fisherman who
lived with his wife in a pig-stye close by the
sea, and every day he went out fishing; and he
fished, and he fished. And once he was sitting
with his rod, looking at the clear water, and
he sat and he sat. Then his line suddenly went
down, far down below, and when he drew it
up again, he brought out a large Flounder. Then

the flounder said to him: "Hark, you Fisherman, I pray you, let me live, I am no Flounder really, but an enchanted prince. What good will it do you to kill me? I should not be good to eat, put me in the water again, and let me go." "Come," said the Fisherman, "there is no need for so many words about it — a fish that can talk I should certainly let go, anyhow." And with that he put him back again into the clear water, and the Flounder went to the bottom, leaving a long streak of blood behind him. Then the Fisherman got up and went home to his wife in the pig-stye.

"Husband," said the woman, "have you caught nothing to-day?" "No," said the man, "I did catch a Flounder, who said he was an enchanted prince, so I let him go again." "Did you not wish for anything first?" said the woman. "No," said the man; "what should I wish for?" "Ah," said the woman, "it is surely hard to have to live always in this pig-stye which stinks and is so disgusting; you might have wished for a little hut for us. Go back and call him. Tell him we want to have a little hut, he will certainly give us that." "Ah," said the man, "why should I go there again?" "Why," said the woman, "you did catch him, and you let him go again; he is sure to do it. Go at once." The man still did not quite like to go, but did not like to oppose his wife either, and went to the sea.

"Flounder, flounder in the sea
  Come, I pray thee, here to me;
  For my wife, good Ilsabil,
  Wills not as I'd have her will."

Then the Flounder came swimming to him and said: "Well, what does she want, then?" "Ah," said the man, "I did catch you, and my wife says I really ought to have wished for something. She does not like to live in a pig-stye any longer; she would like to have a hut." "Go, then," said the Flounder, "she has it already."

When the man went home, his wife was no longer in the stye, but instead of it there stood a hut, and she was sitting on a bench before the door. Then she took him by the hand and said to him: "Just come inside. Look, now isn't this a great deal better?" So they went in, and there was a small porch, and a pretty little parlor and bedroom, and a kitchen and pantry, with the best of furniture, and fitted up with the most beautiful things made of tin and brass, whatsoever was wanted. And behind the hut there was a small yard, with hens and ducks, and a little garden with flowers and fruit. "Look," said the wife, "is not that nice!" "Yes," said the husband, "and so it shall remain — now we will live quite contented." "We will think about that," said the wife. With that they ate something and went to bed.

Everything went well for a week or a fortnight, and then the woman said: "Hark you, husband, this hut is too small for us, and the garden and yard are little; the Flounder might just as well have given us a larger house. I should like to live in a great stone castle; go to the Flounder, and tell him to give us a castle." "Ah, wife," said the man, "the hut is quite good enough; why should we live in a castle?" "What!" said the woman; "just go there, the Flounder can always do that." "No, wife," said the man, "the Flounder has just given us the hut, I do not like to go back so soon, it might

Illustration by Margot Zenach from *The Fisherman and His Wife,* by the Brother's Grimm tr. by Randall Jarrell. Copyright © 1980. Reprinted by permission of Farrar, Straus, Groux Publishers.

make him angry." "Go," said the woman, "he can do it quite easily, and will be glad to do it; just you go to him."

The man's heart grew heavy, and he would not go. He said to himself: "It is not right," and yet he went. And when he came to the sea the water was quite purple and dark-blue, and gray and thick, and no longer so green and yellow, but it was still quiet. And he stood there and said:

"Flounder, flounder in the sea,
　Come, I pray thee, here to me;
　For my wife, good Ilsabil,
　Wills not as I'd have her will."

"Well, what does she want, now?" said the Flounder. "Alas," said the man, half scared, "she wants to live in a great stone castle." "Go to it, then, she is standing before the door," said the Flounder.

Then the man went away, intending to go home, but when he got there, he found a great stone palace, and his wife was just standing in the steps going in, and she took him by the hand and said: "Come in." So he went in with her, and in the castle was a great hall paved with marble, and many servants, who flung wide the doors; and the walls were all bright with beautiful hangings, and in the rooms were chairs and tables of pure gold, and crystal chandeliers hung from the ceiling, and all the rooms and bedrooms had carpets, and food and wine of the very best were standing on all the tables, so that they nearly broke down beneath it. Behind the house, too, there was a great court-yard, with stables for horses and cows, and the very best of carriages; there was a magnificent large garden, too, with the most beautiful flowers and fruit-trees, and a park quite half a mile long, in which were stags, deer, and hares, and everything that could be desired. "Come," said the woman, "isn't that beautiful?" "Yes, indeed," said the man, "now let it be; and we will live in this beautiful castle and be content." "We will consider about that," said the woman, "and sleep upon it;" thereupon they went to bed.

Next morning the wife awoke first, and it was just daybreak, and from her bed she saw the beautiful country lying before her. Her husband was still stretching himself, so she poked him in the side with her elbow, and said: "Get up, husband, and just peep out of the window. Look you, couldn't we be the King over all that land? Go to the Flounder, we will be the King." "Ah, wife," said the man, "why should we be King? I do not want to be King." "Well," said the wife, "if you won't be King, I will; go to the Flounder, for I will be King." "Ah, wife," said the man, "why do you want to be King? I do not like to say that to him." "Why not?" said the woman; "go to him this instant; I must be King!" So the man went, and was quite unhappy because his wife wished to be King. "It is not right; it is not right," thought he. He did not wish to go, but yet he went.

And when he came to the sea, it was quite dark-gray, and the water heaved up from below, and smelt putrid. Then he went and stood by, and said:

"Flounder, flounder in the sea,
　Come, I pray thee, here to me;
　For my wife, good Ilsabil,
　Wills not as I'd have her will."

"Well, what does she want, now?" said the Flounder. "Alas," said the man, "she wants to be King." "Go to her; she is King already."

So the man went, and when he came to the palace, the castle had become much larger, and had a great tower and magnificent ornaments, and the sentinel was standing before the door, and there were numbers of soldiers with kettle-drums and trumpets. And when he went inside the house, everything was of real marble and gold, with velvet covers and great golden tassels. Then the doors of the hall were opened, and there was the court in all its splendor, and his wife was sitting on a high throne of gold and diamonds, with a great crown of gold on her head, and a sceptre of pure gold and jewels in her hand, and on both sides of her stood her maids-in-waiting in a row, each of them always one head shorter than the last.

Then he went and stood before her, and said: "Ah, wife, and now you are King." "Yes," said the woman, "now I am King." So he stood and looked at her, and when he had looked at her thus for some time, he said: "And now that you are King, let all else be, now we will wish for nothing more." "No, husband," said the woman, quite anxiously, "I find time passes very heavily, I can bear it no longer; go to the Flounder — I am King, but I must be Emperor, too." "Oh, wife, why do you wish to be Emperor?" "Husband," said she, "go to the Flounder. I will be Emperor." "Alas, wife," said the man, "he cannot make you Emperor; I may not say that to the fish. There is only one Emperor in the land. An Emperor the Flounder cannot make you! I assure you he cannot."

"What!" said the woman, "I am the King, and you are nothing but my husband; will you go this moment? go at once! If he can make a king he can make an emperor. I will be Emperor; go instantly." So he was forced to go. As the man went, however, he was troubled in mind, and thought to himself: "It will not end well; it will not end well! Emperor is too shameless! The Flounder will at last be tired out."

With that he reached the sea, and the sea was quite black and thick, and began to boil up from below, so that it threw up bubbles, and such a sharp wind blew over it that it curdled, and the man was afraid. Then he went and stood by it, and said:

"Flounder, flounder in the sea,
  Come, I pray thee, here to me;
  For my wife, good Ilsabil,
  Wills not as I'd have her will."

"Well, what does she want, now?" said the Flounder. "Alas, Flounder," said he, "my wife wants to be Emperor." "Go to her," said the Flounder; "she is Emperor already."

So the man went, and when he got there the whole palace was made of polished marble with alabaster figures and golden ornaments, and soldiers were marching before the door blowing trumpets, and beating cymbals and drums; and in the house, barons, and counts, and dukes were going about as servants. Then they opened the doors to him, which were of pure gold. And when he entered, there sat his wife on a throne, which was made of one piece of gold, and was quite two miles high; and she wore a great golden crown that was three yards high, and set with dia-

monds and carbuncles, and in one hand she had the sceptre, and in the other the imperial orb; and on both sides of her stood the yeomen of the guard in two rows, each being smaller than the one before him, from the biggest giant, who was two miles high, to the very smallest dwarf, just as big as my little finger. And before it stood a number of princes and dukes.

Then the man went and stood among them, and said: "Wife, are you Emperor now?" "Yes," said she, "now I am Emperor." Then he stood and looked at her well, and when he had looked at her thus for some time, he said: "Ah, wife, be content, now that you are Emperor." "Husband," said she, "why are you standing there? Now, I am Emperor, but I will be Pope too; go to the Flounder." "Oh, wife," said the man, "what will you not wish for? You cannot be Pope; there is but one in Christendom; he cannot make you Pope." "Husband," said she, "I will be Pope; go immediately, I must be Pope this very day." "No, wife," said the man, "I do not like to say that to him; that would not do, it is too much; the Flounder can't make you Pope." "Husband," said she, "what nonsense! if he can make an emperor he can make a pope. Go to him directly. I am Emperor, and you are nothing but my husband; will you go at once?"

Then he was afraid and went; but he was quite faint, and shivered and shook, and his knees and legs trembled. And a high wind blew over the land, and the clouds flew, and towards evening all grew dark, and the leaves fell from the trees, and the water rose and roared as if it were boiling, and splashed upon the shore; and in the distance he saw ships which were firing guns in their sore need, pitching and tossing on the waves. And yet in the midst of the sky there was still a small patch of blue, though on every side it was as red as in a heavy storm. So, full of despair, he went and stood in much fear and said:

"Flounder, flounder in the sea,
  Come, I pray thee, here to me;
  For my wife, good Ilsabil,
  Wills not as I'd have her will."

"Well, what does she want, now?" said the Flounder. "Alas," said the man, "she wants to be Pope." "Go to her then," said the Flounder; "she is Pope already."

So he went, and when he got there, he saw what seemed to be a large church surrounded by palaces. He pushed his way through the crowd. Inside, however, everything was lighted up with thousands and thousands of candles, and his wife was clad in gold, and she was sitting on a much higher throne, and had three great golden crowns on, and round about her there was much ecclesiastical splendor; and on both sides of her was a row of candles the largest of which was as tall as the very tallest tower, down to the very smallest kitchen candle, and all the emperors and kings were on their knees before her, kissing her shoe. "Wife," said the man, and looked attentively at her, "are you now Pope?" "Yes," said she, "I am Pope." So he stood and looked at her, and it was just as if he was looking at the bright sun. When he had stood looking at her thus for a short time, he said: "Ah, wife, if you are Pope, do let well alone!" But she looked as stiff as a post, and did not move or show any signs of life. Then said he: "Wife, now that you are Pope, be satisfied, you cannot become anything greater now." "I will consider about that," said the woman. Thereupon they both went to bed, but she was not satisfied, and greediness let her have no sleep, for she was continually thinking what there was left for her to be.

The man slept well and soundly, for he had run about a great deal during the day; but the woman could not fall asleep at all, and flung herself from one side to the other the whole night through, thinking always what more was left for her to be, but unable to call to mind anything else. At length the sun began to rise, and when the woman saw the red of dawn, she sat up in bed and looked at it. And when, through the window, she saw the sun thus rising, she said: "Cannot I, too, order the sun and moon to rise?" "Husband," she said, poking him in the ribs with her elbows, "wake up! go to the Flounder, for I wish to be even as God is." The man was still half asleep, but he was so horrified that he fell out of bed. He thought he must have heard amiss, and rubbed his eyes, and said: "Wife, what are you saying?" "Husband," said she, "if I can't order the sun and

moon to rise, and have to look on and see the sun and moon rising, I can't bear it. I shall not know what it is to have another happy hour, unless I can make them rise myself." Then she looked at him so terribly that a shudder ran over him, and said: "Go at once; I wish to be like unto God." "Alas, wife," said the man, falling on his knees before her, "the Flounder cannot do that; he can make an emperor and a pope; I beseech you, go on as you are, and be Pope." Then she fell into a rage, and her hair flew wildly about her head, she tore open her bodice, kicked him with her foot, and screamed: "I can't stand it, I can't stand it any longer! will you go this instant?" Then he put on his trousers and ran away like a madman. But outside a great storm was raging, and blowing so hard that he could scarcely keep his feet; houses and trees toppled over, the mountains trembled, rocks rolled into the sea, the sky was pitch black, and it thundered and lightened, and the sea came in with black waves as high as church-towers and mountains, and all with crests of white foam at the top. Then he cried, but could not hear his own words:

"Flounder, flounder in the sea,
  Come, I pray thee, here to me;
  For my wife, good Ilsabil,
  Wills not as I'd have her will."

"Well, what does she want, now?" said the Flounder. "Alas," said he, "she wants to be like unto God." "Go to her, and you will find her back again in the pig-stye." And there they are still living to this day.

———

"*Get Up and Bar the Door,*" *from* English and Scottish Popular Ballads. *Student's Cambridge Edition (Boston: Houghton, Mifflin, 1904).*

In this favorite comic ballad, the stubbornness of the husband and wife leads to consequences they had not expected. Because of the pride of each, neither will speak in what is potentially a dangerous situation. When at last the husband does speak, the wife is happy that she's won the battle rather than that he's saved both of them from dishonor. The relationship between the couple can be contrasted to that between the fisherman and his wife.

Get Up and Bar the Door

It fell about the Martinmas time,
   And a gay time it was then,
When our good wife got puddings to make,
   And she's boild them in the pan.

The wind sae cauld blew south and north,
   And blew into the floor;
Quoth our goodman to our goodwife,
   'Gae out an bar the door.'

'My hand is in my hussyfskap,
   Goodman, as ye may see;
An it shoud nae be barrd this hundred year,
   It's no be barrd for me.'

They made a paction tween them twa,
   They made it firm and sure,
That the first word whaeer shoud speak,
   Shoud rise and bar the door.

Then by there came two gentlemen,
   At twelve o clock at night,
And they could neither see house nor hall,
   Nor coal nor candle-light.

'Now whether is this a rich man's house,
   Or whether is it a poor?'
But neer a word wad ane o them speak,
   For barring of the door.

And first they ate the white puddings,
   And then they ate the black;
Tho muckle thought the goodwife to hersel,
   yet neer a word she spake.

Then said the one unto the other,
   'Here, man, tak ye my knife;
Do ye tak aff the auld man's beard,
   And I'll kiss the goodwife.'

'But there's nae water in the house,
   And what shall we do than?'
'What ails ye at the pudding-broo,
   That boils into the pan?'

O up then started our goodman,
   An angry man was he:
'Will ye kiss my wife before my een,
   And scad me wi pudding-bree?'

Then up and started our goodwife,
   Gied three skips on the floor:
'Goodman, you've spoken the foremost word,
   Get up and bar the door.'

"Guashi and the Bears," from Hispano Folklife of New Mexico, *by Lorin W. Brown (Albuquerque: University of New Mexico, 1978).*

This story from the Southwest reflects not only the arid landscape of the region, but also the Spanish-American love of tall-tale humor. On the literal level, the hero, Guashi, has a fantastic adventure: he meets bears who follow the cultural patterns of good Catholics, he acts kindly toward them, makes an arduous journey home, and ends up with nothing to show for it but the implied ire of his wife. However, in light of the opening paragraph, it is highly probable that Guashi is a lazy liar. If this is so, the true humor in the story is to be found in the audacity with which he spins his preposterous yarn.

Guashi and the Bears

Guashi had his own flock of sheep which he attended accompanied by one or the other of his two sons. Gossip had it that no sooner was he out of sight of the town with his flock than Guashi threw himself on the ground in a comfortable spot. Leaving his son to take care of the sheep, he set himself to the more serious business of thinking out his *Guashadas.*

One time, so Guashi relates, he had to take his sheep out to graze by himself, neither of his two sons being available. He had his burro with him on this occasion to save himself a lot of walking. At noon when the sheep had eaten their fill and had bedded down as usual during the heat of midday, Guashi also retired to a shady nook for a siesta. He had slept a very short while when he awakened because he was being shaken insistently by the shoulder. Opening his eyes, he was astounded to see that his awakener was a bear. And not only one bear: nearby was a mother bear holding a cub.

"'*Amigo*,' the bear said, 'I want you to do me and my wife a favor. We are going to christen our little son and want you to honor us by being his *padrino*.'

"My mouth was so dry I could only nod my head; I was so afraid and astonished at hearing a bear speak," said Guashi. "But the big bear helped me to my feet so gently that I took courage, especially after the she-bear proudly held out her baby for me to admire. I tried to show no fear and smiled as I patted the cub on the head.

"'Well, let's go, *compadre*. The *padre* is waiting and all my *amigos* also over in my cave,' said my strange *compadre*-to-be.

"So I went along between my two so-strange friends. My knees were kind of weak at first, but they talked so kindly with me, asking me about my family, how many children I had, and so on, that I began to think that bears were not so bad as they were painted. Soon we came to a cave in a ledge of rock overlooking a small stream. I could see three old-looking bears sitting outside who seemed to be talking together about the weather or of the prospects for good hunting. As soon as they saw us one of them bolted inside to tell the rest I guess, and Holy Mother if there weren't about twenty bears who came rushing out to meet us.

"'*Amigos*, I bring here the *padrino* for my son. I introduce to you Don José María,' said the big bear, whose name I might as well tell you was Gorgonio.

"I shook hands all around and really was received most politely. On entering the cave, two bears inside started playing a guitar and a violin. Then I saw the *padre*, a great big silvered bear, much larger than the rest.

"'Well, friends, I am proud to have Don José María christen my son because then I know he will be like his *padrino* and have a tame herd of deer to watch, and he will never go hungry,' was the announcement made by Gorgonio.

"So with my *ahijado* or godson in my arms I stood before the *padre* bear and the baby was baptized. *Seguro*, I had him named José María after myself.

"After the christening we feasted awhile; then we started dancing. I danced first with my *comadre*, Gorgonio's wife, in a *valse redondo*. All the bears danced every piece, stomping their big feet on the floor and clapping their paws together until their claws clicked when they wished the music to continue. The cave was large with a rock floor. I asked for a polka and, seizing a young she-bear, I showed those bears how a polka should be danced. They were very good at the polka, but you fellows know that they had to go some to beat me.

"And the feast! *Hombre*, what a good feast! I ate of everything, but I liked their wild strawberry wine best. Ay! what a wine, very strong, and soon I was feeling very good and felt as if I had known these bears all my life. You should have seen those bears dance the *cuna* and *varsoviana*. Don't ever let anybody tell you the bear is not a graceful animal.

"Once I asked to sing the verses for a *valse cantado*. Here I had a chance to honor all my friends, the bears. I sang a verse first in honor of both my *compadre* and *comadre*, then one for my godchild, to whom I gave my horsehair hatband for a collar. It was all I had to give him. As I sang each verse I was offered a glass of wine, so that by the time I had reached the last one I was feeling very happy. By that time also, it was beginning to get light and I said I had to get back to my sheep.

"I was heartily embraced by both my *compadre* and *comadre*, and after giving my godchild my blessing I said goodbye to the rest. Two young bears took me to the top of a ridge and told me I would find my sheep in the little valley below. And thanks to Santa Inés I soon found my burro and nearby were my sheep.

"But the country was strange to me. I thought I knew every part of the mountains around here, yet I could see no familiar landmarks. Maybe it's the wine, I thought, so I just followed along after my sheep as they grazed, hoping to locate myself soon or recover from the effects of the wine, if that were the cause. I soon began to feel hungry and could find only a few cold tortillas in my lunch sack. So I killed a fat lamb and built a fire on which to roast some meat. I remembered to save the rennet for my wife, who had told me she needed some to make cheese.

"Feeling thirsty, I started looking for water. I found a spring, *amigos*, but what a surprise to see that it ran milk instead of water. Just the same, I stooped over and took a big drink of it; it was cold and quenched my thirst very nicely. As I got up from taking my drink, the rennet, which I was still holding in my hand, fell into the spring. The spring was deep, and I couldn't recover the rennet, especially after the milk began to curdle. Well, I thought, it looks like the good God wants me to help my wife out on the cheesemaking. So I set to work and soon had a large number of cheeses made and hung up to drain on willow shelves.

"Feeling drowsy, I built up a big fire and went to sleep. I must have slept a long time, for when I woke up the fire had crept up and under the cheese. It was hanging in long threads; you know how cheese gets when it is heated. This made me pretty mad, but what could I do?

"Thinking I might have to spend a few more nights out until I found out where I was, I wondered how I could keep warm. so I made a loom like the Navahos use and wove those cheese threads into a large white blanket. That night I slept very comfortably under my new blanket.

"Next morning I ate breakfast and, getting on my burro, tied the blanket on behind me and started after my sheep. They seemed to know where they were going and I just followed them. Soon we were in country I knew and by evening we were home.

"I was anxious to show my wife the blanket I had woven and to tell her about my friends the bears, so I jumped off my burro and thought I would untie the blanket. All I found were a few threads which had caught on the saddle. Somewhere back on the mountain a thread must have caught on a limb of a tree or some stump, and the blanket had unravelled as I rode along. Now I had nothing with which to convince my wife as to where I had been, so I went very sorrowfully into the house.

"I never could find that spring again, and, as for my godson, I once saw a bear that looked like it had a collar on. It must not have been he, because when I tried to get closer he ran away. No godson of mine would treat his *padrino* in that manner."

Nursery Rhymes as Mini-Narratives. Selections from The Oxford Dictionary of Nursery Rhymes, *edited by Iona and Peter Opie (London: Oxford University Press, 1951).*

Many theories have been advanced to explain the origin, purpose, and popularity of the small folk poems known as nursery or "Mother Goose" rhymes. Although some scholars have argued that individual rhymes make implicit reference to specific historical incidents and people, their contentions have not been conclusively proven. It is certain that a large number of these poems originated in the sixteenth and seventeenth centuries and reflect the cultural and physical conditions of England in this period. Their continued popularity can be attributed to the fact that, although brief, they are vivid and emphatic: they present memorable characters and actions with strong rhythmic patterns and rhymes. Many of them are, indeed, superb short narratives. In a few lines, characters are introduced and conflicts (usually arising from the personalities of the actors) are begun and resolved. "Hark, Hark" portrays the terror experienced in small villages as bands of beggars approach; "The Three Wisemen of Gotham," because of their foolishness, make an ironic linear journey: Jack Sprat and his wife find a dietary solution; and the Old Woman of the shoe finds an expedient way of overcoming her difficulties. Two shepherds, Bo-peep and Boy Blue, have problems with their animals , while Mary, because of her loving kindness, cannot lose her lamb.

Little Bo-peep

Little Bo-peep has lost her sheep,
  And can't tell where to find them;
Leave them alone, and they'll come home,
  And bring their tails behind them.

Little Bo-peep fell fast asleep,
  And dreamt she heard them bleating;
But when she awoke, she found it a joke,
  For they were still all fleeting.

Then up she took her little crook,
  Determined for to find them,
She found them indeed, but it made her heart
  bleed,
  For they'd left their tails behind them.

It happened one day, as Bo-peep did stray
  Into a meadow hard by,
There she espied their tails side by side,
  All hung on a tree to dry.

She heaved a sigh, and wiped her eye,
  And over the hillocks went rambling,
And tried what she could, as a shepherdess
  should,
  To tack again each to its lambkin.

Little Boy Blue

Little Boy Blue,
  Come blow your horn,
The sheep's in the meadow,
  The cow's in the corn;
But where is the boy
  Who looks after the sheep?
He's under a haycock,
  Fast asleep.

Will you wake him?
  No, not I,
For if I do,
  He's sure to cry.

Jack Sprat

Jack Sprat could eat no fat,
  His wife could eat no lean,
And so between them both, you see,
  They licked the platter clean.

Hark, Hark

  Hark, hark,
  The dogs do bark,
The beggars are coming to town;
  Some in rags,
  And some in jags,
And one in a velvet gown.

Three Wise Men of Gotham

Three wise men of Gotham,
They went to sea in a bowl,
And if the bowl had been stronger
My song had been longer.

Mary Had a Little Lamb

Mary had a little lamb,
  Its fleece was white as snow;
And everywhere that Mary went
  The lamb was sure to go.

It followed her to school one day,
  That was against the rule;
It made the children laugh and play
  To see a lamb at school.

And so the teacher turned it out,
  But still it lingered near,
And waited patiently about
  Till Mary did appear.

Why does the lamb love Mary so?
  The eager children cry;
Why, Mary loves the lamb, you know,
  The teacher did reply.

The Old Woman
Who Lived in a Shoe

There was an old woman who lived in a shoe,
She had so many children she didn't know
what to do;
She gave them some broth without any bread;
She whipped them all soundly and put them
to bed.

Folktales for Further Reading

COLLECTIONS:

The Arabian Knights: Tales of Wonder and Magnificence, by Padraic Colum. Ill. by Lynd Ward (Macmillan, 1953).
   —a master storyteller gives new life to these tales of magic and adventure.

Australian Legendary Tales, comp. by K. Langloh Parker. Ill. by Rex Backhaus-Smith (Bodley Head, 1978).
   —a reprint of a classic nineteenth century anthology of fifty-four Australian legends.

Badger the Mischief Maker, by Kay Hill. Ill. by John Hamberger (McClelland and Stewart, 1965).
   —episodes about the Micmac Indian trickster are arranged in novelistic fashion, showing the moral growth of the main character.

Beat the Story-Drum, Pum-Pum, by Ashley Bryan (Atheneum, 1980).
   —African animal fables illustrate the virtues of cooperation. The prose style recaptures the speech rhythms of the storyteller.

Bluenose Ghosts, by Helen Creighton (McGraw-Hill Ryerson, 1957).
   —stories of phantom ships, buried treasure, and haunted houses from Atlantic Canada.

The Brocaded Slipper and Other Vietnamese Tales, by Lynette Dyer Vuong. Ill. by Vo-Dinh Mai (Addison-Wesley, 1982).
   —five tales include a Cinderella-like story and the legend of a man who visits fairyland.

The Classic Fairy Tales, by Peter and Iona Opie (Oxford, 1974).
   —the first English versions of twenty-four well-known tales are reprinted, along with scholarly introductions and full color illustrations by well-known artists.

The Cow-Tail Switch and Other West African Stories, by Harold Courlander and George Herzog. Ill. by Madye Lee Chastain (Holt, Rinehart, and Winston, 1947).
   —irony, exaggeration, and satire characterize these stories, several of which deal with the trickster Anansi.

The Demons of Rajpur: Five Tales from Bengal, trans. by Betsy Bang, Ill. by Molly Garrett Bang (Greenwillow, 1980).
   —traditional Bengali motifs are embodied in these five stories, which also show similarities to well-known European tales.

Elijah's Violin and Other Jewish Fairy Tales, by Howard Schwartz. Ill. by Linda Heller (Harper and Row, 1983).
   —thirty-six tales collected from Europe, the Near East, and India.

Eskimo Songs and Stories, trans. by Edward Field. Ill. by Kiakshuk and Pudlo (Delacorte, 1973).
   —based on the collections of Knud Rasmussen, the tales and poems included reflect both the humorous and violent aspects of Inuit life. The illustrators are from the Canadian Arctic.

The Golden Goose Book. Ill. by L. Leslie Brooke (Warne, 1976).
   —inimitable illustrations accompany four classic English tales.

How the People Sang the Mountains Up: How and Why Stories, comp. by Maria Leach. Ill. by Glen Rounds (Viking, 1967).
   —pourquoi tales from around the world explain land formations, animal peculiarities, the formation of constellations, etc.

Jataka Tales, ed. by Nancy De Roin. Ill. by Ellen Lanyon (Dell, 1975).
   —a collection of thirty of the oldest tales in the world, these Indian fables embody the teachings of Buddha.

The Knee-High Man and Other Tales, by Julius Lester. Ill. by Ralph Pinto (Dial, 1972).
   —these seven tales often reflect the master-slave relationships which prevailed in the pre-Civil War era of the United States.

The Magic Fiddler and Other Legends of French Canada, by Claude Aubry. Trans. by Alice E. Kane (Peter Martin Associates, 1968).
   —ten magical tales of French Canada.

Mouse Woman and the Vanished Princesses, by Christie Harris. Ill. by Douglas Tait (McClelland and Stewart, 1976).
   —six stories, based on West Coast legends, all reflect the need for harmonious interrelationships between all beings.

The Road to Canterbury: Tales from Chaucer, by Ian Serraillier. Ill. by John Lawrence (Kestrel, 1979).
   —prose retellings of nine of the fourteenth-century English *Canterbury Tales*, along with profiles of all the pilgrims.

The Silver Chanter: Traditional Scottish Tales and Legends, by Wendy Wood. Ill. by Colin McNaughton (Chatto and Windus, 1980).
   —twenty well-known and lesser legends are vigorously retold.

Tales the Elders Told: Ojibway Legends, by Basil H. Johnston. Ill. by Shirley Cheechoo (Royal Ontario Museum, 1981).
   —nine tales excellently retold and illustrated by Native Ojibways.

Teepee Tales of the American Indian, by Dee Brown (Holt, Rinehart, and Winston, 1979).
   —a variety of tales including animal-people relationships, contacts with Europeans, tricksters and magi-

cians, and ghost stories. Stories are taken from a variety of cultures.

Three Aesop Fox Fables, retold and Ill. by Paul Galdone (Seabury, 1971).
—Galdone's illustrations humorously capture the various emotions of these foxes.

EDITIONS OF INDIVIDUAL TALES:
Titles marked with an asterisk (*) are alternate, illustrated versions of tales found in this anthology.

About Sleeping Beauty, by P. L. Travers. Ill. by Charles Keeping (McGraw-Hill, 1975).
—contains five versions of the tale, including those by Perrault and the Grimms, and an expanded version by Travers. An interpretive essay explores the tale's possible meanings.

Anansi the Spider: a Tale from the Ashanti, retold and ill. by Gerald McDermott (Holt, Rinehart, and Winston, 1972).
—geometric designs and vivid colors highlight this tale of how the well-known West African trickster was rescued by his sons and how the moon was placed in the sky.

The Angry Moon, by William Sleator. Ill. by Blair Lent (Little, Brown, 1970).
—a West Coast Native legend about two small children who climb into the sky on an arrow ladder.

The Bear and the Kingbird, by the Brothers Grimm. Trans. by Lore Segal, ill. by Chris Conover (Farrar, Straus, Giroux, 1979).
—because the bear insults the kingbird's children, a ridiculous war between the winged and four-legged creatures breaks out.

Bo Rabbit Smart for True: Folktales from the Gullah, by Priscilla Jaquith. Ill. by Ed Young (Philomel, 1981).
—four Black American trickster tales from the coastal states.

Chanticleer and the Fox, by Geoffrey Chaucer, retold and ill. by Barbara Cooney (Crowell, 1958).
—vivid and historically accurate illustrations add to the vitality and humor of this English tale of a proud rooster. A Caldecott Medal winner.

Cinderella, by Charles Perrault. Trans. and ill. by Marcia Brown (Scribner's 1954).*
—A Caldecott Medal-winning book in which the grace and delicacy of the illustrations reflect the grace of the French court.

Cinderella, by Charles Perrault. Retold and ill. by Alan Suddon (Dennis Dobson, 1969).*
—a loose adaptation and humorous collage illustrations give a satiric slant to this old tale.

Cinderella, by the Brothers Grimm. Retold and ill. by Nonny Hogrogian (Greenwillow, 1981).*
—the understated colors of the illustrations suggest the gentle, loving nature of the heroine.

The Crane Wife, by Sumiko Yagawo. Trans. by Katherine Paterson, ill. by Suekichi Akaba (Morrow, 1981).
—when a simple Japanese peasant saves an injured crane, he is given a beautiful wife, until greed and curiosity overcome him.

Cricket Boy, by Feenie Ziner. Ill. by Ed Young (Doubleday, 1977).
—a poor Chinese scholar, filled with grief over the death of his son, finds joy in the victory of a champion fighting cricket.

Dick Whittington and His Cat, retold and ill. by Marcia Brown (Scribner's 1950).*
—Brown's woodcut illustrations, in black and gold, depict the changing emotions and economic status of this legendary English hero.

The Donkey Prince, by the Brothers Grimm. Adapted by M. Jean Craig, ill. by Barbara Cooney (Doubleday, 1977).
—Cooney's Renaissance-style illustrations embody the tender pathos evoked by the story.

Duffy and the Devil, by Harve Zemach. Ill. by Margot Zemach (Farrar, Straus, Giroux, 1973).
—in order to win the favor of the Squire, lazy Duffy makes a bargain with the Devil in this English folktale. A Caldecott Medal book.

Fin M'Coul: The Giant of Knockmany Hill, retold and ill. by Tomie De Paola (Holiday House, 1981).*
—De Paola's illustrations capture the many humorous ironies of this story of a not-so-brave Irish giant saved by his wife.

The Fisherman and His Wife, by the Brothers Grimm. Trans. by Randall Jarrell, ill. by Margot Zemach (Farrar, Straus, Giroux, 1980).*
—Zemach's illustrations humorously add to this satire on human wishes.

The Five Sparrows: a Japanese Folktale, retold and ill. by Patricia Montgomery Newton (Antheneum, 1982).
—an old woman is rewarded for giving aid to a wounded sparrow.

The Fool of the World and The Flying Ship, by Arthur Ransome. Ill. by Uri Shulevitz (Farrar, Straus, Giroux, 1968).
—in this Slavic tale, the young simpleton who shows kindness to the people he meets overcomes the treacherous Czar and marries the princess. A Caldecott Medal book.

Goldilocks and the Three Bears, retold and ill. by Lorinda Bryan Cauley (Putnam's, 1981).*
—Goldilocks in this version is merely mischievous.

The illustrations capture the varying emotions of the characters.

The Good-Hearted Youngest Brother, trans. by Emöke de Papp Severo. Ill. by Diane Goode (Bradbury, 1981).
    —in this Hungarian story, three orphaned brothers seeking their fortunes achieve lasting happiness because of the kindness of the youngest.

Hansel and Gretel, by the Brothers Grimm. Trans. by Elizabeth Crawford, ill. by Lisbeth Zwerger (William Morrow, 1979).*
    —the deadly quality of the witch is excellently portrayed by the illustrations.

Henny Penny, by Veronica S. Hutchinson, ill. by Leonard B. Lubin (Little, Brown, 1976).*
    —the devious fox is portrayed in the style of eighteenth century engravings.

The History of Mother Twaddle and the Marvelous Achievements of her Son Jack, retold and ill. by Paul Galdone (Seabury, 1974).*
    —based on an old ballad, this version ends with Jack marrying a damsel he meets at the giant's castle.

Jack and the Wonder Beans, by James Still. Ill. by Margot Tomes (Putnam's, 1977).*
    —an Appalachian version of the famous English tale.

Journey Cake, Ho! by Ruth Sawyer. Ill. by Robert McCloskey (Viking, 1952).
    —McCloskey's illustrations add to the humor of this American version of the Pancake story.

King Krakus and the Dragon, retold and ill. by Janina Domanska (Greenwillow, 1979).
    —in Poland, an apprentice shoemaker cleverly uses his skills to rid the country of a great dragon.

The Little Girl and the Big Bear, by Joanna Galdone. Ill. by Paul Galdone (Houghton, Mifflin, 1980).
    —in this Slavic tale, a little girl lost on a berry-picking expedition uses her wits to outwit her captor and return home.

Little Sister and the Month Brothers, by Beatrice Schenk de Regniers. Ill. by Margot Tomes (Seabury, 1976).
    —an ill-treated girl who fulfills the impossible tasks set by her stepsister and stepmother ends up happily married while the others perish. Slavic.

The Little Wee Tyke: an English Folktale, retold and ill. by Marcia Sewall (Atheneum, 1979).
    —a small, rejected dog finds a home when he saves a poor farming family from the spells of a witch. English.

The Loon's Necklace, by William Toye. Ill. by Elizabeth Cleaver (Oxford, 1977).*
    —collage illustrations capture the West Coast flavor of this version of a widely known Native Indian and Inuit legend.

Lovely Vassilisa, by Barbara Cohen. Ill. by Anatoly Ivanov (Atheneum, 1980).*
    —this version is based on the illustrator's memory of the story as he heard it during his childhood.

The Magic Plum Tree: Based on a Tale from the Jataka, by Freya Littledale. Ill. by Enrico Arno (Crown, 1981).
    —In this fable from India, three brothers are individually shown a plum tree in different seasons. When they see it together during harvest time, they learn the magic of nature.

The Magician of Cracow, retold and ill. by Krystyna Turska (Hamish Hamilton, 1975).
    —a Polish story in which a famous magician makes a bargain with the Devil and finds himself living forever on the moon.

The Mermaid's Cape, by Margaret K. Wetterer. Ill. by Elsie Primavera (Atheneum, 1981).
    —based on Celtic legends of the Selche (seal in water, woman on shore), this Irish story tells of the fisherman who forces a mermaid to be his wife by stealing her magic cloak.

The Miraculous Hind: a Hungarian Legend, retold and ill. by Elizabeth Cleaver (Holt, Rinehart, and Winston, 1973).
    —collage illustrations vividly depict this legend recounting the founding of Hungary. Winner of the Canadian Library Association Book of the Year for Children Medal.

Mother Crocodile, trans. and retold by Rosa Guy. Ill. by John Steptoe (Delacorte, 1981).
    —a Senegalese storyteller explains how a mother crocodile gave wisdom to her doubting children.

The Nine Crying Dolls, retold by Anne Pellowski. Ill. by Charles Mikolaycak (Philomel, 1980).
    —a mother and father take an old grandmother's advice on how to stop her baby from crying, but only succeed in causing all of the other babies in the village to cry.

Once a Mouse . . . , retold and ill. by Marcia Brown (Scribner's, 1961).
    —an Indian fable in which an ungrateful mouse turns upon his benefactor. Vivid woodcuts reflect the changing emotions of the story. A Caldecott Medal book.

One Fine Day, adapted and ill. by Nonny Hogrogian (Macmillan, 1971).
    —in this cumulative Armenian tale, a greedy fox is punished for stealing a pail of milk. A Caldecott Medal book.

The Pied Piper of Hamelin, by Kurt Baumann. Ill. by Jean Claverie (Methuen, 1978).*
    —in this version of the well-known story, the emphasis is on the greed and hypocrisy of the burghers. Brueghelesque illustrations reflect the harsh satire.

The Prince Who Knew His Fate, trans. and ill. by Lise Manniche (Philomel, 1981).
—although the prince may not escape his destiny, he proves his love and courage during his long journey. Detailed explanatory notes relate the story to Egyptian art and culture.

Puss in Boots, by Charles Perrault. Ill. by Paul Galdone (Seabury Press, 1976).
—there's more to this crafty cat than at first appears. Galdone's usual humor enhances the satire.

Rapunzel, retold and ill. by Bernadette Watts (Crowell, 1975).*
—tempera-and-pastel paintings portray the emotions of the lonely, long-haired maiden imprisoned in a tower.

Red Riding Hood, by the Brothers Grimm, retold by Beatrice Schenk de Regniers. Ill. by Edward Gorey (Atheneum, 1972).*
—a verse version for young readers, with Edward Gorey's humorous, grisly illustrations.

Seashore Story, retold and ill. by Taro Yashima (Viking, 1967).
—in this Japanese story, Urashima takes a long undersea journey with a turtle he has rescued, returning home to find himself an old man and his family dead.

The Seven Ravens, by the Brothers Grimm. Retold and ill. by Donna Diamond (Viking, 1979).
—when a father's unthinking curse turns his sons into ravens, the sister must rescue them.

The Shoemaker and the Elves, by the Brothers Grimm. Trans. by Wayne Andrews, ill. by Adrienne Adams (Scribner's, 1960).
—Adams' illustrations reflect the atmosphere of an old German cobbler shop in this story of a poor shoemaker who receives mysterious aid.

Simon and the Golden Sword, retold and ill. by Frank Newfeld (Oxford, 1976).
—the youngest son triumphs in this story from Atlantic Canada.

Snow-White, by the Brothers Grimm. Trans. by Paul Heins, ill. by Trina Schart Hyman (Little Brown, 1974).*
—Hyman's illustrations capture the jealous anger of the stepmother who wishes to destroy the beautiful princess.

Snow-White and the Seven Dwarfs, by the Brothers Grimm. Trans. by Randall Jarrell, ill. by Nancy Ekholm Burkert (Farrar, Straus, Giroux, 1972).*
—Burkert's illustrations are considered among the finest ever to accompany a Brothers Grimm tale.

The Stone-Cutter: a Japanese Folktale, retold and ill. by Gerald McDermott (Viking, 1975).

—envy and ambition lead to the downfall of a lowly stone-cutter.

A Story, a Story, retold and ill. by Gail E. Haley (Atheneum, 1970).
—a Caldecott Medal book which explains how the African trickster Anansi used his wits to bring stories to his people.

The Story of Mr. and Mrs. Vinegar, retold and ill. by Stephen Gammell (Lothrop, Lee, and Shepard, 1982).
—although the husband in this English story is foolish, he and his wife attain much greater happiness than do the fisherman and his wife.

Strega Nona, retold and ill. by Tomie de Paola (Prentice-Hall, 1973).
—in an Italian version of ''The Sorcerer's Apprentice,'' a young man loses control of the magic pasta pot.

Suho and the White Horse, by Yuzo Otsuka. Ill. by Suekichi Akaba (Viking, 1981).
—a Mongolian story of a young shepherd and his love for the horse he rescued is used to explain the origin of the horse-head fiddle.

Tattercoats, by Flora Annie Steel. Ill. by Diane Goode (Bradbury, 1976).*
—delicate illustrations enhance the tenderness and pathos of this story.

The Twelve Dancing Princesses, by the Brothers Grimm. Ill. by Errol Le Cain (Viking, 1978).
—ornate artwork adds many subtleties to this story of how a poor sailor solves a great mystery.

Under the Shade of the Mulberry Tree, retold and ill. by Demi (Prentice-Hall, 1979).
—an arrogant, selfish richman is outwitted by an old beggar.

White Wave, retold by Diane Wolkstein. Ill. by Ed Young (Crowell, 1979).
—a poor Chinese farmer who treats a white snail with kindness is rewarded by the Moon Goddess.

Why Mosquitoes Buzz in People's Ears, by Verna Aardema. Ill. by Leo and Diane Dillon (Dial, 1975).
—this West African cumulative and pourquoi tale traces the disastrous consequences of acting on misinformation and rumor. A Caldecott Medal winner.

Yussel's Prayer: a Yom Kippur Story, by Barbar Cohen. Ill. by Michael J. Deraney (Lothrop, Lee, and Shepard, 1981).
—a simple cowherd teaches his rich and selfish master the true meaning of the Day of Atonement.

Hero Tales

Hero Tales

An Introduction

In *The Hero With a Thousand Faces*, Joseph Campbell writes that regardless of a story's cultural origins, "it will always be the one shape shifting yet marvelously constant story that we find." In his study, Campbell examines hundreds of folktales, hero tales, and myths from around the world to discover the structural similarity underlying them all: what has been called the monomyth. Although there are biographies of many heroes from many cultures, there is, he argues, only one basic life-story: the quest by individuals to discover their own identities and roles in society. This is a quest for individuation and socialization; one must know one's self and find a meaningful place amongst one's fellows.

Many twentieth-century psychologists, most notably Carl Jung, have argued that this quest is taken by all people; moreover, this is why hero tales have been so important in all cultures. We can identify with the aspirations and struggles of an heroic figure, for they are our aspirations and struggles as well. However, unlike the average reader of, or listener to a hero story, heroes enact their dramas on a larger stage. The events of their lives, including the conflicts they experience, affect not only themselves, but also the people they lead. In effect, they are superior to us; they represent a higher level of human potential and achievement. Although we may sympathize with their difficult journeys, we also admire them, for they fulfill their quests — and therefore, ours — in a manner far more grand and heroic than we do.

The hero's life is usually presented as a life-story, a complete biography. The stages within this life-story, as outlined by Campbell, begin with the hero's significant birth. Often mysterious, and always an indication of their special status, the births of heroes are unique events that forever separate them from their peers. Often, they are the product of a union between a god and a mortal, a sky-father and an earth-mother. Perseus, the Greek hero, was the son of Zeus, the King of the Gods, and Danae, daughter of the King of Argos. The hero is, or may appear to be, an orphan: Moses, found hidden in the bullrushes, is raised by Pharoah's daughter; King Arthur is raised as a ward of Sir Ector. The birth may also be marked by marvelous occurrences: in some versions of the legend of John Henry, the moon stops and then moves backwards on the night of his birth.

This pronounced difference from other children often produces difficulties for the hero. Maui the Hawaiian trickster-hero is often rejected by his older brothers. Sir Gareth, the kitchen knight, is reviled by many members of King Arthur's court. The Blackfoot hero Scarface is treated like a social outcast. Heroes also must usually go through an arduous process of education guided by an old, wise tutor, as Arthur is by Merlin, before they are recognized as true leaders.

Having assumed a role as leader, the hero must display courage, wisdom, and must lead through example. Physical tasks appear to be overwhelming, even impossible: David must destroy Goliath, a giant before whom all of the Israelites tremble; Beowulf must kill the dragon. Heroes help their people in times of great need: Robin Hood steals from rich, hypocritical authorities to help England's downtrodden yeomen and peasants; Nanabozho rescues his people who are threatened by a flood caused by the evil Windegos. Scarface brings back from the sun the knowledge of the Medicine Lodge. However, courage or strength such as that exhibited by John Henry or Beowulf is not always in itself enough. Both Robin Hood and Ulysses succeed through trickery and guile; David perceptively realizes that he must employ small, but superior weapons when confronting the heavily armored Philistine giant.

Although superior, heroes are generally not perfect. The love of adventure and trickery displayed by Ulysses and Robin Hood often creates dangers for themselves and their followers. The idealistic King Arthur fails to realize that the greatest threat to his kingdom is man's fallen nature. In fact, a hero's failings can bring about final defeat and death.

The death of the leader is a major element of great hero tales; Beowulf dies killing a fire-drake while all but one of his men hide in terror; John Henry dies of exhaustion after having driven more steel than the steam drill; Robin Hood is betrayed by an hypocritical, evil prioress. Sir Patrick Spens is a victim of his own pride, political treachery, and the elements. Nanabozho and Arthur do not die according to the legends, but leave the world, supposedly to return in times of great need.

Although in general outline the stories of heroes are much the same throughout the world, each hero tale is a unique embodiment of the culture which produced it. In depicting the character and actions of their great leaders, people have celebrated those ideals they most admired. Ulysses affirms the Greek belief in the value and dignity of humanity in an often hostile universe. Beowulf embodies the physical and mental courage so admired by the fierce warriors of northern Europe. Robin Hood possesses the qualities of the ideal English yeoman; King Arthur, those of the chivalrous medieval knight. John Henry, a member of a downtrodden race, is a symbol both of his people's dignity and of modern man's struggle against the encroachments of technology.

There may be only one hero, but this hero wears a thousand faces, a different one for each culture represented. Modern readers should be aware of the basic structure of hero tales *and* the specific cultural forms they take, the superior individuals and great deeds, *and* the story structures, conflicts, and elements of human character also found in stories from other genres in "The Family of Stories."

The hero tales most commonly adapted as children's stories have their origins in traditional epics, sagas, romances, and ballad cycles. The stories contained in these narratives may have originally developed around historical events and actual people. In retellings over the years, these events were magnified until the heroes became larger than life. Totally unrelated stories attached themselves to the original material, and motifs from folklore and mythology were added. At a specific point in time, all of the materials were unified into one coherent narrative. The result, be it the *Odyssey, Beowulf*, or the *Volsunga Saga*, has remained basically constant and represents the form in which the specific story is best-known today.

The hero tales most widely known in the English speaking world are the *Iliad* and the *Odyssey* (Greek), the stories of the Trojan War and the wanderings of Ulysses (Odysseus); *Beowulf* (Anglo-Saxon), the exploits of the killer of monsters and dragons; *Le Morte d'Arthur* (English), the adventures of the Knights of the Round Table; Robin Hood (English), legends of the honest savior of the poor; and several Norse (Icelandic and Scandinavian) sagas, the best-known of which is probably the *Volsunga Saga*, the account of the deeds of the great warriors. Perhaps because it is such a relatively new area, modern North America has fewer clearly developed hero tales. However, such characters as Daniel Boone, John Henry, and Nanabozho are among the better-known pioneer, Black American, and Native Indian heroes.

A consideration of the most popular English heroes, Robin Hood and King Arthur, will illustrate how legends developed and how they have been adapted as children's stories.

It is generally believed that Robin Hood's character and adventures are based on the lives of many people. Outlaws were numerous in the later Middle Ages and many were the subjects of legends. It is argued that these legends gradually coalesced, focusing on one character. It is also hypothesized that the stories about the Sheriff of Nottingham were later added to the Robin Hood collection from tales about such corrupt sheriffs. A third major hypothesis about the Robin Hood stories moves away from the specifically historical. Clad in green, associated with the forest, and buried beneath a tree, Robin was linked to nature myths of a woodland spirit symbolizing the natural and pure against the hypocritical and corrupt. By the fifteenth century, Robin Hood was being portrayed in many ballads as the ideal English yeoman. Handsome, skilled in archery and hand-to-hand combat, courageous and intelligent, he was not against dangerous adventure for its own sake. But more important, he strove to help his people against tyrannical and dishonest secular and ecclesiastical leaders.

Although children have probably always enjoyed Robin Hood stories, it was not until the nineteenth century that versions written specifically for children emerged. In 1883, Howard Pyle, the American author-illustrator, published *The Merry Adventures of Robin Hood*, a work which quickly established itself as a classic. Since then, many well-known authors and illustrators have depicted him. The stories have provided the basis for many television series and motion pictures, the best-known of them being the 1939 *Adventures of Robin Hood*, starring Errol Flynn.

The adventure and basic simplicity of Robin Hood's life may account for the continued popularity of the stories with younger readers. Not only are the tales easy to follow and filled with fast-paced adventure, they also present characters who are free of imposed authority. The Merry Men are like little boys who can come and go as they please, enjoying the fellowship of like-minded individuals, engaging in adventures without their parents' fretting.

If King Arthur was an actual person, he was probably a warrior-chief who fought in the sixth century battles against the invading Saxons. In succeeding centuries, legends developed until he became a larger-than-life hero. Britons fleeing to France took the stories with them, where they developed further before being brought back to England after the Norman invasion of the late eleventh century. Between the twelfth and fifteenth centuries, more stories were written about Arthur, making him the embodiment of the new chivalric ideals. The most important of these retellings was *Le Morte d'Arthur*, written by Sir Thomas Malory in the late fifteenth century and published by William Caxton, England's first printer, in 1485. Nearly all later treatments of the Arthurian legends have been influenced by Malory's book.

As was the case with the Robin Hood legends, the first major children's adaptation of the King Arthur stories was undertaken by Howard Pyle, who referred to the legendary hero as "the most gentle knight who ever lived in the world." Pyle's four volumes are *The Story of King Arthur and His Knights*

(1903), *The Story of the Champions of the Round Table* (1907), *The Story of Sir Lancelot and His Companions* (1907), and *The Story of the Grail and the Passing of Arthur* (1910). Several well-known twentieth century children's authors have retold the legends; among them is Rosemary Sutcliff, who has also adapted the Robin Hood tales. Perhaps the most interesting of the adaptations is T.H. White's *The Sword in the Stone*, which has been made into a full-length Walt Disney animated motion picture. He presents the story of a young boy not conspicuously different in ability from the average reader. There is much humor in the book, but his treatment of the major theme — the education of a future leader — is very serious.

The basic nature of the Arthurian material has made adaptation for younger readers difficult. The original legends contain many sexual elements and deal with complex religious themes. Most retellers emphasize the high adventure, courage, and heroism. Riding through strange and threatening landscapes, dressed in their shining armor, the Knights of the Round Table face dragons, giants, superior numbers, and supernatural adversaries. Often outnumbered, they never shirk confrontations and generally emerge victorious.

Among traditional tales in "The Family of Stories," hero tales occupy a central position. In a sense, they stand between folktales and myths and borrow characteristics from both. Whereas folktales deal with local occurrences and often use magic which is limited in its sphere of influence, hero tales deal with events affecting an entire cultural group, and accordingly, supernatural forces, if any, have wide-reaching influence. Moreover, folktales are usually short, self-contained stories; their events do not generally influence other stories. In hero tales, individual episodes are part of an entire life-story; they occur in relation to earlier and later events. Unlike myths, which deal with an entire world from its creation to its destruction, hero tales are limited to the lifetimes of specific heroes and the areas they influence. Although hero tales often depict gods affecting the lives of mortals, as in myths, the actions of mortals, rather than those of gods, are of prime importance. In spite of the differences, hero tales do use motifs common to myths and folktales. Thus we find unlikely heroes and tricksters, special, often magical objects, cumulative tests, unnatural and supernatural beings, and names that have special significance.

Since hero tales were an early form of history and biography, they can serve as an introduction to those genres when written for children. Although many readers tend to view both history and biography as essentially accurate presentations of facts, they may be critically understood as interpretations of their material. Regarding hero tales as obvious, deliberate structures designed to display or inculcate cultural attitudes will assist the reader in perceiving the implicit structures and interpretations of their modern counterparts.

Such modern writers of fantasy as J.R.R. Tolkien, C.S. Lewis, Lloyd Alexander, Alan Garner, Ursula LeGuin, and Susan Cooper read widely and deeply in traditional hero tales and drew not only specific characters, objects, and incidents, but also general motifs and patterns from them. Such stories as "Sir Gareth, or The Knight of the Kitchen," and "The Fire-Drake's Hoard" thus serve as excellent introductions to such novels as Susan Cooper's *The Dark Is Rising*, Lloyd Alexander's *The High King*, and J.R.R. Tolkien's *The Hobbit*.

Finally, it should be noted that many popular television programs and motion pictures avidly consumed by young people make use, consciously or unconsciously, of elements from the hero tales. For example, the mysterious origin, the silver bullets, and recognizable costume of the Lone Ranger parallel elements from Robin Hood stories. The recent motion pictures about Superman deal with the mysterious birth, the boyhood and education of the young hero, and his ultimate, self-sacrificing leadership. George Lucas, in preparation for his Star Wars films, studied traditional hero tales thoroughly. The orphan Luke Skywalker must go through long, arduous training, guided by Yoda and the spirit of Obiwan Kenobi, before becoming a Jedi Knight. The student who is aware of these traditional patterns and symbols will be able to consider popular modern stories in a new light, and, with a basis for comparison, will be better able to make evaluative judgments about them.

In developing a literature curriculum, hero tales can best be introduced in the upper elementary grades. Robin Hood stories are the least complex of the best-known legends and, in addition to their exciting adventures, they contain a great deal of irony. After a general sampling of hero tales, students are introduced to stories that deal with specific phases in the lives of heroes: birth and childhood, testing and recognition, leadership and death. Over a two- or three-year period, children will acquire a knowledge of a number of stories dealing with several heroes from many cultures. At this point, they can be introduced to the general structure of the hero's life and to the different cultural expressions of this pattern.

It will be noted that only two selections have been included in which women are central heroes. This limitation arises from the fact that in the epics, sagas, and romances which have provided the basis for modern adaptations, female characters generally played minor parts. Moreover, until recently, sex-role stereotyping usually relegated girls and women in children's stories to non-physical, "lady-like" roles. Even unconventional heroines like Anne Shirley of *Anne of Green Gables* and Jo March of *Little Women* became much more demure as they grew older. In Christian thought, women were traditionally seen as secondary to men; as Milton expressed it in *Paradise Lost* when speaking of Adam and Eve: "He for

God; she for God in him." People like Joan of Arc, who acted in aggressive and masculine ways, were generally disapproved of. Often in traditional stories, women who exerted their power, as did Morgan le Fay in Arthurian legends, were presented as being destructive and evil, denying their natural, womanly qualities.

Children's literature of the past twenty years has presented many more heroic women and girls, as seen in such fantasies as Madeleine L'Engle's *A Wrinkle in Time* and Anne McCaffrey's "Dragonsong Trilogy," in realistic novels like Scott O'Dell's *Island of the Blue Dolphins* and Jean George's *Julie of the Wolves*, and in biographies of women athletes, political figures, and scientists. However, as recent collections have emphasized, folktales have always contained many courageous, heroic women.

"Goliath," from Stories from the Bible, *by Walter de la Mare. Illustrated by Edward Ardizzone (London: Faber and Faber, 1977).*

During their early lives, heroes often perform deeds which reveal their differences from others. David, the youngest son of Jesse, scorned by his brothers, bears many resemblances to folktale characters as he begins his linear journey toward heroic status. Like Cinderella, he is constantly made to feel inferior; like Jack, he slays a fearsome giant; like Dick Whittington, he emerges from humble origins to become a great leader. In addition to giving a detailed account of David's battle strategy and emphasizing Goliath's tremendous size, de la Mare develops David's character fully, showing both his ambition and religious zeal. This retelling makes direct use of several passages from II Samuel 17 and follows the measured rhythms of Biblical style.

Goliath

When again the Philistines gathered an army together for war, they marched into the territory of Judah, and pitched their camp above the Valley of Elah, and on the steeps of a mountain ridge west of Bethlehem. And the host of Israel lay on the northern height of the valley, so that the two armies were face to face, and in sight one of another; the Philistines occupying the mountain on the one side, and Saul and his army occupying the mountain on the other side, with the wide valley and ravine between them. Through this ravine a pebbly brook coursed down among its rocks from the mountains above.

Now in the ranks of the Philistines at this time was a giant of prodigious strength and girth and stature, whose name was Goliath. He was of the city of Gath, and his four sons who were as yet in their childhood there, grew up to be giants like him; and one of them had six fingers on either hand, and on either foot six toes. From the crown of his head to the sole of his foot Goliath stood six cubits and a span. And he was the champion of the army of the Philistines.

While the day of battle was still in the balance, and neither army moved, morning and evening this Goliath would issue out from among the tents of the camp of the Philistines, stride down into the valley and there, in full view of both armies, would roar out his challenge, defying all Israel. Unlike his fellows in the ranks who were dressed in kilts with a pleated head-cap strapped under the chin, and who, apart from spear and broad-sword, carried only a two-handled shield or wore a cuirass of leather, he was clad from head to foot in armor of brass. A helmet of bronze was upon his head; a bronze coat of mail loose and supple covered his body, the scales of it overlapping one above another like the scales of a fish; and it weighed five thousand shekels of brass. Greaves also of bronze covered his shins, and a javelin of bronze hung between his shoulders. The haft of the spear he carried was like the beam of a weaver's loom, and the pointed head of iron upon it weighed six hundred shekels. And there went out before him a crookbacked Philistine who in stature was a dwarf by comparison, and he carried the giant's shield.

Now when this champion had bawled his challenge, and no man made answer, he would begin to taunt and mock at the Israelites.

"Why, forsooth," he would shout against them, "have you come out in your rabble against the Philistines, and why have you set yourselves in battle array, seeing that the quarrel between us may be decided here and now. Here stand I, a warrior of the princes of Philistia; and there sit you, servants of Saul. If there be any man among you with the courage of a sheep, drive him down to meet me, face to face. For I swear by Dagon that if he prevail against me and kill me, then shall the Philistines become the slaves of Israel, to hew them wood and draw them water. But if, as I surely shall, I prevail against him, and fell him to the dust with this spear in my hand, then shall Israel be the slaves of the Philistines. Hai, now! Yet again this day I defy the armies of Israel. If man among you there is none to meet me, call on Jehovah to smite me with his thunderbolt! Peradventure he will answer!"

He clashed with his spear upon his breastplate, shouting derision. And the troops of

Israel who heard him were dismayed. There were many men among them of tried valor and skill in battle, but not one ready to go out against this giant in single combat, with even a hope of triumphing over him. And defeat would bring disaster.

So morning and evening, Goliath would come striding down out of the camp of the Philistines, yell aloud his challenge, and pour out his taunts and insults. And the Philistines laughed to hear him.

Now of the eight sons of Jesse, who was himself too old for the hardships of war, the three eldest, Eliab, Abinadab and Shammah, were serving in the ranks of the army under Saul. But David, the youngest, was with his father in Bethlehem, keeping his sheep.

When one evening he returned home, his father bade him set out on the morrow for the camp of the army of Israel to see how his brothers fared.

"And take with thee", he said, "a bushel of this parched corn, and these ten loaves and these ten cheeses; and run to the camp and bring me news, for it is many days since we had word of them."

The parched or roasted corn and the flat round loaves were for David's brothers, and the curd cheeses were for a present to the captain in command of their thousand. For Saul and they themselves and all the men of Israel were above the valley of Elah, confronting the Philistines.

Next morning, then, as soon as the first flush of dawn appeared in the sky, David rose up and having left his sheep in charge of a herdsman, set out for the camp, a journey of twelve miles. He went rejoicing on his way. After the brief time he had spent in the service of the king, he had fretted at remaining at home with his father, keeping his sheep. He pined to be with his brothers, fighting for Israel.

When he came to the hills on which Saul's army was entrenched, the whole camp was astir. For army against army, Israel and the Philistines were ready and in array. He heard that battle might be joined that very morning. On fire with eagerness to see what was afoot, David gave all that he had brought with him into the hands of the keeper who had charge of the baggage, and ran off with all speed to seek out his brothers. Their quarters were in the forefront of the camp. There he found them and saluted them. "Peace be with you!" he said. And he gave them his father's message, and talked with them there.

And as he talked with them, his eyes ranged eagerly over the camp of the Philistines on the heights above and beyond the valley. Their bright-dyed tents in the crystal clear air shone in their colors in the sun. He could even count their chariots with their horses and charioteers. And the mountain-side was thick with men moving — like an ant-hill in midsummer, when its warriors prepare to sally out to attack a neighboring tribe.

Curious and intent, he watched every movement, and at the same time questioned his brothers of what he saw, the numbers, the regiments, the commanders, the chances of the battle.

The day was yet early, and even as he watched, there showed a stir on the outskirts of the enemy's camp, and there issued out of it from among the host of the Philistines, smalled in the distance and alone but for his armor-bearer, the giant, Goliath.

With slow and ponderous tread he advanced down the slope into the valley until he was a little beyond midway between the two camps, and a rabble of his comrades followed after him, though afar off.

He came to a standstill, and brandishing his bronze-tipped spear on high, he cried out as he had cried before, and roared out his challenge against Israel. The hoarse echoes of his voice rang among the hills; the sun beat down upon the burnished fish-scales of his armor, and gleamed upon his helm. David could well-nigh see the glittering of his eyes in his great face.

At sight of him he had fallen silent. He stood stock-still like an image carved out of wood, his gaze fixed on Goliath, his heart wildly beating, while his ears drank in the vile and boastful words he uttered. At sound of his mighty voice the Israelitish troops who had been filling their water-pots at the stream-side and those who were on the fringes of the camp, fled back before him, for they were so afraid. When David saw it, a frown gathered on his brow. He turned to those who stood near.

"Who is this accursed Philistine?" he asked them. "And how comes it that he dare insult and defy the armies of the living God? What man has been chosen to go out to meet him, and what shall be done to him when he hath laid him low, and hath washed away this shame and reproach against Israel?"

The soldiers who stood by told David that no man had yet been chosen or had dared to go out to meet the giant, but that any who accepted his challenge and met him face to face and killed him would not only be enriched with great riches but that the king himself would give him his own daughter in marriage, and from that day onward his father's whole house, whosoever he might be, would be made free men in Israel. And David hearkened, pondering what they said.

But when his eldest brother, Eliab, heard him talking, he turned on him fiercely, hot with anger. He remembered the day when the great prophet Samuel had come to Bethlehem and he himself had been set aside, and this stripling, the youngest of them all, had been blessed by the prophet and anointed with the holy oil. And he had been filled with envy when he heard that David had been summoned to court by the king.

"Who bade thee come idling here," he said, "leaving thy poor little flock of sheep with some herd-boy in the wilds? Oh, but I know thee of old, thy pride and presumption and the naughtiness of thy heart. Thou art puffed up with self-will, and it is not to bring a message from our father that thou hast come into the camp, but to see the fighting."

But David answered him, "What is it I have done amiss? I did but ask a question, and thou canst not deny it is one that needs an answer."

He turned away from his brother, and continued to question those who stood near, and one and all gave him the answer that had been given him already.

"But look now," he adjured them earnestly, "this boaster, monster though he be, is but a man. Weighed down with brass he moves as clumsily as an ox, and his face at least is naked. Why is he allowed to live, defying Jehovah?"

Seeing at length, though he was still little more than a boy, that David's scorn of the champion of the Philistines and his shame for Israel sprang from the courage of his very soul, these men reported the matter to their captain, who himself questioned David, and brought him to the tent of the king.

David stood beside Saul's standard while the captain went within. Then the captain led him into the tent where Saul sat, with Abner and his chief officers in attendance upon him; and David stood before the king. He bowed himself before Saul, and being questioned, said simply what was in his mind. He told the king why he had come into the camp, and how he had chanced to hear the champion of the Philistines shout his challenge against Israel, and that he had spoken only as his own soul had declared.

"Why", he said, "should any heart in Israel be faint with fear because of this man, this enemy of the Lord? Thy servant would himself go out and fight with the Philistine."

The king looked on him and marveled, questioning within himself where he had seen his face before. But there came back no clear remembrance of the shepherd-boy who had sat beside him as he lay sick, and had solaced the dread and horror in his mind with the music of his harp.

"Of a truth," he said, "there is no doubt of thy valor. But what hope hast thou of prevailing against him? Thou art but a youth and hast had no experience in arms, while this Goliath hath been a man of war from the day when he was first able to carry a spear. He would disdain thee, my son, and snap thee in twain between his fingers."

But David pleaded with the king. He said how in days gone by, when he had sat keeping his father's sheep alone in the wild, at one time a bear and at another a young lion had sprung out from its ambush in the rocks and thickets near by, and had seized and carried off a lamb from his flock.

"So I went out after him," he said, "and chased him, and snatched his prey from out of his mouth. And when, raging with fury, he sprang upon me, his paws upon my shoulders, I caught him, like this, by the beard upon his chin, and with my club smote and slew him at a blow. So indeed, my lord, thy servant killed both the lion and the bear, and so will I do unto this accursed Philistine, for I vow, my lord, I have no fear of him, seeing that he hath defied the armies of the living God, and is himself no better than a ravening beast. The Lord God who delivered me from the paw of the lion and the paw of the bear will deliver me from the spear of this Philistine also!''

Watching David close as he stood before him and marking how his face was lit up and transfigured with the faith and courage of the spirit within him, Saul consented at length to let him go. He glanced at Abner; there was a strange influence in this young man that swept all doubts aside and prevailed over his own ripe judgment.

"Go," he said, "and may the Lord be with thee."

Then he bade his servants bring him his coat of mail and his helmet of bronze. "Thou wilt not venture out unarmed," he said.

There in the king's tent David put on Saul's coat of mail, and his helmet on his head, and girded Saul's sword about the armor as he stood. And the king with his own hand aided him. But Saul was a man of a mighty stature; and thus armed, David essayed in vain to take a pace or two, hoping that he might become accustomed to the burden, for he had never worn the like before. But he could not. He turned with a sigh to the king, and entreated that the armor should be put off him.

He said to the king: "It was in truth a grace of kindness that my lord should array me in his armor, but I cannot wear it, for I am not used to it. Be it the king's will that I go to meet Goliath as I am."

So he went out of Saul's tent with nothing in his hand but his shepherd's staff or club and his sling. When he had gone, Saul turned to Abner, the commander-in-chief of his armies, who had watched all that had passed. He asked him, "Abner, whose son is this youth?"

And Abner said: "As thy soul liveth, O king, I cannot tell."

And Saul bade him make inquiry and discover from whence he came. Then the king and Abner with their officers followed after David to see what would come of his ordeal.

And David, having left the king, made his way back between the clustering tents until he had come out beyond the fringes of the camp. As he continued on his way down into the valley he came to the brook of water that flowed between the rocks in the ravine, warbling amid its stones, and gleaming in its blue in the sunbeams. It was as though he moved in a dream, but a dream marvelously clear, and with all his senses alert. He stooped and chose from out of the brook's cold waters five of the smoothest pebbles on its bed, and in so doing saw the image of his own face reflected there, and it was as though he had never seen its like before. He put the pebbles into the scrip or shepherd's bag he carried, then rose and went on his way.

At the shout that had gone up from the men of Israel at sight of him, the giant who had turned back towards the Philistine camp wheeled and looked about, and knitting his shaggy eyebrows in the glare of the sun, fixed his stare on David as he rose from the brookside and, leaping from boulder to boulder, came on down into the valley. Whereat the champion called back a word over his shoulder to his shield-bearer, and advanced to meet him.

And David, his sling in his hand, the sling with which he was wont to drive off the smaller beasts that pestered his flocks, drew near. The men of Israel fell silent, and the armies, clustered black on either height, watched. In the hush of the valley the skirring of the grass-hoppers in the heat of the morning, and the song of the brook-water brawling in its rocky channel, were the only sounds to be heard.

Astounded and rejoiced that after these many fruitless days there had at last come forth a man of Israel valiant enough to take up his challenge, Goliath snatched his shield from the Philistine who carried it, and stood in wait.

But when he could see his foe clearly and what manner of champion this was, little more than a lad, fair and tanned with the sun, in shepherd's clothes and unarmed, his voice pealed out in mocking laughter, and he cursed him by his gods.

"Am I a carrion dog," he cried, "that thou

comest out against me with nought but a staff in they hand? By the gods of my fathers, do but come a little closer, and I will strip the flesh from off thy body and give it to the fowls of the air, and thy bones to the wild beasts to mumble.''

Even as he spoke there showed black specks in the height of the sky above the mountain-tops, and vulture and kite came circling overhead against the blue above the valley.

Warily David watched the Philistine, and he stepped alertly pace with his pace and well beyond javelin cast, and circled about him so that he should bring the giant face to face with him against the dazzle and blaze of the sun. And as he did so, he made answer to Goliath, calling clearly across in the stillness between them.

''Thou hast come out against me, armed with sword and spear and javelin,'' he cried. ''A brazen shield is on thine arm, and thou art hung head to foot with armour of brass. But if this be all thy strength, beware of it! For I am come out against thee in the name of the Lord of Hosts, the God of the armies of Israel, whom thou hast insulted and defied, and this day the Lord will deliver thee into my hand. And I will smite thee and take thy head from off thy shoulders, and not only thy carcass but the carcasses of the host of the Philistines shall be given this day to the fowls of the air and the beasts of the wild. That all the earth may know there is a God in Israel, and that his salvation is not in sword and spear, nor his battle to the strong, but that he giveth victory according as he decree.''

In rage and fury at these words, Goliath raised himself, towering in his might, his blood roaring in his ears, and with lifted spear strode in to smite his enemy down, and his armour clanged as he trod.

And David drew back lightly from before him. He watched every transient look upon the great flushed bony countenance beneath the crested helmet, now full in the glare of noonday. And softly as he sped on, he drew from out his scrip one after another of the pebbles he had chosen from the brook and poised it in his sling. His first stone rang out sharp upon the champion's breastplate; and the next numbed the hand that held his spear; for David could sling a stone at a hair-breadth, and not miss.

Then of a sudden he turned swiftly, and with the speed of an angel sent from God, ran in towards the giant, whirling his sling above his head as he did so, his gaze fixed gravely on the target of his face. And as he looked, Goliath's heart fainted within him and he was cold as stone. He stood bemused. And David lifted his thumb, set free the stone, and slang it straight at its mark. It whistled through the air, and smote the Philistine in the middle of the forehead, clean between the eyes. The stone sank down into his forehead, and into his brain and, without a groan, the giant fell stunned upon his face upon the ground. The noise of his fall was like the clashing of innumerable cymbals, and the dust above his body rose over him in a cloud.

Before he could stir from the swoon in which he lay, David ran in, and stood over him. And with his two hands he drew the giant's bronze two-bladed sword from out of its sheath, wheeled it with all his might above his shoulders and at a blow smote off Goliath's head.

Then with his two hands he snatched up the helmless matted head and held it high aloft before all Israel. And there went up a cry.

When the Philistines, who had been watching the combat from the heights above, saw that their champion had been defeated and lay prone, dead, and headless upon the ground they fled in terror back towards their camp. A wild clamor arose as the news of the champion's downfall sped on from mouth to mouth; cries of astonishment and fear.

Then sounded the trumpets in the camp of Israel. The Lord had wrought a great salvation, and the men of Israel and the men of Judah, shouting their war cry, swept down into the valley and up the slopes beyond, and stormed the heights of Shochoh. Rank on rank they pressed forward, beating down all resistance, and the Philistine army broke and fled. Westward and north-westward the Israelites pursued them though the valleys and ravines until they came out on to the plain and even to the walls of Ekron and of Gath. Throughout the whole way to Shaaraim the ground was strown with their dead and wounded, to the very gates of the two cities.

Thence the pursuers turned back. And when they had come from chasing after the Philistines, they plundered their tents, a rich booty. Laden with their spoil, they returned to their own camp. And the armor of Goliath was stripped from off his body, and with his spear, his javelin and his sword, was afterwards laid up as a trophy in Jerusalem.

When David himself returned from the pursuit of the Philistines he was brought to Abner, and Abner himself took him into the presence of Saul. And Jonathan was with his father the king. David came in and stood before them, the head of the Philistine in his hand. Saul looked from the one face, wan and swarthy and dark and shut by death, to the other, young and bright with life and aware, and he marveled.

He asked David whose son he was, and many another question. David told him that he was the son of Jesse of Bethlehem. And there returned into Saul's mind, as though it were a dream that had faded out after waking, the memory of the hours when he had lain terrified and distraught in the gloom of his tent, and his only solace had been the music of David's harp-strings.

He said nothing of it, but talked long and earnestly with him, and questioned him. And David answered the king simply and openly, while Jonathan who had been absent from his father during his sickness, stood near at hand, his eyes fixed on David's face, as he mutely drank in every word he uttered. His heart welled over with wonder at his simplicity and fearlessness, and his soul went out to David. He loved him — as do all men who love — at first sight. And he continued to love him, friend with friend, until the last hour of his life.

So great was the love of Jonathan for David that he made a covenant of brotherhood with him, a covenant that in Israel knitted two friends together in mind and spirit closer even than if they had been sons of the same mother.

"Whatever thy soul desireth, that I will indeed do for thee," he said. And in token of it he stripped himself of the cloak which he wore, a cloak befitting the son of a king, and he gave it to David, and his armor also, even to his sword and his bow. And he girdled him with his girdle.

From that day forward Saul took David into his service and made him his armor-bearer, and David returned no more to the house of his father.

When the king, with his captains and his army, laden with the spoil they had taken from the Philistines, returned in triumph from their camp above the valley of Elah and marched to Gibeah, a vast concourse of people gathered together to watch them pass.

And the women and maidens of Israel, clad in their brightest colors, scarlet and blue and purple, came out singing and dancing from all the towns and villages on their way to meet and greet King Saul, and to give him welcome.

To the clash of timbrel and of cymbal and the music of diverse instruments they came dancing in two companies, scattering garlands before the king, singing his praises; and as one company chanted their song of victory, so the other answered them again, shrill and wild and sweet; and the refrain of their song was:

"*Saul hath slain his thousands, but David hath slain his tens of thousands.*"

And Saul's heart sank within him. The words displeased him, and he thought, "To David they have given ten times the praise that they have given to me. What more is wanting to his glory than the kingdom itself?"

From that day forward he was filled with envy of David and looked at him askance. Nevertheless, to the joy and satisfaction of the people and of his own officers, Saul made him the captain of a thousand.

And David was renowned and beloved throughout Israel, for he bore himself wisely in all his ways, and the Lord was with him.

————

From The Sword in the Stone, *by T.H. White (New York: Dell, 1963).*

In the penultimate chapter of T.H. White's unusual novel about the boyhood of King Arthur, the true identity of young Wart (as he has been nicknamed) is revealed: he is the new king. This selection illustrates the unique char-

acteristics of White's adaptation of well-known material: his sensitive portrayal of landscape, his humorous use of anachronisms (notice that Sir Ector has "income property" in London), his careful portrayal of Wart, whom he earlier called, "a born follower . . . a hero-worshiper," and his obvious enjoyment of spectacular scenes. When Arthur prepares to withdraw the sword, he is surrounded by the characters who, earlier in the novel, had been his instructors. After his linear journey, Arthur is no longer a child of unknown origins but an acknowledged leader. White's prose style can be compared to the consciously archaic style employed by Sidney Lanier in "Of Sir Gareth of Orkney."

The Sword in the Stone

The knighting took place in a whirl of preparations. Kay's sumptuous bath had to be set up in the box-room, between two towel-horses and an old box of selected games which contained a worn-out straw dart-board — it was called flechette in those days—because all the other rooms were full of packing. The nurse spent the whole time constructing new warm pants for everybody, on the principle that the climate of any place outside the Forest Sauvage must be treacherous to the extreme, and, as for the sergeant, he polished all the armor till it was quite brittle and sharpened the swords till they were almost worn away.

At last it was time to set out.

Perhaps, if you happen not to have lived in the old England of the fifteenth century, or whenever it was, and in a remote castle on the borders of the Marches at that, you will find it difficult to imagine the wonders of their journey.

The road, or track, ran most of the time along the high ridges of the hills or downs, and they could look down on either side of them upon the desolate marshes where the snowy reeds sighed, and the ice crackled, and the duck in the red sunsets quacked loud on the winter air. The whole country was like that. Perhaps there would be a moory marsh on one side of the ridge, and a forest of thirty thousand acres on the other, with all the great branches

weighted in white. They could sometimes see a wisp of smoke among the trees, or a huddle of buildings far out among the impassable reeds, and twice they came to quite respectable towns which had several inns to boast of; but on the whole it was an England without civilization. The better roads were cleared of cover for a bowshot on either side of them, lest the traveler should be slain by hidden thieves.

They slept where they could, sometimes in the hut of some cottager who was prepared to welcome them, sometimes in the castle of a brother knight who invited them to refresh themselves, sometimes in the firelight and fleas of a dirty little hovel with a bush tied to a pole outside it — this was the sign-board used at that time by inns — and once or twice on the open ground, all huddled together for warmth between their grazing chargers. Wherever they went and wherever they slept, the east wind whistled in the reeds, and the geese went over high in the starlight, honking at the stars.

London was full to the brim. If Sir Ector had not been lucky enough to own a little land in Pie Street, on which there stood a respectable inn, they would have been hard put to it to find a lodging. But he did own it, and as a matter of fact drew most of his dividends from this source, so that they were able to get three beds between the five of them. They thought themselves fortunate.

On the first day of the tournament, Sir Kay managed to get them on the way to the lists at least an hour before the jousts could possibly begin. He had lain awake all night, imagining how he was going to beat the best barons in England, and he had not been able to eat his breakfast. Now he rode at the front of the cavalcade, with pale cheeks, and Wart wished there was something he could do to calm him down.

For country people who only knew the dismantled tilting ground of Sir Ector's castle, the scene which now met their eyes was really ravishing. It was a huge green pit in the earth, about as big as the arena at a football match. It lay about ten feet lower than the surrounding country, with sloping banks, and all the snow had been swept off it. It had been kept warm with straw, which had been cleared off that morning, and now all the close-mown grass sparkled green in the white landscape. Round the arena there was a world of color so dazzling and moving and twinkling as to make you blink your eyes. The wooden grandstands were painted in scarlet and white. The silk pavilions of famous people, pitched on every side, were azure and green and saffron and chequered. The pennons and pennoncells which floated everywhere in the sharp wind were flappng with every color of the rainbow, as they strained and slapped at their flag-poles, and the barrier down the middle of the arena itself was done in chessboard squares of black and white. Most of the combatants and their friends had not yet arrived, but you could see from those few who had arrived how the very people would turn the scene into a bank of flowers, and how the armor would flash, and the scalloped sleeves of the heralds jig in the wind, as they raised their brazen trumpets to their lips to shake the fleecy clouds of winter with joyances and fanfares.

"Good heavens!" cried Sir Kay. "I have left my sword at home."

"Can't joust without a sword," said Sir Grummore. "Quite irregular."

"Better go and fetch it," said Sir Ector. "You have time."

"My squire will do," said Sir Kay. "What a damned mistake to make. Here, squire, ride hard back to the inn and fetch my sword. You shall have a shilling if you fetch it in time."

The Wart went as pale as Sir Kay was, and looked as if he were going to strike him. Then he said, "It shall be done, master," and turned his stupid little ambling palfrey against the stream of newcomers. He began to push his way towards their hostelry as best he might.

"To offer me money!" cried the Wart to himself. "To look down at this beastly little donkey-affair off his great charger and to call me Squire! Oh, Merlyn, give me patience with the brute, and stop me from throwing his filthy shilling in his face."

When he got to the inn it was closed. Everybody had thronged out to see the famous tournament, and the entire household had followed after the mob. Those were lawless days and it was not safe to leave your house — or even to go to sleep in it — unless you were certain that it was impregnable. The wooden shutters bolted over the downstairs windows were two inches thick, and the doors were doublebarred.

"Now what do I do," said the Wart, "to earn my shilling?"

He looked ruefully at the blind little inn, and began to laugh.

"Poor Kay," he said. "All that shilling stuff was only because he was scared and miserable, and now he has good cause to be. Well, he shall have a sword of some sort if I have to break into the Tower of London."

"How does one get hold of a sword?" he continued. "Where can I steal one? Could I waylay some knight, even if I am mounted on an ambling pad, and take his weapons by force? There must be some swordsmith or armorer in a great town like this, whose shop would be still open."

He turned his mount and cantered off along the street.

There was a quiet churchyard at the end of it, with a kind of square in front of the church door. In the middle of the square there was a heavy stone with an anvil on it, and a fine new sword was struck through the anvil.

"Well," said the Wart, "I suppose it's some sort of war memorial, but it will have to do. I am quite sure nobody would grudge Kay a war memorial, if they knew his desperate straits."

He tied his reins round a post of the lychgate, strode up the gravel path, and took hold of the sword.

"Come, sword," he said. "I must cry your mercy and take you for a better cause."

"This is extraordinary," said the Wart. "I feel queer when I have hold of this sword, and I notice everything much more clearly. Look at the beautiful gargoyles of this church, and of the monastery which it belongs to. See how splendidly all the famous banners in the aisle are waving. How nobly that yew holds up the red flakes of its timbers to worship God. How clean the snow is. I can smell something like fetherfew and sweet briar — and is that music that I hear?"

It was music, whether of pan-pipes or of recorders, and the light in the churchyard was so clear, without being dazzling, that you could have picked a pin out twenty yards away.

"There is something in this place," said the Wart. "There are people here. Oh, people, what do you want?"

Nobody answered him, but the music was loud and the light beautiful.

"People," cried the Wart. "I must take this sword. It is not for me, but for Kay. I will bring it back."

There was still no answer, and Wart turned back to the sword. He saw the golden letters on it, which he did not read, and the jewels on its pommel, flashing in the lovely light.

"Come, sword," said the Wart.

He took hold of the handles with both hands, and strained against the stone. There was a melodious consort on the recorders, but nothing moved.

The Wart let go of the handles, when they were beginning to bite into the palms of his hands, and stepped back from the anvil, seeing stars.

"It is well fixed," said the Wart.

He took hold of it again and pulled with all his might. The music played more and more excitedly, and the light all about the churchyard glowed like amethysts; but the sword still stuck.

"Oh, Merlyn," cried the Wart, "help me to get this sword."

There was a kind of rushing noise, and a long chord played along with it. All around the churchyard there were hundreds of old friends. They rose over the church wall all together, like the Punch and Judy ghosts of remembered days, and there were otters and nightingales and vulgar crows and hares and serpents and falcons and fishes and goats and dogs and dainty unicorns and newts and solitary wasps and goatmoth caterpillars and corkindrills and volcanoes and mighty trees and patient stones. They loomed round the church wall, the lovers and helpers of the Wart, and they all spoke solemnly in turn. Some of them had come from the banners in the church, where they were painted in heraldry, some from the waters and the sky and the fields about, but all, down to

the smallest shrew mouse, had come to help on account of love. Wart felt his power grow.

"Remember my biceps," said the Oak, "which can stretch out horizontally against Gravity, when all the other trees go up or down."

"Put your back into it," said a Luce (or pike) off one of the heraldic banners, "as you did once when I was going to snap you up. Remember that all power springs from the nape of the neck."

"What about those forearms," asked a Badger gravely, "that are held together by a chest? Come along, my dear embryo, and find your tool."

A Merlin sitting at the top of the yew tree cried out, "Now then, Captain Wart, what is the first law of the foot? I thought I once heard something about never letting go?"

"Don't work like a stalling woodpecker," urged a Tawny Owl affectionately. "Keep up a steady effort, my duck, and you will have it yet."

"Cohere," said a Stone in the church wall.

A Snake, slipping easily along the coping which bounded the holy earth, said, "Now then, Wart, if you were once able to walk with three hundred ribs at once, surely you can co-ordinate a few little muscles here and there? Make everything work together, as you have been learning to do ever since God let the amphibia crawl out of the sea. Fold your powers together, with the spirit of your mind, and it will come out like butter. Come along, homo sapiens, for all we humble friends of yours are waiting here to cheer."

The Wart walked up to the great sword for the third time. He put out his right hand softly and drew it out as gently as from a scabbard.

There was a lot of cheering, a noise like a hurdy-gurdy which went on and on. In the middle of this noise, after a very long time, he saw Kay and gave him the sword. The people at the tournament were making a frightful row.

"But this isn't my sword," said Sir Kay.

"It was the only one I could get," said the Wart. "The inn was locked."

"It is a nice-looking sword. Where did you get it?"

"I found it stuck in a stone, outside a

church."

Sir Kay had been watching the tilting nervously, waiting for his turn. He had not paid much attention to his squire.

"That's a funny place to find a sword," he said.

"Yes, it was stuck through an anvil."

"What? cried Sir Kay, suddenly rounding upon him. "Did you just say this sword was stuck in a stone?"

"It was," said the Wart. "It was a sort of war memorial."

Sir Kay stared at him for several seconds in amazement, opened his mouth, shut it again, licked his lips, then turned his back and plunged through the crowd. He was looking for Sir Ector, and the Wart followed after him.

"Father," cried Sir Kay, "come here a moment."

"Yes, my boy," said Sir Ector. "Splendid falls these professional chaps do manage. Why, what's the matter, Kay? You look as white as a sheet."

"Do you remember that sword which the King of England would pull out?"

"Yes."

"Well, here it is. I have it. It is in my hand. I pulled it out."

Sir Ector did not say anything silly. He looked at Kay and he looked at the Wart. Then he stared at Kay again, long and lovingly, and said, "We will go back to the church."

"Now then, Kay," he said, when they were at the church door. He looked at his first-born again, kindly, but straight between the eyes. "Here is the stone, and you have the sword. It will make you the King of England. You are my son that I am proud of, and always will be, whatever happens. Will you promise me that you took it out by your own might?"

Kay looked at his father. He also looked at the Wart and at the sword.

Then he handed the sword to the Wart quite quietly.

He said, "I am a liar. Wart pulled it out."

As far as the Wart was concerned, there was a time after this in which sir Ector kept telling him to put the sword back into the stone — which he did — and in which Sir Ector and Kay then vainly tried to take it out. The Wart took

it out for them, and struck it back again once or twice. After this, there was another time which was more painful.

He saw that his dear guardian Sir Ector was looking quite old and powerless, and that he was kneeling down with difficulty on a gouty old knee.

"Sir," said poor old sir Ector, without looking up, although he was speaking to his own boy.

"Please don't do this, father," said the Wart, kneeling down also. "Let me help you up, Sir Ector, because you are making me unhappy."

"Nay, nay, my lord," said Sir Ector, with some very feeble old tears. "I was never your father nor of your blood, but I wote well ye are of an higher blood than I wend ye were."

"Plenty of people have told me you are not my father, said the Wart, "but it doesn't matter a bit."

"Sir," said Sir Ector humbly, "will ye be my good and gracious lord when ye are King?"

"Don't!" said the Wart.

"Sir," said Sir Ector, "I will ask no more of you but that you will make my son, your foster-brother, Sir Kay, seneschal of all your lands."

Kay was kneeling down too, and it was more than the Wart could bear.

"Oh, do stop," he cried. "Of course he can be seneschal, if I have got to be this King, and, oh, father, don't kneel down like that, because it breaks my heart. Please get up, Sir Ector, and don't make everything so horrible. Oh, dear, oh, dear, I wish I had never seen that filthy sword at all."

And the Wart also burst into tears.

———

"Of Sir Gareth of Orkney" from The Boy's King Arthur *by Sidney Lanier (New York: Scribner's, 1952).*

Before a young hero achieves full maturity, he must usually undergo a series of tests. In this story, Gareth emerges victorious not only because he has defeated the various knights, but also because he has endured the humiliating taunts of Sir Kay and the Lady Linet. As is the case for many heroes, includ-

ing his own king, Arthur, Gareth's identity is unknown until he has proved himself. Only then does he lose his nickname, Beaumains, applied condescendingly by others. Lanier drew his story from Le Morte d'Arthur *(fifteenth century) by Sir Thomas Malory, adapting it for younger readers. The result is a tale more tightly unified than those generally found in the traditional Arthurian legends.*

Of Sir Gareth of Orkney

When Arthur held his Round Table most fully, it fortuned that he commanded that the high feast of Pentecost should be holden at a city and a castle, the which in those days was called King-Kenadon, upon the sands that marched [*bordered*] nigh Wales. So ever the king had a custom that at the feast of Pentecost, in especial afore other feasts in the year, he would not go that day to meat until he had heard or seen of a great marvel. And for that custom all manner of strange adventures came before Arthur as at that feast before all other feasts. And so Sir Gawaine, a little before noon of the day of Pentecost, espied at a window three men upon horseback and a dwarf on foot. And so the three men alighted, and the dwarf kept their horses, and one of the three men was higher than the other twain by a foot and a half. Then Sir Gawaine went unto the king and said, "Sir, go to your meat, for here at hand come strange adventures."

So Arthur went unto his meat with many other kings. And there were all the knights of the Round Table, save those that were prisoners or slain at a rencounter. Then at the high feast evermore they should be fulfilled the whole number of an hundred and fifty, for then was the Round Table fully accomplished. Right so came into the hall two men well beseen and richly, and upon their shoulders there leaned the goodliest young man and the fairest that ever they all saw, and he was large and long, and broad in the shoulders, and well visaged, and the fairest and the largest handed that ever man saw, but he fared as though he might not go nor bear himself but if he leaned upon their shoulders. Anon as Arthur saw him, there was made peace [*silence*] and room, and right so

they went with him unto the high dais, without saying of any words. Then this big young man pulled him aback, and easily stretched up straight, saying, "King Arthur, God you bless, and all your fair fellowship, and in especial the fellowship of the Table Round. And for this cause I am come hither, to pray you and require you to give me three gifts, and they shall not be unreasonably asked, but that ye may worshipfully and honorably grant them me, and to you no great hurt nor loss. And as for the first gift I will ask now, and the other two gifts I will ask this day twelvemonth wheresoever ye hold your high feast."

"Now ask," said Arthur, "and ye shall have your asking."

"Now, sir, this is my petition for this feast, that ye will give me meat and drink sufficiently for this twelvemonth, and at that day I will ask mine other two gifts."

"My fair son," said Arthur, "ask better, I counsel thee, for this is but a simple asking, for my heart giveth me to thee greatly that thou art come of men of worship, and greatly my conceit faileth me but thou shalt prove a man of right great worship."

"Sir," said he, "thereof be as it may, I have asked that I will ask."

"Well," said the king, "ye shall have meat and drink enough, I never defended that none, neither my friend nor my foe. But what is thy name I would wit?"

"I cannot tell you," said he.

"That is marvel," said the king, "that thou knowest not thy name, and thou art the goodliest young man that ever I saw."

Then the king betook him to Sir Kay, the steward, and charged him that he should give him of all manner of meats and drinks of the best, and also that he had all manner of finding as though he were a lord's son.

"That shall little need," said Sir Kay, "to do such cost upon him; for I dare undertake he is a villain born, and never will make man, for and he had come of gentlemen he would have asked of you horse and armor, but such as he is, so he asketh. And since he hath no name, I shall give him a name: that shall be Beaumains, that is Fairhands, and into the kitchen I shall bring him, and there he shall have fat browis [*broth*] every day, that he shall be as fat by the twelvemonth's end as a pork hog.''

Right so the two men departed, and left him to Sir Kay, that scorned him and mocked him.

Thereat was Sir Gawaine wroth, and in especial Sir Launcelot bade Sir Kay leave his mocking, ''for I dare lay my head he shall prove a man of great worship.''

''Let be,'' said Sir Kay, ''it may not be, by no reason, for as he is, so hath he asked.''

''Beware,'' said Sir Launcelot; ''so ye gave the good knight Brewnor, Sir Dinadan's brother, a name, and ye called him La Cote Mal Taile, and that turned you to anger afterward.''

''As for that,'' said Sir Kay, ''this shall never prove none such; for Sir Brewnor desired ever worship, and this desireth bread and drink, and broth; upon pain of my life he was fostered up in some abbey, and, howsoever it was, they failed meat and drink, and so hither he is come for his sustenance.''

And so Sir Kay bade get him a place and sit down to meat, so Beaumains went to the hall door, and set him down among boys and lads, and there he eat sadly. And then Sir Launcelot after meat bade him come to his chamber, and there he should have meat and drink enough. And so did Sir Gawaine, but he refused them all; he would do none other but as Sir Kay commanded him, for no proffer. But as touching Sir Gawaine, he had reason to proffer him lodging, meat, and drink, for that proffer came of his blood, for he was nearer kin to him than he wist. But that Sir Launcelot did was of his great gentleness and courtesy. So thus he was put into the kitchen, and lay nightly as the boys of the kitchen did. And so he endured all that twelvemonth, and never displeased man nor child, but always he was meek and mild. But ever when he saw any jousting of knights, that would he see and he might. And ever Sir Launcelot would give him gold to spend, and clothes, and so did Sir Gawaine. And where were any masteries done thereat would he be, and there might none cast the bar or stone to him by two yards. Then would Sir Kay say, ''How like you my boy of the kitchen?'' So it passed on till the feast of Pentecost, and at that time the king held it at Caerleon, in the most

royallest wise that might be, like as yearly he did. But the king would eat no meat on the Whitsunday till he had heard of some adventure. And then came there a squire to the king, and said, ''Sir, ye may go to your meat, for here cometh a damsel with some strange adventure.'' Then was the king glad, and set him down. Right so there came in a damsel, and saluted the king, and prayed him for succor.

''For whom?'' said the king: ''what is the adventure?''

''Sir,'' said she, ''I have a lady of great worship and renown, and she is besieged with a tyrant, so that she may not go out of her castle, and because that here in your court are called the noblest knights of the world, I come unto you and pray you for succor.''

''What call ye your lady, and where dwelleth she, and who is he and what is his name that hath besieged her?''

''Sir king,'' said she, ''as for my lady's name, that shall not be known for me as at this time; but I let you wit she is a lady of great worship, and of great lands. And as for the tyrant that besiegeth her and destroyeth her land, he is called the Red Knight of the Red Lawns.''

''I know him not,'' said the king.

''Sir,'' said Sir Gawaine, ''I know him well, for he is one of the perilous knights of the world; men say that he hath seven men's strength, and from him I escaped once full hard with my life.''

''Fair damsel,'' said the king, ''there be knights here that would do their power to rescue your lady, but because ye will not tell her name nor where she dwelleth, therefore none of my knights that be here now shall go with you by my will.''

''Then must I speak further,'' said the damsel.

Then with these words came before the king Beaumains, while the damsel was there; and thus he said: ''Sir king, God thank you, I have been this twelve months in your kitchen, and have had my full sustenance, and now I will ask my two gifts that be behind.''

''Ask upon my peril,'' said the king.

''Sir, these shall be my two gifts: first, that ye will grant me to have this adventure of the damsel, for it belongeth to me.''

"Thou shalt have it," said the king; "I grant it thee."

"Then, sir, this is now the other gift: that ye shall bid Sir Launcelot du Lake to make me a knight, for of him I will be made knight, and else of none; and when I am passed, I pray you let him ride after me, and make me knight when I require him."

"All this shall be done," said the king.

"Fie on thee," said the damsel; "shall I have none but one that is your kitchen page?"

Then was she wroth, and took her horse and departed. And with that there came one to Beaumains, and told him that his horse and armor was come for him, and there was a dwarf come with all things that him needed in the richest manner. Thereat all the court had much marvel from whence came all that gear. So when he was armed, there was none but few so goodly a man as he was. And right so he came into the hall, and took his leave of King Arthur and of Sir Gawaine, and of Sir Launcelot, and prayed him that he would hie after him; and so departed and rode after the damsel.

But there went many after to behold how well he was horsed and trapped in cloth of gold, but he had neither shield nor spear. Then Sir Kay said openly in the hall: "I will ride after my boy of the kitchen, for to wit [*know*] whether he will know me for his better."

Sir Launcelot and Sir Gawaine said, "Yet abide at home."

So Sir Kay made him ready, and took his horse and his spear, and rode after him. And right as Beaumains overtook the damsel, right so came Sir Kay, and said, "Beaumains, what sir, know ye not me?"

Then he turned his horse, and knew it was Sir Kay, that had done him all the despite as ye have heard afore.

"Yea," said Beaumains, "I know you for an ungentle knight of the court, and therefore beware of me."

Therewith Sir Kay put his spear in the rest and ran straight upon him, and Beaumains came as fast upon him with his sword in his hand; and so he put away his spear with his sword, and with a foin [*feint*] thrust him through the side, that Sir Kay fell down as he had been dead, and he alighted down and took

Sir Kay's shield and his spear, and started upon his own horse, and rode his way. All that saw Sir Launcelot, and so did the damsel. And then he bade his dwarf start upon Sir Kay's horse, and so he did. By that Sir Launcelot was come. Then he proffered Sir Launcelot to joust, and either made them ready, and came together so fiercely that either bare down other to the earth, and sore were they bruised. Then Sir Launcelot arose and helped him from his horse. And then Beaumains threw his shield from him, and proffered to fight with Sir Launcelot on foot, and so they rushed together like boars, tracing, racing, and foining, to the mountenance [*amount*] of an hour, and Sir Launcelot felt him so big that he marvelled of his strength, for he fought more like a giant than a knight, and that his fighting was durable and passing perilous. For Sir Launcelot had so much ado with him that he dreaded himself to be shamed, and said, "Beaumains, fight not so sore, your quarrel and mine is not so great but we may leave off."

"Truly, that is truth," said Beaumains, "but it doth me good to feel your might, and yet, my lord, I showed not the uttermost."

"Well," said Sir Launcelot, "for I promise you by the faith of my body I had as much to do as I might to save myself from you unshamed, and therefore have ye no doubt of none earthly knight."

"Hope ye so that I may any while stand a proved knight?" said Beaumains.

"Yea," said Launcelot, "do ye as ye have done, and I shall be your warrant."

"Then, I pray you," said Beaumains, "give me the order of knighthood."

"Then must ye tell me your name," said Launcelot, "and of what kin ye be born."

"Sir, so that ye will not discover me I shall," said Beaumains.

"Nay," said Sir Launcelot, "and that I promise you by the faith of my body, until it be openly known."

"Then, Sir," he said, "my name is Gareth, and brother unto Sir Gawaine, of father and mother."

"Ah! Sir," said Launcelot, "I am more gladder of you than I was, for ever me thought ye should be of great blood, and that ye came not to the court neither for meat nor for drink."

And then Sir Launcelot gave him the order of knighthood. And then Sir Gareth prayed him for to depart, and let him go. So Sir Launcelot departed from him and came to Sir Kay, and made him to be borne home upon his shield, and so he as healed hard with the life, and all men scorned Sir Kay, and in especial Sir Gawaine and Sir Launcelot said it was not his part to rebuke [any] young man, for full little knew he of what birth he is come, and for what cause he came to this court. And so we leave off Sir Kay and turn we unto Beaumains. When he had overtaken the damsel anon she said, "What dost thou there? thou stinkest all of the kitchen, thy clothes be foul of the grease and tallow that thou gainedst in King Arthur's kitchen; weenest thou," said she, "that I allow thee for yonder knight that thou killedst? Nay truly, for thou slewest him unhappily and cowardly, therefore return again, kitchen page. I know thee well, for Sir Kay named thee Beaumains. What art thou but a turner of broaches and a washer of dishes!"

"Damsel," said Sir Beaumains, "say to me what ye list, I will not go from you whatsoever ye say, for I have undertaken of King Arthur for to achieve your adventure, and I shall finish it to the end, or I shall die therefor."

"Fie on thee, kitchen knave. Wilt thou finish mine adventure? thou shalt anon be met withal, that thou wouldest not, for all the broth that ever thou suppest, once look him in the face."

"I shall assay," said Beaumains. So as they thus rode in the wood, there came a man flying all that he might.

"Whither wilt thou?" said Beaumains.

"O Lord," said he, "help me, for hereby in a slade are six thieves which have taken my lord and bound him, and I am afraid lest they will slay him."

"Bring me thither," said Sir Beaumains.

And so they rode together till they came there as the knight was bound; and then he rode unto the thieves, and struck one at the first stroke to death, and then another, and at the third stroke he slew the third thief; and then the other three fled, and he rode after and overtook them, and then those three thieves turned again and hard assailed Sir Beaumains; but at the last he slew them; and then returned and unbound the knight. And the knight thanked him, and prayed him to ride with him to his castle there a little beside, and he should worshipfully reward him for his good deeds.

"Sir," said Sir Beaumains, "I will no reward have; I was this day made knight of the noble Sir Launcelot, and therefore I will have no reward, but God reward me. And also I must follow this damsel."

And when he came nigh her, she bade him ride from her, "for thou smellest all of the kitchen. Weenest thou that I have joy of thee? for all this deed that thou hast done is but mishappened thee. But thou shalt see a sight that shall make thee to turn again, and that lightly."

[Then all the next day] this Beaumains rode with that lady till even-song time, and ever she chid him and would not rest. And then they came to a black lawn, and there was a black hawthorn, and thereon hung a black banner, and on the other side there hung a black shield, and by it stood a black spear and a long, and a great black horse covered with silk, and a black stone fast by it.

There sat a knight all armed in black harness, and his name was the Knight of the Black Lawns. When the damsel saw the black knight, she bade Sir Beaumains flee down the valley, for his horse was not saddled.

"I thank you," said Sir Beaumains, "for always ye will have me a coward."

With that the black knight came to the damsel, and said, "Fair damsel, have ye brought this knight from King Arthur's court to be your champion?"

"Nay, fair knight," said she, "this is but a kitchen knave, that hath been fed in King Arthur's kitchen for alms."

"Wherefore cometh he in such array?" said the knight: "it is great shame that he beareth you company."

"Sir, I cannot be delivered of him," said the damsel, "for with me he rideth maugre [*in spite of*] mine head; would to God ye would put him from me, or else to slay him if ye may, for he is an unhappy knave, and unhappy hath he done to-day through misadventure; for I saw him slay two knights at the passage of the water, and other deeds he did before right marvellous, and all through unhappiness."

"That marvelleth me," said the black knight, "that any man the which is of worship will have to do with him."

"Sir, they know him not," said the damsel, "and because he rideth with me they think he is some man of worship born."

"That may be," said the black knight, "howbeit, as ye say that he be no man of worship, he is a full likely person, and full like to be a strong man; but thus much shall I grant you," said the black knight, "I shall put him down upon his feet, and his horse and his harness he shall leave with me, for it were shame to me to do him any more harm."

When Sir Beaumains heard him say thus, he said, "Sir knight, thou art full liberal of my horse and my harness. I let thee wit it cost thee nought, and whether it liketh thee or not this lawn will I pass, maugre thine head, and horse nor harness gettest thou none of me, but if thou win them with thy hands; and therefore let see what thou canst do."

"Sayst thou that?" said the black knight, "now yield thy lady from thee, for it beseemeth never a kitchen page to ride with such a lady."

"Thou liest," said Beaumains, "I am a gentleman born, and of more high lineage than thou, and that will I prove on thy body."

Then in great wrath they departed with their horses, and came together as it had been the thunder; and the black knight's spear brake, and Beaumains thrust him through both sides, and therewith his spear brake, and the truncheon left still in his side. But nevertheless the black knight drew his sword, and smote many eager strokes and of great might, and hurt Beaumains full sore. But at the last the black knight within an hour and a half he fell down off his horse in a swoon, and there he died. And then Beaumains saw him so well horsed and armed, then he alighted down, and armed him in his armor, and so took his horse, and rode after the damsel. When she saw him come nigh, she said, "Away, kitchen knave, out of the wind, for the smell of thy foul clothes grieveth me. Alas," she said, "that ever such a knave as thou art should by mishap slay so good

Illustration by N.C. Wyeth from *The Boy's King Arthur,* edited by Sidney Lanier. Copyright © 1917 by N.C. Wyeth. Reprinted with the permission of Charles Scribner's Sons.

a knight as thou hast done, but all this is thine unhappiness. But hereby is one shall pay thee all they payment, and therefore yet I counsel thee, flee."

"It may happen me," said Beaumains, "to be beaten or slain, but I warn you, fair damsel, I will not flee away for him, nor leave your company for all that ye can say; for ever ye say that they slay me or beat me, but how soever it happeneth I escape, and they lie on the ground, and therefore it were as good for you to hold you still, than thus to rebuke me all day, for away will I not till I feel the uttermost of this journey, or else I will be slain or truly beaten; therefore ride on your way, for follow you I will, whatsoever happen."

Thus as they rode together they saw a knight come driving by them all in green, both his horse and his harness, and when he came nigh the damsel he asked of her, "Is that my brother, the black knight, that ye have brought with you?"

"Nay, nay," said she, "this unhappy kitchen

knave hath slain your brother through unhappiness.''

"Alas!" said the green knight, "that is great pity that so noble a knight as he was should so unhappily be slain, and namely of a knave's hand, as ye say he is. Ah, traitor!" said the green knight, "thou shalt die for slaying of my brother; he was a full noble knight, and his name was Sir Periard.''

"I defy thee," said Sir Beaumains, "for I let thee to wit I slew him knightly, and not shamefully.''

Therewithal the green knight rode unto an horn that was green, and it hung upon a thorn, and there he blew three deadly notes, and there came three damsels that lightly armed him. And then took he a great horse, and a green shield and a green spear. And then they ran together with all their mights, and brake their spears unto their hands. And then they drew their swords, and gave many sad strokes, and either of them wounded other full ill. And at the last at an overthwart Beaumains' horse struck the green knight's horse upon the side [that] he fell to the earth. And then the green knight avoided his horse lightly, and dressed him upon foot. That saw Beaumains, and therewithal he alighted, and they rushed together like two mighty champions a long while, and sore they bled both. With that came the damsel and said, "My lord the green knight, why for shame stand ye so long fighting with the kitchen knave? Alas, it is shame that ever ye were made knight, to see such a lad match such a knight as the weed overgrew the corn.''

Therewith the green knight was ashamed, and therewithal he gave a great stroke of might, and clave his shield through. When Beaumains saw his shield cloven asunder he was a little ashamed of that stroke, and of her language; and then he gave him such a buffet upon the helm that he fell on his knees; and so suddenly Beaumains pulled him upon the the ground grovelling. And then the green knight cried him mercy, and yielded him unto Sir Beaumains, and prayed him to slay him not.

"All is in vain," said Beaumains, "for thou shalt die, but if this damsel that came with me pray me to save thy life.''

And therewithal he unlaced his helm, like as he would slay him.

"Fie upon thee, false kitchen page, I will never pray thee to save his life, for I never will be so much in thy danger.''

"Then shall he die," said Beaumains.

"Not so hardy, thou foul knave," said the damsel, "that thou slay him.''

"Alas," said the green knight, "suffer me not to die, for a fair word may save my life. O fair knight," said the green knight, "save my life, and I will forgive the death of my brother, and for ever to become thy man, and thirty knights that hold of me for ever shall do you service.''

Said the damsel, "That such a kitchen knave should have thee and thirty knights' service!''

"Sir knight," said Sir Beaumains, "all this availeth not, but if my damsel speak with me for thy life.''

And therewithal he made resemblance to slay him.

"Let be," said the damsel, "thou knave, slay him not, for if thou do, thou shalt repent it.''

"Damsel," said Sir Beaumains, "your charge is to me a pleasure, and at your commandment his life shall be saved, and else not.''

Then he said, "Sir knight with the green arms, I release thee quit [*acquitted*] at this damsel's request, for I will not make her wroth, I will fulfil all that she chargeth me.''

And then the green knight kneeled down and did him homage with his sword.

And always the damsel rebuked Sir Beaumains. And so that night they went unto rest, and all that night the green knight commanded thirty knights privily to watch Beaumains, for to keep him from all treason. And so on the morn they all arose, and heard their mass and brake their fast, and then they took their horses and rode on their way, and the green knight conveyed them through the forest, and there the green knight said, "My lord Beaumains, I and these thirty knights shall be alway at your summons, both early and late, at your calling, and where that ever ye will send us.''

"It is well said," said Beaumains; "when that I call upon you ye must yield you unto King Arthur and all your knights.''

"If that ye so command us, we shall be

ready at all times,'' said the green knight.

"Fie, fie upon thee,'' said the damsel, "that any good knights should be obedient unto a kitchen knave.''

So then departed the green knight and the damsel. And then she said unto Beaumains, "Why followest thou me, thou kitchen boy, cast away thy shield and thy spear and flee away, yet I counsel thee betimes, or thou shalt say right soon, Alas!''

"Damsel,'' said Sir Beaumains, "ye are uncourteous so to rebuke me as ye do, for meseemeth I have done you great service, and ever ye threaten me for I shall be beaten with knights that we meet, but ever for all your boast they lie in the dust or in the mire, and therefore I pray you rebuke me no more; and when ye see me beaten or yielden as recreant, then may ye bid me go from you shamefully, but first I let you wit I will not depart from you, for I were worse than a fool and I would depart from you all the while that I win worship.''

"Well,'' said she, "right soon there shall meet a knight shall pay thee all thy wages, for he is the most man of worship of the world, except King Arthur.''

"I will well,'' said Beaumains; "the more he is of worship the more shall be my worship to have ado with him.''

Then anon they were ware where was before them a city rich and fair. And betwixt them and the city a mile and a half there was a fair meadow that seemed new mown, and therein were many pavilions fair to behold.

"Lo,'' said the damsel, "yonder is a lord that owneth yonder city, and his custom is when the weather is fair to lie in this meadow to joust and tourney; and ever there be about him five hundred knights and gentlemen of arms, and there be all manner of games that any gentleman can devise.''

"That goodly lord,'' said Beaumains, "would I fain see.''

"Thou shalt see him time enough,'' said the damsel.

And so as she rode near she espied the pavilion where he was.

"Lo,'' said she, "seest thou yonder pavilion, that is all of the color of Inde, and all manner of thing that there is about, men and women, and horses trapped, shields and spears, all of the color of Inde, and his name is Sir Persant of Inde, the most lordliest knight that ever thou lookedst on.''

"It may well be,'' said Beaumains, "but be he never so stout a knight, in this field I shall abide till that I see him under his shield.''

"Ah, fool,'' said she, "thou wert better flee betimes.''

"Why,'' said Beaumains, "and he be such a knight as ye make him, he will not set upon me with all his men, or with his five hundred knights. For and there come no more but one at once, I shall him not fail whilst my life lasteth.''

"Fie, fie,'' said the damsel, "that ever such a dirty knave should blow such a boast.''

Damsel,'' he said, "Ye are to blame so to rebuke me, for I had liever do five battles than so to be rebuked; let him come, and then let him do his worst.''

"Sir,'' she said, "I marvel what thou art, and of what kin thou art come: boldly thou speakest, and boldly thou has done, that have I seen: therefore I pray thee save thyself and thou mayest, for thy horse and thou have had great travail, and I dread we dwell over long from the siege, for it is but hence seven mile, and all perilous passages we are past, save all only this passage, and here I dread me sore lest ye shall catch some hurt, therefore I would ye were hence, that ye were not bruised nor hurt with this strong knight. But I let you wit this Sir Persant of Inde is nothing of might nor strength unto the knight that laid the siege about my lady.''

"As for that,'' said Sir Beaumains, "be it as it may; for since I am come so nigh this knight I will prove his might or [*ere*] I depart from him, and else I shall be shamed and [*if*] I now withdraw me from him. And therefore, damsel, have ye no doubt by the grace of God I shall so deal with this knight, that within two hours after noon I shall deliver him, and then shall we come to the siege by daylight.''

"Oh, mercy, marvel have I,'' said the damsel, "what manner a man ye be, for it may never be otherwise but that ye be come of a noble blood, for so foul and shamefully did never woman rule a knight as I have done you, and ever courteously ye have suffered me, and that came never but of a gentle blood.''

"Damsel," said Beaumains, "a knight may little do that may not suffer a damsel; for whatsoever ye said unto me I took none heed to your words, for the more ye said the more ye angered me, and my wrath I wreaked upon them that I had ado withal. And therefore all the missaying that ye missayed me furthered me in my battle, and caused me to think to show and prove myself at the end what I was; for peradventure though I had meat in King Arthur's kitchen, yet I might have had meat enough in other places; but all that I did for to prove my friends; and whether I be a gentleman born or no, fair damsel, I have done you gentleman's service, and peradventure better service yet will I do you or [*before*] I depart from you."

"Alas," said she, "fair Beaumains, forgive me all that I have missaid and misdone against you."

"With all my heart," said Sir Beaumains, "I forgive it you, for ye did nothing but as ye ought to do, for all your evil words pleased me; and, damsel," said Sir Beaumains, "sith [*since*] it liketh you to speak thus fair to me, wit ye well it gladdeth greatly mine heart; and now meseemeth there is no knight living but I am able enough for him."

With this Sir Persant of Inde had espied them, as they hoved [*hovered*] in the field, and knightly he sent to them to know whether he came in war or in peace.

"Say unto thy lord," said Sir Beaumains, "I take no force, but whether as him list himself."

So the messenger went again unto Sir Persant, and told him all his answer.

"Well," said he, "then will I have ado with him to the uttermost;" and so he purveyed him [*prepared himself*], and rode against him. And when Sir Beaumains saw him, he made him ready, and there they met with all the might that their horses might run, and brake their spears either in three pieces, and their horses rashed so together that both their horses fell dead to the earth; and lightly they avoided their horses, and put their shields before them, and drew their swords, and gave each other many great strokes, that sometime they so hurled together that they fell both grovelling on the ground. Thus they fought two hours and more, that their shields and their hauberks were all forhewen [*hewn to pieces*] and in many places they were sore wounded. So at the last Sir Beaumains smote him through the cost [*rib part*] of the body, and then he retrayed him [*drew back*] here and there, and knightly maintained his battle long time. And at the last Sir Beaumains smote Sir Persant on the helm that he fell grovelling to the earth, and then he leaped overthwart [*across*] upon him, and unlaced his helm for to have slain him. Then Sir Persant yielded him, and asked him mercy. With that came the damsel and prayed him to save his life.

"I will well," said Sir Beaumains, "for it were pity that this noble knight should die."

Gramercy," said Sir Persant, "gentle knight and damsel, for certainly now I know well it was you that slew the black knight my brother at the blackthorn; he was a full noble knight, his name was Sir Periard. Also I am sure that ye are he that won mine other brother the green knight: his name was Sir Pertolope. Also ye won the red knight, my brother, Sir Perimones. And now, sir, sith ye have won these knights, this shall I do for to please you: ye shall have homage and fealty of me, and an hundred knights to be always at your command, to go and ride where ye will command us."

And so they went unto Sir Persant's pavilion, and there he drank wine and eat spices. And afterward Sir Persant made him to rest upon a bed till it was supper time, and after supper to bed again. And so we leave him there till on the morrow.

Now leave we the knight and the dwarf, and speak we of Beaumains, that all night lay in the hermitage, and upon the morn he and the damsel Linet heard their mass, and brake their fast. And then they took their horses and rode throughout a fair forest, and then they came to a plain, and saw where many pavilions and tents, and a fair castle, and there was much smoke and great noise. And when they came near the siege Sir Beaumains espied upon great trees, as he rode, how there hung fully goodly armed knights by the neck, and their shields about their necks with their swords, and gilt spurs upon their heels, and so there hung shamefully nigh forty knights with rich arms. Then Sir Beaumains abated his countenance, and said, "What thing meaneth this?"

"Fair sir," saith the damsel, "abate not your cheer for all this sight, for ye must encourage yourself, or else ye be all shent [*ruined*], for all these knights came hither unto this siege to rescue my sister dame Lyoness, and when the red knight of the red lawns had overcome them, he put them to this shameful death, without mercy and pity, and in the same wise he will serve you, but if ye quit [*acquit*] you the better."

"Now Jesu defend me," said Sir Beaumains, "from such a villanous death and shenship [*disgrace*] of arms! for rather than thus I should fare withal, I would rather be slain manfully in plain battle."

"So were ye better," said the damsel, "trust not in him, for in him is no courtesy, but all goeth to the death or shameful murder, and that is great pity, for he is a full likely man and well made of body, and a full noble knight of prowess, and a lord of great lands and possessions."

"Truly," said Sir Beaumains, "he may well be a good knight, but he useth shameful customs, and it is great marvel that he endureth so long, that none of the noble knights of my lord King Arthur's court have not dealt with him."

And then they rode unto the ditches, and saw them double ditched with full strong walls, and there were lodged many great estates and lords nigh the walls, and there was great noise of minstrels, and the sea beat upon the one side of the walls, where as were many ships and mariners' noise with hale and how.[1] And also there was fast by a sycamore tree, and thereon hung an horn, the greatest that ever they saw, of an elephant's bone.

"And this knight of the red lawns hath hanged it up there, that if there come any errant knight, he must blow that horn, and then will he make him ready, and come to him to do battle. But sir, I pray you," said the damsel Linet, "blow ye not the horn till it be

[1] "Hale and how," *haul and ho*: the sailors' cries in hoisting away, &c.

high noon, for now it is about prime, and now increaseth his might, that, as men say, he hath seven men's strength."

"Ah, fie for shame, fair damsel, say ye never so more to me, for, and he were as good a knight as ever was, I shall never fail him in his most might, for either I will win worship worshipfully, or die knightly in the field."

And therewith he spurred his horse straight to the sycamore tree and blew the horn so eagerly that all the siege and the castle rang thereof. And then there leaped our knights out of their tents and pavilions, and they within the castle looked over the walls and out at windows. Then the red knight of the red lawns armed him hastily, and two barons set on his spurs upon his heels, and all was blood-red, his armor, spear, and shield. And an earl buckled his helm upon his head, and then they brought him a red spear and a red steed, and so he rode into a little vale under the castle, that all that were in the castle and at the siege might behold the battle.

"Sir," said the damsel Linet unto Sir Beaumains, "look ye be glad and light, for yonder is your deadly enemy, and at yonder window is my lady my sister, dame Lyoness."

"Where?" said Beaumains.

"Yonder," said the damsel, and pointed with her finger.

"That is truth," said Beaumains. "She seemeth afar the fairest lady that ever I looked upon, and truly," he said, "I ask no better quarrel than now for to do battle, for truly she shall be my lady, and for her I will fight."

And ever he looked up to the window with glad countenance. And the lady Lyoness made courtesy to him down to the earth, with holding up both her hands. With that the red knight of the red lawns called to Sir Beaumains, "Leave, sir knight, thy looking, and behold me, I counsel thee, for I warn thee well she is my lady, and for her I have done many strong battles."

"If thou have so done," said Beaumains, "meseemeth it was but waste labor, for she loveth none of thy fellowship, and thou to love that loveth not thee, is a great folly. For if I understood that she were not glad of my coming, I would be advised or I did battle for her, but I understand by the besieging of this castle she may forbear thy company. And therefore wit thou well, thou red knight of the red lawns, I love her and will rescue her, or else die in the quarrel."

"Sayest thou that?" said the red knight; "me seemeth thou ought of reason to beware by yonder knights that thou sawest hang upon yonder great elms."

"Fie, fie, for shame," said Sir Beaumains, "that ever thou shouldest say or do so evil and such shamefulness, for in that thou shamest thyself and the order of knighthood, and thou mayst be sure there will no lady love thee that knoweth thy detestable customs. And now thou weenest [*thinkest*] that the sight of these hanged knights should fear [*scare*] me and make me aghast, nay truly not so, that shameful sight causeth me to have courage and hardiness against thee, more than I would have had against thee and if thou be a well ruled knight."

"Make thee ready," said the red knight of the red lawns, "and talk no longer with me."

Then Sir Beaumains bade the damsel go from him, and then they put their spears in their rests, and came together with all the might they had, and either smote other in the midst of their shields, that the paytrels [*breast-plates*], surcingles, and cruppers burst, and fell both to the ground with the reins of their bridles in their hands, and so they lay a great while sore astonied, and all they that were in the castle and at the siege wend [*thought*] their necks had been broken, and then many a stranger and other said that the strange knight was a big man and a noble jouster, "for or [*ere*] now we saw never no night match the red knight of the red lawns;" thus they said both within the castle and without. Then they lightly avoided their horses and put their shields afore them, and drew their swords and ran together like two fierce lions, and either gave other such buffets upon their helms that they reeled both backward two strides; and then they recovered both, and hewed great pieces from their harness and their shields that a great part fell in the fields.

And then thus they fought till it was past noon and never would stint till at last they lacked wind both, and then they stood wagging and scattering, panting, blowing and bleeding, that all that beheld them for the most part wept for pity. So when they had rested them a while they went to battle again, tracing, racing, foining [*feinting*], as two boars. And at some time they took their run as it had been two rams, and hurtled together that sometimes they fell grovelling to the earth; and at some time they were so amazed that either took other's sword instead of his own.

Thus they endured till even-song time [*vespers*], that there was none that beheld them might know whether was like to win the battle; and their armor was so far hewn that men might see their naked sides, and in other places they were naked, but ever the naked places they did defend. And the red knight was a wily knight of war, and his wily fighting taught Sir Beaumains to be wise; but he abought [*paid for*] it full sore ere he did espy his fighting. And thus by assent of them both, they granted either other to rest; and so they set them down upon two mole-hills there beside the fighting place, and either of them unlaced his helm, and took the cold wind, for either of their pages was fast by them, to come when they called to unlace their harness and to set it on again at their command. And then when Sir Beaumain's helm was off, he looked up unto the window, and there he saw the fair lady dame Lyoness. And she made to him such countenance that his heart was light and joyful. And therewith he started up suddenly, and bade the red knight make him ready to do the battle to the uttermost.

"I will well," said the red knight.

And then they laced up their helms, and their pages avoided [*got out of the way*], and they stepped together and fought freshly. But the red knight of the red lawns awaited him, and at an overthwart [*crosswise*] smote him within the hand, that his sword fell out of his hand; and yet he gave him another buffet on the helm that he fell grovelling to the earth, and the red knight fell over him for to hold him down.

Then cried the maiden Linet on high, "O Sir Beaumains, where is thy courage become! Alas, my lady my sister beholdeth thee, and she sobbeth and weepeth, that maketh mine heart heavy."

When Sir Beaumains heard her say so, he started up with a great might and gat him upon his feet, and lightly he leaped to his sword and griped it in his hand, and doubled his pace unto the red knight, and there they fought a new battle together. But Sir Beaumains then doubled his strokes, and smote so thick that he smote the sword out of his hand, and then he smote him upon the helm that he fell to the earth, and Sir Beaumains fell upon him, and unlaced his helm to have slain him; and then he yielded him and asked mercy, and said with a loud voice, "O noble knight, I yield me to thy mercy."

Then Sir Beaumains bethought him upon the knights that he had made to be hanged shamefully, and then he said, "I may not with my worship save thy life, for the shameful deaths thou hast caused many full good knights to die."

"Sir," said the red knight of the red lawns, "hold your hand, and ye shall know the causes why I put them to so shameful a death."

"Say on," said Sir Beaumains.

"Sir, I loved once a lady, a fair damsel, and she had her brother slain, and she said it was Sir Launcelot du Lake, or else Sir Gawaine, and she prayed me as that I loved her heartily that I would make her a promise by the faith of my knighthood for to labor daily in arms until I met with one of them, and all that I might overcome I should put them unto a villanous death; and this is the cause that I have put all these knights to death, and so I ensured her to do all the villany unto King Arthur's knights, and that I should take vengeance upon all these knights. And, sir, now I will thee tell that every day my strength increaseth till noon, and all this time have I seven men's strength."

Then came there many earls, and barons, and noble knights, and prayed that knight to save his life, and take him to your prisoner: and all they fell upon their kness and prayed him of mercy, and that he would save his life, and, "Sir," they all said, "it were fairer of him to take homage and fealty, and let him hold his lands of you, than for to slay him: by his death ye shall have none advantage, and his misdeeds that be done may not be undone; and therefore he shall make amends to all parties, and we all will become your men, and do you homage and fealty."

"Fair lords," said Beaumains, "wit you well I am full loth to slay this knight, nevertheless he hath done passing ill and shamefully. But insomuch all that he did was at a lady's request, I blame him the less, and so for your sake I will release him, that he shall have his life upon this covenant, that he go within the castle and yield him there to the lady, and if she will forgive and quit [*acquit*] him, I will well; with this that he make her amends of all the trespass he hath done against her and her lands. And also, when that is done, that ye go unto the court of King Arthur, and there that ye ask Sir Launcelot mercy, and Sir Gawaine, for the evil will ye have had against them."

"Sir," said the red knight of the red lawns, "all this will I do as ye command, and certain assurance and sureties ye shall have."

And so then when the assurance was made, he made his homage and fealty, and all those earls and barons with him. And then the maiden Linet came to Sir Beaumains and unarmed him, and searched his wounds, and stinted his blood, and in likewise she did to the red knight of the red lawns. And so they sojourned ten days in their tents. And the red knight made his lords and servants to do all the pleasure that they might unto Sir Beaumains.

And within a while after, the red knight of the red lawns went unto the castle and put him in the lady Lyoness' grace, and so she received him upon sufficient sureties, and all her hurts were well restored of all that she could complain. And then he departed and went unto the court of King Arthur, and there openly the red knight of the red lawns put him in the mercy of Sir Launcelot and Sir Gawaine, and there he told openly how he was overcome, and by whom, and also he told of all the battles, from the beginning to the ending.

"Jesus, mercy," said King Arthur and Sir Gawaine, "we marvel much of what blood he is come, for he is a full noble knight."

"Have ye no marvel," said Sir Launcelot,

"for ye shall right well wit that he is come of a full noble blood, and, as for his might and hardiness, there be but few now living that is so mighty as he is and so noble of prowess."

"It seemeth by you," said King Arthur, "that ye know his name, and from whence he is come, and of what blood he is."

"I suppose I do so," said Sir Launcelot, "or else I would not have given him the order of knighthood; but he gave me at that time such charge that I should never discover him until he required me, or else it be known openly by some other."

Now return we unto Sir Beaumains, which desired of the damsel Linet that he might see her sister his lady.

"Sir," said she, "I would fain ye saw her."

Then Sir Beaumains armed him at all points, and took his horse and his spear, and rode straight to the castle. And when he came to the gate, he found there many men armed, that pulled up the drawbridge and drew the port close. Then marvelled he why they would not suffer him to enter in. And then he looked up to the window, and there he saw the fair lady dame Lyoness, that said on high: "Go thy way, Sir Beaumains, for as yet thou shalt not wholly have my love, until the time thou be called one of the number of the worthy knights; and therefore go and labor in arms worshipfully these twelve months, and then ye shall hear new tidings; and perdé [per dieu, truly] a twelve-month will be soon gone, and trust you me, fair knight, I shall be true unto you, and shall never betray you, but unto my death I shall love you and none other."

And therewithal she turned her from the window. And Sir Beaumains rode away from the castle in making great moan and sorrow; and so he rode here and there, and wist not whither he rode, till it was dark night; and then it happened him to come to a poor man's house, and there he was harbored all that night. But Sir Beaumains could have no rest, but wallowed and writhed for the love of the lady of the castle. And so on the morrow he took his horse and his armor, and rode till it was noon; and then he came unto a broad water, and thereby was a great lodge, and there he alighted to sleep, and laid his head upon his shield, and betook his horse to the dwarf, and commanded him to watch all night.

Now turn we to the lady of the castle, that thought much upon Sir Beaumains; and then she called unto her Sir Gringamor her brother, and prayed him in all manner, as he loved her heartily, that he would ride after Sir Beaumains, "and ever have him in a wait [look after him] till that ye may find him sleeping, for I am sure in his heaviness he will alight down in some place and lie down to sleep, and therefore have your watch upon him, and, in the priviest wise [softest way] that ye can, take his dwarf from him, and go your way with him as fast as ever ye may or Sir Beaumains awake; for my sister Linet hath showed me that the dwarf can tell of what kindred he is come, and what his right name is; and in the meanwhile I and my sister will ride to your castle to await when ye shall bring with you this dwarf, and then when ye have brought him to your castle, I will have him in examination myself; unto the time I know what his right name is, and of what kindred he is come, shall I never be merry at my heart."

"Sister," said Sir Gringamor, "all this shall be done after your intent." And so he rode all the other day and the night till that he found Sir Beaumains lying by a water, and his head upon his shield, for to sleep. And then when he saw Sir Beaumains fast on sleep, he came stilly stalking behind the dwarf, and plucked him fast under his arm, and so he rode away with him as fast as ever he might unto his own castle. But ever as he rode with the dwarf towards his castle, he cried unto his lord and prayed him of help. And therewith awoke Sir Beaumains, and up he leaped lightly, and saw where Sir Gringamor rode his way with the dwarf, and so Sir Graingamor rode out of his sight.

Then Sir Beaumains put on his helm anon, and buckled his shield, and took his horse and rode after him all that ever he might ride, through marshes and fields and great dales, that many times his horse and he plunged over the head in deep mires, for he knew not the way, but he took the next [nearest] way in that woodness [madness] that many times he was like to perish. [And so he came following his dwarf to Sir Gringamor's castle. But aforetime the lady Lyoness had come and had the dwarf in examination; and the dwarf had told the lady how that Sir Beaumains was the son of a king, and how his mother was sister to King Arthur, and how his right name was Sir Gareth of Orkney.]

And as they sat thus talking, there came Sir Beaumains at the gate with an angry countenance, and his sword drawn in his hand, and cried aloud that all the castle might hear it, saying, "Thou traitor, Sir Gringamor, deliver me my dwarf again, or by the faith that I owe to the order of knighthood, I shall do thee all the harm that I can."

Then Sir Gringamor looked out at a window, and said, "Sir Gareth of Orkney, leave thy boasting words, for thou gettest not thy dwarf again."

"Thou coward knight," said Sir Gareth, "bring him with thee, and come and do battle with me, and win him, and take him."

"So will I do," said Sir Gringamor, "and me list [*if it please me*], but for all thy great words thou gettest him not."

"Ah, fair brother," said dame Lyoness, "I would he had his dwarf again, for I would not he were wroth, for now he hath told me all my desire I will no longer keep the dwarf. And also, brother, he hath done much for me, and delivered me from the red knight of the red lawns, and therefore, brother, I owe him my service afore all knights living; and wit ye well I love him above all other knights, and full fain would I speak with him, but in no wise I would he wist what I were, but that I were another strange lady."

"Well," said Sir Gringamor, "sith [*since*] that I know your will, I will now obey unto him."

And therewithal he went down unto Sir Gareth, and said, "Sir, I cry you mercy, and all that I have misdone against your person I will amend it at your own will, and therefore I pray you that you will alight, and take such cheer as I can make you here in this castle."

"Shall I then have my dwarf again?" said Sir Gareth.

"Yea, sir, and all the pleasure that I can

make you, for as soon as your dwarf told me what ye were and of what blood that ye are come, and what noble deeds ye have done in these marches [*borders*], then I repent me of my deeds."

And then Sir Gareth alighted down from his horse, and therewith came his dwarf and took his horse.

"O my fellow," said Sir Gareth, "I have had many evil adventures for thy sake."

And so Sir Gringamor took him by the hand, and led him into the hall, and there was Sir Gringamor's wife.

And then there came forth into the hall dame Lyoness arrayed like a princess, and there she made him passing good cheer, and he her again. And they had goodly language and lovely countenance together. And Sir Gareth many times thought in himself, "Would to God that the lady of the Castle Perilous were so fair as she is!" There were all manner of games and plays, both of dancing and leaping; and ever the more Sir Gareth beheld the lady, the more he loved her, and so he burned in love that he was past himself in his understanding. And forth towards night they went to supper, and Sir Gareth might not eat, for his love was so hot that he wist not where he was. All these looks Sir Gringamor espied, and after supper he called his sister dame Lyoness unto a chamber, and said: "Fair sister, I have well espied your countenance between you and this knight, and I will, sister, that ye wit that he is a full noble knight, and if ye can make him to abide here, I will do to him all the pleasure that I can, for and ye were better than ye be, ye were well bestowed upon him."

"Fair brother," said dame Lyoness, "I understand well that the knight is good, and come he is of a noble house; notwithstanding I will assay him better, for he hath had great labor for my love, and hath passed many a dangerous passage."

Right so Sir Gringamor went unto Sir Gareth, and said: "Sir, make ye good cheer; for wist [*know*] ye well that she loveth you as well as ye do her, and better if better may be."

"And I wist that," said Sir Gareth, "there lived not a gladder man than I would be."

"Upon my worship," said Sir Gringamor,

"trust unto my promise; and as long as it liketh you ye shall sojourn with me, and this lady shall be with us daily and nightly to make you all the cheer that she can."

"I will well," said Sir Gareth, "for I have promised to be nigh this country this twelvemonth. And well I am sure King Arthur and other noble knights will find me where that I am within this twelvemonth. For I shall be sought and found, if that I be on live."

And then the noble knight Sir Gareth went unto the dame Lyoness, which he then much loved, and kissed her many times, and either made great joy of other. And there she promised him her love, certainly to love him and none other the days of her life. Then this lady, dame Lyoness, by the assent of her brother, told Sir Gareth all the truth what she was, and how she was the same lady that he did battle for, and how she was lady of the Castle Perilous. And there she told him how she caused her brother to take away his dwarf, "For this cause, to know the certainty what was your name, and of what kin ye were come."

And then she let fetch before him Linet the damsel, which had ridden with him many dreary ways. Then was Sir Gareth more gladder than he was tofore. And then they troth plight[1] each other to love, and never to fail while their life lasted.

[1]"Troth," *truth*, and "plight," *wove*: "troth plight," *wove their truth together*.

"Scarface," from Blackfoot Lodge Tales, *by George Bird Grinnell (Lincoln, Nebraska: Univ. of Nebraska Press, 1962).*

This Blackfoot legend, one of the most famous Native tales from the Great Plains, embodies many of the basic features of the hero's life: humble origins and early life, a long, arduous journey, the many tests successfully passed, gifts received from supernatural powers, and the re-integration of the hero back into his culture. Specific aspects of Blackfoot life and customs are incorporated in this tale: the importance of the Sun as the prime source of all life, the close relationship between human beings and animals, and the nature and origin of the Medicine Lodge. Grinnell, who lived among the Plains peoples for over twenty years, collected this and other Blackfoot tales at the end of the nineteenth century.

The circular journey of Scarface can be compared to those of the girl in "The Ghost Owl," Eagle Voice in "Chased by a Cow," the Boy in Arrow to the Sun, *and the young knight in "Of Sir Gareth of Orkney." "Scarface" provided the structural basis for Jamake Highwater's novel* Anpao.

Scarface: Origin of the Medicine Lodge

In the earliest times there was no war. All the tribes were at peace. In those days there was a man who had a daughter, a very beautiful girl. Many young men wanted to marry her, but every time she was asked, she only shook her head and said she did not want a husband.

"How is this?" asked her father. "Some of these young men are rich, handsome, and brave."

"Why should I marry?" replied the girl. "I have a rich father and mother. Our lodge is good. The parfleches are never empty. There are plenty of tanned robes and soft furs for winter. Why worry me, then?"

The Raven Bearers held a dance; they all dressed carefully and wore their ornaments, and each one tried to dance the best. Afterwards some of them asked for this girl, but still she said no. Then the Bulls, the Kit-foxes, and others of the *I-kun-uh'-kah-tsi* held their dances, and all those who were rich, many great warriors, asked this man for his daughter, but to every one of them she said no. Then her father was angry, and said: "Why, now, this way? All the best men have asked for you, and still you say no. I believe you have a secret lover."

"Ah!" said her mother. "What shame for us should a child be born and our daughter still unmarried!" "Father! mother!" replied the girl, "pity me. I have no secret lover, but now hear the truth. That Above Person, the Sun, told me,

'Do not marry any of those men, for you are mine; thus you shall be happy, and live to great age'; and again he said, 'Take heed. You must not marry. You are mine.' "

"Ah!" replied her father. "It must always be as he says." And they talked no more about it.

There was a poor young man, very poor. His father, mother, all his relations, had gone to the Sand Hills. He had no lodge, no wife to tan his robes or sew his moccasins. He stopped in one lodge to-day, and to-morrow he ate and slept in another; thus he lived. He was a good-looking young man, except that on his cheek he had a scar, and his clothes were always old and poor.

After those dances some of the young men met this poor Scarface, and they laughed at him, and said: "Why don't you ask that girl to marry you? You are so rich and handsome!" Scarface did not laugh; he replied: "Ah! I will do as you say. I will go and ask her." All the young men thought this was funny. They laughed a great deal. But Scarface went down by the river. He waited by the river, where the women came to get water, and by and by the girl came along. "Girl," he said, "wait. I want to speak with you. Not as a designing person do I ask you, but openly where the Sun looks down, and all may see."

"Speak then," said the girl.

"I have seen the days," continued the young man. "You have refused those who are young, and rich, and brave. Now, to-day, they laughed and said to me, 'Why do you not ask her?' I am poor, very poor. I have no lodge, no food, no clothes, no robes and warm furs. I have no relations; all have gone to the Sand Hills; yet, now, to-day, I ask you, take pity, be my wife."

The girl hid her face in her robe and brushed the ground with the point of her moccasin, back and forth, back and forth; for she was thinking. After a time she said: "True. I have refused all those rich young men, yet now the poor one asks me, and I am glad. I will be your wife, and my people will be happy. You are poor, but it does not matter. My father will give you dogs. My mother will make us a lodge. My people will give us robes and furs. You will

be poor no longer."

Then the young man was happy, and he started to kiss her, but she held him back, and said: "Wait! The Sun has spoken to me. He says I may not marry; that I belong to him. He says if I listen to him, I shall live to great age. But now I say: Go to the Sun. Tell him, 'She whom you spoke with heeds your words. She has never done wrong, but now she wants to marry. I want her for my wife.' Ask him to take that scar from your face. That will be his sign. I will know he is pleased. But if he refuses, or if you fail to find his lodge, then do not return to me."

"Oh!" cried the young man, "at first your words were good. I was glad. But now it is dark. My heart is dead. Where is that far-off lodge? Where the trail, which no one yet has travelled?"

"Take courage, take courage!" said the girl; and she went to her lodge.

Scarface was very sad. He sat down and covered his head with his robe and tried to think what to do. After a while he got up, and went to an old woman who had been kind to him. "Pity me," he said. "I am very poor. I am going away now on a long journey. Make me some moccasins."

"Where are you going?" asked the old woman. "There is no war; we are very peaceful here."

"I do not know where I shall go," replied Scarface. "I am in trouble, but I cannot tell you now what it is."

So the old woman made him some moccasins, seven pairs, with parfleche soles, and also she gave him a sack of food, — pemmican of berries, pounded meat, and dried back fat; for this old woman had a good heart. She liked the young man.

All alone, and with a sad heart, he climbed the bluffs and stopped to take a last look at the camp. He wondered if he would ever see his sweetheart and the people again. *"Hai' yu!* Pity me, O Sun," he prayed, and turning, he started to find the trail.

For many days he travelled on, over great prairies, along timbered rivers and among the mountains, and every day his sack of food grew lighter; but he saved it as much as he could, and ate berries, and roots, and sometimes he killed an animal of some kind. One night he stopped by the home of a wolf. *"Hai-yah!"* said that one; "what is my brother doing so far from home?"

"Ah!" replied Scarface, "I seek the place where the Sun lives; I am sent to speak with him."

"I have travelled far," said the wolf. "I know all the prairies, the 'valleys, and the mountains, but I have never seen the Sun's home. Wait; I know one who is very wise. Ask the bear. He may tell you."

The next day the man travelled on again, stopping now and then to pick a few berries, and when night came he arrived at the bear's lodge.

"Where is your home?" asked the bear. "Why are you travelling alone, my brother?"

"Help me! Pity me!" replied the young man; "because of her words[1] I seek the Sun. I go to ask him for her."

"I know not where he stops," replied the bear. "I have travelled by many rivers, and I know the mountains, yet I have never seen his lodge. There is some one beyond, that striped-face, who is very smart. Go and ask him."

The badger was in his hole. Stooping over, the young man shouted: "Oh, cunning striped-face! Oh, generous animal! I wish to speak with you."

"What do you want?" said the badger, poking his head out of the hole.

"I want to find the Sun's home," replied Scarface. "I want to speak with him."

"I do not know where he lives," replied the badger. "I never travel very far. Over there in the timber is a wolverine. He is always travelling around, and is of much knowledge. Maybe he can tell you."

Then Scarface went to the woods and looked all around for the wolverine, but could not find him. So he sat down to rest. *"Hai'-yu! Hai'-yu!"* he cried. "Wolverine, take pity on me. My food is gone, my moccasins worn out. Now I must die."

"What is it, my brother?" he heard, and looking around, he saw the animal sitting near.

"She whom I would marry," said Scarface, "belongs to the Sun; I am trying to find where he lives, to ask him for her."

"Ah!" said the wolverine. "I know where he lives. Wait; it is nearly night. To-morrow I will show you the trail to the big water. He lives on the other side of it."

Early in the morning, the wolverine showed him the trail, and Scarface followed it until he came to the water's edge. He looked out over it, and his heart almost stopped. Never before had any one seen such a big water. The other side could not be seen, and there was no end to it. Scarface sat down on the shore. His food was all gone, his moccasins worn out. His heart was sick. "I cannot cross this big water," he said. "I cannot return to the people. Here, by this water, I shall die."

Not so. His Helpers were there. Two swans came swimming up to the shore. "Why have you come here?" they asked him. "What are you doing? It is very far to the place where your people live."

"I am here," replied Scarface, "to die. Far away, in my country, is a beautiful girl. I want to marry her, but she belongs to the Sun. So I started to find him and ask for her. I have travelled many days. My food is gone. I cannot go back. I cannot cross this big water, so I am going to die."

"No," said the swans; "it shall not be so. Across this water is the home of that Above Person. Get on our backs, and we will take you there."

Scarface quickly arose. He felt strong again. He waded out into the water and lay down on the swans' backs, and they started off. Very deep and black is that fearful water. Strange people live there, mighty animals which often seize and drown a person. The swans carried him safely, and took him to the other side. Here was a broad hard trail leading back from the water's edge.

"Kyi," said the swans. "You are now close to the Sun's lodge. Follow that trail, and you will soon see it."

Scarface started up the trail, and pretty soon

---

1 A Blackfoot often talks of what this or that person said, without mentioning names.

he came to some beautiful things, lying in it. There was a war shirt, a shield, and a bow and arrows. He had never seen such pretty weapons; but he did not touch them. He walked carefully around them, and travelled on. A little way further on, he met a young man, the handsomest person he had ever seen. His hair was very long, and he wore clothing made of strange skins. His moccasins were sewn with bright colored feathers. The young man said to him, "Did you see some weapons lying on the trail?"

"Yes," replied Scarface; "I saw them."

"But did you not touch them?" asked the young man.

"No; I thought some one had left them there, so I did not take them."

"You are not a thief," said the young man. "What is your name?"

"Scarface."

"Where are you going?"

"To the Sun."

"My name," said the young man, "is A-pi-su'-ahts.[1] The Sun is my father; come, I will take you to our lodge. My father is not now at home, but he will come in at night."

Soon they came to the lodge. It was very large and handsome; strange medicine animals were painted on it. Behind, on a tripod, were strange weapons and beautiful clothes — the Sun's. Scarface was ashamed to go in, but Morning Star said, "Do not be afraid, my friend; we are glad you have come."

They entered. One person was sitting there, Ko-ko-mik'-e-is,[2] the Sun's wife, Morning Star's mother. She spoke to Scarface kindly, and gave him something to eat. "Why have you come so far from your people?" she asked.

Then Scarface told her about the beautiful girl he wanted to marry. "She belongs to the Sun," he said. "I have come to ask him for her."

When it was time for the Sun to come home, the Moon hid Scarface under a pile of robes. As soon as the Sun got to the doorway, he stopped, and said, "I smell a person."

"Yes, father," said Morning Star; "a good young man has come to see you. I know he is

good, for he found some of my things on the trail and did not touch them."

Then Scarface came out from under the robes, and the Sun entered and sat down. "I am glad you have come to our lodge," he said. "Stay with us as long as you think best. My son is lonesome sometimes; be his friend."

The next day the Moon called Scarface out of the lodge, and said to him: "Go with Morning Star where you please, but never hunt near that big water; do not let him go there. It is the home of great birds which have long sharp bills; they kill people. I have many sons, but these birds have killed them all. Morning Star is the only one left."

So Scarface stayed there a long time and hunted with Morning Star. One day they came near the water, and saw the big birds.

"Come," said Morning Star; "let us go and kill those birds."

"No, no!" replied Scarface; "we must not go there. Those are very terrible birds; they will kill us."

Morning Star would not listen. He ran towards the water, and Scarface followed. He knew that he must kill the birds and save the boy. If not, the Sun would be angry and might kill him. He ran ahead and met the birds, which were coming towards him to fight, and killed every one of them with his spear: not one was left. Then the young men cut off their heads, and carried them home. Morning Star's mother was glad when they told her what they had done, and showed her the birds' heads. She cried, and called Scarface "my son." When the Sun came home at night, she told him about it, and he too was glad. "My son," he said to Scarface, "I will not forget what you have this day done for me. Tell me now, what can I do for you?"

"*Hai'-yu*," replied Scarface. "*Hai'-yu*, pity me. I am here to ask you for that girl. I want to marry her. I asked her, and she was glad; but she says you own her, that you told her not to marry."

"What you say is true," said the Sun. "I have watched the days, so I know it. Now, then, I give her to you; she is yours. I am glad she has been wise. I know she has never done wrong. The Sun pities good women. They shall

1 Early Riser, *i.e.* The Morning Star.
2 Night red light, the Moon.

Illustration by Paul Goble from *Star Boy.* Copyright ©
1983 by Paul Goble. Reprinted by permission of Bradbury Press, an affiliate of Macmillan Inc.

live a long time. So shall their husbands and children. Now you will soon go home. Let me tell you something. Be wise and listen: I am the only chief. Everything is mine. I made the earth, the mountains, prairies, rivers, and forests. I made the people and all the animals. This is why I say I alone am the chief. I can never die. True, the winter makes me old and weak, but every summer I grow young again.''

Then said the Sun: "What one of all animals is smartest? The raven is, for he always finds food. He is never hungry. Which one of all the animals is most *Nat-o'-ye*[1]? The buffalo is. Of all animals, I like him best. He is for the people. He is your food and your shelter. What part of his body is sacred? The tongue is. That is mine. What else is sacred? Berries are. They are mine too. Come with me and see the world." He took Scarface to the edge of the sky, and they looked down and saw it. It is round and flat, and all around the edge is the

jumping-off place [or walls straight down]. Then said the Sun: "When any man is sick or in danger, his wife may promise to build me a lodge, if he recovers. If the woman is pure and true, then I will be pleased and help the man. But if she is bad, if she lies, then I will be angry. You shall build the lodge like the world, round, with walls, but first you must build a sweat house of a hundred sticks. It shall be like the sky [a hemisphere], and half of it shall be painted red. That is me. The other half you will paint black. That is the night."

Further said the Sun: "Which is the best, the heart or the brain? The brain is. The heart often lies, the brain never." Then he told Scarface everything about making the Medicine Lodge, and when he had finished, he rubbed a powerful medicine on his face, and the scar disappeared. Then he gave him two raven feathers, saying: "These are the sign for the girl, that I give her to you. They must always be worn by the husband of the woman who builds a Medicine Lodge."

The young man was now ready to return home. Morning Star and the Sun gave him many beautiful presents. The Moon cried and kissed him, and called him "my son." Then the Sun showed him the short trail. It was the Wolf Road (Milky Way). He followed it, and soon reached the ground.

It was a very hot day. All the lodge skins were raised, and the people sat in the shade. There was a chief, a very generous man, and all day long people kept coming to his lodge to feast and smoke with him. Early in the morning this chief saw a person sitting out on a butte near by, close wrapped in his robe. The chief's friends came and went, the sun reached the middle, and passed on, down towards the mountains. Still this person did not move. When it was almost night, the chief said: "Why does that person sit there so long? The heat has been strong, but he has never eaten nor drunk. He may be a stranger; go and ask him in."

So some young men went up to him, and said: "Why do you sit here in the great heat all day? Come to the shade of the lodges. The chief asks you to feast with him."

Then the person arose and threw off his

1 This word may be translated as "of the Sun," "having Sun power," or more properly, something sacred.

robe, and they were surprised. He wore beautiful clothes. His bow, shield, and other weapons were of strange make. But they knew his face, although the scar was gone, and they ran ahead, shouting, "The scarface poor young man has come. He is poor no longer. The scar on his face is gone."

All the people rushed out to see him. "Where have you been?" they asked. "Where did you get all these pretty things?" He did not answer. There in the crowd stood that young woman; and taking the two raven feathers from his head, he gave them to her, and said: "The trail was very long, and I nearly died, but by those Helpers, I found his lodge. He is glad. He sends these feathers to you. They are the sign."

Great was her gladness then. They were married, and made the first Medicine Lodge, as the Sun had said. The Sun was glad. He gave them great age. They were never sick. When they were very old, one morning, their children said: "Awake! Rise and eat." They did not move. In the night, in sleep, without pain, their shadows had departed for the Sand Hills.

———

"Meleager and Atalanta," from Heroes of Greece and Troy, *by Roger Lancelyn Green. Illustrated by Heather Copley and Christopher Chamberlain (London: Bodley Head, 1960).*

In this story, from what Green calls "the bright, misty morning of legend and literature," a female hero is looked upon as an oddity, one whose life is only fulfilled when she has completed a linear journey through marriage and motherhood. The scorn Atalanta receives because of her hunting prowess and her refusal to marry reflect the male-oriented focus of Greek society. Her refusal can be compared to that in the Inuit myth "Sedna," and contrasted to female characters' desires for happy marriages in many European folktales. In the account of Atalanta's early life are found many traditional motifs: the unwanted child, the unusual upbringing, and the animal helpers.

Meleager and Atalanta

Meleager the Argonaut bore a charmed life. For when he was but seven days old the Three Fates appeared to his mother, Queen Althaea of Calydon, as she lay in the big shadowy room of the palace lit only by the flickerling firelight.

The Fates were the three daughters of Zeus and Themis who presided over the fate of man: and when Althaea saw them, they were busy with the life-thread of her son Meleager.

One Fate spun the thread of life, and that was Clotho, and she was spinning busily, while Lachesis stood by her with her rod to measure it. The third Fate, Atropos, held the shears, and she said to her sisters:

'Why trouble you to spin and measure? As soon as that brand on the hearth yonder is consumed to ashes, I must cut the thread with my shears, and Meleager's life will be ended!'

When Althaea heard this, she leapt out of bed, snatched the burning brand from the hearth and put out the flames. Then she hid it away in a secret chest of which she alone possessed the key.

'Now I defy you, Fates!' she cried. 'I have but to preserve that brand, and my son will live for ever!'

Then the three sisters smiled at Althaea, and there was a secret knowledge in their eyes which made her afraid. After that, they vanished, and only the charred brand in her secret chest remained to prove that she had not dreamed it all.

Years passed and Meleager grew into a brave young prince and went with Jason and the other Argonauts in quest of the Golden Fleece. On his return to Calydon he found a savage wild boar ravaging the land, destroying all the crops and killing any who tried to withstand it.

This great boar, with its wonderful tusks and hide was not to be slain by one man, and Meleager sent for his friends among the Argonauts, Heracles and Theseus, Peleus and Telamon, Admetus, and Nestor, Jason himself, and several others — but in particular he sent for the maiden huntress Atalanta. For Meleager had fallen in love with her during their voyage on the *Argo*, and still hoped to persuade her to be his wife, though she had sworn never to marry.

Atalanta was a princess of Arcadia, but when she was born her father, King Iasus of Tegea, disappointed that she was not a boy, had cast her out onto the wild mountain side. Here a she-bear found the baby and brought her up among her own cubs; and Artemis, the Immortal Huntress, trained her in all matters of the chase and allowed her to join with the nymphs who were her followers.

Now she came eagerly to Calydon, and was welcomed by Meleager and the other Argonauts. But Phexippus and Toxeus, Meleager's uncles, the beloved brothers of Queen Althaea, protested when they saw Atalanta.

'It is an insult,' they cried, 'to expect us to go hunting in company with a woman! She would be weaving at her loom, not mixing with men and pretending to skill in the chase!'

Meleager angrily bade them be silent, and the hunt began, with Atalanta walking at his side—a lovely maiden, simple and boyish with hair falling to her shoulders, a tunic of skins, and a long bow in her hand.

'How happy will the man be who can call himself your husband!' sighed Meleager.

Atalanta blushed and frowned, saying: 'Never by my free will shall any man do so .... But let us give all our thoughts to this fierce boar which we seek.'

They had not far to go, for in a wooded dell overhung by willows and dense with smooth sedge and marshy rushes, the Boar was roused. Out he came in a fury, leveling the young trees and bushes as he went, and scattering the dogs to right and left.

Echion flung a spear, but in his eagerness pinned only the trunk of a maple tree. Jason hurled his weapon, but it too passed over the Boar's back. Squealing with rage, while its eyes flashed fire, it rushed upon young Nestor — who would never have lived to fight at Troy if he had not swung himself quickly into a tree out of harm's way.

Then Telamon rushed at the Boar with his spear ready, but he tripped over an unseen root, and was barely rescued by Peleus. As he staggered to his feet, the Boar charged: and it would have gone hard with them both if Atalanta had not, with quiet skill and courage,

drawn her bow-string and sent an arrow into the Boar's head close to its ear. Yet even her skill could not send an arrow right to the brain, so hard was the creature's skin.

There was no one so delighted as Meleager. 'See!' he cried, 'the Princess Atalanta has taught us men how to hunt boars, and has smitten the creature with a mortal wound!'

Ancaeus, who had also objected to a woman joining in the hunt, was furious at this. 'Watch!' he cried, 'I'll show you how a man settles wild boars! No pin-pricks from a woman will do it. A battle axe is the weapon, and Artemis herself could not defend this Boar against me!'

So saying, he rushed at the maddened creature and struck — but struck short. The next moment he was on his back, and the Boar had killed him. In an effort to save him, Peleus flung his spear; but Eurytion sprang forward at the same moment with his weapon raised, and the spear meant for the Boar passed through his body.

Theseus also launched a spear, but aimed high in his excitement and transfixed only the bough of an oak tree. But Meleager's aim was true, and the Boar fell to the ground, and he dispatched it with a blow of his second spear.

Then the hunters shouted with joy, and stood around gazing in awe at the great creature covering so large a patch of ground. Meleager knelt down and set to work skinning the Boar, and when he had done so, he turned to Atalanta and presented her with the head and hide.

'Lady,' he said, 'take the spoils and share my glory with me. You were the first to wound the Boar and more honour belongs to you than to me or any other one of us.'

Then the rest envied Atalanta her prize, and Phexippus, Meleager's uncle, could not contain his fury:

'This is the worst insult of all!' he shouted. 'My nephew won the skin, and if he did not want it, he should have given it to me, as the most noble person present! As for you, you shameless girl, do not think that we will suffer this dishonor. You may have bewitched Meleager with your beauty, but it has no power on us!'

At that he and his brother Toxeus seized hold of Atalanta and tore the spoils from her as roughly and insultingly as they could.

Then Meleager lost his temper completely. With a yell of rage he drew his sword and stabbed Phexippus to the heart. Next he turned upon Toxeus, who tried to defend himself, but soon lay dead beside his brother. Then the party set out sadly for the city, carrying the dead bodies with them, while Atalanta held the head and hide of the Calydonian Boar.

When Queen Althaea saw that her two brothers were dead, her grief knew no bounds. But when she learnt that Meleager had killed them, her grief turned to a wild frenzy of fury and revenge.

Suddenly she remembered the charred brand which she had snatched from the hearth when Meleager was a baby. Rushing to her room, she drew it from the chest and cast it upon the fire, where it caught quickly, flamed up, and was soon reduced to ashes.

Now Meleager was feasting his friends in the hall and drinking the health of Atalanta. All at once the cup fell from his hand, and with a cry he sank to the ground, writhing there in agony. He cried out that he was burning from within, and that he wished the Boar had killed him instead of Ancaeus; and in a few minutes he lay dead.

Then there was mourning throughout Calydon, and the great Boar Hunt which had begun so happily ended in sadness and tragedy. Queen Althaea, when she came to herself after her frenzy of grief and rage, was so horrified at what she had done that she hanged herself.

But one happy result came of the Calydonian Boar Hunt, for Heracles fell in love with Meleager's sister, the Princess Deianira. Now King Oeneus had promised her, against her will, to the River Achelous, who came to him in the shape of a fierce man and threatened to destroy his land if he refused his suit.

When Heracles heard this, he went to the river bank and cried: 'Noble River Achelous, we both love the same maiden! Come forth, then, in whatever form you choose, and fight with me for her!'

Achelous accepted this daring challenge, took the form of a great, savage bull, and charged at Heracles. But that mighty hero was experienced by now in such contests, and seizing Achelous by one horn he snapped it off at the root. Then Achelous submitted, and Deianira became the wife of Heracles, and they lived happily for a while at Calydon, helping Oeneus until his young son Tydeus should be old enough to rule.

The other hunters had, meanwhile, returned to their homes; but the beautiful Atalanta, famous now for her part in the battle with the Boar, was claimed by her father, King Iasus.

She settled at his home, at Tegea in Arcadia, but still refused to marry.

'But I have no son to succeed me'! lamented Iasus. 'Choose whom you will as husband, and you shall rule here jointly, and your children after you.'

'I will obey you, as a daughter should,' said Atalanta at length. 'But on one condition. Every prince who comes as my suitor must race with me. Only he that is swifter of foot than I shall be my husband. But, those whom I beat in the race shall forfeit their lives.'

Iasus was forced to agree, and sent heralds throughout Greece proclaiming that whoever could outrun his daughter Atalanta, should marry her and be king of Tegea; but that those who lost the race would lose their heads also.

Several princes felt confident that they could run faster than any girl, and came to try their fortune. But each of them in turn left his head to decorate the finishing-post on King Iasus's race-course.

Soon no one else dared to try, and Atalanta smiled happily, for she was determined never to marry.

At length her cousin Prince Melanion fell in love with her and knowing that he could not surpass her in running, he prayed to Aphrodite, the Immortal Queen of Love and Beauty, to assist him.

Aphrodite was angry with Atalanta for scorning love and refusing to marry, and she granted Melanion her help. She lent him the three golden apples which Heracles had brought from the Garden of the Hesperides, and which Athena had passed on to her for this very purpose.

Then Melanion presented himself in Tegea, and in spite of all King Iasus's warnings, insisted on racing for Atalanta.

The course was set, and the race began. At first Atalanta let Melanion gain on her, for she knew that she was twice as fast a runner as he was. When he saw her shadow drawing close to him, he dropped a golden apple which rolled in front of her.

Atalanta saw the apple, and was filled with the desire to possess this wonderful thing. So she stopped quickly, picked it up and then sped after Melanion, certain of overtaking him easily. And so she did, but as she drew level, he dropped a second apple, and again she could not resist the temptation, but stopped and picked it up.

Once more she sped after Melanion, and once more she overtook him. But a third apple rolled across in front of her, and at the sight of its beauty and wonder, Atalanta forgot all else, and stopped to gather it.

'I can still overtake him!' she thought, and sped on like the wind. But Melanion touched the winning-post a moment before she reached him, and so he won her for his wife. And in a little while they were living happily together as king and queen of Tegea, with a small son to be king after them.

Heracles and Deianira were happy too, living quietly at Calydon, though in time they were forced to move again, as Heracles in a quarrel struck a cousin of the king's so hard that he died. So they bade farewell to Oeneus and set out on their travels towards the north of Greece.

Now on their way, they came to the river Evenus where lived the centaur called Nessus who hated Heracles. This centaur was accustomed to carry travelers across the river on his back; and when he had taken Deianira nearly to the other side, he suddenly turned down stream, and began to carry her away. She screamed for help, and Heracles drew his bow and shot Nessus with one of his poisoned arrows.

As he lay dying on the river bank, Nessus gasped:

'Lady Deianira, I will tell you a secret. When I am dead keep a little of the blood from my wound, and if ever you find that Heracles has ceased to love you, soak a robe in it and give it him to wear: that will make him love you more than ever before.'

Then he died, and Deianira did as she was instructed, believing that Nessus had told her this to show how sorry he was for what he had tried to do. But she did not tell Heracles.

After this they came safely to Trachis, a hundred miles north of Thebes, and were welcomed by King Ceyx. And there they settled down safely and happily.

But for Heracles there was never to be any real peace or rest, and indeed he did not wish it, for very soon he set out on a new and dangerous expedition.

"Joan the Maid," from The Red True Storybook, *edited by Andrew Lang. (London: Longmans, Green & Co., 1895).*

This story of the peasant girl who rose to great glory leading the French against the English illustrates how the life of an historical figure (Joan lived in the fifteenth century) takes on legendary aspects. Although Andrew Lang makes use of historical sources, he tends to emphasize the miraculous aspect of Joan's linear journey to a martyr's death: her voices and visions, her discovery of a hidden sword, the miracles she performed, her capture by betrayal, and her heroic death. His references to the Trojan War further add to her heroic stature. It is important to notice the fear Joan created in many people; she was considered unnatural not only because of her visions, but also because she assumed a male role.

The isolation she experienced because of her visionary powers, and the courage with which she defended them, can be compared to similar experiences and qualities exhibited by the title hero of Dennis Lee's poem "Nicholas Knock."

Joan the Maid

Four hundred and seventy years ago, the children of Domremy, a little village near the

Meuse, on the borders of France and Lorraine, used to meet and dance and sing beneath a beautiful beech-tree, 'lovely as a lily.' They called it 'The Fairy Tree,' or 'The Good Ladies' Lodge,' meaning the fairies by the words 'Good Ladies.' Among these children was one named Jeanne (born 1412), the daughter of an honest farmer, Jacques d'Arc. Jeanne sang more than she danced, and though she carried garlands like the other boys and girls, and hung them on the boughs of the Fairies' Tree, she liked better to take the flowers into the parish church, and lay them on the altars of St. Margaret and St. Catherine. It was said among the villagers that Jeanne's godmother had once seen the fairies dancing; but though some of the older people believed in the Good Ladies, it does not seem that Jeanne and the other children had faith in them or thought much about them. They only went to the tree and to a neighbouring fairy well to eat cakes and laugh and play. Yet these fairies were destined to be fatal to Jeanne d'Arc, JOAN THE MAIDEN, and her innocent childish sports were to bring her to the stake and the death by fire. For she was that famed Jeanne la Pucelle, the bravest, kindest, best, and wisest of women, whose tale is the saddest, the most wonderful, and the most glorious page in the history of the world. It is a page which no good Englishman and no true Frenchman can read without sorrow and bitter shame, for the English burned Joan with the help of bad Frenchmen, and the French of her party did not pay a *sou*, or write a line, or strike a stroke to save her.

The English were besieging Orleans; Joan the Maid drove them from its walls. How did it happen that a girl of seventeen, who could neither read nor write, became the greatest general on the side of France? How did a woman defeat the hardy English soldiers who were used to chase the French before them like sheep?

We must say that France could only be saved by a miracle, and by a miracle she was saved. This is a mystery; we cannot understand it. Joan the Maiden was not as other men and women are. But, as a little girl, she was a child among children, though better, kinder, stronger than the rest, and, poor herself, she was always

good and helpful to those who were poorer still.

Joan's parents were not indigent; they had lands and cattle, and a little money laid by in case of need. Her father was, at one time, *doyen*, or head-man, of Domremy. Their house was hard by the church, and was in the part of the hamlet where the people were better off, and had more freedom and privileges than many of their neighbours. They were devoted to the Royal House of France, which protected them from the tyranny of lords and earls further east. As they lived in a village under the patronage of St. Remigius, they were much interested in Reims, his town, where the kings of France were crowned, and were anointed with Holy Oil, which was believed to have been brought in a sacred bottle by an angel.

In the Middle Ages, the king was not regarded as really king till this holy oil had been poured on his head. Thus we shall see, later, how anxious Joan was that Charles VII., then the Dauphin, should be crowned and anointed in Reims, though it was still in the possession of the English. It is also necessary to remember that Joan had once an elder sister named Catherine, whom she loved dearly. Catherine died, and perhaps affection for her made Joan more fond of bringing flowers to the altar of her namesake, St. Catherine, and of praying often to that saint.

Joan was brought up by her parents, as she told her judges, to be industrious, to sew and spin. She did not fear to match herself at spinning and sewing, she said, against any woman in Rouen. When very young she sometimes went to the fields to watch the cattle, like the goose-girl in the fairy tale. As she grew older, she worked in the house, she did not any longer watch sheep and cattle. But the times were dangerous, and, when there was an alarm of soldiers or robbers in the neighbourhood, she sometimes helped to drive the flock into a fortified island, or peninsula, for which her father was responsible, in the river near her home. She learned her creed, she said, from her mother. Twenty years after her death, her neighbours, who remembered her, described her as she was when a child. Jean Morin said that she was a good industrious girl, but that she would often be praying in church when her father and mother did not know it. Beatrix Estellin, an old widow of eighty, said Joan was a good girl. When Domremy was burned, Joan would go to church at Greux, 'and there was not a better girl in the two towns.' A priest, who had known her, called her 'a good, simple, well-behaved girl.' Jean Waterin, when he was a boy, had seen Joan in the fields, 'and when they were all playing together, she would go apart, and pray to God, as he thought, and he and the others used to laugh at her. She was good and simple, and often in churches and holy places. And when she heard the church bell ring, she would kneel down in the fields.' She used to bribe the sexton to ring the bells (a duty which he rather neglected) with presents of knitted wool.

All those who had seen Joan told the same tale: she was always kind, simple, industrious, pious, and yet merry and fond of playing with the others round the Fairy Tree. They say that the singing birds came to her, and nestled in her breast.

Thus, as far as anyone could tell, Joan was a child like other children, but more serious and more religious. One of her friends, a girl called Mengette, whose cottage was next to that of Joan's father, said: 'Joan was so pious that we other children told her she was too good.'

In peaceful times Joan would have lived and married and died and been forgotten. But the times were evil. The two parties of Burgundy and Armagnac divided town from town and village from village. It was as in the days of the Douglas Wars in Scotland, when the very children took sides for Queen Mary and King James, and fought each other in the streets. Domremy was for the Armagnacs — that is, against the English and for the Dauphin, the son of the mad Charles VI. But at Maxey, on the Meuse, a village near Domremy, the people were all for Burgundy and the English. The boys of Domremy would go out and fight the Maxey boys with fists and sticks and stones. Joan did not remember having taken part in those battles, but she had often seen her brothers and the Domremy boys come home all bruised and bleeding.

Once Joan saw more of war than these schoolboy bickers. It was in 1425, when she was a girl of thirteen. There was a kind of robber chief on the English side, a man named Henri d'Orly, from Savoy, who dwelt in the castle of Doulevant. There he and his band of armed men lived and drank and plundered far and near. One day there galloped into Domremy a squadron of spearmen, who rode through the fields driving together the cattle of the villagers, among them the cows of Joan's father. The country people could make no resistance; they were glad enough if their houses were not burned. So off rode Henri d'Orly's men, driving the cattle with their spear-points along the track to the castle of Doulevant. But cows are not fast travellers, and when the robbers had reached a little village called Dommartin le France they rested, and went to the tavern to make merry. But by this time a lady, Madame d'Ogévillier, had sent in all haste to the Count de Vaudemont to tell him how the villagers of Domremy had been ruined. So he called his squire, Barthélemy de Clefmont, and bade him summon his spears and mount and ride. It reminds us of the old Scottish ballad, where Jamie Telfer of the Fair Dodhead has seen all his cattle driven out of his stalls by the English; and he runs to Branxholme and warns the water, and they with Harden pursue the English, defeat them, and recover Telfer's kye, with a great spoil out of England. Just so Barthélemy de Clefmont, with seven or eight lances, galloped down the path to Dommartin le France. There they found the cattle, and d'Orly's men fled like cowards. So Barthélemy with his comrades was returning very joyously, when Henri d'Orly rode up with a troop of horse and followed hard after Barthélemy. He was wounded by a lance, but he cut his way through d'Orly's men, and also brought the cattle back safely — a very gallant deed of arms. We may fancy the delight of the villagers when 'the kye cam' hame.' It may have been now that an event happened, of which Joan does not tell us herself, but which was reported by the king's seneschal, in June 1429, when Joan had just begun her wonderful career. The children of the village, says the seneschal, were running races and leaping in wild joy about the fields;

possibly their gladness was caused by the un-expected rescue of their cattle. Joan ran so much more fleetly than the rest, and leaped so far, that the children believed she actually *flew*, and they told her so! Tired and breathless, 'out of herself,' says the seneschal, she paused, and in that moment she heard a Voice, but saw no man; the Voice bade her go home, because her mother had need of her. And when she came home the Voice said many things to her about the great deeds which God bade her do for France. We shall later hear Joan's own account of how her visions and Voices first came to her.

Three years later there was an alarm, and the Domremy people fled to Neufchâteau, Joan going with her parents. Afterwards her ene-mies tried to prove that she had been a servant at an inn in Neufchâteau, had lived roughly with grooms and soldiers, and had learned to ride. But this was absolutely untrue. An ordi-nary child would have thought little of war and of the sorrows of her country in the flowery fields of Domremy and Vaucouleurs; but Joan always thought of the miseries of *France la bele*, fair France, and prayed for her country and her king. A great road, on the lines of an old Roman way, passed near Domremy, so Joan would hear all the miserable news from trav-ellers. Probably she showed what was in her mind, for her father dreamed that she 'had gone off with soldiers,' and this dream struck him so much, that he told his sons that he, or they, must drown Joan if she so disgraced herself. For many girls of bad character, lazy and rude, followed the soldiers, as they always have done, and always will. Joan's father thought that his dream meant that Joan would be like these women. It would be interesting to know whether he was in the habit of dreaming true dreams. For Joan, his child, dreamed when wide awake, dreamed dreams immortal, which brought her to her glory and her doom.

When Joan was between twelve and thir-teen, a wonderful thing befell her. We have al-ready heard one account of it, written when Joan was in the first flower of her triumph, by the seneschal of the King of France. A Voice spoke to her and prophesised of what she was to do. But about all these marvellous things it is more safe to attend to what Joan always said

herself. She told the same story both to friends and foes; to the learned men who, by her king's desire, examined her at Poictiers, before she went to war (April 1429); and to her deadly foes at Rouen. No man can read her answers to them and doubt that she spoke what she be-lieved. And she died for this belief. Unluckily the book that was kept of what she said at Poictiers is lost. Before her enemies at Rouen there were many things which she did not think it right to say. On one point, after for long re-fusing to speak, she told her foes a kind of par-able, which we must not take as part of her real story.

When Joan was between twelve and thir-teen (1424), so she swore, 'a *Voice came to her from God for her guidance*, but when first it came, she was in great fear. And it came, that Voice, about noonday, in the summer season, she being in her father's garden. And Joan had not fasted the day before that, but was fasting when the Voice came. And she heard the Voice on her right side, towards the church, and rarely did she hear it but she also saw 'a great light.' These are her very words. They asked her if she heard these Voices there, in the hall of judgment, and she answered, 'If I were in a wood, I should well hear these Voices coming to me.' The Voices at first only told her 'to be a good girl, and go to church.' She thought it was a holy Voice, and that it came from God; and the third time she heard it she knew it was the voice of an angel. The Voice told her of 'the great pity there was in France,' and that one day she must go into France and help the coun-try. She had visions with the Voices; visions first of St. Michael, and then of St. Catherine and St. Margaret. She hated telling her hypo-critical judges anything about these heavenly visions, but it seems that she really believed in their appearance, believed that she had em-braced the knees of St. Margaret and St. Cath-erine, and she did reverence to them when they came to her. 'I saw them with my bodily eyes, as I see you,' she said to her judges, 'and when they departed from me I wept, and well I wished that they had taken me with them.'

What are we to think about these visions and these Voices which were with Joan to her death?

It was in 1424 that the Voices first came to Joan the Maid. The years went on, bringing more and more sorrow to France. In 1428 only a very few small towns in the east still held out for the Dauphin, and these were surrounded on every side by enemies. Meanwhile the Voices came more frequently, urging Joan to go into France, and help her country. She asked how she, a girl, who could not ride or use sword and lance, could be of any help? Rather would she stay at home and spin beside her dear mother. At the same time she was encouraged by one of the vague old prophecies which were as common in France as in Scotland. A legend ran 'that France was to be saved by a Maiden from the Oak Wood,' and there was an Oak Wood, *le bois chénu*, near Domremy. Some such prophecy had an influence on Joan, and probably helped people to believe her. The Voices, moreover, instantly and often commanded her to go to Vaucouleurs, a neighbouring town which was loyal, and there meet Robert de Baudricourt, who was captain of the French garrison. Now, Robert de Baudricourt was not what is called a romantic person. Though little over thirty, he had already married, one after the other, two rich widows. He was a gallant soldier, but a plain practical man, very careful of his own interest, and cunning enough to hold his own among his many enemies, English, Burgundian, and Lorrainers. It was to him that Joan must go, a country girl to a great noble, and tell him that she, and she alone, could save France! Joan knew what manner of man Robert de Baudricourt was, for her father had been obliged to visit him, and speak for the people of Domremy when they were oppressed. She could hardly hope that he would listen to her, and it was with a heavy heart that she found a good reason for leaving home to visit Vaucouleurs. Joan had a cousin, a niece of her mother's, who was married to one Durand Lassois, at Burey en Vaux, a village near Vaucouleurs. This cousin invited Joan to visit her for a week. At the end of that time she spoke to her cousin's husband. There was an old saying, as we saw, that France would be rescued by a Maid, and she, as she told Lassois, was that Maid. Lassois listened, and, whatever

he may have thought of her chances, he led her to Robert de Baudricourt.

Joan came, on May 13, 1428, in her simple red dress, and walked straight up to the captain among his men. She knew him, she said, by what her Voices had told her, but she may also have heard him described by her father. She told him that the Dauphin must keep quiet, and risk no battle, for before the middle of Lent next year (1429) God would send him succour. She added that the kingdom belonged, not to the Dauphin, but to her Master, who willed that the Dauphin should be crowned, and she herself would lead him to Reims, to be anointed with the holy oil.

'And who is your Master?' said Robert.

'The King of Heaven!'

Robert, very naturally, thought that Joan was crazed, and shrugged his shoulders. He bluntly told Lassois to box her ears, and take her back to her father. So she had to go home; but here new troubles awaited her. The enemy came down on Domremy and burned it; Joan and her family fled to Neufchâteau, where they stayed for a few days. It was perhaps about this time that a young man declared that Joan had promised to marry him, and he actually brought her before a court of justice, to make her fulfil her promise.

Joan was beautiful, well-shaped, dark-haired, and charming in her manner.

We have a letter which two young knights, André and Guy de Laval, wrote to their mother in the following year. 'The Maid was armed from neck to heel,' they say, 'but unhelmeted; she carried a lance in her hand. Afterwards, when we lighted down from our horses at Selles, I went to her lodging to see her, and she called for wine for me, saying she would soon make me drink wine in Paris' (then held by the English), 'and, indeed, she seems a thing wholly divine, both to look on her and to hear her sweet voice.'

It is no wonder that the young man of Domremy wanted to marry Joan; but she had given no promise, and he lost his foolish lawsuit. She and her parents soon went back to Domremy.

In Domremy they found that the enemy had ruined everything. Their cattle were safe, for they had been driven to Neufchâteau, but when Joan looked from her father's garden to the church, she saw nothing but a heap of smoke ruins. She had to go to say her prayers now at the church of Greux. These things only made her feel more deeply the sorrows of her country. The time was drawing near when she had prophesied that the Dauphin was to receive help from heaven — namely, in the Lent of 1429. On that year the season was held more than commonly sacred, for Good Friday and the Annunciation fell on the same day. So, early in January, 1429, Joan the Maid turned her back on Domremy, which she was never to see again. Her cousin Lassois came and asked leave for Joan to visit him again; she said good-bye to her father and mother, and to her friend Mengette, but to her dearest friend Hauvette she did not even say good-bye, for she could not bear it. She went to her cousin's house at Burey, and there she stayed for six weeks, hearing bad news of the siege of Orleans by the English. Meanwhile, Robert de Baudricourt, in Vaucouleurs, was not easy in his mind, for he was likely to lose the protection of René of Anjou, the Duc de Bar, who was on the point of joining the English. Thus Robert may have been more inclined to listen to Joan than when he bade her cousin box her ears and take her back to her father. A squire named Jean de Nouillompont met Joan one day.

'Well, my lass,' said he, 'is our king to be driven from France, and are we all to become English?'

'I have come here,' said Joan, 'to bid Robert de Baudricourt lead me to the king, but he will not listen to me. And yet to the king I must go, even if I walk my legs down to the knees; for none in all the world — king, nor duke, nor the King of Scotland's daughter — can save France, but myself only. *Certes*, I would rather stay and spin with my poor mother, for to fight is not my calling; but I must go and I must fight, for so my Lord will have it.'

'And who is your Lord?' said Jean de Nouillompont.

'He is God,' said the Maiden.

'Then, so help me God, I shall take you to the king,' said Jean, putting her hands in his. 'When do we start?'

'To-day is better than to-morrow,' said the Maid.

Joan was now staying in Vaucouleurs with Catherine le Royer. One day, as she and Catherine were sitting at their spinning-wheels, who should come in but Robert de Baudricourt with the *curé* of the town. Robert had fancied that perhaps Joan was a witch! He told the priest to perform some rite of the Church over her, so that if she were a witch she would be obliged to run away. But when the words were spoken, Joan threw herself at the knees of the priest, saying, 'Sir, this is ill done of you, for you have heard my confession and know that I am not a witch.'

Robert was now half disposed to send her to the king and let her take her chance. But days dragged on, and when Joan was not working she would be on her knees in the crypt or underground chapel of the chapel Royal in Vaucouleurs. Twenty-seven years later a chorister boy told how he often saw her praying there for France. Now people began to hear of Joan, and the Duke of Lorraine asked her to visit him at Nancy, where she bade him lead a better life. He is said to have given her a horse and some money. On February 12 the story goes that she went to Robert de Baudricourt.

'You delay too long,' she said. 'On this very day, at Orleans, the gentle Dauphin has lost a battle.'

This was, in fact, the Battle of Herrings, so called because the English defeated and cut off a French and Scottish force which attacked them as they were bringing herrings into camp for provisions in Lent. If this tale is true, Joan cannot have known of the battle by any common means; but though it is vouched for by the king's secretary, Joan has told us nothing about it herself.

Now the people of Vaucouleurs bought clothes for Joan to wear on her journey to the Dauphin. They were such clothes as men wear — doublet, hose, surcoat, boots, and spurs — and Robert de Baudricourt gave Joan a sword.

On February 23, 1429, the gate of the little castle of Vaucouleurs, 'the Gate of France,' which is still standing, was thrown open. Seven travellers rode out, among them two squires,

Jean de Nouillompont and Bertrand de Poulengy, with their attendants, and Joan the Maid. 'Go, and let what will come of it come!' said Robert de Baudricourt. He did not expect much to come of it. It was a long journey — they were eleven days on the road—and a dangerous one. But Joan laughed at danger. 'God will clear my path to the king, for to this end I was born.' Often they rode by night, stopping at monasteries when they could. Sometimes they slept out under the sky. Though she was so young and so beautiful, with the happiness of her long desire in her eyes, and the glory of her future shining on her, these two young gentlemen never dreamed of paying their court to her and making love, as in romances they do, for they regarded her 'as if she had been an angel.' 'They were in awe of her,' they said, long afterwards, long after the angels had taken Joan to be with their company in heaven. And all the knights who had seen her said the same. Dunois and d'Aulon and the beautiful Duc d'Alençson, '*le beau Duc*' as Joan called him, all said that she was 'a thing enskied and sainted.' So on they rode, six men and a maid, through a country full of English and Burgundian soldiery. There were four rivers to cross, Marne, Aube, Seine, and Yonne, and the rivers were 'great and mickle o' spate,' running red with the rains from bank to bank, so that they could not ford the streams, but must go by unfriendly towns, where alone there were bridges. Joan would have liked to stay and go to church in every town, but this might not be. However, she heard mass thrice at the church of her favourite saint, Catherine de Fierbois, between Loches and Chinon, in a friendly country. And a strange thing happened later in that church.

From Fierbois Joan made some clerk write to the king that she was coming to help him, and that she would know him among all his men. Probably it was here that she wrote to beg her parents' pardon, and they forgave her, she says. Meanwhile news reached the people then besieged in Orleans that a marvellous Maiden was riding to their rescue. On March 6 Joan arrived in Chinon, where for two or three days the king's advisers would not let him see her. At last they yielded, and she went straight up to him, and when he denied that he was the king, she told him that she knew well who he was.

'There is the king,' said Charles, pointing to a richly dressed noble.

'No, fair sire. You are he!'

Still, it was not easy to believe. Joan stayed at Chinon in the house of a noble lady. The young Duc d'Alençon was on her side from the first, bewitched by her noble horsemanship, which she had never learned. Great people came to see her, but, when she was alone, she wept and prayed. The king sent messengers to inquire about her at Domremy, but time was going on, and Orleans was not relieved.

Weeks had passed, and Joan had never yet seen a blow struck in war. She used to exercise herself in horsemanship, and knightly sports of tilting, and it is wonderful that a peasant girl became, at once, one of the best riders among the chivalry of France. The young Duc d'Alençon, lately come from captivity in England, saw how gallantly she rode, and gave her a horse. He and his wife were her friends from the first, when the politicians and advisers were against her. But, indeed, whatever the Maid attempted, she did better than others, at once, without teaching or practice. It was now determined that Joan should be taken to Poictiers, and examined before all the learned men, bishops, doctors, and higher clergy who still were on the side of France. There was good reason for this delay. It was plain to all, friends and foes, that the wonderful Maid was not like other men and women, with her Voices, her visions, her prophecies, and her powers. All agreed that she had some strange help given to her; but who gave it? This aid must come, people thought then, either from heaven or hell — either from God and his saints, or from the devil and his angels. Now, if any doubt could be thrown on the source whence Joan's aid came, the English might argue (as of course they did), that she was a witch and a heretic. If she was a heretic and a witch, then her king was involved in her wickedness, and so he might be legally shut out from his kingdom. It was necessary, therefore, that Joan should be examined by learned men. They must find out whether she had always been good, and a true believer, and whether her Voices always agreed in everything with the teachings of the Church. Otherwise her angels must be devils in disguise. For these reasons Joan was carried to Poictiers. During three long weeks the learned men asked her questions, and, no doubt, they wearied her terribly. But they said it was wonderful how wisely this girl, who 'did not know A from B,' replied to their puzzling inquiries. She told the story of her visions, of the command laid upon her to rescue Orleans. Said Guillaume Aymeri, 'You ask for men-at-arms, and you say that God will have the English to leave France and go home. If that is true, no men-at-arms are needed; God's pleasure can drive the English out of the land.'

'In God's name,' said the Maid, 'the men-at-arms will fight, and God will give the victory.' Then came the learned Seguin; 'a right sour man was he,' said those who knew him.

Seguin was a Limousin, and the Limousins spoke in a queer accent at which the other French were always laughing.

'In what language do your Voices speak?' asked he.

'In a better language than *yours*, said Joan, and the bishops smiled at the country quip.

'We may not believe in you,' said Seguin, 'unless you show us a sign.'

'I did not come to Poictiers to work miracles,' said Joan; 'take me to Orleans, and I shall show you the signs that I am sent to do.' And show them she did.

Joan never pretended to work miracles. Though, in that age, people easily believed in miracles, it is curious that none worth mentioning were invented about Joan in her own time. She knew things in some strange way sometimes, but the real miracle was her extraordinary wisdom, genius, courage, and power of enduring hardship.

At last, after examining witnesses from Domremy, and the Queen of Sicily and other great ladies to whom Joan was entrusted, the clergy found nothing in her but 'goodness, humility, frank maidenhood, piety, honesty, and simplicity.' As for her wearing a man's dress, the Archbishop of Embrun said to the king, 'It is more becoming to do these things in man's

gear, since they have to be done amongst men.'

The king therefore made up his mind at last. Jean and Pierre, Joan's brothers, were to ride with her to Orleans; her old friends, her first friends, Jean de Nouillompont and Bertrand de Poulengy, had never left her. She was given a squire, Jean d'Aulon, a very good man, and a page, Louis de Coutes, and a chaplain. The king gave Joan armour and horses, and offered her a sword. But her Voices told her that, behind the altar of St. Catherine de Fierbois, where she heard mass on her way to Chinon, there was an old sword, with five crosses on the blade, buried in the earth. That sword she was to wear. A man whom Joan did not know, and had never seen, was sent from Tours, and found the sword in the place which she described. The sword was cleaned of rust, and the king gave her two sheaths, one of velvet, one of cloth of gold, but Joan had a leather sheath made for use in war. She also commanded a banner to be made, with the Lilies of France on a white field. There was also a picture of God, holding the round world, and two angels at the sides, with the sacred words, JHESU MARIA. On another flag was the Annunciation, the Virgin holding a lily, and the angel coming to her. In battle, when she led a charge, Joan always carried her standard, that she might not be able to use her sword. She wished to kill nobody, and said 'she loved her banner forty times more than her sword.' Joan afterwards broke St. Catherine's sword, when slapping a girl (who richly deserved to be slapped) with the flat of the blade. Her enemies, at her trial, wished to prove that her flag was a kind of magical talisman, but Joan had no belief in anything of that kind. What she believed in was God, her Voices, and her just cause. When once it was settled that she was to lead an army to relieve Orleans, she showed her faith by writing a letter addressed to the King of England; Bedford, the Regent; and the English generals at Orleans. This letter was sent from Blois, late in April. It began JHESU MARIA. Joan had no ill-will against the English. She bade them leave France, 'and if you are reasonable, you yet may ride in the Maid's company, where the French will do the fairest feat of arms that ever yet was done for Christentie.' Probably she had in her mind some Crusade. But, before France and England can march together, 'do ye justice to the King of Heaven and the Blood Royal of France. Yield to the Maid the keys of all the good towns which ye have taken and assailed in France.' If they did not yield to the Maid and the king, she will come on them to their sorrow. 'Duke of Bedford, the Maid prays and entreats you not to work your own destruction!'

We may imagine how the English laughed and swore when they received this letter. They threw the heralds of the Maid into prison, and threatened to burn them as heretics. From the very first, the English promised to burn Joan as a witch and a heretic. This fate was always before her eyes. But she went where her Voices called her.

At last the men-at-arms who were to accompany Joan were ready. She rode at their head, as André de Laval and Guy de Laval saw her, and described her in a letter to their mother. She was armed in white armour, but unhelmeted, a little axe in her hand, riding a great black charger, that reared at the door of her lodging and would not let her mount.

' "Lead him to the Cross!" cried she, for a Cross stood on the roadside, by the church. There he stood as if he had been stone, and she mounted. Then she turned to the church, and said, in her girlish voice, "You priests and churchmen, make prayers and processions to God." Then she cried, "Forwards, Forwards!" and on she rode, a pretty page carrying her banner, and with her little axe in her hand." ' And so Joan went to war. She led, she says, ten or twelve thousand soldiers. Among the other generals were Xaintrailles and La Hire. Joan made her soldiers confess themselves; as for La Hire, a brave rough soldier, she forbade him to swear, as he used to do, but, for his weakness, she permitted him to say, *By my bâton*! This army was to defend a great convoy of provisions, of which the people of Orleans stood in sore need. Since November they had been besieged, and now it was late April. The people in Orleans were not yet starving, but food came in slowly, and in small quantities. From the first the citizens had behaved well; a Scottish priest describes their noble conduct. They had burned all the outlying suburbs,

beyond the wall, that they might not give shelter to the English. They had plenty of cannon, which carried large rough stone balls, and usually did little harm. But a gun was fired, it is said by a small boy, which killed Salisbury, the English general, as he looked out of an arrow-slit in a fort that the English had taken.

The French general-in-chief was the famous Dunois, then called the Bastard of Orleans. On the English side was the brave Talbot, who fought under arms for sixty years, and died fighting when he was over eighty. There were also Suffolk, Pole, and Glasdale, whom the French called 'Classidas.' The English had not soldiers enough to surround and take so large a town, of 30,000 people, in ordinary war. But as Dunois said, 'two hundred English could then beat a thousand French' — that is, as the French were before the coming of the Maid.

About half-past six in the morning the fight began. The French and Scottish leaped into the fosse, they set ladders against the walls, they reached the battlements, and were struck down by English swords and axes. Cannon-balls and great stones and arrows rained on them. 'Fight on!' cried the Maid; 'the place is ours.' At one o'clock she set a ladder against the wall with her own hands, but was deeply wounded by an arrow, which pierced clean through between neck and shoulder. Joan wept, but seizing the arrow with her own hands she dragged it out. The men-at-arms wished to say magic spells over the wound to 'charm' it, but this the Maid forbade as witchcraft. 'Yet,' says Dunois, 'she did not withdraw from the battle, nor took any medicine for the wound; and the onslaught lasted from morning till eight at night, so that there was no hope of victory. Then I desired that the army should go back to the town, but the Maid came to me and bade me wait a little longer. Next she mounted her horse and rode into a vine-yard, and there prayed for the space of seven minutes or eight. Then she returned, took her banner, and stood on the brink of the fosse. The English trembled when they saw her, but our men returned to the charge and met with no resistance. The English fled or were slain, and Glasdale, who had insulted the Maid, was drowned' (by the burning of the drawbridge between the redoubt and Les Tourelles. The Maid in vain besought him, with tears, to surrender and be ransomed), 'and we returned gladly into Orleans.' The people of Orleans had a great share in this victory. Seeing the English hard pressed, they laid long beams across the broken arches of the bridge, and charged by this perilous way. The triumph was even more that of the citizens than of the army. Homer tells us how Achilles, alone and unarmed, stood by the fosse and shouted, and how all the Trojans fled. But here was a greater marvel; and the sight of the wounded girl, bowed beneath the weight of her banner, frighted stouter hearts than those of the men of Troy.

Joan returned, as she had prophesied, by the bridge, but she did not make her supper off the fish: she took a little bread dipped in wine and water, her wound was dressed, and she slept. Next day the English drew up their men in line of battle. The French went out to meet them, and would have begun the attack. Joan said that God would not have them fight.

'If the English attack, we shall defeat them; we are to let them go in peace if they will.'

Mass was then said before the French army. When the rite was done, Joan asked: 'Do they face us, or have they turned their backs?'

It was the English backs that the French saw that day: Talbot's men were in full retreat on Meun.

From that hour May 8 is kept a holiday at Orleans in honour of Joan the Maiden. Never was there such a deliverance. In a week the Maid had driven a strong army, full of courage and well led, out of forts like Les Tourelles. The Duc d'Alençon visited it, and said that with a few men-at-arms he would have felt certain of holding it for a week against any strength however great. But Joan not only gave the French her spirit: her extraordinary courage in leading a new charge after so terrible a wound, 'six inches deep,' says d'Alençon, made the English think that they were fighting a force not of this world. And that is exactly what they were doing.

The Maid had shown her sign, as she promised; she had rescued Orleans. Her next desire was to lead Charles to Reims, through a country occupied by the English, and to have him anointed there with the holy oil. Till this was done she could only regard him as Dauphin — king, indeed, by blood, but not by consecration.

Here are the exploits which the Maid and the loyal French did in one week. She took Jargeau on June 11; on June 15 she seized the bridge of Meun; Beaugency yielded to her on June 17; on June 18 she defeated the English army at Pathay. Now sieges were long affairs in those days, as they are even to-day, when cannon are so much more powerful than they were in Joan's time. Her success seemed a miracle to the world.

This miracle, like all miracles, was wrought by faith. Joan believed in herself, in her country, and in God. It was not by visions and by knowing things strangely that she conquered, but by courage, by strength (on one occasion she never put off her armour for six days and six nights), and by inspiring the French with the sight of her valour. Without her visions, indeed, she would never have gone to war. She often said so. But, being at war, her word was 'Help yourselves, and God will help you.' Who could be lazy or a coward when a girl set such an example?

The King of France and his favourites could be indolent and cowards. Had Charles VII been such a man as Charles Stuart was in 1745, his foot would have been in the stirrup, and his lance in rest. In three months the English would have been driven into the sea. But the king loitered about the castles of the Loire with his favourites, La Tremouille, and his adviser, the Archbishop of Reims. They wasted the one year of Joan. There were jealousies against the Constable de Richemont of Brittany who had come with all his lances to follow the lily flag. If once Charles were king indeed and the English driven out, La Tremouille would cease to be powerful. This dastard sacrificed the Maid in the end, as he was ready to sacrifice France to his own private advantage.

At last, with difficulty, Charles was brought to visit Reims, and consent to be crowned like his ancestors. Seeing that he was never likely to move, Joan left the town where he was and went off into the country. This retreat brought Charles to his senses. The towns which he passed by yielded to him; Joan went and summoned each. 'Now she was with the king in the centre, now with the rearguard, now with the van.' The town of Troyes, where there was an English garrison, did not wish to yield. There was a council in the king's army: they said they could not take the place.

'In two days it shall be yours, by force or by good will,' said the Maid.

'Six days will do,' said the chancellor, 'if you are sure you speak truth.'

Joan made ready for an attack. She was calling 'Forward!' when the town surrendered. Reims, after some doubts, yielded also, on July 16, and all the people, with shouts of '*Noel!*' welcomed the king. On July 17 the king was crowned and anointed with the Holy Oil by that very Archbishop of Reims who always opposed Joan. The Twelve Peers of France were not all present — some were on the English side — but Joan stood by Charles, her banner in her hand. 'It bore the brunt, and deserved to share the renown,' she said later to her accusers.

When the ceremony was ended, and the Dauphin Charles was a crowned and anointed king, the Maid knelt weeping at his feet.

'Gentle king,' she said, 'now is accomplished the will of God, who desired that you should come to Reims to be consecrated, and to prove that you are the true king and the kingdom is yours.'

Then all the knights wept for joy.

The king bade Joan choose her reward. Already horses, rich armour, jewelled daggers, had been given to her. These, adding to the beauty and glory of her aspect, had made men follow her more gladly, and for that she valued them. She, too, made gifts to noble ladies, and gave much to the poor. She only wanted money to wage the war with, not for herself. Her family was made noble; on their shield, between two lilies, a sword upholds the crown. Her father was at Reims, and saw her in her glory. What reward, then, was Joan to choose? She chose nothing for herself, but that her native village of Domremy should be free from taxes. This news her father carried home from the splendid scene at Reims.

The name of Joan was now such a terror to the English that men deserted rather than face her in arms. At this time the truce with Burgundy ended, and the duke openly set out to besiege the strong town of Compiègne, held by de Flavy for France. Joan hurried to Compiègne, whence she made two expeditions which were defeated by treachery. Perhaps she thought of this, perhaps of the future, when in the church of Compiègne she declared one day to a crowd of children whom she loved that she knew she was sold and betrayed. Old men who had heard her told this tale long afterwards.

Burgundy had invested Compiègne, when Joan, with four hundred men, rode into the town secretly at dawn. That day Joan led a sally against the Burgundians. Her Voices told her nothing, good or bad, she says. The Burgundians were encamped at Margny and at Clairoix, the English at Venette, villages on a plain near the walls. Joan crossed the bridge on a grey charger, in a surcoat of crimson silk, rode through the redoubt beyond the bridge, and attacked the Burgundians. Flavy in the town was to prevent the English from attacking her in the rear. He had boats on the river to secure Joan's retreat if necessary.

Joan swept through Margny, driving the Burgundians before her; the garrison of Clairoix came to their help; the battle was doubtful. Meanwhile the English came up; they could not have reached the Burgundians, to aid them, but some of the Maid's men, seeing the English standards, fled. The English followed them under the walls of Compiègne; the gate of the redoubt was closed to prevent the English from entering with the runaways. Like Hector under Troy, the Maid was shut out from the town which she came to save.

Joan was with her own foremost line when the rear fled. They told her of her danger, she heeded not. For the last time rang out in that girlish voice: '*Allez avant! Forward, they are ours!*'

Her men seized her bridle and turned her horse's head about. The English held the entrance from the causeway; Joan and a few men (her brother was one of them) were driven into a corner of the outer wall. A rush was made at Joan. 'Yield! yield! give your faith to me!' each man cried.

'I have given my faith to Another,' she said, 'and I will keep my oath.'

Her enemies confess that on this day Joan did great feats of arms, covering the rear of her force when they had to fly.

Some French historians hold that the gates were closed by treason that the Maid might be taken. We may hope that this was not so; the commander of Compiègne held his town successfully for the king, and was rescued by Joan's friend, the brave Pothon de Xaintrailles.

The sad story that is still to tell shall be shortly told. There is no word nor deed of the Maid's, in captivity as in victory, that is not to her immortal honour. But the sight of the wickedness of men, their cowardice, cruelty, greed, ingratitude, is not a thing to linger over.

Joan was now kept in a high tower at Beaurevoir, and was allowed to walk on the leads. She knew she was sold to England, she had heard that the people of Compiègne were to be massacred. She would rather die than fall into English hands, 'rather give her soul to God, than her body to the English.' But she hoped to escape and relieve Compiègne. She, therefore, prayed for counsel to her Saints; might she leap from the top of the tower? Would they not bear her up in their hands? St. Catherine bade her not to leap; God would help her and the people of Compiègne.

Then, for the first time as far as we know, the Maid wilfully disobeyed her Voices. She leaped from the tower. They found her, not wounded, not a limb was broken, but stunned. She knew not what had happened; they told her she had leaped down. For three days she could not eat, 'yet was she comforted by St. Catherine, who bade her confess and seek pardon of God, and told her that, without fail, they of Compiègne should be relieved before Martinmas.' This prophecy was fulfilled.

About the trial and the death of the Maid, I have not the heart to write a long story. Some points are to be remembered. The person who conducted the trial, itself illegal, was her deadly enemy, the false Frenchman, the Bishop of Beauvais, Cauchon, whom she and her men had turned out of his bishoprick. It is most un-

just and unheard of, that any one should be tried by a judge who is his private enemy. Next, Joan was kept in strong irons day and night, and she, the most modest of maidens, was always guarded by five brutal English soldiers of the lowest rank. Again, she was not allowed to receive the Holy Communion as she desired with tears. Thus weakened by long captivity and ill usage, she, an untaught girl, was questioned repeatedly for three months, by the most cunning and learned doctors in law of the Paris University. Often many spoke at once, to perplex her mind. But Joan always showed a wisdom which confounded them, and which is at least as extraordinary as her skill in war. She would never swear an oath to answer *all* their questions. About herself, and all matters bearing on her own conduct, she would answer. About the king and the secrets of the king, she would not answer. If they forced her to reply about these things, she frankly said, she would not tell them the truth. The whole object of the trial was to prove that she dealt with powers of evil, and that her king had been crowned and aided by the devil. Her examiners, therefore, attacked her day by day, in public and in her dungeon, with questions about these visions which she held sacred, and could only speak of with a blush among her friends. Had she answered (as a lawyer said at the time), '*it seemed to me* I saw a saint,' no man could have condemned her. Probably she did not know this, for she was not allowed to have an advocate of her own party, and she, a lonely girl, was opposed to the keenest and most learned lawyers of France. But she maintained that she certainly did see, hear, and touch her Saints, and that they came to her by the will of God. This was called blasphemy and witchcraft. And now came in the fatal Fairies! She was accused of dealing with devils under the Tree of Domremy.

Most was made of her refusal to wear woman's dress. For this she seems to have had two reasons; first, that to give up her old dress would have been to acknowledge that her mission was ended; next, for reasons of modesty, she being alone in prison among ruffianly men. She would wear woman's dress if they would let her take the Holy Communion, but this they refused. To these points she was constant, she would not deny her visions; she would not say one word against her king, 'the noblest Christian in the world' she called him who had deserted her. She would not wear woman's dress in prison. We must remember that, as she was being tried by churchmen, she should have been, as she often prayed to be, in a prison of the church, attended by women. They set a spy on her, a caitiff priest named L'Oyseleur, who pretended to be her friend, and who betrayed her. The English soldiers were allowed to bully, threaten, and frighten away every one who gave her any advice. They took her to the torture-chamber, and threatened her with torture, but from this even these priests shrunk, except a few more cruel and cowardly than the rest. Finally, they put her up in public, opposite a pile of wood ready for burning, and then set a priest to preach at her. All through her trial, her Voices bade her 'answer boldly,' in three months she would give her last answer, in three months 'she would be free with great victory, and come into the Kingdom of Paradise.' In three months from the first day of her trial she went free through the gate of fire. Boldly she answered, and wisely. She would submit the truth of her visions to the Church, that is, to God, and the Pope. But she would *not* submit them to 'the Church,' if that meant the clergy round her. At last, in fear of fire, and the stake before her, and on promise of being taken to a kindlier prison among women, and released from chains, she promised to 'abjure,' to renounce her visions, and submit to the Church, that is to Cauchon, and her other priestly enemies. Some little note on paper she now signed with a cross, and repeated 'with a smile,' poor child, a short form of words. By some trick this signature was changed for a long document, in which she was made to confess all her visions false. It is certain that she did not understand her words in this sense.

Cauchon had triumphed. The blame of heresy and witchcraft was cast on Joan, and on her king as an accomplice. But the English were not satisfied; they made an uproar, they threatened Cauchon, for Joan's life was to be spared. She was to be in prison all her days, on bread and water, but, while she lived, they dared

scarcely stir against the French. They were soon satisfied.

Joan's prison was not changed. There soon came news that she had put on man's dress again. The judges went to her. She told them (they say), that she put on this dress of her own free will. In confession, later, she told her priest that she had been refused any other dress, and had been brutally treated both by the soldiers and by an English lord. In self-defence, she dressed in the only attire within her reach. In any case, the promises made to her had been broken. The judge asked her if her Voices had been with her again?

'Yes.'

'What did they say?'

'God told me by the voices of St. Catherine and St. Margaret of the great sorrow of my treason, when I abjured to save my life; that I was damning myself for my life's sake.'

'Do you believe the Voices come from St. Margaret and St. Catherine?'

'Yes, and that they are from God.'

She added that she had never meant to deny this, had not understood that she had denied it.

All was over now; she was a 'relapsed heretic.'

The judges said that they visited Joan again on the morning of her death, and that she withdrew her belief in her Voices; or, at least, left it to the Church to decide whether they were good or bad, while she still maintained that they were *real*. She had expected release, and, for the first time, had been disappointed. At the stake she understood her Voices: they had foretold her martyrdom, 'great victory' over herself, and her entry into rest. But the document of the judges is not signed by the clerks, as all such documents must be. One of them, Manchon, who had not been present, was asked to sign it; he refused. Another, Taquel, is said to have been present, but he did not sign. The story is, therefore, worth nothing.

Enough. They burned Joan the Maid. She did not suffer long. Her eyes were fixed on a cross which a priest, Martin L'Advenu, held up before her. She maintained, he says, to her dying moment, the truth of her Voices. With a great cry of JESUS! she gave up her breath, and her pure soul was with God.

"The Wanderings of Ulysses," from Tales of Troy and Greece, *by Andrew Lang. Illustrated by Edward Bawden (London: Faber and Faber, 1962).*

Following years of attempting to return home after the Trojan War, Ulysses (Odysseus) has a series of adventures which many scholars believe are derived from earlier folktales which have been adapted to fit into Homer's epic the Odyssey. *Of these, the most famous is the hero's encounter with the one-eyed cyclops Polyphemus. A member of a savage, lawless tribe, the giant is in marked contrast to the clever Ulysses. Always the trickster, Ulysses very nearly brings about his own downfall, for, although he engineers a very crafty escape, he cannot resist revealing his true identity. The story reflects the vengeful quality of Greek gods such as Poseidon, God of the Sea, who redresses the wrongs done to his follower Polyphemus.*

The Wanderings of Ulysses

When Ulysses left Troy the wind carried him to the coast of Thrace, where the people were allies of the Trojans. It was a king of the Thracians that Diomede killed when he and Ulysses stole into the camp of the Trojans in the night, and drove away the white horses of the king, as swift as the winds. Ismarus was the name of the Thracian town where Ulysses landed, and his men took it and plundered it, yet Ulysses allowed no one to harm the priest of Apollo, Maron, but protected him and his wife and child, in their house within the holy grove of the God. Maron was grateful, and gave Ulysses twelve talents, or little wedges, of gold, and a great bowl of silver, and twelve large clay jars, as big as barrels, full of the best and strongest wine. It was so strong that men put into the mixing bowl but one measure of wine to twenty measures of water. These presents Ulysses stored up in his ship, and lucky for him it was that he was kind to Maron.

Meanwhile his men, instead of leaving the town with their plunder, sat eating and drinking till dawn. By that time the people of the town had warned their neighbors in the country farms, who all came down in full armor, and attacked the men of Ulysses. In this fight he lost seventy-two men, six from each of his twelve ships, and it was only by hard fighting that the others were able to get on board their ships and sail away.

A great storm arose and beat upon the ships, and it seems that Ulysses and his men were driven into Fairyland, where they remained for ten years. We have heard that King Arthur and Thomas the Rhymer were carried into Fairyland, but what adventures they met with there we do not know. About Ulysses we have the stories which are now to be told. For ten days his ships ran due south, and, on the tenth, they reached the land of the Lotus Eaters, who eat food of flowers. They went on shore and drew water, and three men were sent to try to find the people of that country, who were a quiet, friendly people, and gave the fruit of the lotus to the strange sailors. Now whoever tastes of that fruit has no mind ever to go home, but to sit between the setting sun and the rising moon, dreaming happy dreams, and forgetting the world. The three men at the lotus, and sat down to dream, but Ulysses went after them, and drove them to the ships, and bound their hands and feet, and threw them on board, and sailed away. Then he with his ships reached the coast of the land of the Cyclopes, which means the round-eyed men, men with only one eye apiece, set in the middle of their foreheads. They lived not in houses, but in caves among the hills, and they had no king and no laws, and did not plow or sow, but wheat and vines grew wild, and they kept great flocks of sheep.

There was a beautiful wild desert island lying across the opening of a bay; the isle was full of wild goats, and made a bar against the waves, so that ships could lie behind it safely, run up on the beach, for there was no tide in that sea. There Ulysses ran up his ships, and the men passed the time in hunting wild goats, and feasting on fresh meat and the wine of Maron, the priest of Apollo. Next day Ulysses left all the ships and men there, except his own ship, and his own crew, and went to see what kind of people lived on the mainland, for as yet none had been seen. He found a large cave close to the sea, with laurels growing on the rocky roof, and a wall of rough stones built round a court in front. Ulysses left all his men but twelve with the ship; filled a goat skin with the strong wine of Maron, put some corn flour in a sack, and went up to the cave. Nobody was there, but there were all the things that are usually in a dairy, baskets full of cheese, pails and bowls full of milk and whey, and kids and lambs were playing in their folds.

All seemed very quiet and pleasant. The men wanted to take as much cheese as they could carry back to the ship, but Ulysses wished to see the owner of the cave. His men, making themselves at home, lit a fire, and toasted and ate the cheese, far within the cave. Then a shadow thrown by the setting sun fell across the opening of the cave, and a monstrous man entered, and threw down a dry trunk of a tree that he carried for firewood. Next he drove in the ewes of his flock, leaving the rams in the yard and he picked up a huge flat stone, and set it so as to make a shut door to the cave, for twenty-four yoke of horses could not have dragged away that stone. Lastly the man milked his ewes, and put the milk in pails to drink at supper. All this while Ulysses and his men sat quiet and in great fear, for they were shut up in a cave with a one-eyed giant, whose cheese they had been eating.

Then the giant, when he had lit the fire, happened to see the men, and asked them who they were. Ulysses said that they were Greeks, who had taken Troy, and were wandering lost on the seas, and he asked the man to be kind to them in the name of their chief God, Zeus.

"We Cyclopes," said the giant, "do not care for Zeus or the Gods, for we think that we are better men than they. Where is your ship?" Ulysses answered that it had been wrecked on the coast, to which the man made no answer, but snatched up two of the twelve, knocked out their brains on the floor, tore the bodies limb from limb, roasted them at his fire, ate them, and, after drinking many pailfuls of milk, lay down and fell asleep. Now Ulysses had a mind to drive his sword-point into the giant's liver, and he felt for the place with his hand. But he remembered that, even if he killed the giant, he could not move the huge stone that

was the door of the cave, so he and his men would die of hunger, when they had eaten all the cheeses.

In the morning the giant ate two more men for breakfast, drove out his ewes, and set the great stone in the doorway again, as lightly as a man would put a quiverlid on a quiver of arrows. Then away he went, driving his flock to graze on the green hills.

Ulysses did not give way to despair. The giant had left his stick in the cave: it was as large as the mast of a great ship. From this Ulysses cut a portion six feet long, and his men cut and rubbed as if they were making a spear shaft: Ulysses then sharpened it to a point, and hardened the point in the fire. It was a thick rounded bar of wood, and the men cast lots to choose four, who should twist the bar in the giant's eye when he fell asleep at night. Back he came at sunset, and drove his flocks into the cave, rams and all. Then he put up his stone door, milked his ewes, and killed two men and cooked them.

Ulysses meanwhile had filled one of the wooden ivy bowls full of the strong wine of Maron, without putting a drop of water into it. This bowl he offered to the giant, who had never heard of wine. He drank one bowl after another, and when he was merry he said that he would make Ulysses a present. "What is your name?" he asked. "My name is *Nobody*," said Ulysses. "Then I shall eat the others first and Nobody last," said the giant. "That shall be your gift." Then he fell asleep.

Ulysses took his bar of wood, and made the point red-hot in the fire. Next his four men rammed it into the giant's one eye, and held it down, while Ulysses twirled it round, and the eye hissed like red-hot iron when men dip it into cold water, which is the strength of iron. The Cyclops roared and leaped to his feet, and shouted for help to the other giants who lived in the neighboring caves. "Who is troubling you, Polyphemus," they answered. "Why do you wake us out of our sleep?" The giant answered, "Nobody is killing me by his cunning, not at all in fair fight." "Then if nobody is harming you nobody can help you," shouted a giant. "If you are ill pray to your father, Poseidon, who is the god of the sea." So the giants all went back to bed, and Ulysses laughed low to see how his cunning had deceived them. Then the giant went and took down his door and sat in the doorway, stretching his arms, so as to catch his prisoners as they went out.

But Ulysses had a plan. He fastened sets of three rams together with twisted withies, and bound a man to each ram in the middle, so that the blind giant's hands would only feel the two outside rams. The biggest and strongest ram Ulysses seized, and held on by his hands and feet to its fleece, under its belly, and then all the sheep went out through the doorway, and the giant felt them, but did not know that they were carrying out the men. "Dear ram!" he said to the biggest, which carried Ulysses, "you do not come out first, as usual, but last, as if you were slow with sorrow for your master, whose eye Nobody has blinded!"

Then all the rams went out into the open country, and Ulysses unfastened his men, and drove the sheep down to his ship and so on board. His crew wept when they heard of the death of six of their friends, but Ulysses made them row out to sea. When he was just so far away from the cave as to be within hearing distance he shouted at the Cyclops and mocked him. Then that giant broke off the rocky peak of a great hill and threw it in the direction of the sound. The rock fell in front of the ship, and raised a wave that drove it back to shore, but Ulysses punted it off with a long pole, and his men rowed out again, far out. Ulysses again shouted to the giant, "If any one asks who blinded you, say that it was Ulysses, Laertes' son, of Ithaca, the stormer of cities."

Then the giant prayed to the Sea God, his father, that Ulysses might never come home, or if he did, that he might come late and lonely, with loss of all his men, and find sorrow in his

Illustration by Edward Bawden, "The Wanderings of Ulysses" from *Tales of Troy and Greece,* by Andrew Lang. Copyright © 1962.

house. Then the giant heaved and threw another rock, but it fell at the stern of the ship, and the wave drove the ship further out to sea, to the shore of the island. There Ulysses and his men landed, and killed some of the giant's sheep, and took supper, and drank wine.

But the Sea God heard the prayer of his son the blind giant.

Ulysses and his men sailed on, in what direction and for how long we do not know, till they saw far off an island that shone in the sea. When they came nearer they found that it had a steep cliff of bronze, with a palace on the top. Here lived Aeolus, the King of the Winds, with his six sons and six daughters. He received Ulysses kindly on his island, and entertained him for a whole month. Then he gave him a leather bag, in which he had bound the ways of all the noisy winds. This bag was fastened with a silver cord, and Aeolus left no wind out except the West Wind, which would blow Ulysses straight home to Ithaca. Where he was we cannot guess, except that he was to the west of his own island.

So they sailed for nine days and nights towards the east, and Ulysses always held the helm and steered, but on the tenth day he fell asleep. Then his men said to each other, "What treasure is it that he keeps in the leather bag, a present from King Aeolus? No doubt the bag is full of gold and silver, while we have only empty hands." So they opened the bag when they were so near Ithaca that they could see people lighting fires on the shore. Then out rushed all the winds, and carried the ship into unknown seas, and when Ulysses woke he was so miserable that he had a mind to drown himself. But he was of an enduring heart, and he lay still, and the ship came back to the isle of Aeolus, who cried, "Away with you! You are the most luckless of living men: you must be hated by the Gods."

Thus Aeolus drove them away, and they sailed for seven days and nights, till they saw land, and came to a harbour with a narrow entrance, and with tall steep rocks on either side. The other eleven ships sailed into the haven, but Ulysses did not venture in; he fastened his ship to a rock at the outer end of the harbour. The place must have been very far north, as it was summer, the sun had hardly set till dawn began again, as it does in Norway and Iceland, where there are many such narrow harbors within walls of rock. These places are called *fiords*. Ulysses sent three men to spy out the country, and at a well outside the town they met a damsel drawing water; she was the child of the king of the people, the Laestrygonians. The damsel led them to her father's house; he was a giant and seized one of the men of Ulysses, meaning to kill and eat him. The two other men fled to the ships, but the Laestrygonians ran along the tops of the cliffs and threw down great rocks, sinking the vessels and killing the sailors. When Ulysses saw this he drew his sword and cut the cable that fastened his ship to the rock outside the harbour, and his crew rowed for dear life and so escaped, weeping for the death of their friends. Thus the prayer of the blind Cyclops was being fulfilled, for now out of twelve ships Ulysses had but one left.

"Robin Hood and Little John," from English and Scottish Popular Ballads, *Student's Cambridge Edition (Boston: Houghton Mifflin, 1904).*

Among the most famous of the Robin Hood tales are those in which Robin encounters men who become members of his band. In this ballad, which is an example of an early form the Robin Hood stories took, we see the hero's love of adventure — his boredom with two weeks of inactivity spurs on his love of fair play — when he agrees to fight Little John with the latter's choice of weapon. We also witness his sense of humor — during the christening, the new recruit is appropriately treated like a baby.

Like Sir Gareth of Orkney and the Norse God Odin, Robin Hood's true identity is not revealed until after he has proved his inner worth. In his circular journey, Robin must travel away from the security of his forest hideout and succeed without the aid of his companions.

1 WHEN Robin Hood was about twenty years
    old,
    With a hey down down and a down
He happened to meet Little John,
    A jolly brisk blade, right fit for the trade,
    For he was a lusty young man.

2 Tho he was calld Little, his limbs they were
    large,
    And his stature was seven foot high;
Where-ever he came, they quak'd at his
    name,
    For soon he would make them to fly.

3 How they came acquainted, I'll tell you in
    brief,
    If you will but listen a while;
For this very jest, amongst all the rest,
    I think it may cause you to smile.

4 Bold Robin Hood said to his jolly bowmen,
    Pray tarry you here in this grove;
And see that you all observe well my call,
    While thorough the forest I rove.

5 We have had no sport for these fourteen
    long days,
    Therefore now abroad will I go;
Now should I be beat, and cannot retreat,
    My horn I will presently blow.

6 Then did he shake hands with his merry
    men all,
    And bid them at present good b'w'ye;
Then, as near a brook his journey he took,
    A stranger he chancd to espy.

7 They happened to meet on a long narrow
    bridge,
    And neither of them would give way;
Quoth bold Robin Hood, and sturdily
    stood,
    I'll show you right Nottingham play.

8 With that from his quiver an arrow he
    drew,
    A broad arrow with a goose-wing:
The stranger reply'd, I'll liquor thy hide,
    If thou offerst to touch the string.

9 Quoth bold Robin Hood, Thou dost prate
    like an ass,
    For were I to bend but my bow,

I could send a dart quite thro thy proud
    heart,
    Before thou couldst strike me one blow.

10 'Thou talkst like a coward,' the stranger
    reply'd;
    'Well armd with a long bow you stand,
To shoot at my breast, while I, I protest,
    Having nought but a staff in my hand.'

11 'The name of a coward,' quoth Robin, 'I
    scorn,
    Wherefore my long bow I'll lay by;
And now, for thy sake, a staff will I take,
    The truth of thy manhood to try.'

12 Then Robin Hood stept to a thicket of trees,
    And chose him a staff of ground-oak;
Now this being done, away he did run
    To the stranger, and merrily spoke:

13 'Lo! see my staff, it is lusty and tough,
    Now here on the bridge we will play;
Whoever falls in, the other shall win
    The battel, and so we'll away.'

14 'With all my whole heart,' the stranger
    reply'd;
    'I scorn in the least to give out;'
This said, they fell to 't without more
    dispute,
    And their staffs they did flourish about.

15 And first Robin he gave the stranger a bang,
    So hard that it made his bones ring:
The stranger he said, This must be repaid,
    I'll give you as good as you bring.

16 So long as I'm able to handle my staff,
    To die in your debt, friend, I scorn:
Then to it each goes, and followd their
    blows,
    As if they had been threshing of corn.

17 The stranger gave Robin a crack on the
    crown,
    Which caused the blood to appear;
Then Robin, enrag'd, more fiercely
    engag'd,
    And followd his blows more severe.

18 So thick and so fast did he lay it on him,
    With a passionate fury and ire,
At every stroke, he made him to smoke,
    As if he had been all on fire.

19 O then into fury the stranger he grew,
       And gave him a damnable look,
    And with it a blow that laid him full low,
       And tumbld him into the brook.

20 'I prithee, good fellow, O where art thou
          now?'
       The stranger, in laughter, he cry'd;
    Quoth bold Robin Hood, Good faith, in the
          flood,
       And floating along with the tide.

21 I needs must acknowledge thou art a brave
          soul;
       With thee I'll no longer contend;
    For needs must I say, thou hast got the day,
       Our battel shall be at an end.

22 Then unto the bank he did presently wade,
       And pulld himself out by a thorn;
    Which done, at the last, he blowd a loud
          blast
       Straitway on his fine bugle-horn.

23 The eccho of which through the vallies did
          fly,
       At which his stout bowmen appeard,
    All cloathed in green, most gay to be seen;
       So up to their master they steerd.

24 'O what's the matter?' quoth William
          Stutely;
       'Good master, you are wet to the skin:'
    'No matter,' quoth he; 'the lad which you
          see,
       In fighting, hath tumbld me in.'

25 'He shall not go scot-free,' the others
          reply'd;
       So strait they were seizing him there,
    To duck him likewise; but Robin Hood
          cries,
       He is a stout fellow, forbear.

26 There's no one shall wrong thee, friend,
          be not afraid;
       These bowmen upon me do wait;
    There's threescore and nine; if thou wilt
          be mine,
       Thou shalt have my livery strait.

27 And other accoutrements fit for a man;
       Speak up, jolly blade, never fear;

    I'll teach you also the use of the bow,
       To shoot at the fat fallow-deer.'

28 'O here is my hand,' the stranger reply'd,
       'I'll serve you with all my whole heart;
    My name is John Little, a man of good
          mettle;
       Nere doubt me, for I'll play my part.'

29 'His name shall be alterd,' quoth William
          Stutely,
       'And I will his godfather be;
    Prepare then a feast, and none of the least,
       For we will be merry,' quoth he.

30 They presently fetchd in a brace of fat does,
       With humming strong liquor likewise;
    They lovd what was good; so, in the
          greenwood,
       This pretty sweet babe they baptize.

31 He was, I must tell you, but seven foot high,
       And, may be, an ell in the waste;
    A pretty sweet lad; much feasting they had;
       Bold Robin the christning grac'd,

32 With all his bowmen, which stood in a
          ring,
       And were of the Notti[n]gham breed;
    Brave Stutely comes then, with seven
          yeomen,
       And did in this manner proceed.

33 'This infant was called John Little,' quoth
          he,
       'Which name shall be changed anon;
    The words we'll transpose, so wherever
          he goes,
       His name shall be calld Little John.'

34 They all with a shout made the elements
          ring,
       So soon as the office was ore;
    To feasting they went, with true merri-
          ment,
       And tippld strong liquor gillore.

35 Then Robin he took the pretty sweet babe,
       And cloathd him from top to the toe
    In garments of green, most gay to be seen,
       And gave him a curious long bow.

36 'Thou shalt be an archer as well as the best,
       And range in the greenwood with us;

Where we'll not want gold nor silver,
    behold,
  While bishops have ought in their purse.

37 'We live here like squires, or lords of
    renown,
  Without ere a foot of free land;
  We feast on good cheer, with wine, ale,
    and beer,
  And evry thing at our command.'

38 Then musick and dancing did finish the
    day;
  At length, when the sun waxed low,
  Then all the whole train the grove did
    refrain,
  And unto their caves they did go.

39 And so ever after, as long as he livd,
  Altho he was proper and tall,
  Yet nevertheless, the truth to express,
  Still Little John they did him call.

"Robin Hood Turns Butcher," from The Merry
  Adventures of Robin Hood. *Written and
  illustrated by Howard Pyle (New York:
  Scribner's, 1946).*

*Among Robin Hood's most significant
deeds are his fights against evil oppressors.
Like Ulysses, he is a trickster, often disguising
himself to outwit his enemies. Frequently, as is
the case in this circular journey, his escapades
result as much from his restless, adventure-
loving spirit as from necessity. The ironies
arise not only because of Robin's clever mani-
pulations, but also because of the character
of the Sheriff who, led by his greed, agrees to
travel to the home of his unknown dinner
guest. As in all of the Robin Hood tales, Sherwood Forest is seen in double perspective. For
the hero and his honest outlaws, it is a sanctuary and home; for the conniving Sheriff and
other evil hypocrites, it is a place to be feared.
Howard Pyle, the well-known nineteenth century American author-illustrator, has consciously used an archaic style to capture the
medieval flavor of the original Robin Hood
stories.*

Robin Hood Turns Butcher

Now after all these things had happened, and
it became known to Robin Hood how the Sheriff had tried three times to make him captive,
he said to himself: "If I have the chance, I will
make our worshipful Sheriff pay right well for
that which he hath done to me. Maybe I may
bring him some time into Sherwood Forest, and
have him to a right merry feast with us." For
when Robin Hood caught a baron or a squire,
or a fat abbot or bishop, he brought them to
the greenwood tree and feasted them before
he lightened their purses.

But in the mean time Robin Hood and his
band lived quietly in Sherwood Forest, without showing their faces abroad, for Robin knew
that it would not be wise for him to be seen in
the neighborhood of Nottingham, those in authority being very wroth with him. But though
they did not go abroad, they lived a merry life
within the woodlands, spending the days in
shooting at garlands hung upon a willow wand
at the end of the glade, the leafy aisles ringing
with merry jests and laughter: for whoever
missed the garland was given a sound buffet,
which, if delivered by Little John, never failed
to topple over the unfortunate yeoman. Then
they had bouts of wrestling and of cudgel play,
so that every day they gained in skill and
strength.

Thus they dwelt for nearly a year, and in
that time Robin Hood often turned over in his
mind many means of making an even score
with the Sheriff. At last he began to fret at his
confinement; so one day he took up his stout
cudgel and set forth to seek adventure, strolling blithely along until he came to the edge of
Sherwood. There, as he rambled along the sunlit road, he met a lusty young Butcher driving
a fine mare, and riding in a stout new cart, all
hung about with meat. Merrily whistled the
Butcher as he jogged along, for he was going
to the market, and the day was fresh and sweet,
making his heart blithe within him.

"Good morrow to thee, jolly fellow,"
quoth Robin; "thou seemest happy this merry
morn."

"Ay, that am I," quoth the jolly Butcher;
"and why should I not be so? Am I not hale in

wind and limb? Have I not the bonniest lass in all Nottinghamshire? And lastly, am I not to be married to her on Thursday next in sweet Locksley Town?"

"Ha," said Robin, "comest thou from Locksley Town? Well do I know that fair place for miles about, and well do I know each hedge-row and gentle pebbly stream, and even all the bright little fishes therein, for there I was born and bred. Now, where goest thou with thy meat, my fair friend?"

"I go to the market at Nottingham Town to sell my beef and my mutton," answered the Butcher. "But who art thou that comest from Locksley Town?"

"A yeoman am I, good friend, and men do call me Robin Hood."

"Now, by Our Lady's grace," cried the Butcher, "well do I know thy name, and many a time have I heard thy deeds both sung and spoken of. But Heaven forbid that thou shouldst take ought of me! An honest man am I, and have wronged neither man nor maid; so trouble me not, good master, as I have never troubled thee."

"Nay, Heaven forbid, indeed," quoth Robin, "that I should take from such as thee, jolly fellow! Not so much as one farthing would I take from thee, for I love a fair Saxon face like thine right well; more especially when it cometh from Locksley Town, and most especially when the man that owneth it is to marry a bonny lass on Thursday next. But come, tell me for what price thou wilt sell all thy meat and thy horse and cart."

"At four marks do I value meat, cart, and mare," quoth the Butcher; "but if I do not sell all my meat I will not have four marks in value."

Then Robin Hood plucked the purse from his girdle, and quoth he, "Here in this purse are six marks. Now, I would fain be a butcher for the day and sell my meat in Nottingham Town, wilt thou close a bargain with me and take six marks for thine outfit?"

"Now may the blessings of all the saints fall on thine honest head!" cried the Butcher right joyfully, as he leaped down from his cart and took the purse that Robin held out to him.

"Nay," quoth Robin, laughing loudly, "many do like me and wish me well, but few call me honest. Now get thee gone back to thy lass, and give her a sweet kiss from me." So saying, he donned the Butcher's apron, and, climbing into the cart, he took the reins in his hands, and drove off through the forest to Nottingham Town.

When he came to Nottingham, he entered that part of the market where butchers stood, and took up his inn[1] in the best place he could find. Next, he opened his stall and spread his meat upon the bench, then, taking his cleaver and steel and clattering them together, he trolled aloud, in merry tones: —

> *"Now come, ye lasses, and eke, ye dames,*
> *And buy your meat from me;*
> *For three pennyworths of meat I sell*
> *For the charge of one penny.*
>
> *"Lamb have I that hath fed upon nought*
> *But the dainty daisies pied,*
> *And the violet sweet, and the daffodil*
> *That grow fair streams beside.*
>
> *"And beef have I from the heathery wolds,*
> *And mutton from dales all green,*
> *And veal as white as a maiden's brow,*
> *With its mother's milk, I ween.*
>
> *"Then come ye lasses, and eke, ye dames,*
> *Come, buy your meat from me;*
> *For three pennyworths of meat I sell*
> *For the charge of one penny."*

Thus he sang blithely, while all who stood near listened amazedly; then, when he had finished, he clattered the steel and cleaver still more loudly, shouting lustily, "Now, who'll buy? who'll buy? Four fixed prices have I. Three pennyworths of meat I sell to a fat friar or priest for sixpence, for I want not their custom; stout aldermen I charge threepence, for it doth not matter to me whether they buy or not; to buxom dames I sell three pennyworths of meat for one penny, for I like their custom well; but to the bonny lass that hath a liking for a good tight butcher I charge nought but one fair kiss, for I like her custom the best of all."

Then all began to stare and wonder, and crowd around, laughing, for never was such

[1] Stand for selling.

Illustration by Howard Pyle from *The Merry Adventures of Robin Hood* Published by Charles Scribrer's Sons, 1946.

selling heard of in all Nottingham Town; but when they came to buy they found it as he had said, for he gave good wife or dame as much meat for one penny as they could buy elsewhere for three, and when a widow or a poor woman came to him, he gave her flesh for nothing; but when a merry lass came and gave him a kiss, he charged not one penny for his meat; and many such came to his stall, for his eyes were as blue as the skies of June, and he laughed merrily, giving to each full measure. Thus he sold his meat so fast that no butcher that stood near him could sell anything.

Then they began to talk among themselves, and some said, "This must be some thief who has stolen cart, horse, and meat"; but others said, "Nay, when did ye ever see a thief who parted with his goods so freely and merrily? This must be some prodigal who hath sold his father's land, and would fain live merrily while the money lasts." And these latter being the greater number, the others came round, one by one, to their way of thinking.

Then some of the butchers came to him to make his acquaintance. "Come, brother," quoth one who was the head of them all, "we be all of one trade, so wilt thou go dine with us? For this day the Sheriff hath asked all the Butcher Guild to feast with him at the Guild Hall. There will be stout fare, and much to drink, and that thou likest, or I much mistake thee."

"Now, beshrew his heart," quoth jolly Robin, "that would deny a butcher. And, moreover, I will go dine with you all, my sweet lads, and that as fast as I can hie." Whereupon, having sold all his meat, he closed his stall, and went with them to the great Guild Hall.

There the Sheriff had already come in state, and with him many butchers. When Robin and those that were with him came in, all laughing at some merry jest he had been telling them, those that were near the Sheriff whispered to him, "Yon is a right mad blade, for he hath sold more meat for one penny this day than we could sell for three, and to whatsoever merry lass gave him a kiss he gave meat for nought." And others said, "He is some prodigal that hath sold his land for silver and gold, and meaneth to spend all right merrily."

Then the Sheriff called Robin to him, not knowing him in his butcher's dress, and made him sit close to him on his right hand; for he loved a rich young prodigal — especially when he thought that he might lighten that prodigal's pockets into his own most worshipful purse. So he made much of Robin, and laughed and talked with him more than with any of the others.

At last the dinner was ready to be served and the Sheriff bade Robin say grace, so Robin stood up and said: "Now Heaven bless us all and eke good meat and good sack within this house, and may all butchers be and remain as honest men as I am."

At this all laughed, the Sheriff loudest of all, for he said to himself, "Surely this is indeed some prodigal, and perchance I may empty his purse of some of the money that the fool throweth about so freely." Then he spake aloud to Robin, saying: "Thou art a jolly young blade, and I love thee mightily''; and he smote Robin upon the shoulder.

Then Robin laughed loudly too. "Yea," quoth he, "I know thou dost love a jolly blade, for didst thou not have jolly Robin Hood at thy shooting-match and didst thou not gladly give him a bright golden arrow for his own?''

At this the Sheriff looked grave and all the guild of butchers too, so that none laughed but Robin, only some winked slyly at each other.

"Come, fill us some sack!'' cried Robin. "Let us e'er be merry while we may, for man is but dust, and he hath but a span to live here till the worm getteth him, as our good gossip Swanthold sayeth; so let life be merry while it lasts, say I. Nay, never look down i' the mouth, Sir Sheriff. Who knowest but that thou mayest catch Robin Hood yet if thou drinkest less good sack and Malmsey, and bringest down the fat about thy paunch and the dust from out thy brain. Be merry, man.''

Then the Sheriff laughed again, but not as though he liked the jest, while the butchers said, one to another, "Before Heaven, never have we seen such a mad rollicking blade. Mayhap, though, he will make the Sheriff mad.''

"How now, brothers," cried Robin, "be merry! nay, never count over your farthings, for by this and by that I will pay this shot myself, e'en though it cost two hundred pounds. So let no man draw up his lip, nor thrust his forefinger into his purse, for I swear that neither butcher nor Sheriff shall pay one penny for this feast.''

"Now thou are a right merry soul," quoth the Sheriff, "and I wot thou must have many a head of horned beasts and many an acre of land, that thou dost spend thy money so freely.''

"Ay, that have I," quoth Robin, laughing loudly again, "five hundred and more horned beasts have I and my brothers, and none of them have we been able to sell, else I might not have turned butcher. As for my land, I have never asked my steward how many acres I have.''

At this the Sheriff's eyes twinkled, and he chuckled to himself. "Nay, good youth," quoth he, "if thou canst not sell thy cattle it may be I will find a man that will lift them from thy hands; perhaps that man may be myself, for I love a merry youth and would help such a one along the path of life. Now how much dost thou want for thy horned cattle?''

"Well," quoth Robin, "they are worth at least five hundred pounds.''

"Nay," answered the Sheriff, slowly, and as if he were thinking within himself; "well do I love thee, and fain would I help thee along, but five hundred pounds in money is a good round sum; beside I have it not by me. Yet I will give thee three hundred pounds for them all, and that in good hard silver and gold.''

"Now thou old Jew!" quoth Robin; "well thou knowest that so many horned cattle are worth seven hundred pounds and more, and even that is but small for them, and yet thou, with thy gray hairs and one foot in the grave, wouldst trade upon the folly of a wild youth.''

At this the Sheriff looked grimly at Robin. "Nay," quoth Robin, "look not on me as though thou hadst sour beer in thy mouth, man. I will take thine offer, for I and my brothers do need the money. We lead a merry life, and no one leads a merry life for a farthing, so I will close the bargain with thee. But mind that thou bringest a good three hundred pounds with thee, for I trust not one that driveth so shrewd a bargain.''

"I will bring the money," said the Sheriff. "But what is thy name, good youth?''

"Men call me Robert o'Locksley," quoth bold Robin.

"Then, good Robert o'Locksley," quoth the Sheriff, "I will come this day to see thy horned beasts. But first my clerk shall draw up a paper in which thou shalt be bound to the sale, for thou gettest not my money without I get thy beasts in return.''

Then Robin Hood laughed again. "So be it," he cried, smiting his palm upon the Sheriff's hand. "Truly my brothers will be thankful to thee for thy money.''

Thus the bargain was closed; but many of the butchers talked among themselves of the Sheriff, saying that it was but a scurvy trick to beguile a poor spendthrift youth in this way.

The afternoon had come when the Sheriff mounted his horse and joined Robin Hood, who stood outside the gateway of the paved court waiting for him, for he had sold his horse and cart to a trader for two marks. Then they set forth upon their way, the Sheriff riding upon his horse and Robin running beside him. Thus they left Nottingham Town and travelled forward along the dusty highway, laughing and jesting together as though they had been old friends; but all the time the Sheriff said within himself, "Thy jest to me of Robin Hood shall cost thee dear, good fellow, even four hundred pounds, thou fool." For he thought he would make at least that much by his bargain.

So they journeyed onward till they came within the verge of Sherwood Forest, when presently the Sheriff looked up and down and to the right and to the left of him and then grew quiet and ceased his laughter. "Now," quoth he, "may Heaven and its saints preserve us this day from a rogue men call Robin Hood."

Then Robin laughed aloud. "Nay," said he, "thou mayst set thy mind at rest, for well do I know Robin Hood and well do I know that thou art in no more danger from him this day than thou are from me."

At this the Sheriff looked askance at Robin, saying to himself, "I like not that thou seemest so well acquainted with this bold outlaw, and I wish that I were well out of Sherwood Forest."

But still they travelled deeper into the forest shades, and the deeper they went the more quiet grew the Sheriff. At last they came to where the road took a sudden bend, and before them a herd of dun deer went tripping across the path. Then Robin Hood came close to the Sheriff and pointing his finger he said, "These are my horned beasts, good Master Sheriff. How dost thou like them? Are they not fat and fair to see?"

At this the Sheriff drew rein quickly. "Now fellow," quoth he, "I would I were well out of this forest, for I like not thy company. Go thou thine own path, good friend, and let me but go mine."

But Robin only laughed and caught the Sheriff's bridle rein. "Nay," cried he, "stay a while, for I would thou shouldst see my brothers who own these fair horned beasts with me." So saying he clapped his bugle to his mouth and winded three merry notes, and presently up the path came leaping fivescore good stout yeomen with Little John at their head.

"What wouldst thou have, good master?" quoth Little John.

"Why," answered Robin, "dost thou not see that I have brought goodly company to feast with us to-day? Fye, for shame! do you not see our good and worshipful master, The Sheriff of Nottingham? Take thou his bridle, Little John, for he has honored us to-day by coming to feast with us."

Then all doffed their hats humbly, without smiling, or seeming to be in jest, whilst Little John took the bridle rein and led the palfrey still deeper into the forest, all marching in order, with Robin Hood walking beside the Sheriff, hat in hand.

All this time the Sheriff said never a word but only looked about him like one suddenly awakened from sleep; but when he found himself going within the very depth of Sherwood his heart sank within him, for he thought, "Surely my three hundred pounds will be taken from me, even if they take not my life itself, for I have plotted against their lives more than once." But all seemed humble and meek and not a word was said of danger, either to life or money.

So at last they came to that part of Sherwood Forest where a noble oak spread its branches wide, and beneath it was a seat all made of moss, on which Robin sat down, placing the Sheriff at his right hand. "Now busk ye, my merry men all," quoth he, "and bring forth the best we have, both of meat and wine, for his worship, the sheriff, hath feasted me in Nottingham Guild Hall to-day, and I would not have him go back empty."

All this time nothing had been said of the Sheriff's money, so presently he began to pluck up heart. "For," said he to himself, "maybe Robin Hood hath forgotten all about it."

Then, whilst beyond in the forest bright fires crackled and savory smells of sweetly roasting venison and fat capons filled the glade, and brown pasties warmed beside the blaze, did Robin Hood entertain the Sheriff right royally. First, several couples stood forth at quarterstaff, and so shrewd were they at the game, and so quickly did they give stroke and parry, that the Sheriff, who loved to watch all lusty sports of the kind, clapped his hands, forgetting where he was, and crying aloud, "Well struck! well struck, thou fellow with the black beard!" little knowing that the man he called upon was the Tinker that tried to serve his warrant upon Robin Hood.

Then the best archers of the band set up a fair garland of flowers at eightscore paces distance, and shot at it with the cunningest archery practice. But the Sheriff grew grave, for he did not like this so well, the famous meeting at the butts in Nottingham Town being still green in his memory, and the golden arrow that had been won there hanging close behind him. Then, when Robin saw what was in the Sheriff's mind, he stopped the sport, and called forth some of his band, who sang merry ballads, while others made music upon the harp.

When this was done, several yeomen came forward and spread cloths upon the green grass, and placed a royal feast; while others still broached barrels of sack and Malmsey and good stout ale, and set them in jars upon the cloth, with drinking-horns about them. Then all sat down and feasted and drank merrily together until the sun was low and the half-moon glimmered with a pale light betwixt the leaves of the trees overhead.

Then the Sheriff arose and said, "I thank you all, good yeomen, for the merry entertainment ye have given me this day. Right courteously have ye used me, showing therein that ye have much respect for our glorious King and his deputy in brave Nottinghamshire. But the shadows grow long, and I must away before darkness comes, lest I lose myself within the forest."

Then Robin Hood and all his merry men arose also, and Robin said to the Sheriff, "If thou must go, worshipful sir, go thou must; but thou has forgotten one thing."

"Nay, I forgot nought," said the Sheriff; yet all the same his heart sank within him.

"But I saw thou has forgot something," quoth Robin. "We keep a merry inn here in the greenwood, but whoever becometh our guest must pay his reckoning."

Then the Sheriff laughed, but the laugh was hollow. "Well, jolly boys," quoth he, "we have had a merry time together to-day, and even if ye had not asked me, I would have given you a score of pounds for the sweet entertainment I have had."

"Nay," quoth Robin seriously, "it would ill beseem us to treat your worship so meanly. By my faith, Sir Sheriff, I would be ashamed to show my face if I did not reckon the King's deputy at three hundred pounds. Is it not so, my merry men all?"

Then "Ay!" cried all, in a loud voice.

"Three hundred devils!" roared the Sheriff. "Think ye that your beggarly feast was worth three pounds, let alone three hundred?"

"Nay," quoth Robin gravely. "Speak not so roundly, your worship. I do love thee for the sweet feast thou hast given me this day in merry Nottingham Town; but there be those here who love thee not so much. If thou wilt look down the cloth thou wilt see Will Stutely, in whose eyes thou hast no great favor; then two other stout fellows are there here that thou knowest not, that were wounded in a brawl nigh Nottingham Town, some time ago—thou wottest when; one of them was sore hurt in one arm, yet he hath got the use of it again. Good Sheriff, be advised by me; pay thy score without more ado, or maybe it may fare ill with thee."

As he spoke the Sheriff's ruddy cheeks grew pale, and he said nothing more but looked upon the ground and gnawed his nether lip. Then slowly he drew forth his fat purse and threw it upon the cloth in front of him.

"Now take the purse, Little John," quoth Robin Hood, "and see that the reckoning be right. We would not doubt our Sheriff, but he might not like it if he should find he had not paid his full score."

Then Little John counted the money, and found that the bag held three hundred pounds in silver and gold. But to the Sheriff it seemed as if every clink of the bright money was a drop of blood from his veins; and when he saw it all counted out in a heap of silver and gold, filling a wooden platter, he turned away and silently mounted his horse.

"Never have we had so worshipful a guest before!" quoth Robin; "and, as the day waxeth late, I will send one of my young men to guide thee out of the forest depths.''

"Nay, heaven forbid!'' cried the Sheriff, hastily. "I can find mine own way, good man, without aid.''

"Then I will put thee on the right track mine own self,'' quoth Robin; and, taking the Sheriff's horse by the bridle rein, he led him into the main forest path; then, before he let him go, he said, "Now, fare thee well, good Sheriff, and when next thou thinkest to despoil some poor prodigal, remember thy feast in Sherwood Forest. 'Ne'er buy a horse, good friend, without first looking into its mouth,' as our good gaffer Swanthold says. And so, once more, fare thee well.'' Then he clapped his hand to the horse's back, and off went nag and Sheriff through the forest glades.

Then bitterly the Sheriff rued the day that first he meddled with Robin Hood, for all men laughed at him and many ballads were sung by folk throughout the country, of how the Sheriff went to shear and came home shorn to the very quick. For thus men sometimes overreach themselves through greed and guile.

"Nanabozho's Revenge" and "How Nanabozho Remade the Earth," from Tales of Nanabozho, *by Dorothy M. Reid. Illustrated by Donald Grant (Toronto: Oxford University Press, 1963).*

Son of the Moon's granddaughter and the West Wind, Nanabozho (also called Nanabush, Manabozho, and Nanna Bijou) was the major hero of the Ojibwa people of the Great Lakes region. Like Ulysses, his cleverness often lands him in trouble, but in many stories he helps his people by using his magic powers. This tale, in which are found many short pourquoi stories explaining the origin of natural phenomena, is one of many Native legends dealing with a great flood and the building or rebuilding of the world. It can be compared to the myths "God Wash the World" and "The Dawn of the World." The narration begins shortly after the evil windegoes have killed Nanabozho's brother Nahpootie.

Nanabozho's Revenge

For some time after the death of Nahpootie, the Kingfisher went about his fishing in a melancholy mood. Though he had escaped from Nanabozho and had obtained a handsome belt into the bargain, he was troubled because the Big Man was angry with him and he pondered how to make peace with Nanabozho.

One day, as he sat high up in a tree, watching for a fish to break the surface of the water, an idea came to him. He gave one of his loudest, noisiest calls, startling the fish and sending them all to the bottom of the lake. But the Kingfisher did not notice, for already he was flying off to seek Nanabozho.

He found the Big Man walking sadly along the shore of the lake where his brother had been drowned.

"O Mighty One," said the Kingfisher, "it was an evil day when I mocked you. Let there be peace between us. It may be that I have knowledge that will help you."

"The whereabouts of the *windigoes* who captured Nahpootie is the only knowledge I desire," replied Nanabozho. "This would be worth the price of peace between us, O Loud-voiced Fisherman."

"Know then that those you seek dwell beneath the lake. Each day, when the sun is high in the heavens, they come out to lie on the sandy shore on the east side of the lake."

The Big Man was grateful to the Kingfisher. Understanding his vanity, he rewarded the bird by ruffling the feathers on his head to form a handsome crest.

Then Nanabozho hastened to the east shore of the lake. He hid his great war-club, changed himself into an old pine stump, and settled down to wait.

He had not been there long when the monsters began to crawl out of the water, all of them beautiful glistening shades of red and green and yellow. One of them, larger than all the rest and pure white in colour, was their prince.

As the monsters stretched and frolicked on the warm sand, the white prince noticed the stump. He was sure it had not been there before, and he wondered if it was an enemy disguise. One after another his followers wound around the stump and squeezed hard. Twice Nanabozho almost cried out, but each time the monster gave up just as the Big Man was about to reveal himself.

The prince decided that he must have been mistaken about the tree stump, so he contented himself with basking in the sun. At last the warmth made him sleepy. He dozed off, and the others grouped around him did the same.

Changing himself back into an Indian brave, Nanabozho picked up his great war-club from where it was hidden and, stepping lightly between the sleeping monsters, struck and killed the white prince. Then, uttering a loud shout, he sped away.

There was a dreadful outcry on the beach and the monsters set out to capture and punish the slayer of their prince. Though Nanabozho ran with mile-long strides, the monsters also had magic powers and were soon close on his heels. But just when they were about to capture him, they were forced to return to their natural place — they had travelled as far away from the lake as they dared to go. Using their strongest magic, they sent the waters of the lake rushing after the Big Man to drown him.

Nanabozho was forced to climb a mountain, and when he reached the summit he climbed its tallest tree. He looked down and saw the great flood of water rushing in his direction. Soon it covered the mountain he was on.

"Brother Tree," shouted Nanabozho, "grow taller or the water will drown me." The tree stretched upwards. "Higher yet!" the Big Man called, and the tree obeyed. "Still higher!" came the cry. But the tree could grow no more.

The water rose until it reached the top of the tree. It rose until it touched Nanabozho's chin. Then it stopped.

How Nanabozho
Remade the Earth

Nanabozho saw the Eagle flying high above him and cried out, "Great bird, go swiftly and warn my people of their danger! Tell them to get in their canoes so that they may ride safely on the water. Tell them also that I shall return to them as soon as I am able, and stay with them to give them courage and help."

Flying over the flooded country, the Eagle saw that the waters, which had first travelled in the direction of Nanabozho's flight, were slowly spreading in all directions. Because the Ojibwa encampment was built on high ground, the flood had not yet reached it; but the dugout canoes, which had been beached along the shore of the lake, had all been carried away by the rising water.

The Eagle found the people in the camp preparing their evening meal, unaware of their peril. He gave Nanabozho's message to Nokomis and to the chiefs, and told them of the loss of the canes. The people were filled with despair when the Eagle told them that there was no time to build new canoes, or even a raft.

Silently Nokomis walked to the water's edge and gazed at the rising moon. Lifting her arms in supplication, she cried out, "Listen, O Moon, to the voice of your daughter Nokomis. Since I came to dwell on earth, I have borne hardships and trials without complaint. Now I ask a favour for my people and for their children. Hold back the waters, I beg you, until we can escape."

The Moon heard the voice of her daughter. She cast her beam in a silver pathway and held back the water so that it could not flood the encampment. (Since that time the Moon has always had power over the great bodies of water on the earth.)

At once the people set to work. The men cut down trees and the boys trimmed off the branches. Then the young women and the girls lashed them together to make a great raft. Nokomis instructed the women to make handholds of cedar rope on the logs. Then she showed the grandmothers how to protect the babies against the weather. She wrapped one of them in doeskin, lined with cat-tail down and laced up the front. Then she padded a thick piece of bark with deerskin and laid the baby on it, with a shelf across the bottom for his feet to rest on and a hoop of wood projecting from the top to protect his face in case the *tikinagan*[1] was upset.

Nokomis showed the mothers how to carry the cradleboards safely on their backs, with a carrying strap going around their own forehead. In this way their hands would be free to hold onto the raft.

Suddenly the Eagle called out that the Moon's power was waning and that the water was breaking free. The people climbed quickly on the raft, placing the young children in the centre, with the old women to care for them. The mothers sat next, in a circle facing outward, with their babies protected behind their backs. Then came the other women and the young girls sitting shoulder to shoulder. Last of all, in the outer circle, were the men and the older boys, ready for any danger.

As the last man took his place, a great wall of water swept down upon the raft and the people clung to the rope-holds. The raft tipped so steeply that for a moment it seemed as if it might overturn. But the fury of the water was spent, and the raft rode out upon the flood.

The babies looked out with their dark brown eyes at this strange new world of water, or slept, lulled by the swaying motion. Some men fished and shared their catch with the others.

Thus the people waited patiently for Nanabozho to rescue them.

Nanabozho had been swept away from the tree-top and was floating on a great body of water, with no land visible. He saw other creatures swimming desperately about, and realized that he would have to do something to help them.

"Brother Beaver!" he called. "Go down into the water and bring up some earth so that I may make the world anew."

The Beaver obeyed, slapping the water with his tail. (Since then beavers have always slapped the surface of the water as a signal of danger.) Down, down, down he went into the watery depths. Time passed. Just when Nanabozho feared that the animal had been drowned, he reappeared, almost dead but without any earth.

1 Cradleboard.

Next Nanabozho and the other animals persuaded the Otter that he should try. He was gone even longer than the Beaver, but he had no more success.

Nanabozho was almost resigned to floating about forever when the Muskrat, who had been swimming nearby, propelled himself swiftly towards the Big Man, using his long tail as a rudder.

"Nanabozho, Nanabozho!" he called. "Let me try to get some earth. I am not as large or as strong as the Beaver or the Otter, but I would like to help you and so gain some measure of fame for myself."

"Very well, you may have your chance. But remember that both the Beaver and the Otter were close to death when they returned, and yet neither was able to reach the bottom."

"No matter what may happen, O Mighty One, be sure to examine my paws carefully when I return." And the Muskrat disappeared from sight, leaving only an eddy of ripples to mark where he had been.

Everyone waited anxiously. At last, after a day and a night had passed, the Muskrat's body rose to the surface of the water.

Nanabozho pried open the small paws and, under one of the claws, found a tiny lump of mud. He called the Turtle to him and put the mud on its shell. When it was almost dry he began to knead it, turning it over and over. Under his skill the ball of mud grew larger until it became a mountain which broke up and spread all about, making a raft of mud on the face of the waters.

Nanabozho sent the Bear to trample on the world and smooth it down. But the Bear was too heavy. Water oozed up with every step he took, making the land swampy. If Nanabozho had not called him back, all the earth would have been *muskeg*.

Now the Raven was sent to find Nokomis and the people. When he did not come back, Nanabozho ordered the swift-flying Hawk to find him. The Hawk returned and told Nanabozho that he had seen the Raven feasting on the dead bodies of animals which were lying along the shore.

Nanabozho flew into a rage.

"Never again shall the Raven have anything

to eat except what he steals!'' the Big Man shouted.

Then he sent the Caribou to inspect the earth. After a long time the animal returned, quite exhausted, and Nanabozho knew that the world was large enough.

"O Mighty One,'' said the Caribou when he had recovered his breath, ''far out on the water I saw Nokomis and the people on a raft.''

Nanabozho sent the Moose to fetch them and waited anxiously. At last he saw a speck in the distance. It grew larger and larger until he recognized the raft; it was being pushed by the Moose.

Soon Nokomis and the others thankfully stepped once more upon solid ground.

Nanabozho took the trees of which the raft had been built and used them to create forests on the new earth. The birds that for so long had been flying wearily about came down and settled in the tree tops, and the animals found shelter and rest beneath the branches.

Gitche Manitou was proud of his people who had shown themselves brave and steadfast. His smile broke forth like bright sunshine after a storm. It sparkled on the waters and danced on the leaves of the trees, dappling the ground beneath them.

All the world was warmed by it.

───

"The Biggest Fish of All," and "The Secret of Fire," from Maui Mischievous Hero, *by Barbara Lyons (Hilo: Petroglyph Press, 1969).*

A trickster and culture hero whose adventures are known from New Zealand to Hawaii, Maui is the son of a mortal woman and a sea god. The youngest of several brothers, he is often rejected by them and, in reaction, uses his magical powers to create mischief. However, he also uses these powers to perform good deeds, as in his discovery of the way to make fire. The story of the magic fishhook used to pull up an island from the ocean floor is often retold to explain the origin of the Hawaiian Islands. Maui's gift of fire can be compared to the Greek myth "Fire" and the literary myth Little Badger and the Fire Spirit.

The Biggest Fish of All

Maui loved to go with his brothers in their canoe when they went fishing. But he scarcely ever caught a fish, and was apt to do mischievous things like rocking the boat. Finally, the others decided that they had had enough of Maui as a fisherman.

"You just take up room in the canoe,'' they said. "And you're a nuisance to us with your tricks. Stay home with our mother, and perhaps she can find something useful for you to do.''

Maui felt very sad at being left behind, and he didn't want to do a woman's work. He hid from his mother by climbing a tall coconut tree and snuggling down among the long green fronds at its top.

Hina called to him, but when he didn't answer, went back to her chores.

As he lay there in his secret green place, with a breeze from the sea gently stirring the fronds and cooling him, he thought about fishhooks. It seemed to him that with another sort of fishhook, many more fish could be caught. Maui hadn't forgotten that the sea creatures had befriended him, but now that he was older and would soon be a man, he realized that people must fish in order to live. And he knew that he could always warn the ones that were his special friends.

If there were something about a hook that made it harder for the fish to slip off . . . Yes, that was what was needed. After a while, he slid down the slim trunk of the palm and went to the place where his family kept bone and other materials for making their tools and weapons. He searched about for a bit and found a likely looking curved bone, which he cut to the length he wanted with a piece of flaked stone. Then he picked up a coral rasp and set to work at smoothing the bone and shaping it into a hook that he thought would hold the fish. It was a quite new design — a fishhook with a barb.

The next morning, when the brothers were ready to start off in their canoe, Maui went up to them eagerly and showed them what he held in his hand. "It's a new kind of fishhook,'' he explained. "See, it has a barb, and it should catch lots more fish than the kind you've been using.''

"H'm," said the brothers. "Well, well. Give it here and we'll try it out."

Did they mean to go without him when he had made this new hook for them? "Let me come, too!" cried Maui.

"Oh, you," the others said. "You couldn't catch a mullet in the king's fish pond—even if this does prove to be a good hook, which we doubt."

It was, in fact, a very good hook indeed, and the brothers returned with their canoe loaded with fish. But still, they wouldn't take Maui with them when they went again.

Maui was hurt about this, when it was he who had fashioned the splendid new hook. He resolved to show his brothers that he was really the best fisherman of all—and he thought he knew how he could do it. He had heard of an ancestress of his who lived in the underworld, who was dead on one side and alive on the other. If only she will agree to what I want, Maui thought, I will be able to make a magic fishhook.

He went on the dark, frightening journey to the underworld, and there in a great, gloomy cavern he found his ancestress.

"Old Woman," he said, "I beg you to give me a bone from your jaw on the side of you that is dead, so that I can make a magic fishhook." He told her who he was and of how his brothers had behaved, and that he wanted to prove that he too could fish.

"Is this so important to you, boy?" She sat looking him up and down as he stood before her, straight and as tall as he could make himself.

"It's the most important thing in life to me, right now. And I'll tell you a secret. The fish I catch with my magic hook will be like none ever caught before."

The old woman grinned. "I love secrets," she said. "I'll remember that." There was a gleam of kindness in her ancient eye as she added, "You're a nice boy, and of my family. I will give you what you ask." She took a bone from her jaw, on the dead side.

"Oh, thank you, my Ancestress! You won't be sorry, when you hear of the fish this has caught."

He went back up into the world of light, and made his fishhook. Then he sought his mother.

"Oh Hina, dear mother, I have made a magic fishhook, but I need bait for it. Will you let me have one of your sacred *'alae* birds?"

Hina knew that Maui was capable of making a magic hook, because his father was a god. "Yes, son," she said, "I will give you a nice fat one." She picked a bird out from under the great wooden calabash where she kept her sacred *'alae*, and Maui hid it beneath his *malo*, the brief garment he wore.

Then he ran to his brothers, who were about to go off in the canoe. "Let me go with you," he called.

But they shoved off without him and he stood at the edge of the sea, hearing their laughter float back to him and watching as the canoe grew smaller and smaller. At last it was hidden by the waves. Standing in water to his knees, Maui uttered a chant, sending a message to the kinds of fish his brothers hoped to catch.

The fishermen came home early this time, discouraged because they had found nothing but sharks. Maui could have told them why.

"I will show you where the biggest fish of all is," he said. "Set out again, and take me along."

"All right," said the eldest. "Why not, brothers? There's still plenty of daylight left, and perhaps he really will show us where the *pimoe* and *ulua* are."

Maui urged them on and on, farther and farther beyond the reef, until the ocean was very dark blue. Waves splashed over the side of the canoe, and when they looked toward shore, Haleakala was a long, low mound, pale and far away. The brothers were frightened; never had they paddled out so far. "Let's go back now," they said. "Maui is playing a joke on us."

"No, wait," Maui said. He baited his magic hook with the *'alae* and let the line fall into the water. Down, down it went, until it must have reached the bottom of the sea. There it caught fast on something.

Now the brothers were excited. They paddled with all their strength, and said, "Maui must have hooked the biggest fish in the ocean!'' How heavy the fish was — would they ever pull it from the depths of the sea?

When the canoe was lifted by an enormous swell, the boys had to paddle furiously to keep the craft upright. After the wave had gone by and they could see it rippling on into the distance, one of the brothers, exhausted, paused to look back. He gave a cry of terror.

When the others turned, it was to see a new island floating on the sea behind them.

The Secret of Fire

''This is really a great nuisance,'' Hina said as she put out the bananas for breakfast. ''How do you suppose I managed to let my fire go out? I must be the most absent-minded woman on the island.''

''It isn't so bad at breakfast-time,'' said Maui consolingly. ''I like bananas, and coconut milk too.'' He took a swallow from his coconut shell. ''I must say, though, that I prefer the fish to be cooked for dinner.''

''Me too,'' chorused his four brothers.

''We're all getting tired of raw fish,'' went on the eldest. ''If only there were something we could do about it!''

''Maybe there is,'' Maui said thoughtfully. ''Perhaps we just have to think of what it is.''

''Oh you! You're always full of bright ideas,'' said his brothers.

The secret of fire was lost in the mists of long-ago. Hina's mother had given her some live coals and cautioned her to keep them burning, for no one knew how to light a fire again when it had gone out. For years Hina had tended her fire-pit with care — but now, she had forgotten it, and the coals had become mere dead ashes.

That morning, when Maui was out fishing in the canoe with his brothers, he sat looking back toward Haleakala. He was thinking deeply, and at first didn't realize what it meant when he saw a slim pillar of smoke rising from the crater at the top of the mountain. Then he gave a shout.

''There's our answer!'' he cried. ''Someone has a fire in the crater, and we'll go and get some of it for our mother.''

''Maybe it's Pele,'' said one of the boys in a scared voice. They all looked dubious, except Maui.

''It can't be,'' he replied confidently. ''Do you think the fire goddess would light such a small fire? Hers would be a volcano, with great clouds of smoke. Come, let's go!''

The boys knew that Maui was a demigod because his father, unlike their own, was a god. They were jealous of the deeds he was able to perform and belittled them, but still they were inclined to accept his word when it concerned another deity. They beached their canoe and started to walk up the mountain.

On the way they watched the column of smoke, fearful lest it disappear before they could reach it. But it was still there, scarcely moving in the quiet air, when finally they came to the great rift in the mountain's side.

They climbed up through this gap, where rivers of lava once had spilled out of the crater and down the mountainside to the sea. The smoke was just beyond a hill now, one of the volcanic cones of pinkish sand. As they walked across the rocky crater floor, it seemed to be vanishing right before their eyes . . . .

The boys broke into a run, and rounded the hill. There was an old *'alae* hen — scratching out the fire as fast as she could! Only embers were left.

''Wait!'' cried Maui, rushing forward. ''Don't put it out until you've given us a flame for our mother. Her fire has gone out.''

The *'alae* hen cackled to herself and kicked some sand over the last glowing coal. ''Fire is my secret,'' she said to Maui. ''I don't intend to give away either my secret or any of my coals.'' And she waddled off.

Discouraged and weary now after their long, fruitless climb, the boys limped down over the hills, back to their dinner of raw fish.

''The hen will light her fire again,'' Maui said, ''and next time I'll go alone while the rest of you fish. I'll surprise her yet. Wait and see!''

Sure enough, a few days later the brothers again saw the thin spiral of smoke above the mountain top. Maui hurried up the slope and arrived panting, only to find that the hen had once more put out her fire before he could reach it. She's a smart old girl, he thought. She must have seen that there were only four boys in our canoe.

On the long downhill trek, he thought hard. When he reached home, he asked his mother for a tall calabash and a length of *tapa* cloth.

"Whatever do you want them for?" asked Hina, rather annoyed at being called from her *tapa*-making house.

"I have an idea, Ma," said Maui excitedly. "I think I know now how to outwit that old hen." He set to work, winding the *tapa* around and around the calabash.

Curious, Hina stayed to watch.

Maui made a final twist of the material and said, "There! Now what does that look like? Or what would it look like if it were in a canoe with my brothers, and you saw it from the top of the mountain?"

"Why — it would look just like one of them."

"You see!" cried Maui, hugging her and swinging her around. "That's how I'm going to fool the old *'alae* hen."

The next morning he placed the calabash in the canoe with his brothers and said, "You all go out fishing as usual — and see what happens." He set off on the long hike.

The *'alae* hen was fooled, just as he had planned, and her fire was burning brightly when Maui reached the gap in the crater's wall. How does she light it? he wondered. I'll either have to steal some coals, or find out how she does it. And I'd better learn the secret, in case Mother's fire ever goes out again.

He approached cautiously, then leaped out and grabbed the hen by the neck. "Teach me how to make a fire, old hen!" he shouted.

"Not so tight," clucked the hen, trying to wriggle free. "How can I tell you when I can scarcely breathe?"

Maui loosened his hold, and she nearly got away. "I'll have to hold you tight, if you're going to do that," he said.

She shook her feathers as best she could and looked about, as if for help. But no one was in sight. At length she said, "All you have to do is to rub the stalk of a *taro* plant with a hard stick." She nodded toward a *lauhala* basket of wood and another of things she was going to cook.

Maui kept his grasp on her while he picked up some *taro* and a stick of wood, and did as she had said. No sparks came, but to this day the *taro* stalk has a groove in it.

Maui tightened his hold again, nearly choking the hen.

"Be careful!" she croaked. "I can hardly breathe — much less talk."

He said, "Tell me quickly!" and held her more gently.

"Try rubbing two reeds together."

Nothing happened. In anger, then, he rubbed the top of that hen's head until it was red — as the *'alae* hen's has been ever since.

"All right," she cackled at last. "I'll tell you because I have no other choice. You must rub a stick of hard sandalwood upon one of soft *bau*, and you will have fire."

Maui found these two kinds of wood in her basket, and rubbed them together. Sparks flew in all directions!

"Thank you, old hen," he said. "If you hadn't been so stubborn, I wouldn't have had to hurt you."

Down the mountainside he went, with the gift of firemaking for his mother. Cooked fish for dinner! he thought as he ran.

"The Fire-Drake's Hoard" and "The Death of Beowulf," from Dragon Slayer, *by Rosemary Sutcliff. Illustrated by Charles Keeping (Harmondsworth: Puffin, 1966).*

The death of the hero is the final stage of the linear journey. Although he possesses superhuman strength, Beowulf, hero of the great Anglo-Saxon epic, is mortal. Now an aging king, he is called on to fight the evil dragon who is devastating the countryside. In addition to depicting vividly the hero's final battle, this selection clearly indicates the nature of the comitatus *bond, the mutually supportive relationship between a leader and his followers. While Beowulf and Wiglaf fulfill their obligations, the other followers of the king do not. In her retelling, Rosemary Sutcliff, a well-known British writer of historical nov-*

els for children, approximates the alliterative rhythms and word-kennings (combinations) of the original Old English poetry.

In describing Bilbo's encounter with the dragon Smaug in The Hobbit, *J.R.R. Tolkien was drawing on his knowledge of Beowulf's encounter with the dragon.*

The Fire-Drake's Hoard

The years went by and the years went by, bringing as they passed great changes to the two kingdoms. In Denmark Hrothgar died and was howe-laid, and Hrethric his son ruled in his place. Hygelac fell in an expedition against the Frisians, and Beowulf, still his chief thane, avenged him worthily on the enemy and then, sore wounded himself, fought his way back to the seashore and the waiting war-galleys, and so escaped to carry the sad tidings back to Hygd the Queen. Heardred the King's son was still only a boy, too young to lead his people in war or guide them wisely in peace, and so the Queen called together the Councillors and foremost chieftains of the land, and with their consent offered the gold collar of the Kingship to Beowulf in his stead. But Beowulf, true to his House-Lord, would have nothing to say to this, and so Heardred, young as he was, was raised to the High Seat with his mighty cousin to stand ever at his side as counsellor and protector.

Alas! It was all to no avail, for in his young manhood Heardred fell in battle as his father had done. And this time, when the Kingship was offered to him again Beowulf took it, though with a heavy heart, for he was the rightful next of kin.

Long and gloriously he ruled, holding his people strongly and surely as in the hollow of his great sword hand. Fifty times the wild geese flew south in the autumn, fifty times the birch buds quickened in the spring and the young men ran the war keels down from the sheds; and in all that time Geatland prospered as never before.But when the fiftieth year was over, a terror fell upon the land.

And this was the way of it.

Many hundreds of years before, a family of mighty warriors had gathered by inheritance and by strength in war an immense store of treasure, gold cups and crested helmets, arm-rings of earls and necklaces of queens, ancient swords and armour wrought with magic spells by the dwarf-kind long ago. A great war of many battles had carried away all this kinsfolk save one, and he, lonely and brooding on the fate of the precious things that he and his kin had gathered with such joy when he also should have gone by the Dark Road, made ready a secret fastness that he knew of, a cave under the headland that men called the Whale's Ness. And there, little by little, he carried all his treasures and hid them within sounding of the sea, and made a death-song over them as over slain warriors, lamenting for the thanes who would drink from the golden cups and wield the mighty swords no more, for the hearths grown cold and the harps fallen silent and the halls abandoned to the foxes and the ravens.

When the man died the hoard was forgotten and lay unknown under the flank of the hill while the slow centuries went by, until at last a fire-dragon, seeking a lair among the rocks, came upon the hidden entrance to the cave and, crawling within, found the treasure. Because he had found it the fire-drake thought that it was his, and he loved it, heavy arm-ring and jewelled dagger and gold-wrought cup; and he flung his slithering coils about it, and lay brooking over it for three hundred years.

But at the end of that time a man who had angered his chieftain in some way and was fleeing from his wrath also found the hidden entrance among the rocks, and the golden hoard, and the dragon sleeping.

Now through all those three hundred years the dragon had been slowly growing, until from snout to tail tip he was ten times as long as a man is tall. Yet still he was not long enough completely to encircle the mound of treasure, and between snout and tail tip as he lay was a gap just wide enough to let through a man.

The fugitive saw the golden glimmer of the hoard, and even while his brain swam at the sight it seemed to him that here might be a way out of his desperate plight. Creeping between snout and tail tip of the sleeping dragon, he caught up a golden cup, one great cup glowing like the sun with which to buy off his chieftain's wrath, and, clutching it to his breast, fled back the way he had come.

Presently the fire-drake woke, and knew in the moment of his waking that he had been robbed. Blindly, in grief and fury, he snuffed about his beloved hoard, and knew by the smell that a man had been there. He crawled outside and padded about the entrance to the cave and among the rocks, and found man's footprints; and when the dusk came down he spread his great wings and flew out in search of the thief.

Night after night from that time forward he flew out, filled with hatred, and seeking not only the thief but to wreak his vengeance on all men because it was a man who had robbed him. Far and wide he flew, from coast to coast of Geatland, wrapped in his own fiery breath as though in mists of flame. Houses, men, trees and cattle, even the King's Hall itself, shrivelled up as his angry breath blew upon them, and at each sunrise when he returned to his lair, he left the trail of his night's flying marked in black and smoking desolation across the land.

Beowulf was old now, a grey warrior who had once been golden, but a warrior still. Also he was the King; and for him in the last resort was the duty and the privilege of dying for the life of his people. And so, as he had done so many times before, he made himself ready for battle. Well he knew that he would not be able to come to grips with the dragon as he had done in his youth with Grendel the Night-Stalker, for now he had to fight not only strength but fire, and his familiar war-gear would not serve him, for how long could a shield of linden-wood withstand flame? So he sent for the Warsmith to come to him in his sleeping quarters — now that his hall was no more than a blackened shell — and said to him, 'Forge me a shield of iron, strong to withstand fire. And be quick in the forging of it, for the people cannot endure many more such nights of desolation.' And he chose twelve thanes of his own bodyguard, among them Wiglaf, grandson of that Waegmund who had sailed with him for Denmark fifty roving-seasons ago, and bade them make ready to accompany him.

There was a thirteenth of their company also, for the chieftain for whom the cup had been stolen had handed over the thief to Beowulf when he saw the evil that the theft had caused; and to him Beowulf said, quietly terrible, 'You and you alone of all living men know in what place the Terror-that-flies-by-Night has his lair; and if you lead us to the spot, it may be that you shall continue among living men. Your chances shall be no better and no worse than those of my companions who come with me. But if you fail to lead us truly to the place, then you may escape the fire-drake, but assuredly *you shall not escape me!*'

So next morning the King put on his grey ring-mail sark, and sheathed at his side the ancient sword that had been his companion in every fight since Hrothgar gave it to him. And he took the heavy iron shield that was still warm from the anvil, and bidding the rest of his warhost to follow on behind he rode out with his twelve chosen thanes on his last adventure.

Illustration by Charles Keeping, "The Dragon Slayer" from *Beowulf* by Rosemary Sutcliff. Copyright © 1966. Reprinted with the permission of The Bodley Head.

The cave below the Whale's Ness was more than two days' ride from the royal village, but they pressed on with desperate speed, by dark as well as by day, and on the next morning, having left the weary horses behind them among the trees, they came over a wooded ridge and found themselves looking down upon what must once have been a fair and pleasant valley, dipping to low sea-cliffs at one end and at the other running up to meet the high moors where the bees droned among the heather bloom. It was blackened and desolate now, a landscape of despair, fanged with the stumps of charred tree trunks. On the far side of the valley the blunt turf slope of the Ness upheaved itself and thrust its great head out to sea. And against the flank of the Whale's Ness the ground was tumbled and broken up into low cliffs and rocky outcrops over which a faint smoke hung.

The thief halted on the edge of the trees and pointed, trembling. 'There, down there where the smoke curls among the rocks; that is where the fire-drake has his lair and guards his treasure. I have brought you to the place as you bade me, and there is no further use that you can have for such as I am. Now be merciful as you are mighty, my lord Beowulf, and let me go.'

Beowulf glanced at him in scorn. 'Even as you say, I have no further use for such as you. Go where you will, then; your part is done.' And when the man had scurried back into the woods, he seated himself on a fallen tree bole, to rest and gather strength, his elbows on his knees, his gaze going down into the valley and across it to the tumble of rocks under the green flank of the Whale's Ness. And sitting there he felt Wyrd touch him, like a shadow passing across the sun. He had been young and confident, glorying in his own strength when he fought his battle with Grendel, but now he was old and he knew that this would be his last fight. And suddenly lifting his head he began as the wild swans are said to do to sing his own death-song. 'I have lived a long life, and all since before I was seven summers old, I remember.' He sang of his contest with Breca son of Beanstan, and of Hygelac his House-Lord, and the companions who had been his war-boat's crew and sailed with him for Denmark, and the fights with Grendel and his Dam. He sang of the death of Hygelac and the death of Heardred, and his own coming to the Kingship. 'The Frankish warrior who slew Hygelac my King, him I slew Grendel the Night-Stalker,' and with the words, he sighed, and it seemed that all at once he had come to the end of his song. 'But this fight that waits for me now is a different thing,' and I am old. Yet the battlepower is not yet fallen away from me, and I am still the King.' He looked about him at the warriors gathered on the woodshore, and slowly got to his feet, holding out his hand for the great iron shield.

Wiglaf gave it to him, stammering in desperate eagerness, 'My King and House-Lord — I beg you let me come with you!'

Beowulf shook his head, but his eyes were kindly as he looked at the young warrior. 'Na, na, did I not say that I am the King? This is a fight, not for a war-host but for one man, even as my fight with Grendel was for one man. But stay here, all of you, with your weapons ready, and watch to see how it goes with me down yonder.'

And he took up the heavy shield and walked out from among them, out from among the charred trees and down into the valley of desolation, his sword naked in his hands.

The Death of Beowulf

As Beowulf drew near to the gigantic rock-tumble under the Whale's Ness, he saw in the midst of it the dark mouth of a cave about which the smoke hung more thickly than elsewhere. A stream broke out from the darkness of it, flowing away down the slope of the valley, the water boiling as it came, and flickered over with the vaporous flame of dragon's breath; and Beowulf, with his shield before his face, forced his way up beside it until he reached the trampled ground before the cave mouth and could go no further for the choking fumes and smoke that poured out from the darkness under the flank of the hill.

There he stood, and beat sword upon shield and shouted his defiance to the fire-drake within. His shout rose like a storm, the war-cry that his thanes had heard above the clamour of many and many a battlefield; it pierced in through the opening among the rocks, and the fire-drake heard it and awoke. A great cloud of fiery breath belched out from the cave mouth, and within there sounded the clapping of mighty wings; and even as the King flung up his shield to guard his face, the earth shook and roared and the dragon came coiling from its lair.

Heat played over its scales so that they changed colour, green and blue and gold, as the colours play on a sword-blade heated for tempering, and all the air danced and quivered about him. Fire was in his wings and a blasting flame leapt from his eyes. With wings spread, he half-flew half-sprang at Beowulf, who stood firm to meet him and swung up his sword for a mighty blow. The bright blade flashed down, wounding the monster in the head: but though the skin gaped and the stinking blood sprang forth, the bones of the skull turned the blow so that the wound was not mortal. Bellowing, the creature crouched back, then sprang again, and Beowulf was wrapped from head to heel in a cloud of fire. The iron rings of his mail seared him to the bone and the great shield of smith's work glowed redhot as he strove to guard his face and bring up his blade for another blow.

On the hill above the watching thanes saw the terrible figure of their lord in its rolling shroud of flame, and brave men though they had been in battle, terror seized them and they turned to fly; all save one. Wiglaf, grandson of Waegmund, and the youngest of them all, stood firm. For one despairing moment he tried to rally the rest, crying after them to remember their loyalty to their House-Lord. 'Brave things we promised in the King's hall when we drank his mead and took the gifts he gave us! Often we swore ourselves his men to the death—and now the death comes, we forget! Shame to us for ever if we bear home our shields in safety from this day; but I will not share the shame!' And snatching up his shield and dragging his sword from its sheath, he began to run also, not back towards the safety of the woods, but forward and down into the smoke-filled valley.

Head down and shield up, he plunged into the fiery reek, shouting, 'Beowulf, beloved lord, I come! Remember the battles of your youth and stand strong—I am here beside you!'

Beowulf heard his young kinsman's voice and felt him at his shoulder, yellow linden shield beside that of glowing iron, and his heart took new strength within him. But the sound of another voice roused the dragon to yet greater hatred, and the earth groaned and the rocks shivered to his fury, while he drove out blast on blast of searing flame. Wiglaf's shield blackened and flamed like a torch, and he flung the blazing remnant from him and sprang to obey his lord as Beowulf shouted to him, 'Here! Behind my targe — it shall serve to cover us both!' And steady and undismayed they fought on behind the red-hot shield of iron.

But at last, as it came whistling down in mighty blow, Beowulf's sword that had seen the victory in a hundred battles shivered into fragments on the dragon's head.

With a great cry, the King threw the useless hilt away from him, but before he could snatch the saex from his belt, the fire-drake was upon him, rearing up under the flailing darkness of its wings, the poisonous foreclaws slashing at his throat above the golden collar.

In the same instant, while the King's life blood burst out in a red wave, Wiglaf sprang clear of the iron targe and, diving low under the fire-drake, stabbed upward with shortened blade into its scaleless underparts.

A convulsive shudder ran through all the lashing coils of the dragon's body, and instantly the fire began to fade, and as it faded, Beowulf with the last of his battle strength, tore the saex from his belt and hurling himself forward, hacked the great brute almost in two.

The dragon lay dead, with the brightness of its fires darkening upon it. But Beowulf also had got his death hurt, and now as he stood swaying above the huge carcass, his wounds began to burn and swell, the venom from the monster's talons boiled in his breast and all his limbs seemed on fire. Blindly he staggered towards a place where the rocks made a natural couch close beside the cave entrance, and sank down upon it, gasping for air.

Wiglaf with his own burns raw upon him

bent over his lord, loosened the thongs of his helmet and lifted it away so that the cool sea wind was on his forehead; brought water in his own helmet from the stream, which now ran cool and clear, to bathe Beowulf's face and wounds, all the while calling to him, calling him back from somewhere a long way off. By and by Beowulf's head cleared a little, and for a while the scalding tide of poison seemed to ebb, and the old King gathered up strength to speak, knowing that his time for speaking would soon be done. 'Now I wish in my heart that the All-Father had granted me a son to take my war-harness after me; but since that may not be, you must be son to me in this, and take my helm and good saex, and my battle-sark from my body after I am dead, and wear them worthily for my sake.'

He felt Wiglaf's tears upon his face and gathered himself again. 'Na, na, here is no cause for weeping. I am an old man and have lived my life and fought my battles. Fifty winters I have held rule over my people and made them strong so that never a war-host dared to cross our frontiers. I have not sought out feuds, nor sworn many oaths and lightly broken them; and when my life goes out from my body I shall not have to answer to the All-Father for slain kinsfolk or unjust rule.'

He propped himself on to his elbow and looked about him, and his gaze came to rest on the carcass of the fire-drake lying sprawled before the entrance to the cave. 'I have paid away my life to slay the thing which would have slain my people, and now I see it lying dead before me. But if the thief's tale be true, then I have won for them in my last battle some store of treasure also, and that too I would see before the light goes from my eyes. Go now, Wiglaf, my kinsman, and bring out to me what you can carry.'

Wiglaf, who had been kneeling at his lord's side, got to his feet and stumbling past the still twitching coils of the dead monster, went into the cave.

Within the entrance he came to a halt, staring with scarce-believing eyes at the piled-up wonders of the fire-drake's hoard. Golden cups and pitchers, jewelled collars for a king's throat, ancient ring-mail and boar-masked helmets and swords eaten through with rust; and upreared high above the rest, a golden banner curiously wrought with long-forgotten magic, which shone of itself, and shed about it a faint light in which he saw all the rest. But he had neither the time nor the heart for much marvelling. In frantic haste he loaded himself with cups and armrings and weapons, and the banner last of all, and carried them out into the daylight and flung them clanging down at the old man's feet.

Beowulf lay still with his eyes closed, and the blood still flowing from his wounds. But when Wiglaf fetched more water from the stream and again bathed his face he revived once more, and opened his eyes to gaze upon the treasure as it lay glittering among the rocks. 'A fine bright gleam of gold to light me on my way,' he said. 'Glad am I that since the time has come for me to go I may leave behind me such treasure for my people.' Then his gaze abandoned the glitter of the dragon's hoard, and went out and upward to where the great bluff forehead of the Whale's Ness upreared itself against the sky. 'After the bale-fire is burned out, bid them raise me a burial howe on the Whale's Ness yonder, a tall howe on the cliff edge, that it may serve as a mark for sea-faring men such as I was in my youth. So they may see it from afar as they pass on the Sail-Road, and say, "There stands Beowulf's Barrow" and remember me.'

For the last time his gaze went to young Wiglaf's face, and his hands were at his wounded throat, fumbling off the golden collar of the Kingship. 'Take this also, with my war-gear.' His voice was only a whisper now. 'Use it well, for you are the last of our kindred. One by one, Wyrd has swept them all away at their fated hour; and now it is time for me to go to them.'

And with the words scarce spoken, a great sigh broke from him and he fell back into the young warrior's arms. And Wiglaf laid him down.

He was still sitting at his dead lord's shoulder when a shadow fell across them both and, looking up slowly, he saw that the King's Hearth Companions had come stealing down from the high woods of their refuge, and were standing about him staring down in shame at slain hero and slain monster. He did not trouble to rise, but sitting drearily where he was, stony-eyed, he flayed them with all the bitter scorn that was in his heart. 'So you come, do you, now that the fire is spent! Well may men say, seeing you safe and unmarked in the war-gear that Beowulf gave you, that he made a bad bargain with his gifts. When his sorest need came upon him he had no cause to boast of his companions in arms. Small honour will Geatland have in her foremost warriors, when the princes of other lands hear of this day's work! Aye, you have kept whole your skins under your bright battle-sarks; but it may be that death is better for a warrior than a life of shame!'

And the thanes stood silent about their dead lord, enduring the lash of Wiglaf's scorn, for there was nothing that they could say.

Presently a scout sent out by the following war-host came riding over the wooded ridge and looked down into the valley. One long look was enough, and then wheeling his horse he galloped back to tell what he had seen. 'The fight is over, and our King lies dead among the rocks with the fire-drake dead beside him. Now the joy and honour that he gave us are fled from the land, and the War Chieftains will come against us as they have not dared to do for fifty years, and Beowulf who should have led us against them is dead.'

A groan ran through the host at his words, and at an increased pace they pressed on towards the dragon's lair.

When they came down into the blackened valley they found all as the messenger had told them, the grey-headed King lying dead with his broken sword beside him, and the carcass of the fire-drake outstretched on the burned and bloodsoaked turf nearby; the shamed thanes standing at a distance, and Wiglaf sitting bowed with grief at his lord's shoulder; the golden gleam of the dragon's hoard among the rocks and, upreared over all, the great gold-wrought banner curving to the sea wind like the curved sail of a ship.

Sadly the warriors gathered about their King, and then at last Wiglaf stirred and rose to his feet, stiffly as though he too were an old man. He took up the golden collar of the King-ship, stained as it was with the dead hero's blood, and standing there before the sorrowing war-host he fastened it about his own neck. And with it he put on the King's authority. 'Beowulf is dead, and plainly you may see how he met his end. Gladly he paid away his life to save his people from the Terror-that-flew-by-Night, and in his dying he bade me greet you and pray you, after the bale-fire is burned out, to build him a worthy barrow for his resting-place — a great barrow high on the Whale's Ness, to be a guiding-mark hereafter for all who sail the sea. Now make ready the funeral pyre, and bring something to serve as a bier, that we may carry our old King to his chosen place. And meanwhile let seven of you come with me into the cave and bring out into the daylight all that yet remains there of the fire-drake's hoard.'

So while Wiglaf and the seven toiled to and fro, bringing out from the dark the treasure that had not seen the sun for a thousand years, others set themselves to gather wood and build a pyre high on the Whale's Ness and hang it round with war helms and fine weapons and ring-mail sarks, as befitted a King's funeral pyre. And yet others dragged the carcass of the fire-drake to the cliff's edge and heaved it over into the surf that creamed below. They brought a farm wain drawn by oxen and hung it round with shields as though its sides were the bulwarks of a warboat, and when all was ready they laid the dead King in it, and piled about him the wrought gold and wondrous weapons of the dragon's hoard — for Wiglaf said, 'As Beowulf alone won all these things, so let them go back with him into the dark from which they came,' and in all the war-host no man lifted a voice against him.

Then they set the four slow yoke of oxen straining up the steep slope to the headland, where the pyre stood waiting against the sky. They laid the body of Beowulf on the stacked brushwood and thrust in the torches, and presently all men far and wide saw the red fire on the Whale's Ness, and knew that Beowulf had gone to join his kindred.

All night long the fire burned, and when it sank at dawn they piled about the ashes the precious things of the dragon's hoard, and up-reared the golden banner over all. Then they set themselves to raise the barrow as the old King had bidden them. For ten days they laboured, building it high and strong for the love that they had borne him, and on the tenth day the great howe of piled stones stood finished, notching the sky for all time on the uttermost height of the Whale's Ness, where the cliffs plunged sheer to the sea.

Then twelve chieftains of his bodyguard rode sunwise about it, singing the death song that the harpers had made for him. And when the song was sung, all men went away, and left Beowulf's barrow alone with the sea wind and the wheeling gulls and the distant ships that passed on the Sail-Road.

"Sir Patrick Spens," from English And Scottish Popular Ballads, *Student's Cambridge Edition (Boston: Houghton, Mifflin, 1904).*

This Medieval ballad has been called "a tragedy in miniature." Sir Patrick is drowned, a victim of the weather, political intrigue, and his own character flaws. The circumstances, the writing of the King's letter and Sir Patrick's reaction to it, suggest that the Right Hand Man has used the occasion to send a feared rival on a voyage which might be fatal. He quickly and innocuously suggests Patrick as the ideal person to take an untested ship out in dangerous weather. However, Spens, even though he recognizes the threat, immediately acts on his instructions, ignoring the warnings of an adviser, and what was intended as a circular journey becomes tragically linear.

Sir Patrick Spens

The king sits in Dumferling toune,
  Drinking the blude-reid wine;
'O whar will I get gaid sailor,
  To sail this schip of mine?'
Up and spak an eldern knicht,
  Sat at the kings richt kne:
'Sir Patrick Spence is the best sailor
  That sails upon the se.'
The king has written a braid letter
  And signd it wi his hand,

And sent it to Sir Patrick Spence,
  Was walking on the sand.
The first line that Sir Patrick red,
  A loud lauch lauched he;
The next line that Sir Patrick red,
  The teir blinded his ee.
'O wha is this has don this deid,
  This ill deid don to me,
To send me out this time o' the yeir,
  To sail upon the se!
'Mak hast, mak haste, my mirry men all,
  Our guid schip sails the morne:'
'O say na sae, my master deir,
  For I feir a deadlie storme.
'Late late yestree I saw the new moone,
  Wi the auld moone in hir arme,
And I feir, I feir, my deir master,
  That we will cum to harme.'
O our Scots nobles we richt laith
  To weet their cork-heild schoone;
Bot lang owre a' the play wer playd,
  Thair hats they swam aboone.
O lang, lang may their ladies sit,
  Wi thair fans into their hand,
Or eir they se Sir Patrick Spence
  Cum sailing to the land.
O lang, lang may the ladies stand,
  Wi thair gold kems in their hair,
Waiting for thair ain deir lords,
  For they'll se thame na mair.
Haf owre, haf owre to Aberdour,
  It's fiftie fadom deip,
And their lies guid Sir Patrick Spence,
  Wi the Scots lords at his feit.

"Of the Death of Arthur," from The Boy's King Arthur. *Edited by Sidney Lanier, illustrated by N.C. Wyeth (New York: Scribner's, 1952).*

In addition to being embodiments of Medieval beliefs of chivalry and religious purity, the legends of King Arthur are also stories of high idealism finally destroyed by human corruption. Arthur receives his fatal wound at the hands of Mordred, his illegitimate son, and is twice deceived by Sir Bedivere, whom he has charged to throw his famed sword Excalibur into the lake. It should be noted that Arthur does not die, but is transported to the enchan-

ted land of Avalon, from whence, according to some legends, he will return in England's time of greatest need. This story is taken from a book entitled The Boy's King Arthur — *an indication of nineteenth and early twentieth century attitudes, which were that adventure stories were best suited for young male audiences.*

Of the Death of Arthur

Then the king looked about him, and then was he ware that of all his host, and of all his good knights, were left no more alive but two knights, that was Sir Lucan the Butler and Sir Bedivere his brother, and they were right sore wounded.

"Jesu mercy!" said King Arthur, "where are all my noble knights become? Alas! that ever I should see this doleful day; for now," said King Arthur, "I am come unto mine end; but would to God that I wist where that traitor Sir Mordred is, which hath caused all this mischief."

Then was King Arthur ware where Sir Mordred leaned upon his sword among a great heap of dead men.

"Now give me my spear," said King Arthur to Sir Lucan, "for yonder I have espied the traitor which hath wrought all this woe."

"Sir, let him be," said Sir Lucan, "for he is unhappy; and if ye pass this unhappy day ye shall be right well revenged upon him. My good lord, remember well your dream that ye had this night, and what the spirit of Sir Gawaine told you this night; yet God of his great goodness hath preserved you hitherto, therefore, for God's sake, my lord, leave off by this, for blessed be God ye have won the field; for here we be three on live, and with Sir Mordred is none alive. And if ye leave off now, this wicked day of destiny is done."

"Betide me death, betide me life," said the king, "now I see him yonder alone he shall never escape my hands, for at a better vantage shall I never have him."

"God speed you well," said Sir Bedivere.

Then the king gat his spear in both his hands, and ran towards Sir Mordred, crying, "Traitor, now is thy death day come."

And when Sir Mordred heard King Arthur, he ran unto him with his sword drawn in his hand. And then King Arthur smote Sir Mordred under the shield with a foin of his spear throughout the body more than a fathom. And when Sir Mordred felt that he had his death's wound, he thrust himself, with the might that he had, up to the bur of King Arthur's spear. And right so he smote [the king] with his sword holden in both his hands, on the side of the head, that the sword pierced the helmet and the brain-pan. And therewithal Sir Mordred fell stark dead to the earth. And the noble Arthur fell in a swoon to the earth, and there he swooned ofttimes. And Sir Lucan the Butler and Sir Bedivere offtimes heaved him up, and so weakly they led him betwix them both to a little chapel not far from the sea side. And when the king was there, he thought him well eased. Then heard they people cry in the field.

"Now go thou, Sir Lucan," said the king, "and do me to wit what betokens that noise in the field."

So Sir Lucan departed, and he was grievously wounded in many places. And so as he went, he saw and hearkened by the moonlight, how the pillers [pillagers] and robbers were come into the field to pill and to rob many a full noble knight of broaches and beads, of many a good ring, and of many a rich jewel; and who that were not dead all out [entirely], there they slew them for their harness and their riches. When Sir Lucan understood this work, he came to the king as soon as he might, and told him all what he had heard and seen.

"Therefore by mine advice," said Sir Lucan, "it is best that we bring you to some town."

"I would it were so," said the king.

"But I may not stand. Ah, Sir Launcelot," said King Arthur, "this day have I sore missed thee. Alas, that ever I was against thee, for now have I my death, whereof Sir Gawaine me warned in my dream."

Then Sir Lucan took up the king the one part, and Sir Bedivere the other part, and in the lifting, the king swooned, and Sir Lucan fell in a swoon with the lift, and therewith the noble knight's heart brast. And when King Arthur came to himself again, he beheld Sir Lucan how he lay foaming at the mouth.

"Alas," said the king, "this is unto me a full heavy sight to see this noble duke so die for my sake, for he would have holpen me, that had more need of help than I. Alas, he would not complain him, his heart was so set to help me. Now Jesu have mercy upon his soul."

Then Sir Bedivere wept for the death of his brother.

"Leave this mourning and weeping," said the king, "for all this will not avail me: for, wit thou well, and I might live myself the death of Sir Lucan would grieve me evermore: but my time hieth fast," said the king. "Therefore," said King Arthur, "take thou Excalibur, my good sword, and go with it to yonder water side, and when thou comest there, I charge thee throw my sword in that water, and come again, and tell me what thou shalt see there."

"My lord," said Sir Bedivere, "your command shall be done, and lightly bring you word again."

And so Sir Bedivere departed; and by the way he beheld that noble sword where the pommel and the haft were all of precious stones, and then he said to himself, "If I throw this rich sword into the water, thereof shall never come good, but harm and loss."

And then Sir Bedivere hid Excalibur under a tree, and as soon as he might he came again unto King Arthur, and said he had been at the water, and had thrown the sword into the water.

"What sawest thou there?" said the king.

"Sir," said he, "I saw nothing but waves and wind."

"That is untruly said of thee," said King Arthur, "therefore go thou lightly and do my command, as thou art to me lief [*beloved*] and dear; spare not, but throw it in."

Then Sir Bedivere returned again, and took the sword in his hand; and then him thought it sin and shame to throw away that noble sword. And so he hid the sword, and returned again and told to the king that he had been at the water and done his command.

"What saw ye there?" said the king.

"Sir," said he, "I saw nothing but the water wap and waves wane."[1]

[1]"*Water wap and waves wane*," *water laps and waves ebb.*

"Ah, traitor untrue!" said King Arthur, "now hast thou betrayed me two times. Who would have wend that thou that hast been unto me so self [*loved like myself*] and dear, and thou art named a noble knight, and wouldest betray me for the rich sword? But now go again lightly, for thy long tarrying putteth me in great jeopardy of my life, for I have taken cold; and but if thou do as I command thee, and if ever I may see thee, I shall slay thee with my own hands, for thou wouldst for my rich sword see me dead."

Then Sir Bedivere departed, and went to the sword, and lightly took it up, and went to the water's side; and there he bound the girdle about the hilts, and then he threw the sword into the water as far as he might; and there came an arm and an hand above the water, and met it and caught it, and so shook it thrice and brandished.

And then the hand vanished away with the sword in the water. So Sir Bedivere came again to the king, and told him what he had seen.

"Alas!" said the king, "help me from hence, for I dread me I have tarried over long."

Then Sir Bedivere took King Arthur upon his back, and so went with him to the water's side. And when they were at the water's side, even fast by the bank hoved a little barge, with many fair ladies in it, and among them all was a queen, and all they had black hoods, and they wept and shrieked when they saw King Arthur.

"Now put me into the barge," said the king; and so he did softly; and there received him three queens with great mourning, and so these three queens [whereof one was King Arthur's sister Morgen le Fay, the other was the queen of Northgalis, and the third was the queen of the waste lands] set them down, and in one of their laps King Arthur laid his head. And then that queen said, "Ah! dear brother, why have ye tarried so long from me? Alas! this wound on your head hath taken overmuch cold."

And so then they rowed from the land, and Sir Bedivere beheld all those ladies go from him; then Sir Bedivere cried, "Ah! my lord Arthur, what shall become of me now ye go from me, and leave me here alone among mine enemies?"

"Comfort thyself," said King Arthur, "and

do as well as thou mayest, for in me is no trust for to trust in; for I will into the vale of Avalon for to heal me of my grievous wound; and if thou never hear more of me, pray for my soul."

But evermore the queens and the ladies wept and shrieked that it was pity for to hear them. And as soon as Sir Bedivere had lost the sight of the barge, he wept and wailed, and so took the forest; and so he went all the night, and in the morning he was ware between two hills of a chapel and an hermitage.

——

"The Death of John Henry" from John Henry and His Hammer *by Harold W. Felton, illustrated by Aldren A. Watson (New York: Knopf, 1950).*

The threat of machines and progress has been a major theme in literature since the Industrial Revolution; it can be observed in such children's books as Virginia Lee Burton's The Little House *and Jean Craighead George's* Julie of the Wolves. *In this well-known story from Black American folklore, John Henry, a railroad construction worker, is determined to assert the dignity of man in the face of the new steam drills. Ironically, he is a victim of the progress he helps to create; he collapses after having completed the driving of steel through the Big Bend Tunnel. His hammer, with which he was born, with which he labors, and with which he dies, symbolizes not only John Henry's physical strength, but also the great pride he brings to his work, a pride which in the end contributes to his death.*

The Death of John Henry

"You all hear," asked Friday, " 'bout that new steam drill engine they got down at the east heading?"

"No," said Steve.

"They tell that they's goin' to use a engine for steel drivin'. "

"How they goin' to do that?" John Henry asked.

"Don't right know. All I know is they got a steam drill."

"No steam engine ever goin' to drive steel like a man. That takes muscle, not steam."

The Captain walked past down near the shaft and John Henry left the group and hurried toward him.

"Cap'n," he said, "what's this I hear 'bout a steam drill for drivin' steel?"

"That's right, John Henry. It's all set up at the east heading and ready to go."

"Cap'n, that steam drill ain't no good. It cain't drive more steel than I can."

"That's what we are going to try and find out," the Captain replied as Li'l Bill, Steve, Murphy, Friday and the others drew near.

"You mean that I's goin' to work 'gainst that steam drill engine?"

"Well, we hadn't thought about it that way. The inventor claims it will do more work than a man, but we hadn't thought about a contest."

John Henry scratched his head. "Then how you goin' to tell if it can do more work than a man if they ain't no man there?"

"Seems to me you got to have a man," said Li'l Bill.

"Sure," said Friday. "If they ain't no man there, how you goin' to tell?"

"Cap'n," said John Henry seriously, "it cain't do it. They's got to be a contest."

"Well — "

"I can show you no steam drill can drive as much steel as I can."

"I'm going down to the east heading now," the Captain replied. "Want to come and look at it?"

"Sure 'nuff do," John Henry replied quickly.

The Captain turned and went down the steep incline and the others followed. At the heading they saw the steam drill, a giant machine covered with gauges and gears and surrounded with hose, and with men swarming around it.

The Captain talked for a few moments with several men who were standing nearby. John Henry and his comrades examined the machine. Soon the Captain returned.

"Still want to have a contest with the steam drill?" he asked.

"Cap'n, I know steam engines. I heaved coal in 'em. I's a natural man. I ain't nothin' but a man. But I knows I can drive more steel than that steam drill engine. That takes muscle, not steam. An' I's itchin' to have me a contest with that steam drill!''

"Then a contest you have. Be down here in the morning."

"Can I bring Li'l Bill for my shaker?"

"Certainly."

Li'l Bill squared his shoulders, and his face became lost in a grin of pride.

John Henry looked the steam drill up and down. Then he turned back to the Captain and said: "Cap'n, I'll be here in the mornin'. Just have me plenty of good sheepnose hammas handy, an' I'll drive more steel than that steam drill — if it's the last thing I ever do!"

The news spread through the camp and in the morning when John Henry and Li'l Bill showed up at the east heading, a big crowd was there. John Henry went into the tunnel and with him went Li'l Bill his shaker. The steam engine had been moved in and it was throbbing softly and powerfully. Two men were there to shovel coal. The engineer was near.

The Captain stepped forward in the dim, flickering light and his shadow trembled on the wall. "Ready?" he asked.

"Ready," said the engineer.

"I's ready, Cap'n," said John Henry.

"Go!"

Li'l Bill leaped to the wall and held the drill. John Henry's hammer flew through the air and fell with a clang!

There was a roar from the engine, a clash of gears, a hiss of steam, and the crash of the drill.

The contest was on! Man against machine!

The roar of the engine filled the air as the drill beat against the rock and the dust swelled up.

John Henry's hammer rose and fell, rose and fell. Li'l Bill shook the drill and turned it in the hole. Now and then he glanced away to watch the steam drill. It was ahead. There was no time to stop and talk, so he sang to John Henry to give him the news, and he sang so that the fall of the hammer marked the time for the song:

"That machine am sure goin' fast.
It's ahead, an' we are last."

John Henry heard. He increased the speed of his stroke and Li'l Bill nodded encouragement and bent to his task. Then John Henry sang:

"How we doin' there, Li'l Bill?
Is we behind that engine still?"

Li'l Bill glanced aside at the steam drill, and answered:

"We're still behin' a li'l bit.
We speeded up, an' so did it."

John Henry swung the hammer with the same powerful and steady rhythm. He answered back:

"This nine-pound hamma am too light.
A twenty-pounder would be right."

Murphy rushed to the tool box and picked up a twenty-pound hammer. He thrust it into John Henry's hands at the end of a stroke. John Henry's big hands closed on the handle and the heavy hammer crashed down on the drill. Li'l Bill flashed up a grin of pride and encouragement. The roar of the steam drill increased, and the fight went on with Li'l Bill and John Henry singing the songs of the hammer men to mark the time.

Then John Henry sang:

"That ol' steam drill am still ahead.
I'll fight an' fight 'til I drop dead.
This hamma handle's gettin' hot.
An' now I'm goin' to tell you what;
This hamma, it won't never do,
So reach down there an' get me two."

Murphy and Steve quickly brought up two twenty-pound hammers. John Henry dropped the one he had been using and took the two hammers, one in each hand, and banged them one after the other against the steel drill. The handle of the discarded hammer smoked and smouldered for a moment on the rocky floor. Then it broke into flame.

The steam engine trembled with anger. Smoke, sparks and steam surged from it and its boiler glowed red with fire and rage. Its gears clashed louder in defiance.

Hour after hour the fight went on. First the steam drill was ahead. Then John Henry. Then the steam drill. The giant machine roared and swayed on its foundation. It devoured tons of coal and barrels of water.

The smooth and even rhythm of John Henry's twenty-pound hammers rang out above the confused violence of the machine. Often the endless songs of the big steel driver and of Li'l Bill could not be heard above the wild rage of the mechanical monster, but the songs were there, for there was always a song in John Henry's heart, and when there was a hammer in his hand, there was always a song on his lips.

The hours went on and never did John Henry pause, or miss, or turn a stroke. Not even when the heavy hammers grew hot and glowed red from the friction and the terrific pounding. Then Murphy and Steve thrust two more hammers in his hands. John Henry seized them, and the great contest went on without pause.

The noise was intense, and strange. The Captain listened. He made a sudden start. "What's that noise?" he said.

"What noise?" Murphy shouted.

"That strange noise! It might be a cave-in!"

John Henry heard, and he sang:

"Ain't no worry, Cap'n.
The tunnel won't cave in.
That noise am just the hammas
A whistlin' in the win.''

Great drops of sweat formed on John Henry's face and back and fell in little rivers to the floor. The constant, never-ending blows jarred him from head to toe and shook the nails loose in his shoes. The soles and heels fell off, but there was no pause. Both man and machine were giving all that was in them, and John Henry sang:

"Oh, the mountain is so tall
An' John Henry is so small.
But I's goin' to beat that steam drill down.
A man's nothin' but a man.

Got to do the best he can.
So I's goin' to beat that steam drill down.
If it's the death of me
The whole world's got to see
John Henry beat that steam drill down.''

Illustration by Aldren Watson from *John Henry and His Hammer,* by Harold Felton. Copyright © 1950 by Alfred A. Knopf Inc. Reprinted by permission of the publisher.

John Henry's drill sank deeper and deeper into the rock. The steam drill worked and labored, groaned and roared. It throbbed and pounded in a desperate attempt to win. But it could not. It had reached the end. There was a sickening mechanical thud and the gears gave way. The hose crumbled, the valves blew out, the gauges dropped, the boiler split wide open, and the machine ground to a noisy stop.

There was silence in the tunnel except for the steady clang, clang, clang of John Henry's hammers. He was singing the song that was in his heart.

Li'l Bill's grimy and sweaty face, covered with a happy grin, looked up at John Henry. The crowd broke into a roar. John Henry had won!

But John Henry did not stop. A dozen more hammer blows and the drill sank out of sight into the wall. John Henry had broken through again! He had broken through from the east heading to shaft number three! The Big Bend Tunnel was finished! John Henry had struck the first blow — and the last!

He turned away from the hard rock wall of the mountain and he walked down the tunnel toward the east heading and the sunlight. Li'l Bill was at his side. The crowd followed.

John Henry stood at the heading and he looked down at the river turning and churning far below. His gaze rose from the leafy carpet that spread over the valley to the mountain tops far beyond. Then he turned and looked into the deep, black, yawning entrance of the tunnel. There was a big white smile on his face as his friends gathered around laughing and slapping his back with joy and pride.

He wavered a moment, put his hand to his head and sank down on a rock near the heading.

The Captain came up to him. "Well, John Henry," he said, "you did it. You lasted longer than the steam drill, and you drove more steel. It drove only twenty-seven inches, and you drove eighty-nine!"

"I knowed I could, Cap'n. It takes muscle to drive steel, not steam."

"What's the matter, John Henry?" asked Li'l Bill.

"My head's a bustin'," he said as he leaned back against the rocky slope. "I think I's goin' to die."

"Get a doctor!" the Captain said.

"Ain't no use, Cap'n. I done all I's supposed to do. I started this here Big Bend Tunnel, and I finished it. I had me a contest with the steam drill. An' I drove more steel than the steam drill. An' now I's done." He pulled his hammer up close to him.

His eyes closed and he sighed deeply and life went from him. John Henry was dead, and he died with a hammer in his hand.

They buried him there at the east heading of the Big Bend Tunnel. They buried him with his hammer in his hand.

They say that John Henry's spirit still moves in the Big Bend Tunnel, and that his spirit moves in all of the tunnels in the land of his birth, and that his spirit protects the trains and the people who use the tunnels. They say that it is a kindly, helpful spirit, and a determined one, and strong.

The spirit is sometimes heard, but never seen, for the tunnels are black, and John Henry was black. As black as the strange night was black when he was born. But sometimes a strange light is seen, only for a fleeting moment. It looks like nothing of this world. More like the flash of an angel's wing.

And when men say they hear music in the tunnels, it may be true. It may be John Henry singing, for John Henry always had a song in his heart.

Hero Tales for Further Reading

COLLECTIONS

The Faber Book of Greek Legends, ed. by Kathleen Lines. Ill. by Faith Jaques (London: Faber and Faber, 1973).
  —includes major episodes from *The Illiad, The Odyssey*, and *The Aeneid*, along with several Greek myths.

The Hamish Hamilton Book of Heroes, ed. by William Mayne. Ill. by Krystyna Turska (London: Hamish Hamilton, 1967).
  —Twenty-two tales, several by the editor, including stories of Hiawatha, Paul Jones, Fin Maccumhail, and Horatius.

Hero Tales from Many Lands, comp. by Alice I. Hazeltine. Ill. by Gordon Laite (New York: Abingdon, 1961).
  —Thirty stories from Europe, North America, and the East, including, in addition to old favorites, several lesser-known tales.

Heroes of Greece and Troy, by Roger Lancelyn Green (London: Bodley Head, 1960).
  —Thirty-five legends, one third of which are based on the Homeric epics. Green unifies the stories "as that single whole which the Greeks believed it to be."

TALES OF INDIVIDUAL HEROES

Titles marked with an asterisk (*) are alternate versions of those found in this anthology.

The Adventures of Nanabush: Ojibway Indian Stories, comp. by Elizabeth and David Coatsworth. Ill. by Francis Kagige (Toronto: Doubleday, 1979).*
—the tales in this collection emphasize the disruptive nature of the Native trickster-hero.

Beowulf, by Charles Kevin Crossley-Holland. Ill. by Charles Keeping (Oxford: Oxford University Press, 1982).*
—a fine condensed adaptation of the Anglo-Saxon epic, with powerful illustrations which capture the grim and heroic qualities of the story.

Bows Against the Barons, by Geoffrey Trease. Ill. by C. Walter Hodges (Leicester: Brockhampton Press, 1934).*
—an ironic novel of Robin Hood emphasizing the hardships of the hero's life.

The Children's Homer: The Adventures of Odysseus and the Tale of Troy, by Padraic Colum. Ill. by Willy Pogany (New York: Macmillan, 1962).*
—simple, dignified, and rhythmic prose captures the style and flavor of the Homeric originals.

David, by Maud and Miska Petersham (New York: Macmillan, 1938).*
—the classic giant-killer story is recreated by a major husband-and-wife author/illustrator team.

The Days of the Dragon's Seed, by Norma Johnston (New York: Atheneum, 1982).
—the story of Oedipus is retold in novelistic fashion.

Gilgamesh: Man's First Story, written and ill. by Bernarda Bryson (New York: Holt, Rinehart, Winston, n.d.).
—this 5000-year-old Sumerian epic describes the deeds of Gilgamesh and his monster companion, Enkidu. Stylized drawings and a simplified text diminish the epic scope somewhat.

Glooscap and His Magic: Legends of the Wabanaki Indians, by Kay Hill. Ill. by Robert Frankenberg (Toronto: McClelland and Stewart, 1963).
—Nineteen short legends in which the Eastern Woodlands Indian hero helps people to help themselves.

The Golden Fleece and the Heroes Who Lived Before Achilles, by Padraic Colum. Ill. by Willy Pogany (New York: Macmillan, 1921).
—a master reteller details the adventures of Jason and the Argonauts.

The Golden Shadow: a Recreation of the Greek Legends, by Leon Garfield and Edward Blishen. Ill. by Charles Keeping (New York: Pantheon, 1973).

—in novelistic fashion, the authors retell the adventures of the tragic Heracles.

The Green Hero: Early Adventures of Finn McCool, by Bernard Evslin. Illus. by Barbara Bascove (New York: Four Winds, 1975).
—recounts the youth of the Celtic hero who was known for his human weaknesses.

I Am Joseph, by Barbara Cohen. Ill. by Charles Mikolaycak (New York: Lothrop, Lee, and Shepard, 1980).
—the troubled life of the Old Testament hero is brought vividly to life in words and pictures.

The Illiad and the Odyssey: the Heroic Story of the Trojan War and the Famous Adventures of Odysseus, by Jane Werner Watson. Ill. by Alice and Martin Provensen (New York: Golden Press, 1956).*
—short but readable versions of the main adventures along with superb illustrations by a major illustration team.

The Knight of the Lion, by Gerald McDermott (New York: Four Winds, 1979).
—stark illustrations enhance this story of Yvain, the knight who must struggle to overcome deep inner weaknessess.

Moses, by Opal Wheeler. Ill. by Linford Donovan (New York: E.P. Dutton, 1962).
—a simple, but not simplistic, retelling.

Perseus, by Compton Mackenzie. Ill. by William Stobbs (New York: World Publishing, 1972).
—one of a series of excellent retellings of Greek hero tales by a major novelist and significant illustrator. Others in the series are about Theseus, Jason, and Achilles.

Raven-Who-Sets-Things-Right: Indian Tales of the Northwest Coast, by Fran Martin. Ill. by Dorothy McEntee (New York: Harper and Row, 1975).
—Ten traditional tales focusing on the trickster-hero who sometimes performs good deeds and sometimes merely nourishes his mischievous ego.

Robin Hood, by Paul Creswick. Ill. by N.C. Wyeth (New York: Charles Scribner's Sons, 1984).*
—this edition is noteworthy for its reproductions of nine full-color paintings by one of America's best-known illustrators.

Saint George and the Dragon, by Margaret Hodges. Ill. by Trina Schart Hyman (Boston: Little, Brown, 1984).
—this brief retelling of Edmund Spenser's *The Faerie Queene: Book One* is notable for Hyman's Caldecott Medal-winning illustrations.

Sir Gawain and the Green Knight, by Selina Hastings. Ill. by Juan Wijngaard (New York: Lothrop, Lee, and Shepard, 1981).

—the young knight faces inner and outer tests as he proves himself worthy of being a member of King Arthur's court. A good adaptation of a complex medieval romance with fine illustrations in the style of old manuscripts.

Sir Orfeo, by Anthea Davis. Ill. by Errol LeCain (London: Faber and Faber, 1970).
—based on the Greek legend of Orpheus and Eurydice, this Middle English romance tells of the search by a harper-king for his missing wife. LeCain incorporates a variety of medieval styles into his illustrations.

Song of Robin Hood, comp. and ed. by Anne Malcolmson. Music arranged by Grace Castagnetta, designed and ill. by Virgina Lee Burton (Boston: Houghton, Mifflin, 1947).*
—Eighteen of the old ballads set to music and illustrated in medieval manuscript style.

Star Boy, retold and ill. by Paul Goble (Scarsdale, N.Y.: Bradbury Press, 1983).*
—Goble's illustrations accurately embody the spiritual and cultural dimensions of the Scarface Legend.

The Story of King Arthur and His Knights, written and ill. by Howard Pyle (New York: Scribner's, 1903).
—the first of four volumes of retellings of Arthurian legends that are still considered by many to be the finest adaptations for children. Others in the series are *The Story of the Champions of the Round Table* (1905), *Sir Lancelot and His Companions* (1907), and *The Story of the Grail and the Passing of Arthur* (1910).

The Surprising Things Maui Did, by Jay Williams. Ill. by Charles Mikolaycak (New York: Four Winds Press, 1979).*
—a vividly illustrated account of the adventures of the Polynesian trickster-hero.

The Sword and the Grail, by Constance Hieatt. Ill. by David Palladini (New York: Crowell, 1972).
—a smooth-flowing, generally fast-paced and easy-to-follow narration about Sir Perceval's quest for the Holy Grail.

The Treasure of Siegfried, by E.M. Almedingen. Ill. by Charles Keeping (London: Bodley Head, 1964).
—an adaptation of the German *Nibelungenlied*, in which Siegfried woos Princess Kremhild and fights against the jealousy of Brunhild.

Myths

Myths

An Introduction

The word "myth" is frequently misused to refer to a story which is not true. For example, hearing an account of escapades of a celebrity, a person might remark: "Oh, that's just a myth! It couldn't possibly have happened." However, correctly used, the term "myth" refers to a religious story, generally one involving the actions of gods. Although to a reader who doesn't hold the religious beliefs of the people who created the story a myth may be considered untrue, it was most likely true to those who originally told it.

A mythology is the collection of the sacred stories of a specific culture. Often, as in the case of the Norse myths or the Bible, mythologies are highly structured, beginning with the creation and concluding with the end of the world as it is known within the mythology.

Mythological stories have been found in cultures, both primitive and sophisticated, around the world. However, how they were created and formed are not known. Since the time of the ancient Greeks, numerous theories have been advanced. In the third century B.C., the Greek Euhemeris stated that myths were based on reports of historical events and people; over the generations these gradually acquired supernatural elements, and the characters achieved the status of gods. Other Greek thinkers argued that the myths were allegorical, with the characters and actions personifying moral qualities. Since the late nineteenth century, when mythology became an object of serious academic study, a variety of conflicting theories have been advanced to explain their origins. Myths have been seen as primitive science: lacking modern, empirical knowledge, people attributed natural occurences to the actions of supernatural beings. Myths have been related to basic human psychology: because human nature is the same everywhere, similar stories have developed around the world reflecting the inner concerns and emotions of all people. Others have argued that all myths can be traced back to a single origin: one culture in a specific region and time creates a basic mythology which is then carried to different places and takes on different characteristics in new cultures. Yet others have advanced the theory that myths are stories developed to explain or accompany the religious rituals which primitive human beings enacted.

While each of these viewpoints has its advocates, most contemporary scholars agree with folklorist Stith Thompson who has stated that "the origins of myth and folktale over the world must be extremely diverse, so that it is not safe to posit any simple origin even for those of a particular people."[1] He goes on to suggest that studies should focus on the actual nature of myths themselves and notes that "that actual reason for the existence of stories about the gods . . . is the fact that there are certain psychological compulsions which impel people to tell stories of particular kinds."[2] Certainly, when we look at myths from around the world, we find a number of common characteristics. First, the majority of them are sacred in purpose and content. The myth of Demeter and Persephone has been related to the Greek agricultural rituals, and the story of the birth, crucifixion, and resurrection of Christ embodies the central beliefs of Christianity.

Myths also represent quests for psychological security; each culture explains its gods in terms of itself. The Bible states that God created people in His image and likeness. However, it may be said that the way in which people have described their supernatural beings indicates that they have portrayed their gods in their *own* images and likenesses. Even if these beings are terrifying, the fact that their emotions resemble those experienced by humans is in itself comforting.

In many ways, myths do not represent the world, but a people's way of viewing it. It is a human response to, rather than a description of, reality. Literary critic Northrop Frye has written that "man lives, not directly or nakedly in nature like the animals, but within a mythological universe, a body of assumptions and beliefs developed from his existential concerns."[3] In other words, myths take shape within the human mind; the people within a culture believe the same myths and thus have a shared way of seeing themselves in relation to the natural and supernatural world surrounding them. Philosopher Ernst Cassirer compares mythic to scientific perceptions of reality. Whereas science is objective and often abstract and static, myth is dynamic. "The world of myth is a dramatic world — a world of action, of forces, of conflicting powers. In every phenomenon of nature it sees the collision of these powers. Mythical perception is always impregnated with these emotional qualities."[4] Both Frye and Cassirer emphasize the integrative, social importance of myths. For Frye, "a mythology rooted in a specific culture transmits a heritage of shared allusion and verbal experience in time, and so mythology helps to create a cultural history."[5] Cassirer refers to the ideas of French philosopher E. Durkheim: "Not nature but society is the true model of myth. All its fundamental motives are projections of man's social life. By these projections nature becomes the image of the social world."[6]

French anthropologist Claude Levi-Strauss advanced the theory that myths were developed in order to provide reconciliations between seemingly irreconcilable human emotions; in myths, opposing forces achieve harmony.

In many cultures, particularly those of several Native North American groups, myths have not coalesced to create unified mythologies. However, in the best-known myths of the Western world — Greek, Norse, and Biblical — a clearly structured mythology exists. An examination of these reveals the social aspects of myths noted above. The mythologies of these cultures form what can be called a sacred world history and reflect clearly the cultures which created them.

As sacred world history, a mythology explains the creation of the world by a divine power, the relationships between the supernatural beings and between them and human beings, the nature of the world as it exists, the reasons for the existence of sin, disease, and death, and often, the destruction of the world. In a sense, a mythology can be called encylopedic; that is, it considers and accounts for all aspects of life on earth. Herein exists one of the major differences between myths and folktales or hero tales. Folktales are brief and self-contained; they deal with actions of consequence only to the few characters in the specific story. Hero tales, while larger in scope, consider the life of one figure, the culture hero, and how the actions which have occurred in his lifetime influence his cultural group. Mythology, in addition to focussing extensively on supernatural beings, encompasses all time and all space. It is the history of the world as interpreted by one culture; and, although it may only be believed by the people of that culture, these people generally hold it to be true for all of the world. For many Christians, the Bible is the literal record of God's influence on the world and the history of his dealings with the chosen people. The Zuni people distinguish between *telapnaawe*, or *tales*, which are regarded as fiction, and stories of the *chimiky'ana'kowa*, or "The Beginning," which are regarded as historical truth."[7]

The most widespread type of myth describes the creation of the world, the event which, in essence, marks the beginning of history. In *Sun Songs: Creation Myths from Around the World*, Raymond van Over notices that six basic themes recur frequently:

> (1) The idea of a primeval abyss (which is sometimes simply space, but often is an infinite watery deep) .... (2) The originating god (or gods) is frequently awakened or eternally existing in this abyss .... (3) The originating god broods over the water. (4) Another common theme is the cosmic egg or embryo .... (5) Life was also created through sound, or a sacred word spoken by the original god .... (6) A peculiar theme, but quite common, is the creation of life from the corpse or parts of the primeval god's body."

In the creation myths included in this anthology, the Native American "Dawn of the World" is of the first type. The Biblical account is of the fifth type, and the Inuit story "Sedna," of the sixth. Of the three best-known Western creation myths, that contained in the first chapter of Genesis is the most simple and straightforward. Only sin and death are absent. The Greek and Norse myths are much more complex.

According to Greek mythology, in the beginning, Gaea (the Earth) and Uranus (the Sky) loved, producing three different groups of children: six titans (immortal giants) and their sister-wives; three one-eyed monsters, the cyclopi; and three fifty-headed giants. Uranus, fearing these last two groups, imprisoned them in Tartarus. Meanwhile, the Titan Cronus turned upon his father, who fled. Assuming leadership, Cronus fathered several children, the gods, all of whom he ate except the sixth born, Zeus, who was hidden by his mother. Grown to maturity, Zeus forced Cronus to vomit up the other five children, and, with the aid of two titans, Prometheus and Epimetheus, overthrew Cronus and established his own kingdom on Mount Olympus. He divided the rule of the universe between himself, as lord of the heavens and earth, his brother Poseidon, to whom he gave the sea, and Hades, who ruled the underworld.

In Norse mythology, there first existed the darkness out of which emerged Nifflheim, the North, a land of ice and cold, and Muspelheim, the south, a land of fire and heat. Then the giant Ymir was born, and shortly after there appeared a giant cow which provided him with food. Over a long period of time, three generations of giants were created, with Odin, a member of the third generation, becoming the most powerful. He killed Ymir, whose body provided the materials for the heavens, the earth, and the oceans, and caused Asgard, the great home of the gods (often called the Aesir), to be built. In another region was Jotenhem, the land of the giants, enemies of the gods.

The main body of stories within a mythology describes the interrelationships amongst the supernatural beings and between them and human beings. These myths may be said to contain key elements in the world history of the specific culture, and can be divided into two categories. In existential myths, the interactions of the gods exemplify the moral and psychological qualities approved or disapproved of by the people. In etiological or pourquoi myths, the actions of the gods on earth help to explain the physical characteristics of the world, the existence of sin, disease, and death, and the origin of important religious observances. Some myths contain elements of both types.

Two central elements of mythic world history, both found in the Bible, are the occurrence of a world-destroying flood and the human incarnation of God. The story of Noah and the Great Flood represents God's judgment on sinful mortals;

the appearance of the rainbow is an etiological myth explaining the origin and significance of that natural phenomenon. The birth, crucifixion, and resurrection of Christ provide direct evidence of God's desire to provide salvation for all who believe in Him.

The most widespread pourquoi myths explain the stages by which the world assumed its present state and human beings their present methods of living. Two of the most common of these explain the acquisition of fire and the cycle of the seasons. Humanity's discovery and use of fire has often been called its most important step toward achieving its unique status in creation. The fire-bearers of the various myths generally embody characteristics most admired by their cultures. For agrarian societies, the alternation of the seasons was of vital importance, and accordingly they attributed this phenomenon to the actions of supernatural beings. The Greek story of Demeter and Persephone is such a myth. Many Native American pourquoi myths explain the acquisition of unique features of certain animal species as events which took place after the creation had been completed. Thus, for the Blackfoot people, Thunder created horses; the Inuit goddess Sedna was a human being before the sea mammals were created from her amputated digits.

Existential myths deal with those inner problems which most concern humanity. Why is there sin in the world? Why are we afflicted with disease? Why do we die? For the Greeks, the inquisitiveness of Pandora explained the troubles of the world. In the Bible, the disobedience of Adam and Eve led to their expulsion from Eden and the toil and pain which have oppressed humanity since. In "The Dawn of the World," the dissatisfaction of a foolish mortal leads to death. Often the troubles experienced by people are caused by the actions and characters of the gods. Zeus' anger with Prometheus leads to humanity's ultimate miserable condition; Demeter's grief for her lost daughter similarly causes human suffering In their actions, the gods have very human personalities. Thor has a quick temper, Loki is malicious, Sedna is bitter over mistreatment by her father, Epimetheus (whose name means "after thought") is short-sighted.

The final element in the cosmic history of many mythologies is the end of the world. The Biblical accounts in the Book of Revelations and the Norse description of Ragnorak or the "Twilight of the Gods" are the most famous of these. Time and space are seen as moving to an inevitable conclusion; after the dissolution of the world, there will be a newer, better existence, one not subject to the vicissitudes and imperfections of the one lived in by the believers. Frequently, the end of the world is described with winter and wasteland imagery, a contrast to the spring and garden imagery associated with paradise.

In addition to providing a narrative framework embodying the beliefs of the specific culture, individual myths and the mythologies they form reveal the intellectual, religious, and social characteristics of that culture. From the Greek myths can be seen a sense of a people much concerned with the dignity of humanity. If, in fact, it can be said that people describe gods in terms of themselves, the Greeks must indeed have considered people noble in potential at least, for the gods, though not perfect, did lead magnificent lives on their beautiful Mount Olympus. Their frequent, difficult moral choices and responsibilities reflect the high value the Greeks placed on these aspects of life.

Norse mythology, by contrast, is far harsher and much more physical. It is somber and fatalistic. Unlike Mount Olympus where the Greek gods, no matter how imperfect, lived in relative ease and fulfillment, Asgard, home of the Norse gods, contained "no radiancy of joy . . . , no assurance of bliss. It is a grave and solemn place, over which hangs the threat of an inevitable doom."[9] Knowing that Ragnorak (although it could be postponed) was inevitable, the gods asserted their dignity through physical heroism. Courage, loyalty, and relentless struggle against the evil Frost Giants gave meaning to their lives and lessened their despair. The mortal Aesir—whereas Greek gods were immortal—were prepared to lay down their lives whenever necessary, for the righteousness of their cause made the dangers worthwhile. One can see how this mythology reflected the culture of the Northern peoples who created it. Life in a rugged landscape where bitter winters and violent storms made physical survival a constant struggle, and combat against enemies equally as fierce and brave as they were resulted in a projection on their gods of those qualities they most admired.

With the exception of Biblical stories and some Native American legends, none of the myths represented in this anthology embody religious beliefs currently held. In fact, even when the "Poetic Edda" and the "Prose Edda," the major sources for Norse mythology, were written around the thirteenth century A.D., Christianity was the established Icelandic religion. But if these tales are not commonly believed in, then why have mythological stories been retold century after century?

An answer can be found in a statement from a notable nineteenth-century adaptor of Greek myths, American novelist Nathaniel Hawthorne: "No epoch of time can claim a copyright in these immortal fables. They seem never to have been made; and certainly so long as man exists, they can never perish; but, by their indestructability itself, they are legitimate subjects for any age to clothe with its own garniture of manners and sentiment, and to imbue with its own morality."[10] Retelling the stories in the 1850s, Hawthorne discovered what most writers have, that at a deeper level, myths reveal universal concerns and patterns of human nature. Although human nature does express itself differently from society to society, and from age to age, basic psychological elements seem to remain constant.

A brief survey of the history of retelling Greek myths will indicate how they have changed and survived over the centuries. In their best-known forms, the Greek myths were recorded by a variety of writers between the tenth and sixth centuries B.C. However, modern researchers have advanced the theory that these versions were adaptations of earlier works. In *Lost Goddesses of Early Greece*, Charlene Spretnak argues that groups which invaded Greece between 2500 and 1000 B.C. ''found . . . a firmly rooted religion of Goddess worship.''[11] The newer, male oriented society transformed the existing goddesses, making them inferior to those gods introduced into the pantheon. With the ascendancy of Roman civilization, the myths were again adapted, lessening their intensity. During the Middle Ages, those classical myths which were consistent with Christian teachings were retold, while in the Renaissance, with the rediscovery of many ancient manuscripts, interest in mythology increased and the Greek emphasis on the dignity of the human spirit became attractive to contemporary humanists. The Romantic writers of the early nineteenth century were fascinated with the old myths and legends; the poet Percy Shelley saw Prometheus as the prototypical rebel against unjust authority. Modern psychologists have re-examined the traditional materials to demonstrate that these are consistent with their own theories on the nature of the human mind.

Since the middle of the nineteenth century, with the growth in publishing for children, a large number of retellings of myths from around the world has appeared. At first, the Greek, Norse, and Biblical myths were the most frequently retold; more recently, with an increased awareness of minority groups and Third World cultures, a wider range of mythological stories has been presented; Native North American, African, and Oriental myths have been sensitively retold. Since World War II, the attitudes toward foreign religious beliefs have altered considerably also. With greater awareness of cultural relativity, myths which embody customs and beliefs different from those of either the writer or the intended audience are treated with respect. Recent sensitivity to sexual stereotyping has led to the discovery and presentation of myths which do not present women as inferior beings playing secondary roles.

Writers who select myths for younger readers face many challenges and difficulties. A major responsibility is to tell a good story, one that can be understood and enjoyed by the audience. Because not all myths can be understood by all children, the age level of the readers must be taken into account. The story of

Prometheus with its emphasis on moral responsibility and leadership is not generally accessible to children under the age of ten. To reduce it to a simple plot outline for younger children is to rob it of the themes and characterization which make it so great a myth. However, these children can respond to straightforward allegorical myths like "Midas." The Norse myths, particularly those involving the adventures of Thor and the less malevolent tricks of Loki are enjoyed by children in the middle elementary grades. Similarly, etiological Native American myths are suitable for children of this age. The more complex Greek myths are best appreciated by junior-high and high-school students.

The second responsibility of the adaptor is to present the myths accurately and with respect for the originating cultures. In addition to engaging in the requisite background research, the adaptor must again consider the ages of the intended audience. If a story reflects important and fairly complex cultural or religious beliefs, these should not be ignored, but should be presented in a manner comprehensible to the reader. If a story cannot be understood by readers of a specific age group, it should not be told to them.

When introducing myths and mythologies to elementary and junior-high-school children, it is useful to develop a systematic, step-by-step method of presentation. Beginning in the early elementary grades, children can read and listen to individual myths related to other works in the literature curriculum. They can be considered as stories, not specifically as myths. However, over a period of three or four years, students will become familiar with a large number and wide variety of myths. In the upper elementary grades, the literature curriculum can consider the differences between genres. After having read "East o' the Sun and West o' the Moon" and "Cupid and Psyche," students discuss the fact that although the stories have similarities in plot and character, they also contain significant differences. After considering these, the terms "myth" and "folktale" can be introduced and lists of folktales and myths made up. These lists form the basis for introducing the unique characteristics of each genre.

In junior high school, two or more steps can be taken. First, by considering a large number of myths from several culture groups, myths can be subdivided into a number of categories, basically those outlined above in the discussion of mythology as cosmological history. Finally, the myths of a specific culture can be studied as an integral unit, as a mythology which reflects the culture producing it. This procedure allows students to develop gradually their understanding of mythology, moving from the specific to the general as their abilities to comprehend develop. The reverse method requires students to engage in a process of structuring which, in most cases, they are not initially capable of performing.

Notes

1 Stith Thompson, "Myth and Folktales," in *Myth: A Symposium*, ed. by Thomas A. Sebeok (Bloomington: Indiana Univ. Press, 1965), p. 170.

2 Thompson, p. 171.

3 Northrop Frye, *The Great Code: the Bible and Literature* (Toronto: Academic Press, 1982), p. xviii.

4 Ernst Cassirer, *An Essay on Man: an Introduction to a Philosophy of Human Culture* (New York: Bantam, 1970), p. 84.

5 Frye, p. 34.

6 Cassirer, p. 87.

7 Dennis Tedlock, translator, *Finding the Center: Narrative Poetry of the Zuni Indians* (Lincoln: University of Nebraska Press, 1970), p. xvi.

8 Raymond van Over, *Sun Songs: Creation Myths from Around the World* (New York: New American Library, 1980), p. 10.

9 Hamiltion, p. 14.

10 Nathaniel Hawthorne, *A Wonder Book and Tanglewood Tales* (Columbus: Ohio State University Press, 1972), p. 3.

11 Charlene Spretnak, *Lost Goddesses of Early Greece: a Collection of Pre-Hellenic Myths* (Boston: Beacon, 1981), p. 21.

Illustration by Edward Ardizzone, "The Garden of Eden" from *Stories from the Bible*, by Walter de la Mare. Copyright © 1929. Reprinted by permission of the publisher.

"The Garden of Eden," from Stories from the Bible, *by Walter de la Mare (London: Faber and Faber, 1929).*

The most famous of the Western creation myths is the one contained in the first three chapters of the Book of Genesis, which emphasizes both man's position midway between the beasts and the angels, and his superiority to woman — these beliefs being dominant until recently. Walter de la Mare follows his Biblical source closely, using its words and phrases and imitating its prose rhythms and style. However, he has expanded on the original through his descriptions, dialogue, and character development. The purpose of the additions, as he notes in his "Introduction," was to recapture "what the matchless originals in the Bible itself meant to me when I was a child." De la Mare's adaptation also reflects Christian interpretations of man's fall from grace, equating the serpent to the fallen angel Satan and making reference to the arrival of "one to defeat his [Satan's] evil and to redeem man's sin." This myth can be compared to the Greek myth of Pandora as retold by Garfield and Blishen in "An Ordinary Woman" and to the Native North American accounts of creation adapted by Jamake Highwater in "The Dawn of the World." Adam and Eve's situation — ejected from their home, beginning an arduous and frightening linear journey—can be compared to that of the children in "The New Mother" and "A Child in Prison Camp."

The Creation of Man

In the beginning the Lord God created the heaven and the earth. And the earth was without form, and void. All was darkness, confusion and watery chaos. But the spirit of the Lord God, in whose sight a thousand years are but as yesterday, brooded in divine creation upon the dark face of the waters. And God said: "Let there be light." And there was light. And God saw the light, that it was good.

And he divided the wondrous light called Day from the darkness that he called Night. And he parted asunder the waters of the firmament called heaven from the waters beneath upon the earth. And the dry land appeared, its desolate plains and drear ice-capped mountains. And he made the green seeding grass to grow, and the herb and tree yielding fruit; and he saw that it was good.

In the heaven above, for sign of the seasons and of days and of years, and to divide the day from the night, he set the sun and the moon to shine and to lighten the whole earth. The sun, the greater light, ruled the day, and the moon, the lesser light, that waxes and wanes in radiance ever changing, ruled the night; and the wandering planets had each its circuit in heaven, and the stars their stations in the depth and height of space.

Then said the Lord God: "Let the waters bring forth abundantly moving creatures that have life, and winged birds of the air that may fly above the earth under the firmament of heaven." So there were fishes in the deep sea, and great whales had their habitation therein, and the air was sweet with birds.

And when the heavens and the earth and all the host of them were finished in the days that the Lord God appointed, he for ever blessed and hallowed the seventh day, because in joy and love he had stayed then and rested from all his work which he had created and made.

Of the power and wisdom of God was everything to which he had given life — tree and plant and flower and herb, from the towering cedar to the branching moss. All the beasts of the earth also, the fishes of the sea, the fowls of the air, the creeping things and the insects, each in the place where was its natural food and what was needful for its strength and ways and wants; from beasts so mighty and ponderous that they shook the ground with their tread, to the grasshopper shrilling in the sunshine on his blade of grass and the silent lovely butterfly sipping her nectar in the flower; from the eagle in the height of the skies to the wren flitting from thicket to thicket, each after its own kind.

The Lord God saw everything that he had made, and behold, it was very good. He blessed it, and bade all things living grow and increase and multiply upon the earth, wheresoever it was meet for them. But still in his power and wisdom he was not satisfied with the earth that he had created until, last of all things living, he made man. And he called him by name, Adam.

For dwelling-place meet for this man that he had made the Lord God planted a garden. It was a paradise of all delight, wherein he intended him to have bliss in body and soul without end. And though it was of the earth, it was yet of a beauty and peace celestial, wherein even the angels of heaven might find joy to stray.

This garden lay eastward in Eden; and a river went out of Eden to water it. Flowing thence, and beyond it, its waters were divided, and they became the four great rivers of the world, whose names have been many.

The name of the first river was Pison, which flows about and encompasses the whole land of Havilah, where there is gold. And the gold of that land is fine gold. There also is found the gum spicery called bdellium, sweet to the taste and bitter to the tongue, and the clear green onyx or berle stone. The name of the second river was Gihon, whose windings encompass the whole land of Ethiopia. And the name of the third river was Hiddekel, or Tigris, that flows eastward of the land Assyria. And the fourth great river of the world is the Euphrates.

But by any device of knowledge, desire, or labour, to return from beyond Eden by any one of these rivers into that Garden is now for man a thing impossible. Its earthly paradise is no more.

Then, every beast and living thing that was in the Garden, and roved its shades and valleys and drank of its waters, was at peace in the life that had been given it, without fear or disquietude or wrong. But as yet they had no names. Trees grew in abundance on the hills and in the valleys of the Garden, and every tree that sprang forth out of the earth was fair in sight and good to eat.

In the crystal waters of its river swam fish curious and marvellous in scale and fin and in their swift motion in the water; and flowers of every shape and hue grew so close in company upon its banks that the air was coloured with the light cast back from their clear loveliness. The faintest breeze that stirred was burdened with their fragrance. And at certain seasons a mist went up out of the Garden; and night-tide shed its dews, watering the whole face of the ground, refreshing all things.

And in the very midst of the Garden were two trees, secret and wondrous; the Tree of Life, and the Tree of the Knowledge of Good and Evil. Their branches rose in a silence so profound that no cry of bird or beast was heard there, and no living thing shaped by the Lord God out of the dust of the earth ever drew near.

Now the man whom the Lord God had created was different from every other living thing upon the earth. Miraculous in grace and life and strength, his lighted eyes, his hair, his hands, the motion of his limbs, the mystery of his beating heart, his senses to touch and taste and smell and hear and see — miraculous also in the wonder of his mind that reflected in little all things of the great world around him — he too, like all else that had life in the Garden, had been fashioned and shaped of the dust. Yet was he in the image and likeness of the divine; the Lord God had breathed into him breath of life, and he became a living soul.

Since his body, like theirs, was also of the earth, Adam was at peace with all living creatures in the Garden. Nevertheless because in mind and spirit he was man and no beast, God made him the lord and master of the Garden, sovereign even to the fishes of the water, to the birds of heaven and the unreasonable beasts of earth. He had dominion over them all. And as the free and harmless creatures that for a happy dwelling-place shared the Garden with him were less than he, so he himself was a little lower than the angels of heaven, who are not of the earth, but of a different being and nature, and dwell in glory beyond thought or imagination in the presence of the Lord God.

Thus Adam, shaped of the dust and given life of the divine, came into this earthly paradise, and his eyes were opened, and the light of day shone in upon him as through windows, and joy and amazement filled his mind. He heard the voice of beast and bird and wind and water, and with his fingers he touched the flowers. He was clothed in the light and heat of the sun, and stood erect and moved his limbs and stretched his arms above his head. The Lord God looked on him with love and talked with him in the secrecy of his heart.

"Lo, all things that I have made to be of thy company I give into thy charge to keep and tend and to use. Do with them as thy heart desires. And behold, I have given thee also for food every herb whose seed is in itself of its own kind, and every tree yielding fruit and seed. Of every tree thou mayest freely eat except only the fruit of the Tree of the Knowledge of Good and Evil that is in the midst of the Garden. Of that thou mayest not eat. It is denied thee. For if thou eat of it, it will bring thee only grief and misery; deadly of its nature is this fruit unto thee, and in the day that thou eatest thereof thou shalt surely die."

Adam hearkened to these words with all his understanding, and in the will of the Lord God he found freedom and his peace. The days of his life went by, and the Lord God brought to him in his own season every beast of the field and every fowl of the air that he had made out of the dust, to see what Adam would call it, and to see which of them was most meet to him for company. And Adam gazed at them, marvelling as they moved before him, each in its own kind following the instinct and desire that was the secret of its life.

And as Adam watched them, it seemed that of his own insight and divination he shared in the life and being of each one of them in turn. They wandered amid the branching trees, browsing in the herbage, and on the gentle slopes at the river's brink stooped their heads to quench their thirst, or stretched themselves to drowse in the sunshine, or lay cleaning and preening their sleek coats, or sported in play one with another, and leaped and exulted.

Adam watched too the birds among the green-leafed branches, and the prudent and loving ways of the waterfowl. The swan with plumage markless as the snow was there, and the goose on high at evening arrowed the still air, winging in company of her kind. In the hush of dark the little owl called *a-whoo* into the warm silence, and the nightingale sang on whether the moon shone in the dark or no,

though all through the day it had been singing too.

Adam listened, never wearying of their cries and songs. And whatsoever — according to the exclamations of wonder, surprise or delight that came to his lips at sight or hearing of them — Adam called them, such were their names. To every living thing he gave a name. Its image and its name were of one memory in his mind. At call of its name the creature to whom he had given it came fearlessly to his side. He rejoiced to see it, and at sound of his laughter the Garden itself seemed also to rejoice and to renew its life.

At evenfall the Lord God would return into the Garden and talk with Adam, communing with him in the secrecy of his heart. And even when Adam slept, his divine presence haunted him in dreams, and when he awoke to day again his love enfolded him. As naturally as the birds in their singing, Adam praised the Lord God in all that he did.

But though he had joy in the company of the creatures around him in the Garden, Adam had none like to himself with whom to share his own spirit and nature. He was in this apart from them and was alone. And the Lord God read this secret in Adam's heart and had compassion on his solitude.

"It is not good," he said, "that the man whom I have created should be alone; I will make him a help meet for him."

In the darkness of night he caused a deep sleep or trance to fall upon Adam, and out of his side as he slept he took a rib, and with a touch closed again and healed the wounded side. And as he had made all things living and Adam himself out of the dust, so in the mystery of his wisdom he made woman out of man. He breathed into her body the breath of life, and in the stillness of night she lay, as yet unawakened, beside Adam as he slept.

When daybreak lightened again over Eden and the shafts of sunrise pierced its eastern skies, the voice of the bird of morning stole sweet and wildly in upon Adam's dreams, and the very rocks resounded. He awoke, and saw the woman. She lay quiet as a stone, the gold of the sun mingling with the gold of her hair, her countenance calm and marvellous.

Adam stooped in awe and wonder and with his finger touched her hand, as in the beginning the Lord God had with his divine touch bidden him rise and live. So too the woman's eyes opened and looked upon Adam, and out of one paradise he gazed into another. And love breathed in him, seeing that she was of his own form and likeness. As he looked upon her, he cried with joy: "This, this is now bone of my bones and flesh of my flesh!"

So Adam was no longer alone in the Garden. She whom he called woman because she had been created by the Lord God out of man, was his continual company and delight. She was Eve, Adam's wife. They two were one, and this is the reason why a man, leaving even his father and his mother, cleaves to his wife. And in the paradise of earth and mind which had been made for them, Adam and Eve were both of them naked, for they were of all innocence as are children, and they were not ashamed.

Happy and at peace together beyond the heart of man now to dream of or conceive, Adam and Eve dwelt in the Garden of Eden, tending and dressing it to keep it fair and well.

The Fall from Grace

Now of all living creatures in Eden the serpent was more subtle than any other which the Lord God had made. And because of his subtlety there entered into him the knowledge and malice of an angel fallen because of pride from grace, and banished from the presence of the Lord God. This fallen angel's evil influence found harbourage within the serpent; and Adam knew it not.

Couched in his beauty upon his coils, cold and stealthy, the changing colour of his scales rippling his whole length through, the serpent with lifted head would of his subtlety seek their company and share with them a knowledge that was his only. He would drowse beside them in the sun's heat while they talked together, and as he listened, envy sprang up in him, and he hated them for their innocence and their peace in their happy obedience to him who had made them and set them free.

There came an hour in the fullness of morning when Adam was away from the woman, and the serpent, seeing it, approached her and

was with Eve alone. She sat in dappled shade from the sun, whose light was on all around them, and whose heat was pleasant to her after the cold of the waters in which she had bathed. There she had seen her own image or reflex in its glass; and she had praised the Lord God at the thought she was so fair. The serpent lifted up his flat-browed heat, fixed his eyes upon her as she sat sleeking her hair, and he said: "Where, now, is the man Adam?"

Eve told the serpent that he was gone into the glades of the Garden near at hand to gather fruit for them to eat.

The serpent couched lower, rimpling the scales upon his skin. "But is it not", he said, "that the Lord God hath forbidden thee and the man Adam, saying, 'You shall not eat of any of the trees in the Garden'?"

Eve smiled, marvelling that the serpent should so speak.

"Nay," she said, "we may eat of the fruit of any of the trees in the Garden. Except only the fruit of the Tree that is in the midst of it. Of that the Lord God hath said: 'You shall not eat of it. Taste it not lest you die!'"

The Garden was still. Above them the wondrous blue of morning was brimmed with the light of day, and the shadows of tree and mountain moved with the sun. Except for the warbling of birds, there came no sound of any other voice between them, and the serpent drew back his head, and from his cold and changeless eyes steadfastly looked upon Eve, loveliest of all things on earth that the Lord God had made.

"Yea," he answered, "and so the Lord God has said! But of a surety thou shalt not die. For he himself knows well that in the day that thou eat of the fruit of this Tree, then shall thine eyes be opened to his wisdom and thou shalt be as the divine ones, the angels of heaven, knowing both good and evil. It is no wonder that the fruit of the Tree hath been forbidden thee, for even though thou share it not with me, thou hast thine own secret wisdom. I did but desire to show thee how sweet and delectable are the fruits that grow upon this strange Tree's branches."

Eve listened to the guile of the serpent. She stooped her head upon her shoulders and thought deeply within herself of what he had said. And the serpent watching her, held his peace.

At length she answered him. "I know not", she said, "where grows the Tree. And Adam my husband expressly told me not even to seek to look upon it unless he were with me. It is well that the Lord God hath forbidden us the Tree, if only evil come of it."

"Yea," said the serpent. "But verily Adam thy husband hath seen it. I know well where grows this Tree of Knowledge. Come, now, let us go together, and thou thyself shalt see with thine own eyes how harmless it is. Yea, verily, it far surpasses every other tree that is in the Garden; and when I myself quaffed in its fragrance there was none to say me nay. But it may be thou hast no thirst for this wisdom, and thy husband himself would keep it from thee."

The woman rose with trembling hands and looked hither and thither, seeking Adam. But in vain, and the serpent was already gone from her. With a faint cry she followed after him, and the serpent went on before her.

The way became strange to her. It narrowed in beneath lofty trees whose upper branches, interlacing their leaves together under the noon, shut out the day. The ground rose steeply, crag and boulder, but smooth with moss and pleasant to the foot. They descended into a ravine where streams of water brawled among rocks, meeting to part again. Birds of smouldering and fiery plumage, so small they seemed to be of flame, and butterflies, with damasked wings, hovered over the wide-brimmed flowers.

But soon these were few and showed no more. And there were now no birds or any living thing, and in silence they continued on their way ever going up now through the secret places of the Garden, and hidden in a shade so deep no star of night could pierce it, or the moon shine in. The air was cold as water from a well, and there was not even sighing of wind in the midst of the forest to cool Eve's cheek. But it seemed to her that she heard the music of voices afar off and as it were out of the midst of the morning, between the earth and the firmament.

She stayed her steps to listen. And the ser-

pent tarried beside her while she rested, for she was weary with the steepness of the way. Her eyes entreated him, for her mind was troubled, but speech was over between them, and she followed again after him, to discover whence the music of the voices she heard was sounding.

They came out from the verge and shade of the forest into a hollow space of a marvellous verdure that fell away, then rose in slope towards a mountain that towered high beyond it, transfigured with a light that seemed too rare and radiant to be only the light of day. On either side of this mountain, its rocks illumined with the colours of their own bright stone and of the multitudinous flowers that mantled over them, Eve gazed into the vacancy of space. It was as though they had come to the earth's end.

And midway on the green of the mountain slope there was a Tree, the Tree of the Knowledge of Good and Evil, while above it, but well-nigh invisible in the light that dwelt upon it, there was another Tree, and that on the heights beyond.

The sounds as of voices and instruments of music faint and far, and of the rapture of thousands upon thousands beyond telling, had ceased; and it was as though the radiant blue were agaze with the eyes of a great multitude, lost to vision in the light of heaven.

"Lo, now," the serpent whispered in Eve's ear, "methought I heard the sound of voices, but all is still, and there is none to watch or hear us."

And Eve approached and drew near to the Tree, whose branches as of crystal shone in the light of day, ravishing her eyes. Buds and petalled flowers lay open upon them, and they were burdened also with their fruit, both ripening and ripe. A nectar-like fragrance lay upon the air, and the Tree was of a beauty and strangeness that made her heart pine within her.

And behold, the fruit that was upon the Tree seemed sweet and pleasant and desirable to the sight, a fruit to make one wise. Eve looked upon it, and thirsted, though a voice in her own mind called in warning to her of the deathly and infinite danger she was in. And though she remembered the words of Adam that the Lord God had spoken, yet she heeded them not.

The eyes of the serpent were fixed upon her, stealthy with malice, and an envy came upon her senses. She put out her hand and plucked one of the fruits that hung low upon the Tree, and raised it to her lips. Its odour filled her with desire of it. She tasted and did eat, and shuddering at its potency that coursed into her veins, she stayed without motion and as if in sleep.

With her long gentle hand she drew back her hair that lay heavy as gold upon her shoulders, and supple as the serpent himself languished in her own beauty. She raised her head and stared with her eyes, exulting and defiant, yet the radiance of the mountain now smote upon her eyes and dazzled her mind not as with light but with darkness. Dread and astonishment came upon her, and in fear even of herself she turned for help to the serpent that had persuaded her there with his false and evil counsel. And behold, she was alone. She was alone and knew herself forsaken. With the fruit that she had plucked from the forbidden branches she drew back cowering from beneath the Tree; and she fled away.

The darkness of the forest smote cold upon her body as she fled on by the way she had come, stumbling and falling and rising again, seeking she knew not what, but only to escape from the wild tumult of her mind. Her naked limbs bruised, her breath spent, she came into the presence of Adam her husband who had come forth to seek her. With countenance bleak and strange, she crouched kneeling before him, thrust the fruit into his hand, and said: "See, see, the wonder the serpent hath made known to us! Taste and see!"

Her voice rang falsely on his ear. At sight of her face he trembled and, utterly loth and because he loved her, he took the fruit, and deaf to the voice within him, did eat.

In that moment they knew that they had sinned. Their eyes were opened; they looked out upon the Garden, and all things that were familiar in it were now become estranged and remote from them. Power was in their minds, but of knowledge, not of love. A grief no speech could reveal had veiled its beauty. In fear and horror they gazed on one another. Shame overshadowed them. They saw that they were naked, yet knew not where to turn to hide from their own shame. They plucked off leaves from a fig-tree and sewing them together made themselves aprons.

Smitten with doubt, they turned away each from each, and the love that was between them faded from out of their faces like the dew that vanishes in the heat of the day. Burning, mute, shaken with fear, yet on fire with life, they sat, their minds in torment; then, not daring to raise their horror-stricken eyes to sight, they turned again as if for refuge one to another. And Eve hid her face in Adam's hands, and they wept.

At sound of it a fawn that was browsing in a green hollow beneath the branches of a cedar tree lifted its eyes towards them, and, as if in fear, sped away and fled.

Night drew near; the level rays of the sun barred with shadow the vale in which they sat, and the milk-white flowers at their feet were dyed with its red. The firmament above them was flooded as if with flame, that as they looked ebbed out and was quenched. And the song of a multitude of birds in their green haunts rose to a wild babbling rapture that now was desolation to them to hear, then died away and all was stilled.

And behold the serpent was of their company. "Hail, wise and happy!" he whispered with flickering tongue.

But even as they gazed on him with horror and loathing in their eyes, they heard in the silence the sound of the Lord God walking in the Garden in the cool of the day, in the sweet fresh air that comes with evening. They were sore afraid, and hid themselves from his presence amongst the trees of the Garden. But even as they stood together, seeking in vain for refuge where none could be, there came the voice of the Lord calling to Adam.

"Adam, where art thou?"

And the sound of the voice that had been their life and joy stilled their hearts with terror. They came forth from out of their hiding-place, and Adam bowed his head, for he dared not look upon the Lord God.

He said: "I heard thy voice in the Garden, and I was afraid, because I was naked; and I hid myself.''

And the Lord God said: ''Who told thee that thou wast naked? Hast thou then eaten of the fruit of the Tree, whereof I commanded thee that thou shouldst not eat?''

Adam bowed his head yet lower, hiding his face, his eyes fixed upon the ground.

''The woman'', he said, ''whom thou thyself gavest to be with me, she gave me of the Tree, and I did eat.''

And the Lord God said unto the woman: ''What is this that thou hast done?''

And the woman said, weeping: ''The serpent beguiled me — and I did eat.''

Then said the Lord God to the serpent: ''Because thou hast done this thing, thou art from henceforth accursed among all living things upon the earth. Upon thy belly shalt thou crawl, both thou and thy kind, and dust shalt thou eat all the days of thy life, and all that come after thee. And I will put enmity between thee and the woman, and between thy seed, and all that shall spring out of thee, and her seed. And it shall bruise and crush thee, and thou shalt lie in wait to bruise her heel.''

The serpent, the all-subtle one, the sower of mischief, sorrow and malice, looked stonily upon the Lord God, hearing his doom, in evil cold and corrupt. And this Satan went forth from out of his presence, eternal foe of man, though in the loving-kindness of the Lord God there should arise one to defeat his evil and to redeem man's sin, and paradise shall be restored to him again.

When the serpent was gone his way, the Lord God said to the woman: ''Because of this that thou hast done, thy griefs shall be many. In sorrow and anguish thou shalt bring forth children. Yet the desire of thine own nature shall bind thee to thy husband. In him shall be thy strength and refuge, and he shall rule over thee.''

And unto Adam he said: ''Because thou hast hearkened to the voice of thy wife, and hast eaten of the Tree of which I commanded thee, saying, 'Thou shalt not eat of it,' cursed shall be the ground for thy sake and by reason of thy sin. Thorns also and thistles shall it bring forth, and weeds shall cumber thy labour, and thou shalt eat the green herb that springs there-from. But in toil and in weariness and in the sweat of thy brow shalt thou find thy bread all the days of thy life, until thou lay down thy body in death, and be turned again into the earth whence thou wast taken. For dust thou art and unto dust shalt thou return.''

And Adam and Eve, smitten to the soul, fled away from the presence of the Lord God into the night, and returned into the darkness of their hiding-place in the Garden.

The Lord God was grieved to the heart because of their sin and sorrow, and communing in his wisdom he said within himself: ''Behold, this man is become like unto one that is divine, seeing that, though it is not for his own peace, he hath attained the knowledge of good and evil. And now it may be in pride and disobedience he may sin yet again, and put forth his hand and pluck of the fruit of the Tree of Life, and eat and live for ever in shame and grief.''

Therefore did the Lord God, though he was never to leave them utterly alone or abandon them, determine to cast Adam and Eve forth from out of the Garden of Eden, and to exile them into a world that could be no more a paradise, and where there could be no peace except that which their love and desire of him could bring them, for solace of their bitter banishment.

In the darkness that is before dawn they awoke where they lay, but into the sorrow where sleep had found them. They arose, and behold, there stood in watch round about them Cherubim of heaven whose eyes were like flames in the light of their countenances, unendurable to their gaze.

Adam and Eve fled from before them, stricken with dread, cold with anguish, and came through chasms to where in the sea-like gold of the risen sun the river of Eden flowed out beyond the Garden, falling in foam with sound of thunder from height to height. And the vast circuit of the earth lay spread out beneath them where they stood, dense with enormous forests, parched with sand, chequered with ice-capped mountains, through whose valleys the four rivers rolled their waters, which are the four great rivers of the world.

Thither they went down out of Eden, and dared not rest, until, looking back, even the verges of the Garden that had been their joy and peace were hidden from them. And night fell, cold and dark, and they were alone.

And at the east of the paradise whence God had cast out Adam, he set Cherubim, angels of heaven, and in their hands were flaming swords, turned every way, to keep and guard the way of the Tree of Life.

—————

"The Dawn of the World," from Anpao: an American Indian Odyssey, *by Jamake Highwater (New York: Crowell, 1977).*

There are many different Native North American creation myths. However, four types appear most frequently: the creation of the world from nothing by an All-being who has existed eternally; the earth diver story, in which a bird dives beneath the all-encompassing waters to bring up a small lump of dirt which is then enlarged and made into land; the emergence theme in which human beings come from beneath the ground; and episodes in which a culture hero travels about creating plants and animals, giving them the characteristics they now possess. Some cultures emphasize only one aspect, others combine several. However, in all Native creation myths, human beings are represented as a part of *rather than* apart from *the rest of the creation; all living things are meant to help each other.*

Contemporary American writer Jamake Highwater, in his novel Anpao, *draws upon the myths of a variety of cultures, particularly Blackfoot and Cheyenne, to create a story which he believes reflects the common quality of spiritual belief underlying all Native cultures.*

The Dawn of the World

At the place where all things began, there was first the black world. And Old Man, the all-spirit, lived in this void, silently and without motion. For he was he.

The all-spirit was also her and all that exists between the her and the him, like the snail which from itself brings new life. For Old Man was without mother or father, being together something and nothing.

He looked around him, but there was nothing but himself to see. He listened carefully, but there was only silence. Nothing was born and nothing grew. Nothing was new and nothing old. There was only Old Man, alone in an unthinkable forever.

Because he was everything, Old Man was not lonely. But as he radiated through the endless time of nothingness, it seemed to him that something might be more interesting than nothing. Here and there within his immensity were specks of his power.

So he drew himself inward like a vast breath. And all that he was came together in one place, like the place in the acorn which imagines the tree. There he glowed with power until suddenly he was ignited by an idea of being. And from this mysterious center of the all-spirit came a light into the blankness which was so great that it illuminated all that had been in darkness, reaching beyond the farthest specks of him that is called everything.

First came white—of the brightness of him.

Then he made a great water filled to its depths with all that he knew. And from the sea could come all life that ever would be, so deep and so rich was that great water which Old Man had made.

Then came green — of the waters of him.

Because Old Man was each thing and also everything, he could feel the coolness of the water and he could taste on his lips the salt from it. And just as he was thinking that this water which he had made was good, his thoughts shattered by accident and broke into fragments which fell through him and into the water. From this dazzling shower of bright yellow thoughts came the beings of the water, first so small that they could scarcely be called anything at all and then larger, until the fish, swimming in the deep, appeared one at a time. And then the snails and crawfish, the mussels, and the grass that grew beneath the water.

And blue was the sky where the water and the light mingled. And brown and russet and black the creatures in the sea he had made.

"Hmm," said Old Man. "I am forever, but

still I grow older and older. Since I have made so beautiful a reflection of myself on this green water, perhaps I should also make something that will continue to live on the surface of the water when my reflection has gone. For I also created youth and old age when I created time." And so it happened. Now there were snow geese and mallards and teal and coots and terns and loons, living and swimming about on the water's surface. Old Man could hear the splashing of their feet and the flapping of their wings.

Then the snow goose paddled to where she believed Old Man was, and she said, "I do not see you, but I know you are within me and outside of me everywhere. Listen to me, Old Man. This is very good water that you have made. But birds are not like fish. Sometimes we get tired of swimming around. Sometimes we would like to get out of the water."

"Then fly!" Old Man rejoiced, and he waved his arms so that a wind came and all the water birds flew, skittering along the surface of the deep green sea until they moved fast enough to soar into the air.

And the sky was dark with them and full of their clatter.

"How beautiful these flying birds are, and what a good idea that they should fly!" said Old Man.

The loon was the first to glide back to the surface of the water. "Old Man," he said — looking all around, for he knew that Old Man was everywhere around and within him — "Old Man, you have made us a fine sky and bright light in which to fly, and you have made us water to swim in, but still, though it must sound ungrateful to want more, there is something we need. When we are tired of swimming and also tired of flying, we should like a dry place where we can walk around and sleep. Old Man, give us a place to build our nests, please, and we will make many blue and white and speckled eggs for you to look at!"

"Well," Old Man said slowly, "that is not too easy. To make such a place, I must have your help. By myself, I have already made four difficult things: the green water, the white light, and the blue sky, not to mention the people of the water. Now I must have help if I am to create more, for I am very old and cannot do it by myself."

"We will help!" exclaimed all the water-people. "We are ready to do what you say!"

Old Man stretched out his hands and beckoned. "Let the fastest and also the biggest of you try to help me find land," he said.

"I am ready to try," the snow goose said, and she drove herself along the water until the wake behind her grew to a point that drove her up high into the air. She flew into the sky until she was no more than a speck against the bright light. Then she turned and, plummeting down like an arrow, dived into the water.

Down, down, down she went, into the deep green water until she could not be seen — not even by the eyes of Old Man. She was gone a very long time. Old Man counted slowly to four hundred four times before she rose to the surface of the water, where she gasped for air.

"What have you found?" Old Man asked her.

"Nothing. I have brought nothing," the goose said sadly.

Then the loon tried, and after him, the mallard. Each bird flew high into the sky and then turned and dived down, down, into the water. And then each rose wearily from the depths and murmured, "Nothing," when Old Man asked what had been found.

And Old Man shook his head and sighed. Only the little coot was left. He paddled busily in the water, dipping his head under the surface and making his happy gibberish.

"Old Man," the little coot whispered, "when I dip my head into the green water I think that I see something there, very, very far below in the dark. I am small, I know, but perhaps I can swim deep enough to reach it. I cannot fly high into the sky, nor can I dive like my brothers and sisters; I can only swim. But I will try my best to swim deep into the water and find what we are looking for. May I try, Old Man?"

"Little brother coot, I have asked for help, and certainly every one of the water-people is welcome to try. It is possible that what those who can fly and those who can dive cannot accomplish, the coot, who can only swim, may yet achieve. Try, little brother, and see how well you can do.''

"Ah-ho!" the little coot exclaimed. "Thank you, Old Man!" And he tipped smoothly under the water and swam down, down, and farther down into the deepest green of the green water, until at last he was out of sight.

Little coot was under the water a very long time, longer than any of his brothers or sisters. Just as Old Man and the other water-people were afraid that he had vanished forever, a very small dark spot appeared far beneath the water's surface, but none of them could see what it was. The tiny spot rose and rose until at last Old Man and the birds saw that it was the little coot, desperately swimming up from the very bottom of the salty green water in which everything that would ever be already was.

The coot splashed to the surface and stretched his neck for breath, but he would not open his beak to gasp for air.

"Ah, give me what you have brought, little coot," Old Man said, holding his hand under the coot's beak. A small ball of mud fell into his palm. "Thank you, little brother, for what you have brought."

Then Old Man looked at the bit of mud and he smiled and began to roll it slowly in his hands. Then he smiled once again. And the ball of mud grew and grew until even Old Man could not hold it. So he looked around for a good place to put this muddy world, but there was only water and air, for nothing else yet existed.

"Come, brothers and sisters, you must help me again, for I must find a place for this land which you have asked me to create for you." All the people of the water came to Old Man, and he tried to find among them the right creature to carry the large ball of mud. But the mussels and the snails and the crawfish were too small, and they lived much too deep in the water to keep the island afloat. And the fish were too narrow. No, the fish would never do. And when Old Man looked around for someone else to carry the land which he had created, he saw that only one water-person was left. "Ah, Grandmother Turtle," he said, "you are very slow, but you are strong and perhaps you can help me."

Grandmother Turtle feebly swam to Old Man and waited patiently while he piled the mud on her back and made a shape of it which completely covered her. "Ah," said Old Man, "we have done it!"

Now there were earth and water and there was the great blue sky. But on the Earth there was nothing.

Old Man looked around and shook his head. There seemed always to be something else that needed to be created.

"Our beautiful Earth should be fruitful," said Old Man. "Let it begin to bear life!"

When Old Man said this, trees and grass and flowers sprang up to become the fragrant hair of the Earth. The flowers rose upon her hills, and the fruits and the seeds glowed in the Sun and blew perfume into the wind. The many birds of the sky came to sleep in her palms when they were tired, and the fish came close to her side to nibble the tender roots.

Old Man said, "Ah," and smiled as he looked at Earth, for she was very beautiful — truly the most beautiful thing he had made so far. "The Earth should not be alone," Old Man thought. "I shall give her something of myself so she will know that I am near and that I love her dearly."

And Old Man reached into himself and from his body he pulled out a rib and breathed upon it, then laid it softly on the Earth. The bone moved slightly and then gradually it came to life and it stood up and walked upon the Earth. And so it was that people were made.

As the days passed, and the Moon rose and circled the Earth, and the Sun glowed and set, the children of these first people were born. And they wandered over the Earth and ate of her fruitfulness and were born into many generations, until at last all the animals had come from them, as well as all the men and women of the Earth.

The animals heard and knew Old Man, and all the birds of the air heard and knew him also. All things that he had made loved him and understood him when he spoke to them — the birds, the animals, and also the people.

The years passed and Old Man became older and older. As he traveled around the sweet Earth, the animals would help him climb the mountains, and the birds would flutter around his head to cool his brow. Snakes led him safely though the jungle, where the spiders wove a glistening hammock for him to sleep in.

The moons came, one after the other, and Old Man grew still older. One day he was traveling about, making people as he went, making stones and turquoise and silver as he stumbled along. He busied himself making the mountains, the prairies, the forests, the deserts, and the redwoods, which he blessed with very long life and with branches that reached into the bluest of the blue sky. So he went along, humming merrily and making things as he went: putting rivers here, and waterfalls there, putting red paint and brown paint here and there into the hills, and tossing armfuls of snow upon the tips of the great mountains. And he smiled and said, "Ah, it is better to make something than to do nothing. It is better to be something than to be nothing. It is better to know than not to know. It is better to be than not to be." Then he continued on his way, covering the plains with tall grass for the animal-people to eat, putting roses on the rosebushes and ferny tops on the orange spikes he pressed into the Earth to make carrots. While he was in the prairie, he made the bighorn and let it go free. But it tripped and fell down and did not seem able to manage in the tall grass. So Old Man impatiently took it by one of its horns and led it up into the mountains and turned it loose there. Immediately it skipped away, stepping easily from rock to rock and going up terrifying slopes where other animals would not venture. Then he said, "I can see, Bighorn, that this place suits you well. Stay here and be happy."

While Old Man was in the mountains, he made the antelope and turned it loose, to see what it would do. It ran so fast that it constantly fell over rocks and hurt itself. Old Man knew that this would not do, so he took the antelope down to the prairie and set it free. It ran off as gracefully and as fast as a bird in the sky, and Old Man smiled and said, "Ah, no matter how great you are, you must be willing to make a few mistakes if you would be the kind of person who creates new things."

One day Old Man came upon a river and found a woman and a man standing there watching the dead leaves floating past in the swift current.

"How is it, Old Man?" the woman asked. "Will we always live; will there be no end to it?"

Old Man said, "I have never thought of that. We will have to try to decide it now. I tell you what, I will throw this chip of wood into the water. If it floats, people will die, but they will die for only four days, after which time they will come back to life." When he threw the chip into the river, it floated, and Old Man smiled.

But the woman seemed displeased. "No," she said, "I will throw this stone into the river. If it floats, we will always live, and if it sinks, then we must die forever." Before Old Man could stop her, the woman had thrown the stone into the river, where it immediately sank to the bottom.

"Ah," said Old Man. "My daughter, you have chosen death. Now there must be an end to all the people of Earth."

And Old Man walked away sadly, nodding his head.

A few nights later the woman's only child died in its sleep, and she cried out and threw her body on the ground. "Oh! Old Man, listen to me, please! I did not know that death would be so terrible. Let us change this to the way it was first when the chip of wood floated on the water!" she said, and wept.

But Old Man sighed and said, "Not so. What you have done is done. We can undo nothing that we have done. The child is dead; therefore people will have to die. Even I must grow old. Nothing is permanent and nothing can remain unchanged and something must become nothing as it was in the beginning."

And Old Man went into the mountains to get away from the terrible sorrow of the woman. He tried to sleep, but his bones were too old and his breath was too short, and before the dawn, Old Man began to sink into nothing just as the stone had sunk into the water of the river.

"I do not wish to leave these things which I have made. I do not wish to leave the sight of the beautiful Earth and all her people, or of the sky and the river and the sea. But I must go.'' And he smiled and nodded his head.

"Gentle ... gentle, little coot, dig a bed for Old Man so he can sleep with Earth about him. And before I sleep, I will create one last thing so that women who weep for the dead will also be happy. From such women will come children who hunger for the stars and who will climb the mountains to be close to them. From such women will come creatures of so vast a hunger that they will raise themselves in spirit until they fly above death in the memories of all their people.''

And Old Man fell to his knees in the newly turned soil of the Earth and, as the first light of the new day came into the sky, a great river began to flow from him and he was gradually covered by the water. His last word came from his watery mouth as his hand reached to take the glowing Sun into his palm.

"*Anpao!*" he whispered. "It is the dawn of the world!"

And he was gone.

"Sedna" by Jon C. Stott.

The story of Sedna, the mother of the sea mammals on whom the Inuit (Eskimos) depend for food, fuel, and clothing, is known across the Arctic. In a land where poor hunting meant starvation, the people believed that if they broke one of the taboos imposed by Sedna, she would not allow her children to give themselves to the harpoons of the hunters. The story, which portrays her linear journey and explains the origins of the sea creatures, is a violent and harsh one. Adaptations for children frequently omit this violence and portray Sedna as less angry and malevolent than she is in the original sources. In this retelling, an attempt has been made to retain the flavor of the originals, and respect the spiritual beliefs the story embodies, many of which are still held by the Inuit.

Sedna

"You must remember, children,'' the wise old man said to the boys and girls sitting around

him, "to honor the laws of Sedna. She is the mother of the sea creatures and it is she who allows them to give themselves to our hunters. When we offend her by breaking her laws, she keeps the sea creatures in her home beneath the sea. Then our people starve and many of them die.''

"But why would she do this to the people?'' asked one of the children.

"It is because she knows that the lives of all beings are valuable and should be respected. And when people do not treat her children well, she is very angry, for she remembers that her own people were cruel to her when she was a person like you and I.''

"Please tell us about her,'' another child asked. This little girl knew the story well and so did the other children. But she wanted to hear it again so that she could feel the power of Sedna and not forget the laws by which the people lived.

"When she lived as you and I do, Sedna was very beautiful,'' began the old man. "But she was also very proud. The other girls of her village had all married. They had husbands to catch the animals whose bodies gave people food, clothing, and oil for the lamps, and they worked in their igloos sewing and taking care of their children. But Sedna still lived with her father. She refused to marry any of the men who came to her; she had no one to sew for and no children. And she didn't care.

"One day, as she walked at the edge of the great sea, she saw a kayak in the distance, a tiny speck on the cold, shimmering waters. As it came closer, she could not recognize the man who paddled. But he was handsome, finer than any man she had ever seen before. Her heart stirred. This would be the husband she had hoped for.

" 'Come with me,' he said to her. 'I will give you wonderful furs to make parkas with. My home is a fine one, the best in my village. I am a great hunter. We will have the best meat to eat, and our lamps will always burn brightly. We will have beautiful children.'

"Sedna did not speak, but stepped quietly into his kayak. Surely this man is better than the men of my village, she thought to herself. I will always be happy. And so they traveled across the sea to the distant island where his village was.

"At first Sedna was happy. In fact, she had never been so happy in her life. Her husband was a good provider; and he loved her well.

"But one day, Sedna made a frightening discovery. She had been tricked. Her husband was not a man. He was a petrel, a sea bird; and he had great spirit powers. He had made himself look like a man so that she would live with him. He lived on a rocky island. His home was on a windswept ledge. It only looked like a warm, cozy home.

"Sedna did not know what to do. It was nearly winter; the winds were churning the sea into a dangerous chop; soon the ice would form and the blizzards would come. She was trapped.

"All that winter Sedna lived with her bird husband. She felt frightened and lonely and she knew that she was being punished for her pride. If only she were at home and safe, she would be happy to live with one of the men in her village. Even if he were not handsome, he would be good and kind.

"When the spring arrived, Sedna thought constantly of her village, and in her soul she prayed that her father would come to rescue her.

"So strong were the prayers in her soul that her father heard them. So he traveled over the sea in his umiak to find his daughter. When he arrived at the windswept, rocky island, the petrel was not home. Quickly he took Sedna to the boat and they began the long journey home.

"When the petrel returned from his hunting, he discovered that his wife was gone. He knew in his heart that she was leaving him to return to her village. He flew high above the seas searching for the boat. The anger grew and grew within him and he was filled with a terrible rage.

"Finally, he saw the umiak with his wife and her father. His body grew and grew until he was of gigantic size. He swooped down, beating his tremendous wings furiously, turning the ocean waters into mountainous waves.

"Sedna's father looked up. The bird seemed to fill the sky, and anger shone from his eyes.

The man felt panic seize him and he thought only about saving himself. He grabbed his daughter and, made strong by his fear, he shoved her into the churning, icy waters.

"Sedna struggled, but his strength was too great, and she felt the chill of the sea as she fell beneath the waves. The water made her furs heavy and she felt herself being pulled toward the bottom of the sea. She struggled and came to the surface. Her father had grabbed a paddle and was trying to escape. Her hands were numb, but she reached up and clutched at the edge of the boat.

"When he felt her weight pulling against the boat, her father turned. His terror had transformed him into a madman. If he did not get away, the petrel would capsize the boat and he would drown. He lifted his paddle over his head and swung it down on his daughter's hands.

"So strong was the blow that it chopped her fingers off at the first knuckles and they dropped into the churning, grey water and sank from sight. Desperately, Sedna kept clinging to the boat and her father again struck down with his paddle. Now her fingers were completely severed from her hands and sank into the sea. She began to feel herself slipping, but she hooked her thumbs over the edge of the boat. With a final chop, her father took these off.

"Sedna could no longer grip the boat and she slowly sank into the sea. The pain in her hands was great; the pain in her heart was greater.

"In a few moments, the waters grew dark; but soon, a strange green light seemed to shine everywhere, and before her eyes she saw a wonderful thing.

"The parts of her fingers and hands which were floating down around her began to grow and change in shape. The smaller pieces became seals, the large ones, sea lions, and the thumbs, whales. And as she kept sinking, the new animals swam about, rubbing gently against her.

"Her feet touched the floor of the sea and she walked about. The animals stayed with her, as tame as sled dogs around an igloo and much friendlier. She discovered that she could breathe and she moved around, the seals, walruses, and whales following her.

"Suddenly Sedna understood. These animals were her children; they had been created from her body. At last she had a family, even if it was very different from the one she had hoped for when she was a girl.

"Sedna was a mother, and like all mothers she had to protect her children. As she looked at them, she knew that the people would want to hunt them. Their meat would give food; their fat, oil for the lamps; and their skins, fur for clothing and coverings for boats. Their bones could be made into harpoon heads.

"Sedna had lived on the land and she knew that the people would need her children to survive. She would give her children as gifts to them. But she also knew that people could be cruel and that sometimes they did not respect life. She remembered what her father had done to her.

" 'My children have souls just as all living creatures do. The people must respect the souls of my children. If they do not show respect, I will not give them the gift of my children's bodies. I will let them starve.'

The old man looked at the children sitting around him. They sat very quietly. He knew that they were thinking about Sedna and about how they must obey their laws. If they did not respect the souls of her children, there would be great hardship for everyone. Many of the people would die.

The old man did not speak for a long time. He remembered the time he had first learned about Sedna. He had been frightened because he had learned how dangerous it was to anger Sedna.

Finally he broke the silence. "Children," he said, "if you are good to Sedna's children, you will not have to fear. But if you are not good to them, she will know. In her home at the bottom of the sea, she knows all that happens to her creatures. She is very powerful. She can bring life or death to us. It all depends on how we think and what we do."

"How the Thunder Made Horses," from The Bear Who Stole the Chinook and Other Stories, *by Frances Fraser (Toronto: Macmillan, 1959).*

Although stereotyped presentations suggest that Native peoples have been riding horses since earliest times, the horse is actually a relatively recent addition to Native culture, specifically on the Great Plains from the seventeenth to nineteenth centuries. As important as they were to the physical lives of the various tribes, horses had an equally profound spiritual impact. They were regarded as gifts from supernatural beings, possessing great spiritual powers. Retelling a tale she heard from the Blackfoot people of northern Montana and southern Alberta, Frances Fraser emphasizes these supernatural origins by associating the horses with the spiritually powerful forces of thunder and lightning. She also explains the nature of the animals' physical charateristics and includes an important moral: the necessity of people's treating their horses well. Like "Sedna," this story expresses the North American Native belief in the importance of people living harmoniously with other creatures.

How the Thunder Made Horses

One fine day, when the Moon of Frogs was rising, Ka-tsi-tís-kuma, the Thunder, had nothing to do. And he was very bored. He sat up there in the Sky Country, looking about for some way of amusing himself.

Down on the earth he saw a lake, shining in the sunlight. He leaned away over, and reached down to get a big handful of mud out of the middle of it. Then he sat by his fire, making little figures, and baking them in the ashes. When they were well baked, he took them out, and sat idly turning them over and over in his hands. One caught his eye.

"Aie!" said the Thunder, delighted. "Here is something good! Something useful! Maybe pretty, too! I must make this one better, and make more like it!" He threw some more sticks on the fire and reached down into the lake again.

All day long the Thunder worked hard, making horses. He made big ones, and little ones, mares, and stallions. When he had gotten them all modelled and baked, he lined them up evenly, and looked at them again.

"Sometimes it is cold," he said. "They must have fur, or hair, to keep them warm." But how to get it, and put it on?

Ka-tsi-tís-kuma looked down to earth again, and his eyes brightened. There were a great many animals down there with the kind of hair he wanted. So he took the hair from the white dogs, from the gophers, from the moose, and the deer, and even the little grey mice, and all these colours of horses he made. Sometimes he had bits of two colours left, and with these he made pintos. Some of the hair fell into the soot by the fire, and that made the black horses.

Ka-tsi-tís-kuma was very happy. He lined up all the horses he had made, and the lightning went flickering down the row, touching each one in turn, and the little horses came alive, and began to cavort around. Ka-tsi-tís-kuma sat, smoking his pipe, and watching them. He was very proud of what he had done.

Suddenly, he noticed that his beautiful horses weren't running and jumping any more. They were limping, slowly, and painfully. He had forgotten to make hooves for them! They had to have hooves to protect the tender parts of their feet, but what to make them of?

Ka-tsi-tís-kuma sighed, and set to work to find something that could be made to serve as hooves. First, he tried making hooves out of buckskins, like moccasins. These were not bad, but then he thought, "No. These animals will have to travel over rough and stony ground. Moccasins would wear out."

Then he tried making the hooves out of rock. But the poor little horses limped worse than ever. He tried a lot of other things, but nothing worked. So, up in the Sky Country, Ka-tsi-tís-kuma sat with his chin on his hand, looking gloomily down to the earth.

Down on the lake-shore, queer little creatures were crawling in the mud. Thunder reached down and snatched a handful of them. And the hooves of his horses were made from the shells of the turtle. (That, say the Old Ones, is why there are no turtles around this part of the country, now. The Thunder used every one of them for the hooves of his horses.)

Then the Thunder dropped the horses one by one down to earth for the Indians to use. And he watches them, even to this day. For if you are cruel to your horses, and run them hard, till they sweat, in a thunderstorm you are likely to lose them. Ka-tsi-tís-kuma will send lightning to strike them, and take them back to the Sky Country. Ka-tsi-tís-kuma does not like his gifts to be abused.

"E-ma-ne-ya! True!" say the Old Ones.

———

God Wash the World and Start Again, *by Lorenz Graham (New York: Crowell, 1946).*

Deluge myths — stories of Earth-destroying floods — are found all around the world. No geological evidence exists for such an event, yet these stories are found in cultures that have no contact with each other. It is generally believed, therefore, that individual versions of this type of myth emerged as an attempt to embody moral and religious beliefs. This seems to be the case with the Genesis story of Noah and the Ark.

The flood marks the end of the first era of Biblical history. God's decision to destroy humanity, His first major intrusion into the lives of His people since the expulsion from Eden, stems from human wickedness and their failure to listen to His word. Noah, a symbol of the truly faithful servant of God, is presented in direct contrast to his scorning neighbors. The account of God's covenant with mankind and His creation of the rainbow concludes a pourquoi myth of significant meaning.

Lorenz Graham, an American Methodist minister, adapted this myth while serving as a missionary in Liberia. In it, he uses detail, vocabulary, and speech patterns that are familiar to his African audience. He has, however, remained true to the details and religious meanings of his Biblical source.

God Wash the World and Start Again

You talking bout the time!
You think you see some rain!
You vex to see the water falling so
On the house!

God make the time for Him Own Self.
He make the rain
He make the dry and wet.
He make the sunny day
And dark of night for rest.
This time He make it good for we
And rainy day can come and go
And all be dry again
And people live.

But was a time
When all the world be young,
And so-so long time past,
That God let all the rain fall down
And cover up the land
And every house and tree
And every hill and mountain.
The rain done fall that time for true.

First time God make the world
And all the mens
And all the thing that move about.
First time Him heart lay down
But bye-m-bye He look and see
The people no be fit to hear Him Word
And things that walk be bad too much
And God want try again.

God see mens that grow like trees
And elephants like mountains walk about
And leopards big like elephant
And monkey mens what eat the people
And snakes what carry fire in their mouth
To cook the mens they eat.

And God no like to see
    the world be so.

In all the world He see one man
What mind Him Word.
God go down and speak
He say

"Noah, O Noah!
Hear My Word.
I want you cut down plenty trees
And make a ship.
I want it be the biggest ship
Men ever see.
I want it be from here to there
And plenty tight
And when you finish so
I come again."

Now Noah call him people,
All him sons and all the mens they got.
They set to cut down trees
And lay to build a ship
And people come and laugh.
They say
    "How now?
    This old man Noah build him ship
    Far from the sea.
    How now?
    Who going carry ship to water for him
    When he finish?
    He be fool!"

The people come and laugh
But Noah and him people build
And make it tight with pitch.
God come walk about inside the ship
And Noah hear God's Word and mind.
God say like this
    "Noah, O Noah,
    You make it here rooms
    And here you make a cargo space
    Just so."
Nother time God say
    "Noah, O Noah,
    That side you got bad board,
    Make it your son take that one out."
And how God say, that way Old Noah do.
One day the ship be finish
All the people come to see.
The ship be big past anything before
And no water there.

God walk about with Noah on the ship.
He say
    "Noah, O Noah,
    You hear My Word
    You make My heart lay down.

Now see what you must do.
Go take up in all the land
The things what walk
The things what crawl
The things what fly
Go catch them two by two.''

So Noah call him people,
And him sons and all the mens they got,
They set to bring the living things
That walk and crawl and fly
They bring the man and woman kind
They bring them two by two
They bring in corn and rice for chop.
They bring in elephant
They bring in cow and horse
And fowl and snake and goat
And dog and leopard,
Deer and monkey
And everything that move in bush
And in the air
They bring.
And God look on and call for something else
And something else they bring.
And God look on and know
The thing be good.

He say
   "Noah, O Noah
   You done mind me good!
   Now go aboard and take you people,
   Seal the door and seal the hatch
   And wait!''

That time God open up the sky
And let the water fall
And all the world see water.
It no fall in rain that time
It pour down till all the world be full.
And rivers run in every road
And every field be like a lake
And every lake be like a sea
And all the low land fill.
And hills stand up like islands
And then the islands self done cover
And only mountains stand.
And soon the mountains cover up
And all the land and all the sea be all the same.
Where be all the people what done laugh?
Where be the giants what walk like trees?

Where be the leopards big like elephants?
And all the elephants standing up like mountains?
Where they be?

God look down on all the water
And then He hold the rain.
God look down and all he find
Be Noah's one ship on the sea.
In that one ship live everything that live
Above the water.

God say
   "Now!
   My old world done finish
   I make new start
   And everything I do
   I look him good.''

God open new holes down in the sea.
To drain the land.
He make the sun shine bright
And send dry winds
To sweep the world.
He put the ship down softly
And see Noah with His people
And all the things what walk
And things what crawl
And things what fly
Go out again.

He smile
And in the sky He set Him bow
And turn to make a better world.

▬▬▬

"Odin Goes to Mimir's Well," from The Children of Odin: a Book of Northern Myths, *by Padraic Colum (New York: Macmillan, 1948).*

   Unlike Zeus, the tyrannical, bad-tempered, and selfish leader of the Greek Gods, Odin, the king of the Aesir, or Norse, gods, took his responsibilities very seriously. In addition to being the god of War, he was the god of Wisdom, and he used this wisdom to be a good ruler. Again unlike Zeus, he was mortal, and thus in his adventures he faced very real danger.

Nowhere are his bravery and sense of responsibility better seen than in "Odin Goes to Mimir's Well." In order to be able to foresee the future by drinking at Mimir's well of wisdom, he undergoes great physical pain by sacrificing an eye. Symbolically speaking, he trades physical sight for inner sight or wisdom. During the early part of his quest, Odin travels in disguise; he must succeed on his own merits rather than on the strength of his name. In this respect, he is like Odysseus or Robin Hood. One of Odin's major tests involves answering riddles. Failure to answer them means certain death; by giving correct answers he indicates that he has the cleverness necessary to continue his journey. This adaptation, by Irish-born novelist and playwright Padraic Colum, has been praised for its faithfulness to the original Norse sources, in both details and style.

Odin Goes to Mimir's Well

And so Odin, no longer riding on Sleipner, his eight-legged steed; no longer wearing his golden armor and his eagle-helmet, and without even his spear in his hand, traveled through Midgard, the World of Men, and made his way toward Jötunheim, the Realm of the Giants.

No longer was he called Odin All-Father, but Vegtam the Wanderer. He wore a cloak of dark blue and he carried a traveler's staff in his hands. And now, as he went toward Mimir's Well, which was near to Jötunheim, he came upon a Giant riding on a great Stag.

Odin seemed a man to men and a giant to giants. He went beside the Giant on the great Stag and the two talked together. "Who art thou, O brother?" Odin asked the Giant.

"I am Vafthrudner, the wisest of the Giants," said the one who was riding on the Stag. Odin knew him then. Vafthrudner was indeed the wisest of the Giants, and many went to strive to gain wisdom from him. But those who went to him had to answer the riddles Vafthrudner asked, and if they failed to answer the Giant took their heads off.

"I am Vegtam the Wanderer," Odin said, "and I know who thou art, O Vafthrudner. I would strive to learn something from thee."

The Giant laughed, showing his teeth. "Ho, ho," he said, "I am ready for a game with thee. Dost thou know the stakes? My head to thee if I cannot answer any question thou wilt ask. And if thou canst not answer any question that I may ask, then thy head goes to me. Ho, ho, ho. And now let us begin."

"I am ready," Odin said.

"Then tell me," said Vafthrudner, "tell me the name of the river that divides Asgard from Jötunheim?"

"Ifling is the name of that river," said Odin. "Ifling that is dead cold, yet never frozen."

"Thou hast answered rightly, O Wanderer," said the Giant. "But thou hast still to answer other questions. What are the names of the horses that Day and Night drive across the sky?"

Odin Goes To Mimir's Well; His Sacrifice For Wisdom

Illustration by Willy Pogany from *The Children of Odin* by Padraic Colum. Copyright © 1920 by Macmillan Publishing Company, renewed © 1948 by Willy Pogany.

"Skinfaxe and Hrimfaxe," Odin answered. Vafthrudner was startled to hear one say the names that were known only to the Gods and to the wisest of the Giants. There was only one question now that he might ask before it came to the stranger's turn to ask him questions.

"Tell me," said Vafthrudner, "what is the name of the plain on which the last battle will be fought?"

"The Plain of Vigard," said Odin, "the

plain that is a hundred miles long and a hundred miles across.''

It was now Odin's turn to ask Vafthrudner questions. "What will be the last words that Odin will whisper into the ear of Baldur, his dear son?'' he asked.

Very startled was the Giant Vafthrudner at that question. He sprang to the ground and looked at the stranger keenly.

"Only Odin knows what his last words to Baldur will be," he said, "and only Odin would have asked that question. Thou art Odin, O Wanderer, and thy question I cannot answer."

"Then," said Odin, "if thou wouldst keep thy head, answer me this: what price will Mimir ask for a draught from the Well of Wisdom that he guards?''

"He will ask thy right eye as a price, O Odin," said Vafthrudner.

"Will he ask no less a price than that?'' said Odin.

"He will ask no less a price. Many have come to him for a draught from the Well of Wisdom, but no one yet has given the price Mimir asks. I have answered thy question, O Odin. Now give up thy claim to my head and let me go on my way."

"I give up my claim to thy head," said Odin. Then Vafthrudner, the wisest of the Giants, went on his way, riding on his great Stag.

It was a terrible price that Mimir would ask for a draught from the Well of Wisdom, and very troubled was Odin All-Father when it was revealed to him. His right eye! For all time to be without the sight of his right eye! Almost he would have turned back to Asgard, giving up his quest for wisdom.

He went on, turning neither to Asgard nor to Mimir's Well. And when he went toward the South he saw Muspelheim, where stood Surtur with the Flaming Sword, a terrible figure, who would one day join the Giants in their war against the Gods. And when he turned North he heard the roaring of the cauldron Hvergelmer as it poured itself out of Niflheim, the place of darkness and dread. And Odin knew that the world must not be left between Surtur, who would destroy it with fire, and Niflheim, that would gather it back to Darkness and Nothingness. He, the eldest of the Gods, would have to win the wisdom that would help to save the world.

And so, with his face stern in front of his loss and pain, Odin All-Father turned and went toward Mimir's Well. It was under the great root of Ygdrassil — the root that grew out of Jötunheim. And there sat Mimir, the Guardian of the Well of Wisdom, with his deep eyes bent upon the deep water. And Mimir, who had drunk every day from the Well of Wisdom, knew who it was that stood before him.

"Hail, Odin, Eldest of the Gods," he said.

Then Odin made reverence to Mimir, the wisest of the world's beings. "I would drink from your well, Mimir," he said.

"There is a price to be paid. All who have come here to drink have shrunk from paying that price. Will you, Eldest of the gods, pay it?''

"I will not shrink from the price that has to be paid, Mimir," said Odin All-Father.

"Then drink," said Mimir. He filled up a great horn with water from the well and gave it to Odin.

Odin took the horn in both his hands and drank and drank. And as he drank all the future became clear to him. He saw all the sorrows and troubles that would fall upon Men and Gods. But he saw, too, why the sorrows and troubles had to fall, and he saw how they might be borne so that Gods and Men, by being noble in the days of sorrow and trouble, would leave in the world a force that one day, a day that was far off indeed, would destroy the evil that brought terror and sorrow and despair into the world.

Then when he had drunk out of the great horn that Mimir had given him, he put his hand to his face and he plucked out his right eye. Terrible was the pain that Odin All-Father endured. But he made no groan nor moan. He bowed his head and put his cloak before his face, as Mimir took the eye and let it sink deep, deep into the water of the Well of Wisdom. And there the Eye of Odin stayed, shining up through the water, a sign to all who came to that place of the price that the Father of the Gods had paid for his wisdom.

━━━

"The Apples of Iduna," from Thunder of the Gods, *by Dorothy Hosford (New York: Holt, Rinehart, and Winston, 1952).*

This brief story emphasizes the mortality of the Norse gods and the malicious character of the trickster Loki who precipitates the crisis that leads to this circular journey. Unless the gods eat the apples of Iduna, they will lose their youth and strength. Loki, who is one of the Frost Giants — the enemies of the gods — has become a blood brother of Odin and often travels with the Aesir, who enjoy his quick wit and mischievousness. However, his trickery becomes progressively more evil as his fundamental selfishness and animosity toward the gods develop. Many scholars believe that the emphasis of these aspects of Loki's nature reflect the influence of Christianity on Norse myths, particularly its presentation of the Devil as an evil trickster. Dorothy Hosford's retelling of this and other myths has been praised for its "strength, clarity, and cohesion."

The Apples of Iduna

Odin often traveled forth from Asgard to take part in the affairs of men and to see what was going on in all the wide expanses of the world. One day he set out on such a journey, taking Loki and Hoenir with him. They wandered a long way over mountains and waste land and at length they grew hungry. But food was hard to find in that lonely country.

They had walked many miles when they saw a herd of oxen grazing in a valley.

"There is food for us at last," said Hoenir.

They went down into the valley and it was not long before they had one of the oxen roasting on a fire. While their meal cooked they stretched out on the ground to rest. When they thought the meat had cooked long enough they took it off the fire. But it was not yet ready. So they put it back over the embers and waited.

"I can wait no longer," cried Loki at last. "I am starving. Surely the meat is ready."

The gods scattered the fire once more and pulled forth the ox, but it seemed as though it had not even begun to cook. It was certainly not fit for eating.

This was a strange thing and not even Odin knew the meaning of it. As they wondered among themselves, they heard a voice speak from the great oak tree above them.

"It is because of me," said the voice, "that there is no virtue in your fire and your meat will not cook."

They looked up into the branches of the tree and there sat a huge eagle.

"If you are willing to give me a share of the ox, then it will cook in the fire," said the eagle.

There was little the gods could do but agree to this. The eagle let himself float down from the tree and alighted by the fire. In no time at all the ox was roasted. At once the eagle took to himself the two hindquarters and two forequarters as well.

This greediness angered Loki. He snatched up a great pole, brandished it with all his strength, and struck the eagle with it. The eagle plunged violently at the blow and whirled into the air. One end of the pole stuck fast to the eagle's back and Loki's hands stuck fast to the other end. No matter how he tried he could not free them. Swooping and turning, the eagle dragged Loki after him in his flight, flying just low enough that Loki's feet and legs knocked against stones and rock heaps and trees. Loki thought his arms would be torn from his shoulders. He cried out for mercy.

"Put me down! Put me down!" begged Loki. "Free me and you shall have the whole ox for your own."

"I do not want the ox," cried the eagle. "I want only one thing — Iduna and her apples. Deliver them into my power and I will set you free."

Iduna was the beautiful and beloved wife of the god Bragi. She guarded the most precious possession of the gods, the apples of youth. Unless they might eat of them the gods would grow old and feeble like mortal men. They kept the gods ever young. Iduna and her apples were priceless beyond words.

"Iduna and her apples! Such a thing cannot be done," shouted Loki.

"Then I will fly all day," screamed the eagle. "I will knock you against the rocks until you die." And he dragged Loki through rough tree branches and against the sides of mountains and over the rocky earth. Loki could endure it no longer.

"I will do as you ask," he cried. "I will bring Iduna to you, and her apples as well."

"Give me your oath," said the eagle. Loki gave his oath. A time was set when Loki should put Iduna in the eagle's power.

The eagle straightway made Loki free and flew off into the sky. A much-bruised Loki returned to his companions and all three set off on their homeward journey. But Odin and Hoenir did not know the promise which Loki had made.

Loki pondered how he could keep his word to the eagle, whom he now knew to be the giant Thjazi in disguise. When the appointed day came Loki approached Iduna.

"Iduna," he said, speaking gently, "yesterday I found a tree on which grow wondrous apples. It is in the wood to the north of Asgard. They are like your apples in color and shape. Surely they must have the same properties. Should we not gather them and bring them to Asgard?"

"There are no apples anywhere," said Iduna, "like to my apples."

"These are," said Loki. "They are very like. Come and look for yourself. If you bring your apples we can put them side by side and you will see."

So Iduna went with Loki to the wood, taking her apples with her. While they were in the wood the giant Thjazi swooped down in his eagle's plumage and carried Iduna and her apples off to his abode.

The gods soon missed Iduna. And they knew her apples were gone, for the signs of old age began to show among them. They grew bent and stiff and stooped.

Odin called a hasty council of the gods. They asked each other what they knew of Iduna.

"Where was she last seen?" asked Odin.

Heimdal had seen her walking out of Asgard with Loki. That was the last that was known of her.

Odin sent Thor to seize Loki and to bring him to the council. When Loki was brought the gods threatened him with tortures and death unless he told what he knew of Iduna. Loki grew frightened and admitted that Iduna had been carried off to Jotunheim.

"I will go in search of her," he cried, "if Freyja will lend me her falcon wings."

Freyja was more than willing. When Loki had put on the feather dress he flew to the north in the direction of Jotunheim.

He flew for a long time before he came to the home of Thjazi, the giant. Then he circled slowly overhead and saw Iduna walking below. She carried in her arms her golden casket of apples. Thjazi was nowhere to be seen, for he had rowed out to sea to fish. Loki quickly alighted on the ground beside Iduna.

"Hasten, Iduna," he cried, "I will rescue you." And he changed Iduna into the shape of a nut and flew off with her in his claws.

Loki had no sooner gone than Thjazi arrived home. At once he missed Iduna and her precious apples. Putting on his eagle's plumage, he flew into the air. Far off in the distance he saw the falcon flying. Instantly he took after him. The eagle's wings beat powerfully, making a deep rushing sound like a great wind. Thjazi drew nearer and nearer to Loki. Loki flew with all his might, but the eagle was bearing down upon the falcon just as the towers of Asgard came into view. With a last burst of strength Loki hastened toward the shining battlements.

The gods were on watch for Loki's return. They saw the falcon bearing the nut between his claws, with the eagle in close pursuit. Quickly they built a great pile of wood shavings just outside the wall of Asgard. As Loki came near he swooped down low over the shavings. Thjazi swooped down too, hoping to seize the falcon before he reached the safety of Asgard. Just as the eagle came close to the pile the gods set fire to the shavings. Instantly the fire blazed up, but Thjazi could not stop himself. He plunged into the flames and the feathers of his wings took fire. Then he could fly no more and the gods slew him where he was.

There was great rejoicing within the walls of Asgard to have Iduna safe once more. And the gods grew young and bright again.

Demeter and Persephone, *translated and
adapted by Penelope Proddow (New York:
Doubleday, 1972), and "The Myth of
Demeter and Persephone," from* Lost God-
desses of Early Greece, *by Charlene Spretnak
(Boston: Beacon, 1981).*

*As Edith Hamilton has noted of the Greek
gods, "for the most part [they] were of little
use to human beings and often they were quite
the reverse of useful." One of the exceptions
was Demeter, the corn goddess who gave human beings the gift of agriculture. The most
important myth associated with her describes
the origin of the seasonal cycles. Winter is
said to be caused by the grieving of Demeter
over the loss of her daughter Persephone to
Hades, the God of the Underworld, for four
months each year. However, recent research
has indicated that earlier versions of this story make no references to Hades at all. Carol
Spretnak has written: "Whatever the impulse
portraying Persephone as a rape victim, evidence indicates that this twist to the story was
added after the societal shift from matrifocal
to patriarchal, and that it was not part of the
original mythology." Spretnak's adaptation
presents Persephone as the willing queen of
the dead who, upon her return to the world
above, causes the springtime growth. Penelope Proddow's poetic adaptation of the more
widely known myth reflects the psychological richness so characteristic of Greek mythology.*

*In retelling this circular journey, she cap-
tures the emotional intensity of the angry and
grieving mother, and the tensions which often
exist between a mother and son-in-law as they
compete for the affections of a daughter. For
her part, the daughter must search for her
own identity. Demeter reveals two aspects of
womanhood: she is the giving mother (bringing agriculture) and the grieving mother,
angrily withholding her gifts. In most folktales
these two aspects are split into two characters:
the mother and the stepmother.*

*Demeter's gift of life to the arid landscape
can be compared to the youngest son's gift in
the African folktale "The Fortune Hunt."
Persephone's descent into the underworld as*

*described by Spretnak can be compared to
that of Inanna in "From the Great Above to
the Great Below."*

Demeter and Persephone

Now I will sing
of golden-haired Demeter,
the awe-inspiring goddess,
and of her trim-ankled daughter,
Persephone,
who was frolicking in a grassy meadow.

She was far away
from her mother.

With the deep-girdled daughters of Ocean,
the maiden was gathering flowers —
crocuses, roses and violets,
irises and lovely hyacinths
growing profusely together,
with one narcissus . . .
This was the snare
for the innocent maiden.

She knelt in delight
to pluck the astonishing bloom
when, all of a sudden, the wide-wayed earth
split open
down the Nysian meadow.

Out sprang a lord
with his deathless horses.
It was He Who Receives Many Guests,
He Who Has Many Names.

Seizing Persephone,
he caught her up in his golden chariot
despite her laments.

Her screams were shrill
as she shrieked for her father, Zeus,
but no one heard
except kind-hearted Hecate
from her cave
and Helios, the sun.

Still glimpsing the earth,
the brilliant sky,
the billowing, fish-filled sea

and the rays of the sun,
Persephone vainly hoped to see her beloved
mother again.

The peaks of the mountains
and the ocean depths
resounded
with her immortal voice.

And her stately mother heard.
A sudden pang
went through Demeter's heart.

She set off like a bird
wildly
over the bodies of water
and the dry stretches of land,
but no one would tell her the truth —
not a god,
not a mortal,
not even a long-winged bird of omen.

She circled the earth
for nine days
steadily
brandishing shining torches.

At the dawning
of the tenth,
Hecate approached,
holding a pine torch in her hands.

"Demeter!" she said.
"Bringer of the Seasons!
Giver of Rich Gifts!
What god in heaven,
what mortal,
has caused your heart such torment
and taken your daughter?

I heard her cries
but I did not see
who he was!"

They both hurried on
to the sun,
the watchman of gods and of men.

"Helios!" cried Demeter.
"Have pity on me — goddess that I am.
I bore a child

whose frantic voice I heard
through the barren air
as if she had been overpowered,
but I saw nothing.
Tell me,
was it a god or a mortal
who stole away my daughter
against her will — and mine?"

"Fair-tressed Demeter!" Helios replied.
"No one is guilty
among the immortals
but Zeus,
who gave her to Hades
to be his youthful bride.

"Now, goddess,
you must stop this violent weeping!

"The Ruler of Many is not undesirable
as a son-in-law.
He wields great power,
for he is king over the dead,
with whom he lives
in the underworld."

Anguish
rent the goddess' heart —
savage and terrible.

Embittered with black-clouded Zeus,
she departed broad Olympus
and the gatherings of the gods.
From that time forth,
she sought the villages and fields of mortal men
with her face disguised.

No one knew her
until she reached the palace of prudent Celeus,
lord over fragrant Eleusis.

There by the roadside
she sank down
at the Well of the Maiden
in sorrow —
seemingly some poor old woman,
fit only for nursing a wise king's children
or keeping his shadowy halls.

The king's four daughters
saw her

when they came up with their golden pitchers
to draw the sparkling water.

"Where have you come from,
elderly mortal?"
they cried.

"Lovely maidens!" Demeter replied.
"Pirates seized me
and bore me over the broad sea's back
by force — but I escaped
and came hither.

"On me, young girls, have pity!
Where can I go
to take up the tasks
allotted to elderly women — like myself —
such as nursing a newborn child in my arms?"

"Gentle woman!" said Callidice,
the fairest of Celeus' children.

"Wait,
while we go to our mother,
for she has a newborn child."

Swiftly the four
sped to their mother
and she bade them bring the woman
at once
and promise a generous reward.

Back they bounded,
holding their full skirts high,
barely touching
the shady paths,
and their hair streamed over their shoulders —
the color of yellow crocuses.

Her heart aching for Persephone,
Demeter covered her head with a veil
and followed
behind the maidens.

When they came to
the palace of god-favored Celeus,
the goddess stepped on the portal
and her head came up to the rafters.
The splendor of an immortal
shone
in the doorway.

Awe seized their mother, Metaneira.

"Good Lady,
your birth cannot be lowly,"
she exclaimed.

"Here is my only son —
Damophon —
whom the gods bestowed upon me
as a companion for my old age.
If you nurse him
and he grows up handsomely,
then women throughout the land will envy
  you,
so great will be your reward."

"Great Lady," replied Demeter.
"May the gods grant you riches!
I will bring up your son wisely."

His mother rejoiced.

The boy then grew like a god.
He never ate food
nor drank any milk —
Demeter was feeding him ambrosia
by day,
as if he were the child of a goddess.

And, without the knowledge of his doting
parents,
she put him to sleep
by night
in the embers of the fire.

The goddess would have made him
deathless and immortal
in this fashion,
had not Mateneira,
foolishly peeping out from her chamber,
spied her one night.

"My son!" she shrieked.
"This stranger is putting you in the fire!"

The bright goddess turned about.

Furious at the mother,
Demeter took the child
from the fire

and thrust him from her
with immortal hands.

"Senseless mortals!" she raged.
"You cannot see whether your fate
is good or bad,
even when it comes upon you!
I would have made your boy —
deathless and immortal
all his days.

For I am dread Demeter!
Now, let this land build me a temple
and a broad altar
to win back my favor."

Then the great goddess flung off her disguise
and her beauty appeared.
The light in her eyes
filled up the strong halls
like a flash of lightning.

She departed from the chamber.

Quickly, the Eleusians
built the temple.
When they had finished,
they all returned to their homes.

But golden-haired Demeter
remained
enthroned within,
far from all of the festive gods,
wasting away with longing
for her graceful daughter.

She made that year
most shocking and frightening
for mortals
who lived on the nourishing earth.

The soil did not yield a single seed —
Demeter kept them all
underground.

In vain,
oxen hauled many curved ploughs
over the meadows.

Now, she was about to cause
the race of chattering men

to die out
altogether
from frightful hunger,
depriving those who lived on Olympus
of their lavish gifts and sacrifices.

Then Zeus noticed . . .

He sent golden-winged Iris first
to summon her.
On swift feet,
Iris spanned the distance
to Eleusis — now laden with incense —
and found Demeter
within her temple,
clad in a dark gown.

"Demeter!" she announced.
"Father Zeus
in his infinite wisdom
calls you back to the family
of the undying gods."

Demeter's heart was unmoved.

Thereupon Zeus
sent forth all the gods —
the joyous beings who live forever.

Demeter scorned their speeches.
She vowed
she would not set foot on Olympus
nor let a fruit spring upon the earth
until she had seen
with her own eyes
the lovely face of her daughter.

Then Zeus dispatched Hermes
with his staff of gold.

Setting off from the Olympian seat,
Hermes dashed down
at once
into the depths of the earth.

He found Hades
in his halls
on a couch with his tender bride —
who was listless
out of longing for her mother.

Illustration by Barbara Cooney from *Demeter and Persephone*, tr. by Penelope Proddow. Copyright © 1972. Reprinted by permission of Doubleday and Co. Publishers.

"Dark-haired Hades!" said Hermes,
"Zeus commands me
to bring back fair Persephone.
Her mother is planning a horrible deed —
to starve the tribes
of earth-dwelling mortals
and so, to deprive the gods
of their offerings!"

The king of the dead
raised his eyebrows,
but he did not disobey Zeus' order.

"Go, Persephone," he said,
"back to your dark-robed mother!"
Persephone smiled,
as joyfully she sprang up from the couch,
but stealthily the lord of the dead
spread out about her
delicious pomegranate seeds
to make sure she would not remain
forever
at the side of her noble mother.

Soon after, Hades
harnessed up his deathless horses
to the golden chariot.

Persephone leapt into the car.
Hermes seized the whip and the reins
in his skillful hands
and they drove off together
away from the land of the dead.

Hermes guided the horses
to Eleusis where Demeter sat
waiting,
and they drew to a halt
in front of her incense-filled temple.
Demeter,
catching sight of Persephone,
flew forward
like a maenad on a mountain.

But, as she clasped her daughter,
she suspected treachery.

"My child!" she cried in fear,
"Could you have eaten anything
in the land of the dead?"

"Truthfully, Mother!"
exclaimed Persephone.
"When Hermes arrived from Zeus,
I arose with joy.
Then Hades brought out delicious pomegranate seeds
and urged me to eat them."

"In that case,
you must return
to the land of the dead," said Demeter,
"for one third of the rolling seasons.

"But when you come back
to me
for the other two,
the earth will burst into bloom
with flocks of sweet-smelling, spring flowers —
a great marvel to all men."

At that moment,
Wide-ruling Zeus

sent a messenger —
Rhea
with a golden band in her hair.

"Demeter, my daughter," said Rhea,
"Zeus wishes you
to return to the company of the gods.
Yield to him,
lest you carry your anger
toward dark-clouded Zeus
too far.

"And now,
bestow some nourishing fruit
on mortal men!"

Bright-garlanded Demeter
did not disobey.

Immediately, she caused the fruit
to grow in the fertile fields
and soon the wide earth
was weighed down
with buds and blossoms.

Hail to you, Demeter,
lady of Fragrant Eleusis,
Leader of the Seasons and Giver of Shining
Gifts,
you and your most beautiful daughter
Persephone,
look kindly on me
and in return for my song,
grant abundant life to follow.

The Myth of Demeter and Persephone

There once was no winter. Leaves and vines, flowers and grass grew into fullness and faded into decay, then began again in unceasing rhythms.

Men joined with other men of their mother's clan and foraged in the evergreen woods for game. Women with their children or grandchildren toddling behind explored the thick growth of plants encircling their homes. They learned eventually which bore fruits that sated hunger, which bore leaves and roots that chased illness and pain, and which worked magic on the eye, mouth, and head.

The Goddess Demeter watched fondly as the mortals learned more and more about Her plants. Seeing that their lives were difficult and their food supply sporadic, She was moved to give them the gift of wheat. She showed them how to plant the seed, cultivate, and finally harvest the wheat and grind it. Always the mortals entrusted the essential process of planting food to the women, in the hope that their fecundity of womb might be transferred to the fields they touched.

Demeter had a fair-born Daughter, Persephone, who watched over the crops with Her Mother. Persephone was drawn especially to the new sprouts of wheat that pushed their way through the soil in Her favorite shade of tender green. She loved to walk among the young plants, beckoning them upward and stroking the weaker shoots.

Later, when the plants approached maturity, Persephone would leave their care to Her Mother and wander over the hills, gathering narcissus, hyacinth, and garlands of myrtle for Demeter's hair. Persephone Herself favored the bold red poppies that sprang up among the wheat. It was not unusual to see Demeter and Persephone decked with flowers dancing together through open fields and gently sloping valleys. When Demeter felt especially fine, tiny shoots of barley or oats would spring up in the footprints She left.

One day They were sitting on the slope of a high hill looking out in many directions over Demeter's fields of grain. Persephone lay on Her back while Her Mother stroked Her long hair idly.

"Mother, sometimes in my wanderings I have met the spirits of the dead hovering around their earthly homes and sometimes the mortals, too, can see them in the dark of the moon by the light of their fires and torches."

"There are those spirits who drift about restlessly, but they mean no harm."

"I spoke to them, Mother. They seem confused and many do not even understand their own state. Is there no one in the netherworld who receives the newly dead?"

Demeter sighed and answered softly, "It is I who have domain over the underworld. From beneath the surface of the earth I draw forth the crops and the wild plants. And in pits beneath the surface of the earth I have instructed the mortals to store My seed from harvest until sowing, in order that contact with the spirits of My underworld will fertilize the seed. Yes, I know very well the realm of the dead, but My most important work is here. I must feed the living.''

Persephone rolled over and thought about the ghostly spirits She had seen, about their faces drawn with pain and bewilderment.

''The dead need us, Mother. I will go to them.''

Demeter abruptly sat upright as a chill passed through Her and rustled the grass around Them. She was speechless for a moment, but then hurriedly began recounting all the pleasures they enjoyed in Their world of sunshine, warmth, and fragrant flowers. She told Her Daughter of the dark gloom of the underworld and begged Her to reconsider.

Persephone sat up and hugged Her Mother and rocked Her with silent tears. For a long while They held each other, radiating rainbow auras of love and protection. Yet Persephone's response was unchanged.

They stood and walked in silence down the slope toward the fields. Finally They stopped, surrounded by Demeter's grain, and shared weary smiles.

''Very well. You are loving and giving and We cannot give only to Ourselves. I understand why You must go. Still, You are My Daughter and for every day that You remain in the underworld, I will mourn Your absence.''

Persephone gathered three poppies and three sheaves of wheat. Then Demeter led Her to a long, deep chasm and produced a torch for Her to carry. She stood and watched Her Daughter go down farther and farther into the cleft in the earth.

In the crook of Her arm Persephone held Her mother's grain close to Her breast, while Her other arm held the torch aloft. She was startled by the chill as She descended, but She was not afraid. Deeper and deeper into the darkness She continued, picking Her way slowly along the rocky path. For many hours She was surrounded only by silence. Gradually She became aware of a low moaning sound. It

grew in intensity until She rounded a corner and entered an enormous cavern, where thousands of spirits of the dead milled about aimlessly, hugging themselves, shaking their heads, and moaning in despair.

Persephone moved through the forms to a large, flat rock and ascended. She produced a stand for Her torch, a vase for Demeter's grain, and a large shallow bowl piled with pomegranate seeds, the food of the dead. As She stood before them, Her aura increased in brightness and in warmth.

''I am Persephone and I have come to be your Queen. Each of you has left your earthly body and now resides in the realm of the dead. If you come to Me, I will initiate you into your new world.''

She beckoned those nearest to step up onto the rock and enter Her aura. As each spirit crossed before Her, Persephone embraced the form and then stepped back and gazed into the eyes. She reached for a few of the pomegranate seeds, squeezing them between Her fingers. She painted the forehead with a broad swatch of the red juice and slowly pronounced:

You have waxed into the fullness
   of life
And waned into darkness;
May you be renewed in tranquility
   and wisdom.

For months Persephone received and renewed the dead without ever resting or even growing weary. All the while Her Mother remained disconsolate. Demeter roamed the earth hoping to find Her Daughter emerging from one of the secret clefts. In Her sorrow She withdrew Her power from the crops, the trees, and plants. She forbade any new growth to blanket the earth. The mortals planted their seed, but the fields remained barren. Demeter was consumed with loneliness and finally settled on a bare hillside to gaze out at nothing from sunken eyes. For days and nights, weeks and months She sat waiting.

One morning a ring of purple crocus quietly pushed their way through the soil and surrounded Demeter. She looked with surprise at the new arrivals from below and thought what a shame it was that She was too weakened to feel rage at Her injunction being broken. Then She leaned forward and heard them whisper in the warm breeze: "Persephone returns! Persephone returns!"

Demeter leapt to Her feet and ran down the hill through the fields into the forests. She waved Her arms and cried: "Persephone returns!" Everywhere Her energy was stirring, pushing, bursting forth into tender greenery and pale young petals. Animals shed old fur and rolled in the fresh, clean grass while birds sang out: "Persephone returns! Persephone returns!"

When Persephone ascended from a dark chasm, there was Demeter with a cape of white crocus for Her Daughter. They ran to each other and hugged and cried and laughed and hugged and danced and danced and danced. The mortals saw everywhere the miracles of Demeter's bliss and rejoiced in the new life of spring. Each winter they join Demeter in waiting through the bleak season of Her Daughter's absence. Each spring they are renewed by the signs of Persephone's return.

―――――

"The Descent of Inanna: From the Great Above to the Great Below," from Inanna: Queen of Heaven and Earth. *Trans. by Samuel Noah Kramer, retold by Diane Wolkstein (New York: Harper and Row Publishers, 1983).*

The ancient civilization of Sumeria, the first from which we have written texts, worshipped the goddess Inanna and composed hymns in her praise. According to Samuel Noah Kramer, "Inanna played a greater role in myth, epic, and hymn than any other deity, male or female." Inanna begins her divine existence as a young woman who is courted. Later, as Queen of Heaven, she enjoys her female powers to the fullest. At last, to complete her identity, she must face death in the underworld. "From the Great Above to the Great Below" dramatizes Inanna's relinquishment of all that she has until she stands naked before her sister to face death; the poignant love between Inanna and her faithful servant, Ninshubur; and Inanna's triumphant rebirth.

The Descent of Inanna: From the Great Above to the Great Below

From the Great Above she opened her ear to the Great Below.
From the Great Above the goddess opened her ear to the Great Below.
From the Great Above Inanna opened her ear to the Great Below.

My Lady abandoned heaven and earth to descend to the underworld.
Inanna abandoned heaven and earth to descend to the underworld.
She abandoned her office of holy priestess to descend to the underworld.

In Uruk she abandoned her temple to descend to the underworld.
In Badtibira she abandoned her temple to descend to the underworld.
In Zabalam she abandoned her temple to descend to the underworld.
In Adab she abandoned her temple to descend to the underworld.
In Nippur she abandoned her temple to descend to the underworld.
In Kish she abandoned her temple to descend to the underworld.
In Akkad she abandoned her temple to descend to the underworld.

She gathered together the seven *me*.
She took them into her hands.
With the *me* in her possession, she prepared herself:

She placed the *shugurra*, the crown of the steppe, on her head.
She arranged the dark locks of hair across her forehead.
She tied the small lapis beads around her neck,
Let the double strand of beads fall to her breast,
And wrapped the royal robe around her body.
She daubed her eyes with ointment called "Let him come,
    Let him come,"
Bound the breastplate called "Come, man, come!" around her chest,
Slipped the gold ring over her wrist,

And took the lapis measuring rod and line in her hand.

Inanna set out for the underworld.
Ninshubur, her faithful servant, went with her.
Inanna spoke to her, saying:
   "Ninshubur, my constant support,
   My *sukkal* who gives me wise advice,
   My warrior who fights by my side,
   I am descending to the *kur*, to the underworld.
   If I do not return,
   Set up a lament for me by the ruins.
   Beat the drum for me in the assembly places.
   Circle the houses of the gods.
   Tear at your eyes, at your mouth, at your thighs.
   Dress yourself in a single garment like a beggar.
   Go to Nippur, to the temple of Enlil.
   When you enter his holy shrine, cry out:
   'O Father Enlil, do not let your daughter
   Be put to death in the underworld.
   Do not let your bright silver
   Be covered with the dust of the underworld.
   Do not let your precious lapis
   Be broken into stone for the stoneworker.
   Do not let your fragrant boxwood
   Be cut into wood for the woodworker.
   Do not let the holy priestess of heaven
   Be put to death in the underworld.'

   If Enlil will not help you,
   Go to Ur, to the temple of Nanna.
   Weep before Father Nanna.
   If Nanna will not help you,
   Go to Eridu, to the temple of Enki.
   Weep before Father Enki.
   Father Enki, the God of Wisdom, knows the food of life,
   He knows the water of life;
   He knows the secrets.
   Surely he will not let me die."

Inanna continued on her way to the underworld.
Then she stopped and said:
   "Go now, Ninshubur —
   Do not forget the words I have commanded you."

When Inanna arrived at the outer gates of the underworld,

She knocked loudly.

She cried out in a fierce voice:
   "Open the door, gatekeeper!
   Open the door, Neti!
   I alone would enter!"

Neti, the chief gatekeeper of the *kur*, asked:
   "Who are you?"

She answered:
   "I am Inanna, Queen of Heaven,
   On my way to the East."

Neti said:
   "If you are truly Inanna, Queen of Heaven,
   On your way to the East,
   Why has your heart led you on the road
   From which no traveler returns?"

Inanna answered:
   "Because . . . of my older sister, Ereshkigal,
   Her husband, Gugalanna, the Bull of Heaven, has died.
   I have come to witness the funeral rites.
   Let the beer of his funeral rites be poured into the cup.
   Let it be done."

Neti spoke:
   "Stay here, Inanna, I will speak to my queen.
   I will give her your message."

Neti, the chief gatekeeper of the *kur*,
Entered the palace of Ereshkigal, the Queen of the Underworld, and said:
   "My queen, a maid
   As tall as heaven,
   As wide as the earth,
   As strong as the foundations of the city wall,
   Waits outside the palace gates.

   She has gathered together the seven *me*.
   She has taken them into her hands.
   With the *me* in her possession, she has prepared herself:

   On her head she wears the *shugurra*, the crown of the steppe.
   Across her forehead her dark locks of hair

are carefully
    arranged.
  Around her neck she wears the small lapis
    beads.
    At her breast she wears the double strand
    of beads.
    Her body is wrapped with the royal robe.
    Her eyes are daubed with the ointment
    called, 'Let him come,
      let him come.''
  Around her chest she wears the breastplate
    called 'Come, man,
      come!''
  On her wrist she wears the gold ring.
  In her hand she carries the lapis measuring
    rod and line.''

When Ereshkigal heard this,
She slapped her thigh and bit her lip.
She took the matter into her heart and dwelt
on it.
Then she spoke:
  "Come, Neti, my chief gatekeeper of the *kur*.
  Heed my words:
  Bolt the seven gates of the underworld.
  Then, one by one, open each gate a crack.
  Let Inanna enter.
  As she enters, remove her royal garments.
    Let the holy priestess of heaven enter
    bowed low.''

Neti heeded the words of his queen.
He bolted the seven gates of the underworld.
Then he opened the outer gate.
He said to the maid:
  "Come, Inanna, enter.''

When she entered the first gate,
From her head, the *shugurra*, the crown of the
steppe, was removed.

Inanna asked:
  "What is this?''

She was told:
  "Quiet, Inanna, the ways of the underworld
    are perfect.
  They may not be questioned.''

When she entered the second gate,
From her neck the small lapis beads were re-

moved.
Inanna asked:
  "What is this?''

She was told:
  "Quiet, Inanna, the ways of the underworld
    are perfect.
  They may not be questioned.''

When she entered the third gate,
From her breast the double strand of beads was
removed.

Inanna asked:
  "What is this?''

She was told:
  "Quiet, Inanna, the ways of the underworld
    are perfect.
  They may not be questioned.''

When she entered the fourth gate,
From her chest the breastplate called "Come,
man, come!''
was removed.

Inanna asked:
  "What is this?''

She was told:
  "Quiet, Inanna, the ways of the underworld
    are perfect.
  They may not be questioned.''

When she entered the fifth gate,
From her wrist the gold ring was removed.

Inanna asked:
  "What is this?''

She was told:
  "Quiet, Inanna, the ways of the underworld
    are perfect.
  They may not be questioned.''

When she entered the sixth gate,
From her hand the lapis measuring rod and line
was removed.

Inanna asked:
  "What is this?''

She was told:
   "Quiet, Inanna, the ways of the underworld
      are perfect.
   They may not be questioned."

When she entered the seventh gate,
From her body the royal robe was removed.

Inanna asked:
   "What is this?"

She was told:
   "Quiet, Inanna, the ways of the underworld
      are perfect.
   They may not be questioned."

Naked and bowed low, Inanna entered the
throne room.
Ereshkigal rose from her throne.
Inanna started toward the throne.
The Annuna, the judges of the underworld, sur-
rounded her.
They passed judgment against her.

Then Ereshkigal fastened on Inanna the eye of
death.
She spoke against her the word of wrath.
She uttered against her the cry of guilt.

She struck her.

Inanna was turned into a corpse,
A piece of rotting meat,
And was hung from a hook on the wall.

When, after three days and three nights, Inanna
had not returned,
Ninshubur set up a lament for her by the ruins.
She beat the drum for her in the assembly
places.
She circled the houses of the gods.
She tore at her eyes; she tore at her mouth; she
tore at her thighs.
She dressed herself in a single garment like a
beggar.
Alone, she set out for Nippur and the temple
of Enlil.

When she entered the holy shrine,
She cried out:

   "O Father Enlil, do not let your daughter
   Be put to death in the underworld.
   Do not let your bright silver
   Be covered with the dust of the underworld.
   Do not let your precious lapis
   Be broken into stone for the stoneworker.
   Do not let your fragrant boxwood
   Be cut into wood for the woodworker.
   Do not let the holy priestess of heaven
   Be put to death in the underworld."

Father Enlil answered angrily:
   "My daughter craved the Great Above.
   Inanna craved the Great Below.
   She who receives the *me* of the underworld
      does not return.
   She who goes to the Dark City stays there."

Father Enlil would not help.

Ninshubur went to Ur and the temple of Nanna.
When she entered the holy shrine,
She cried out:
   "O Father Nanna, do not let your daughter
   Be put to death in the underworld.
   Do not let your bright silver
   Be covered with the dust of the underworld.
   Do not let your precious lapis
   Be broken into stone for the stoneworker.
   Do not let your fragrant boxwood
   Be cut into wood for the woodworker.
   Do not let the holy priestess of heaven
   Be put to death in the underworld."

Father Nanna answered angrily:
   "My daughter craved the Great Above.
   Inanna craved the Great Below.
   She who receives the *me* of the underworld
      does not return.
   She who goes to the Dark City stays there."

Father Nanna would not help.

Ninshubur went to Eridu and the temple of
Enki.
When she entered the holy shrine,
She cried out:
   "O Father Enki, do not let your daughter
   Be put to death in the underworld.
   Do not let your bright silver

Be covered with the dust of the underworld.
Do not let your precious lapis
Be broken into stone for the stoneworker.
Do not let your fragrant boxwood
Be cut into wood for the woodworker.
Do not let the holy priestess of heaven
Be put to death in the underworld.''

Father Enki said:
   ''What has happened?
What has my daughter done?
Inanna! Queen of All the Lands! Holy Priest-
   ess of Heaven!
What has happened?
I am troubled. I am grieved.''

From under his fingernail Father Enki brought
forth dirt.
He fashioned the dirt into a *kurgarra*, a crea-
ture neither male nor
   female.
From under the fingernail of his other hand he
brought forth dirt.
He fashioned the dirt into a *galatur*, a crea-
ture neither male nor female
He gave the food of life to the *kurgarra*.
He gave the water of life to the *galatur*.
Enki spoke to the *kurgarra* and *galatur*,
saying:
   ''Go to the underworld,
Enter the door like flies.
Ereshkigal, the Queen of the Underworld,
   is moaning
With the cries of a woman about to give
   birth.
No linen is spread over her body.
Her breasts are uncovered.
Her hair swirls about her head like leeks.
When she cries, 'Oh! Oh! My inside!'
Cry also, 'Oh! Oh! Your inside!'
When she cries, 'Oh! Oh! My outside!'
Cry also, 'Oh! Oh! Your outside!'
The queen will be pleased.
She will offer you a gift.
Ask her only for the corpse that hangs from
   the hook on the wall.
One of you will sprinkle the food of life on
   it.
The other will sprinkle the water of life.
Inanna will arise.''

The *kurgarra* and the *galatur* heeded Enki's
words.
They set out for the underworld.
Like flies, they slipped through the cracks of
the gates.
They entered the throne room of the Queen
of the Underworld.
No linen was spread over her body.
Her breasts were uncovered.
Her hair swirled around her head like leeks.

Ereshkigal was moaning:
   ''Oh! Oh! My inside!''

They moaned:
   ''Oh! Oh! Your inside!''

She moaned:
   ''Ohhhh! Oh! My outside!''

They moaned:
   ''Ohhhh! Oh! Your outside!''

She groaned:
   ''Oh! Oh! My belly!''

They groaned:
   ''Oh! Oh! Your belly!''

She groaned:
   ''Oh! Ohhhh! My back!!''

They groaned:
   ''Oh! Ohhhh! Your back!!''

She sighed:
   ''Ah! Ah! My heart!''

They sighed:
   ''Ah! Ah! Your heart!''

She sighed:
   ''Ah! Ahhhh! My liver!''

They sighed:
   ''Ah! Ahhhh! Your liver!''

Ereshkigal stopped.
She looked at them.
She asked:

"Who are you,
Moaning — groaning — sighing with me?
If you are gods, I will bless you.
If you are mortals, I will give you a gift.
I will give you the water-gift, the river in its
    fullness.''

The *kurgarra* and *galatur* answered:
    "We do not wish it."

Ereshkigal said:
    "I will give you the grain-gift, the fields in
    harvest.''

The *kurgarra* and *galatur* said:
    "We do not wish it."

Ereshkigal said:
    "Speak then! What do you wish?"

They answered:
    "We wish only the corpse that hangs from
    the hook on the wall.''

Ereshkigal said:
    "The corpse belongs to Inanna."

They said:
    "Whether it belongs to our queen,
    Whether it belongs to our king,
    That is what we wish.''

The corpse was given to them.

The *kurgarra* sprinkled the food of life on the
corpse.
The *galatur* sprinkled the water of life on the
corpse.
Inanna arose . . . .

Inanna was about to ascend from the
underworld
When the Annuna, the judges of the underworld, seized her.
They said:
    "No one ascends from the underworld un-
    marked.
    If Inanna wishes to return from the under-
    world,
    She must provide someone in her place.''

As Inanna ascended from the underworld,
The *galla*, the demons of the underworld,
clung to her side.
The *galla* were demons who know no food,
who know no drink,
Who eat no offerings, who drink no libations,
Who accept no gifts.
They enjoy no lovemaking.
They have no sweet children to kiss.
They tear the wife from the husband's arms,
They tear the child from the father's knees,
They steal the bride from her marriage home.

The demons clung to Inanna.
The small *galla* who accompanied Inanna
Were like reeds the size of low picket fences.
The large *galla* who accompanied Inanna
Were like reeds the size of high picket fences.

The one who walked in front of Inanna was
not a minister,
Yet he carried a sceptre.
The one who walked behind her was not a
warrior,
Yet he carried a mace.
Ninshubur, dressed in a soiled sackcloth,
Waited outside the palace gates.
When she saw Inanna
Surrounded by the *galla*,
She threw herself in the dust at Inanna's feet.

The *galla* said:
    "Walk on, Inanna,
    We will take Ninshubur in your place.''

Inanna cried:
    "No! Ninshubur is my constant support.
    She is my *sukkal* who gives me wise advice.
    She is my warrior who fights by my side.
    She did not forget my words.

    She set up a lament for me by the ruins.
    She beat the drum for me at the assembly
        places.
    She circled the houses of the gods.
    She tore at her eyes, at her mouth, at her
        thighs.
    She dressed herself in a single garment like a
        beggar.

    Alone, she set out for Nippur and the tem-
        ple of Enlil.

She went to Ur and the temple of Nanna.
She went to Eridu and the temple of Enki.
Because of her, my life was saved.
I will never give Ninshubur to you."

The *galla* said:
  "Walk on, Inanna,
  We will accompany you to Umma."

In Umma, at the holy shrine,
Shara, the son of Inanna, was dressed in a soiled
sackcloth.
When he saw Inanna
Surrounded by the *galla*,
He threw himself in the dust at her feet.

The *galla* said:
  "Walk on to your city, Inanna,
  We will take Shara in your place."

Inanna cried:
  "No! Not Shara!
  He is my son who sings hymns to me.
  He is my son who cuts my nails and smooths
    my hair.
  I will never give Shara to you."

The *galla* said:
  "Walk on, Inanna,
  We will accompany you to Badtibira."

In Badtibira, at the holy shrine,
Lulal, the son of Inanna, was dressed in a soiled
sackcloth.
When he saw Inanna
Surrounded by the *galla,*
He threw himself in the dust at her feet.

The *galla* said:
  "Walk on to your city, Inanna,
  We will take Lulal in your place."

Inanna cried:
  "Not Lulal! He is my son.
  He is a leader among men.
  He is my right arm. He is my left arm.
  I will never give Lulal to you."

The *galla* said:
  "Walk on to your city, Inanna.

We will go with you to the big apple tree in
  Uruk."

In Uruk, by the big apple tree,
Dumuzi, the husband of Inanna, was dressed
in his shining *me*-garments.
He sat on his magnificent throne; (he did not
move).

The *galla* seized him by his thighs.
They poured milk out of his seven churns.
They broke the reed pipe which the shepherd
was playing.

Inanna fastened on Dumuzi the eye of death.
She spoke against him the word of wrath.
She uttered against him the cry of guilt:
  "Take him! Take Dumuzi away!"

The *galla*, who know no food, who know no
drink,
Who eat no offerings, who drink no libations,
Who accept no gifts, seized Dumuzi.
They made him stand up; they made him sit
down.
They beat the husband of Inanna.
They gashed him with axes.
Dumuzi let out a wail.
He raised his hands to heaven to Utu, the god
of Justice,
    and beseeched him:
  "O Utu, you are my brother-in-law,
  I am the husband of your sister.
  I brought cream to your mother's house,
  I brought milk to Ningal's house.
  I am the one who carried food to the holy
    shrine.
  I am the one who brought wedding gifts to
    Uruk.
  I am the one who danced on the holy knees,
    the knees of Inanna.

  Utu, you who are a just god, a merciful god,
  Change my hands into the hands of a snake.
  Change my feet into the feet of a snake.
  Let me escape from my demons;
  Do not let them hold me."

The merciful Utu accepted Dumuzi's tears.
He changed the hands of Dumuzi into snake
hands.

He changed the feet of Dumuzi into snake feet.
Dumuzi escaped from his demons.
They could not hold him . . . .

———

"Fire," and "An Ordinary Woman," from
The God Beneath the Sea, by Edward Blishen
and Leon Garfield (London: Longmans,
1970).

Probably the best-known of the classical
myths, the story of Prometheus is, on its sim-
plest level, a pourquoi myth about how peo-
ple acquired fire. But if the fire is symbolic of
knowledge, Prometheus, the Titan who helped
Zeus establish himself as king in his rebellion
against Cronos, becomes the being who denies
the authority of gods to give mankind the
knowledge it needs to rise above the level of
animals. For his punishment, Prometheus be-
comes a sacrificial god who, like Odin and
Christ, suffers for the good of his people. One
can see in the myth the Greek emphasis on the
dignity of struggle in the face of fate.

In the version selected here, Garfield and
Blishen use novelistic techniques to capture
the rich human complexity they found embod-
ied in the Greek myths. In their adaptation,
they have also incorporated the story of Pan-
dora, who, like the Biblical Eve, was believed
to have introduced evil into the world.

Fire

'My father bids me tell you to destroy them,
great Prometheus; or he will do so himself.'

Thus spoke Hermes, messenger of the gods,
as he stood, piercing bright, in the Titan's garden, washed by the morning sun.

'Why? Why? How have they offended?
What is their crime?'

'Who knows what is in the mind of Zeus?
Perhaps he is offended, Lord Prometheus? Perhaps he finds what you have made too close
in aspect to the gods? Perhaps he sees them as
a mockery? Gods who are subject to the Fates
. . . . Destroy them, Prometheus. So my father
says.'

'And you, good Hermes? Is it your wish,
too?'

The god looked sideways, avoiding the Titan's despairing eyes; shifted from foot to
winged foot and smiled as his shadow seemed
to dance off into the trees.

'Between you and me, Prometheus . . . no.
Not particularly, that is. I think they have a certain charm. Personally, I like them. I assure you,
Prometheus, that such messages as, from time
to time, I bring from this great god or that, do
not necessarily reflect my own opinions.'

Hermes, ever politic, ever unwilling to offend, watched the mighty Titan curiously; he
continued, 'Believe me, my friend — I understand your affection and your sorrow. When I
summoned the shade of the one that died, I
was troubled, Prometheus. As we entered the
grove of black poplars, this shade and I, it asked
me: Why, why? And I could not answer. Then,
when I led it to the dark river and dragged it
aboard the evil, rotting boat, and it saw there
was no one else there but bony Charon, again it
begged me: Why, why?

'We came to the further bank, and still there
was no one else by. And so to the Field of Asphodel: empty, empty . . . .

'It clung to me, Prometheus, as I left it, still
begging me to tell it why.

'It knew nothing; had not lived more than
the winking of an eye — yet it sensed the vastness of its loss. I looked back, and never in all
the universe have I seen anything so lonely as
that single, frightened shade wandering over
the ashy ground and crying: Why, why?'

The Titan listened and groaned in anguish;
then Hermes added softly: 'They are so frail,
Prometheus. Your creatures are so pitifully
frail. Are they worth their labour?'

Eagerly the Titan laid his hand on Hermes'
ribboned staff — as if to deflect or soften the
god's terrible message.

'But I will strengthen them! I will refine the
substance, purify it and pluck out the seeds that
menace. I — '

'It is too late, Prometheus. They are doomed.'

'By Zeus?'

'If not by my father, then by every wind
that blows. How could they endure, never
knowing when Atropos might take it into her
blind head to slit the thread of their lives?'

How indeed? And the more Hermes argued,

the more intolerable seemed the burden Prometheus' fragile creatures would have to bear.

Yet their very frailty stung the Titan's heart and strengthened his great will. He begged bright Hermes to plead with his father for a little respite. If the creatures were destined to flicker out — then let them perish of their own accord. But spare them the dreadful thunderbolt. Let them see and love the gods, however briefly, and, maybe, find some favour in their sight —

Here, subtle Hermes pursed his lips and tapped his staff against his head.

'Between you and me, my friend, I fancy you've hit on something. I don't promise — I never promise — but if your creatures were to find favour in great Zeus's eyes . . . that is to say, if they were to go out of their way to please, then who knows? Think on that, Lord Prometheus; and I will undertake to delay my father's hand.'

Between Arcadia and Attica, there was a place called Sicyon where the creatures of Prometheus had begun to make a home.

It was here, in a myrtle grove — once dear to Hermes — that Prometheus put it into men's minds to honour the gods. A rich, red bull, sleek and portly, was sacrificed and the Titan cupped his hands to his vast mouth and shouted up to Olympus for almighty Zeus to descend and be mankind's first guest.

'See, great god! My creatures honour you and worship you! Come down so they may behold you and give you the best of the earth!'

He shaded his eyes and stared desperately up towards the curtains of cloud that veiled the mountain's divine summit.

Even as he watched, a finger of lightning crooked round them and drew them briefly apart. Then came a roll of thunder. The god had heard. The god would come.

Eagerly Prometheus stripped the blood-dappled skin from the bull and divided the carcass, laying the bones and fat beneath one part of the hide, and the steaming flesh beneath the other; but in his haste he had not detached the stomach . . . . Two portions: one for the god — and one for mankind.

Wide-eyed and innocent that they were, poised on the edge of extinction, the Titan's creatures watched as their great creator toiled and struggled to save them.

Suddenly they shrank back. A fearful radiance seared their naked eyes and scorched their skin. They cried out and fled into the shadows of the myrtles, hiding their faces in their hands. The blaze had been unendurable. It lingered on the inner eye where it burned its vision. Within the scalding radiance had been a shape. A shimmering fluent shape, part man-like, part immeasurably greater. Eyes had seen them — eyes like merciless suns.

It had been the god . . . .

'Welcome, mighty Zeus. Welcome, father of the gods, lord of the sky! Your feast is ready. Mankind awaits.'

The Titan stood back as the fiery god stared round the grove. Then, seeing that Prometheus' poor creatures were blasted by his light, Zeus veiled his lustre and smiled.

He saw the covered portions of the slaughtered bull. He nodded. They had not skimped their offering. The beast had been of the finest.

He touched one portion, lifted a corner of the hide. The stomach: it reeked of offal. He turned to the other. He glimpsed rich fat. Prometheus trembled; all-seeing Zeus nodded.

He pointed to the second portion.

'I have chosen,' the mighty god decreed. 'From now through all eternity, in feast and holy sacrifice, this portion is for the immortal gods, and that for mankind.'

He flung back the skin he had chosen. Beneath the rich layer of fat lay nothing but the animal's wretched, meatless bones. The divine portion . . . .

Prometheus bowed his head to hide a helpless smile. He awaited the enraged god's thunderbolt. But Zeus' anger took a subtler form.

'Let them eat their flesh raw,' he said. 'I forbid them the use of fire.'

Without fire, they would die. Their slender limbs would freeze, their blood congeal and their bright eyes glaze and film like scum on a quiet pond. The angry god had doomed them as surely as if he'd hurled his thunderbolt and scorched them in an instant.

Prometheus wept slow, bitter tears. It had been his own smile that had brought it about: mighty Zeus had taken this way of punishing him. The smile of the father was to be the death's-head grin of his children.

For a while, fury took hold of him — and his gentle brother watched with terror and awe as great Prometheus paced their garden, bursting asunder the well-tended trees as if they'd been straw. Then the Titan passed into despair. War and violence had ever been hateful to him, The mighty struggles his nature demanded had all been in the mind.

He knew he could not storm Olympus and drag down the father of the gods. He lacked both Zeus' strength and Zeus' instant passion. Thinking had ever held him back.

For long it had preserved him — and saved him from the fearful fate of all his race. But now that power had reached its end — the limits of his mind. Thought stared into soul; and soul stared back at thought. They were the same; and the tragic Titan knew that he must destroy himself to save his children: men.

Some time during the night, mankind saw him shining among the thick trees that cloaked the northern slopes of Mount Olympus. His light pierced the branches so that it seemed as if some star had fallen and been caught in a vast black net.

Then his light was snuffed in a deep cleft in the rock, and the Titan mounted unseen.

An owl flew out of the trees, screeched several times, then fluttered uncertainly, hovering as if seeking its moment to pounce. It screeched again, and began to pursue a devious path in the night air, leading higher and higher up the mountain.

It was the owl of the goddess Athene.

The hidden Titan saw it and knew that the goddess had not turned against him. She had sent her owl to lead him secretly into the fortress of the gods. This was the most she could do for him. Mighty though she was, even she feared her blazing father's wrath.

Now came another bird out of the night. A crane perched in the Titan's twisting path. It stared at him with bright, inquisitive eyes.

'Though I will not help you, Prometheus,' whispered the voice of cunning Hermes, 'I will not stand in your path.' The crane flew off and its soft cry came back to the mounting Titan. 'There is what you seek in my brother Hephaestus' forge.'

Flames gleamed and danced on the twenty golden bellows as they rose and fell like twenty gigantic beating hearts. They breathed on the forge, increasing its fire till the lip of its rocky prison shivered and ran.

Shadows loomed and lumbered against the huge smithy's walls. Rods and crucibles made the shapes of nodding beasts; and in their midst crouched the shadow of a misshapen monster on bird-thin legs that were broken sharply by the angle of the floor and walls. Hephaestus was at work. He was making a wedding gift for Aphrodite, his wife. He scowled tempestuously as he beat out the gold on the black anvil with a loud, regular clang. He was fashioning the clasp of a girdle . . . .

Suddenly the god's heat-inflamed eyes quickened. A strange shadow had crossed his on the wall. It moved secretly among the beast-like shadows of the rods and crucibles which seemed to nod and swear at it, then crowd it under their own dangerous night.

Hephaestus turned. He saw a hand, holding an unkindled torch. He saw it reach forward, plunge in and out of the fire. The torch flared. It was alight.

The god looked up. Prometheus stood before him.

'For my children,' whispered the despairing Titan. 'For mankind.'

The two great outcasts stared at one another.

'Take it and be gone,' muttered the god.

For long after the Titan had departed, Hephaestus brooded over his anvil. His mighty hammer leaned against his knee . . . and the beaten gold grew cool. Then the god began again. His hammer rose and fell till fountains of sparks leaped up and seemed to engulf him in robes of broken fire.

At last he rested. The smithy grew quiet and the ugly god examined the clasp he had made. It was a golden hand holding a torch. It seemed to be caressing it, and the torch was spurting its vital fire. So delicately wrought was this hand that it seemed to tremble — to move, even with tenderness . . . .

The god nodded. Here in this eternal clasp was his own fierce love for Aphrodite — and Prometheus' aching love for mankind.

He fastened it to the girdle with rivets as fine as hair and hobbled off to the laughing goddess of his dreams.

An Ordinary Woman

Still Zeus did not strike the defiant Titan down. Prometheus had opposed him, set his command aside. Fire flickered below and strengthened the new, aspiring life.

Time and again Prometheus turned his eyes to heaven so that he might see his destruction blazing forth. But the lord of the sky seemed to have turned his back. Had grave Athene pleaded with her father? Had subtle Hermes put a case?

The Titan's uncertainty grew agonised as his time ran out. Nonetheless, he still laboured for his creatures, teaching them what he could to widen their narrow foothold between the fates and the gods. At night he brooded in the mysterious room where man had been born. Already he had begun to refine the precious substance of Chaos. Strange spots and scales he'd discovered on the bright seeds. These he scraped away and confined in a small jar which he sealed and hid. He suspected them to be some malignant rot . . . .

'Can you fashion a woman, my clever, ugly son? Can you make her as skilfully as Prometheus made his creatures below?'

The father of the gods stared down from his gold and ivory throne in the great council chamber. 'Not of gold, nor silver, nor imperishable bronze; but of the self-same clay the Titan used — the soft wet clay of Attica?'

Hephaestus shuffled and blinked his reddened eyes away from Zeus' radiance. The fire of his forge was as night beside the blazing noon of Zeus.

'Fetch me the clay and I will make such a woman.'

Zeus nodded; and swift as thought Hermes sped down, twisting through the cloudy swarms of bees that sang above the lower slopes of Mount Hymettus.

Hephaestus waited; and presently, the thieving god returned with Prometheus' clay.

Hephaestus set about his task and Hermes, leaning against the lintel post of the smithy door, watched the great artificer at his work.

Unlike Prometheus, the god worked slowly. He seemed to seek the form within the dull shapeless clay. Even as Hermes watched, his burnt and twisted fingers probed and dragged at hair, cheeks, lips, breasts and limbs and as if he was freeing rather than creating them. He tore the clay away from her eyes as if it had been a blindfold; and suddenly a woman stared at Hermes in the doorway. Even though he knew his ill-tempered brother's marvellous skill, Hermes was startled by this strange new evidence of it.

Her height was perhaps a finger's breadth below Aphrodite's; but otherwise her beauty was not of Olympus. It had the darker, richer colours of the earth. Hephaestus had fashioned a woman far beyond the Titan's skill.

She stood beside the mighty anvil and as the twenty golden bellows breathed on the fire, the heat drew tears of moisture out of the clay so that she seemed to be weeping before she had life. Then Zeus bade Acolus, warder of the four winds, breathe life into her nostrils and mouth.

She stirred; she moved; she stared about her with a sweet vacancy, understanding nothing — feeling nothing.

Being formed from unseeded clay, she had neither passions nor qualities.

So life-giving Zeus commanded the immortal gods to enrich her with their gifts.

First Hestia, gentlest of the children of Cronus, gave this woman a gentleness and generosity not unlike her own; and the vacant eyes took on a soft and tender gleam. But Ares, roughly elbowing forward, forced on her a touch of himself, so that behind the tender gleam there glinted the flicker of a savage fire.

Next great Apollo gave her sweet and tempting grace of movement — such as he himself delighted in; but straightway his moon-sister Artemis gave her defensive quickness, modesty and virginity.

Glorious Demeter shook her head. Never quite in sympathy with Artemis, she blessed the woman with a richly fertile womb — and the knowledge of it. This knowledge now glinted mysteriously from under the downcast lashes that the mighty huntress's gift had imposed.

'And I will give her wisdom,' said Athene suddenly. She had divined the danger there lurked in this woman, compounded as she was of so many opposing passions. 'I will give her wisdom so that her gifts may be well-used.'

Zeus frowned; but could not deny the powerful goddess her right. So he bade Hermes give Athene's gift a double edge, with curiosity and deceit.

Now the woman turned and smiled gratefully at each of the gods in turn; her eyes seemed to linger so that her last look was always sideways . . . till imperious Hera hastened to cover her nakedness with fine, cloudy robes. This woman was curiously disturbing. Beside her, the hot nymphs were but as children — their amorous leapings and twinings as children's games . . . . Then Zeus gave her a name: Pandora — all giving.

·She bowed her head. 'Great goddess,' she murmured, raising her face now to lovely Aphrodite while her eyes lingered timidly on smiling Zeus. 'Is there no gift from you? Are you displeased with me? Have I unknowingly offended you? If so, I beg forgiveness . . . and plead for your gift. For without it, I think, all would wither away unused.'

So Aphrodite laughed — and lent Pandora the girdle that Hephaestus had made for her — the girdle that kindled desire.

'With such a piece of work,' murmured the king of the gods as he brooded down on Pandora, 'what need have I of thunderbolts?'

It was Hermes who led her down the slopes of Mount Olympus; and as the gods watched, none was sorry to see her go.

'What harsh message do you bring from Olympus now, Hermes?'

Prometheus and his brother were in their orchard, securing the well-filled branches with stout props, when the great herald rippled through the trees.

'No message, Lord Prometheus,' answered the god courteously. He had plucked an apple in passing and now speared it idly on his ribboned staff. He stared at it as if surprised. 'I bring a gift. Indeed, Prometheus, there is no need to look at me so angrily, as if you would refuse. The gift does not concern you. It is for your brother, Epimetheus.'

He pointed his staff, with the red apple on its head, at the second Titan, the ever-gentle, not over-wise Epimetheus.

'The gift of the gods is for you.'

Epimetheus came forward with a pleased smile. His heart was open; his nature unsuspecting. Such happy beings as he are always the last of their race.

'Beware of gods bearing gifts,' muttered his great brother whom he never understood.

Epimetheus looked uncertain. Hermes stretched out his staff. 'Come,' he called. 'Pandora!'

She came from behind the trees in the cloudy gown of Hera. She walked with graceful yet uncertain steps. Her eyes were downcast — though from time to time they glimmered with a curious sideways glance that lingered in Epimetheus' heart.

'Here is your new gift, Epimetheus. Pandora — gift of the Olympian gods.'

Epimetheus was entranced. Never had their orchard seen a richer fruit.

'Beware, brother — '

'Lord Prometheus, this is no concern of yours.' Hermes spoke calmly, but there was an edge to his voice. Then he laughed disarmingly. 'Epimetheus — your deep brother is too anxious. He mistrusts good fortune. Between you and me, I suspect a little envy. And who could blame him? See — '

He touched the trembling Pandora with his staff, laying its appled tip on her breast. She smiled timidly. 'She bears the gifts of us all.'

'She is the gift of Zeus, brother. Old Cronus once had such a gift. Do you remember a cup of honied drink — ?'

Epimetheus hesitated; gazed uneasily from brother to the god. He avoided Pandora's eyes. He thanked Olympus, but begged time to consider. . . .

Prometheus smiled triumphantly.

'Do you refuse me, Epimetheus?' Pandora's voice was low . . . even pleading. The gentle Titan glanced at her. Modestly she cast her eyes down to Aphrodite's kindling girdle. Epimetheus felt desire rise like the all-covering sea.

Then briefly Pandora lifted her eyes and stared at Prometheus. Her look was still gentle and partly timid. She seemed to be bewildered and curious as to why this mighty being should bid his brother send her away. What had she done? Why did he stare at her as if to pierce her through and through? Why did his great brows furrow till his eyes were no more than pools of troubled shadow? Was it only because she had come between brother and brother? Was it as the bright god had said — that this vast soul was stabbed with envy for his brother's blessing?

If so, then it was not of her doing . . .

See — he was drawing Epimetheus aside, talking with him — while the god who had brought her looked on with the strangest smile. What was to become of her, with all her beauty and gifts?

Why had the gods made her so?

'Do not refuse me, Epimetheus,' she pleaded; and such was her power that Epimetheus' heart faltered within him. She promised him such joy and fierce delight that even the gods would envy him. Epimetheus' eyes began to gleam. Whereupon the blessing of Hestia, momentarily conquering the passions of Aphrodite and Ares, prompted Pandora to speak of ease and sweet companionship, and the speaking silences of harmonious kinds . . . .

'Can there be danger in such a gift?' asked simple Epimetheus of his brother.

'Nor will their lives be fruitless, Lord Prometheus,' murmured Hermes, drifting close and leaning towards the Titan's ear. 'Glorious Demeter has blessed her, too. Even as your well-tended trees bear fine fruit, so will Pandora bear children to your home. Mark my words, Prometheus, her children will inherit our immortal gifts — for the god's gifts do not die — and these children will mingle with mankind. Thus does my father mean well, Prometheus. He seeks to improve on your charming but fragile creation with some more durable qualities of the gods. Believe me, my friend — '

Suddenly the Titan turned with terror on the murmuring god of lies. His eyes were wild — his vast comprehension tilted so that all ran down into the pit of dismay. He had divined dread Zeus' purpose and creatures that he loved — the creatures who might have inherited the earth as neither gods nor Titans were permitted to do — were to be crippled before they had begun.

Even as in Pandora the passions of the gods opposed each other, so they would in men. All aspiration would be lamed, all achievement warped as man eternally fought within himself a battle that could be neither lost nor won.

The great Titan raised his eyes to Mount Olympus and cursed immortal Zeus.

He lifted up his voice and hurled his curses till they echoed in the far corners of the universe. Even in hateful Tartarus they were heard, like thin, high whispers over the ceaseless weeping and groaning of the Titans who were chained there.

Close by the dreary Fields of Asphodel, there is a pool beside which grows a bone-white poplar tree. It is the pool of memory. Here strayed the solitary shade of the man who had died. Vainly it drank of the pool; but what memories could it recapture of a life so fleeting, save an aching glimpse of a garden by night?

It heard Prometheus' curses and shook its thin head. 'Why? Why?' it wailed — and flittered away into the lonely gloom.

Grim Hades in his palace heard them — and nodded in expectation of his vast brother's revenge.

As in a dream, Prometheus saw Hermes flicker away; and with a last stab of anguish he saw his brother and Pandora retreat with frightened faces, and run from the orchard. Their hands had been clasped — and there was no undoing them now.

Prometheus bowed his mighty head. He heard a rushing in the air. It was coming; and he was almost glad of it — the thunderbolt of Zeus!

The trees blazed and, for an instant, their

blackened branches reached up like imploring arms with fingers charred and flaming.

A radiance that seared even the Titan's ancient eyes stood in the ruined orchard like a fiery sword. Zeus in all his unendurable glory was come for his revenge.

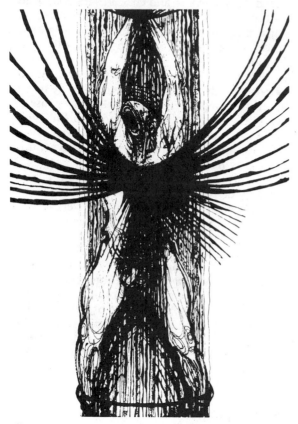

Illustration by Charles Keeping from Leon Garfield and Edward Blisher, *The God Beneath The Sea* (Hangman Books 1970) Copyright © 1970 by Charles Keeping. Reprinted by permission of Penquin Books Ltd.

Far, far to the north, amid the freezing mountains of the Caucasus, there stood a tall, cold pillar. Chains of unburstable iron hung from its base and capital. Here the naked Titan was manacled by wrists and ankles, stretched so that he could scarcely twist his body or avert his head.

He waited — then a shadow fell across his face. He rolled his eyes to see what had come between him and the pale, bitter sun.

A vulture with hooked talons and greedy beak hung in the air. Its stony eyes met his. Then it swooped and the Titan writhed and screamed till the mountains cracked. His agony had begun. Again and again the hungry bird flew at him and tore at his undefended liver. When night came with biting frosts and whirling snow, the Titan's wounds healed and he grew whole again. But when the cold sun rose, the self-same shadow fell across his face and the Titan waited for his agony to begin once more. Such was the punishment of Prometheus, marker of men.

Epimetheus, the last of the Titans, wept for his mighty brother — whom he had never understood. In his great sadness Pandora comforted him, and little by little, Epimetheus began to think his brother had misjudged her. She was so quick to understand and minister to his every need. She never crossed nor questioned him; nor did she plead to enter his lost brother's mysterious room. For Prometheus, in his last moments of liberty, had charged his brother most urgently never to enter it or disturb what was hidden there.

Pandora nodded. Though she had not liked Prometheus, she was sensible of her husband's affection and was anxious for him to feel that she was of a like mind. For a while it seemed that the gifts of Hestia and Athene were uppermost.

Then, thanks to the rich soil of Attica, the black scars in the orchard healed over, and the reason for the great Titan's fall faded from Pandora's mind. More and more she came round to the view that the whole unlucky affair had blown up out of jealousy. Why else had her husband's brother so taken against her?

She gazed at her reflection in a pool. Certainly she was beautiful enough to stir envy in any one. After all, the gods had made her. She sighed. It had been tragic; but jealousy was an evil passion and Prometheus had paid for it. She only hoped it would serve as a lesson.

She stood up and thoughts of Prometheus slid into thoughts of the forbidden room. What was so particular about it? She suspected jealousy was at the root of it again. A jealous spirit is jealous in everything. Most likely the room was very handsome and Prometheus had forbidden it to her out of spite. The more she thought of it, the more she was convinced. It irritated her like a crumb in her bed. Wherever she turned for comfort, there it was, scratching away. Agitatedly she left the garden and entered the house. She paced the hall, pausing each time before the closed door. It was ridiculous. She felt she couldn't call her home her own. She laid her hand on the engraved bolt. Epimetheus would get over it. Naturally he'd be hurt at first and grieve for his brother again. But it would pass and then there'd be nothing to come between them. A shadow would have been removed . . . .

Pandora nodded. All in all, it would be for the best. She opened the door.

As she'd suspected, the room was the best in the house. A little dark, perhaps, and certainly dusty . . . but the fig-tree and its polished branches gave it great character and atmosphere.

She ran her finger along the wide bench that stretched from wall to wall. Idly she drew the shape of a baby in the dust. She smiled. The room would make a fine nursery . . . .

No sooner had she thought of it than she set to work. She swept and polished and transformed the shadowy room into a shining joy. She cleared out the cupboards of all old stone jars — but did not open them.

Here she respected her husband's wishes; besides, the jars seemed quite useless.

Then, quite by chance, she came upon a smaller one, tucked underneath the bench. She held it up. It was a pretty jar. Cleaned out, it would hold jewels or perfume . . . . She shook her head. No. She would defer to her husband's wish, foolish as it was.

Then she thought of Prometheus. How like him to keep such a jar himself! What could he possibly want with it now? After all, it wasn't as though she intended to open *all* the jars.

She had her principles and would not have abandoned them for anything. She was perfectly certain that her husband would come to see it her way. He would admire her for leaving the other jars and so honouring his selfish brother's memory.

She shook the pretty little jar gently. There was something inside. She listened. It gave a dry rattling sound. She shrugged her shoulders. She'd put up with the sacred memory of Prometheus for long enough. She opened the jar.

She screamed; she shrieked; she dropped the jar. Gentle Epimetheus came running to her cries.

There seemed to be a cloud about Pandora: a whirling, malignant veil that glittered with ten thousand furious wings. They seemed to be insects of extraordinary venom and ferocity. They bit and stung and beat against his crouching wife; then they turned on him and he felt their wicked little spears in every part of his body. He cried out:

'Prometheus, Prometheus! What have we done?'

Far in the north a fiercer pain than the vulture's beak stabbed at the chained Titan. From his icy place of punishment he saw what had befallen his children. His deep eyes filled with tears as a more terrible vulture tore at his heart.

Nor did this phantom bird depart with its bloody brother when healing night came. High in the freezing mountains, striped with the purple glaciers of his blood, Prometheus wept. His labours and his fall had been in vain.

The strange spots and scales he had imprisoned in the jar had been malignant indeed. Unhindered by the divine substance from which they'd been scraped, they had grown into hideous little furies. He had seen them fly out of his house in a wicked cloud to sting his helpless children. Madness, vice, old age and crippling sickness had been let out upon the world as a birthright for man.

Prometheus raised his eyes and stared across the world's night. His eyes met those of bitter Atlas; and these two giants who had opposed the gods looked long and deep at each other from their separate high prisons of pain.

'Mankind,' whispered great Prometheus, 'forgive me; I have failed. Better that I never made you . . . for what is there left to you now?'

Pandora gazed down at the shattered jar. It was past repairing. She felt awkward. Her husband, inflamed from the strange insects' attacks, had looked at her reproachfully.

So, as mildly as she was able, she remarked that Prometheus was to blame. He should never have kept such things in a jar. She bent down and began to gather the broken pieces. Suddenly she came upon a curious stone. She picked it up. It was not a stone. She looked at it carefully. I seemed to be a chrysalis . . . .

She shivered as she tried to throw it away before it hatched. But it stuck to her fingers.

At last she scraped it off on a fragment of the jar. She rubbed her hands to rid herself of the gum-like substance the chrysalis had left. Her eyes brightened in surprise. The pain of the bites and stings seemed soothed. Eagerly she told Epimetheus. The chrysalis was a balm — a wondrous healing balm.

Pandora was delighted. She smiled at her husband. Was it not a good thing after all that she'd opened the jar? As she'd always told him, everything turned out for the best.

A sudden movement aloft distracted her. She looked up. A bird had been perched in the polished rafters, looking down with bright, inquisitive eyes. It flapped its wings and flew away. It had been a crane. She watched it through the casement as it flew with amazing speed towards the north. It pierced the colder air and crossed the mountains till at last it saw below it the pillar of Prometheus.

'What is there left to mankind now?' cried the despairing Titan as he saw the sideways-dropping god.

'Hope,' answered great Hermes. 'For better or worse for who knows what may unfold from a chrysalis? — hope was left behind.'

———

"Cupid and Psyche," from Mythology, *by Edith Hamilton (Boston: Little, Brown, 1942).*

The story of Cupid and Psyche is one of the most complex and sophisticated of the Greek myths. It is basically allegorical, representing the union of love (Cupid) and the soul (Psyche), a concept as important for us today as it was for the Ancient Greeks. Furthermore, it is a highly stylized and very compelling story due to the depth of emotions presented.

The hostile relationship between Psyche and Venus reveals the jealous nature of the Gods and their domineering attitudes toward mortals, the eternal jealousy of an older woman toward a younger, more beautiful rival, and a mother's protective instinct for a son whose lover she feels is inferior. The story focuses on Psyche's character development as she journeys from her unhappy life on earth to her final union as an immortal with Cupid on Mount Olympus. This myth closely resembles the Scandinavian folktale "East o' the Sun and West o' the Moon."

Cupid and Psyche

There was once a king who had three daughters, all lovely maidens, but the youngest, Psyche, excelled her sisters so greatly that beside them she seemed a very goddess consorting with mere mortals. The fame of her surpassing beauty spread over the earth, and everywhere men journeyed to gaze upon her with wonder and adoration and to do her homage as though she were in truth one of the immortals. They would even say that Venus herself could not equal this mortal. As they thronged in ever-growing numbers to worship her loveliness no one any more gave a thought to Venus herself. Her temples were neglected; her altars foul with cold ashes; her favorite towns deserted and falling in ruins. All the honors once hers were now given to a mere girl destined some day to die.

It may well be believed that the goddess would not put up with this treatment. As always when she was in trouble she turned for help to her son, the beautiful winged youth whom some call Cupid and others Love, against whose arrows there is no defense, neither in heaven nor on the earth. She told him her wrongs and as always he was ready to do her bidding. "Use your power," she said, "and make the hussy fall madly in love with the vilest and most despicable creature there is in the whole world." And so no doubt he would have done, if Venus had not first shown him Psyche, never thinking in her jealous rage what such beauty might do even to the God of Love himself. As he looked upon her it was as if he had shot one of his arrows into his own heart.

He said nothing to his mother, indeed he had no power to utter a word, and Venus left him with the happy confidence that he would swiftly bring about Psyche's ruin.

What happened, however, was not what she had counted on. Psyche did not fall in love with a horrible wretch, she did not fall in love at all. Still more strange, no one fell in love with her. Men were content to look and wonder and worship — and then pass on to marry someone else. Both her sisters, inexpressibly inferior to her, were splendidly married, each to a king. Psyche, the all-beautiful, sat sad and solitary, only admired, never loved. It seemed that no man wanted her.

This was, of course, most disturbing to her parents. Her father finally traveled to an oracle of Apollo to ask his advice on how to get her a good husband. The god answered him, but his words were terrible. Cupid had told him the whole story and had begged for his help. Accordingly Apollo said that Psyche, dressed in deepest mourning, must be set on the summit of a rocky hill and left alone, and that there her destined husband, a fearful winged serpent, stronger than the gods themselves, would come to her and make her his wife.

The misery of all when Psyche's father brought back this lamentable news can be imagined. They dressed the maiden as though for her death and carried her to the hill with greater sorrowing then if it had been to her tomb. But Psyche herself kept her courage. "You should have wept for me before," she told them, "because of the beauty that has drawn down upon me the jealousy of Heaven. Now go, knowing that I am glad the end has come." They went in despairing grief, leaving the lovely helpless creature to meet her doom alone, and they shut themselves in their palace to mourn all their days for her.

On the high hilltop in the darkness Psyche sat, waiting for she knew not what terror. There, as she wept and trembled, a soft breath of air came through the stillness to her, the gentle breathing of Zephyr, sweetest and mildest of winds. She felt it lift her up. She was floating away from the rocky hill and down until she lay upon a grassy meadow soft as a bed and fragrant with flowers. It was so peaceful there,

all her trouble left her and she slept. She woke beside a bright river, and on its bank was a mansion stately and beautiful as though built for a god, with pillars of gold and walls of silver and floors inlaid with precious stones. No sound was to be heard; the place seemed deserted and Psyche drew near, awestruck at the sight of such splendor. As she hesitated on the threshold, voices sounded in her ear. She could see no one, but the words they spoke came clearly to her. The house was for her, they told her. She must enter without fear and refresh herself. Then a banquet table would be spread for her. "We are your servants," the voices said, "ready to do whatever you desire."

The bath was the most delightful, the food the most delicious, she had ever enjoyed. While she dined, sweet music breathed around her: a great choir seemed to sing to a harp, but she could only hear, not see, them. Throughout the day, except for the strange companionship of the voices, she was alone, but in some inexplicable way she felt sure that with the coming of the night her husband would be with her. And so it happened. When she felt him beside her and heard his voice softly murmuring in her ear, all her fears left her. She knew without seeing him that here was no monster or shape of terror, but the lover and husband she had longed and waited for.

This half-and-half companionship could not fully content her; still she was happy and the time passed swiftly. One night, however, her dear though unseen husband spoke gravely to her and warned her that danger in the shape of her two sisters was approaching. "They are coming to the hill where you disappeared, to weep for you," he said, "but you must not let them see you or you will bring great sorrow upon me and ruin to yourself." She promised him she would not, but all the next day she passed in weeping, thinking of her sisters and herself unable to comfort them. She was still in tears when her husband came and even his caresses could not check them. At last he yielded sorrowfully to her great desire. "Do what you will," he said, "but you are seeking your own destruction." Then he warned her solemnly not to be persuaded by anyone to try to see him, on pain of being separated from him forever. Psyche cried out that she would never do so. She would die a hundred times over rather than live without him. "But give me this joy," she said: "to see my sisters." Sadly he promised her that it should be so.

The next morning the two came, brought down from the mountain by Zephyr. Happy and excited, Psyche was waiting for them. It was long before the three could speak to each other; their joy was too great to be expressed except by tears and embraces. But when at last they entered the palace and the elder sisters saw its surpassing treasures; when they sat at the rich banquet and heard the marvelous music, bitter envy took possession of them and a devouring curiosity as to who was the lord of all this magnificence and their sister's husband. But Psyche kept faith; she told them only that he was a young man, away now on a hunting expedition. Then filling their hands with gold and jewels, she had Zephyr bear them back to the hill. They went willingly enough, but their hearts were on fire with jealousy. All their own wealth and good fortune seemed to them as nothing compared with Psyche's and their envious anger so worked in them that they came finally to plotting how to ruin her.

That very night Psyche's husband warned her once more. She would not listen when he begged her not to let them come again. She never could see him, she reminded him. Was she also to be forbidden to see all others, even her sisters so dear to her? He yielded as before, and very soon the two wicked women arrived, with their plot carefully worked out.

Already, because of Psyche's stumbling and contradictory answers when they asked her what her husband looked like, they had become convinced that she had never set eyes on him and did not really know what he was. They did not tell her this, but they reproached her for hiding her terrible state from them, her own sisters. They had learned, they said, and knew for a fact, that her husband was not a man, but the fearful serpent Apollo's oracle had declared he would be. He was kind now, no doubt, but he would certainly turn upon her some night and devour her.

Psyche, aghast, felt terror flooding her heart instead of love. She had wondered so often why he would never let her see him. There must be some dreadful reason. What did she really know about him? If he was not horrible to look at, then he was cruel to forbid her ever to behold him. In extreme misery, faltering and stammering, she gave her sisters to understand that she could not deny what they said, because she had been with him only in the dark. "There must be something very wrong," she sobbed, "for him so to shun the light of day." And she begged them to advise her.

They had their advice all prepared beforehand. That night she must hide a sharp knife and a lamp near her bed. When her husband was fast asleep she must leave the bed, light the lamp, and get the knife. She must steel herself to plunge it swiftly in the body of the frightful being the light would certainly show her. "We will be near," they said, "and carry you away with us when he is dead."

Then they left her torn by doubt and distracted what to do. She loved him; he was her dear husband. No; he was a horrible serpent and she loathed him. She would kill him — She would not. She must have certainty — She did not want certainty. So all day long her thoughts fought with each other. When evening came, however, she had given the struggle up. One thing she was determined to do: she would see him.

When at last he lay sleeping quietly, she summoned all her courage and lit the lamp. She tiptoed to the bed and holding the light high above her she gazed at what lay there. Oh, the relief and the rapture that filled her heart. No monster was revealed, but the sweetest and fairest of all creatures, at whose sight the very lamp seemed to shine brighter. In her first shame at her folly and lack of faith, Psyche fell on her knees and would have plunged the knife into her own breast if it had not fallen from her trembling hands. But those same unsteady hands that saved her betrayed her, too, for she hung over him, ravished at the sight of him and unable to deny herself the bliss of filling her eyes with his beauty, some hot oil fell from the lamp upon his shoulder. He started awake; he saw the light and knew her faithlessness, and without a word he fled from her.

She rushed out after him into the night. She could not see him, but she heard his voice speaking to her. He told her who he was, and sadly bade her farewell. "Love cannot live where there is no trust," he said, and flew away. "The God of Love!" she thought. "He was my husband, and I, wretch that I am, could not keep faith with him. Is he gone from me forever? . . . At any rate," she told herself with rising courage, "I can spend the rest of my life searching for him. If he has no more love left for me, at least I can show him how much I love him." And she started on her journey. She had no idea where to go; she knew only that she would never give up looking for him.

He meanwhile had gone to his mother's chamber to have his wound cared for, but when Venus heard his story and learned that it was Psyche whom he had chosen, she left him angrily alone in his pain, and went forth to find the girl of whom he had made her still more jealous. Venus was determined to show Psyche what it meant to draw down the displeasure of a goddess.

Poor Psyche in her despairing wanderings was trying to win the gods over to her side. She offered ardent prayers to them perpetually, but not one of them would do anything to make Venus their enemy. At last she perceived that there was no hope for her, either in heaven or on earth, and she took a desperate resolve. She would go straight to Venus; she would offer herself humbly to her as her servant, and try to soften her anger. "And who knows," she thought, "if he himself is not there in his mother's house." So she set forth to find the goddess who was looking everywhere for her.

When she came into Venus' presence the goddess laughed aloud and asked her scornfully if she was seeking a husband since the one she had had would have nothing to do with her because he had almost died of the burning wound she had given him. "But really," she said, "you are so plain and ill-favoured a girl that you will never be able to get you a lover except by the most diligent and painful service. I will therefore show my good will to you by training you in such ways." With that she took a great quantity of the smallest of the seeds, wheat and poppy and millet and so on, and mixed them all together in a heap. "By nightfall these must all be sorted," she said. "See to it for your own sake," And with that she departed.

Psyche, left alone, sat still and stared at the heap. Her mind was all in a maze because of the cruelty of the command; and indeed, it was of no use to start a task so manifestly impossible. But at this direful moment she who had awakened no compassion in mortals or immortals was pitied by the tiniest creatures of the field, the little ants, the swift-runners. They cried to each other, "Come, have mercy on this poor maid and help her diligently." At once they came, waves of them, one after another, and they labored separating and dividing, until what had been a confused mass lay all ordered, every seed with its kind. This was what Venus found when she came back, and very angry she was to see it. "Your work is by no means over," she said. Then she gave Psyche a crust of bread and bade her sleep on the ground while she herself went off to her soft, fragrant couch. Surely if she could keep the girl at hard labor and half starve her, too, that hateful beauty of hers would soon be lost. Until then she must see that her son was securely guarded in his chamber where he was still suffering from his wound. Venus was pleased at the way matters were shaping.

The next morning she devised another task for Psyche, this time a dangerous one. "Down there near the riverbank," she said, "where the bushes grow thick, are sheep with fleeces of gold. Go fetch me some of their shining wool." When the worn girl reached the gently flowing stream, a great longing seized her to throw herself into it and end all her pain and despair. But as she was bending over the water she heard a little voice from near her feet, and looking down saw that it came from a green reed. She must not drown herself, it said. Things were not as bad as that. The sheep were indeed very fierce, but if Psyche would wait until they came out of the bushes toward evening to rest beside the river, she could go into the thicket and find plenty of the golden wool hanging on the sharp briars.

So spoke the kind and gentle reed, and Psyche, following the directions, was able to carry back to her cruel mistress a quantity of the shining fleece. Venus received it with an evil smile. "Someone helped you," she said sharply. "Never did you do this by yourself. However, I will give you an opportunity to prove that you really have the stout heart and the singular prudence you make such a show of. Do you see that black water which falls from the hill yonder? It is the source of the terrible river which is called hateful, the river Styx. You are to fill this flask from it." That was the worst task yet, as Psyche saw when she approached the waterfall. Only a winged creature could reach it, so steep and slimy were the rocks on all sides, and so fearful the on-rush of the descending waters. But by this time it must be evident to all the readers of this story (as, perhaps, deep in her heart it had become evident to Psyche herself) that although each of her trials seemed impossibly hard, an excellent way out would always be provided for her. This time her savior was an eagle, who poised on his great wings beside her, seized the flask from her with his beak and brought it back full of the black water.

But Venus kept on. One cannot but accuse her of some stupidity. The only effect of all that had happened was to make her try again. She gave Psyche a box which she was to carry to the underworld and ask Proserpine to fill with some of her beauty. She was to tell her that Venus really needed it, she was so worn-out from nursing her sick son. Obediently as always Psyche went forth to look for the road to Hades. She found her guide in a tower she passed. It gave her careful directions how to get to Proserpine's palace, first through a great hole in the earth, then down to the river of death, where she must give the ferryman, Charon, a penny to take her across. From there the road led straight to the palace. Cerberus, the three-headed dog, guarded the doors, but if she gave him a cake he would be friendly and let her pass.

All happened, of course, as the tower had foretold. Proserpine was willing to do Venus a service, and Psyche, greatly encouraged, bore back the box, returning far more quickly than she had gone down.

Her next trial she brought upon herself through her curiosity and, still more, her vanity. She felt that she must see what that beauty-charm in the box was; and, perhaps, use a little of it herself. She knew quite as well as Venus did that her looks were not improved by what she had gone through, and always in her mind was the thought that she might suddenly meet Cupid. If only she could make herself more lovely for him! She was unable to resist the temptation; she opened the box. To her sharp disappointment she saw nothing there; it seemed empty. Immediately, however, a deadly languor took possession of her and she fell into a heavy sleep.

At this juncture the God of Love himself stepped forward. Cupid was healed of his wound by now and longing for Psyche. It is a difficult matter to keep Love imprisoned. Venus had locked the door, but there were the windows. All Cupid had to do was to fly out and start looking for his wife. She was lying almost beside the palace, and he found her at once. In a moment he had wiped the sleep from her eyes and put it back into the box. Then waking her with just a prick from one of his arrows, and scolding her a little for her curiosity, he bade her take Proserpine's box to his mother and he assured her that all thereafter would be well.

While the joyful Psyche hastened on her errand, the god flew up to Olympus. He wanted to make certain that Venus would give them no more trouble, so he went straight to Jupiter himself. The Father of Gods and Men consented at once to all that Cupid asked — "Even though," he said, "you have done me great harm in the past — seriously injured my good name and my dignity by making me change myself into a bull and a swan and so on . . . . However, I cannot refuse you."

Then he called a full assembly of the gods, and announced to all, including Venus, that Cupid and Psyche were formally married, and that he proposed to bestow immortality upon the bride. Mercury brought Psyche into the palace of the gods, and Jupiter himself gave her the ambrosia to taste which made her immortal. This, of course, completely changed the situation. Venus could not object to a goddess for her daughter-in-law; the alliance had become eminently suitable. No doubt she reflected also that Psyche, living up in heaven with a husband and children to care for, could not be much on the earth to turn men's heads and interfere with her own worship.

So all came to a most happy end. Love and the Soul (as that is what Psyche means) had sought and, after sore trials, found each other; and that union could never be broken.

"The Death of Baldur," from Heroes of Asgard: Tales from Scandinavian Mythology, *by A. and E. Keary (London: Macmillan, 1930).*

The mortality of the Norse gods is brought tragically home with the death of the beloved Baldur, God of Light and Joy, through the agency of the malicious Loki. The event marks the beginning of the end of their world. Loki's evil is at its fullest in this story; Baldur has done him no ill, but Loki harbors a great hatred for the god's goodness. Baldur's death has been interpreted as symbolizing the end of summer and the arrival of winter in the north. In linking emotions and the external landscape, this myth is not unlike "Demeter and Persephone" and "Beauty and the Beast." The role of Baldur's mother, Frigga, can be compared to the roles of the mothers of Persephone and Cupid.

The Death of Baldur

PART I: THE DREAM

Upon a summer's afternoon it happened that Baldur the Bright and Bold, beloved of men and Æsir, found himself alone in his palace of Broadblink. Thor was walking low down among the valleys, his brow heavy with summer heat; Frey and Gerda sported on still waters in their cloud-leaf ship; Odin, for once, slept on the top of Air Throne; a noon-day stillness pervaded the whole earth; and Baldur in Broadblink, the wide-glancing most sunlit of palaces, dreamed a dream.

Now the dream of Baldur was troubled. He knew not whence nor why; but when he awoke he found that a most new and weighty care was within him. It was so heavy that Baldur could scarcely carry it, and yet he pressed it closely to his heart, and said, "Lie there, and do not fall on any one but me." Then he rose up, and walked out from the expanded splendour of his hall, that he might seek his own mother, Frigga, and tell her what had happened to him. He found her in her crystal saloon, calm and kind, waiting to listen, and ready to sympathise; so he walked up to her, his hands pressed closely on his heart, and lay down at her feet sighing.

"What is the matter, dear Baldur?" asked Frigga, gently.

"I do not know, mother," answered he. "I do not know what the matter is; but I have a shadow in my heart."

"Take it out, then, my son, and let me look at it," replied Frigga.

"But I fear, mother, that if I do it will cover the whole earth.

Then Frigga laid her hand upon the heart of her son that she might feel the shadow's shape. Her brow became clouded as she felt it; her parted lips grew pale, and she cried out, "Oh! Baldur, my beloved son! the shadow is the shadow of death!"

Then said Baldur, "I will die bravely, my mother."

But Frigga answered, "You shall not die at all; for I will not sleep to-night until everything on earth has sworn to me that it will neither kill nor harm you."

So Frigga stood up, and called to her everything on earth that had power to hurt or slay. First she called all metals to her; and heavy iron-ore came lumbering up the hill into the crystal hall, brass and gold, copper, silver, lead, and steel, and stood before the Queen, who lifted her right hand high in the air, saying, "Swear to me that you will not injure Baldur;" and they all swore, and went. Then she called to her all stones; and huge granite came with crumbling sand-stone, and white lime, and the round, smooth stones of the sea-shore, and Frigga raised her arm, saying, "Swear that you will not injure Baldur;" and they swore, and went. Then Frigga called to her the trees; and wide-spreading oak-trees, with tall ash and sombre firs came rushing up the hill, with long branches, from which green leaves like flags were waving, and Frigga raised her hand, and said, "Swear that you will not hurt Baldur;" and they said, "We swear," and went. After this Frigga called to her the diseases, who came blown thitherward by poisonous winds on wings of pain, and to the sound of moaning. Frigga said to them, "Swear:" and they sighed, "We swear," then flew away. Then Frigga called to her all beasts, birds, and venomous snakes, who came to her and swore, and disappeared. After this she stretched out her hand to Baldur, whilst a smile spread over her face, saying, "And now, my son, you cannot die."

But just then Odin came in, and when he had heard from Frigga the whole story, he looked even more mournful than she had done; neither did the cloud pass from his face when he was told of the oaths that had been taken.

"Why do you still look so grave, my lord?" demanded Frigga, at last. "Baldur cannot now die."

But Odin asked very gravely, "Is the shadow gone out of our son's heart, or is it still there?"

"It cannot be there," said Frigga, turning away her head resolutely, and folding her hands before her.

But Odin looked at Baldur, and saw how it was. The hands pressed to the heavy heart, the beautiful brow grown dim. Then immediately he arose, saddled Sleipnir, his eight-footed steed, mounted him, and, turning to Frigga, said, "I know of a dead Vala,* Frigga, who, when she was alive, could tell what was going to happen; her grave lies on the east side of Helheim, and I am going there to awake her, and ask whether any terrible grief is really coming upon us."

So saying Odin shook the bridle in his hand, and the Eight-footed, with a bound, leapt forth, rushed like a whirlwind down the mountain of Asgard, and then dashed into a narrow defile between rocks.

Sleipnir went on through the defile a long way, until he came to a place where the earth opened her mouth. There Odin rode in and down a broad, steep, slanting road which led

him to the cavern Gnipa, and the mouth of the cavern Gnipa yawned upon Niflheim. Then thought Odin to himself, "My journey is already done." But just as Sleipnir was about to leap through the jaws of the pit, Garm, the voracious dog who was chained to the rock, sprang forward, and tried to fasten himself upon Odin. Three times Odin shook him off, and still Garm, as fierce as ever, went on with the fight. At last Sleipnir leapt, and Odin thrust just at the same moment; then horse and rider cleared the entrance, and turned eastward toward the dead Vala's grave, dripping blood along the road as they went; while the beaten Garm stood baying in the cavern's mouth.

When Odin came to the grave he got off his horse, and stood with his face northwards looking through barred enclosures into the city of Helheim itself. The servants of Hela were very busy there making preparations for some new guest — hanging gilded couches with curtains of anguish and splendid misery upon the walls. Then Odin's heart died within him and he began to repeat mournful runes in a low tone to himself.

The dead Vala turned heavily in her grave at the sound of his voice, and, as he went on, sat bolt upright. "What man is this," she asked, "who dares disturb my sleep?"

Then Odin, for the first time in his life, said what was not true; the shadow of Baldur dead fell upon his lips, and he made answer, "My name is Vegtam, the son of Valtam."

"And what do you want from me?" asked the Vala.

"I want to know," replied Odin, "for whom Hela is making ready that gilded couch in Helheim?"

"That is for Baldur the Beloved," answered the dead Vala. "Now go away, and let me sleep again, for my eyes are heavy."

But Odin said, "Only one word more. Is Baldur going to Helheim?"

"Yes, I've told you that he is," answered the Vala.

"Will he never come back to Asgard again?"

"If everything on earth should weep for him," answered she, "he will go back; if not, he will remain in Helheim."

*Vala — a prophetess.

Then Odin covered his face with his hands, and looked into darkness.

"Do go away," said the Vala, "I'm so sleepy; I cannot keep my eyes open any longer."

But Odin raised his head, and said again, "Only tell me this one thing. Just now, as I looked into darkness, it seemed to me as if I saw one on earth who would not weep for Baldur. Who was it?"

At this the Vala grew very angry and said, "How couldst *thou* see in darkness? I know of only one who, by giving away his eye, gained light. No Vegtam art thou, but Odin, chief of men."

At her angry words Odin became angry too, and called out as loudly as ever he could, "No Vala art thou, nor wise woman, but rather the mother of three giants."

"Go, go!" answered the Vala, falling back in her grave; "no man shall waken me again until Loki have burst his chains and Ragnarök be come." After this Odin mounted the Eight-footed once more, and rode thoughtfully towards home.

"The Death of Baldur" from *Heroes of Asgard: Tales From Scandinavian Mythology* by A. and E. Keary. Copyright © 1930. Reprinted by permission of Macmillan Publishers, London.

PART II: THE PEACESTEAD

When Odin came back to Asgard, Hermod took the bridle from his father's hand, and told him that the rest of the Æsir were gone to the Peacestead — a broad, green plain which lay just outside the city. Now this was, in fact, the playground of the Æsir, where they practised trials of skill one with another, and held tournaments and sham fights. These last were always conducted in the gentlest and most honourable manner; for the strongest law of the Peacestead was, that no angry blow should be struck, or spiteful word spoken, upon the sacred field, and for this reason some have thought it might be well if children also had a Peacestead to play in.

Odin was too much tired by his journey from Helheim to to to the Peacestead that afternoon; so he turned away, and shut himself up in his palace of Gladsheim. But when he was gone, Loki came into the city by another way, and hearing from Hermod where the Æsir were, set off to join them.

When he got to the Peacestead, Loki found that the Æsir were standing round in a circle shooting at something, and he peeped between the shoulders of two of them to find out what it was. To his surprise he saw Baldur standing in the midst, erect and calm, whilst his friends and brothers were aiming their weapons at him. Some hewed at him with their swords — others threw stones at him — some shot arrows pointed with steel, and Thor continually swung Miölnir at his head. "Well," said Loki to himself, "if this is the sport of Asgard, what must that of Jötunheim be? I wonder what Father Odin and Mother Frigga would say if they were here?" But as Loki still looked, he became even more surprised, for the sport went on, and Baldur was not hurt. Arrows aimed at his very heart glanced back again untinged with blood. The stones fell down from his broad bright brow, and left no buries there. Swords clave, but did not wound him; Miölnir struck him, and he was not crushed. At this Loki grew perfectly furious with envy and hatred. "And why is Baldur to be so honoured," said he, "that even steel and stone shall not hurt him?" Then Loki changed himself into a little, dark, bent, old woman, with a stick in his hand, and hobbled away from the Peacestead to Frigga's cool saloon. At the door he knocked with his stick.

"Come in!" said the kind voice of Frigga, and Loki lifted the latch.

Now when Frigga saw, from the other end of the hall, a little, bent crippled, old woman, come hobbling up her crystal floor, she got up with true queenliness, and met her half way, holding out her hand, and saying in the kindest manner, "Pray sit down, my poor old friend; for it seems to me that you have come from a great way off."

"That I have, indeed," answered Loki in a tremulous, squeaking voice.

"And did you happen to see anything of the Æsir," asked Frigga, "as you came?"

"Just now I passed by the Peacestead, and saw them at play."

"What were they doing?"

"Shooting at Baldur."

Then Frigga bent over her work with a pleased smile on her face. "And nothing hurt him?" she said.

"Nothing," answered Loki, looking keenly at her.

"No, nothing," murmured Frigga, still looking down and speaking half musingly to herself; "for all things have sworn to me that they will not."

"Sworn!" exclaimed Loki, eagerly; "what is that you say? Has everything sworn then?"

"Everything," answered she, "excepting, indeed, the little shrub mistletoe, which grows, you know, on the west side of Valhalla, and to which I said nothing, because I thought it was too young to swear."

"Excellent!" thought Loki; and then he got up.

"You're not going yet, are you?" said Frigga, stretching out her hand and looking up at last into the eyes of the old woman.

"I'm quite rested now, thank you," answered Loki in his squeaky voice, and then he hobbled out at the door, which clapped after him, and sent a cold gust into the room. Frigga shuddered, and thought that a serpent was gliding down the back of her neck.

When Loki had left the presence of Frigga, he changed himself back to his proper shape, and went straight to the west side of Valhalla, where the mistletoe grew. Then he opened his knife, and cut off a large branch, saying these words, "Too young for Frigga's oaths, but not too weak for Loki's work." After which he set off for the Peacestead once more, the mistletoe in his hand. When he got there he found that the Æsir were still at their sport, standing round, taking aim, and talking eagerly, and Baldur did not seem tired.

But there was one who stood alone, leaning against a tree, and who took no part in what was going on. This was Hödur, Baldur's blind twin-brother; he stood with his head bent downwards, silent, whilst the others were speaking, doing nothing when they were most eager; and Loki thought that there was a discontented expression on his face, just as if he were saying to himself, "Nobody takes any notice of me," So Loki went up to him, and put his hand upon his shoulder.

"And why are you standing here all alone, my brave friend?" said he. "Why don't *you* throw something at Baldur? Hew at him with a sword, or show him some attention of that sort."

"I haven't got a sword," answered Hödur, with an impatient gesture; "and you know as well as I do, Loki, that Father Odin does not approve of my wearing warlike weapons, or joining in sham fights, because I am blind."

"Oh! is that it?" said Loki. "Well, I only know I shouldn't like to be left out of everything. However, I've got a twig of mistletoe here which I'll lend you if you like; a harmless little twig enough, but I shall be happy to guide your arm if you would like to throw it, and Baldur might take it as a compliment from his twin-brother."

"Let me feel it," said Hödur, stretching out his uncertain hands.

"This way, this way, my dear friend," said Loki, giving him the twig. "Now, as hard as ever you can, to do *him honour*; throw!"

Hödur threw — Baldur fell, and the shadow of death covered the whole earth.

PART III: BALDUR DEAD
One after another they turned and left the Peacestead, those friends and brothers of the slain. One after another they turned and went towards the city; crushed hearts, heavy footsteps, no word amongst them, a shadow upon all. The shadow was in Asgard too, — had walked through Frigga's hall, and seated itself upon the threshold of Gladsheim. Odin had just come out to look at it, and Frigga stood by in mute despair as the Æsir came up.

"Loki did it! Loki did it!" they said at last in confused, hoarse whispers, and they looked from one to another, upon Odin, upon Frigga, upon the shadow which they saw before them, and which they felt within. "Loki did it! Loki, Loki!" they went on saying; but it was no use repeating the name of Loki over and over again when there was another name they were too sad to utter which yet filled all their hearts — Baldur. Frigga said it first, and then they all went to look at him lying down so peacefully on the grass — dead, dead.

"Carry him to the funeral pyre!" said Odin, at length; and four of the the Æsir stooped

down, and lifted their dead brother.

With scarcely any sound they carried the body tenderly to the sea-shore, and laid it upon the deck of that majestic ship called Ringhorn, which had been *his*. Then they stood round waiting to see who would come to the funeral. Odin came, and on his shoulders sat his two ravens, whose croaking drew clouds down over the Asa's face, for Thought and Memory sang one sad song that day. Frigga came, — Frey, Gerda, Freyja, Thor, Hœnier, Bragi and Idūna Heimdall came sweeping over the tops of the mountains on Golden Mane, his swift, bright steed. Ægir the Old groaned from under the deep, and sent his daughters up to mourn around the dead. Frost-giants and mountain-giants came crowding round the rimy shores of Jötunheim to look across the sea upon the funeral of an Asa. Nanna came, Baldur's fair young wife; but when she saw the dead body of her husband her own heart broke with grief, and the Æsir laid her beside him on the stately ship. After this Odin stepped forward, and placed a ring on the breast of his son, whispering something at the same time in his ear; but when he and the rest of the Æsir tried to push Ringhorn into the sea before setting fire to it, they found that their hearts were so heavy they could lift nothing. So they beckoned to the giantness Hyrrokin to come over from Jötunheim and help them. She, with a single push, set the ship floating, and then, whilst Thor stood up holding Miölnir high in the air, Odin lighted the funeral pile of Baldur and of Nanna.

So Ringhorn went out floating towards the deep, and the funeral fire burnt on. Its broad red flame burst forth towards heaven; but when the smoke would have gone upward too, the winds came sobbing and carried it away.

Myths for Further Reading

COLLECTIONS:
Beginnings: Creation Myths of the World, comp. by Penelope Farmer, ill, by Antonio Frasconi (New York: Atheneum, 1979).

— in addition to creation myths, this volume also includes a section entitled "The End of the World," and over eighty selections, ranging from a paragraph to several pages.

Book of Greek Myths, by Ingri and Edgar Parin d'Aulaire (Garden City, N.Y.: Doubleday, 1962).
— not as successful as their companion collection of Norse myths. This book nonetheless captures, in words and pictures, the flavor of ancient Greek culture.

A Book of Myths, by Roger Lancelyn Green. Ill. by Joan Kiddell-Monroe (London: J.M. Dent, 1965).

— Greek, Roman, Norse, and Mideastern myths are retold by a well-known British editor/adaptor.

City of Gold and Other Stories from the Old Testament, by Peter Dickinson. Ill. by Michael Foreman (London: Victor Gollancz, 1980).
— an award-winning British novelist retells the Bible stories as he imagines they might have been orally delivered in a time before they were written down.

The Earth Is on a Fish's Back: Tales of Beginnings, by Natalia Belting. Ill. by Esta Nesbitt (New York: Holt, Rinehart, and Winston, 1965).
— twenty-one pourquoi and creation myths. Each is short and includes a great deal of dialogue.

The Four Ages of Man: the Classical Myths, by Jay Macpherson (Toronto: Macmillan, 1962).
— the author notes that the stories "are told in a sequence which, though not strictly historical, has some analogy to history." There are useful appendices of family trees, a mythology-history chart, and a full index of mythological characters.

Gods and Men: Myths and Legends from the World's Religions, by John Bailey, Kenneth McLeish, and David Spearman. Ill. by Derek Collard, Charles Keeping, and Jerod Roy (Oxford: Oxford University Press, 1981).
— thirty stories from around the world gathered under the headings "Creation Myths," "Good and Evil," and "Heroes and Prophets."

Greek Myths, by Olivia Coolidge. Ill. by Edouard Sandoz (Boston: Houghton, Mifflin, 1949).
— a fairly simple retelling of the major myths. Coolidge seems to like these because "they are good stories" and tends to omit the religious qualities of the originals.

Hawaiian Myths of Earth, Sea, and Sky, by Vivian L. Thompson. Ill. by Leonard Weisgard (New York: Holiday House, 1966).
— twelve myths, including the Creation, and several pourquoi and trickster stories.

The Hungry Woman: Myths and Legends of the Aztecs, edited by John Bierhorst (New York: William Morrow, 1984).
— creation myths, stories of Montezuma, and myths introduced after the coming of Cortez are illustrated by sixteenth-century Aztec artists.

Myths of Ancient Greece, by Robert Graves. Ill. by Joan Kiddell-Monroe (London: Cassell, 1960).
— a well-known British poet retells the ancient myths, revealing the imperfections of the Gods. It concludes, interestingly enough, with a chapter entitled "The End of the Olympians." With the coming of Christianity, "the Olympians were forced to hide in woods and caves, and have not been seen for centuries."

Norse Gods and Giants, by Ingri and Edgar Parin d'Aulaire (Garden City, N.Y.: Doubleday, 1967).
— a highly readable account of Norse mythology with full-color illustrations which capture the rough and robust quality of the myths.

The Other World: Myths of the Celts, by Margaret Hodges. Ill. by Eros Keith (New York: Farrar, Straus, and Giroux, 1973).
— ten stories, chosen because they release "in the listener or the reader a sense of strength and of joy that overrides sorrow."

Tales of the Norse Gods and Heroes, by Barbara Leonie Picard. Ill. by Joan Kiddell-Monroe (London: Oxford University Press, 1953).
— the main myths and legends, vigorously retold.

A Wonder-Book for Girls and Boys and Tanglewood Tales, by Nathaniel Hawthorne (Garden City, N.Y.: Doubleday, n.d.).
— although the style may be old fashioned for modern readers, Hawthorne's nineteenth-century retellings of Greek myths and legends were among the first adapted for children.

RETELLINGS OF INDIVIDUAL MYTHS:
Titles marked with an asterisk (*) indicate alternate versions to those included in this anthology.

Apollo, by Katherine Miller. Ill. by Vivian Berger (Boston: Houghton, Mifflin, 1970).
— the "biography" of the Sun God is interspersed with background information about the "history" of the Greek Gods. An easily read adaptation.

Balder and the Mistletoe, a Story for the Winter Holidays, by Edna Barth. Ill. by Richard Cuffari (New York: Seabury, 1979).*
— although the text is true to the Old Icelandic sagas, the illustrations tend to create too gentle a mood.

The Christ Child, by Maud and Miska Petersham (Garden City, N.Y.: Doubleday, 1931).
— Biblical style and stone lithography illustrations capture the tenderness and dignity of the Christmas story.

Cupid and Psyche, by Walter Pater. Ill. by Errol LeCain (London: Faber and Faber, 1977).
— Pater's adaptation and LeCain's illustrations embody the elegance of the Aesthetic period.*

Daughter of the Earth: a Roman Myth, retold and ill. by Gerald McDermott (New York: Delacorte, 1984).
— in his illustrations, McDermott emphasizes the darker, tempestuous emotions of the story of Ceres and Proserpina (Demeter and Persephone).*

The Hammer of Thunder, by Ann Pyk. Ill by Jan Pyk (New York: G.P. Putnam's, 1972).
— the story of the theft of Thor's hammer is debased by the banality of the language and the exaggerated cartoon-like quality of the illustrations.

Jonah and the Great Fish, retold and ill. by Warwick Hutton (New York: Atheneum, 1983).
— the illustrations emphasize the smallness of Jonah in contrast to the forces of nature and God.

Lord of the Sky: Zeus, by Doris Gates. Ill. by Robert Handville (New York: Viking, 1972).
— the first of six volumes retelling the Greek myths and legends. Retold in a slightly simplified style, the stories capture both specific cultural aspects of Ancient Greece and universal human emotions. Others in the series are *The Warrior Goddess* (1972), *The Golden God: Apollo* (1973), *Two Queens of Heaven: Aphrodite, Demeter* (1974), *The Mightiest of Mortals: Heracles* (1975), and *A Fair Wind for Troy* (1976).

Noah's Ark. Ill. by Peter Spier (Garden City, N.Y.: Doubleday, 1977).
— using a seventeenth-century Dutch poem as his starting point, Spier mixes both humor and reverence in his illustrations.*

Pegasus, by Krystyna Turska (London: Hamish Hamilton, 1970).
— the story of Bellerophon and his winged steed is retold in a simple, yet stately style. Turska's full-color illustrations add to the majesty of the story.

Sedna: an Eskimo Myth, adapted and ill. by Beverly Brodsky McDermott (New York: Viking, 1975).
— using elements of Eskimo design and only two colors in the illustrations, McDermott communicates the harshness and violence of this myth.*

The Serpent's Teeth: the Story of Cadmus, by Penelope Farmer. Ill. by Chris Connor (London: William Collins, 1971).
— Cadmus' many adventures, climaxed by his slaying of a three-headed serpent, are vividly recreated in words and pictures.

Spirit Child: a Story of the Nativity, trans. by John Bierhorst. Ill. by Barbara Cooney (New York: William Morrow, 1984).
— in his translation, Bierhorst captures characteristics of Aztec storytelling. Cooney's illustrations embody both Aztec culture and the universal spiritual meanings of the story.

Sun Flight, by Gerald McDermott (New York: Four Winds, 1980).
— the intense emotions of the tragic story of Daedalus and his son Icarus are conveyed by the vivid illustrations.

The Voyage of Osiris: a Myth of Ancient Egypt, retold and ill. by Gerald McDermott (New York: E.P. Dutton, 1977).
— the death and rebirth of this savior god are retold in the style of ancient Egyptian prayers and illustrated with Egyptian motifs that reinforce the story's symbolic meaning.

Literary Folktales

Literary Folktales

An Introduction

In some important respects folktales become literature once they are transmitted in writing. The folktale, like other types of folklore, is an oral phenomenon. Hence its formulaic qualities, its repetitious phrases, and its structural patterns result from its origins in oral, rather than written, culture. Today most folklorists insist that to retain the purity of the folktale, it must be recorded from an oral telling, as the manner of the storyteller is essential to the tale's meaning and significance. In his recently published book, *One Fairy Tale Too Many*, John Ellis has stressed that Jakob and Wilhelm Grimm modified their tales significantly from the oral versions they supposedly recorded from folk storytellers. Other scholars also insist that the folktale rarely exists in a pure form. Translators, editors, and persons retelling tales inevitably modify details, introduce differences in tone, and vary shades of meaning according to their own cultural values and those of their audiences.

Despite such qualifications, one can make some distinctions between the folktale and the literary folktale. First, the author of the folktale is anonymous. We may know who first wrote the tale. We may even know a storyteller who told the tale upon a specific occasion, but we do not know who first told the story or who first created it. The folktale is a product of the collective imagination of folk culture. On the other hand the literary folktale, though modeled on the folktale, is written by a specific author in a particular social and historical context. The literary folktale will not only resemble the folktale in its structure, themes, and motifs, it will also share qualities of literature written in the same period. Thus while the literary folktale may use such formulaic phrases as "Once upon a time..." and "...happily ever after," it will also employ more complex figures of speech, more elaborate imagery, and a more sophisticated presentation of character, setting, and plot. The literary folktale is more likely to particularize physical scenes and depict the psychological states of characters in more depth and detail than the folktale.

In distinguishing between the traditional folktale and the literary folktale, C.N. Manlove has written that in the more recently told stories written by specific authors, there "is the sense of a mind creating, separate from the material."[1] Manlove qualifies this statement, however, noting that the nineteenth-century writer of literary folktales, George MacDonald, attempts "to remove all his consciousness and become wholly one with his material in a kind of mystical self-surrender."[2] MacDonald's need to diminish the distance between himself and his material, however, is an important indication of a crucial difference between the oral folktale and the written literary folktale. The folktale is passed on from a largely unself-conscious imagination. The literary folktale is the product of the conscious artistry of the writer.

One of the most interesting and potent controversies in nineteenth-century British children's literature centered upon the so-called "battle of the fairy tale." This struggle between those who advocated folktales as suitable for children and those who bitterly opposed them had begun, according to historians of children's literature, centuries earlier. A resurgence of this hostility toward folktales and their "literary" offspring occurred as recently as the 1960s, when some overly zealous parents and educators carried their ideas on non-violence into the realm of children's book selection. Controversy about the violence and implicit sexism of folktales continues today.

In England as early as the Middle Ages, fairies were associated with the powers of darkness and evil. This identification of fairyland with the realm of darkness no doubt accounts in part for the failure of the native tradition of British folktales to flourish in England. Harvey Darton has written that the folktale had appeared "but scrappily between the covers of printed books before 1744 and for a long while afterwards."[3] Both Hobbes and Locke, eighteenth-century British philosophers, had attacked the fairy tale as unsuitable reading for children. Later in the eighteenth century, children's writers Sarah Fielding and Maria Edgeworth reinforced this negative view of fairy tales. Also the first notable publisher of children's books in England, John Newbery, had shown little interest in such tales, probably because they were considered merely vulgar tales of peasants and unworthy of middle-class attention. Hobbes, Locke, Fielding, and Edgeworth disapproved of the tales because they told "lies" and violated reason in depicting supernatural and fantastic events. Early in nineteenth-century England, Mrs. Sarah Trimmer re-ignited the controversy with her 1803 review of Charles Perrault's "Cinderella." Eventually, however, some of the most prestigious names in nineteenth-century English literature were to defend the fairy tale and to write fairy tales themselves: Charles Lamb, Charles Dickens, and John Ruskin. The controversy continued and continues today. However, by the end of the nine-teenth century, Andrew Lang was able finally to make the fairy tale an acceptable middle-class form of reading with the publication of his popular rainbow of fairy books.

It would be a mistake, however, to assume that children did not read or hear fairy tales during this period. Such English tales were told by generations of servants and nurses and were available in vulgar chapbooks and cheap reprints. Unlike the tradition of fairy tales in France, which had been adapted by the eighteenth-century courtier, Charles Perrault, and written by such courtly ladies as Marie Catherine La Mothe, Countess D'Aulnoy, and Jeanne le Prince de Beaumont, native English folktales enjoyed no such aristocratic patronage. Therefore, they had no substantial literary status and did not exercise a signifi-cant influence on writers of children's books until much later in the nineteenth century. Instead, literary folktales entered the world of children's literature in Britain from France, with the support of such fashionable names as Perrault, Mme. D'Aulnoy, and Mme. le Prince de Beaumont.

Charles Perrault's fairy tales, as we have noted in a previous section, were first published in England in 1719. In the same period Countess D'Aulnoy wrote a collection of tales; they were translated into English and published under the title *Diverting Works* in 1707. This volume included such favorites as "The Yellow Dwarf," "Goldylocks," and "The White Cat." Jeanne le Prince de Beaumont, whose collection of stories included the famous "Beauty and the Beast," also influenced the tradition of literary folktales in England. (While the term "fairy tale" is generally not accepted by folklorists, it was the term used at that time to describe such stories, whether actual fairies were present in the tale or not.)

In the French tradition of *contes*, which was itself influenced by the much earlier courtly Italian *favole*, the teller of the tale comes across as urbane, witty, and sophisticated. The teller assumes a slight superiority to the tale being narrated. In his essay on fairy stories, J.R.R. Tolkien was to criticize this self-consciousness on the part of the narrator, accusing Andrew Lang, for example, of "sniggering over the heads of children," to appeal to the adult reader in his *The Chronicles of Pantouflia*. This tradition of literary folktale, which may be called the "fairy-court tradition," was practiced by several mid-nineteenth-century writers for children in England: F.E. Paget, *The Hope of the Katzekopfs*, (1844); Thomas Hood, *Petsetilla's Posy* (1871); William Makepeace Thackeray, *The Rose and the Ring*, (1854); Charles Dickens, *The Magic Fishbone*, (1868); Andrew Lang, *The Chronicles of Pantouflia*, (1889 and 1891); and George MacDonald, *The Light*

Princess, (1868). This tradition makes extensive use of the conventions of folktales and often burlesques these conventions for humorous purposes. Edwardian children's writer, E. Nesbit, was also to write in this tradition. She used the fairy court tradition to present new and vital images of female identity in such literary folktales as "The Island of Nine Whirl Pools" (1899). She also called into question some of the conventions such tales help to perpetuate, such as the proper role for princesses. Today such writers as Tanith Lee, Judith Viorst, and others continue the practice of writing "feminist fairy tales." Two such tales are represented in this anthology: John Gardner's "Gudgekin the Thistle Girl" and Jay Williams' "The Practical Princess."

English writers of literary folktales owe a double debt to Germany. First and most important, or course, was the work of German philologists, Jakob and Wilhelm Grimm (see introduction to the section on folktales). Also in Germany in the late eighteenth and early nineteenth centuries, there arose to prominence the literary folktale or *Künstmarchen*. The history of the German "Romantic fairy tale" begins with Wackenroder's work, *Outpourings of the Heart of an Art-loving Monastic* in 1797. For such German Romantics as Wackenroder, Novalis, Tieck, Brentano, and Hoffman, the form was ideal for expressing a mystical spirituality in revolt against an unromantic age. While the Romantic fairy tale was populated with the kings, princesses, witches, and dangerous adventures of the folktale, its form was more complex and its tone more serious. These German Romantic stories were not published for children, though children have enjoyed such stories as Hoffman's "The Nutcracker." Although the Romantic literary fairy tales of these German writers were not as well-known as the folktales of the Brothers Grimm, an important British children's writer, George MacDonald, was directly influenced by these German stories. Thus, the German Romantic literary folktale helped to establish an important precedent for subsequent writers by evaluating and extending the artistic and spiritual potential of literary folktales.[4]

After the translation into English in 1823, and subsequent popularity of the Grimms' folktales, British writers of moral tales apparently recognized the powerful effect of such tales on the minds and imaginations of the young. As early as the 1830s and 1840s and as late as the 1890s, moralists employed the conventions of folktales to teach moral lessons. Apparently influenced by the medieval *exemplum* (later the moral tale for children) and the eighteenth-century Gothic romance, these didactic literary folktales generally feature a superficial use of folktale conventions, convey moral lessons explicitly, and employ terrifying effects to frighten children. While many of these didactic fairy tales exhibit little literary value, they reveal an important transition between the predominance of the moral tale, with its narrowly focused didacticism, and more complex forms of children's literature, whose lessons are woven more skillfully and subtly into the texture of the story and whose design upon the reader is not so explicit.

Most of the earliest English literary folktales written for children from 1840 until 1850 were concerned with diagnosing, treating, and curing the moral ailments of children, as were writers of explicitly moral and matter-of-fact tales. Such literary folktales as Catherine Sinclair's "Uncle David's Story about Giants and Fairies," an interpolated tale in Catherine Sinclair's realistic novel *Holiday House* (1839), Francis Edward Paget's *The Hope of the Katzekopfs* (1844), Mark Lemon's *The Enchanted Doll* (1849), Christina Rossetti's *Speaking Likenesses* (1873), George MacDonald's *The Wise Woman* (1875), and Lucy Clifford's *The New Mother*, all employed the structural patterns of folktales to teach moral lessons through sometimes riveting and terrifying scenes.

While many of these writers consciously espoused the imagination and championed its function in the lives of children and their literature, none of these writers sustained a commitment to the pleasure of fantasy all the way through the story. In Paget's *The Hope of the Katzekopfs*, for example, the first half of the story is lively and humorous. This spirited story becomes at last only a dreary and preachy moral lesson. These didactic fairy tales thus reflect a split in the creative purposes of these writers between their avowed attitudes toward children and the imagination on one hand and their practices on the other, a division often manifested in the split structures of the stories themselves.

Much more important than either the French or German influences on writers of literary folktales, however, was the Danish writer of classic fairy tales for children, Hans Christian Andersen. Harvey Darton wrote that the literary folktale and fantasy for children emerged triumphantly with the publication of Andersen's *Wonderful Stories for Children* (1846). Andersen blended elements of folklore and fantasy to present a variety of moods and themes. Some of his tales appeal to the child's sense of humor; some satirize the pretentions of human folly and pride; others, such as "The Snow Queen" and "The Little Match Girl" present Romantic idealizations of the child, who redeems or transcends a sadly fallen and imperfect world.

The work of the Romantic poets William Blake, William Wordsworth, and Samuel Taylor Coleridge were also to exert a powerful impact upon writers of literary fairy tales. In endorsing the importance of the imagination and in presenting revolutionary images of the child, the Romantics encouraged the writing of imaginative literature for children, of which the literary fairy tale was one of the most important forms. The influence of Hans Christian Andersen, the English Romantic poets, along with the influence of the less well-known German writers of *Künstamarchen*, helped to establish the tradition which we may call the Romantic literary folktale. These tales reveal a Romantic idealization of the child as an agent capable of redeeming a fallen adult world. This tradition inspired dozens of literary fairy tales in nineteenth-century Britain: John Ruskin's *The King of the Golden River* (1869); George MacDonald's literary fairy tales for children, as well as his longer fantasies, *The Princess and the Goblin* and *The Princess and Curdie*; Jean Ingelow's *Mopsa the Fairy* (1869); Dinah Mulock's *The Little Lame Prince*; Mrs. Molesworth's fantasies for children, among many others.

In late nineteenth-century England, the Romantic fairy tale, like other expressions of Romanticism, became excessively precious. These tales, perhaps in response to the excessively materialistic values of an industrial society, expressed a longing for the transcendent world of the marvelous and often depicted escape into a spiritual world. Oscar Wilde's *The Happy Prince and Other Tales* (1888) and *A House of Pomegranates* (1891) and Laurence Housman's several volumes of ornate fairy tales are characteristic examples of these excessively ornate literary folktales. Because of their elaborate language and their consciously aesthetic themes, most of Wilde's stories are unsuitable for child readers. Two, however, ''The Happy Prince'' and ''The Selfish Giant,'' remain popular with children. Most contemporary writers of literary fairy tales do not write in this ''Romantic'' mode, although American children's writer Jane Yolen clearly belongs in the tradition of Andersen, Ruskin, MacDonald, and Wilde.

In classifying folktales in Section One, the concept of linear and circular journeys is used to describe their structures. In some respects these basic structural patterns resemble those of the romantic comedy and the romance in literature. It is also noticed that some folktales reversed these patterns to achieve ironic or comic effects.

In this chapter the literary folktale has been classified as ''the didactic literary folktale,'' the ''French-Court tradition,'' and the ''Romantic literary folktale,'' in order to show connections with literary history. It is also possible, however, to classify literary folktales according to the linear and circular journeys. Finally, it is believed that any system of classification, though useful as a conceptual framework, is somewhat reductive and that the tales themselves will offer rich dimensions for discussion and enjoyment not encompassed by any system of classification. However, in studying the literary fairy tales, students may acquire an enlarged and enriched sense of the linear and circular journeys in literature.

These journeys, as we have noted, may be allegorical or symbolic, as well as literal. Several of the following stories may be viewed as symbolic linear journeys in which characters progress toward maturity or spiritual transcendence. Hans Christian Andersen's "Inchelina" undergoes severe trials of physical endurance and moral character, all of which she passes triumphantly. In "The Ugly Duckling," Andersen stresses the transformation of the homely fowl into the lovely swan — its linear progress from an outcast and alienated state to one of integration and belonging in a community. "The Little Match Girl" features the poor child's sufferings in an uncaring society and her spiritual transcendence of pain and hunger in the end. In John Gardner's "Gudgekin the Thistle Girl" and Jay Williams' "The Practical Princess," the characters' "linear" journeys assume a larger significance, since the princesses ascend from a state of passive acceptance of their roles to one of active initiative in pursuing their own identities.

Circular journeys also feature prominently among the following selections. Mme. La Comtesse D'Aulnoy's tale, "The White Cat," depicts the youngest son's embarking upon a quest, and, with the help of the charming white cat, returning home in the end to assume his rightful place in the kingdom. While the circular journey in this tale closely resembles those of traditional folktales, the details of the story are intricately complex; also, the female white cat seems to be the true protagonist of the story. Lucy Clifford's haunting and terrifying tale, "The New Mother," reverses the reader's expectations rather dramatically. The children encounter strange new characters when they leave home, but ultimately they do not grow or change. Rather they are locked out of home and locked into an endless cycle of regret. The circular journey in this strange story, then, may be seen as essentially tragic. The children lose paradise, and it is not to be regained. Christina Rossetti's famous fairy tale in verse, "Goblin Market," features the journeys of two sisters; one leads to destruction and annihilation of the self, while the other results in life and independence for both girls.

Thus, as the reader examines structural patterns and archetypal characters in more sophisticated literary fairy tales and other works for children, these patterns will assume much more sophisticated and subtle dimensions. "Journeys" become internalized as characters make the most perilous trip of all — the inward journey of self-discovery.

Notes

1 C.N. Manlove, *The Impulse of Fantasy Literature* (Kent, Ohio: The Kent State University Press, 1983), p. 14.

2 *Ibid.*

3 F.J. Harvey Darton, *Children's Books in England: Five Centuries of Social Life* (Rpt. Cambridge: Cambridge University Press, 1970), p. 85.

4 For a thorough account of the Romantic fairy tale in early nineteenth-century Germany, see Marianne Thalmann, *The Romantic Fairy Tale*, Trans. by Mary B. Corcoran (Ann Arbor: University of Michigan Press, 1964).

Didactic Literary Folktales

"Granny's Wonderful Chair," from Granny's Wonderful Chair and Its Tales of Fairy Times, *by Frances Browne. (New York: E.P. Dutton and Company, Inc., 1916).*

Frances Browne, a popular poet of the nineteenth century, was blind from birth and wrote perhaps the best of the didactic literary folktales. The most popular of her collection of literary folk tales was Granny's Wonderful Chair, *written in 1856. Although the work was well-received at the time of publication, it unaccountably went out of print and was not reprinted until 1880. In 1887, Frances Hodgson Burnett, author of such major children's classics as* The Secret Garden, *published it with a preface, calling it "Stories from the Lost Fairy Book."*

This charming work centers upon the adventures of a lovely girl called Snowflower, who lives in a cottage in the forest with her grandmother, Dame Frostyface. Once, Dame Frostyface has to leave her grandchild for a time. She gives the girl instructions about housekeeping and also reveals the secret of her wonderful chair: "As you have been a good girl, I'll tell you what to do when you feel lonely. Lay your head gently down on the cushion of the arm chair, and say, 'Chair of my Grandmother, tell me a story.' It was made by a cunning fairy, who lived in the forest when I was young, and she gave it to me be-cause she knew nobody could keep what they got hold of better. Remember, you must never ask a story more than once a day; and if there should be any occasion to travel, you have only to seat yourself in it and say, 'Chair of my Grandmother, take me such a way'. It will carry you to wherever you wish."

The chair eventually takes Snowflower to the Court of King Winwealth. For quite a long time, Granny's Wonderful chair entertains the court with stories. The last tale in the collection, "Prince Wisewit's Return," presents moral lessons as well as exhibiting such typical folk motifs as the breaking of an evil magical spell. While the tale is didactic, Frances Browne breaks out of the narrow preachment characteristic of most didactic fairy tales. The capacity of the chair to entertain the court and to prolong Snowflower's life reminds the reader of Scheherazade's ability to tell tales and to prolong her life in The Arabian Nights.

Granny's Wonderful Chair

PRINCE WISEWIT'S RETURN

Snowflower was delighted at the promise of feasting with those noble lords and ladies, whose wonderful stories she had heard from the chair. Her courtesy was twice as low as usual, and she thanked King Winwealth from the bottom of her heart. All the company were glad to make room for her, and when her golden girdle was put on, little Snowflower looked as fine as the best of them.

"Mamma," whispered the Princess Greedalind, while she looked ready to cry for spite, "only see that low little girl who came here in a coarse frock and barefooted, what finery and favour she has gained by her story-telling chair! All the court are praising her and overlooking me, though the feast was made in honour of my birthday. Mamma, I must have that chair from her. What business has a common little girl with anything so amusing?"

"So you shall, my daughter," said Queen Wantall — for by this time she saw that King Winwealth had, according to custom, fallen asleep on his throne. So calling two of her pages, Screw and Hardhands, she ordered them to bring the chair from the other end of the hall where Snowflower sat, and directly made it a present to Princess Greedalind.

Nobody in that court ever thought of disputing Queen Wantall's commands, and poor Snowflower sat down to cry in a corner; while Princess Greedalind, putting on what she thought a very grand air, laid down her head on the cushion, saying:

"Chair of my grandmother, tell me a story."

"Where did you get a grandmother?" cried the clear voice from under the cushion; and up went the chair with such force as to throw Princess Greedalind off on the floor, where she lay screaming, a good deal more angry than hurt.

All the courtiers tried in vain to comfort her. But Queen Wantall, whose temper was still worse, vowed that she would punish the impudent thing, and sent for Sturdy, her chief woodman, to chop it up with his axe.

At the first stroke the cushion was cut open, and, to the astonishment of everybody, a bird, whose snow-white feathers were tipped with purple, darted out and flew away through an open window.

"Catch it! catch it!" cried the queen and the princess; and all but King Winwealth, who still slept on his throne, rushed out after the bird. It flew over the palace garden and into a wild common, where houses had been before Queen Wantall pulled them down to search for a gold mine, which her majesty never found, though three deep pits were dug to come at it. To make the place look smart at the feast time these pits had been covered over with loose boughs and turf. All the rest of the company remembered this but Queen Wantall and Princess Greedalind. They were nearest to the bird, and poor Snowflower, by running hard, came close behind them, but Fairfortune, the king's first page, drew her back by the purple mantle, when coming to the covered pit, boughs and turf gave way, and down went the queen and the princess.

Everybody looked for the bird, but it was nowhere to be seen; but on the common where they saw it alight, there stood a fair and royal prince, clad in a robe of purple and a crown of changing colours, for sometimes it seemed of gold and sometimes of forest leaves.

Most of the courtiers stood not knowing what to think, but all the fairy people and all the lords and ladies of the chair's stories, knew him, and cried, "Welcome to Prince Wisewit!"

King Winwealth heard that sound where he slept, and came out glad of heart to welcome back his brother. When the lord high chamberlain and her own pages came out with ropes and lanthorns to search for Queen Wantall and Princess Greedalind, they found them safe and well at the bottom of the pit, having fallen on a heap of loose sand. The pit was of great depth, but some daylight shone down, and whatever were the yellow grains they saw glittering among the sand, the queen and the princess believed it was full of gold.

They called the miners false knaves, lazy rogues, and a score of bad names beside, for leaving so much wealth behind them, and utterly refused to come out of the pit; saying, that since Prince Wisewit was come, they could find no pleasure in the palace, but would stay there and dig for gold, and buy the world with it for themselves. King Winwealth thought the plan was a good one for keeping peace in his palace. He commanded shovels and picks to be lowered to the queen and the princess. The two pages, Screw and Hardhands, went down to help them, in hopes of halving the profits, and there they stayed, digging for gold. Some of the courtiers said they would find it; others believed they never could; and the gold was not found when this story was written.

As for Prince Wisewit, he went home with the rest of the company, leading Snowflower by the hand, and telling them all how he had been turned into a bird by the cunning fairy Fortunetta, who found him off his guard in the forest; how she had shut him up under the cushion of that curious chair, and given it to old Dame Frostyface; and how all his comfort had been in little Snowflower, to whom he told so many stories.

King Winwealth was so rejoiced to find his brother again, that he commanded another feast to be held for seven days. All that time the gates of the palace stood open; all comers were welcome, all complaints heard. The houses and lands which Queen Wantall had taken away were restored to their rightful owners. Everybody got what they most wanted. There were no more clamours without, nor discontents within the palace; and on the seventh day of the feast who should arrive but Dame Frostyface, in her grey hood and mantle.

Snowflower was right glad to see her grandmother — so were the king and prince, for they had known the dame in her youth. They kept the feast for seven days more; and when it was ended everything was right in the kingdom. King Winwealth and Prince Wisewit reigned once more together; and because Snowflower was the best girl in all that country, they chose her to be their heiress, instead of Princess Greedalind. From that day forward she wore white velvet and satin; she had seven pages, and lived in the grandest part of the palace. Dame Frostyface, too, was made a great lady. They put a new velvet cushion on her chair, and she sat in a gown of grey cloth, edged with gold, spinning on an ivory wheel in a fine painted parlour. Prince Wisewit built a great summer-house covered with vines and roses, on the spot where her old cottage stood. He also made a highway through the forest, that all good people might come and go there at their leisure; and the cunning fairy Fortunetta, finding that her reign was over in those parts, set off on a journey round the world, and did not return in the time of this story. Good boys

and girls, who may chance to read it, that time is long ago. Great wars, work, and learning, have passed over the world since then, and altered all its fashions. Kings make no seven-day feasts for all comers now. Queens and princesses, however greedy, do not mine for gold. Chairs tell no tales. Wells work no wonders; and there are no such doings on hills and forests, for the fairies dance no more. Some say it was the hum of schools — some think it was the din of factories that frightened them; but nobody has been known to have seen them for many a year, except, it is said, one Hans Christian Andersen, in Denmark, whose tales of the fairies are so good that they must have been heard from themselves.

It is certain that no living man knows the subsequent history of King Winwealth's country, nor what became of all the notable characters who lived and visited at his place. Yet there are people who believe that the monarch still falls asleep on his throne, and into low spirits after supper; that Queen Wantall and Princess Greedalind have found the gold, and begun to buy; that Dame Frostyface yet spins — they cannot tell where; that Snowflower may still be seen at the new year's time in her dress of white velvet, looking out for the early spring; that Prince Wisewit has somehow fallen under a stronger spell and a thicker cushion, that he still tells stories to Snowflower and her friends, and when both cushion and spell are broken by another stroke of Sturdy's hatchet — which they expect will happen some time — the prince will make all things right again, and bring back the fairy times to the world.

"The New Mother," from Anyhow Stories: Moral and Otherwise, *by Mrs. W.K. Clifford (London: MacMillan and Company, 1882; rpt. New York and London: Garland Publishing, Inc., 1977).*

Like many other writers of her time, Lucy Lane Clifford (1853?-1929), wrote to support her family after the death of her husband, William Kingdon Clifford. Mrs. Clifford was well known in her own day as a successful novelist, dramatist, poet, and author of some of the strangest and most haunting of late Victorian literary fairy tales. "The New Mother," according to Alison Lurie, is not only one of the strangest but "one of the most brilliant." While "The New Mother" is ostensibly a moral tale warning children to mind their parents and not to be naughty, the story transcends narrow preachment because of its psychological sophistication. The "strange wild-looking girl" tempts the two children, Turkey and Blue Eyes (pet names of Mrs. Clifford's own children) with her peardrum and its little dancing couple, suggesting that the little man and woman can tell the children mysterious secrets. The children's fall from innocence into a lost and alienated state, the horrific "New Mother" with her terrifying glass eyes and long wooden tail, the image of the cheerful little cottage situated so near the dark forboding forest — all of these features endow the tale with exceptional emotional power. In structure, "The New Mother" offers an ironic variation of the circular journey, since the children cannot go home again. Historian of children's literature F.J. Harvey Darton rightly describes the story as full of "pity and terror."

The New Mother

The children were always called Blue-Eyes and the Turkey, and they came by the names in this manner. The elder one was like her dear father who was far away at sea, and when the mother looked up she would often say, "Child, you have taken the pattern of your father's eyes;" for the father had the bluest of blue eyes, and so gradually his little girl came to be called after them. The younger one had once, while she was still almost a baby, cried bitterly because a turkey that lived near to the cottage, and sometimes wandered into the forest, suddenly vanished in the middle of the winter; and to console her she had been called by its name.

Now the mother and Blue-Eyes and the Turkey and the baby all lived in a lonely cottage on the edge of the forest. The forest was so near that the garden at the back seemed a part of it, and the tall fir-trees were so close that their big black arms stretched over the little

thatched roof, and when the moon shone upon them their tangled shadows were all over the white-washed walls.

It was a long way to the village, nearly a mile and a half, and the mother had to work hard and had not time to go often herself to see if there was a letter at the post-office from the dear father, and so very often in the afternoon she used to send the two children. They were very proud of being able to go alone, and often ran half the way to the post-office. When they came back tired with the long walk, there would be the mother waiting and watching for them, and the tea would be ready, and the baby crowing with delight; and if by any chance there was a letter from the sea, then they were happy indeed. The cottage room was so cosy: the walls were as white as snow inside as well as out, and against them hung the cake-tin and the baking-dish, and the lid of a large saucepan that had been worn out long before the children could remember, and the fish-slice, all polished and shining as bright as silver. On one side of the fireplace, above the bellows hung the almanac, and on the other the clock that always struck the wrong hour and was always running down too soon, but it was a good clock, with a little picture on its face and sometimes ticked away for nearly a week without stopping. The baby's high chair stood in one corner, and in another there was a cupboard hung up high against the wall, in which the mother kept all manner of little surprises. The children often wondered how the things that came out of that cupboard had got into it, for they seldom saw them put there.

"Dear children," the mother said one afternoon late in the autumn, "it is very chilly for you to go to the village, but you must walk quickly, and who knows but what you may bring back a letter saying that dear father is already on his way to England." Then Blue-Eyes and the Turkey made haste and were soon ready to go. "Don't be long," the mother said, as she always did before they started. "Go the nearest way and don't look at any strangers you meet, and be sure you do not talk with them."

"No, mother," they answered; and then she kissed them and called them dear good children, and they joyfully started on their way.

The village was gayer than usual, for there had been a fair the day before, and the people who had made merry still hung about the street as if reluctant to own that their holiday was over.

"I wish we had come yesterday," Blue-Eyes said to the Turkey; "then we might have seen something."

"Look there," said the Turkey, and she pointed to a stall covered with gingerbread; but the children had no money. At the end of the street, close to the Blue Lion where the coaches stopped, an old man sat on the ground with his back resting against the wall of a house, and by him, with smart collars round their necks, were two dogs. Evidently they were dancing dogs, the children thought, and longed to see them perform, but they seemed as tired as their master, and sat quite still beside him, looking as if they had not even a single wag left in their tails.

"Oh, I *do* wish we had been here yesterday,' Blue-Eyes said again as they went on to the grocer's, which was also the post-office. The post-mistress was very busy weighing out half-pounds of coffee, and when she had time to attend to the children she only just said "No letter for you to-day," and went on with what she was doing. Then Blue-Eyes and the Turkey turned away to go home. They went back slowly down the village street, past the man with the dogs again. One dog had roused himself and sat up rather crookedly with his head a good deal on one side, looking very melancholy and rather ridiculous; but on the children went towards the bridge and the fields that led to the forest.

They had left the village and walked some way, and then, just before they reached the bridge, they noticed, resting against a pile of stones by the wayside, a strange dark figure. At first they thought it was some one asleep, then they thought it was a poor woman ill and hungry, and then they saw that it was a strange wild-looking girl, who seemed very unhappy, and they felt sure that something was the matter. So they went and looked at her, and thought they would ask her if they could do anything to help her, for they were kind children and sorry indeed for any one in distress.

The girl seemed to be tall, and was about fifteen years old. She was dressed in very ragged clothes. Round her shoulders there was an old brown shawl, which was torn at the corner that hung down the middle of her back. She wore no bonnet, and an old yellow handkerchief which she had tied round her head had fallen backwards and was all huddled up round her neck. Her hair was coal black and hung down uncombed and unfastened, just anyhow. It was not very long, but it was very shiny, and it seemed to match her bright black eyes and dark freckled skin. On her feet were coarse gray stockings and thick shabby boots, which she had evidently forgotten to lace up. She had something hidden away under her shawl, but the children did not know what it was. At first they thought it was a baby, but when, on seeing them coming towards her, she carefully put it under her and sat upon it, they thought they must be mistaken. She sat watching the children approach, and did not move or stir till they were within a yard of her; then she wiped her eyes just as if she had been crying bitterly, and looked up.

The children stood still in front of her for a moment, staring at her and wondering what they ought to do.

"Are you crying?" they asked shyly.

To their surprise she said in a most cheerful voice,

"Oh dear, no! quite the contrary. Are you?"

They thought it rather rude of her to reply in this way, for any one could see that they were not crying. They felt half in mind to walk away; but the girl looked at them so hard with her big black eyes, they did not like to do so till they had said something else.

"Perhaps you have lost yourself?" they said gently.

But the girl answered promptly, "Certainly not. Why, you have just found me. Besides," she added, "I live in the village."

The children were surprised at this, for they had never seen her before, and yet they thought they knew all the village folk by sight.

"We often go to the village," they said, thinking it might interest her.

"Indeed," she answered. That was all; and again they wondered what to do.

Then the Turkey, who had an inquiring mind, put a good straightforward question.

"What are you sitting on?" she asked.

"On a peardrum," the girl answered, still speaking in a most cheerful voice, at which the children wondered, for she looked very cold and uncomfortable.

"What is a peardrum?" they asked.

"I am surprised at your not knowing," the girl answered. "Most people in good society have one." And then she pulled it out and showed it to them. It was a curious instrument, a good deal like a guitar in shape; it had three strings, but only two pegs by which to tune them. The third string was never tuned at all, and thus added to the singular effect produced by the village girl's music. And yet, oddly, the peardrum was not played by touching its strings, but by turning a little handle cunningly hidden on one side.

But the strange thing about the peardrum was not the music it made, or the strings, or the handle, but a little square box attached to one side. The box had a little flat lid that appeared to open by a spring. That was all the children could make out at first. They were most anxious to see inside the box, or to know what it contained, but they thought it might look curious to say so.

"It really is a most beautiful thing, is a peardrum," the girl said, looking at it, and speaking in a voice that was almost affectionate.

"Where did you get it?" the children asked.

"I bought it,' the girl answered.

"Didn't it cost a great deal of money?" they asked.

"Yes," answered the girl slowly, nodding her head, "it cost a great deal of money. I am very rich," she added.

And this the children thought a really remarkable statement, for they had not supposed that rich people dressed in old clothes, or went about without bonnets. She might at least have done her hair, they thought; but they did not like to say so.

"You don't look rich," they said slowly, and in as polite a voice as possible.

"Perhaps not," the girl answered cheerfully.

At this the children gathered courage, and ventured to remark, "You look rather shabby"

— they did not like to say ragged.

"Indeed?" said the girl in the voice of one who had heard a pleasant but surprising statement. "A little shabbiness is very respectable," she added in a satisfied voice. "I must really tell them this," she continued. And the children wondered what she meant. She opened the little box by the side of the peardrum, and said, just as if she were speaking to some one who could hear her, "They say I look rather shabby; it is quite lucky, isn't it?"

"Why, you are not speaking to any one!" they said, more surprised than ever.

"Oh dear, yes! I am speaking to them both."

"Both?" they said, wondering.

"Yes. I have here a little man dressed as a peasant, and wearing a wide slouch hat with a large feather, and a little woman to match, dressed in a red petticoat, and a white handkerchief pinned across her bosom. I put them on the lid of the box, and when I play they dance most beautifully. The little man takes off his hat and waves it in the air, and the little woman holds up her petticoat a little bit — on one side with one hand, and with the other sends forward a kiss."

"Oh! let us see; do let us see!" the children cried, both at once.

Then the village girl looked at them doubtfully.

"Let you see!" she said slowly. "Well, I am not sure that I can. Tell me, are you good?"

"Yes, yes," they answered eagerly, "we are very good!"

"Then it's quite impossible," she answered, and resolutely closed the lid of the box.

They stared at her in astonishment.

"But we are good," they cried, thinking she must have misunderstood them. "We are very good. Mother always says we are."

"So you remarked before," the girl said, speaking in a tone of decision.

Still the children did not understand.

"Then can't you let us see the little man and woman?" they asked.

"Oh dear, no!" the girl answered. "I only show them to naughty children."

"To naughty children!" they exclaimed.

"Yes, to naughty children," she answered; "and the worse the children the better do the man and woman dance."

She put the peardrum carefully under her ragged cloak, and prepared to go on her way.

"I really could not have believed that you were good," she said, reproachfully, as if they had accused themselves of some great crime. "Well, good day."

"Oh, but do show us the little man and woman," they cried.

"Certainly not. Good day," she said again.

"Oh, but we will be naughty," they said in despair.

"I am afraid you couldn't," she answered, shaking her head. "It requires a great deal of skill, especially to be naughty well. Good day," she said for the third time. "Perhaps I shall see you in the village to-morrow."

And swiftly she walked away, while the children felt their eyes fill with tears, and their hearts ache with disappointment.

"If we had only been naughty," they said, "we should have seen them dance; we should have seen the little woman holding her red petticoat in her hand, and the little man waving his hat. Oh, what shall we do to make her let us see them?"

"Suppose," said the Turkey, "we try to be naughty to-day; perhaps she would let us see them to-morrow."

"But, oh!" said Blue-Eyes, "I don't know how to be naughty; no one ever taught me."

The Turkey thought for a few minutes in silence. "I think I can be naughty if I try," she said. "I'll try to-night."

And then poor Blue-Eyes burst into tears.

"Oh, don't be naughty without me!" she cried. "It would be so unkind of you. You know I want to see the little man and woman just as much as you do. You are very, very unkind." And she sobbed bitterly.

And so, quarrelling and crying, they reached their home.

Now, when their mother saw them, she was greatly astonished, and, fearing they were hurt, ran to meet them.

"Oh, my children, oh, my dear, dear children," she said; "what is the matter?"

But they did not dare tell their mother about the village girl and the little man and woman, so they answered, "Nothing is the matter; nothing at all is the matter," and cried all the more.

"But why are you crying?" she asked in surprise.

"Surely we may cry if we like," they sobbed. "We are very fond of crying."

"Poor children!" the mother said to herself. "They are tired, and perhaps they are hungry; after tea they will be better." And she went back to the cottage, and made the fire blaze, until its reflection danced about on the tin lids upon the wall; and she put the kettle on to boil, and set the tea-things on the table, and opened the window to let in the sweet fresh air, and made all things look bright. Then she went to the little cupboard, hung up high against the wall, and took out some bread and put it on the table, and said in a loving voice, "Dear little children, come and have your tea; it is all quite ready for you. And see, there is the baby waking up from her sleep; we will put her in the high chair, and she will crow at us while we eat."

But the children made no answer to the dear mother, they only stood still by the window and said nothing.

"Come, children," the mother said again. "Come, Blue-Eyes, and come, my Turkey; here is nice sweet bread for tea."

Then Blue-Eyes and the Turkey looked round, and when they saw the tall loaf, baked crisp and brown, and the cups all in a row, and the jug of milk, all waiting for them, they went to the table and sat down and felt a little happier, and the mother did not put the baby in the high chair after all, but took it on her knee, and danced it up and down, and sang little snatches of songs to it, and laughed, and looked content, and thought of the father far away at sea, and wondered what he would say to them all when he came home again. Then suddenly she looked up and saw that the Turkey's eyes were full of tears.

"Turkey!" she exclaimed, "my dear little Turkey! what is the matter? Come to mother, my sweet, come to own mother." And putting the baby down on the rug, she held out her arms, and the Turkey, getting up from her chair, ran swiftly into them.

"Oh, mother," she sobbed, "oh, dear

mother! I do so want to be naughty.''

"My dear child!" the mother exclaimed.

"Yes, mother," the child sobbed, more and more bitterly. "I do so want to be very, very naughty."

And then Blue-Eyes left her chair also, and, rubbing her face against the mother's shoulder, cried sadly. "And so do I, mother. Oh, I'd give anything to be very, very naughty."

"But, my dear children," said the mother, in astonishment, "why do you want to be naughty?"

"Because we do; oh, what shall we do?" they cried together.

"I should be very angry if you were naughty. But you could not be, for you love me," the mother answered.

"Why couldn't we be naughty because we love you?" they asked.

"Because it would make me very unhappy; and if you love me you couldn't make me unhappy."

"Why couldn't we?" they asked.

Then the mother thought a while before she answered; and when she did so they hardly understood, perhaps because she seemed to be speaking rather to herself than to them.

"Because if one loves well," she said gently, "one's love is stronger than all bad feelings in one, and conquers them. And this is the test whether love be real or false, unkindness and wickedness have no power over it."

"We don't know what you mean," they cried; "and we do love you; but we want to be naughty."

"Then I should know you did not love me," the mother said.

"And what should you do?" asked Blue-Eyes.

"I cannot tell. I should try to make you better."

"But if you couldn't? If we were very, very, very naughty, and wouldn't be good, what then?"

"Then," said the mother sadly — and while she spoke her eyes filled with tears, and a sob almost choked her — "then," she said, "I should have to go away and leave you, and to send home a new mother, with glass eyes and wooden tail."

"You couldn't," they cried.

"Yes, I could," she answered in a low voice; "but it would make me very unhappy, and I will never do it unless you are very, very naughty, and I am obliged."

"We won't be naughty," they cried; "we will be good. We should hate a new mother; and she shall never come here." And they clung to their own mother, and kissed her fondly.

But when they went to bed they sobbed bitterly, for they remembered the little man and woman, and longed more than ever to see them; but how could they bear to let their own mother go away, and a new one take her place?

"Good-day," said the village girl, when she saw Blue-Eyes and the Turkey approach. She was again sitting by the heap of stones, and under her shawl the peardrum was hidden. She looked just as if she had not moved since the day before. "Good day," she said, in the same cheerful voice in which she had spoken yesterday; "the weather is really charming."

"Are the little man and woman there?" the children asked, taking no notice of her remark.

"Yes; thank you for inquiring after them," the girl answered; "they are both here and quite well. The little man is learning how to rattle the money in his pocket, and the little woman has heard a secret — she tells it while she dances."

"Oh, do let us see," they entreated.

"Quite impossible, I assure you," the girl answered promptly. "You see, you are good."

"Oh!" said Blue-Eyes, sadly; "but mother says if we are naughty she will go away and send home a new mother, with glass eyes and a wooden tail."

"Indeed," said the girl, still speaking in the same unconcerned voice, "that is what they all say."

"What do you mean?" asked the Turkey.

"They all threaten that kind of thing. Of course really there are no mothers with glass eyes and wooden tails; they would be much too expensive to make." And the common sense of this remark the children, especially the Turkey, saw at once, but they merely said, half crying —

"We think you might let us see the little

man and woman dance."

"The kind of thing you would think," remarked the village girl.

"But will you if we are naughty?" they asked in despair.

"I fear you could not be naughty — that is, really — even if you tried," she said scornfully.

"Oh, but we will try; we will indeed," they cried; "so do show them to us."

"Certainly not beforehand," answered the girl, getting up and preparing to walk away.

"But if we are very naughty to-night, will you let us see them to-morrow?"

"Questions asked to-day are always best answered to-morrow," the girl said, and turned around as if to walk on. "Good day," she said blithely; "I must really go and play a little to myself; good day," she repeated, and then suddenly she began to sing —

"Oh, sweet and fair's the lady-bird,
And so's the bumble-bee,
But I myself have long preferred
The gentle chimpanzee,
The gentle chimpanzee-e-e,
The gentle chim ——"

"I beg your pardon," she said, stopping, and looking over her shoulder; "it's very rude to sing without leave before company. I won't do it again."

"Oh, do go on," the children said.

"I'm going," she said, and walked away.

"No, we meant go on singing," they explained, "and do let us just hear you play," they entreated, remembering that as yet they had not heard a single sound from the peardrum.

"Quite impossible," she called out as she went along. "You are good, as I remarked before. The pleasure of goodness centres in itself; the pleasures of naughtiness are many and varied. Good day," she shouted, for she was almost out of hearing.

For a few minutes the children stood still looking after her, then they broke down and cried.

"She might have let us see them," they sobbed.

The Turkey was the first to wipe away her tears.

"Let us go home and be very naughty," she said; "then perhaps she will let us see them to-morrow."

"But what shall we do?" asked Blue-Eyes, looking up. Then together all the way home they planned how to begin being naughty. And that afternoon the dear mother was sorely distressed, for, instead of sitting at their tea as usual with smiling happy faces, and then helping her to clear away and doing all she told them, they broke their mugs and threw their bread and butter on the floor, and when the mother told them to do one thing they carefully went and did another, and as for helping her to put away, they left her to do it all by herself, and only stamped their feet with rage when she told them to go upstairs until they were good.

"We won't be good," they cried. "We hate being good, and we always mean to be naughty. We like being naughty very much."

"Do you remember what I told you I should do if you were very very naughty?" she asked sadly.

"Yes, we know, but it isn't true," they cried. "There is no mother with a wooden tail and glass eyes, and if there were we should just stick pins into her and send her away; but there is none."

Then the mother became really angry at last, and sent them off to bed, but instead of crying and being sorry at her anger they laughed for joy, and when they were in bed they sat up and sang merry songs at the top of their voices.

The next morning quite early, without asking leave from the mother, the children got up and ran off as fast as they could over the fields towards the bridge to look for the village girl. She was sitting as usual by the heap of stones with the peardrum under her shawl.

"Now please show us the little man and woman," they cried, "and let us hear the peardrum. We were very naughty last night. But the girl kept the peardrum carefully hidden. "We were very naughty," the children cried again.

"Indeed,' she said in precisely the same tone in which she had spoken yesterday.

"But we were," they repeated; "we were indeed."

"So you say," she answered. "You were not half naughty enough."

"Why, we were sent to bed!"

"Just so," said the girl, putting the other corner of the shawl over the peardrum. "If you had been really naughty you wouldn't have gone; but you can't help it, you see. As I remarked before, it requires a great deal of skill to be naughty well."

"But we broke our mugs, we threw our bread and butter on the floor, we did everything we could to be tiresome.

"Mere trifles," answered the village girl scornfully. "Did you throw cold water on the fire, did you break the clock, did you pull all the tins down from the walls, and throw them on the floor?"

"No!" exclaimed the children, aghast, "we did not do that."

"I thought not," the girl answered. "So many people mistake a little noise and foolishness for real naughtiness; but, as I remarked before, it wants skill to do the thing properly. Well, good day," and before they could say another word she had vanished.

"We'll be much worse," the children cried, in despair. "We'll go and do all the things she says;" and then they went home and did all these things. They threw water on the fire; they pulled down the baking-dish and the cake-tin, the fish-slice and the lid of the saucepan they had never seen, and banged them on the floor; they broke the clock and danced on the butter; they turned everything upside down; and then they sat still and wondered if they were naughty enough. And when the mother saw all that they had done she did not scold them as she had the day before or send them to bed, but she just broke down and cried, and then she looked at the children and said sadly —

"Unless you are good to-morrow, my poor Blue-Eyes and Turkey, I shall indeed have to go away and come back no more, and the new mother I told you of will come to you."

They did not believe her; yet their hearts ached when they saw how unhappy she looked, and they thought within themselves that when they once had seen the little man and woman dance, they would be good to the dear mother for ever afterwards; but they could

not be good now till they had heard the sound of the peardrum, seen the little man and woman dance, and heard the secret told—then they would be satisfied.

The next morning, before the birds were stirring, before the sun had climbed high enough to look in at their bedroom window, or the flowers had wiped their eyes ready for the day, the children got up and crept out of the cottage and ran across the fields. They did not think the village girl would be up so very early, but their hearts had ached so much at the sight of the mother's sad face that they had not been able to sleep, and they longed to know if they had been naughty enough, and if they might just once hear the peardrum and see the little man and woman, and then go home and be good for ever.

To their surprise they found the village girl sitting by the heap of stones, just as if it were her natural home. They ran fast when they saw her, and they noticed that the box containing the little man and woman was open, but she closed it quickly when she saw them, and they heard the clicking of the spring that kept it fast.

"We have been very naughty," they cried. "We have done all the things you told us; now will you show us the little man and woman?" The girl looked at them curiously, then drew the yellow silk handkerchief she sometimes wore round her head out of her pocket, and began to smooth out the creases in it with her hands.

"You really seem quite excited," she said in her usual voice. "You should be calm; calmness gathers in and hides things like a big cloak, or like my shawl does here, for instance;" and she looked down at the ragged covering that hid the peardrum.

"We have done all the things you told us," the children cried again, "and we do so long to hear the secret;" but the girl went on smoothing out her handkerchief.

"I am so very particular about my dress," she said. They could hardly listen to her in their excitement.

"But do tell if we may see the little man and woman," they entreated again. "We have been so very naughty, and mother says she will go away to-day and send home a new mother if we are not good."

"Indeed," said the girl, beginning to be interested and amused. "The things that people say are most singular and amusing. There is an endless variety in language." But the children did not understand, only entreated once more to see the little man and woman.

"Well, let me see," the girl said at last, just as if she were relenting. "When did your mother say she would go?"

"But if she goes what shall we do?" they cried in despair. "We don't want her to go; we love her very much. Oh! what shall we do if she goes?"

"People go and people come; first they go and then they come. Perhaps she will go before she comes; she couldn't come before she goes. You had better go back and be good," the girl added suddenly; "you are really not clever enough to be anything else; and the little woman's secret is very important; she never tells it for make-believe naughtiness."

"But we did do all the things you told us," the children cried, despairingly.

"You didn't throw the looking-glass out of window, or stand the baby on its head."

"No, we didn't do that," the children gasped.

"I thought not," the girl said triumphantly. "Well, good-day. I shall not be here to-morrow. Good-day."

"Oh, but don't go away," they cried. "We are so unhappy; do let us see them just once."

"Well, I shall go past your cottage at eleven o'clock this morning," the girl said. "Perhaps I shall play the peardrum as I go by."

"And will you show us the man and woman?" they asked.

"Quite impossible, unless you have really deserved it; make-believe naughtiness is only spoilt goodness. Now if you break the looking-glass and do the things that are desired ——"

"Oh, we will," they cried. "We will be very naughty till we hear you coming."

"It's waste of time, I fear," the girl said politely; "but of course I should not like to interfere with you. You see the little man and woman, being used to the best society, are very particular. Good-day," she said, just as she always said, and then quickly turned away, but she looked back and called out, "Eleven o'clock, I shall be quite punctual; I am very particular about my engagements."

Then again the children went home, and were naughty, oh, so very very naughty that the dear mother's heart ached, and her eyes filled with tears, and at last she went upstairs and slowly put on her best gown and her new sun-bonnet, and she dressed the baby all in its Sunday clothes, and then she came down and stood before Blue-Eyes and the Turkey, and just as she did so the Turkey threw the looking-glass out of window, and it fell with a loud crash upon the ground.

"Good-bye, my children," the mother said sadly, kissing them. "Good-bye, my Blue-Eyes; good-bye, my Turkey; the new mother will be home presently. Oh, my poor children!" and then weeping bitterly the mother took the baby in her arms and turned to leave the house.

"But, mother," the children cried, "we are —— " and then suddenly the broken clock struck half-past ten, and they knew that in half an hour the village girl would come by playing on the peardrum. "But, mother, we will be good at half-past eleven, come back at half-past eleven," they cried, "and we'll both be good, we will indeed; we must be naughty till eleven o'clock." But the mother only picked up the little bundle in which she had tied up her cotton apron and a pair of old shoes, and went slowly out at the door. It seemed as if the children were spellbound, and they could not follow her. They opened the window wide, and called after her —

"Mother! mother! oh, dear mother, come back again! We will be good, we will be good now, we will be good for evermore if you will come back." But the mother only looked round and shook her head, and they could see the tears falling down her cheeks.

"Come back, dear mother!" cried Blue-Eyes; but still the mother went on across the fields.

"Come back, come back!" cried the Turkey; but still the mother went on. Just by the corner of the field she stopped and turned, and waved her handkerchief, all wet with tears, to the children at the window; she made the baby kiss its hand; and in a moment mother and baby had vanished from their sight.

Then the children felt their hearts ache with sorrow, and they cried bitterly just as the mother had done, and yet they could not believe that she had gone. Surely she would come back, they thought; she would not leave them altogether; but, oh, if she did — if she did — if she did. And then the broken clock struck eleven, and suddenly there was a sound — a quick, clanging, jangling sound, with a strange discordant one at intervals; and they looked at each other, while their hearts stood still, for they knew it was the peardrum. They rushed to the open window, and there they saw the village girl coming towards them from the fields, dancing along and playing as she did so. Behind her, walking slowly, and yet ever keeping the same distance from her, was the man with the dogs whom they had seen asleep by the Blue Lion, on the day they first saw the girl with the peardrum. He was playing on a flute that had a strange shrill sound; they could hear it plainly above the jangling of the peardrum. After the man followed the two dogs, slowly waltzing round and round on their hind legs.

"We have done all you told us," the children called, when they had recovered from their astonishment. "Come and see; and now show us the little man and woman."

The girl did not cease her playing or her dancing, but she called out in a voice that was half speaking half singing, and seemed to keep time to the strange music of the peardrum.

"You did it all badly. You threw the water on the wrong side of the fire, the tin things were not quite in the middle of the room, the clock was not broken enough, you did not stand the baby on its head."

Then the children, still standing spellbound by the window, cried out, entreating and wringing their hands, "Oh, but we have done everything you told us, and mother has gone away. Show us the little man and woman now, and let us hear the secret."

As they said this the girl was just in front of the cottage, but she did not stop playing. The sound of the strings seemed to go through their hearts. She did not stop dancing; she was already passing the cottage by. She did not stop

singing, and all she said sounded like part of a terrible song. And still the man followed her, always at the same distance, playing shrilly on his flute; and still the two dogs waltzed round and round after him — their tails motionless, their legs straight, their collars clear and white and stiff. On they went, all of them together.

"Oh, stop!" the children cried, "and show us the little man and woman now."

But the girl sang out loud and clear, while the string that was out of tune twanged above her voice.

"The little man and woman are far away. See, their box is empty."

And then for the first time the children saw that the lid of the box was raised and hanging back, and that no little man and woman were in it.

"I am going to my own land," the girl sang, "to the land where I was born." And she went on towards the long straight road that led to the city many many miles away.

"But our mother is gone," the children cried; "our dear mother, will she ever come back?"

"No," sang the girl; "she'll never come back, she'll never come back. I saw her by the bridge: she took a boat upon the river; she is sailing to the sea; she will meet your father once again, and they will go sailing on, sailing on to the countries far away."

And when they heard this, the children cried out, but could say no more, for their hearts seemed to be breaking.

Then the girl, her voice getting fainter and fainter in the distance, called out once more to them. But for the dread that sharpened their ears they would hardly have heard her, so far was she away, and so discordant was the music.

"Your new mother is coming. She is already on her way; but she only walks slowly, for her tail is rather long, and her spectacles are left behind; but she is coming, she is coming — coming — coming."

The last word died away; it was the last one they ever heard the village girl utter. On she went, dancing on; and on followed the man, they could see that he was still playing, but they could no longer hear the sound of his flute; and on went the dogs round and round and round. On they all went, farther and farther away, till they were separate things no more, till they were just a confused mass of faded colour, till they were a dark misty object that nothing could define, till they had vanished altogether, — altogether and for ever.

Then the children turned, and looked at each other and at the little cottage home, that only a week before had been so bright and happy, so cosy and so spotless. The fire was out, and the water was still among the cinders; the baking-dish and cake-tin, the fish-slice and the saucepan lid, which the dear mother used to spend so much time in rubbing, were all pulled down from the nails on which they had hung so long, and were lying on the floor. And there was the clock all broken and spoilt, the little picture upon its face could be seen no more; and though it sometimes struck a stray hour, it was with the tone of a clock whose hours are numbered. And there was the baby's high chair, but no little baby to sit in it; there was the cupboard on the wall, and never a sweet loaf on its shelf; and there were the broken mugs, and bits of bread tossed about, and the greasy boards which the mother had knelt down to scrub until they were white as snow. In the midst of all stood the children, looking at the wreck they had made, their hearts aching, their eyes blinded with tears, and their poor little hands clasped together in their misery.

"Oh, what shall we do?" cried Blue-Eyes. "I wish we had never seen the village girl and the nasty, nasty peardrum."

"Surely mother will come back," sobbed the Turkey. "I am sure we shall die if she doesn't come back."

"I don't know what we shall do if the new mother comes," cried Blue-Eyes. "I shall never, never like any other mother. I don't know what we shall do if that dreadful mother comes."

"We won't let her in," said the Turkey.

"But perhaps she'll walk in," sobbed Blue-Eyes.

Then Turkey stopped crying for a minute, to think what should be done.

"We will bolt the door," she said, "and shut the window; and we won't take any notice when she knocks."

So they bolted the door, and shut the window, and fastened it. And then, in spite of all they had said, they felt naughty again, and longed after the little man and woman they had never seen, far more than after the mother who had loved them all their lives. But then they did not really believe that their own mother would not come back, or that any new mother would take her place.

When it was dinner-time, they were very hungry, but they could only find some stale bread, and they had to be content with it.

"Oh, I wish we had heard the little woman's secret," cried the Turkey; "I wouldn't have cared then."

All through the afternoon they sat watching and listening for fear of the new mother; but they saw and heard nothing of her, and gradually they became less and less afraid lest she should come. Then they thought that perhaps when it was dark their own dear mother would come home; and perhaps if they asked her to forgive them she would. And then Blue-Eyes thought that if their mother did come she would be very cold, so they crept out at the back door and gathered some wood, and at last, for the grate was wet, and it was a great deal of trouble to manage it, they made a fire. When they saw the bright fire burning, and the little flames leaping and playing among the wood and coal, they began to be happy again, and to feel certain that their own mother would return; and the sight of the pleasant fire reminded them of all the times she had waited for them to come from the post-office, and of how she had welcomed them, and comforted them, and given them nice warm tea and sweet bread, and talked to them. Oh, how sorry they were they had been naughty, and all for the nasty village girl! They did not care a bit about the little man and woman now, or want to hear the secret.

They fetched a pail of water and washed the floor; they found some rag, and rubbed the tins till they looked bright again, and, putting a footstool on a chair, they got up on it very carefully and hung up the things in their places; and then they picked up the broken mugs and made the room as neat as they could, till it looked more and more as if the dear mother's hands had been busy about it. They felt more and more certain she would return, she and the dear little baby together, and they thought they would set the tea-things for her, just as she had so often set them for her naughty children. They took down the tea-tray, and got out the cups, and put the kettle on the fire to boil, and made everything look as home-like as they could. There was no sweet loaf to put on the table, but perhaps the mother would bring something from the village, they thought. At last all was ready, and Blue-Eyes and the Turkey washed their faces and their hands, and then sat and waited, for of course they did not believe what the village girl had said about their mother sailing away.

Suddenly, while they were sitting by the fire, they heard a sound as of something heavy being dragged along the ground outside, and then there was a loud and terrible knocking at the door. The children felt their hearts stand still. They knew it could not be their own mother, for she would have turned the handle and tried to come in without any knocking at all.

"Oh, Turkey!" whispered Blue-Eyes, "if it should be the new mother, what shall we do?"

"We won't let her in," whispered the Turkey, for she was afraid to speak aloud, and again there came a long and loud and terrible knocking at the door.

"What shall we do? oh, what shall we do?" cried the children, in despair. "Oh, go away!" they called out. "Go away; we won't let you in; we will never be naughty any more; go away, go away!"

But again there came a loud and terrible knocking.

"She'll break the door if she knocks so hard," cried Blue-Eyes.

"Go and put your back to it," whispered the Turkey, "and I'll peep out of the window and try to see if it is really the new mother."

So in fear and trembling Blue-Eyes put her back against the door, and the Turkey went to the window, and, pressing her face against one side of the frame, peeped out. She could just see a black satin poke bonnet with a frill round the edge, and a long bony arm carrying a black leather bag. From beneath the bonnet there flashed a strange bright light, and Turkey's heart sank and her cheeks turned pale, for she knew it was the flashing of two glass eyes. She crept up to Blue-Eyes. "It is — it is — it is!" she whispered, her voice shaking with fear, "it is the new mother! She has come, and brought her luggage in a black leather bag that is hanging on her arm!"

"Oh, what shall we do?" wept Blue-Eyes; and again there was the terrible knocking.

"Come and put your back against the door too, Turkey," cried Blue-Eyes; "I am afraid it will break."

So together they stood with their two little backs against the door. There was a long pause. They thought perhaps the new mother had made up her mind that there was no one at home to let her in, and would go away, but presently the two children heard through the thin wooden door the new mother move a little, and then say to herself — "I must break open the door with my tail."

For one terrible moment all was still, but in it the children could almost hear her lift up her tail, and then, with a fearful blow, the little painted door was cracked and splintered.

With a shriek the children darted from the spot and fled through the cottage, and out at the back door into the forest beyond. All night long they stayed in the darkness and the cold, and all the next day and the next, and all through the cold, dreary days and the long dark nights that followed.

They are there still, my children. All through the long weeks and months have they been there, with only green rushes for their pillows and only the brown dead leaves to cover them, feeding on the wild strawberries in the summer, or on the nuts when they hang green; on the blackberries when they are no longer sour in the autumn, and in the winter on the little red berries that ripen in the snow. They wander about among the tall dark firs or beneath the great trees beyond. Sometimes they stay to rest beside the little pool near the copse where the ferns grow thickest, and they long and long, with a longing that is greater than words can say, to see their own dear mother again, just once again, to tell her that they'll be good for evermore — just once again.

And still the new mother stays in the little cottage, but the windows are closed and the doors are shut, and no one knows what the inside looks like. Now and then, when the darkness has fallen and the night is still, hand in hand Blue-Eyes and the Turkey creep up near to the home in which they once were so happy, and with beating hearts they watch and listen; sometimes a blinding flash comes through the window, and they know it is the light from the new mother's glass eyes, or they hear a strange muffled noise, and they know it is the sound of her wooden tail as she drags it along the floor.

French Court Tradition Literary Folktales

"The White Cat," from The White Cat and Other Old French Fairy Tales by Mme. La Comtesse D'Aulnoy, *by Rachel Field. Ill. by E. MacKinstry (New York: The Macmillan Company, 1928).*

In the age of Louis XIV, members of the court took delight in the witty, ornately written variety of French contes *or literary fairy tales. Charles Perrault adapted traditional folk tales and presented them in a fashion that appealed to courtly society. Certainly one of the most popular writers of the French* contes *was Marie Catherine Le Jumelle De Berneville, known afterward as Mme. La Comptesse D'Aulnoy. Although most of Mme. D'Aulnoy's stories are too precious and ornate to appeal much to child readers, "The White Cat" blends courtly charm with the motifs of traditional folk tables. Thus, while the youngest and most virtuous of three sons goes on a quest at the behest of his father, the king, he encounters a White Cat whose manners are as graceful and charming as those of a great and courtly lady. Such whimsical details as the rainbow-coated dogs, who dance the tarantella with the grace of a Spanish dancer, and an orchestra composed of cats, though often criticized by adults as excessive, are apt to charm children. As in so many other tales, "The White Cat" features the circular journey, the quest, the presence of three tests, the undoing of an evil spell, and the radical transformation of an animal character into a human being of royal ancestry.*

The White Cat

Once upon a time there was a King who had three sons. The day came when they were grown so big and strong that he began to fear they would be planning to rule in his place. This would cause trouble among themselves and his subjects. Now the King was not so young as he once had been but nevertheless he had no notion of giving up his kingdom then and there. So after much thought he hit upon a scheme which should keep them too busily occupied to interfere in the affairs of state. Accordingly he called the three into his private apartments where he spoke to them with great kindliness and concern of his plans for their future.

"I am planning to retire from the affairs of state. But I do not wish my subjects to suffer from this change. Therefore, while I am still alive, I shall transfer my crown to one of you. I shall not follow the usual custom of leaving the crown to my eldest son, but whichever one of you shall bring me the handsomest and most intelligent little dog shall become my heir."

The Princes were greatly surprised by this

strange request, but they could not very well refuse to humor their father's whim; and since there was luck in it for the two younger sons and the elder of the three was a timid, rather spiritless fellow, they agreed readily enough. The King then bade them farewell after first distributing jewels and money among them and adding that a year from that day at the same place and hour they should return to him with their little dogs.

Within sight of the city gates stood a castle where the three often spent many days in company with their young companions. Here they agreed to part and to meet again in a year before proceeding with their trophies to the King; and so having pledged their good faith, and changing their names that they might not be known, each set off upon a different road.

It would take far too long to recount the adventures of all three Princes so I shall tell only of those that befell the youngest, for a more gay and well-mannered Prince never lived, nor one so handsome and accomplished.

Scarcely a day passed that he did not buy a dog or two, greyhounds, mastiffs, bloodhounds, pointers, spaniels, water dogs, lapdogs; but the instant he found a handsomer one he let the first go and kept the new purchase, since it would have been impossible for him to carry them all on his journeyings. He went without fixed plan or purpose and so he continued for many days until at last darkness and a terrible storm overtook him at nightfall in a lonely forest. Thunder and lightning rumbled and flashed; rain fell in torrents; the trees seemed to close more densely about him until at last he could no longer find his way. When he had wandered thus for some time he suddenly saw a glint of light between the tree trunks. Feeling certain that this must mean a shelter of some sort he pressed on till he found himself approaching the most magnificent castle he had ever seen. The gate was of gold and covered with jewels of such brilliance that it was their light which had guided him to the spot. In spite of the rain and storm he caught glimpses of walls of finest porcelain decorated with pictures of the most famous fairies from the beginning of the world up to that very day: Cinderella, Graciosa, Sleeping Beauty, and a

hundred others. As he admired all this magnificence he noticed a rabbit's foot fastened to the golden gates by a chain of diamonds. Marveling greatly at such a lavish display of precious gems, the young Prince pulled at the rabbit's foot and straightway an unseen bell of wonderful sweetness rang; the gate was opened by hundreds of tiny hands and others pushed him forward while he hesitated amazed upon the threshold. He moved on wonderingly, his hand on the hilt of his sword until he was reassured by two voices singing a welcome. Again he felt himself being pushed, this time toward a gate of coral opening upon an apartment of mother-of-pearl from which he passed into others still more richly decorated and alight with wax candles and great chandeliers sparkling with a thousand rainbows.

He had passed through perhaps sixty such rooms when the hands that guided him made a sign for him to stop. He saw a large armchair moving by itself toward a fireplace at the same moment that the fire began to blaze and the hands, which he now observed to be very small and white, carefully drew off his wet clothes and handed him others so fine and richly embroidered they seemed fit for a wedding day. The hands continued to dress him, until at last, powdered and attired more handsomely than he had ever been in his life before, the Prince was led into a banquet hall. Here the four walls were decorated solely with paintings representing famous cats, Puss-in-Boots and others whom he was quick to recognize. Even more astonishing than this was the table set for two with its gold service and crystal cups.

There was an orchestra composed entirely of cats. One held a music book with the strangest notes imaginable; another beat time with a little baton; and all the rest strummed tiny guitars.

While the Prince stared in amazement, each cat suddenly began to mew in a different key and to claw at the guitar strings. It was the strangest music ever heard! The Prince would have thought himself in bedlam had not the palace itself been so marvelously beautiful. So he stopped his ears and laughed heartily at the various poses and grimaces of these strange musicians. He was meditating upon the extraordinary sights he had already seen in the castle, when he beheld a little figure entering the hall. It was scarcely more than two feet in height and wrapped in a long gold crêpe veil. Before it walked two cats dressed in deep mourning and wearing cloaks and swords, while still others followed, some carrying rat-traps full of rats and mice in cages.

By this time the Prince was too astonished to think. But presently the tiny pink figure approached him and lifted its veil. He now beheld the most beautiful little white cat that ever was or ever will be. She had such a very youthful and melancholy air and a mewing so soft and sweet that it went straight to the young Prince's heart.

"Son of a King," she said to him, "thou art welcome; my mewing Majesty beholds thee with pleasure."

"Madam," responded the Prince, bowing as low as possible before her, "it is very gracious of you to receive me with so much attention, but you do not appear to me to be an ordinary little cat. The gift of speech which you have and this superb castle you inhabit are certainly evidence to the contrary."

"Son of a King," rejoined the White Cat, "I pray that you will cease to pay me compliments. I am plain in my speech and manners, but I have a kind heart. Come," she added, to her attendants, "let them serve supper and bid the concert cease, for the Prince does not understand what they are singing."

"And are they singing words, madam?" he asked incredulously.

"Certainly," she answered, "we have very gifted poets here, as you will see if you remain long enough."

Supper was then served to them by the same hands that had guided him there, and a very strange meal it was. There were two dishes of each course — one soup, for instance, being of savory pigeons while the other had been made of nicely fattened mice. The sight of this rather took away the Prince's appetite until his hostess, who seemed to guess what was passing in his mind, assured him that his own dishes had been specially prepared and contained no rats and mice of any kind. Her charming manners convinced the Prince that

the little Cat had no wish to deceive him, so he began to eat and drink with great enjoyment. During their meal he happened to observe that on one paw she wore a tiny miniature set in a bracelet. This surprised him so that he begged her to let him examine it more closely. He had supposed it would be the picture of Master Puss, but what was his astonishment to find it the portrait of a handsome young man who bore a strange resemblance to himself! As he stared at it, the White Cat was heard to sigh so deeply and with such profound sadness that the Prince became even more curious; but he dared not question one so affected. Instead he entertained her with tales of court life, with which, to his surprise, he found her well acquainted.

After supper the White Cat led her guest into another Hall, where upon a little stage twelve cats and twelve monkeys danced in the most fantastic costumes. So the evening ended in great merriment; and after the Cat had bade the Prince a gracious good night the same strange hands conducted him to his own apartment, where in spite of the softness of his bed he spent half the night trying to solve the mystery of the castle and his extraordinary little hostess.

But when morning came he was no nearer to an answer to his questionings, so he allowed the pair of hands to help him dress and lead him into the palace courtyard. Here a vast company of cats in hunting costume were gathering to the sound of the horn. A fête day indeed! The White Cat was going to hunt and wished the Prince to accompany her. Now the mysterious hands presented him with a wooden horse. He made some objection to mounting it, but it proved to be an excellent charger, and a tireless galloper. The White Cat rode beside him on a monkey, the handsomest and proudest that ever was seen. She had thrown off her long veil and wore a military cap which made her look so bold that she frightened all the mice in the neighborhood. Never was there a more successful hunt. The cats outran all the rabbits and hares and a thousand skillful feats were performed to the gratification of the entire company. Tiring of the hunt at last the White Cat took up a horn no bigger than the

Prince's little finger and blew upon it with so loud and clear a tone it could be heard ten leagues away. Scarcely had she sounded two or three flourishes when all the cats in the countryside seemed to appear. By land and sea and through the air they all came flocking to her call, dressed in every conceivable costume. So, followed by this extraordinary train, the Prince rode back with his hostess to the castle.

That night the White Cat put on her gold veil again and they dined together as before. Being very hungry the Prince ate and drank heartily, and this time the food had a strange effect upon him. All recollection of his father and the little dog he was to find for him slipped from his mind. He no longer thought of anything but of gossiping with the White Cat and enjoying her kind and gracious companionship. So the days passed in pleasant sport and amusement and the nights in feasting and conversation. There was scarcely one in which he did not discover some new charm of the little White Cat. Now he had forgotten even the land of his birth. The hands continued to wait upon him and supply every want till he began to regret that he could not become a cat himself to live forever in such pleasant company.

"Alas," he confessed to the White Cat at last, "how wretched it makes me even to think of leaving you! I have come to love you so dearly. Could you not become a woman or else make me a cat?"

But though she smiled at his wish, the look she turned upon him was very strange.

A year passes away quickly when one has neither pain nor care, when one is merry and in good health. The Prince took no thought of time, but the White Cat was not so forgetful.

"There are only three days left to look for the little dog you were to bring to the King, your father," she reminded him. "Your two brothers have already found several very beautiful ones."

At her words the Prince's memory returned to him and he marveled at his strange forgetfulness.

'What spell would have made me forget what was most important to me in the whole world?" he cried in despair. "My honor and my fortune are lost unless I can find a dog that will win a kingdom for me and a horse swift enough to carry me home again in this short time!"

So, believing this to be impossible, he grew very sorrowful. Then the White Cat spoke to him with great reassurance.

"Son of a King," she said, "do not distress yourself so. I am your friend. Remain here another day, and though it is five hundred leagues from here to your country the good wooden horse will carry you there in less than twelve hours' time."

"But it is not enough for me to return to my father, dear Cat," said the Prince. "I must take him a little dog as well."

"And so you shall," replied she. "Here is a walnut which contains one more beautiful than the Dog Star."

"Your Majesty jests with me," he protested.

"Put the walnut to your ear then," insisted the Cat, "and you will hear it bark."

He obeyed her, and as he held the walnut to his ear a faint "Bow-wow" came from within, more tiny and shrill than a cricket on a winter night. The Prince could scarcely believe his ears or contain his curiosity to see so diminutive a creature. But he was wise enough to follow the White Cat's advice not to open the walnut till he should reach his father's presence.

It was a sad leave-taking between the Prince and the White Cat. A thousand times he thanked her, but though he urged her to return to court with him, she only shook her head and sighed deeply as upon the night of his arrival. So he galloped away at last on the wooden horse, which bore him more swiftly than the wind to the appointed place.

He reached the castle even before his two brothers and enjoyed the sight of their surprise at seeing a wooden horse champing at the bit in the courtyard. The two brothers were so busy telling of their various adventures that they took little note of their younger brother's silence concerning his, but when the time came to show one another their dogs the two were vastly amused at sight of an ugly cur which the young Prince had brought along, pretending to consider it a marvel of beauty. Needless to say the elder Princes smiled with secret satisfaction to think how far superior were their own dogs, for though they wished their brother no ill luck, they had no wish to see him ruling over the kingdom.

Next morning the three set out together in the same coach. The two eldest brothers carried baskets filled with little dogs too delicate and beautiful to be touched, while the youngest carried the poor cur as if it also was precious. By no outward sign did he betray the presence of the walnut with its precious occupant which was safely hidden in his pocket. No sooner did the three set foot in the palace than all the court crowded around to welcome the returned travelers and see the results of their journeyings. The King received them with great joy, professing delight over the little dogs his two elder sons brought out for his inspection. But the more he studied their merits, the more puzzled he became, so nearly were they alike in beauty and grace. The two brothers were already beginning to dispute with one another as to which deserved the crown when the younger Brother stepped forward, holding upon the palm of his hand the walnut so lately presented to him by the White Cat. Opening it without more ado, he revealed a tiny dog lying upon cotton. So perfectly formed was it and so small that it could pass through a little finger ring without touching any part of it. It was more delicate than thistledown and its coat shone with colors of the rainbow. Nor was this all; immediately it was released from its kennel, the little creature arose on its hind legs and began to go through the steps of a tarantella, with tiny castanets and all the airs and graces of a Spanish dancer!

The King was dumbfounded and even the two brothers were forced to acknowledge that such a beautiful and gifted little dog had never been seen before. But their father was in no mood to give up his kingdom, so he announced that he had decided upon another test of their skill. This time he would give them a year to travel over land and sea in search of a piece of cloth so fine it would pass through the eye of the finest Venetian-point lace needle.

So the Prince remounted his wooden horse and set off at full speed, for now he knew exactly where he wanted to go. So great was his eagerness to see the beautiful White Cat once more that he could scarcely contain himself until her castle came into view. This time every window was alight to welcome him and the faithful pair of hands which had waited on him so well before were ready to take the bridle of the wooden horse and lead it back to the stable while the Prince hurried to the White Cat's private apartments.

He found her lying on a little couch of blue satin with many pillows. Her expression was sad until she caught sight of him. Then she sprang up and began to caper about him delightedly.

"Oh, dear Prince," cried she, "I had scarcely dared to hope for your return. I am generally so unfortunate in matters that concern me."

A thousand times must the grateful Prince caress her and recount his adventures, which perhaps she knew more about than he guessed. And now he told her of his father's latest whim —how he had set his heart upon having a piece of cloth that could pass through the eye of the finest needle. For his own part he did not believe it was possible to find such a thing, but he believed that if any one could help him in this quest it would be his dear White Cat. She listened attentively to all he told her and finally explained with a thoughtful air that this was a matter demanding careful consideration. There were, it seemed, some cats in her castle who could spin with extraordinary skill, and she added that she would also put a paw to the work herself so that he need not trouble himself to search farther.

The Prince was only too delighted to accept this offer and he and his charming hostess sat down to supper together, after which a magnificent display of fireworks was set off in his honor. And once more the days passed in enchanted succession. The ingenious White Cat knew a thousand different ways of entertaining her guest, so that he never once thought of missing human society. Indeed, he was probably the first person in the world to spend a whole year of complete contentment with only cats for company.

The second year slipped away as pleasantly as the first. The Prince could scarcely think of anything that the tireless hands did not instantly supply, whether books, jewels, pictures, old things or new. In short, he had but to say, "I want a certain gem that is in the cabinet of the Great Mogul, or the King of Persia, or such and such a statue in Corinth or any part of Greece," and he saw it instantly before him, without knowing how it came or who brought it. It is not unpleasant at all to find oneself able to possess any treasure in the world. No wonder our Prince was happy!

But the White Cat who was ever watchful of his welfare, warned him that the hour of departure was approaching and that he might make himself easy in his mind about the piece of cloth, for she had a most wonderful one for him. She added that it was her intention this time to furnish him with an equipage worthy of his high birth, and without waiting for his reply, beckoned him to the window overlooking the castle courtyard. Here he saw an open coach of gold and flame-color with a thousand gallant devices to please the mind and eye. It was drawn by twelve horses as white as snow, four-and-four abreast, with harnesses of flaming velvet embroidered with diamonds and gold. A hundred other coaches, each with eight horses and filled with superbly attired noblemen followed, escorted by a thousand bodyguards whose uniforms were so richly embroidered you could not see the material beneath. But the most remarkable part of this cavalcade was that a portrait of the White Cat was to be seen everywhere, in coach device, uniform, or worn as a decoration on the doublets of those who rode in the train, as if it were some newly created order that had been conferred upon them.

"Go now," said the White Cat to the Prince. "Appear at the court of the King, your father, in such magnificence that he cannot fail to be impressed and to bestow upon you the crown which you deserve. Here is another walnut. Crack it in his presence and you will find the piece of cloth you asked of me."

"Oh, dear White Cat," he answered tenderly, "I am so overcome by your goodness that I would gladly give up my hopes of power and future grandeur to stay here with you the rest of life."

"Son of a King," she answered, "I am convinced of your kindness of heart. A kind heart is a rare thing among princes who would be loved by all, yet not love any one themselves. But you are the proof that there is an exception to this rule. I give you credit for the affection you have shown to a little white cat that after all is good for nothing but to catch mice."

So the Prince kissed her paw and departed.

This time the two brothers arrived at their father's palace before him, congratulating themselves that their young brother must be dead or gone for good. They lost no time in displaying the cloths they had brought, which were indeed so fine that they could pass through the eye of a large needle but not through the small eye of the needle the King had already selected. At this there arose a great murmuring at court. The friends of the two Princes took sides among themselves as to which had fulfilled the bargain better. But this was interrupted by a flourish of trumpets announcing the arrival of their younger brother.

The magnificence of his train fairly took away the breath of the King and his court, but their astonishment grew even greater when, after saluting his father, the young Prince brought out the walnut. This he cracked with great ceremony only to find, instead of the promised piece of cloth, a cherry stone. At sight of this the King and the court exchanged sly smiles. Nothing daunted, the Prince cracked the cherry stone, only to find a kernel inside. Jeers and murmurs ran through the great apartment. The Prince must be a fool indeed! He made no answer to them, but even he began to doubt the White Cat's words as he found next a grain of wheat and within that the smallest millet seed. "Oh, White Cat, White Cat! Have you betrayed me?" he muttered between his teeth. Even as he spoke he felt a little scratch upon his hand, so sharp that it drew blood. Taking this to be some sort of sign, the Prince proceeded to open the millet seed. Before the incredulous eyes of the whole court he drew out of it a piece of cloth four hundred yards long and marvelously embroidered with colored birds and beasts, with trees and fruits and flowers, with shells and jewels and even with suns and moons and countless stars. There were also portraits of Kings and Queens of the past upon it and of their children and children's children, not forgetting the smallest child, and each dressed perfectly in the habit of his century.

The sight of this was almost too much for the King. He could scarcely find the needle. Through its eye the wonderful piece of cloth was able to pass not only once but six times, before the jealous gaze of the two older Princes. But the King was still far from ready to give up his kingdom. Once more he turned to his children.

"I am going to put your obedience to a new and final test," he told them. "Go and travel for another year and whichever one of you brings back with him the most beautiful Princess shall marry her and be crowned King on his wedding day. I pledge my honor that after this I shall ask no further favors of you."

So off the three went again, the youngest Prince still in a good humor although he had the least cause to be since he had twice been the acknowledged winner of the wager. But he was not one to dispute his father's will, so soon he and all his train were taking the road back to his dear White Cat. She knew the very day and hour of his arrival, and all along the way flowers had been strewn and perfume made the air sweet. Once more the castle gate was opened to him and the strange hands took him in charge while all the cats climbed into the trees to welcome their returning visitor.

"So, my Prince," said the White Cat when he reached her side at last, "once more you have returned without the crown. But no matter," she added as he opened his lips to explain, "I know that you are bound to take back the most beautiful Princess to court and I will find one for you, never fear. Meantime, let us amuse ourselves and be merry."

The third year passed for the young Prince as had the two others, and since nothing runs away faster than time passed without trouble or care, it is certain that he would have completely forgotten the day of his return to court had not the White Cat reminded him of it. This time, however, she told him that upon him alone depended his fate. He must promise to do whatever she asked of him. The Prince

agreed readily enough until he heard her command him to cut off her head and tail and fling them into the fire.

"I!" cried the Prince, aghast, "I be so barbarous as to kill my dear White Cat? This is some trick to try my heart, but you should be sure of its gratitude."

"No, no, Son of a King," she answered, "I know your heart too well for that. But fate is stronger than either of us, and you must do as I bid you. It is the only way; and you must believe me, for I swear it on the honor of a Cat."

Tears came into the eyes of the Prince at the mere thought of cutting off the head of so amiable and pretty a creature. He tried to say all the most tender things he could think of, hoping to distract her. But she persisted that she wished to die by his hand because it was the only means of preventing his brothers from winning the crown. So piteously did she beg him that at last, all of a tremble, he drew his sword. With faltering hand he cut off the head and tail of his dear White Cat.

Next moment the most remarkable transformation took place before his very eyes. The body of the little White Cat suddenly changed into that of a young girl, the most graceful ever seen. But this was as nothing compared to the beauty and sweetness of her face, where only the shining brightness of the eyes gave any hint of the cat she had so recently been. The Prince was struck dumb with surprise and delight. He opened his eyes wider still to look at her, and what was his amazement to behold a troop of lords and ladies entering the apartment, each with a cat's skin flung over an arm. They advanced and, throwing themselves at the feet of their Queen, expressed their joy at seeing her once more restored to her natural form. She received them with great affection, but presently she desired them to leave her alone with the Prince.

"Behold, my dear Prince," she said as soon as they had done so, "I am released of a terrible enchantment, too long a tale to tell you now. Suffice it to say that this portrait which you saw upon my paw when I was a cat, was given to me by my guardian fairies during the time of my trial. I supposed it was of my first, unhappy love who was so cruelly taken from

me and whose resemblance to you was so striking. Conceive my joy then, to find that it is
of the Prince who has my entire heart and
who was destined to rescue me from my
enchantment."

And she bowed low before our Prince, who
was so filled with joy and wonder that he
would have remained there forever telling her
of his love, had she not reminded him that the
hour for his return to his father's court was
almost upon them. Taking him by the hands,
she led him into the courtyard to a chariot even
more magnificent than the one she had provided before. The rest were equally gorgeous,
the horses shod with emeralds held in place
by diamond nails, with such gold and jeweled
trappings as were never seen before or since.
But the young Prince had eyes for nothing
beyond the beauty of his companion.

Just before they reached the outskirts of the
city, they sighted the Prince's two brothers
with their trains driving toward them from opposite directions. At this the Princess hid herself in a small throne of rock crystal and
precious gems, while the Prince remained
alone in the coach. His two brothers, each
accompanied by a charming lady, greeted him
warmly but expressed surprise and curiosity
that he should be alone. To these questions he
replied that he had been so unfortunate as not
to have met with any lady of sufficient beauty
to bring with him to court. He added, however, that he had instead a very rare and gifted
White Cat. At this the brothers laughed loudly
and exchanged pleased glances, for now they
were convinced that he was indeed a simpleton and they need have no fears of his outwitting them a third time.

Through the streets of the city the two elder Princes rode with their ladies in open carriages, while the youngest Prince came last.
Behind him was borne the great rock crystal,
at which every one gazed in wonder.

The two Princes eagerly charged up the
palace stairs with their Princesses, so anxious
were they for their father's approval. The King
received them graciously, but once more had
difficulty in deciding which should have the
prize. So he turned to his youngest son, who
stood alone before him.

"Have you returned empty-handed this
time?" he asked.

"In this rock your Majesty will find a little
White Cat," he answered, "one which mews
so sweetly and has such velvet paws that you
cannot but be delighted with it."

But before the surprised King could reach
the crystal, the Princess touched an inner
spring. It flew open revealing her in all her
beauty, more dazzling than the sun itself. Her
hair fell in golden ringlets; she was crowned
with flowers and she moved with incompara-
ble grace in her gown of white and rose-colored
gauze. Even the King himself could not resist
such loveliness, but hastened to acknowledge
her undisputed right to wear the crown.

"But I have not come to deprive your Majesty of a throne which you fill so admirably,"
she said, bowing before him graciously. "I was
born the heiress to six kingdoms of my own,
so permit me to offer one to you and to each
of your elder sons. I ask no other favors of you
than your friendship and that your youngest
son shall be my husband. Three kingdoms will
be quite enough for us."

And so in truth they found them.

▬▬▬▬

"Beauty and the Beast," from Blue Fairy Book.
*Collected by Andrew Lang. Edited by Brian
Alderson. Illustrated by John Lawrence.
Longmans Green Company, Ltd., 1889; Re-
printed: Kestral Books, 1975.*

*In 1740 Madame Gabrielle—Suzanne de
Villeneuve—published her rendering of the
famous literary fairy tale, "Beauty and the
Beast," in* Les Contes Marins. *Madame Le
Prince de Beaumont published a much shorter
version of the tale in 1756. It is Mme. de Beaumont's story which has been so often translated into English. One of the best translations
of "Beauty and the Beast" is that of Andrew
Lang, who published the tale in his famous*
Blue Fairy Book *(1889). While the splendid details concerning the palace are characteristic
of the French* contes, *"Beauty and the Beast"
is rich in the archetypes of the folk tale: the
heroine is the youngest and best of three sisters;
the transformation of the Beast through Beau-*

*ty's love; and the linear structure of the hero-
ine's passage from childhood into maturity.*

Beauty and the Beast

Once upon a time, in a far-off country, there
lived a merchant who had been so lucky in all
his undertakings that he was enormously rich.
As he had, however, six sons and six daughters, he found that his money was not too much
to let them all have everything they fancied,
as they were accustomed to do.

But one day a most unexpected misfortune
befell them. Their house caught fire and was
speedily burnt to the ground, with all the splendid furniture, the books, pictures, gold, silver,
and precious goods it contained; and this was
only the beginning of their troubles. Their father, who had until this moment prospered in
all ways, suddenly lost every ship he had upon
the sea, either by dint of pirates, shipwreck,
or fire. Then he heard that his clerks in distant
countries, whom he trusted entirely, had
proved unfaithful; and at last from great wealth
he fell into the direst poverty.

All that he had left was a little house in a
desolate place at least a hundred leagues from
the town in which he had lived, and to this he
was forced to retreat with his children, who
were in despair at the idea of leading such a
different life. Indeed, the daughters at first
hoped that their friends, who had been so numerous while they were rich, would insist on
their staying in their houses now they no longer
possessed one. But they soon found that they
were left alone, and that their former friends
even attributed their misfortunes to their own
extravagance, and showed no intention of offering them any help. So nothing was left for
them but to take their departure to the cottage,
which stood in the midst of a dark forest, and
seemed to be the most dismal place upon the
face of the earth. As they were too poor to have
any servants, the girls had to work hard, like
peasants, and the sons, for their part, cultivated
the fields to earn their living. Roughly clothed,
and living in the simplest way, the girls regret-
ted unceasingly the luxuries and amusements
of their former life; only the youngest tried to
be brave and cheerful. She had been as sad as

anyone when misfortune first overtook her father, but, soon recovering her natural gaiety,
she set to work to make the best of things, to
amuse her father and brothers as well as she
could, and to try to persuade her sisters to join
her in dancing and singing. But they would do
nothing of the sort, and, because she was not
as doleful as themselves, they declared that this
miserable life was all she was fit for. But she
was really far prettier and cleverer than they
were; indeed, she was so lovely that she was
always called Beauty. After two years, when
they were all beginning to get used to their new
life, something happened to disturb their tranquillity. Their father received the news that one
of his ships, which he had believed to be lost,
had come safely into port with a rich cargo.
All the sons and daughters at once thought that
their poverty was at an end, and wanted to set
out directly for the town; but their father, who
was more prudent, begged them to wait a little, and, though it was harvest-time, and he
could ill be spared, determined to go himself
first, to make inquiries. Only the youngest
daughter had any doubt but that they would
soon again be as rich as they were before, or at
least rich enough to live comfortably in some
town where they would find amusement and
gay companions once more. So they all loaded
their father with commissions for jewels and
dresses which it would have taken a fortune
to buy; only Beauty, feeling sure that it was of
no use, did not ask for anything. Her father,
noticing her silence, said: 'And what shall I
bring for you, Beauty?'

'The only thing I wish for is to see you come
home safely,' she answered.

But this reply vexed her sisters, who fancied she was blaming them for having asked
for such costly things. Her father, however, was
pleased, but as he thought that at her age she
certainly ought to like pretty presents, he told
her to choose something.

'Well, dear father,' she said, 'as you insist
upon it, I beg that you will bring me a rose. I
have not seen one since we came here, and I
love them so much.'

So the merchant set out and reached the
town as quickly as possible, but only to find
that his former companions, believing him to

be dead, had divided between them the goods which the ship had brought; and after six months of trouble and expense he found himself as poor as when he started, having been able to recover only just enough to pay the cost of his journey. To make matters worse, he was obliged to leave the town in the most terrible weather, so that by the time he was crossing the hills near his home he was almost exhausted with cold and fatigue. Though he knew it would take some hours to get through the forest, he was so anxious to be at his journey's end that he resolved to go on; but night overtook him, and the deep snow and bitter frost made it impossible for his horse to carry him any further. Not a house was to be seen; the only shelter he could get was the hollow trunk of a great tree, and there he crouched all the night, which seemed to him the longest he had ever known. In spite of his weariness the howling of the wolves kept him awake, and even when at last the day broke he was not much better off, for the falling snow had covered up every path, and he did not know which way to turn.

At length he made out some sort of track, and though at the beginning it was so rough and slippery that he fell down more than once, it presently became easier, and led him into an avenue of trees which ended in a splendid castle. It seemed to the merchant very strange that no snow had fallen in the avenue, which was entirely composed of orange trees, covered with flowers and fruit. When he reached the first court of the castle he saw before him a flight of agate steps, and went up them, and passed through several splendidly furnished rooms. The pleasant warmth of the air revived him, and he felt very hungry; but there seemed to be nobody in all this vast and splendid palace whom he could ask to give him something to eat. Deep silence reigned everywhere, and at last, tired of roaming through empty rooms and galleries, he stopped in a room smaller than the rest, where a clear fire was burning and a couch was drawn up cosily close to it. Thinking that this must be prepared for someone who was expected, he sat down to wait till he should come, and very soon fell into a sweet sleep.

When his extreme hunger wakened him after several hours, he was still alone; but a little table, upon which was a good dinner, had been drawn up close to him, and, as he had eaten nothing for twenty-four hours, he lost no time in beginning his meal, hoping that he might soon have an opportunity of thanking his considerate host, whoever it might be. But no one appeared, and even after another long sleep, from which he awoke completely refreshed, there was no sign of anybody, though a fresh meal of dainty cakes and fruit was prepared upon the little table at his elbow. Being naturally timid, he began to be terrified by the silence, and resolved to search once more through all the rooms; but it was of no use. Not even a servant was to be seen; there was no sign of life in the palace! He began to wonder what he should do, and to amuse himself by pretending that all the treasures he saw were his own, and considering how he would divide them among his children. Then he went into the garden, and though it was winter everywhere else, here the sun shone, and the birds sang, and the flowers bloomed, and the air was soft and sweet. The merchant, in ecstacies with all he saw and heard, said to himself:

'All this must be meant for me. I will go this minute and bring my children to share all these delights.'

In spite of being so cold and weary when he reached the castle, he had taken his horse to the stable and fed it. Now he thought he would saddle it for his homeward journey, and he turned down the path which led to the stable. This path had a hedge of roses on each side of it, and the merchant thought he had never seen or smelt such exquisite flowers. They reminded him of his promise to Beauty, and he stopped and had just gathered one to take to her when he was startled by a strange noise behind him. Turning round, he saw a frightful Beast, which seemed to be very angry and said, in a terrible voice:

'Who told you that you might gather my roses? Was it not enough that I allowed you to be in my palace and was kind to you? This is the way you show your gratitude, by stealing my flowers! But your insolence shall not go unpunished.' The merchant, terrified by these furious words, dropped the fatal rose, and, throwing himself on his knees, cried: 'Pardon me, noble sir. I am truly grateful to you for your hospitality, which was so magnificent that I could not imagine that you would be offended by my taking such a little thing as a rose.' But the Beast's anger was not lessened by this speech.

'You are very ready with excuses and flattery,' he cried; 'but that will not save you from the death you deserve.'

'Alas!' thought the merchant, 'if my daughter Beauty could only know what danger her rose has brought me into!'

And in despair he began to tell the Beast of his misfortunes, and the reason of his journey, not forgetting to mention Beauty's request.

'A king's ransom would hardly have procured all that my other daughters asked,' he said; 'but I thought that I might at least take Beauty her rose. I beg you to forgive me, for you see I meant no harm.'

The Beast considered for a moment, and then he said, in a less furious tone:

"I will forgive you on one condition — that is, that you will give me one of your daughters.'

'Ah!' cried the merchant, 'if I were cruel enough to buy my own life at the expense of one of my children's, what excuse could I invent to bring her here?'

'No excuse would be necessary,' answered the Beast. 'If she comes at all she must come willingly. On no other condition will I have her. See if any one of them is courageous enough, and loves you well enough to come and save your life. You seem to be an honest man, so I will trust you to go home. I give you a month to see if any of your daughters will come back with you and stay here, to let you go free. If none of them is willing, you must come alone, after bidding them good-bye for ever, for then you will belong to me. And do not imagine that you can hide from me, for if you fail to keep your word I will come and fetch you!' added the Beast grimly.

The merchant accepted this proposal, though he did not really think any of his daughters would be persuaded to come. He promised to return at the time appointed, and then, anxious to escape from the presence of the Beast, he asked permission to set off at once. But the Beast answered that he could not go until the next day.

'Then you will find a horse ready for you,' he said. 'Now go and eat your supper, and await my orders.'

The poor merchant, more dead than alive, went back to his room, where the most delicious supper was already served on the little table which was drawn up before a blazing fire. But he was too terrified to eat, and only tasted a few of the dishes, for fear the Beast should be angry if he did not obey his orders. When he had finished he heard a great noise in the next room, which he knew meant that the Beast was coming. As he could do nothing to escape his visit, the only thing that remained was to seem as little afraid as possible; so when the Beast appeared and asked roughly if he had supped well, the merchant answered humbly that he had, thanks to his host's kindness. Then the Beast warned him to remember their agreement, and to prepare his daughter exactly for what she had to expect.

'Do not get up to-morrow,' he added, 'until you see the sun and hear a golden bell ring. Then you will find your breakfast waiting for you here, and the horse you are to ride will be ready in the courtyard. He will also bring you back again when you come with your daughter a month hence. Farewell. Take a rose to Beauty, and remember your promise!'

The merchant was only too glad when the Beast went away, and though he could not sleep for sadness, he lay down until the sun rose. Then, after a hasty breakfast, he went to gather Beauty's rose, and mounted his horse, which carried him off so swiftly that in an instant he had lost sight of the palace, and he was still wrapped in gloomy thoughts when it stopped before the door of the cottage.

His sons and daughters, who had been very uneasy at his long absence, rushed to meet him, eager to know the result of his journey, which, seeing him mounted upon a splendid horse and wrapped in a rich mantle, they supposed to be favourable. But he hid the truth from them at first, only saying sadly to Beauty as he gave her the rose:

'Here is what you asked me to bring you;

you little know what it has cost.'

But this excited their curiosity so greatly that presently he told them his adventures from beginning to end, and then they were all very unhappy. The girls lamented loudly over their lost hopes, and the sons declared that their father should not return to this terrible castle, and began to make plans for killing the Beast if it should come to fetch him. But he reminded them that he had promised to go back. Then the girls were very angry with Beauty, and said it was all her fault, and that if she had asked for something sensible this would never have happened, and complained bitterly that they should have to suffer for her folly.

Poor Beauty, much distressed, said to them:

'I have indeed caused this misfortune, but I assure you I did it innocently. Who could have guessed that to ask for a rose in the middle of summer would cause so much misery? But as I did the mischief it is only just that I should suffer for it. I will therefore go back with my father to keep his promise.'

At first nobody would hear of this arrangement, and her father and brothers, who loved her dearly, declared that nothing should make them let her go; but Beauty was firm. As the time drew near she divided all her little possessions between her sisters, and said goodbye to everything she loved, and when the fatal day came she encouraged and cheered her father as they mounted together the horse which had brought him back. It seemed to fly rather than gallop, but so smoothly that Beauty was not frightened; indeed, she would have enjoyed the journey if she had not feared what might happen to her at the end of it. Her father still tried to persuade her to go back, but in vain. While they were talking the night fell, and then, to their great surprise, wonderful coloured lights began to shine in all directions, and splendid fireworks blazed out before them; all the forest was illuminated by them, and even felt pleasantly warm, though it had been bitterly cold before. This lasted until they reached the avenue of orange trees, where were statues holding flaming torches, and when they got nearer to the palace they saw that it was illuminated from the roof to the ground, and music sounded softly from the courtyard. 'The

Beast must be very hungry,' said Beauty, trying to laugh, 'if he makes all this rejoicing over the arrival of his prey.'

But, in spite of her anxiety, she could not help admiring all the wonderful things she saw.

The horse stopped at the foot of the flight of steps leading to the terrace, and when they had dismounted her father led her to the little room he had been in before, where they found a splendid fire burning, and the table daintily spread with a delicious supper.

The merchant knew that this was meant for them, and Beauty, who was rather less frightened now that she had passed through so many rooms and seen nothing of the Beast, was quite willing to begin, for her long ride had made her very hungry. But they had hardly finished their meal when the noise of the Beast's footsteps was heard approaching, and Beauty clung to her father in terror, which became all the greater when she saw how frightened he was. But when the Beast really appeared, though she trembled at the sight of him, she made a great effort to hide her horror, and saluted him respectfully.

This evidently pleased the Beast. After looking at her he said, in a tone that might have struck terror into the boldest heart, though he did not seem to be angry:

'Good-evening, old man. Good-evening, Beauty.'

The merchant was too terrified to reply, but Beauty answered sweetly:

'Good-evening, Beast.'

'Have you come willingly?' asked the Beast. 'Will you be content to stay here when your father goes away?'

Beauty answered bravely that she was quite prepared to stay.

'I am pleased with you,' said the Beast. As you have come of your own accord, you may stay. As for you, old man,' he added, turning to the merchant, 'at sunrise to-morrow you will take your departure. When the bell rings get up quickly and eat your breakfast, and you will find the same horse waiting to take you home; but remember that you must never expect to see my palace again.'

Then turning to Beauty, he said:

'Take your father into the next room, and

Illustration by Errol LeCain from *Beauty and the Beast*, retold by Rosemary Harris.
Copyright © 1979.

help him to choose everything you think your brothers and sisters would like to have. You will find two travelling-trunks there; fill them as full as you can. It is only just that you should send them something very precious as a remembrance of yourself.'

Then he went away, after saying, 'Good-bye, Beauty; good-bye old man;' and though Beauty was beginning to think with great dismay of her father's departure, she was afraid to disobey the Beast's orders: and they went into the next room, which had shelves and cupboards all round it. They were greatly surprised at the riches it contained. There were splendid dresses fit for a queen, with all the ornaments that were to be worn with them; and when Beauty opened the cupboards she was quite dazzled by the gorgeous jewels that lay in heaps upon every shelf. After choosing a vast quantity, which she divided between her sisters — for she had made a heap of the wonderful dresses for each of them — she opened the last chest, which was full of gold.

'I think, father,' she said, 'that, as the gold will be more useful to you, we had better take out the other things again, and fill the trunks with it.' So they did this; but the more they put in, the more room there seemed to be, and at last they put back all the jewels and dresses they had taken out, and Beauty even added as many more of the jewels as she could carry at once; and then the trunks were not too full, but they were so heavy that an elephant could not have carried them!

'The Beast was mocking us,' cried the merchant; 'he must have pretended to give us all these things, knowing that I could not carry them away.'

'Let us wait and see,' answered Beauty. 'I cannot believe that he meant to deceive us. All we can do is to fasten them up and leave them ready.'

So they did this and returned to the little room, where, to their astonishment, they found breakfast ready. The merchant ate his with a good appetite, as the Beast's generosity made him believe that he might perhaps venture to come back soon and see Beauty. But she felt sure that her father was leaving her for ever, so she was very sad when the bell rang sharply for the second time, and warned them that the time was come for them to part. They went down into the courtyard, where two horses were waiting, one loaded with the two trunks, the other for him to ride. They were pawing the ground in their impatience to start, and the merchant was forced to bid Beauty a hasty farewell; and as soon as he was mounted he went off at such a pace that she lost sight of him in an instant. Then Beauty began to cry, and wandered sadly back to her own room. But she soon found that she was very sleepy, and as she had nothing better to do she lay down and instantly fell asleep. And then she dreamed that she was walking by a brook bordered with trees, and lamenting her sad fate, when a young prince, handsomer than anyone she had ever seen, and with a voice that went straight to her heart, came and said to her, 'Ah, Beauty! you are not so unfortunate as you suppose. Here you will be rewarded for all you have suffered elsewhere. Your every wish shall be gratified. Only try to find me out, no matter how I may be disguised, for I love you dearly, and in making me happy you will find your own happiness. Be as true-hearted as you are beautiful, and we shall have nothing left to wish for.'

'What can I do, Prince, to make you happy?' said Beauty.

'Only be grateful,' he answered, 'and do not trust too much to your eyes. And, above all, do not desert me until you have saved me from my cruel misery.'

After this she thought she found herself in a room with a stately and beautiful lady, who said to her:

'Dear Beauty, try not to regret all you have left behind you, for you are destined to a better fate. Only do not let yourself be deceived by appearances.'

Beauty found her dreams so captivating that she was in no hurry to awake, but presently the clock roused her by calling her name softly twelve times, and then she got up and found her dressing-table set out with everything she could possibly want; and when her toilet was finished she found dinner was wait-

ing in the room next to hers. But dinner does not take very long when you are all by yourself, and very soon she sat down cosily in the corner of a sofa, and began to think about the charming Prince she had seen in her dream.

'He said I could make him happy,' said Beauty to herself. 'It seems, then, that this horrible Beast keeps him a prisoner. How can I set him free? I wonder why they both told me not to trust to appearances? I don't understand it. But, after all, it was only a dream, so why should I trouble myself about it? I had better go and find something to do to amuse myself.'

So she got up and began to explore some of the many rooms of the palace.

The first she entered was lined with mirrors, and Beauty saw herself reflected on every side, and thought she had never seen such a charming room. Then a bracelet which was hanging from a chandelier caught her eye, and on taking it down she was greatly surprised to find that it held a portrait of her unknown admirer, just as she had seen him in her dream. With great delight she slipped the bracelet on her arm, and went on into a gallery of pictures, where she soon found a portrait of the same handsome Prince, as large as life, and so well painted that as she studied it he seemed to smile kindly at her. Tearing herself away from the portrait at last, she passed through into a room which contained every musical instrument under the sun, and here she amused herself for a long while in trying some of them, and singing until she was tired. The next room was a library, and she saw everything she had ever wanted to read, as well as everything she had read, and it seemed to her that a whole lifetime would not be enough even to read the names of the books, there were so many. By this time it was growing dusk, and wax candles in diamond and ruby candlesticks were beginning to light themselves in every room.

Beauty found her supper served just at the time she preferred to have it, but she did not see anyone or hear a sound, and, though her father had warned her that she would be alone, she began to find it rather dull.

But presently she heard the Beast coming, and wondered trembling if he meant to eat her up now.

However, as he did not seem at all ferocious, and only said gruffly:

'Good-evening, Beauty.' She answered cheerfully and managed to conceal her terror. Then the Beast asked her how she had been amusing herself, and she told him all the rooms she had seen.

Then he asked if she thought she could be happy in his palace; and Beauty answered that everything was so beautiful that she would be very hard to please if she could not be happy. And after about an hour's talk Beauty began to think that the Beast was not nearly so terrible as she had supposed at first. Then he got up to leave her, and said in his gruff voice:

'Do you love me, Beauty? Will you marry me?'

'Oh! what shall I say?' cried Beauty, for she was afraid to make the Beast angry by refusing.

'Say "yes" or "no" without fear,' he replied.

'Oh! no, Beast,' said Beauty hastily.

'Since you will not, good-night, Beauty,' he said. And she answered:

'Good-night Beast,' very glad to find that her refusal had not provoked him. And after he was gone she was very soon in bed and asleep, and dreaming of her unknown Prince. She thought he came and said to her:

'Ah, Beauty! why are you so unkind to me? I fear I am fated to be unhappy for many a long day still.'

And then her dreams changed, but the charming Prince figured in them all; and when morning came her first thought was to look at the portrait and see if it was really him, and she found that it certainly was.

This morning she decided to amuse herself in the garden, for the sun shone, and all the fountains were playing; but she was astonished to find that every place was familiar to her, and presently she came to the brook where the myrtle trees were growing where she had first met the Prince in her dream, and that made her think more than ever that he must be kept a prisoner by the Beast. When she was tired she went back to the palace, and found a new room full of materials for every kind of work — ribbons to make into bows, and silks to work into flowers. Then there was an aviary full of rare birds, which were so tame that they flew to Beauty as soon as they saw her, and perched upon her shoulders and her head.

'Pretty little creatures,' she said, 'how I wish that your cage was nearer to my room, that I might often hear you sing!'

So saying she opened a door, and found to her delight that it led into her own room, though she had thought it was quite the other side of the palace.

There were more birds in a room farther on, parrots and cockatoos that could talk, and they greeted Beauty by name; indeed, she found them so entertaining that she took one or two back to her room, and they talked to her while she was at supper; after which the Beast paid her his usual visit, and asked the same questions as before, and then with a gruff 'good-night' he took his departure, and Beauty went to bed to dream of her mysterious Prince. The days passed swiftly in different amusements, and after a while Beauty found out another strange thing in the palace, which often pleased her when she was tired of being alone. There was one room which she had not noticed particularly; it was empty, except that under each of the windows stood a very comfortable chair; and the first time she had looked out of the window it had seemed to her that a black curtain prevented her from seeing anything outside. But the second time she went into the room, happening to be tired, she sat down in one of the chairs, when instantly the curtain was rolled aside, and a most amusing pantomime was acted before her; there were dances, and coloured lights, and music, and pretty dresses, and it was all so gay that Beauty was in ecstacies. After that she tried the other seven windows in turn, and there was some new and surprising entertainment to be seen from each of them, so that Beauty never could feel lonely any more. Every evening after supper the Beast came to see her, and always before saying good-night asked her in his terrible voice:

'Beauty, will you marry me?'

And it seemed to Beauty, now she understood him better, that when she said, 'No, Beast,' he went away quite sad. But her happy dreams of the handsome young Prince soon made her forget the poor Beast, and the only thing that at all disturbed her was to be constantly told to distrust appearances, to let her heart guide her, and not her eyes, and many other equally perplexing things, which, consider as she would, she could not understand.

So everything went on for a long time, until at last, happy as she was, Beauty began to long for the sight of her father and her brothers and sisters; and one night, seeing her look very sad, the Beast asked her what was the matter. Beauty had quite ceased to be afraid of him. Now she knew that he was really gentle in spite of his ferocious looks and his dreadful voice. So she answered that she was longing to see her home once more. Upon hearing this the Beast seemed sadly distressed, and cried miserably:

'Ah! Beauty, have you the heart to desert an unhappy Beast like this? What more do you want to make you happy? Is it because you hate me that you want to escape?'

'No, dear Beast,' answered Beauty softly, 'I do not hate you, and I should be very sorry never to see you any more, but I long to see my father again. Only let me go for two months, and I promise to come back to you and stay for the rest of my life.'

The Beast, who had been sighing dolefully while she spoke, now replied:

'I cannot refuse you anything you ask, even though it should cost me my life. Take the four boxes you will find in the room next to your own, and fill them with everything you wish to take with you. But remember your promise and come back when the two months are over, or you may have cause to repent it, for if you do not come in good time you will find your faithful Beast dead. You will not need any chariot to bring you back. Only say good-bye to all your brothers and sisters the night before you come away, and when you have gone to bed turn this ring round upon your finger and say firmly: "I wish to go back to my palace and see my Beast again." Good-night, Beauty. Fear nothing, sleep peacefully, and before long you shall see your father once more.'

As soon as Beauty was alone she hastened to fill the boxes with all the rare and precious things she saw about her, and only when she was tired of heaping things into them did they seem to be full.

Then she went to bed, but could hardly sleep for joy. And when at last she did begin to dream of her beloved Prince she was grieved to see him stretched upon a grassy bank sad and weary, and hardly like himself.

'What is the matter?' she cried.

But he looked at her reproachfully, and said:

'How can you ask me, cruel one? Are you not leaving me to my death perhaps?'

'Ah! don't be so sorrowful,' cried Beauty; 'I am only going to assure my father that I am safe and happy. I have promised the Beast faithfully that I will come back, and he would die of grief if I did not keep my word!'

'What would that matter to you?' said the Prince. 'Surely you would not care?'

'Indeed I should be ungrateful if I did not care for such a kind Beast,' cried Beauty indignantly. 'I would die to save him from pain. I assure you it is not his fault that he is so ugly.'

Just then a strange sound woke her — someone was speaking not very far away; and opening her eyes she found herself in a room she had never seen before, which was certainly not nearly so splendid as those she was used to in the Beast's palace. Where could she be? She got up and dressed hastily, and then saw that the boxes she had packed the night before were all in the room. While she was wondering by what magic the Beast had transported them and herself to this strange place she suddenly heard her father's voice, and rushed out and greeted him joyfully. Her brothers and sisters were all astonished at her appearance, as they had never expected to see her again, and there was no end to the questions they asked her. She had also much to hear about what had happened to them while she was away, and of her father's journey home. But when they heard that she had only come to be with them for a short time, and then must go back to the Beast's palace for ever, they lamented loudly. Then Beauty asked her father what he thought could be the meaning of her strange dreams, and why the Prince constantly begged her not to trust appearances. After much consideration he answered: 'You tell me yourself that the Beast, frightful as he is, loves you dearly, and deserves your love and gratitude for his gentleness and kindness; I think the Prince must mean you to understand that you ought to reward him by doing as he wishes you to, in spite of his ugliness.'

Beauty could not help seeing that this seemed very probable; still, when she thought of her dream Prince who was so handsome, she did not feel at all inclined to marry the Beast. At any rate, for two months she need not decide, but could enjoy herself with her sisters. But though they were rich now, and lived in a town again, and had plenty of acquaintances, Beauty found that nothing amused her very much; and she often thought of the palace, where she was so happy, especially as at home she never once dreamed of her dear Prince, and she felt quite sad without him.

Then her sisters seemed to have got quite used to being without her, and even found her rather in the way, so she would not have been sorry when the two months were over but for her father and brothers, who begged her to stay, and seemed so grieved at the thought of her departure that she had not the courage to say good-bye to them. Every day when she got up she meant to say it at night, and when night came she put it off again, until at last she had a dismal dream which helped her to make up her mind. She thought she was wandering in a lonely path in the palace gardens, when she heard groans which seemed to come from some bushes hiding the entrance of a cave, and running quickly to see what could be the matter, she found the Beast stretched out upon his side, apparently dying. He reproached her faintly with being the cause of his distress, and at the same moment a stately lady appeared, and said very gravely:

'Ah! Beauty, you are only just in time to save his life. See what happens when people do not keep their promises! If you had delayed one day more, you would have found him dead.'

Beauty was so terrified by this dream that the next morning she announced her intention of going back at once, and that very night she said good-bye to her father and all her brothers and sisters, and as soon as she was in bed she turned her ring round upon her finger, and said firmly:

'I wish to go back to my palace and see my Beast again,' as she had been told to do.

Then she fell asleep instantly, and only woke up to hear the clock saying, 'Beauty, Beauty,' twelve times in its musical voice, which told her at once that she was really in the palace once more. Everything was just as before, and her birds were so glad to see her! but Beauty thought she had never known such a long day, for she was so anxious to see the Beast again that she felt as if supper-time would never come.

But when it did come and no Beast appeared she was really frightened; so, after listening and waiting for a long time, she ran down into the garden to search for him. Up and down the paths and avenues ran poor Beauty, calling him in vain, for no one answered, and not a trace of him could she find; until at last, quite tired, she stopped for a minute's rest, and saw that she was standing opposite the shady path she had seen in her dream. She rushed down it, and, sure enough, there was the cave, and in it lay the Beast — asleep, as Beauty thought. Glad to have found him, she ran up and stroked his head, but to her horror he did not move or open his eyes.

'Oh! he is dead; and it is all my fault,' said Beauty, crying bitterly.

But then, looking at him again, she fancied he still breathed, and, hastily fetching some water from the nearest fountain, she sprinkled it over his face, and to her great delight he began to revive.

'Oh! Beast, how you frightened me!' she cried. 'I never knew how much I loved you until just now, when I feared I was too late to save your life.'

'Can you really love such an ugly creature as I am?' said the Beast faintly. 'Ah! Beauty, you only came just in time. I was dying because I thought you had forgotten your promise. But go back now and rest, I shall see you again by-and-by.'

Beauty, who had half expected that he would be angry with her, was reassured by his gentle voice, and went back to the palace, where supper was awaiting her; and afterwards the Beast came in as usual, and talked about the time she had spent with her father, asking if she had enjoyed herself, and if they had all been very glad to see her.

Beauty answered politely, and quite enjoyed telling him all that had happened to her. And when at last the time came for him to go, and he asked, as he had so often asked before:

'Beauty, will you marry me?' she answered softly:

'Yes, dear Beast.'

As she spoke a blaze of light sprang up before the windows of the palace; fireworks crackled and guns banged, and across the avenue of orange trees, in letters all made of fireflies, was written: 'Long live the Prince and his Bride.'

Turning to ask the Beast what it could all mean, Beauty found that he had disappeared, and in his place stood her long-loved Prince! At the same moment the wheels of a chariot were heard upon the terrace, and two ladies entered the room. One of them Beauty recognized as the stately lady she had seen in her dreams; the other was also so grand and queenly that Beauty hardly knew which to greet first.

But the one she already knew said to her companion:

'Well, Queen, this is Beauty, who has had the courage to rescue your son from the terrible enchantment. They love one another, and only your consent to their marriage is wanting to make them perfectly happy.'

'I consent with all my heart,' cried the Queen. 'How can I ever thank you enough for having restored my dear son to his natural form?'

And then she tenderly embraced Beauty and the Prince, who had meanwhile been greeting the Fairy and receiving her congratulations.

'Now,' said the Fairy to Beauty, 'I suppose you would like me to send for all your brothers and sisters to dance at your wedding?'

And so she did, and the marriage was celebrated the very next day with the utmost splendour, and Beauty and the Prince lived happily ever after.

"The Emperor's New Clothes," from Hans Christian Andersen: The Complete Fairy Tales and Stories, *Trans. by Erik Christian Haugaard. Forward by Virginia Haviland. (Garden City, New York: Doubleday and Company, 1974).*

In 1846 a volume of Hans Christian Andersen's tales was translated into English and published as Wonderful Stories for Children. *With this publication, Harvey Darton notes, the triumph of the fairy tale in English children's literature was secure. Andersen's stories have been read and told to children all over the world and have exerted a powerful influence upon subsequent writers of literary folk tales.*

"The Emperor's New Clothes" is a tale which endorses the clear-eyed honesty of the child and deflates adult hypocrisy. It features the child as seer and visionary in contrast to the moral blindness of the emperor and the court. "The Emperor's New Clothes" is economical and spare in style, unlike the French contes. *Yet its humorously satirical tone and those of the French* contes *probably influenced the development of such comic burlesques of folk tales as William Makepeace Thackeray's* The Rose and the Ring *(1854).*

The Emperor's New Clothes

Many, many years ago there was an emperor who was so terribly fond of beautiful new clothes that he spent all his money on his attire. He did not care about his soldiers, or attending the theater, or even going for a drive in the park, unless it was to show off his new clothes. He had an outfit for every hour of the day. And just as we say, "The king is in his council chamber," his subjects used to say, "The emperor is in his clothes closet."

In the large town where the emperor's palace was, life was gay and happy; and every day new visitors arrived. One day two swindlers came. They told everybody that they were weavers and that they could weave the most marvelous cloth. Not only were the colors and the patterns of their material extraordinarily beautiful, but the cloth had the strange quality of being invisible to anyone who was unfit for his office or unforgivably stupid.

"This is truly marvelous," thought the emperor. "Now if I had robes cut from that material, I should know which of my councilors was unfit for his office, and I would be able to pick out my clever subjects myself. They must weave some material for me!" And he gave the swindlers a lot of money so they could start working at once.

They set up a loom and acted as if they were weaving, but the loom was empty. The fine silk and gold threads they demanded from the emperor they never used, but hid them in their own knapsacks. Late into the night they would sit before their empty loom, pretending to weave.

"I would like to know how they are getting along," thought the emperor; but his heart beat strangely when he remembered that those who were stupid or unfit for their office would not be able to see the material. Not that he was really worried that this would happen to him. Still, it might be better to send someone else the first time and see how he fared. Everybody in town had heard about the cloth's magic quality and most of them could hardly wait to find out how stupid or unworthy their neighbors were.

'I shall send my faithful prime minister over to see how the weavers are getting along," thought the emperor. "He will know how to judge the material, for he is both clever and fit for his office, if any man is."

The good-natured old man stepped into the room where the weavers were working and saw the empty loom. He closed his eyes, and opened them again. "God preserve me!" he thought. "I cannot see a thing!" But he didn't say it out loud.

The swindlers asked him to step a little closer to the loom so that he could admire the intricate patterns and marvelous colors of the material they were weaving. They both pointed to the empty loom, and the poor old prime minister opened his eyes as wide as he could; but it didn't help, he still couldn't see anything.

"Am I stupid?" he thought. "I can't believe it, but if it is so, it is best no one finds out about it. But maybe I am not fit for my office. No,

that is worse, I'd better not admit that I can't see what they are weaving."

"Tell us what you think of it," demanded one of the swindlers.

"It is beautiful. It is very lovely," mumbled the old prime minister, adjusting his glasses. "What patterns! What colors! I shall tell the emperor that it pleases me ever so much."

"That is a compliment," both the weavers said; and now they described the patterns and told which shades of color they had used. The prime minister listened attentively, so that he could repeat their words to the emperor; and that is exactly what he did.

The two swindlers demanded more money, and more silk and gold thread. They said they had to use it for their weaving, but their loom remained as empty as ever.

Soon the emperor sent another of his trusted councilors to see how the work was progressing. He looked and looked just as the prime minister had, but since there was nothing to be seen, he didn't see anything.

"Isn't it a marvelous piece of material?" asked one of the swindlers; and they both began to describe the beauty of their cloth again.

"I am not stupid," thought the emperor's councilor. "I must be unfit for my office. That is strange; but I'd better not admit it to anyone." And he started to praise the material, which he could not see, for the loveliness of its patterns and colors.

"I think it is the most charming piece of material I have ever seen," declared the councilor to the emperor.

Everyone in town was talking about the marvelous cloth that the swindlers were weaving.

At last the emperor himself decided to see it before it was removed from the loom. Attended by the most important people in the empire, among them the prime minister and the councilor who had been there before, the emperor entered the room where the weavers were weaving furiously on their empty loom.

Isn't it *magnifique*?" asked the prime minister.

"Your Majesty, look at the colors and the patterns," said the councilor.

And the two old gentlemen pointed to the

empty loom, believing that all the rest of the company could see the cloth.

"What!" thought the emperor. "I can't see a thing! Why, this is a disaster! Am I stupid? Am I unfit to be emperor? Oh, it is too horrible!" Aloud he said, "It is very lovely. It has my approval," while he nodded his head and looked at the empty loom.

All the councilors, ministers, and men of great importance who had come with him stared and stared; but they saw no more than the emperor had seen, and they said the same thing that he had said, "It is lovely." And they advised him to have clothes cut and sewn, so that he could wear them in the procession at the next great celebration.

"Is is magnificent! Beautiful! Excellent! All of their mouths agreed, though none of their eyes had seen anything. The two swindlers were decorated and given the title "Royal Knight of the Loom."

The night before the procession, the two swindlers didn't sleep at all. They had sixteen candles lighting up the room where they worked. Everyone could see how busy they were, getting the emperor's new clothes finished. They pretended to take the cloth from the loom; they cut the air with their big scissors, and sewed with needles without thread. At last they announced: "The emperor's clothes are ready!"

Together with his courtiers, the emperor came. The swindlers lifted their arms as if they were holding something in their hands, and said, "These are the trousers. This is the robe, and here is the train. They are all as light as if they were made of spider webs! It will be as if Your Majesty had almost nothing on, but that is their special virtue."

"Oh yes," breathed all the courtiers; but they saw nothing, for there was nothing to be seen.

"Will Your Imperial Majesty be so gracious as to take off your clothes?" asked the swindlers. "Over there by the big mirror, we shall help you put your new ones on."

The emperor did as he was told; and the swindlers acted as if they were dressing him in the clothes they should have made. Finally they tied around his waist the long train which two of his most noble courtiers were to carry.

The emperor stood in front of the mirror admiring the clothes he couldn't see.

"Oh, how they suit you! A perfect fit!" everyone exclaimed. "What colors! What patterns! The new clothes are magnificent!"

"The crimson canopy, under which Your Imperial Majesty is to walk, is waiting outside," said the imperial master of court ceremony.

"Well, I am dressed. Aren't my clothes becoming?" The emperor turned around once more in front of the mirror, pretending to study his finery.

The two gentlemen of the imperial bedchamber fumbled on the floor, trying to find the train which they were supposed to carry. They didn't dare admit that they didn't see anything, so they pretended to pick up the train and held their hands as if they were carrying it.

The emperor walked in the procession under his crimson canopy. And all the people of the town, who had lined the streets or were looking down from the windows, said that the emperor's clothes were beautiful. "What a magnificent robe! And the train! How well the emperor's clothes suit him!"

None of them were willing to admit that they hadn't seen a thing; for if anyone did, then he was either stupid or unfit for the job he held. Never before had the emperor's clothes been such a success.

"But he doesn't have anything on!" cried a little child.

"Listen to the innocent one," said the proud father. And the people whispered among each other and repeated what the child had said.

"He doesn't have anything on. There's a little child who says that he has nothing on."

"He has nothing on!" shouted all the people at last.

The emperor shivered, for he was certain that they were right; but he thought, "I must bear it until the procession is over." And he walked even more proudly, and the two gentlemen of the imperial bedchamber went on carrying the train that wasn't there.

The Magic Fishbone, *by Charles Dickens. Illustrated by Louis Slobodkin. (The Vanguard Press, 1953).*

*In his famous article, "Frauds on the Fairies," Charles Dickens eloquently defended the value of the fairy tale as appropriate reading for the young and reprehended Victorian illustrator, George Cruikshank, for editing such traditional tales. He concluded the essay by advocating "a little more fancy and a little less fact," warning the "frauds on the fairies" that "the world is too much with us early and late. Leave this precious old escape from it" (*Household Words, 1853*).*

"The Magic Fishbone" is probably Dickens' most famous literary folk tale. First published in an American children's magazine, "The Magic Fishbone" appeared as Alice Rainbird's story in A Holiday Romance *(1868). In this comic tale, Dickens endorses the fairy tale as the kind of story which communicates useful truths to children, while also gently mocking the conventions of the fairy tale: the magic talisman is not a golden apple, a cap of darkness, an enchanted purse, but a lowly fishbone. Prince Certainpersonio is not a dashing, handsome hero, but a retiring young man who sits by himself "eating barley-sugar, and waiting to be ninety." Princess Alicia does not wait for a fairy-godmother but "cuts and contrives," doing the best she can with her own initiative before she asks for help. While Dickens clearly enjoys mocking the conventions of "fairy business," he witholds his irony from the child and from the form itself, directing it instead toward the foolish, immature adults in the tale. Princess Alicia follows the linear pattern of moving from childhood home to her husband's home. Yet Dickens presents an ironic variation of this linear structure; Princess Alicia is merely leaving a childish father to live with an equally childish husband.*

The Magic Fishbone

There was once a king, and he had a queen; and he was the manliest of his sex, and she was the loveliest of hers. The king was, in his private profession, under government. The queen's father had been a medical man out of town.

They had nineteen children, and were always having more. Seventeen of these children took care of the baby; and Alicia, the eldest, took care of them all. Their ages varied from seven to seven months.

Let us now resume our story.

One day the king was going to the office, when he stopped at the fishmonger's to buy a pound and a half of salmon not too near the tail, which the queen (who was a careful housekeeper) had requested him to send home. Mr. Pickles, the fishmonger, said, "Certainly, sir; is there any other article? Good morning."

The king went on towards the office in a melancholy mood; for quarter-day was such a long way off, and several of the dear children were growing out of their clothes. He had not proceeded far, when Mr. Pickles's errand-boy came running after him, and said, "Sir, you didn't notice the old lady in our shop."

"What old lady?" inquired the king. "I saw none."

Now, the king had not seen any old lady, because this old lady had been invisible to him, though visible to Mr. Pickles's boy. Probably because he messed and splashed the water about to that degree, and flopped the pairs of soles down in that violent manner, that, if she had not been visible to him, he would have spoiled her clothes.

Just then the old lady came trotting up. She was dressed in shot-silk of the richest quality, smelling of dried lavender.

"King Watkins the First, I believe?" said the old lady.

"Watkins," replied the king, "is my name."

"Papa, if I am not mistaken, of the beautiful Princess Alicia?" said the old lady.

"And of eighteen other darlings," replied the king.

"Listen. You are going to the office," said the old lady.

It instantly flashed upon the king that she must be a fairy, or how could she know that?

"You are right," said the old lady, answering his thoughts. "I am the good Fairy Grandmarina. Attend! When you return home to dinner, politely invite the Princess Alicia to have some of the salmon you bought just now.''

"It may disagree with her," said the king. The old lady became so very angry at this absurd idea, that the king was quite alarmed, and humbly begged her pardon.

"We hear a great deal too much about this thing disagreeing and that thing disagreeing," said the old lady, with the greatest contempt it was possible to express. "Don't be greedy. I think you want it all yourself."

The king hung his head under this reproof, and said he wouldn't talk about things disagreeing any more.

"Be good, then," said the Fairy Grandmarina, "and don't! When the beautiful Princess Alicia consents to partake of the salmon — as I think she will — you will find she will leave a fishbone on her plate. Tell her to dry it, and to rub it, and to polish it, till it shines like mother-of-pearl, and to take care of it as a present from me."

"Is that all?" asked the king.

"Don't be impatient, sir," returned the Fairy Grandmarina, scolding him severely. "Don't catch people short before they have done speaking. Just the way with you grownup persons. You are always doing it."

The king again hung his head and said he wouldn't do so any more.

"Be good, then," said the Fairy Grandmarina, "and don't! Tell the Princess Alicia, with my love, that the fishbone is a magic present which can only be used once; but that it will bring her, that once, whatever she wishes for, PROVIDED SHE WISHES FOR IT AT THE RIGHT TIME. That is the message. Take care of it." The king was beginning, "Might I ask the reason?" when the fairy became absolutely furious.

"*Will* you be good, sir?" she exclaimed, stamping her foot on the ground. "The reason for this, and the reason for that, indeed! You are always wanting the reason. No reason. There! Hoity toity me! I am sick of your grownup reasons."

The king was extremely frightened by the old lady's flying into such a passion, and he said he was very sorry to have offended her, and he wouldn't ask for reasons any more.

"Be good, then," said the old lady, "and don't!"

With those words, Grandmarina vanished, and the king went on and on and on, till he came to the office. There he wrote and wrote and wrote, till it was time to go home again. Then he politely invited the Princess Alicia, as the fairy had directed him, to partake of the salmon. And when she had enjoyed it very much, he saw the fishbone on her plate, as the fairy told him he would, and he delivered the Fairy's message, and the Princess Alicia took care to dry the bone, and to rub it, and to polish it, till it shone like mother-of-pearl.

And so, when the queen was going to get up in the morning, she said, "Oh, dear me, dear me; my head, my head!" and then she fainted away.

The Princess Alicia, who happened to be looking in at the chamber door, asking about breakfast, was very much alarmed when she saw her royal mamma in this state, and she rang the bell for Peggy, which was the name of the lord chamberlain. But remembering where the smelling-bottle was, she climbed on a chair and got it; and after that she climbed on another chair to the bedside, and held the smelling-bottle to the queen's nose; and after that she jumped down and got some water; and after that she jumped up again and wetted the queen's forehead; and, in short, when the lord chamberlain came in, that dear old woman said to the little princess, "What a trot you are! I couldn't have done it better myself!"

But that was not the worst of the good queen's illness. Oh, no! She was very ill indeed, for a long time.

The Princess Alicia kept the seventeen young princes and princesses quiet, and dressed and undressed and danced the baby, and made the kettle boil, and heated the soup, and swept the hearth, and poured out the medicine, and nursed the queen, and did all that ever she could, and was as busy, busy, busy, as busy as could be; for there were not many servants at that palace for three reasons: because the king was short of money, because a rise in his office never seemed to come, and because quarter-day was so far off that it looked almost as far off and as little as one of the stars.

But on the morning when the queen fainted away, where was the magic fishbone? Why, there it was in the Princess Alicia's pocket! She had almost taken it out to bring the queen to life again, when she put it back, and looked for the smelling-bottle.

After the queen had come out of her swoon that morning and was dozing, the Princess Alicia hurried upstairs to tell a most particular secret to a most particular confidential friend of hers, who was a duchess. People did suppose her to be a doll; but she was really a duchess, though nobody knew it except the princess.

This most particular secret was the secret about the magic fishbone, the history of which was well-known to the duchess, because the princess told her everything. The princess kneeled down by the bed on which the duchess was lying, full-dressed and wide-awake, and whispered the secret to her. The duchess smiled and nodded. People might have supposed that she never smiled and nodded; but she often did, though nobody knew it except the princess.

Then the Princess Alicia hurried downstairs again to keep watch in the queen's room. She often kept watch by herself in the queen's room; but every evening, while the illness lasted, she sat there watching with the king. And every evening the king sat looking at her with a cross look, wondering why she never brought out the magic fishbone.

As often as she noticed this, she ran upstairs, whispered the secret to the duchess over again, and said to the duchess besides, "They think we children never have a reason or a meaning!" And the duchess, though the most fashionable duchess that ever was heard of, winked her eye.

"Alicia," said the king, one evening, when she wished him good night.

"Yes, papa."

"What has become of the magic fishbone?"

"In my pocket, papa!"

"I thought you had lost it!"

"Oh, no, papa!"

"Or forgotten it?"

"No, indeed, papa."

And so another time the dreadful little snapping pug dog next door made a rush at one of the young princes as he stood on the steps coming home from school, and terrified him out of his wits; and he put his hand through a pane of glass and bled, bled, bled. When the seventeen other young princes and princesses saw him bleed, bleed, bleed, they were terrified out of their wits too, and screamed themselves black in their seventeen faces all at once.

But the Princess Alicia put her hands over all their seventeen mouths, one after another, and persuaded them to be quiet because of the sick queen. And then she put the wounded prince's hand in a basin of fresh cold water, while they stared with their twice seventeen are thirty-four, put down four and carry three, eyes, and then she looked in the hand for bits of glass, and there were fortunately no bits of glass there. And then she said to two chubby-legged princes, who were sturdy though small, "Bring me in the royal rag-bag: I must snip and stitch and cut and contrive." So the two young princes tugged at the royal rag-bag and lugged it in; and the Princess Alicia sat down on the floor, with a large pair of scissors and a needle and thread, and snipped and stitched and cut and contrived, and made a bandage, and put it on, and it fitted beautifully; and so when it was all done, she saw the king her papa looking on by the door.

"Alicia."

"Yes, papa."

"What have you been doing?"

"Snipping, stitching, cutting, and contriving, papa."

"Where is the magic fishbone?"

"In my pocket, papa."

"I thought you had lost it."

"Oh, no, papa!"

"Or forgotten it?"

"No, indeed, papa."

After that, she ran upstairs to the duchess, and told her what had passed, and told her the secret over again; and the duchess shook her flaxen curls and laughed with her rosy lips.

Well! and so another time the baby fell under the grate. The seventeen young princes and princesses were used to it, for they were almost always falling under the grate or down the stairs; but the baby was not used to it yet, and it gave him a swelled face and a black eye.

The way the poor little darling came to tumble was, that he was out of the Princess

Alicia's lap just as she was sitting, in a great coarse apron that quite smothered her, in front of the kitchen fire, beginning to peel the turnips for the broth for dinner; and the way she came to be doing that was, that the king's cook had run away that morning with her own true love, who was a very tall but very tipsy soldier.

Then the seventeen young princes and princesses, who cried at everything that happened, cried and roared. But the Princess Alicia (who couldn't help crying a little herself) quietly called to them to be still, on account of not throwing back the queen upstairs, who was fast getting well, and said, "Hold your tongues, you wicked little monkeys, every one of you, while I examine baby!"

Then she examined baby and found that he hadn't broken anything; and she held cold iron to his poor dear eye, and smoothed his poor dear face, and he presently fell asleep in her arms. Then she said to the seventeen princes and princesses, "I am afraid to let him down yet, lest he should wake and feel pain; be good, and you shall all be cooks."

They jumped for joy when they heard that, and began making themselves cooks' caps out of old newspapers. So to one she gave the salt-box, and to one she gave the barley, and to one she gave the herbs, and to one she gave the turnips, and to one she gave the carrots, and to one she gave the onions, and to one she gave the spice-box, till they were all cooks, and all running about at work, she sitting in the middle, smothered in the great coarse apron, nursing baby.

By and by the broth was done; and the baby woke up, smiling like an angel, and was trusted to the sedatest princess to hold, while the other princes and princesses were squeezed into a far-off corner to look at the Princess Alicia turning out the saucepanful of broth, for fear (as they were always getting into trouble) they should get splashed and scalded. When the broth came tumbling out, steaming beautifully, and smelling like a nosegay good to eat, they clapped their hands. That made the baby clap his hands; and that, and his looking as if he had a comic toothache, made all the princes and princesses laugh. So the Princess Alicia said, "Laugh and be good; and after dinner we will

make him a nest on the floor in a corner, and he shall sit in his nest and see a dance of eighteen cooks."

That delighted the young princes and princesses, and they ate up all the broth, and washed up all the plates and dishes, and cleared away, and pushed the table into a corner; and then they in their cooks' caps, and the Princess Alicia in the smothering coarse apron that belonged to the cook that had run away with her own true love that was the very tall but very tipsy soldier, danced a dance of eighteen cooks before the angelic baby, who forgot his swelled face and his black eye and crowed with joy.

And so then, once more, the Princess Alicia saw King Watkins the First, her father, standing in the doorway looking on, and he said, "What have you been doing, Alicia?"

"Cooking and contriving, papa."

"What else have you been doing, Alicia?"

"Keeping the children lighthearted, papa."

"Where is the magic fishbone, Alicia?"

"In my pocket, papa."

"I thought you had lost it?"

"Oh, no, papa!"

"Or forgotten it?"

"No, indeed, papa."

The king then sighed so heavily, and seemed so low-spirited, and sat down so miserably, leaning his head upon his hand, and his elbow upon the kitchen table pushed away in the corner, that the seventeen princes and princess crept softly out of the kitchen and left him alone with the Princess Alicia and the angelic baby.

"What is the matter, papa?"

"I am dreadfully poor, my child."

"Have you no money at all, papa?"

"None, my child."

"Is there no way of getting any, papa?"

"No way," said the king. "I have tried very hard, and I have tried all ways." When she heard those last words, the Princess Alicia began to put her hand into the pocket where she kept the magic fishbone.

"Papa," said she. "When we have tried very hard, and tried all ways, we must have done our very, very best?"

"No doubt, Alicia."

"When we have done our very, very best, papa, and that is not enough, then I think the right time must have come for asking help of others." This was the very secret connected with the magic fishbone, which she had found out for herself from the good Fairy Grandmarina's words, and which she had so often whispered to her beautiful and fashionable friend, the duchess.

So she took out of her pocket the magic fishbone, that had been dried and rubbed and polished till it shone like mother-of-pearl; and she gave it one little kiss, and wished it was quarter-day. And immediately it *was* quarter-day; and the king's quarter's salary came rattling down the chimney and bounced into the middle of the floor.

But this was not half of what happened — no, not a quarter; for immediately afterwards the good Fairy Grandmarina came riding in, in a carriage and four (peacocks), with Mr. Pickles's boy up behind, dressed in silver and gold, with a cocked hat, powdered hair, pink silk stockings, a jewelled cane, and a nosegay. Down jumped Mr. Pickles's boy, with his cocked hat in his hand, and wonderfully polite (being entirely changed by enchantment), and handed Grandmarina out; and there she stood, in her rich shot silk smelling of dried lavender, fanning herself with a sparkling fan.

"Alicia, my dear," said this charming old fairy, "how do you do? I hope I see you pretty well. Give me a kiss."

The Princess Alicia embraced her; and then Grandmarina turned to the king and said rather sharply, "Are you good?"

The king said he hoped so.

"I suppose you know the reason *now* why my goddaughter here," kissing the princess again, "did not apply to the fishbone sooner?" said the fairy.

The king made a shy bow.

"Ah! but you didn't *then*?" said the fairy.

The king made a shyer bow.

"Any more reasons to ask for?" said the fairy. The king said No, and he was very sorry.

"Be good, then," said the fairy, "and live happy ever afterwards."

Then Grandmarina waved her fan, and the queen came in most splendidly dressed; and the seventeen young princes and princesses, no longer grown out of their clothes, came in, newly fitted out from top to toe, with tucks in everything to admit of its being let out. After that, the fairy tapped the Princess Alicia with her fan; and the smothering coarse apron flew away, and she appeared exquisitely dressed, like a little bride, with a wreath of orange-flowers and a silver veil. After that, the kitchen dresser changed of itself into a wardrobe, made of beautiful woods and gold and looking-glass, which was full of dresses of all sorts, all for her and all exactly fitting her. After that, the angelic baby came in running alone, with his face and eye not a bit the worse, but much the better. Then Grandmarina begged to be introduced to the duchess; and, when the duchess was brought down, many compliments passed between them.

A little whispering took place between the fairy and the duchess; and then the fairy said out loud. "Yes, I thought she would have told you." Grandmarina then turned to the king and queen, and said. "We are going in search of Prince Certainpersonio. The pleasure of your company is requested at church in half an hour precisely." So she and the Princess Alicia got into the carriage; and Mr. Pickles's boy handed in the duchess, who sat by herself on the opposite seat; and then Mr. Pickles's boy put up the steps and got up behind, and the peacocks flew away with their tails behind.

Prince Certainpersonio was sitting by himself, eating barley-sugar, and waiting to be ninety.

When he saw the peacocks, followed by the carriage, coming in at the window, it immediately occurred to him that something uncommon was going to happen.

"Prince," said Grandmarina, "I bring you your bride."

The moment the fairy said those words, Prince Certainpersonio's face left off being sticky, and his jacket and corduroys changed to peach-bloom velvet, and his hair curled, and a cap and feather flew in like a bird and settled on his head.

He got into the carriage by the fairy's invitation; and there he renewed his acquaintance with the duchess, whom he had seen before.

In the church were the prince's relations and friends, and the Princess Alicia's relations and friends, and the seventeen princes and princesses, and the baby, and a crowd of the neighbours. The marriage was beautiful beyond expression. The duchess was bridesmaid, and beheld the ceremony from the pulpit, where she was supported by the cushion of the desk.

Grandmarina gave a magnificent wedding feast afterwards, in which there was everything and more to eat, and everything and more to drink. The wedding cake was delicately ornamented with white satin ribbons, frosted silver, and white lilies, and was forty-two yards round.

When Grandmarina had drunk her love to the young couple, and Prince Certainpersonio had made a speech, and everybody cried, Hip, hip, hip hurrah! Grandmarina announced to the king and queen that in the future there would be eight quarter-days in every year, except in leap year, when there would be ten. She then turned to Certainpersonio and Alicia and said, "My dears, you will have thirty-five children, and they will be all good and beautiful. Seventeen of your children will be boys, and eighteen will be girls. The hair of the whole of your children will curl naturally. They will never have the measles, and will have recovered from the whooping-cough before being born."

On hearing such good news, everybody cried out "Hip, hip, hip, hurrah!" again.

"It only remains," said Grandmarina in conclusion, "to make an end of the fishbone."

So she took it from the hand of the Princess Alicia, and it instantly flew down the throat of the dreadful little snapping pug-dog next door and choked him, and he expired in convulsions.

———

"Gudgekin the Thistle Girl," from Gudgekin the Thistle Girl and Other Tales, *by John Gardner (New York: Alfred A. Knopf, 1976).*

Obviously inspired by such traditional favorites as "Cinderella," John Gardner presents a linear tale about Gudgekin, a fairy tale heroine with so much pride and self-respect (as well as goodness) that her prince must trick her into marriage. Gardner reverses the heroine's passiveness and endows the usually slow-witted fairy tale prince with unusual cleverness.

Gudgekin the Thistle Girl

In a certain kingdom there lived a poor little thistle girl. What thistle girls did for a living —that is, what people did with thistles—is no longer known, but whatever the reason that people gathered thistles, she was one of those who did it. All day long, from well before sunrise until long after sunset, she wandered the countryside gathering thistles, pricking her fingers to the bone, piling the thistles into her enormous thistle sack and carrying them back to her stepmother. It was a bitter life, but she always made the best of it and never felt the least bit sorry for herself, only for the miseries of others. The girl's name was Gudgekin.

Alas! The stepmother was never satisfied. She was arrogant and fiercely competitive, and when she laid out her thistles in her market stall, she would rather be dead than suffer the humiliation of seeing that some other stall had more thistles than she had. No one ever did, but the fear preyed on her, and no matter how many sacks of thistles poor Gudgekin gathered, there were never enough to give the stepmother comfort. "You don't earn your keep," the stepmother would say, crossing her arms and closing them together like scissors. "If you don't bring more thistles tomorrow, it's away you must go to the Children's Home and good riddance!"

Poor Gudgekin. Every day she brought more than yesterday, but every night the same. "If you don't bring more thistles tomorrow, it's away to the Home with you." She worked feverishly, frantically, smiling through her tears, seizing the thistles by whichever end came first, but never to her stepmother's satisfaction. Thus she lived out her miserable childhood, blinded by burning tears and pink with thistle pricks, but viewing her existence in the best light possible. As she grew older she grew more and more beautiful, partly because she was always smiling and refused to pout, whatever the provocation; and soon she was as lovely as any princess.

One day her bad luck changed to good. As she was jerking a thistle from between two rocks, a small voice cried, "Stop! You're murdering my children!"

"I beg your pardon?" said the thistle girl. When she bent down she saw a beautiful little fairy in a long white and silver dress, hastily removing her children from their cradle, which was resting in the very thistle that Gudgekin had been pulling.

"Oh," said Gudgekin in great distress.

The fairy said nothing at first, hurrying back and forth, carrying her children to the safety of the nearest rock. But then at last the fairy looked up and saw that Gudgekin was crying. "Well," she said. "What's this?"

Illustration by Michael Sporn from *Gudgekin the Thistle Girl and Other Tales*, by John Gardner, Copyright © 1976 Michael Sporn. Reprinted by permission of Alfred A. Knopf Inc.

"I'm sorry," said Gudgekin. "I always cry. It's because of the misery of others, primarily. I'm used to it."

"Primarily?" said the fairy and put her hands on her hips.

"Well," sniffled Gudgekin, "to tell the truth, I do sometimes imagine I'm not as happy as I might be. It's shameful, I know. Everyone's miserable, and it's wrong of me to whimper."

"Everyone?" said the fairy," — miserable? Sooner or later an opinion like that will make a fool of you!"

"Well, I really don't know," said Gudgekin, somewhat confused. "I've seen very little of the world, I'm afraid."

"I see," said the fairy thoughtfully, lips pursed. "Well, that's a pity, but it's easily fixed. Since you've spared my children and taken pity on my lot, I think I should do you a good turn."

She struck the rock three times with a tiny golden straw, and instantly all the thistles for miles around began moving as if by their own volition toward the thistle girl's sack. It was the kingdom of fairies, and the beautiful fairy with whom Gudgekin had made friends was none other than the fairies' queen. Soon the fairies had gathered all the thistles for a mile around, and had filled the sack that Gudgekin had brought, and had also filled forty-three more, which they'd fashioned on the spot out of gossamer.

"Now," said the queen, "it's time that you saw the world."

Immediately the fairies set to work all together and built a beautiful chariot as light as the wind, all transparent gossamer woven like fine thread. The chariot was so light that it needed no horses but flew along over the ground by itself, except when it was anchored with a stone. Next they made the thistle girl a gown of woven gossamer so lovely that not even the queen of the kingdom had anything to rival it; indeed, no one anywhere in the world had such a gown or has ever had, even to this day. For Gudgekin's head the fairies fashioned a flowing veil as light and silvery as the lightest, most silvery of clouds, and they sprinkled both the veil and the gown with dew so they glittered as if with costly jewels.

Then, to a tinny little trumpeting noise, the

queen of the fairies stepped into the chariot and graciously held out her tiny hand to the thistle girl.

No sooner was Gudgekin seated beside the queen than the chariot lifted into the air lightly, like a swift little boat, and skimmed the tops of the fields and flew away to the capital.

When they came to the city, little Gudgekin could scarcely believe her eyes. But there was no time to look at the curious shops or watch the happy promenading of the wealthy. They were going to the palace, the fairy queen said, and soon the chariot had arrived there.

It was the day of the kingdom's royal ball, and the chariot was just in time. "I'll wait here," said the kindly queen of the fairies. "You run along and enjoy yourself, my dear."

Happy Gudgekin! Everyone was awed by her lovely gown and veil; and even the fact that the fairies had neglected to make shoes for her feet, since they themselves wore none, turned out to be to Gudgekin's advantage. Barefoot dancing immediately became all the rage at court, and people who'd been wearing fine shoes for years slipped over to the window and shyly tossed them out, not to be outdone by a stranger. The thistle girl danced with the prince himself, and he was charmed more than words can tell. His smile seemed all openness and innocence, yet Gudgekin had a feeling he was watching her like a hawk. He had a reputation throughout the nine kingdoms for subtlety and shrewdness.

When it was time to take the thistle sacks back to her cruel stepmother, Gudgekin slipped out, unnoticed by anyone, and away she rode in the chariot.

"Well, how was it?" asked the queen of the fairies happily.

"Wonderful! Wonderful!" Gudgekin replied. "Except I couldn't help but notice how gloomy people were, despite their merry chatter. How sadly they frown when they look into their mirrors, fixing their make-up. Some of them frown because their feet hurt, I suppose; some of them perhaps because they're jealous of someone; and some of them perhaps because they've lost their youthful beauty. I could have wept for them!"

The queen of the fairies frowned pensively.

"You're a good-hearted child, that's clear," she said, and fell silent.

They reached the field, and the thistle girl, assisted by a thousand fairies, carried her forty-four sacks to her wicked stepmother. The stepmother was amazed to see so many thistle sacks, especially since some of them seemed to be coming to the door all by themselves. Nevertheless, she said—for her fear of humiliation so drove her that she was never satisfied —"A paltry forty-four, Gudgekin! If you don't bring more thistles tomorrow, it's away to the Home with you!"

Little Gudgekin bowed humbly, sighed with resignation, forced to her lips a happy smile, ate her bread crusts, and climbed up the ladder to her bed of straw.

The next morning when she got to the field, she found eighty-eight thistle sacks stuffed and waiting. The gossamer chariot was standing at anchor, and the gossamer gown and veil were laid out on a rock, gleaming in the sun.

"Today," said the queen of the fairies, "we're going on a hunt."

They stepped into the chariot and flew off light as moonbeams to the royal park, and there, sure enough, were huntsmen waiting, and huntswomen beside them, all dressed in black riding-pants and riding-skirts and bright red jackets. The fairies made the thistle girl a gossamer horse that would sail wherever the wind might blow, and the people all said she was the most beautiful maiden in the kingdom, possibly an elf queen. Then the French horns and bugles blew, and the huntsmen were off. Light as a feather went the thistle girl, and the prince was so entranced he was beside himself, though he watched her, for all that, with what seemed to her a crafty smile. All too soon came the time to carry the thistle sacks home, and the thistle girl slipped from the crowd, unnoticed, and rode her light horse beside the chariot where the queen of the fairies sat beaming like a mother.

"Well," called the queen of the fairies, "how was it?"

"Wonderful!" cried Gudgekin, "it was truly wonderful! I noticed one thing, though. It's terrible for the fox!"

The queen of the fairies thought about it.

"Blood sports," she said thoughtfully, and nodded. After that, all the rest of the way home, she spoke not a word.

When the thistle girl arrived at her stepmother's house, her stepmother threw up her arms in amazement at sight of those eighty-eight thistle-filled sacks. Nonetheless, she said as sternly as possible, "Eighty-eight! Why not a hundred? If you don't bring in more sacks tomorrow, it's the Home for you for sure!"

Gudgekin sighed, ate her dry crusts, forced a smile to her lips, and climbed the ladder.

The next day was a Sunday, but Gudgekin the thistle girl had to work just the same, for her stepmother's evil disposition knew no bounds. When she got to the field, there stood two times eighty-eight thistle sacks, stuffed to the tops and waiting. "That ought to fix her," said the queen of the fairies merrily. "Jump into your dress."

"Where are we going?" asked Gudgekin, as happy as could be.

"Why, to church, of course!" said the queen of the fairies. "After church we go to the royal picnic, and then we dance on the bank of the river until twilight."

"Wonderful!" said the thistle girl, and away they flew.

The singing in church was thrilling, and the sermon filled her heart with such kindly feelings toward her friends and neighbors that she felt close to dissolving in tears. The picnic was the sunniest in the history of the kingdom, and the dancing beside the river was delightful beyond words. Throughout it all the prince was beside himself with pleasure, never removing his eyes from Gudgekin, for he thought her the loveliest maiden he'd met in his life. For all his shrewdness, for all his aloofness and princely self-respect, when he danced with Gudgekin in her bejeweled gown of gossamer, it was all he could do to keep himself from asking her to marry him on the spot. He asked instead, "Beautiful stranger, permit me to ask you your name."

"It's Gudgekin," she said, smiling shyly and glancing at his eyes.

He didn't believe her.

"Really," she said, "it's Gudgekin." Only now did it strike her that the name was rather odd.

"Listen," said the prince with a laugh, "I'm serious. What is it really?"

"I'm serious too," said Gudgekin bridling. "It's Gudgekin the Thistle Girl. With the help of the fairies I've been known to collect two times eighty-eight sacks of thisles in a single day."

The prince laughed more merrily than ever at that. "Please," he said, "don't tease me, dear friend! A beautiful maiden like you must have a name like bells on Easter morning, or like songbirds in the meadow, or children's laughing voices on the playground! Tell me now. Tell me the truth. What's your name?"

"Puddin Tane," she said angrily, and ran away weeping to the chariot.

"Well," said the queen of the fairies, "how was it?"

"Horrible," snapped Gudgekin.

"Ah!" said the queen. "Now we're getting there!"

She was gone before the prince was aware that she was leaving, and even if he'd tried to follow her, the gossamer chariot was too fast, for it skimmed along like wind. Nevertheless, he was resolved to find and marry Gudgekin — he'd realized by now that Gudgekin must indeed be her name. He could easily understand the thistle girl's anger. He'd have felt the same himself, for he was a prince and knew better than anyone what pride was, and the shame of being made to seem a fool. He advertised far and wide for information on Gudgekin the Thistle Girl, and soon the news of the prince's search reached Gudgekin's cruel stepmother in her cottage. She was at once so furious she could hardly see, for she always wished evil for others and happiness for herself.

"I'll never in this world let him find her," thought the wicked stepmother, and she called in Gudgekin and put a spell on her, for the stepmother was a witch. She made Gudgekin believe that her name was Rosemarie and sent the poor baffled child off to the Children's Home. Then the cruel stepmother changed herself, by salves and charms, into a beautiful young maiden who looked exactly like Gudgekin, and she set off for the palace to meet the prince.

"Gudgekin!" cried the prince and leaped forward and embraced her. "I've been looking for you everywhere to implore you to forgive me and be my bride!"

"Dearest prince," said the stepmother disguised as Gudgekin, "I'll do so gladly!"

"Then you've forgiven me already, my love?" said the prince. He was surprised, in fact, for it had seemed to him that Gudgekin was a touch more sensitive than that and had more personal pride. He'd thought, in fact, he'd have a devil of a time, considering how he'd hurt her and made a joke of her name. "Then you really forgive me?" asked the prince.

The stepmother looked slightly confused for an instant but quickly smiled as Gudgekin might have smiled and said, "Prince, I forgive you everything!" And so, though the prince felt queer about it, the day of the wedding was set.

A week before the wedding, the prince asked thoughtfully, "Is it true that you can gather, with the help of the fairies, two times eighty-eight thistle sacks all in one day?"

"Haven't I told you so?" asked the stepmother disguised as Gudgekin and gave a little laugh. She had a feeling she was in for it.

"You did say that, yes," the prince said, pulling with two fingers at his beard. "I'd surely like to see it!"

"Well," said the stepmother, and curtsied, "I'll come to you tomorrow and you shall see what you shall see."

The next morning she dragged out two times eighty-eight thistle sacks, thinking she could gather in the thistles by black magic. But the magic of the fairies was stronger than any witch's, and since they lived in the thistles, they resisted all her fiercest efforts. When it was late afternoon the stepmother realized she had only one hope: she must get the real Gudgekin from the Children's Home and make her help.

Alas for the wicked stepmother, Gudgekin was no longer an innocent simpleton! As soon as she was changed back from simple Rosemarie, she remembered everything and wouldn't touch a thistle with an iron glove. Neither would she help her stepmother now, on account of all the woman's cruelty before, nor

would she do anything under heaven that might be pleasing to the prince, for she considered him coldhearted and inconsiderate. The stepmother went back to the palace empty-handed, weeping and moaning and making a hundred excuses, but the scales had now fallen from the prince's eyes — his reputation for shrewdness was in fact well founded — and after talking with his friends and advisers, he threw her in the dungeon. In less than a week her life in the dungeon was so miserable it made her repent and become a good woman, and the prince released her. "Hold your head high," he said, brushing a tear from his eye, for she made him think of Gudgekin. "People may speak of you as someone who's been in prison, but you're a better person now than before." She blessed him and thanked him and went her way.

Then once more he advertised far and wide through the kingdom, begging the real Gudgekin to forgive him and come to the palace.

"Never!" thought Gudgekin bitterly, for the fairy queen had taught her the importance of self-respect, and the prince's offense still rankled.

The prince mused and waited, and he began to feel a little hurt himself. He was a prince, after all, handsome and famous for his subtlety and shrewdness, and she was a mere thistle girl. Yet for all his beloved Gudgekin cared, he might as well have been born in some filthy cattle shed! At last he understood how things were, and the truth amazed him.

Now word went far and wide through the kingdom that the handsome prince had fallen ill for sorrow and was lying in his bed, near death's door. When the queen of the fairies heard the dreadful news, she was dismayed and wept tears of remorse, for it was all, she imagined, her fault. She threw herself down on the ground and began wailing, and all the fairies everywhere began at once to wail with her, rolling on the ground, for it seemed that she would die. And one of them, it happened, was living among the flowerpots in the bedroom of cruel little Grudgekin.

When Gudgekin heard the tiny forlorn voice wailing, she hunted through the flowers and found the fairy and said, "What in heaven's name is the matter, little friend?"

"Ah, dear Gudgekin," wailed the fairy, "our queen is dying, and if she dies we will all die of sympathy, and that will be that."

"Oh, you mustn't!" cried Gudgekin, and tears filled her eyes. "Take me to the queen at once, little friend, for she did a favor for me and I see I must return it if I possibly can!"

When they came to the queen of the fairies, the queen said, "Nothing will save me except possibly this, my dear: ride with me one last time in the gossamer chariot for a visit to the prince."

"Never!" said Gudgekin, but seeing the heartbroken looks of the fairies, she instantly relented.

The chariot was brought out from its secret place, and the gossamer horse was hitched to it to give it more dignity, and along they went skimming like wind until they had arrived at the dim and gloomy sickroom. The prince lay on his bed so pale of cheek and so horribly disheveled that Gudgekin didn't know him. If he seemed to her a stranger it was hardly surprising; he'd lost all signs of his princeliness and lay there with his nightcap on sideways and he even had his shoes on.

"What's this?" whispered Gudgekin. "What's happened to the music and dancing and the smiling courtiers? And where is the prince?"

"Woe is me," said the ghastly white figure on the bed. "I was once that proud, shrewd prince you know, and this is what's become of me. For I hurt the feelings of the beautiful Gudgekin, whom I've given my heart and who refuses to forgive me for my insult, such is her pride and uncommon self-respect."

"My poor beloved prince!" cried Gudgekin when she heard this, and burst into a shower of tears. "You have given your heart to a fool, I see now, for I am your Gudgekin, simpleminded as a bird! First I had pity for everyone but myself, and then I had pity for no one but myself, and now I pity all of us in this miserable world, but I see by the whiteness of your cheeks that I've learned too late!" And she fell upon his bosom and wept.

"You give me your love and forgiveness forever and will never take them back?" asked the poor prince feebly, and coughed.

"I do," sobbed Gudgekin, pressing his frail, limp hand in both of hers.

"Cross your heart?" he said.

"Oh, I do, I do!"

The prince jumped out of bed with all his wrinkled clothes on and wiped the thick layer of white powder off his face and seized his dearest Gudgekin by the waist and danced around the room with her. The queen of the fairies laughed like silver bells and immediately felt improved. "Why you fox!" she told the prince. All the happy fairies began dancing with the prince and Gudgekin, who waltzed with her mouth open. When she closed it at last it was to pout, profoundly offended.

"Tr-tr-tricked!" she spluttered.

"Silly goose," said the prince, and kissed away the pout. "It's true, I've tricked you, I'm not miserable at all. But you've promised to love me and never take it back. My advice to you is, make the best of it!" He snatched a glass of wine from the dresser as he merrily waltzed her past, and cried out gaily, "As for myself, though, I make no bones about it: I intend to watch out for witches and live happily ever after. You must too, my Gudgekin! Cross your heart!"

"Oh, very well," she said finally, and let a little smile out. "It's no worse than the thistles."

And so they did.

"The Practical Princess," from The Practical Princess and Other Liberating Fairy Tales, *by Jay Williams (New York: Scholastic Book Services, 1978).*

When Jay Williams' "practical princess" says, "Rubbish!... Dragons can't tell the difference between princesses and anyone else. Use your common sense. He's just asking for me because he's a snob," the author satirizes the class distinctions so prominent in the French court tradition as well as makes fun of European dragon legends. Unlike the pas-

sive fairy tale heroines of the past, Princess Bedelia takes matters into her own hands, refuses to become a victim of rigid and meaningless conventions, and manages to rescue the prince of her dreams. Her intelligence and courage thus save her from being consumed by a dragon or destroyed by a horrid marriage. Williams thus reverses well-known conventions of familiar fairy tales in order to show the reader that the conventions of story (and by extension of society in general) can be modified and changed in accordance with the changing needs of readers. Jack Zipes has written that writers of liberating fairy tales achieve "transfiguration that does not obliterate the recognizable features or values of the classical fairy tale but cancels their negativity by showing how a different aesthetic and social setting relativizes all values."

The Practical Princess

Princess Bedelia was as lovely as the moon shining upon a lake full of waterlilies. She was as graceful as a cat leaping. And she was also extremely practical.

When she was born, three fairies had come to her cradle to give her gifts as was usual in that country. The first fairy had given her beauty. The second had given her grace. But the third, who was a wise old creature, had said, "I give her common sense."

"I don't think much of that gift," said King Ludwig, raising his eyebrows. "What good is common sense to a princess? All she needs is charm."

Nevertheless, when Bedelia was eighteen years old, something happened which made the king change his mind.

A dragon moved into the neighborhood. He settled in a dark cave on top of a mountain, and the first thing he did was to send a message to the king. "I must have a princess to devour," the message said, "or I shall breathe out my fiery breath and destroy the kingdom."

Sadly, King Ludwig called together his councilors and read them the message. "Perhaps," said the Prime Minister, "we had better advertise for a knight to slay the dragon? That is what is generally done in these cases."

"I'm afraid we haven't time," answered the king. "The dragon has only given us until tomorrow morning. There is no help for it. We shall have to send him the princess." Princess Bedelia had come to the meeting because, as she said, she liked to mind her own business and this was certainly her business.

"Rubbish!" she said. "Dragons can't tell the difference between princesses and anyone else. Use your common sense. He's just asking for me because he's a snob."

"That may be so," said her father, "but if we don't send you along, he'll destroy the kingdom."

"Right!" said Bedelia. "I see I'll have to deal with this myself." She left the council chamber. She got the largest and gaudiest of her state robes and stuffed it with straw, and tied it together with string. Into the center of the bundle she packed about a hundred pounds of gunpowder. She got two strong young men to carry it up the mountain for her. She stood in front of the dragon's cave, and called, "Come out! Here's the princess!"

The dragon came blinking and peering out of the darkness. Seeing the bright robe covered with gold and silver embroidery, and hearing Bedelia's voice, he opened his mouth wide.

At Bedelia's signal, the two young men swung the robe and gave it a good heave, right down the dragon's throat. Bedelia threw herself flat on the ground, and the two young men ran.

As the gunpowder met the flames inside the dragon, there was a tremendous explosion.

Bedelia got up, dusting herself off. "Dragons," she said, "are not very bright."

She left the two young men sweeping up the pieces, and she went back to the castle to have her geography lesson.

The lesson that morning was local geography. "Our kingdom, Arapathia, is bounded on the north by Istven," said the teacher. "Lord Garp, the ruler of Istven, is old, crafty, rich, and greedy." At that very moment, Lord Garp of Istven was arriving at the castle. Word of Bedelia's destruction of the dragon had reached him. "That girl," said he, "is just the wife for me." And he had come with a hundred finely-dressed courtiers and many presents to ask King Ludwig for her hand.

The king sent for Bedelia. "My dear," he said, clearing his throat nervously, "just see who is here."

"I see. It's Lord Garp," said Bedelia. She turned to go.

"He wants to marry you," said the king.

Bedelia looked at Lord Garp. His face was like an old napkin, crumpled and wrinkled. It was covered with warts, as if someone had left crumbs on the napkin. He had only two teeth. Six long hairs grew from his chin, and none on his head. She felt like screaming.

However, she said, "I'm very flattered. Thank you, Lord Garp. Just let me talk to my father in private for a minute." When they had retired to a small room behind the throne, Bedelia said to the king, "What will Lord Garp do if I refuse to marry him?"

"He is rich, greedy, and crafty," said the king unhappily. "He is also used to having his own way in everything. He will be insulted. He will probably declare war on us, and then there will be trouble."

"Very well," said Bedelia. "We must be practical."

She returned to the throne room. Smiling sweetly at Lord Garp, she said, "My lord, as you know, it is customary for a princess to set tasks for anyone who wishes to marry her. Surely you wouldn't like me to break the custom. And you are bold and powerful enough, I know, to perform any task."

"That is true," said Lord Garp smugly, stroking the six hairs on his chin. "Name your task."

"Bring me," said Bedelia, "a branch from the Jewel Tree of Paxis."

Lord Garp bowed, and off he went. "I think," said Bedelia to her father, "that we have seen the last of him. For Paxis is a thousand miles away, and the Jewel Tree is guarded by lions, serpents, and wolves."

But in two weeks, Lord Garp was back. With him he bore a chest, and from the chest he took a wonderful twig. Its bark was a rough gold. The leaves that grew from it were of fine silver. The twig was covered with blossoms, and each blossom had petals of mother of pearl and centers of sapphires, the color of the evening sky.

Bedelia's heart sank as she took the twig. But then she said to herself, "Use your common sense, my girl! Lord Garp never travelled two thousand miles in two weeks, nor is he the man to fight his way through lions, serpents, and wolves."

She looked carefully at the branch. Then she said, "My lord, you know that the Jewel Tree of Paxis is a living tree, although it is all made of jewels."

"Why, of course," said Lord Garp. "Everyone knows that."

"Well," said Bedelia, "then why is it that these blossoms have no scent?"

Lord Garp turned red.

"I think," Bedelia went on, "that this branch was made by the jewelers of Istven, who are the best in the world. Not very nice of you, my lord. Some people might even call it cheating."

Lord Garp shrugged. He was too old and rich to feel ashamed. But like many men used to having their own way, the more Bedelia refused him, the more he was determined to have her.

"Never mind all that," he said. "Set me another task. This time, I swear I will perform it."

Bedelia sighed. "Very well. Then bring me a cloak made from the skins of salamanders who live in the Volcano of Scoria."

Lord Garp bowed, and off he went. "The Volcano of Scoria," said Bedelia to her father, "is covered with red-hot lava. It burns steadily with great flames, and pours out poisonous smoke so that no one can come within a mile of it."

"You have certainly profited by your geography lessons," said the king, with admiration.

Nevertheless, in a week Lord Garp was back. This time, he carried a cloak that shone and rippled like all the colors of fire. It was made of scaly skins, stitched together with golden wire as fine as a hair; and each scale was red and orange and blue, like a tiny flame.

Bedelia took the splendid cloak. She said to herself, "Use your head, miss! Lord Garp never climbed the red-hot slopes of the Volcano of Scoria."

A fire was burning in the fireplace of the throne room. Bedelia hurled the cloak into it. The skins blazed up in a flash, blackened, and fell to ashes.

Lord Garp's mouth fell open. Before he could speak, Bedelia said, "That cloak was a fake, my lord. The skins of salamanders who can live in the Volcano of Scoria wouldn't burn in a little fire like that one."

Lord Garp turned pale with anger. He hopped up and down, unable at first to do anything but splutter.

"Ub — ub — ub!" he cried. Then, controlling himself, he said, "So be it. If I can't have you, no one shall!"

He pointed a long, skinny finger at her. On the finger was a magic ring. At once, a great wind arose. It blew through the throne room. It sent King Ludwig flying one way and his guards the other. It picked up Bedelia and whisked her off through the air. When she could catch her breath and look about her, she found herself in a room at the top of a tower.

Bedelia peered out of the window. About the tower stretched an empty, barren plain. As she watched, a speck appeared in the distance. A plume of dust rose behind it. It drew nearer and became Lord Garp on horseback.

He rode to the tower and looked up at Bedelia. "Aha!" he croaked. "So you are safe and snug, are you? And will you marry me now?"

"Never," said Bedelia, firmly.

"Then stay there until never comes," snarled Lord Garp.

Away he rode.

For the next two days, Bedelia felt very sorry for herself. She sat wistfully by the window, looking out at the empty plain. When she was hungry, food appeared on the table. When she was tired, she lay down on the narrow cot and slept. Each day, Lord Garp rode by and asked if she had changed her mind, and each day she refused him. Her only hope was that, as so often happens in old tales, a prince might come riding by who would rescue her.

But on the third day, she gave herself a shake.

"Now, then, pull yourself together," she said, sternly. "If you sit waiting for a prince to rescue you, you may sit here forever. Be practical! If there's any rescuing to be done, you're going to have to do it yourself."

She jumped up. There was something she had not yet done, and now she did it. She tried the door.

It opened.

Outside, were three other doors. But there was no sign of a stair, or any way down from the top of the tower.

She opened two of the doors and found that they led into cells just like hers, but empty.

Behind the fourth door, however, lay what appeared to be a haystack.

From beneath it came the sound of snores. And between snores, a voice said, "Sixteen million and twelve . . . snore . . . sixteen million and thirteen . . . snore . . . sixteen million and fourteen . . . "

Cautiously, she went closer. Then she saw that what she had taken for a haystack was in fact an immense pile of blond hair. Parting it, she found a young man, sound asleep.

As she stared, he opened his eyes. He blinked at her. "Who — ?" he said. Then he said, "Sixteen million and fifteen," closed his eyes, and fell asleep again.

Bedelia took him by the shoulder and shook him hard. He awoke, yawning, and tried to sit up. But the mass of hair made this difficult.

"What on earth is the matter with you?" Bedelia asked. "Who are you?"

"I am Prince Perian," he replied, "the rightful ruler of — oh, dear, here I go again. Sixteen million and . . . " His eyes began to close.

Bedelia shook him again. He made a violent effort and managed to wake up enough to continue," — of Istven. But Lord Garp has put me under a spell. I have to count sheep jumping over a fence, and this puts me to slee — ee — ee — "

He began to snore lightly.

"Dear me," said Bedelia. "I must do something."

She thought hard. Then she pinched Perian's ear, and this woke him with a start. "Listen," she said. "It's quite simple. It's all in your mind, you see. You are imagining the sheep jumping over the fence — No! Don't go to sleep again!

"This is what you must do. Imagine them jumping backward. As you do, *count* them backwards and when you get to *one*, you'll be wide awake."

The prince's eyes snapped open. "Marvelous!" he said. "Will it work?"

"It's bound to," said Bedelia. "For if the sheep going one way will put you to sleep, their going back again will wake you up."

Hastily, the prince began to count, "Six million and fourteen, six million and thirteen, six million and twelve . . ."

"Oh, my goodness," cried Bedelia, "count by hundreds, or you'll never get there."

He began to gabble as fast as he could, and with each moment that passed, his eyes sparkled more brightly, his face grew livelier, and he seemed a little stronger, until at last, he shouted, "Five, four, three, two, ONE!" and awoke completely.

He struggled to his feet, with a little help from Bedelia.

"Heavens!" he said. "Look how my hair and beard have grown. I've been here for years. Thank you, my dear. Who are you, and what are you doing here?"

Bedelia quickly explained.

Perian shook his head. "One more crime of Lord Garp's," he said. "We must escape and see that he is punished."

"Easier said than done," Bedelia replied. "There is no stair in this tower, as far as I can tell, and the outside wall is much too smooth to climb."

Perian frowned. "This will take some thought," he said. "What we need is a long rope."

"Use your common sense," said Bedelia. "We haven't any rope."

Then her face brightened, and she clapped her hands. "But we have your beard," she laughed.

Perian understood at once, and chuckled. "I'm sure it will reach almost to the ground," he said. "But we haven't any scissors to cut it off with."

"That is so," said Bedelia. "Hang it out of the window and let me climb down. I'll search the tower and perhaps I can find a ladder, or a hidden stair. If all else fails, I can go for help."

She and the prince gathered up great armfuls of the beard and staggered into Bedelia's room, which had the largest window. The prince's long hair trailed behind and nearly tripped him.

He threw the beard out of the window, and sure enough the end of it came to within a few feet of the ground.

Perian braced himself, holding the beard with both hands to ease the pull on his chin. Bedelia climbed out of the window and slid down the beard. She dropped to the ground and sat for a moment, breathless.

And as she sat there, out of the wilderness came the drumming of hoofs, a cloud of dust, and then Lord Garp on his swift horse.

With one glance, he saw what was happening. He shook his fist up at Prince Perian.

"Meddlesome fool!" he shouted. "I'll teach you to interfere."

He leaped from the horse and grabbed the beard. He gave it a tremendous yank. Headfirst came Perian, out of the window. Down he fell, and with a thump, he landed right on top of old Lord Garp.

This saved Perian, who was not hurt at all. But it was the end of Lord Garp.

Perian and Bedelia rode back to Istven on Lord Garp's horse.

In the great city, the prince was greeted with cheers of joy — once everyone had recognized him after so many years and under so much hair.

And of course, since Bedelia had rescued him from captivity, she married him. First, however, she made him get a haircut and a shave so that she could see what he really looked like.

For she was always practical.

Romantic Literary Folktales

"Inchelina," The Ugly Duckling," and "The Little Match Girl," from Hans Christian Andersen: The Complete Fairy Tales and Stories. *Translated by Erik Christian Haugaard. (Garden City: Doubleday, Inc., 1974).*

While Hans Christian Andersen's vision penetrates adult hypocrisy, his writing also reveals many characteristics of the Romantic period. "Inchelina" (most often translated "Thumbelina") reveals the heroine's triumphant linear quest for love and transcendence, the result of her goodness and her close association with nature. "The Ugly Duckling" depicts the little duckling's quest for acceptance in an uncaring society and exemplifies the archetype of the outsider or scapegoat. He is unspoiled by his transformation because of his goodness and shyness. "The Little Match Girl," often considered too allegorical to be suitable for child readers, reveals the child's linear journey towards spiritual transcendence and shows up the child's innocence in a cruel and fallen society.

Inchelina

Once upon a time there was a woman whose only desire was to have a tiny little child. Now she had no idea where she could get one; so she went to an old witch and asked her: "Please, could you tell me where I could get a tiny little child? I would so love to have one."

"That is not so difficult," said the witch. "Here is a grain of barley; it is not the kind that grows in the farmer's fields or that you can feed to the chickens. Plant it in a flowerpot and watch what happens."

"Thank you," said the woman. She handed the witch twelve pennies, and she went home to plant the grain of barley. No sooner was it in the earth than it started to sprout. A beautiful big flower grew up; it looked like a tulip that was just about to bloom.

"What a lovely flower," said the woman, and kissed the red and yellow petals that were closed so tightly. With a snap they opened and one could see that it was a real tulip. In the center of the flower on the green stigma sat a tiny little girl. She was so beautiful and so delicate, and exactly one inch long. "I will call her Inchelina," thought the woman.

The lacquered shell of a walnut became Inchelina's cradle, the blue petals of violets her mattress, and a rose petal her cover. Here she slept at night; in the daytime she played on the table by the window. The woman had put a bowl of water there with a garland of flowers around it. In this tiny "lake" there floated a tulip petal, on which Inchelina could row from one side of the plate to the other, using two white horsehairs as oars; it was an exquisite sight. And Inchelina could sing, as no one has ever sung before — so clearly and delicately.

One night as she lay sleeping in her beautiful little bed a toad came into the room through a broken windowpane. The toad was big and wet and ugly; she jumped down upon the table where Inchelina was sleeping under her red rose petal.

"She would make a lovely wife for my son," said the toad; and grabbing the walnut shell in which Inchelina slept, she leaped through the broken window and down into the garden.

On the banks of a broad stream, just where it was muddiest, lived the toad with her son. He had taken after his mother and was very ugly. "Croak . . . Croak . . . Croak!" was all he said when he saw the beautiful little girl in the walnut shell.

"Don't talk so loud or you will wake her," scolded the mother. "She could run away and we wouldn't be able to catch her, for she is as light as the down of a swan. I will put her on a water-lily leaf, it will be just like an island to her. In the meantime, we shall get your apartment, down in the mud, ready for your marriage."

Out in the stream grew many water lilies, and all of their leaves looked as if they were floating in the water. The biggest of them was the farthest from shore; on that one the old toad put Inchelina's little bed.

When the poor little girl woke in the morning and saw where she was — on a green leaf with water all around her — she began to cry bitterly. There was no way of getting to shore at all.

The old toad was very busy down in her mud house, decorating the walls with reeds and yellow flowers that grew near the shore. She meant to do her best for her new daughter-in-law. After she had finished, she and her ugly son swam out to the water-lily leaf to fetch Inchelina's bed. It was to be put in the bridal chamber. The old toad curtsied and that is not easy to do while you are swimming; then she said, "Here is my son. He is to be your husband; you two will live happily down in the mud."

"Croak! . . . Croak!" was all the son said. Then they took the bed and swam away with it. Poor Inchelina sat on the green leaf and wept and wept, for she did not want to live with the ugly toad and have her hideous son as a husband. The little fishes that were swimming about in the water had heard what the old toad said; they stuck their heads out of the water to take a look at the tiny girl. When they saw how beautiful she was, it hurt them to think that she should have to marry the ugly toad and live in the mud. They decided that they would not let it happen, and gathered around the green stalk that held the leaf anchored to the bottom of the stream. They all nibbled on the stem, and soon the leaf was free. It drifted down the stream, bearing Inchelina far away from the ugly toad.

As Inchelina sailed by, the little birds on the shore saw her and sang, "What a lovely little girl." Farther and farther sailed the leaf with its little passenger, taking her on a journey to foreign lands.

For a long time a lovely white butterfly flew around her, then landed on the leaf. It had taken a fancy to Inchelina. The tiny girl laughed, for she was so happy to have escaped the toad; and the stream was so beautiful, golden in the sunshine. She took the little silk ribbon which she wore around her waist and tied one end of it to the butterfly and the other to the water-lily leaf. Now the leaf raced down the stream — and so did Inchelina, for she was standing on it.

At that moment a big May bug flew by; when it spied Inchelina, it swooped down and with its claws grabbed the poor girl around her tiny waist and flew up into a tree with her. The leaf floated on down the stream, and the butterfly had to follow it.

Oh God, little Inchelina was terrified as the May bug flew away with her, but stronger than her fear was her grief for the poor little white butterfly that she had chained to the leaf with her ribbon. If he did not get loose, he would starve to death.

The May bug didn't care what happened to the butterfly. He placed Inchelina on the biggest leaf on the tree. He gave her honey from the flowers to eat, and told her that she was the loveliest thing he had ever seen, even though she didn't look like a May bug. Soon all the other May bugs that lived in the tree came visiting. Two young lady May bugs — they were still unmarried — wiggled their antennae and said: "She has only two legs, how wretched. No antennae and a thin waist, how disgusting! She looks like a human being: how ugly!"

All the other female May bugs agreed with them. The May bug who had caught Inchelina still thought her lovely; but when all the others kept insisting that she was ugly, he soon was convinced of it too. Now he didn't want her any longer, and put her down on a daisy at the foot of the tree and told her she could go wherever she wanted to, for all he cared. Poor Inchelina cried; she thought it terrible to be so ugly that even a May bug would not want her, and that in spite of her being more beautiful than you can imagine, more lovely than the petal of the most beautiful rose.

All summer long poor Inchelina lived all alone in the forest. She wove a hammock out of grass and hung it underneath a dock leaf so that it would not rain on her while she slept. She ate the honey in the flowers and drank the dew that was on their leaves every morning.

Summer and autumn passed. But then came winter: the long, cold winter. All the birds that had sung so beautifully flew away. The flowers withered, the trees lost their leaves; and the dock leaf that had protected her rolled itself up and became a shriveled yellow stalk. She was so terribly cold. Her clothes were in shreds; and she was so thin and delicate.

Poor Inchelina, she was bound to freeze to death. It started to snow and each snowflake that fell on her was like a whole shovelful of snow would be to us, because we are so big, and she was only one inch tall.

She wrapped herself in a wizened leaf, but it gave no warmth and she shivered from the cold.

Not far from the forest was a big field where grain had grown; only a few dry stubbles still rose from the frozen ground, pointing up to the heavens. To Inchelina these straws were like a forest. Trembling, she wandered through them and came to the entrance of a field mouses's house. It was only a little hole in the ground. But deep down below the mouse lived in warmth and comfort, with a full larder and a nice kitchen. Like a beggar child, Inchelina stood outside the door and begged for a single grain of barley. It was several days since she had last eaten.

"Poor little wretch," said the field mouse, for she had a kind heart. "Come down into my warm living room and dine with me."

The field mouse liked Inchelina. "You can stay the winter," she said. "But you must keep the room tidy and tell me a story every day, for I like a good story." Inchelina did what the kind old mouse demanded, and she lived quite happily.

"Soon we shall have a visitor," said the mouse. "Once a week my neighbor comes. He lives even more comfortably than I do. He has a drawing room, and wears the most exquisite black fur coat. If only he would marry you, then you would be well provided for. He can't see you, for he is blind, so you will have to tell him the very best of your stories."

But Inchelina did not want to marry the mouse's neighbor, for he was a mole. The next day he came visiting, dressed in his black velvet fur coat. The field mouse had said that he was both rich and wise. His house was twenty times as big as the mouse's; and learned he was, too; but he did not like the sun and the beautiful flowers, he said they were "abominable," for he had never seen them. Inchelina had to sing for him; and when she sang *"Frère Jacques, dormez vous?"* he fell in love with her because of her beautiful voice; but he didn't show it, for he was sober-minded and never made a spectacle of himself.

He had recently dug a passage from his own house to theirs, and he invited Inchelina and the field mouse to use it as often as they pleased. He told them not to be afraid of the dead bird in the corridor. It had died only a few days before. It was still whole and had all its feathers. By chance it had been buried in his passageway.

The mole took a piece of dry rotten wood in his mouth; it shone as brightly as fire in the darkness; then he led the way down through the long corridor. When they came to the place where the dead bird lay, the mole made a hole with his broad nose, up through the earth, so that light could come through. Almost blocking the passageway was a dead swallow, with its beautiful wings pressed close to its body, its feet almost hidden by feathers, and its head nestled under a wing. The poor bird undoubtedly had frozen to death. Inchelina felt a great sadness; she had loved all the birds that twittered and sang for her that summer. The mole kicked the bird with one of his short legs and said, "Now it has stopped chirping. What a misfortune it is to be born a bird. Thank God, none of my children will be born birds! All they can do is chirp, and then die of starvation when winter comes."

"Yes, that's what all sensible people think," said the field mouse. "What does all that chirping lead to? Starvation and cold when winter comes. But I suppose they think it is romantic."

Inchelina didn't say anything, but when the mouse and the mole had their backs turned, she leaned down and kissed the closed eye of the swallow. "Maybe that was one of the birds that sang so beautifully for me this summer," she thought. "How much joy you gave me, beautiful little bird."

The mole closed the hole through which

the daylight had entered and then escorted the ladies home. That night Inchelina could not sleep; she rose and wove as large a blanket as she could, out of hay. She carried it down in the dark passage and covered the little bird with it. In the field mouse's living room she had found bits of cotton; she tucked them under the swallow wherever she could, to protect it from the cold earth.

"Good-by, beautiful bird," she said. "Good-by, and thank you for the songs you sang for me when it was summer and all the trees were green and the sun warmed us."

She put her head on the bird's breast; then she jumped up! Something was ticking inside: it was the bird's heart, for the swallow was not really dead, and now the warmth had revived it.

In the fall all the swallows fly to warm countries. If one tarries too long and is caught by the first frost, he lies down on the ground as if he were dead, and the cold snow covers him.

Inchelina shook with fear. The swallow was huge to a girl so tiny that she only measured an inch. But she gathered her courage and pressed the blanket closer to the bird's body. She even went to fetch the little mint leaf that she herself used as a cover and put it over the bird's head.

The next night she sneaked down to the passageway again; the bird was better although still very weak. He opened his eyes just long enough to see Inchelina standing in the dark with a little piece of dry rotten wood in her hand, as a lamp.

"Thank you, you sweet little child," said the sick swallow, "I feel so much better. I am not cold now. Soon I shall be strong again and can fly out into the sunshine."

"Oh no," she said. "It is cold and snowing outside now and you would freeze. Stay down here in your warm bed, I will nurse you."

She brought the swallow water on a leaf. After he had drunk it, he told her his story. He had torn his wing on a rosebush, and therefore could not fly as swiftly as the other swallows, so he had stayed behind when the others left; then one morning he had fainted from cold. That was all he could remember. He did not know how he came to be in the mole's passageway.

The bird stayed all winter. Inchelina took good care of him, grew very fond of him, and breathed not a word about him to either the mole or the field mouse, for she knew that they didn't like the poor swallow.

As soon as spring came and the warmth of the sun could be felt through the earth, the swallow said good-by to Inchelina, who opened the hole that the mole had made. The sun shone down so pleasantly. The swallow asked her if she did not want to come along with him; she could sit on his back and he would fly with her out into the great forest. But Inchelina knew that the field mouse would be sad and lonely if she left.

"I cannot," she said.

The bird thanked her once more. "Farewell .... Farewell, lovely girl," he sang, and flew out into the sunshine.

Inchelina's eyes filled with tears as she watched the swallow fly away, for she cared so much for the bird.

"Tweet ... tweet," he sang, and disappeared in the forest.

Poor Inchelina was miserable. Soon the grain would be so tall that the field would be in shade, and she would no longer be able to enjoy the warm sunshine.

"This summer you must spend getting your trousseau ready," said the field mouse, for the sober mole in the velvet coat had proposed to her. "You must have both woolens and linen to wear and to use in housekeeping when you become Mrs. Mole."

Inchelina had to spin by hand and the field mouse hired four spiders to weave both night and day. Every evening the mole came visiting, but all he talked about was how nice it would be when the summer was over. He didn't like the way the sun baked the earth; it made it so hard to dig in. As soon as autumn came they would get married. But Inchelina was not happy; she thought the mole was dull and she did not love him. Every day, at sunrise and at sunset, she tiptoed to the entrance of the field mouse's house, so that when the wind blew and parted the grain, she could see the blue sky above her. She thought of how light and beautiful it was out there, and she longed for her friend the swallow but he never came back. "He is probably far away in the wonderful green forest!" she thought.

Autumn came and Inchelina's trousseau was finished.

"In four weeks we shall hold your wedding," said the field mouse.

Inchelina cried and said she did not want to marry the boring old mole.

"Fiddlesticks!" squeaked the field mouse. "Don't be stubborn or I will bite you with my white teeth. You are getting an excellent husband; he has a velvet coat so fine that the queen does not have one that is better. He has both a larder and kitchen, you ought to thank God for giving you such a good husband."

The day of the wedding came; the mole had already arrived. Inchelina grieved. Now she would never see the warm sun again. The mole lived far down under the ground, for he didn't like the sun. While she lived with the field mouse, she at least had been allowed to walk as far as the entrance of the little house and look at the sun.

"Farewell.... Farewell, you beautiful sun!" Inchelina lifted her hands up toward the sky and then took a few steps out upon the field. The harvest was over and only the stubbles were left. She saw a little red flower. Embracing it, she said: "Farewell! And give my love to the swallow if you ever see him."

"Tweet ... Tweet ... "something said in the air above her.

She looked up. It was the little swallow. As soon as he saw Inchelina he chirped with joy. And she told the bird how she had to marry the awful mole, and live forever down under the ground, and never see the sun again. The very telling of her future brought tears to her eyes.

"Now comes the cold winter," said the swallow, "and I fly far away to the warm countries. Why don't you come with me? You can sit on my back; tie yourself on so you won't fall off and we will fly far away from the ugly mole and his dismal house; across the great mountains, to the countries where the sun shines more beautifully than here and the loveliest flowers grow and it is always summer. Fly

with me, Inchelina. You saved my life when I lay freezing in the cold cellar of the earth."

"Yes, I will come," cried Inchelina, and climbed up on the bird's back. She tied herself with a ribbon to one of his feathers, and the swallow flew high up into the air, above the forests and lakes and over the high mountains that are always snow-covered. Inchelina froze in the cold air, but she crawled underneath the warm feathers of the bird and only stuck her little head out to see all the beauty below her.

They came to the warm countries. And it was true what the swallow had said: the sun shone more brightly and the sky seemed twice as high. Along the fences grew the loveliest green and blue grapes. From the trees in the forests hung oranges and lemons. Along the roads the most beautiful children ran, chasing many-colored butterflies. The swallow flew even farther south, and the landscape beneath them became more and more beautiful.

Near a forest, on the shores of a lake, stood the ruins of an ancient temple; ivy wound itself around the white pillars. On top of these were many swallows' nests and one of them belonged to the little swallow that was carrying Inchelina.

"This is my house," he said. "Now choose for yourself one of the beautiful flowers down below and I will set you down on it, it will make a lovely home for you."

"How wonderful!" exclaimed Inchelina, and clapped her hands. Among the broken white marble pillars grew tall, lovely white flowers. The swallow sat her down on the leaves of one of them; and to Inchelina's astonishment, she saw a little man sitting in the center of the flower. He was white and almost transparent, as if he were made of glass. On his head he wore a golden crown. On his back were a pair of wings. He was no taller than Inchelina. In every one of the flowers there lived such a tiny angel; and this one was the king of them all.

"How handsome he is!" whispered Inchelina to the swallow.

The tiny little king was terrified of the bird, who was several times larger than he was. But when he saw Inchelina he forgot his fear. She was the loveliest creature he had ever seen; and so he took the crown off his own head and put it on hers. Then he asked her what her name was and whether she wanted to be queen of the flowers.

Now here was a better husband than old mother toad's ugly son or the mole with the velvet coat. Inchelina said yes; and from every flower came a lovely little angel to pay homage to their queen. How lovely and delicate they all were; and they brought her gifts, and the best of these was a pair of wings, so she would be able to fly, as they all did, from flower to flower.

It was a day of happiness. And the swallow, from his nest in the temple, sang for them as well as he could. But in his heart he was ever so sad, for he, too, loved Inchelina and had hoped never to be parted from her.

"You shall not be called Inchelina any longer," said the king. "It is an ugly name. From now on we shall call you Maja."

"Farewell! Farewell!" called the little swallow. He flew back to the north, away from the warm countries. He came to Denmark; and there he has his nest, above the window of a man who can tell fairy tales.

"Tweet . . . tweet," sang the swallow. And the man heard it and wrote down the whole story.

The Ugly Duckling

It was so beautiful out in the country. It was summer. The oats were still green, but the wheat was turning yellow. Down in the meadow the grass had been cut and made into haystacks; and there the storks walked on their long red legs talking Egyptian, because that was the language they had been taught by their mothers. The fields were enclosed by woods, and hidden among them were little lakes and pools. Yes, it certainly was lovely out there in the country!

The old castle, with its deep moat surrounding it, lay bathed in sunshine. Between the heavy walls and the edge of the moat there was a narrow strip of land covered by a whole forest of burdock plants. Their leaves were large and some of the stalks were so tall that a child could stand upright under them and imagine that he was in the middle of the wild and lonesome woods. Here a duck had built her nest. While she sat waiting for the eggs to hatch, she felt a little sorry for herself because it was taking so long and hardly anybody came to visit her. The other ducks preferred swimming in the moat to sitting under a dock leaf and gossiping.

Finally the eggs began to crack. "Peep . . . Peep," they said one after another. The egg yolks had become alive and were sticking out their heads.

"Quack . . . Quack . . . " said their mother. "Look around you." And the ducklings did; they glanced at the green world about them, and that was what their mother wanted them to do, for green was good for their eyes.

"How big the world is!" piped the little ones, for they had much more space to move around in now than they had had inside the egg.

"Do you think that this is the whole world?" quacked their mother. "The world is much larger than this. It stretches as far as the minister's wheat fields, though I have not been there. . . . Are you all here?" The duck got up and turned around to look at her nest. "Oh no, the biggest egg hasn't hatched yet; and I'm so tired of sitting here! I wonder how long it will take?" she wailed, and sat down again.

"What's new?" asked an old duck who had come visiting.

"One of the eggs is taking so long," complained the mother duck. "It won't crack. But take a look at the others. They are the sweetest little ducklings you have ever seen; and every one of them looks exactly like their father. That scoundrel hasn't come to visit me once."

"Let me look at the egg that won't hatch," demanded the old duck. "I am sure that it's a turkey egg! I was fooled that way once. You can't imagine what it's like. Turkeys are afraid of the water. I couldn't get them to go into it. I quacked and I nipped them, but nothing helped. Let me see that egg! . . . Yes, it's a turkey egg. Just let it lie there. You go and teach your young ones how to swim, that's my advice."

"I have sat on it so long that I guess I can sit a little longer, at least until they get the hay in," replied the mother duck.

"Suit yourself," said the older duck, and went on.

At last the big egg cracked too. "Peep . . . Peep," said the young one, and tumbled out. He was big and very ugly.

The mother duck looked at him. "He's awfully big for his age," she said. "He doesn't look like any of the others. I wonder if he could be a turkey? Well, we shall soon see. Into the water he will go, even if I have to kick him to make him do it."

The next day the weather was gloriously beautiful. The sun shone on the forest of burdock plants. The mother duck took her whole brood to the moat. "Quack . . . Quack . . ." she ordered.

One after another, the little ducklings plunged into the water. For a moment their heads disappeared, but then they popped up again and the little ones floated like so many corks. Their legs knew what to do without being told. All of the new brood swam very nicely, even the ugly one.

"He is no turkey," mumbled the mother. "See how beautifully he uses his legs and how straight he holds his neck. He is my own child and, when you look closely at him, he's quite handsome. . . . Quack! Quack! Follow me and I'll take you to the henyard and introduce you to everyone. But stay close to me, so that no one steps on you, and look out for the cat."

They heard an awful noise when they arrived at the henyard. Two families of ducks had got into a fight over the head of an eel. Neither of them got it, for it was swiped by the cat.

"That is the way of the world," said the mother duck, and licked her bill. She would have liked to have the eel's head herself. "Walk nicely," she admonished them. "And remember to bow to the old duck over there. She has Spanish blood in her veins and is the most aristocratic fowl here. That is why she is so fat and has a red rag tied around one of her legs. That is the highest mark of distinction a duck can be given. It means so much that she will never be done away with; and all the other fowl and the human beings know who she is. Quack! Quack! . . . Don't walk, waddle like well-brought-up ducklings. Keep your legs far apart,

just as your mother and father have always done. Bow your heads and say, 'Quack!' " And that was what the little ducklings did.

Other ducks gathered about them and said loudly, "What do we want that gang here for? Aren't there enough of us already? Pooh! Look how ugly one of them is! He's the last straw!" And one of the ducks flew over and bit the ugly duckling on the neck.

"Leave him alone!" shouted the mother. "He hasn't done anyone any harm."

"He's big and he doesn't look like everybody else!" replied the duck who had bitten him. "And that's reason enough to beat him."

"Very good-looking children you have," remarked the duck with the red rag around one of her legs. "All of them are beautiful except one. He didn't turn out very well. I wish you could make him over again."

"That's not possible, Your Grace," answered the mother duck. "He may not be handsome, but he has a good character and swims as well as the others, if not a little better. Perhaps he will grow handsomer as he grows older and becomes a bit smaller. He was in the egg too long, and that is why he doesn't have the right shape." She smoothed his neck for a moment and then added, "Besides, he's a drake; and it doesn't matter so much what he looks like. He is strong and I am sure he will be able to take care of himself."

"Well, the others are nice," said the old duck. "Make yourself at home, and if you should find an eel's head, you may bring it to me."

And they were "at home."

The poor little duckling, who had been the last to hatch and was so ugly, was bitten and pushed and made fun of both by the hens and by the other ducks. The turkey cock (who had been born with spurs on, and therefore thought he was an emperor) rustled his feathers as if he were a full-rigged ship under sail, and strutted up to the duckling. He gobbled so loudly at him that his own face got all red.

The poor little duckling did not know where to turn. How he grieved over his own ugliness, and how sad he was! The poor creature was mocked and laughed at by the whole henyard.

That was the first day; and each day that followed was worse than the one before. The poor duckling was chased and mistreated by everyone, even his own sisters and brothers, who quacked again and again, "If only the cat would get you, you ugly thing!"

Even his mother said, "I wish you were far away." The other ducks bit him and the hens pecked at him. The little girl who came to feed the fowls kicked him.

At last the duckling ran away. It flew over the tops of the bushes, frightening all the little birds so that they flew up into the air. "They, too, think I am ugly," thought the duckling, and closed his eyes — but kept on running.

Finally he came to a great swamp where wild ducks lived; and here he stayed for the night, for he was too tired to go any farther.

In the morning he was discovered by the wild ducks. They looked at him and one of them asked, "What kind of bird are you?"

The ugly duckling bowed in all directions, for he was trying to be as polite as he knew how.

"You are ugly," said the wild ducks, "but that is no concern of ours, as long as you don't try to marry into our family."

The poor duckling wasn't thinking of marriage. All he wanted was to be allowed to swim among the reeds and drink a little water when he was thirsty.

He spent two days in the swamp; then two wild geese came — or rather, two wild ganders, for they were males. They had been hatched not long ago; therefore they were both frank and bold.

"Listen, comrade," they said. "You are so ugly that we like you. Do you want to migrate with us? Not far from here there is a marsh where some beautiful wild geese live. They are all lovely maidens, and you are so ugly that you may seek your fortune among them. Come along."

"Bang! Bang!" Two shots were heard and both the ganders fell down dead among the reeds, and the water turned red from their blood.

"Bang! Bang!" Again came the sound of shots, and a flock of wild geese flew up.

The whole swamp was surrounded by hunters; from every direction came the awful noise. Some of the hunters had hidden behind bushes or among the reeds but others, screened from sight by the leaves, sat on the long, low branches of the trees that stretched out over the swamp. The blue smoke from the guns lay like a fog over the water and among the trees. Dogs came splashing through the marsh, and they bent and broke the reeds.

The poor little duckling was terrified. He was about to tuck his head under his wing, in order to hide, when he saw a big dog peering at him through the reeds. The dog's tongue hung out of its mouth and its eyes glistened evilly. It bared its teeth. Splash! It turned away without touching the duckling.

"Oh, thank God!" he sighed. "I am so ugly that even the dog doesn't want to bite me."

The little duckling lay as still as he could while the shots whistled through the reeds. Not until the middle of the afternoon did the shooting stop; but the poor little duckling was still so frightened that he waited several hours longer before taking his head out from under his wing. Then he ran as quickly as he could out of the swamp. Across the fields and the meadows he went, but a wind had come up and he found it hard to make his way against it.

Toward evening he came upon a poor little hut. It was so wretchedly crooked that it looked as if it couldn't make up its mind which way to fall and that was why it was still standing. The wind was blowing so hard that the poor little duckling had to sit down in order not to be blown away. Suddenly he noticed that the door was off its hinges, making a crack; and he squeezed himself through it and was inside.

An old woman lived in the hut with her cat and her hen. The cat was called Sonny and could both arch his back and purr. Oh yes, it could also make sparks if you rubbed its fur the wrong way. The hen had very short legs and that was why she was called Cluck Lowlegs. But she was good at laying eggs, and the old woman loved her as if she were her own child.

In the morning the hen and the cat discovered the duckling. The cat meowed and the hen clucked.

"What is going on?" asked the old woman, and looked around. She couldn't see very well, and when she found the duckling she thought it was a fat, full-grown duck. "What a fine catch!" she exclaimed. "Now we shall have duck eggs, unless it's a drake. We'll give it a try."

So the duckling was allowed to stay for three weeks on probation, but he laid no eggs. The cat was the master of the house and the hen the mistress. They always referred to themselves as "we and the world," for they thought that they were half the world — and the better half at that. The duckling thought that he should be allowed to have a different opinion, but the hen did not agree.

"Can you lay eggs?" she demanded.

"No," answered the duckling.

"Then keep your mouth shut."

And the cat asked, "Can you arch your back? Can you purr? Can you make sparks?"

"No."

"Well, in that case, you have no right to have an opinion when sensible people are talking."

The duckling was sitting in a corner and was in a bad mood. Suddenly he recalled how lovely it could be outside in the fresh air when the sun shone: a great longing to be floating in the water came over the duckling, and he could not help talking about it.

"What is the matter with you?" asked the hen as soon as she had heard what he had to say. "You have nothing to do, that's why you get ideas like that. Lay eggs or purr, and such notions will disappear."

"You have no idea how delightful it is to float in the water, and to dive down to the bottom of a lake and get your head wet," said the duckling.

"Yes, that certainly does sound amusing," said the hen. "You must have gone mad. Ask the cat—he is the most intelligent being I know — ask him whether he likes to swim or dive down to the bottom of a lake. Don't take my word for anything. . . . Ask the old woman, who is the cleverest person in the world; ask her whether she likes to float and to get her

head all wet."

"You don't understand me!" wailed the duckling.

"And if I don't understand you, who will? I hope you don't think that you are wiser than the cat or the old woman — not to mention myself. Don't give yourself airs! Thank your Creator for all He has done for you. Aren't you sitting in a warm room among intelligent people whom you could learn something from? While you, yourself, do nothing but say a lot of nonsense and aren't the least bit amusing! Believe me, that's the truth, and I am only telling it to you for your own good. That's how you recognize a true friend: it's someone who is willing to tell you the truth, no matter how unpleasant it is. Now get to work: lay some eggs, or learn to purr and arch your back."

"I think I'll go out into the wide world," replied the duckling.

"Go right ahead!" said the hen.

And the duckling left. He found a lake where he could float in the water and dive to the bottom. There were other ducks, but they ignored him because he was so ugly.

Autumn came and the leaves turned yellow and brown, then they fell from the trees. The wind caught them and made them dance. The clouds were heavy with hail and snow. A raven sat on a fence and screeched, "Ach! Ach!" because it was so cold. When just thinking of how cold it was is enough to make one shiver, what a terrible time the duckling must have had.

One evening just as the sun was setting gloriously, a flock of beautiful birds came out from among the rushes. Their feathers were so white that they glistened; and they had long, graceful necks. They were swans. They made a very loud cry, then they spread their powerful wings. They were flying south to a warmer climate, where the lakes were not frozen in the winter. Higher and higher they circled. The ugly duckling turned round and round in the water like a wheel and stretched his neck up toward the sky; he felt a strange longing. He screeched so piercingly that he frightened himself.

Oh, he would never forget those beautiful birds, those happy birds. When they were out of sight the duckling dove down under the water to the bottom of the lake; and when he came up again he was beside himself. He did not know the name of those birds or where they were going, and yet he felt that he loved them as he had never loved any other creatures. He did not envy them. It did not even occur to him to wish that he were so handsome himself. He would have been happy if the other ducks had let him stay in the henyard: that poor, ugly bird!

The weather grew colder and colder. The duckling had to swim round and round in the water, to keep just a little space for himself that wasn't frozen. Each night his hole became smaller and smaller. On all sides of him the ice creaked and groaned. The little duckling had to keep his feet constantly in motion so that the last bit of open water wouldn't become ice. At last he was too tired to swim any more. He sat still. The ice closed in around him and he was frozen fast.

Early the next morning a farmer saw him and with his clogs broke the ice to free the duckling. The man put the bird under his arm and took it home to his wife, who brought the duckling back to life.

The children wanted to play with him. But the duckling was afraid that they were going to hurt him, so he flapped his wings and flew right into the milk pail. From there he flew into a big bowl of butter and then into a barrel of flour. What a sight he was!

The farmer's wife yelled and chased him with a poker. The children laughed and almost fell on top of each other, trying to catch him; and how they screamed! Luckily for the duckling, the door was open. He got out of the house and found a hiding place beneath some bushes, in the newly fallen snow; and there he lay so still, as though there were hardly any life left in him.

It would be too horrible to tell of all the hardship and suffering the duckling experienced that long winter. It is enough to know that he did survive. When again the sun shone warmly and the larks began to sing, the duckling was lying among the reeds in the swamp. Spring had come!

He spread out his wings to fly. How strong and powerful they were! Before he knew it, he was far from the swamp and flying above a beautiful garden. The apple trees were blooming and the lilac bushes stretched their flower-covered branches over the water of a winding canal. Everything was so beautiful: so fresh and green. Out of a forest of rushes came three swans. They ruffled their feathers and floated so lightly on the water. The ugly duckling recognized the birds and felt again that strange sadness come over him.

"I shall fly over to them, those royal birds! And they can hack me to death because I, who am so ugly, dare to approach them! What difference does it make? It is better to be killed by them than to be bitten by the other ducks, and pecked by the hens, and kicked by the girl who tends the henyard; or to suffer through the winter."

And he lighted on the water and swam toward the magnificent swans. When they saw him they ruffled their feathers and started to swim in his direction. They were coming to meet him.

"Kill me," whispered the poor creature, and bent his head humbly while he waited for death. But what was that he saw in the water? It was his own reflection; and he was no longer an awkward, clumsy, gray bird, so ungainly and so ugly. He was a swan!

It does not matter that one has been born in the henyard as long as one has lain in a swan's egg.

He was thankful that he had known so much want, and gone through so much suffering, for it made him appreciate his present happiness and the loveliness of everything about him all the more. The swans made a circle around him and caressed him with their beaks.

Some children came out into the garden. They had brought bread with them to feed the swans. The youngest child shouted, "Look, there's a new one!" All the children joyfully clapped their hands, and they ran to tell their parents.

Cake and bread were cast on the water for the swans. Everyone agreed that the new swan was the most beautiful of them all. The older swans bowed toward him.

He felt so shy that he hid his head beneath his wing. He was too happy, but not proud, for a kind heart can never be proud. He thought of the time when he had been mocked and persecuted. And now everyone said that he was the most beautiful of the most beautiful birds. And the lilac bushes stretched their branches right down to the water for him. The sun shone so warm and brightly. He ruffled his feathers and raised his slender neck, while out of the joy in his heart, he thought, "Such happiness I did not dream of when I was the ugly duckling."

The Little Match Girl

It was dreadfully cold, snowing, and turning dark. It was the last evening of the year, New Year's Eve. In this cold and darkness walked a little girl. She was poor and both her head and feet were bare. Oh, she had had a pair of slippers when she left home; but they had been too big for her — in truth, they had belonged to her mother. The little one had lost them while hurrying across the street to get out of the way of two carriages that had been driving awfully fast. One of the slippers she could not find, and the other had been snatched by a boy who, laughingly, shouted that he would use it as a cradle when he had a child of his own.

Now the little girl walked barefoot through the streets. Her feet were swollen and red from the cold. She was carrying a little bundle of matches in her hand and had more in her apron pocket. No one had bought any all day, or given her so much as a penny. Cold and hungry, she walked through the city; cowed by life, the poor thing!

The snowflakes fell on her long yellow hair that curled so prettily at the neck, but to such things she never gave a thought. From every window of every house, light shone, and one could smell the geese roasting all the way out in the street. It was, after all, New Year's Eve; and this she did think about.

In a little recess between two houses she sat down and tucked her feet under her. But now she was even colder. She didn't dare go home because she had sold no matches and was frightened that her father might beat her. Besides, her home was almost as cold as the street.

She lived in an attic, right under a tile roof. The wind whistled through it, even though they had tried to close the worst of the holes and cracks with straw and old rags.

Her little hands were numb from cold. If only she dared strike a match, she could warm them a little. She took one and struck it against the brick wall of the house; it lighted! Oh, how warm it was and how clearly it burned like a little candle. She held her hand around it. How strange! It seemed that the match had become a big iron stove with brass fixtures. Oh, how blessedly warm it was! She stretched out her legs so that they, too, could get warm, but at that moment the stove disappeared and she was sitting alone with a burned-out match in her hand.

She struck another match. Its flame illuminated the wall and it became as transparent as a veil: she could see right into the house. She saw the table spread with a damask cloth and set with the finest porcelain. In the center, on a dish, lay a roasted goose stuffed with apples and prunes! But what was even more wonderful: the goose — although a fork and knife were stuck in its back — had jumped off the table and was waddling toward her. The little girl stretched out her arms and the match burned out. Her hands touched the cold, solid walls of the house.

She lit a third match. The flame flared up and she was sitting under a Christmas tree that was much larger and more beautifully decorated than the one she had seen through the glass doors at the rich merchant's on Christmas Eve. Thousands of candles burned on its green branches, and colorful pictures like the ones you can see in store windows were looking down at her. She smiled up at them; but then the match burned itself out, and the candles of the Christmas tree became the stars in the sky. A shooting star drew a line of fire across the dark heavens.

"Someone is dying," whispered the little girl. Her grandmother, who was dead, was the only person who had ever loved or been kind to the child; and she had told her that a shooting star was the soul of a human being traveling to God.

She struck yet another match against the

wall and in its blaze she saw her grandmother, so sweet, so blessedly kind.

"Grandmother!" shouted the little one. "Take me with you! I know you will disappear when the match goes out, just like the warm stove, the goose, and the beautiful Christmas tree." Quickly, she lighted all the matches she had left in her hand, so that her grandmother could not leave. And the matches burned with such a clear, strong flame that the night became as light as day. Never had her grandmother looked so beautiful. She lifted the little girl in her arms and flew with her to where there is neither cold nor hunger nor fear: up to God.

In the cold morning the little girl was found. Her cheeks were red and she was smiling. She was dead. She had frozen to death on the last evening of the old year. The sun on New Year's Day shone down on the little corpse; her lap was filled with burned-out matches.

"She had been trying to warm herself," people said. And no one knew the sweet visions she had seen, or in what glory she and her grandmother had passed into a truly new year.

▬▬

"Goblin Market," by Christina Rossetti. *Illustrated by Laurence Housman (London: MacMillan, 1874; rpt. New York and London: Garland Publishing, 1976).*

According to R. Loring Taylor, "Goblin Market" was not written for children: "It was apparently Victorian culture rather than the author's intention which identified the work as children's verse, although it is hard to determine what audience, if any, was originally intended." Christina Rossetti (1830–1894), however, insisted on calling the poem a fairy tale, implying that its prime function was for the amusement of children. Though the poem functions on one level as a moral tale, its macabre goblins, its hinted terrors and pleasures, its archetypes of temptation, fall, and redemption, as well as death and rebirth, its lush and sensuous language, and its lilting music place it in the tradition of Romantic literary fairy tales. As one critic argues, "... only by view-

ing "Goblin Market," as a tale for children, a tale which is structurally based on the interweaving of the predominant nineteenth-century strands of children's literature — the fairy tale and the moral tale — can the poem's true moral ... be understood." Thus, while the moral aspects of the poem made it acceptable to Victorian adults, the poem's fast-paced narrative, its remarkable music, and its subversive fairy tale dimensions made it appealing to children.

Illustration by Arthur Backham from *Goblin Market*, by Christina Rossetti. Copyright © 1933. Reprinted by permission of Harrap Limited.

Goblin Market

Morning and evening
Maids heard the goblins cry
"Come buy our orchard fruits,
Come buy, come buy:
Apples and quinces,

Lemons and oranges,
Plump unpecked cherries,
Melons and raspberries,
Bloom-down-cheeked peaches,
Wild free-born cranberries,
Swart-headed mulberries,
Crab-apples, dewberries,
Pine-apples, blackberries,
Apricots, strawberries; —
All ripe together
In summer weather, —
Morns that pass by,
Fair eves that fly;
Come buy, come buy:
Our grapes fresh from the vine,
Pomegranates full and fine,
Dates and sharp bullaces,
Rare pears and greengages,
Damsons and bilberries,
Taste them and try:
Currants and gooseberries,
Bright-fire-like barberries,
Figs to fill your mouth,
Citrons from the South,
Sweet to tongue and sound to eye;
Come buy, come buy.''

Evening by evening
Among the brookside
rushes,
Laura bowed her head to hear,
Lizzie veiled her blushes:
Crouching close together
In the cooling weather,
With clasping arms and cautioning lips,
With tingling cheeks and finger tips.
"Lie close,"
"Lie close," Laura said,
Pricking up her golden head:
"We must not look at goblin men,
We must not buy their fruits:
Who knows upon what soil they fed
Their hungry thirsty roots?"
"Come buy," call the goblins
Hobbling down the glen.
"Oh," cried Lizzie, "Laura, Laura,
You should not peep at goblin men."
Lizzie covered up her eyes,
Covered close lest they should look;
Laura reared her glossy head,
And whispered like the restless brook:

"Look, Lizzie, look, Lizzie,
Down the glen tramp little men.
One hauls a basket,
One bears a plate,
One lugs a golden dish
Of many pounds weight.
How fair the vine must grow
Whose grapes are so luscious;
How warm the wind must blow
Through those fruit bushes."
"No," said Lizzie: "No, no, no;
Their offers should not charm us,
Their evil gifts would harm us."
She thrust a dimpled finger
In each ear, shut eyes and ran:
Curious Laura chose to linger
Wondering at each merchant man.
One had a cat's face,
One whisked a tail,
One tramped at a rat's pace,
One crawled like a snail,
One like a wombat prowled obtuse and furry,
One like a ratel tumbled hurry skurry.
She heard a voice like voice of doves
Cooing all together:
They sounded kind and full of loves
In the pleasant weather.

Laura stretched her gleaming neck
Like a rush-imbedded swan,
Like a lily from the beck,
Like a moonlit poplar branch.
Like a vessel at the launch
When its last restraint is gone.
Backwards up the mossy glen
Turned and trooped the goblin men,
With their shrill repeated cry,
"Come buy, come buy."
When they reached where Laura was
They stood stock still upon the moss,
Leering at each other,
Brother with queer brother;
Signalling each other,
Brother with sly brother.
One set his basket down,
One reared his plate;
One began to weave a crown
Of tendrils, leaves, and rough nuts brown
(Men sell not such in any town);
One heaved the golden weight
Of dish and fruit to offer her:

"Come buy, come buy," was still their cry.
Laura stared but did not stir,
Longed but had no money:
The whisk-tailed merchant bade her taste
In tones as smooth as honey,
The cat-faced purr'd,
The rat-paced spoke a word
Of welcome, and the snail-paced even was
    heard;
One parrot-voiced and jolly
Cried "Pretty Goblin" still
    for "Pretty Polly;" —
One whistled like a bird.

But sweet-tooth Laura spoke in haste:
"Good Folk, I have no coin;
To take were to purloin:
I have no copper in my purse,
I have no silver either,
And all my gold is on the furze
That shakes in windy weather
Above the rusty heather."
"You have much gold upon your head,"
They answered all together:
"Buy from us with a golden curl."
She clipped a precious golden lock,
She dropped a tear more rare than pearl,
Then sucked their fruit globes fair or red:
Sweeter than honey from the rock,
Stronger than man-rejoicing wine,
Clearer than water flowed that juice;
She never tasted such before,
How should it cloy with length of use?
She sucked and sucked and sucked the more
Fruits which that unknown orchard bore;
She sucked until her lips were sore;
Then flung the emptied rinds away
But gathered up one kernel-stone,
And knew not was it night or day
As she turned home alone.

Lizzie met her at the gate
Full of wise upbraidings:
"Dear, you should not stay so late,
Twilight is not good for maidens;
Should not loiter in the glen
In the haunts of goblin men.
Do you not remember Jeanie,
How she met them in the moonlight,
Took their gifts both choice and many,
Ate their fruits and wore their flowers

Plucked from bowers
Where summer ripens at all hours?
But ever in the moonlight
She pined and pined away;
Sought them by night and day,
Found them no more, but dwindled and
    grew grey;
Then fell with the first snow,
While to this day no grass will grow
Where she lies low:
I planted daisies there a year ago
That never blow.
You should not loiter so."
"Nay, hush," said Laura:
"Nay, hush, my sister:
I ate and ate my fill,
Yet my mouth waters still;
To-morrow night I will
Buy more;" and kissed her:
"Have done with sorrow;
I'll bring you plums to-morrow
Fresh on their mother twigs,
Cherries worth getting;
You cannot think what figs
My teeth have met in,
What melons icy-cold
Piled on a dish of gold
Too huge for me to hold,
What peaches with a velvet nap,
Pellucid grapes without one seed:
Odorous indeed must be the mead
Whereon they grow, and pure the wave they
    drink
With lilies at the brink,
And sugar-sweet their sap."

Golden head by golden head,
Like two pigeons in one nest
Folded in each other's wings,
They lay down in their curtained bed:
Like two blossoms on one stem,
Like two flakes of new-fall'n snow,
Like two wands of ivory
Tipped with gold for awful kings.
Moon and stars gazed in at them,
Wind sang to them lullaby,
Lumbering owls forbore to fly,
Not a bat flapped to and fro
Round their rest:
Cheek to cheek and breast to breast
Locked together in one nest.

Early in the morning
When the first cock crowed his warning,
Neat like bees, as sweet and busy,
Laura rose with Lizzie:
Fetched in honey, milked the cows,
Aired and set to rights the house,
Kneaded cakes of whitest wheat,

Cakes for dainty mouths to eat,
Next churned butter, whipped up cream,
Fed their poultry, sat and sewed;
Talked as modest maidens should:
Lizzie with an open heart,
Laura in an absent dream,
One content, one sick in part;
One warbling for the mere bright day's delight,
One longing for the night.
    At length slow evening came:
They went with pitchers to the reedy brook;
Lizzie most placid in her look,
Laura most like a leaping flame.
They drew the gurgling water from its deep;
Lizzie plucked purple and rich golden flags,
Then turning homeward said: "The sunset
        flushes
Those furthest loftiest crags;
Come, Laura, not another maiden lags,
No wilful squirrel wags,
The beasts and birds are fast asleep."
But Laura loitered still among the rushes
    And said the bank was steep.
And said the hour was early still,
The dew not fall'n, the wind not chill;
Listening ever, but not catching
The customary cry,
"Come buy, come buy,"
With its iterated jingle
Of sugar-baited words:
Not for all her watching
Once discerning even one goblin
Racing, whisking, tumbling, hobbling;
Let alone the herds
That used to tramp along the glen,
In groups or single,
Of brisk fruit-merchant men.
    Till Lizzie urged, "Oh Laura, come;
I hear the fruit-call, but I dare not look:
You should not loiter longer at this brook:
Come with me home.
The stars rise, the moon bends her arc,
Each glowworm winks her spark,

Let us get home before the night grows dark:
For clouds may gather
Though this is summer weather,
Put out the lights and drench us through;
Then if we lost our way what should we do?"

    Laura turned cold as stone
To find her sister heard that cry alone,
That goblin cry,
"Come buy our fruits, come buy."
Must she then buy no more such dainty fruit?
Must she no more such succous pasture find,
Gone deaf and blind?
Her tree of life drooped from the root:
She said not one word in her heart's sore ache;
But peering thro' the dimness, nought
        discerning,
Trudged home, her pitcher dripping all the
        way;
So crept to bed, and lay
Silent till Lizzie slept;
Then sat up in a passionate yearning,
And gnashed her teeth for baulked desire, and
        wept
As if her heart would break.
Day after day, night after night,
Laura kept watch in vain
In sullen silence of exceeding pain.
She never caught again the goblin cry:
"Come buy, come buy;" —
She never spied the goblin men
Hawking their fruits along the glen:
But when the noon waxed bright
Her hair grew thin and grey;
She dwindled, as the fair full moon doth turn
To swift decay and burn
Her fire away.
    One day remembering her kernel-stone
She set it by a wall that faced the south;
Dewed it with tears, hoped for a root.
Watched for a waxing shoot,
But there came none;
It never saw the sun,
It never felt the trickling moisture run:
While with sunk eyes and faded mouth
She dreamed of melons, as a traveller sees
False waves in desert drouth
With shade of leaf-crowned trees,
And burns the thirstier in the sandful breeze.
    She no more swept the house,
Tended the fowls or cows,

Fetched honey, kneaded cakes of wheat,
Brought water from the brook:
But sat down listless in the chimney-nook
And would not eat.

Tender Lizzie could not bear
To watch her sister's cankerous care
Yet not to share.
She night and morning
Caught the goblins' cry:
"Come buy our orchard fruits,
Come buy, come buy:" —
Beside the brook, along the glen,
She heard the tramp of goblin men,
The voice and stir
Poor Laura could not hear;
Longed to buy fruit to comfort her,
But feared to pay too dear.
She thought of Jeanie in her grave,
Who should have been a bride;
But who for joys brides hope to have
Fell sick and died
In her gay prime,
In earliest Winter time,
With the first glazing rime,
With the first snow-fall of crisp Winter time.
    Till Laura dwindling
Seemed knocking at Death's door:
Then Lizzie weighed no more
Better and worse;
But put a silver penny in her purse,
Kissed Laura, crossed the heath with clumps
    of furze
At twilight, halted by the brook:
And for the first time in her life
Began to listen and look.
    Laughed every goblin
When they spied her peeping:
Came towards her hobbling,
Flying, running, leaping,
Puffing and blowing,
Chuckling, clapping, crowing,
Clucking and gobbling,
Mopping and mowing,
Full of airs and graces,
Pulling wry faces,
Demure grimaces,
Cat-like and rat-like,
Ratel- and wombat-like,
Snail-paced in a hurry,
Parrot-voiced and whistler,

Helter skelter, hurry skurry,
Chattering like magpies,
Fluttering like pigeons,
Gliding like fishes, —
Hugged her and kissed her:
Squeezed and caressed her:
Stretched up their dishes,
Panniers, and plates:
"Look at our apples
Russet and dun,
Bob at our cherries,
Bite at our peaches,
Citrons and dates,
Grapes for the asking,
Pears red with basking
Out in the sun,
Plums on their twigs;
Pluck them and suck them,
Pomegranates, figs." —

    "Good folk," said Lizzie,
Mindful of Jeanie:
"Give me much and many:" —
    Held out her apron,
Tossed them her penny.
"Nay, take a seat with us,
Honour and eat with us,"
They answered grinning:
"Our feast is but beginning,
Night yet is early,
Warm and dew pearly,
Wakeful and starry:
Such fruits as these
No man can carry;
Half their bloom would fly,
Half their dew would dry,
Half their flavour would pass by.
Sit down and feast with us,
Be welcome guest with us,
Cheer you and rest with us." —
"Thank you," said Lizzie: "But one waits
At home alone for me:
So without further parleying,
If you will not sell me any
Of your fruits though much and many,
Give me back my silver penny
I tossed you for a fee." —
They began to scratch their pates,
No longer wagging, purring,
But visibly demurring,
Grunting and snarling.

One called her proud,
Cross-grained, uncivil;
Their tones waxed loud,
Their looks were evil.
Lashing their tails
They trod and hustled her,
Elbowed and jostled her,
Clawed with their nails,
Barking, mewing, hissing, mocking,
Tore her gown and soiled her stocking,
Twitched her hair out by the roots,
Stamped upon her tender feet,
Held her hands and squeezed their fruits
Against her mouth to make her eat.

White and golden Lizzie stood,
Like a lily in a flood, —
Like a rock of blue-veined stone
Lashed by tides obstreperously, —
Like a beacon left alone
In a hoary roaring sea,
Sending up a golden fire, —
Like a fruit-crowned orange-tree
White with blossoms honey-sweet
Sore beset by wasp and bee, —
Like a royal virgin town
Topped with gilded dome and spire
Close beleaguered by a fleet
Mad to tug her standard down.
One may lead a horse to water,
Twenty cannot make him drink.
Though the goblins cuffed and caught her,
Coaxed and fought her,
Bullied and besought her,
Scratched her, pinched her black as ink,
Kicked and knocked her,
Mauled and mocked her,
Lizzie uttered not a word;
Would not open lip from lip
Lest they should cram a mouthful in:
But laughed in heart to feel the drip
Of juice that syrupped all her face,
And lodged in dimples of her chin,
And streaked her neck which quaked like curd.
At last the evil people,
Worn out by her resistance,
Flung back her penny, kicked their fruit
Along whichever road they took,
Not leaving root or stone or shoot;
Some writhed into the ground,
Some dived into the brook

With ring and ripple,
Some scudded on the gale without a sound,
Some vanished in the distance.
In a smart, ache, tingle,
Lizzie went her way;
Knew not was it night or day;
Sprang up the bank, tore thro' the furze,
Threaded copse and dingle,
And heard her penny jingle
Bouncing in her purse,
Its bounce was music to her ear.
She ran and ran
As if she feared some goblin man
Dogged her with gibe or curse
Or something worse:
But not one goblin skurried after,
Nor was she pricked by fear;
The kind heart made her windy-paced
That urged her home quite out of breath with
     haste
And inward laughter.

She cried, "Laura," up the garden,
"Did you miss me?
Come and kiss me.
Never mind my bruises,
Hug me, kiss me, suck my juices
Squeezed from goblin fruits for you,
Goblin pulp and goblin dew.
Eat me, drink me, love me;
Laura, make much of me;
For your sake I have braved the glen
And had to do with goblin merchant men."
Laura started from her chair,
Flung her arms up in the air,
Clutched her hair:
"Lizzie, Lizzie, have you tasted
For my sake the fruit forbidden?
Must your light like mine be hidden,
Your young life like mine be wasted,
Undone in mine undoing,
And ruined in my ruin,
Thirsty, cankered, goblin-ridden?" —
She clung about her sister,
Kissed and kissed and kissed her:
Tears once again
Refreshed her shrunken eyes,
Dropping like rain
After long sultry drouth;
Shaking with anguish, fear, and pain,
She kissed and kissed her with a hungry mouth.

Her lips began to scorch,
That juice was wormwood to her tongue,
She loathed the feast:
Writhing as one possessed she leaped and sung,
Rent all her robe, and wrung
Her hands in lamentable haste,
And beat her breast.
Her locks streamed like the torch
Borne by a racer at full speed,
Or like the mane of horses in their flight,
Or like an eagle when she stems the light
Straight toward the sun,
Or like a caged thing freed,
Or like a flying flag when armies run.

Swift fire spread through her veins, knocked
    at her heart,
Met the fire smouldering there
And overbore its lesser flame;
She gorged on bitterness without a name:
Ah! fool, to choose such part
Of soul-consuming care!
Sense failed in the mortal strife:
Like the watch-tower of a town
Which an earthquake shatters down,
Like a lightning-stricken mast,
Like a wind-uprooted tree
Spun about,
Like a foam-topped waterspout
Cast down headlong in the sea,
She fell at last;
Pleasure past and anguish past,
Is it death or is it life?
Life out of death.
That night long Lizzie watched by her,
Counted her pulse's flagging stir,
Felt for her breath,
Held water to her lips, and cooled her face
With tears and fanning leaves:
But when the first birds chirped about their
eaves,
And early reapers plodded to the place
Of golden sheaves,
And dew-wet grass
Bowed in the morning winds so brisk to pass,
And new buds with new day
Opened of cup-like lilies on the stream,
Laura awoke as from a dream,
Laughed in the innocent old way,
Hugged Lizzie but not twice or thrice;
Her gleaming locks showed not one thread of
grey
Her breath was sweet as May
And light danced in her eyes.

Days, weeks, months, years
Afterwards, when both were wives
With children of their own;
Their mother-hearts beset with fears,
Their lives bound up in tender lives;
Laura would call the little ones
And tell them of her early prime,
Those pleasant days long gone
Of not-returning time:
Would talk about the haunted glen,
The wicked, quaint fruit-merchant men,
Their fruits like honey to the throat
But poison in the blood;
(Men sell not such in any town):
Would tell them how her sister stood
In deadly peril to do her good,
And win the fiery antidote:
Then joining hands to little hands
Would bid them cling together,
"For there is no friend like a sister
In calm or stormy weather;
To cheer one on the tedious way,
To fetch one if one goes astray,
To lift one if one totters down,
To strengthen whilst one stands."

"Little Daylight," from The Gifts of the Child Christ: Fairytales and Stories for the Childlike*, by George MacDonald. (Grand Rapids, Michigan: William B. Eerdman's, 1976).*

In "Little Daylight," George MacDonald, who earlier read and translated German Romantic Künstmarchen*, reveals his affinities with the Romantic movement. Little Daylight, who "might have come from the sun," exemplifies the Romantic idealization of childhood. In her close association with nature, in the hint that she has divine origins, and in her innocent joy in song and dance, she embodies many Romantic conceptions. The tale also reveals many traditional folktale motifs: the evil spell visited on the innocent girl-child by the evil fairy; the archetype of death and rebirth; the presence of a nurturing maternal* *figure; and the undoing of the evil spell through the love and goodness of the prince. The tale's structure is perhaps most evident in its pattern of oppositions, though it is also revealed through the young girl's linear movement toward mature love. In its carefully wrought structure and its effortless prose style, "Little Daylight" is one of George MacDonald's finest literary folktales. Like "The Light Princess," this tale appeared originally in the 1867 publication, Dealings with the Fairies.*

Little Daylight

No house of any pretension to be called a palace is in the least worthy of the name, except it has a wood near it — very near it — and the nearer the better. Not all round it — I don't mean that, for a palace ought to be open to the sun and wind, and stand high and brave, with weathercocks glittering and flags flying; but on one side of every palace there must be a wood. And there was a very grand wood indeed beside the palace of the king who was going to be Daylight's father; such a grand wood, that nobody yet had ever got to the other end of it. Near the house it was kept very trim and nice, and it was free of brushwood for a long way in; but by degrees it got wild, and it grew wilder, and wilder, and wilder, until some said wild beasts at last did what they liked in it. The king and his courtiers often hunted, however, and this kept the wild beasts far away from the palace.

One glorious summer morning, when the wind and sun were out together, when the vanes were flashing and the flags frolicking against the blue sky, little Daylight made her appearance from somewhere — nobody could tell where — a beautiful baby, with such bright eyes that she might have come from the sun, only by and by she showed such lively ways that she might equally have come out of the wind. There was great jubilation in the palace, for this was the first baby the queen had had, and there is as much happiness over a new baby in a palace as in a cottage.

But there is one disadvantage of living near a wood: you do not know quite who your neighbours may be. Everybody knew there were in it several fairies, living within a few miles of the palace, who always had had something to do with each new baby that came; for fairies live so much longer than we, that they can have business with a good many generations of human mortals. The curious houses they lived in were well known also, — one, a hollow oak; another, a birch-tree, though nobody could ever find how that fairy made a house of it; another, a hut of growing trees intertwined, and patched up with turf and moss. But there was another fairy who had lately come to the place, and nobody even knew she was a fairy except the other fairies. A wicked old thing she was, always concealing her power, and being as disagreeable as she could, in order to tempt people to give her offence, that she might have the pleasure of taking vengeance upon them. The people about thought she was a witch, and those who knew her by sight were careful to avoid offending her. She lived in a mud house, in a swampy part of the forest.

In all history we find that fairies give their remarkable gifts to prince or princess, or any child of sufficient importance in their eyes, always at the christening. Now this we can understand, because it is an ancient custom amongst human beings as well; and it is not hard to explain why wicked fairies should choose the same time to do unkind things; but it is difficult to understand how they should be able to do them, for you would fancy all wicked creatures would be powerless on such an occasion. But I never knew of any interference on the part of a wicked fairy that did not turn out a good thing in the end. What a good thing, for instance, it was that one princess should sleep for a hundred years! Was she not saved from all the plague of young men who were not worthy of her? And did she not come awake exactly at the right moment when the right prince kissed her? For my part, I cannot help wishing a good many girls would sleep till just the same fate overtook them. It would be happier for them, and more agreeable to their friends.

Of course all the known fairies were invited to the christening. But the king and queen never thought of inviting an old witch. For the power of the fairies they have by nature; whereas a witch gets her power by wickedness. The other fairies, however, knowing the danger thus run, provided as well as they could against accidents from her quarter. But they could neither render her powerless, nor could they arrange their gifts in reference to her beforehand, for they could not tell what those might be.

Of course the old hag was there without being asked. Not to be asked was just what she wanted, that she might have a sort of a reason for doing what she wished to do. For somehow even the wickedest of creatures likes a pretext for doing the wrong thing.

Five fairies had one after the other given the child such gifts as each counted best, and the fifth had just stepped back to her place in the surrounding splendour of ladies and gentlemen, when, mumbling a laugh between her toothless gums, the wicked fairy hobbled out into the middle of the circle, and at the moment when the archbishop was handing the baby to the lady at the head of the nursery department of state affairs, addressed him thus, giving a bite or two to every word before she could part with it:

"Please your Grace, I'm very deaf: would your Grace mind repeating the princess's name?"

"With pleasure, my good woman," said the archbishop, stooping to shout in her ear: "the infant's name is little Daylight."

"And little daylight it shall be," cried the fairy, in the tone of a dry axle, "and little good shall any of her gifts do her. For I bestow upon her the gift of sleeping all day long, whether she will or not. Ha, ha! He, he! Hi, hi!"

Then out started the sixth fairy, who, of course, the others had arranged should come after the wicked one, in order to undo as much as she might.

"If she sleep all day," she said, mournfully, "she shall, at least, wake all night."

"A nice prospect for her mother and me!" thought the poor king; for they loved her far too much to give her up to nurses, especially at night, as most kings and queens do — and are sorry for it afterwards.

"You spoke before I had done," said the wicked fairy. "That's against the law. It gives me another chance."

"I beg your pardon," said the other fairies, all together.

"She did. I hadn't done laughing," said the crone. "I had only got to Hi, hi! and I had to go through Ho, ho! and Hu, hu! So I decree that if she wakes all night she shall wax and wane with its mistress the moon. And what that may mean I hope her royal parents will live to see. Ho, ho! Hu, hu!"

But out stepped another fairy, for they had been wise enough to keep two in reserve, because every fairy knew the trick of one.

"Until," said the seventh fairy, "a prince comes who shall kiss her without knowing it."

The wicked fairy made a horrid noise like an angry cat, and hobbled away. She could not pretend that she had not finished her speech this time, for she had laughed Ho, ho! and Hu, hu!

"I don't know what that means," said the poor king to the seventh fairy.

"Don't be afraid. The meaning will come with the thing itself," said she.

The assembly broke up, miserable enough —the queen, at least, prepared for a good many sleepless nights, and the lady at the head of the nursery department anything but comfortable in the prospect before her, for of course the queen could not do it all. As for the king, he made up his mind, with what courage he could summon, to meet the demands of the case, but wondered whether he could with any propriety require the First Lord of the Treasury to take a share in the burden laid upon him.

I will not attempt to describe what they had to go through for some time. But at last the household settled into a regular system — a very irregular one in some respects. For at certain seasons the palace rang all night with bursts of laughter from little Daylight, whose heart the old fairy's curse could not reach; she was Daylight still, only a little in the wrong place, for she always dropped asleep at the first hint of dawn in the east. But her merriment was of short duration. When the moon was at the full, she was in glorious spirits, and as beautiful as it was possible for a child of her age to be. But as the moon waned, she faded, until at last she was wan and withered like the poorest, sickliest child you might come upon in the streets of a great city in the arms of a homeless mother. Then the night was quiet as the day, for the little creature lay in her gorgeous cradle night and day with hardly a motion, and indeed at last without even a moan, like one dead. At first they often thought she was dead, but at last they got used to it, and only consulted the almanac to find the moment when she would begin to revive, which, of course, was with the first appearance of the silver thread of the crescent moon. Then she would move her lips, and they would give her a little nourishment; and she would grow better and better and better, until for a few days she was splendidly well. When well, she was always merriest out in the moonlight; but even when near her worst, she seemed better when, in warm summer nights, they carried her cradle out into the light of the waning moon. Then in her sleep she would smile the faintest, most pitiful smile.

For a long time very few people ever saw her awake. As she grew older she became such a favourite, however, that about the palace there were always some who would contrive to keep awake at night, in order to be near her. But she soon began to take every chance of getting away from her nurses and enjoying her moonlight alone. And thus things went on until she was nearly seventeen years of age. Her father and mother had by that time got so used to the odd state of things that they had ceased to wonder at them. All their arrangements had reference to the state of the Princess Daylight, and it is amazing how things contrive to accommodate themselves. But how any prince was ever to find and deliver her, appeared inconceivable.

As she grew older she had grown more and more beautiful, with the sunniest hair and the loveliest eyes of heavenly blue, brilliant and profound as the sky of a June day. But so much more painful and sad was the change as her bad time came on. The more beautiful she was in the full moon, the more withered and worn did she become as the moon waned. At the time at which my story has now arrived, she looked, when the moon was small or gone, like an old woman exhausted with suffering. This was the more painful that her appearance was unnatural; for her hair and eyes did not change. Her wan face was both drawn and wrinkled, and had an eager hungry look. Her skinny hands moved as if wishing, but unable, to lay hold of something. Her shoulders were bent forward, her chest went in, and she stooped as if she were eighty years old. At last she had to be put to bed, and there await the flow of the tide of life. But she grew to dislike being seen, still more being touched by any hands, during this season. One lovely summer evening, when the moon lay all but gone upon the verge of the horizon, she vanished from her attendants, and it was only after searching for her a long time in great terror, that they found her fast asleep in the forest, at the foot of a silver birch, and carried her home.

A little way from the palace there was a great open glade, covered with the greenest and softest grass. This was her favourite haunt; for here the full moon shone free and glorious, while through a vista in the trees she could generally see more or less of the dying moon as it crossed the opening. Here she had a little rustic house built for her, and here she mostly resided. None of the court might go there without leave, and her own attendants had learned by this time not to be officious in waiting upon her, so that she was very much at liberty. Whether the good fairies had anything to do with it or not I cannot tell, but at last she got into the way of retreating further into the wood every night as the moon waned, so that sometimes they had great trouble in finding her; but as she was always very angry if she discovered they were watching her, they scarcely dared to do so. At length one night they thought they had lost her altogether. It was morning before they found her. Feeble as she was, she had wandered into a thicket a long way from the glade, and there she lay — fast asleep, of course.

Although the fame of her beauty and sweetness had gone abroad, yet as everybody knew she was under a bad spell, no king in the neighbourhood had any desire to have her for a daughter-in-law. There were serious objections to such a relation.

About this time in a neighbouring kingdom, in consequence of the wickedness of the nobles, an insurrection took place upon the death of the old king, the greater part of the nobility was massacred, and the young prince was compelled to flee for his life, disguised like a peasant. For some time, until he got out of the country, he suffered much from hunger and fatigue; but when he got into that ruled by the princess's father, and had no longer any fear of being recognized, he fared better, for the people were kind. He did not abandon his disguise, however. One tolerable reason was that he had no other clothes to put on, and another that he had very little money, and did not know where to get any more. There was no good in telling everybody he met that he was a prince, for he felt that a prince ought to be able to get on like other people, else his rank only made a fool of him. He had read of princes setting out upon adventure; and here he was out in similar case, only without having had a choice in the matter. He would go on, and see what would come of it.

For a day or two he had been walking through the palace-wood, and he had next to nothing to eat, when he came upon the strangest little house, inhabited by a very nice tidy motherly old woman. This was one of the good fairies. The moment she saw him she knew quite well who he was and what was going to come of it; but she was not at liberty to interfere with the orderly march of events. She received him with the kindness she would have shown to any other traveller, and gave him bread and milk, which he thought the most delicious food he had ever tasted, wondering that they did not have it for dinner at the palace sometimes. The old woman pressed him to stay all night. When he awoke he was amazed to find how well and strong he felt. She would not take any of the money he offered, but begged him, if he found occasion of continuing in the neighbourhood, to return and occupy the same quarters.

"Thank you much, good mother," answered the prince: "but there is little chance of that. The sooner I get out of this wood the better."

"I don't know that," said the fairy.

"What do you mean?" asked the prince.

"Why how *should* I know?" returned she.

"I can't tell," said the prince.

"Very well," said the fairy.

"How strangely you talk!" said the prince.

"Do I?" said the fairy.

"Yes, you do," said the prince.

"Very well," said the fairy.

The prince was not used to being spoken to in this fashion, so he felt a little angry and turned and walked away. But this did not offend the fairy. She stood at the door of her little house looking after him till the trees hid him quite. Then she said "At last!" and went in.

The prince wandered and wandered, and got nowhere. The sun sank and sank and went out of sight, and he seemed no nearer the end of the wood than ever. He sat down on a fallen tree, ate a bit of bread the old woman had given him, and waited for the moon; for, although he was not much of an astronomer, he knew the moon would rise some time, because she had risen the night before. Up she came, slow and slow, but of a good size, pretty nearly round indeed; whereupon, greatly refreshed with his piece of bread, he got up and went — he knew not whither.

After walking a considerable distance, he thought he was coming to the outside of the forest; but when he reached what he thought the last of it, he found himself only upon the edge of a great open space in it, covered with grass. The moon shone very bright, and he thought he had never seen a more lovely spot. Still it looked dreary because of its loneliness, for he could not see the house at the other side. He sat down weary again, and gazed into the glade. He had not seen so much room for several days.

All at once he espied something in the middle of the grass. What could it be? It moved; it came nearer. Was it a human creature, gliding across — a girl dressed in white, gleaming in the moonshine? She came nearer and nearer. He crept behind a tree and watched, wondering. It must be some strange being of the wood —a nymph whom the moonlight and the warm dusky air had enticed from her tree. But when she came close to where he stood, he no longer doubted she was human — for he had caught sight of her sunny hair, and her clear blue eyes, and the loveliest face and form that he had ever seen. All at once she began singing like a nightingale, and dancing to her own music, with her eyes ever turned towards the moon. She passed close to where he stood, dancing on by the edge of the trees and away in a great circle towards the other side, until he could see but a spot of white in the yellowish green of the moonlit grass. But when he feared it would vanish quite, the spot grew, and became a figure once more. She approached him again, singing and dancing and waving her arms over her head, until she had completed the circle. Just opposite his tree she stood, ceased her song, dropped her arms, and broke out into a long clear laugh, musical as a brook. Then, as if tired, she threw herself on the grass, and lay gazing at the moon. The prince was almost afraid to breathe lest he should startle her, and she should vanish from his sight. As to venturing near her, that never came into his head.

She had lain for a long hour or longer, when the prince began again to doubt concerning her. Perhaps she was but a vision of his own fancy. Or was she a spirit of the wood, after all? If so, he too would haunt the wood, glad to have lost kingdom and everything for the hope of being near her. He would build him a hut in the forest, and there he would live for the pure chance of seeing her again. Upon nights like this at least she would come out and bask in the moonlight, and make his soul blessed. But while he thus dreamed she sprang to her feet, turned her face full to the moon, and began singing as if she would draw her down from the sky by the power of her entrancing voice. She looked more beautiful than ever. Again she began dancing to her own music, and danced away into the distance. Once more she returned in a similar manner; but although he was watching as eagerly as before, what with fatigue and what with gazing, he fell fast asleep before she came near him. When he awoke it was broad daylight, and the princess was nowhere.

He could not leave the place. What if she should come the next night! He would gladly endure a day's hunger to see her yet again: he would buckle his belt quite tight. He walked round the glade to see if he could discover any

prints of her feet. But the grass was so short, and her steps had been so light, that she had not left a single trace behind her.

He walked half-way round the wood without seeing anything to account for her presence. Then he spied a lovely little house, with thatched roof and low eaves, surrounded by an exquisite garden, with doves and peacocks walking in it. Of course this must be where the gracious lady who loved the moonlight lived. Forgetting his appearance, he walked towards the door, determined to make inquiries, but as he passed a little pond full of gold and silver fishes, he caught sight of himself, and turned to find the door to the kitchen. There he knocked, and asked for a piece of bread. The good-natured cook brought him in, and gave him an excellent breakfast, which the prince found nothing the worse for being served in the kitchen. While he ate, he talked with his entertainer, and learned that this was the favourite retreat of the Princess Daylight. But he learned nothing more, both because he was afraid of seeming inquisitive, and because the cook did not choose to be heard talking about her mistress to a peasant lad who had begged for his breakfast.

As he rose to take his leave, it occurred to him that he might not be so far from the old woman's cottage as he had thought, and he asked the cook whether she knew anything of such a place, describing it as well as he could. She said she knew it well enough, adding with a smile —

"It's there you're going, is it?"

"Yes, if it's not far off."

"It's not more than three miles. But mind what you are about, you know."

"Why do you say that?"

"If you're after any mischief, she'll make you repent it."

"The best thing that could happen under the circumstances," remarked the prince.

"What do you mean by that?" asked the cook.

"Why, it stands to reason," answered the prince, "that if you wish to do anything wrong, the best thing for you is to be made to repent of it."

"I see," said the cook. "Well, I think you

may venture. She's a good old soul.''

''Which way does it lie from here?'' asked the prince.

She gave him full instructions; and he left her with many thanks.

Being now refreshed, however, the prince did not go back to the cottage that day: he remained in the forest, amusing himself as best he could, but waiting anxiously for the night, in the hope that the princess would again appear. Nor was he disappointed, for, directly the moon rose, he spied a glimmering shape far across the glade. As it drew nearer, he saw it was she indeed — not dressed in white as before: in a pale blue like the sky, she looked lovelier still. He thought it was that the blue suited her yet better than the white; he did not know that she was really more beautiful because the moon was nearer the full. In fact the next night was full moon, and the princess would then be at the zenith of her loveliness.

The prince feared for some time that she was not coming near his hiding-place that night; but the circles in her dance ever widened as the moon rose, until at last they embraced the whole glade, and she came still closer to the trees where he was hiding than she had come the night before. He was entranced with her loveliness, for it was indeed a marvellous thing. All night long he watched her but dared not go near her. He would have been ashamed of watching her too, had he not become almost incapable of thinking of anything but how beautiful she was. He watched the whole night long, and saw that as the moon went down she retreated in smaller and smaller circles, until at last he could see her no more.

Weary as he was, he set out for the old woman's cottage, where he arrived just in time for her breakfast, which she shared with him. He then went to bed, and slept for many hours. When he awoke, the sun was down, and he departed in great anxiety lest he should lose a glimpse of the lovely vision. But, whether it was by the machinations of the swamp-fairy or merely that it is one thing to go and another to return by the same road, he lost his way. I shall not attempt to describe his misery when the moon rose, and he saw nothing but tree, trees, trees. She was high in the heavens before he reached the glade. Then indeed his troubles vanished, for there was the princess coming dancing towards him, in a dress that shone like gold, and with shoes that glimmered through the grass like fire-flies. She was of course still more beautiful than before. Like an embodied sunbeam she passed him, and danced away into the distance.

Before she returned in her circle, clouds had begun to gather about the moon. The wind rose, the trees moaned, and their lighter branches leaned all one way before it. The prince feared that the princess would go in, and he should see her no more that night. But she came dancing on more jubilant than ever, her golden dress and her sunny hair streaming out upon the blast, waving her arms towards the moon, and in the exuberance of her delight ordering the clouds away from off her face. The prince could hardly believe she was not a creature of the elements, after all.

By the time she had completed another circle, the clouds had gathered deep, and there were growlings of distant thunder. Just as she passed the tree where he stood, a flash of lightning blinded him for a moment, and when he saw again, to his horror, the princess lay on the ground. He darted to her, thinking she had been struck; but when she heard him coming, she was on her feet in a moment.

''What do you want?'' she asked.

''I beg your pardon. I thought — the lightning — '' said the prince, hesitating.

''There is nothing the matter,'' said the princess, waving him off rather haughtily.

The poor prince turned and walked towards the wood.

''Come back,'' said Daylight; ''I like you. You do what you are told. Are you good?''

''Not so good as I should like to be,'' said the prince.

''Then go and grow better,'' said the princess.

Again the disappointed prince turned and went.

''Come back,'' said the princess.

He obeyed, and stood before her waiting.

''Can you tell me what the sun is like?'' she asked.

''No,'' he answered. ''But where's the good

of asking what you know?"

"But I don't know," she rejoined.

"Why, everybody knows."

"That's the very thing: I'm not everybody. I've never seen the sun."

"Then you can't know what it's like till you do see it."

"I think you must be a prince," said the princess.

"Do I look like one?" said the prince.

"I can't quite say that."

"Then why do you think so?"

"Because you both do what you are told and speak the truth. — Is the sun so very bright?"

"As bright as the lightning."

"But it doesn't go out like that, does it?"

"Oh no. It shines like the moon, rises and sets like the moon, is much the same shape as the moon, only so bright that you can't look at it for a moment."

"But I *would* look at it," said the princess.

"But you couldn't," said the prince.

"But I could," said the princess.

"Why don't you, then?"

"Because I can't."

"Why can't you?"

"Because I can't wake. And I never shall wake until — "

Here she hid her face in her hands, turned away, and walked in the slowest, stateliest manner towards the house. The prince ventured to follow her at a little distance, but she turned and made a repellent gesture, which, like a true gentleman-prince, he obeyed at once. He waited a long time, but as she did not come near him again, and as the night had now cleared, he set off at last for the old woman's cottage.

It was long past midnight when he reached it, but, to his surprise, the old woman was paring potatoes at the door. Fairies are fond of doing odd things. Indeed, however they may dissemble, the night is always their day. And so it is with all who have fairy blood in them.

"Why, what are you doing there, this time of the night, mother?" said the prince; for that was the kind way in which any young man in his country would address a woman who was much older than himself.

"Getting your supper ready, my son," she answered.

"Oh! I don't want any supper," said the prince.

"Ah! you've seen Daylight," said she.

"I've seen a princess who never saw it," said the prince.

"Do you like her?" asked the fairy.

"Oh! don't I?" said the prince. "More than you would believe, mother."

"A fairy can believe anything that ever was or ever could be," said the old woman.

"Then are you a fairy?" asked the prince.

"Yes," said she.

"Then what do you do for things not to believe?" asked the prince.

"There's plenty of them — everything that never was nor ever could be."

"Plenty, I grant you," said the prince. "But do you believe there could be a princess who never saw the daylight? Do you believe that, now?"

This the prince said, not that he doubted the princess, but that he wanted the fairy to tell him more. She was too old a fairy, however, to be caught so easily.

"Of all people, fairies must not tell secrets. Besides, she's a princess."

"Well, I'll tell *you* a secret. I'm a prince."

"I know that."

"How do you know it?"

"By the curl of the third eyelash on your left eyelid."

"Which corner do you count from?"

"That's a secret."

"Another secret? Well, at least, if I am a prince, there can be no harm in telling me about a princess."

"It's just princes I can't tell."

"There's ain't any more of them — are there?" said the prince.

"What! you don't think you're the only prince in the world, do you?"

"Oh, dear, no! not at all. But I know there's one too many just at present, except the princess — "

"Yes, yes, that's it," said the fairy.

"What's *it*?" asked the prince.

But he could get nothing more out of the fairy, and had to go to bed unanswered, which was something of a trial.

Now wicked fairies will not be bound by the laws which the good fairies obey, and this always seems to give the bad the advantage over the good, for they use means to gain their ends which the others will not. But it is all of no consequence, for what they do never succeeds; nay, in the end it brings about the very thing they are trying to prevent. So you see that somehow, for all their cleverness, wicked fairies are dreadfully stupid, for, although from the beginning of the world they have really helped instead of thwarting the good fairies, not one of them is a bit the wiser for it. She will try the bad thing just as they all did before her; and succeed no better of course.

The prince had so far stolen a march upon the swamp-fairy that she did not know he was in the neighbourhood until after he had seen the princess those three times. When she knew it, she consoled herself by thinking that the princess must be far too proud and too modest for any young man to venture even to speak to her before he had seen her six times at least. But there was even less danger than the wicked fairy thought; for, however much the princess might desire to be set free, she was dreadfully afraid of the wrong prince. Now, however, the fairy was going to do all she could.

She so contrived it by her deceitful spells, that the next night the prince could not by any endeavour find his way to the glade. It would take me too long to tell her tricks. They would be amusing to us, who know that they could not do any harm, but they were something other than amusing to the poor prince. He wandered about the forest till daylight, and then fell fast asleep. The same thing occurred for seven following days, during which neither could he find the good fairy's cottage. After the third quarter of the moon, however, the bad fairy thought she might be at ease about the affair for a fortnight at least, for there was no chance of the prince wishing to kiss the princess during that period. So the first day of the fourth quarter he did find the cottage, and the next day he found the glade. For nearly another week he haunted it. But the princess never came. I have little doubt she was on the farther edge of it some part of every night, but at this period she always wore black, and there being little or no light, the prince never saw her. Nor would he have known her if he had seen her. How could he have taken the worn decrepit creature she was now, for the glorious Princess Daylight?

At last, one night when there was no moon at all, he ventured near the house. There he heard voices talking, although it was past midnight; for her women were in considerable uneasiness, because the one whose turn it was to watch her had fallen asleep, and had not seen which way she went, and this was a night when she would probably wander very far, describing a circle which did not touch the open glade at all, but stretched away from the back of the house, deep into that side of the forest — a part of which the prince knew nothing. When he understood from what they said that she had disappeared, and that she must have gone somewhere in the said direction, he plunged at once into the wood to see if he could find her. For hours he roamed with nothing to guide him but the vague notion of a circle which on one side bordered on the house, for so much had he picked up from the talk he had overheard.

It was getting towards the dawn, but as yet there was no streak of light in the sky, when he came to a great birch-tree, and sat down weary at the foot of it. While he sat — very miserable, you may be sure — full of fear for the princess, and wondering how her attendants could take it so quietly, he bethought himself that it would not be a bad plan to light a fire, which, if she were anywhere near, would attract her. This he managed with a tinder-box, which the good fairy had given him. It was just beginning to blaze up, when he heard a moan, which seemed to come from the other side of the tree. He sprung to his feet, but his heart throbbed so that he had to lean for a moment against the tree before he could move. When he got round, there lay a human form in a little dark heap on the earth. There was light enough from his fire to show that it was not the princess. He lifted it in his arms, hardly heavier than a child, and carried it to the flame. The countenance was that of an old woman, but it had a fearfully strange look. A black hood concealed her hair, and her eyes were closed. He laid her down as comfortably as he could, chafed her hands, put a little cordial from a bottle, also the gift of the fairy, into her mouth; took off his coat and wrapped it about her, and in short did the best he could. In a little while she opened her eyes and looked at him — so pitifully! The tears rose and flowed down her gray wrinkled cheeks, but she said never a word. She closed her eyes again, but the tears kept on flowing, and her whole appearance was so utterly pitiful that the prince was very near crying too. He begged her to tell him what was the matter, promising to do all he could to help her; but still she did not speak. He thought she was dying, and took her in his arms again to carry her to the princess's house, where he thought the good-natured cook might be able to do something for her. When he lifted her, the tears flowed yet faster, and she gave such a sad moan that it went to his very heart.

"Mother, mother!" he said — "Poor mother!" and kissed her on the withered lips.

She started; and what eyes they were that opened upon him! But he did not see them, for it was still very dark, and he had enough to do to make his way through the trees towards the house.

Just as he approached the door, feeling more tired than he could have imagined possible — she was such a little thin old thing — she began to move, and became so restless that, unable to carry her a moment longer, he thought to lay her on the grass. But she stood upright on her feet. Her hood had dropped, and her hair fell about her. The first gleam of the morning was caught on her face: that face was bright as the never-ageing Dawn, and her eyes were lovely as the sky of darkest blue. The prince recoiled in over-mastering wonder. It was Daylight herself whom he had brought from the forest! He fell at her feet, nor dared look up until she laid her hand upon his head. He rose then.

"You kissed me when I was an old woman: there! I kiss you when I am a young princess." murmured Daylight. — "Is that the sun coming?"

"The Happy Prince," from Complete Writings of Oscar Wilde. The House of Pomegranates. *(New York: The Nottingham Society, 1905.)*

In "The Happy Prince" Oscar Wilde reveals his affinities with Hans Christian Andersen, as he employs the conventions of fairytales to depict the redeeming quality of innocence in the context of a fallen world. The Happy Prince sacrifices his gold, his sapphire eyes, and his ruby mouth in order that the poor of the city may be fed. The swallow sacrifices his life of joy among the other birds in order to minister to his friend, the prince. In the end, they achieve a transcendence and spiritual purity. The tale, in its linear structure toward spiritual transcendence, is reminiscent of Andersen's "Little Match Girl."

The Happy Prince

High above the city, on a tall column, stood the statue of the Happy Prince. He was gilded all over with thin leaves of fine gold, for eyes he had two bright sapphires, and a large red ruby glowed on his sword-hilt.

He was very much admired indeed. 'He is as beautiful as a weathercock,' remarked one of the Town Councillors who wished to gain a reputation for having artistic tastes; 'only not quite so useful,' he added, fearing lest people should think him unpractical, which he really was not.

'Why can't you be like the Happy Prince?' asked a sensible mother of her little boy who was crying for the moon. 'The Happy Prince never dreams of crying for anything.'

'I am glad there is some one in the world who is quite happy,' muttered a disappointed man as he gazed at the wonderful statue.

'He looks just like an angel,' said the Charity Children as they came out of the cathedral in their bright scarlet cloaks and their clean white pinafores.

'How do you know?' said the Mathematical Master, 'you have never seen one.'

'Ah! but we have, in our dreams,' answered the children; and the Mathematical Master frowned and looked very severe, for he did not approve of children dreaming.

One night there flew over the city a little Swallow. His friends had gone away to Egypt six weeks before, but he had stayed behind, for he was in love with the most beautiful Reed. He had met her early in the spring as he was flying down the river after a big yellow moth, and had been so attracted by her slender waist that he had stopped to talk to her.

'Shall I love you?' said the Swallow, who liked to come to the point at once, and the Reed made him a low bow. So he flew round and round her, touching the water with his wings, and making silver ripples. This was his courtship, and it lasted all through the summer.

'It is a ridiculous attachment,' twittered the other Swallows; 'she has no money, and far too many relations'; and indeed the river was quite full of Reeds. Then, when the autumn came, they all flew away.

After they had gone he felt lonely, and began to tire of his lady-love. 'She has no conversation,' he said, 'and I am afraid that she is a coquette, for she is always flirting with the wind.' And certainly, whenever the wind blew, the Reed made the most graceful curtseys. 'I admit that she is domestic,' he continued, 'but I love travelling, and my wife, consequently, should love travelling also.'

'Will you come away with me?' he said finally to her; but the Reed shook her head, she was so attached to her home.

'You have been trifling with me,' he cried. 'I am off to the Pyramids. Good-bye!' and he flew away.

All day long he flew, and at night-time he arrived at the city. 'Where shall I put up?' he said; 'I hope the town has made preparations.' Then he saw the statue on the tall column.

'I will put up there,' he cried; 'it is a fine position with plenty of fresh air.' So he alighted just between the feet of the Happy Prince.

'I have a golden bedroom,' he said softly to himself as he looked round, and he prepared to go to sleep; but just as he was putting his head under his wing a large drop of water fell on him. 'What a curious thing!' he cried; 'there is not a single cloud in the sky, the stars are quite clear and bright, and yet it is raining. The climate in the north of Europe is really dreadful. The Reed used to like the rain, but that was merely her selfishness.'

Then another drop fell.

'What is the use of a statue if it cannot keep the rain off?' he said; 'I must look for a good chimney-pot,' and he determined to fly away.

But before he had opened his wings, a third drop fell, and he looked up, and saw — Ah! what did he see?

The eyes of the Happy Prince were filled with tears, and tears were running down his golden cheeks. His face was so beautiful in the moonlight that the little Swallow was filled with pity.

'Who are you?' he said.

'I am the Happy Prince.'

'Why are you weeping then?' asked the Swallow; 'you have quite drenched me.'

'When I was alive and had a human heart,' answered the statue, 'I did not know what tears were, for I lived in the Palace of Sans-Souci, where sorrow is not allowed to enter. In the daytime I played with my companions in the garden, and in the evening I led the dance in the Great Hall. Round the garden ran a very lofty wall, but I never cared to ask what lay beyond it, everything about me was so beautiful. My courtiers called me the Happy Prince, and happy indeed I was, if pleasure be happiness. So I lived, and so I died. And now that I am dead they have set me up here so high that I can see all the ugliness and all the misery of my city, and though my heart is made of lead yet I cannot choose but weep.'

'What! is he not solid gold?' said the Swallow to himself. He was too polite to make any personal remarks out loud.

'Far away,' continued the statue in a low musical voice, 'far away in a little street there is a poor house. One of the windows is open, and through it I can see a woman seated at a table. Her face is thin and worn, and she has coarse, red hands, all pricked by the needle, for she is a seamstress. She is embroidering passion-flowers on a satin gown for the loveliest of the Queen's maids-of-honour to wear at the next Court-ball. In a bed in the corner of the room her little boy is lying ill. He has a fever, and is asking for oranges. His mother has nothing to give him but river water, so he is crying. Swallow, Swallow, little Swallow, will you not bring her the ruby out of my sword-hilt? My feet are fastened to this pedestal and I cannot move.'

'I am waited for in Egypt,' said the Swallow. 'My friends are flying up and down the Nile, and talking to the large lotus-flowers. Soon they will go to sleep in the tomb of the great King. The King is there himself in his painted coffin. He is wrapped in yellow linen, and embalmed with spices. Round his neck is a chain of pale green jade, and his hands are like withered leaves.'

'Swallow, Swallow, little Swallow,' said the Prince, 'will you not stay with me for one night, and be my messenger? The boy is so thirsty, and the mother so sad.'

'I don't think I like boys,' answered the Swallow. 'Last summer, when I was staying on the river, there were two rude boys, the miller's sons, who were always throwing stones at me. They never hit me, of course; we swallows fly far too well for that, and besides I come of a family famous for its agility; but still, it was a mark of disrespect.'

But the Happy Prince looked so sad that the little Swallow was sorry. 'It is very cold here,' he said; 'but I will stay with you for one night, and be your messenger.'

'Thank you, little Swallow,' said the Prince.

So the Swallow picked out the great ruby from the Prince's sword, and flew away with it in his beak over the roofs of the town.

He passed by the cathedral tower, where the white marble angels were sculptured. He passed by the palace and heard the sound of dancing. A beautiful girl came out on the balcony with her lover. 'How wonderful the stars are,' he said to her, 'and how wonderful is the power of love!'

'I hope my dress will be ready in time for the State-ball,' she answered; 'I have ordered passion-flowers to be embroidered on it; but the seamstresses are so lazy.'

He passed over the river, and saw the lanterns hanging to the masts of the ships. He passed over the Ghetto, and saw the old Jews bargaining with each other, and weighing out money in copper scales. At last he came to the poor house and looked in. The boy was tossing feverishly on his bed, and the mother had fallen asleep, she was so tired. In he hopped, and laid the great ruby on the table beside the woman's thimble. Then he flew gently round the bed, fanning the boy's forehead with his wings. 'How cool I feel,' said the boy, 'I must be getting better'; and he sank into a delicious slumber.

Then the Swallow flew back to the Happy Prince, and told him what he had done. 'It is curious,' he remarked, 'but I feel quite warm now, although it is so cold.'

'That is because you have done a good action,' said the Prince. And the little Swallow began to think, and then he fell asleep. Thinking always made him sleepy.

When day broke he flew down to the river and had a bath. 'What a remarkable phenomenon,' said the Professor of Ornithology as he was passing over the bridge. 'A swallow in winter!' And he wrote a long letter about it to the local newspaper. Every one quoted it, it was full of so many words that they could not understand.

'To-night I go to Egypt,' said the Swallow, and he was in high spirits at the prospect. He visited all the public monuments, and sat a long time on top of the church steeple. Wherever he went the Sparrows chirruped, and said to each other, 'What a distinguished stranger!' so he enjoyed himself very much.

When the moon rose he flew back to the Happy Prince. 'Have you any commissions for Egypt?' he cried; 'I am just starting.'

'Swallow, Swallow, little Swallow,' said the Prince, 'will you not stay with me one night longer?'

'I am waited for in Egypt,' answered the Swallow. 'To-morrow my friends will fly up to the Second Cataract. The river-horse couches there among the bulrushes, and on a great granite throne sits the God Memnon. All night long he watches the stars, and when the morning star shines he utters one cry of joy, and then he is silent. At noon the yellow lions come down to the water's edge to drink. They have eyes like green beryls, and their roar is louder than the roar of the cataract.'

'Swallow, Swallow, little Swallow,' said the Prince, 'far away across the city I see a young man in a garret. He is leaning over a desk covered with papers, and in a tumbler by his side there is a bunch of withered violets. His hair is brown and crisp, and his lips are red as a pomegranate, and he has large and dreamy eyes. He is trying to finish a play for the Director of the Theatre, but he is too cold to write any more. There is no fire in the grate, and hunger has made him faint.'

'I will wait with you one night longer,' said the Swallow, who really had a good heart. 'Shall I take him another ruby?'

'Alas! I have no ruby now,' said the Prince; 'my eyes are all that I have left. They are made of rare sapphires, which were brought out of India a thousand years ago. Pluck out one of them and take it to him. He will sell it to the jeweller, and buy food and firewood, and finish his play.'

'Dear Prince,' said the Swallow, 'I cannot do that'; and he began to weep.

'Swallow, Swallow, little Swallow,' said the Prince, 'do as I command you.'

So the Swallow plucked out the Prince's eye, and flew away to the student's garret. It was easy enough to get in, as there was a hole in the roof. Through this he darted, and came into the room. The young man had his head buried in his hands, so he did not hear the flutter of the bird's wings, and when he looked up he found the beautiful sapphire lying on the withered violets.

'I am beginning to be appreciated,' he cried; 'this is from some great admirer. Now I can finish my play,' and he looked quite happy.

The next day the Swallow flew down to the harbour. He sat on the mast of a large vessel and watched the sailors hauling big chests out of the hold with ropes. 'Heave a-hoy!' they shouted as each chest came up. 'I am going to Egypt,' cried the Swallow, but nobody minded, and when the moon rose he flew back to the Happy Prince.

'I am come to bid you good-bye,' he cried.

'Swallow, Swallow, little Swallow,' said the Prince, 'will you not stay with me one night longer?'

'It is winter,' answered the Swallow, 'and the chill snow will soon be here. In Egypt the sun is warm on the green palm-trees, and the crocodiles lie in the mud and look lazily about

them. My companions are building a nest in the Temple of Baalbec, and the pink and white doves are watching them, and cooing to each other. Dear Prince, I must leave you, but I will never forget you, and next spring I will bring you back two beautiful jewels in place of those you have given away. The ruby shall be redder than a red rose, and the sapphire shall be as blue as the great sea.'

'In the square below,' said the Happy Prince, 'there stands a little match-girl. She has let her matches fall in the gutter, and they are all spoiled. Her father will beat her if she does not bring home some money, and she is crying. She has no shoes or stockings, and her little head is bare. Pluck out my other eye, and give it to her, and her father will not beat her.'

'I will stay with you one night longer,' said the Swallow, 'but I cannot pluck out your eye. You would be quite blind then.'

'Swallow, Swallow, little Swallow,' said the Prince, 'do as I command you.'

So he plucked out the Prince's other eye, and darted down with it. He swooped past the match-girl and slipped the jewel into the palm of her hand. 'What a lovely bit of glass,' cried the little girl; and she ran home, laughing.

Then the Swallow came back to the Prince. 'You are blind now,' he said, 'so I will stay with you always.'

'No, little Swallow,' said the poor Prince, 'you must go away to Egypt.'

'I will stay with you always,' said the Swallow, and he slept at the Prince's feet.

All the next day he sat on the Prince's shoulder, and told him stories of what he had seen in strange lands. He told him of the red ibises, who stand in long rows on the banks of the Nile, and catch gold-fish in their beaks; of the Sphinx, who is as old as the world itself, and lives in the desert, and knows everything; of the merchants, who walk slowly by the side of their camels, and carry amber beads in their hand; of the King of the Mountains of the Moon, who is as black as ebony, and worships a large crystal; of the great green snake that sleeps in a palm-tree, and has twenty priests to feed it with honey-cakes; and of the pygmies who sail over a big lake on large flat leaves, and are always at war with the butterflies.

'Dear little Swallow,' said the Prince, 'you tell me of marvellous things, but more marvellous than anything is the suffering of men and women. There is no Mystery so great as Misery. Fly over my city, little Swallow, and tell me what you see there.'

So the Swallow flew over the great city, and saw the rich making merry in their beautiful houses, while the beggars were sitting at the gates. He flew into dark lanes, and saw the white faces of starving children looking out listlessly at the black streets. Under the archway of a bridge two little boys were lying in one another's arms to try and keep themselves warm. 'How hungry we are!' they said. 'You must not lie here,' shouted the Watchman, and they wandered out into the rain.

Then he flew back and told the Prince what he had seen.

'I am covered with fine gold,' said the Prince, 'you must take it off, leaf by leaf, and give it to my poor; the living always think that gold can make them happy.'

Leaf after leaf of the fine gold the Swallow picked off, till the Happy Prince looked quite dull and grey. Leaf after leaf of the fine gold he brought to the poor, and the children's faces grew rosier, and they laughed and played games in the street. 'We have bread now!' they cried.

Then the snow came, and after the snow came the frost. The streets looked as if they were made of silver, they were so bright and glistening; long icicles like crystal daggers hung down from the eaves of the houses, everybody went about in furs, and the little boys wore scarlet caps and skated on the ice.

The poor little Swallow grew colder and colder, but he would not leave the Prince, he loved him too well. He picked up crumbs outside the baker's door when the baker was not looking, and tried to keep himself warm by flapping his wings.

But at last he knew that he was going to die. He had just strength to fly up to the Prince's shoulder once more. 'Good-bye, dear Prince!' he murmured, 'will you let me kiss your hand?

'I am glad that you are going to Egypt at last, little Swallow,' said the Prince, 'you have stayed too long here; but you must kiss me on the lips, for I love you.'

'It is not to Egypt that I am going,' said the Swallow, 'I am going to the House of Death. Death is the brother of Sleep, is he not?'

And he kissed the Happy Prince on the lips, and fell down dead at his feet.

At that moment a curious crack sounded inside the statue, as if something had broken. The fact is that the leaden heart had snapped right in two. It certainly was a dreadfully hard frost.

Early the next morning the Mayor was walking in the square below in company with the Town Councillors. As they passed the column he looked up at the statue: 'Dear me! how shabby the Happy Prince looks!' he said.

'How shabby indeed!' cried the Town Councillors, who always agreed with the Mayor; and they went up to look at it.

'The ruby has fallen out of his sword, his eyes are gone, and he is golden no longer,' said the Mayor; 'in fact, he is little better than a beggar!'

'Little better than a beggar,' said the Town Councillors.

'And here is actually a dead bird at his feet!' continued the Mayor. 'We must really issue a proclamation that birds are not to be allowed to die here.' And the Town Clerk made a note of the suggestion.

So they pulled down the statue of the Happy Prince. 'As he is no longer beautiful he is no longer useful,' said the Art Professor at the University.

Then they melted the statue in a furnace, and the Mayor held a meeting of the Corporation to decide what was to be done with the metal. 'We must have another statue, of course,' he said, 'and it shall be a statue of myself.'

'Of myself,' said each of the Town Councillors, and they quarrelled. When I last heard of them they were quarrelling still.

'What a strange thing!' said the overseer of the workmen at the foundry. 'This broken lead heart will not melt in the furnace. We must throw it away.' So they threw it on a dust-heap where the dead Swallow was also lying.

'Bring me the two most precious things in the city,' said God to one of His Angels; and the Angel brought Him the leaden heart and the dead bird.

'You have rightly chosen,' said God, 'for in my garden of Paradise this little bird shall sing for evermore, and in my city of gold the Happy Prince shall praise me.'

"The Moon Ribbon", from The Moon Ribbon and Other Tales, *by Jane Yolen. Illustrated by David Palladini. (New York: Thomas Y. Crowell Company, 1976.)*

Contemporary American writer of literary folktales, Jane Yolen, acknowledges the influence of George MacDonald's stories upon "The Moon Ribbon." Like Cinderella and Snow White, the tale's heroine, Sylva, is beleaguered by an evil stepmother and two waspish step-sisters. Unlike other fairy tale heroines but very much like MacDonald's Princess Irene in The Princess and the Goblin, *Sylva is saved, not by a prince, but through the majestic and divine influence of her goddess-like mother and grandmother, who have left her a magical ribbon woven of strands of their silver hair. Sylva's circular journey — to the spiritual realm of her mother and back again — enables her to assert her own will and allow the evil ones to destroy themselves.*

The Moon Ribbon

There was once a plain but goodhearted girl named Sylva whose sole possession was a ribbon her mother had left her. It was a strange ribbon, the color of moonlight, for it had been woven from the gray hairs of her mother and her mother's mother and her mother's mother's mother before her.

Sylva lived with her widowed father in a great house by the forest's edge. Once the great house had belonged to her mother, but when she died, it became Sylva's father's house to do with as he willed. And what he willed was to live simply and happily with his daughter without thinking of the day to come.

But one day, when there was little enough to live on, and only the great house to recommend him, Sylva's father married again, a beautiful widow who had two beautiful daughters of her own.

It was a disastrous choice, for no sooner were they wed when it was apparent the woman was mean in spirit and meaner in tongue. She dismissed most of the servants and gave their chores over to Sylva, who followed her orders without complaint. For simply living in her mother's house with her loving father seemed enough for the girl.

After a bit, however, the old man died in order to have some peace, and the house passed on to the stepmother. Scarcely two days had passed, or maybe three, when the stepmother left off mourning the old man and turned on Sylva. She dismissed the last of the servants without their pay.

"Girl," she called out, for she never used Sylva's name, "you will sleep in the kitchen and do the charring." And from that time on it was so.

Sylva swept the floor and washed and mended the family's clothing. She sowed and hoed and tended the fields. She ground the wheat and kneaded the bread, and she waited on the others as though she were a servant. But she did not complain.

Yet late at night, when the stepmother and her own two daughters were asleep, Sylva would weep bitterly into her pillow, which was nothing more than an old broom laid in front of the hearth.

One day, when she was cleaning out an old desk, Sylva came upon a hidden drawer she had never seen before. Trembling, she opened the drawer. It was empty except for a silver ribbon with a label attached to it. *For Sylva* read the card. *The Moon Ribbon of Her Mother's Hair.* She took it out and stared at it. And all that she had lost was borne in upon her. She felt the tears start in her eyes, and so as not to cry she took the tag off and began to stroke the ribbon with her hand. It was rough and smooth at once and shone like the rays of the moon.

At that moment her stepsisters came into the room.

"What is that?" asked one. "Is it nice? It is mine."

"I want it. I saw it first," cried the other.

The noise brought the stepmother to them. "Show it to me," she said.

Illustration by David Balladini, "The Moon Ribbon" from *The Moon Ribbon and Other Tales,* by Jane Yalen. Copyright © 1976. Reprinted by permission of Crowell Inc.

Obediently, Sylva came over and held the ribbon out to her. But when the stepmother picked it up, it looked like no more than strands of gray hair woven together unevenly. It was prickly to the touch.

"Disgusting," said the stepmother dropping it back into Sylva's hand. "Throw it out at once."

"Burn it," cried one stepsister.

"Bury it," cried the other.

"Oh, please. It was my mother's. She left it for me. Please let me keep it," begged Sylva.

The stepmother looked again at the gray strand. "Very well," she said with a grim smile. "It suits you." And she strode out of the room, her daughters behind her.

Now that she had the silver ribbon, Sylva thought her life would be better. But instead it became worse. As if to punish her for speaking out for the ribbon, her sisters were at her to wait on them both day and night. And whereas before she had to sleep by the hearth, she now had to sleep outside with the animals. Yet she did not complain or run away, for she was tied by her memories for her mother's house.

One night, when the frost was on the grass turning each blade into a silver spear, Sylva threw herself to the ground in tears. And the silver ribbon, which she had tied loosely about her hair, slipped off and lay on the ground before her. She had never seen it in the moonlight. It glittered and shone and seemed to ripple.

Sylva bent over to touch it and her tears fell upon it. Suddenly the ribbon began to grow and change, and as it changed the air was filled with a woman's soft voice speaking these words:

> *"Silver ribbon, silver hair,*
> *Carry Sylva with great care,*
> *Bring my daughter home."*

And there at Sylva's feet was a silver river that glittered and shone and rippled in the moonlight.

There was neither boat nor bridge, but Sylva did not care. She thought the river would wash away her sorrows, and without a single word, she threw herself in.

But she did not sink. Instead she floated like a swan and the river bore her on, on past houses and hills, past high places and low. And strange to say, she was not wet at all.

At last she was carried around a great bend in the river and deposited gently on a grassy slope that came right down to the water's edge.

Sylva scrambled up onto the bank and looked about. There was a great meadow of grass so green and still it might have been painted on. At the meadow's rim, near a dark forest, sat a house that was like and yet not like the one in which Sylva lived.

"Surely someone will be there who can tell me where I am and why I have been brought here," she thought. So she made her way across the meadow and only where she stepped down did the grass move. When she moved beyond, the grass sprang back and was the same as before. And though she passed larkspur and meadowsweet, clover and rye, they did not seem like real flowers, for they had no smell at all.

"Am I dreaming?" she wondered, "or am I dead?" But she did not say it out loud, for she was afraid to speak into the silence.

Sylva walked up to the house and hesitated at the door. She feared to knock and yet feared equally not to. As she was deciding, the door opened of itself and she walked in.

She found herself in a large, long, dark hall with a single crystal door at the end that emitted a strange glow the color of moonlight. As she walked down the hall, her shoes made no clatter on the polished wood floor. And when she reached the door, she tried to peer through into the room beyond, but the crystal panes merely gave back her own reflection twelve times.

Sylva reached for the doorknob and pulled sharply. The glowing crystal knob came off in her hand. She would have wept then, but anger stayed her; she beat her fist against the door and it suddenly gave way.

Inside was a small room lit only by a fireplace and a round white globe that hung from the ceiling like a pale, wan moon. Before the fireplace stood a tall woman dressed all in white. Her silver-white hair was unbound and cascaded to her knees. Around her neck was a silver ribbon.

"Welcome, my daughter," she said.

"Are you my mother?" asked Sylva wonderingly, for what little she remembered of her mother, she remembered no one as grand as this.

"I am if you make me so," came the reply.

"And how do I do that?" asked Sylva.

"Give me your hand."

As the woman spoke, she seemed to move away, yet she moved not at all. Instead the floor between them moved and cracked apart. Soon they were separated by a great chasm which was so black it seemed to have no bottom.

"I cannot reach," said Sylva.

"You must try," the woman replied.

So Sylva clutched the crystal knob to her breast and leaped, but it was too far. As she fell, she heard a woman's voice speaking from behind her and before her and all about her, warm with praise.

"Well done, my daughter. You are halfway home."

Sylva landed gently on the meadow grass, but a moment's walk from her house. In her hand she still held the knob, shrunk now to the size of a jewel. The river shimmered once before her and was gone, and where it had been was the silver ribbon, lying limp and damp in the morning frost.

The door to the house stood open. She drew a deep breath and went in.

"What is that?" cried one of the stepsisters when she saw the crystalline jewel in Sylva's hand.

"I want it," cried the other, grabbing it from her.

"I will take that," said the stepmother, snatching it from them all. She held it up to the light and examined it. "It will fetch a good price and repay me for my care of you. Where did you get it?" she asked Sylva.

Sylva tried to tell them of the ribbon and the river, the tall woman and the black crevasse. But they laughed at her and did not believe her. Yet they could not explain away the jewel. So they left her then and went off to the city to sell it. When they returned it was late. They thrust Sylva outside to sleep and went themselves to their comfortable beds to dream of their new riches.

Sylva sat on the cold ground and thought about what had happened. She reached up and took down the ribbon from her hair. She stroked it, and it felt smooth and soft and yet hard, too. Carefully she placed it on the ground.

In the moonlight, the ribbon glittered and shone. Sylva recalled the song she had heard, so she sang it to herself:

> *"Silver ribbon, silver hair,*
> *Carry Sylva with great care,*
> *Bring my daughter home."*

Suddenly the ribbon began to grow and change, and there at her feet was a silver highway that glittered and glistened in the moonlight.

Without a moment's hesitation, Sylva got up and stepped out onto the road and waited for it to bring her to the magical house.

But the road did not move.

"Strange," she said to herself. "Why does it not carry me as the river did?"

Sylva stood on the road and waited a moment more, then tentatively set one foot in front of the other. As soon as she had set off on her own, the road set off, too, and they moved together past fields and forests, faster and faster, till the scenery seemed to fly by and blur into a moon-bleached rainbow of yellows, grays, and black.

The road took a great turning and then quite suddenly stopped, but Sylva did not. She scrambled up the bank where the road ended and found herself again in the meadow. At the far rim of the grass, where the forest began, was the house she had seen before.

Sylva strode purposefully through the grass, and this time the meadow was filled with the song of birds, the meadowlark and the bunting and the sweet jug-jug-jug of the nightingale. She could smell fresh-mown hay and the pungent pine.

The door of the house stood wide open, so Sylva went right in. The long hall was no longer dark but filled with the strange moonglow. And when she reached the crystal door at the end, and gazed at her reflection twelve times in the glass, she saw her own face set with strange gray eyes and long gray hair. She put her hand up to her mouth to stop herself from crying out. But the sound came through, and the door opened of itself.

Inside was the tall woman all in white, and the globe above her was as bright as a harvest moon.

"Welcome, my sister," the woman said.

"I have no sister," said Sylva, "but the two stepsisters I left at home. And you are none of those."

"I am if you make me so."

"How do I do that?"

"Give me back my heart which you took from me yesterday."

"I did not take your heart. I took nothing but a crystal jewel."

The woman smiled. "It was my heart."

Sylva looked stricken. "But I cannot give it back. My stepmother took it from me."

"No one can take unless you give."

"I had no choice."

"There is always a choice," the woman said.

Sylva would have cried then, but a sudden thought struck her. "Then it must have been your choice to give me your heart."

The woman smiled again, nodded gently, and held out her hand.

Sylva placed her hand in the woman's and there glowed for a moment on the woman's breast a silvery jewel that melted and disappeared.

"Now will you give me your heart?"

"I have done that already," said Sylva, and as she said it, she knew it to be true.

The woman reached over and touched Sylva on her breast and her heart sprang out onto the woman's hand and turned into two fiery red jewels. "Once given, twice gained," said the woman. She handed one of the jewels back to Sylva. "Only take care that you give each jewel with love."

Sylva felt the jewel warm and glowing in her hand and at its touch felt such comfort as she had not in many days. She closed her eyes and a smile came on her face. And when she opened her eyes again, she was standing on the meadow grass not two steps from her own door. It was morning, and by her feet lay the silver ribbon, limp and damp from the frost.

The door to her house stood open.

Sylva drew in her breath, picked up the ribbon, and went in.

"What has happened to your hair?" asked one stepsister.

"What has happened to your eyes?" asked the other.

For indeed Sylva's hair and eyes had turned as silver as the moon.

But the stepmother saw only the fiery red jewel in Sylva's hand. "Give it to me," she said, pointing to the gem.

At first Sylva held out her hand, but then quickly drew it back. "I *can* not," she said.

The stepmother's eyes became hard. "Girl, give it here."

"I *will* not," said Sylva.

The stepmother's eyes narrowed. "Then you shall tell me where you got it."

"That I shall, and gladly," said Sylva. She told them of the silver ribbon and the silver road, of the house with the crystal door. But strange to say, she left out the woman and her words.

The stepmother closed her eyes and thought. At last she said, "Let me see this wondrous silver ribbon, that I may believe what you say."

Sylva handed her the ribbon, but she was not fooled by her stepmother's tone.

The moment the silver ribbon lay prickly and limp in the stepmother's hand, she looked up triumphantly at Sylva. Her face broke into a wolfish grin. "Fool," she said, "the magic is herein. With this ribbon there are jewels for the taking." She marched out of the door and the stepsisters hurried behind her.

Sylva walked after them, but slowly, stopping in the open door.

The stepmother flung the ribbon down. In the early morning sun it glowed as if with a cold flame.

"Say the words, girl," the stepmother commanded.

From the doorway Sylva whispered:

> *"Silver ribbon, silver hair,*
> *Lead the ladies with great care,*
> *Lead them to their home."*

The silver ribbon wriggled and writhed in the sunlight, and as they watched, it turned into a silver-red stair that went down into the ground.

"Wait," called Sylva. "Do not go." But it was too late.

With a great shout, the stepmother gathered up her skirts and ran down the steps, her daughters fast behind her. And before Sylva could move, the ground had closed up after them and the meadow was as before.

On the grass lay the silver ribbon, limp and dull. Sylva went over and picked it up. As she did so, the jewel melted in her hand and she felt a burning in her breast. She put her hand up to it, and she felt her heart beating strongly beneath. Sylva smiled, put the silver ribbon in her pocket, and went back into her house.

After a time, Sylva's hair returned to its own color, except for seven silver strands, but her eyes never changed back. And when she was married and had a child of her own, Sylva plucked the silver strands from her own hair and wove them into the silver ribbon, which she kept in a wooden box. When Sylva's child was old enough to understand, the box with the ribbon was put into her safekeeping, and she has kept them for her own daughter to this very day.

Literary Folktales for Further Reading

Titles marked with an asterisk (*) are alternate versions to those found in this anthology.

Allumette, by Tomi Ungerer. Ill. by author. (Four Winds Press, 1982.)
    —A literary fairy tale which reinterprets H.C. Andersen's "The Little Match Girl."

The Animal Family, by Randall Jarrell. Ill. by Maurice Sendak. (New York: Pantheon, 1965.)
    —A lonely hunter and a lovely mermaid establish a family in the wilderness.

At the Back of the North Wind, by George Macdonald. Ill. by George and Doris Hauman. (London and New York: MacMillan, 1964.)
    —Reminiscent of Andersen's fairy tales, this features a fairy godmother-like character, the North Wind, who takes the little boy Diamond on fantastic journeys. The last trip is a transcendent journey to the back of the North Wind.

The Best Tales of Hoffmann, ed. and trans. by E.F. Bleiler. (New York: Dover, 1967.)
—Three of the nineteenth-century German writer's literary folktales: ''The Golden Flower Pot,'' ''The Nutcracker and the King of Mice,'' and ''The King's Betrothed.''

Beyond the Looking Glass: Extraordinary Works of Fairy Tale and Fantasy, ed. by Jonathan Cott; intro. by Leslie Fiedler. (New York: Stonehill, 1973.)
—The anthology includes some of the finest Victorian literary fairy tales: John Ruskin's ''King of the Golden River,'' Tom Hood's ''Petsetilla's Posy,'' Lucy Clifford's ''Wooden Tony,'' Mary de Morgan's ''Through the Fire,'' and many other fine selections.

Birdsong, by Gail E. Haley. Ill. by author. (New York: Crown, 1984.)
—An orphan girl is lured into the home of a witch, Jorinella, who wants the girl to trap birds. The birds rescue the girl and transport her to a secret kingdom where musicians and artists work in a beautiful garden.

The Blue Book of Hob Stories, by William Mayne. Ill. by Patrick Penson. (New York: Philomel, 1984.)
—Tiny goblins keep busy and enjoy adventures in a British home.

Broomsticks and Other Tales, by Walter de la Mare. (London: Constable, 1925.)
—Twelve of de la Mare's literary folktales and fantasies; one of the best is ''The Dutch Cheese,'' which depicts a comic contest between a young farmer and a troupe of fairies.

The Brothers Lionheart, by Astrid Lindgren. Trans. by Joan Tate; ill. by J.K. Lambert. (New York: Viking, 1975.)
—After death Joathan and Karl enter a strange land, where they liberate the people from a vicious tyrant and his dragon.

The Complete Fairy Tales and Stories of Hans Christian Andersen, trans, by Erik Haugaard; forward by Virginia Haviland. (Garden City: Doubleday, 1974.)
—This volume is probably the most comprehensive source of Andersen's fairy tales, as it includes many little-known stories as well as the enduringly popular selections.

The Cuckoo Clock and *The Tapestry Room*, by Mary Louisa Molesworth. Preface by Angela Bull. (London and New York: Garland Pub, 1976.)
—A cuckoo clock initiates Grislda into magical adventure in *The Cuckoo Clock*; in the *Tapestry Room* two children go to fairy land guided by a proud raven.

The Dark Princess, by Richard Kennedy. Ill. by Donna Diamond. (Holiday, 1978.)
—The court fool risks blindness to win the love of the dark princess.

The Devil's Storybook, by Natalie Babbitt. Ill. by author. (New York: Farrar, Straus, and Giroux, 1974.)
—Inspired by traditional tales about the devil, the author writes comic stories about encounters between human beings and the devil; the humans always get the best of the old rogue.

The Door in the Hedge, by Robin McKinley. (New York: Greenwillow, 1981.)
—Volume includes two original literary folktales — ''The Hunting of the Hind,'' and ''The Stolen Princess'' — and retellings of ''The Twelve Dancing Princesses'' and ''The Prince and the Frog.''

Dragon, Dragon, and Other Tales, by John Gardner. (New York: Knopf, 1975.) Ill. by Charles Shields.
—Comic parodies of traditional tales about dragons, giants, and magic.

The Dragon of Og, by Rumer Godden. Ill. by Pauline Baynes. (New York: Viking, 1981.)
—Angus Og is horrified to learn that his dragon dines on a bullock now and then and hires a courtly knight to slay the fabulous beast; the dragon is saved in the end.

Dulac's The Snow Queen and Other Stories from Hans Christian Andersen. Ill. by Edmund Dulac. 1911; Rpt. (Garden City, N.Y.: Doubleday, 1976.)
—Includes five of Andersen's tales: ''The Snow Queen,'' ''The Emperor's New Clothes,'' ''The Winter's Tale,'' ''The Nightingale,'' and ''The Little Mermaid;'' a beautifully illustrated edition.

The Emperor's New Clothes, by Hans Christian Andersen. Adapted and Ill. by Nadine Bernard Westcott. (Boston: Little Brown, 1984.)
—Westcott has simplified the language of the tale to make it appropriate for young readers. *

The Emperor's New Clothes, by Hans Christian Andersen. Ill. by Jack Delano and Irene Delano; Adapted by Jean Van Leuwen. (New York: Random House, 1971.)
—Con artists pretend to weave exquisite clothing for the emperor; a small boy tells the truth about the invisible clothing. Other illustrated versions of Andersen's popular story: Ill. by Monika Laimgruber (Reading, Penn.: Addison -Wesley, 1973); Ill. by and trans. by Erik Blegvad (New York: Harcourt, 1959), and ill. by Virginia Lee Burton (Boston: Houghton, 1949). *

Fairy Tales, by E.E. Cummings. Ill. by John Eaton. (New York and London: Harcourt, 1950.) Voyager Edition (paper), 1975.
—This volume includes several lyrical and whimsical literary folktales told by Cummings to his daughter: ''The Old Man Who Said, 'Why?','' ''The Elephant and the Butterfly,'' ''The House that Ate Mosquito Pie,'' and ''The Little Girl Named I.''

The Faithless Lollybird, by Joan Aiken. Ill. by Eros Keith. (Garden City, N.Y.: Doubleday, 1978.)
   —Thirteen modern fairy tales featuring witches, ghosts, and mermaids.

The Gifts of the Child Christ: Fairy Tales and Stories for the Childlike (Two Volumes), by George MacDonald; ed. by Glenn Edward Sadler. (Grand Rapids. MI: Eerdmans, 1973.)
   —Each of the two volumes contains some of MacDonald's finest literary fairy tales, including "The Light Princess," "The Little Day Light," "The Day Boy and the Night Girl," and "The Giant's Heart."

The Girl Who Cried Flowers and Other Tales, by Jane Yolen. Ill. by David Palladini. (New York: Crowell, 1974.)
   —Five romantic and mystical literary fairy tales, reminiscent of those of George MacDonald.

The Golden Key, by George MacDonald. Ill. by Maurice Sendak. Orig. pub. 1868; Rpt. (New York: Farrar, Straus, and Giroux, Inc. 1967.) New York: Dell, 1978 (paper edition).
   —Mossy and Tangle, a young boy and girl, enter fairyland and embark upon a quest for a golden key. Each character undergoes trials, rites of passage, and finally attains spiritual transcendence.

The Green Book of Hob Stories, by William Mayne. Ill. by Patrick Benson. (New York: Philomel, 1984.)
   —Episodic tale about a plump goblin in a British household; author draws upon traditional legend and lore to create comic effects.

Gudgekin the Thistle Girl and Other Stories, by John Gardner. (New York: Alfred A. Knopf, 1976.)
   —Volume includes four literary folktales — "Gudgekin the Thistle Girl," "The Griffin and the Wise Old Philosopher," "The Shape-Shifters of Shorm," and "The Sea Gulls." Each story is a humorous parody of a traditional folktale.

The Happy Prince, by Oscar Wilde. Ill. by Kaj Beckman. 1888; Rpt. (New York: Methuen, 1977.)
   —Looking out over the city, the golden prince with sapphire eyes, ruby lips, and a kind heart grieves for the misery he sees; a swallow takes all of the prince's jewels and gold to the poor.

The Happy Prince and Other Stories, by Oscar Wilde. Ill. by Peggy Fortrum. (London: Dent, 1977.)
   —A collection of Wilde's literary fairy tales, including "The Selfish Giant."

A Harp of Fishbones and Other Stories, by Joan Aiken. (London: Cape, 1972; New York: Puffin, 1975 (paper).)
   —A collection of humorous literary folktales which exhibit Aiken's blend of humor, fantasy, and ordinary reality.

The Hope of the Katzekopfs: *A Fairy Tale*, by Francis Edward Paget. 1844; Rpt. (New York: Johnson Reprint Corporation, 1968.)
   —King Katzekopf and Queen Ninnilinda spoil their child, Prince Eigenwillig. At last Fairy Abracadabra fetches him, takes him to fairyland, and transforms the prince into an exemplary boy.

The King of the Golden River, or the Black Brothers, by John Ruskin. Ill. by Krystyna Turska. 1841; Rpt. (New York: Greenwillow, 1978.)
   —Gluck's older brothers misuse holy water and become two black stones; Gluck restores paradise to his valley with the aid of two wise old men, the King of the Golden River and the South-West Wind.

Kristin and Boone, by Karen Rose. (Boston: Houghton Mifflin, 1983.)
   —A reinterpretation of "Beauty and the Beast."

The Land Beyond, by Maria Gripe. Trans. by Sheila La Farge. Ill. by Harald Gripe. (New York: Delacorte, 1974.)
   —An explorer, a young king, and a maladjusted princess discover an imaginary world.

The Light Princess, by George MacDonald. Ill. by Maurice Sendak. 1868; Rpt. (New York: Farrar, Straus, and Giroux, 1969; New York: Dell, 1978 (paper).)
   —A delightful reworking of "Sleeping Beauty." An evil fairy deprives the princess of her gravity in all senses; she floats about and she cannot cry. The love and sacrifice of a prince breaks the evil spell.

The Little Lame Prince by Dinah Mulock (Mrs. Craik). 1874; Rpt. (New York: Collins, 1975.)
   —Prince Dolor's kingdom has been stolen by an evil uncle; Dolor, having been banished to a tower with his nurse, enjoys adventures on a magic carpet and eventually overthrows the usurping uncle.

The Little Match Girl, by Hans Christian Andersen. Ill. by Blair Lent. (Boston: Houghton Mifflin, 1968.)
   —The hungry and freezing little match seller must strike all her matches to keep warm. As the last flames go out, she transcends her death as she envisions happiness in heaven with her grandmother. *

Little Witch's Big Night, by Deborah Hautzig. Ill. by Marc Brown. (New York: Random House, 1984.)
   —A little witch is left out at Hallowe'en because she has been too good.

The Magic Fishbone, by Charles Dickens. Ill. by Louis Slobodkin. (New York: Vanguard, 1953.)
   —Princess Alicia resorts to using her magic fishbone only when her own resourcefulness no longer works. *

Many Moons, by James Thurber. Ill. by Louis Slobodkin. (New York: Harcourt, 1943.)
   —The spoiled Princess Lenore demands the moon; only the court fool is wise enough to grant her wish.

The Magic World, by E. Nesbit. Ill. by H.R. Millar and Spencer Pryse. 1916; Rpt. (London: the British Book Center, 1974.) (Facsimile Edition available from Mayflower Books).
—Volume includes some of Nesbit's most delightful magical tales: "The Cathood of Maurice," "Accidental Magic," "Kenneth and the Carp," and "The White Cat."

Molly McCollough and Tom the Rogue, by Kathleen Stevens. Ill. by Margot Zemach. (New York: Crowell, 1983.)
—Tom, a clever trickster, meets his match in Molly, who outwits him and wins him.

The Moon Ribbon and Other Tales, by Jane Yolen. Ill. by David Palladini. (New York: Crowell, 1976.)
—Six romantic and mystical tales — "The Moon Ribbon," "The Moon Child," "Somewhen," "Rosechild," and "Honey-Stick Boy."

Mopsa the Fairy, by Jean Ingelow. London: Longmans, 1869. Rpt. (New York: Garland, 1976.)
—Booklength Victorian work about Jack, who enters fairyland through the hollow of a tree and finds four tiny fairies in a bird's nest. Jack and Mopsa the Fairy find that they cannot escape their destinies.

The Mouldy, by William Mayne. Ill. by Nicola Bayley. (New York: Knopf, 1983.)
—Mouldy the Mole proposes to the king's daughter but decides to marry a hedgepig instead.

A Necklace of Raindrops and Other Stories, by Joan Aiken. Ill. by Jan Pienkowski. 1969; Rpt. (New York: Dell, 1971.)
—Eight literary folktales blending elements of fantasy and reality and rendered in Aiken's characteristically comic mode.

The Nightingale, by Hans Christian Andersen. Trans. by Eva Le Gallienne. Ill. by Nancy Ekholm Burkert. 1896; (New York: Harper and Row, 1965.)
—The nightingale from nature is banished when the emperor receives a golden one instead. Ultimately the natural bird saves the emperor's life.

Nutcracker, by E.T.A. Hoffman. Ill. by Maurice Sendak. (New York: 1984.)
—Translation of Hoffman's famous tale about the animated nutcracker and his encounter with the Mouse King.

The Ordinary Princess, by M.M. Kaye. Ill. by author. (Garden City, N.Y.: Doubleday, 1984.)
—Amethyst has been cursed at her christening to be ordinary.

The Princess and the Lion, by Elizabeth Coatsworth. Ill. by Evaline Ness. (New York: Pantheon, 1963.)
—Princess Miriam journeys to the Prison of Princes to prevent Prince Michael, the heir to the throne, from escaping.

Princess Hynchatti and Some Other Surprises, by Tanith Lee. Ill. by Velma Ilsly. (New York: Farrar, Straus, and Giroux, 1973.)
—A collection of comic literary fairy tales with strong feminist dimensions.

Princess Kalina and the Hedgehog, by Jeanette B. Flot. Adapted by Frances Marshall and ill. by Dorothee Duntze. (London: Faber, 1981.)
—The princesses's helpful hedgehog proves to be a prince; the tale is strongly reminiscent of E. Nesbit's "The Princess and the Hedgepig."

The Plain Princess, by Phyllis McGinley. Ill. by Helen Storr. (New York: Lippincott, 1945.)
—In this didactic literary folktale Dame Goodwit transforms a selfish princess.

The Princess and the Pea, by Hans Christian Andersen. Ill. by Paul Galdone. (New York: Seabury Press, 1978.)
—Humorous tale in which the prince's mother tests a princess by placing a pea beneath a pile of mattresses to see if the girl is truly royal.

The Princess on the Nut: *Or the Curious Courtship of the Son of the Princess on the Pea*, by Michelle Nikly. Trans. by Lucy Meredith. (London: Faber, 1981.)
—A spoof on Andersen's famous story, the tale dramatizes Prince Caspar's search for a real princess; he finds her and almost allows her to get away.

The Practical Princess and Other Liberating Fairy Tales, by Jay Williams. Ill. by Rick Schreiter. (Parents, 1978.)
—Six comic tales featuring strong heroines.

Prince Prigio and Prince Ricardo of Pantouflia, by Andrew Lang. Preface by Peter Neumeyer. Bristol: J.W. Arrowsmith, 1889, 1893; Rpt. (New York: Garland, 1976.)
—Lang presents a humorous burlesque of fairy tale conventions. Prince Prigio was cursed to be too clever. Prince Ricardo wears himself out rescuing princesses.

Prince Sparrow, by Mordicai Gerstein. Ill. by author. (New York: Four Winds, 1984.)
—Comic treatment of a bratty princess, who loves fairy tales. When a sparrow flies into her room, she believes the bird is a prince in disguise.

The Rat Catcher's Daughter: *A Collection of Stories*, by Laurence Housman. Ed. by Ellin Greene. Ill. by Julia Noonan. Rpt. (New York: Atheneum, 1974.)
—Twelve whimsical literary folk tales.

The Rose and the Ring; *or the History of Prince Giglio and Prince Bulbo*, by William Makepeace Thackeray. 1855, Rpt. (New York: Garland, 1976.)
—Fairy Blackstick helps to restore Princess Rosealba and Prince Giglio to their rightful thrones; Thackeray burlesques fairy tale conventions and satirizes human nature.

The Selfish Giant, by Oscar Wilde. Ill. by Michael Foreman and Freire Wright. 1888; Rpt. (New York and London: Methuen, 1978.)
— The selfish giant allows the children to play in his garden; a special child accompanies him to heaven.

Sleeping Ugly, by Jane H. Yolen. Ill. by Diane Stanley. (New York: Coward, 1981.)
An amusing parody of "The Sleeping Beauty."

The Snow Parlor and Other Bedtime Stories, by Elizabeth Coatsworth. Ill. by Charles Robinson. (New York: Grosset and Dunlap, 1972.)
— Five lively tales featuring animated toys, a walking pine tree, and talking animals.

The Snow Queen, by Hans Christian Andersen. Trans. by R.P.Keigwin. Ill. by Errol Le Cain. (New York: Viking, 1979.)
— Gerda embarks upon a perilous quest to rescue her friend Kay from the evil and icy Snow Queen; she succeeds after many dangerous adventures.

The Steadfast Tin Soldier, by Hans Christian Andersen. Ill. by Marcia Brown. Trans. by M.R. James. (New York: Scribner's, 1953.)
— A toy soldier with one leg undergoes many dangerous adventures before he is joined at last with the toy ballerina whom he loves.

The Strange Child, E.T.A Hoffman. Trans. and adapted by Anthea Bell; Ill. by Lisbeth Zwerger. (Neugebauer/Alphabet, 1984.)
— First published in 1817, this is the tale of two children who play happily with a mysterious child, who comforts them when they are troubled.

A Tale of Three Wishes, by Isaac Bashevis Singer. Ill. by Irene Lieblich. (New York: Farrar, Straus, and Giroux, 1976.)
— The wishes of three children create trouble on the night of Hoshanah Rabbah.

The Thirteen Clocks, by James Thurber. Ill. by Marc Simont. (New York: Simon, 1950.)
— In order to win his princess Prince Zorn searches for a thousand jewels to start the silent clocks in the land.

Thistle, by Walter Wangerin. Ill. by Marcia Sewall. (New York: Harper, 1983.)
— The youngest child saves her family by kissing an ugly witch.

Thumbelina, by Hans Christian Andersen. Ill. by Adrienne Adams. Trans. by R.P. Keigwin. (New York: Scribner's, 1961.)*

The Touchstone, by Robert Louis Stevenson. Ill. by Uri Shulevitz. (New York: Morrow, 1976.)
— Two rival princes look for the "touchstone of truth;" each finds a surprising solution.

The Town Cats and Other Tales, by Lloyd Alexander. Ill. by Laszle Kubiny. (New York: Dutton, 1977.)
— Heroic cats undergo adventures in eight literary fairy tales.

The Ugly Duckling, by Hans Christian Andersen. Ill. by Adrienne Adams. Trans. by R.P. Keigwin. (New York: Scribner's, 1965.)
— The ugly duckling is transformed into a lovely swan after enduring suffering and ridicule.*

The Ugly Princess, by Nancy Luenn. Ill. by David Wiesner. (Boston: Little Brown, 1981.)
— Princess Saralinde is cursed by ugliness; she wisely chooses an ugly but kind suitor who breaks the evil spell.

Undine, by Baron de La Motte Fouque. (London: Bell and Daldy, 1859; Rpt. Westport Ct: Hyperion, 1978.)
— Undine, a lovely water sprite, loves an undeserving knight. Though Undine loses her knight's love, she acquires a human soul.

Unicorn Moon by Gale Cooper. Ill. by author. (New York: Dutton, 1984.)
— In her dreams the princess falls in love with a young man in the land of the unicorn moon.

The Unicorn and the Plow, by Louise Moeri. Ill. by Diane Good. (New York: Dutton, 1982.)
— A farmer's crop fails, and he must get rid of his oxen. The oxen promise and deliver a miracle — a unicorn and a plow.

The White Cat and Other Old French Fairy Tales by Mme. La Comtesse D'Aulnoy. Arranged by Rachel Field. Ill. by E. MacKinstry. (New York: Macmillan, 1967.)
— Volume contains "The White Cat," "Graciosa and Percinet," "The Pot of Carnations," "Prince Sprite," and "The Good Little Mouse;" all of the stories exhibit Mme. D'Aulnoy's characteristic witty and whimsical style.

The White Deer, by James Thurber. 1945 Rpt. (New York: Harcourt, 1968.) Ill. by author and Don Freeman.
— King Cade married a princess who emerged from a forest in the form of a white deer. When the king and his sons wish to hunt in the forest, another deer appears.

The Wild Swans, by Hans Christian Andersen. Adapted by Amy Ehrlich; ill. by Susan Jeffers. (New York: Dial, 1981.)
— A sister sacrifices herself to release her brothers from an evil enchantment.

Literary
Hero Tales

Literary Hero
Tales

An Introduction

In Section Two, the outstanding features of traditional hero tales and how these were revealed in stories specifically adapted for younger readers were examined. Since the middle of the nineteenth century, many writers of children's books have consciously incorporated many of these features into their own stories and have created a genre known as the literary hero tale. Elements of traditional hero tales as they are found in writings of the last century, the relationship between popular modern heroes and the traditional, and the nature of the parody of the literary hero tale, in which aspects of traditional heroism are inverted or otherwise reinterpreted, will be examined in this section.

The traditional characteristics of heroes likewise apply to the protagonists of literary hero tales. Most often male, the hero is preceded by legends predicting his extraordinary birth and miraculous deeds. Often conceived miraculously, the hero is born amid unusual portents or supernatural events. Like Lloyd Alexander's hero, Dallben, in the short tale in the following selections, the hero's origins may be mysterious. Like Dallben, Superman, and many other heroes of traditional tales, literary hero tales, and the heroes of popular culture, the hero may be an orphan. Since his father's identity is often unknown, the hero may be nameless. If so, he may have to acquire his name as a significant part of his quest.[1]

In some stories the hero is a twin or a part of a multiple birth. In such an instance one may act as a foil or double to the twin. The archetype of the good and the bad brother is pervasive in traditional folklore and myth and is often expressed in literary hero tales and in popular culture. Robert Louis Stevenson's *The Master of Ballantrae*, and J.R. and the late Bobby Ewing of ''Dallas'' are examples of modern works which feature the evil and unscrupulous brother against the ethical and forthright one, a traditional pattern found, for example, in the Old Testament story of Cain and Abel.

The apprenticeship of the hero is crucial in almost all hero tales — traditional and literary. He is often taught in a pastoral setting by a Wise Old Man or perhaps a wise animal. Even at birth the hero exhibits unusual feats of strength or cleverness, but the teaching received from supernatural beings is essential. One recalls King Arthur's apprenticeship with Merlin the wizard. Luke Skywalker of "Star Wars" is taught the mysteries of the Force by the wise old man Ben Kenobi, and in the later film, "The Empire Strikes Back," by the wise and wizened Yoda. Whatever the nature of the apprenticeship, it prepares the hero for a series of arduous tests, which may involve physical strength, intelligence, identity, character, or spiritual wisdom.

The tests or trials endured by the hero constitute an inititation into heroic status. In the process of proving oneself, the hero may acquire extraordinary weapons. Once the identity of the hero is securely established, the heroic life assumes several distinguishing characteristics. He may be a wanderer and forever in quest. Because of their extraordinary qualities, heroes may need to disguise their true identities — perhaps by adopting an antithetical persona (Batman as Bruce Wayne, Superman as Clark Kent, The Shadow as Lamont Cranston). Once the hero settles down or marries, the heroic life often ends.

Although often a loner, the hero may enjoy the close friendship of a companion. As medieval knights shared their adventures with the young squires, so the hero may take on a youthful apprentice, a wild man, a fool, or a wise animal. Cervantes' famous characters Don Quizote and Sancho Panza have inspired many famous duos — The Lone Ranger and Tonto, Batman and Robin, the Cisco Kid and Pancho, Huck Finn and Jim, and many others. These characters often possess different aspects of character and suggest the need for balance and wholeness in the hero's life.

Often the hero comes into conflict with formidable foes, who are in many respects equal to himself. These antagonists may possess all of the virtues of the hero, but these heroic qualities are misused by the antagonist — usually to secure the power or wealth or status of the evil one. These evil or Satanic heroes may begin on the side of light and goodness and succumb to the temptations of greed, power, or lust. Such is the case with John Milton's Satan and with Darth Vader of "Star Wars." Examples of these fallen heroes abound in the works of modern fantasy writers — Sauron of Tolkien's *The Lord of the Rings*; Arawn, Lord of Death, of Lloyd Alexander's *Prydain* series; and Grimnir of Alan Garner's *The Weirdstone of Brisingamen*. Perhaps one of the most sophisticated expressions of this dark hero appears in Ursula Le Guin's *A Wizard of Earthsea*, in which the heroic wizard, Ged, must confront and conquer the most dangerous antagonist of all—the Shadow, whose name is also Ged. Thus Le Guin makes explicit what is implicit in the presence of evil heroes—the potential for evil within all human beings.

The central and climactic event in the hero's life is the quest, which may involve a night journey to another world, perhaps the nether world of death. In the course of achieving his quest, the hero presents a gift to his culture. He may save the society from destruction; thus, the hero of Western films often rids the town of the evil banker or lawyer before riding off alone to confront other foes and save other towns. A similar pattern occurs in William Steig's children's fantasy, *Dominic*, in which a lovable heroic dog rids his community of the anarchic Doomsday Gang. On the other hand, the hero's gift may be something more tangible, such as a holy treasure. (Indiana Jones retrieves the lost ark in the film "Raiders of the Lost Ark," and Alan Garner's child heroes, Susan and Colin, in *The Weirdstone of Brisingamen* retrieve the magical stone, Firefrost, for the Wizard Cadellin.) The gift may be one of agriculture or wealth. For example, Tolkien's Bilbo Baggins retrieves the treasure for his friends by struggling successfully with the dragon Smaug.

Despite successes and friendships, the hero is doomed to be essentially lonely. A love life is apt to be tragic or non-existent. Frequently the hero's achievements inspire jealousy and betrayal among friends. Despite extraordinary strengths and accomplishments, the traditional hero is likely to be vulnerable in one spot — Achilles' heel, Samson's hair, etc. This vulnerability may bring about the hero's untimely death.

As the hero's life is characterized by supernatural events and unusual circumstances, so the hero's death is usually obscured by mystery. In traditional tales the death may be sacrificial; many heroes die young in battle. They may be executed or assassinated — martyrs to their culture's idealistic causes. Like the hero's birth, his or her death may be attended by signs and portents. Dismemberment and burial may be performed in preparation for rebirth and resurrection. After death, legends abound predicting a return, and a cult may emerge to celebrate both the hero's life and death.[2] Dell McCormick's account of Paul Bunyan's death in "The Last Camp of Paul Bunyan" demonstrates characteristic features of the hero's passing.

The archetype of the hero, or as Joseph Campbell calls it, "the monomyth," is one of the most pervasively universal kind of story. Ordinary human beings find their hopes and desires thwarted in the face of arduous difficulties. It is no wonder that the human imagination continues to create heroic figures who perform miraculous feats of which most of us are incapable.

Because the structure of the hero tale described here and in Section Two is easily adapted to the adventure story, many nineteenth and twentieth-century children's writers have used it as a vehicle for their narratives. Writing about the tradition of "heroic romance" as it came to contemporary writers of literary hero tales, Lloyd Alexander, the well-known author of the *Prydain* series, has stated that while the most distant origins of heroic stories remain a mystery, "we can still trace mythology's historical growth into an art form: through the epic poetry, the *chansons de geste*, the Icelandic sagas, the medieval romances and works of prose in the Romance languages. Its family tree includes *Beowulf*, the *Eddas, The Song of Roland, Amades de Gaule,* the *Perceval* of Chretien de Troyes, and *The Faerie Queen*."[4] Alexander adds that in modern literature the "one form that draws most directly from the fountainhead of mythology and does it consciously and deliberately, is the heroic romance, which is a form of high fantasy . . . ."[5]

According to Alexander and other critics of heroic fantasy, William Morris, a nineteenth-century British poet, artisan, translator of sagas, and author of several prose romances (*The Well at the World's End, The Sundering Flood,* among others) was the writer who rediscovered heroic romance as we know it today in the works of Lord Dunsany, Eric Eddison, James Branch Cabell, C.S. Lewis, T.H. White, J.R.R. Tolkien, Ursula Le Guin, Anne McCaffrey, Susan Cooper, Lloyd Alexander, Alan Garner, and many others. One can also argue that Morris had models for the quest romance in the Romantic and Victorian poets and in the children's stories of George MacDonald (*The Princess and the Goblin* and *The Princess and Curdie*). Contemporary writers of heroic romance, Alexander remarks, "work directly in the tradition and within the conventions of an earlier body of literature and legend and draw from a common source: the 'Pot of Soup,' as Tolkien calls it, the 'cauldron of story,' which has been simmering away since time immemorial."[6]

Among the truly outstanding examples of contemporary writers of fantasy who work directly in this tradition of heroic literature are Ursula Le Guin's *A Wizard of Earthsea* (1968), Lloyd Alexander's *Prydain* series, and Alan Garner's *The Weirdstone of Brisingamen* (1960), and *The Moon of Gomrath* (1963).

Both Alan Garner and Lloyd Alexander draw heavily upon the Celtic tradition (that is, the folk literature associated with the ancient inhabitants of Scotland, Ireland, and Wales) in creating their contemporary fantasies. However, these writers renew and enrich the tradition by imparting their individual styles, and their own textures and images to the traditional material. In explaining how he came to write his books *The Weirdstone of Brisingamen* and *The Moon of Gomrath*, Garner has stated: "Most of the elements and entities in the book are to be seen, in one shape or another, in traditional folk-lore. . . . The more I learn, the more I am convinced that there are no original stories . . . . Originality now means the personal coloring of existing themes, and some of the richest ever expressed are in the folk-lore of Britain. But this very richness makes the finding of a way to any understanding of the imagery and incident impossible without the help of scholarship.''[7] Hence, Garner's two heroic fantasies contain highly traditional conventions and characteristics. In both *The Weirdstone of Brising-amen* and *The Moon of Gomrath*, Garner's protagonists, Susan and Colin, become involved in supernatural adventure and must undertake arduous and dangerous quests to defeat the forces of evil. In *The Weirdstone of Brisingamen* the two children must help the wizard Cadellin to retrieve a powerful magical stone, Firefrost, from the evil hero Grimnir. As in many heroic stories, Grimnir perhaps represents the dark side of Cadellin's nature, since the two wizards are finally revealed to be brothers. In *The Moon of Gomrath* the two children once more become involved in the struggle between the forces of White Magic led by Cadellin and the forces of Black Magic represented by the evil witch, Selina Place. Evil is also represented in this fantasy by the terrifying formless and speechless Brollachan, which can possess the body of another. Again the children are assisted by supernatural beings. One notable feature of Garner's heroic fantasies is that the girl Susan plays perhaps a more important role than Colin, an unusual feature in a genre traditionally associated with male identity.

While much of the material for Garner's two fantasies is taken from such sources as the Welsh mythology *The Mabinogion*, Garner creates a vivid sense of Alderley Edge, a real place inhabited by quite real and substantial people, such as Gowther and Bess Mossock, the sturdy folk residents who care for Susan and Colin. In imparting a vivid sense of the speech and the presence of his characters and in brilliantly describing the magical ambience of actual places, Garner gives new and vital life to ancient hero tales.

Like Alan Garner, Lloyd Alexander has drawn upon Celtic heroic literature in creating his fantasies, *The Book of Three* (1964), *The Black Cauldron* (1965), *The Castle of Llyr* (1966), *Taran Wanderer* (1967), and *The High King* (1968). In the course of this series, Alexander's protagonist, Taran, moves from the lowly position of assistant pig keeper to that of the high king. Repeatedly Taran must prove his heroic stature through physical and mental trials, and finally, through painful moral choices as well. Though Alexander also uses Celtic sources as the basis of his literary hero tales, he has made these stories uniquely his own through his strong characterization. Critics have also noted that though these tales are set in the British Isles, Alexander nevertheless imparts a strongly American quality to them.

In contrast to the practices of Garner and Alexander, Ursula Le Guin creates an entirely imaginary landscape (and seascape) in her *Earthsea* trilogy. Though she clearly draws upon traditional heroic literature for the structural and thematic aspects of her heroic fantasy, she does not rework a specific body of mythic material. Her hero, Ged, is gifted with great magical powers. In the first book of the trilogy, *The Wizard of Earthsea* (1968), Ged discovers these magical powers and must learn to use them wisely. Like the tragic Greek and Shakespearean heroes, he is flawed with excessive pride. After misusing his great power in a foolish contest with his friend and fellow student, Jasper, Ged must endure many tests and trials. He learns from wise teachers and from his own bitter experiences to confront the evil shadow within himself. In the *Tombs of Atuan* (1971) Le Guin also focuses upon the growth and maturity of a young protagonist. Arha must discover her true name in order to reject a false identity and to be reborn as a "child of light." In the final book of the series, *The Farthest Shore* (1972), Ged must accept his mortality and the impermanence of his power. In all of these books Le Guin introduces an unusual degree of complexity to the characters of her heroes. Rather than locating Ged's antagonist outside himself in the form of an evil hero, she shows that the most serious obstacle to his full potential as a great wizard lies within himself. The *Earthsea* trilogy, then, exhibits many traditional characteristics of the hero tale: the quest, the presence of Wise Old Men and Women, the presence of such supernatural characters as shapeshifting witches and wizards, magical talismen, etc. Yet Le Guin's hero tales are powerfully original because of her intensely concentrated and poetic language and the degree of complexity with which she creates a remarkable sense of an entire imaginary world and its inhabitants.

One important trait shared by Tolkien, Alexander, and Le Guin is the tone with which their narrators tell their heroic tales. Though there is humor in many of these fantasies, it is not ironically directed towards the conventions of the form itself. In some variations of the hero tale, however, writers do treat these conventions ironically. The degree of this irony may range from an amused and affectionate parody of the conventions of the heroic tradition all the way to a rather bitter treatment of the tradition which calls the genre itself into question.

In his two animal fantasies *Dominic* (1972) and *Abel's Island* (1976), for example, William Steig uses the heroic tradition humorously. His adventurous dog Dominic loves adventure for its own sake and wears different hats for their various effects. Dominic receives his cunning spear, not from a lady in the lake, but from a catfish in the pond. His quest is presided over not by a powerful wizard, but by an amiable witch-alligator, and Dominic battles the evil Doomsday Gang to make the world safe for the conventional values represented by a loving couple of wild boars — Pearl and Barney Swain. At last, like traditional heroes, Dominic undergoes a death-and-rebirth and awakens to find his own Sleeping Beauty, a lovely dog named Evelyn, waiting in her castle. While Dominic's linear quest and the pattern of his adventures closely conform to those of the traditional hero tale, Steig's tone suggests an ironic but affectionate parody of those conventions. In so doing Steig calls his readers' attention to the fictionality of his tale and acknowledges that his story is made from other stories. Finally, Steig implies, the hero tale is not a rendering of life as it is but as one wishes it to be.

Natalie Babbitt also uses the conventions of the hero tale ironically. In *Goody Hall* (1971) Babbitt's central character, Hercules Feltwright, humorously reinacts the twelve labors of the Greek hero Heracles: he mashes an earthworm flat in his cradle, he kills and skins a mad cat, secures a sack of big yellow apples (a bit like Heracles' Golden Apples of the Hesperides), rescues a man tied up in a cornfield persecuted by crows (a comic rendering of the rescue of Prometheus). Eventually Hercules Feltwright even confronts a humorous version of the terrible three-headed dog, Cerberus. The function of Babbitt's rather outrageous parody is to characterize Hercules Feltwright and draw attention to what may be a new kind of heroism. A gentle and intelligent peacemaker, Hercules Feltwright eventually helps to reconcile an estranged family.

In the spare, fable-like book *Knee-Knock Rise* (1971), Babbitt burlesques the conventions of the hero tale with more serious purpose than she does in *Goody Hall*. A young boy, Egan, runs away and climbs the mountain Knee-Knock Rise, in hopes of killing the monstrous Megrimum. As he departs from the village of In-Step on this dangerous quest, he dreams that he will be rewarded and recognized as a hero when he returns with the monster's head. But Egan finds no Megrimum; he finds only a hot spring whistling and moaning through a hole in a cave. The people of In-Step, however, refuse to give up believing in their monster. Instead of receiving the praise he had expected, Egan is ridiculed. In *Knee-Knock Rise*, then, Babbitt employs the characteristic patterns of the hero tale ironically. Her character's expectations are upset and reversed, just as are those of her reader. Babbitt thus suggests that our perceptions of literature and the world are strongly shaped by convention; she would have both her characters and her readers question these conventions, even as she reshapes them. In the following selections similar ironic uses of the conventions of the hero tale may be observed in E. Nesbit's "The Last of the Dragons."

Perhaps one of the most striking examples of an ironic use of the hero tale is Paula Fox's *The Slave Dancer* (1973), a winner of the Newbery Award. When the novel's central character, Jessie Bollier, is kidnapped and forced to serve aboard a slave ship, the reader expects that he will undergo a growth from innocence to experience, that the journey will mark his heroic maturity, like that of Jim Hawkins in Robert Louis Stevenson's *Treasure Island*. Jessie moves into a terrifying state of experience as he confronts the darkest evil of which human beings are capable, yet unlike traditional heroes, Jessie is broken by his quest. (See a more extended discussion of *The Slave Dancer* in the appendix on the Children's Novel.)

The hero tale may also be expressed in realistic works of children's and adolescents' fiction. Notable examples are William Armstrong's *Sounder* (1969), which portrays in epic-like fashion a young boy's struggle to hold his family together in the face of racial hatred and a quest for his father. The almost supernatural quality of the dog Sounder is reminiscent of the archetype of the Wise Animal, which serves as helper in many hero tales. Likewise Armstrong Sperry's Newbery Award-winning novel, *Call It Courage* (1940) presents the heroic quest of Mafatu, a chief's son, to overcome his fear of the sea. Mafatu's circular journey conforms to that of the traditional hero tale in every respect. Biographers also make use of the outstanding features of the hero tale to depict the lives of historical characters, sports figures, and other celebrities. In Parson Weems' famous biography, *The Life of Washington*, the author stresses the early teaching of Washington, and his outstanding talents. Parson Weems suggests that Washington is destined to become a hero — by special appointment from God and through the excellent teaching Washington receives from his father.

The genre variously known as the literary hero tale, the heroic romance, or heroic fantasy, comprises a large and significant portion of children's literature. Since the broad characteristics of the form have been appropriated by the creators of children's popular culture, young readers are apt to be especially receptive to it. Short literary hero tales can be introduced to children in middle elementary school, preferably after they have studied a variety of traditional hero tales. Once children have acquired a basic familiarity with the traditional hero tales, they will then be able to appreciate ironic and humorous treatments of the hero tale. Upper elementary and early junior high students can then be introduced to the longer and more complex literary hero tales of such writers as Lloyd Alexander, Susan Cooper, C.S. Lewis, Natalie Babbitt, and Madeleine L'Engle. Junior high students, if they have had sufficient literary experience, will enjoy reading and studying the more complex fantasies of Alan Garner, Ursula Le Guin, and J.R.R. Tolkien. Although the genre has been dominated by male protagonists in the past, such writers as Andre Norton and Anne McCaffrey are creating compelling female heroes.

Notes

1 See Bill Butler, *The Myth of the Hero* (London: Rider and Company, 1979), pp. 1-11 especially. Also see Joseph Campbell, *The Hero with a Thousand Faces* (Princeton: Princeton University Press, 1949).

2 See Paul Zweig, *The Adventurer* (Princeton: Princeton University Press, 1974). Zweig distinguishes between the true hero, whose efforts and struggles are on behalf of establishing and securing a home (like Aeneas) and the adventurer, whose efforts and adventures are done for their own sake (like Odysseus).

3 Bill Butler, p. 11.

4 Lloyd Alexander, "High Fantasy and Heroic Romance," *Cross Currents of Criticism: Horn Book Essays 1968-1977*, ed. by Paul Heins (Boston: The Horn Book, Inc., 1977), p. 171.

5 *Ibid.*

6 *Ibid.*

7 Alan Garner, Concluding "Note," *The Moon of Gomrath* (London: William Collins Sons and Co. Ltd., 1963), pp. 154-55.

"The Foundling," from The Foundling and Other Tales, *by Lloyd Alexander. Illustrated by Margot Zemach (New York and Chicago: Holt, Rinehart, and Winston, 1973).*

In this short literary hero tale Lloyd Alexander tells the story of the apprenticeship of Dallben, destined to become the greatest wizard in all of Prydain. Dallben's story resembles that of many other heroes: his birth and parentage remain mysterious; his childhood is guided by three supernatural sisters, Orddu, Orwen, and Orgoch (similar to the Three Fates in Greek mythology); and he is blessed with a great gift which he must learn to use wisely. "The Foundling" shows Dallben's initiation from innocence into wisdom, a transformation which he finds exceptionally painful. In this short tale, then, Dallben completes the first important stage on his linear quest to become a great wizard of heroic vision.

The Foundling

This is told of Dallben, greatest of enchanters in Prydain: how three black-robed hags found him, when he was still a baby, in a basket at the edge of the Marshes of Morva. "Oh, Orddu, see what's here!" cried the one named Orwen, peering into the wicker vessel floating amid the tall grasses. "Poor lost duckling! He'll catch his death of cold! Whatever shall we do with him?"

"A sweet morsel," croaked the one named Orgoch from the depths of her hood. "A tender lamb. I know that I should do."

"Please be silent, Orgoch," said the one named Orddu. "You've already had your breakfast." Orddu was a short, plump woman with a round, lumpy face and sharp black eyes. Jewels, pins, and brooches glittered in her tangle of weedy hair. "We can't leave him here to get all soggy. I suppose we shall have to take him home with us."

"Oh, yes!" exclaimed Orwen, dangling her string of milky white beads over the tiny figure in the basket. "Ah, the darling tadpole! Look at his pink cheeks and chubby little fingers! He's smiling at us, Orddu! He's waving! But what shall we call him? He mustn't go bare

and nameless."

"If you ask me —" began Orgoch.

"No one did," replied Orddu. "You are quite right, Orwen. We must give him a name. Otherwise, how shall we know who he is?"

"We have so many names lying around the cottage," said Orwen. "Some of them never used. Give him a nice, fresh, unwrinkled one."

"There's a charming name I'd been saving for a special occasion," Orddu said, "but I can't remember what I did with it. No matter. His name — his name: Dallben."

"Lovely!" cried Orwen, clapping her hands. "Oh, Orddu, you have such good taste."

"Taste, indeed!" snorted Orgoch. "Dallben? Why call him Dallben?"

"Why not?" returned Orddu. "It will do splendidly. Very good quality, very durable. It should last him a lifetime."

"It will last him," Orgoch muttered, "as long as he needs it."

And so Dallben was named and nursed by these three, and given a home in their cottage near the Marshes of Morva. Under their care he grew sturdy, bright, and fair of face. He was kind and generous, and each day handsomer and happier.

The hags did not keep from him that he was a foundling. But when he was of an age to wonder about such matters, he asked where indeed he had come from, and what the rest of the world was like.

"My dear chicken," replied Orddu, "as to where you came from, we haven't the slightest notion. Nor, might I say, the least interest. You're here with us now, to our delight, and that's quite enough to know."

"As to the rest of the world," Orwen added, "don't bother your pretty, curly head about it. You can be sure it doesn't bother about you. Be glad you were found instead of drowned. Why, this very moment you might be part of a school of fish. And what a slippery, scaly sort of life that would be!"

"I like fish," muttered Orgoch, "especially eels."

"Do hush, dear Orgoch," said Orddu. "You're always thinking of your stomach."

Despite his curiosity, Dallben saw there was no use in questioning further. Cheerful and willing, he went about every task with eagerness and good grace. He drew pails of water from the well, kept the fire burning in the hearth, pumped the bellows, swept away the ashes, and dug the garden. No toil was too troublesome for him. When Orddu spun thread, he turned the spinning wheel. He helped Orwen measure the skeins into lengths and held them for Orgoch to snip with a pair of rusty shears.

One day, when the three brewed a potion of roots and herbs, Dallben was left alone to stir the huge, steaming kettle with a long iron spoon. He obeyed the hags' warning not to taste the liquid, but soon the potion began boiling so briskly that a few drops bubbled up and by accident splashed his fingers. With a cry of pain, Dallben let fall the spoon and popped his fingers into his mouth.

His outcry brought Orddu, Orwen, and Orgoch hurrying back to the cottage.

"Oh, the poor sparrow!" gasped Orwen, seeing the boy sucking at his blistered knuckles. "He's gone and burned himself. I'll fetch an ointment for the sweet fledgling, and some spider webs to bandage him. What did you do with all those spiders, Orgoch? They were here only yesterday."

"Too late for all that," growled Orgoch. "Worse damage is done."

"Yes, I'm afraid so," Orddu sighed. "There's no learning without pain. The dear gosling has had his pain; and now, I daresay, he has some learning to go along with it."

Dallben, meanwhile, had swallowed the drops of liquid scalding his fingers. He licked his lips at the taste, sweet and bitter at the same time. And in that instant he began to shake with fear and excitement. All that had been common and familiar in the cottage he saw as he had never seen before.

Now he understood that the leather bellows lying by the hearth commanded the four winds; the pail of water in the corner, the seas and oceans of the world. The earthen floor of the cottage held the roots of all plants and trees. The fire showed him the secrets of its flame, and how all things come to ashes. He gazed awestruck at the enchantresses, for such they were.

"The threads you spin, and measure, and cut off," Dallben murmured, "these are no threads, but the lives of men. I know who you truly are."

"Oh, I doubt it," Orddu cheerfully answered. "Even we aren't always sure of that. Nevertheless, one taste of that magical brew and you know as much as we do. Almost as much, at any rate."

"Too much for his own good," muttered Orgoch.

"But what shall we do?" moaned Orwen. "He was such a sweet, innocent little robin. If only he hadn't swallowed the potion! Is there no way to make him unswallow it?"

"We could try," said Orgoch.

"No," declared Orddu. "What's done is done. You know that as well as I. Alas, the dear duckling will have to leave us. There's nothing else for it. So many people, knowing so much, under the same roof? All that knowledge crammed in, crowded, bumping and jostling back and forth? We'd not have room to breathe!"

"I say he should be kept," growled Orgoch.

"I don't think he'd like your way of keeping him," Orddu answered. She turned to Dallben. "No, my poor chicken, we must say farewell. You asked us once about the world? I'm afraid you'll have to see it for yourself."

"But, Orddu," protested Orwen, "we can't let him march off just like that. Surely we have some little trinket he'd enjoy? A going-away present, so he won't forget us?"

"I could give him something to remember us by," began Orgoch.

"No doubt," said Orddu. "But that's not what Orwen had in mind. Of course, we shall offer him a gift. Better yet, he shall choose one for himself."

As Dallben watched, the enchantress unlocked an iron-bound chest and rummaged inside, flinging out all sorts of oddments until there was a large heap on the floor.

"Here's something," Orddu at last exclaimed. "Just the thing for a bold young chicken. A sword!"

Dallben caught his breath in wonder as Orddu put the weapon in his hands. The hilt, studded with jewels, glittered so brightly that he was dazzled and nearly blinded. The blade flashed, and a thread of fire ran along its edges.

"Take this, my duckling," Orddu said, "and you shall be the greatest warrior in Prydain. Strength and power, dear gosling! When you command, all must obey even your slightest whim."

"It is a fine blade," Dallben replied, "and comes easily to my hand."

"It shall be yours," Orddu said. "At least, as long as you're able to keep it. Oh, yes," the enchantress went on, "I should mention it's already had a number of owners. Somehow, sooner or later, it wanders back to us. The difficulty, you see, isn't so much getting power as holding on to it. Because so many others want it, too. You'd be astonished, the lengths to which some will go. Be warned, the sword can be lost or stolen. Or bent out of shape — as, indeed, so can you, in a manner of speaking."

"And remember," put in Orwen, "you must never let it out of your sight, not for an instant."

Dallben hesitated a moment, then shook his head. "I think your gift is more burden than blessing."

"In that case," Orddu said, "perhaps this will suit you better."

As Dallben laid down the sword, the enchantress handed him a golden harp, so perfectly wrought that he no sooner held it than it seemed to play of itself.

"Take this, my sparrow," said Orddu, "and be the greatest bard in Prydain, known throughout the land for the beauty of your songs."

Dallben's heart leaped as the instrument thrilled in his arms. He touched the sweeping curve of the glowing harp and ran his fingers over the golden strings. "I have never heard such music," he murmured. "Who owns this will surely have no lack of fame."

"You'll have fame and admiration a-plenty," said Orddu, "as long as anyone remembers you."

"Alas, that's true," Orwen said with a sigh. "Memory can be so skimpy. It doesn't stretch very far; and, next thing you know, there's your fame gone all crumbly and mildewed."

Sadly, Dallben set down the harp. "Beau-tiful it is," he said, "but in the end, I fear, little help to me."

"There's nothing else we can offer at the moment," said Orddu, delving once more into the chest, "unless you'd care to have this book."

The enchantress held up a large heavy tome and blew away the dust and cobwebs from its moldering leather binding. "It's a bulky thing for a young lamb to carry. Naturally, it would be rather weighty, for it holds everything that was ever known, is known, and will be known."

"It's full of wisdom, thick as oatmeal," added Orwen. "Quite scarce in the world — wisdom, not oatmeal — but that only makes it the more valuable."

"We have so many requests for other items," Orddu said. "Seven-league boots, cloaks of invisibility, and such great nonsense. For wisdom, practically none. Yet whoever owns this book shall have all that and more, if he likes. For the odd thing about wisdom is the more you use it the more it grows; and the more you share, the more you gain. You'd be amazed how few understand that. If they did, I suppose, they wouldn't need the book in the first place."

"Do you give this to me?" Dallben asked. "A treasure greater than all treasures?"

Orddu hesitated. "Give? Only in a manner of speaking. If you know us as well as you say you do, then you also know we don't exactly *give* anything. Put it this way: We shall *let* you take that heavy, dusty old book if that's what you truly want. Again, be warned: The greater the treasure, the greater the cost. Nothing is given for nothing; not in the Marshes of Morva — or anyplace else, for the matter of that."

"Even so," Dallben replied, "this book is my choice."

"Very well," said Orddu, putting the ancient volume in his hands. "Now you shall be on your way. We're sorry to see you go, though sorrow is something we don't usually feel. Fare well, dear chicken. We mean this in the polite sense, for whether you fare well or ill is entirely up to you."

So Dallben took his leave of the enchantress and set off eagerly, curious to see what lay in store not only in the world but between the covers of the book. Once the cottage was well out of sight and the marshes far behind him, he curbed his impatience no longer, but sat down by the roadside, opened the heavy tome, and began to read.

As he scanned the first pages, his eyes widened and his heart quickened. For here was knowledge he had never dreamed of: the pathways of the stars, the rounds of the planets, the ebb and flow of time and tide. All secrets of the world and all its hidden lore unfolded to him.

Dallben's head spun, giddy with delight. The huge book seemed to weigh less than a feather, and he felt so lighthearted he could have skipped from one mountaintop to the next and never touched the ground. He laughed and sang at the top of his voice, bursting with gladness, pride, and strength in what he had learned.

"I chose well!" he cried, jumping to his feet. "But why should Orddu have warned me? Cost? What cost can there be? Knowledge is joy!"

He strode on, reading as he went. Each page lightened and sped his journey, and soon he came to a village where the dwellers danced and sang and made holiday. They offered him meat and drink and shelter for the coming night.

But Dallben thanked them for their hospitality and shook his head, saying he had meat and drink enough in the book he carried. By this time he had walked many miles, but his spirit was fresh and his legs unweary.

He kept on his way, hardly able to contain his happiness as he read and resolving not to rest until he had come to the end of the book. But he had finished less than half when the pages, to his horror, began to grow dark and stained with blood and tears.

For now the book told him of the other ways of the world; of cruelty, suffering, and death. He read of greed, hatred, and war; of men striving against one another with fire and sword; of the blossoming earth trampled underfoot, of harvests lost and lives cut short. And the book told that even in the same village he had passed, a day would come when no house would stand; when women would

weep for their men, and children for their parents; and where they had offered him meat and drink, they would starve for lack of a crust of bread.

Each page he read pierced his heart. The book, which had seemed to weigh so little, now grew so heavy that his pace faltered and he staggered under the burden. Tears blinded his eyes, and he stumbled to the ground.

All night he lay shattered by despair. At dawn he stirred and found it took all his efforts even to lift his head. Bones aching, throat parched, he crept on hands and knees to quench his thirst from a puddle of water. There, at the sight of his reflection, he drew back and cried out in anguish.

His fair, bright curls had gone frost-white and fell below his brittle shoulders. His cheeks, once full and flushed with youth, were now hollow and wrinkled, half hidden by a long, gray beard. His brow, smooth yesterday, was scarred and furrowed, his hands gnarled and knotted, his eyes pale as if their color had been wept away.

Dallben bowed his head. "Yes, Orddu," he whispered, "I should have heeded you. Nothing is given without cost. But is the cost of wisdom so high? I thought knowledge was joy. Instead, it is grief beyond bearing."

The book lay nearby. Its last pages were still unread and, for a moment, Dallben thought to tear them to shreds and scatter them to the wind. Then he said:

"I have begun it, and I will finish it, whatever else it may foretell."

Fearfully and reluctantly, he began to read once more. But now his heart lifted. These pages told not only of death, but of birth as well; how the earth turns in its own time and in its own way gives back what is given to it; how things lost may be found again; and how one day ends for another to begin. He learned that the lives of men are short and filled with pain, yet each one a priceless treasure, whether it be that of a prince or a pig-keeper. And, at the last, the book taught him that while nothing was certain, all was possible.

"At the end of knowledge, wisdom begins," Dallben murmured. "And at the end of wisdom there is not grief, but hope."

He climbed to his withered legs and hobbled along his way, clasping the heavy book. After a time a farmer drove by in a horse-drawn cart, and called out to him:

"Come, Grandfather, ride with me if you like. That book must be a terrible load for an old man like you."

"Thank you just the same," Dallben answered, "but I have strength enough now to go to the end of my road."

"And where might that be?"

"I do not know," Dallben said. "I go seeking it."

"Well, then," said the farmer, "may you be lucky enough to find it."

"Luck?" Dallben answered. He smiled and shook his head. "Not luck, but hope. Indeed, hope."

"The Last Camp of Paul Bunyan," from Paul Bunyan Swings his Axe, *by Dell McCormick (Caldwell, Idaho: Caxton Printers, 1968).*

Like the heroes of traditional epic and legend, the most famous character in the American tall-tale tradition lives to see the passing of the old order. Like King Arthur's death, that of Paul Bunyan remains a mystery. The important aspect of Paul Bunyan's character, however, is that he is faithful to his heroic codes until the end. In this respect he resembles such traditional heroes as the Anglo-Saxon Beowulf.

The Last Camp of Paul Bunyan

It was late in the summer when Paul and his faithful moose hound Elmer started back to Paul's camp on Tadpole Creek. Paul was tired after hunting the Giant Moose. In spite of his great size he could average only forty or fifty miles a day.

One day as he was resting in the Bitter Root Mountains of Idaho, he noticed Elmer sniffing in the air and acting very strange.

"What's the matter, Old Boy?" asked Paul. "Are there grizzly bears in these woods?"

In answer, the moose hound only ran forward and back in front of Paul as if urging his master to continue the homeward journey at once. Every once in awhile he would point his nose toward the sky and growl and whine in terror!

Paul climbed the nearest mountain to investigate. What a sight met his horror-stricken eyes? For miles and miles, as far as he could see, the forest was afire! Great clouds of black smoke rolled upward. Leaping swiftly from treetop to treetop, the angry flames rushed toward Paul!

Paul never thought of himself or the danger. In the center of that raging fire was his camp on Tadpole Creek! What had happened to his men? Where were Tiny Tim and Ole and Johnnie Inkslinger and all his brave crew? Had they perished in the flames?

Without a thought for himself, he ran toward that raging wall of fire. Over rivers and lakes he leaped, and on through the forests, stopping only to soak his great handkerchief in a mountain lake. With this tied over his nose and mouth so that he could breathe more easily, he plunged into the blazing forest fire!

The smoke blinded him, and the fire burned great holes in his leather boots. On he ran through the forest fire that scorched his hands and burned his clothing. It was like a fiery furnace! At times he stumbled and fell and the heat burned his beard to a crisp. Pulling himself to his feet by a mighty effort, he would stagger on.

Soon, he came to the blackened remains of his camp on Tadpole Creek. The great camp that covered so many acres was only a smoldering mass of ashes! The giant griddle that was the pride of Hot Biscuit Slim and all the cooks lay in the center of the ruins. It was bent out of shape by the intense heat. In all that fire-swept country there was no trace of his brave men.

Sadly, and with tears in his eyes, Paul Bunyan gazed over the blackened land that had once been the great forest that he loved so well. His brave crew had disappeared. What had happened to them as the raging forest fire surrounded the camp? Most of all, he missed Babe, his great Blue Ox, who had been his companion on all his many adventures.

Although his feet were blistered with the great heat and his clothing hung in shreds, Paul went back to see if he could find Elmer, his faithful moose hound. By that time, the great forest fire had died out, and all the vast mountain country was covered with blackened stumps.

Paul found Elmer with some loggers on the upper Snake River. The loggers looked at Paul in wonder. "Are you the great Paul Bunyan we have heard so much about? The man who has the largest logging camp in the world?"

"I am Paul Bunyan," he said, "but alas, my camp has burned, and all my men destroyed in the great fire."

The loggers spoke up:

"Your men are safe. We saw them escape. A great Blue Ox that was a hundred times larger than any ox we had ever seen came through the woods. All the men followed him as he cut a path through the trees with his great hoofs. They built rafts here on the Snake River and floated down into the Oregon Country."

Paul Bunyan cried with joy as he heard the great news! His men were safe! Burned and weary as he was, Paul laughed and shouted with joy. Elmer barked happily by his side.

"What happened to Babe the Blue Ox?" asked Paul.

"The Blue Ox disappeared, after leading the men to safety," said the loggers.

Paul lay down to rest and was soon fast asleep. It was the first night's sleep he had had since the fire. In the morning, a soft wet nose nudged his ear. Then a large rough tongue licked his cheek. It was Babe the Blue Ox who had found his master! The faithful animal had searched far and near until he had found Paul!

The loggers were amazed at the great size of Paul Bunyan and his Blue Ox and the enormous breakfast they ate together. They asked Paul if he were going down into the Oregon Country.

"No," said Paul, "my work is over. My men can join other logging camps in Oregon. I am tired and weary, and my beloved forest is burned to the ground. I am going to take Babe the Blue Ox and go up into the mountains where I can hunt and fish with my faithful dog."

No more do the woods resound with the sharp blows of the Seven Axemen. Tiny Tim is no longer the water boy. Hot Biscuit Slim and Cream Puff Fatty are cooking in other camps in the Oregon woods. Brimstone Bill and Ole the Big Swede were last seen in a logging camp near Bend, Oregon. They passed their later years telling of the brave deeds and mighty exploits of Paul Bunyan and of Babe, his Blue Ox.

Paul Bunyan has disappeared from the woods. Some say he is still roaming the forest of the West. No one has seen him, but the woodsmen say the low rumbling thunder in the mountains on a summer night is Paul Bunyan calling to his faithful ox. Others say that the wind whistling through the treetops is the sound of Paul Bunyan striding through the forests as of old.

▬▬▬

From Hockey in My Blood, *by Johnny Bucyk, with Russ Conway (Toronto: Scholastic-TAB, 1973).*

During the twentieth century, many athletic and entertainment stars have been viewed by children as heroes, and many books have been written emphasizing this heroic status. What is interesting about these books is that the stories are often shaped around the "rags to riches" linear journey pattern. Although events of Boston Bruin hockey star Johnny Bucyk's life are typical of people in his profession, the "autobiography," ghost-written by a Boston sportswriter, emphasizes the humble origins, the determination, the aid of wise helpers, and the ultimate achievement of success—all in a manner not unlike that of "The History of Whittington."

Hockey in My Blood

They say to be a good hockey player and to be a pro hockey player in the National Hockey League you've got to come from Canada, so I guess I got off on the right foot. You see, I was born in Edmonton, Alberta, and that's in western Canada.

I can remember playing street hockey when I was a kid, maybe seven or eight years old. In those days you couldn't afford to buy hockey sticks, nobody in our group could. I was from a poor family and I really didn't know what it was to own a hockey stick, so I didn't care. I played a lot of street hockey and we used brooms for sticks. We couldn't afford pucks either, so we'd follow the milk wagon which was pulled by a couple horses, waiting until the horses did their job, dropping a good hunk of manure. Usually it would be a cold day, any time between the start of October through the end of April, and we'd let it freeze up solid. We'd use it as a hockey puck.

Most of the time we were able to use a softball or a tennis ball for a puck. The horse manure was only in case of an emergency. I didn't get my first pair of skates until I was about 10 years old. It was a pair of my older brother Bill's, which he outgrew. That's when I finally started skating. I wasn't any Bobby Orr either.

Then I got involved in pee-wee hockey. I started off as a goalie and I didn't like it because I found out I didn't get enough space in the local newspaper. All that I ever read about was the guys scoring goals. So then I played defense for a little while but it was the same thing all over again. All I read in the newspaper was about a few players who were scoring all the goals. It made me wonder if anybody was watching me at all.

So then I figured I wasn't a defenseman. Who ever watches a defenseman? I guess there's a few around they watch now! I finally decided I wanted to be a forward so I started playing left wing and I've stayed there ever since. My brother Bill played, too. He's a couple years older than me but he played in the same leagues as I did, except I continued on and he stopped in the Western League. When he was playing hockey he hated me. I've got another brother and two step-sisters but Bill was the only one who really was interested in hockey like I was.

We used to have outdoor rinks in our own backyard. All we had to do was keep scraping the snow off the ice. That's why Canadians have the advantage over Americans. There's always some place to skate nearby from October to late April and there's so many hockey organizations you find yourself playing almost all of the time.

It was all outdoor hockey, just like most any kid plays in the States, until I broke into Junior A. That's when I finally got to play hockey indoors. When I first played the game everyone would bring their sticks to school and we'd play during lunch hours. If we had half an hour, we'd be playing street hockey. We'd find a nice smooth slippery part of the street where it hadn't been sanded and make that the rink. But I got away from that when I started to skate. Right off the bat I was a rink rat.

Whenever it snowed it was my job to scrape the ice. I always wanted to skate, to play hockey, so I'd usually be the first one out to get the snow off the ice. For doing that I could always use the ice free, saving the usual service charge. I had to do it that way because I couldn't afford to pay.

After I played pee-wee hockey I got involved with midget hockey. A couple of school buddies of mine were playing and I told them I'd like to get into it, too. They were short a few players so they told me to try out for the team. I was pretty shy, though, and afraid of what would happen. But things turned out pretty well. I was scouted by the Edmonton Oil Kings who belonged to the Detroit Red Wings. They kept an eye on me and I kept progressing. I was 12 years old when I first started in midgets. Little did I know then that I'd go on to juvenile hockey when I was 14 and turn professional with Detroit when I was 19.

I'll never forget my first two games in Junior A hockey with the Edmonton Oil Kings. During warm-up our goaltender got hurt and we didn't have a spare goalie. Every one looked at each other. So I just put the pads on and we won the game 4-2. I was as surprised as anybody else that we won but just a little glad it was over with. We were going back to Edmonton, and the spare goalie was back home.

So what happens at the next game? The spare goalie gets sick and who gets the chance to flip-flop in front of the goal? You guessed it . . . Bucyk in goal. So I put the pads on and we won it 4-0. I'd say I had a pretty good goals-against average but our spare goalie was better for the next game and I went back to left wing. I was glad of that.

Ken McCauley, a fellow who used to be with the New York Rangers, was our coach then, and I have to say that he certainly helped me a lot in becoming a better player. He taught me how to handle the puck better and gave me a lot of encouragement.

When I was playing juvenile hockey I played in more than one organization. I played for an intermediate team that was competing just in tournaments. Then I played with the juvenile league, and when I found time I'd play three or four hours a day with the kids after school. My mother always knew where to find me if I wasn't home. I always was at the rink just three blocks away from our home.

I was playing so much hockey I was missing a lot of School. When the time came, during grade 11, that I had the chance to play junior league hockey I had to make a big decision. Detroit offered me a contract which wasn't very much money. $1,500 for a season, and they also found me a job. So I told my mother I thought I should quit school. She said it was my decision but something I would always have to live with. She wasn't working then, she couldn't work because of her health and I wanted to help the family as much as I could so I decided to become a professional hockey player and that's what I did.

Probably my biggest disappointment as a youngster came when I was 10 years old. My father, Sam, died leaving the kids and my mother Pearl alone. It's unfortunate that he never got to see me play hockey in the NHL. My mother never remarried. She just decided to help us get through school as far as we wanted to go. Since then, my brother, Bill and I have been looking after her.

Ma has seen me play in a few games. A couple years ago she came down to Boston and spent a little time with us in Boxford, a suburb of Boston where I now live. Back home, she watches quite a few games on television but she gets awfully nervous.

When I was young we were a very poor family. The holidays weren't very exciting for us and I can remember that Christmas wasn't too grand either. We used to have a big Christmas dinner and perhaps get a couple of presents.

I always wanted a present to do with hockey. I can remember as a youngster we couldn't afford shin pads so I'd get magazines and roll them up and put them underneath my pants. We didn't have gloves either, just ordinary mittens. I never really had any good hockey equipment until I got into organized hockey.

The best present I ever received was my first pair of skates. You see, up until then I was using an old pair of my brother's skates or I'd borrow a pair from somebody. It was just something else to get a *Brand New* pair of skates. Imagine, not having a used pair of skates or not having to borrow skates from somebody else. It sounds funny now, but at that time it was the biggest thrill of my life.

My brother, among several other people, helped me get my start in hockey. Bill had been playing for a while and was a couple years ahead of me. I started playing hockey when I was 10 and that was the average age then. Some difference from today. It seems as though now kids are born wearing skates. The first contact I had with a scout was a fellow by the name of Clarence Moore. He was with the Detroit Red Wings at the time and I was playing juvenile hockey. Back in those days they could talk to you, it didn't matter how old you were, and they could sign you up right away for a pro contract. The scouts used to follow a lot of our juvenile games. They had scouts in every little town and that's how Clarence Moore saw me.

I've been lucky to have been associated with some good teams during my career. We had a good team when I was in juvenile hockey and we really had a powerhouse when I was in junior hockey with the Edmonton Oil Kings. We just lost one game during the regular season then. We walked away with the Western Division championship and came East to play St. Catharine's in Toronto. We sat there in Toronto for a month waiting for the other series to finish and it got into May. Believe me, it wasn't hockey season then and we got stale, ended up losing the championship playoffs and made the long trip back home. That was a major disappointment for me.

I wasn't the only Bucyk playing hockey then; my brother Bill also played junior hockey. When I went up to play pro with the Edmonton Flyers, he was playing for Victoria. We played against each other during the 1954–55 season, the same year I won the Western Hockey League's Rookie of The Year award and set a new league rookie record scoring 30 goals and 58 assists for 88 points in 70 games. Bill had a pretty good career. Besides Victoria, he played professionally with Regina and for Eddie Shore in Springfield.

Bill was a defenseman. Of course, we ended up playing each other, and at times things could get a little rough. It's not easy at first to play against your own brother but I got used to it. I can feel a little something for the Espositos when they play against each other. I know when Bill and I played against each other we played extra hard. I can remember a time when he came to hit me and I ducked. I got the best of him because he flew right over me and came down hard.

His skate bent upwards and caught him in the thigh when he fell. He had to go to the hospital to get stitched up. I'll never forget it because I was really upset, I could tell that he was in severe pain. He ended up in a cast with torn tendons and was out of action for two months. It really wasn't my fault but it wasn't what you'd call brotherly love, either. Eventually I went up with the Red Wings for good and he stayed in the minors for a couple more years.

Hockey took up the fall, winter and most of the spring for me when I was working my way through the Edmonton Oil Kings and Edmonton Flyers. I spent most of my summers working in a service station. I did auto body work, drove the tow truck, greased cars, pumped gas, just about everything. I was what you call a regular handy man and it worked out well because I love working with cars.

Maybe for two weeks I'd wash cars and for another two weeks the grease monkey would go away for vacation, so I'd be greasing cars. It went that way all summer long. I drove the tow truck a lot and did estimates on wrecked cars, even the office work. I worked there for 13 years during the summers, even when I played with Detroit and the Bruins. That was one of the steadiest jobs I've ever had.

You've heard about the kid who grew up on the bad side of the tracks, the bad part of town ... well, that's me. I lived in the North End of Edmonton and everybody used to call it the rough part of town. We weren't all that rough, at least I didn't think so, but it had that brand name. I lived at 12941 65th St., and my mother still lives there. Actually, as a youngster, we lived in four houses at one time or another but they were all in the same general area. My father was married before, so my step-brother and step-sisters are much older than I am. My brother Bill was closest of all to me. He was my hockey brother, too, and that may have had something to do with it.

I never saw a National Hockey League game until I went to the Detroit Red Wings camp but I followed what was going on as much as I could in the newspapers and magazines. I always idolized Gordie Howe.

Finally, when I went to training camp with Detroit, I made it a point to meet Gordie right off the bat. He was with Ted Lindsay at the time. It was my very first pro camp and when I met them I stuttered something like "Hi" and that was about it. But Gordie was something else. I was just a kid but he didn't care if you were young or not. He made me feel wanted, he made everybody feel wanted, and that meant a heck of a lot to somebody just coming up.

The Last of the Dragons, *by E. Nesbit. Illustrated by Peter Firmin (New York: McGraw-Hill, 1980).*

On one level, this story is a parody of the traditional European dragon-slayer legend. The princess is brave, unconventional, and athletic; the prince is a dreamy philosopher; and the dragon, who would rather be left alone, is tame. Underneath the humor of the parody there is a serious theme: each of the characters is expected to fulfill socially imposed roles. Real happiness is achieved only when individuals are allowed to fulfill their true natures. The conclusion of the story parodies the pourquoi story, giving a tall-tale explanation for the origin of the aeroplane.

The Last of the Dragons

Of course you know that dragons were once as common as buses are now, and almost as dangerous. But as every well-brought-up prince was expected to kill a dragon and rescue a princess, the dragons grew fewer and fewer, till it was often quite hard for a princess to find a dragon to be rescued from. And at last there were no more dragons in France and no more dragons in Germany, or Spain, or Italy, or Russia. There were some left in China, and are still, but they are cold and bronzy, and there were never any, of course, in America. But the last real live dragon left was in England, and of course that was a very long time ago, before what you call English History began. This dragon lived in Cornwall in a cave amidst the rocks, and a very fine dragon it was, quite seventy feet long from the tip of its fearful snout to the end of its terrible tail. It breathed fire and smoke, and rattled when it walked, because its scales were made of iron. Its wings were like half-umbrellas — or like bat's wings, only several thousand times bigger. Everyone was very frightened of it, and well they might be.

Now the King of Cornwall had one daughter, and when she was sixteen, of course she would have to go and face the dragon: such tales are always told in royal nurseries at twilight, so the Princess knew what she had to expect. The dragon would not eat her, of course — because the prince would come and rescue her. But the Princess could not help thinking it would be much pleasanter to have nothing to do with the dragon at all — not even to be rescued from him.

"All the princes I know are such very silly little boys," she told her father. "Why must I be rescued by a prince?"

"It's always done, my dear," said the King, taking his crown off and putting it on the grass, for they were alone in the garden, and even kings must unbend sometimes.

"Father, darling," said the Princess presently, when she had made a daisy chain and put it on the King's head, where the crown ought to have been. "Father, darling, couldn't we tie up one of the silly little princes for the

Illustration by Peter Firmin from *The Last of the Dragons,* by E. Nesbit. Copyright © 1980. Reprinted by permission of Macdonald General Books.

dragon to look at — and then I could go and kill the dragon and rescue the Prince? I fence much better than any of the princes we know."

"What an unladylike idea!" said the King, and put his crown on again, for he saw the Prime Minister coming with a basket of new-laid Bills for him to sign. "Dismiss the thought, my child. I rescued your mother from a dragon, and you don't want to set yourself up above her, I should hope?"

But this is the *last* dragon. It is different from all other dragons."

"How?" asked the King.

"Because he *is* the last," said the Princess, and went off to her fencing lessons, with which she took great pains. She took great pains with all her lessons — for she could not give up the idea of fighting the dragon. She took such pains that she became the strongest and boldest and most skillful and most sensible princess in Europe. She had always been the prettiest and nicest.

And the days and years went on, till at last the day came which was the day before the Princess was to be rescued from the dragon. The Prince who was to do this deed of valor was a pale prince, with large eyes and a head full of mathematics and philosophy, but he had unfortunately neglected his fencing lessons. He was to stay the night at the palace, and there was a banquet.

After supper the Princess sent her pet parrot to the Prince with a note. It said:

"Please, Prince, come on to the terrace. I want to talk to you without anybody else hearing. — The Princess."

So, of course, he went — and he saw her gown of silver a long way off shining among the shadows of the trees like water in starlight. And when he came quite close to her he said:

"Princess, at your service," and bent his cloth-of-gold-covered knee and put his hand on his cloth-of-gold-covered heart.

"Do you think," said the Princess earnestly, "that you will be able to kill the dragon?"

"I will kill the dragon," said the Prince firmly, "or perish in the attempt."

"It's no use your perishing," said the Princess.

"It's the least I can do," said the Prince.

"What I'm afraid of is that it'll be the most you can do," said the Princess.

"It's the only thing I can do," said he, "unless I kill the dragon."

"Why you should do anything for me is what I can't see," said she.

"But I want to," he said. "You must know that I love you better than anything in the world."

When he said that he looked so kind that the Princess began to like him a little.

"Look here," she said, "no one else will go out tomorrow. You know they tie me to a rock, and leave me — and then everybody scurries home and puts up the shutters and keeps them shut till you ride through the town in triumph shouting that you've killed the dragon, and I ride on the horse behind you weeping for joy."

"I've heard that this is how it is done," said he.

"Well, do you love me well enough to come very quickly and set me free — and we'll fight the dragon together?"

"It wouldn't be safe for you."

"Much safer for both of us for me to be free, with a sword in my hand, than tied up and helpless. *Do* agree."

He could refuse her nothing. So he agreed. And next day everything happened as she had said.

When he had cut the cords that tied her to the rocks they stood on the lonely mountainside looking at each other.

"It seems to me," said the Prince, "that this ceremony could have been arranged without the dragon."

"Yes," said the Princess, "but since it has been arranged with the dragon —"

"It seems such a pity to kill the dragon — the last in the world," said the Prince.

"Well, then, don't let's," said the Princess, "let's tame it not to eat princesses but to eat out of their hands. They say everything can be tamed by kindness."

"Taming by kindness means giving them things to eat," said the Prince. "Have you got anything to eat?"

She hadn't, but the Prince owned that he had a few biscuits. "Breakfast was so very early," said he, "and I thought you might have felt faint after the fight."

"How clever," said the Princess, and they took a biscuit in each hand. And they looked here and they looked there, but never a dragon could they see.

"But here's its trail," said the Prince, and pointed to where the rock was scarred and scratched so as to make a track leading to the mouth of a dark cave. It was like cart-ruts in a Sussex road, mixed with the marks of sea gulls' feet on the sea-sand. "Look, that's where it's dragged its brass tail and planted its steel claws."

"Don't let's think how hard its tail and its claws are," said the Princess, "or I shall begin to be frightened — and I know you can't tame anything, even by kindness, if you're frightened of it. Come on. Now or never."

She caught the Prince's hand in hers and they ran along the path towards the dark mouth of the cave. But they did not run into it. It really was so very *dark*.

So they stood outside, and the Prince shouted: "What ho! Dragon there! What ho within!" And from the cave they heard an answering voice and great clattering and creaking. It sounded as though a rather large cotton mill were stretching itself and waking up out of its sleep.

The Prince and the Princess trembled, but they stood firm.

"Dragon — I say, Dragon!" said the Princess, "do come out and talk to us. We've brought you a present."

"Oh yes — I know your presents," growled the dragon in a huge rumbling voice. "One of those precious princesses, I suppose? And I've got to come out and fight for her. Well, I tell you straight, I'm not going to do it. A fair fight I wouldn't say no to — a fair fight and no favor — but one of these put-up fights where you've got to lose — No. So I tell you. If I wanted a princess I'd come and take her, in my own time — but I don't. What do you suppose I'd do with her, if I'd got her?"

"Eat her, wouldn't you?" said the Princess in a voice that trembled a little.

"Eat a fiddlestick end," said the dragon

very rudely. "I wouldn't touch the horrid thing."

The Princess's voice grew firmer.

"Do you like biscuits?" she asked.

"No," growled the dragon.

"Not the nice little expensive ones with sugar on the top?"

"*NO*," growled the dragon.

"Then what *do* you like?" asked the Prince.

"You go away and don't bother me," growled the dragon, and they could hear it turn over, and the clang and clatter of its turning echoed in the cave like the sound of steam-hammers in the Arsenal at Woolwich.

The Prince and Princess looked at each other. What *were* they to do? Of course it was no use going home and telling the King that the dragon didn't want princesses — because His Majesty was very old-fashioned and would never have believed that a new-fashioned dragon could ever be at all different from an old-fashioned dragon. They could not go into the cave and kill the dragon. Indeed, unless he attacked the Princess it did not seem fair to kill him at all.

"He must like something," whispered the Princess, and she called out in a voice as sweet as honey and sugarcane:

"Dragon! Dragon dear!"

"*WHAT?*" shouted the dragon. "Say that again!" and they could hear the dragon coming towards them through the darkness of the cave. The Princess shivered, and said in a very small voice:

"Dragon — Dragon dear!"

And then the dragon came out. The Prince drew his sword, and the Princess drew hers — the beautiful silver-handled one that the Prince had brought in his motor-car. But they did not attack; they moved slowly back as the dragon came out, all the vast scaly length of him, and lay along the rock — his great wings half-spread and his silvery sheen gleaming like diamonds in the sun. At last they could retreat no farther — the dark rock behind them stopped their way — and with their backs to the rock they stood swords in hand and waited.

The dragon drew nearer and nearer — and now they could see that he was not breathing fire and smoke as they had expected—he came crawling slowly towards them wriggling a little as a puppy does when it wants to play and isn't quite sure whether you're not cross with it.

And then they saw that great tears were coursing down its brazen cheek.

"Whatever's the matter?" said the Prince.

"Nobody," sobbed the dragon, "ever called me 'dear' before!"

"Don't cry," said the Princess. "We'll call you 'dear' as often as you like. We want to tame you."

"I *am* tame," said the dragon—"that's just it. That's what nobody but you has ever found out. I'm so tame that I'd eat out of your hands."

"Eat what, dragon dear?" said the Princess. "Not biscuits?"

The dragon slowly shook its heavy head.

"Not biscuits?" said the Princess tenderly. "What then, dragon dear?"

"Your kindness quite undragons me," it said. "No one has ever asked any of us what we like to eat—always offering us princesses, and then rescuing them — and never once, 'What'll you take to drink the King's health in?' Cruel hard I call it," and it wept again.

"But what would you like to drink our health in?" said the Princess. "We're going to be married today, aren't we, Princess?"

She said that she supposed so.

"What'll I take to drink your health in?" asked the dragon. "Ah, you're something like a gentleman, you are, sir. I don't mind if I do, sir. I'll be proud to drink your and your good lady's health in a tiddy drop of" — its voice faltered — "to think of you asking me so friendly like," it said. "Yes, sir, just a tiddy drop of puppuppuppuppupetrol—tha—that's what does a dragon good, sir —"

I've lots in the car," said the Prince, and was off down the mountain like a flash. He was a good judge of character, and he knew that with this dragon the Princess would be safe.

"If I might make so bold," said the dragon, "while the gentleman's away — p'raps just to pass time you'd be so kind as to call me 'dear' again, and if you'd shake claws with a poor old dragon that's never been anybody's enemy but his own — well, the last of the dragons'll

be the proudest dragon there's ever been since the first of them."

It held out an enormous paw, and the great steel hooks that were its claws closed over the Princess's hand as softly as the claws of the Himalayan bear will close over the bit of bun you hand it through the bars at the Zoo.

And so the Prince and Princess went back to the palace in triumph, the dragon following them like a pet dog. And all through the wedding festivities no one drank more earnestly to the happiness of the bride and bridegroom than the Princess's pet dragon — whom she had at once named Fido.

And when the happy pair were settled in their own kingdom, Fido came to them and begged to be allowed to make himself useful.

"There must be some little thing I can do," he said, rattling his wings and stretching his claws. "My wings and claws and so on ought to be turned to some account — to say nothing of my grateful heart."

So the Prince had a special saddle or howdah made for him — very long it was — like the tops of many tramcars fitted together. One hundred and fifty seats were fitted to this, and the dragon, whose greatest pleasure was now to give pleasure to others, delighted in taking parties of children to the seaside. It flew through the air quite easily with its hundred and fifty little passengers — and would lie on the sand patiently waiting till they were ready to return.

The children were very fond of it and used to call it "dear," a word which never failed to bring tears of affection and gratitude to its eyes. So it lived, useful and respected, till quite the other day — when some one happened to say, in his hearing, that dragons were out-of-date, now so much new machinery had come in. This so distressed him that he asked the King to change him into something less old-fashioned, and the kindly monarch at once changed him into a mechanical contrivance. The dragon, indeed, became the first aeroplane.

——

"Casey at the Bat," from The Annotated Casey at the Bat, *by Martin Gardner (New York: Clarkson N. Potter, 1967).*

The ability of the hero to lead his followers to victory against great odds is parodied in this well-known sports poem. In the eyes of the crowd and himself, Casey is clearly expected to be superior to the inept batters who preceded him to the plate. With two men out and runners in scoring position, Casey should have attempted only a base hit, which would have driven in the tying runs. Instead, he strikes out seeking personal glory instead of the well-being of his team.

Casey at the Bat

The outlook wasn't brilliant for the Mudville nine that day;
The score stood four to two with but one inning more to play.
And then when Cooney died at first, and Barrows did the same,
A sickly silence fell upon the patrons of the game.

A straggling few got up to go in deep despair the rest.
Clung to that hope which springs eternal in the human breast;
They thought if only Casey could but get a whack at that —
We'd put up even money now with Casey at the bat.

But Flynn preceded Casey, as did also Jimmy Blake,
And the former was a lulu and the latter was a cake;
So upon that stricken multitude grim melancholy sat,
For there seemed but little chance of Casey's getting to the bat.

But Flynn let drive a single, to the wonderment of all,
And Blake, the much despis-ed, tore the cover off the ball;

And when the dust had lifted, and the men saw what had occurred,
There was Johnnie safe at second and Flynn a-hugging third.

Then from 5,000 throats and more there rose a lusty yell;
It rumbled through the valley, it rattled in the dell;
It knocked upon the mountain and recoiled upon the flat,
For Casey, mighty Casey, was advancing to the bat.

There was ease in Casey's manner as he stepped into his place;
There was pride in Casey's bearing and a smile on Casey's face.
And when, responding to the cheers, he lightly doffed his hat,
No stranger in the crowd could doubt 'twas Casey at the bat.

Ten thousand eyes were on him as he rubbed his hands with dirt;
Five thousand tongues applauded when he wiped them on his shirt.
Then while the writhing pitcher ground the ball into his hip,
Defiance gleamed in Casey's eye, a sneer curled Casey's lip.

And now the leather-covered sphere came hurtling through the air,
And Casey stood a-watching it in haughty grandeur there.
Close by the sturdy batsman the ball unheeded sped —
"That ain't my style," said Casey. "Strike one," the umpire said.

From the benches, black with people, there went up a muffled roar,
Like the beating of the storm-waves on a stern and distant shore.
"Kill him! Kill the umpire!" shouted some one on the stand;
And it's likely they'd have killed him had not Casey raised his hand.

With a smile of Christian charity great Casey's
   visage shone;
He stilled the rising tumult; he bade the game
   go on;
He signaled to the pitcher, and once more the
   spheroid flew;
But Casey still ignored it, and the umpire said,
   "Strike two."

"Fraud!" cried the maddened thousands, and
   echo answered fraud;
But one scornful look from Casey and the audience was awed.
They saw his face grow stern and cold, they
   saw his muscles strain,
And they knew that Casey wouldn't let that ball
   go by again.

The sneer is gone from Casey's lip, his teeth
   are clenched in hate;
He pounds with cruel violence his bat upon
   the plate.
And now the pitcher holds the ball, and now
   he lets it go,
And now the air is shattered by the force of
   Casey's blow.

Oh, somewhere in this favored land the sun is
   shining bright;
The band is playing somewhere, and somewhere hearts are light,
And somewhere men are laughing, and somewhere children shout;
But there is no joy in Mudville—mighty Casey
   has struck out.

Literary Hero Tales for Further Reading

Alone in the Wild Forest, by Isaac Bashevis Singer. Trans. by author and illustrated by Margot Zemach. (New York: Farrar, Straus, and Giroux, 1971.)
   —the orphaned Joseph dreams of winning Princess Chassidah, but Bal Makane plots against him.

The Blue Hawk, by Peter Dickinson. (New York: Atlantic-Little, 1976.)
   —in ancient Egypt, Tran angers high priests when he saves a sacrificial hawk.

The Book of Three (1964), *The Black Cauldron* (1965), *The Castle of Llyr* (1966), *Taran Wanderer* (1967), and *The High King* (1968). (New York and Toronto: Holt, Rinehart and Winston.)
   —in this series of heroic fantasies, Taran, an assistant pig-keeper, battles the Horned King and other foes. Eventually he becomes the celebrated "High King" and a true hero.

But We are Not of Earth, by Jean E. Karl. (New York: Dutton, 1981.)
   —Romula Linders and her three best friends go on a mission in outer space and experience dangerous adventures.

Call It Courage, by Armstrong Sperry. (New York and London: Macmillan, 1943.)
   —set in the Polynesian Islands, the story recounts Mafatu's quest to acquire courage and to overcome his fear of the sea.

Cart and Cwidder, by Dianna Wynne Jones. (New York: Atheneum, 1977.)
   —Moril's lutelike magical instrument saves his family from murderous warriors. Sequels: *Drowned Ammet* (1978), and *The Spellcoats* (1979).

The Cats of Seroster, by Robert Westall. (New York: Greenwillow, 1984.)
   —Cam fights for a country, saves the cats, and acquires the title "Seroster," the name of a legendary hero who is periodically replaced.

Coll and his White Pig, by Lloyd Alexander. Ill. by Evaline Ness. (New York: Holt, Rinehart and Winston, 1965.)
   —the account of Coll's adventures to rescue the magical pig, Hen Wen. When evil horsemen steal Hen Wen, Coll depends upon several wise animal helpers to complete his quest.

The Complete Book of Dragons, by E. Nesbit. Ill. by Erik Blegvad. 1899: Rpt. (New York and London: Macmillan, 1973.)
   —nine tales about child heroes who encounter and tame dragons in clever and unusual ways; many of these heroes are princesses.

The Crystal Gryphon, by Andre Norton (psud. of Alice Mary Norton). (New York: Atheneum, 1972.)
   —Kerovan and wife battle the Dark Powers for the throne of Urm. Companion volume: *The Jargoon Pard* (1974).

The Dark Is Rising, by Susan Cooper. (New York: Aladdin, 1976.)
—young Will Stanton discovers his true identity as the last of the "Old Ones," who are destined to battle the evil forces of the Dark. Will proves himself by completing his quest to find four powerful signs to be used in the service of the light.

The Diamond in the Window, by Jane Langton. (New York: Harper and Row, 1962.)
—two children, Edward and Eleanor Hall, live with Aunt Lily in an old Victorian house. The children enter upon an heroic adventure to find their aunt and uncle, who have disappeared mysteriously in an attic room.

The Donkey Prince, by Angela Carter. (New York: Simon, 1970.)
—Prince Bruno has been transformed into a donkey; he searches for a magic apple to save the queen's life.

Dragon's Blood, by Jane Yolen. (New York: Delacorte, 1982.)
—Jakkin decides to earn his freedom by fighting a dragon.

Dragonsong, by Anne McCaffrey. (New York: Atheneum, 1976.)
—central character Menolly resents her limited female identity and runs away to join a family of fire dragons.
Sequels: *Dragonsinger* (1977) and *Dragondrums* (1979)

Dragon of the Lost Sea, by Laurence Yep. (New York: Harper and Row, 1982.)
—a boy and a dragon engage in a quest for the evil Civit, who has stolen the waters of the dragons; author has blended and reinterpreted several Chinese myths.

Elidor, by Alan Garner. (London: Collins, 1965; Cleveland: Collins-World, 1979.)
—the four Watson children enter a fantasy world through a crumbling church as they follow a strange fiddler. In Elidor the children acquire and keep symbols which later help restore the light to the strange fantasy world.

Farmer Giles of Ham, by J.R.R. Tolkien. (London: Allen and Unwin, 1949). Rpt. (Boston: Houghton Mifflin, 1978.)
—Farmer Giles likes his pastoral existence; reluctantly he is called to become a hero when dragons attack his village.

The Farthest Away Mountain, by Lynn Reid Banks. Ill. by Victor Ambrus. (Garden City, N.Y.: Doubleday, 1977.)
—Dakin and her enchanted frog-prince try to free a mountain from a witch's spell.

The Forgotten Beasts of Eld, by Patricia McKillip. (New York: Atheneum, 1974.)
—a sorceress, Sybel, raises an abandoned baby; later she learns that his father is the enemy of her lover.

The Foundling and Other Tales of Prydain, by Lloyd Alexander. (New York and Toronto; Holt, Rinehart and Winston, 1973.)
—six tales about Prydain that include various heroic adventures; "The Foundling" is printed in this anthology.

The Great Alexander the Great, by Joe Lasker. Ill. by author. (New York: Viking, 1983.)
—this biography features characteristics of the hero tale.

Greenwitch, by Susan Cooper. New York: Atheneum, 1974. (New York: Aladdin, 1977 (paper).)
—this quest to retrieve the golden chalice centers upon Jane's love of the Greenwitch, a female image fashioned by women in a South Cornwall village out of green foliage. The Greenwitch is cast into the sea to insure bountiful fishing. (This volume is the third book of the *Dark Is Rising* series.)

The Grey King, by Susan Cooper. (New York: Atheneum, 1975.) (New York: Aladdin, 1978 (paper).)
—the fourth volume in the *Dark Is Rising* series, this book centers upon Bran and Will Stanton, who must complete several difficult tasks to insure the victory of the Old Ones against the Dark.

In the Hand of the Goddess, by Tamora Pierce. (New York: Atheneum, 1984.)
—Alanna, who disguises herself as a boy and trains for knighthood, must fight a wicked wizard.

Heart of Ice, by De Caylus. Adapted by Benjamin Appel, ill. by J.K. Lambert. (New York: Pantheon, 1977.)
—a tiny prince climbs Ice Mountain to win Princess Sabella's hand.

The Hero and the Crown, by Robin McKinley. (New York: Greenwillow, 1984.)
—Arien wins fame by slaying a dragon, but she must learn her true history and discover her real power to complete her identity. (The first book of this series was *The Blue Sword*, 1983).

The Hobbit; or There and Back Again, by J.R.R. Tolkien. (London: Allen and Unwin, 1937.)
—Bilbo Baggins is hired by a group of dwarves to retrieve a treasure from Smaug, a fierce dragon. Bilbo succeeds with the aid of a ring which renders him invisible.

Kneeknock Rise, by Natalie Babbitt. Ill. by author. (New York: Farrar, Straus, Giroux, 1970.)
—Egan climbs Kneeknock Rise to kill the terrible Megrimum, but he makes a surprising discovery.

The Knight of the Golden Plain, by Mollie Hunter. Ill. by Marc Simont. (New York: Harper and Row, 1983.)
—Sir Dauntless searches for a tiny golden bird held captive by an evil magician. The tale spoofs the heroic tradition.

Legend Days, by Jamake Highwater. (New York: Harper and Row, 1984.)
—a young woman, Anmana, possesses the heart of a warrior. She struggles for heroic identity even as Native Americans are destroyed.

Legend of Tarik, by Walter Dean Myers. (New York: Viking, 1981.)
—set in medieval Africa, this literary hero tale features a black protagonist, Tarik, who must conquer the evil warrior El Muerte.

The Lion the Witch and the Wardrobe, by C.S. Lewis. (London: Bles, 1950; New York: Collier, 1979 (paper).)
—in the first book of the *Chronicles of Narnia*, the four Pevensie children enter Narnia through a wardrobe and help the great lion Aslan to conquer the White Witch.

The Dragon and the George, by Gordon R. Dickson. (New York: Ballantine, 1976.)
—a comic hero tale about Jim Eckert, a history professor who is transformed into a dragon.

Moon-Flash, by Patricia McKillip. (New York: Atheneum, 1984.)
—Kyreal, a young girl, is a dreamer. She questions her primitive world and discovers that her tribe is an anomaly in a highly technological world of the future.

The Moon of Gomrath, by Alan Garner. (London: Collins, 1963.)
—Susan and Colin aid the wizard Cadellin in his struggle against dark forces. Susan is almost destroyed when the evil Brollachan possesses her body.

The Nargun and the Stars, by Patricia Wrightson. (New York: Atheneum, 1974.)
Sequels: *The Ice Is Coming* (1977) and *The Dark Bright Water* (1979).
—Simon Brent and his elderly cousins struggle against a monster from the past.

The Nearsighted Knight, by Mary Shura. Ill. by Adrienne Adams. (New York: Knopf, 1964.)
—Prince Todd helps the nearsighted knight kill a dragon and win his sister's hand.

Out There, by Elisabeth Mace. (New York: Greenwillow, 1978.)
—an unnamed main character searches for a legendary utopian colony.

Prince Caspian, by C.S. Lewis. (London: Bles, 1951; New York: Collier, 1970.)
—in Book II of the *Chronicles of Narnia* the Pevensie children are pulled from a railway station back into Narnia to help Prince Caspian claim his rightful throne from the usurping Telmarine.

The Prince in Waiting, by John Christopher. (London: Macmillan, 1970.)
—Luke endures the destruction of the world and becomes involved with a wizard in a struggle for control of an emerging civilization.

Quag Keep, by Andre Norton. (New York: Atheneum, 1978.)
—seven strangers wearing identical bracelets confront the power that has enslaved them.

The Reluctant Dragon, by Kenneth Grahame. Ill. by Gregorio Prestopino. 1898; Rpt. (New York: Grosset and Dunlap, 1968.)
—Grahame humorously parodies traditional dragon lore by creating a poetry-loving dragon; the boy in the story tries to reconcile the town and the dragon.

The Riddle Master of Hed, by Patricia McKillip. (New York: Ballantine, 1978.)
—Morgan quests to find the meaning of the three stars on his forehead.
Sequels: *Heir of Sea and Fire* (1977) and *Harpist in the Wind* (1979).

The Search for Delicious, by Natalie Babbitt. (New York: Farrar, Straus, and Giroux, 1969.)
—the prologue to this tale is a literary myth and is printed in the literary myth section of this anthology. The remainder of the tale concerns young Gaylen's attempt to discover the true meaning of the word "delicious."

Seaward, by Susan Cooper. (New York: Atheneum, 1983.)
—Cooper dramatizes the eternal struggle between good and evil. Two young people cross the borders of time to achieve their goals.

Seven Spells to Farewell, by Betty Baker. (London: Macmillan, 1982.)
—Drucilla, a slave at her uncle's inn, yearns to become a true sorceress. She achieves her quest with the help of a talking raven and a performing pig.

The Shadow of the Gloom-World, by Roger Eldridge. (New York: Dutton, 1978.)
—Fernfeather and Harebell explore a deadly world when they are cast out of their underground land.

The Shattered Stone, by Robert Newman. Ill. by John Gretzer. (New York: Atheneum, 1975.)
—two children seek a stone inscription that will bring peace to their land.

The Silver Chair, by C.S. Lewis. (London: Bles, 1953; New York: Collier, 1970.)
—book IV of the *Chronicles of Narnia*; this is the story of how Eustace Scrubb and Jill Pole enter Narnia and free Prince Rilian from an evil enchantment.

Silver on the Tree, by Susan Cooper. (New York, Atheneum, 1977.)
—final volume of the *Dark Is Rising* series; Will, Merriman, the Drews, and Bran engage in the final contest with the forces of the Dark.

The Stolen Lake, by Joan Aiken. (New York: Delacorte, 1981.)

—Dido Trite, aged twelve, must assist the Queen of New Cumbria to retrieve her lake. Dido confronts a series of villains and heroes in achieving her quest.

A String in the Harp, by Nancy Bond. (New York: Atheneum, 1976.)

—twelve-year-old Peter finds the harp key of Taliessen, the sixth-century Welsh bard. Peter experiences both inner and outer quests when his family moves to Wales.

The Tapestry Warriors, by Cherry Wilder. (New York: Atheneum, 1983.)

—fifteen-year-old Ravan embarks on a mission for his master, Orath Veer, only to discover that the wizard is aligned with evil powers.

Tatsinda, by Elizabeth Enright. Ill by Irene Haas. (New York: Harcourt, 1963.)

—Prince Tackatan tries to rescue an outcast girl, Tatsinda, from an evil giant.

The Truthful Harp, by Lloyd Alexander. (New York and Toronto: Holt, Rinehart & Winston, 1967.)

—a comic hero tale about the adventurous minstrel, Fflewddur Flam; a string of his harp breaks whenever he lies.

Over Sea, Under Stone, by Susan Cooper. (New York: Harcourt, 1966.)

—the first of the *Dark Is Rising* series, the story recounts the adventures of Simon, Jane, and Barney, who spend the summer with their Uncle Merriman Lyon. They find an ancient map which leads them to a golden chalice and a struggle with evil forces.

The Voyage of the Dawn Treader, by C.S. Lewis. (London: Bles, 1952; New York: Collier, 1970.)

—Edmund and Lucy and their cousin Eustace Scrubb find themselves aboard the Dawn Treader as they are looking at a picture of a sailing ship. They embark upon a perilous voyage with Prince Caspian.

A Walk Out of the World, by Ruth Nichols. Ill. by Trina Schart Hyman. (New York: Harcourt, 1969.)

—a mysterious light leads Judith and Tobit into another world, where they help to overthrow the wicked King Hagerrak.

The Weathermonger, by Peter Dickinson. (Boston and Toronto: Little Brown, 1969.)

—Geoffrey Tinker possesses magical powers enabling him to control the weather. He returns to the Middle Ages to uncover the cause of the enchantment.

The Weirdstone of Brisingamen, by Alan Garner. (London: Collins, 1960; Cleveland: Collins-World, 1979.)

—Susan and Colin assist the wizard Cadellin Silverbrow to retreive the powerful stone, Firefrost, from the evil Nastrond.

The Wizard's Daughter, by Chris Conover. Ill. by author. (Boston and Toronto: Little Brown, 1984.)

—a wizard's apprentice rescues his master's beautiful daughter from an evil undersea kingdom.

A Wizard of Earthsea, by Ursula Le Guin. Ill. by Ruth Robbins. (Parnassus, 1968.)

—Ged, an apprentice wizard, unleashes a terrible shadow when he misuses his power; his quest is to conquer the shadow and thus save himself and Earthsea. Sequels: *The Tombs of Atuan* (1971) and *The Farthest Shore* (1972).

Literary Myths

Literary Myths

An Introduction

In our introduction to mythology, theories about the nature and origins of myths were examined; also discussed was the modern children's writer's fascination with great myths from around the world. In addition to their study of ancient myths and their adaptations of these, modern writers for both children and adults have been influenced by mythology in another way. Just as they have created literary folktales and hero tales, consciously adapting the styles, themes, structures, and motifs of oral literature, so too, many writers have created literary myths, based on their studies of the nature of mythology in general and their interest in the myths of specific cultures.

The importance of mythology to nineteenth- and twentieth-century literature can scarcely be overestimated. Some critics assert that a search for a coherent myth is in fact a prime characteristic of modern literature. The Romantic poets in England, feeling that Dante and Milton had already given definitive literary expression to the Judeo-Christian myth in the *Divine Comedy* and *Paradise Lost*, searched for a new mythology to reinvigorate literature. Thus we find William Wordsworth creating his own myths of the marriage of mind and nature in *The Prelude*, William Blake forging his own highly personal and visionary myths of the self, Samuel Taylor Coleridge and John Keats turning to medieval myth and legend, and Percy Bysshe Shelley writing his reinterpretation of the Promethean myth in *Prometheus Unbound*. This trend continued throughout the nineteenth century, and it has continued in the twentieth.

At the beginning of the twentieth century the great anthropologist Sir James George Frazer collected and compared such universal myths as "the scapegoat" in his massive study *The Golden Bough*: *A Study of Magic and Religion* (1911—1915). Jessie L. Weston's study *From Ritual to Romance* (1919) suggested the potent mythic implications of the Arthurian legends, in particular the Grail legends. Both of these important works in turn exerted a powerful influence upon modernist writers such as T.S. Eliot (particularly in the long poem *The Waste Land*), James Joyce in his novels *A Portrait of the Artist as a Young Man* and *Ulysses*, and William Butler Yeats in many of his poems.

In writing what is considered by many critics as the best poetry of the twentieth century, Yeats consciously used several varieties of myth for various literary purposes. From the rich but largely unfamiliar body of Irish mythology Yeats sought to create his own myths of contemporary Ireland in the hope that he could create a sense of national identity and purpose among the Irish people, whose culture had largely been forgotten. To elevate his love for the actress Maude Gonne above the merely personal, Yeats often compared her to Helen of Troy. He also turned to other sources of myth, including studies in mystical and occult literature and the ancient civilization of Byzantium. Eventually Yeats's quest for a unifying myth led him to elaborate on his own private mythical system in his prose work *A Vision*.

Among the most famous modern examples of a writer's use of ancient myth to tell a contemporary story is James Joyce's *Ulysses*. Joyce had used the Greek myth of the artificer Daedalus in the earlier novel *A Portrait of the Artist as a Young Man*, in which he equates the central character's development as an artist with that of the ancient Greek creator. T.S. Eliot explained what he considered to be the importance of Joyce's example of using Homer's *The Odyssey* to structure the episodes of the novel *Ulysses*:

> In using the myth, in manipulating a continuous parallel between contemporaneity and antiquity, Mr. Joyce is pursuing a method which others must pursue after him. They will not be imitators. It is simply a way of controlling, of ordering, of giving a shape and a significance to the immense panorama of futility and anarchy which is contemporary history . . . . It is, I seriously believe, a step toward making the modern world possible for art . . . .[1]

As we shall see, children's writers have also participated in this quest for mystic structures to enlarge and to enrich their children's stories. Many children's writers create literary myths in which they quite literally borrow the form and function of specific myths. Many others incorporate mythic structures and themes in both fantasy and realist works for children.

As we noted in the second section, scholars of mythology have posed several theories and definitions of myth. While definitions vary, and while critics take an endless interest in distinguishing myths from hero tales, folktales, and other forms of folk literature, in general, myths are stories which tell of the dealings of gods with human beings, the origins of all things in nature and human civilization, and the ultimate destiny of the gods and humanity. In many respects, however, myths, folktales, and hero tales strongly resemble one another. As Elizabeth Cook has explained in discussing myth, folktales, hero tales, and other types of folk literature:

> The common reader is more struck by the ways in which they all look rather

like each other, and indeed merge into one another . . . . They are not realistic; they are almost unlocalized in time and space; they are often supernatural or at least fantastic in character; and the human beings in them are not three-dimensional people with complex motives and temperaments. These stories do hold a mirror up to nature, but they do not reflect the world as we perceive it with our senses at the present moment.[2]

Like Cook, prominent psychologist Carl Jung perceived what he called archetypes not only in myth but in literature as well. His theories have thus provided an effective method for studying the relationship between myth and literature. For Jung myths reveal universal symbols — characters, settings, and patterns of experience which arise from the primordial images of what Jung calls "the collective unconscious." He describes such characters as the Earthmother, who appears in such myths as the Greek "Demeter and Persephone," as well as in contemporary children's novels such as Katherine Paterson's *The Great Gilly Hopkins*. A true earthmother, Paterson's character "Trotter" nourishes foster children both physically and spiritually.

Other archetypal characters include the Fatal Woman or Temptress, the male fantasy of the perilously beautiful woman who enslaves and destroys men, as she lures them into her power with her exceptional beauty and charm. Circe in Homer's *The Odyssey* is a good example of this archetype, as she lures Odysseus' men into her home with her beauty and hospitality and then transforms them into swine. The Fatal Woman likewise appears as the White Witch in C.S. Lewis's *The Lion, the Witch and the Wardrobe*, as she lures Edmund into her power with promises of Turkish Delight. In the same story Mrs. Beaver clearly represents the Earthmother, while the old Professor embodies many traits of the archetypal Wise Old Man, since he combines rational, imaginative, and intuitive ways of knowing.

Other mythic characters include, as we have already seen, the Hero, the Trickster, who must, of course, trick others to stay alive, and the Wise Animal or Holy Fool, an innocent character whose goodness and resourcefulness usually prevail against much more worldly and shrewd characters.

Many of these archetypal characters appear in stories with highly symbolic settings, such as the garden, the wasteland or difficult landscape, and various symbolic bodies of water. Likewise these characters often undergo mythic patterns of experience. They may occupy a golden age in a state of innocence and fall into painful experience, which forces them to learn and grow. Many such characters go through initiations of one kind or another as they develop and mature. They may experience death (or perhaps a symbolic death, such as a serious illness) and rebirth. Or they may fail to grow and may desire, at least metaphorically, a return to the womb.

Although these Jungian archetypes — which appear in their purest state in myth, folktales, and hero tales—provide an excellent conceptual framework for the study of literature, Jung himself has cautioned against an excessively mechanical approach to the study of archetypes. An archetype is a rich symbol, not a reductive stereotype. Thus, the reader must attend carefully to the distinctions and differences with which these mythic patterns find new and vital expression in literary works.

Northrop Frye's theories on myths and their relationship to literature are also of great practical use to students of literature for both adults and children. He argues that literature is "displaced mythology," that "archetypes" may be regarded as the structural units of literature, and that these mythic patterns may in fact comprise a "grammar of literary archetypes." Frye explains that: "In myth we see the structural principles of literature isolated; in realism we see the same structural principles . . . . fitting into a context of plausibility."[3] At the same time Frye carefully stresses that a mythical theme or "archetype" is not to be regarded as a Platonic absolute which all later treatments of the myth must approximate, but rather, a flexible and informing principle of literature. In his essay "Literature and Myth," Frye writes that "the more we study the literary development of a myth the more we learn about the myth."[4] In the same essay he suggests strongly that the real meaning of a myth is revealed not by its origin but by its destiny — by what happens to it in later literary treatments.

Although defining myth remains a problematic task, one may follow Frye's example and examine how children's writers have handled mythic materials in their own creative practices. Reading mythology has exerted a profound influence upon the imaginations of many writers for both children and adults. In interviews and essays too numerous to cite, writers for children have indicated that mythology comprised some of their most potent and meaningful childhood reading. British poet Ted Hughes has written that "Greek mythology presents a working anatomy of our psychic life in a very complete and profound way . . . . It enriches our sense of ourselves with genuine additions, new openings and recognitions. It is a whole system of keys and passwords and introductions to energies and relationships between energies, within ourselves."[5] Hughes exhibits mythic patterns in his poetry for children and especially in his children's fantasy, *The Iron Man*, which powerfully reveals the archetypal pattern of death, dismemberment, and rebirth.

Children's writer, Alan Garner, also writes of the power of myth in his creative and imaginative life:

Myth is no escapist entertainment. It is distilled and violent truth. Anyone who

reads it is handling spiritual gelignite. There are three basic ways of handling
the [mythic] material. The writer may re-absorb and transmute (often unconsciously) the elements of the myth; or he may translate existing texts; or he
may retell . . . . Hardest of all is the absorption of myth, not the shape but the
spirit, and making it relevant to the present moment. This absorption, if it
works, is the most positive form for the myth to take, because the life of the
myth is handed forward.[6]

Retellings and translations of myths from all over the world flood the children's book market each year. Many of these are excellent. Those who retell
myths for children have learned in recent years to respect cultural differences
and to interpret the myths in their retellings in light of the specific cultures
represented. Garner's books provide excellent examples of the practice he describes. In his complex and compelling fantasy *The Owl Service* (1967), Garner
shows how a violent and passionate Celtic myth is reenacted in the lives of three
British children. According to the myth, a great wizard creates a lovely woman
from flowers as a wife for Lleu Llaw Gyffes. Called Blodeuwedd, the woman
betrays her husband, who then kills her lover, Gronw. Because of her betrayal,
Blodeuwedd is doomed to live as an owl rather than returning to her original
state. When Roger, Allison, and Gwyn find a set of china with a curious owl
pattern on it, strange forces are unleashed in the Welsh valley. The myth,
however, is not merely reenacted; the children must reinterpret the myth in
accordance with their own characters and circumstances in order to transcend
some of the fatal errors their parents have made in their past reenactment of the
myth. Garner expresses with powerful intensity the passionate emotions which
exist between parents and children and between men and women.

In his *Chronicles of Narnia* C.S. Lewis has created an entire mythic world of
his own. In *The Magician's Nephew*, for example, Lewis recounts how Narnia
was created and reveals young Digory's discovery of this new world. In *The Last
Battle*, a portion of which is among the following selections, Lewis dramatizes
the destruction of an old order and the apocalyptic creation of a new and transcendent Narnia.

Afro-American writer Virginia Hamilton has created one of the most remarkable and rich literary myths in children's literature. In *The Magical Adventures
of Pretty Pearl*, Hamilton blends elements of black legend, myth, and folklore to
tell how the god child Pretty Pearl stepped down from Mount Highness in Africa
to discover her godly powers and to help her people enslaved in America. Pretty
Pearl's older brother John de Conquer gives Pearl a magical necklace made of
John de Conquer root, well known in black folk medicine, to help her people
find freedom. This mythical story also features Mother Pearl, a middle-aged

godmother, and another aspect of Pretty Pearl herself, John Henry Roustabout, the oldest brother of Pretty Pearl and the famous steel-driving man of black folk legend. As well, four spirits who aid Pretty Pearl in leading the people to freedom are also present. Like many other literary myths, then, *The Magical Adventures of Pretty Pearl* draws upon a body of myth and folk belief to create an intricate and highly original literary work.

Thus, in an important sense many contemporary writers of fantasy, literary folktale, and literary myth have absorbed both the form and the spirit of ancient myth in order to become mythmakers in their own right. In his famous essay "On Fairy-Stories," Tolkien describes the activity of such mythmakers:

What really happens is that the storymaker proves a successful 'sub-creator'. He makes a Secondary World which your mind can enter. Inside it, what he relates is 'true'; it accords with the laws of that world. You therefore believe it, while you are, as it were, inside. The moment disbelief arises, the spell is broken . . . . You are out in the Primary World again.[7]

For Tolkien, "fantasy (in this sense) is . . . not a lower but a higher form of Art, indeed the most nearly pure form, and so (when achieved) the most potent."[8]

Tolkien's conception of a mythic Secondary World strongly resembles the mythic cosmos described by Northrop Frye as, "an abstract or purely literary world of fictional and thematic design, unaffected by canons of plausible adaptation to familiar experience. In terms of narrative, myth is the initiation of actions near or at the conceivable limits of desire. The gods enjoy beautiful women, fight one another with prodigious strength, comfort and assist men, or else watch his miseries from the height of their immortal freedom . . . ."[9]

The literary myths among the following selections include contemporary mythmakers who have created their own plausible Secondary Worlds. They reveal essential patterns of myth because they have absorbed both the shape and the spirit of ancient mythology. Several writers — Natalie Babbitt, Richard Adams, Maria Campbell, and C.S. Lewis — depict elemental aspects of myth: the creation of the world; the relationship of the mortal to the immortal; the gift of fire, perhaps the most essential element of human civilization; and the apocalypse, that is, the end of an old and corrupt order and the beginning of a new creation. The literary myths of Rudyard Kipling and Virginia Hamilton, however, come close to parody because of their comic, mildly ironic tones. Nevertheless, these stories are examples of myths which are only slightly "displaced." That is, the writers have followed the conventions of myths rather closely in creating their literary myths. In a later section of this anthology we shall examine mythic patterns in fantasy and realistic fiction which provide significantly new interpretations of ancient patterns or "archetypes" of literature. In children's literature one can find almost every conceivable use of myth to enlarge the symbolic and emotional emphases of the stories. For example, Cynthia Voight, in writing her two novels, *Homecoming* and its Newbery-award winning sequel, *Dicey's Song*, draws explicitly upon the myth of the lost child with specific allusions to "Hansel and Gretel," to the myth of Odysseus and his wanderings, and perhaps most compellingly to the myth of Demeter and Persephone to reveal the troubled and poignant relationship between mothers and daughters. In her moving fantasy *Tuck Everlasting*, Natalie Babbitt deliberately calls into question the myth of a deathless, pastoral "golden age." Her fantasy asks hard questions concerning the place of death in human existence and thus can be viewed as an ironic treatment of the myth it embodies and expresses.

As mythic patterns or the "archetypes" of literature are examined, one must remember that although two stories share identical mythical patterns and structures, they are by no means the same story. As Tolkien reminds us, "It is precisely the colouring, the atmosphere, the unclassifiable individual details of a story, and above all, the general purport, that informs with life the undissected bones of the plot, that really count."[10]

In the conclusion to our introduction to mythology in section two, we emphasized that teachers, parents, and librarians should begin reading myths to children in early to middle elementary school. Recent studies in theories of reading suggest that how well children read depends upon the extent to which they have internalized the conventions of literature, since these conventions help the students to predict outcome by establishing a pattern of reading expectations. If, as Northrop Frye suggests, myths comprise the structural units of literature, early experience with these stories is essential to promote critical reading skills among students. We noted that some myths, such as the tragic story of Prometheus are too complex for early elementary school and are best introduced in upper elementary and junior high. In any event, children should be exposed to a variety of myths from different cultures suited to their particular stage of development.

Once they have experienced many different myths, children will recognize and enjoy the ironic and humorous treatments which appear in literary myths. Once again, adults sharing literary myths with children must use their own judgment as to which literary myths are appropriate for a particular class. Hamilton's "How Jahdu Took Care of Trouble" can be understood and enjoyed by early to middle elementary-school children if the teacher reads it aloud and discusses it. Babbitt's *The Search for Delicious*, Kipling's "The Elephant's Child," McCormick's "The Last Camp of Paul Bunyan," and C.S. Lewis's *The Last Battle* are appropriate for upper elementary and junior high students.

Once children have internalized the conventions of myth, teachers can begin to teach mythic patterns in literature. Rather than isolating the study of myth, teachers may wish to integrate it by studying a particular myth in relation to a "displaced" version of the story. For example, a middle elementary teacher may wish to introduce the trickster character in a Jahdu story, a Brer Rabbit tale, and to conclude the unit by studying the "displaced" trickster in Evaline Ness's fine realistic children's book *Sam, Bang, and Moonshine*, and E.B. White's fantasy, *Charlotte's Web*. This does not mean, of course, that the class would look only at the trickster characters. The archetype should always be studied in the context of other literary elements in the book. Ultimately the purpose of locating archetypes is not only to examine similarities with other stories, but also to highlight the differences in order to appreciate the unique qualities of each book.

Notes

1 T.S. Eliot, "*Ulysses*, Order, and Myth" (1923), *Selected Prose of T.S. Eliot*, ed. and intro. by Frank Kermode (London: Faber and Faber, 1975), p. 177.

2 Elizabeth Cook, *The Ordinary and the Fabulous: An Introduction to Myth, Legends and Fairy Tales for Teachers and Storytellers* (Cambridge: University Press, 1971), p. 1.

3 Northrop Frye, *Anatomy of Criticism* (Princeton, N.J.: Princeton University Press, 1957; Rpt. Atheneum, 1966), p. 136.

4 Northrop Frye, "Literature and Myth," in *Relations of Literary Study*, ed. James Thorpe (New York: MLA, 1967), p. 38.

5 Ted Hughes, "Review of *The God Beneath the Sea*," *Children's Literature in Education*, 3 (1970), pp. 66-67.

6 Alan Garner, "The Death of Myth," *Children's Literature in Education*, 3 (1970), pp. 69-71.

7 J.R.R. Tolkien, "On Fairy-Stories," *Tree and Leaf* (London: George Allen and Unwin, Ltd., 1964), p. 36.

8 *Ibid.*, p. 45.

9 Frye, *Anatomy of Criticism*, p. 136.

10 Tolkien, "On Fairy-Stories," pp. 21-22.

From The Search for Delicious, *by Natalie Babbitt (New York: Farrar, Straus, and Giroux, 1969).*

One of the strengths of Natalie Babbitt's books for children is her powerful use of mythic patterns. She has stated in interviews that reading the Greek myths was central to the growth of her creative imagination. In her fantasy The Search for Delicious *Babbitt includes a literary creation myth to frame the ironic quest of Gaylen for the most delicious food in the kingdom. In this mythic prologue Babbitt focuses upon the essential elements of nature — earth, air, water, and the forests — to reveal their immaculate condition at the time of creation. In the story of Gaylen's quest for "delicious," Babbitt reveals with humor and wry wit the poignance of a fallen creation in which human beings have lost touch with the sacramental significance of myth, as well as the truth of poetry, song, and story.*

The Search for Delicious

There was a time once when the earth was still very young, a time some call the oldest days. This was long before there were any people about to dig parts of it up and cut parts of it off. People came along much later, building their towns and castles (which nearly always fell down after a while) and plaguing each other with quarrels and supper parties. The creatures who lived on the earth in that early time stayed each in his own place and kept it beautiful. There were dwarfs in the mountains, woldwellers in the forests, mermaids in the lakes, and, of course, winds in the air.

There was one particular spot on the earth where a ring of mountains enclosed a very dry and dusty place. There were winds and dwarfs there, but no mermaids because there weren't any lakes, and there were no woldwellers either because forests couldn't grow in so dry a place.

Then a remarkable thing happened. Up in the mountains one day a dwarf was poking about with a sharp tool, looking for a good spot to begin mining. He poked and poked until he had made a very deep hole in the earth. Then

he poked again and clear spring water came spurting up in the hole. He hurried in great excitement to tell the other dwarfs and they all came running to see the water. They were so pleased with it that they built over it a fine house of heavy stones and they made a special door out of a flat rock and balanced it in its place very carefully on carved hinges. Then one of them made a whistle out of a small stone which blew a certain very high note tuned to just the right warble so that when you blew it, the door of the rock house would open, and when you blew it again, the door would shut. They took turns being in charge of the whistle and they worked hard to keep the spring clean and beautiful.

But the spring they had discovered was in a cup of land surrounded by cliffs and eventually the spring began to fill up the cup, until after a while there was a little lake there with the top of the spring house standing out in the center like an island. And the lake kept getting higher and higher. After a few years the spring house was completely submerged and the dwarfs could no longer get down to it, although they could see it easily through the clear water and could still make the door open and close with the whistle, just the same as before.

The water in the lake began in time to fill up with creatures of its own, as water has a way of doing, and one of these creatures was a lovely little mermaid. The dwarfs named her Ardis and one of them made her a pretty doll out of linked stones with a trailing fern fastened to its head for hair. Ardis loved the doll very much and played with it all the time, and in exchange she promised to keep watch over the spring in the house of rocks, now far down under the water. So the dwarfs gave her the special whistle and she kept it hanging by a chain on a sharp bit of rock at the water's edge. Every morning she would blow the whistle to open the door and then she would dive down and play with her doll inside among the bubbles. At night she would come up and blow the whistle again to close the door, and swim away to sleep.

While all this was happening, the water in the lake had risen so high that it began to spill over in one spot where there was a V-shaped gap in the cliffs, and it tumbled down into the dry and dusty placer ringed by the mountains. It fingered itself into a great many streams and watered the land so well that everything was soon green and fresh. Forests sprang up and woldwellers came there to watch over the trees. And then, later, the people began to arrive. They built towns and they crowned a king and they enjoyed a great many quarrels and troubles, all of which they created quite by themselves. The dwarfs withdrew deep under the mountains where they wouldn't have to watch and they went on mining and almost never came out. In time they separated into groups of two or three, each group mining where it chose, and they never lived all together again. The woldwellers, who were admired by the people for their knowledge, stayed in their trees and came down to answer questions from time to time, but after a while they grew irritated by the foolishness of these questions and wouldn't always answer. Eventually the people stopped coming to ask.

And something very sad happened to Ardis. One day, while she was in the spring house playing with her doll, she heard a new and pleasing kind of sound. She put down the doll and swam up to the top of the lake. There on the bank sat a man, the first she had ever seen, making pretty music on a round box with strings pulled tight across it. Ardis stayed to listen, hiding behind a water lily, with only her eyes and ears out of the water. After a while the man put the round box aside and, leaning over to drink from the lake, noticed the whistle hanging from its sharp bit of rock. He picked it up and blew through it, but he was only a man and couldn't hear the sound it made. As Ardis watched in dismay, he started to toss it away, paused, looked at it again, and finally hung it around his neck. Then he picked up his strange instrument and wandered off. She cried to him to come back, but he didn't hear.

Ardis dove trembling to the spring house, but the blast the man had blown on the whistle had made the door swing shut. The house was locked. Ardis could peer through the cracks between the rocks and see her doll lying inside, but there was no way to get it out. After that, she was sad all the time. At night she

would swim up to the spot where the whistle had hung, and weep for hours. Someone heard her once and made a song about her, but no one could help her, for the dwarfs were far away.

And in the meantime, in the land below, towns were built and burned and built again and kings and their people lived and died and enjoyed their troubles for years and years and years. Ardis and the dwarfs and the woldwellers were largely forgotten except in stories and songs. Nobody believed they were real any more except for an occasional child or an even more occasional worker of evil, these being the only ones with imagination enough to admit to the possibility of something even more amazing in the world than those commonplace marvels which it spreads so carelessly before us every day.

___

"The Story of the Blessing of El-ahrairah," from Watership Down, *by Richard Adams (New York: Macmillan, 1972).*

Richard Adams' novel Watership Down *is interspersed with stories about El-ahrairah, the culture hero of rabbits and a favorite of the creator Frith. Adams writes that "what Robin Hood is to the English and John Henry to the American Negroes . . . El-ahrairah — the Prince with a Thousand Enemies — is to rabbits. . . . Odysseus himself might have borrowed a trick or two from the rabbit hero, for he is very old and was never at a loss to deceive his enemies." Early in the novel a group of rabbits who have fled from their warren sit trembling in the woods and ask one of their number to tell them this creation and pourquoi myth.*

The Story of the Blessing of El-ahrairah

Why should he think me cruel
Or that he is betrayed?
I'd have him love the thing that was
Before the world was made.
                    W.B. Yeats, *A Woman Young and Old*

"Long ago, Frith made the world. He made all the stars, too, and the world is one of the stars. He made them by scattering his droppings over the sky and this is why the grass and the trees grow so thick on the world. Frith makes the rivers flow. They follow him as he goes through the sky, and when he leaves the sky they look for him all night. Frith made all the animals and birds, but when he first made them they were all the same. The sparrow and the kestrel were friends and they both ate seeds and flies. And the fox and the rabbit were friends and they both ate grass. And there was plenty of grass and plenty of flies, because the world was new and Frith shone down bright and warm all day.

"Now, El-ahrairah was among the animals in those days and he had many wives. He had so many wives that there was no counting them, and the wives had so many young that even Frith could not count them, and they ate the grass and the dandelions and the lettuces and the clover, and El-ahrairah was the father of them all." (Bigwig growled appreciatively.) "And after a time," went on Dandelion, "after a time the grass began to grow thin and the rabbits wandered everywhere, multiplying and eating as they went.

"Then Frith said to El-ahrairah, 'Prince Rabbit, if you cannot control your people, I shall find ways to control them. So mark what I say.' But El-ahrairah would not listen and he said to Frith, 'My people are the strongest in the world, for they breed faster and eat more than any of the other people. And this shows how much they love Lord Frith, for of all the animals they are the most responsive to his warmth and brightness. You must realize, my lord, how important they are and not hinder them in their beautiful lives.'

"Frith could have killed El-ahrairah at once, but he had a mind to keep him in the world, because he needed him to sport and jest and play tricks. So he determined to get the better of him, not by means of his own great power but by means of a trick. He gave out that he would hold a great meeting and that at that meeting he would give a present to every animal and bird, to make each one different from the rest. And all the creatures set out to go to the meeting place. But they all arrived at different times, because Frith made sure that it

would happen so. And when the blackbird came, he gave him his beautiful song, and when the cow came, he gave her sharp horns and the strength to be afraid of no other creature. And so in their turn came the fox and the stoat and the weasel. And to each of them Frith gave the cunning and the fierceness and the desire to hunt and slay and eat the children of El-ahrairah. And so they went away from Frith full of nothing but hunger to kill the rabbits.

"Now, all this time El-ahrairah was dancing and mating and boasting that he was going to Frith's meeting to receive a great gift. And at last he set out for the meeting place. But as he was going there, he stopped to rest on a soft, sandy hillside. And while he was resting, over the hill came flying the dark swift, screaming as he went, 'News! News! News!' For you know, this is what he has said ever since that day. So El-ahrairah called up to him and said, 'What news?' 'Why,' said the swift, 'I would not be you, El-ahrairah. For Frith has given the fox and the weasel cunning hearts and sharp teeth, and to the cat he has given silent feet and eyes that can see in the dark, and they are gone away from Frith's place to kill and devour all that belongs to El-ahrairah.' And he dashed on over the hills. And at that moment El-ahrairah heard the voice of Frith calling. 'Where is El-ahrairah? For all the others have taken their gifts and gone and I have come to look for him.'

"Then El-ahrairah knew that Frith was too clever for him and he was frightened. He thought that the fox and the weasel were coming with Frith and he turned to the face of the hill and began to dig. He dug a hole, but he had dug only a little of it when Frith came over the hill alone. And he saw El-ahrairah's bottom sticking out of the hole and the sand flying out in showers as the digging went on. When he saw that, he called out, 'My friend, have you seen El-ahrairah, for I am looking for him to give him my gift?' 'No,' answered El-ahrairah, without coming out, 'I have not seen him. He is far away. He could not come.' So Frith said, 'Then come out of that hole and I will bless you instead of him.' 'No, I cannot,' said El-ahrairah, 'I am busy. The fox and the weasel are coming. If you want to bless me you can bless my bottom, for it is sticking out of the hole.' "

All the rabbits had heard the story before: on winter nights, when the cold draft moved down the warren passages and the icy wet lay in the pits of the runs below their burrows; and on summer evenings, in the grass under the red may and the sweet, carrion-scented elder bloom. Dandelion was telling it well, and even Pipkin forgot his weariness and danger and remembered instead the great indestructibility of the rabbits. Each one of them saw himself as El-ahrairah, who could be impudent to Frith and get away with it.

"Then," said Dandelion, "Frith felt himself in friendship with El-ahrairah, because of his resourcefulness, and because he would not give up even when he thought the fox and the weasel were coming. And he said, 'Very well, I will bless your bottom as it sticks out of the hole. Bottom, be strength and warning and speed forever and save the life of your master. Be it so!' And as he spoke, El-ahrairah's tail grew shining white and flashed like a star: and his back legs grew long and powerful and he thumped the hillside until the very beetles fell off the grass stems. He came out of the hole and tore across the hill faster than any creature in the world. And Frith called after him, 'El-ahrairah, your people cannot rule the world, for I will not have it so. All the world will be your enemy, Prince with a Thousand Enemies, and whenever they catch you, they will kill you. But first they must catch you, digger, listener, runner, prince with the swift warning. Be cunning and full of tricks and your people shall never be destroyed.' And El-ahrairah knew then that although he would not be mocked, yet Frith was his friend. And every evening, when Frith has done his day's work and lies calm and easy in the red sky, El-ahrairah and his children and his children's children come out of their holes and feed and play in his sight, for they are his friends and he has promised them that they can never be destroyed."

"How Jahdu Took Care of Trouble," from The Time-Ago Tales of Jahdu, *by Virginia Hamilton. Ill. by Nonny Hogrogian (New York: Macmillan, 1969).*

In her stories about the trickster figure Jahdu, Virginia Hamilton has combined elements from a number of African trickster stories and Kiowa Indian trickster stories about Sayanday. Jahdu, like so many tricksters, often gets into trouble. In this story, he ignores the warnings of the tumbleweeds and, at the end of the tale, he disbelieves Trouble's statements. Each of the Jahdu stories has a contemporary framework: a small boy listens to the tales of his old babysitter as the two sit in a Harlem apartment.

How Jahdu Took Care of Trouble

Mama Luka liked to eat red licorice candy better than any other kind of candy. One day she sat in her room with a jar of red licorice beside her.

Mama Luka held out a red licorice twist to Lee Edward, who sat on the floor. She took a piece for herself and ate it slowly. Then Mama Luka sat on her plait and looked at Lee Edward.

Lee Edward pointed to a space in the air about a foot in front of him. Mama Luka reached for the space. She almost dropped the space before she finally got it on her lap.

Mama Luka said, "You picked a heavy Jahdu story out of the air this time, you surely did, Lee Edward."

Mama Luka patted and shaped whatever it was in her lap that Lee Edward couldn't see. "I don't think I'll taste this one," Mama Luka said, "for I know it can't taste good."

"Why is this Jahdu story a heavy one," asked Lee Edward, "and why won't it taste good?"

"Well, because, child," Mama Luka said, "after what happened to Jahdu in this story, Jahdu was different."

"How was he different?" asked Lee Edward.

Mama Luka smiled to herself and patted

whatever it was in her lap that Lee Edward couldn't see. "Little Brother, I sure wish you hadn't picked this story out of the air," she said.

"Well, tell it so I can know how Jahdu was different," said Lee Edward.

"I'm getting myself ready," said Mama Luka.

THIS IS THE HEAVY JAHDU STORY THAT MAMA LUKA TOLD ONE DAY TO THE CHILD, LEE EDWARD.

Jahdu was running along. He had been running all over for many a year. Now Jahdu was hurrying southward through an empty land. And he whispered to himself as he ran.

"Woogily!" whispered Jahdu. "This empty land takes Jahdu too long to run through. I've seen a few trees but I haven't seen anything else."

Just then, a strong wind blew in Jahdu's face. Jahdu heard a swishing sound. Coming out of the south he saw thirty-two members of a tumbleweed family. They were heading north and they passed Jahdu in a hurry.

"Hey, there!" Jahdu called after the tumbleweeds. "What's the big hurry? Wait up a minute." Jahdu started running northward. But the wind helped the tumbleweeds more than it did him. Jahdu soon found there was no catching those thirty-two tumbleweeds.

"Jahdu, you're a long way from home," one tumbleweed shouted back.

"I like to be always running along," Jahdu told him. "But what's your hurry?"

"We're the last to leave here," the tumbleweed shouted. "We want to reach the mountains in the north before nightfall."

"You were lucky to catch such a swift wind," called Jahdu. "If you'll wait just a minute, I'll go along with you. I'm pretty much tired of this long, empty land."

"We can't wait for you," all the tumbleweeds called. "But do follow us north, Jahdu, for southward lies trouble."

"Trouble?" said Jahdu. He stopped running. "Hey, tumbleweeds," shouted Jahdu. "What is it you said?"

The tumbleweeds called from far away. "Follow us, Jahdu, for southward lies trouble . . . lies trouble . . . " And the tumbleweeds were gone to the north.

"Woogily!" said Jahdu. "Those tumbleweeds surely were in a hurry. I wonder what kind of thing is trouble. I'd better go southward and see."

So Jahdu went hurrying on. He ran and he ran southward through the long, empty land. He saw a few tall trees but not one sound did he hear.

"Woogily!" Jahdu said. "There are mountains to southward. Those thirty-two tumbleweeds need not have gone north. Jahdu likes mountains much better than empty land."

Jahdu ran more softly as he came closer to the mountains. The mountains were not like any he had known. When Jahdu was quite close, the mountains moved. Yes, they did.

The mountains sat up with a great creaking sound. Then they stared hard at Jahdu.

"Woogily!" said Jahdu, coming to a stop. "What in the world kind of sitting mountains are *you*!"

The mountains shook all over. They made a noise like thunder that made Jahdu tremble. "I'm no mountains, friend. I'm the giant, Trouble. Come up closer, friend, so Trouble can see what you're made of."

"Oh, no, thank you," said Jahdu. "I'm really just passing through. I've known all kinds of mountains and a number of tumbleweeds," added Jahdu, "but I've never known anything called the giant, Trouble."

"Well, now you do," said Trouble in a voice like drums. "And what might you be called, little friend?"

"You mean to say you've never heard of Jahdu?" asked Jahdu.

"Never in my life," said the giant, Trouble.

"Everyone knows me," said Jahdu. "I am Jahdu who is always running along. I'm three feet tall. I live in a tupelo tree when I'm at home. And I have magic which I keep to myself."

Trouble laughed loudly. "You come too close to Trouble, Jahdu," said the giant. "I think I'll just keep you from running along."

The great right hand of Trouble swooped down. Yes, it did. But Jahdu had already started running away. Jahdu ran and he ran. The great right hand of Trouble just missed him.

The great left hand of Trouble swooped down. Jahdu managed to slip through its fingers. Trouble laughed in a thunderous roar. He stretched himself out along the southward landscape and propped himself up on his elbow.

Jahdu stayed out of the reach of Trouble without letting Trouble out of his sight. He could see that Trouble was no kind of mountain. For Trouble was bigger than fifty-two mountains.

The giant, Trouble, was clothed in gray. His eyes were rain-cloud dark and his face had about it the anger of a storm.

"Trouble's teeth flash like lightning," thought Jahdu. "And what a large earring he wears on his right ear."

"What are you staring at, Jahdu?" the giant, Trouble, asked. "You like my ears? Oh, it's my earring you stare at. Come closer, Jahdu, and I'll show it to you."

"Oh, no thank you," said Jahdu. "I really have to be running on."

But Jahdu kept right on staring at the giant, Trouble. Trouble's feet were as big as steamships. His legs were as long as highways.

Attached to Trouble's ear was a gold loop as round and bright as the moon. An upright blue keg hung from the gold loop. The keg was as large as a water tower and screams and cries came from inside it.

"What in the world are those sounds from your earring?" asked Jahdu.

"Why, Jahdu, old friend, that's Trouble's barrel," said the giant. "I love all my friends, so I keep them with me!" Then Trouble laughed like thunder.

"Well, the friends you love are screaming," said Jahdu to the giant. "I'm sure they want you to let them out."

"Screams and cries are sounds I like best," said the giant. "Besides, no one I put in my barrel has ever got out again."

"But what sort of friends would even a giant like you treat so badly?" asked Jahdu.

"All kinds of friends," Trouble said. "I don't care if they are good or bad or big or little. Trouble treats every kind of folks just the same. I never bother them but they seek me out and swarm over me like flies."

"Woogily!" said Jahdu. "I surely wouldn't want to end up like a fly in your barrel!"

"Oh, come, come!" said Trouble. "Take a look. I've got a whole bunch of fine folks traveling with me."

With one huge finger, Trouble tipped his barrel so Jahdu could see inside. Staying out of Trouble's reach, Jahdu climbed the tallest tree he could find to have a look.

"That's about the worst sight I've ever seen," said Jahdu.

Jahdu saw all manner of flying birds in the barrel. He saw forest animals. He saw a lion. He saw mothers and fathers and babies and donkeys. He saw all kinds of life in that awful barrel of Trouble.

Now Jahdu grew angry. His face looked fierce. He knew he didn't like the giant, Trouble, at all. Suddenly Jahdu thought of a plan to free all those who were in Trouble's barrel.

Jahdu climbed down the tree and started running along close to the giant.

"You must set them loose," Jahdu said to Trouble. "If you don't put that barrel down on the ground and let everybody out, I will have to free them myself!"

"Come ahead, little Jahdu," said the giant. "Come right on in." When Jahdu came close to the giant, Trouble's hand swooped down in a rush of wind and scooped him up.

"Oh, please, giant, Trouble, don't put me in your barrel," said Jahdu. "I was really just running along." He pretended to be frightened and moaned as loudly as he could.

"You won't run along ever again," said Trouble. And, plop! He dropped Jahdu into his barrel.

"It's Jahdu!" shouted everybody in the barrel. "Trouble's caught Jahdu! It's the end of us for sure!"

"Hi, everybody!" said Jahdu. "I want all of you to gather around close to me, please. We're getting out of here!"

"We are?" everybody asked.

"Of course," said Jahdu. "Do you think I would have allowed Trouble to catch me if I wasn't planning to get free again?"

"Oh, Jahdu, you're wonderful!" everybody said.

Jahdu felt so good he said, "Woogily!" in

a loud voice. Then Jahdu told everybody what they must do.

"Mothers and fathers, dig under the walls of this barrel. Babies, you scratch at the sides. Birds, you peck away. Donkeys, you kick. You, lion, use your claws to tear at the floors. We've got to make lots of holes. Now, cows and horses, set up a mooing and neighing so Trouble won't know what's going on."

Everybody did what Jahdu said to do. After an hour not one of them had made a dent in Trouble's barrel.

"Woogily!" whispered Jahdu. "It will take forever to get us out of *this* barrel of Trouble. I see I'm going to have to outsmart that giant if I'm to free his friends."

While everybody was busy digging and neighing and scratching and clawing, Jahdu started running around the barrel. He ran faster and faster. Yes, he did. Soon the dust of himself rose up in the barrel. The Jahdu dust settled on everybody. And one by one, everybody in the barrel fell fast asleep. When everybody was asleep, Jahdu lay down and pretended he was asleep also.

Now Trouble still lay across the southward landscape listening to the screams and cries from his barrel. The screams and cries were like music to his ears. But after a time, Trouble didn't hear even one scream or cry.

"Hey, friends," Trouble called out of the side of his mouth. "Sing a little louder. I can't hear you."

Not one sound came from Trouble's barrel. Trouble took off his earring and peered inside the barrel. He couldn't believe his eyes. No, he couldn't. For he found everybody stretched out at the bottom of the barrel.

"Why, they've all fainted from the heat. Even the last one's fainted — little Jahdu," said the giant.

Carefully Trouble gathered everybody and Jahdu from the bottom of the barrel. And he laid everybody and Jahdu out on the ground.

"They need to lie down by a cool mountain lake for awhile," Trouble said. "Let's see. There's a lake in the mountains northward. I'll lay them over there."

Trouble picked up everybody and Jahdu in one hand. He stood up and held out his arm aross the long, empty land to the mountains in the north. Then Trouble set everybody and Jahdu down beside a cool mountain lake.

Said the giant, "I'll give my friends a chance to cool themselves now so they will feel more like screaming and crying later."

Again, Trouble lay down across the southward landscape. At once Jahdu got up and began running along. He ran as slowly as he knew how. Soon Jahdu dust rose off everybody and settled back into Jahdu. Everybody woke up. Yes, they did.

"We are in the mountains in the north," Jahdu told everybody. "I've outsmarted Trouble," added Jahdu. "He still lies resting, so be quiet and hear what I say."

"Those who live in water, dive deep under water and stay hidden as long as you can. Those who like holes, go hide in holes. Everybody else, follow the lion, for he knows where to find the oldest mountain cave. Trouble is sure to come searching for all of us soon, so hurry!"

It was not long before Trouble stood up and looked across the long, empty land for his friends beside the mountain lake. He saw only Jahdu, who was running along just out of the reach of Trouble's long arm.

"Little Jahdu," Trouble said, "that's the first time anybody has ever tricked me."

"I didn't trick you at all," said Jahdu. "I used my head and my magic. I thought of a plan to outsmart you. There's no need for you to search for your friends either," Jahdu added. "You might find two or three of them but you'll never find everybody."

The giant shook with laughter, making the earth tremble. "I don't need to go looking for them, little friend," he said to Jahdu. "I've never had to go looking for anybody. For it's the truth that everybody comes looking for Trouble and they always will."

"Not *me*!" said Jahdu. "I'll not come looking for you ever again!"

"Oh, sure you will," said Trouble. "You won't be able to help yourself. So, good-bye, little friend, until the next time." Trouble turned away. With three of his giant steps he was out of sight beyond the long, empty land.

"Woogily!" whispered Jahdu. "I hope I

never run into Trouble again!''

So it was that Jahdu met Trouble and was able to outsmart him. And Jahdu came to believe he was smarter than anyone.

THIS IS THE END OF THE HEAVY JAHDU STORY MAMA LUKA TOLD ONE DAY TO THE CHILD, LEE EDWARD.

▬▬▬

Little Badger and the Fire Spirit, *by Maria Campbell. Ill. by David Maclagan (Toronto: McClelland and Stewart, 1977).*

Canadian Metis writer Maria Campbell has written that she created this literary pourquoi myth because she wished to examine the Native belief in guardian spirits. In the circular journey of Little Badger are found several elements also seen in traditional Native stories: the four-fold testing pattern, the necessity of a solitary journey, and the rapport between human beings and animals. The story's framework represents an important aspect of contemporary Native life: the attempts of young people to discover their cultural heritage by learning from old people. This story can be contrasted with the Greek myth of Prometheus, an embodiment of the spirit of Greek humanism.

Little Badger and the Fire Spirit

GLOSSARY

Ahsinee	Stone
	Her name is Red Stone Woman.
Kookoom	Grandmother
Mooshoom	Grandfather
Ma-he-kun	Wolf
Waa-hi	Exclamation
	i.e. Good Gracious
Mas-cha-can-is una	He was a coyote, that one.
Ni-kis-kis-in aqua	I remember now.

Ahsinee was going to visit her grandparents, Mooshoom and Kookoom. She was so happy she could hardly wait to get there. It was her eighth birthday and for a present she could spend the whole summer with them. How lucky could a little girl be!

Mooshoom and Kookoom lived in a little log house right beside a huge lake called Lac La Biche. Here Mooshoom spent his days mending nets for the fishermen who fished in the big lake, and making snow shoes for the trappers who went far into the wilderness to trap when the first snows came.

Kookoom, too, had much work to keep her busy. She had a small garden to look after, and fish and meat to smoke and dry on the racks set up outside. She also had hides to tan, and plenty of sewing and beading to do. She had many grandchildren who wore the beautiful moccasins she sewed and decorated with dyed porcupine quills and beads.

Ahsinee lived only ten miles from Mooshoom and Kookoom. For a little girl, it was like a million miles away.

She talked excitedly as she and her father bounced along the rough dirt road in the old pick-up truck. They arrived just as the sun was going down over the lake, the last rays casting a golden glow over the calm water.

Mooshoom's old dog, Ma-he-kun, limped out to meet them as they stopped in the yard. He wagged his tail in welcome. There was a light in the kitchen window, and as Ahsinee jumped from the truck, she could smell freshly baked bannock and rabbit stew, which was her very favourite. She had not realized she was so hungry.

Kookoom bustled around the old black wood stove warming the stew and bannock, which she served with steaming cups of tea. Ahsinee sat down and ate and ate, until Mooshoom reminded her that Kookoom had baked some fresh Saskatoon pie. Ahsinee was so full she could only smile and nod her head. Yes, she had room for pie.

Soon they were all done and Kookoom got up to wash the dishes and clean the table. This was the time of day that Ahsinee loved best.

It was always the same in the evening with the two old people. When Kookoom finished cleaning the supper dishes, she took her sewing to the table and began her work. Mooshoom built up the fire to take away the chill of evening. Then he sat across from Kookoom to mend his nets. Kookoom smiled at Ahsinee because they both knew that Mooshoom would soon fall asleep.

Ahsinee sat between them, and after a time of silence, she would go to the cupboard where Mooshoom kept his pipe and tobacco. Giving the pipe to the old man, she would ask for a story.

This evening Ahsinee could hardly wait. She had something special to ask Mooshoom. Maybe the old man would not have a story for this question, but Ahsinee rushed over to the cupboard for the pipe and tobacco. In her hurry, she forgot old Ma-he-kun lying by the stove, and tripped over him. What a commotion! The old dog yelped so loudly that Mooshoom, who was sleeping soundly, woke up with a start. Kookoom began to laugh.

"Waa-hi," said Mooshoom, as he helped Ahsinee up. "You always be in such a hurry. Here, sit down and rest before you get us all tired. We are old, remember, and our days of hurry are over."

Old Ma-he-kun growled in agreement.

Kookoom smiled as she bit the thread from the needle and said, "Speak for yourself and your dog, Old Man."

Mooshoom filled his pipe. As he packed the tobacco, he looked at Ahsinee.

"Your Kookoom makes jokes about my old bones. Pay her no mind for she has loved them for many years now."

Kookoom smiled and did not reply.

"Now, my girl," said Mooshoom, "what is it you want to know? It must be very important if you could not sit still for a moment and let your belly rest."

"Fire, Mooshoom," said Ahsinee at last. "How did our people get fire?"

"Aaah . . . that is a good question. Let me think for a while. Perhaps I will remember."

The old man sat back and puffed on his pipe.

He puffed and puffed. Finally he laid down his pipe and began to mend the net. He worked for a long time, then he looked across at Kookoom.

"Do you remember the animal's name?" he asked her.

Animal? Ahsinee looked at them. What did animals have to do with fire? perhaps Mooshoom had forgotten.

"Mas-cha-can-is una," Kookoom replied.

"Aaah," interrupted Mooshoom, raising his hand. "Ni-kis-kis-in aqua, the Grey Coyote." He took a big puff from his pipe and began to speak.

It was a long time ago when our mother, the earth, was young. In those days, people and animals all spoke one language. There was one animal who was a very good friend of the people and he often came to visit them. His name was Grey Coyote.

Now, Grey Coyote was a gentle and considerate creature. He was also very wise. When he visited, the people all gathered around and listened to him speak. Grey Coyote had one friend who was special, a boy named Little Badger.

Grey Coyote and Little Badger spent many hours talking. You see, Little Badger was blind. Grey Coyote took him on many long walks in the forest. He taught Little Badger about the earth he could not see, and how to smell, hear and touch all the things around him. He taught him that everything on the earth—human, animal, insect or plant—had a purpose. This purpose was to serve and help each other.

Little Badger's people lived in a world of plenty. Mother earth gave them all they needed. There was never any want. However, with so much good, there had to be some bad. For Little Badger's people, the bad was the long, cold winters. On winter days, the people took refuge in their teepees, huddled together for warmth.

One cold day, as Little Badger shivered under his robe, he thought: *There must be some way for us to be warm. But how? Grey Coyote will know what to do. I will go and find him.*

And he set off to find Grey Coyote.

Outside, the wind howled in rage and blew snow around Little Badger's head. He pulled his robe tightly around himself and started for the forest.

Grey Coyote told me if I ever needed him, I was to sit under this pine tree and think very hard. He said he would hear me and come, thought Little Badger. He sat down under the tall pine and began to concentrate on Grey

Coyote.

Grey Coyote was trotting through the forest when he heard a voice calling to him. He stopped and listened.

It is Little Badger, he thought. *I must hurry. He sounds very weak.*

Grey Coyote headed for the pine tree as fast as he could run. When he arrived, Little Badger was so cold his teeth rattled when he tried to talk.

"What is wrong, Little Brother?" asked Grey Coyote.

"My people are freezing to death," chattered Little Badger. "You must help us."

"How thoughtless of me," said Grey Coyote. "I have a warm coat, and I never thought of my brothers and sisters. Here, I will shield you from the cold." Grey Coyote wrapped himself around Little Badger.

"You must help us, Grey Coyote," Little Badger pleaded. "You are wise. There must be some way for us to keep warm in the winter."

Grey Coyote thought and thought. Slowly he said, "Yes, there is a way, Little Brother, but it is very dangerous."

"Tell me, Grey Coyote, before my people perish," cried Little Badger.

"There is a mountain far away from our land. Inside the mountain is fire. This fire is strange. It feeds on wood and rock and it burns forever. It would provide warmth for the people. But someone must go inside the mountain to get it."

"I will go," said Little Badger.

"Wait. I am not finished," warned Grey Coyote. "Inside the mountain lives the Fire Spirit. He has four strange creatures who stand guard for him.

"There is Mountain Goat who can stab you with his horns, Mountain Lion who can tear you apart with his claws, Grizzly Bear who can kill you with one slap of his mighty paw, and Rattlesnake whose teeth hold deadly poison. And remember, Little Brother, you are blind and will not be able to see these dangers."

"I will still go," insisted Little Badger. "Will you take me to this place?"

Grey Coyote thought for a while.

"Yes, I will take you. Go back to your people. Find among them one hundred of the fastest runners. Bring them here tomorrow when the sun comes up."

"Where are you going?" asked Little Badger as Grey Coyote turned to leave.

"I am going to call the spirits to help us," said Grey Coyote as he trotted away.

The next morning, when Little Badger met Grey Coyote by the pine tree, he had with him one hundred of the fastest runners and the wise men of the tribe. They held council, and the wise men asked the Great Spirit for strength, endurance and courage for Little Badger, Grey Coyote and the runners.

Then Grey Coyote spoke.

"I have talked to the spirits and they have given me guidance for our journey. They will do all in their power to help us reach the great mountain. Once we are there, Little Badger must go into the mountain alone. No power can help him until he has climbed back outside with the fire."

Now Grey Coyote said to the runners: "You must follow the direction in which I am pointing. That is where the mountain is."

He turned to the first runner. "You must run with Little Badger on your shoulders. When you have run as far as you can, the second runner will take Little Badger and do the same thing. You must wait where you are. When the last runner has gone as far as he can, I will meet him. From there, Little Badger and I will go on alone.

"I have told you of the journey there," continued Grey Coyote. "Now I will tell you of the journey back. Instead of carrying Little Badger, you will carry a stick of burning wood. You will bring it back here the same way you carried Little Badger. When you arrive here, the people of the tribe will feed the fire with small pieces of wood and keep it burning until Little Badger and I return."

The runners nodded and, picking up Little Badger, the first one started off. He ran so fast Little Badger felt he was flying through the air.

Finally, after many days, the last runner went as far as he could go. When he stopped, Grey Coyote appeared and led Little Badger to the foot of the mountain.

"Here is the mountain, Little Brother," said Grey Coyote. "From here the spirits will guide and help you to the top. Once you reach the top, you must climb down the hole and get the fire yourself. When you have the fire and have climbed out, the spirits will help you down again. I will beat this drum and sing until you return."

Little Badger took a deep breath. He was frightened, but he knew that if he failed, his people would continue to die from the cold. He listened to the beat of the drum. Suddenly, he did not feel frightened anymore and he began to climb. As he climbed, he felt the spirit of the wind steadying him, and the spirit of the rocks made the way smooth. When he reached the top, he stopped to rest. He felt a last breath of air, then it was gone and he knew he was alone. The spirits had left him.

Little Badger stood wondering how he was going to find the opening in the mountain. He began to move around slowly and to feel with his hands. A wave of warm air touched him and he knew he had found the entrance to the place of fire. He stopped and listened for a moment. When he again heard the drum Grey Coyote was beating, he carefully started down.

Suddenly, Little Badger heard a gruff voice: "WHAT ARE YOU DOING HERE? THIS PLACE IS FORBIDDEN TO YOU!"

Almost paralyzed with fear, he stayed very still. He knew he had come upon one of the guardians of the fire as it was told to him by Grey Coyote, but he did not know which one.

"I have come to see the Fire Spirit," he said, his voice shaking. "My people are cold and he is the only one who can help us."

NO ONE CAN SEE THE FIRE SPIRIT," said the gruff voice. "YOU CANNOT PASS BY ME. IF YOU TRY, THEN I WILL KILL YOU."

Little Badger's heart pounded with fear. He had no weapons. He could not even see his enemy. As he clung to the rock ledge, he could hear Grey Coyote's drum beating. The sound comforted him, and his fear was gone. He reached out towards the voice. When he touched the creature, it trembled, and Little Badger could feel coarse hair.

"WHY DO YOU DO THAT?" grumbled the creature. "NO ONE TOUCHES ME. MY HORNS COULD TEAR YOU APART." The words were angry, but the voice was frightened.

"Do not be afraid," said Little Badger gently. "I will not hurt you. As you can see, I have no weapons. I am blind. To know who you are, I must touch you. Ah, you are the Mountain Goat."

When Little Badger touched the Mountain Goat, he felt peace come over them. He told the creature of his mission.

The goat listened, then said, "I WILL LET YOU GO BY, BUT I CANNOT HELP YOU GO BACK. BEWARE. THERE ARE THREE MORE GUARDIANS YOU MUST PASS BEFORE YOU REACH THE FIRE SPIRIT. I WISH YOU GOOD FORTUNE, LITTLE BROTHER."

Little Badger continued climbing down inside the mountain. As he descended, he could feel the heat of the fire. When he heard a soft growl, he knew he had met the Mountain Lion.

Little Badger reached out and touched the animal. As he stroked the smooth fur, he told the Lion of his people. They could hear the drum far off in the distance and again peace settled over both of them.

Little Badger continued his slow climb down. He knew he still had to meet the Grizzly Bear and the Rattlesnake, but he was no longer afraid. If things went on as they had, he knew he would make two new friends.

It was true. When he met the Grizzly Bear and touched him, they became friends. The Bear warned him that the Rattlesnake was very dangerous.

"YOU MUST BE VERY CAREFUL, LITTLE BROTHER," he rumbled in his great voice, as the boy turned to go. "YOU MUST USE WISDOM TO GET BY RATTLER, FOR HIS MEDICINE IS VERY POWERFUL."

Little Badger continued his climb down towards the fire. Soon he met the Rattlesnake. The Snake coiled, rattled his tail and raised his mighty head up to strike.

When Little Badger heard the sound of the rattle, he quickly said, "You must be the Snake. What a beautiful rattle you have."

Rattlesnake was so surprised that someone, especially a small boy, would dare to talk to him, and find him beautiful, that he relaxed without even realizing he had done so.

"WHY ARE YOU NOT AFRAID OF ME?" he hissed.

"I do not want to hurt you, so why should you want to hurt me?" replied Little Badger.

Rattlesnake was astonished at the little boy's words. He was thinking about what the boy had said and did not notice him leave to continue his climb.

Little Badger had almost finished his journey to meet the Fire Spirit. It was so hot, he felt his braids must be singed. He was also very tired and he stumbled. As he tried to catch his balance, a voice crackled, "NO HUMAN BEING HAS EVER SEEN THE HOME OF THE FIRE SPIRIT. WHY ARE YOU HERE?"

Little Badger knew that at last he had met the Fire Spirit.

"I cannot see your home," replied Little Badger, "for I am blind. It is very warm. If my people lived here, they would never be cold."

"COLD? COLD?" said the Fire Spirit. "WHAT IS COLD?"

As he talked, he flamed up and all the colours of the rainbow seemed to glow around him.

Little Badger could not see the flames but he felt a gust of warm air as the Spirit spoke.

"When the snows come," explained Little Badger, "my people are very cold. There is not enough warmth from the sun, so many of them die. I have come to ask you for fire to warm my people."

"TELL ME MORE," said the Fire Spirit. "I HAVE NEVER TALKED TO A HUMAN BEFORE AND THERE IS MUCH I DO NOT KNOW."

Little Badger sat down. He told the Fire Spirit about his land and his people. He told of his journey into the heart of the mountain and of the friends he had made along the way. The Fire Spirit was quiet for a long time. All that Little Badger could hear was the hiss of his flames.

Finally the Spirit spoke: "HOW LONG HAVE YOU BEEN BLIND?"

"All my life," replied Little Badger. "But I can feel and hear very well. Grey Coyote has taught me. He is like my eyes."

"GREY COYOTE? WHO IS HE?" asked the Spirit.

"Grey Coyote is my friend," said Little Badger. He told the Fire Spirit how his friend had taught him about the world.

"He brought me to this mountain and he is waiting for me now. Listen. Can you hear him? He is beating a drum."

The Fire Spirit listened. "YES, I CAN HEAR HIM," he replied.

"The drum gave me courage and strength," said Little Badger. "It helped me make new friends."

Little Badger and the Fire Spirit sat together for a long time and listened to the faint beating of the drum.

"IT IS STRONG AND BEAUTIFUL MUSIC," said the Fire Spirit. "I WILL NEVER FORGET IT. . . . HERE, TAKE THIS BURNING STICK. IT IS THE WARMTH OF FRIENDSHIP THAT YOU BROUGHT TO THIS PLACE. IT WILL KEEP YOUR PEOPLE WARM FOREVER."

Little Badger was bursting with gratitude.

"DO NOT THANK ME FOR IT, LITTLE BROTHER. YOU SHARED YOUR WARMTH WITH ME, AND I WILL SHARE MINE WITH YOU. WHEN YOU REACH THE TOP OF THE MOUNTAIN, YOU WILL NO LONGER BE BLIND. YOU WILL SEE THE WORLD THAT YOUR FRIEND, GREY COYOTE, HAS TAUGHT YOU ABOUT. GO NOW, HE WAITS FOR YOU."

Little Badger took the stick, said goodbye to the Fire Spirit and began to climb up out of the mountain. As he climbed, he met his friends and said goodbye to them also.

When he reached the top, with the stick of fire in his hand, he saw a great light. He saw the world for the first time in his life.

He stopped for a long time and looked and looked at the world. It was so beautiful. His eyes filled with tears of happiness. He felt the Spirit of the wind touch his hair gently and whisper, "Listen, Little Brother."

From far below, at the foot of the mountain, came the beating of the drum. As Little Badger listened, he heard two drums, then three.

How can there be three drums? he wondered. He listened again. Now there were four, five, then six drums. Soon the air was filled with the sound of many drums, all of different sizes, making different and beautiful sounds.

Suddenly Little Badger smiled. He knew. Grey Coyote's magic drum was his heartbeat.

The other drums were the beating hearts of all living things.

Little Badger laughed as he climbed down the mountain. Around him was the sound of the drums, the pulse of the world, the music of the universe.

. . . THE MUSIC OF THE UNIVERSE.

The story was finished, and Ahsinee's eyes were shining as she said, "Oh, Mooshoom, it was a beautiful story. But what happened to the fire?"

Mooshoom struck a match to light his pipe, then answered her.

"Little Badger brought the fire home to his people, and we have it to this day."

"Tell me another story about Little Badger," Ahsinee pleaded.

"It is time for bed, my girl," Kookoom said. "There will be many more stories later. We have all summer, remember."

Ahsinee could hear a loon calling from across the lake as she snuggled down in the soft feather bed.

Yes, they had all summer together, and Mooshoom and Kookoom had so many stories to tell.

"The Elephant's Child," from Just So Stories, *by Rudyard Kipling (London and Basingstoke: MacMillan Children's Books, 1902; rpt. 1983).*

Rudyard Kipling's famous Just So Stories *offer the reader humorous pourquoi myths. In the following tale the "elephant's child," so full of "'satiable curtiosity" goes on a quest to discover what the crocodile eats for dinner. He not only learns the answer but returns home with a new and useful, if homely, nose. Kipling's self-conscious use of the conventions of pourquoi myths not only achieves humorous effects but also functions satirically to show up the foolishness of human beings through animal characters.*

The Elephant's Child

In the High and Far-Off Times the Elephant, O Best Beloved, had no trunk. He had only a blackish, bulgy nose, as big as a boot, that he could wriggle about from side to side; but he couldn't pick up things with it. But there was one Elephant—a new Elephant—an Elephant's Child—who was full of 'satiable curtiosity, and that means he asked ever so many questions. *And* he lived in Africa, and he filled all Africa with his 'satiable curtiosities. He asked his tall aunt, the Ostrich, why her tail-feathers grew just so, and his tall aunt the Ostrich spanked him with her hard, hard claw. He asked his tall uncle, the Giraffe, what made his skin spotty, and his tall uncle, the Giraffe, spanked him with his hard, hard hoof. And still he was full of 'satiable curtiosity! He asked his broad aunt, the Hippopotamus, why her eyes were red, and his broad aunt, the Hippopotamus, spanked him with her broad, broad hoof; and he asked his hairy uncle, the Baboon, why melons tasted just so, and his hairy uncle, the Baboon, spanked him with his hairy, hairy paw. And *still* he was full of 'satiable curtiosity! He asked questions about everything that he saw, or heard, or felt, or smelt, or touched, and all his uncles and his aunts spanked him. And still he was full of 'satiable curtiosity!

One fine morning in the middle of the Precession of the Equinoxes this 'satiable Elephant's Child asked a new fine question that he had never asked before. He asked, 'What does the Crocodile have for dinner?' Then everybody said, 'Hush!' in a loud and dretful tone, and they spanked him immediately and directly, without stopping, for a long time.

By and by, when that was finished, he came upon Kolokolo Bird sitting in the middle of a wait-a-bit thorn-bush, and he said, 'My father has spanked me, and my mother has spanked me; all my aunts and uncles have spanked me for my 'satiable curtiosity; and *still* I want to know what the Crocodile has for dinner!'

Then Kolokolo Bird said, with a mournful cry, 'Go to the banks of the great grey-green, greasy Limpopo River, all set about with fever-trees, and find out.'

That very next morning, when there was nothing left of the Equinoxes, because the Precession had preceded according to precedent, this 'satiable Elephant's Child took a hundred pounds of bananas (the little short red kind), and a hundred pounds of sugar-cane (the long

"The Elephant's Child" from *Just So Stories,* by Rudyard Kipling. Copyright © 1902. Reprinted by permission of The National Trust for Places of Historic Interest or Natural Beauty and Macmillan London Ltd.

purple kind), and seventeen melons (the greeny-crackly kind), and said to all his dear families, 'Good-bye. I am going to the great grey-green, greasy Limpopo River, all set about with fever-trees, to find out what the Crocodile has for dinner.' And they all spanked him once more for luck, though he asked them most politely to stop.

Then he went away, a little warm, but not at all astonished, eating melons, and throwing the rind about, because he could not pick it up.

He went from Graham's Town to Kimberley, and from Kimberley to Khama's Country, and from Khama's Country he went east by north, eating melons all the time, till at last he came to the banks of the great grey-green, greasy Limpopo River, all set about with fever-trees, precisely as Kolokolo Bird had said.

Now you must know and understand, O Best Beloved, that till that very week, and day, and hour, and minute, this 'satiable Elephant's Child had never seen a Crocodile, and did not know what one was like. It was all his 'satiable curtiosity.

The first thing that he found was a Bi-Coloured-Python-Rock-Snake curled round a rock.

' 'Scuse me,' said the Elephant's Child most politely, 'but have you seen such a thing as a Crocodile in these promiscuous parts?'

'*Have* I seen a Crocodile?' said the Bi-Coloured-Python-Rock-Snake, in a voice of dretful scorn. 'What will you ask me next?'

''Scuse me,' said the Elephant's Child, 'but could you kindly tell me what he has for dinner?'

Then the Bi-Coloured-Python-Rock-Snake uncoiled himself very quickly from the rock, and spanked the Elephant's Child with his scalesome, flailsome tail.

'That is odd,' said the Elephant's Child, 'because my father and my mother, and my uncle and my aunt, not to mention my other aunt, the Hippopotamus, and my other uncle, the Baboon, have all spanked me for my 'satiable curtiosity — and I suppose this is the same thing.'

So he said good-bye very politely to the Bi-Coloured-Python-Rock-Snake, and helped to coil him up on the rock again, and went on, a little warm, but not at all astonished, eating melons, and throwing the rind about, because he could not pick it up, till he trod on what he thought was a log of wood at the very edge of the great grey-green, greasy Limpopo River, all set about with fever-trees.

But it was really the Crocodile, O Best Beloved, and the Crocodile winked one eye — like this!

''Scuse me,' said the Elephant's Child most politely, 'but do you happen to have seen a Crocodile in these promiscuous parts?'

Then the Crocodile winked the other eye, and lifted half his tail out of the mud; and the Elephant's Child stepped back most politely, because he did not wish to be spanked again.

'Come hither, Little One,' said the Crocodile. 'Why do you ask such things?'

''Scuse me,' said the Elephant's Child most politely, 'but my father has spanked me, my mother has spanked me, not to mention my tall aunt, the Ostrich, and my tall uncle, the Giraffe, who can kick ever so hard, as well as my broad aunt, the Hippopotamus, and my hairy uncle, the Baboon, *and* including the Bi-Coloured-Python-Rock-Snake, with the scalesome, flailsome tail, just up the bank, who spanks harder than any of them; and *so*, if it's quite all the same to you, I don't want to be spanked any more.'

'Come hither, Little One,' said the Crocodile, 'for I am the Crocodile,' and he wept crocodile-tears to show it was quite true.

Then the Elephant's Child grew all breathless, and panted, and kneeled down on the bank and said, 'You are the very person I have been looking for all these long days. Will you please tell me what you have for dinner?'

'Come hither, Little One,' said the Crocodile, 'and I'll whisper.'

Then the Elephant's Child put his head down close to the Crocodile's musky, tusky mouth, and the Crocodile caught him by his little nose, which up to that very week, day, hour, and minute, had been no bigger than a boot, though much more useful.

'I think,' said the Crocodile — and he said

it between his teeth, like this — 'I think to-day I will begin with Elephant's Child!'

At this, O Best Beloved, the Elephant's Child was much annoyed, and he said, speaking through his nose, like this, 'Led go! You are hurtig be!'

Then the Bi-Coloured-Python-Rock-Snake scuffled down from the bank and said, 'My young friend, if you do not now, immediately and instantly, pull as hard as ever you can, it is my opinion that your acquaintance in the large-pattern leather ulster' (and by this he meant the Crocodile) 'will jerk you into yonder limpid stream before you can say Jack Robinson.'

This is the way Bi-Coloured-Python-rock-Snakes always talk.

Then the Elephant's Child sat back on his little haunches, and pulled, and pulled, and pulled, and his nose began to stretch. And the Crocodile floundered into the water, making it all creamy with great sweeps of his tail, and *he* pulled, and pulled, and pulled.

And the Elephant's Child's nose kept on stretching; and the Elephant's Child spread all his little four legs and pulled, and pulled, and pulled, and his nose kept on stretching; and the Crocodile threshed his tail like an oar, and *he* pulled, and pulled, and pulled, and at each pull the Elephant's nose grew longer and longer — and it hurt him hijjus!

Then the Elephant's Child felt his legs slipping, and he said through his nose, which was now nearly five feet long, 'This is too butch for be!'

Then the Bi-Coloured-Python-Rock-Snake came down from the bank, and knotted himself in the double-clove-hitch round the Elephant's Child's hind-legs, and said, 'Rash and inexperienced traveller, we will now seriously devote ourselves to a little high tension, because if we do not, it is my impression that yonder self-propelling man-of-war with the armour-plated upper deck' (and by this, O Best Beloved, he meant the Crocodile) 'will permanently vitiate your future career.'

That is the way all Bi-Coloured-Python-Rock-Snakes always talk.

So he pulled, and the Elephant's Child pulled, and the Crocodile pulled; but the Elephant's Child and the Bi-Coloured-Python-Rock-Snake pulled hardest; and at last the Crocodile let go of the Elephant's Child's nose with a plop that you could hear all up and down the Limpopo.

Then the Elephant's Child sat down most hard and sudden; but first he was careful to say 'Thank you' to the Bi-Coloured-Python-Rock-Snake; and next he was kind to his poor pulled nose, and wrapped it all up in cool banana leaves, and hung it in the great grey-green, greasy Limpopo to cool.

'What are you doing that for?' said the Bi-Coloured-Python-Rock-Snake.

''Scuse me,' said the Elephant's Child, 'but my nose is badly out of shape, and I am waiting for it to shrink.'

'Then you will have to wait a long time,' said the Bi-Coloured-Python-Rock-Snake. 'Some people do not know what is good for them.'

The Elephant's Child sat there for three days waiting for his nose to shrink. But it never grew any shorter, and, besides, it made him squint. For, O Best Beloved, you will see and understand that the Crocodile had pulled it out into a really truly trunk same as all Elephant's have to-day.

At the end of the third day a fly came and stung him on the shoulder, and before he knew what he was doing he lifted up his trunk and hit that fly dead with the end of it.

''Vantage number one!' said the Bi-Coloured-Python-Rock-Snake. 'You couldn't have done that with a mere-smear nose. Try and eat a little now.'

Before he thought what he was doing the Elephant's Child put out his trunk and plucked a large bundle of grass, dusted it clean against his fore-legs, and stuffed it into his own mouth.

''Vantage number two!' said the Bi-Coloured-Python-Rock-Snake. 'You couldn't have done that with a mere-smear nose. Don't you think the sun is very hot here?'

'It is,' said the Elephant's Child, and before he thought what he was doing he schlooped up a schloop of mud from the banks of the great grey-green, greasy Limpopo, and slapped it on his head, where it made a cool schloopy-sloshy mud-cap all trickly behind his ears.

''Vantage number three!' said the Bi-Coloured-Python-Rock-Snake. 'You couldn't have done that with a mere-smear nose. Now how do you feel about being spanked again?'

''Scuse me,' said the Elephant's Child, 'but I should not like it at all.'

'How would you like to spank somebody?' said the Bi-Coloured-Python-Rock-Snake.

'I should like it very much indeed,' said the Elephant's Child.

'Well,' said the Bi-Coloured-Python-Rock-Snake, 'you will find that new nose of yours very useful to spank people with.'

'Thank you,' said the Elephant's Child. 'I'll remember that; and now I think I'll go home to all my dear families and try.'

So the Elephant's Child went home across Africa frisking and whisking his trunk. When he wanted fruit to eat he pulled fruit down from a tree, instead of waiting for it to fall as he used to do. When he wanted grass he plucked grass up from the ground, instead of going on his knees as he used to do. When the flies bit him he broke off the branch of a tree and used it as a fly-whisk; and he made himself a new, cool, slushy-squshy mud-cap whenever the sun was hot. When he felt lonely walking through Africa he sang to himself down his trunk, and the noise was louder than several brass bands. He went specially out of his way to find a broad Hippopotamus (she was no relation of his), and he spanked her very hard, to make sure that the Bi-Coloured-Python-Rock-Snake had spoken the truth about his new trunk. The rest of the time he picked up the melon-rinds that he had dropped on his way to the Limpopo — for he was a Tidy Pachyderm.

One dark evening he came back to all his dear families, and he coiled up his trunk and said, 'How do you do?' They were very glad to see him, and immediately said, 'Come here and be spanked for your 'satiable curtiosity.'

'Pooh!' said the Elephant's Child. 'I don't think you peoples know anything about spanking; but *I* do, and I'll show you.'

Then he uncurled his trunk and knocked two of his dear brothers head over heels.

'Oh Bananas!' said they, 'where did you learn that trick, and what have you done to your nose?'

'I got a new one from the Crocodile on the banks of the great grey-green, greasy Limpopo River,' said the Elephant's Child. 'I asked him what he had for dinner, and he gave me this to keep.'

'It looks very ugly,' said his hairy uncle, the Baboon.

'It does,' said the Elephant's Child. 'But it's very useful,' and he picked up his hairy uncle, the Baboon, by one hairy leg, and hove him into a hornets' nest.

Then that bad Elephant's Child spanked all his dear families for a long time, till they were very warm and greatly astonished. He pulled out his tall Ostrich aunt's tail-feathers; and he caught his tall uncle, the Giraffe, by the hind leg, and dragged him through a thorn-bush; and he shouted at his broad aunt, the Hippopotamus, and blew bubbles into her ear when she was sleeping in the water after meals; but he never let any one touch Kolokolo Bird.

At last things grew so exciting that his dear families went off one by one in a hurry to the banks of the great grey-green, greasy Limpopo River, all set about with fever-trees, to borrow new noses from the Crocodile. When they came back nobody spanked anybody any more; and ever since that day, O Best Beloved, all the Elephants you will ever see, besides all those that you won't, have trunks precisely like the trunk of the 'satiable Elephant's Child.

"Night Falls on Narnia," from The Last Battle, *by C.S. Lewis (New York: MacMillan Publishing Company, 1956).*

Few writers of any age have achieved such a comprehensive literary myth as C.S. Lewis's The Chronicles of Narnia. *This series of seven fantasies features the creation of Narnia, the gift of speech for Narnian animals, the coming of evil into Narnia, the death and resurrection of Aslan, the great divine Lion, and many other mythic episodes. In the final book, Lewis shows the sorrowful passing of Narnia and the joyful creation of a new and redeemed creation — the apocalyptic fulfillment of the prophecy of a "New Heaven and a New Earth."*

Night Falls on Narnia

They all stood beside Aslan, on his right side, and looked through the open doorway.

The bonfire had gone out. On the earth all was blackness: in fact you could not have told that you were looking into a wood, if you had not seen where the dark shapes of the trees ended and the stars began. But when Aslan had roared yet again, out on their left they saw another black shape. That is, they saw another patch where there were no stars: and the patch rose up higher and higher and became the shape of a man, the hugest of all giants. They all knew Narnia well enough to work out where he must be standing. He must be on the high moorlands that stretch away to the North beyond the River Shribble. Then Jill and Eustace remembered how once long ago, in the deep caves beneath those moors, they had seen a great giant asleep and been told that his name was Father Time, and that he would wake on the day the world ended.

"Yes," said Aslan, though they had not spoken. "While he lay dreaming his name was Time. Now that he is awake he will have a new one."

Then the great giant raised a horn to his mouth. They could see this by the change of the black shape he made against the stars. After that — quite a bit later, because sound travels so slowly — they heard the sound of the horn: high and terrible, yet of a strange, deadly beauty.

Immediately the sky became full of shooting stars. Even one shooting star is a fine thing to see; but these were dozens, and then scores, and then hundreds, till it was like silver rain: and it went on and on. And when it had gone on for some while, one or two of them began to think that there was another dark shape against the sky as well as the giant's. It was in a different place, right overhead, up in the very roof of the sky as you might call it. "Perhaps it is a cloud," thought Edmund. At any rate, there were no stars there: just blackness. But all around, the downpour of stars went on. And then the patch began to grow, spreading further and further out from the centre of the sky. And presently a quarter of the whole sky was black, and then a half, and at last the rain of shooting stars was going on only low down near the horizon.

With a thrill of wonder (and there was some terror in it too) they all suddenly realized what was happening. The spreading blackness was not a cloud at all: it was simply emptiness. The black part of the sky was the part in which there were no stars left. All the stars were falling: Aslan had called them home.

The last few seconds before the rain of stars had quite ended were very exciting. Stars began falling all round them. But stars in that world are not the great flaming globes they are in ours. They are people (Edmund and Lucy had once met one). So now they found showers of glittering people, all with long hair like burning silver and spears like white-hot metal, rushing down to them out of the black air, swifter than falling stones. They made a hissing noise as they landed and burnt the grass. And all these stars glided past them and stood somewhere behind, a little to the right.

This was a great advantage, because otherwise, now that there were no stars in the sky, everything would have been completely dark and you could have seen nothing. As it was, the crowd of stars behind them cast a fierce, white light over their shoulders. They could see mile upon mile of Narnian woods spread out before them, looking as if they were floodlit. Every bush and almost every blade of grass had its black shadow behind it. The edge of every leaf stood out so sharp that you'd think you could cut your finger on it.

On the grass before them lay their own shadows. But the great thing was Aslan's shadow. It streamed away to their left, enormous and very terrible. And all this was under a sky that would now be starless for ever.

The light from behind them (and a little to their right) was so strong that it lit up even the slopes of the Northern Moors. Something was moving there. Enormous animals were crawling and sliding down into Narnia: great dragons and giant lizards and featherless birds with wings like bat's wings. They disappeared into the woods and for a few minutes there was si-

Illustration by Pauline Baynes, ''Night Falls on Narnia'' from *The Last Battle* by C.S. Lewis. Copyright © 1956. Reprinted by permission of the Bodley Head.

lence. Then there came—at first from very far off—sounds of wailing and then, from every direction, a rustling and a pattering and a sound of wings. It came nearer and nearer. Soon one could distinguish the scamper of little feet from the padding of big paws, and the clack-clack of light little hoofs from the thunder of great ones. And then one could see thousands of pairs of eyes gleaming. And at last, out of the shadow of the trees, racing up the hill for dear life, by thousands and by millions, came all kinds of creatures — Talking Beasts, Dwarfs, Satyrs, Fauns, Giants, Calormenes, men from Archenland, Monopods and strange unearthly things from the remote islands or the unknown Western lands. And all these ran up to the doorway where Aslan stood.

This part of the adventure was the only one which seemed rather like a dream at the time and rather hard to remember properly afterwards. Especially, one couldn't say how long it had taken. Sometimes it seemed to have lasted only a few minutes, but at others it felt as if it might have gone on for years. Obviously, unless either the Door had grown very much larger or the creatures had suddenly grown as small as gnats, a crowd like that couldn't ever have tried to get through it. But no one thought about that sort of thing at the time.

The creatures came rushing on, their eyes brighter and brighter as they drew nearer and nearer to the standing Stars. But as they came right up to Aslan one or other of two things happened to each of them. They all looked straight in his face; I don't think they had any choice about that. And when some looked, the expression of their faces changed terribly — it was fear and hatred: except that, on the faces of Talking Beasts, the fear and hatred lasted only for a fraction of a second. You could see that they suddenly ceased to be *Talking* Beasts. They were just ordinary animals. And all the creatures who looked at Aslan in that way swerved to their right, his left, and disappeared into his huge black shadow, which (as you have heard) streamed away to the left of the doorway. The children never saw them again. I don't know what became of them. But the others looked in the face of Aslan and loved him, though some of them were very frightened at the same time. And all these came in at the Door, in on Aslan's right. There were some queer specimens among them. Eustace even recognised one of those very Dwarfs who had helped to shoot the Horses. But he had no time to wonder about that sort of thing (and anyway it was no business of his) for a great joy put everything else out of his head. Among the happy creatures who now came crowding round Tirian and his friends were all those whom they had thought dead. There was Roonwit the Centaur and Jewel the Unicorn, and the good Boar and the good Bear and Farsight the Eagle, and the dear Dogs and the Horses, and Poggin the Dwarf.

"Further in and higher up!" cried Roonwit and thundered away in a gallop to the West. And though they did not understand him, the words somehow set them tingling all over. The Boar grunted at them cheerfully. The Bear was just going to mutter that he still didn't understand, when he caught sight of the fruit trees behind them. He waddled to those trees as fast

as he could and there, no doubt, found something he understood very well. But the Dogs remained, wagging their tails and Poggin remained, shaking hands with everyone and grinning all over his honest face. And Jewel leaned his snowy white head over the King's shoulder and the King whispered in Jewel's ear. Then everyone turned his attention again to what could be seen through the Doorway.

The Dragons and Giant Lizards now had Narnia to themselves. They went to and fro tearing up the trees by the roots and crunching them up as if they were sticks of rhubarb. Minute by minute the forests disappeared. The whole country became bare and you could see all sorts of things about its shape — all the little humps and hollows — which you had never noticed before. The grass died. Soon Tirian found that he was looking at a world of bare rock and earth. You could hardly believe that anything had ever lived there. The monsters themselves grew old and lay down and died. Their flesh shrivelled up and the bones appeared: soon they were only huge skeletons that lay here and there on the dead rock, looking as if they had died thousands of years ago. For a long time everything was still.

At last something white — long, level line of whiteness that gleamed in the light of the standing stars — came moving towards them from the eastern end of the world. A widespread noise broke the silence: first a murmur, then a rumble, then a roar. And now they could see what it was that was coming, and how fast it came. It was a foaming wall of water. The sea was rising. In that treeless world you could see it very well. You could see all the rivers getting wider and the lakes getting larger, and separate lakes joining into one, and valleys turning into new lakes, and hills turning into islands, and then those islands vanishing. And the high moors to their left and the higher mountains to their right crumbled and slipped down with a roar and a splash into the mounting water; and the water came swirling up to the very threshold of the Doorway (but never passed it) so that the foam splashed about Aslan's forefeet. All now was level water from where they stood to where the water met the sky.

And out there it began to grow light. A streak of dreary and disastrous dawn spread along the horizon, and widened and grew brighter, till in the end they hardly noticed the light of the stars who stood behind them. At last the sun came up. When it did, the Lord Digory and the Lady Polly looked at one another and gave a little nod: those two, in a different world, had once seen a dying sun, and so they knew at once that this sun also was dying. It was three times — twenty times — as big as it ought to be, and very dark red. As its rays fell upon the great Time-giant, he turned red too: and in the reflection of that sun the whole waste of shoreless waters looked like blood.

Then the Moon came up, quite in her wrong position, very close to the sun, and she also looked red. And at the sight of her the sun began shooting out great flames, like whiskers or snakes of crimson fire, towards her. It is as if he were an octopus trying to draw her to himself in his tentacles. And perhaps he did draw her. At any rate she came to him, slowly at first, but then more and more quickly, till at last his long flames licked round her and the two ran together and became one huge ball like a burning coal. Great lumps of fire came dropping out of it into the sea and clouds of steam rose up.

Then Aslan said, "Now make an end."

The giant threw his horn into the sea. Then he stretched out one arm — very black it looked, and thousands of miles long — across the sky till his hand reached the Sun. He took the Sun and squeezed it in his hand as you would squeeze an orange. And instantly there was total darkness.

Everyone except Aslan jumped back from the ice-cold air which now blew through the Doorway. Its edges were already covered with icicles.

"Peter, High King of Narnia," said Aslan. "Shut the Door."

Peter, shivering with cold, leaned out into the darkness and pulled the Door to. It scraped over ice as he pulled it. Then, rather clumsily (for even in that moment his hands had gone numb and blue) he took out a golden key and locked it.

They had seen strange things enough through that Doorway. But it was stranger than any of them to look round and find themselves in warm daylight, the blue sky above them, flowers at their feet, and laughter in Aslan's eyes.

He turned swiftly round, crouched lower, lashed himself with his tail and shot away like a golden arrow.

"Come further in! Come further up!" he shouted over his shoulder. But who could keep up with him at that pace? They set out walking westward to follow him.

"So," said Peter, "Night falls on Narnia. What, Lucy! You're not *crying*? With Aslan ahead, and all of us here?"

"Don't try to stop me, Peter," said Lucy, "I am sure Aslan would not. I am sure it is not wrong to mourn for Narnia. Think of all that lies dead and frozen behind that door."

"Yes and I *did* hope," said Jill, "that it might go on for ever. I knew *our* world couldn't. I did think Narnia might."

"I saw it begin," said the Lord Digory. "I did not think I would live to see it die."

"Sirs," said Tirian. "The ladies do well to weep. See I do so myself. I have seen my mother's death. What world but Narnia have I ever known? It were no virtue, but great discourtesy, if we did not mourn."

They walked away from the Door and away from the Dwarfs who still sat crowded together in their imaginary Stable. And as they went they talked to one another about old wars and old peace and ancient Kings and all the glories of Narnia.

The Dogs were still with them. They joined in the conversation but not very much because they were too busy racing on ahead and racing back and rushing off to sniff at smells in the grass till they made themselves sneeze. Suddenly they picked up a scent which seemed to excite them very much. They all started arguing about it — "Yes it is — No it isn't — That's just what I said — anyone can smell what *that* is — Take your great nose out of the way and let someone else smell."

"What is it, cousins?" said Peter.

"A Calormene, Sire," said several Dogs at once.

"Lead on to him, then," said Peter. "Whether he meets us in peace or war, he shall be welcome."

The Dogs darted on ahead and came back a moment later, running as if their lives depended on it, and barking loudly to say that it really was a Calormene. (Talking Dogs, just like the common ones, behave as if they thought whatever they are doing at the moment, immensely important.)

The others followed where the Dogs led them and found a young Calormene sitting under a chestnut tree beside a clear stream of water. It was Emeth. He rose at once and bowed gravely.

"Sir," he said to Peter, "I know not whether you are my friend or my foe, but I should count it my honour to have you for either. Has not one of the poets said that a noble friend is the best gift and a noble enemy the next best?"

"Sir," said Peter, "I do not know that there need be any war between you and us."

"Do tell us who you are and what's happened to you," said Jill.

"If there's going to be a story, let's all have a drink and sit down," barked the Dogs. "We're quite blown."

"Well of course you will be, if you keep tearing about the way you have done," said Eustace.

So the humans sat down on the grass. And when the Dogs had all had a very noisy drink out of the stream they all sat down, bolt upright, panting, with their tongues hanging out of their heads a little on one side, to hear the story. But Jewel remained standing, polishing his horn against his side.

"Know, O Warlike Kings," said Emeth, "and you O Ladies, whose beauty illuminates the universe, that I am Emeth, the seventh son of Harpa Tarkaan of the city of Tehishbaan, Westward beyond the desert. I came lately into Narnia with nine and twenty others under the command of Rishda Tarkaan. Now when I first heard that we should march upon Narnia, I rejoiced; for I had heard many things of your Land and desired greatly to meet you in battle. But when I found that we were to go in disguised as merchants (which is a shameful dress for a warrior and the son of a Tarkaan) and to work by lies and trickery, then my joy departed from me. And most of all when I found we must wait upon a monkey, and when it began to be said that Tash and Aslan were one, then the world became dark in my eyes. For always since I was a boy, I have served Tash and my great desire was to know more of him and, if it might be, to look upon his face. But the name of Aslan was hateful to me.

"And, as you have seen, we were called together outside the straw-roofed hovel, night after night, and the fire was kindled, and the Ape brought forth out of the hovel something upon four legs that I could not well see. And the people and the Beasts bowed down and did honour to it. But I thought, the Tarkaan is deceived by the Ape: for this thing that comes out of the stable is neither Tash nor any other god. But when I watched the Tarkaan's face, and marked every word that he said to the Monkey, then I changed my mind: for I saw that the Tarkaan did not believe in it himself. And then I understood that he did not believe in Tash at all: for if he had, how could he dare to mock him?

"When I understood this, a great rage fell upon me and I wondered that the true Tash did not strike down both the Monkey and the Tarkaan with fire from heaven. Nevertheless I hid my anger and held my tongue and waited to see how it would end. But last night, as some of you know, the Monkey brought forth not the yellow thing, but said that all who desired to look upon Tashlan — for so they mixed the two words to pretend that they were all one — must pass one by one into the hovel. And I said to myself, Doubtless this is some other deception. But when the Cat had gone in and had come out again in a madness of terror, then I said to myself, Surely the true Tash, whom they called on without knowledge or belief, has now come among us, and will avenge himself. And though my heart was turned into water inside me because of the greatness and terror of Tash, yet my desire was stronger than my fear, and I put force upon my knees to stay them from trembling, and on my teeth that they should not chatter, and resolved to look upon the face of Tash, though he should slay me. So I offered myself to go into the hovel, and the Tarkaan, though unwillingly, let me go.

"As soon as I had gone through the door, the first wonder was that I found myself in this great sunlight (as we all are now) though the inside of the hovel had looked dark from outside. But I had no time to marvel at this, for immediately I was forced to fight for my head against one of our own men. As soon as I saw him I understood that the Monkey and the Tarkaan had set him there to slay any who came in if he were not in their secrets: so that this man also was a liar and a mocker and no true servant of Tash. I had the better will to fight him; and having slain the villain, I cast him out behind me through the door.

"Then I looked about me and saw the sky and the wide lands and smelled the sweetness. And I said, By the Gods, this is a pleasant place: it may be that I am come into the country of Tash. And I began to journey into the strange country and to seek him.

"So I went over much grass and many flowers and among all kinds of wholesome and delectable trees till lo! in a narrow place between two rocks there came to meet me a great Lion. The speed of him was like the ostrich, and his size was an elephant's; his hair was like pure gold and the brightness of his eyes, like gold that is liquid in the furnace. He was more terrible than the Flaming Mountain of Lagour, and in beauty he surpassed all that is in the world, even as the rose in bloom surpasses the dust of the desert. Then I fell at his feet and thought, Surely this is the hour of death, for the Lion (who is worthy of all honour) will know that I have served Tash all my days and not him. Nevertheless, it is better to see the Lion and die than to be Tisroc of the world and live and not to have seen him. But the Glorious One bent down his golden head and touched my forehead with his tongue and said, Son, thou art welcome. But I said, Alas, Lord, I am no son of Thine but the servant of Tash. He answered, Child, all the service thou hast done to Tash, I account as service done to me. Then by reason of my great desire for wisdom and understanding, I overcame my fear and questioned the Glorious One and said, Lord, is it then true, as the Ape said, that thou and Tash are one? The Lion growled so that the earth shook (but his

wrath was not against me) and said, It is false. Not because he and I are one, but because we are opposites, I take to me the services which thou hast done to him, for I and he are of such different kinds that no service which is vile can be done to me, and none which is not vile can be done to him. Therefore if any man swear by Tash and keep his oath for the oath's sake, it is by me that he has truly sworn, though he know it not, and it is I who reward him. And if any man do a cruelty in my name, then though he says the name Aslan, it is Tash whom he serves and by Tash his deed is accepted. Dost thou understand, Child? I said, Lord, thou knowest how much I understand. But I said also (for the truth constrained me), Yes, I have been seeking Tash all my days. Beloved, said the Glorious One, unless thy desire had been for me thou wouldst not have sought so long and so truly. For all find what they truly seek.

"Then he breathed upon me and took away the trembling from my limbs and caused me to stand upon my feet. And after that, he said not much but that we should meet again, and I must go further up and further in. Then he turned him about in a storm and flurry of gold and was gone suddenly.

"And since then, O Kings and Ladies, I have been wandering to find him and my happiness is so great that it even weakens me like a wound. And this is the marvel of marvels, that he called me, Beloved, me who am but as a dog — "

"Eh? What's that?" said one of the Dogs.

"Sir," said Emeth. "It is but a fashion of speech which we have in Calormen."

"Well, I can't say it's one I like very much," said the Dog.

"He doesn't mean any harm," said an older Dog. "After all, *we* call our puppies, *Boys*, when they don't behave properly."

"So we do," said the first Dog. "Or, *girls*."

"S-s-sh!" said the Old Dog. "That's not a nice word to use. Remember where you are."

"Look!" said Jill suddenly. Someone was coming, rather timidly, to meet them; a graceful creature on four feet, all silvery-grey. And they stared at him for a whole ten seconds before five or six voices said all at once, "Why, it's old Puzzle!" They had never seen him by day light with the lionskin off, and it made an extraordinary difference. He was himself now: a beautiful donkey with such a soft, grey coat and such a gentle, honest face that if you had seen him you would have done just what Jill and Lucy did — rushed forward and put your arms round his neck and kissed his nose and stroked his ears.

When they asked him where he had been, he said he had come in at the door along with all the other creatures but he had — well, to tell the truth, he had been keeping out of their way as much as he could; and out of Aslan's way. For the sight of the real Lion had made him so ashamed of all that nonsense about dressing up in a lionskin that he did not know how to look anyone in the face. But when he saw that all his friends were going away westward, and after he had had a mouthful or so of grass ("And I've never tasted such good grass in my life," said Puzzle), he plucked up his courage and followed. "But what I'll do if I really have to meet Aslan, I'm sure I don't know," he added.

"You'll find it will be all right when you really do," said Queen Lucy.

Then they all went forward together, always westward, for that seemed to be the direction Aslan had meant when he cried out "Further up and further in." Many other creatures were slowly moving the same way, but that grassy country was very wide and there was no crowding.

It still seemed to be early and the morning freshness was in the air. They kept on stopping to look round and to look behind them, partly because it was so beautiful but partly also because there was something about it which they could not understand.

"Peter," said Lucy, "where is this, do you suppose?"

"I don't know," said the High King. "It reminds me of somewhere but I can't give it a name. Could it be somewhere we once stayed for a holiday when we were very, very small?"

"It would have to have been a jolly good holiday," said Eustace. "I bet there isn't a country like this anywhere in *our* world. Look at the colours? You couldn't get a blue like the blue on those mountains in our world."

"Is it not Aslan's country?" said Tirian.

"Not like Aslan's country on top of that mountain beyond the eastern end of the world," said Jill. "I've been there."

"If you ask me," said Edmund, "It's like somewhere in the Narnian world. Look at those mountains ahead — and the big ice-mountains beyond them. Surely they're rather like the mountains we used to see from Narnia, the ones up Westward beyond the Waterfall?"

"Yes, so they are," said Peter. "Only these are bigger."

"I don't think *those* ones are so very like anything in Narnia," said Lucy. "But look there." She pointed southward to their left, and everyone stopped and turned to look. "Those hills," said Lucy, "the nice woody ones and the blue ones behind — aren't they very like the southern border of Narnia?"

"Like!" cried Edmund after a moment's silence. "Why they're exactly like. Look, there's Mount Pire with his forked head and there's the pass into Archenland and everything!"

"And yet they're not like," said Lucy. "They're different. They have more colours on them and they look further away than I remembered and they're more ... more ... oh, I don't know ...."

"More like the real thing," said the Lord Digory softly.

Suddenly Farsight the Eagle spread his wings, soared thirty or forty feet up into the air, circled round and then alighted on the ground.

"Kings and Queens," he cried, "we have all been blind. We are only beginning to see where we are. From up there I have seen it all — Ettinsmuir, Beaversdam, the Great River, and Cair Paravel still shining on the edge of the Eastern Sea. Narnia is not dead. This is Narnia."

"But how can it be?" said Peter. "For Aslan told us older ones that we should never return to Narnia, and here we are."

"Yes," said Eustace. "And we saw it all destroyed and the sun put out."

"And it's all so different," said Lucy.

"The Eagle is right," said the Lord Digory. "Listen, Peter. When Aslan said you could never go back to Narnia, he meant the Narnia you were thinking of. But that was not the real Narnia. That had a beginning and an end. It was only a shadow or a copy of the real Narnia, which has always been here and always will be here: just as our own world, England and all, is only a shadow or copy of something in Aslan's real world. You need not mourn over Narnia, Lucy. All of the old Narnia that mattered, all the dear creatures, have been drawn into the real Narnia through the Door. And of course it is different; as different as a real thing is from a shadow or as waking life is from a dream.'' His voice stirred everyone like a trumpet as he spoke these words: but when he added under his breath "It's all in Plato, all in Plato: bless me, what *do* they teach them at these schools!'' the older ones laughed. It was so exactly like the sort of thing they had heard him say long ago in that other world where his beard was grey instead of golden. He knew why they were laughing and joined in the laugh himself. But very quickly they all became grave again: for, as you know, there is a kind of happiness and wonder that makes you serious. It is too good to waste on jokes.

It is as hard to explain how this sunlit land was different from the old Narnia, as it would be to tell you how the fruits of that country taste. Perhaps you will get some idea of it, if you think like this. You may have been in a room in which there was a window that looked out on a lovely bay of the sea or a green valley that wound away among mountains. And in the wall of that room opposite to the window there may have been a looking glass. And as you turned away from the window you suddenly caught sight of that sea or that valley, all over again, in the looking glass. And the sea in the mirror, or the valley in the mirror, were in one sense just the same as the real ones: yet at the same time they were somehow different — deeper, more wonderful, more like places in a story: in a story you have never heard but very much want to know. The difference between the old Narnia and the new Narnia was like that. The new one was a deeper country: every rock and flower and blade of grass looked as if it meant more. I can't describe it any bet-

ter than that: if you ever get there, you will know what I mean.

It was the Unicorn who summed up what everyone was feeling. He stamped his right fore-hoof on the ground and neighed and then cried:

"I have come home at last! This is my real country! I belong here. This is the land I have been looking for all my life, though I never knew it till now. The reason why we loved the old Narnia is that it sometimes looked a little like this. Bree-hee-hee! Come further up, come further in!''

He shook his mane and sprang forward into a great gallop — a Unicorn's gallop which, in our world, would have carried him out of sight in a few moments. But now a most strange thing happened. Everyone else began to run, and they found, to their astonishment, that they could keep up with him: not only the Dogs and the humans but even fat little Puzzle and short-legged Poggin the Dwarf. The air flew in their faces as if they were driving fast in a car without a windscreen. The country flew past as if they were seeing it from the windows of an express train. Faster and faster they raced, but no one got hot or tired or out of breath. If one could run without getting tired, I don't think one would often want to do anything else. But there might be special reasons for stopping, and it was a special reason which made Eustace presently shout:

"I say! Steady! Look what we're coming to!''

And well he might. For now they saw before them Caldron Pool and beyond the Pool, the high unclimbable cliffs and, pouring down the cliffs, thousands of tons of water every second, flashing like diamonds in some places and dark, glassy green in others, the Great Waterfall; and already the thunder of it was in their ears.

"Don't stop! Further up and further in,'' called Farsight, tilting his flight a little upwards.

"It's all very well for *him*,'' said Eustace, but Jewel also cried out:

"Don't stop. Further up and further in! Take it in your stride.''

His voice could only just be heard above

the roar of the water but next moment every-one saw that he had plunged into the Pool. And helter-skelter behind him, with splash after splash, all the others did the same. The water was not bitingly cold as all of them (and especially Puzzle) expected, but of a delicious foamy coolness. They all found they were swimming straight for the Waterfall itself.

"This is absolutely crazy," said Eustace to Edmund.

"I know. And yet — " said Edmund.

"Isn't it wonderful?" said Lucy. "Have you noticed one can't feel afraid, even if one wants to? Try it."

"By Jove, one can't," said Eustace after he had tried.

Jewel reached the foot of the Waterfall first, but Tirian was only just behind him. Jill was last, so she could see the whole thing better than the others. She saw something white moving steadily up the face of the Waterfall. That white thing was the Unicorn. You couldn't tell whether he was swimming or climbing, but he moved on, higher and higher. The point of his horn divided the water just above his head, and it cascaded out in two rainbow-coloured streams all round his shoulders. Just behind him came King Tirian. He moved his legs and arms as if he were swimming but he moved straight upwards: as if one could swim up a wall.

What looked funniest was the Dogs. During the gallop they had not been at all out of breath, but now, as they swarmed and wriggled upwards, there was plenty of spluttering and sneezing among them; that was because they would keep on barking, and every time they barked they got their mouths and noses full of water. But before Jill had time to notice all these things fully, she was going up the Waterfall herself. It was the sort of thing that would have been quite impossible in our world. Even if you hadn't been drowned, you would have been smashed to pieces by the terrible weight of water against the countless jags of rock. But in that world you could do it. You went on, up and up, with all kinds of reflected lights flashing at you from the water and all manner of coloured stones flashing through it, till it seemed as if you were climbing up

light itself — and always higher and higher till the sense of height would have terrified you if you could be terrified, but here it was only gloriously exciting. And then at last one came to the lovely, smooth green curve in which the water poured over the top and found that one was out on the level river above the waterfall. The current was racing away behind you, but you were such a wonderful swimmer that you could make headway against it. Soon they were all on the bank, dripping but happy.

A long valley opened ahead and great snowmountains, now much nearer, stood up against the sky.

"Further up and further in," cried Jewel and instantly they were off again.

They were out of Narnia now and up into the Western Wild which neither Tirian nor Peter nor even the Eagle had ever seen before. But the Lord Digory and the Lady Polly had. "Do you remember? Do you remember?" they said — and said it in steady voices too, without panting, though the whole party was now running faster than an arrow flies.

"What, Lord?" said Tirian. "Is it then true, as stories tell, that you two journeyed here on the very day the world was made?"

"Yes," said Digory, "and it seems to me as if it were only yesterday."

"And on a flying horse?" asked Tirian. "Is that part true?"

"Certainly," said Digory. But the Dogs barked, "Faster, faster!"

So they ran faster and faster till it was more like flying than running, and even the Eagle overhead was going no faster than they. And they went through winding valley after winding valley and up the steep sides of hills and, faster than ever, down the other sides, following the river and sometimes crossing it and skimming across mountain-lakes as if they were living speedboats, till at last at the far end of one long lake, which looked as blue as a turquoise, they saw a smooth green hill.Its sides were as steep as the sides of a pyramid and round the very top of it ran a green wall: but above the wall rose the branches of trees, whose leaves looked like silver and their fruit like gold.

"Further up and further in!" roared the

Unicorn, and no one held back. They charged straight at the foot of the hill and then found themselves running up it almost as water from a broken wave runs up a rock out at the point of some bay. Though the slope was nearly as steep as the roof of a house and the grass was smooth as a bowling green, no one slipped. Only when they had reached the very top did they slow up; that was because they found themselves facing great golden gates. And for a moment none of them was bold enough to try if the gates would open. They all felt just as they had felt about the fruit — "Dare we? Is it right? Can it be meant for *us*?"

But while they were standing thus a great horn, wonderfully loud and sweet, blew from somewhere inside that walled garden and the gates swung open.

Tirian stood holding his breath and wondering who would come out. And what came out was the last thing he had expected: a little, sleek, bright-eyed Talking Mouse with a red feather stuck in a circlet on its head and its left paw resting on a long sword. It bowed, a most beautiful bow, and said in its shrill voice:

"Welcome, in the Lion's name. Come further up and further in."

Then Tirian saw King Peter and King Edmund and Queen Lucy rush forward to kneel down and greet the Mouse and they all cried out, "Reepicheep!" And Tirian breathed fast with the sheer wonder of it, for now he knew that he was looking at one of the great heroes of Narnia, Reepicheep the Mouse, who had fought at the great Battle of Beruna and afterwards sailed to the World's end with King Caspian the Seafarer. But before he had had much time to think of this, he felt two strong arms thrown about him and felt a bearded kiss on his cheeks and heard a well-remembered voice saying:

"What, lad? Art thicker and taller since I last touched thee?"

It was his own father, the good King Erlian: but not as Tirian had seen him last when they brought him home pale and wounded from his fight with the giant, nor even as Tirian remembered him in his later years when he was a grey-headed warrior. This was his father young and merry as he could just remember him from very

early days, when he himself had been a little boy playing games with his father in the castle garden at Cair Paravel, just before bedtime on summer evenings. The very smell of the bread-and-milk he used to have for supper came back to him.

Jewel thought to himself, "I will leave them to talk for a little and then I will go and greet the good King Erlian. Many a bright apple did he give me when I was but a colt." But next moment he had something else to think of, for out of the gateway there came a horse so mighty and noble that even a Unicorn might feel shy in its presence: a great winged horse. It looked a moment at the Lord Digory and the Lady Polly and neighed out "What, cousins!" and they both shouted "Fledge! Good old Fledge!" and rushed to kiss it.

But by now the Mouse was again urging them to come in. So all of them passed in through the golden gates, into the delicious smell that blew towards them out of that garden and into the cool mixture of sunlight and shadow under the trees, walking on springy turf that was all dotted with white flowers. The very first thing which struck everyone was that the place was far larger than it had seemed from outside. But no one had time to think about that for people were coming up to meet the newcomers from every direction.

Everyone you had ever heard of (if you knew the history of those countries) seemed to be there. There was Glimfeather the Owl and Puddleglum the Marshwiggle, and King Rilian the Disenchanted, and his mother, the Star's daughter, and his great father, Caspian himself. And close beside him were the Lord Drinian and the Lord Berne and Trumpkin the Dwarf and Trufflehunter, the Good Badger, with Glenstorm the Centaur and a hundred other heroes of the great War of Deliverance. And then from another side came Cor the King of Archenland with King Lune, his father, and his wife, Queen Aravis and the brave prince, Corin Thunder-Fist, his brother and Bree the Horse and Hwin the Mare. And then — which was a wonder beyond all wonders to Tirian — there came from further away in the past, the two good Beavers and Tumnus the Faun. And there was greeting and kissing and handshaking and old jokes revived (you've no idea how good an old joke sounds when you take it out again after a rest of five or six hundred years) and the whole company moved forward to the centre of the orchard where the Phoenix sat in a tree and looked down upon them all and at the foot of that tree were two thrones and in those two thrones, a King and Queen so great and beautiful that everyone bowed down before them. And well they might, for these two were King Frank and Queen Helen from whom all the most ancient Kings of Narnia and Archenland are descended. And Tirian felt as you would feel if you were brought before Adam and Eve in all their glory.

About half an hour later — or it might have been half a hundred years later, for time there is not like time here — Lucy stood with her dear friend, her oldest Narnian friend, the Faun Tumnus, looking down over the wall of that garden, and seeing all Narnia spread out below. But when you looked down you found that this hill was much higher than you had thought: it sank down with shining cliffs, thousands of feet below them and trees in that lower world looked no bigger than grains of green salt. Then she turned inward again and stood with her back to the wall and looked at the garden.

"I see," she said at last, thoughtfully. "I see now. This garden is like the Stable. It is far bigger inside than it was outside."

"Of course, Daughter of Eve," said the Faun. "The further up and the further in you go, the bigger everything gets. The inside is larger than the outside."

Lucy looked hard at the garden and saw that it was not really a garden at all but a whole world, with its own rivers and woods and sea and mountains. But they were not strange: she knew them all.

"I see," she said. "This is still Narnia, and, more real and more beautiful than the Narnia down below, just as *it* was more real and more beautiful than the Narnia outside the Stable door! I see . . . world within world, Narnia within Narnia . . . ."

"Yes," said Mr. Tumnus, "like an onion: except that as you continue to go in and in, each circle is larger than the last."

And Lucy looked this way and that and

soon found that a new and beautiful thing had happened to her. Whatever she looked at, however far away it might be, once she had fixed her eyes steadily on it, became quite clear and close as if she were looking through a telescope. She could see the whole southern desert and beyond it the great city of Tashbaan: to eastward she could see Cair Paravel on the edge of the sea and the very window of the room that had once been her own. And far out to sea she could discover the islands, island after island to the end of the world, and, beyond the end, the huge mountain which they had called Aslan's country. But now she saw that it was part of a great chain of mountains which ringed round the whole world. In front of her it seemed to come quite close. Then she looked to her left and saw what she took to be a great bank of brightly-coloured cloud, cut off from them by a gap. But she looked harder and saw that it was not a cloud at all but a real land. And when she had fixed her eyes on one particular spot of it, she at once cried out, "Peter! Edmund! Come and look! Come quickly." And they came and looked, for their eyes also had become like hers.

"Why!" exclaimed Peter. "It's England. And that's the house itself — Professor Kirke's old home in the country where all our adventures began!"

"I thought that house had been destroyed," said Edmund.

"So it was," said the Faun. "But you are now looking at the England within England, the real England just as this is the real Narnia. And in that inner England no good thing is destroyed."

Suddenly they shifted their eyes to another spot, and then Peter and Edmond and Lucy gasped with amazement and shouted out and began waving: for there they saw their own father and mother, waving back at them across the great, deep valley. It was like when you see people waving at you from the deck of a big ship when you are waiting on the quay to meet them.

"How can we get at them?" said Lucy.

"That is easy," said Mr. Tumnus. "That country and this country — all the *real* countries — are only spurs jutting out from the great mountains of Aslan. We have only to walk along the ridge, upward and inward, till it joins on. And listen! There is King Frank's horn: we must all go up.''

And soon they found themselves all walking together — and a great, bright procession it was — up towards mountains higher than you could see in this world even if they were there to be seen. But there was no snow on those mountains: there were forests and green slopes and sweet orchards and flashing waterfalls, one above the other, going up for ever. And the land they were walking on grew narrower all the time, with a deep valley on each side: and across that valley the land which was the real England grew nearer and nearer.

The light ahead was growing stronger. Lucy saw that a great series of many-coloured cliffs led up in front of them like a giant's staircase. And then she forgot everything else, because Aslan himself was coming, leaping down from cliff to cliff like a living cataract of power and beauty.

And the very first person whom Aslan called to him was Puzzle the Donkey. You never saw a donkey look feebler and sillier than Puzzle did as he walked up to Aslan; and he looked, beside Aslan, as small as a kitten looks beside a St. Bernard. The Lion bowed down his head and whispered something to Puzzle at which his long ears went down; but then he said something else at which the ears perked up again. The humans couldn't hear what he had said either time. Then Aslan turned to them and said:

"You do not yet look so happy as I mean you to be."

Lucy said, "We're so afraid of being sent away, Aslan. And you have sent us back into our own world so often."

"No fear of that," said Aslan. "Have you not guessed?"

Their hearts leaped and a wild hope rose within them.

"There *was* a real railway accident," said Aslan softly. "Your father and mother and all of you are — as you used to call it in the Shadow-Lands — dead. The term is over: the holidays have begun. The dream is ended: this is the morning."

And as he spoke He no longer looked to them like a lion; but the things that began to happen after that were so great and beautiful that I cannot write them. And for us this is the end of all the stories, and we can most truly say that they all lived happily ever after. But for them it was only the beginning of the real story. All their life in this world and all their adventures in Narnia had only been the cover and the title page: now at last they were beginning Chapter One of the Great Story, which no one on earth has read: which goes on for ever: in which every chapter is better than the one before.

Literary Myths for Further Reading

Titles marked by an asterisk (*) are alternate versions to those contained in this anthology.

The Elephant's Child, by Rudyard Kipling. Ill. by Lorinda Bryan Cauley. (New York: Harcourt, 1983.)*
        — the humorous tale of how the elephant got his trunk.

The Feathered Serpent, by Scott O'Dell. (Boston: Houghton Mifflin, 1981.)
        — Julian Escobar comes to the New World from Spain; the citizens of the City of Seven Serpents proclaim him the god Kukulcan. O'Dell blends history and Mayan myth in this compelling novel.

The Good Giants and the Bad Pukudgies, by Jean Fritz.

Ill. by Tomie de Paola. (Putnam, 1982.)
        — author blends several tales of the Wampanoag Indians of Massachusetts to form a creation myth of Buzzard's Bay, Nantucket, and Martha's Vinyard.

Greedy Zebra, by Mwenye Hadithi. Ill. by Adrienne Kennaway. (Boston: Little, Brown, 1984.)
        — A "pourquoi" myth about the beginning of the world and how the Zebra got his black and white stripes.

Just So Stories, by Rudyard Kipling. Ill. by Etienne Delessert. Orig. published 1897-1902; Rpt. (Garden City, N.Y.: Doubleday, 1972.)
        — Twelve comic literary myths, including such favorites as "How the Camel Got His Hump," "How the

Leopard Got His Spots,'' and "The Cat Who Walked by Himself.''

The Last Battle, by C.S. Lewis. (London: Lane, 1956; New York: Collier, 1970.)*
— The final book of the *Chronicles of Narnia* depicts the apocalyptic destruction of Old Narnia and the creation of a new and redeemed one.

The Magical Adventures of Pretty Pearl, by Virginia Hamilton. (New York: Harper and Row, 1983.)
— How Pretty Pearl, god child, came down to Africa from Mount Kenya, received a magical necklace from her older god brother, John de Conquer, and accompanied her suffering people to Georgia, where she had to wait for freedom time. Author draws upon black legend, myth, and folklore to create a comprehensive literary myth about the struggles of Afro-Americans for freedom.

The Magician's Nephew, by C.S. Lewis. (London: Lane, 1955; New York: Collier, 1970.)
— Book VI of the *Chronicles of Narnia* describes the actual creation of Narnia by the great lion, Aslan, and young Digory's discovery of the fantasy world.

The Master of Miracle: A New Novel of the Golem, by Sulamith Ish-Kishor. Ill. by Arnold Lobel. (New York: Harper, 1971.)
— author reinterprets ancient Jewish myth of the golem, a being created to protect the Jews of Prague from anti-semitic attacks.

The Morning the Sun Refused to Rise, by Glen Rounds. Ill. by author. (Holiday House, 1984.)
— Rounds tells a Paul Bunyan myth — how the world stopped turning and how Paul Bunyan got it spinning again.

Mr. Noah and the Second Flood, by Sheila Burnford. Ill. by Michael Foreman, (Washington Square, 1974.)
— The myth of Noah's ark with its apocalyptic flood is reinterpreted in a contemporary myth about the dangers of pollution and the possible extinction of the animal world.

The Owl Service, by Alan Garner. (New York: Walck, 1967.)
— Alison, her stepbrother, Roger, and the housekeeper's son, Gwyn, find a mysterious dinner service decorated with a pattern of owls. This discovery releases the ancient Welsh myth of Blodeuwedd, the woman made out of flowers by the wizard Gwydion. Garner treats themes of obsessive love and betrayal with remarkable power and insight.

Rootabaga Stories, by Carl Sandburg. 1922; Rpt. (New York: Harcourt, 1951.)
— forty-nine whimsical tales which reveal Sandburg's Middle-American myth.

Spirit Child: A Story of the Nativity, trans. by John Bierhorst. Ill. by Barbara Cooney. (New York: Morrow, 1984.)
— author and illustrator combine medieval lore and Aztec culture to create a myth of the nativity.

The Story of Old Mrs. Brubeck and How She Looked for Trouble and Where She Found Him, by Lore Segal. Ill. by Marcia Sewell. (New York: Pantheon, 1981.)
— Mrs. Brubeck finds trouble and gets rid of him.

The Silmarillion, by J.R.R. Tolkien. Boston: Houghton Mifflin, 1977. (New York: Ballantine, 1979.)
— the "prequel" of *The Hobbit* and *The Lord of the Rings* trilogy, this volume presents a mythic account of the creation of Middle Earth, its cosmology and history.

The Time-Ago Tales of Jahdu, by Virginia Hamilton. Ill. by Nonny Hogrogian. (New York: Macmillan Company, 1969.)
— author creates original literary myths which draw upon her vast knowledge of African legend and folklore; volume tells "How Jahdu Found His Power," "How Jahdu Took Care of Trouble," "How Young Owl and Almost Everybody Grew Tired of Jahdu," and "How Jahdu Became Himself."

Time-Ago Lost: More Tales of Jahdu, by Virginia Hamilton. Ill. by Ray Prather. (New York: The Macmillan Company, 1973.)
— author creates more literary myths featuring Jahdu: "How Jahdu Ran Through Darkness In No Time at All," "How Jahdu Found a Fire to Light His Way," "How Jahdu Discovered the Light and Found Enough Time," and "How Lee Edward Went Running Along with Jahdu."

Tuck Everlasting, by Natalie Babbitt. (New York: Farrar, Straus, and Giroux, 1975; New York: Bantam, 1976 (paper).)
— author reinterprets the myth of the golden age. The Tuck family has unwittingly drunk from a spring which has stopped death and change. Ten-year-old Winnie Foster matures through her encounter with the Tucks and surprises the reader with her choices.

Watership Down, by Richard Adams. (London and New York: Macmillan, 1974.)
— This heroic fantasy features a central hero, Hazel, who inspires several other rabbits to found a new home. Striking features of this book are its many interpolated literary myths about the rabbits' origins and their relation to the Great Rabbit, El-Ahrairah.

Modern Stories

Modern Stories

An Introduction

When one approaches the stories of the past century, the period of what might be called Modern Children's Literature, the first impression is that of their incredible variety. There are adventure stories and historical novels; stories presenting families existing in relative harmony and families struggling against the many pressures and stresses of modern life; there are stories about animals realistically described and animals portrayed with human characteristics; there are fantasies recounting journeys into strange, alien worlds and into the worlds of dreams and the subconscious; and there are stories about the incursions of strange and powerful forces and beings into the everyday world.

A survey of lists of subjects, characters, and settings once again reveals great diversity. The selections that follow include encounters with a red fox, a parentless girl of extraordinary physical strength, a boat-rowing river rat, a wooden doll, a pioneering family, a New York City boy and his grandmother, and a nineteenth-century Plains Indian, among others. Actions take place on a downtown Toronto street, in Central Park, in the midst of a buffalo herd, in the Hundred Acre Wood, and in an elderly woman's bedroom. Subjects include death, parent-child conflicts, self-pity, threats to the security of home, visits to strange places, and a search for treasure.

However, from beneath this great variety, two important patterns emerge. First, the stories reflect the changing social attitudes of the last one hundred years, and, consequently the changing notions of what is suitable reading for children. Second, these stories embody many of the same themes and structures found in both traditional stories and those works that have imitated them.

Until well into the nineteenth century, the adults who created or purchased most of the literature for children believed that stories should provide either moral or factual instruction. While it was agreed by some theorists that pleasurable works might effectively achieve this goal, the utilitarian view was dominant. Writing in 1803, Mrs. Sara Trimmer, an influential critic of the period, rejected fairy tales, noting: "Neither do the generality of tales of this kind supply any moral instruction level to the infantine capacity."[1] Although she approved of those passages of *Robinson Crusoe* which inculcated the virtues of industry and ingenuity, she worried that overimaginative readers might be led to "an early taste for a rambling life and a desire of adventures."[2]

As child literacy increased and changes in printing technology made books less expensive, many new types of stories appeared. Lewis Carroll's *Alice's Adventures in Wonderland* (1865) and George MacDonald's *The Princess and the Goblins* (1871) and other novels created fantasies in which the adventures themselves and the development of character were most important. The same is true in the adventure stories of such novelists as Robert Ballantyne (*The Coral Island*, 1883) and Robert Louis Stevenson (*Treasure Island*, 1883). In the United States, Louisa May Alcott developed the family story — episodes in the lives of normal children — in *Little Women* (1868–9), while Samuel Clemens (Mark Twain) combined the daily activities of average boys and girls with high adventure in *The Adventures of Tom Sawyer* (1876). At the beginning of the twentieth century, British author E. Nesbit combined the family story, the adventure novel, and the fantasy in a series of three books: *Five Children and It* (1902), *The Phoenix and the Carpet* (1904), and *The Story of the Amulet* (1906). While these authors did not emphasize morality, their prevailing attitudes were nonetheless those of the dominant white, Anglo-Saxon middle class.

During the later part of the nineteenth century, increased scientific study of animals, combined with a growing interest in Darwin's theories of "survival of the fittest," and humanitarian efforts to ameliorate the conditions of domestic animals, contributed to the development of the realistic animal story. This form of story reached its fulfillment in the works of Canadian writer Sir Charles G.D. Roberts and American Ernest Thompson Seton. Although based on the authors' careful observations of animals, the central characters were often presented as being superior to the animals around them; in short, they were heroes. As Roberts noted in the introduction to *Red Fox* (1905): "Once in a while such exceptional strength and such exceptional intelligence may be combined in one animal. This combination is apt to result in just such a fox as I have made the hero of my story."

The same period saw one of the great flowerings of animal fantasies. Beatrix Potter in *The Tale of Peter Rabbit* (1902) and several other books, Rudyard Kipling in *The Jungle Books* (1894–1950), and Kenneth Grahame in *The Wind in the Willows* (1908) created a gallery of animal characters who combined traits of their own species with qualities of human, and specifically British, nature.

So many stories have been written and published in the twentieth century that it is difficult to provide little more than a general overview of trends. Two distinct periods can be noted. Up until the 1960s, many of the traditional types of stories continued to be published. Although they portrayed a variety of adventures and characters, the view of the family as the focal point of children's lives prevailed. While minority groups such as Native Indians and Afro-Americans were presented, they were generally viewed from the outside, from the moral and cultural standpoint of the white middle class, be it British, American, or Canadian.

Since the 1960s, a considerable shift in emphasis has occurred. The world of childhood has not been viewed as totally safe and secure. Death, social violence, racial prejudice, drugs, genocide, and sex have been viewed by many adults as acceptable subject matter for children's stories. While some writers have handled these subjects as a way as to reinforce their own moral points of view, others have honestly examined the very real tensions and conflicts children must face in the difficult process of growing up. Moreover, a greater awareness of the multicultural diversity of North American society has also developed. For example, in the United States such gifted Afro-American writers as Virginia Hamilton, Sharon Bell Mathis, and Mildred Taylor have examined their cultural heritage and the contemporary nature of Black life.

While women have been traditionally viewed as mothers and wives, the influence of the feminist movements of the late 1960s and early 1970s changed the picture. Girls, as well as boys, are represented heroically. Isabel, in Ogden Nash's "The Adventures of Isabel," faces adversaries every bit as dangerous as those confronted by boys. Takashima's character in *A Child in Prison Camp* grimly and bravely faces an uncertain future. In novels such as Jean George's *Julie of the Wolves*, Madeline L'Engle's *A Wrinkle in Time*, and Barbara Smucker's *Underground to Canada*, heroines occupy the center stage.

"The more things change," the old saying notes, "the more they remain the same." Or, as the Biblical Solomon stated: "There is nothing new under the sun." This is certainly true of children's stories. While modern Children's Literature has reflected changing social conditions and views on what constitutes acceptable reading material for young people, it also embodies timeless themes, presenting character types and situations not dissimilar to those found in traditional literature. This is probably because all literature attempts to present the universal embodied in the particular. In his great plays, Shakespeare retold stories from a variety of cultures and periods. However, in interpreting those stories he reflected the concerns of Elizabethan England. His greatness lies in the fact that he also communicated universal concerns of human nature. That is why his plays are still read.

While the stories included in this section represent many of the subjects and themes of the past century, they are, nonetheless, members of "The Family of

Stories,'' and embody journey patterns, motifs, and character types found in the traditional stories and their literary imitations. Of course, in traditional stories the symbols and patterns are found at their purest. In more complex modern fantasies and realistic stories, these patterns and symbols become, to use Northrop Frye's term, "displaced." Displacement, as explained in the Myth section of this anthology, involves presenting traditional symbols and patterns in more superficially realistic forms. "By displacement, I mean the techniques a writer uses to make his story credible, logically motivated or morally acceptable — lifelike, in short."[3] Symbols or patterns are disguised or concealed beneath or within recognizable characters, situations, and settings. However, the reader who recognizes the patterns and symbols underlying the surface will be better able to understand the stories employing them.

The selections in this section can be categorized as either linear or circular journeys. As was the case in traditional stories, home is the first setting for each story. For a variety of reasons characters leave either to find new homes or return to their previous homes somehow matured. In linear journeys characters are often like the orphans in folktales who must enter into new worlds to find secure homes. In many circular journeys, characters engage in actions which enable them to reestablish themselves in the homes from which they departed. In several stories, the journeys are ironic. For example, Peter Rabbit does not achieve maturity; he reveals his childishness and is subsequently punished. Unlike the romantic heroes and heroines of many folktales, the Yonghy-Bonghy-Bò and the Highway Man conclude their quests tragically.

Linear Journey selections begin with a chapter from Takashima's *A Child in Prison Camp*, which begins with the violent displacement of the narrator and her family from their home. Like Takashima, the mongoose Rikki-tikki-tavi, and the Mole, from "The River Bank," leave their homes, but, unlike her, they achieve happiness and a sense of fulfillment in their new dwellings. Like Rikki-tikki-tavi, Isabel, in "The Adventures of Isabel," proves her bravery by slaying threatening characters. Nicholas Knock possesses imaginative vision; however, he searches longingly, but, it is implied, hopelessly, for the object of this power. In *The Hundred Penny Box*, "Jim Who Ran Away from his Nurse," "The Highway Man," and "The Price of His life," death concludes the linear journey. For "Jim" and the lovers in "The Highway Man," irony takes the shape of unexpected death.

Circular Journey selections begin with four stories centering on the home and the relationships between children and parents. In "The Wolf-Pack," Pa provides security for the family when it is threatened. Ramona, in "Pay Day," is able to accept the disruption of family security and plans ways to restore it. The Armitage children rescue their bewitched father and drive the wizards out of their home in "The Frozen Cuckoo."

In "Tottie Meets the Queen," "Pippi Goes to the Circus," and "Nothing New Under the Sun (Hardly)," children briefly leave the known and secure confines of home and, while they are away, prove superior to the adults they confront. Several of the circular journeys deal with initiation. In Harry Behn's "The Errand," the young boy traveling alone across a deserted landscape acquires a sense of maturity and self-worth. This poem provides a standard against which the following stories and their major characters can be measured. Although the Bastable children believe they are in search of riches, it is questionable whether they mature or not as a result of their experiences. While Peter Rabbit and Eagle Voice learn lessons during their misadventures, they do not succeed in achieving their goals and return home still children. "Stopping by Woods" and "The Night of the Leonids" are circular journeys that focus on a character's relation to death. In the former, the speaker realizes that the responsibilities of life must be faced and death rejected. In the latter, Lewis understands his grandmother better when he realizes her awareness of her own mortality.

In specific selections characters, actions, and settings perform functions similar to those seen in many traditional tales. Rikki-tikki-tavi can be compared to the victorious underdogs of hero tales; the aging fox in "The Price of his Life," is similiar to the hero who dies saving his people; Uncle Albert, in "Digging for Treasure," resembles a fairy godmother or father; and Isabel can be compared to the self-possessed heroine Molly Whuppie. The boys in Harry Behn's "The Errand" and John Neihardt's "Chased by a Cow" can be compared to the heroes in "Of Sir Gareth of Orkney" and *Arrow to the Sun*, for, like them, they are engaged in circular journeys of initiation.

In the selection and presentation of modern stories, adults should consider the comprehension level and literary experience of children as well as the relationship between a specific story and other modern and traditional stories. A selection like Harry Behn's "The Errand" will probably be too sophisticated for seven or eight year olds and it could present some difficulty for children in upper elementary or junior high school. However, students in the latter age group who have developed a familiarity with the circular journey pattern and the symbolic uses of landscape will bring to the poem literary experiences which can assist them in their comprehension.

It is very important to present stories in relation to other stories, enabling children to use past literary experiences to provide frameworks for understanding stories currently being considered. For example, in the early elementary grades, the fear of wolves found in "The Wolf-Pack" is not unlike that conveyed by "Little Red Riding Hood," and the heroism of the tiny Rikki-tikki-tavi can be compared to that of Inchelina.

In upper elementary grades the experiences in "Nothing New Under the Sun (Hardly)" acquire greater dimension when read with "The Pied Piper of Hamelin," and the quest for riches in "Digging for Treasure" can be compared to that in the folktale "The Fisherman and His Wife." In junior high school, "The Highway Man" can be studied in relation to the traditional ballad "Sir Patrick Spens" and the loneliness of Nicholas Knock can be compared to that of the Greek Titan Prometheus.

Along with traditional stories, short modern stories can be used as lead-ins to the study of novels. The circular journey in *The Tale of Peter Rabbit* is not unlike that in Mordecai Richler's *Jacob Two-Two Meets the Hooded Fang*. The theme of growth in self-knowledge and self-respect which is examined in Madeline L'Engle's *A Wrinkle in Time* is also considered in Harry Behn's "The Errand" and Gerald McDermott's *Arrow to the Sun*.

The key point is that modern stories should not be read in isolation either from each other or from traditional stories or novels. By seeing how these stories fit into the overall pattern of "The Family of Stories," children will increase their general literary experience and their appreciation and enjoyment of specific tales.

Notes

1 Sara Trimmer, from *The Guardian of Education*, included in *Suitable for Children*, ed. by Nicholas Tucker (London: Sussex University Press, 1976), p. 38.

2 Ibid., p. 39

3 Northrop Frye, *Fables of Identity* (New York: Harcourt, Brace and World, 1963), p. 36.

Linear Journeys

From A Child in Prison Camp, *by Takashima (Montreal: Tundra, 1971).*

Leaving the security of home is an event often treated in children's stories. When the departure means the disruption of an entire way of life, the insecurities and fears are magnified. Writing of her childhood experiences in Vancouver, artist Takashima captures the emotions experienced by thousands of Canadians and Americans of Japanese origin who, during World War II, were viewed as security threats and moved far inland to internment camps.

A Child in Prison Camp

Vancouver, British Columbia
March 1942

Japan is at war with the United States, Great Britain and all the Allied Countries, including Canada, the country of my birth. My parents are Japanese, born in Japan, but they have been Canadian citizens for many, many years, and have become part of this young country. Now, overnight our rights as Canadians are taken away. Mass evacuation for the Japanese!

"All the Japanese," it is carefully explained to me, "whether we were born in Tokyo or in Vancouver are to be moved to distant places. Away from the west coast of British Columbia — for security reasons."

We must all leave, my sister Yuki, my older brother David, my parents, our relatives — all.

The older men are the first to go. The government feels that my father, or his friends, might sabotage the police and their buildings. Imagine! I couldn't believe such stories, but there is my father packing just his clothes in a small suitcase.

Yuki says, "They are going to the foothills of the Rockies, to Tête Jaune. No one's there, and I guess they feel father won't bomb the mountains."

The older people are very frightened. Mother

is so upset; so are all her friends. I, being only eleven, seem to be on the outside.

One March day, we go to the station to see father board the train.

At the train station

An empty bottle is tossed in the air.
I stand away, hold my mother's hand.
Angry, dark curses, a scream. A train window
    is broken.

Most of the men have been drinking.
An angry man is shouting.
The men are dragged violently into the trains.
Father can be seen. He is being pushed onto
    the train.
He is on the steps, turns. His head is above the
shouting crowd. I see his mouth opening;
    he shouts
to his friends, waves his clenched fist.
But the words are lost in all the noise.
Mother holds my hand tightly.

A sharp police whistle blows.
My blood stops. We see a uniformed Mounted
    Police drag
an old man and hurl him into the train.
More curses, threats. The old train bellows
its starting sound. White, hellish smoke appears
from the top of its head. It grunts, gives another
shrill blast. Slowly, slowly, the engine comes
    to life.
I watch from where we stand, fascinated.
The huge, black, round, ugly wheels begin
to move slowly, then faster, and faster.
Finally, the engine, jet dark,
rears its body and moves with a lurch.
The remaining men rush toward the train,
scramble quickly into the moving machine.

Men crowd at the windows. Father is still on
    the steps,
he seems to be searching the crowd, finally sees
us, waves.
Mother does not move. Yuki and I wave. Most
    remain still.
The dark, brown faces of the men become
    small.

Some are still shouting. Yuki moves closer to
    mother.

The long, narrow, old train quickly picks up
    speed
as it coils away along the tracks
away from all of us who are left at the station.

Mother is silent. I look at her.
I see tears are slowly falling. They remain
on her cheeks. I turn away, look around. The
    women
and the children stare at one another. Some
    women
cry right out loud. A bent old woman breaks
    out
into a Buddhist prayer, moves her orange beads
in her wrinkled hands, prays aloud to her God.
Mother and the other women bow their heads.
The silent God seems so far away.

Summer 1942

From March to September, 1942, my mother, my sister Yuki and I are alone in Vancouver. David, our brother, is taken away, for he is over eighteen and in good health. It's hard for me to understand. Our David, who is so gentle, considered an enemy of his own country. I wondered what he thought as his time came to leave us. He spoke very little, but I do remember him saying, "In a way it's better we leave. I am fired from my job. The white people stare at me. The ways things are, we'd starve to death!"

Now our house is empty. What we can sell, we do for very little money. Our radio, the police came and took away. Our cousins who have acres of berry farm had to leave everything. Trucks, tractors, land, it was all taken from them. They were moved with only a few days notice to Vancouver.

Strange rumors are flying. We are not supposed to own anything! The government takes our home.

Mother does not know what to do now that father is not here and David too is taken. She does not speak very much; she is too worried how we are to eat with all her men gone. So finally, Yuki goes to work. She is sixteen; she becomes help for an elderly lady. She comes home once a week to be with us and seems so grown up.

I grow very close to my mother. Because we are alone, I often go to different places with her. Many Japanese families who were moved from the country towns such as Port Hammond and Steveston on the west coast of B.C., are now housed in the Exhibition grounds in Vancouver, waiting to be evacuated.

One very hot summer day mother and I visit a friend of hers who has been moved there.

A visit to the Exhibition grounds

The strong, summer July sun is over our heads
as we near the familiar Exhibition grounds.
But the scene is now quite different from the
    last time I saw it.
The music, the rollercoasters, the hawkers
with their bright balloons and sugar candy are
    not there.
Instead, tension and crying children greet us
as we approach the grounds. A strong odor hits
    us
as we enter: the unmistakable foul smell of
    cattle,
a mixture from their waste and sweat.
The animals were removed, but their stink
    remains.
It is very strong in the heat. I look at mother.
She exclaims, "We are treated like animals!"
I ask mother, "How can they sleep in such a
    stink?"
She looks at me. "Thank our Lord, we don't
    have to
live like them. So this is where they are.
They used to house the domestic animals here.
Such a karma!"

As we draw close to the concrete buildings,
    the stench
becomes so powerful in the hot, humid heat,
I want to turn and run. I gaze at my mother.
She only quickens her steps. It seems as if

we are visiting the hell-hole my Sunday school
teacher spoke of with such earnestness.

White, thin sheets are strung up
carelessly to block the view of prying eyes.
Steel bunkbeds, a few metal chairs, suitcases,
boxes, clothes hanging all over the place
to dry in the hot sour air, greet our eyes.
Mother sits on a chair, looks at her friend.
Mrs. Abe sits on the bed, nursing her baby.
The child, half asleep, noisily sucks her breast.
Mrs. Abe looks down at it, smiles,
looks at mother and says, "The food is much
    better now.
We complained every day, refused to eat one
    day.
They take all our belongings, even our
    husbands,
and house us like pigs, even try to feed us pigs'
    food!"

Mrs. Abe opens her heart to mother.
I look around. The children's voices
echo through the huge concrete buildings.
Some of them are running around. The cement
    floor
smells of strong chemical. I stare at
the gray, stained floor. Mrs. Abe seeing this,
    says
"They wash it every week with some cleaner.
As if they cared whether we lived or died."

A curious head pokes in from the drawn, frail
    curtain.
Mrs. Abe sees this, becomes angry, "Nosy
    bitch!"
she says aloud. The dark head disappears.
Mrs. Abe turns to me, glares into my eyes,
forgetting for a moment that I do not live here,
that I am still a child and am not responsible
for her unhappiness. I begin to feel
    uncomfortable.
I gently nudge my mother. She reads my sign,
rises to take her leave, bowing, speaking words
    of
encouragement. Mrs. Abe bows, thanks
    mother,
"You are lucky. You can still live in your house.
And your children are older. They are a
    comfort."

Her words trail off. She bursts into tears.
Her child awakens, startled; she begins to cry.
Several heads appear from behind the curtains,
eyes peer with curiosity. Mrs. Abe holds the
    child
close to her and weeps into its small neck.
I quietly walk away.

From the corner of my eye
I can see sweaty children; they gape at me.
They know I am from the outside. I pretend I
    do
not see them, I quicken my steps, I am outside.
Here the animal stench again overwhelms me.
I turn. Mother is behind me.
"You are rude to leave like that," she scolds.
Her dark eyes search mine. I feel bad,
I look down. The concrete ground seems to
    melt
from the blazing heat. I curl my toes in my
white, summer shoes. They are dusty from the
    walk.
I look up, "I'm sorry. I couldn't help it.
Her crying, and the smell. . . . ''
Mother takes my hand and we begin to walk
to the tram stop. "Someday, you'll understand.
Mrs. Abe is much younger than me. She is new
in this country, misses her family in Japan.
You know she has only her husband.''

All the way home in the noisy tram, mother
    says
very little. I, happy to leave the smelly,
unhappy grounds, daydream. I think of the film
    with
Tyrone Power Yuki promised to take me to one
    day.

Vancouver
September 1942

Now we have curfew. All Japanese have to be
indoors by ten. The war with Japan is fierce.
People in the streets look at us anger. My sister
Yuki has to quit her job. No reason is given by
the elderly lady. We wait, mother, Yuki and I,
for our notice to go to the camps. Already
    many families have left.

A night out

Yuki holds my hand, begins to run.
"We have to hurry, Shichan. It's close to ten.
Can you run a bit?" "I'll try," I say.
but my limp makes it hard for me to keep up.
Yuki slows down. I wish mother were with us.
Everything seems so dark. An old man comes
towards us, peers at us in the dim light.
His small eyes narrow, he shouts, "Hey, you!
Get off our streets!" He waves his thin arms,
"I'll have the police after you."
Yuki pulls my arm, ignoring him, and we run
    faster
towards our house. The man screams after us.

Mother is at the door when we arrive.
She looks worried, "You are late." She sees us
    panting.
"Did you two have trouble?" She closes the
    door quickly.
"You know I worry when you're late, Yuki."
Yuki sits on a chair, looks at mother.
"I'm sorry. The film was longer than I thought.
It was so great we forgot about the curfew."

Mother pours Japanese green tea. It smells nice.
I sit beside her and drink the hot tea.
I look around. The rooms are bare.
Boxes are piled for storage in the small room
    upstairs.

Our suitcases are open, they are slowly being
    filled.
We are leaving for camp next week.

A siren screams in the night. Air-raid practice.
I go to the window. All our blinds are tightly
    drawn.
I peek out, carefully lifting them. I see
one by one the lights in the city vanish. Heavy
darkness and quiet covers Vancouver. It looks
    weird.
But the stars, high, high above, still sparkle,
not caring, still beautiful and happy. I feel sad
to be leaving the mountains, the lovely sea.
I have grown with them always near me.

"Come away from the window, Shichan."
    mother's voice
reaches me. I turn. I feel sadness come from
    her too.

She has lived here for so long:
"Over twenty-five years — hard to believe —
I was a young girl, full of dreams.
America! Canada! all sounded so magical in
    Japan.
Remember, we had no radio in those days, so
    all our
knowledge of this country came from books.
My own mother had come to Canada long
    before
other women. She was brave, not knowing the
    language,
young, adventurous, a widow with three
    children.
She took your uncle Fujiwara with her.
He was thirteen. I went to my grandmother's;
my sister, to an aunt. It seems so long ago."

Mother often talks of the past. Her life
on the tiny island sounds lovely, for she had
a happy childhood, so full of love.
I go to see her. I see her hands folded neatly
on her lap. She always sits like this,
very quiet, calm. Her warm eyes behind her
round glasses are dark and not afraid.

An end to waiting

We have been waiting for months now. The
Provincial Government keeps changing the
dates of our evacuation, first from April, then
from June, for different reasons: lack of trains,
the camps are not ready. We are given another
final notice. We dare not believe this is the one.

Mother is so anxious. She has just received a
letter from father that he is leaving his camp
with others; the families will be back together. I
feel so happy. He writes that he is being moved
to a new camp, smaller than others, but it is
supposed to be located in one of the most beautiful spots in British Columbia. It's near a small
village, 1800 feet above sea level. The Government wants the Japanese to build their own san-
atorium for the T.B. patients. I hear there are
many Japanese who have this disease, and the
high altitude and dry air are supposed to be
good for them. I feel secretly happy for I love
the mountains. I shall miss the roaring sea, but
we are to be near a lake. Yuki says, "They

decided all the male heads of families are to
rejoin their wives, but not the single men."
So, of course, David will remain in his camp,
far away.

We rise early, very early, the morning we are
    to leave.
The city still sleeps. The fresh autumn air feels
    nice.
We have orders to be at the Exhibition grounds.
The train will leave from there, not from the
    station
where we said good-bye to father and to David.
We wait for the train in small groups scattered
alongside the track. There is no platform.
It is September 16. School has started. I think
of my school friends and wonder if I shall ever
    see
them again. The familiar mountains, all pur-
    ple and
splendid, watch us from afar. The yellowy-
    orangy
sun slowly appears. We have been standing
for over an hour. The sun's warm rays reach
    us,

touch a child still sleeping in its
mother's arms, touch a tree, blades of grass.
All seems magical. I study the thin yellow rays
of the sun. I imagine a handsome prince will
    come and
carry us all away in a shining, gold carriage with
white horses. I daydream, and feel nice as long
    as I don't
think about leaving this city where I was born.
The crisp air becomes warmer. I shift my feet,
    restless.
Mother returns; she has been speaking to her
    friend,
"Everyone says we will have to wait for hours."
She bends, moves the bundles at our feet:
food, clothes for the journey. I am excited. This
is my first train ride! Yuki smiles, she too feels
    the
excitement of our journey. Several children cry,
weary of waiting. Their mothers' voices are
    heard, scolding.

Now the orange sun is far above our heads.
I hear the twelve o'clock whistle blow from a

nearby factory. Yuki asks me if I am tired.
I nod, "I don't feel tired yet, but I'm getting
  hungry."
We haven't eaten since six in the morning.
Names are being called over the loudspeaker.
One by one, families gather their belongings
  and
move towards the train. Finally, ours is called.

Yuki shouts, "That's us!" I shout, "Hooray!"
I take a small bag. Yuki and mother, the larger
ones and the suitcases. People stare as we walk
towards the train. It is some distance away.
I see the black, dull colored train. It looks
quite old. Somehow I had expected a shiny new
  one.
Yuki remarks, "I hope it moves. You never
  know
with the government." Mother looks, smiles,
"Never mind, as long as we get there. We aren't
going on vacation; we are being evacuated."

Bang . . . bang . . . psst . . . the old train gurgles,
makes funny noises. I, seated by the window,
feel the wheels move, stop, move, stop.
Finally, I hear them begin to move in an
even rhythm slowly.

I look out the dusty window.
A number of people still wait their turn.
We wave. Children run after the train.
Gradually, it picks up speed. We pass the gray
granaries, tall and thin against the blue Van-
  couver sky.
The far mountains, tall pines, follow us
for a long time, until finally they are gone.

Mother sits opposite; she has her eyes closed,
her hands are on her lap. Yuki stares out the
  window.
A woman across the aisle quietly dabs her
tears with a white cloth. No one speaks.

_____

"The River Bank," from The Wind in the Willows, *by Kenneth Grahame (New York:
Charles Scribner's 1954).*

The first chapter of The Wind in the
Willows *is a classic portrayal of the innocent
individual's first encounter with the world*
*beyond his own home. Naive but enthusias-
tic, Mole feels new life in him as spring
approaches. Like the three little pigs, the
heroine of "Beauty and the Beast," and Mary
Lennox in* The Secret Garden, *Mole must successfully "relocate" if he is to mature. By the
end of the chapter, he has made the first step
toward maturity by discovering new places,
making new friends, and finding a new home.
In this chapter, as throughout the book,
Grahame presents the river as a symbol of the
ideal place to live; it is rural without being
wild, and it possesses all the necessary domestic comforts.*

The River Bank

The Mole had been working very hard all the
morning, spring cleaning his little home. First
with brooms, then with dusters; then on ladders and steps and chairs, with a brush and a
pail of whitewash; till he had dust in his throat
and eyes, and splashes of whitewash all over
his black fur, and an aching back and weary
arms. Spring was moving in the air above and
in the earth below and around him, penetrat-
ing even his dark and lowly little house with
its spirit of divine discontent and longing. It
was small wonder, then, that he suddenly flung
down his brush on the floor, said 'Bother!' and
'O blow!' and also 'Hang spring-cleaning!' and
bolted out of the house without even waiting
to put on his coat. Something up above was
calling him imperiously, he made for the steep
little tunnel which answered in his case to the
gravelled carriage-drive owned by animals
whose residences are nearer to the sun and air.
So he scraped and scratched and scrabbled and
scrooged, and then he scrooged again and
scrabbled and scratched and scraped, working
busily with his little paws and muttering to himself, 'Up we go! Up we go!' till at last, pop! his
snout came out into the sunlight, and he found
himself rolling in the warm grass of a great
meadow.
  'This is fine!' he said to himself. 'This is better than whitewashing!' The sunshine struck
hot on his fur, soft breezes caressed his heated
brow, and after the seclusion of the cellarage
he had lived in so long the carol of happy birds

fell on his dulled hearing almost like a shout. Jumping off all his four legs at once, in the joy of living and the delight of spring without its cleaning, he pursued his way across the meadow till he reached the hedge on the further side.

'Hold up!' said an elderly rabbit at the gap. 'Sixpence for the privilege of passing by the private road!' He was bowled over in an instant by the impatient and contemptuous Mole, who trotted along the side of the hedge chaffing the other rabbits as they peeped hurriedly from their holes to see what the row was about. 'Onion-sauce! Onion-sauce!' he remarked jeeringly, and was gone before they could think of a thoroughly satisfactory reply. Then they all started grumbling at each other. 'How *stupid* you are! Why didn't you tell him —' 'Well, why didn't *you* say —' 'You might have reminded him —' and so on, in the usual way; but, of course, it was then much too late, as is always the case.

It all seemed too good to be true. Hither and thither through the meadows he rambled busily, along the hedgerows, across the copses, finding everywhere birds building, flowers budding, leaves thrusting — everything happy, and progressive, and occupied. And instead of having an uneasy conscience pricking him and whispering 'Whitewash!' he somehow could only feel how jolly it was to be the only idle dog among all these busy citizens. After all, the best part of a holiday is perhaps not as much to be resting yourself, as to see all the other fellows busy working.

He thought his happiness was complete when, as he meandered aimlessly along, suddenly he stood by the edge of a full-fed river. Never in his life had he seen a river before — this sleek, sinuous, full-bodied animal, chasing and chuckling, gripping things with a gurgle and leaving them with a laugh, to fling itself on fresh playmates that shook themselves free, and were caught and held again. All was a-shake and a-shiver — glints and gleams and sparkles, rustle and swirl, chatter and bubble. The Mole was bewitched, entranced, fascinated. By the side of the river as he trotted as one trots, when very small, by the side of a man who holds one spellbound by exciting stories; and when tired at last, he sat on the bank, while the river still chattered on to him, a babbling procession of the best stories in the world, sent from the heart of the earth to be told at last to the insatiable sea.

As he sat on the grass and looked across the river, a dark hole in the bank opposite, just above the water's edge, caught his eye, and dreamily he fell to considering what a nice snug dwelling-place it would make for an animal with few wants and fond of a bijou riverside residence, above flood level and remote from noise and dust. As he gazed, something bright and small seemed to twinkle down in the heart of it, vanished, then twinkled once more like a tiny star. But it could hardly be a star in such an unlikely situation; and it was too glittering and small for a glow-worm. Then, as he looked, it winked at him, and so declared itself to be an eye; and a small face began gradually to grow up round it, like a frame round a picture.

A brown little face, with whiskers.

A grave round face, with the same twinkle in its eye that had first attracted his notice.

Small neat ears and thick silky hair.

It was the Water Rat!

Then the two animals stood and regarded each other cautiously.

'Hullo, Mole!' said the Water Rat.

'Hullo, Rat!' said the Mole.

'Would you like to come over?' inquired the Rat presently.

'Oh, it's all very well to *talk*,' said the Mole rather pettishly, he being new to a river and riverside life and its ways.

The Rat said nothing, but stooped and unfastened a rope and hauled on it; then lightly stepped into a little boat which the Mole had not observed. It was painted blue outside and white within, and was just the size for two animals; and the Mole's whole heart went out to it at once, even though he did not yet fully understand its uses.

The Rat sculled smartly across and made fast. Then he held up his fore-paw as the Mole stepped gingerly down. 'Lean on that!' he said. 'Now then, step lively!' and the Mole to his surprise and rapture found himself actually seated in the stern of a real boat.

'This has been a wonderful day!' said he,

as the Rat shoved off and took to the sculls again. 'Do you know, I've never been in a boat in all my life.'

'What?' cried the Rat, open-mouthed: 'Never been in a — you never — well, I — what have you been doing, then?'

'Is it so nice as all that?' asked the Mole shyly, though he was quite prepared to believe it as he leant back in his seat and surveyed the cushions, the oars, the row-locks, and all the fascinating fittings, and felt the boat sway lightly under him.

'Nice? It's the *only* thing,' said the Water Rat solemnly, as he leant forward for his stroke. 'Believe me, my young friend, there is *nothing* — absolutely nothing — half so much worth doing as simply messing about in boats. Simply messing,' he went on dreamily: 'messing — about — in — boats; messing —'

'Look ahead, Rat!' cried the Mole suddenly.

It was too late. The boat struck the bank full tilt. The dreamer, the joyous oarsman, lay on his back at the bottom of the boat, his heels in the air.

'— about in boats — or *with* boats,' the Rat went on composedly, picking himself up with a pleasant laugh. 'In or out of' em, it doesn't matter. Nothing seems really to matter, that's the charm of it. Whether you get away, or whether you don't; whether you arrive at your destination or whether you reach somewhere else, or whether you never get anywhere at all, you're always busy, and you never do anything in particular; and when you've done it there's always something else to do, and you can do it if you like, but you'd much better not. Look here! If you've really nothing else on hand this morning, supposing we drop down the river together, and have a long day of it?'

The Mole waggled his toes from sheer happiness, spread his chest with a sigh of full contentment, and leaned back blissfully into the soft cushions. '*What* a day I'm having!' he said. 'Let us start at once!'

'Hold hard a minute, then!' said the Rat. He looped the painter through a ring in his landing-stage, climbed up into his hole above, and after a short interval reappeared staggering under a fat, wicker luncheon-basket.

'Shove that under your feet,' he observed to the Mole, as he passed it down into the boat. Then he untied the painter and took the sculls again.

'What's inside it?' asked the Mole, wiggling with curiosity.

'There's cold chicken inside it,' replied the Rat briefly; 'coldtonguecoldhamcoldbeef-pickledgherkinssaladfrenchrollscresssand-widgespottedmeatgingerbeerlemonadesoda-water —'

'O stop, stop,' cried the Mole in ecstasies: 'This is too much!'

'Do you really think so?' inquired the Rat seriously. 'It's only what I always take on these little excursions; and the other animals are always telling me that I'm a mean beast and cut it *very* fine!'

The Mole never heard a word he was saying. Absorbed in the new life he was entering upon, intoxicated with the sparkle, the ripple, the scents and the sounds and the sunlight, he trailed a paw in the water and dreamed long waking dreams. The Water Rat, like the good little fellow he was, sculled steadily on and forbore to disturb him.

'I like your clothes awfully, old chap,' he remarked after some half an hour or so had passed. 'I'm going to get a black velvet smoking suit myself some day, as soon as I can afford it.'

'I beg your pardon,' said the mole, pulling himself together with an effort. 'You must think me very rude; but all this is so new to me. So — this — is — a — River!'

'*The* River,' corrected the Rat.

'And you really live by the river? What a jolly life!'

'By it and with it and on it and in it,' said the Rat. 'It's brother and sister to me, and aunts, and company, and food and drink, and (naturally) washing. It's my world, and I don't want any other. What it hasn't got is not worth having, and what it doesn't know is not worth knowing. Lord! the times we've had together! Whether in winter or summer, spring or autumn, it's always got its fun and its excitements. When the floods are on in February, and my cellars and basement are brimming with drink that's no good to me, and the brown water runs by my best bedroom window; or again when it all drops away and shows patches of mud that smells like plum-cake, and the rushes and weed clog the channels, and I can potter about dry-shod over most of the bed of it and find fresh food to eat, and things careless people have dropped out of boats!'

'But isn't it a bit dull at times?' the Mole ventured to ask. 'Just you and the river, and no one else to pass a word with?'

'No one else to — well, I mustn't be hard on you,' said the Rat with forbearance. 'You're new to it, and of course you don't know. The bank is so crowded nowadays that many people are moving away altogether. O no, it isn't what it used to be, at all. Otters, kingfishers, dabchicks, moorhens, all of them about all day long and always wanting you to do something — as if a fellow had no business of his own to attend to!'

'What lies over *there*?' asked the Mole, waving a paw towards a background of woodland that darkly framed the water-meadows on one side of the river.

'That? O, that's just the Wild Wood,' said the Rat shortly. 'We don't go there very much, we river-bankers.'

'Aren't they — aren't they very *nice* people in there?' said the Mole a trifle nervously.

'W-e-ll,' replied the Rat, 'let me see. The squirrels are all right. *And* the rabbits — some of 'em, but rabbits are a mixed lot. And then there's Badger, or course. He lives right in the heart of it; wouldn't live anywhere else, either, if you paid him to do it. Dear old Badger! Nobody interferes with *him*. They'd better not,' he added significantly.

'Why, who *should* interfere with him?' asked the Mole.

'Well, of course — there — are others,' explained the Rat in a hesitating sort of way. 'Weasels — and stoats — and foxes — and so on. They're all right in a way — I'm very good friends with them — pass the time of day when we meet, and all that — but they break out sometimes, there's no denying it, and then — well, you can't really trust them, and that's the fact.'

The Mole knew well that it is quite against animal-etiquette to dwell on possible trouble ahead, or even to allude to it; so he dropped the subject.

'And beyond the Wild Wood again?' he asked: 'Where it's all blue and dim, and one sees what may be hills or perhaps they mayn't, and something like the smoke of towns, or is it only cloud-drift?'

'Beyond the Wild Wood comes the Wide World,' said the Rat. 'And that's something that doesn't matter, either to you or me. I've never been there, and I'm never going, nor you either, if you've got any sense at all. Don't ever refer to it again, please. Now then! Here's our backwater at last, where we're going to lunch.'

Leaving the main stream, they now passed into what seemed at first sight like a little land-locked lake. Green turf sloped down to either edge, brown snaky tree-roots gleamed below the surface of the quiet water, while ahead of them the silvery shoulder and foamy tumble of a weir, arm-in-arm with a restless dripping mill-wheel, that held up in its turn a grey-gabled mill-house, filled the air with a soothing murmur of sound, dull and smothery, yet with little clear voices speaking up cheerfully out of it at intervals. It was so very beautiful that the Mole could only hold up both fore-paws and gasp, 'O my! O my! O my!'

The Rat brought the boat alongside the bank, made her fast, helped the still awkward Mole safely ashore, and swung out the luncheon-basket.

The Mole begged as a favour to be allowed to unpack it all by himself; and the Rat was very pleased to indulge him, and to sprawl at full length on the grass and rest, while his excited friend shook out the tablecloth and spread it, took out all the mysterious packets one by one and arranged their contents in due order, still gasping, 'O my! O my!' at each fresh revelation. When all was ready, the Rat said, 'Now, pitch in, old fellow!' and the Mole was indeed very glad to obey, for he had started his spring cleaning at a very early hour that morning, as people *will* do, and had not paused for bite or sup; and he had been through a very great deal since that distant time which now seemed so many days ago.

'What are you looking at?' said the Rat presently, when the edge of their hunger was somewhat dulled, and the Mole's eyes were able to wander off the tablecloth a little.

'I am looking,' said the Mole, 'at a streak of bubbles that I see traveling along the surface of the water. That is a thing that strikes me as funny.'

'Bubbles? Oho!' said the Rat, and chirruped cheerily in an inviting sort of way.

A broad glistening muzzle showed itself above the edge of the bank, and the Otter hauled himself out and shook the water from his coat.

Illustration by Ernest Shepard, ''The River Bank'' from *The Wind in the Willows* by Kenneth Grahame. Copyright © 1933, 1953, 1954 Charles Scribner's Sons; Copyright renewed © 1961 Ernest H. Shepard. Used by permission of Charles Sribner's Sons.

'Greedy beggars!' he observed, making for the provender. 'Why didn't you invite me, Ratty?'

'This was an impromptu affair,' explained the Rat. 'By the way — my friend Mr. Mole.'

'Proud, I'm sure,' said the Otter, and the two animals were friends forthwith.

'Such a rumpus everywhere!' continued the Otter. 'All the world seems out on the river today. I came up this backwater to try and get a moment's peace, and then stumble upon you fellows! — At least — I beg pardon — I don't exactly mean that, you know.'

There was a rustle behind them, proceeding from a hedge wherein last year's leaves still clung thick, and a stripy head, with high shoulders behind it, peered forth on them.

'Come on, old Badger,' shouted the Rat.

The Badger trotted forward a pace or two; then grunted, 'H'm! Company,' and turned his back and disappeared from view.

'That's *just* the sort of fellow he is!' observed the disappointed Rat. 'Simply hates Society! Now we shan't see any more of him today. Well, tell us *who's* out on the river?'

'Toad's out, for one,' replied the Otter. 'In his brand-new wager-boat; new togs, new everything!'

The two animals looked at each other and laughed.

'Once, it was nothing but sailing,' said the Rat. 'Then he tired of that and took to punting. Nothing would please him but to punt all day and every day, and a nice mess he made of it. Last year it was house-boating, and we all had to go and stay with him in his house-boat, and pretend we liked it. He was going to spend the rest of his life in a house-boat. It's all the same whatever he takes up; he gets tired of it, and starts on something fresh.'

'Such a good fellow, too,' remarked the Otter reflectively. 'But no stability — especially in a boat!'

From where they sat they could get a glimpse of the main stream across the island that separated them; and just then a wager-boat flashed into view, the rower — a short, stout figure — splashing badly and rolling a good deal, but working his hardest. The Rat stood up and hailed him, but Toad — for it was he — shook his head and settled sternly to his work.

'He'll be out of the boat in a minute if he rolls like that,' said the Rat, sitting down again.

'Of course he will,' chuckled the Otter. 'Did I ever tell you that good story about Toad and the lock-keeper? It happened this way. Toad . . .

An errant May-fly swerved unsteadily athwart the current in the intoxicated fashion affected by young bloods of May-flies seeing life. A swirl of water and a 'cloop!' and the May-fly was visible no more.

Neither was the Otter.

The Mole looked down. The voice was still in his ears, but the turf whereon he had sprawled was clearly vacant. Not an Otter to be seen, as far as the distant horizon.

But again there was a streak of bubbles on the surface of the river.

The Rat hummed a tune, and the Mole recollected that animal-etiquette forbade any sort of comment on the sudden disappearance of one's friends at any moment, for any reason or no reason whatever.

'Well, well,' said the Rat, 'I suppose we ought to be moving. I wonder which of us had better pack the luncheon-basket?' He did not speak as if he was frightfully eager for the treat.

'O, please let me,' said the Mole. So, of course, the Rat let him.

Packing the basket was not quite such pleasant work as unpacking the basket. It never is. But the Mole was bent on enjoying everything, and although just when he had got the basket packed and strapped up tightly he saw a plate staring up at him from the grass, and when the job had been done again the Rat pointed out a fork which anybody ought to have seen, and last of all, behold! the mustard pot, which he had been sitting on without knowing it — still, somehow, the thing got finished at last, without much loss of temper.

The afternoon sun was getting low as the Rat sculled gently homewards in a dreamy mood, murmuring poetry-things over to himself, and not paying much attention to Mole. But the Mole was very full of lunch, and self-satisfaction, and pride, and already quite at home in a boat (so he thought) and was getting a bit restless besides: and presently he said, 'Ratty! Please, I want to row, now!'

The Rat shook his head with a smile. 'Not yet, my young friend,' he said — 'wait till you've had a few lessons. It's not so easy as it looks.'

The Mole was quiet for a minute or two. But he began to feel more and more jealous of Rat, sculling so strongly and so easily along, and his pride began to whisper that he could do it every bit as well. He jumped up and seized the sculls so suddenly, that the Rat, who was gazing out over the water and saying more poetry-things to himself, was taken by surprise and fell backwards off his seat with his legs in the air for the second time, while the triumphant Mole took his place and grabbed the sculls with entire confidence.

'Stop it, you *silly* ass!' cried the Rat, from the bottom of the boat. 'you can't do it! You'll have us over!'

The Mole flung his sculls back with a flourish, and made a great dig at the water. He missed the surface altogether, his legs flew up above his head, and he found himself lying on the top of the prostrate Rat. Greatly alarmed, he made a grab at the side of the boat, and the next moment — Sploosh!

Over went the boat, and he found himself struggling in the river.

O my, how cold the water was, and O, how *very* wet it felt. How it sang in his ears as he went down, down, down! How bright and welcome the sun looked as he rose to the surface coughing and spluttering! How black was his despair when he felt himself sinking again! Then a firm paw gripped him by the back of his neck. It was the Rat, and he was evidently laughing — the Mole could *feel* him laughing, right down his arm and through his paw, and so into his — the Mole's — neck.

The Rat got hold of a scull and shoved it under the Mole's arm; then he did the same by the other side of him and, swimming behind, propelled the helpless animal to shore, hauled him out, and set him down on the bank, a squashy, pulpy lump of misery.

When the Rat had rubbed him down a bit, and wrung some of the wet out of him, he said, 'Now, then, old fellow! Trot up and down the towing-path as hard as you can, till you're warm and dry again, while I dive for the luncheon-basket.'

So the dismal Mole, wet without and ashamed within, trotted about till he was fairly dry, while the Rat plunged into the water again, recovered the boat, righted her and made her fast, fetched his floating property to shore by degrees, and finally dived successfully for the luncheon-basket and struggled to land with it.

When all was ready for a start once more, the Mole, limp and dejected, took his seat in the stern of the boat; and as they set off, he said in a low voice, broken with emotion, 'Ratty, my generous friend! I am very sorry indeed for my foolish and ungrateful conduct. My heart quite fails me when I think how I might have lost that beautiful luncheon-basket. Indeed, I have been a complete ass, and I know it. Will you overlook it this once and forgive me, and let things go on as before?'

'That's all right, bless you!' responded the Rat cheerily. 'What's a little wet to a Water Rat? I'm more in the water than out of it most days. Don't you think any more about it; and, look here! I really think you had better come and stop with me for a little time. It's very plain and rough, you know — not like Toad's house at all — but you haven't seen that yet; still, I can make you comfortable. And I'll teach you to row, and to swim and you'll soon be as handy on the water as any of us.'

The Mole was so touched by his kind manner of speaking that he could find no voice to answer him; and he had to brush away a tear or two with the back of his paw. But the Rat kindly looked in another direction, and presently the Mole's spirits revived again, and he was even able to give some straight back-talk to a couple of moorhens who were sniggering to each other about his bedraggled appearance.

When they got home, the Rat made a bright fire in the parlour, and planted the Mole in an armchair in front of it, having fetched down a dressing-gown and slippers for him, and told him river stories till supper-time. Very thrilling stories they were, too, to an earth-dwelling animal like Mole. Stories about weirs, and sudden floods, and leaping pike, and steamers that flung hard bottles — at least bottles were certainly flung, and *from* steamers, so presumably by them; and about herons, and how particular they were whom they spoke to; and about adventures down drains, and nightfishings with Otter, or excursions far afield with Badger. Supper was a most cheerful meal; but very shortly afterwards a terrible sleepy Mole had to be escorted upstairs by his considerate host, to the best bedroom, where he soon laid his head on his pillow in great peace and contentment, knowing that his new found friend the River was lapping the sill of his window.

This day was only the first of many similar ones for the emancipated Mole, each of them longer and fuller of interest as the ripening summer moved onward. He learnt to swim and to row, and entered into the joy of running water; and with his ear to the reed-stems he caught, at intervals, something of what the wind went whispering so constantly among them.

_____

"Rikki-tikki-tavi," from The Jungle Books, *by Rudyard Kipling (Garden City, N.Y.: Doubleday, 1948).*

Kipling's story of the unlikely hero, Rikki-tikki-tavi, combines realistic accounts of mongoose behaviour with a portrayal of human characteristics. In many ways, the mongoose resembles Kenneth Grahame's Mole, especially in his trying to take his place in the larger world as he grows in experience. Like the Biblical David and Bilbo Baggins in J.R. Tolkien's The Hobbit, *this hero succeeds in spite of his size.*

Rikki-tikki-tavi

At the hole where he went in
  Red-Eye called to Wrinkle-Skin.
Hear what little Red-Eye saith:
  "Nag, come up and dance with death!"
Eye to eye and head to head,
  (Keep the measure, Nag.)
This shall end when one is dead;
  (At thy pleasure, Nag.)
Turn for turn and twist for twist —
  (Run and hide thee, Nag.)
Hah! The hooded Death has missed!
  (Woe betide thee, Nag!)

This is the story of the great war that Rikki-tikki-tavi fought single-handed, through the bath-rooms of the big bungalow in Segowlee cantonment. Darzee, the tailor-bird, helped him, and Chuchundra, the musk-rat, who never comes out into the middle of the floor, but always creeps round by the wall, gave him advice; but Rikki-tikki did the real fighting.

He was a mongoose, rather like a little cat in his fur and his tail, but quite like a weasel in his head and his habits. His eyes and the end of his restless nose were pink; he could scratch himself anywhere he pleased, with any leg, front or back, that he chose to use; he could fluff up his tail till it looked like a bottle-brush, and his war-cry, as he scuttled through the long grass, was: "*Rikk-tikk-tikki-tikki-tchk*!"

One day, a high summer flood washed him out of the burrow where he lived with his father and mother, and carried him, kicking and clucking, down a roadside ditch. He found a little wisp of grass floating there, and clung to it till he lost his senses. When he revived, he was lying in the hot sun on the middle of a garden path, very draggled indeed, and a small boy was saying: "Here's a dead mongoose. Let's have a funeral."

"No," said his mother; "let's take him in and dry him. Perhaps he isn't really dead."

They took him into the house, and a big man picked him up between his finger and thumb, and said he was not dead but half choked; so they wrapped him in cotton-wool, and warmed him, and he opened his eyes and sneezed.

"Now," said the big man(he was an Englishman who had just moved into the bungalow); "don't frighten him, and we'll see what he'll do."

It is the hardest thing in the world to frighten a mongoose, because he is eaten up from nose to tail with curiosity. The motto of all the mongoose family is, "Run and find out"; and Rikki-tikki was a true mongoose. He looked at the cotton-wool, decided that it was not good to eat, ran all round the table, sat up and put his fur in order, scratched himself, and jumped on the small boy's shoulder.

"Don't be frightened, Teddy," said his father. "That's his way of making friends."

"Ouch! He's tickling under my chin," said Teddy.

Rikki-tikki looked down between the boy's collar and neck, snuffed at his ear, and climbed down to the floor, where he sat rubbing his nose.

"Good gracious," said Teddy's mother, "and that's a wild creature! I suppose he's so tame because we've been kind to him."

"All mongooses are like that," said her husband. "If Teddy doesn't pick him up by the tail, or try to put him in a cage, he'll run in and out of the house all day long. Let's give him something to eat."

They gave him a little piece of raw meat. Rikki-tikki liked it immensely, and when it was finished he went out into the verandah and sat in the sunshine and fluffed up his fur to make it dry to the roots. Then he felt better.

"There are more things to find out about in this house," he said to himself, "than all my family could find out in all their lives. I shall certainly stay and find out."

He spent all that day roaming over the house. He nearly drowned himself in the bathtubs, put his nose into the ink on a writing table, and burnt it on the end of the big man's cigar, for he climbed up in the big man's lap to see how writing was done. At nightfall he ran into Teddy's nursery to watch how kerosene-lamps were lighted, and when Teddy went to bed Rikki-tikki climbed up too; but he was a restless companion, because he had to get up and attend to every noise all through the night, and find out what made it. Teddy's mother and father came in, the last thing, to look at their boy, and Rikki-tikki was awake on the pillow. "I don't like that," said Teddy's mother; "he may bite the child." "He'll do no such thing," said the father. "Teddy's safer with that little beast than if he had a bloodhound to watch him. If a snake came into the nursery now—"

But Teddy's mother wouldn't think of anything so awful.

Early in the morning Rikki-tikki came to early breakfast in the verandah riding on Teddy's shoulder, and they gave him banana and some boiled egg; and he sat on all their laps one after the other, because every well-brought-up mongoose always hopes to be a house-mongoose some day and have rooms to run about in, and Rikki-tikki's mother (she used to live in the General's house at Segowlee) had carefully told Rikki what to do if ever he came across white men.

Then Rikki-tikki went out into the garden

to see what was to be seen. It was a large garden, only half cultivated, with bushes as big as summer-houses of Marshal Niel roses, lime and orange trees, clumps of bamboos, and thickets of high grass. Rikki-tikki licked his lips. ''This is a splendid hunting-ground,'' he said, and his tail grew bottle-brushy at the thought of it, and he scuttled up and down the garden, snuffing here and there till he heard very sorrowful voices in a thorn-bush.

It was Darzee, the tailor-bird, and his wife. They had made a beautiful nest by pulling two big leaves together and stitching them up the edges with fibres, and had filled the hollow with cotton and downy fluff. The nest swayed to and fro, as they sat on the rim and cried.

''What is the matter?'' asked Rikki-tikki.

''We are very miserable,'' said Darzee. ''One of our babies fell out of the nest yesterday, and Nag ate him.''

''H'm!'' said Rikki-tikki, ''that is very sad — but I am a stranger here. Who is Nag?''

Darzee and his wife only cowered down in the nest without answering, for from the thick grass at the foot of the bush there came a low hiss — a horrid cold sound that made Rikki-tikki jump back two clear feet. Then inch by inch out of the grass rose up the head and spread hood of Nag, the big black cobra, and he was five feet long from tongue to tail. When he had lifted one-third of himself clear of the ground, he stayed balancing to and fro exactly as a dandelion-tuft balances in the wind, and he looked at Rikki-tikki with the wicked snake's eyes that never change their expression, whatever the snake may be thinking of.

''Who is Nag?'' said he. ''*I* am Nag. The great god Brahm put his mark upon all our people when the first cobra spread his hood to keep the sun off Brahm as he slept. Look, and be afraid!''

He spread out his hood more than ever, and Rikki-tikki saw the spectacle-mark on the back of it that looks exactly like the eye part of a hook-and-eye fastening. He was afraid for the minute; but it is impossible for a mongoose to stay frightened for any length of time, and though Rikki-tikki had never met a live cobra before, his mother had fed him on dead ones, and he knew that all a grown mongoose's business in life was to fight and eat snakes. Nag knew that too, and at the bottom of his cold heart he was afraid.

''Well,'' said Rikki-tikki, and his tail began to fluff up again, ''marks or no marks, do you think it is right for you to eat fledglings out of a nest?''

Nag was thinking to himself, and watching the least little movement in the grass behind Rikki-tikki. He knew that mongooses in the garden meant death sooner or later for him and his family, but he wanted to get Rikki-tikki off his guard. So he dropped his head a little, and put it on one side.

''Let us talk,'' he said. ''You eat eggs. Why should not I eat birds?''

''Behind you! Look behind you!'' sang Darzee.

Rikki-tikki knew better than to waste time in staring. He jumped up in the air as high as he could go, and just under him whizzed by the head of Nagaina, Nag's wicked wife. She had crept up behind him as he was talking, to make an end of him; and he heard her savage hiss as the stroke missed. He came down almost across her back, and if he had been an old mongoose he would have known that then was the time to break her back with one bite; but he was afraid of the terrible lashing return-stroke of the cobra. He bit, indeed, but did not bite long enough, and he jumped clear of the whisking tail, leaving Nagaina torn and angry.

''Wicked, wicked Darzee!'' said Nag, lashing up as high as he could reach toward the nest in the thornbush; but Darzee had built it out of reach of snakes, and it only swayed to and fro.

Rikki-tikki felt his eyes growing red and hot (when a mongoose's eyes grow red, he is angry), and he sat back on his tail and hind legs like a little kangaroo, and looked all round him, and chattered with rage. But Nag and Nagaina had disappeared into the grass. When a snake misses its stroke, it never says anything or gives any sign of what it means to do next. Rikki-tikki did not care to follow them, for he did not feel sure that he could manage two snakes at once. So he trotted off to the gravel path near the house, and sat down to think. It was a serious matter for him.

If you read the old books of natural history, you will find they say that when the mongoose fights the snake and happens to get bitten, he runs off and eats some herb that cures him. That is not true. The victory is only a matter of quickness of eye and quickness of foot, — snake's blow against mongoose's jump, — and as no eye can follow the motion of a snake's head when it strikes, that makes things much more wonderful than any magic herb. Rikki-tikki knew he was a young mongoose, and it made him all the more pleased to think that he had managed to escape a blow from behind. It gave him confidence in himself, and when Teddy came running down the path, Rikki-tikki was ready to be petted.

But just as Teddy was stooping, something flinched a little in the dust, and a tiny voice said: "Be careful. I am death!" It was Karait, the dusty brown snakeling that lies for choice on the dusty earth; and his bite is as dangerous as the cobra's. But he is so small that nobody thinks of him, and so he does the more harm to people.

Rikki-tikki's eyes grew red again, and he danced up to Karait with the peculiar rocking, swaying motion that he had inherited from his family. It looks very funny, but it is so perfectly balanced a gait that you can fly off from it at any angle you please; and in dealing with snakes this is an advantage. If Rikki-tikki had only known, he was doing a much more dangerous thing than fighting Nag, for Karait is so small, and can turn so quickly, that unless Rikki bit him close to the back of the head, he would get the return-stroke in his eye or lip. But Rikki did not know: his eyes were all red, and he rocked back and forth, looking for a good place to hold. Karait struck out. Rikki jumped sideways and tried to run in, but the wicked little dusty gray head lashed within a fraction of his shoulder, and he had to jump over the body, and the head followed his heels close.

Teddy shouted to the house: "Oh, look here! Our mongoose is killing a snake"; and Rikki-tikki heard a scream from Teddy's mother. His father ran out with a stick, but by the time he came up, Karait had lunged out once too far, and Rikki-tikki had sprung, jumped on the snake's back, dropped his head far between his fore-legs, bitten as high up the back as he could get hold, and rolled away. That bite paralysed Karait, and Rikki-tikki was just going to eat him up from the tail, after the custom of his family at dinner, when he remembered that a full meal makes a slow mongoose, and if he wanted all his strength and quickness ready, he must keep himself thin.

He went away for a dust-bath under the castor-oil bushes, while Teddy's father beat the dead Karait. "What is the use of that?" thought Rikki-tikki. "I have settled it all"; and then Teddy's mother picked him up from the dust and hugged him, crying that he had saved Teddy from death, and Teddy's father said that he was a providence, and Teddy looked on with big scared eyes. Rikki-tikki was rather amused at all the fuss, which, of course, he did not understand. Teddy's mother might just as well have petted Teddy for playing in the dust. Rikki was thoroughly enjoying himself.

That night, at dinner, walking to and fro among the wine-glasses on the table, he could have stuffed himself three times over with nice things; but he remembered Nag and Nagaina, and though it was very pleasant to be patted and petted by Teddy's mother, and to sit on Teddy's shoulder, his eyes would get red from time to time, and he would go off into his long war-cry of "*Rikk-tikk-tikki-tikki-tchk!*"

Teddy carried him off to bed, and insisted on Rikki-tikki sleeping under his chin. Rikki-tikki was too well bred to bite or scratch, but as soon as Teddy was asleep he went off for his nightly walk round the house, and in the dark he ran up against Chuchundra, the musk-rat, creeping round by the wall. Chuchundra is a broken-hearted little beast. He whimpers and cheeps all the night, trying to make up his mind to run into the middle of the room, but he never gets there.

"Don't kill me," said Chuchundra, almost weeping. "Rikki-tikki, don't kill me."

"Do you think a snake-killer kills musk-rats?" said Rikki-tikki scornfully.

"Those who kill snakes get killed by snakes," said Chuchundra, more sorrowfully than ever. "And how am I to be sure that Nag won't mistake me for you some dark night?"

"There's not the least danger," said Rikki-tikki; "but Nag is in the garden, and I know you don't go there."

"My cousin Chua, the rat, told me—" said Chuchundra, and then he stopped.

"Told you what?"

"H'sh! Nag is everywhere, Rikki-tikki. You should have talked to Chua in the garden."

"I didn't — so you must tell me. Quick, Chuchundra, or I'll bite you!"

Chuchundra sat down and cried till the tears rolled off his whiskers. "I am a very poor man," he sobbed. "I never had spirit enough to run out into the middle of the room. H'sh! I mustn't tell you anything. Can't you *hear*, Rikki-tikki?"

Rikki-tikki listened. The house was as still as still, but he thought he could just catch the faintest *scratch-scratch* in the world, — a noise as faint as that of a wasp walking on a window-pane, — the dry scratch of a snake's scales on brick-work.

"That's Nag or Nagaina," he said to himself; "and he is crawling into the bath-room sluice. You're right, Chuchundra; I should have talked to Chua."

He stole off to Teddy's bath-room, but there was nothing there, and then to Teddy's mother's bath-room. At the bottom of the smooth plaster wall there was a brick pulled out to make a sluice for the bath-water, and as Rikki-tikki stole in by the masonry curb where the bath is put, he heard Nag and Nagaina whispering together outside in the moonlight.

"When the house is emptied of people," said Nagaina to her husband, "*he* will have to go away, and then the garden will be our own again. Go in quietly, and remember that the big man who killed Karait is the first one to bite. Then come out and tell me, and we will hunt for Rikki-tikki together."

"But are you sure that there is anything to be gained by killing the people?" said Nag.

"Everything. When there were no people in the bungalow, did we have any mongoose in the garden? So long as the bungalow is empty, we are king and queen of the garden; and remember that as soon as our eggs in the melon-bed hatch (as they may to-morrow), our children will need room and quiet."

"I had not thought of that," said Nag. "I will go, but there is no need that we should hunt for Rikki-tikki afterward. I will kill the big man and his wife, and the child if I can, and come away quietly. Then the bungalow will be empty, and Rikki-tikki will go."

Rikki-tikki tingled all over with rage and hatred at this, and then Nag's head came through the sluice, and his five feet of cold body followed it. Angry as he was, Rikki-tikki was very frightened as he saw the size of the big cobra. Nag coiled himself up, raised his head, and looked into the bath-room in the dark, and Rikki could see his eyes glitter.

"Now, if I kill him there, Nagaina will know; and if I fight him on the open floor, the odds are in his favour. What am I to do?" said Rikki-tikki-tavi.

Nag waved to and fro, and then Rikki-tikki heard him drinking from the biggest water-jar that was used to fill the bath. "That is good," said the snake. "Now, when Karait was killed, the big man had a stick. He may have that stick still, but when he comes in to bathe in the morning he will not have a stick. I shall wait here till he comes. Nagaina — do you hear me? — I shall wait here in the cool till daytime."

There was no answer from outside, so Rikki-tikki knew Nagaina had gone away. Nag coiled himself down, coil by coil, round the bulge at the bottom of the water-jar, and Rikki-tikki stayed still as death. After an hour he began to move, muscle by muscle, toward the jar. Nag was asleep, and Rikki-tikki looked at his big back, wondering which would be the best place for a good hold. "If I don't break his back at the first jump," said Rikki!, "he can still fight; and if he fights — O Rikki!" He looked at the thickness of the neck below the hood, but that was too much for him; and a bite near the tail would only make Nag savage.

"It must be the head," he said at last; "the head above the hood; and when I am once there, I must not let go."

Then he jumped. The head was lying a little clear of the water-jar, under the curve of it; and, as his teeth met, Rikki braced his back against the bulge of the red earthenware to hold down the head. This gave him just one second's purchase, and he made the most of it. Then he was battered to and fro as a rat is shaken by a dog — to and fro on the floor, up and down, and round in great circles; but his eyes were red, and he held on as the body cart-whipped over the floor, up-setting the tin dipper and the soap-dish and the fleshbrush, and banged against the tin side of the bath. As he held he closed his jaws tighter and tighter, for he made sure he would be banged to death, and, for the honour of his family, he preferred to be found with his teeth locked. He was dizzy, aching, and felt shaken to pieces when something went off like a thunderclap just behind him; a hot wind knocked him senseless, and red fire singed his fur. The big man had been wakened by the noise, and had fired both barrels of a shot-gun into Nag just behind the hood.

Rikki-tikki held on with his eyes shut, for now he was quite sure he was dead; but the head did not move, and the big man picked him up and said: "It's the mongoose again, Alice; the little chap has saved *our* lives now." Then Teddy's mother came in with a very white face, and saw what was left of Nag, and Rikki-tikki dragged himself to Teddy's bed-room and spent half the rest of the night shaking himself tenderly to find out whether he really was broken into forty pieces, as he fancied.

When morning came he was very stiff, but well pleased with his doings. "Now I have Nagaina to settle with, and she will be worse than five Nags, and there's no knowing when the eggs she spoke of will hatch. Goodness! I must go and see Darzee," he said.

Without waiting for breakfast, Rikki-tikki ran to the thorn-bush where Darzee was singing a song of triumph at the top of his voice. The news of Nag's death was all over the garden, for the sweeper had thrown the body on the rubbish-heap.

"Oh, you stupid tuft of feathers!" said Rikki-tikki angrily. "Is this the time to sing?"

"Nag is dead — is dead — is dead!" sang Darzee. "The valiant Rikki-tikki caught him by the head and held fast. The big man brought the bang-stick, and Nag fell in two pieces! He will never eat my babies again."

"All that's true enough; but where's Nagaina?" said Rikki-tikki, looking carefully round him.

"Nagaina came to the bath-room sluice and called for Nag," Darzee went on; "and Nag came out on the end of a stick — the sweeper picked him up on the end of a stick and threw him upon the rubbish-heap. Let us sing about the great, the red-eyed Rikki-tikki!" and Darzee filled his throat and sang.

"If I could get up to your nest, I'd roll all your babies out!" said Rikki-tikki. "You don't know when to do the right thing at the right time. You're safe enough in your nest there, but it's war for me down here. Stop singing a minute, Darzee."

"For the great, the beautiful Rikki-tikki's sake I will stop," said Darzee. "What is it, O Killer of the terrible Nag?"

"Where is Nagaina, for the third time?"

"On the rubbish-heap by the stables, mourning for Nag. Great is Rikki-tikki with the white teeth."

"Bother my white teeth! Have you ever heard where she keeps her eggs?"

"In the melon-bed, on the end nearest the wall, where the sun strikes nearly all day. She hid them there weeks ago."

"And you never thought it worth while to tell me? The end nearest the wall, you said?"

"Rikki-tikki, you are not going to eat her eggs?"

"Not eat exactly; no. Darzee, if you have a grain of sense you will fly off to the stable and pretend that your wing is broken, and let Nagaina chase you away to this bush. I must get to the melon-bed, and if I went there now she'd see me."

Darzee was a feather-brained little fellow who could never hold more than one idea at a time in his head; and just because he knew that Nagaina's children were born in eggs like his own, he didn't think at first that it was fair to kill them. But his wife was a sensible bird, and she knew that cobra's eggs meant young cobras later on; so she flew off from the nest, and left Darzee to keep the babies warm, and continue his song about the death of Nag. Darzee was very like a man in some ways.

She fluttered in front of Nagaina by the rubbish-heap, and cried out, "Oh, my wing is broken! The boy in the house threw a stone at me and broke it." Then she fluttered more desperately than ever.

Nagaina lifted up her head and hissed, "You warned Rikki-tikki when I would have killed him. Indeed and truly, you've chosen a bad place to be lame in." And she moved toward Darzee's wife, slipping along over the dust.

"The boy broke it with a stone!" shrieked Darzee's wife.

"Well! It may be some consolation to you when you're dead to know that I shall settle accounts with the boy. My husband lies on the rubbish-heap this morning, but before night the boy in the house will lie very still. What is the use of running away? I am sure to catch you. Little fool, look at me!"

Darzee's wife knew better than to do *that*, for a bird who looks at a snake's eyes gets so frightened that she cannot move. Darzee's wife fluttered on, piping sorrowfully, and never leaving the ground, and Nagaina quickened her pace.

Rikki-tikki heard them going up the path from the stables, and he raced for the end of the melon-patch near the wall. There, in the warm litter about the melons, very cunningly hidden, he found twenty-five eggs, about the size of a bantam's eggs, but with whitish skin instead of shell.

"I was not a day too soon." he said; for he could see the baby cobras curled up inside the skin, and he knew that the minute they were hatched they could each kill a man or a mongoose. He bit off the tops of the eggs as fast as he could, taking care to crush the young cobras, and turned over the litter from time to time to see whether he had missed any. At last there were only three eggs left, and Rikki-tikki began to chuckle to himself, when he heard Darzee's wife screaming:

"Rikki-tikki, I led Nagaina toward the house, and she has gone into the verandah, and — oh, come quickly — she means killing!"

Rikki-tikki smashed two eggs, and tumbled backward down the melon-bed with the third egg in his mouth, and scuttled to the verandah as hard as he could put foot to the ground. Teddy and his mother and father were there at early breakfast; but Rikki-tikki saw that they were not eating anything. They sat stone-still, and their faces were white. Nagaina was coiled up on the matting by Teddy's chair, within easy striking-distance of Teddy's bare leg, and she was swaying to and fro singing a song of triumph.

"Son of the big man that killed Nag," she hissed, "stay still. I am not ready yet. Wait a little. Keep very still, all you three. If you move I strike, and if you do not move I strike. Oh, foolish people, who killed my Nag!"

Teddy's eyes were fixed on his father, and all his father could do was to whisper, "Sit still, Teddy. You mustn't move. Teddy, keep still."

Then Rikki-tikki came up and cried: "Turn around, Nagaina; turn and fight!"

"All in good time," said she, without moving her eyes. "I will settle my account with *you* presently. Look at your friends, Rikki-tikki. They are still and white; they are afraid. They dare not move, and if you come a step nearer I strike."

"Look at your eggs," said Rikki-tikki, "in the melon-bed near the wall. Go and look, Nagaina."

The big snake turned half round, and saw the egg on the verandah. "Ah-h! Give it to me," she said.

Rikki-tikki put his paws one on each side of the egg, and his eyes were blood-red. "What price for a snake's egg? For a young cobra? For a young king-cobra? For the last — the very last of the brood? The ants are eating all the others down by the melon-bed."

Nagaina spun clear round, forgetting everything for the sake of one egg; and Rikki-tikki saw Teddy's father shoot out a big hand, catch Teddy by the shoulder, and drag him across the little table with the tea-cups, safe and out of reach of Nagaina.

"Tricked! Tricked! Tricked! *Rikk-tck-tck!*" chuckled Rikki-tikki. "The boy is safe, and it was I—I—I that caught Nag by the hood last night in the bathroom." Then he began to jump up and down, all four feet together, his head close to the floor. "He threw me to and fro, but he could not shake me off. He was dead before the big man blew him in two. I did it. *Rikki-tikki-tck-tck!* Come then, Nagaina. Come and fight with me. You shall not be a widow long."

Nagaina saw that she had lost her chance

of killing Teddy and the egg lay between Rikki-tikki's paws. "Give me the egg, Rikki-tikki. Give me the last of my eggs, and I will go away and never come back," she said, lowering her hood.

"Yes, you will go away, and you will never come back; for you will go to the rubbish-heap with Nag. Fight, widow! The big man has gone for his gun! Fight!"

Rikki-tikki was bounding all round Nagaina, keeping just out of reach of her stroke, his little eyes like hot coals. Nagaina gathered herself together, and flung out at him. Rikki-tikki jumped up and backward. Again and again and again she struck, and each time her head came with a whack on the matting of the verandah, and she gathered herself together like a watch-spring. Then Rikki-tikki danced in a circle to get behind her, and Nagaina spun round to keep her head to his head, so that the rustle of her tail on the matting sounded like dry leaves blown along by the wind.

He had forgotten the egg. It still lay on the verandah, and Nagaina came nearer and nearer to it, till at last, while Rikki-tikki was drawing breath, she caught it in her mouth, turned to the verandah steps, and flew like an arrow down the path, with Rikki-tikki behind her. When the cobra runs for her life, she goes like a whip-lash flicked across a horse's neck.

Rikki-tikki knew that he must catch her, or all the trouble would begin again. She headed straight for the long grass by the thorn-bush, and as he was running Rikki-tikki heard Darzee still singing his foolish little song of triumph. But Darzee's wife was wiser. She flew off her nest as Nagaina came along, and flapped her wings about Nagaina's head. If Darzee had helped they might have turned her; but Nagaina only lowered her hood and went on. Still, the instant's delay brought Rikki-tikki up to her, and as she plunged into the rat-hole where she and Nag used to live, his little white teeth were clenched on her tail, and he went down with her — and very few mongooses, however wise and old they may be, care to follow a cobra into its hole. It was dark in the hole; and Rikki-tikki never knew when it might open out and give Nagaina room to turn and strike at him. He held on savagely, and struck out his feet to act as brakes on the dark slope of the hot, moist earth.

Then the grass by the mouth of the hole stopped waving, and Darzee said: "It is all over with Rikki-tikki! We must sing his death song. Valiant Rikki-tikki is dead! For Nagaina will surely kill him underground."

So he sang a very mournful song that he made up on the spur of the minute, and just as he got to the most touching part the grass quivered again, and Rikki-tikki, covered with dirt, dragged himself out of the hole leg by leg, licking his whiskers. Darzee stopped with a little shout. Rikki-tikki shook some of the dust out of his fur and sneezed. "It is all over," he said. "The widow will never come out again." And the red ants that live between the grass stems heard him, and began to troop down one after another to see if he had spoken the truth.

Rikki-tikki curled himself up in the grass and slept where he was — slept and slept till it was late in the afternoon, for he had done a hard day's work.

"Now," he said, when he awoke, "I will go back to the house. Tell the Coppersmith, Darzee, and he will tell the garden that Nagaina is dead."

The Coppersmith is a bird who makes a noise exactly like the beating of a little hammer on a copper pot; and the reason he is always making it is because he is the town-crier to every Indian garden, and tells all the news to everybody who cares to listen. As Rikki-tikki went up the path, he heard his "attention" notes like a tiny dinner-gong; and then the steady "*Ding-dong-tock!* Nag is dead — *dong!* Nagaina is dead! *Ding-dong-tock!*" That set all the birds in the garden singing, and the frogs croaking; for Nag and Nagaina used to eat frogs as well as little birds.

When Rikki got to the house, Teddy and Teddy's mother (she still looked very white, for she had been fainting) and Teddy's father came out and almost cried over him; and that night he ate all that was given him till he could eat no more, and went to bed on Teddy's shoulder, where Teddy's mother saw him when she came to look late at night.

"He saved our lives and Teddy's life," she said to her husband. "Just think, he saved all our lives!''

Rikki-tikki woke up with a jump, for all the mongooses are light sleepers.

''Oh, it's you,'' said he. ''What are you bothering for? All the cobras are dead; and if they weren't, I'm here.''

Rikki-tikki had a right to be proud of himself; but he did not grow too proud, and he kept that garden as a mongoose should keep it, with tooth and jump and spring and bite, till never a cobra dared show its head inside the walls.

DARZEE'S CHAUNT

(Sung in honour of Rikki-tikki-tavi)

Singer and tailor am I —
  Doubled the joys that I know —
Proud of my lilt through the sky,
  Proud of the house that I sew —
Over and under, so weave I my music — so
  weave I the house that I sew.

Sing to your fledglings again,
  Mother, oh lift up your head!
Evil that plagued us is slain,
  Death in the garden lies dead.
Terror that hid in the roses is impotent — flung
  on the dung-hill and dead!

Who hath delivered us, who?
  Tell me his nest and his name.
Rikki, the valiant, the true,
  Tikki, with eyeballs of flame,
Rik-tikki-tikki, the ivory-fangéd, the hunter
  with eyeballs of flame.

Give him the Thanks of the Birds,
  Bowing with tail-feathers spread!
Praise him with nightingale-words —
  Nay, I will praise him instead.
Hear! I will sing you the praise of the bottle-
  tailed
Rikki, with eyeballs of red!

(Here Rikki-tikki interrupted, and the rest of the song is lost.)

''The Adventures of Isabel,'' from Custard and Company, *by Ogden Nash (Boston: Little, Brown, 1980).*

In ''The Adventures of Isabel,'' Ogden Nash has created a very memorable female hero. In each of her encounters, Isabel is faced with a dangerous opponent, yet in every instance she maintains her poise, and easily defeats him with a nonchalant attitude. Like folktale heroine Molly Whuppie, or Pippi Longstocking, Isabel does not behave according to accepted codes of feminine behavior.

The Adventures of Isabel

Isabel met an enormous bear,
Isabel, Isabel, didn't care;
The bear was hungry, the bear was ravenous,
The bear's big mouth was cruel and cavernous.
The bear said, Isabel, glad to meet you,
How do, Isabel, now I'll eat you!
Isabel, Isabel, didn't worry,
Isabel didn't scream or scurry,
She washed her hands and she straightened her
  hair up,
Then Isabel quietly ate the bear up.

Once in a night as black as pitch
Isabel met a wicked witch.
The witch's face was cross and wrinkled,
The witch's gums with teeth were sprinkled.
Ho ho, Isabel! the old witch crowed,
I'll turn you into an ugly toad!
Isabel, Isabel, didn't worry,
Isabel didn't scream or scurry,
She showed no rage, she showed no rancor,
But she turned the witch into milk and drank
  her.

Isabel met a hideous giant,
Isabel continued self-reliant.
The giant was hairy, the giant was horrid,
He had one eye in the middle of his forehead.
Good morning, Isabel, the giant said,
I'll grind your bones to make my bread.
Isabel, Isabel didn't worry,
Isabel didn't scream or scurry.
She nibbled the zwieback that she always fed
  off,

And when it was gone, she cut the giant's head
    off.

Isabel met a troublesome doctor,
He punched and he poked till he really shocked
    her.
The doctor's talk was of coughs and chills
And the doctor's satchel bulged with pills.
The doctor said unto Isabel,
Swallow this, it will make you well.
Isabel, Isabel, didn't worry,
Isabel didn't scream or scurry.
She took those pills from the pill concoctor,
And Isabel calmly cured the doctor.

Isabel once was asleep in bed
When a horrible dream crawled into her head.
It was worse than a dinosaur, worse than a
    shark,
Worse than an octopus oozing in the dark.
'Boo!' said the dream, with a dreadful grin,
'I'm going to scare you out of your skin!'
Isabel, Isabel didn't worry,
Isabel didn't scream or scurry,
Isabel had a cleverer scheme;
She just woke up and fooled that dream.

Whenever you meet a bugaboo
Remember what Isabel used to do.
Don't scream when the bugaboo says 'Boo!'
Just look it in the eye and say, 'Boo to you!'
That's how to banish a bugaboo;
Isabel did it and so can you!
Booooo to you.

___

"Nicholas Knock," from Nicholas Knock and
    Other People, *by Dennis Lee (Toronto: Mac-
    millan, 1974).*

*Nicholas Knock, in his confrontation with
adult authority figures, represents the older
child asserting his integrity. His relationship
to the Silver Honkabeest symbolizes his imaginative creativity, a quality he strives to
maintain in spite of all attempts to crush it.
The grown-ups' reactions to Nicholas and his
friend reveal adult fears of a power they no
longer possess. Award-winning Canadian
poet Dennis Lee skillfully varies verse forms*
*and rhythmic patterns to indicate the variety
of emotions experienced by his hero, who
does not achieve fulfillment by exercising his
talents.*

Nicholas Knock

PART ONE
Nicholas Knock was a venturesome boy.
    He lived at Number Eight.
He went for walks in the universe
    And generally got home late.

But Nicholas Knock was always around
    When the ice-cream truck went *ching*.
He dug up flowers, to watch them grow
    And he mended them with string.

He found a chipmunk, shivering like a
    Fur-cube in the snow.
He nursed it through to the end of March
    And then he let it go.

Acres of grass and acres of air —
    Acres of acres everywhere:
The sun shone high, and the moon shone low
    And Nicholas didn't care.

So Nicholas Knock went doodling
    Through summer & winter & spring.
His mind had funny edges
    And the ice-cream truck went *ching*.

PART TWO
One year it was Tuesday; Nicholas Knock
Went noodling off for a bit of a walk.
He hid on his brother, he raced a dog;
He helped a little kid catch a frog.
Then at the curb and walking east
He spied the silver honkabeest.

A trick, a flicker of the light;
The tiny creature, like a flight
Of warblers, seemed to ride the air
And shed a frisky lustre there.
And yet it did not move a hair.

Its eyes were dusky, deep, and clear.
It rose; it flew, it settled near

And Nicholas stood by its delicate side,
Nicholas stood and almost cried.

He left it then, but all that night
He dreamed of its radiant arc in flight.
And when he returned in the morning, the air
Was dimpled with light and the creature was
    there!
And every day, for a month at least,
He met the silver honkabeest.

PART THREE

"O mother, dear mother
    Prepare us a feast;
I'm friends with the silver
    Honkabeest!

"Oh father come quickly,
    I want you to see
For it's shiny and gentle as
    Gentle can be."

"Nicholas Knock!"
    His parents hissed,
"That honkabeast
    Does not exist!"

But Nicholas whinnied,
    And Nicholas sang,
And Nicholas hopped
    Till his bell-bottoms rang.

"I've seen it! I've seen it!
    I'm practically sure:
We meet every morning
    At Brunswick and Bloor."

His parents sat down,
    Exchanging a glance —
Alas for their son
    With his weirdo dance!

Even the neighbours
    Were starting to talk:
What was the matter
    With Nicholas Knock?

His mother declared,
    "I wish I was dead!"

And all in a fury
    His father said,

"This neighbourhood
    Should be policed
To get that vicious
    Honkabeast!"

But Nicholas figured
    Their tempers would mend,
So Nicholas tore off
    To visit his friend.

PART FOUR

"Frisky, most silver, serene —
bright step at the margins of air, you
tiny colossus and
winsome and
master me, easy in sunlight, you
gracious one come to me, live in
my life."

PART FIVE

Well —

They took him to
    A specialist
Who soon prescribed
    An oculist
And then a child
    Psychologist
And last a demon-
    Ologist,
Who knew about
    Astrology
And dabbled in
    Phrenology.

Their diagnoses
    Disagreed
But on one thing
    They all agreed:
If Nicholas Knock's
    Delusion ceased
(He thought he saw
    A honkabeast),
The boy would mend
    Within a year;

But otherwise
   His fate was clear —
A life in hospitals,
   Designed
To pacify
   The deviant mind,
A life in
   Institutions, meant
To exorcize
   Such devilment;
But still the boy
   Could be released
If he gave up
   His honkabeast.

Their words were kind,
   Their eyes sincere,
Their arguments
   Were strong and clear:
Because the honka-
   Beast was not,
He ought to kill it
   On the spot;
Because it was
   An utter fraud,
He ought to offer
   It to God.

Yet heartless, witless,
   Stubborn and slow,
Nicholas Knock
   Kept murmuring, "No."
They yelled at him,
   They shed real tears
Till Nicholas finally
   Plugged his ears;
The more they told him
   "Kill it dead!"
The harder Nicholas
   Shook his head.

At last they cried,
   "His time is short.
Take him away, to
   Supreme Court."

PART SIX

Snort! went the
Court clerk, and

Pounded on the table-top.
"Stand!" cried the
Bailiff with a
Steely-eyed stare.
"Name?" shrilled the
Registrar, and
Poked him with a fountain-pen.
"Swear!" boomed the
Justice with a glare.

"Please," stammered
Nicholas, "I've seen the silver
Honkabeest — "
"Silence!" roared His
Lordship, "that's a
Rumour and a lie!
Poppycock and
Insolence! The
Honkabeast is *not* a beast —
How are we to know it's not a
Pervert, or a spy?
Eh?
It's probably a pervert *and* a spy.

"Unless you sign a declaration
That the honkabeast is fiction,
Then I must — as a precaution,
To preserve Confederation —
Place a legal limitation
On your circumambulation
With a minor operation
Which we call decapitation."

   Nicholas, Nicholas
   Nicholas Knock
   Do what he says
   Or you'll go to the block.

   Nicholas, Nicholas
   Living or dead
   Sign what he says
   Or they'll chop off your head.

Nicholas stood,
He quivered with fear,
As he uttered the words
Which I set down here:

"I'm frightened of burglars,
I shake in the dark,

And I'm scared of your sharp sharp knife;
But I love the silver
Honkabeest
More than I love my life.

"I will not sign your paper.
I will not sign your bill.
I've seen him every day for a month
And I hope I always will."

Nicholas Knock,
You'll soon be deceased —
Why should you die
For a honkabeest?

PART SEVEN

His Lordship was raging,
    He sputtered and said,
"Take out the rascal
    And chop off his head! —
And by midnight tonight
    There'll be two of them dead!

"For the army, the navy,
    The Mounted Police,
The bailiff, the sheriff,
    And I
Will personally go
    To the honkabeast's den,
Preparing to do
    Or to die.
With thousands of soldiers,
    And guns in each hand,
With bombers and
    Submarines —
To safeguard our children
    We'll blast it and blitz it
To billions of
    Smithereens!!
And at last this land
    Will be released
From the threat of the terrible
    Honkabeast!"

Now, Nicholas had
Listened with a
Very meek expression;
Nicholas had heard him
with a look of

Meek dismay.
But when His Lordship spoke about
The bombing
Of the honkabeest,
Nicholas's meekness seemed to
All
Go
Away.

"Thump!" went his
Fist upon the
Forehead of the clerk of court —
"Crack!" went his shoes against the
Registrar's shin —
"Squelch!" as his head
Hit the lawyer's bulgy
Stomach, and —
"Sssmrtch!" as he caved His Lordship's
Hearing-aid in.

Then Nicholas whizzed
    And Nicholas whanged
And Nicholas knocked
    Till their craniums rang.

He rolled them up in table-cloths,
    He dumped them in the sink,
He covered them with prune-juice
    Till their eyeballs ran like ink.
He hung them from the curtain-rods,
    He slathered them in foam
And told them, gently, "Leave the silver
    Honkabeest alone."
And then he pulled the ceiling down
    And made his way back home.

PART EIGHT

The sky was as blue as a clear blue sky,
    The sun was hot and high,
When Nicholas came with a flick in his step
    And a fidgety glint in his eye.

The city hung around him, like a
    Quick and dirty scrawl:
The traffic lights, the neon lights,
    And the Bank of Montreal.

He never looked to left or right;
    He came home straightaway

To where the silver honkabeest
    Had met him every day.

He watched the stores; he watched the cars;
    He spied a silver light
That winked at him, and blinked at him —
    And disappeared from sight!

And hunting round to find the thing
    He thought he heard a hoof
That clickered like a honkabeest's,
    But vanished without proof.

And here a snort, and there a tail,
    And silver without end:
He spent a day and night that way,
    But he couldn't find his friend.

But neither could he give it up
    (And this is what was queer),
For every time he started to,
    The thing would reappear.

And if you take a walk on Bloor
    You still can see a boy
Whose face is sometimes in despair
    And sometimes full of joy.

You'll see him stalk and whirl around
    A hundred times at least.
Don't bother him! He's hunting for
    A silver honkabeest.

The Hundred Penny Box, *by Sharon Bell
Mathis (New York: Viking, 1975).*

*Just as death marks the end of life, under-
standing the reality of death is believed by
many to mark the end of childhood innocence
and the beginning of maturity. Mike, fiercely
defending his aging relative's hundred penny
box and with it her dignity and sense of independence, is learning about the old lady's past
and about the continuity of youth and age,
life and death. As in E.L. Konigsburg's "The
Night of the Leonids," the focus in this story
is on the growing awareness of the child.*

The Hundred Penny Box

In your shadow I have grown up . . . .
    And your beauty strikes me to the heart like
        the flash of an eagle.
                Leopold Sedar Senghor
                      Black Woman

Michael sat down on the bed that used to be his
and watched his great-great-aunt, Aunt Dew,
rocking in the rocking chair.

He wanted to play with the hundred penny
box — especially since it was raining outside
— but Aunt Dew was singing that long song
again. Sometimes when she sang it she would
forget who he was for a whole day.

Then she would call him John.

John was his father's name. Then his
mother would say, "He's Mike, Aunt Dew. His
name is Michael. John's name is John. His name
is Michael." But if his father was home, Aunt
Dew would just say "Where's my boy?" Then
it was hard to tell whether she meant him or
his father. And he would have to wait until she
said something more before he knew which
one she meant.

Aunt Dew didn't call his mother any name
at all.

Michael had heard his father and mother
talking in bed late one night. It was soon after
they had come from going to Atlanta to bring
back Aunt Dew. "She won't even look at me
— won't call my name, nothing," his mother
had said, and Michael could tell she had been
crying. "She doesn't like me. I know it. I can
tell. I do everything I can to make her
comfortable —" His mother was crying hard.
"I rode half the way across this city — all the
way to Mama Dee's — to get some homemade
ice cream, some decent ice cream. Mama Dee
said, 'The ice cream be melted fore you get
home.' So I took a cab back and made her lunch
and gave her the ice cream. I sat down at the
table and tried to drink my coffee — I mean, I
wanted to talk to her, say something. But she
sat there and ate that ice cream and looked
straight ahead at the wall and never said nothing to me. So talks to Mike and if I come around
she even stops talking sometime." His mother
didn't say anything for a while and then he

heard her say, "I care about her. But she's making me miserable in my own house."

Michael heard his father say the same thing he always said about Aunt Dew. "She's a one-hundred-year-old lady, baby." Sometimes his father would add, "And when I didn't have nobody, she was there. Look here — after Big John and Junie drowned, she gave me a home. I didn't have one. I didn't have nothing. No mother, no father, no nobody. Nobody but her. I've loved her all my life. Like I love you. And that tough beautiful boy we made — standing right outside the door listening for all he's worth — and he's supposed to be in his room sleep."

Michael remembered he had run back to his room and gotten back into bed and gotten up again and tiptoed over to the bedroom door to close it a little and shut off some of the light shining from the bathroom onto Aunt Dew's face. Then he looked at Aunt Dew and wished she'd wake up and talk to him like she did when she felt like talking and telling him all kinds of stories about people.

"Hold tight, Ruth," he had heard his father say that night. "She knows we want her. She knows it. And baby, baby — sweet woman, you doing fine. Everything you doing is right." Then Michael could hear the covers moving where his mother and father were and he knew his father was putting his arms around his mother because sometimes he saw them asleep in the morning and that's the way they looked.

But he was tired of remembering now and he was tired of Aunt Dew singing and singing and singing.

"Aunt Dew," Michael whispered close to his great-great-aunt's wrinkled face. "Can we play with the hundred penny box?"

Precious Lord —"

"Aunt Dew! Let's count the pennies out."

"Take my hand —,"

"Aunt Dew!"

"Lead me on —"

Michael thought for a moment. He knew the large scratched wooden box was down beside the dresser, on the floor where he could easily get it.

Except it was no fun to count the pennies alone.

It was better when Aunt Dew whacked him a little and said, "Stop right there, boy. You know what that penny means?" And he'd say, "You tell me," and she would tell him.

But when she started singing it was hard to stop her. At least when she was dancing what she called "moving to the music," she'd get tired after a while. Then she would tell him about the pennies and help count them too.

Michael cupped his large hands — everybody talked about how large his hands were for his age — around his great-great-aunt's ear. "Aunt Dew!" he said loudly.

Aunt Dew stopped rocking hard and turned and looked at him. But he didn't say anything and she didn't say anything. Aunt Dew turned her head and began to sing again. Exactly where she had left off. *"Let me stand —"*

Michael moved away from the rocking chair and sat back down on the bed. Then he got up and went to the dresser. He reached down and picked up the heavy, scratched-up hundred penny box from the floor, walked to the bedroom door, and stood there for a moment before he went out.

There was no way to stop Aunt Dew once she started singing that long song.

Michael walked down the hall and held the huge box against his stomach. He could still hear Aunt Dew's high voice.

"I am weak. I am worn."

"What's wrong?" his mother asked when he walked into the kitchen and sat down on a chair and stared at the floor.

He didn't want to answer.

"Oh," his mother said and reached for the hundred penny box in his arms. "Give me that thing," she said. "That goes today! Soon as Aunt Dew's sleep, that goes in the furnace."

Michael almost jumped out of the chair. He wouldn't let go of the big, heavy box. He could hear his great-great-aunt's voice. She was singing louder. *"Lead me through the night, precious Lord. Take my hand."*

"You can't take the hundred penny box," Michael cried. "I'll tell Daddy if you take it and burn it up in the furnace like you burned up all the rest of Aunt Dew's stuff!" Then Michael thought of all the things he and Aunt Dew had hidden in his closet, and almost told his mother.

5

His mother walked closer to him and stood there but he wasn't afraid. Nobody was going to take Aunt Dew's hundred penny box. Nobody. Nobody. Nobody.

"Aunt Dew's like a child," his mother said quietly. "She's like you. Thinks she needs a whole lot of stuff she really doesn't. I'm not taking her pennies — you know I wouldn't take her pennies. I'm just getting rid of that big old ugly wooden box always under foot!"

Michael stood up. "No," he said.

"Mike, did you say no to me?" his mother asked. She put her hands on her hips.

"I mean," Michael said and tried to think fast. "Aunt Dew won't go to sleep if she doesn't see her box in the corner. Can I take it back and then you can let her see it? And when she goes to sleep, you can take it."

"Go put it back in her room then," his mother said. "I'll get it later."

"Okay," Michael said and held the heavy box tighter and walked slowly back down the hall to the small bedroom that used to be his. He opened the door and went in, put the hundred penny box down on the floor and sat down on it, staring at his aunt. She wasn't singing, just sitting. "John-boy," she said.

"Yes, Aunt Dew," Michael answered and didn't care this time that she was calling him John again. He was trying to think.

"Put my music on."

The music wasn't going to help him think because the first thing she was going to do was to make him "move" too.

But Michael got off the hundred penny box and reached under his bed and pulled out his blue record player that he had got for his birthday. He had already plugged it in the wall when he heard her say, "Get mine. My own Victrola, the one your father give me."

"Momma threw it out," Michael said and knew he had told her already, a lot of times. "It was broken."

Aunt Dew squeezed her lips real tight together. "Your momma gonna throw me out soon," she said.

Michael stood still and stared at his great-great-aunt. "Momma can't throw *people* out," he said.

"Put my music on, boy," Aunt Dew said again. "And be quick about it."

"Okay," Michael said and turned the record player on and got the record, Aunt Dew's favorite, that they had saved and hidden in the bottom drawer.

The dusty, chipped record was of a lady singing that long song, "*Precious Lord, Take My Hand.*" Michael turned it down low.

Aunt Dew started humming and Michael sat down on the bed and tried to think about what he'd do with the hundred penny box.

Aunt Dew got up from her rocking chair and stood up. She kept her arms down by her sides and made her thin hands into fists and clenched her lips tight and moved real slow in one spot. Her small shoulders just went up and down and up and down. "Get up, John-boy," she said, "and move with me. Move with Dew-bet Thomas!"

"I don't feel like dancing," Michael said and kept sitting on the bed. But he watched his great-great-aunt move both her thin arms to one side and then to the other and move her hands about and hold her dress. Then she stopped and started all of a sudden again, just swinging her arms and moving her shoulders up and down and singing some more. Every time the record ended, he'd start it again.

When he was playing it for the third time, he said, "Aunt Dew, where will you put your hundred pennies if you lose your hundred penny box?"

"When I lose my hundred penny box, I lose me," she said and kept moving herself from side to side and humming.

"I mean maybe you need something better than an old cracked-up, wacky-dacky box with the top broken."

"It's *my* old cracked-up, wacky-dacky box with the top broken," Aunt Dew said. And Michael saw her move her shoulders real high that time. "Them's my years in that box," she said. "That's me in that box."

"Can I hide the hundred penny box, Aunt Dew," Michael asked, hoping she'd say yes and not ask him why. He'd hide it like the other stuff she had asked him to and had even told him where to hide it most of the time.

"No, don't hide my hundred penny box!" Aunt Dew said out loud. "Leave my hundred penny box right alone. Anybody takes my hundred penny box takes me!''

"Just in case," Michael said impatiently and wished his great-great-aunt would sit back down in her chair so he could talk to her. "Just in case Momma puts it in the furnace when you go to sleep like she puts all your stuff in the furnace in the basement."

"What your momma name?"

"Oh, no," Michael said. "You keep *on* forgetting Momma's name!" That was the only thing bad about being a hundred years old like Aunt Dew — you kept *on* forgetting things that were important.

"Hush, John-boy," Aunt Dew said and stopped dancing and humming and sat back down in the chair and put the quilt back over her legs.

"You keep on forgetting."

"I don't."

"You do, you keep on forgetting!"

"Do I forget to play with you when you worry me to death to play?"

Michael didn't answer.

"Do I forget to play when you want?"

"No."

"Okay. What your momma name? Who's that in my kitchen?"

"Momma's name is Ruth, but this isn't your house. Your house is in Atlanta. We went to get you and now you live with us."

"Ruth."

Michael saw Aunt Dew staring at him again. Whenever she stared at him like that, he never knew what she'd say next. Sometimes it had nothing to do with what they had been talking about.

"You John's baby," she said, still staring at him. "Look like John just spit you out."

"That's my father."

"My great-nephew," Aunt Dew said. "Only one ever care about me." Aunt Dew rocked hard in her chair then and Michael watched her. He got off the bed and turned off the record player and put the record back into the bottom drawer. Then he sat down on the hundred penny box again.

"See that tree out there?" Aunt Dew said and pointed her finger straight toward the window with the large tree pressed up against it.

Michael knew exactly what she'd say.

"Didn't have no puny-looking trees like that near my house," she said. "Dewbet Thomas — that's me, and Henry Thomas — that was my late husband, had the biggest, tallest, prettiest trees and the widest yard in all Atlanta. And John, that was your daddy, liked it most because he was city and my five sons, Henry, Jr., and Truke and Latt and the twins — Booker and Jay — well, it didn't make them no never mind because it was always there. But when my oldest niece Junie and her husband — we called him Big John — brought your daddy down to visit every summer, they couldn't get the suitcase in the house good before he was climbing up and falling out the trees. We almost had to feed him up them trees!"

"Aunt Dew, we have to hide the box."

"Junie and Big John went out on that water and I was feeling funny all day. Didn't know what. Just feeling funny. I told big John, I said, 'Big John, that boat old. Nothing but a piece of junk.' But he fooled around and said, 'We taking it out.' I looked and saw him and Junie on that water. Then it wasn't nothing. Both gone. And the boat turned over, going downstream. Your daddy, brand-new little britches on, just standing there looking, wasn't saying nothing. No hollering. I try to give him a big hunk of potato pie. But he just looking at me, just looking and standing. Wouldn't eat none of that pie. Then I said, 'Run get Henry Thomas and the boys.' He looked at me and then he looked at that water. He turned round real slow and walked toward the west field. He never run. All you could see was them stiff little britches — red they was — moving through the corn. Bare-waisted, he was. When we found the boat later, he took it clean apart — what was left of it — every plank, and pushed it back in that water. I watched him. Wasn't a piece left of that boat. Not a splinter."

"Aunt Dew, where can we hide the box!"

"What box?"

"The hundred penny box."

"We can't hide the hundred penny box and if she got to take my hundred penny box — she might as well take me!"

"We have to hide it!"

"No — 'we' don't. It's *my* box!"

"It's *my* house. And I said we have to hide it!"

"How you going to hide a house, John?"

"Not the house! Our hundred penny box!"

"It's *my* box!"

Michael was beginning to feel desperate. But he couldn't tell her what his mother had said. "Suppose Momma takes it when you go to sleep?"

Aunt Dew stopped rocking and stared at him again. "Like John just spit you out," she said. "Go on count them pennies, boy. Less you worry me in my grave if you don't. Dewbet Thomas's hundred penny box. Dewbet Thomas a hundred years old and I got a penny to prove it — each year!"

Michael got off the hundred penny box and sat on the floor by his great-great-aunt's skinny feet stuck down inside his father's old slippers. He pulled the big wooden box toward him and lifted the lid and reached in and took out the small cloth roseprint sack filled with pennies. He dumped the pennies out into the box.

He was about to pick up one penny and put it in the sack, the way they played, and say, "One," when his great-great-aunt spoke.

"Why you want to hide my hundred penny box?"

"To play," Michael said, after he thought for a moment.

"Play now," she said. "Don't hide my hundred penny box. I got to keep looking at my box and when I don't see my box I won't see me neither."

"One!" Michael said and dropped the penny back into the old print sack.

"18 and 74," Aunt Dew said. "Year I was born. Slavery over! Black men in Congress running things. They was in charge. It was the Reconstruction."

Michael counted twenty-seven pennies back into the old print sack before she stopped talking about Reconstruction. "19 and 01," Aunt Dew said. "I was twenty-seven years. Birthed my twin boys. Hattie said, 'Dewbet, you got two babies.' I asked Henry Thomas, I said 'Henry Thomas, what them boys look like?' "

By the time Michael had counted fifty-six pennies, his mother was standing at the door.

"19 and 30," Aunt Dew said. "Depression. Henry Thomas, that was my late husband, died. Died after he put the fifty-six penny in my box. He had the double pneumonia and no decent shoes and he worked too hard. Said he was going to sweat the trouble out his lungs. Couldn't do it. Same year I sewed that fancy dress for Rena Coles. She want a hundred bows all over that dress. I was sewing bows and tieing bows and twisting bows and cursing all the time. Was her *fourth* husband and she want a dress full of bow-ribbons. Henry the one started that box, you know. Put the first thirty-one pennies in it for me and it was my birthday. After fifty-six, I put them all in myself."

"Aunt Dew, time to go to bed," his mother said, standing at the door.

"Now, I'm not sleepy," Aunt Dew said. "John-boy and me just talking. Why you don't call him John? Look like John just spit him out. Why you got to call that boy something different from his daddy?"

Michael watched his mother walk over and open the window wide. "We'll get some fresh air in here," she said. "And then, Aunt Dew, you can take your nap better and feel good when you wake up." Michael wouldn't let his mother take the sack of pennies out of his hand. He held tight and then she let go.

"I'm not sleepy," Aunt Dew said again. "This child and me just talking."

"I know," his mother said, pointing her finger at him a little. "But we're just going to take our nap anyway."

"I got a long time to sleep and I ain't ready now. Just leave me sit here in this little narrow piece a room. I'm not bothering anybody."

"Nobody said you're bothering anyone but as soon as I start making that meat loaf, you're going to go to sleep in your chair and fall out again and hurt yourself and John'll wonder where I was and say I was on the telephone and that'll be something all over again."

"Well, I'll sit on the floor and if I fall, I'll be there already and it won't be nobody's business but my own."

"Michael," his mother said and took the sack of pennies out of his hand and laid it on the dresser. Then she reached down and closed the lid of the hundred penny box and pushed it against the wall. "Go out the room, honey, and let Momma help Aunt Dew into bed."

"I been putting Dewbet Thomas to bed a long time and I can still do it," Aunt Dew said.

"I'll just help you a little," Michael heard his mother say through the closed door.

As soon as his mother left the room, he'd go in and sneak out the hundred penny box.

But where would he hide it?

Michael went into the bathroom to think, but his mother came in to get Aunt Dew's washcloth. "Why are you looking like that?" she asked. "If you want to play go in my room. Play there, or in the living room. And don't go bothering Aunt Dew. She needs her rest."

Michael went into his father's and his mother's room and lay down on the big king bed and tried to think of a place to hide the box.

He had an idea!

He'd hide it down in the furnace room and sneak Aunt Dew downstairs to see it so she'd know where it was. Then maybe they could sit on the basement steps inside and play with it sometimes. His mother would never know. And his father wouldn't care as long as Aunt Dew was happy. He could even show Aunt Dew the big pipes and the little pipes.

Michael heard his mother close his bedroom door and walk down the hall toward the kitchen.

He'd tell Aunt Dew right now that they had a good place to hide the hundred penny box. The best place of all.

Michael got down from the huge bed and walked quietly back down the hall to his door and knocked on it very lightly. Too lightly for his mother to hear.

Aunt Dew didn't answer.

"Aunt Dew," he whispered after he'd opened the door and tiptoed up to the bed. "It's me. Michael."

Aunt Dew was crying.

Michael looked at his great-great-aunt and tried to say something but she just kept crying. She looked extra small in his bed and the covers were too close about her neck. He moved them down a little and then her face didn't look so small. He waited to see if she'd stop crying but she didn't. He went out of the room and down the hall and stood near his mother. She

was chopping up celery. "Aunt Dew's crying," he said.

"That's all right," his mother said. "Aunt Dew's all right."

"She's crying real hard."

"When you live long as Aunt Dew's lived, honey — sometimes you just cry. She'll be all right."

"She's not sleepy. You shouldn't make her go to sleep if she doesn't want to. Daddy never makes her go to sleep."

"You say you're not sleepy either, but you always go to sleep."

"Aunt Dew's bigger than me!"

"She needs her naps."

"Why?"

"Michael, go play please," his mother said. "I'm tired and I'm busy and she'll hear your noise and never go to sleep."

"She doesn't have to if she doesn't want!" Michael yelled and didn't care if he did get smacked. "We were just playing and then you had to come and make her cry!"

"Without a nap, she's irritable and won't eat. She has to eat. She'll get sick if she doesn't eat."

"You made her cry!" Michael yelled.

"Michael John Jefferson," his mother said too quietly. "If you don't get away from me and stop that yelling and stop that screaming and leave me alone —!"

Michael stood there a long time before he walked away.

"Mike," his mother called but he didn't answer. All he did was stop walking.

His mother came down the hall and put her arm about him and hugged him a little and walked him back into the kitchen.

Michael walked very stiffly. He didn't feel like any hugging. He wanted to go to back to Aunt Dew.

"Mike," his mother said, leaning against the counter and still holding him.

Michael let his mother hold him but he didn't hold her back. All he did was watch the pile of chopped celery.

"Mike, I'm going to give Aunt Dew that tiny mahogany chest your daddy made in a woodshop class when he was a teen-ager. It's really perfect for that little sack of pennies and when she sees it on that pretty dresser scarf she made — the one I keep on her dresser — she'll like it just as well as that big old clumsy box. She won't even miss that big old ugly thing!''

"The hundred penny box isn't even *bothering* you!''

His mother didn't answer. But Michael heard her sigh. ''You don't even care about Aunt Dew's stuff,'' Michael yelled a little. He even pulled away from his mother. He didn't care at all about her hugging him. Sometimes it seemed to him that grown-ups never cared about anything unless it was theirs and nobody else's. He wasn't going to be like that when he grew up and could work and could do anything he wanted to do.

"Mike,'' his mother said quietly. ''Do you remember that teddy bear you had? The one with the crooked head? We could never sit him up quite right because of the way you kept him bent all the time. You'd bend him up while you slept with him at night and bend him up when you hugged him, played with him. Do you remember that, Mike?''

Why did she have to talk about a dumb old teddy bear!

"You wouldn't let us touch that teddy bear. I mean it was all torn up and losing its stuffing all over the place. And your daddy wanted to get rid of it and I said, 'No. Mike will let us know when he doesn't need that teddy bear anymore.' So you held onto that teddy bear and protected it from all kinds of monsters and people. Then, one day, you didn't play with it anymore. I think it was when little Corky moved next door.''

"Corky's not little!''

"I'm sorry. Yes — Corky's big. He's a very big boy. But Corky wasn't around when you and I cleaned up your room a little while back. We got rid of a lot of things so that Aunt Dew could come and be more comfortable. That day, you just tossed that crooked teddy bear on top of the heap and never even thought about it —''

"I *did* think about it,'' Michael said.

"But you knew you didn't need it anymore,'' his mother whispered and rubbed his shoulder softly. ''But it's not the same with

Aunt Dew. She will hold onto everything that is hers — just to hold onto them! She will hold them tighter and tighter and she will not go forward and try to have a new life. This is a new life for her, Mike. You must help her have this new life and not just let her go backward to something she can never go back to. Aunt Dew does *not* need that huge, broken, half-rotten wooden box that you stumble all over the house with — just to hold one tiny little sack of pennies!''

"I don't stumble around with it!''

His mother reached down then and kissed the top of his head. ''You're the one that loves that big old box, Mike. I think that's it.''

Michael felt the kiss in his hair and he felt her arms about him and he saw the pile of celery. His mother didn't understand. She didn't understand what a hundred penny box meant. She didn't understand that a new life wasn't very good if you had to have everything old taken away from you — just for a dumb little stupid old funny-looking ugly little red box, a shiny ugly nothing box that didn't even look like it was big enough to hold sack of one hundred pennies!

Mike put his arms around his mother. Maybe he could make her understand. He hugged her hard. That's what she had done — hugged him. ''All Aunt Dew wants is her hundred penny box,'' Michael said. ''That's the only thing —''

"And all you wanted was that teddy bear,'' his mother answered.

"You can't burn it,'' Michael said and moved away from his mother. ''You can't burn any more of Aunt Dew's stuff. You can't take the hundred penny box. I said you can't take it!''

"Okay,'' his mother said.

Michael went down the hall and opened the door to his room.

"No, Mike,'' his mother said and hurried after him. ''Don't go in there now.''

"I am,'' Michael said.

His mother snatched him and shut the door and pulled him into the living room and practically threw him into the stuffed velvet chair. ''You're as stubborn as your father,'' she said. ''Everything your way or else!'' She was really angry. "Just sit there," she said. "And don't move until I tell you!"

As soon as Michael heard his mother chopping celery again, he got up from the chair.

He tiptoed into his room and shut the door without a sound.

Aunt Dew was staring at the ceiling. There was perspiration on her forehead and there was water in the dug-in places around her eyes.

"Aunt Dew?"

"What you want, John-boy?"

"I'm sorry Momma's mean to you."

"Ain't nobody mean to Dewbet Thomas — cause Dewbet Thomas ain't mean to nobody," Aunt Dew said, and reached her hand out from under the cover and patted Michael's face. "Your Momma Ruth. She move around and do what she got to do. First time I see her — I say, 'John, she look frail but she ain't.' He said, 'No, she ain't frail.' I make out like I don't see her all the time." Aunt Dew said, and winked her eye. "But she know I see her. If she think I don't like her that ain't the truth. Dewbet Thomas like everybody. But me and her can't talk like me and John talk — cause she don't know all what me and John know."

"I closed the door," Michael said. "You don't have to sleep if you don't want to."

"I been sleep all day, John," Aunt Dew said.

Michael leaned over his bed and looked at his great-great-aunt. "You haven't been sleep all day," he said. "You've been sitting in your chair and talking to me and then you were dancing to your record and then we were counting pennies and we got to fifty-six and then Momma came."

"Where my hundred penny box?"

"I got it," Michael answered.

"Where you got it?"

"Right here by the bed."

"Watch out while I sleep."

He'd tell her about the good hiding place later. "Okay," he said.

Aunt Dew was staring at him. "Look like John just spit you out," she said.

Michael moved away from her. He turned his back and leaned against the bed and stared at the hundred penny box. All of a sudden it looked real *real* old and beat up.

"Turn round. Let me look at you."

Michael turned around slowly and looked at his great-great-aunt.

"John!"

"It's me," Michael said. "Michael."

He went and sat down on the hundred penny box.

"Come here so I can see you," Aunt Dew said.

Michael didn't move.

"Stubborn like your daddy. Don't pay your Aunt Dew no never mind!"

Michael still didn't get up.

"Go on back and do your counting out my pennies. Start with fifty-seven — where you left off. 19 and 31. Latt married that schoolteacher. We roasted three pigs. Just acting the fool, everybody. Latt give her a pair of yellow shoes for her birthday. Walked off down the road one evening just like you please, she did. Had on them yellow shoes. Rode a freight train clean up to Chicago. Left his food on the table and all his clothes ironed. Six times she come back and stay for a while and then go again. Truke used to say, 'Wouldn't be *my* wife.' But Truke never did marry nobody. Only thing he care about was that car. He would covered it with a raincoat when it rained, if he could."

"First you know me, then you don't." Michael said.

"Michael John Jefferson what your name is," Aunt Dew said. "Should be plain John like your daddy and your daddy's daddy — stead of all this new stuff. Name John and everybody saying 'Michael.' " Aunt Dew was smiling. "Come here, boy," she said. "Come here close. Let me look at you. Got a head full of hair."

Michael got up from the hundred penny box and stood at the foot of the bed.

"Get closer," Aunt Dew said.

Michael did.

"Turn these covers back little more. This little narrow piece a room don't have the air the way my big house did."

"I took a picture of your house," Michael said and turned the covers back some more.

"My house bigger than your picture." Aunt Dew said. "Way bigger."

Michael leaned close to her on his bed and propped his elbows up on the large pillow under her small head. "Tell me about the barn again," he said.

"Dewbet and Henry Thomas had the biggest, reddest barn in all Atlanta, G-A!"

"And the swing Daddy broke," Michael asked and put his head down on the covers. Her chest was so thin under the thick quilt that he hardly felt it. He reached up and pushed a few wispy strands of her hair away from her closed eyes.

"Did more pulling it down than he did swinging."

"Tell me about the swimming pool," Michael said. He touched Aunt Dew's chin and covered it up with only three fingers.

It was a long time before Aunt Dew answered. "Wasn't no swimming pool," she said. "I done told you was a creek. Plain old creek. And your daddy like to got bit by a cottonmouth."

"Don't go to sleep, Aunt Dew," Michael said. "Let's talk."

"I'm tired, John."

"I can count the pennies all the way to the end if you want me to."

"Go head and count."

"When your hundred and one birthday comes, I'm going to put in the new penny like you said."

"Yes, John."

Michael reached up and touched Aunt Dew's eyes. "I have a good place for the hundred penny box, Aunt Dew," he said quietly.

"Go way. Let me sleep." she said.

"You wish you were back in your own house, Aunt Dew?"

"I'm going back," Aunt Dew said.

"You sad?"

"Hush, boy!"

Michael climbed all the way up on the bed and put his whole self alongside his great-great-aunt. He touched her arms. "Are your arms a hundred years old?" he asked. It was their favorite question game.

"Um-hm," Aunt Dew murmured and turned a little away from him.

Michael touched her face. "Is your face and your eyes and fingers a hundred years old too?"

"John, I'm tired," Aunt Dew said. "Don't talk so."

How do you get to be a hundred years old?"

Michael asked and raised up from the bed on one elbow and waited for his great-great-aunt to answer.

"First you have to have a hundred penny box," his great-great-aunt finally said.

"Where you get it from?" Michael asked.

"Somebody special got to give it to you," Aunt Dew said. "And soon as they give it to you, you got to be careful less it disappear."

"Aunt Dew —"

"Precious Lord —"

"Aunt Dew?"

"Take my hand —"

Michael put his head down on Aunt Dew's thin chest beneath the heavy quilt and listened to her sing her long song.

"The Courtship of the Yonghy-Bonghy-Bò," from The Complete Nonsense of Edward Lear, *ed. and intro. by Holbrook Jackson (London: Faber, 1947; Rpt. New York: Dover, 1951).*

First published in Laughable Lyrics (1877), *Edward Lear's poem "The Courtship of the Yonghy-Bonghy-Bò," is characteristic of his longer nonsense verse, which treats the themes of wandering and loss. Scholars concur that the Bò is Edward Lear, and Lady Jingly Jones is Gussie Bethell, and that the poem refers to their painful romance, one which did not succeed. Studies of children's humor suggest, however, that children themselves often create humorous stories about impossible marriages and thus give expression to their own impossible wishes. Through the comic nonsense of this poem, the reader apprehends the poignant sadness of a futile and ironic quest.*

The Courtship of the Yonghy-Bonghy-Bò

On the Coast of Coromandel
Where the early pumpkins blow,
In the middle of the woods
     Lived the Yonghy-Bonghy-Bò.
Two old chairs, and half a candle, —
One old jug without a handle, —
     These were all his worldly goods:

In the middle of the woods,
These were all the worldly goods,
Of the Yonghy-Bonghy-Bò,
Of the Yonghy-Bonghy-Bò.

Once, among the Bong-trees walking
    Where the early pumpkins blow,
    To a little heap of stones.
    Came the Yonghy-Bonghy-Bò.
There he heard a Lady talking,
To some milk-white Hens of Dorking, —
    ''Tis the Lady Jingly Jones!
    'On that little heap of stones
    'Sits the Lady Jingly Jones!'
    Said the Yonghy-Bonghy-Bò,
    Said the Yonghy-Bonghy-Bò.

'Lady Jingly! Lady Jingly!
    'Sitting where the pumpkins blow,
    'Will you come and be my wife?'
    Said the Yonghy-Bonghy-Bò.
'I am tired of living singly, —
'On this coast so wild and shingly, —
    'I'm a-weary of my life:
    'If you'll come and be my wife,
    'Quite serene would be my life!' —
    Said the Yonghy-Bonghy-Bò,
    Said the Yonghy-Bonghy-Bò.

'On this Coast of Coromandel,
    'Shrimps and watercresses grow,
    'Prawns are plentiful and cheap,'
    Said the Yonghy-Bonghy-Bò.
'You shall have my Chairs and candle,
'And my jug without a handle! —
    'Gaze upon the rolling deep
    ('Fish is plentiful and cheap)
    'As the sea, my love is deep!'
    Said the Yonghy-Bonghy-Bò,
    Said the Yonghy-Bonghy-Bò.

Lady Jingly answered sadly,
    And her tears began to flow, —
    'Your proposal comes too late,
    'Mr. Yonghy-Bonghy-Bò!
'I would be your wife most gladly!'
(Here she twirled her fingers madly,)
    'But in England I've a mate!
    'Yes! you've asked me far too late,
    'For in England I've a mate,

    'Mr. Yonghy-Bonghy-Bò!
    'Mr. Yonghy-Bonghy-Bò!'

'Mr. Jones — (his name is Handel, —
    'Handel Jones, Esquire & Co.)
    'Dorking fowls delights to send,
    'Mr. Yonghy-Bonghy-Bò!
'Keep, oh! keep your chairs and candle,
'And your jug without a handle, —
    'I can merely be your friend!
    '— Should my Jones more Dorkings send,
    'I will give you three, my friend!
    'Mr. Yonghy-Bonghy-Bò!
    'Mr. Yonghy-Bonghy-Bò!'

'Though you've such a tiny body,
    'And your head so large doth grow, —
    'Though your hat may blow away
    'Mr. Yonghy-Bonghy-Bò!
'Though you're such a Hoddy Doddy —
'Yet I wish that I could modi-
    'fy the words I needs must say!
    'Will you please to go away?
    'That is all I have to say —
    'Mr. Yonghy-Bonghy-Bò!
    'Mr. Yonghy-Bonghy-Bò!'

Down the slippery slopes of Myrtle,
    Where the early pumpkins blow,
    To the calm and silent sea
    Fled the Yonghy-Bonghy-Bò.
There, beyond the Bay of Gurtle,
Lay a large and lively Turtle; —
    'You're the Cove,' he said, 'for me
    'On your back beyond the sea,
    'Turtle, you shall carry me!'
    Said the Yonghy-Bonghy-Bò,
    Said the Yonghy-Bonghy-Bò.

Through the silent-roaring ocean
    Did the Turtle swiftly go;
    Holding fast upon his shell
    Rode the Yonghy-Bonghy-Bò.
With a sad primaeval motion
Towards the sunset isles of Boshen
    Still the Turtle bore him well.
    Holding fast upon his shell,
    'Lady Jingly Jones, farewell!'
    Sang the Yonghy-Bonghy-Bò,
    Sang the Yonghy-Bonghy-Bò.

From the Coast of Coromandel,
    Did that Lady never go;
    On that heap of stones she mourns
    For the Yonghy-Bonghy-Bò.
On that Coast of Coromandel,
In his jug without a handle
    Still she weeps, and daily moans;
    On that little heap of stones
    To her Dorking Hens she moans,
    For the Yonghy-Bonghy-Bò,
    For the Yonghy-Bonghy-Bò.

"The Highwayman," from Collected Poems *(in one volume), by Alfred Noyes (New York: J.B. Lippincott Company, 1906).*

Alfred Noyes has created a highly romantic narrative poem in the ballad tradition. The poem's strong rhythms and vivid, figurative language, together with its exciting and finally tragic narrative, make it abidingly popular with young readers. Though the lovers die, they transcend the limits of mortality through the heroic intensity of their love.

The Highwayman

The wind was a torrent of darkness among the
    gusty trees.
The moon was a ghostly galleon tossed upon
    cloudy seas.
The road was a ribbon of moonlight over the
    purple moor,
And the highwayman came riding —
    Riding — riding —
The highwayman came riding, up to the old
    inn-door.

He'd a French cocked-hat on his forehead, a
    bunch of lace at his chin,
A coat of the claret velvet, and breeches of
    brown doe-skin.
They fitted with never a wrinkle. His boots
    were up to the thigh.
And he rode with a jewelled twinkle,
    His pistol butts a-twinkle,
His rapier hilt a-twinkle, under the jewelled
    sky.

Over the cobbles he clattered and clashed in
    the dark inn-yard.
He tapped with his whip on the shutters, but
    all was locked and barred.
He whistled a tune to the window, and who
    should be waiting there
But the landlord's black-eyed daughter,
    Bess, the landlord's daughter,
Plaiting a dark red love-knot into her long black
    hair.

And dark in the dark old inn-yard a stable-
    wicket creaked
Where Tim the ostler listened. His face was
    white and peaked.
His eyes were hollows of madness, his hair like
    mouldy hay,
But he loved the landlord's daughter, The land-
    lord's red-lipped daughter.
Dumb as a dog he listened, and he heard the
    robber say —

"One kiss, my bonny sweetheart, I'm after a
    prize to-night,
But I shall be back with the yellow gold before
    the morning light;
Yet, if they press me sharply, and harry me
    through the day,
Then look for me by moonlight, Watch for me
    by moonlight,
I'll come to thee by moonlight, though hell
    should bar the way."

He rose upright in the stirrups. He scarce could
    reach her hand,
But she loosened her hair in the casement. His
    face burnt like a brand
As the black cascade of perfume came tumbling
    over his breast;
And he kissed its waves in the moonlight, (O,
    sweet black waves in the moonlight!)
Then he tugged at his rein in the moonlight,
    and galloped away to the west.

He did not come in the dawning. He did not
    come at noon;
And out of the tawny sunset, before the rise of
    the moon,
When the road was a gypsy's ribbon, looping
    the purple moor,

A red-coat troop came marching —
  Marching — marching —
King George's men came marching, up to the
  old inn-door.

They said no word to the landlord. They drank
  his ale instead.
But they gagged his daughter, and bound her,
  to the foot of her narrow bed.
Two of them knelt at her casement, with mus-
  kets at their side!
There was death at every window;
  And hell at one dark window;
For Bess could see, through her casement, the
  road that *he* would ride.

They had tied her up to attention, with many
  a sniggering jest.
They had bound a musket beside her, with the
  muzzle beneath her breast!
"Now, keep good watch!" and they kissed her.
  She heard the doomed man say —
Look for me by moonlight; Watch for me by
  moonlight;
I'll come to thee by moonlight, though hell
  should bar the way!

She twisted her hands behind her; but all the
  knots held good!
She writhed her hands till her fingers were wet
  with sweat or blood!
They stretched and strained in the darkness,
  and the hours crawled by like years,
Till, now, on the stroke of midnight,
  Cold, on the stroke of midnight,
The tip of one finger touched it! The trigger at
  least was hers!

The tip of one finger touched it. She strove no
  more for the rest.
Up, she stood up to attention, with the muzzle
  beneath her breast.
She would not risk their hearing; she would
  not strive again;
For the road lay bare in the moonlight; Blank
  and bare in the moonlight;
And the blood of her veins, in the moonlight,
  throbbed to her love's refrain.

Tlot-tlot; tlot-tolt! Had they heard it? The
  horse-hoofs ringing clear;
Tlot-Tlot, tlot-tlot, in the distance? Were they
  deaf that they did not hear?
Down the ribbon of moonlight, over the brow
  of the hill,
The highwayman came riding —
  Riding — riding —
The red-coats looked to their priming! She
  stood up, straight and still.

Tlot-tlot, in the frosty silence! *Tlot-tlot*, in the
  echoing night!
Nearer he came and nearer. Her face was like a
  light.
Her eyes grew wide for a moment; she drew
  one last deep breath.
Then her finger moved in the moonlight, Her
  musket shattered the moonlight,
Shattered her breast in the moonlight and
  warned him — with her death.

He turned. He spurred to the west; he did not
  know who stood
Bowed, with her head o'er the musket,
  drenched with her own blood!
Not till the dawn he heard it, and his face grew
  grey to hear
How Bess, the landlord's daughter,
  The landlord's black-eyed daughter,
Had watched for her love in the moonlight,
  and died in the darkness there.

Back, he spurred like a madman, shouting a
  curse to the sky
With the white road smoking behind him and
  his rapier brandished high.
Blood-red were his spurs in the golden noon;
  wine-red was his velvet coat;
When they shot him down on the highway,
  Down like a dog on the highway,
And he lay in his blood on the highway, with a
  bunch of lace at his throat.

And still of a winter's night, they say, when
  the wind is in the trees,
When the moon is a ghostly galleon tossed
  upon cloudy seas,
When the road is a ribbon of moonlight over
  the purple moor,

A highwayman comes riding —
   Riding — riding —
A highwayman comes riding, up to the old
   inn-door.

Over the cobbles he clatters and clangs in the
   dark inn-yard.
He taps with his whip on the shutters, but all
   is locked and barred.
He whistles a tune to the window, and who
   should be waiting there
But the landlord's black-eyed daughter, Bess,
   the landlord's daughter,
Plaiting a dark red love-knot into her long
   black hair.

━━━

"Jim, Who Ran Away from His Nurse, and Was Eaten by a Lion," from Cautionary Tales for Children, *by Hilaire Belloc (London: Eveleigh Nash, 1907).*

   English writer Hilaire Belloc wrote four volumes of humorous poetry for children. In Cautionary Tales for Children *Belloc satirizes the "awful warning story" popular in nineteenth-century England and written by moralist writers. In this tale Belloc treats a boy's disobedience and its awful consequences, yet he treats the subject in a comic and jaunty manner reminiscent of the nonsense poems of Edward Lear and Lewis Carroll. "The New Mother," "The Story of the Three Bears," and, to a much lesser degree,* The Tale of Peter Rabbit *belong to the tradition Belloc is parodying.*

Jim, Who ran away from his Nurse, and was eaten by a Lion.

There was a Boy whose name was Jim;
His Friends were very good to him.
They gave him Tea, and Cakes, and Jam,
And slices of delicious Ham,
And Chocolate with pink inside,
And little Tricycles to ride,
And read him Stories through and through,
And even took him to the Zoo —
But there it was the dreadful Fate
Befel him, which I now relate.

You know — at least you *ought* to know,
For I have often told you so —
That Children never are allowed
To leave their Nurses in a Crowd;

Now this was Jim's especial Foible,
He ran away when he was able,
And on this inauspicious day
He slipped his hand and ran away!
He hadn't gone a yard when —

                              Bang!
With open Jaws, a Lion sprang,
And hungrily began to eat
The Boy: beginning at his feet.

Now, just imagine how it feels
When first your toes and then your heels,
And then by gradual degrees,
Your shins and ankles, calves and knees,
Are slowly eaten, bit by bit.

No wonder Jim detested it!
No wonder that he shouted "Hi!"
The Honest Keeper heard his cry,
Though very fat

                    he almost ran
To help the little gentleman.
"Ponto!" he ordered as he came
(For Ponto was the Lion's name),
"Ponto!" he cried,

                    with angry Frown.
"Let go, Sir! Down, Sir! Put it down!"

The Lion made a sudden Stop,
He let the Dainty Morsel drop,
And slunk reluctant to his Cage,
Snarling with Disappointed Rage.
But when he bent him over Jim,
The Honest Keeper's

                    Eyes were dim.
The Lion having reached his Head,
The Miserable Boy was dead!

When Nurse informed his Parents, they
Were more Concerned than I can say: —
His Mother, as She dried her eyes,

Said, "Well — it gives me no surprise,
He would not do as he was told!"
His Father, who was self-controlled,
Bade all the children round attend

To James' miserable end,
And always keep a-hold of Nurse
For fear of finding something worse.

———

"The Price of His Life," from Red Fox, *by Sir Charles G.D. Roberts (Toronto: Ryerson Press, 1948).*

Although Canadian naturalist and writer Sir Charles G.D. Roberts is painstakingly accurate in his portrayal of animals, he makes heroes of the superior animals he chooses as subjects, The father of Red Fox is referred to as "stronger and cleverer than the average run of foxes" and as being "a very Odysseus of his kind for valour and guile." In Roberts' presentation of the death of the old fox, one can find similarities to the death of Beowulf: age and fate combine to bring about the end; however, the hero dies for the well-being of others. This selection also emphasizes the continuity of life: although the father is dead, it is springtime and the newly born foxes now have the chance for a full life.

The hero of this story can be contrasted to the fox in "Henny Penny" and, in his ability as a trickster, to Coyote in "Coyote Loses His Dinner."

The Price of His Life

Two voices, a mellow, bell-like baying and an excited yelping, came in chorus upon the air of the April dawn. The musical and irregularly blended cadence, now swelling, now diminishing, seemed to fit accompaniment to the tender, thin-washed colouring of the landscape which lay spread out under the gray and lilac lights of approaching sunrise. The level country, of mixed woodland and backwoods farm, still showed a few white patches here and there where the snow lingered in the deep hollows; but all over the long, wide southward-facing slope of the uplands, with their rough woods broken by occasional half-cleared, hillocky pastures, the spring was more advanced. Faint green films were beginning to show on the birch and popular thickets, and over the pasture hillocks; and every maple hung forth a rosy veil that seemed to imitate the flush of morning.

The music of the dog's voices, melodious though it was, held something sinister in its sweetness, — a sort of menacing and implacable joy. As the first notes of it came floating up from the misty lowlands, an old red fox started up from his sleep under a squat juniper-bush on the top of a sunny bank. Wide-awake on the instant, he stood listening critically to the sound. Then he came a few paces down the bank, which was open, dotted with two or three bushes and boulders, and its turf already green through the warmth of its sandy soil. He paused beside the mouth of a burrow which was partly screened by the evergreen branches of a juniper. The next moment another and somewhat smaller fox appeared, emerging briskly from the burrow, and stood beside him, intently listening.

The thrilling clamour grew louder, grew nearer, muffled now and then for a few moments as the trail which the dogs were following led through some dense thicket of spruce or fir. Soon an uneasy look came over the shrewd, grayish-yellow face of the old fox, as he realized that the trail in question was the one which he had himself made but two hours earlier, on his return from a survey of a neighbouring farmer's hen-roost. He had taken many precautions with that homeward trail, tangling and breaking it several times; but he knew that ultimately, for all its deviations and subtleties, it might lead the dogs to this little warm den on the hillside, wherein his mate had but yesterday given birth to five blind, helpless whimpering puppies. As the slim red mother realized the same fact, her fangs bared themselves in a silent snarl, and, backing up against the mouth of the burrow, she stood there an image of savage resolution, a dangerous adversary for any beast less powerful than bear or panther.

To her mate, however, it was obvious that something more than valour was needed to avert the approaching peril. He knew both the dogs whose chiming voices came up to him so unwelcomely on the sweet spring air. He knew that both were formidable fighters, strong and woodswise. For the sake of those five helpless, sprawling ones at the bottom of the den, the mother must not be allowed to fight. Her death, or even her serious injury, would mean their death. With his sharp ears cocked very straight, one paw lifted alertly, and an expression of confident readiness in his whole attitude, he waited a moment longer, seeking to weigh the exact nearness of the menacing cries. At length a wandering puff of air drawing up from the valley brought the sound startlingly near and clear. Like a flash the fox slipped down the bank and darted into the underbrush, speeding to intercept the enemy.

A couple of hundred yards away from the den in the bank a rivulet, now swollen and noisy with spring rains, ran down the hillside. For a little distance the fox followed its channel, now on one side, now on the other, now springing from rock to rock amid the foamy darting of the waters, now making brief, swift excursions among the border thickets. In this way he made his trail obscure and difficult. Then, at what he held a fitting distance from home, he intersected the line of his old trail, and halted upon it ostentatiously, that the new scent might unmistakably overpower the old.

The baying and yelping chorus was now very close at hand. The fox ran on slowly, up an open vista between the trees, looking over his shoulder to see what the dogs would do on reaching the fresh trail. He had not more than half a minute to wait. Out from a greening poplar thicket burst the dogs, running with noses to the ground. The one in the lead, baying conscientiously, was a heavy-shouldered, flop-eared, much dewlapped dog of a tawny yellow colour, a half-bred foxhound whose cur mother had not obliterated the instincts bequeathed him by his pedigreed and well-trained sire. His companion, who followed at his heels and paid less scrupulous heed to the trail, looking around excitedly every other minute and yelping to relieve his exuberance, was a big black and white mongrel, whose long jaw and wavy coat seemed to indicate a strain of collie blood in his much mixed ancestry.

Arriving at the point where the trail was crossed by the hot, fresh scent, the leader stopped so abruptly that his follower fairly fell over him. For several seconds the noise of their voices was redoubled, as they sniffed wildly at the pungent turf. Then they wheeled, and took up the new trail. The next moment they saw the fox, standing at the edge of a ribbon of spruce woods and looking back at them superciliously. With a new and wilder note in their cries, they dashed forward frantically to seize him. But his white-tipped, feathery brush flickered before their eyes for a fraction of a second, and vanished into the gloom of the spruce wood.

The chase was now full on, the quarry near, and the old trail forgotten. In a savage intoxication, reflected in the wildness of their cries, the dogs tore ahead through brush and thicket, ever farther and farther from that precious den on the hillside. Confident in his strength as well as his craft, the old fox led them for a couple of miles straight away, choosing the roughest ground, the most difficult gullies, the most tangled bits of underbrush for his course. Fleeter of foot and lighter than his foes, he had no difficulty in keeping ahead of them. But it was not his purpose to distance them or run any risk of discouraging them, lest they should give up and go back to their first venture. He wanted to utterly wear them out, and leave them at last so far from home that, by the time they should be once more ready to go hunting, his old trail leading to the den should be no longer decipherable by eye or nose.

By this time the rim of the sun was above the horizon, mounting into a rose-fringed curtain of tender April clouds, and shooting long beams of rose across the level country. These beams seemed to find vistas ready everywhere, open lines of roadway, or cleared fields, or straight groves, or gleaming river reaches all appearing to converge toward the far-off fount of radiance. Down one of these lanes of pink glory the fox ran in plain sight, looking strangely large and dark in the mystic glow. Very close behind him came the two pursuers, fantastic, leaping, ominous shapes. For several minutes the chase fled on into the eye of the morning, then vanished down an unseen cross-corridor of the woods.

And now it seemed to the brave and crafty old fox, a very Odysseus of his kind for valour and guile, that he had led the enemy almost far enough from home. It was time to play with them a little. Lengthening out his stride till he had secured a safer lead, he described two or three short circles, and then ran on more slowly. His pursuers were quite out of sight, hidden by the trees and bushes; but he knew very well by his hearing just when they ran into those confusing loops in the trail. As the sudden, excited confusion in their cries reached him, he paused and looked back with his grayish-ruddy head cocked to one side; and, if laughter had been one of the many vulpine accomplishments, he certainly would have laughed at that moment. But presently the voices showed him that their owners had successfully straightened out the little snarl and were once more after him. So once more he ran on, devising further shifts.

Coming now to a rocky brook of some width, the fox stepped out upon the stones, then leaped back upon his own trail, ran a few steps along it, and finally jumped aside as far as he could, alighting upon a log in the heart of a blueberry scrub. Slipping down from the log, he raced back a little way parallel with his tracks and lay down on the top of a dry hillock to rest. A drooping screen of hemlock branches here gave him effective hiding, while his sharp eyes commanded the brookside and perhaps a hundred yards of the back trail.

In a moment or two the dogs rushed by, their tongues hanging far out, but their voices still eager and fierce. Not thirty paces away the old fox watched them cynically, wrinkling his narrow nose with aversion as the light breeze brought him their scent. As he watched, the pupils of his eyes contracted to narrow, upright slits of liquid black, then rounded out again as anger yielded to interest. It filled him with interest, indeed, to watch the frantic bewilderment and haste of his pursuers when the broken trail at the edge of the brook baffled them. First they went splashing across to the other bank, and rushed up and down sniffing savagely for the scent. Next they returned to the near bank and repeated the same tactics. Then they seemed to conclude that the fugitive had attempted to cover his tracks by travelling in the water, so they traced the water's edge exactly, on both sides, for about fifty yards up and down. Finally they returned to the point where the trail was broken, and silently began to work around it in widening circles. At that the yellow half-breed gave voice. He had recaptured the scent on the log in the blueberry patch. As the noisy chorus rose again upon the morning air, the old fox got up, stretched himself somewhat contemptuously, and stood out in plain view with a shrill bark of defiance. Joyously the dogs accepted the challenge and hurled themselves forward; but in the same instant the fox vanished, leaving behind him a streak of pungent, musky scent that clung in the bushes and on the air.

And now for an hour the eager dogs found themselves continually overrunning or losing the trail. More than half their time and energy were spent in solving the riddles which their quarry kept propounding to them. Once they lost fully ten minutes racing up and down and round and round a hillocky sheep-pasture, utterly baffled, while the fox, hidden in the cleft of a rock on the other side of the fence, lay comfortably eyeing their performances. The sheep, huddling in a frightened mass in one corner of the pasture, scared by the noise, had given him just the chance he wanted. Leaping lightly upon the nearest, he had run over the thick-fleeced backs of the whole flock, and gained the top of the rail fence, from which he had sprung easily to the cleft in the rock. To the dogs it was as if their quarry had suddenly grown wings and soared into the air. The chase would have ended there but for the mischance of the shifting of the wind. The light breeze which had been drawing up from the southwest all at once, without warning, veered over to the east; and with it came a musky whiff which told the puzzled dogs the whole story. As they raced joyously and clamorously toward the fence, the fox slipped down the other side of the rock and fled away.

A fox's wits are full of resource, and he seldom cares to practise all his accomplishments in one run. But this was a unique occasion; and this fox was determined to make his work complete and thoroughly dishearten his pursuers. He now conceived a stratagem which might, possibly, prove discouraging. Minutely familiar with every inch of his range, he remembered a certain deep deadwater on the brook, bridged by a fallen sapling. The sapling was now old and partly rotted away. He had crossed it often, using it as a bridge for his convenience; and he had noticed just a day or two ago that it was growing very insecure. He would see if it was yet sufficiently insecure to serve his purpose.

Without any more circlings and twistings, he led the way straight to the deadwater, leaving a clear trail. The tree was still there. It seemed to yield, almost imperceptibly, as he leaped upon it. His shrewd and practised perceptions told him that its strength would just suffice to carry him across, but no more. Lightly and swiftly, and not without some apprehension (for he loathed a wetting), he ran over, and halted behind a bush to see what would happen.

Arrived at the fallen tree, the dogs did not hesitate. The trail crossed. They would go where it went. But the tree had something to say in the matter. As the double weight sprang up it, it sagged ominously, but the excited hunters were in no mood to heed the warning. The next moment it broke in the middle with a punky, crumbling sound; and the dogs plunged, splashing and yelping into the middle of the icy stream.

If the fox, however, had imagined that this unexpected bath would be cold enough to chill the ardour of his pursuers, he was speedily disillusioned. Neither dog seemed to have his attention for one single moment distracted by the incident. Both swam hurriedly to land, scrambled up the bank, and at once resumed the trail. The fox was already well away through the underbrush.

By this time he was tired of playing tricks. He made up his mind to lead the enemy straight, distance them completely, and lose them in the rocky wilderness on the other side of the hill, where their feet would soon get sore on the sharp stones. Then he could rest awhile

in safety, and later in the day return by a devious route to the den in the bank and his slim red mate. The plan was a good one, and in all ways feasible. But the capricious fate of the woodfolk chose to intervene.

It chanced that, as the fox passed down an old, mossy wood-road, running easily and with the whole game well in hand, a young farmer carrying a gun was approaching along a highway which intersected the wood-road. Being on the way to a chain of shallow ponds along the foot of the uplands, he had his gun loaded with duck shot, and was unprepared for larger game. The voices of the dogs — now much subdued by weariness and reduced to an occasional burst of staccato clamour — gave him warning of what was afoot. His eyes sparkled with interest, and he reached for his pocket to get a cartridge of heavier shot. But just as he did so the fox appeared.

There was no time to change cartridges. The range was long for B B, but the young farmer was a good shot and had confidence in his weapon. Like a flash he lifted his gun and fired. As the heavy report went banging and flapping among the hills, and the smoke blew aside, he saw the fox dart lightly into the bushes on the other side of the way, apparently untouched. With a curse, devoted impartially to his weapon and his marksmanship, he ran forward and carefully examined the tracks. There was no smallest sign of blood. "Clean miss, by gum!" he ejaculated; and strode on without further delay. He knew the dogs could never overtake that seasoned old fox. They might waste their time, if they cared to. He would not. They crossed the road just as he disappeared around the next turning.

But the fox, though he had vanished from view so nonchalantly and swiftly, had not escaped unscathed. With the report, he had felt a sudden burning anguish, as of a white-hot needle-thrust, go through his loins. One stray shot had found its mark; and now, as he ran, fierce pains racked him, and every breath seemed to cut. Slower and slower he went, his hind legs reluctant to stretch out in the stride, and utterly refusing to propel him with their old springy force. Nearer and nearer came the cries of the dogs, till presently he realized that he could run no farther. At the foot of a big granite rock he stopped, and turned, and waited, with bare, dangerous fangs gleaming from his narrow jaws.

The dogs were within a dozen yards of him before they saw him, so still he stood. This was what they had come to seek; yet now, so menacing were his looks and attitude, they stopped short. It was one thing to catch a fugitive in flight. It was quite another to grapple with a desperate and cunning foe at bay. The old fox knew that fate had come upon him at last. But there was no coward nerve in his lithe body, and the uncomprehended anguish that gripped his vitals added rage to his courage. The dogs rightly held him dangerous, though his weight and stature were scarcely half what either one of them could boast.

Their hesitation, however, was but momentary. Together they flung themselves upon him, to get lightning slashes, almost simultaneously, on neck and jaw. Both yelped angrily, and bit wildly, but found it impossible to hold down their twisting foe, who fought in silence and seemed to have the strength and irrepressibility of steel springs in his slender body. Presently his teeth met through the joint of the hound's fore paw, and the hound, with a shrill *ki yi*, jumped backward from the fight. But the black and white mongrel was of better grit. Though one eye was filled with blood, and one ear slit to the base, he had no thought of shirking the punishment. Just as the yelping hound withdrew from the mix-up, his long, powerful jaws secured a fair grip on the fox's throat, just back of the jawbone. There was a moment of breathless, muffled, savage growling, of vehement and vindictive shaking. Then the valorous red body straightened itself out at the foot of the rock, and made no more resistance as the victors mauled and tore it. At a price the little family in the burrow had been saved.

Circular Journeys

"The Wolf-Pack," from Little House on the Prairie, *by Laura Ingalls Wilder. Ill. by Garth Williams (New York: Harper and Brothers, 1935; rpt. 1953).*

Laura Ingalls Wilder emphasizes for her young readers the rigorous but satisfying struggle to establish a home and community on the frontier. Quietly strong and confident, Laura's father confronts dangers, while protecting and reassuring his family. In this episode we see Laura's eager response to the thrilling dangers of prairie life, as well as the special closeness between her and her father. Wilder is especially adept at creating a vivid sense of the child's experience of home — the snug coziness within the little house and the lonely vastness without.

The strong role played by Laura's father can be contrasted to the weak role played by Hansel and Gretel's father. "Pa" is, in some ways, like the dragonslayer who protects his people from great danger.

The Wolf-Pack

All in one day Pa and Mr. Edwards built the stable for Pet and Patty. They even put the roof on, working so late that Ma had to keep supper waiting for them.

There was no stable door, but in the moonlight Pa drove two stout posts well into the ground, one on either side of the doorway. He put Pet and Patty inside the stable, and then he laid small, split logs one above another, across the door space. The posts held them, and they made a solid wall.

"Now!" said Pa. "Let those wolves howl! I'll sleep, tonight."

When Pet was on the picket-line, with Bunny frisking around her and wondering at the big world, Laura must watch Baby Carrie carefully. If anyone but Pa came near Bunny, Pet squealed with rage and dashed to bite that little girl.

Early that Sunday afternoon Pa rode Patty away across the prairie to see what he should see. There was plenty of meat in the house, so he did not take his gun.

He rode away through the tall grass, along

the rim of the creek bluffs. Birds flew up before him and circled and sank into the grasses. Pa was looking down into the creek bottoms as he rode; perhaps he was watching deer browsing there. Then Patty broke into a gallop, and swiftly she and Pa grew smaller. Soon there was only waving grass where they had been.

Late that afternoon Pa had not come home. Ma stirred the coals of the fire and laid chips on them, and began to get supper. Mary was in the house, minding the baby, and Laura asked Ma, "What's the matter with Jack?"

Jack was walking up and down, looking worried. He wrinkled his nose at the wind, and the hair rose up on his neck and lay down, and then rose up again. Pet's hoofs suddenly thudded. She ran around the circle of her picket-rope and stood still, whickering a low whicker. Bunny came close to her.

"What's the matter, Jack?" Ma asked. He looked up at her, but he couldn't say anything. Ma gazed around the whole circle of earth and sky. She could not see anything unusual.

"Likely it isn't anything, Laura," she said. She raked coals around the coffee-pot and the spider and onto the top of the bake oven. The prairie hen sizzled in the spider and the corncakes began to smell good. But all the time Ma kept glancing at the prairie all around. Jack walked about restlessly, and Pet did not graze. She faced the north-west, where Pa had gone, and kept her colt close beside her.

All at once Patty came running across the prairie. She was stretched out, running with all her might, and Pa was leaning almost flat on her neck.

She ran right past the stable before Pa could stop her. He stopped her so hard that she almost sat down. She was trembling all over and her black coat was streaked with sweat and foam. Pa swung off her. He was breathing hard, too.

"What is the matter, Charles?" Ma asked him. Pa was looking toward the creek, so Ma and Laura looked at it, too. But they could see only the space above the bottom lands, with a few tree-tops in it, and the distant tops of the earthen bluffs under the High Prairie's grasses.

"What is it?" Ma asked again. "Why did you ride Patty like that?"

Pa breathed a long breath. "I was afraid the wolves would beat me here. But I see everything's all right."

"Wolves!" she cried. "What wolves?"

"Everything's all right, Caroline," said Pa. "Let a fellow get his breath."

When he had got some breath, he said, "I didn't ride Patty like that. It was all I could do to hold her at all. Fifty wolves, Caroline, the biggest wolves I ever saw. I wouldn't go through such a thing again, not for a mint of money."

A shadow came over the prairie just then because the sun had gone down, and Pa said, "I'll tell you about it later."

"We'll eat supper in the house," said Ma.

"No need of that," he told her. "Jack will give us warning in plenty of time."

He brought Pet and her colt from the picket-line. He didn't take them and Patty to drink from the creek, as he usually did. He gave them the water in Ma's washtub, which was standing full, ready for the washing next morning. He rubbed down Patty's sweaty sides and legs and put her in the barn with Pet and Bunny.

Supper was ready. The camp fire made a circle of light in the dark. Laura and Mary stayed close to the fire, and kept Baby Carrie with them. They could feel the dark all around them, and they kept looking behind them at the place where the dark mixed with the edge of the firelight. Shadows moved there, as if they were alive.

Jack sat on his haunches beside Laura. The edges of his ears were lifted, listening to the dark. Now and then he walked a little way into it. He walked all around the camp fire, and came back to sit beside Laura. The hair lay flat on his thick neck and he did not growl. His teeth showed a little, but that was because he was a bulldog.

Laura and Mary ate their corncakes and the prairie hen's drumsticks, and they listened to Pa while he told Ma about the wolves.

He had found some more neighbors. Settlers were coming in and settling along both sides of the creek. Less than three miles away, in a hollow on the High Prairie, a man and his wife were building a house. Their name was

Scott, and Pa said they were nice folks. Six miles beyond them, two bachelors were living in one house. They had taken two farms, and built the house on the line between them. One man's bunk was against one wall of the house, and the other man's bunk was against the other wall. So each man slept on his own farm, although they were in the same house and the house was only eight feet wide. They cooked and ate together in the middle of the house.

Pa had not said anything about the wolves yet. Laura wished he would. But she knew that she must not interrupt when Pa was talking.

He said that these bachelors did not know that anyone else was in the country. They had seen nobody but Indians. So they were glad to see Pa, and he stayed there longer than he had meant to.

Then he rode on, and from a little rise in the prairie he saw a white speck down in the creek bottoms. He thought it was a covered wagon, and it was. When he came to it, he found a man and his wife and five children. They had come from Iowa, and they had camped in the bottoms because one of their horses was sick. The horse was better now, but the bad night air so near the creek had given them fever 'n' ague. The man and his wife and the three oldest children were too sick to stand up. The little boy and girl, no bigger than Mary and Laura, were taking care of them.

So Pa did what he could for them, and then he rode back to tell the bachelors about them. One of them rode right away to fetch that family up on the High Prairie, where they would soon get well in the good air.

One thing had led to another, until Pa was starting home later than he had meant. He took a short cut across the prairie, and as he was loping along on Patty, suddenly out of a little draw came a pack of wolves. They were all around Pa in a moment.

"It was a big pack," Pa said. "All of fifty wolves, and the biggest wolves I ever saw in my life. Must be what they call buffalo wolves. Their leader's a big gray brute that stands three feet at the shoulder, if an inch. I tell you my hair stood straight on end."

"And you didn't have your gun," said Ma.

"I thought of that. But my gun would have been no use if I'd had it. You can't fight fifty wolves with one gun. And Patty couldn't outrun them."

"What did you do?" Ma asked.

"Nothing," said Pa. "Patty tried to run. I never wanted anything worse than I wanted to get away from there. But I knew if Patty even started, those wolves would be on us in a minute, pulling us down. So I held Patty to a walk."

"Goodness, Charles!" Ma said under her breath.

"Yes. I wouldn't go through such a thing again for any money. Caroline, I never saw such wolves. One big fellow trotted along, right by my stirrup. I could have kicked him in the ribs. They didn't pay any attention to me at all. They must have just made a kill and eaten all they could.

"I tell you, Caroline, those wolves just closed in around Patty and me and trotted along with us. In broad daylight. For all the world like a pack of dogs going along with a horse. They were all around us, trotting along, and jumping and playing and snapping at each other, just like dogs."

Illustration by Garth Williams, "The Wolf-Pack" from *The Little House on the Prairie,* by Laura Ingalls Wilder. Copyright © 1953.

"Goodness, Charles!" Ma said again. Laura's heart was thumping fast, and her mouth and her eyes were wide open, staring at Pa.

"Patty was shaking all over, and fighting the bit," said Pa. "Sweat ran off her, she was so scared. I was sweating, too. But I held her down to a walk, and we went walking along among those wolves. They came right along with us, a quarter of a mile or more. That big fellow trotted my stirrup as if he were there to stay.

"Then we came to the head of a draw, running down into the creek bottoms. The big gray leader went down it, and all the rest of the pack trotted down into it, behind him. As soon as the last one was in the draw, I let Patty go.

"She headed straight for home, across the prairie. And she couldn't have run faster if I'd been cutting into her with a rawhide whip. I was scared the whole way. I thought the wolves might be coming this way and they might be making better time than I was. I was glad you had the gun, Caroline. And glad the house is built. I knew you could keep the wolves out of the house, with the gun. But Pet and the colt were outside."

"You need not have worried, Charles," Ma said. "I guess I would manage to save our horses."

"I was not fully reasonable, at the time," said Pa. "I know you would save the horses, Caroline. Those wolves wouldn't bother you, anyway. If they had been hungry, I wouldn't be here to —"

"Little pitchers have big ears," Ma said. She meant that he must not frighten Mary and Laura.

"Well, all's well that ends well," Pa replied. "And those wolves are miles from here by now."

"What made them act like that?" Laura asked him.

"I don't know, Laura," he said. "I guess they had just eaten all they could hold, and they were on their way to the creek to get a drink. Or perhaps they were out playing on the prairie, and not paying any attention to anything but their play, like little girls do sometimes. Perhaps they saw that I didn't have my gun and couldn't do them any harm. Or perhaps they

had never seen a man before and didn't know that men can do them any harm. So they didn't think about me at all."

Pet and Patty were restlessly walking around and around, inside the barn. Jack walked around the camp fire. When he stood still to smell the air and listen, the hair lifted on his neck.

"Bedtime for little girls!" Ma said, cheerfully. Not even Baby Carrie was sleepy yet, but Ma took them all into the house. She told Mary and Laura to go to bed, and she put Baby Carrie's little nightgown on and laid her in the big bed. Then she went outdoors to do the dishes. Laura wanted Pa and Ma in the house. They seemed so far away outside.

Mary and Laura were good and lay still, but Carrie sat up and played by herself in the dark. In the dark Pa's arm came from behind the quilt in the doorway and quietly took away his gun. Out by the camp fire the tin plates rattled. Then a knife scraped the spider. Ma and Pa were talking together and Laura smelled tobacco smoke.

The house was safe, but it did not feel safe because Pa's gun was not over the door and there was no door; there was only the quilt.

After a long time Ma lifted the quilt. Baby Carrie was asleep then. Ma and Pa came in very quietly and very quietly went to bed. Jack lay across the doorway, but his chin was not on his paws. His head was up, listening. Ma breathed softly, Pa breathed heavily, and Mary was asleep, too. But Laura strained her eyes in the dark to watch Jack. She could not tell whether the hair was standing up on his neck.

Suddenly she was sitting straight up in bed. She had been asleep. The dark was gone. Moonlight streamed through the window hole and streaks of moonlight came through every crack in that wall. Pa stood black in the moonlight at the window. He had his gun.

Right in Laura's ear a wolf howled.

She scringed away from the wall. The wolf was on the other side of it. Laura was too scared to make a sound. The cold was not in her backbone only, it was all though her. Mary pulled the quilt over her head. Jack growled and showed his teeth at the quilt in the doorway.

"Be still, Jack," Pa said.

Terrible howls curled all around inside the

house, and Laura rose out of bed. She wanted to go to Pa, but she knew better than to bother him now. He turned his head and saw her standing in her nightgown.

"Want to see them, Laura?" he asked, softly. Laura couldn't say anything, but she nodded, and padded across the ground to him. He stood his gun against the wall and lifted her up to the window hole.

There in the moonlight sat half a circle of wolves. They sat on their haunches and looked at Laura in the window, and she looked at them. She had never seen such big wolves. The biggest one was taller than Laura. He was taller even than Mary. He sat in the middle, exactly opposite Laura. Everything about him was big —his pointed ears, and his pointed mouth with the tongue hanging out, and his strong shoulders and legs, and his two paws side by side, and his tail curled around the squatting haunch. His coat was shaggy gray and his eyes were glittering green.

Laura clutched her toes into a crack of the wall and she folded her arms on the window slab, and she looked and looked at that wolf. But she did not put her head through the empty window space into the outdoors where all those wolves sat so near her, shifting their paws and licking their chops. Pa stood firm against her back and kept his arm tight around her middle.

"He's awful big," Laura whispered.

"Yes, and see how his coat shines," Pa whispered into her hair. The moonlight made little glitters in the edges of the shaggy fur, all around the big wolf.

"They are in a ring clear around the house," Pa whispered. Laura pattered beside him to the other window. He leaned his gun against that wall and lifted her up again. There, sure enough, was the other half of the circle of wolves. All their eyes glittered green in the shadow of the house. Laura could hear their breathing. When they saw Pa and Laura looking out, the middle of the circle moved back a little way.

Pet and Patty were squealing and running inside the barn. Their hoofs pounded the ground and crashed against the walls.

After a moment Pa went back to the other window, and Laura went, too. They were just in time to see the big wolf lift his nose till it pointed straight at the sky. His mouth opened, and a long howl rose toward the moon.

Then all around the house the circle of wolves pointed their noses toward the sky and answered him. Their howls shuddered through the house and filled the moonlight and quavered away across the vast silence of the prairie.

"Now go back to bed, little half-pint," Pa said. "Go to sleep. Jack and I will take care of you all."

So Laura went back to bed. But for a long time she did not sleep. She lay and listened to the breathing of the wolves on the other side of the log wall. She heard the scratch of their claws on the ground, and the snuffling of a nose at a crack. She heard the big gray leader howl again, and all the others answering him.

But Pa was walking quietly from one window hole to the other, and Jack did not stop pacing up and down before the quilt that hung in the doorway. The wolves might howl, but they could not get in while Pa and Jack were there. So at last Laura fell asleep.

"Pay Day," from Ramona and Her Father, *by Beverly Cleary. Ill. by Alan Tiegreen (New York: William Morrow and Company, 1977).*

Among Beverly Cleary's many books for children, none have enjoyed more popularity than her "Ramona" books: Ramona the Brave, Ramona the Pest, Ramona and Her Mother, *and most recently* Ramona and Her Father. *High-spirited Ramona is not really naughty — merely inventive, energetic, and irrepressible. In the following incident Cleary demonstrates her gifts for writing humorous and effective dialogue and for creating fine characters, as Ramona and her sister confront a common and extremely difficult family problem.*

The failure of the father is a frequent situation in children's stories. In "Beauty and the Beast" and Julie of the Wolves *the heroines mature as they realize that their fathers are not perfect.*

Pay Day

"Ye-e-ep!" sang Ramona Quimby one warm September afternoon, as she knelt on a chair at the kitchen table to make out her Christmas list. She had enjoyed a good day in second grade, and she looked forward to working on her list. For Ramona a Christmas list was a list of presents she hoped to receive, not presents she planned to give. "Ye-e-ep!" she sang again.

"Thank goodness today is payday," remarked Mrs. Quimby, as she opened the refrigerator to see what she could find for supper.

"Ye-e-ep!" sang Ramona, as she printed *mice or ginny pig* on her list with purple crayon. Next to Christmas and her birthday, her father's payday was her favorite day. His payday meant treats. Her mother's payday from her part-time job in a doctor's office meant they could make payments on the bedroom the Quimbys had added to their house when Ramona was in first grade.

"What's all this yeeping about?" asked Mrs. Quimby.

"I'm making a joyful noise until the Lord like they say in Sunday school," Ramona explained. "Only they don't tell us what the joyful noise sounds like so I made up my own." *Hooray* and *wow*, joyful noises to Ramona, had not sounded right, so she had settled on *yeep* because it sounded happy but not rowdy. "Isn't that all right?" she asked, as she began to add *myna bird that talks* to her list.

"Yeep is fine if that's the way you feel about it," reassured Mrs. Quimby.

Ramona printed *coocoo clock* on her list while she wondered what the treat would be this payday. Maybe, since this was Friday, they could all go to a movie if her parents could find one suitable. Both Ramona and her big sister, Beezus, christened Beatrice, wondered what went on in all those other movies. They planned to find out the minute they were grown-up. That was one thing they agreed on. Or maybe their father would bring presents, a package of colored paper for Ramona, a paperback book for Beezus.

"I wish I could think of something interesting to do with leftover pot roast and creamed cauliflower," remarked Mrs. Quimby.

Leftovers — yuck!, thought Ramona. "Maybe Daddy will take us to the Whopperburger for supper for payday," she said. A soft, juicy hamburger spiced with relish, French fries crisp on the outside and mealy inside, a little paper cup of cole slaw at the Whopperburger Restaurant were Ramona's favorite payday treat. Eating close together in a booth made Ramona feel snug and cozy. She and Beezus never quarreled at the Whopperburger.

"Good idea." Mrs. Quimby closed the refrigerator door. "I'll see what I can do."

Then Beezus came into the kitchen through the back door, dropped her books on the table, and flopped down on a chair with a gusty sigh.

"What was that all about?" asked Mrs. Quimby, not at all worried.

"Nobody is any fun anymore," complained Beezus. "Henry spends all his time running around the track over at the high school getting ready for the Olympics in eight or twelve years, or he and Robert study a book of world records trying to find a record to break, and Mary Jane practices the piano all the time." Beezus sighed again. "And Mrs. Mester says we are going to do lots of creative writing, and I hate creative writing. I don't see why I had to get Mrs. Mester for seventh grade ayway."

"Creative writing can't be as bad as all that," said Mrs. Quimby.

"You just don't understand," complained Beezus. "I can never think of stories, and my poems are stuff like, 'See the bird in the tree. He is singing to me.'"

"Tee-hee, tee-hee," added Ramona without thinking.

"Ramona," said Mrs. Quimby, "that was not necessary."

Because Beezus had been so grouchy lately, Ramona could manage to be only medium sorry.

"Pest!" said Beezus. Noticing Ramona's work, she added, "Making out a Christmas list in September is silly."

Ramona calmly selected an orange crayon.

She was used to being called a pest. "If I am a pest, you are a rotten dinosaur egg," she informed her sister.

"Mother, make her stop," said Beezus.

When Beezus said this, Ramona knew she had won. The time had come to change the subject. "Today's payday," she told her sister. "Maybe we'll get to go to the Whopperburger for supper."

"Oh, Mother, will we?" Beezus's unhappy mood disappeared as she swooped up Picky-picky, the Quimbys' shabby old cat, who had strolled into the kitchen. He purred a rusty purr as she rubbed her cheek against his yellow fur.

"I'll see what I can do," said Mrs. Quimby.

Smiling, Beezus dropped Picky-picky, gathered up her books, and went off to her room. Beezus was the kind of girl who did her homework on Friday instead of waiting until the last minute on Sunday.

Ramona asked in a quiet voice, "Mother, why is Beezus so cross lately?" Letting her sister overhear such a question would lead to real trouble.

"You mustn't mind her," whispered Mrs. Quimby. "She's reached a difficult age."

Ramona thought such an all-purpose excuse for bad behavior would be a handy thing to have. "So have I," she confided to her mother.

Mrs. Quimby dropped a kiss on the top of Ramona's head. "Silly girl," she said. "It's just a phase Beezus is going through. She'll outgrow it."

A contented silence fell over the house, as three members of the family looked forward to supper at the Whopperburger, where they would eat, close and cozy in a booth, their food brought to them by a friendly waitress who always said, "There you go," as she set down their hamburgers and French fries.

Ramona had decided to order a cheeseburger when she heard the sound of her father's key in the front door. "Daddy, Daddy!" she shrieked, scrambling down from the chair and running to meet her father as he opened the door. "Guess what?"

Beezus, who had come from her room, answered before her father had a chance to guess. "Mother said maybe we could go to the Whopperburger for dinner!"

Mr. Quimby smiled and kissed his daughters before he held out a small white paper bag. "Here, I brought you a little present." Somehow he did not look as happy as usual. Maybe he had had a hard day at the office of the van-and-storage company where he worked.

Illustration by Alan Tiegreen, "Pay Day" from *Ramona and Her Father* by Beverly Cleary. Reprinted by permission of William Morrow and Company.

His daughters pounced and opened the bag together. "Gummybears!" was their joyful cry. The chewy little bears were the most popular sweet at Glenwood School this fall. Last spring powdered Jell-o eaten from the package had been the fad. Mr. Quimby always remembered these things.

"Run along and divide them between you," said Mr. Quimby. "I want to talk to your mother."

"Don't spoil your dinner," said Mrs. Quimby.

The girls bore the bag off to Beezus's room,

where they dumped the gummybears onto the bedspread. First they divided the cinnamon-flavored red bears, one for Beezus, one for Ramona. Then they divided the orange bears and the green, and as they were about to divide the yellow bears, both girls were suddenly aware that their mother and father were no longer talking. Silence filled the house. The sisters looked at one another. There was something unnatural about this silence. Uneasy, they waited for some sound, and then their parents began to speak in whispers. Beezus tiptoed to the door to listen.

Ramona bit the head off a red gummybear. She always ate toes last. "Maybe they're planning a big surprise," she suggested, refusing to worry.

"I don't think so," whispered Beezus, "but I can't hear what they are saying."

"Try listening through the furnace pipes," whispered Ramona.

"That won't work here. The living room is too far away." Beezus strained to catch her parents' words. "I think something's wrong."

Ramona divided her gummybears, one heap to eat at home, the other to take to school to share with friends if they were nice to her.

"Something is wrong. Something awful," whispered Beezus. "I can tell by the way they are talking."

Beezus looked so frightened that Ramona became frightened, too. What could be wrong? She tried to think what she might have done to make her parents whisper this way, but she had stayed out of trouble lately. She could not think of a single thing that could be wrong. This frightened her even more. She no longer felt like eating chewy little bears. She wanted to know why her mother and father were whispering in a way that alarmed Beezus.

Finally the girls heard their father say in a normal voice, "I think I'll take a shower before supper." This remark was reassuring to Ramona.

"What'll we do now?" whispered Beezus. "I'm scared to go out."

Worry and curiosity, however, urged Beezus and Ramona into the hall.

Trying to pretend they were not concerned about their family, the girls walked into the kitchen where Mrs. Quimby was removing leftovers from the refrigerator. "I think we'll eat at home after all," she said, looking sad and anxious.

Without being asked, Ramona began to deal four place mats around the dining-room table, laying them all right side up. When she was cross with Beezus, she laid her sister's place mat face down.

Mrs. Quimby looked at the cold creamed cauliflower with distaste, returned it to the refrigerator, and reached for a can of green beans before she noticed her silent and worried daughters watching her for clues as to what might be wrong.

Mrs. Quimby turned and faced Beezus and Ramona. "Girls, you might as well know. Your father has lost his job."

"But he liked his job," said Ramona, regretting the loss of that hamburger and those French fries eaten in the coziness of a booth. She had known her father to change jobs because he had not liked his work, but she had never heard of him losing a job.

"Was he fired?" asked Beezus, shocked at the news.

Mrs. Quimby opened the green beans and dumped them into a saucepan before she explained. "Losing his job was not your father's fault. He worked for a little company. A big company bought the little company and let out most of the people who worked for the little company."

"But we won't have enough money." Beezus understood these things better than Ramona.

"Mother works," Ramona reminded her sister.

"Only part time," said Mrs. Quimby. "And we have to make payments to the bank for the new room. That's why I went to work."

"What will we do?" asked Ramona, alarmed at last. Would they go hungry? Would the men from the bank come and tear down the new room if they couldn't pay for it? She had never thought what it might be like not to have enough money — not that the Quimbys ever had money to spare. Although Ramona had often heard her mother say that house payments, car payments, taxes, and groceries seemed to eat up money, Mrs. Quimby some-how managed to make their money pay for all they really needed with a little treat now and then besides.

"We will have to manage as best we can until your father finds work," said Mrs. Quimby. "It may not be easy."

"Maybe I could baby-sit," volunteered Beezus.

As she laid out knives and forks, Ramona wondered how she could earn money, too. She could have a lemonade stand in front of the house, except nobody ever bought lemonade but her father and her friend Howie. She thought about pounding rose petals and soak-ing them in water to make perfume to sell. Un-fortunately, the perfume she tried to make always smelled like rotten rose petals, and any-way the roses were almost gone.

"And girls," said Mrs. Quimby, lowering her voice as if she was about to share a secret, "you mustn't do anything to annoy your fa-ther. He is worried enough right now."

But he remembered to bring gummybears, thought Ramona, who never wanted to annoy her father or her mother either, just Beezus, although sometimes, without even trying, she succeeded in annoying her whole family. Ra-mona felt sad and somehow lonely, as if she were left out of something important, because her family was in trouble and there was noth-ing she could do to help. When she had fin-ished setting the table, she returned to the list she had begun, it now seemed, a long time ago. "But what about Christmas?" she asked her mother.

"Right now Christmas is the least of our worries." Mrs. Quimby looked sadder than Ra-mona had ever seen her look. "Taxes are due in November. And we have to buy groceries and make car payments and a lot of other things."

"Don't we have any money in the bank?" asked Beezus.

"Not much," admitted Mrs. Quimby, "but your father was given two weeks' pay."

Ramona looked at the list she had begun so happily and wondered how much the pres-ents she had listed would cost. Too much, she knew. Mice were free if you knew the right per-son, the owner of a mother mouse, so she might get some mice.

Slowly Ramona crossed out *ginny pig* and the other presents she had listed. As she made black lines through each item, she thought about her family. She did not want her father to be worried, her mother sad, or her sister cross. She wanted her whole family, including Picky-picky, to be happy.

Ramona studied her crayons, chose a pinky-red one because it seemed the happiest color, and printed one more item on her Christmas list to make up for all she had crossed out. *One happy family*. Beside the words she drew four smiling faces and beside them, the face of a yel-low cat, also smiling.

"The Frozen Cuckoo," from All But a Few, *by Joan Aiken. Ill. by Pat Marriott (published from* All and More, *Jonathan Cape, Ltd., 1971; stories first appeared in* All You've Ever Wanted *(1953) and* More than You Bar-gained For *(1955); Rpt. London: Puffin Books, 1974).*

Known for blending elements of fantasy and humor, British author Joan Aiken creates here a farcical fantasy similar to those of F. Anstey and E. Nesbit. In this tale Aiken relies on a stock character, Sarah, the "good" bad-girl prankster who has descended from such characters as Mark Twain's Tom Saw-yer, Peck's Bad Boy, and Booth Tarkington's Penrod. *Ludicrous magical transforma-tions, near disasters, and misunderstandings are all confronted and vanquished by Aiken's other plucky child characters, Mark and Harriet Armitage. Aiken also has fun at the expense of the conventional "moral tale," since the adult rather than the child is taught a lesson about the folly of writing unkind reviews. As in "Hansel and Gretel," "Noth-ing New Under the Sun (Hardly)," and "Molly Whuppie," it is the child rather than the adult who brings about the successful resolution to the conflict.*

The Frozen Cuckoo

There was a good deal of trouble at breakfast. To begin with, Mr. Armitage was late, and that made Mrs. Armitage cross, as she always liked to have the meal over quickly on Mondays, so that the dining-room could be turned out. Then she began reading her letters, and suddenly inquired:

'What is the date today?'

'The second,' said Harriet.

'I thought so. Then that means she is coming today. How very inconsiderate.'

'Who is coming today?'

'Your cousin Sarah.'

'Oh no!' said Mark and Harriet together, in deep dismay. It is dreadful to have to say it of anybody, but their cousin Sarah was really a horrible girl. The only thing she seemed to enjoy was playing practical jokes, which she did the whole time. Nobody minds an occasional joke, but an endless course of sand in the brown-sugar bowl, grease on the stairs, and plastic spiders on the pillow-cases soon becomes tiresome.

'It'll be apple-pie beds, apple-pie beds all the way,' said Mark gloomily. 'Can't you put her off?'

'No, Aunt Rachel has to go into hospital for an operation, so I'm afraid you'll just have to bear with her. She's coming at lunch time.'

Here Mr. Armitage arrived, and sat down rubbing his hands and saying: 'The Christmas roses will be out any minute now.'

'Your bacon's cold,' said his wife crossly. 'Here are your letters.'

He opened a long, important-looking one which had a lot of printed headings on it, and instantly began to puff and blow with rage. 'Evicted? Requisitioned? What's this? Notice to quit forthwith, before 11 a.m., December 2nd. Who the dickens is this from?'

'Good gracious my dear,' said his wife, 'what have you got there?'

'It's from the Board of Incantation,' he replied, throwing the letter to her. 'They've requisitioned this house, if you please, to make a seminary for young magicians, and we have notice to quit immediately.'

'A. Whizzard,' murmured Mrs. Armitage, looking at the signature. 'Wasn't that the name of the man whose book you were so rude about in your review?'

'Yes, of course. I knew the name seemed familiar. A shockingly bad book on spells and runes.'

'Oh dear,' sighed Mrs. Armitage. 'I do wish you'd learn to be more tactful. Now we have to find somewhere else to live, and just before Christmas, too. It really is too bad.'

'Do we really have to be out by eleven o'clock?' asked Mark, who with Harriet had been listening round-eyed.

'I shall contest it,' said his father. 'It's the most monstrous tyranny. They needn't think they can ride over me roughshod.'

However, Mrs. Armitage who was a quiet but practical person, at once sent Harriet along the village to ask if they could borrow the house of Mrs Foster, who was going off to the south of France, while they looked around for somewhere else to live. Then with the help of Mrs Epis she packed up all their clothes and put them in the car. Mr Armitage refused to leave with the rest of the family, and remained behind to tackle the invaders.

Sharp at eleven o'clock several men who looked like builders' labourers arrived. They rode on rather battered, paint-stained old broomsticks, and carried hammers, saws, and large sheets of beaver-board.

'Morning, Guvner,' said one who seemed to be the foreman, advancing up the front steps.

Mr Armitage stood in the way with his arms folded. 'I protest against this unseemly intrusion!' he cried. 'It is entirely contrary to the British Constitution.'

'Ah,' said the foreman, waving a screwdriver at him in a pitying manner, 'you're cuckoo.'' At once Mr Armitage vanished, and in his place a large bird flapped in a dazed manner round the front door.

Just then an enormous, sleek dark man stepped out and came up the steps, swinging an elegant umbrella.

'Excellent, Wantage, excellent. I see you have arrived,' he said, glancing about. 'I trust you have had no trouble?'

'Only a little, sir,' said the foreman, respectfully, indicating the bird, which let out a hoarse and indignant 'Cuckoo'!

'Dear me,' said the sleek gentleman. 'Can this be my unfortunate friend Mr Armitage? Such a pleasant person — perhaps just a *little* hot-tempered, just a *little* unkind in his reviews? However it would certainly be unkind to wrest him from this old home; we must find some accommodation for him. Hawkins!' The chauffeur's head looked out from the car. 'Bring the case, will you.'

A large glass dome was brought, of the kind which is placed over skeleton clocks, with the hours and minutes marked on one side.

'There,' said the gentleman, tucking Mr Armitage under one arm. 'Now, in the study, perhaps? On one's desk, for inspiration. When I place the bird in position, Hawkins, pray cover him with the case. Thank you. A most tasteful ornament, I flatter myself, and perhaps in time we may even teach him to announce the hours.'

'Your father's being a long time,' said Mrs Armitage rather anxiously to the children. 'I do hope he isn't getting into trouble.'

'Oh, I don't suppose it's worth expecting him before lunch,' said Mark. 'He'll argue with everybody and then probably to for a walk and start drafting a letter to *The Times*.'

So they sat down to lunch in Mrs. Foster's house, but just as they were raising the first bites to their mouths, Harriet gave a little squeak and said:

'Goodness! We!ve forgotten all about Sarah! She'll arrive at the house and won't know what's happened to us.'

'Oh, she's sure to see Father somewhere around, and he'll bring her along,' Mark pointed out. 'I wouldn't worry. We can go along afterwards and see, if they don't turn up soon.'

At this moment Sarah was walking onward to her doom. She found the front door of the Armitage house open, and nobody about. This seemed to her a good moment to plant some of her practical jokes, so she opened her suitcase and stole into the dining-room. The long table was already set for tea. There were thirteen places, which puzzled her, but she supposed her aunt and uncle must be giving a party. Some plates of sandwiches and cakes covered with damp napkins were standing on a side table, so she doctored them with sneez-

ing powder, and placed Fizz-bangs in some of the teacups.

She was surprised to see that the rooms had been split in two by partitions of beaver-board, and wondered where the family were, and what was going on. Hearing hammering upstairs she decided to tiptoe up and surprise them. Feeling around in her suitcase again, she dug out her water pistol, and charged it from a jug which stood on the sideboard. Then she went softly up the stairs.

The door facing the top of the stairs was open, and she stole through it. This was Mr Armitage's study, which Mr Whizzard had decided should be his private office. Just now, however, he was out having his lunch, and the room was empty. Sarah went to work at once. She laid a few drawing-pins carefully on what she supposed to be her uncle's chair, and was just attaching a neat little contrivance to the telephone, when there came an interruption. The huge black cat, Walrus, who had stayed behind when the family left, had strolled into the study after Sarah, and taken a deep interest in the dejected-looking cuckoo sitting under the glass dome. While Sarah was busy laying the drawing-pins he leapt on to the desk, and after a moment's reflection, knocked the glass case off the desk with one sweep of his powerful paw.

'Sarah!' cried Mr Armitage in terror. 'Save me from this murdering beast!'

Completely startled, thinking that her uncle must have come in unheard while her back was turned, Sarah spun round and let fly with her water pistol. The jet caught the unfortunate bird in mid-air, and at once (for the weather was very cold) he turned to a solid block of ice, and fell to the ground with a heavy thud. The cat pounced at once, but his teeth simply grated on the ice, and he sprang back with a hiss of dismay.

At that moment Mr Whizzard returned from lunch.

'Dear me!' he said peevishly. 'What is all this? Cats? Little girls? And who has been meddling with my cuckoo?' But when he saw Mr Armitage's frozen condition he began to laugh uncontrollably.

'Warlock! Warlock! Come and look at this,'

he shouted, and another man came in, wearing a mortarboard and magician's gown.

'The lads have just arrived in the dragon-bus,' he said. 'I told them to go straight in to tea, as the workmen haven't quite finished dividing up the classrooms. What have you got there?'

'Poor Armitage has become quite seized up,' said Mr Whizzard. 'If we had a deep-freeze—'

Before he could finish, several young student-magicians dashed into the room, with cries of complaint. They were all sneezing.

'Really it's too bad, when we're all tired from our journey! Sneezing powder in everything, and tea all over the floor. A joke's a joke, but this is going too far. Someone ought to get the sack for this.'

'What is the matter, my lads?' inquired Mr Whizzard.

'Someone's been playing a lot of rotten practical jokes.'

Sarah quailed, and would gladly have slipped away, but she was jammed in a corner. She tried to squeeze past the desk, but one of the drawers was open and caught her suitcase. A small bomb fell out and exploded on the carpet, amid yelps of terror from the students.

'Seize that child,' commanded Mr Whizzard. Two of them unwillingly did so, and stood her before him. He cast his eye over the diabolical contents of her suitcase, and then the label attracted his attention.

'Armitage. Ah, just so, this is plainly an attempt at sabotage from the evicted family. They shall pay dearly for it. Nightshade, fetch an electric fire, will you. There's one in the front hall.'

While they were waiting, Mr Whizzard sat down in his chair, but shot up again at once, with a murderous look at Sarah.

Nightshade returned with the fire, and plugged it in.

'Good. Now place the bird before it, in this pencil tray, so as not to damp the carpet. The cat sits at hand on this chair, ready for when the thawing process commences. It should not be long, I fancy. Now my young friends, you may return to your interrupted meal, and as for you,' with a savage glance at Sarah, 'a little solitary confinement will do you no harm,

while I reflect on how to dispose of you.'

Sarah was dragged away and locked into a beaver-board cell, which had once been part of Harriet's bedroom.

'Now I think we deserve a quiet cup of tea, after all this excitement,' said Mr Whizzard to Mr Warlock, when they were left alone. 'We can sip it as we watch poor Armitage melt. I'll ring down to the kitchen.' He lifted the telephone, and instantly a flood of ink poured into his ear.

Meanwhile Mark and Harriet had decided to come in search of their father and cousin.

'It might be wise not to go in the front way, don't you think,' said Harriet. 'After all, it's rather odd that we haven't heard *something* of them by now. I feel there must have been some trouble.'

So they went stealthily round through the shrubbery, and climbed up the wistaria to Harriet's window. The first thing they saw when they looked in was Sarah, pacing up and down in a distracted manner.

'Good gracious—' Harriet began, but Sarah made frantic gestures to silence her. They climbed in as quietly as they could.

'Thank heaven you've come,' she whispered. 'Uncle Armitage is being roasted to death in the study, or else eaten by Walrus. You must rescue him at once.' They listened in horror, as she explained the position, and then hurriedly climbed out again. Sarah was no climber, so she hung out anxiously watching them, and thinking of the many times her uncle had given her half-crowns and pats on the head.

Harriet ran to the back door, where the cat's tin plate still lay, and began to rattle it, calling 'Walrus, Walrus, Walrus! Dinner! Walrus! Fish!'

Mark climbed along the wistaria to the study window, to wait for the result of this move.

He saw the cat Walrus, who was still sitting on the chair, attentively watching the melting process, suddenly pick up his ears and look towards the door. Then as Harriet's voice came faintly again he shot out of it and disappeared.

'Confound that animal!' exclaimed Mr Whizzard. 'Catch him, Warlock!' They both ran out of the door, looking to right and left. Mark wasted no time. He clambered through the window, grabbed the cuckoo, and was out again before the two men returned, frustrated and angry.

'Good heavens, now the bird's gone,' cried Mr Warlock. 'What a fool you were to leave the window open. It must have flown out.'

'Impossible! This is some more of that wretched child's doing. I'm going along to see her, right away.'

He burst in on Sarah, looking so ferocious that she instinctively caught up the first weapon she could see, to defend herself. It was a screwdriver, left lying on the floor by one of the workmen.

'What have you done with the cuckoo?' Mr Whizzard demanded.

'I haven't touched it,' Sarah truthfully replied.

'Nonsense. Do you deny that you enticed the cat away by black arts, and then kidnapped the cuckoo?' He approached her threateningly.

Sarah retreated as far as she could and clutched the screwdriver. 'You're crackers,' she said. 'I tell you I haven't —' Her mouth dropped open in astonishment. For where Mr Whizzard had been standing there was nothing but a large white cardboard box, with a red and blue picture on the lid. At this moment Mark and Harriet came climbing back through the window.

Downstairs in the dining-room the young wizards, having cleared away tea, were enjoying a sing-song.

'Ha, ha ha, he he he,' they sang,
'Little broom stick, how I love thee.'

They were interrupted by Mr Warlock.

'Have any of you boys seen Mr Whizzard?' he inquired. 'He went to interview the young female prisoner, and I haven't seen him since.'

'No, sir, he hasn't been in here,' the eldest one said. 'Won't you come and play for us, Mr Warlock? You do play so beautifully.'

'Well, just for five minutes, if you insist.' They began to sing again,

'Necromancers come away, come away, come come away,

This is wizards' holiday,'

when suddenly they were aware of the three children, Mark, Harriet, and Sarah, standing inside the door, holding red and blue crackers in their hands.

'What is the meaning of this?' said Mr Warlock severely. 'You are trespassing on private property.'

'Yes,' said Mark. '*Our* property. This is our house, and we would like you to get out of it at once.'

'Vacate it,' whispered Harriet.

'Vacate it at once.'

'We shall do no such thing.'

'Very well then. Do you know what we have here?' he held up one of the crackers. 'Your Mr Whizzard. And if you don't get out — vacate — at once, we shall *pull* them. So you'd better hurry up.'

The wizards looked at each other in consternation, and then, slowly at first, but with gathering speed, began to put their things together and take them out to the dragon coach. The children watched them, holding their crackers firmly.

'And you must take down all that beaverboard partitioning,' said Harriet firmly. 'I don't know *what* Mummy would say if she saw it.'

'The workmen have all gone home.'

'Then you must manage on your own.'

The house began to resound with amateurish bangs and squeaks. 'O, Nightshade, you clumsy clot, you dropped that board on my toe.' 'Well get out of the way then, you nitwit necromancer.'

At last it was all done, and at the front gate the children handed over the twelve red-and-blue parts of Mr Whizzard.

'And it's more than you deserve,' said Harriet, 'seeing how you were going to treat our poor Pa.'

'We should also like that screwdriver, with which I perceive you have armed yourself, or we shall not be able to restore our Director to his proper shape,' said Mr Warlock coldly.

'Oh, dear me, no. You're nuts if you think we're going to let you get away with that,' said Sarah. 'We shall want it in case of any further trouble. Besides, what about poor uncle — oh dear —' she stopped in dismay. For Mr War-lock had disappeared, and his place had been taken by a sack of coconuts.

'Oh, never mind,' said Harriet. 'You didn't mean to do it. Here, do for goodness' sake hurry up and go.' She shoved the sack into the arms of Nightshade, and bundled him into the coach, which slowly rolled off. 'We must simply dash along to Mrs Foster's. I'm sure Mummy will be worrying.'

They burst in on Mrs Armitage with their story. 'And where is your Father?' she said immediately.

'Oh goodness.' Mark looked guilty. 'I'd forgotten all about him.' He carefully extracted the half-stifled looking cuckoo from his trouser pocket.

'Out with the screwdriver, Sarah.'

Sarah obediently pointed it at him and said, 'You're Uncle' and he was restored to himself once more, but looking much rumpled and tattered. He glared at them all.

'I must say, that's a fine respectful way to treat your Father. Carried in your trouser pocket, indeed . . . '

'Well, I hope this will cure you once and for all of writing those unkind reviews,' said Mrs Armitage coldly. 'Now we have all the trouble of moving back again, and just when I was beginning to feel settled.'

'And talking of cures,' said Mr Armitage, turning on his niece, 'we won't say anything *this* time, seeing it's all turned out for the best, but if ever I catch you playing any of your practical pranks again —'

'Oh, I never, never will,' Sarah assured him. 'I only thought people enjoyed them.'

'Not in this family,' said Mark.

———

"Tottie Meets the Queen," from The Dolls' House *by Rumer Godden. Ill. by Tasha Tudor (New York: The Vicking Press, 1947; Rpt. 1962).*

*Writing in the tradition of such authors of animated toy stories as Hans Christian Andersen (*The Steadfast Tin Soldier*), E.T.A. Hoffman (*The Nutcracker*) and Collodi (*Pinocchio*), Rumer Godden has created several* *volumes of charming doll stories. The Doll's House concerns the adventures of the five dolls in the Plantagenet family and the children who love them, Emily and Charlotte Dane. The precarious lives of Godden's dolls may often resemble the emotional lives of some children. In the following episode from* The Dolls' House *Godden creates a vivid sense of Tottie's smallness and aloneness among so many larger, more beautiful dolls. That the Queen chooses Tottie precisely because of these qualities is an especially appealing feature to most child readers. The situation of the unlikely heroine, surrounded by haughty, critical dolls, can be compared to the situations of Cinderella, the Greek heroine Psyche, and Beauty.*

Tottie Meets the Queen

When Tottie was next taken out of her box she found herslf in a large cold room that had long tables, covered with blue cloth, against each wall, and a number of ladies all busy unpacking dolls.

Tottie had never seen so many ladies and so many dolls, particularly so many dolls. There was every kind of doll: baby dolls, little girl dolls, boy dolls, lady and gentleman dolls, soldier dolls, sailor dolls, acting dolls, dancing dolls, clockwork dolls, fairy dolls, Chinese dolls, Polish, Japanese, French, German, Russian. There was a white wax doll with exquisite white china hands, and a Dutch fisherman with a basket on his back, and a Flemish doll in market clothes, and her cook sitting down with her basket. There were Japanese dolls with blank white faces, and Chinese dolls whose faces were as alive as snakes, with painted snaky eyebrows and long noses; they were dancers and ceremonial dolls with satin trousers and red-painted shoes. There were two little German dolls with yellow fringes and gentle brown eyes and peasant clothes, and a Polichinelle, very old, with his legs drawn up and a carved, frightening, evil face. There was every kind and sort of doll and they filled the room, each standing in its place and showing what kind of doll it was. Some of them were very handsome and imposing; all of them, without exception, were far, far larger than Tottie.

She felt small and shy and longed to go home. "But I can't go home," said Tottie. "I shall never go home again," and her secret trouble filled her so strongly that, if wood could have drooped, Tottie would have drooped. "Oh! Oh! Oh!" cried poor little Tottie, and she thought of them all at home: Mr. Plantaganet, Birdie, Darner, Apple; when she thought of Apple she felt as if she must break into splinters, but of course, being made of such good wood, she gave no outward sign.

A lady took her up in her hand. "Where shall we put this darling little thing?" she asked. "Look. She goes with this sampler."

"What a charming idea," said another, but Tottie did not think it was in the least bit charming.

"A farthing doll!" said another lady. "Why, I should think she must be unique."

Tottie did not know what "unique" meant (if you don't, go and look it up in the dictionary), for all she could tell it might be something rude, and she wished she could hang her head, but of course a wooden neck will never, never bend and so she stayed, staring as woodenly as possible, straight in front of her. The ladies took her and set her up on the center of one of the long tables, with the sampler behind her and two square cards and one longer one in front of her. From Tottie's point of view, these cards were upside down, so that she could not read them. They looked like this:

LITTLE GIRL OF 1846   IN 1846
DRESSED BY SAME   BY A LITTLE GIRL
FARTHING DOLL   SAMPLER WORKED
IN 1946
EMILY AND CHARLOTTE DANE
LENT BY HER GREAT-GRAND-DAUGHTERS,

On the table opposite Tottie were four dolls under a glass-domed cover. Next to her, on her right side, was a wax doll with a satin dress, and on the other side a walking doll dressed in blue satin with a bustle behind and white flounces. She held, tiptilted, a blue parasol, and

in the other tiny hand, a fan.

"Who—who are those in the case?" asked Tottie.

"They were Queen Victoria's dolls when she was a child," said the wax doll.

"O-ooh!" said Tottie. She remembered Queen Victoria of course.

"La! We 'ave been put in one of ze best positions, is it you say? in ze room," said the walking doll.

"Why does she talk like that?" asked Tottie in a whisper of the wax doll.

"She is French," said the wax doll. "She is very proud."

The walking doll held her tiptilted parasol and her fan and glanced at Tottie. "What ees is you are made of?" she asked. "*Pardonnez-moi*, but la! I do not recognize ze substance."

"I am made of wood," answered Tottie with dignity.

"Wood? La! La! La! Tee-hee-hee." Her laughing sounded as if it were wound up. "Tee-hee. La! La! I thought doorknobs and broom 'andles and bedposts and clothes-pegs were made of wood, not dolls."

"So they are," said Tottie, "and so are the masts of ships and flagpoles and violins — and trees," said Tottie.

She and the walking doll looked at one another and, though the walking doll was quite ten inches taller than Tottie, Tottie did not flinch.

"I am made of keed and porcelain," said the walking doll. "Inside I 'ave a leetle set of works. Wind me up and I walk."

"Walk, walk, walk," cried the other dolls.

Merci! Je ne marcherai pas que si ça me chante," which means she could not walk unless someone wound her up.

"I once knew a kid doll," said Tottie. "I did not like her."

"Who is talking about kid dolls?" came a voice from the opposite table. "Who did not like kid dolls?"

"I don't," said Tottie firmly though, at the sound of that voice, she felt as if instead of being wood all through, she might have been made hollow inside.

"And who are you?" said the voice.

"It is a leetle object," said the walking doll,

"that 'as found its way in 'ere. La! It is made of wood."

"Of wood?" said the voice. "Once I knew a little doll made of wood and I did not like her at all!"

"I 'ave nevaire see one," said the walking doll.

"They were sold in the cheaper shops. A shilling a dozen or four for a penny. The children, silly little things, would waste their money on them."

"La! Children! *Merci. Je ne mange pas de ce pain là.* 'Orrible leetle creatures. *Je les déteste.*"

"Silly little things! Little creatures! Those are children they are talking of!" said the wax doll, shocked. Her voice, after the others, was meltingly soft. "How dare they!" said the wax doll. "They don't deserve the name of 'doll.' But tell me about those things you were talking of — the ships and flagpoles. It must be good to be made of something hard," said the wax doll.

"It is," said Tottie. At the moment all the good wood in her was standing firmly against the things the voice and the haughty doll had said. Tottie knew that voice. She looked across at the other table and she saw whom she had expected to see. She saw Marchpane. Marchpane saw her.

"Oh, it's you," said Marchpane.

"Yes," said Tottie.

"Strange!" said Marchpane. "I thought you would have been broken or thrown away long, long ago."

"No," said Tottie.

"What is it they used to call you?" asked Marchpane. "Spotty. Dotty. Surely it was Dotty."

"Tee! Tee-hee! Tee-hee! giggled the walking doll. "Tee-hee-hee! Tee-hee!"

"My name is Tottie," said Tottie. "It always has been."

"I couldn't be expected to remember," said Marchpane. "There were so many of you."

"Not in our family," said Tottie. "I was the only one."

"She is the only one now," said the wax doll. "The only one of her kind in the Exhibition. I heard them say so."

For some time there had been whispers going on among the dolls and now the walking doll was listening. "La! Is it possible?" she asked. "*Non. Non. Je m'en doute.*"

"What is it?" asked Marchpane.

"Dey say that some of the dolls 'ere are to be sold, sold out of their families."

"What? Sold by your own family?"

"Sold!"

"Sold!"

"Sold!" ran the whisper among the dolls. *La! Quel malheur!*" said the walking doll. "My museum would nevaire part with me."

"Nor mine," said Marchpane quickly.

"Nor mine," said the wax doll, but she said it with a fluttering sigh.

You notice that Tottie had said nothing all this time. This was Tottie's secret trouble. Yes, Tottie thought that Emily and Charlotte had sold her to Mrs. Innisfree. If you look back to page 51 of this book you will see why. "We pay for some of the dolls," Mrs. Innisfree had said. "I should like to pay you for Tottie."

"How much would you pay?" Charlotte had asked. Oh, Charlotte! "Would you pay a whole pound?"

Tottie shuddered when she remembered that.

"We should pay a guinea," said Mrs. Innisfree.

Of course Tottie did not know that Emily and Charlotte had given the guinea back to Mrs. Innisfree. She thought she was sold and would presently be sold again. She was filled with shame.

"It must be there on those cards," thought Tottie. "Only they can't read them because they are upside down and Marchpane is too far away on the other table. But soon they must know! thought Tottie.

"La! I am glad I am not standing next to such a one," said the walking doll.

"But you are. You are," thought Tottie. She wished she could sink through the table.

The other dolls were longing for the Exhibition to open. Marchpane, of course, was eager for the people to come and admire her, and so was the haughty doll. The wax doll was excited. She had been packed away in a box so long.

"Do you think there will be any children?"

asked the wax doll with longing in her voice.

"Children? I hope not!" said Marchpane.

"I 'ope zey will not touch," said the haughty doll.

"They had better not touch me," said Marchpane. "That must certainly not be allowed."

"But — were you not meant to be played with?" asked the wax doll. "I was. I was."

"La! You are un'appy?"

"I am shut away in a box. Away from children, and it is children who give us life," said the wax doll.

"And tumble one about and spoil one," said Marchpane, and the walking doll shuddered to the tip of her parasol.

"Isn't that life?" asked Tottie.

"I want children," cried the wax doll. "I — I —" She stopped. It had been on the tip of her tongue to say, "I wish I could be sold." She wished she dared say this aloud, but wax is not very brave stuff and so she remained quiet.

Tottie wished the Exhibition would never open. "But it will," thought Tottie, "and then — then — someone will buy me. I shall be sold and when the Exhibition closes I shall go away to a new home. Oh!" cried Tottie. "Oh Apple! Darner! Birdie! Mr. Plantaganet! My little home! Oh! Oh! Oh!" But no sign of grief showed on her wooden face. She stood as firm as ever.

"Is it true, it is true," said one of the dolls, "that this Exhibition is to be opened by a Queen."

"Queen Victoria?" asked the wax doll, looking at the dolls in the glass case. Tottie whispered to her that Queen Victoria had been dead long, long ago.

"Forgive me," said the wax doll. "I have been shut away so long."

"A Queen?" said Marchpane with great satisfaction. "How right and proper. She will be sure to notice me. They always do," she said, though Tottie was sure she had never seen a queen before. "I am so glad I have been cleaned."

"I always stay clean," said Tottie. "Wood can be washed and be none the worse."

"So can scrubbing brushes," said March-

pane tartly. "I am afraid Her Majesty will have rather a disagreeable surprise," said Marchpane. "She can't have been told that there are farthing dolls in this Exhibition. Why, I don't suppose," said Marchpane, opening her china-blue eyes wide, "that she knows that such things exist."

"Even queens can learn," said Tottie quietly.

Every evening, when the Exhibition room was shut, a child came to look at the dolls.

"A child! A child! A child!" The whisper would go through the room because so many of the dolls through being rare and precious had been for a long while put away in boxes or kept on shelves or in museums. They had not been near children for so long. They yearned toward this little girl who crept in to look at them. None of them yearned more than the wax doll.

The child was thin, with poor clothes, and she kept her hands behind her as if she had been told not to touch. She went from one doll to the other and stared with eyes that looked large in her thin face.

"La! You would think she'ad nevaire see a doll before!" said the walking doll.

"Perhaps she hasn't, as close as this," said Tottie. "Dolls are scarce now and very expensive."

"Quite right. They should never be given to children to be played with," said Marchpane.

The wax doll looked at the child as if her heart would melt. "Little darling!" she said. "How good she is! How gentle! See, she doesn't even touch."

At that moment the child took one hand from behind her back and stretched it out to the wax doll and, with a finger, very gently touched her satin dress. The wax doll trembled with pleasure from head to toe. After that the child came most often to look at the wax doll.

"I believe she is the caretaker's child," said Marchpane.

"She is my child," breathed the wax doll.

Now the day came for the Exhibition to be open. By eleven o'clock everything was dusted and ready; the ladies were waiting, the dolls were waiting, and a great number of other ladies and gentlemen and a few children, invited guests, were waiting. Marchpane and the haughty doll were preening their necks to hold them to the greatest advantage and setting off their dresses; the wax doll was looking at the children and thinking they were not as good as the caretaker's child; Tottie stood dreading and fearing the moment when someone would buy her and her secret must be told.

The Exhibition ladies kept coming along the tables and shifting and tidying what was arranged and neat already, and putting straight what was straight before.

"I do wish they wouldn't," sighed Tottie.

"They are showing us every attention, naturally," said Marchpane. "We are very important — at least," she corrected herself, "some of us are."

"I don't like attention," said Tottie who had been dusted and flicked with a feather broom and stood up and down until she felt giddy.

There was a stir, a pause, the Queen had come. Presently they heard her voice. The Queen's voice was as clear, her words as distinct, as separate drops of water. "*Clear and cool, clear and cool.*" Tottie had heard that about water once, and the Queen's voice sounded to her like that.

"I have great pleasure in declaring this Exhibition open," said the Queen's voice, and there was an immediate clapping of hands.

"Why are they clapping?" asked the wax doll.

"They are clapping us, of course," said Marchpane.

"They are clapping the Queen," said Tottie.

Now the ladies and gentlemen, following the Queen, who was attended by the ladies of the Exhibition and her own lady-in-waiting, began to come down the tables, looking at the dolls. The lady-in-waiting carried a bouquet of chrysanthemums. "That is for us, I expect," said Marchpane.

"How could it be for us? It's too big," said Tottie, but by now Marchpane was so far gone in conceit that nothing looked big to her.

"But — she isn't wearing a crown!" said the wax doll, disappointed.

"She only wears a crown when she goes to Parliament and places like that," said Tottie, who had learned about kings and queens when her little girls, from Great-Grandmother down to Charlotte, learned their history.

"She has the most elegant hat with gray feathers," said Marchpane. "I shall have one copied for myself. S-sh. She is coming this way."

"La! I am nairvous," said the walking doll. "*Je ne me sens pas bien du tout,*" which means she did not feel well. The wax doll trembled, but the people thought it was their footsteps shaking the room. Tottie remained woodenly staring in front of her.

On the Queen came, stopping, looking, touching, this doll or that, asking questions. Then she stopped directly in front of Marchpane, as Marchpane had known she would.

"What a beautiful little doll," said the Queen. "Surely she is the smallest in the Exhibition?"

Now in Marchpane's ears, the Queen could not have asked a more unfortunate question. Marchpane was not the smallest doll in the Exhibition, Tottie was, and Marchpane hated her for that. She almost cracked her china as she heard Mrs. Innisfree say, "There is one even smaller, Ma'am. This little farthing doll," and saw the Queen turn away to Tottie.

"Oh!" said the Queen. "Oh! I used to play with wooden dolls like this when I was a little girl."

"A Queen! With wooden dolls! How *very* surprising!" said the other dolls.

"*La! Comme c'est drôle!*" said the walking doll. As for Marchpane she said nothing. She was afraid she really would crack if she did.

"I haven't seen one for years and years," said the Queen. "My nurse used to buy them for me." And then she asked the very question Tottie was dreading to hear. "Is she for sale?" asked the Queen.

Every knot and grain in Tottie hardened as she waited for the answer to come. Whispers ran up and down among the dolls.

"I should like to buy her if she is," said the Queen.

"Birdie, Emily, Charlotte, Mr. Plantaganet, Apple, Darner, Apple, good-by," whispered

Tottie. She wished she could close her eyes to shut out the faces but, naturally, she had to keep them woodenly open. But—what was this that Mrs. Innisfree was saying?

"I'm afraid not, Ma'am," said Mrs. Innisfree. "She isn't for sale. She is the very dear possession of two little girls," and she pointed to the card.

The Queen picked up the cards and read them out:

"'*Sampler, worked by a little girl in 1846.*' '*Farthing doll dressed by the same little girl in 1846.*' '*Lent by her great-granddaughters, Emily and Charlotte Dane, in 1946.*'"

"Of course," said the Queen, "she must be a great treasure. May I look at her?"

And Tottie was picked up in the pale gray glove of the Queen, who examined her and examined her clothes.

"Dear little thing," said the Queen, and gave Tottie back to Mrs. Innisfree and passed on down the tables.

"My dear, you 'ave 'ad a *succès fou*!" said the haughty doll. Tottie did not ask what a *succès fou* was. For the first time her wood neck felt weak, bending, and then one of the ladies ran forward with a cry. "Oh dear!" she said, "the little farthing doll has fallen over and rolled down right off the table."

───

"Pippi Goes to the Circus," from Pippi Longstocking, *by Astrid Lindgren. Trans. by Florence Lamborn (New York: Viking, 1950).*

A popular character in literature is the individual who successfully defies social conventions or expectations. Such a character embodies impulses which are generally suppressed within the reader. Pippi Longstocking is such a character. Living alone, without parental guidance or restriction, she controls her own destiny, often shocking adults, but delighting and arousing the admiration of her ordinary child friends Tommy and Annika. In this selection, her ingenuous spontaneity contrasts with the structured and artificial gaiety of the circus. Pippi's self-confidence can be compared to that of Ogden Nash's Isabel and her independent life, and to the life of Robin Hood.

Pippi Goes to the Circus

A circus had come to the little town, and all the children were begging their mothers and fathers for permission to go. Of course Tommy and Annika asked to go too, and their kind father immediately gave them some money.

Clutching it tightly in their hands, they rushed over to Pippi's. She was on the porch with her horse, braiding his tail into tiny pigtails and tying each one with red ribbon.

"I think it's his birthday today," she announced, "so he has to be all dressed up."

"Pippi," said Tommy, all out of breath because they had been running so fast, "Pippi, do you want to go with us to the circus?"

"I can go with you most anywhere," answered Pippi, "but whether I can go to the surkus or not I don't know, because I don't know what a surkus is. Does it hurt?"

"Silly!" said Tommy, "of course it doesn't hurt; it's fun. Horses and clowns and pretty ladies that walk the tightrope."

"But it costs money," said Annika, opening her small fist to see if the shiny half-dollar and the quarter were still there.

"I'm rich as a troll," said Pippi, "so I guess I can buy a surkus all right. But it'll be crowded here if I have more horses. The clowns and the pretty ladies I could keep in the laundry, but it's harder to know what to do with the horses."

"Oh, don't be so silly," said Tommy, "you don't buy a circus. It costs money to go and look at it—see?"

"Preserve us!" cried Pippi and shut her eyes tightly. "It costs money to *look*? And here I go around goggling all day long. Goodness knows how much money I've goggled up already!"

Then, little by little, she opened one eye very carefully, and it rolled round and round in her head. "Cost what it may," she said, "I must take a look!"

At last Tommy and Annika managed to explain to Pippy what a circus really was, and she took some gold pieces out of her suitcase. Then she put on her hat, which was as big as a millstone, and off they all went.

There were crowds of people outside the circus tent and a long line at the ticket window. But at last it was Pippi's turn. She stuck her head through the window and stared at the dear old lady sitting there.

"How much does it cost to look at you?" Pippi asked.

But the old lady was a foreigner who did not understand what Pippi meant and answered in broken Swedish.

"Little girl, it costs a dollar and a quarter in the grandstand and seventy-five cents on the benches and twenty-five cents for standing room."

Now Tommy interrupted and said that Pippi wanted a seventy-five-cent ticket. Pippi put down a gold piece and the old lady looked suspiciously at it. She bit it too, to see if it was genuine. At last she was convinced that it really was gold and gave Pippi her ticket and a great deal of change in silver.

"What would I do with all those nasty little white coins?" asked Pippi disgustedly. "Keep them and then I can look at you twice. In the standing room."

As Pippi absolutely refused to accept any change, the lady changed her ticket to one for the grandstand and gave Tommy and Annika grandstand tickets too without their having to pay a single penny. In that way Pippi, Tommy, and Annika came to sit on some beautiful red chairs right next to the ring. Tommy and Annika turned around several times to wave to their schoolmates, who were sitting much farther away.

"This is a remarkable place," said Pippi, looking around in astonishment. "But, see, they've spilled sawdust all over the floor! Not that I'm overfussy myself, but that does look careless to me."

Tommy explained that all circuses had sawdust on the floor for the horses to run around in.

On a platform nearby the circus band suddenly began to play a thundering march. Pippi clapped her hands wildly and jumped up and down with delight.

"Does it cost money to hear too?" she asked, "or can you do that for nothing?"

At that moment the curtain in front of the performers' entrance was drawn aside, and the ringmaster in a black frock coat, with a whip in his hand, came running in, followed by ten white horses with red plumes on their heads.

The ringmaster cracked his whip, and all the horses galloped around the ring. Then he cracked it again, and all the horses stood still with their front feet up on the railing around the ring.

One of them had stopped directly in front of the children. Annika didn't like to have a horse so near her and drew back in her chair as far as she could, but Pippi leaned forward and took the horse's right foot in her hands.

"Hello, there," she said, "my horse sent you his best wishes. It's his birthday today too, but he has bows on his tail instead of on his head."

Luckily she dropped the foot before the ringmaster cracked his whip again, because then all the horses jumped away from the railing and began to run around the ring.

When the number was over, the ringmaster bowed politely and the horses ran out. In an instant the curtain opened again for a coal-black horse. On its back stood a beautiful lady dressed in green silk tights. The program said her name was Miss Carmencita.

The horse trotted around in the sawdust, and Miss Carmencita stood calmly on his back and smiled. But then something happened; just as the horse passed Pippi's seat, something came swishing through the air — and it was none other than Pippi herself. And there she stood on the horse's back, behind Miss Carmencita. At first Miss Carmencita was so astonished that she nearly fell off the horse. Then she got mad. She began to strike out with her hands behind her to make Pippi jump off. But that didn't work.

"Take it easy," said Pippi. "Do you think you're the only one who can have any fun? Other people have paid too, haven't they?"

Then Miss Carmencita tried to jump off herself, but that didn't work either, because Pippi was holding her tightly around the waist. At that the audience couldn't help laughing. They thought it was so funny to see the lovely Miss Carmencita held against her will by a little red-headed youngster who stood there on the horse's back in her enormous shoes and looked as if she had never done anything except perform in a circus.

But the ringmaster didn't laugh. He turned toward an attendant in a red uniform and made a sign to him to go and stop the horse.

"Is this number already over," asked Pippi in a disappointed tone, "just when we were having so much fun?"

"Horrible child!" hissed the ringmaster between his teeth. "Get out of here!"

Pippi looked at him sadly. "Why are you mad at me?" she asked. "What's the matter? I thought we were here to have fun."

She skipped off the horse and went back to her seat. But now two huge guards came to throw her out. They took hold of her and tried to lift her up.

They couldn't do it. Pippi sat absolutely still, and it was impossible to budge her although they tried as hard as they could. At last they shrugged their shoulders and went off.

Meanwhile the next number had begun. It was Miss Elvira about to walk the tightrope. She wore a pink tulle skirt and carried a pink parasol in her hand. With delicate little steps she ran out on the rope. She swung her legs gracefully in the air and did all sorts of tricks. It looked so pretty. She even showed how she could walk backwards on the narrow rope. But when she got back to the little platform at the end of the rope, there stood Pippi.

"What are you going to do now?" asked Pippi, delighted when she saw how astonished Miss Elvira looked.

Miss Elvira said nothing at all but jumped down from the rope and threw her arms around the ringmaster's neck, for he was her father. And the ringmaster once more sent for his guards to throw Pippi out. This time he sent for five of them, but all the people shouted, "Let her stay! We want to see the red-headed girl." And they stamped their feet and clapped their hands.

Pippi ran out on the rope; and Miss Elvira's tricks were as nothing compared with Pippi's. When she got to the middle of the rope she stretched one leg straight up in the air, and her big shoe spread out like a roof over her head. She bent her foot a little so that she could tickle herself with it back of her ear.

The ringmaster was not at all pleased to have Pippi performing in his circus. He wanted to get rid of her, and so he stole up and loosened the mechanism that held the rope taut, thinking surely Pippi would fall down.

But Pippi didn't. She set the rope a-swinging instead. Back and forth it swayed, and Pippi swung faster and faster, until suddenly she leaped out into the air and landed right on the ringmaster. He was so frightened he began to run.

"Oh, what a jolly horse!" cried Pippi. "But why don't you have any pompoms in your hair?"

Now Pippi decided it was time to go back to Tommy and Annika. She jumped off the ringmaster and went back to her seat. The next number was about to begin, but there was a brief pause because the ringmaster had to go out and get a drink of water and comb his hair.

Then he came in again, bowed to the audience, and said, "Ladies and gentlemen, in a moment you will be privileged to see the Greatest Marvel of all time, the Strongest Man in the World, the Mighty Adolf, whom no one has yet been able to conquer. Here he comes, ladies and gentlemen, Allow me to present to you THE MIGHTY ADOLF."

And into the ring stepped a man who looked as big as a giant. He wore flesh-coloured tights and had a leopard skin draped around his stomach. He bowed to the audience and looked very pleased with himself.

"Look at these muscles," said the ringmaster and squeezed the Mighty Adolf's arm where the muscles stood out like balls under the skin.

"And now, ladies and gentlemen, I have a very special invitation for you. Who will challenge the Mighty Adolf in a wrestling match? Who of you dares to try his strength against the World's Strongest Man? A hundred dollars for anyone who can conquer the Mighty Adolf! A hundred dollars, ladies and gentlemen! Think of that! Who will be the first to try?"

Nobody came forth.

"What did he say?" asked Pippi.

"He says that anybody who can lick that big man will get a hundred dollars," answered Tommy.

"I can," said Pippi, "but I think it's too bad to, because he looks nice."

"Oh, no you couldn't," said Annika, "he's

the strongest man in the world.''

"*Man*, yes," said Pippi, "but I am the strongest girl in the world, remember that."

Meanwhile the Mighty Adolf was lifting heavy iron weights and bending thick iron rods in the middle just to show how strong he was.

"Oh, come now, ladies and gentlemen," cried the ringmaster, "is there really nobody here who wants to earn a hundred dollars? Shall I really be forced to keep this myself?" And he waved a bill in the air.

"No, that you certainly won't be forced to do," said Pippi and stepped over the railing into the ring.

The ringmaster was absolutely wild when he saw her. "Get out of here! I don't want to see any more of you," he hissed.

"Why do you always have to be so unfriendly?" said Pippi reproachfully. "I just want to fight with Mighty Adolf."

"This is no place for jokes," said the ringmaster. "Get out of here before the Mighty Adolf hears your impudent nonsense."

But Pippi went right by the ringleader and up to Mighty Adolf. She took his hand and shook it heartily.

"Shall we fight a little, you and I?" she asked.

Mighty Adolf looked at her but didn't understand a word.

"In one minute I'll begin," said Pippi.

And begin she did. She grabbed Mighty Adolf around the waist, and before anyone knew what was happening she had thrown him on the mat. Mighty Adolf leaped up, his face absolutely scarlet.

"Atta girl, Pippi!" shrieked Tommy and Annika, so loudly that all the people at the circus heard it and began to shriek "Atta girl, Pippi!" too. The ringmaster sat on the railing, wringing his hands. He was mad, but Mighty Adolf was madder. Never in his life had he experienced anything so humiliating as this. And he certainly intended to show that red-headed girl what kind of a man Mighty Adolf really was. He rushed at Pippi and caught her round the waist, but Pippi stood firm as a rock.

"You can do better than that," she said to encourage him. Then she wriggled out of his grasp, and in the twinkling of an eye Mighty

Adolf was on the mat again. Pippi stood beside him, waiting. She didn't have to wait long. With a roar he was up again, rushing at her.

"Tiddelipom and piddeliday," said Pippi.

All the people in the tent stamped their feet and threw their hats in the air and shouted, "Hurrah, Pippi!"

When Mighty Adolf came rushing at her for the third time, Pippi lifted him high in the air and, with her arms straight above her, carried him clear around the ring. Then she laid him down on the mat again and held him there.

"Now, little fellow," said she, "I don't think we'll bother about this any more. We'll never have any more fun than we've had already."

"Pippi is the winner! Pippi is the winner!" cried all the people.

Mighty Adolf stole out as fast as he could, and the ringmaster had to go up and hand Pippi the hundred dollars, although he looked as if he'd much prefer to eat her.

"Here you are, young lady, here you are," said he. "One hundred dollars."

"That thing!" said Pippi scornfully. "What would I want with that old piece of paper. Take it and use it to fry herring on if you want to." And she went back to her seat.

"This is certainly a long surkus," she said to Tommy and Annika. "I think I'll take a little snooze, but wake me if they need my help about anything else."

And then she lay back in her chair and went to sleep at once. There she lay and snored while the clowns, the sword swallowers, and the snake charmers did their tricks for Tommy and Annika and all the rest of the people at the circus.

"Just the same, I think Pippi was best of all," whispered Tommy to Annika.

———

"Nothing New Under the Sun (Hardly)," from Homer Price, *by Robert McCloskey (New York: Viking, 1943).*

Robert McCloskey's short stories mix memories of his small town Ohio boyhood with elements of the American tall tale: exaggeration, unusual characters, and humor. In

addition, they contain echoes of many tradi-
tional stories. "Nothing New Under the Sun
(Hardly)" is a modern version of an episode
in Homer's Odyssey *in which the hero avoids*
being enchanted by the music of the sirens by
plugging his ears. There are also many par-
allels between this story and the German folk-
tale The Pied Piper of Hamelin. *As in all of*
the Homer Price stories, the adults appear
foolish while the children are in control of the
situations.

Nothing New Under the Sun (Hardly)

After the County Fair, life in Centerburg eases
itself back to normal. Homer and the rest of
the children concentrate on arithmetic and bas-
ketball, and the grown-ups 'tend to business
and running the town in a peaceful, democratic
way. Election time still being a month away,
the Democrats and the Republicans are still
speaking to each other. The Ladies' Aid hasn't
anything to crusade about at the moment, and
Uncle Ulysses hasn't bought any new-fangled
equipment for his lunchroom recently. There
is nothing for people to gossip about, or speculate on, or argue about.

There's always the weather, the latest books
and movies, and ladies' hats. But, of course,
that doesn't provide nearly enough to talk and
think about for a whole month until election
time. Uncle Ulysses, the sheriff, and the men
around the barbershop usually run out of things
to talk about toward the middle of the month.
Sometimes during the mornings the conversation is lively. Like today, the sheriff came in
beaming and said, "Well, I put on long ullen
wonderwear, I mean woolen underwear, this
morning."

"Soo?" said Uncle Ulysses. "Guess I'll have
to ask Aggy to get mine out of mothballs this
week."

"Humph," said the barber, "I wouldn't
wear woolen underwear for anything on earth.
It *itches!*"

Well, that was something to argue about
for almost an hour. Then the subject changed

to woolen socks, to shoes, to overshoes, to
mud, to mud in roads, mud in barnyards and
barns, chicken coops. Then there was a long
pause. Only ten-thirty by the town hall clock,
and conversation had already dwindled to
nothing at all. Nothing to do but look out of
the barbershop window.

"There goes Doc Pelly," said the barber,
"I wonder who's sick?"

"Judge's wife having a fainting spell,
maybe," suggested the sheriff.

"Colby's wife is expectin' a baby," said Uncle Ulysses. "I'll ask Aggy this noon, she'll
know all about it."

"There's Dulcey Dooner," said the sheriff. "He hasn't worked for three years," added
the barber disapprovingly.

A few children came into view. "School's
out for lunch," pronounced the sheriff.

The door opened and Homer came in
saying, "Hello everybody. Uncle Ulysses, Aunt
Aggy sent me over to tell you to stir yourself
over to the lunchroom and help serve blue-
plate specials."

Uncle Ulysses sighed and prepared to leave.
The sheriff cupped a hand behind his ear and
said, "What's that?" Uncle Ulysses stopped
sighing and everybody listened.

The noise (it was sort of a rattle) grew
louder, and then suddenly an old car swung
into the town square. The sheriff, the barber,
Uncle Ulysses, and Homer watched it with gap-
ing mouths as it rattled around the town square
once — twice — and on the third time slowed
down and shivered to a stop right out front of
Uncle Ulysses' lunchroom.

It wasn't because this car was old, old
enough to be an *antique*, or because some
strange business was built onto it; or that the
strange business was covered with a large canvas. No, that wasn't what made Homer and the
sheriff and Uncle Ulysses and the barber stare
so long. It was the car's *driver*.

"Gosh what a beard!" said Homer.

"And what a head of hair!" said the barber. "That's a two-dollar cutting job if I ever
saw one!"

"Could you see his face?" asked the sheriff.

"Nope," answered Uncle Ulysses, still staring across the square.

They watched the stranger untangle his beard from the steering wheel and go into the lunchroom.

Uncle Ulysses promptly dashed for the door, saying, "See you later."

"Wait for me!" the sheriff called, "I'm sort of hungry."

Homer followed and the barber shouted, "Don't forget to come back and tell me the news!"

"O.K., and if I bring you a new customer I get a commission."

The stranger was sitting at the far end of the lunch counter, looking very shy and embarrassed. Homer's Aunt Aggy had already served him a blue-plate special and was eyeing him with suspicion. To be polite, Homer and Uncle Ulysses pretended to be busy behind the counter, and the sheriff pretended to study the menu — though he knew every single word on it by heart. They just glanced in the stranger's direction once in a while.

Finally Uncle Ulysses' curiosity got the best of him and he sauntered down to the stranger and asked, "Are you enjoying your lunch? Is everything all right?"

The stranger appeared to be very embarrassed, and you could easily tell that he was blushing underneath his beard and all his hair. "Yes, sir, it's a very good lunch," he replied with a nod. When he nodded a stray whisp of beard accidentally got into the gravy. This made him more embarassed than ever.

Uncle Ulysses waited for the stranger to start a conversation, but he didn't.

So Uncle Ulysses said, "Nice day today."

The stranger said, "Yes, nice day," and dropped a fork. Now the stranger *really* was embarrassed. He looked as though he would like to sink right through the floor.

Uncle Ulysses quickly handed the man another fork, and eased himself away, so as not to embarrass him into breaking a plate or falling off his stool.

After he finished lunch, the stranger reached into the pocket of his ragged, patched coat and drew out a leather moneybag. He paid for his lunch, nodded good-by, and crept out of the door and down the street with everyone staring after him.

Aunt Aggy broke the silence by bouncing on the marble counter the coin she had just received.

"It's good money," she pronounced, "but it looks as though it had been *buried* for *years!*"

"Shyest man I ever laid eyes on!" said Uncle Ulysses.

"Yes!" said the sheriff. "My as a shouse, I mean shy as a mouse!"

"Gosh what a beard!" said Homer.

"Humph!" said Aunt Aggy. "Homer, it's time you started back to school!"

By mid-afternoon every man, woman, and child in Centerburg had something to gossip about, speculate on, and argue about.

Who was this stranger? Where did he come from?

Where was he going? How long was his beard, and his hair? What was his name? Did he have a business? What could be on the back of his car that was so carefully covered with the large canvas?

Nobody knew. Nobody knew anything about the stranger except that he parked his car in the town parking space and was spending considerable time walking about town. People reported that he paused in his walking and whistled a few bars of some strange tune, a tune nobody had ever heard of. The stranger was shy when grown-ups were near, and he would cross the street or go around a block to avoid speaking to someone. However, he did not avoid children. He smiled at them and seemed delighted to have them follow him.

People from all over town telephoned the sheriff at the barbershop asking about the stranger and making reports as to what was going on.

The sheriff was becoming a bit uneasy about the whole thing. He couldn't get near enough to the stranger to ask him his intentions, and if he *did* ask the stranger would be too shy to give him an answer.

As Homer passed by the barbershop on his way home from school the sheriff called him in. "Homer," he said, "I'm gonna need your help. This stranger with the beard has got me worried. You see, Homer, I can't find out who he is or what he is doing here in town. He's probably a nice enough fellow, just an individualist. But, then again, he might be a fugitive in disguise or something.'' Homer nodded. And the sheriff continued, ''Now, what I want you to do is gain his confidence. He doesn't seem to be afraid of children, and you might be able to find out what this is all about. I'll treat you to a double raspberry sundae.''

''It's a deal sheriff!'' said Homer. ''I'll start right now.''

At six o'clock Homer reported to the sheriff. ''The stranger seems like a nice person, Sheriff,'' Homer began. ''I walked down Market Street with him. He wouldn't tell me who he is or what he's doing, but he did say he'd been away from people for a great many years. He asked me to recommend a place for him to stay, and I said the Strand Hotel, so that's where he went just now when I left him. I'll have to run home for dinner now, Sheriff, but I'll find out some more tomorrow. Don't forget about that raspberry sundae,'' said Homer.

''I won't,'' replied the sheriff, ''and, Homer, don't forget to keep me posted on this fellow.''

After Homer had gone, the sheriff turned to the barber and said, ''Goll durnitt! We don't know one blessed thing about this fellow except that he's shy, and he's been away from people for quite a spell. For all we know he might be a fugitive, or a lunatic, or maybe one of these amnesia cases.''

''If he didn't have so much hair I could tell in a second what kind of a fellow he is,'' complained the sheriff. ''Yep! Just one look at a person's ears and _I_ can _tell_!''

''Well,'' said the barber, ''_I_ judge people by their _hair_, and I've been thinking. This fellow looks like somebody I've heard about, or read about somewhere. Like somebody out of a book, you understand, Sheriff?''

''Well, yes, in a way, but I could tell you definite with a good look at his ears!'' said the sheriff. ''Here comes Ulysses, let's ask him what _he_ thinks.''

Uncle Ulysses considered a second and said, ''Well, _I_ judge a person by his _waistline_ and his _appetite_. Now I'm not saying I'm right, Sheriff, because I couldn't tell about his waistline under the old coat, but judging from his

appetite I'd say he's a sort of person that I've read about somewhere. I can't just put my finger on it. Seems as though it must have been in a book.''

''U-m-m,'' said the sheriff.

Just then Tony the shoe repairman came in for a haircut. After he was settled in the barber chair, the sheriff asked him what he thought about the mysterious stranger.

''Well, Sheriff, _I_ judge everybody by their _feet_ and their _shoes_. Nobody's worn a pair of gaiters like his for twenty-five years. It seems as though those shoes must have just up and walked right out of the pages of some old dusty book.''

''There!'' said the sheriff. ''_Now_ we're getting somewhere!''

He rushed to the phone and called Mr. Hirsh of the Hirsh Clothing Store, and asked, ''Say, Sam , what do _you_ think about this stranger? . . . Yes, the one bith the weard, I mean beard! . . . uh-huh . . . storybook clothes, eh? . . . Thanks a lot, Sam, good night.''

Then he called the garage and said, ''Hello, Luke, this is the sheriff talking. What do you make of this stranger in town . . . Yes? . . . literature, eh? Durn'd if I kin see how you can judge a man by the car he drives, but I'll take your word for it. Good night, Luke, and thanks a lot.''

The sheriff looked very pleased with himself. He paced up and down and muttered, ''Getting somewhere! Getting somewhere at last!'' Then he surprised everyone by announcing that he was going over to the _library_!

In a few minutes he was back, his mustache twitching with excitement. ''I've solved it!'' he shouted. ''The librarian knew right off just what book to look in! It's _Rip Van Winkle_! It's Rip Van Winkle this fellow's like. He must have driven up into the hills some thirty years ago and fell asleep, or got amnesia, or something!''

''Yeah! That's it!'' agreed the barber along with Uncle Ulysses and the shoemaker.

Then Uncle Ulysses asked, ''_But_ how about that 'whatever-it-is' underneath the canvas on the back of his car?''

''Now look here, Ulysses,'' shouted the sheriff, ''you're just trying to complicate my deduction! Come on, let's play checkers!''

Bright and early the next morning the Rip-Van-Winklish stranger was up and wandering around Centerburg.

By ten o'clock everyone was referring to him as "Old Rip," and remarking how clever the sheriff was at deducting things.

The sheriff tried to see what was under the canvas, but couldn't make head or tail of what it was. Uncle Ulysses peeked at it too and said, "Goodness only knows! But never mind, Sheriff. If anybody can find out what this thing is, Homer will do the finding!"

That same afternoon after school was dismissed Uncle Ulysses and the sheriff saw Homer strolling down the street with "Old Rip."

"Looks like he's explaining something to Homer," said the sheriff.

"Homer'll find out!" said Uncle Ulysses proudly. Then they watched through the barbershop window while the stranger took Homer across the square to the parking lot and showed him his car. He lifted one corner of the canvas and pointed underneath, while Homer looked and nodded his head. They shook hands and the stranger went to his hotel, and Homer headed for the barbershop.

"Did he talk?" asked the sheriff the minute Homer opened the door.

"What's his name?" asked Uncle Ulysses.

"What is he doing?" asked the barber.

"Yes, he told me everything!" said Homer. "It sounds just like a story out of a book!"

"Yes, son did he get amnesia up in the hills?" asked the sheriff.

"Well no, not exactly, Sheriff, but he did *live* in the hills for the past thirty years."

"Well, what's he doing here now?" the barber demanded.

"I better start at the beginning," said Homer.

"That's a good idea, son," said the sheriff. "I'll take a few notes just for future reference."

"Well, to begin with," Homer stated, "his name is Michael Murphy — just plain Michael Murphy. About thirty years ago he built himself a small vacation cabin out in the hills, some place on the far side of the state forest reserve. Then, he liked living in the cabin so much he decided to live there all of the time. He packed his belongings on his car and moved out to the hills."

"He cided ta be a dermit?" asked the sheriff.

"Not exactly a *hermit*," Homer continued. "But yesterday was the first time that he came out of the hills and saw people for thirty years. That's why he's so shy."

"Then he's moving back to civilization," suggested Uncle Ulysses.

"That comes later," said Homer, "I've only told as far as twenty-nine years ago."

"Can't you skip a few years, son, and get to the point?" demanded the sheriff.

"Nope! Twenty-nine years ago," Homer repeated firmly, "Mr. Murphy read in an almanac that if a man can make a better mousetrap than anybody else, the world will beat a path to his house — even if it is way out in the hills. "So-o-o he started making *mousetraps*."

There was a pause, and then the sheriff said, "Will you repeat that again, son?"

"I said, Mr. Murphy started making *mousetraps*. He made good ones too — the very best — and when one of Mr. Murphy's traps caught a mouse, that was the end of that mouse for all time."

The sheriff forgot all about taking notes as Homer continued, "But nobody came to buy the traps. But that was just as well, you see, because twenty-eight years ago Mr. Murphy began to feel *sorry* for the mice. He came to realize that he would have to change his whole approach. He thought and thought, and finally he decided to build mouse traps that wouldn't hurt the mice.

"He spent the next fifteen years doing research on what was the pleasantest possible way for a mouse to be caught. He discovered that being caught to music pleased mice the most, even more than cheese. Then," said Homer, "Mr. Murphy set to work to make a *musical* mousetrap."

"That wouldn't hurt the mice?" inquired Uncle Ulysses.

"That wouldn't hurt the mice," Homer started. "It was a long, hard job too, because first he had to build an organ out of reeds that the mice liked the sound of, and then he had to compose a tune that the mice couldn't possibly resist. Then he incorporated it all into a mousetrap . . ."

"That wouldn't hurt the mice?"

interrupted the barber.

"That wouldn't hurt the mice," Homer went on. "The mousetrap caught mice, all right. The only trouble was, it was too big. What with the organ and all, and sort of impractical for general use because somebody had to stay around and pump the organ."

"Yes, I can see that wouldn't be practical," said Uncle Ulysses, stroking his chin — "But with a small electric motor . . . "

"But he solved it, Uncle Ulysses! The whole idea seems very practical after you get used to it. He decided since the trap was too large to use in a house, he would fasten it onto his car, which he hadn't used for so long anyway. Then he could drive it to a town and make a bargain with the mayor to remove all the mice. You see he would start the musical mousetrap to working, drive up and down the streets and alleys. Then all of the mice would run out of the houses to get themselves caught in this trap that plays music that no mouse ever born can possibly resist. After the trap is full of mice, Mr. Murphy drives them out past the city limits, somewhere where they can't find their way home, and lets them go."

"Still without hurting them?" suggested the barber.

"Of course," said Homer.

The sheriff chewed on his pencil, Uncle Ulysses stroked on his chin, and the barber ran his fingers through his hair.

Homer noticed the silence and said, "I guess the idea *is* sort of startling when you first hear about it. But if a town has a water truck to sprinkle streets, and a street-sweeping truck to remove dirt, why shouldn't they, maybe, just hire Mr. Murphy's musical mousetrap once in a while to remove mice?" Uncle Ulysses stroked his chin again and then said, "By gum! This man Murphy is a genius!"

"I told Mr. Murphy that *you* would understand, Uncle Ulysses!" said Homer with a grin. "I told him the mayor was a friend of yours, and you could talk him into anything, even hiring a musical mousetrap."

"Whoever heard of a micical moostrap!" said the sheriff.

"That doesn't hurt the *mice*!" added the barber as Homer and Uncle Ulysses went off

arm in arm to see the mayor.

It scarcely took Uncle Ulysses and Homer half an hour to convince the mayor that Mr. Murphy's musical mousetrap should be hired to rid Centerburg of mice. While Uncle Ulysses chatted on with the mayor, Homer dashed over to the hotel to fetch Mr. Murphy.

Homer came back with the bearded inventor and introduced him to the mayor and to Uncle Ulysses. The mayor opened a drawer of his desk and brought out a bag of jelly beans. "Have one," he said to Mr. Murphy, to sort of break the ice and make his shy visitor feel at home. Mr. Murphy relaxed and answered the mayor's questions without blushing too much.

"How do we know this *thing of a jig* of yours will do what you say it will?" asked the mayor.

Mr. Murphy just whistled a few bars "*Tum tidy ay dee*" and a couple of mice jumped right out of the mayor's desk!

"Of course," Homer explained, "the mice come *quicker* and get *removed* when the mousetrap plays that tune through the streets. Mr. Murphy guarantees to remove every single mouse from Centerburg for only thirty dollars."

"It's a bargain!" said the mayor, "I wondered where my jelly beans were disappearing to!" and he shook hands with Mr. Murphy. Then he proclaimed Saturday as the day for demousing Centerburg. By this time everyone knew that the shy stranger's name was Michael Murphy, but people still spoke of him as Rip Van Winkle (Rip for short), because of the sheriff's deduction. Everybody talked about the musical mousetrap (that didn't hurt the mice) and the mayor's demousing proclamation.

The children, especially, were looking forward to the great event. They watched with interest while Mr. Murphy went over his car and his musical trap to be sure everything was in perfect working order. Homer and Freddy and most of the other children were planning to follow the trap all around town Saturday, and see the mice come out and get caught in Michael Murphy's musical trap.

"Gosh, Homer," said Freddy, "let's follow him until he lets them loose out in the country! That *will* be a sight, seeing all those mice let loose at once!''

''Well, Freddy, I've been thinking it might not be a good idea to follow the mousetrap past the city limits,'' said Homer to Freddy's surprise.

''You know, Freddy, I've been over at the library reading up on mice and music — music can do funny things sometimes. It can soothe savage beasts and charm snakes and *lots* of things. If we're going to follow this musical trap till the mice are let loose, we better make some plans.''

Homer and Freddy spent all Friday recess period making plans. They decided that all the children should meet in the school yard before the demousing started on Saturday. They arranged a signal, thumbs up, if everything was going along all right, and thumbs down if anyone was in trouble.

''It's just to be on the safe side,'' Homer explained.

Saturday dawned a beautiful crisp fall day, fine weather for the grand demousing of Centerburg. Mr. Michael Murphy came forth from the Strand Hotel, and after carefully slinging his long gray beard over his shoulder he cranked his car and warmed up the engine. He carefully removed the canvas covering from the musical mousetrap and ever so painstakingly arranged the spiral ramps and runways so that no mouse, no matter how careless, could stub a toe or bump a nose. He then climbed behind the steering wheel and the musical mousetrap was underway!

A loud cheer arose from the crowd of children as Mr. Murphy yanked a lever and the reed organ started to play. Even before the cheering stopped the mice began to appear!

Through the streets of Centerburg rolled Mr. Michael Murphy and his musical mousetrap. The mice came running from every direction! Fat, doughnut-fed mice from Uncle Ulysses' lunchroom, thin mice from the churches, ordinary mice from the houses and homes, mice from the stores, and mice from the town hall.

They all went running up the ramps and runways, and disappeared in Michael Murphy's musical mousetrap. The children followed behind, enjoying the whole thing almost as much as the mice.

''Nothing New Under the Sun (Hardley)'' from *Homer Price,* by Robert McCloskey. Copyright © 1943. Reprinted by permission of Viking Press.

After traveling down every street in town, the procession came to a stop in front of the town hall, and the mayor came out and presented Mr. Murphy with his thirty-dollar fee — thirty bright, crisp new one-dollar bills.

Just as the mayor finished counting out the bills into Mr. Murphy's hand, the sheriff stepped up and said, ''Mr. Murphy, I hope this won't embarrass you too much, in fact I hate to mention it at all, but this here misical moostrap, I mean mouse trap of yours, has got a license plate that is thirty years old . . . A *new* license will cost you just exactly thirty dollars.''

Mr. Murphy blushed crimson under his beard. ''It's the law, you know, and *I* can't help it!'' apologized the sheriff.

Poor Mr. Murphy, poor *shy* Mr. Murphy! He handed his thirty dollars to the sheriff, took his new license plates and crept down the city hall steps. He climbed into his car and drove slowly away toward the edge of town, with the musical mousetrap playing its reedy music. The children followed along to see Mr. Murphy release all of the mice.

''I really hated to do that, Mayor,'' said the sheriff as the procession turned out of sight on route 56A. ''It's the law you know, and if I hadn't reminded him he might have been arrested in the next town he visits.'' There's no telling how this demousing would have ended if the children's librarian hadn't come shouting ''Sheriff! Sheriff! Quick! *We guessed the wrong book*!''

"What?" shouted the sheriff and the mayor and Uncle Ulysses.

"Yes!" gasped the children's librarian, "not *Rip Van Winkle*, but *another* book, *The Pied Piper of Hamelin*!"

"Geeminy Christmas!" yelled the sheriff, "and almost every child in town is followin' him this very minute!"

The sheriff and the librarian and the mayor and Uncle Ulysses all jumped into the sheriff's car and roared away after the procession. They met up with the children just outside the city limits. "Come back! Turn around, children!" they shouted.

"I'll treat everybody to a doughnut!" yelled Uncle Ulysses.

The children didn't seem to hear, and they kept right on following the musical mousetrap.

"The music must have affected their minds," cried the librarian.

"Sheriff, we can't lose all these children with election time coming up next month!" mourned the mayor. "Let's give Murphy another thirty dollars!"

"That's the idea," said Uncle Ulysses. "Drive up next to him, Sheriff, and I'll hand him the money."

The sheriff's car drew alongside the musical mousetrap, and Uncle Ulysses tossed a wad of thirty dollar bills onto the seat next to the shy Mr. Murphy.

"Please don't take them away!" pleaded the librarian.

"Come, Murphy, let's be reasonable," shouted the mayor.

Mr. Murphy was very flustered, and his steering was distinctly wobbly.

Then the sheriff got riled and yelled at the top of his lungs, "*Get'em low! Get'em go! Durnit, Let'em go!*"

And that's exactly what Mr. Murphy did. He let them go. He pulled a lever and every last mouse came tumbling out of the bottom of the musical mousetrap. And *such* a *sight* it was, well worth walking to the city limits to see. The mice came out in a torrent. The reedy organ on the musical mousetrap stopped playing, and the squeaking of mice and the cheering of children filled the air.

The torrent of mice paused, as if sensing

direction, and then each Centerburg mouse started off in a straight, straight line to his own Centerburg mousehole. Mr. Murphy didn't pause. He stepped on the gas, and the musical mousetrap swayed down the road. The mayor, the children's librarian, the sheriff, Uncle Ulysses, and the children watched as it grew smaller and smaller and finally disappeared.

Then Uncle Ulysses remembered the children. He turned around and noticed them grinning at each other and holding their thumbs in the air. They paid no attention whatever when they were called!

"That music has pixied these children!" he moaned.

"No, it hasn't, Uncle Ulysses," said Homer who had just come up. "There's not a thing the matter with them that Doc Pelly can't cure in two shakes! Just to be on the safe side, Freddy and I asked Doc Pelly to come down to the school yard this morning and put cotton in all the children's ears. You know, just like Ulysses — not you, Uncle Ulysses, but the ancient one, the one that Homer wrote about. Not me, but the ancient one."

"You mean to say Doc Pelly is mixed up in this?" asked the mayor.

"Yes, he thought it was awfully funny, our being so cautious."

Uncle Ulysses laughed and said "Round'em up and we'll all go down to the lunchroom for doughnuts and milk."

"Sheriff," said the mayor, "with election time coming next month *we* gotta put our heads together and cook up a good excuse for spending sixty dollars of the taxpayers' money."

―――

"The Errand," from The Golden Hive, *by Harry Behn (New York: Harcourt, Brace, 1966).*

On one level, Harry Behn's poem is a simple account of a boy's trip across the southwest desert to perform a task. However, it is also a circular journey of initiation. The boy riding to a new geographical area has also entered a new realm of experience. Along the way, he learns self-reliance and responsibility and returns to his home a changed person.

The Errand

I rode my pony one summer day
Out to a farm far away
Where not one of the boys I knew
Had ever wandered before to play,

Up to a tank on top of a hill
That drips into a trough a spill
That when my pony drinks it dry
Its trickling takes all day to fill;

On to a windmill a little below
That brings up rusty water slow,
Squeaking and pumping only when
A lazy breeze decides to blow;

Then past a graveyard overgrown
With gourds and grass, where every stone
Leans crookedly against the sun,
Where I had never gone alone.

Down a valley I could see
Far away, one house and one tree
And a flat green pasture out to the sky,
Just as I knew the farm would be!

I was taking a book my father sent
Back to the friendly farmer who lent
It to him, but who wasn't there;
I left it inside, and away I went!

Nothing happened. The sun set,
The moon came slowly up, and yet
When I was home at last, I knew
I'd been on an errand I'd never forget.

"Digging for Treasure," from The Story of the Treasure Seekers, *by E. Nesbit (1899; Rpt. Middlesex, England: Puffin Books, 1958).*

E. Nesbit is remembered for her achievements in the area of fantasy, literary fairy tales, and realistic stories for children. Perhaps her most enduringly popular book is The Story of the Treasure Seekers, *in which the Bastables (Dora, Oswald, Dicky, Alice, Noel, and H.O.) seek to restore their fallen fortunes.*

In the following episode the Bastables attempt to regain their fortune by digging for treasure but only succeed in planting their neighbor Albert. This humorous incident was probably inspired by a similar event from Nesbit's childhood, since her older brothers once planted her in the flower garden. The authentic rendering of the child's voice and her memorable depiction of a group of imaginative children at play are among Nesbit's lasting contributions to children's literature.

The idea of searching for treasure can be compared to the African folktale "The Fortune Hunt" and Robert Louis Stevenson's Treasure Island. *Albert's uncle plays a role similar to that of the fairy godmother or the wise teacher in traditional stories.*

Digging for Treasure

I am afraid the last chapter was rather dull. It is always dull in books when people talk and talk, and don't do anything, but I was obliged to put it in, or else you wouldn't have understood all the rest. The best part of books is when things are happening. That is the best part of real things too. This is why I shall not tell you in this story about all the days when nothing happened. You will not catch me saying, 'thus the sad days passed slowly by' — or 'the years rolled on their weary course' — or 'time went on' —,because it is silly; of course time goes on—whether you say so or not. So I shall just tell you the nice, interesting parts — and in between you will understand that we had our meals and got up and went to bed, and dull things like that. It would be sickening to write all that down, though of course it happens. I said so to Albert-next-door's uncle, who writes books, and he said, 'Quite right, that's what we call selection, a necessity of true art.' And he is very clever indeed. So you see.

I have often thought that if the people who write books for children knew a little more it would be better. I shall not tell you anything about us except what I should like to know about if I was reading the story and you were writing it. Albert's uncle says I ought to have put this in the prefaces, but I never read prefaces, and it is not much good writing things just for people to skip. I wonder other authors have never thought of this.

Well, when we had agreed to dig for treasure we all went down into the cellar and lighted the gas. Oswald would have liked to dig there, but it is stone flags. We looked among the old boxes and broken chairs and fenders and empty bottles and things, and at last we found the spades we had to dig in the sand with when we went to the seaside three years ago. They are not silly, babyish, wooden spades, that split if you look at them, but good iron, with a blue mark across the top of the iron part, and yellow wooden handles. We wasted a little time getting them dusted, because the girls wouldn't dig with spades that had cobwebs on them. Girls would never do for African explorers or anything like that, they are too beastly particular.

It was no use doing the thing by halves. We marked out a sort of square in the mouldy part of the garden, about three yards across, and began to dig. But we found nothing except worms and stones — and the ground was very hard.

So we thought we'd try another part of the garden, and we found a place in the big round flower bed, where the ground was much softer. We thought we'd make a smaller hole to begin with, and it was much better. We dug and dug and dug, and it was jolly hard work! We got very hot digging, but we found nothing.

Presently Albert-next-door looked over the wall. We do not like him very much, but we let him play with us sometimes, because his father is dead, and you must not be unkind to orphans, even if their mothers are alive. Albert is always very tidy. He wears frilly collars and velvet knickerbockers. I can't think how he can bear to.

So we said, 'Hallo!'

And he said, 'What are you up to?'

'We're digging for treasure,' said Alice; 'an ancient parchment revealed to us the place of concealment. Come over and help us. When we have dug deep enough we shall find a great pot of red clay, full of gold and precious jewels.'

Albert-next-door only sniggered and said, 'What silly nonsense!' He cannot play properly at all. It is very strange, because he has

a very nice uncle. You see, Albert-next-door doesn't care for reading, and he has not read nearly so many books as we have, so he is very foolish and ignorant, but it cannot be helped, and you just have to put up with it when you want him to do anything. Besides, it is wrong to be angry with people for not being so clever as you are yourself. It is not always their faults.

So Oswald said, 'Come and dig! Then you shall share the treasure when we've found it.'

But he said, 'I shan't — I don't like digging — and I'm just going in to my tea.'

'Come along and dig, there's a good boy,' Alice said. 'You can use my spade. It's much the best —'

So he came along and dug, and when once he was over the wall we kept him at it, and we worked as well, of course, and the hole got deep. Pincher worked too — he is our dog and he is very good at digging. He digs for rats in the dustbin sometimes, and gets very dirty. But we love our dog, even when his face wants washing.

'I expect we shall have to make a tunnel,' Oswald said, 'to reach the rich treasure.' So he jumped into the hole and began to dig at one side. After that we took it in turns to dig at the tunnel, and Pincher was most useful in scraping the earth out of the tunnel — he does it with his back feet when you say 'Rats!' and he digs with his front ones, and burrows with his nose as well.

At last the tunnel was nearly a yard long, and big enough to creep along to find the treasure, if only it had been a bit longer. Now it was Albert's turn to go in and dig, but he funked it.

'Take your turn like a man,' said Oswald — nobody can say that Oswald doesn't take his turn like a man. But Albert wouldn't. So we had to make him, because it was only fair.

'It's quite easy,' Alice said. 'You just crawl in and dig with your hands. Then when you come out we can scrape out what you've done, with the spades. Come — be a man. You won't notice it being dark in the tunnel if you shut your eyes tight. We've all been in except Dora — and she doesn't like worms.'

'I don't like worms neither.' Albert-next-door said this; but we remembered how he had picked a fat red and black worm up in his fingers and thrown it at Dora only the day before.

So we put him in.

But he would not go in head first, the proper way, and dig with his hands as we had done, and though Oswald was angry at the time, for he hates snivellers, yet afterwards he owned that perhaps it was just as well. You should never be afraid to own that perhaps you were mistaken — but it is cowardly to do it unless you are quite sure you are in the wrong.

'Let me go in feet first,' said Albert-next-door. 'I'll dig with my boots — I will truly, honour bright.'

So we let him get in feet first — and he did it very slowly and at last he was in, and only his head sticking out into the hole; and all the rest of him in the tunnel.

'Now dig with your boots,' said Oswald; 'and, Alice, do catch hold of Pincher, he'll be digging again in another minute, and perhaps it would be uncomfortable for Albert if Pincher threw the mould into his eyes.'

You should always try to think of these little things. Thinking of other people's comfort makes them like you. Alice held Pincher, and we all shouted, 'Kick! dig with your feet, for all you're worth!'

So Albert-next-door began to dig with his feet, and we stood on the ground over him, waiting — and all in a minute the ground gave way, and we tumbled together in a heap: and when we got up there was a little shallow hollow where we had been standing, and Albert-next-door was underneath, stuck quite fast, because the roof of the tunnel had tumbled in on him. He is a horribly unlucky boy to have anything to do with.

It was dreadful the way he cried and screamed, though he had to own it didn't hurt, only it was rather heavy and he couldn't move his legs. We would have dug him out all right enough, in time, but he screamed so we were afraid the police would come, so Dicky climbed over the wall, to tell the cook there to tell Albert-next-door's uncle he had been buried by mistake, and to come and help dig him out.

Dicky was a long time gone. We wondered what had become of him, and all the while the screaming went on and on, for we had taken the loose earth off Albert's face so that he could scream quite easily and comfortably.

Presently Dicky came back and Albert-next-door's uncle came with him. He has very long legs, and his hair is light and his face is brown. He has been to sea, but now he writes books. I like him.

He told his nephew to stow it, so Albert did, and then he asked him if he was hurt — and Albert had to say he wasn't, for though he is a coward, and very unlucky, he is not a liar like some boys are.

'This promises to be a protracted if agreeable task,' said Albert-next-door's uncle, rubbing his hands and looking at the hole with Albert's head in it. 'I will get another spade,' so he fetched the big spade out of the next-door garden tool-shed, and began to dig his nephew out.

'Mind you keep very still,' he said, 'or I might chunk a bit out of you with the spade.' Then after a while he said —

'I confess that I am not absolutely insensible to the dramatic interest of the situation. My curiosity is excited. I own that I should like to know how my nephew happened to be buried. But don't tell me if you'd rather not. I suppose no force was used?'

'Only moral force,' said Alice. They used to talk a lot about moral force at the High School where she went, and in case you don't know what it means I'll tell you that it is making people do what they don't want to, just by slanging them, or laughing at them, or promising them things if they're good.

'Only moral force, eh? said Albert-next-door's uncle, 'Well?'

'Well,' Dora said, 'I'm very sorry it happened to Albert — I'd rather it had been one of us. It would have been my turn to go into the tunnel, only I don't like worms, so they let me off. You see we were digging for treasure.'

'Yes,' said Alice, 'and I think we were just coming to the underground passage that leads to the secret hoard, when the tunnel fell in on Albert. He *is* so unlucky,' and she sighed.

Then Albert-next-door began to scream again, and his uncle wiped his face — his own face, not Albert's — with his silk handkerchief, and then he put it in his trousers pocket. It seems a strange place to put a handkerchief, but he wanted the handkerchief handy. Digging is warm work.

He told Albert-next-door to drop it, or he wouldn't proceed further in the matter, so Albert stopped screaming, and presently his uncle finished digging him out. Albert did look so funny, with his hair all dusty and his velvet suit covered with mould and his face muddy with earth and crying.

We all said how sorry we were, but he wouldn't say a word back to us. He was most awfully sick to think he'd been the one buried, when it might just as well have been one of us. I felt myself that it was hard lines.

'So you were digging for treasure,' said Albert-next-door's uncle, wiping his face again with his handkerchief. 'Well, I fear that your chances of success are small. I have made a careful study of the whole subject. What I don't know about buried treasure is not worth knowing. And I never knew more than one coin buried in any one garden — and that is generally — Hullo — what's that?'

He pointed to something shining in the hole he had just dragged Albert out of. Oswald picked it up. It was a half-crown. We looked at each other, speechless with surprise and delight, like in books.

'Well, that's lucky, at all events,' said Albert-next-door's uncle. 'Let's see, that's fivepence each for you.'

'It's fourpence — something; I can't do fractions,' said Dicky; 'there are seven of us, you see.'

'Oh, you count Albert as one of yourselves on this occasion, eh?'

'Of course,' said Alice; 'and I say he was buried after all. Why shouldn't we let him have the odd somethings, and we'll have fourpence each.'

We all agreed to do this, and told Albert-next-door we would bring his share as soon as we could get the half-crown changed. He cheered up a little at that, and his uncle wiped his face again — he did look hot — and began to put on his coat and waistcoat.

When he had done it he stooped and picked up something. He held it up, and you will hardly believe it, but it is quite true — it was

another half-crown!

'To think that there should be two!' he said; 'in all my experience of buried treasure I never heard of such a thing!'

I wish Albert-next-door's uncle would come treasure-seeking with us regularly; he must have very sharp eyes: for Dora says she was looking just the minute before at the very place where the second half-crown was picked up from, and *she* never saw it.

———

The Tale of Peter Rabbit, *by Beatrix Potter (London: Warne, 1902),*

Whereas Kipling's Rikki-tikki-tavi made a garden safe against invaders, Peter Rabbit wrongly invades Mr. McGregor's garden, where his character flaws, particularly his gluttony, very nearly lead to his death. Potter presents Peter as the quintessential naughty boy who, after his adventures, learns the dangers of his reckless ways. Her story is notable not only for its skillful portrayal of character, but also for its stylistic excellence, particularly in its use of understatement.

The Tale of Peter Rabbit

Once upon a time there were four little Rabbits, and their names were —

> Flopsy,
> Mopsy,
> Cotton-tail,
> and Peter.

They lived with their Mother in a sand-bank, underneath the root of a very big fir-tree.

'Now, my dears,' said old Mrs. Rabbit one morning, 'you may go into the fields or down the lane, but don't go into Mr. McGregor's garden: your Father had an accident there; he was put in a pie by Mrs. McGregor.'

'Now run along, and don't get into mischief. I am going out.'

Then old Mrs. Rabbit took a basket and her umbrella, and went through the wood to the baker's. She bought a loaf of brown bread and five currant buns.

Flopsy, Mopsy, and Cotton-tail, who were good little bunnies, went down the lane to gather blackberries:

But Peter, who was very naughty, ran straight away to Mr. McGregor's garden, and squeezed under the gate!

First he ate some lettuces
and some French beans; and then he ate some radishes;

And then, feeling rather sick, he went to look for some parsley.

But round the end of a cucumber frame, whom should he meet but Mr. McGregor!

Mr. McGregor was on his hands and knees planting out young cabbages, but he jumped up and ran after Peter, waving a rake and calling out, 'Stop thief!'

From *The Tale of Peter Rabbit* by Beatrix Potter London: Warne, 1902.

Peter was most dreadfully frightened; he rushed all over the garden, for he had forgotten the way back to the gate.

He lost one of his shoes among the cabbages, and the other shoe amongst the potatoes.

After losing them, he ran on four legs and went faster, so that I think he might have got away altogether if he had not unfortunately run into a gooseberry net, and got caught by the large buttons on his jacket. It was a blue jacket with brass buttons, quite new.

Peter gave himself up for lost, and shed big tears; but his sobs were overheard by some friendly sparrows, who flew to him in great excitement, and implored him to exert himself.

Mr. McGregor came up with a sieve, which he intended to pop upon the top of Peter; but Peter wriggled out just in time, leaving his jacket behind him.

And rushed into the toolshed, and jumped into a can. It would have been a beautiful thing to hide in, if it had not had so much water in it.

Mr. McGregor was quite sure that Peter was somewhere in the tool-shed, perhaps hidden underneath a flower-pot. He began to turn them over carefully, looking under each.

Presently Peter sneezed—'Kertyschoo!' Mr. McGregor was after him in no time.

And tried to put his foot upon Peter, who jumped out of a window, upsetting three plants. The window was too small for Mr. McGregor, and he was tired of running after Peter. He went back to his work.

Peter sat down to rest; he was out of breath and trembling with fright, and he had not the least idea which way to go. Also he was very damp with sitting in that can.

After a time he began to wander about, going lippity — lippity — not very fast, and looking all round.

He found a door in a wall; but it was locked, and there was no room for a fat little rabbit to squeeze underneath.

An old mouse was running in and out over the stone doorstep, carrying peas and beans to her family in the wood. Peter asked her the way to the gate, but she had such a large pea in her mouth that she could not answer. She only shook her head at him. Peter began to cry.

Then he tried to find his way straight across the garden, but he became more and more puzzled. Presently, he came to a pond where Mr. McGregor filled his water-cans. A white cat was staring at some gold-fish, she sat very, very still, but now and then the tip of her tail twitched as if it were alive. Peter thought it best to go away without speaking to her; he had heard about cats from his cousin, little Benjamin Bunny.

He went back towards the tool-shed, but suddenly, quite close to him, he heard the noise of a hoe — scr-r-ritch, scratch, scratch, scritch. Peter scuttered underneath the bushes. But presently, as nothing happened, he came out, and climbed upon a wheelbarrow and peeped over. The first thing he saw was Mr. McGregor hoeing onions. His back was turned towards Peter, and beyond him was the gate!

Peter got down very quietly off the wheelbarrow, and started running as fast as he could go, along a straight walk behind some black-currant bushes.
Mr. McGregor caught sight of him at the corner, but Peter did not care. He slipped underneath the gate, and was safe at last in the wood outside the garden.

Mr. McGregor hung up the little jacket and the shoes for a scare-crow to frighten the blackbirds.

Peter never stopped running or looked behind him till he got home to the big fir-tree.
He was so tired that he flopped down upon the nice soft sand on the floor of the rabbit-hole and shut his eyes. His mother was busy cooking; she wondered what he had done with his clothes. It was the second little jacket and pair of shoes that Peter had lost in a fortnight!

I am sorry to say that Peter was not very well during the evening.
His mother put him to bed, and made some camomile tea; and she gave a dose of it to Peter!

'One table-spoonful to be taken at bed-time.'

But Flopsy, Mopsy, and Cotton-tail had bread and milk and blackberries for supper.

"Chased by a Cow," from Eagle Voice: an Authentic Tale of the Sioux Indians, *by John G. Neihardt (London: Andrew Melrose, 1953).*

For the people of the Plains, the hunting of the buffalo, which was the primary source of meat and clothing, was accompanied by strictly observed sacred rituals. John Neihardt, who lived with the Plains people for many years and who wrote the autobiography of the holy man Black Elk, captures a young boy's excitement at his first buffalo hunt. In addition to accurately presenting Plains' cuture, he humorously depicts the ironic circular journey of Eagle Voice as he is chased by a buffalo cow and returns home empty-handed.

Chased by a Cow

The old man chuckled after one of his long silences. "Yes," he said "I wondered if the great voice was angry when it called to me on the pointed hill. But my grandfather was not angry about the pipe, and maybe the great voice was not either. I thought and thought about this. Maybe that was the only voice Wakon Tonka had, and it only sounded angry because it was so big. Maybe it was cheering me for making the offering.

"Everybody was getting ready for the big hunt, and something wonderful was going to happen. I might even get a cow, a lame one; and then everybody would praise me. Anyway, it would be a calf—one that got lost, maybe in a draw to one side away from the herd. When I had killed it, I would find my mother and grandmother, and they would come and butcher it. Then we would pack the meat on Whirlwind, and when we came into the village with the meat, people would notice and my grandmother would tell the other old women: 'See what my grandson did, and he is going to give it all to the old people.'

"The scouts had gone out to look for a bison herd over towards where the sun comes up, and one day the criers went about the village, calling: 'Make moccasins for your children! Look after the children's moccasins!' And that meant to be ready, for we were going to move. Then early next morning the criers went around, calling: 'Councillors, come to the centre! Councillors, come to the centre and bring your fires!' They did this because in the old days, a long time ago, the people had no matches or flint and steel. They could make fire another way in dry rotten wood by rubbing sticks together, but that was hard and could not always be done. Fire was sacred then, and had to be kept alive when the people moved. Then when they camped again, everybody came to the centre and got fire for their own tepees. They did not have to do it this time, but it was part of living in a sacred manner, and that was good for the people.

"When the councillors had brought their fires to the centre, the criers shouted to the people: 'Take it down! Take it down!' And the women all began taking down the tepees and packing everything on pony-drags. Then when everything was ready we began moving towards where the sun comes up, for that way the scouts had gone. First were the six councillors on foot; then came the chiefs with the criers behind them, then the *akichita*, and after them were the people with the loaded pony-drags. If there were enemies to be feared, there would be riders out there on our flanks and some ahead and behind; but there was no enemy to fear the way we were going; and we were so many that no band of Crows would attack us moving.

"There were four *teoshpaiay* going together on this hunt, one after the other in a long line; and it makes me feel good to remember how it looked. The *akichita* were not very strict before we came near the bison, and the children could play along the way. Maybe the girls would pick pretty flowers or dig up some wild turnips, or there might be a clump of rabbit berry bushes looking smoky with the ber-

ries getting red in them, like sparks; or, if it was late enough, plums might be getting good to eat, and the children would pick them while the people were passing. The bigger boys could play 'throwing them off their horses'. That was a rough game, but it was good for boys because it helped them to be brave warriors later on. They would divide up into little bands and charge each other, wrestling from the horses' backs, and sometimes a boy would get hurt. I was not big enough yet for that game, but I had a good time on Whirlwind, and sometimes I would get on a high place and see all the people travelling in a sacred manner. They were happy, and you could hear them singing here and there along the line. Maybe a drag pony would lift his head and neigh because the singing of the people made him want to sing too; and then the other ponies would lift their heads and sing down along the line.

"That was the next time I saw Tashina. I was riding up and down the line with some other boys; and when we came to where the Miniconjou were, I heard somebody cry out: '*Shonka 'kan! Shonka 'kan*! Come and pull my tepee!' And it was Tashina looking up at me. I was getting to be a big boy, for I had mourned and wandered, and I had killed a deer. Also I was going to kill a bison cow pretty soon, or anyway a calf. So I was too big to play with girls any more, and I did not say anything back. I wanted to talk to her, because I liked her; but I just made Whirlwind prance and rear. And when I rode away, I could see her sticking her tongue out at me and I heard her cry: 'Yah! Yah! Go and eat grass! Go and eat grass, *Shonka 'kan sheetsha*!'"[1]

With a chuckle the old man went into one of his reveries, gazing at me with eyes that saw what wasn't there. "She *was* a pretty little girl," he said, more to himself than to me; "a very pretty little girl." Then the focus of his gaze shortened to include me, and he continued:

"It was a time for the people to be happy, so we travelled slowly. And when the sun stood high above us, it would be time to rest awhile and let the ponies graze. The councillors would

1 Bad horse.

choose a place where there was water and good grass. Then the criers would call out to the people: 'Take off your loads and rest your horses! Take them off and rest your horses.' And if wild turnips were growing there, they would say: 'Take your sticks and dig some turnips for yourselves!' And the women would do this while the ponies drank and grazed and the councillors sat on a hillside watching the people. And when they had smoked together maybe two or three pipes, it would be time to move again, and the criers would call: 'Now put on your loads! Put them on!' And we would move, as before, until the sun was getting low.

"By that time the councillors would know a good place to camp for the night where there was plenty of wood, water, and grass, and the criers would tell the people to make camp.

"We were all camped the sacred way, in a big hoop of four hoops with the opening towards where you are always facing,[2] and the tepee-thrown-over-together was in the centre. The drags were all outside the circle, and, all around, the horses were grazing with the horse guards watching them. Smokes were standing above the tepees, for it was morning and the people were eating.

"Then there was a crier shouting: 'They are returning! The scouts I have seen. They are returning!' And all the people came out of the tepees to look. Three horsebacks were coming over the hill towards where the sun comes up, and they had something good to tell, for as they galloped down the hillside we could hear them singing together.

"When they had entered the hoop where you are always facing, they turned to the left and rode single file about the circle from left to right, looking straight ahead and saying nothing; and the people waited and were still. And when they had come again to the opening, they turned to the right and rode towards the centre where the councillors and chiefs were waiting in the tepee-thrown-over-together. And as the riders came near, a crier spoke for the scouts, calling to the chiefs and councillors: 'Come forth and make haste! I have

protected you, and you shall give to me in return.'

"Then the chiefs and councillors came forth, and the scouts sat down in front of them, facing the tepee, and all the people crowded around to see and hear.

"Then the chief filled a pipe and lit it; and when he had presented it to the Six Powers, first to the four quarters of the earth, then to the Great Mystery above, and last to the ground, which is the mother of all living things, he placed it on a buffalo chip in front of him, with the stem towards the scouts. There was bison hide on the mouthpiece of the pipe, and it was sacred; for it was through the bison that Earth, the mother of all, fed the people, and whoever smoked the pipe was nursing at his mother's breast like a little child. The chip was sacred too, for it meant the bison. They were the life and the shelter of the people's hoop, and when they died, the sacred hoop was broken.

"Then the chief spoke to the scouts: 'The nation has depended upon you. Whatever you have seen, maybe it is for the good of the people you have seen it.' And when he had said this, he offered the pipe to the scouts. They took it, smoking in turn, and that was a sacred vow that what they told would be the truth.

"Then the chief spoke again, and said: 'At what place have you stood and seen the good? Report it to me and I shall be glad. You have been raised on this earth, and every corner of it you know. So tell me the truth.'

"The first scout was so anxious to tell that he forgot the sacred rules and held up his thumb to the Great Mysterious One. But before he spoke, the chief shook his head and said: '*Hunh unh*! The first finger! The first finger for the truth!' So the first scout raised his first finger and said: 'You know where we started from. We came to a hill yonder, and there in the next valley we saw some bison.'

"The chief stood up when he heard this, and said: 'Maybe you have seen more farther on. Report it to me and I shall be glad.' And the second scout raised his first finger, saying: 'Beyond this hill there is another, and there we saw a small herd grazing in a valley.' And the chief spoke again: 'I shall be thankful if you will tell me more of the good that you have seen.' And the third scout said: 'From still another hill farther on, there we saw a big herd grazing in a valley and on the hillsides.'

"Then the chief spoke again, saying: 'Maybe you have not told me all the good that you have seen. Tell it now, and all the people will be glad.' When he had said this, the scouts forgot the rules and all began talking together: 'There is still another hill! *Wasichu! Wasichu!* There was nothing but bison all over the prairie! More than many looks could see! *Wasichu! Wasichu!*'

"When they said that, they did not mean white men. They meant very, very much of something, more than could be told or counted, like a great fatness. Then the chief cried out: '*Hetchetu alóh!*'[1] And all the people shouted, '*hi-yay, hi-yay*,' and the grazing horses out yonder, hearing the people, sent forth voices, neighing for gladness; and dogs raised their snouts and howled.

"Then the criers went forth and the people were still to hear them: 'Many bison I have heard! Many bison I have heard! Your knives you must sharpen! Your arrows make sharp. Make ready, make haste, your horses make ready. We shall go forth with arrows. Plenty of meat we shall make!'

"I had already sharpened my arrows so often that if I sharpened them much more, I wouldn't have any left. While the people were all getting ready for the big killing of meat, the council sent for certain young men who were being noticed by the people, and to these the chief said: 'Good young warriors, my relatives, your work I know is good. What you do is good always. So today you will feed the helpless and the old and feeble. Maybe there is an old woman or an old man who has no son. Or there may be a woman who has little children but no man. You will know these and hunt only for them. Today you belong to the needy.' This made the young men very proud, for it was a great honour.

"Then as the people were taking their places for going to the hunt, the criers shouted: 'Your children, take care of them! Your chil-

dren, take care of them!' After that the children must stay close to their mothers and not run around, for they might scare the bison; also, they might get hurt.

"Then we started off towards the big herd. First went the three scouts, riding abreast to show the way. Then came the councillors and the chiefs with the criers; and after them came all the *akichita* riding twenty abreast, and next were all the hunters, four or five abreast. If any hunter rode ahead of the *akichita*, he would be knocked off his horse and he would get no meat that day. Also, he would see shame in all eyes. The killing was for the nation, and everyone must have the same chance to kill. After the hunters were the women and older men, who would follow up and butcher the kill. Each hunter knew his arrows by the marks, and so he claimed his meat. And if two should claim a kill, then an *akichita* could decide between them or have the meat divided.

"We did not stop to rest that day, and when the sun was getting high, we began to see bison. Sometimes they were scattered out and sometimes there were small herds, but nobody was allowed to shoot at them or to cry out in a loud voice. They might get frightened, and the running fear might spread like fire in dry grass, until the big herd yonder caught the fear and started running. It was hard for the younger hunters riding behind the *akichita* up there; but no one pulled a bow or raised a voice; and all the children kept close to their mothers with the drags in the rear.

"The sun was high and had started down a little, when we saw that those ahead up yonder had stopped on a ridge to look. And while they were looking, voices came running all along the line down to us: 'Many bison they have seen! Make ready, make haste! Make ready to follow with your knives! They are going to charge!'

"Then just when the voices had come running back to us, we could see the hunters and *akichita* up younder splitting into two big bands; one to the right and one to the left.''

With a hand at his brow the old man peered narrow-eyed at the head of the column on the ridge that was a lifetime away. Then, clapping his hands high above his head, he cried: ''They

---

1 So be it.

are charging over the hill! They are all charging! The hunters and *akichita* are charging! *Hoka-hey! hoka-hey!*

"Everybody was excited, and the people were hurrying towards the hunt, except the very old ones and the women who stayed back to take care of the drag ponies and the children and to set up the tepees; for that was a good place to camp and there would soon be plenty of meat to dry and many hides to tan.

"Nobody was noticing me, and there were no *akichita* around there, so when I saw the hunters charge I charged too — not towards where the hunters had gone, but away from the people to the right where there was a big patch of buffalo berry bushes to help me. When Whirlwind and I got behind them, we started on the run towards where there was a break in the ridge ahead, to the right of where the hunters went over. While we were crossing the valley, my calf grew so fast that when I rode into the ravine, it wasn't a calf at all any more, but a big fat cow, and maybe even two cows.

"The ravine was full of thunder that was coming from a rolling storm of dust ahead. And when we got close over there and stopped to look down, we were a little scared. Whirlwind snorted and wanted to go back, but I had made an offering and I had to do something.

"Dust and thunder, dust and steady thunder with bull voices roaring in it! And wherever the dust blew thinner in the wind or lifted a little, there were backs, backs, backs of galloping bison bobbing up and down; bison beyond counting and more and more. And here and there over to the left I could see horsebacks charging in and out along the flanks of the herd, killing and killing, lost in the dust and appearing, lost and appearing. And while I looked, a big man on a big Wasichu horse that he must have taken from the soldiers came charging out of the dust. He was after a big bull with only a spear. Just as he was coming in front of me, he rode close and leaned far over. Then I saw him drive the spear with both hands in behind the bull's front leg. I forgot that I should not be where I was, and I yelled and yelled; but the man did not know I was there. I could see that his mouth was wide open and I knew he was shouting for a kill, but he did not make

any sound in the steady thunder. Then the bull stopped and turned and charged the horseback; but the man did not run away. He was very brave. Also he knew how to handle his horse, and the horse was wise too. They dodged and reared and circled until the man got hold of his spear again. Then with both hands he drove it deeper and pried it back and forth. The bull's mouth gushed blood, and when he started running again, he wobbled; and I could see the man prying the spear back and forth until the dust hid them.

"Just then, right down there not far away, a cow came loping with my calf! I did not wait. I charged. It is not easy to put an arrow where you want it from a galloping horse's back and the horse all excited. I was yelling, '*yu-hoo*', already, because I had one arrow sticking in the calf's hump and was pulling the bow for another try at the right place behind the front leg, when Whirlwind squealed and reared and wheeled away. For a long time after that it made me feel a little better when I blamed him for running away with me just as I was really getting my calf. But I was as scared as he was when I saw the cow charging us, and I did not look around until we were far up the side of the ridge. By that time the cow was loping back to find her calf.

"When I got Whirlwind to stand still, I was a little scared yet, and I was ashamed too. Nobody but the cow saw me running away, but Wakon Tonka could see everything, and I had made an offering. So I thought, there are plenty of calves, and when Whirlwind is not afraid any more I will charge again. Maybe it will be better next time.

"But that part of the herd was getting thinner as it passed to the right, and I could see more and more hunters among them, killing and killing. Sometimes I could even hear their cries above the rumbling sound when they killed: '*Ohee! Yuhoo!*' Then I said to myself, 'If I go down there now they will see me and the *akichita* will get me.' So I did not go down. Anyway, it was good to watch the hunters killing, and that is what I did. Afterwhile, when the dust and rumbling had passed, I could see the people yonder scattered in spots all over the prairie butchering the kill. That made me very hungry, so I galloped down there where the grass was beaten to dust; and wherever I came to a butchering they would give me something to eat — a chunk of liver, maybe with gall poured over it, or a piece of the strip of fat that runs along the backbone. It is good raw, but it is even better roasted a little. By the time I found my grandmother and grandfather, they had a fat cow all cut up on the stretched-out hide. They told me to ride over to a draw and to get some dry brush; and when I got back, my grandmother made a little fire. Then she roasted pieces of fat hump meat, and some old people came over to help us eat it.

"When the sun was getting low people were going back to camp with their horse-loads and drag-loads of meat and hides; and they kept on coming in with their loads long after it was dark. Before the feasting began, all the councillors and chiefs went into the tepee-thrown-over-together, and people came from all over the village with gifts of the best meat. This is how they gave thanks for good leading. Then the councillors cried, '*hiya-hiya*,' and sang all together to the bringers of food. And when the councillors had eaten awhile, the criers went about the village again, calling: 'All come home, for it is more than we can eat. Come home! There is plenty for all!' Then the people came with their cups and crowded about the tepee-thrown-over-together that all might have some of the councillors' meat; and after that the feasting began — feasting and dancing all night long. I can see the circle of the village yet with all the fires and the happy people feasting and singing. It makes me want to sing, too, for that is the way the Grandfather meant we should live. It was the sacred way and it kept the people good.

"That was near the Rosebud River, and it was a big killing; for we stayed there and killed until there was plenty for all. We had no hunter in our tepee, but the chosen young men offered us more than we could use, and my father's brother-friend, Looks Twice, took care of us. He brought the meat to my grandparents; but I know now that he was thinking most of my mother, because he wanted to be my father; and afterwhile he was.

"Next day there were drying racks all over the village, and I can see the stripped red meat turning brown in the bright sunlight, and the brown turning black. And I can see the happy women sitting in little circles with their sharp knives, unwinding the chunks of meat in their laps. They are joking and laughing and holding up their strips of meat to see whose is thinnest and longest. And outside the village raw hides are pegged out everywhere, and the old women are scraping and beating them for the soft tanning that made them good to wear and to sleep in on the coldest night.

"But I kept thinking and thinking about the calf I did not kill and of the way I got chased by the cow. If it had only been a bull I might have felt better. It helped me a little to blame Whirlwind for running away; but then I would remember the big voice that called to me on the pointed hill when I offered my grandfather's pipe, and I began to feel sure the voice was angry at me.

"Some of us boys made a war-game of sneaking up to the racks at night and stealing meat without getting caught. It was like going on the warpath for enemy horses. We had war councils out in the brush before we went and kill-talks around the fire if we got back safe with the meat. That was fun; but I kept thinking and thinking about the angry voice, and I was not quite happy. I wanted to try for a calf again, but I was afraid to try because I kept hearing the great voice scolding me for stealing the pipe from my grandfather.

"When my grandmother noticed how I was acting, she said: 'I wonder what is the matter with our grandson. He looks queer and he does not say anything.' Then my mother looked at me and said: 'I think he has been eating too much again. He is always eating.' "

——————

"Stopping by Woods on a Snowy Evening,"
by Robert Frost, from The Poetry of Robert
Frost. *Ed. by Edward Connery Lathem (New*
York: Holt, Rinehart and Winston, 1969).

Of Robert Frost's many poems, "Stopping
by Woods" is probably his best-known. The
solitary traveler, hypnotized by the darkness
and the deepening snow, is lulled in to a dan-
gerous peace by his surroundings, a peace he

nearly gives into until the spell is broken. In its use of symbol, as well as its circular pattern, this poem is similar to Harry Behn's "The Errand."

Stopping by Woods on a Snowy Evening

Whose woods these are I think I know.
His house is in the village, though;
He will not see me stopping here
To watch his woods fill up with snow.

My little horse must think it queer
To stop without a farmhouse near
Between the woods and frozen lake
The darkest evening of the year.

He gives his harness bells a shake
To ask if there is some mistake.
The only other sound's the sweep
Of easy wind and downy flake.

The woods are lovely, dark, and deep,
But I have promises to keep,
And miles to go before I sleep,
And miles to go before I sleep.

———

"The Night of the Leonids," from Altogether, One at a Time *by E.L. Konigsburg. Ill. by Laurel Schindelman (New York: Atheneum, 1971).*

Elaine Konigsburg is well known for creating intelligent and sensitive child characters, who are often intellectually curious and eager to grow. In this short story young Lewis experiences an important initiation with his grandmother, a woman who, though eccentric, is not unlike the wise old teachers of traditional stories. Expressing a serious theme in deft, light-textured and humorous prose, Konigsburg quietly dramatizes Lewis's first apprehension of mortality, time, and the smallness of human life in the universe.

The Night of the Leonids

I arrived at Grandmother's house in a taxi. I had my usual three suitcases, one for my pil-low and my coin collection. The doorman helped me take the suitcases up, and I helped him; I held the elevator button so that the door wouldn't close on him while he loaded them on and off. Grandmother's new maid let me in. She was younger and fatter than the new maid was the last time. She told me that I should unpack and that Grandmother would be home shortly.

Grandmother doesn't take me everywhere she goes and I don't take her everywhere I go; but we get along pretty well, Grandmother and I.

She doesn't have any pets, and I don't have any other grandmothers, so I stay with her whenever my mother and my father go abroad; they send me post cards.

My friend Clarence has the opposite: three Eiffels and two Coliseums. My mother and my father are very touched that I save their post cards. I also think that it is very nice of me.

I had finished unpacking, and I was wondering why Grandmother didn't wait for me. After all, I am her only grandchild, and I am named Lewis. Lewis was the name of one of her husbands, the one who was my grandfather. Grandmother came home as I was on my way to the kitchen to see if the new maid believed in eating between meals better than the last new maid did.

"Hello, Lewis," Grandmother said.

"Hello, Grandmother," I replied. Sometimes we talk like that, plain talk. Grandmother leaned over for us to kiss her cheek. Neither one of us adores slobbering, or even likes it.

"Are you ready?" I asked.

"Just as soon as I get out of this girdle and these high heels," she answered.

"Take off your hat, too, while you're at it," I suggested. "I'll set things up awhile."

Grandmother joined me in the library. I have taught her double solitaire, fish, cheat, and casino. She has taught me gin rummy; we mostly play gin rummy.

The maid served us supper on trays in the library so that we could watch the news on color TV. Grandmother has only one color TV set, so we watch her programs on Mondays, Wednesday, Fridays and every other Sunday; we watch mine on Tuesdays, Thursdays, Saturdays and the leftover Sundays. I thought that she could have given me *every* Sunday since I am her only grandchild and I am named Lewis, but Grandmother said, "Share and share alike." And we do. And we get along pretty well, Grandmother and I.

After the news and after supper Grandmother decided to read the newspaper; it is delivered before breakfast but she only reads the ads then. Grandmother sat on the sofa, held the newspaper at the end of her arm, then she squinted and then she tilted her head back and farther back so that all you could see were nostrils, and then she called, "Lewis, Lewis, please bring me my glasses."

I knew she would.

I had to look for them. I always have to look for them. They have pale blue frames and are shaped like sideways commas, and they are never where she thinks they are or where I think they should be: *on the nose of her head*. You should see her trying to dial the telephone without her glasses. She practically stands in the next room and points her finger, and she still gets wrong numbers. I only know that in case of fire, I'll make the call.

I found her glasses. Grandmother began reading messages from the paper as if she were sending telegrams. It is one of her habits I wonder about; I wonder if she does it even when I'm not there. "Commissioner of Parks invites everyone to Central Park tonight," she read.

"What for?" I asked. "A mass mugging?"

"No. Something else."

"What else?"

"Something special."

I waited for what was a good pause before I asked, "What special?"

Grandmother waited for a good pause before she answered, "Something spectacular," not even bothering to look up from the newspaper.

I paused. Grandmother paused. I paused. Grandmother paused. I paused, I paused, I paused, and I won. Grandmother spoke first. "A spectacular show of stars," she said.

"Movie stars or rock and roll?" I inquired politely.

"Star stars," she answered.

"You mean like the sky is full of?"

"Yes, I mean like the sky is full of."

"You mean that the Commissioner of Parks has invited everyone out just to enjoy the night environment?" We were studying environment in our school.

"Not any night environment. Tonight there will be a shower of stars."

"Like a rain shower?" I asked.

"More like a thunderstorm."

"Stars falling like rain can be very dangerous and pollute our environment besides." We were also studying pollution of the environment in our school.

"No, they won't pollute our environment," Grandmother said.

"How do you know?" I asked.

"Because they will burn up before they fall all the way down. Surely you must realize that," she added.

I didn't answer.

"You must realize that they always protect astronauts from burning up on their reentry into the earth's atmosphere."

I didn't answer.

"They give the astronauts a heat shield. Otherwise they'd burn up."

I didn't answer.

"The stars don't have one. A heat shield, that is."

I didn't answer.

"That's why the stars burn up. They don't have a shield. Of course, they aren't really stars, either. They are Leonids."

Then I answered.

"Why don't you tell me about the shower of stars that isn't really a shower and isn't really stars?" She wanted to explain about them. I could tell. That's why I asked.

Grandmother likes to be listened to. That's one reason why she explains things. She prefers being listened to when she *tells* things: like get my elbow off the table and pick up my feet when I walk. She would tell me things like that all day if I would listen all day. When she *explains*, I listen. I sit close and listen close, and that makes her feel like a regular grandmother. She likes that, and sometimes so do I. That's one reason why we get along pretty well.

Grandmother explained about the Leonids.

The Leonids are trash that falls from the comet called Temple-Tuttle. Comets go around the sun just as the planet Earth does. But not quite just like the planet Earth. Comets don't make regular circles around the sun. They loop around the sun, and they leak. Loop and leak. Loop and leak. The parts that leak are called the tail. The path that Earth takes around the sun and the path that Temple-Tuttle takes around the sun were about to cross each other. Parts of the tail would get caught in the earth's atmosphere and light up as they burn up as they fall down. Little bits at a time. A hundred little bits at a time. A thousand little bits at a time. A million bits.

The parts that burn up look like falling stars. That is why Grandmother and the Commissioner of Parks called it a Shower of Stars. The falling stars from Temple-Tuttle are called the Leonids. Leonids happen only once every thirty-three and one-third years. The whole sky over the city would light up with them. The reason that everyone was invited to the park was so that we city people could see a big piece of sky instead of just a hallway of sky between the buildings.

It would be an upside-down Grand Canyon of fireworks.

I decided that we ought to go. Grandmother felt the same way I did. Maybe even more so.

Right after we decided to go, Grandmother made me go to bed. She said that I should be rested and that she would wake me in plenty of time to get dressed and walk to Central Park. She promised to wake me at eleven o'clock.

And I believed her.

I really did believe her.

Grandmother said to me, "Do you think that I want to miss something that happens only three times in one century?"

"Didn't you see it last time?" I asked. After all, there was a Shower of Leonids thirty-three and one-third years ago when she was only thirty, and I'll bet there was no one making her go to bed.

"No, I didn't see it last time," she said.

"What was the matter? Didn't the Commissioner of Parks invite you?"

"No, that was not the matter."

"Why didn't you see it then?"

"Because," she explained.

"Because you forgot your glasses and you didn't have Lewis, Lewis to get them for you?"

"I didn't even wear glasses when I was thirty."

"Then why didn't you see it?"

"Because," she said, "because I didn't bother to find out about it, and I lost my chance."

I said, "Oh." I went to bed. I knew about lost chances.

Illustration by Laurel Schindelman from "The Night of the Leonids" in *Altogether, One at a Time*. Copyright © 1971 by E.L. Konigsburg. Reprinted with the permission of Atheneum Publishers Inc.

Grandmother woke me. She made me bundle up. She was bundled, too. She looked sixty-three years lumpy. I knew that she wouldn't like it if I expressed an opinion, so I didn't. Somehow.

We left the apartment.

We found the place in the park. The only part that wasn't crowded was up. Which was all right because that was where the action would be.

The shower of stars was to begin in forty-five minutes.

We waited.

And waited.

And saw.

"What are you crying about?" Grandmother asked. Not kindly.

"I have to wait thirty-three and one-third years before I can see a big spectacular Shower of Stars.

"You add it up," Grandmother said. Not kindly.

So I did. I added it up. Sixty-three and thirty-three don't add up to another chance.

I held Grandmother's hand on the way back to her apartment. She let me even though neither one of us adores handholding. I held the hand that hit me.

Modern Stories for Further Reading

NOVELS

Note: Many of the novels in this list have won major children's literature awards, which are indicated in parentheses following the annotations. Symbols for the awards are as follows: NB — Newbery Medal, awarded annually for "the most distinguished contribution to American literature for children"; CG — Carnegie Medal, awarded annually for the most outstanding British children's book; CLA — Canadian Library Association Book-of-the-Year for Children award. Listings of other novels are included in the bibliographies for literary folktales, hero tales, and myths.

Abel's Island, by William Steig (New York: Farrar, Straus, and Giroux, 1976).
— a wealthy dandy of a mouse survives for a year on a wilderness island onto which he has been cast during a storm.

Are You There God? It's Me, Margaret, by Judy Blume (Englewood Cliffs, N.J.: Bradbury, 1970).
— in what is probably the best of Blume's novels about growing up in the modern world, the title heroine deals with the problems of moving to a new town, with religious doubts, and with anxieties about puberty.

The Borrowers, by Mary Norton (London: Dent, 1952).
— in this first book in a series of five, the Clock Family, tiny people living beneath the floorboards of a country estate, must flee when they are discovered by "human beans." (CG)

Caddie Woodlawn, by Carol Brink (New York: Macmillan, 1935).
— based on the Wisconsin childhood of the author's grandmother, this novel traces a year in the life of the title heroine, a tomboy who matures. (NB)

Call It Courage, by Armstrong Sperry (Philadelphia: Winston, 1940).
— the cowardly son of a chief, Mafatu leaves his Pacific island on a long journey during which he acquires courage and a sense of self-worth. (NB)

Carrie's War, by Nina Bawden (London: Gollancz, 1973).
— evacuated to Wales during the bombings of World War II, a brother and sister become involved in the family struggles between their mean and puritanical guardian and his widowed sister.

The Court of the Stone Children, by Eleanor Cameron (New York: Dutton, 1973).
— unhappy because her family has moved to San Francisco from a small town, Nina Harmsworth becomes fascinated with a private museum where she makes contact with the spirit of Dominique, a girl from the Napoleonic era.

Dear Mr. Henshaw, by Beverly Cleary (New York: William Morrow, 1983).
— a lonely, troubled sixth grader writes a series of letters to his favorite author. (NB)

Dicey's Song, by Cynthia Voigt (New York: Atheneum, 1982).
— the relationships between thirteen-year-old Dicey and the grandmother who has cared for her are described. (NB)

From the Mixed Up Files of Mrs. Basil E. Frankweiler, by E.L. Konigsburg (New York: Atheneum, 1967).
— wanting to feel different, Claudia Kincaid runs away with her brother to New York's Metropolitan Museum of Art. (NB)

A Gathering of Days: a New England Girl's Journal, 1830-32, by Joan Blos (New York: Scribner's, 1979).
— an account of a teenaged girl's daily life and the extraordinary events, such as giving aid to an escaped slave, which help her to mature. (NB)

A Glass Rope, by William Mayne (London: Oxford University Press, 1957).
— Nan Owland, her sister, and a neighbor boy solve the mystery of the old legend of hounds and a unicorn which mysteriously disappeared on the night that an innkeeper eloped with the daughter of Lord Owland. (CG)

Hans Brinker, or the Silver Skates, by Mary Mapes Dodge (New York: O'Kane, 1865).
— a classic novel about a poor but honest brother and sister and their invalid family, who recover the wealth their father had hidden long ago.

The House of Arden, by E. Nesbit (London: Unwin, 1908).
— two children who are heirs to a titled estate must travel through time to overcome the difficulties which obstruct their inheritance.

The Incredible Journey, by Sheila Burnford (Boston: Little Brown, 1961).
— two dogs and a cat travel across the Canadian wilderness to return to their home and human family. (CLA)

Island of the Blue Dolphins, by Scott O'Dell (Boston: Houghton, Mifflin, 1960).
— maroooned when her tribe abandons their California island home, Karena survives alone, physically and psychologically, for eighteen years. (NB)

Johnny Tremain, by Esther Forbes (Boston: Houghton, Mifflin, 1943).
— during the Revolutionary War, an apprentice silversmith becomes involved in the struggle for independence. (NB)

The Lantern Bearers, by Rosemary Sutcliff (London: Oxford University Press, 1959).
— Aquila deserts as the last Roman legion departs Britain. He later serves as a lieutenant to Ambrosius, who fights to keep the Saxon invaders at bay. (CG)

Listen for the Fig Tree, by Sharon Bell Mathis (New York: Viking, 1974).
— a blind girl must fend for herself and must help her mother, still distraught over the murder of her husband a year earlier.

The Little House in the Big Woods, by Laura Ingalls Wilder (New York: Harper, 1932).
— the first book in the famous series describes pioneer life as seen through the eyes of five-year-old Laura.

Little Women, by Louisa May Alcott (Boston: Roberts, 1868-69).
— after over a century this family story of four sisters living during the War Between the States remains a great favorite.

The Marrow of the World, by Ruth Nichols (New York: Atheneum, 1972).
— teenage cousins Linda and Philip are transported to an alternate universe where Linda must exorcise the evil within herself and must choose between conflicting loyalties. (CLA)

Mistress Masham's Repose, by T. H. White (New York: Putnam's, 1946).

— Maria, a ten-year-old orphan controlled by her villainous guardians, discovers tiny people on an island in the ruinous estate she is to inherit.

The Moffats, by Eleanor Estes (New York: Harcourt, Brace, 1941).
— set during World War I, the book tells of the adventures and misadventures of four children who worry that their widowed mother will be forced to sell their house.

Mom, the Wolf Man, and Me, by Norma Klein (New York: Pantheon, 1972).
— during a peace march in Washington, Brett and her unwed mother meet a man whom the mother eventually marries.

Mrs. Frisby and the Rats of NIMH, by Robert O'Brian, pseudonym of Robert Conly (New York: Atheneum, 1971).
— the relationships between a widowed mouse and a group of super rats who have developed a highly mechanized civilization. (NB)

Otto of the Silver Hand, by Howard Pyle (New York: Scribner's, 1888).
— a young man of gentle spirit confronts the physical and mental violence of the European Middle Ages.

The Owl Service, by Alan Garner (London: Collins, 1967).
— three emotionally troubled teenagers in an isolated Welsh valley are caught up in forces from the past. (CG)

Pinocchio, by Collodi, pseudonym of Carlo Lorenzini. Translated by M. L. Rosenthal (New York: Lothrop, Lee and Shepard, 1983).
— a new, authorized translation of the 1883 Italian classic about the wooden puppet who, in the course of his adventures, matures into a thoughtful human being.

Peter Pan, by J. M. Barrie. Illustrated by Trina Schart Myman (New York: Scribner's, 1980).
— a reprint, with new illustrations, of the 1911 novel *Peter and Wendy*, about the Darling children and their fantastic night adventures with the boy who never grew up.

Rabbit Hill, by Robert Lawson (New York: Viking, 1944).
— the reactions of the country animals to the arrival of new human beings to a nearby rundown farm house. (NB)

River Runners, by James Houston (Toronto: McClelland and Stewart, 1979).
— a Native boy and his white companion learn mutual respect while struggling to survive in the northern Canadian wilderness. (CLA)

Roll of Thunder, Hear My Cry, by Mildred Taylor (New York: Dial, 1976).
— the Logan family fights increasing racial hostility in the South of the 1930s. (NB)

The Root Cellar, by Janet Lunn (New York: Scribner's, 1981).

— a lonely orphan, sent to live with relatives in Canada, discovers where she belongs after she has traveled in time to the period of the War Between the States. (CLA)

Smith, by Leon Garfield (London: Constable, 1967).

— a London pickpocket's life is endangered when he witnesses a murder.

Sounder, by William Armstrong (New York: Harper Row, 1969).

— an account of the courageous life of a Black sharecropping family after the father has been sent to prison for stealing a ham to feed his children. (NB)

A Stranger at Green Knowe, by L. M. Boston (London: Faber and Faber, 1961).

— the fourth in the Green Knowe series tells of the friendship between a young Oriental refugee and a gorilla which has escaped from a London zoo. (CG)

The Summer of the Swans, by Betsy Byers (New York: Viking, 1970).

— when her mentally retarded brother is lost, Sara discovers love and a focus for her conflicting emotions. (NB)

Time of Trial, by Hester Burton (London: Oxford University Press, 1963).

— in a time of social unrest at the beginning of the Nineteenth Century, Margaret Pargeter struggles to defend her radical father and tries to cope with her love for the "socially superior" Robert Kerridge. (CG)

Tom's Midnight Garden, by Philippa Pearce (London: Oxford University Press, 1958).

— while spending a summer away from his parents, Tom is mysteriously transported to a time in which the old lady who owns the house he is staying in is a girl. (CG)

The Twenty-One Balloons, by William Pene duBois (New York: Viking, 1947).

— a retired professor who decides to fly around the world in a giant balloon lands on the island of Krakatoa just before the great volcanic eruption. (NB)

Up a Road Slowly, by Irene Hunt (Chicago: Follett, 1966).

— living with a loving but proper maiden aunt and an alcoholic uncle, Julie Trelling matures as she learns to adjust to her guardians.

Watership Down, by Richard Adams (London: Rex Collings, 1972).

— the depiction of the heroics and power struggles of a group of rabbits who flee their warren in the face of encroaching technology. (CG)

The Westing Game, by Ellen Raskin (New York: Dutton, 1978).

— sixteen heirs to the Westing fortune gather to receive the clues they need to claim the great wealth. (NB)

The Witch of Blackbird Pond, by Elizabeth Speare (Boston: Houghton, Mifflin, 1958).

— in colonial Connecticut, lonely Kit Tyler discovers friendship and danger in her relationship with a solitary old woman. (NB)

The Wolves of Willoughby Chase, by Joan Aiken (New York: Doubleday, 1963).

— in an imaginary English kingdom ruled by James III, Bonnie Green and her cousin fight to save her absent father's estate from the clutches of the evil Miss Slighcarp.

The Wonderful Wizard of Oz, by L. Frank Baum. Illustrated by D.W. Denslow (Chicago: George Hill, 1900).

— the first of the popular Oz books, this novel tells of the actual journey (not a dream as in the movie) Dorothy takes as she learns to appreciate the gray land of Kansas and her aunt and uncle.

PICTURE BOOKS
Note: Many of the picture books in this reading list have won major children's literature awards, which are indicated in parentheses following the annotation. Symbols for the various awards are as follows: CD — Caldecott Medal, awarded annually for the best American children's picture book; KG — Kate Greenaway, awarded annually for the best illustrations in a British children's book; AFH — the Amelia Frances Howard-Gibbon Illustrators Award, presented annually for "outstanding illustrations" in a Canadian book for children. Listings of other picture books can be found in the bibliographies at the conclusions of earlier chapters.

Andy and the Lion, by James Daugherty (New York: Viking, 1938).

— a humorous, tall-tale version of the classical story of the boy who helped a lion.

Bear Party, by William Pene duBois (New York: Viking, 1951).

— a wise old Koala devises a means of ending the constant quarrelling of his companions.

The Beast of Monsieur Racine, by Tomi Ungerer (Farrar, Straus, and Giroux, 1971).

— a retired tax collector discovers a monster eating his prize pears and befriends it, only to discover that it is really two children in a costume.

The Biggest Bear, by Lynd Ward (Boston: Houghton, Mifflin, 1952).

— going into the woods to shoot the biggest bear, Johnny Orchard returns to the farm with a cub which, as it grows, creates havoc. (CD)

Charley, Charlotte, and the Golden Canary, by Charles Keeping (London: Oxford University Press, 1967).

— separated from his best friend, who is moved during urban renewal, Charley rediscovers her when he chases his pet canary, which has escaped from its cage. (KG)

Chin Chaing and the Dragon's Dance, by Ian Wallace (Toronto: Groundwood, 1984).
— as he prepares for his first traditional ceremony, a small Chinese boy feels very frightened. (AFH)

Come Away from the Water Shirley, by John Burningham (London: Jonathan Cape, 1977).
— facing pictures contrast the parent's hum-drum view of a day at the beach with their daughter's imaginative, adventurous perspective.

Crow Boy, by Taro Yashima (New York: Viking, 1955).
— a lonely boy in a tiny Japanese village is discovered possessing special talents.

Daisy, by Brian Wildsmith (New York: Oxford University Press, 1984).
— a cow, after discovering fame and fortune as a Hollywood movie star, realizes that there's no place like home.

Dawn. by Uri Shulevitz (New York: Farrar, Straus, and Giroux, 1974).
— keeping his text to an absolute minimum, Shulevitz uses dark hues and then the colors of sunrise to evoke the mood of early morning on a lake.

Deep in the Forest, by Trinton Turkle (New York: Dutton, 1976).
— a wordless picture book in which the traditional story of Goldilocks is reversed.

The Desert is Theirs, by Byrd Baylor. Illustrated by Peter Parnall (New York: Scribner's, 1975).
— the theme of the total integration of all life for the southwest Indians is captured by the skillful design of the illustrations.

Dogger, by Shirley Hughes (London: Bodley Head, 1977). Published in the United States as *David and Dog*.
— a little boy is extremely upset when he loses his favorite stuffed animal. (KG)

The Dragon of an Ordinary Family, by Margaret Mahy. Illustrated by Helen Oxenbury (London: Heinemann, 1969).
— an unusual pet rewards his human owners by taking them on a vacation to a miraculous land. (KG)

Drummer Hoff, by Ed and Barbara Emberley (Englewood Cliffs, N.J.: Prentice Hall, 1967).
— in this cumulative rhyme about the loading and firing of a cannon, military pomposity is satirized. (CD)

Fables, by Arnold Lobel (New York: Harper and Row, 1980).

— superb illustrations enhance the author's easy-to-read, but often very profound, little stories.

Father Christmas, by Raymond Briggs (London: Hamish Hamilton, 1976).
— an overworked, somewhat cranky old man is awakened from a dream of warm summer sunshine and must put up with a cold outhouse, miserable weather, tight chimneys, and rooftop antennas as he performs his annual duties.

Fly High, Fly Low, by Don Freeman (New York: Viking, 1937).
— two pigeons build their nest in the curves of a letter in a giant sign atop a San Francisco building.

Frederick, by Leo Lionni (New York: Pantheon, 1967).
— criticized by the other mice for not working during the autumn, Frederick becomes a hero when his poetic abilities help the mice get through the long winter.

The Funny Little Woman, by Arlene Mosel. Illustrated by Blair Lent (New York: Dutton, 1972).
— when she chases her dumpling which has fallen into a hole in the ground, the little woman is captured by the wicked Oni, who make her their cook. (CD)

Johnny Crow's Garden, by L. Leslie Brooke (London: Warne, 1903).
— the perfect host, Johnny Crow caters to the whims of the egocentric guests who visit his garden.

Jumanji, by Chris Van Allsburg (Boston: Houghton, Mifflin, 1980).
— a mysterious game found in the park comes to life when the children bring it home and begin to play it. (CD)

The King's Flower, by Mitsumasa Anno (London: Bodley Head, 1976).
— the king believes that biggest is best, until he discovers the beauty of a little flower.

Madeline's Rescue, by Ludwig Bemelmans (New York: Viking, 1953).
— when the dog Genevieve rescues Madeline from drowning, it is adopted by the convent, until the trustees object. (CD)

Make Way for Ducklings, by Robert McCloskey (New York: Viking, 1941).
— a mother duck raising her children in and around the pond of the Boston Common experiences many trials and tribulations. (CD)

Mike Mulligan and His Steam Shovel, by Virginia Lee Burton (Boston: Houghton, Mifflin, 1939).
— rendered obsolete by the new types of machines, Mike and Mary Ann find contentment and a sense of usefulness in a small rural village.

Mishka, by Victor Ambrus (London: Oxford University Press, 1975).

— seeking fame, eight-year-old Mishka joins the circus, only to discover that he must work as an odd-job man. (KG)

Moja Means One: Swahili Counting Book, by Tom and Muriel Feelings (New York: Dial, 1971).

— sensitive illustrations relate the Swahili numbers to aspects of traditional African life.

Nana Upstairs and Nana Downstairs, by Tomie dePaola (New York: Putnam's, 1972).

— sensitive portrayal of a litle boy's relationship with his ninety-four-year-old great-grandmother and his adjustment to her death.

Nine Days to Christmas: a Story of Mexico, by Marie Hall Ets (New York: Viking, 1959).

— a small child waits anxiously for her first Posada, or Christmas party. (CD)

Outside Over There, by Maurice Sendak (New York: Harper and Row, 1981).

— when the baby sister she is watching over is stolen by goblins, Ida makes a long and dangerous journey to effect a rescue.

Ox-Cart Man, by Donald Hall. Illustrated by Barbara Cooney (New York: Viking, 1979).

— American Primitive style illustrations depict the journey to town of a New England farmer who trades his goods for supplies for his family. (CD)

The Post Office Cat, by Gail Haley (New York: Scribner's, 1976).

— a lonely cat wanders into London where he becomes famous by ridding the post office of the rats which plague it. (KG)

A Salmon for Simon, by Betty Waterton. Illustrated by Ann Blades (Vancouver, B.C.: Douglas and McIntyre, 1978).

— unhappy because he cannot catch a fish, a West Coast Native boy achieves a sense of self-worth when he rescues a trapped salmon. (AFH)

Sam, Bangs, and Moonshine, by Evaline Ness (New York: Holt, Rinehart, and Winston, 1966).

— a lonely, motherless child nearly causes a tragedy because of her habit of telling lies. (CD)

The Snowy Day, by Ezra Jack Keats (New York: Viking, 1962).

— a little boy goes outdoors to explore his first snowfall, responding with wonder and curiosity. (CD)

The Story About Ping, by Marjorie Flack. Illustrated by Kurt Wiese (New York: Viking, 1933).

— when a runaway duck nearly becomes soup, he realizes that it is best to be at home and accept punishment.

The Story of Babar the Little Elephant, by Jan de Brunhoff (New York: Random House, 1933).

— after the death of his mother, Babar lives fashionably in Paris before returning to the jungle to marry and assume the role of king.

The Story of Ferdinand, by Monro Leaf. Illustrated by Robert Lawson (New York: Viking, 1936).

— when he reacts to a bee he sits on, Ferdinand is mistakenly identified as the most ferocious fighting bull in Spain.

Tim All Alone, by Edward Ardizzone (London: Oxford University Press, 1956).

— returning from a sea voyage, the youthful hero begins a lonely, sometimes tearful, but finally successful search for his missing mother. (KG)

Unbuilding, by David Macaulay (Boston: Houghton, Mifflin, 1980).

— set in the future, this book portrays the demolition of the Empire State Building. The drawings are both accurate and satirical.

The Wind Blew, by Pat Hutchins (London: Bodley Head, 1974).

— unsuspecting adults and children lose balloons, umbrellas, top hats, and wigs to the wind, which then mixes the objects up before dumping them on the wrong people. (KG)

Appendix A:
The Picture Book

An Introduction

Pictures have always been an important element of children's books. One of the earliest children's books, *Orbis Pictus* (1659), used crude woodcuts to instruct children about natural sciences; the Golden Age of Children's Literature, as the last half of the nineteeth century has been called, was highlighted by the art work of Randolph Caldecott, Kate Greenaway, Walter Crane, Sir John Tenniel, and Howard Pyle; during the twentieth century, hundreds of artists contributed to thousands of books for children. Because pictures are so immediate to the adults who buy children's books and to the children who receive them, they are often considered to be the major distinguishing feature of books for younger readers. Yet the nature and importance of pictures in children's books is often only partially understood by most adults, and because of this, children who look at books are often imperfectly assisted in coming to a full appreciation of the pictures they encounter. By clearly understanding, firstly, the ways in which picture books work, secondly, the history of children's picture books, and lastly, the significance of the artistry in specific books, adults will be better prepared to bring children and picture books together.

Pictures in children's books cannot be easily classified. However, by placing them on a spectrum in which words dominate the page at one extreme and pictures at the other, we may see certain categories. In the illustrated book, there are generally not too many pictures. The text is most important. One associates the books of Howard Pyle (*Otto of the Silver Hand* or *The Merry Adventures of Robin Hood*), or Lewis Carroll (*Alice's Adventures in Wonderland*), with the illustrations of Sir John Tenniel; A. A. Milne's "Winnie the Pooh" books are associated with Ernest Shepard's illustrations, and E. B. White's *Charlotte's Web*, with Garth Williams' pictures. While the illustrations are excellent, the texts of these novels could stand on their own. In such wordless books as Brinton Turkle's *Deep in the Forest*, Jean Jacques Loup's *The Architect*, or Lynd Ward's *The Silver Pony*, the entire meaning is communicated by the pictures. Between these extremes are books in which either the words or the pictures can assume greater importance. In the discussion which follows, we shall define picture books as those books in which a great deal, if not all of the meaning — action, theme, mood, characterization — is created by the pictorial elements.

Just as the selection and order of the words must be carefully studied in a purely verbal narrative, so too, specific visual details and their arrangement must be studied in stories in which the pictures communicate a great deal, if not all, of the meaning of a story. In approaching a given book one must examine and evaluate the artist's use of color, design, and detail, the choice of media, and the artistic style employed. These elements all contribute to the impact of a given page and the relationship between the specific pages in creating the overall impression of a book.

From *Deep in the Forest* by Brinton Turkle. Copyright © 1976. Reprinted by permission of E.P. Dutton Inc.

Since artists generally conceive of picture books as complete units, they should be considered as such by readers. All elements of a book—cover, endpapers, title page, size and texture of paper, and type face, as well as the words and illustrations —should be carefully examined. To pick up a book and turn immediately to the page on which the story begins is to miss the mood and thematic anticipations created by the introductory material. With mass marketed adult paperbacks it is not wise to judge a book by its cover; with a good children's book, the reverse is true. Taro Yashima's *Crow Boy* is a case in point. The cover, both front and back, depicts both the hero and the crows he has carefully studied. The endpapers, in the style of a Japanese screen decoration, show a cherry blossom and a butterfly;

these are not only favorite Japanese objects, but also symbols of transformation, which, we will see, is a major theme in the book. The title page, with a school bell, blackboard, and Japanese characters for the title, indicates the story's central setting.

The essential ingredient of color is, for most readers, the most obvious element in a picture book. It can be used to indicate characters' emotions: bright and light colors often suggest happiness; sombre colors, the opposite. In Leo Lionni's *Frederick*, the general sense of well-being experienced by the mice during the late summer and early fall is reflected by the greens and yellows of the illustrations. In Elizabeth Cleaver's *The Mountain Goats of Temlaham*, the sense of impending doom is conveyed by a gradual darkening of colors, which reaches deep purple just before the catastrophe.

From *The Green Man* by Gail E. Haley, Copyright © 1979 by Gail E. Haley. Reprinted with the permission of Charles Scribner's Sons.

In some stories, color is used symbolically. In Gail Haley's *The Green Man*, for example, green embodies the goodness of a life lived in close harmony with nature. The central character, who at the beginning of the story is described as arrogant, vain, and selfish, becomes more sensitive to nature and the woodland creatures, and consequently, more green appears in his clothing. Finally, it should be noticed that the use of color does not mean reliance on bright or sharply contrasting hues. In *The Biggest Bear*, Lynd Ward uses different shades of sepia to emphasize significant details. In Chris Van Allsburg's *Jumanji*, subtle gradations of light and shade capture the strangeness which invades a normal house while parents are away.

Details of a story present not only factual information about the characters,

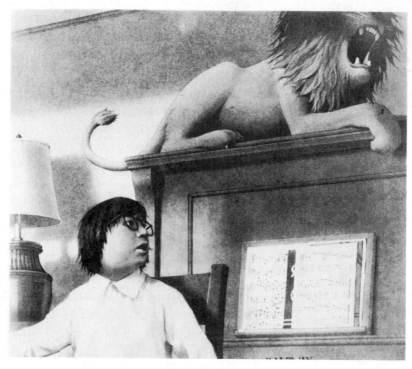

From *Jumanyi* by Chris Van Allsburg. Copyright © 1981 by Chris Van Allsburg. Reprinted by permission of Houghton Mifflin Company.

the actions, and the settings, but also the implications of these. Some of the implications conveyed by the details are obvious: body language and facial expressions communicate emotions. Others are more subtle: for example, the size and position of a character in an illustration may indicate the nature of his relationship with his peers. Both Frederick and Crow Boy are depicted as being very small and peripheral to the activities when rejected by their fellows; when they are accepted and given recognition for their talents, they assume more central positions in the illustrations. In many picture books, details have a specific symbolic significance that viewers should be aware of if they are to understand fully the implied meanings of specific illustrations. In *The Gift of the Sacred Dog*, Paul Goble's adaptation of the Native legend regarding the coming of the horse to the Plains, many of the details have cultural meanings. For example, as a boy climbs a hill to seek the wisdom necessary for him to assist his starving people, he becomes smaller on successive pages. This, Goble has explained, reflects the traditional vision quest of the Plains' people where the individual loses his sense of self-importance as he gradually comes into contact with the great spirit powers of the universe.

In many picture books, visual details are placed in contrast to the words found on the same page; the reader is expected to notice the difference. A notable example is Ellen Raskin's *Nothing Ever Happens on My Block*. A boy sits on the curb, lamenting that nothing ever happens on his block; but the pictures show that all kinds of marvelous events are taking place behind his back. Clearly the discrepancy between what the boy says and what the pictures reveal serves as a comment on his character.

ferocious lions and tigers,

Illustration by Ellen Raskin from *Nothing Ever Happens on My Block*. Copyright © 1966 by Ellen Raskin. Reprinted by permission of Atheneum Publishers, Inc.

Design refers both to the layout of individual pages and to the overall pattern created by the interrelationships between the pages. In Maria Campbell's *Little Badger and the Fire Spirit*, David Maclagan's illustrations emphasize the title hero's unhappiness early in the story, not merely through the use of a cold blue coloring and in the depiction of facial expressions, but also by page design, in which the lines flow downward and to the corner. The hillside, the branches of the tree, and the slope of the shoulders of Badger all move downward. Similarly, in *Mike Mulligan and His Steamshovel*, Virginia Lee Burton captures the sense of rejection experienced by Mike and his machine by arranging the words, the fence, the steam from the shovel, and Mike on a diagonal axis moving downward to the lower right hand corner of the page.

In the overall design of a book, color, page design, and details often form a structure intended to show changing moods and conflicts. In *The Mountain Goats of Temlaham*, pictures dominated by gently flowing lines and colors reflecting the gold of the sunshine and the green of the forest are replaced by pictures in which sharp jagged lines and darker colors prevail. This overall pattern parallels the emotional movement of the story: in the earlier part, the people live in harmony with the animals they hunt; however, when they violate the hunting rules, they invoke the anger of the mountain goats who later avenge themselves. In *The Bear Who Wanted to be a Bear*, by Jörg Steiner and Jörg Müller — the story of a bear who is mistaken for a lazy laborer and forced to work in a factory — the early pictures contain only details from the natural world. As the bear is forced into the factory and onto the assembly line, fewer natural details appear until nature disappears completely and he is shown in a windowless room surrounded by gigantic machines.

From *The Bear Who Wanted to be a Bear* by Jorg Steiner and Jorg Muller. Copyright © 1977 by Atheneum Publishers, Inc. Reprinted with the permission of Atheneum Publishers, Inc.

In creating their illustrations, artists use those styles best suited to achieving the effects they wish. Caldecott Medal-winning author-illustrator Maurice Sendak has written: "Style is purely a means to an end, and the more styles you have, the better."[1] In addition to Sendak, who has evolved through several stylistic phases, each appropriate for the works that embody them, three artists notable for employing a variety of styles are Marcia Brown, Barbara Cooney, and Gail Haley. In her adaptation of Charles Perrault's *Cinderella*, Brown uses pen, ink, and washes to create an elaborate and intricate style evocative of the elegance of the late-seventeenth-century French court. In *Once a Mouse . . .* , the retelling of an ancient East Indian fable, she creates woodcuts and limits herself to three colors, thereby communicating the formal simplicity of the story. Gail Haley, in *A Story, a Story*, also uses woodcuts in her retelling of a West African pourquoi tale and incorporates designs from the art work of that area. However, in *The Green Man*, in which she creates her own literary legend, one based on medieval traditions, her art is like that of the tapestries of the Middle Ages. Barbara Cooney has imitated a variety of styles: for the illustrated Greek myth *Dionysus and the Pirates*, she used Greek artistic styles; the pictures for Jean Craig's adaptation of *The Donkey Prince* are like those of the fifteenth century Renaissance; for her illustrations of Donald Hall's *Ox-Cart Man*, she copied the style of American primitive painting. Many artists creating picture books do not have such a variety of styles, and many, such as Brian Wildsmith, have only one (which is easily recognizable from book to book). The fact remains that in all good picture books, style is an important vehicle of tone and meaning, and should be carefully considered.

In wordless picture books, pictoral elements can be used to create a considerable range of effects and meanings. In Mercer Meyer's *The Great Cat Chase*, the humorous cause-and-effect relationships in a simple sequence of events are emphasized by Meyer's links between sequential illustrations. In *The Architect*, by Jean Jacques Loup, the central figure appears very small on each page. However, by noticing his physical appearance, facial expressions, and body language, readers can better understand his changing reactions to the city he has created. Without words to draw a reader's attention to important aspects of the story, these wordless picture books require considerable alertness on the part of the reader, who must perceive significant visual details and the relationships between illustrations.

While a survey of illustrations in children's books published over the centuries reveals that the devices, styles, and media discussed above have been used in a variety of ways and with varying degrees of success, two important elements can be noted. First, artistic success has been related not only to the talent of the individual creating the illustrations, but also to the state of printing technology. Second, the illustrations, in contributing to the total effect of the books of which they are a part, reflect prevailing adult notions of what constitutes a suitable picture book for children.

The earliest illustrations were printed from crudely carved engravings. Artistic excellence was not important: if the illustrations assisted in the moral or intellectual education of children, they fulfilled their purpose. Occasionally illustrations had little direct relationship with the texts they appeared with and were used mainly as decoration. However, in the later eighteenth and early nineteenth centuries, skilled engravers made it possible to create meticulously detailed illustrations that not only depicted events but also enhanced mood and explained character. Techniques of color printing were not sufficiently developed, and therefore commercially viable, until well into the nineteenth century. However, there were colored pictures in children's books. Scores of children were employed to paint appropriate colors in pictures printed from engravings.

The Golden Age of children's book illustration commenced in the late 1850s and was largely the result of the collaboration between one of the finest engravers of his day, Edmund Evans, and three great illustrators: Randolph Caldecott, Walter Crane, and Kate Greenaway. Evans developed a technique which faithfully reproduced the subtleties of color and delicacies of line in original paintings; he was then able to capture the surfaces and, through them, the essences of the works of the three artists. At the same time, children's books were gradually being freed of excessive moral and instructional intent which had previously been so stifling. Edmund Lear's limericks and nonsense narratives had helped to make foolishness and laughter acceptable, and, in the 1860s, Lewis Carroll was, among other things, to parody the dreary seriousness of earlier books.

In such volumes as *The Baby's Opera* (1877) and *The Sleeping Beauty in the Wood* (1876), Walter Crane practiced his belief that children deserved quality art work and excellent design in their books. He stated that "the best of designing for children is that the imagination and fancy may be let loose and roam freely, and there is always room for humor and even pathos, sure of being followed by that ever-living sense of wonder and romance in the child heart."[2] Kate Greenaway was one of the first children's author-illustrators to achieve best-seller status. Total sales of such books as *Under the Window* (1898) and *An Apple Pie* (1886) reached the hundreds of thousands, and the clothing styles of the children in her books influenced fashions in England and Europe. However, her popularity waned at the turn of the century and her influence on later artists was not so great as that of Crane and Caldecott.

Of the three, Randolph Caldecott was indubitably the greatest children's book illustrator; he exerted the greatest influence, and his books are still widely enjoyed today. Beginning in 1878 with *The Diverting History of John Gilpin* and *The House That Jack Built*, he published a series of sixteen picture books which exploited as fully as anyone has done before or since the narrative potentials of illustration. His achievement can be seen in his treatment of the traditional four-line nursery rhyme "Bye Baby Bunting." Ten illustrations humorously reveal the predicament of a father who, unsuccessful in his hunting expedition, must go to a store to purchase a fur for his child. Unlike Greenaway, who presented her characters generally in static poses, Caldecott emphasized action, freezing motion in a manner not unlike that of modern photography. In *A Frog He Would*

Illustration by Walter Crane, ''Beauty and the Beast'' reproduced from *Walter Crane as Book Illustrator*, by Rodney K. Engen. Copyright © 1975. Reprinted by permission of St. Martin's Press.

A-Wooing Go, Caldecott employed anatomical accuracy and human-like movement in his illustration of the gallant suitor, the frog. Such twentieth-century artists as Maurice Sendak have acknowledged their enormous debt to Caldecott, and the American Library Association has named the Caldecott Medal, awarded annually for the best American picture book, after him.

"A Frog He Would a Wooing Go" from *Randolph Caldecott's John Gilpin and Other Stories*, by Randolph Caldecott. Copyright © 1977. A Fredrick Warne Book. Reprinted by permission by Viking Penguin Inc.

During the late nineteenth century and into the twentieth century, the high quality of children's book illustration continued. Arthur Rackham, Leslie Brooke, Beatrix Potter, and Ernest Shepard in Great Britain, and Howard Pyle and N. C. Wyeth in the United States are the best-known names of this period.

In the twentieth century, the picture book has been the dominant form of children's literature. Countless artists have used a variety of styles and media to illustrate traditional folktales and to create original stories. Critic Sheila Egoff, surveying the field in her study *Thursday's Child*, has noted two distinct trends. Until the 1950s, she has written, the books produced "a single vision of a secure childhood and an abiding social order," [3] and refers, among others, to the works of Wanda Gág, Virginia Lee Burton, and Robert McCloskey. Works of the last two decades, she states, have shattered this security as uncertainty, unpleasantness, and fear have been accepted as legitimate subjects for picture books. In addition, the range of subject matter has broadened considerably: racial and sexual stereotypes have been attacked; minority cultures and members of both sexes are now being depicted more openly and honestly.

Although picture books are often categorized in libraries under the heading "E" for "easy," it is a mistake to consider them suitable only for preschool or early elementary children. Certainly, many picture books are accessible to consumers in this age group. However, these books also contain levels of meaning best understood by older children; moreover, they generally have a reading level of Grade Three or higher. In addition, there are many picture books specifically created for older readers. In creating literature programs, teachers and librarians should keep these facts in mind.

The object of teaching picture books to elementary school children is to provide them with the skills necessary to understand how the pictorial aspects make important contributions to meaning and total effect. Books like Pat Hutchins's *The Wind Blew* can be used to help young children notice details in specific illustrations and the relationships between details on adjacent pages. In Keats's *Whistle for Willie*, color, page design, facial expressions, and body language are important indications of the hero's emotions. By mid Grade Two, the overall visual patterns of books like *Frederick*, *Little Badger and the Fire Spirit*, and *The Little House* can be studied so students can see how these patterns contribute to the development of character and conflict. Grade Three students should be able to notice visual ironies in such works as *The Biggest Bear* (Lynd Ward), *Blueberries for Sal* (Robert McCloskey), and *Dick Whittington and His Cat* (Marcia Brown).

In the upper elementary grades, as children's skills of literary interpretation become more sophisticated and their powers of conceptualization increase, more complex picture books can be introduced and stories studied earlier can be reconsidered at a deeper level. For example, ironies of character can be studied in Tomie de Paola's *Fin M'Coul: the Giant of Knockmany Hill* and Paul Galdone's *The Little Girl and the Big Bear*. The illustrations in Jean Jacques Loup's *The Architect* and Jörg Steiner and Jörg Müller's *The Bear Who Wanted to Be a Bear* can be examined for the light they cast on the conflict between nature and civilization. Toshi Maruki's *Hiroshima No Pika*, an account of the explosion of the atomic bomb in Japan in 1945, can provide an excellent introduction to discussions of nuclear war. *Sedna* (Beverly Brodsky McDermott), *Arrow to the Sun* (Gerald McDermott), and *Buffalo Woman* (Paul Goble) provide visually accurate representations of historical Native cultures. Different illustrated versions of traditional folktales such as the Grimm Brothers' *Hansel and Gretel* and Charles Perrault's *Cinderella* can be compared, with students discussing which artist they consider to be most successful in communicating character, mood, and conflict.

In the pages that follow, we shall consider in some detail a number of picture books which have received high critical acclaim, shall examine how the illustrations in them communicate elements of characterization, mood, and theme, and shall relate them to other members of "The Family of Stories."

Notes

1 Quoted in Jon C. Stott, *Children's Literature from A to Z: a Guide for Parents and Teachers* (New York: McGraw-Hill, 1984), p. 249.

2 Quoted in Stott, p. 85.

3 Sheila Egoff, *Thursday's Child: Trends and Patterns in Contemporary Children's Literature* (Chicago: American Library Association, 1981), p. 249.

Rosie's Walk

by Pat Hutchins (New York: Macmillan, 1968).

On a first reading, *Rosie's Walk* appears to be a very simple book. The text consists of only thirty-two words presented in one long, yet simple sentence. The illustrations are clear: there is no mistaking the fox's motivation or the results of his actions. But like most good picture books, the simplicity is deceptive: a great deal more is implied than is explicitly presented, and the text and illustrations can be read on many levels.

The book is the creation of Pat Hutchins, an English artist who began producing picture books while living in New York City. Although in such picture books as *Rosie's Walk; Changes, Changes*; and *The Wind Blew*, she deals with different subjects, in each of these she uses a common approach: her narrative progresses in a steady, step-by-step manner with the details of each picture preparing the reader for what happens when the page is turned. "To me,"

The introductory material presents two main characters, a fox and a hen, in a barnyard setting. It also raises false expectations for the reader. The position of the fox on the cover indicates his predatory intentions; Rosie's movement away from her hen house suggests her increasing vulnerability. The placement of the fox above the lettering on the half title page and Rosie below again emphasizes his intentions and her vulnerability. However, the events of the circular journeys made by both characters do not fulfill expectations: Rosie returns home unscathed; the wet, battered, and beestung fox makes a hasty retreat from the barnyard. Hutchins has used her cover and half title page to play a deliberate trick on the reader.

Reading the thirty-two word text in relation to the pictures, the reader discovers that another trick has been played. It makes no reference to the fox at all; only Rosie's progress past the various objects in the barnyard is men-

From *Rosie's Walk,* by Pat Hutchins. Copyright © 1968 by author. Reprinted with permission of Macmillan Publishing Co.

Hutchins has stated, "the most important thing about a children's picture book is that it should be logical, not only the story, but the layout too .... I like to build my stories up, so that the reader can understand what is happening and, in some cases, anticipate what is likely to happen on the next page."[1]

tioned. Perhaps no mention of the fox is made to indicate Rosie's ignorance of his presence. Certainly, however, the pictures must be read if the full story is to be understood. The fox is so intent on his intended victim that he fails to notice objects which will injure him and impede his progress. However, the pictures are designed to draw the viewer's attention to these objects; the viewer is thus invited to anticipate what will happen when the page is turned. Hutchins subtly increases the complexity of the events which take place. At first, there are simple actions and results: the fox leaps and lands on the rake, leaps and lands in the pond, leaps and lands on the haystack. However, between the time Rosie catches her leg on the rope as she passes the mill and the flour lands on the fox's head, several actions take place. Rosie's next stride tightens the rope, causing the knot to come undone, the rope slides through the pulley, the bag tips, and, finally, the flour spills out on the fox. In the page depicting the fox leaping over the fence, the reader is invited to anticipate a series of events which will take place over a longer period of time and will be presented in several pictures.

A young reader, after viewing the first two incidents, can generally predict the future events with little difficulty. A slightly older reader can perceive the character of the fox. So intent is he on capturing Rosie that he does not take the time to survey the terrain before making his leaps. Nor after two or three unfortunate leaps does he learn greater caution. His greed seems to be so great that he becomes even more reckless. If, in the end, he is badly hurt, it is just punishment, not only for his greed, but also for his reckless stupidity. Children usually laugh at his ignominious plight, for they recognize that he is a fool.

Rosie's Walk acquires new dimensions of meaning when it is placed within a centuries-old tradition of stories about sly foxes. In such stories as "Henny Penny," the fox generally symbolizes cleverness and evil, and, in the Middle Ages, he was often compared to the Devil. He is a death-dealing figure who preys on the innocent and weak. He is also an invader entering the sanctuary of the barnyard, and his plan is often to lure his victims as far as possible from the protection of their homes. In *Rosie's Walk* the fox possesses the characteristics of the fox of traditional stories, but with two significant exceptions: he is reckless and stupid. In this respect, the picture book is a parody of the main tradition. Perhaps Rosie is also a parody of the traditional victim. It could be argued that, rather than being a naive victim, unaware of the danger lurking behind her, she may be feigning ignorance, deliberately leading the fox past the objects which will thwart him and finally cause him to leave the barnyard without having achieved his goal.

Chanticleer and the Fox

adapted and illustrated by Barbara Cooney (New York: Crowell, 1958).

The idea for writing a picture book adaptation of Geoffrey Chaucer's fourteenth-century story "The Nun's Priest's Tale" came to Barbara Cooney as a result of two interests: as an artist, she became interested in sketching chickens; at about the same time she read a modernization of Chaucer's poem. She wished to combine the two and to "convey in my pictures what Chaucer conveys in his words: that people . . . in this case chickens . . . can be beautiful and lovable even when they are being ridiculous."[1] However, before *Chanticleer and the Fox* was published, Cooney had to engage in a great deal of research and preliminary art work. She thoroughly studied the various aspects of life in fourteenth-century England. She then carefully examined the herbs and flowers growing in her New England garden. When she discovered which of these had also been found in Chaucer's England, she included them in her illustrations. Finally, she borrowed chickens and roosters from her neighbors, sketching them in a variety of activities. Then she was ready to work on the book, adapting a modern English version to picture-book length and creating the illustrations.

The finished product, which was awarded the Caldecott Medal, is in some ways like *Rosie's Walk*: both stories recount the encounter of a fox and a barnyard fowl, and in both, the fowl is not captured or eaten. However, there are differences. Cooney carefully and accurately depicts a medieval setting appropriate to the story, and her illustrations contribute in more subtle ways to the meaning of the story.

Chaucer's fable, which was based on a well-known tale found throughout Europe, emphasized the dangers of false pride and flattery and suggested that the best defense against trickery was alertness and even greater trickery. In her illustrations, Cooney emphasizes the mes-

1 Quoted in Jon C. Stott, *Children's Literature from A to Z: a Guide for Parents and Teachers* (New York: McGraw-Hill, 1984), p. 83.

Illustration by Barbara Cooney from *Chanticleer and the Fox,* Copyright © 1958.
Reprinted with permission of Crowell Co. Publishers.

sage of the text. The illustrations of the cover, half title page, and the title page present not only the main characters and setting, but also hint at the characters of the two main actors. On the cover, Chanticleer struts along, and, because his head is thrust proudly into the air, cannot see the fox concealed in a nearby bush. The farmyard is protected by a stick fence, but, as we shall see, it provides little protection for so proud a rooster against a fox so sly. The title page seems to suggest that the rooster is stupid as well as proud, for although he curiously looks at the fox's tail protruding from the bush, he fails to think about the head which is at the opposite end.

The first three illustrations for the story, depicting the life of the family which owns the farm, are designed to create a contrast with the picture of Chanticleer which immediately follows. They are simply dressed, industrious, and orderly. Mother and daughters gather food, tend the livestock, and prepare the meals. Their home is poor, but tidy, and the family appears to enjoy its life. The picture of Chanticleer comes as somewhat of a surprise. He dominates the double page spread with his regal bearing. Significantly, there is no background, for Chanticleer in his pride considers himself superior to his surroundings. Indeed, it might be questioned whether or not he even notices them.

In the pages portraying Chanticleer's life with Partlet and the other hens, the rooster is again the dominant figure. He exists in blissful peace and, as indicated by the floral borders on two of the pages, Chanticleer is protected from the harsh influence of the outside world. However, sorrow is not far away, and the first picture of the lurking fox is almost completely black, with only the blood-red tongue providing any contrast. Not only the darkness of the picture with its hint of blood, but also the abrupt change from full-color illustrations indicates the impending disaster. Although in the depiction of the first encounter between the fox and the rooster full color is used, two elements indicate that a change has taken place. The fox occupies the dominant position on the page, just as he controls the relationship by means of his flattery. Moreover, there is no protective floral border around the page; evil forces have intruded into the barnyard.

The design of the pictures depicting the chase scene moves the reader's eye diagonally upward to the right hand corner, anticipating the eventual position of Chanticleer after he has escaped from the fox. The fox moves out of the yard, up the hill toward the woods; the widow, her children, and the animals follow; the geese fly over the trees; and, finally, Chanticleer flutters into the branches of an oak. Now he assumes the dominant position in the pictures and, although he is the largest object in the double spread, he is neither as large nor as haughty looking as before. At this point, he is safe and wiser, and a protective border of oak leaves and acorns surrounds him. The final picture of the book, in which the mother, flanked by her two daughters, lovingly holds Chanticleer, who has completed a circular journey, communicates the security which has been reestablished at the conclusion of the story.

Although *Chanticleer and the Fox* could have been told without the illustrations, the sense of Chanticleer's pride, the power struggle taking place between the rooster and the fox, the idea of the violation of the barnyard security by the intruder, and the final tone of harmony would not have been so fully communicated.

Hansel and Gretel

by the Brothers Grimm. Trans. by Charles Scribner, Jr. Ill. by Adrienne Adams (New York: Charles Scribner's Sons, 1975).

Few fairy tales have received more critical attention than "Hansel and Gretel," by the Brothers Grimm, and for good reason. The principal characters are children, not the adolescents who appear in most folk tales. The tale works extremely well at the level of story. Hansel and Gretel face the most fearful situation a child can imagine—being abandoned by their parents deep in the woods. The shelter they find turns out to be a perilous one indeed—

the gingerbread cottage is set in the woods by a wicked witch to lure innocent children into her power. Gretel's cunning, however, enables her to trick the witch into the oven, where Gretel leaves her to roast. The children take the witch's jewels, are helped across a stream by a white duck, and return to their father's house, where they give him the witch's jewels and so restore him to his proper role.

The structure of the tale is truly satisfying to most readers. Essentially circular, the tale features child characters who strongly resemble the heroes of romance. Hansel exercises initiative in the first part of the tale. He uses white pebbles to find his way home the first time that he and Gretel are lost in the forest. The second time his plan fails, as the birds have devoured the bread crumbs he has dropped. Why are the children abandoned twice? Psychologists suggest that this feature of the tale emphasizes the necessity for children to be separate from their parents in order to grow and to secure their own identities. Other interpretations work well. Perhaps Hansel reveals his immaturity by trying the same plan twice. Perhaps the children are wrong to want to return to such a home in the first place.

Hansel does not abdicate his male role, however; even after his plan has failed, he continues to protect and to comfort Gretel in the forest. Once having arrived at the witch's cottage, Hansel finds himself a prisoner, totally in the power of the witch. He is pinned in a cage, and fed fattening food in order to gratify the gluttony of the witch. Using his wits to survive, he uses a bone to fool the witch into thinking he is still too thin to eat.

In the second half of the tale, Gretel becomes the more active and resourceful character. She saves her life and Hansel's by tricking the witch; she also secures the witch's jewels. Bruno Bettelheim has written that one of his child patients, a little girl with several brothers, demanded that "Hansel and Gretel" be read to her repeatedly. [1] Bettelheim speculates that the girl was gratified to read about a female character apparently just as strong and resourceful as her brothers.

1 Bruno Bettelheim, *The Uses of Enchantment*.

Max Luthi has observed that the helping animal, the duck, did not appear in the earliest versions of "Hansel and Gretel."[2] It is interesting to speculate upon why the Brothers Grimm chose to add this detail. Why should such independent and resourceful children suddenly need help from an animal? Until this point in the story Hansel and Gretal have been thrown entirely upon their own resources. The teller of the tale suggests perhaps that nature can be beneficent as well as malevolent. Heretofore the children have experienced a terrible famine, have been lost in the woods, and lured into the witch's power by an innocent-looking white bird. The presence of the helping animal helps to balance the notion that the natural world is entirely hostile and alien.

Many illustrators have been attracted to this popular Grimms' tale. One of the most effectively illustrated versions of the tale is that of Adrienne Adams. Her book is not technically a picture book, since the text alone can tell the story. The illustrations in this book do, however, interpret the tale in a significant way. Adams uses several techniques to emphasize the symbolic and emotional aspects of the story: symbolic uses of color and shapes, among others.

In her first illustration Adams has drawn the stepmother and the father in bed. Shades of brown and yellow dominate the scene. The stepmother's night cap, however, is unnaturally white, a detail which foreshadows the ghostly white of the witch's face. Angles and conical shapes dominate. The noses of the mother and father are pointed. The stepmother's eyes are slanted to points; her teeth are pointed. The window panes divide the full yellow moon into pie-shaped pieces. The vertical lines and formal balance of the composition emphasize the trapped situation which the father apparently feels acutely. The cones — phallic-like — reinforce the wife's power over the weak husband. Implicitly the artist suggests that the trouble is caused by the father's inability to fulfill his patriarchal role.

The first illustration of the children contrasts sharply with the previous one. The composition is informally balanced; horizontal lines predominate. The round moon corresponds to the rounded golden heads of the children and the shining round pebbles on the ground.

In the next scene the sun shines huge and orange behind the trees of the forest. The trees do not seem frightening; they are painted in comforting shades of gold, brown, and orange. However, the trees are disproportionately large in contrast with the human figures. Gretel is shown between two large trees, separated both from Hansel and the parents. The stepmother's cap and apron are once again unnaturally white in contrast with the prevailing browns of the forest.

Among Adams's most effective illustrations in the book are the forest scenes with Hansel and Gretel lost and alone. Huddled together before the fire, the two children are surrounded by darkness and enormous trees. The stark branches of the trees pick up the reflections of the flames of the fire and resemble gigantic fingers as they seem to grope threateningly toward the children. This illustration brilliantly captures the emotional situation of the children and emphasizes the symbolic dimension of the forest: that is, the children occupy both a physical and an emotional wilderness.

In a doublespread illustration the children make their way through the dark forest by following the shining pebbles. The round silver moon again corresponds to the luminous shining pebbles and the shining round heads of Hansel and Gretel. The moon transforms the trees into ghostly blue shapes.

Once the children have arrived at the witch's gingerbread cottage, conical images and triangular shapes prevail. The roof of the cottage is conical; the oven's chimney is pointed. The criss-crossing branches of trees form numerous triangles. When the witch appears, she too is all points and angles: pointed nose, chin, hat, and teeth. Her arms are angular. She is framed sharply in the doorway, as if to suggest her isolation from the children and from nature. The whiteness associated earlier with the step-mother appears again in the horrid white of the witch's face and hands.

Illustration by Adrienne Adams from *Hansel and Gretel.* Copyright © 1975 by Adreinne Adams. Reprinted with the permission of Charles Scribner's Sons.

As the children run away from the witch's cottage, their pockets full of jewels and pearls, a ghostly white smoke issues prominently from the chimney of the oven — the dreadful white witch is quite literally going up in smoke. In the final scene inside the father's cottage, rounded shapes have replaced pointed ones. The father's nose and head are no longer pointed. Round pans, pitchers, and plates adorn the walls. The children shower their father with round jewels — white and gleaming. The white cat dashes forward to meet the children. Adams thus suggests through her symbolic use of white that the children have transformed an evil energy into a beneficent one. Through their own efforts, Hansel and Gretel have solved the problem of poverty and reestablished their home.

In his recent book *Fairy Tales and the Art of Subversion* Jack Zipes argues that the tales of the Brothers Grimm essentially reinforce the prevailing system of patriarchal power: "The wandering protagonist always leaves home to reconstitute home."[3] That is, the hero or heroine returns home not to change the system but to reinforce it. Adams's illustrations reinforce such an interpretation. At the beginning of the tale the father has failed in his role as provider, and his wife has taken advantage of his weakness to secure what there is of his wealth and property for herself and to disenfranchise the children. In a caricature of greed, the witch hoards treasure and food to excess; rather than abandoning the children, she wishes to devour them and to incorporate their youth and energy as a part of herself. Implicitly the tale expresses a fear of female power. Though Gretel shows much resourcefulness and energy, in the end she yields her wealth, acquired by her own efforts, to her father. The father's power and property have been restored; home has been reconstructed in accordance with the prevailing system of patriarchy.

Hansel and Gretel's circular journey with its dangers and its establishment of a securer, happier home at the conclusion can be compared to the experiences in *Sylvester and the Magic Pebble* and can be contrasted to the experiences of the children in "The New Mother."

3 Jack Zipes, *Fairy Tales and the Art of Subversion* (New York: Wildman Press, 1983), p. 57.

Sylvester and the Magic Pebble

by William Steig (New York: Simon and Schuster, 1969).

William Steig, the son of two painters, was born in New York City and began reading and drawing as a young child. For years Steig was well-known for his *New Yorker* covers and cartoons and for such adult books as *Small Fry* and *The Lonely Ones*. He entered the field of children's books at age 61 with the publication of *Roland, the Minstrel Pig* (1968). The following year he earned a national reputation as a creator of picture books with the publication of *Sylvester and the Magic Pebble*, winner of the Caldecott Medal. Since then, Steig has continued to write and to illustrate distinguished children's books.

Steig's animal stories are strongly influenced by the conventions of folk tale and romance. In his Caldecott acceptance speech, Steig stated: "Among the things that affected me most profoundly as a child and consequently as an adult were certain works of art: Grimm's fairy tales, Charlie Chaplin movies, Humperdinck's opera 'Hansel and Gretel,' the Katzenjammer Kids, *Pinocchio*. Pinocchio especially. I can still remember after this long stretch of time, the turmoil of emotions, the excitement, the fears, the delights, and the wonder with which I followed Pinocchio's adventures. . . . And it is very likely that Sylvester became a rock and then a live donkey because I had once been so deeply impressed with Pinocchio's longing to have his spirit enclosed in flesh instead of wood."

In *Sylvester and the Magic Pebble*, Steig employs an appealing cartoon style of art, delicate watercolors, strong lines to enlarge and to enrich the poignant story of Sylvester, and an anthropomorphic donkey whose hobby is collecting pebbles. When Sylvester finds a magic red pebble and encounters a vicious lion, he wishes to become a rock to save himself.

After this violent transformation, Sylvester undergoes a kind of spiritual death. As spring and summer yield to autumn and winter, Sylvester sinks into a deathlike sleep while his parents look frantically for him and then sadly grieve for him. With the coming of spring, Mr. and Mrs. Duncan, Sylvester's parents, decide to go for a picnic. Mr. Duncan notices the red pebble near the large rock they are using for a table. When Mrs. Duncan sighs and wishes that Sylvester were there, he awakes and thinks, "I wish I were myself again, I wish I were my real self again!" Instantly Sylvester is himself, and the family rejoices amid the delicately beautiful colors of early spring.

Every aspect of the illustrations reinforces the values celebrated in this picture book: the closeness of the family, the sadness of separation and loss, and the joy of rebirth and a reunited family.

The picture book begins with an illustration of Sylvester in the living room with his parents. He plays with his pebbles as his father reads and his mother sweeps. The colors suggest warmth and coziness. The three characters look happy and contented. Fresh flowers grace the mantel. The mother is central in the informally balanced illustration, a detail suggesting the comfort and security that only a mother can provide.

The next two pages illustrate Sylvester equally at home in the natural world. On the first page it is raining. Sylvester picks up his magic pebble and wishes the rain would stop. On the opposite page the sun is shining. Two ducks on the pond have lifted their beaks to enjoy the sun; in the previous illustration their heads had been drooping slightly. The contrast between these two illustrations seems to foreshadow Sylvester's experience of symbolic death and rebirth.

One of the strengths of Steig's illustrations is his ability to suggest such a great range of emotions on his characters' faces. Steig's lion, for example, appears in three illustrations. In the first he seems ferocious, in the second puzzled, and in the final one befuddled and amused as he walks away from the rock that is Sylvester.

One of the loveliest illustrations in the picture book is a doublespread night scene. Shades of blue dominate; flowers and trees take on a blue-green hue, and stars brilliantly illuminate the sky. Strong lines create gently the curving shapes of the hills in the distance, and both the color and the shape of the rock, situated on the extreme right of the illustration, blend with the landscape. In this scene, a serene and lovely natural setting, Sylvester experiences the anguish of his situation; he struggles in this dark night of despair and yields finally to rest and oblivion. The text depicts Sylvester's anguish, while the illustrations suggest a larger reality which finally subsumes all suffering and anguish.

In contrast to this peaceful pastoral scene, Steig depicts the struggles of Sylvester's parents in the social reality of institutions. One of the most controversial of the illustrations in the book shows Sylvester's parents seeking help from the police, who are drawn as ineffectual-looking pigs. The stillness and serenity of Sylvester's existence in any event contrast sharply with his parents' frenetic activity.

Subsequent illustrations seem to be inspired by the pastoral tradition in literature in which the seasons of the year often serve as a structural principle. The blue-green of summer yields to the amber and gold of fall, and as winter approaches, Sylvester goes "into an endless sleep." In the winter landscape, the rock is almost entirely lost in the bleakness of the snow. Spring comes, however, bringing life, color, shape, rebirth, identity, and the reunited family. In the final illustration Sylvester has completed his circular journey, and he and his parents are cuddled together on the sofa. The curving lines of the donkeys are enfolded by the curving lines of the sofa. Line and shape reinforce the notion of a sheltered haven protecting the little family.

Arrow to the Sun

by Gerald McDermott (New York: Viking, 1974).

Gerald McDermott's Caldecott Medal-winning picture book *Arrow to the Sun* provides an excellent example of how an author illustrator can use illustrations to integrate a personal vision with a study of both a specific culture and the work of an important cultural anthropologist and literary critic. *Arrow to the Sun* embodies McDermott's interest in "the idea of the individual who goes out on a quest of self-fulfillment," major features of traditional Pueblo culture, and concepts about worldwide hero tales developed by Joseph Campbell in his highly influential *The Hero With a Thousand Faces*.[1] Although there are nearly four hundred words to the story, meaning is conveyed, to a great extent, through the visuals. As McDermott has said, he believes in "the powerful potential of art to communicate what cannot be expressed in words."[2]

On one level, the color, design, and details communicate a theme found in many children's stories, that of a rejected or dissatisfied child who must leave home, work out the problems confronting him, and return home with a fuller sense of belonging. The gradual introduction

1 See Gerald McDermott, "On the Rainbow Trail," *Horn Book*, 51 (April 1975), p. 127.
2 Joseph Campbell, *The Hero With a Thousand Faces* (Princeton, N.J: Princeton University Press, 1949), p. 37.

of a full spectrum of color from the middle of the story onward indicates the growth of the Boy's sense of fulfillment and, therefore, happiness. The transformation of the ribbon pattern running across the pages from predominantly orange to multicolored as the hero emerges from the Kiva of Lightning indicates the moment of fulfillment. Details in the depiction of the Boy also indicate the changes. Rejected by his peers, he appears quite small on a two-page spread, and is located in the corner of the page with a frown on his face. In the final spread, as he leads the people in the Dance of Life, he is located front and center, the dominant figure on the page, a smile on his face. Moreover, his appearance has changed. Instead of a small wisp of hair leaning to the side, he sports a full headdress in the form of a stylized arrow, and instead of a black garment, he wears a robe of many colors.

On a deeper level, McDermott's visuals invest his story with implicit meanings which specifically link it to the cultural and religious beliefs of the traditional Pueblo people. An agrarian people whose main harvest was corn, the Pueblo believed that a successful crop depended not only on rain, but also on the achievement of a good relationship with the spiritual powers. At the beginning of the book, the Boy, whose logo is a stylized cross-section of an ear of corn, lives in an arid land symbolized by the dominant color orange. To this land he brings the rainbow, symbol of sun and rain. The manner in which he proves himself worthy of bringing the rain, an embodiment of the power of the sun, is deeply rooted in elements of Pueblo belief. These elements are implicitly presented in the illustrations depicting his experiences in the four Kivas: mountain lions, symbolizing war, are tamed; the Boy has established the peace necessary for agriculture. Rattlesnakes, used in rainmaking ceremonies, are formed into a circle; the Boy has accorded them spiritual respect. By forcing the bees to order themselves into a functioning hive, he establishes the organization necessary for the process of pollination. Finally, by submitting to the power of lightning, he is able to bring his father's powers to the earth.

The visual elements also reveal the influence of Campbell's *The Hero with a Thousand Faces* on McDermott's interpretation of the traditional Pueblo tale. Early in his life, Campbell writes, the typical hero "finds himself [in a world which] suffers from a symbolic deficiency."[3] The dominant orange color of the

The people celebrated his return in the Dance of Life.

From *Arrow to the Sun* by Gerald McDermott. Copyright © 1974. Reprinted by permission of Viking Press.

first part of the book reflects this deficiency. It depicts the arid land which parallels the spiritual state of the people who jeer at and reject the Boy. His search for his father fits well with the patterns of the quest as described by Campbell: "the child of destiny has to face a long period of obscurity. . . . He is thrown inward to his own depths or outward to the unknown . . . . Alone in some little room the young world-apprentice learns the lesson of the seed powers."[4] For the Boy this involves traveling through the dark heavens and entering the four Kiva chambers. After having been transformed by the lightning, he brings the full rainbow to the earth, a gift of life for his people. Campbell writes: "The effect of the successful adventure of the hero is the unlocking and release again of the flow of life into the body of the world. The miracle of this flow may be represented in physical terms as the circulation of food substance, dynamically as a streaming of energy, or spiritually as the manifestation of grace. . . . Abundant harvest as the sign of God's grace; God's grace is the food of the soul, the lightning bolt is the harbinger of fertilizing rain, and at the same time the manifestation of the released energy of God."[5]

After being struck by the lightning, the Boy trails the rainbow behind him, the emanation of his new power. On the final spread, he dances on the rainbow, surrounded by figures representing the spiritual powers of the Kivas on the one side and figures representing the growing corn on the other. The circular designs and the abundance of color indicate the unity and new physical and spiritual vitality he has given to the people who once rejected him.

His circular journey is not unlike those experienced by the heroes in "Scarface" and *A Story, a Story*, as each character concludes his quest by giving gifts to his people.

3 Campbell, p. 37
4 Campbell, pp. 326-7.
5 Campbell, p. 40.

A Story, A Story

retold from an African folk tale and illustrated by Gail E. Haley (New York: Atheneum, 1970).

While Gail Haley lived in the Caribbean she became interested in the African origins of Caribbean folklore and immersed herself in African culture and oral traditions. In her Caldecott acceptance speech for *A Story, A Story,* Haley describes this study and its importance to her work:

> My interest in African folk tales stems in large part from the role they play in the education of children. The African storyteller, like the live reader of children's books, invites questions, and he answers them. He adapts his tales to the understanding and experience of his audience, and he repeats or explains what is difficult. He is marvelously well-informed and he has a prodigious memory. He recalls heroic deeds of whole dynasties of chiefs, back through three or four centuries. He is the keeper of the tribe's traditions, conscience, and identity. He is the poser of riddles and conundrums. He is the spontaneous teacher. . . . The African folk tale and the modern children's book are very closely related.

In her Caldecott medal-winning picture book Haley has created bold, large-scale forms in vivid color reminiscent of the designs in the folk art of West Africa. Done in woodcuts, the illustrations complement the story of Ananse the "spider man," who tricks the Sky God out of his golden box of stories. In the preface to the book, the author illustrator explains that "spider" stories in Africa "tell how small, defenseless men or animals outwit others and succeed against great odds."

The opening illustration depicts the African storyteller, Ananse, sitting surrounded by a circle of enraptured children and one curious dog. Though Haley has used details sparingly, they nevertheless convey a vivid sense of African setting.

Ananse spins a web to the sky, where he

Ananse ran along the jungle path—
yiridi, yiridi, yiridi—till he came
to Osebo the leopard-of-the-terrible-teeth.

"Oho, Ananse," said the leopard,
"you are just in time to be my lunch."

Ananse replied: "As for that, what will
happen will happen. But first let us play
the binding binding game."

The leopard, who was fond of games,
asked: "How is it played?"

"With vine creepers," explained Ananse.
"I will bind you by your foot and foot.
Then I will untie you, and you can tie me up."

"Very well," growled the leopard,
who planned to eat Ananse
as soon as it was his turn to bind him.

Illustration by Gail E. Haley from *A Story, a Story*. Copyright © 1970 by Gail E. Haley. Reprinted with the permission of Atheneum Publishers, Inc.

intends to buy Nyame's stories. The strands of the web parallel Ananse's wispy white beard and hair; silhouettes of villagers, huts, and palm trees appear in the background. Ananse's body suggests agility and quickness of movement in contrast to the static silhouettes. The composition of the illustration, with Ananse dominating the figures behind him, emphasizes his actions on behalf of the community; the storyteller plays a vital role of leadership in the African village.

The Sky God demands three items: "Osebo, the leopard of the terrible-teeth; Mmboro the hornet who-stings-like-fire; and Mmoatia the fairy whom-men-never-see."

The text contains several African words, a feature contributing to the authentic cultural ambience of the book. Ananse runs, "yiridi, yiridi, yiridi;" Nyame laughs, "twe, twe, twe." Many African dialects use repetition to signify intensity; thus Ananse ties the leopard "by his foot, by his foot, by his foot, by his foot." And Mmoatia the fairy comes "dancing, dancing, dancing."

The design and layout of the book also complement the text of *A Story, A Story*. As Ananse approaches the Sky God, he appears obeisant,

looking frail and defenseless on the left page, while Nyame sits with haughty expression on his colorful throne. His substantial, handsomely robed body contrasts dramatically with the frail, scantily clad Ananse. Nyame is also solidly flanked with the dark silhouettes of the guards.

In his confrontation with Osebo, however, the illustration is formally balanced; Ananse and the leopard face one another near the center of the two pages; text is laid out neatly and precisely on either side, and a green figured background stretches beneath each block of text. Haley's illustrations are composed to suggest the nature of the contest. Osebo is superior in physical strength and size; Ananse is superior in intelligence. Thus Haley draws them as if equal in size and strength, each possessing a fighting chance to win the "binding, binding" game. On the following page, however, the bound shape of Osebo is disproportionately large, a detail emphasizing Ananse's small physical power and Osebo's physical bulk. Implicitly, the illustrations celebrate the power of Ananse's ability to outwit much larger and stronger adversaries.

Ananse similarly tricks the hornets into his

Calabash by pretending that it is raining. To capture the fairy Mmoatia, Ananse fashions a "gum baby," and puts a dish of yams before her. Having eaten the yams, Mmoatia grows angry, slaps and kicks the gum baby (like Joel Chandler Harris's Tar Baby), and becomes hopelessly stuck. Ananse then takes the captured creatures to Nyame, who gives up his stories to Ananse, who then spreads the stories all over the world.

As a *pourquoi* tale about the origin of stories, Haley's picture book is especially appealing to children because it features the trickster. The familiar three tasks characteristic of many folk tales make the tale easy to remember. A fascinating dimension of the book is its insight into the power of both story and storyteller.

Ananse can be compared to such trickster figures as Robin Hood and Brer Rabbit. The tests he experiences on his circular journey are similar in purpose to those found in *Arrow to the Sun* and *Little Badger and the Fire Spirit*.

Millions of Cats

written and illustrated by Wanda Gág (New York: Coward, McCann, and Geoghegan, 1928).

When *Millions of Cats* was published in 1928, Gág's editor, Ernestine Evans, wrote in the *Nation* (21 November 1928):

> *Millions of Cats* is as important as the librarians say it is. Not only does it bring to bookmaking one of the most talented and original of American lithographers, an artist who has a following both here and abroad, but it is a marriage of picture and tale that is perfectly balanced. And the story pattern, so cunningly devised with such hearty and moral simplicity, is told in a prose as skillful as jingle.

Since the publication of *Millions of Cats* (Newbery Honor Book, 1928), critics have consistently praised its nearly perfect blend of text and illustration to tell a story reminiscent of the cumulative tale in folk literature. The hand-lettered text and black-and-white lithographs contribute to the folk-like atmosphere of the tale. Gág has used this folk art style to tell the story of a gentle peasant and his wife, and how they finally acquired one little cat.

The story begins with a situation similar to that of many folktales. An old man and woman live in a nice, comfortable house, yet they are lonely. Details in the opening illustration are spare. The old man is dressed as a peasant of the Middle Ages and puffs on his pipe vigorously. The old woman is plump and appears round and amiable. The stone house with its slanted roof suggests home, comfort, and security.

On the second page the old man begins his quest for a little cat to keep the couple company. The flowing lines of the double-page illustration are strongly horizontal and convey a sense of movement and direction, a feature which reinforces the experience of the old man's journey. The shapes in the illustration are pleasingly rounded — round hills, round trees, round clouds.

An odd contradiction appears in the illustration: the old man's beard, the clouds, and the trees appear to be blowing in the direction of the journey, while the smoke from the chimney blows in the opposite direction, a detail which may emphasize the opposition between home with its peaceful stasis and the journey with its adventurous action.

At last the old man reaches a hill covered with "Hundreds of Cats, Thousands of Cats, Millions and billions and trillions of Cats." Gág has crowded this illustration with cats as far as the eye can see. The old man has his back to the reader with his hands thrown up. His surprise parallels that of the reader, who can scarcely have imagined so many cats. In the following double-page spread, text divides the illustration as the old man attempts to sort out the cats and decide upon just one. The rather congested quality of text and illustration reinforces the congestion of cats, and the old man's impossible choice.

Unable to make the choice, the old man returns home, his arms loaded with cats, the path before and behind him crowded with "those hundreds and thousands and millions and billions and trillions of cats." Even trees and flowers seems to blend with the cats. Gág repeats her use of horizontal lines and rounded shapes to convey a sense of the homeward journey.

On the way home the cats drink an entire

Illustration by Wanda Gág from *Millions of Cats*. Copyright © 1928 by Coward-McCann Inc.; copyright renewed © 1956 by Robert Janssen.

pond of water and devour an entire hillside of grass, though the old peasant still looks happy and content. Once home, however, the problem dawns upon him. The old woman is illustrated standing in front of the house; the lines of the house and the figure of the old woman are strongly vertical in contrast to the horizontal lines of the cats. The vertical lines emphasize the sudden barrier to the cats.

The following page features an illustration crowded with quarreling cats, all virtually indistinguishable from one another, as the old man and woman flee into their little house. Once inside, the couple watch the fight going on outside from the window, the pair tightly framed by the window, their backs to the reader. The readers' expectations are temporarily overturned here, since the old man and woman appear to be as lonely and as isolated as they had been at the beginning of the story.

This anxiety quickly diminishes when the old couple go outside to discover one "thin and scraggly" cat hiding in some tall grass. He has hidden himself there because he knows that he is not the prettiest. The smallest, homeliest, and most unassuming cat thus gets the reward of a happy comfortable home with people who love him.

In the final illustration, the old man sits comfortably in his chair, puffing his pipe, his slippered feet on a stool. The old woman sits knitting in a chair opposite. The table between them contains coffee and cake; the lamp illuminates the happy circle as the little cat plays on the floor between the couple. Rounded shapes dominate the scene to reinforce a sense of an enclosed and cozy shelter. The fluffy kitten is round; he plays with a ball on a round rug with round flowers on it. The table is round; so are the dishes and the lamp. All of these rounded images strongly suggest an impression of wholeness. The end paper contains an illustration of the cat curved into a tight, sleeping ball of fur.

Structurally *Millions of Cats* resembles the circular journey and completed quest of many folktales and hero tales. The happiness experienced by the old couple at the end of the story can be compared to that found in the Japanese folktale "New Year's Hats for the Statues" and contrasted to the unhappiness of the husband and wife in the Grimm Brothers' "The Fisherman and His Wife."

Another satisfying structural pattern can be seen in its oppositions: stasis versus travel; loneliness and isolation versus crowdedness and confusion—all these oppositions are happily reconciled in the end. Book design, illustrations, and text work harmoniously in this picture book. The result is a tale enduringly pleasing to very young readers. The repetition of the language, the delightful exaggeration, and the comforting resolution of the tale all contribute to the picture book's lasting appeal.

Where the Wild Things Are

by Maurice Sendak (New York: Harper and Row, 1963).

Where the Wild Things Are, winner of the Caldecott Medal in 1964, is Maurice Sendak's most popular picture book and surely one of the most popular as well as critically acclaimed books ever published. While some early reviewers expressed apprehension that the book would frighten children, critical response to the work since then has been overwhelmingly favorable. Indeed, few works in the history of Children's Literature possess such a combination of superb artistry with insight into the inner world of childhood. Sendak has stated that he remains obsessed with his own childhood. He has also written that a central concern in his picture books is his "great curiosity about childhood as a state of being, and how all children manage to get through childhood from one day to the next, how they defeat boredom, fear, pain, and anxiety, and find joy. It is a constant miracle to me that children manage to grow up."[1]

The plot of *Where the Wild Things Are* appears to be simple enough. A high-spirited boy of four or five, Max puts on his wolf suit and makes "mischief of one kind and another." The pictures reveal that this mischief is ordinary enough: Max hammers nails where he should not and chases a dog with a fork. The reader gets only the slightest hint of the monsters to

come in the first illustration, in which a stuffed bear hangs from a clothesline. Of course, Max in his wolf suit is also a little monster. The bedspread hanging over the line may also foreshadow the tent which appears later when Max becomes King of the Wild Things.

The second hint of the monsters to come appears as a drawing "by Max" in the second illustration. Max himself with his wolf suit and wild ways becomes a monster when he provokes his mother to call him "wild thing." When Max threatens to eat his mother, he is banished to his bedroom without supper. A forest grows; Max sails off "where the wild things are" and becomes king. After participating in a "wild rumpus" with the wild things, Max grows lonely and returns to his bedroom where he finds supper "still hot."

While the text of the tale provides a simple enough story, the design of the book, the full-colour doublespreads done in India ink line over tempera, and the offset lithography work perfectly with the text to reveal an exceptionally powerful story about a child's use of dream and fantasy, which compensates for his sense of powerlessness, and helps to release the rage he feels towards the restraints of an adult world.

In the opening scene of the book, text appears on one page and a relatively small illustration appears on the opposite one. Max's range of activity is severely circumscribed by a

1 Selma Lanes, *The Art of Maurice Sendak* (New York: Harry N. Abrams, Inc. Publishers, 1981), p. 85.

wide white border. In successive pages the illustrations grow progressively larger, a feature obvious even upon a first reading of the book. As Max enters his bedroom and stares in angry defiance at the closed door, the room is sparsely furnished. A misty crescent moon shines distantly through the window. One small green plant sits on the table. The white border frames Max tightly and precisely. Max himself appears rigidly still; indeed, the dominance of vertical lines contributes to a fixed, static, imprisoned effect.

In the following illustration Max appears to be in a trance — eyes closed, mouth tightly shut, hands behind him, a foot slightly raised. The moon seems slightly fuller and nearer; the stars shine through the window as well. The lines on the door and the bedposts have become trees. Leaves from the trees spill over into the white border, as if to suggest that Max's imagination can transcend the constraints of everyday reality he dislikes so much. The dominance of brown in the first illustration has now yielded to a luminous blue-green. The illustration grows larger and the white border steadily recedes.

As the forest continues to grow, the reader can barely discern the shape of the bed and the faint outlines of the door. The plant on the table has grown into a bush and the table has disappeared. The moonlight casts a golden glow over the blue-green room, and the foliage has grown rich and strange; still more leaves spill into the still narrower white border. Max is drawn on a line with the moon, which illumines his white wolf suit. Max now looks as if he is about to dance; his left foot is raised high. His face bears an expression of delight.

In the next illustration all signs of the room have disappeared. The moon seems still fuller, and Max, like a wolf, seems to raise his hands and dance in obeisance to the moon. The white border has totally disappeared, and the forest spills literally off the page. Illustration is still confined to the right page, text is to the left. On the following page, however, as Max sails off "through night and day," a tree and part of an ocean move onto the left page. Gradually the imaginary world grows larger and subsumes the ordinary world; the luminous colors of dream and fantasy push out the white blankness of everyday life. Max looks happily, smugly in command of his red boat with yellow sails.

From *Where The Wild Thins Are* by Maurice Sendak. Copyright © 1963.

On the next page, however, a sea monster rises ominously from the left page. Although the text does not mention this monster, Max appears frightened and raises his hands as if to tame it. The sudden appearance of this monster with its sharp horns, teeth, and claws suggests that the journey into the imaginary world brings with it perils as well as pleasures.

When Max meets the wild things, he no longer seems frightened. He faces them with a defiant frown. The points of his ears and the pointed prow of his boat suggest that he is a match for the horns and teeth of the wild things. Illustrations now cover both left and right pages; the white border and text are at the bottom of the pages.

Max tames the wild things, just as St. George tamed the dragon. The moon is pale green but growing bright again. The wild things collapse on the ground like helpless babies. On the following page the moon is brighter and the wild things appear to be much larger. Max has become a king with crown, scepter, and a grassy mound for a throne; the pointed ears of his wolf suit have metamorphosed into the points of his crown. The white border at the bottom of the page is much narrower.

For the next three doublespreads Max and the wild things celebrate in the exuberant anarchy of the "wild rumpus." The moon has become brilliantly full. The blue-green hues of the illustrations shine with silver. Max's wolf suit and the moon appear to be made of the same substance. Vertical lines have all but disappeared, and the illustrations seem to pulse with life, dance, and animated joy.

In his Caldecott acceptance speech Sendak stated that he was trying to capture a sense of music and dance in these illustrations, a feature which he had always admired in the art of the renowned nineteenth-century illustrator Randolph Caldecott. The wild things themselves, according to Sendak, were at least in part inspired by the original King Kong film.[2]

Sendak also indicates that the book is totally concerned with the way children learn to control dangerous energies in themselves — the wild beasts within: "To master these forces,

children turn to fantasy; that imagined world where disturbing emotional situations are solved to their satisfaction. Through fantasy, Max, the hero of my book, discharges his anger against his mother, and returns to the real world sleepy, hungry, and at peace with himself."[3]

After the joyous wild rumpus, Max sits alone in his tent. White border and printed text have reappeared at the bottom of the page; the moon has disappeared. A rosy glow, suggesting dawn and daylight, illumines the background. The vertical lines of trees have reappeared, and vertical lines also frame Max in his tent.

As Max becomes increasingly anxious with the fantasy world, he sails away. The wild things seem to have become threatening: "Please don't go," they shout at Max. "We'll eat you up, we love you so." The white border grows wider at the bottom of the page. On the next page the illustration is still smaller. The moon, though still full, seems shadowy as it casts a silvery glitter over the ocean's waves. With his eyes closed, Max appears to be in a revery. In the final illustration the moon again shines from a distance through Max's bedroom window. Since the fantasy begins with a crescent moon, and the reader knows from Max's sleepy expression that all of the adventure takes place in the time of one evening and in the space of a bedroom, the full moon suggests that the fantasy experience has helped Max to grow and to mature emotionally. The plant is in place on the table. Bed posts and door frames have assumed their ordinary appearance. A sleepy Max stands with the hood of his wolf suit off for the first time, a detail suggesting that he can now put off his "wild thing" role for a time and take pleasure in the everyday comforts of home — such as a still-warm supper and a safe, warm bed.

A careful study of Sendak's outstanding picture book, then, reveals that every dimension of the book — its design and layout, its use of color, space, detail, proportion, line, and shape — contributes to the artistry of the work

3 Maurice Sendak, Caldecott Acceptance Speech, *Newbery and Caldecott Medal Books: 1956-1965* (Boston: The Horn Book, Inc.), p. 250.

2 *Ibid.*

as well as to its emotional power to appeal to young children. In structure the book resembles a romance; the hero undertakes a journey, tames monsters, and returns home for his reward. Max's circular journey, however, is clearly an internalized quest, the one all children must undertake each day to survive in a world of bewildering adult rules and restraints. Max's rebelliousness can be compared to that of the central character in Beatrix Potter's *The Tale of Peter Rabbit*.

Blueberries for Sal

by Robert McCloskey (New York: Viking, 1948).

Blueberries for Sal, which grew out of McCloskey's summers with his family in Maine, has been praised for its superb line drawings, printed in the deep blue of blueberries. Both the text and the pictures of this book are lithographed in dark blue on white. When the book was published in 1948, it was unequivocally praised by reviewers for its splendid design and artistry and for its vivid evocation of the Maine landscape. The book was a runner-up for the Caldecott Medal.

The story begins with Little Sal and her mother (characters modeled on McCloskey's wife and little daughter) visiting Blueberry Hill to pick berries for the winter. Little Sal and her mother are prominent on the extreme right of the double-page illustration. Their car is parked before a dense grove of spiked fir trees, and the community recedes in the distance on the extreme left. McCloskey's art style is essentially representational: Little Sal wears realistically drawn overalls and buckle-up shoes and happily swings a tin pail in her hand.

The next few illustrations show Little Sal happily picking berries. She drops a few in the pail but eats most of them. She eats some of her mother's berries, but her mother reminds Sal to pick her own berries. Sal sits among the blueberry bushes, picking berries, and eating them; clearly she thinks that her mother is nearby.

On the other side of the hill Little Bear and his mother are also eating blueberries, storing up for the long winter ahead. The mother bear dominates the page with her massive round body; the rounded shape of Little Bear is close behind as the two move up toward the top of Blueberry Hill. The reader's eyes are drawn toward the top, and the reader knows what the bears do not: that there are people up there.

Little Bear follows his mother and eats blueberries, just as Little Sal does. Tired, he sits down to eat, thinking that his mother is also nearby. The illustrations show the reader, however, that Little Bear is quite alone on Blueberry Hill. He is surrounded, practically hidden, in blueberry bushes.

On the next page, Little Sal is also quite alone. She is no longer prominent but appears small in contrast to the large hill and fir trees. The illustration thus suggests sudden apprehension, a feeling of smallness and aloneness because Sal cannot find her mother. Sal expects that she will find her mother, but the reader expects that she will find the bear; this dramatic irony is unusual in a children's book. In fact both Little Bear and Little Sal find the wrong mothers. At the climax of the story the narrator explains that "Little Bear and Little Sal's mother and Little Sal and Little Bear's mother were all mixed up with each other among the blueberries on Blueberry Hill."

Finally Little Sal and Little Bear each find their right mothers. The story ends felicitously and the circular journeys are completed with each mother and child descending opposite sides of the mountain both with plenty of blueberries for the winter.

Child readers will find the mix-up humorous and will delight in the reversal of Sal's and Little Bear's expectations, even as their own are confirmed. The endpapers show Little Sal helping her mother can the blueberries. The cheerful, busy scene is full of comforting details: a warm stove with bubbling pots on top; a counter cluttered with canisters and sacks; a curious kitten; Sal, who is playing with rubber canning rings; and Mother, who is pouring the blueberries into glass jars. Pointed fir trees and Blueberry Hill can be seen in the distance through the kitchen window.

Little Sal and her mother have foraged for food in a slightly dangerous setting and have returned to the safe comfort of their own kitchen.

Blueberries for Sal continues to be a popular book for quite young children. The illustrations perfectly complement the structure of the story by emphasizing the parallels between Little Bear and Little Sal. The text is admirable for its vivid details and for its rhythm, which perfectly captures the pace of the story.

The confrontations between the little girl and a bear can be compared to those found in "The Adventures of Isabel" and in "The Story of the Three Bears."

From *Blueberries for Sal,* by Robert McCloskey. Copyright © 1948. Reprinted by permission of Viking Press.

Mary of Mile 18

by Ann Blades (Montreal: Tundra, 1971).

Although many children's stories have been written for a specific audience, only a few of these ever achieve wide recognition. That is because most are quite localized. Those that do succeed generally do so because they capture universal themes. One such book is Ann Blades's *Mary of Mile 18*. Originally, this story was created for school children taught by the author in northern British Columbia. It has since become one of the best selling and most highly acclaimed Canadian picture books.

The content of the story was definitely familiar to Blades's initial audience, since it tells of a poor Mennonite family struggling to make a living off of the rugged land. The illustrations for the book depict the locale in which Blades was teaching. The school house, for example, was hers; Mary is based on sketches made of one of the students. How then, does the author-illustrator create a universal story from these very local materials?

First, Blades gives the reader a symbolic setting. The northern landscape represents a wilderness in the midst of which Mary and her family, like the family in Laura Ingalls Wilder's *The Little House in the Big Woods*, must struggle to make a living. The opening paragraph emphasizes the inhospitable quality of the environment: "It was a cold winter in northern British Columbia. At the Fehr's farm snow has covered the ground since early November and it will not melt until May." The story begins on a night when the temperature is 40 degrees below zero. The nearest neighbors are two miles away and the father works every day clearing land so the family can receive a deed of ownership from the government. In sixteen of the book's seventeen illustrations, the landscape dominates the page: white, grey, and pale blue colors prevail, emphasizing the bleakness and the cold; bare trees in columns convey an impression of dreariness. The only variety of color comes from man-made objects: a red tractor, green outhouses, and a purple flag at the school. For the Fehr family, making a living in this setting is extremely difficult. They live without modern conveniences; the cold hampers their clearing efforts; and wild animals threaten their chickens.

Against this universal conflict of human beings versus the wilderness, Mary's two conflicts, both of which relate to the larger conflict, are superimposed. First, she hopes that the Northern Lights she has seen will bring something special; this hope is often thwarted. Second, Mary's father initially refuses to allow her to keep a half-wolf pup she finds. Mary thinks the pup might be the special thing promised by the Northern Lights. The illustrations reveal her changing emotions in the face of these two conflicts. She is first seen trudging through the snow. Her purple coat, which is too small, her green leotards and scarf, and her blue dress appear shabby, and reinforce rather than contrast with the dreariness of the landscape of white snow, white tree trunks, and grey sky. She slouches with her hands in her pockets, and her head is bent pensively forward. She appears listless and bored.

When she first discovers the wolf pup along the roadside, her mood brightens. Kneeling in front of it, she extends her hands, which are covered in bright yellow mittens. The sky is blue and the trees are in the distance; their trunks no longer reinforce the dreary mood as they did earlier. However, Mary cannot keep the pup, and, as she walks into the woods to abandon it, the tree trunks are again dominant, surrounding her. Her gloves are no longer visible, and her back is turned.

At the story's conclusion, Mary is permitted to keep the dog because it has proven its usefulness; it warns the family of a coyote breaking into the henhouse. In the final drawing, Mary sits in her bed smiling and cradling the puppy in her arms. Her gold-blond hair flows to her shoulders, a multicolored quilt covers her, and the log walls and bedposts provide a rich brown background. For the first time in the book, no trace of the winter landscape can be seen. Mary's circular journey is complete and her conflicts have been resolved. These resolutions are part of the resolution of

From *Mary of Mile 18* by Ann Blades. Copyright © 1971 by Ann Blades. Reprinted by permission of Tundra Books.

conflict for the Fehr family against the wilderness. With Wolf's assistance, they have won one round in an ongoing struggle. Wolf's relationship with the family is not unlike that between the mongoose and the human beings in Kipling's "Rikki-Tikki-Tavi", and the family's situation in the wilderness can be compared to that portrayed in Wilder's "The Wolf-Pack."

Joseph's Yard

by Charles Keeping (Oxford, 1969).

In his stories Charles Keeping combines memories of his childhood experiences and feelings with his artistic skills and techniques to create picture books which represent the everyday world as it is perceived by a child. Keeping has noted that the setting of *Joseph's Yard* is based on his backyard in Lambeth, a working class area of London, England, where he spent much of his time as a small child. He has also said that *Joseph's Yard* deals with such things as loneliness, love, jealousy, and death. "These are the things which I found as a boy were all terribly important to me."

Keeping has deliberately kept his text simple, allowing the colors and designs of the illustrations to evoke the many emotions of the story. The words introduce us to the only character, briefly describe the setting, account for the boy's acquisition of the rose, and portray his actions and their results. The setting is deceptively simple. At the beginning of the book, we are told, "and this is Joseph's Yard. A brick wall, a wooden fence, stone paving, and rusty old iron—that's all there was in the yard. There were no insects, no birds, no cats." At the conclusion, Keeping writes: "In time the plant filled the yard. Insects flew among its flowers, birds perched in its branches, cats lay in its shade."

The illustrations emphasize the great change which has taken place in the garden. The opening statement is accompanied by a one-page illustration. The background is dominated by a dingy brown fence. One of the boards has a yellow circle, suggesting that the sun reaches the area only with difficulty. In the foreground is a pile of iron scraps, unnaturally colored crimson and purple. There is nothing else in the yard. The final picture of the garden occupies a double spread. The fence is no longer visible, and bright green colors and dozens of roses in full bloom dominate the scene. Birds, insects, and a cat are among the flowers.

These contrasting illustrations indicate the changes not only in the garden, but also within Joseph. When we consider that gardens and

From *Joseph's Yard* by Charles Keeping. Copyright © 1969. Reprinted by permission of Oxford University Press.

roses have a long history of symbolic significance, these changes assume greater importance. The enclosed garden has long symbolized the soul and the actions of the gardener reflected his own inner development. Roses are often used as symbols of earthly beauty and their fragility parallels the fragility of life. What Joseph does in his garden and how the state of the garden changes serve as manifestations of his growth as an individual.

Joseph's world is bounded by the fence which surrounds the yard. The endpapers, depicting the fence, enclose the book and indicate his perspective. However, even though he does not leave the yard, the outside world enters into it. His reactions to these incursions are important. In the early part of the story, the garden is "invaded" by the forces of nature. But as the seasons progess, little changes until the boy takes steps to initiate change. Like the garden, there is little vitality in the boy at the opening of the story. When Joseph receives a plant in exchange for the junk he's cleaned out of the yard, he is at first extremely protective, a fact reflected by the circles and rectangles that enclose the illustrations. His selfish love destroys the rose and the resultant sorrow is conveyed by the darkening colors in the pictures. When the rose revives the following year, insects, birds, and cats enter the garden. The yard is no longer isolated; in fact, the presence of the flower has created an interdependence among several living creatures. Joseph cannot accept this fact, and the illustrations depicting his eviction of the unwanted visitors exposes the negative nature of his response. His body language and facial expressions show his anger; the only color is purple, symbolic of his rage. In an illustration devoid of blues and greens, he covers the plant with his coat, stifling the natural forces of nature. However, he comes to understand his faults and his face reveals his shame: he is on the verge of tears and he holds his hands before his mouth in a gesture which suggests supplication.

During the ensuing winter, Joseph stands beside the plant, watching it. Significantly, he does not touch it; he is concerned but not as stiflingly protective as he had been before. By allowing it to grow over several seasons and of its own accord, he is accepting natural patterns, something he had not been willing to do before. That there are birds, insects, and a cat on the final double spread is an explicit indication that he has recognized that the garden cannot be isolated, that the world beyond the fence must enter if the garden is to thrive. His own perspectives on life have grown. He has begun his linear journey toward maturity.

Like the picture books of Ezra Jack Keats, those of Charles Keeping present the ever-widening perspectives of the growing child. In works such as *Alfie and the Ferry Boat* and *Shaun and the Cart Horse*, Keeping presents his young heroes exploring areas far beyond the secure confines of home. Also like Keats, Keeping creates a balance between realistic and impressionistic visual communication. As we have seen in *Joseph's Yard*, key objects are represented, but major emotional implications are conveyed by color and design. As is the case in Virginia Lee Burton's *The Little House* and Frances Hodgson Burnett's *The Secret Garden*, the settings and the changes they undergo are used to symbolize human emotions.

Whistle for Willie

by Ezra Jack Keats (New York: Viking, 1964).

Events which may seem trivial to adults and older children may be very important to a young child. As the child attempts to understand and cope with his increasingly widening world and to develop a strong self concept, such an apparently small failing as the inability to whistle can assume very large proportions. Such a failing is the subject of Ezra Jack Keat's *Whistle for Willie*. Using a simple text and employing vivid colors and the technique of collage, Keats is able convincingly to present a universal theme: the child's sense of achievement after struggling to overcome what, to him, was a serious limitation.

Keats has made collage his major vehicle of expression because "collage is distinguished from other art forms in that its *harmonious fusion of independent shapes and colors* makes for a more unusual balance between illusion and reality." The texture of the various materials used gives a tactile quality to the illustrations, as opposed to the flat, two-dimensional feel of most representations. In addition to differently colored and textured papers, Keats also uses wallpaper to depict the various emotions experienced by his hero during his quest.

The opening double spread simply states the nature of the conflict: "Oh, how Peter wished he could whistle!" The language of the conclusion and final spread is also simply factual: "Peter's mother asked him and Willie to go on an errand to the grocery store. He whistled all the way there, and he whistled all the way home." The language is in accordance with Keats's stated goal "to imply rather than overstate." The rich emotional content of these two scenes is communicated visually rather than verbally, and when they are contrasted, they illustrate the emotional polarities of the story. At the outset, Peter stands at the side of the page. His head is down, he is frowning, and he slouches, leaning disconsolately against a lamp post. A large brick wall dominates the picture, dwarfing Peter. The orange square behind him also leans, reinforcing his body language. Even the red zigzag pattern of his sweater seems to be leaning. His dog, for whom he would like to whistle, is absent from the picture.

The setting at the conclusion is the same; however, Peter's attitude is completely different. As a reward for his achievement, his mother gives him the responsibility of going to the store. As a result Peter occupies a more central position in the picture, and his head is held high as he whistles happily. Willie, the dog, is now in the picture; his ears flop and his tail is jaunty and high as he happily follows his master. The colors of the brick wall and the sky are more subdued. And Peter no longer needs the lamp post to lean upon.

During the course of the story, Peter tries five times to whistle, before finally succeeding. His reactions to his failures, recounted sparingly in the words and fully in the illustrations, are consistent with the emotions of young children. After having failed to emulate an older boy who successfully whistles for his dog, Peter escapes his disappointment by whirling himself into dizziness. The page design shows the horizon tilting, lights appear to pop out of the lamp post, the colored blocks representing buildings seem to lean, and patterns swirl in the yellow-colored sky. The failure of Peter's second attempt is emphasized by the location of the boy and his dog on different colored squares of paper, with the dog facing away from him. Later, wearing his father's hat does not increase Peter's esteem either. Facing his mother, he seems very small on the page, and the green hat blends him into the light green wallpaper which Keats uses for a background.

Peter will finally succeed; that is visually predicted in the page preceding his first whistle. As the boy reaches a corner, he sees his dog approaching on a side street. He hides under a box, but this time he and Willie are placed on the same rather than different colored squares of paper. As he stands up to take the box from his shoulders, the implicit lines of force on the page project him and the dog toward each other. The double spread depicting his triumphant whistle in front of his family is in marked contrast to the scene in which he wore his father's hat and faced his mother. His profile dominates the illustration. His lips curl as he

From *Whistle For Willie*, by Ezra Jack Keats. Copyright © 1964. Reprinted by permission of Viking Press.

simultaneously smiles and whistles; although his eyes are closed, they show a happy wrinkle. His head tilts upward. Facing him, his mother, father, and dog are small by contrast. His father is smiling; his mother applauds; the dog sits up on its hind legs. The pallid green wallpaper has been replaced by a bright yellow sunflower design. Just as Peter is the center of his family's attention and happiness fills the room, so too he is the main figure in the illustration and brightness permeates the picture.

Peter's emotional growth can be compared to that of the central character in Charles Keep-

ing's *Joseph's Yard*.

To read the words of *Whistle for Willie* without viewing the illustrations with their varied colors and subtle collage backgrounds is to be aware only of the actions. To read these along with the pictures is to understand the changing and, for Peter, very important emotions. Through the illustrations, Keats transforms a very simple narrative into a story embodying universal human feelings.

The Little House

by Virginia Lee Burton (Boston: Houghton, Mifflin, 1942).

The object of a good picture book, the expression of its vision or theme through a "marriage" of its visual and linguistic components, is completely achieved in *The Little House*. Virginia Lee Burton presents, through text, design, color, and detail, the reactions of a house to

house, its human occupants, and the environment. The only change is the succession of generations and nature's cycles. The tone of this section is created in part by the illustrations, all of which are variations on one picture — the Little House sitting on her hill surrounded

Illustration by Virginia Lee Burton from *The Little House. Copyright* © 1942 by Virginia Lee Demetrios. Copyright © renewed 1969 by George Demetrios. Reprinted by permission of Houghton Mifflin.

the loss and restoration of its contentment and harmony within the cycles of nature.

The opening third of *The Little House* contains little plot development, but emphasizes the harmony which has long existed in the

by the large curving lines of the other hills and fields. Details and activities may alter, but the all-encompassing pattern of life for the Little House remains the same.

These ideas are reinforced by the visual

aspects. The use of circular and curving patterns, both in overall page design and within illustrations, convey impressions of the health, sweetness, and freshness of country life. Page layout parallels the structure of the illustrations. The text, the easy tempo and even, recurrent rhythmic phrases that reinforce meaning, is made to fit within the harmoniously sweeping curves of the illustrations.

Only two pages are required to describe and illustrate the destruction of a mood built up by the opening third of the book. With assembly line quickness and efficiency, a highway is built, slashing diagonally across and through the gentle curves of the rural landscape. The change is represented by the replacement of the blues, greens, and pinks of nature with the dingy greys and browns of the city, and it is further reflected in the tempo of the prose which, no longer incorporated into the illustrations but arranged diagonally across the page like the new road, achieves an almost breathless, frenzied pace.

The following illustrations reveal how the Little House, now shabby and dirty, is totally divorced from the natural rhythms of her former rural life. Advancing with the buildings are the spreading clouds of smog, gradually settling down into the city. Each page also represents a new and supposedly progressive aspect of the transportation revolution: automobiles, trolleys, elevated trains, and subways. The negative effect that urbanization has on the physical environment is equalled by the effect it has on the people, who rush about frantically and apparently without purpose.

Significantly, rescue for the Little House arrives with the Spring, when, everywhere but in the city, there is a bringing forth of new life. The woman who carries out the rescue stands with her family, their hands joined in unity. They are the only people on the street who are standing still and they remind us of earlier times when people moved more slowly and in harmony with the natural rhythms. Ironically, urban activities are halted for hours as the Little House is moved out of the city. Such a state of affairs is fitting: the frenzied urban life is unnatural, and the older, slower life, one closer to nature, reasserts itself in the personage of the humble Little House

The final pages, in which the house is relocated in a country setting closely resembling that of the first section, are characterized by the use of colors, page designs, and prose rhythms which parallel those of the opening pages and reinforce the sense of new harmony between the house and its environment. The house makes a journey back in time from the skyscrapers of now, past tenements, small houses, and roadside gas stations, off the black-topped highway onto a road curving past farmhouses like those of the Little House's earlier years. All of the details of the first section of the book are reintroduced to emphasize the resolution of conflict and the return to a happier way of life.

Why Mosquitoes Buzz in People's Ears

retold by Verna Aardema. Ill. Leo and Diane Dillon (New York: The Dial Press, 1975).

Why Mosquitoes Buzz in People's Ears is a West African folk tale retold by Verna Aardema. Leo and Diane Dillon have illustrated the story with water color and pastels. The stylized illustrations, inspired by the designs of African fabrics, complement the text perfectly.

In the first part of the story the illustrations, painted on a white background, feature an animated jungle world; even the sun has eyes, nose, and mouth as it shines brightly on an iguana. A mosquito informs him, "I saw a farmer digging yams that were almost as big as I am." Irritated with the mosquito's lies, the iguana puts sticks in his ears. When the python hears the iguana complaining, he decides the iguana is angry and crawls into a rabbit hole. The rabbit dashes out in terror. A crow sees the rabbit and spreads an alarm indicating danger. A monkey hears the crow, leaps through the trees, and breaks a limb that falls and kills an owlet.

Illustration by Leo and Diane Dillon from *Why Mosquitoes Buzz in People's Ears* by Verna Aardema. Copyright © 1975. Reprinted by permission of E.P. Dutton Inc.

Mother Owl, who wakes the sun each day, therefore fails to hoot in the morning.

The jungle night grows longer and longer. At this point in the story the illustrations are painted on a luminous black background. The darkness envelops the animals. Their eyes glow with a sinister yellow light.

At last the Lion, King of the Beasts, calls a council to find out why the owl will not wake the sun. First the monkey is called, then the crow, the rabbit, the python, and then, the iguana.

Each animal explains the reason for his or her behavior. At last the Lion determines, "So it was the mosquito who annoyed the iguana, who frightened the python, who scared the rabbit, who startled the crow, who alarmed the monkey, who killed the owlet — and now Mother Owl won't wake the sun so that day can come."

This cumulative refrain has been repeated each time an animal has been questioned. The illustration at this point in the tale shows the mosquito looking crafty but alarmed. Mother Owl, satisfied that mosquito will be punished, wakes the sun. All seems to be well, but the tale features a surprise *pourquoi* ending. Although the mosquito hides under a leaf to escape the council's punishment, he retains a guilty conscience and buzzes in people's ears. The last page of the book contains no text but shows a man slapping a mosquito with his hand, "kpao."

This tale, with its cumulative refrain and its surprise ending, has a strong narrative which works well even without the illustrations. The text possesses poetic rhythms and sound devices — for example, the onomatopoeic "kpao." The illustrations, however, enrich and enlarge the text by presenting a vividly exotic sense of the jungle — the iguana is brilliantly, gaudily green; the purple-striped python undulates across a double-page spread. The lion's mouth reveals prominently his white sharp teeth. Also, though the illustrations are stylized, the Dillons nevertheless manage to give the animals an interesting range of facial expressions — irritation on the iguana, mischief in the mosquito, alarm in the rabbit and monkey, sorrow on the owl, and the dignified indignation of the lion. In the last two illustrations, narrative meaning is carried entirely by the illustrations. The sidewise expression in the eyes of the man helps prepare the reader for the surprise ending on the final page.

Verna Aardema helps to convey a sense of the West African cultural atmosphere by using African words to describe the movement of the animals: the iguana goes "mek, mek, mek;" the rabbit hops "krik, krik, krik." Like West African dialect, Aardema uses the device of repetition as an intensifier; hence, the owl sits in her tree, "so sad, so sad, so sad." The Dillons' illustrations also enhance the cultural atmosphere of West Africa by capturing the expansive and exuberant quality of African art.

Appendix B: The Children's Novel

An Introduction

Critics have long argued about the date when literature for children actually emerged as a distinct body of writing. If children's literature is defined as works written and published exclusively for children, then it appeared first as seventeenth-century Puritan tracts in England. Some scholars feel that this development was not altogether fortunate. That is, before the seventeenth century, children shared a variety of books with their parents, from *Tom Thumb* to John Foxe's *The Book of Martyrs* (1563).[1] At this time both children and adults enjoyed ballads, folk tales, such romances as *Guy of Warwick*, such chap books as *Jack the Giant Killer, Aesop's Fables*, and other popular forms of literature. After the seventeenth century adults began writing books designed to shape the behavior of children strictly in accordance with the wishes of adults.

In the seventeenth century the Puritans began to institutionalize modern conceptions of the nuclear family, to preach the notion of original sin, and to emphasize the need to save the child's soul; at the same time they promoted the idea that economic prosperity was a token of God's blessing. The need to establish these views as powerful cultural and religious values led to the Puritans' creation of a separate category of works for children. Such stories constituted awful warnings to child readers and urged children to repent, since death could strike at any time. The most famous and influential of these books was the Reverend James Janeway's *A Token for Children, being an exact account of the conversion, holy and exemplary lives and joyful deaths of several young children* (1671). The book featured saintly children who converted their elders and died in a transport of joy. Janeway's book continued to be popular throughout the nineteenth century and inspired many imitators. Eventually the form of children's literature known as the moral tale evolved from this tradition and remained an important kind of children's story throughout the nineteenth century, and survives even today in church school stories and in books designed to teach social lessons at the expense of literary excellence.

Another significant Puritan work in the history of children's literature was John Bunyan's *Pilgrim's Progress* (1678). Although the book was not written specifically for children, this work was enormously popular with children, since it closely resembles the Cinderella story. *Pilgrim's Progress* influenced a host of nineteenth-century quest fantasies by such writers as Charles Kingsley, George MacDonald, and Lewis Carroll.[2] The book was also to figure prominently in numerous realistic works for children. In Louisa May Alcott's *Little Women*, for example, the four girls play "Pilgrims" near the beginning of the novel. Subsequently each girl confronts her flaws, which are similar to those that Christian encounters. Each character struggles to become the perfect little woman, just as Christian strives to reach the Celestial City.

In addition to the potent Puritan influence upon children's literature, two eighteenth-century philosophers were to exert a powerful impact upon the history of children's literature — John Locke and Jean Jacques Rousseau. Locke's work, *Some Thoughts Concerning Education* (1693) undercut the entrenched notion of the child's depravity; he argued that the child's mind resembled a blank tablet to be filled in by sensory and rational experience, the famous *tabula rasa* theory presented in *Essay on Human Understanding*. Locke recommended that adults treat children as rational beings. He argued that teachers and parents should present lessons in the form of entertaining stories and endorsed *Aesop's Fables* as one of the most desirable books for children to read. He discouraged the use of fairy tales and other imaginative stories, since such tales were mere "lies."

Locke's ideas influenced two important publishers of children's books in eighteenth-century England — Thomas Boreman and John Newbery. Newbery was the most important figure in children's literature of the century.[3] A shrewd businessman, he thoroughly understood his market, the rising middle class. From 1744 to 1767, Newbery published and sold books for children, as well as gingerbread, Cephalic snuff, and patent medicines.

Newbery's books for children were attractive, small, and "neatly bound and gilt" to appeal to the child. Such books as *A Little Pretty Pocket-Book* (1744), *The Lilliputian Magazine* (1751), and many other books appeared in Mr. Newbery's shop, but the most important was *The History of Little Goody Two Shoes* (1765), a work which has gone through hundreds of editions and remains in print today.

The History of Little Goody Two Shoes recounts the social ascent of the orphan Miss Margery Meanwell and her brother Tommy. Margery's father dies of a fever, apparently the result of sufferings inflicted by the avaricious Farmer Graspall and Sir Timothy Gripe. Margery and Tommy are taken in and cared for by a virtuous clergyman and his wife. Margery receives her first pair of shoes and exclaims, "See two shoes," the incident providing her with her nickname.

Eventually brother Tommy goes off to sea, while Goody learns to read by following other children home from school. After completing this difficult education, Goody establishes her own school, an enlightened one based upon Locke's principles of education. At last she marries a gentleman and lives comfortably as Lady Jones. Tommy returns finally — handsome and rich.

The identity of the author of *The History of Little Goody Two Shoes* is still not certain. Critics speculate that Oliver Goldsmith or perhaps Newbery himself may have written the book. In many respects the children's novel shares characteristics with other eighteenth-century novels. A poor but virtuous young woman is rewarded with a fine marriage, a title, and economic well-being. As her author describes Margery's remarkable ascent:

Who from a State of Rags and Care
and having Shoes but half a Pair;
Their Fortune and their Fame would fix,
And gallop in a Coach and Six.

Margery's identity, then, depends upon her finding an appropriate place in society. Many imitations of this early popular children's novel flourished in the latter years of the eighteenth century.

Like the works of John Locke, Jean Jacques Rousseau's *Emile* was extraordinarily influential on British children's writers, as well as upon the history of education. In *Emile* Rousseau insists that children are by nature good. Though children need protection, they must also face danger from the beginning of life and learn to solve problems rationally. The child, according to Rousseau, must be allowed to learn by experience, though a patient tutor may guide the child's education. Perhaps most important for children's literature, Rousseau discouraged the use of all books except Daniel Defoe's *Robinson Crusoe*. As a result of Rousseau's endorsement, Defoe's novel became enormously popular and inspired hundreds of imitations. All over Europe, the *Robinsonade* flourished, the most famous of which was Johann Wyss's *The Swiss Family Robinson*. Crusoe, cast up on a deserted island after his ship wrecks, uses all his rational powers to survive until he is rescued. Such survival stories remain popular today. (See discussion of the adventure story below for further information on the importance of *Robinson Crusoe* to the development of children's literature.)

Rousseau exerted a direct influence upon two late eighteenth-century British children's writers — Thomas Day (1748-1789) and Maria Edgeworth (1767-1849). Day was an ardent admirer of Rousseau's *Emile* and consciously incorporated the French philosopher's ideas in his children's book *Sandford and Merton* (3 vols., 1783-1789). Indeed, Day was so fanatically devoted to Rousseau's ideas that he adopted orphan girls and raised them according to Rousseau's precepts.

Sandford and Merton features a spoiled youth, Tommy Merton, the son of a wealthy Jamaican planter. The wise Mr. Barlow takes young Tommy in hand, along with the exemplary Harry Sandford. Improving stories promoting the values of reason and nature, interspersed with descriptions of English country life, are among the highlights of the book. Day contrasts the spoiled and weak Tommy with the active and strong Harry, who completes all assigned tasks and treats all animals kindly. After Tommy has acquired these sensible character traits and other useful lessons, he becomes quite "another boy," an altered child altogether. Mr. Merton fetches his transformed son home to assume his rightful place as a gentleman of property.

Sandford and Merton introduced elements which became standard features of matter-of-fact tales and moral tales: the contrast between an exemplary child and spoiled one, the presence of a wise and patient teacher, and the transformation of the spoiled child.

Maria Edgeworth was the most talented writer for children of the eighteenth century. Indeed she was perhaps the most celebrated woman writer of her era. The second of her famous father's twenty-two children, Edgeworth assumed an active role in educating her younger siblings. Working with her father, Richard Lovell Edgeworth, and her talented stepmother Honoria, Maria Edgeworth began designing lessons scientifically. The result of this educational collaboration appeared in *Practical Education* (1798), a text which remains important in the history of education. The best and most famous of Edgeworth's children's books was her three-volume *The Parent's Assistant* (1796), which features stories to improve the child mentally and morally. "The Purple Jar," for example, centers upon a little girl's conflict as she decides whether to purchase a lovely purple jar or a sensible pair of shoes. Having chosen the purple jar, the child discovers that it is only colored scented water in an ordinary glass jar. Meanwhile the disappointed girl must wear her shoes until they are total ruins because of her unwise choice.

The most popular writer of the moral tale in the early nineteenth century was Martha Mary Butt, later known as Mrs. Sherwood. Married to a missionary stationed in India, Mrs. Sherwood wrote moral tales with the earnest purpose of saving the child's soul. In her most famous work, *The Fairchild Family* (4 vols. pub. from 1818 to 1847), Mrs. Sherwood dramatizes the efforts of the worthy

Mr. and Mrs. Fairchild to save the souls of their three lively children — Lucy, Emily, and Henry. The parents constantly remind their children of original sin, the need for salvation, the ever-present threat of death, and the horrors of hell. The book contains many Bible verses, prayers, and interpretations of scripture. In one of the most famous and horrifying scenes in the history of children's literature, Mr. Fairchild takes his children to view the tattered remains of a gibbeted corpse. This unfortunate person, Mr. Fairchild gravely explains, had first despised and later murdered his brother. The lesson was not without effect; the chastened children kneel and implore God's forgiveness for quarreling

Despite its insistent preaching, *The Fairchild Family* also contains some fine scenes of the family's interacting with one another, and many readers remember Mrs. Sherwood's vivid descriptions of food. Moreover, many child readers admitted that the terrifying scenes fascinated them, a fact which may account for the book's enduring popularity.

In most instances, though, the moral tale and matter-of-fact tale presented essentially shallow portaits of the child's life. Characters were highly stereotyped. If the child characters were not unbearably pious, they were unspeakably evil little wretches who gorged on sweets and tortured innocent animals. Nevertheless, the moral tale has continued to be an important influence throughout the nineteenth century; the didactic impulse has by no means disappeared today.

During the latter part of the nineteenth century and for the first thirty or forty years of the nineteenth, children's books in England and America were firmly committed to moral, religious, and educational didacticism. Such books sternly repressed the imagination and imaginative literature. The fairy tale in particular continued to be the focus of vehement attacks by moralists and educators. Maria Edgeworth expressed the prevailing view regarding children's fiction in the preface to *The Parent's Assistant*:

To prevent the precepts of morality from tiring the ear and the mind, it was necessary to make stories in which they are introduced in some measure dramatic; to keep alive hope and fear and curiosity, by some degree of intricacy. At the same time, care has been taken to avoid inflaming the imagination, or exciting a restless spirit of adventure, by exhibiting false views of life, and creating hopes which, in the ordinary course of things, cannot be realized.[4]

In 1803, Mrs. Sarah Trimmer, the editor of *The Guardian of Education*, also attacked the fairy tale as a pernicious influence upon young minds, and Mrs. Sherwood observed that fairy tales were inappropriate for teaching Christian principles. (For a fuller account of "the battle of the fairy tales," see the introduction to section four.)

Matter-of-fact tales and moral tales for children also flourished in America.

Using the pen name "Peter Parley," Samuel Goodrich wrote factual tales for children because he had been frightened by fairy tales and Mother Goose rhymes as a child. Beginning in 1827, Goodrich produced around 170 books, the first of which was *The Tales of Peter Parley about America*. Jacob Abbott, a congregational minister, attempted to inculcate religious and moral lessons in the young with his Rollo books — *Rollo at Work*, and *The Way for A Boy to Be Industrious* were among his titles. Beginning in 1834, Abbott eventually published over 200 such volumes.

Children's fiction, then, was dreary fare for almost the first half of the nineteenth century, although a few delights such as William Roscoe's *The Butterfly's Ball* (1807) and Charles Lamb's *Tales from Shakespeare* (1807) did enliven the scene from time to time. However, powerful imaginative and intellectual currents were stirring that were to change the course of children's literature. The Romantic movement in English poetry was to introduce radically new ideas about childhood and the imagination, which would later find expression in the great Victorian children's classics.

Two sources eventually changed prevailing ideas about childhood and imagination and hence changed the moral and educational emphases in children's literature. The first was a shift in emotional emphasis late in the eighteenth century; that is, poets and writers reinstated the validity of emotion and imagination as opposed to excessive reliance upon rationalism. The second was Rousseau's emphasis upon the importance of the child's early experience as a shaping force on the mind and character, an idea Wordsworth later expressed as "The child is father of the man."[5]

English poets William Blake and William Wordsworth wrote major poems treating child figures as symbols of redeeming and transforming power. No longer was the child considered only a "brand of hell" or else an empty vessel to be crammed with useful facts. Rather, Wordsworth wrote of childhood as the "seed-time" of the soul. The child, Wordsworth wrote, was a "seer," "a prophet," and the "best Philosopher." In *The Prelude* Wordsworth depicted the importance of the child's freedom to play and to grow amid the green freedom of the natural world as an essential part of the poet's development. Childhood provided intense visionary moments of experience, or "spots of time," which could nourish the creative imagination for a life time. Wordsworth also helped to create an atmosphere in which complex and richly symbolic works of children's literature could be written by featuring child characters and childlike characters in such poems as "We Are Seven," "Lucy Gray," "The Idiot Boy," and many others.

William Blake also enhanced the status of childhood as an important source of literary inspiration. Blake believed profoundly in imaginative man; for him, Bacon, Newton, and Locke were pernicious influences on the history of ideas, since they promoted a mechanistic view of the universe and espoused only rational ways of knowing the world. Blake believed that the imagination was the only way of knowing the truth about ourselves and the world. His poetry indicts the killing materialistic rationalism which informed so many children's books written at the time. In *Songs of Innocence* Blake affirms and celebrates the innocence of children — their imaginative lives, their capacity for joy in nature, and their power to redeem a fallen world. In *Songs of Experience* he indicts a society that not only inhibits an expression of innocent joy but actively persecutes it. Thus Blake uses the child as a vehicle for expressing some of his most potent and profoundly felt ideas.

Romantic poet and critic Samuel Taylor Coleridge also exerted an important influence on children's literature by writing significant essays on the nature and function of the imagination. He reprehended the excessive didacticism in children's literature and described the importance of fairy tales and other forms of romance in helping to shape his own creative imagination. Both Coleridge and John Keats set important examples for children's writers in turning to legend, fairy tale, and other forms of romance as important sources for their poetry.

In promoting the importance of childhood, of nature, and the imagination, and in their search for the origins of the self, the Romantics provided essential theoretical defenses for a rich and imaginative, rather than simplistically didactic, children's literature. In defending the fairy tale and in writing romances, the Romantic poets provided children's writers with important literary models. Eventually such Victorian writers as Charles Dickens, John Ruskin, and William Makepeace Thackeray wrote both fairy tales and essays defending their value. Dickens, for example, featured the child figure as a redeeming force in the lives of weary adults and integrated fairy tale elements into his major novels for adults. Charlotte and Emily Bronte also fused fairy tale structures and romantic elements with realistic features in their novels *Jane Eyre* and *Wuthering Heights*, and ultimately directly influenced children's literature.

As a result of new philosophical, social, and literary forces and as a result of the public acceptance of imaginative stories for children, the stage was set by the mid-nineteenth century for the development of the children's novel. Wordsworthian ideas of childhood and nature are reflected in the great fantasies of George MacDonald, Lewis Carroll, and E. Nesbit. Children's writers not only wrote literary fairy tales but eventually fused fairy tale structures with the conventions of realistic novels to produce such classics as E. Nesbit's *The Story of the Treasure Seekers* (1899) and Frances Hodgson Burnett's *The Secret Garden* (1911).

By the end of the nineteenth century, then, the major types of children's novels had emerged.

The following types of children's novels are traditional classifications based upon the subject treated by the authors. Within these categories, however, you will find that the structural and archetypal patterns used in organizing this anthology apply to different types of novels. For example the circular structures of romance and the linear structure of comedy underlie such animal stories as William Steig's *Abel's Island* and Rudyard Kipling's *The Jungle Book*. The linear structure of comedy also appears in E. B. White's classic, *Charlotte's Web*, in which Wilbur grows from an innocent and naive child into a mature parent figure. While the fantasy includes the sad event of Charlotte's death, the emphasis upon rebirth and renewal at the end are in keeping with the emotional emphases of romantic comedies.

Similarly, a realistic school novel may be structured as a "displaced" romance. In Thomas Hughes' *Tom Brown's School Days* the hero must prove himself on the playing field rather than in a battle or a hunt. Yet Robert Cormier's controversial school novel for young adults, *The Chocolate War*, exhibits features of tragedy and irony, since the novel's protagonist, Jerry Renault, does not succeed in his rebellion against the power-abusing assistant principal, Brother Leon, and the school's secret gang, the Vigils. In a tragic recognition scene Jerry renounces his own quest.

Archetypal characters likewise appear in all types of children's novels. In *Charlotte's Web* Charlotte appears as a clever trickster, while Templeton the Rat resembles the lovable scoundrel or rogue, who also inhabits Robert Louis Stevenson's adventure novel, *Treasure Island*, in the character of Long John Silver.

Thus teachers may design a literature curriculum based upon the structural principles of literature and upon archetypal characters and patterns of experience which may include several different types of children's novels.

A. THE FAMILY STORY OR DOMESTIC NOVEL

One of the most influential British family stories of the early Victorian period was Catherine Sinclair's *Holiday House*. Born in 1800, the daughter of a Scottish gentleman, Sinclair wrote one of the best and most original children's books which had yet appeared. In her preface to *Holiday House* Sinclair states that she wishes to champion the liberation of childhood imagination and play. While she expresses enlightened ideas about childhood in her preface, notions close to the Romantic treatments of childhood, she nevertheless does not sustain a commitment to these values throughout her children's novel. *Holiday House* concludes as a moral tale.

Sinclair's child characters, Harry and Laura Graham, have no mother. Their father, though living, has departed to Europe to grieve for his dead wife and has left the children in the care of their uncle, Major David Graham, and their grandmother, Lady Harriet. Their outwardly severe but inwardly kind house-keeper, Mrs. Crabtree, helps to rear these lively and sometimes over-exuberant children. The children's older brother, an exemplary young man who has taken all the school prizes, departs for a career at sea. The most convenient aspect of Harry and Laura's home is that they have much freedom to play without adult intrusion.

Harry and Laura are naughty even by modern standards. They invite a house-ful of children to tea without permission; the children subsequently smash china and overturn furniture. Harry and Laura ruin their best clothing and even set the house on fire. At the same time they always admit their faults and never sneak. In its conclusion the novel reverts with a vengeance to the moral tale tradition. When their older brother dies, Harry and Laura believe that God is punishing them for their naughtiness. They repent and become the pious children preferred by early Victorian audiences.

Sinclair's *Holiday House*, despite its divided structure and strong element of religious didacticism, became a significant model for later writers of children's family stories. The most appealing aspect of the book is the fact that the children are free to play apart from adults. This kind of children's story has been com-pared to the bucolic tradition of literature in which innocent characters enjoy a life of play within a green and protected shelter.[6] Mark Twain's child characters enjoy this kind of play in *The Adventures of Tom Sawyer* (1876). E. Nesbit's child characters also participate in adventures without adult supervision in *The Story of the Treasure Seekers* (1899). Many modern children's writers also make vivid use of this convention.

Children in this kind of family story are not neglected; rather they are spon-sored by caring adults. Hence, Claudia and her brother in Elaine Konigsburg's Newbery award-winning novel *From the Mixed-Up Files of Mrs. Basil E. Frankweiler* (1969) can enjoy their adventure in the Metropolitan Museum of Art because their family loves and misses them. In Louise Fitzhugh's *Harriet the Spy* (1964), however, Harriet is thrown terribly upon her own emotional re-sources. Harriet resembles the abandoned children who appear in many folk tales. While folk tale characters must battle for physical survival, Harriet must write desperately in her notebook as a stay against emotional chaos.

Another type of family story, sometimes called the domestic novel, reveals child characters interacting within a family, rather than featuring the child char-acters at play apart from adults. Many Victorian novels for adults and children presented home as a domestic paradise presided over by a protecting, nurturing mother. Matriarchal symbols of hearth, garden, and orchard are prominent in such family stories. The family lives in a comfortable, if shabby, house with a kindly servant. Perhaps Louisa May Alcott's *Little Women* (Part I, 1868; Part II, 1869) is the finest example of such domestic novels; in any event it is the most popular. The March girls — Meg, Jo, Beth, and Amy — undergo a linear quest to become perfect "little women," largely because Marmee, an idealized earthmother who helps each daughter conquer her specific character flaw, sets a model for them. She helps Jo to master her bad temper. She teaches Meg how to be a responsible wife and mother. The bounteous matriarchal March household eventually helps to redeem even the sternly patriarchal Mr. Laurence next door. Yet Alcott reveals that such a family asks a dear price of its members. Marmee's sternly set jaw and tightly compressed lips suggest the cost she must pay to establish a home. Nevertheless *Little Women* presents an ideal of family life which influenced many other writers of family stories.

Sentimental and idealized treatments of family life prevailed in America until the 1930s. The family story emerging in that era remained dominant, particularly in American children's literature, until the 1960s and the advent of social changes resulting in the so-called "New Realism" in children's literature. Many family stories of this time, such as those of Laura Ingalls Wilder, depicted the family in an agrarian setting and revealed the family engaged in the difficult business of farming the land, settling a frontier, and making a home through their cooperative efforts. Such frontier stories as Rose Wilder Lane's *Let the Hurricane Roar*, Carol Brink's *Caddie Woodlawn* (1935), as well as the family stories of Eleanor Estes, Elizabeth Enright, and Lois Lenski, all created realistic family stories of this kind. More recent works for children featuring the efforts of the family in a rural community celebrating agrarian values are Mildred Taylor's *Roll of Thunder, Hear My Cry!*, Suellen Bridger's *Home Before Dark*, and the fiction of Robert Burch, Vera and Bill Cleaver, among others.

In the 1960s and 1970s British and North American books for children and young adults began to depict the problems and frustrations of family life in much more starkly, realistic terms. Known as examples of "New Realism" or "the problem novel," such fiction began to treat working-class families and families of various ethnic backgrounds. While older examples of the family story featured wise and benevolent parents, in recent works the parents themselves may be presented as the problem. Divorce, child abuse, alcohol and drug abuse, and other serious social problems are openly treated in family stories. A good example of this kind of family story is Louise Fitzhugh's *Nobody's Family Is Going to Change* (1974), in which Emma Sheridan, an overweight black girl who wants to be a lawyer, recognizes that her father hates her, that she must free herself from her father and her weak, passive mother. Since the family will not change, Emma realizes that she must change. Similarly Patty Bergen in Bette Greene's *The Summer of My German Soldier* must free herself from a cruel, abusive father, hopelessly crippled by his own emotional insecurities.

Fortunately not all contemporary family stories for children present such a bleak view of family life. Some reveal the positive nature of unusual and unconventional families, such as Norma Klein's *Mom, the Wolf Man and Me* and Katherine Paterson's *The Great Gilly Hopkins*. And in Beverly Cleary's *Ramona and her Father* the family deals successfully with the father's unemployment.

B. THE ADVENTURE STORY

Although not written for children, Daniel Defoe's *Robinson Crusoe* (1719) and Jonathan Swift's *Gulliver's Travels* (1726) became immediately popular with youthful audiences and have remained so. Both works were printed in summary chapbook versions early in the eighteenth century and hence were available to a large popular audience of children. Eighteenth-century editions of the *Arabian Nights* also appealed to the taste for adventure stories among young readers.

Classical literature and epic hero tales have provided excellent models for writers of adventure stories from ancient times. Homer's *The Odyssey* is clearly one of the oldest and most popular adventure stories. Structurally *Robinson Crusoe* closely resembles the hero tale. A hero embarks upon a voyage fraught with peril. Cast upon an island, he must endure mental, moral, and physical tests of character. *Robinson Crusoe* celebrates not only the qualities of a traditional hero, but also those of the rising British mercantile class. Crusoe's careful organization of supplies, his thrifty and economic use of material goods, and his ability to survive in the wilderness as a civilized person were all features that appealed to a large audience. As we have noted, specific imitations of the work, called *Robinsades*, appeared all over Western Europe after Rousseau's praise of the novel. One of the first imitations was published in Hamburg in 1779; its author, Joachim Heinrich Campe, acknowledged his debt to Defoe and Rousseau.[7] An English translation of the work entitled *The New Robinson Crusoe* appeared in 1789 and became quite popular. A century later Johann David Rudolph Wyss, pastor of Swiss troops in Berne, produced *The Swiss Family Robinson* (two parts, 1812; 1813).

The Swiss Family Robinson, translated into English in 1814, inspired Captain Frederick Marryat to write his own *Robinsonade* in reaction to the nautical mistakes he discovered in Wyss' work. Captain Marryat's first work of adventure, *Masterman Ready* (3 vols., 1841), blended typical features of the moral tale with the survival story. The faithful Ready serves the Seagrave family as moral, educational, and spiritual guide. At last he even sacrifices his life that the family may survive.

Marryat's most important sea adventure story was *Mr. Midshipman Easy* (3 vols., 1836), which was later to influence the great adult sea stories of Joseph Conrad. Jack Easy has been given a poor education. His father, an irresponsible gentleman devoted to a pursuit of "the rights of man" and a fanatical study of phrenology, has spoiled his son. To cure his flaws, Jack is sent to sea, where he experiences adventure, acquires an African servant, Mephistopheles, and eventually learns to be a responsible gentleman capable of returning home and asssuming his rightful position as a gentleman of property.

Eventually adventure stories of this kind were popularized even more by the establishment of magazines designed to publish wild adventure stories for boys. In the first number of *The Boys of England* (Nov. 29, 1866), Charles Stevens wrote, "Our aim is to enthral you by wild and wonderful but healthy fiction."[8] Such tales, as well as Robert Ballantyne's *The Coral Island* (1858), a work featuring several school boys marooned on an island, inspired Robert Louis Stevenson's classic adventure story, *Treasure Island*. The work features a young hero, Jim Hawkins, who goes on a sea journey in search of treasure and encounters "blood-and-thunder" adventures any young reader would devour: buried treasure, pirates, and the difficulties of sea faring. After his encounters with such characters as the memorable Long John Silver, Jim Hawkins matures into a defiant, fearless, and resourceful young hero. Stevenson's novel also treats such serious themes as greed and betrayal vs. courage and loyalty.

In England in the 1880s there was a revival of romance represented in the many adventure stories of Robert Louis Stevenson, Jules Verne, Rider Haggard, and others. At this time also, the novelist and critic Henry James attempted to enhance the artistic status of the novel by expressing his theory in a famous essay, "The Art of Fiction." What followed was an intense critical controversy between James and Stevenson.

James argues for the serious, high art of the novel, noting that it should portray life realistically and complexly. Hence James became the defender of realism in the novel. Stevenson defended the value of romance. Eventually James argued that the novel could no longer be regarded as merely family reading or written with the young reader in mind as it had been from its origins in the eighteenth century. This controversy eventually led to a much sharper split between children's literature and literature for adults. The unfortunate result was that both children's literature, romance, and fantasy came to be regarded with less critical esteem.[9] In the aftermath of this controversy adventure stories were written much more seriously for adults by such writers as Joseph Conrad; they also became increasingly formulaic in popular works and in writing for young readers.

In America the dime novel satisfied young readers' appetite for fast-paced adventures. In 1860 Edward S. Ellis published *Seth Jones*, an adventure about the rescue of a white girl from wild Indians. From 1860 to 1875, the dime novel flourished. Characterized by breathless action, cliffhanging scenes, improbable plots, and daring heroes, the dime novel often depicted adventures on the frontier and thus became the ancestor of the later Western stories, which were highly popular in Europe and in North America in the 1880s and 1890s.

At this time in England prodigious numbers of adventure stories treating various exotic settings appeared. George Alfred Henty produced over eight historical adventures; John Meade Falkner treated smuggling operations in *Moonfleet* (1898). Arthur Conan Doyle popularized the mystery story, and Jules Verne created exciting science fiction adventure stories.

E. Nesbit created another kind of adventure story. After the popularity of her Bastable stories, she began writing fantasy for children. In *Five Children and It, The Phoenix and the Carpet*, and *The Story of the Amulet*, she created magical adventures as well as stories involving time travel.

Comtemporary children's writers draw upon the conventions of these adventure stories. Scott O'Dell creates a kind of survival story in his award-winning *Island of the Blue Dolphin*, in which Karana, a young girl, must survive alone on an island after her tribe has left. O'Dell describes her attempts to survive physically and psychologically, while empasizing her growth in character. Similarly, in *Julie of the Wolves* (1972), winner of the Newbery Medal, Jean George depicts the struggles of a young Inuit girl to survive on an Arctic Tundra, where the delicate ecological balance is being disturbed by the ravages of civilization. Since the adventure story is the most masculine of literary *genres*, these two works are noteworthy for creating strong female heroes.

C. FANTASY

1. Nineteenth Century Development of Fantasy

With the triumph of fantasy in mid-nineteenth century England, several writers produced classic works in this genre. Charles Kingsley's *The Water Babies* (1863) depicts the sorrows of Tom the Chimney Sweep who seeks cleansing relief from his miserable existence in a nearby river. Although Tom is believed to be drowned, the kindly, if pious, narrator assures his readers that Tom has been transformed into a water baby, complete with a charming necklace of gills. As a water baby Tom undergoes a process of spiritual and physical evolution until he is at last reincarnated as a British gentleman.

Although we can speak in general terms about a "triumph of fantasy," the didactic impulse by no means disappeared suddenly. Indeed, we see it in many children's books today. While *The Water Babies* contains strong elements of fantasy, it also exhibits strongly didactic features. Kingsley was concerned that the reader learn scientific facts and moral lessons; he often interrupts the narrative to introduce and to explain scientific vocabulary or to stress a moral precept. Nevertheless, in its humorous characterizations of sea creatures, its comic satiric treatment of social class, and its use of the structure of the linear quest, *The Water Babies* helped to pave the way for the great fantasies of George MacDonald and Lewis Carroll. As Edwardian writer E. Nesbit was to do in many of her fantasies at the beginning of the twentieth century, Kingsley strongly suggests that creation and science are themselves fantastic miracles.

The story of Charles Lutwidge Dodgson's famous friendship with Alice Liddell, the young daughter of the Dean of Christ Church, and the picnic on the river which initiated the adventures of Alice are by now widely known. On this excursion along the river Dodgson began to tell Alice and her two sisters about Alice's adventures underground. Eventually these adventures were published as *The Adventures of Alice in Wonderland* under Dodgson's pen name, Lewis Carroll. In 1871 Carroll published the sequel to the fantasy, *Through the Looking-Glass and What Alice Found There*.

In his children's classic Carroll combines conventions of dream vision, fairy tale, and quest romance to create one of the most complex and provocative children's fantasies ever written. The book has been called "the spiritual volcano" of children's books because it turns the didactic tradition inside out; its humor subverts and deflates adult authority and celebrates the child's inventive efforts to master inner and outer reality through the ordering processes of language, games, and fantasy.

The *Alice* books have been analyzed by adult critics and scholars from every conceivable perspective — as evidence of Lewis Carroll's psychological problems, as allegories of religious doubt, as parables about sexual maturation, as a manifestation of Lewis Carroll's views on logic, among others. One of the most convincing treatments of the fantasy explores it as Alice's quest for maturity. The classic remains notable for its presentation of the inner wishes and terrors of the child, its comic characterizations, its delightfully outrageous nonsense, inventive use of language, and verbal jokes. We find powerful resonances of Carroll's fantasies in such nineteenth-century works as Jean Ingelow's *Mopsa the Fairy* (1869), Christina Rossetti's *Speaking Likenesses* (1874), and others, as well as such twentieth-century fantasies as Maurice Sendak's picture book *Where the Wild Things Are* (1963) and Norton Juster's *The Phantom Tollbooth*.

The other important name in the development of nineteenth-century British fantasy for children is George MacDonald. Besides writing important literary fairy tales, such as "The Light Princess," "Little Daylight," and many others, he also created three booklength fantasies for children: *At the Back of the North Wind* (1871), *The Princess and the Goblin* (1872), and its sequel *The Princess and Curdie*. All three of these works are strongly indebted to the Romantic movement. In their presentation of child characters, they draw heavily upon the notion that the child is not only innocent but also has special insight and ways of knowing, and that the child possesses a special affinity with the natural world.

In *At the Back of the North Wind* Little Diamond endures in actual life terrible poverty and illness. In an imaginary realm of faith, however, Diamond experiences magical adventures with the North Wind, presented as a beautiful goddess-like woman. Diamond is an idealized child whose goodness can redeem the fallen adults around him. When Diamond dies at the end of the novel, the narrator suggests that Diamond transcends his finite existence and enters a luminous world of spirit at the Back of the North Wind. Though cruel poverty has in part been responsible for Diamond's death, the book suggests that his death and transcendence represent a happy ending.

In *The Princess and the Goblin* and *The Princess and Curdie* MacDonald uses the conventions of fairy tale and quest romance and draws upon such visionary works as Dante's *The Divine Comedy* to show its child protagonists, Princess Irene and miner boy Curdie, undergoing quests of the spirit and the imagination. Both books are remarkable for their poetic prose and for their depiction of the goddess-like maternal figure who appears in many of MacDonald's works.

George MacDonald's fantasies directly influenced several nineteenth-century writers of children's fantasy and helped to establish the modern tradition known as "sacred" or "ethical fantasy." Mrs. Molesworth created her own visionary fairylands in such books as *The Tapestry Room* (1879), *Chrismas-Tree Land* (1884), and many others. Mrs. Craik's *The Little Lame Prince* (1874) reflects MacDonald's idealization of the child and his conceptions of nature. In the twentieth century such writers as E. Nesbit, C.S. Lewis, and J.R.R. Tolkien have all acknowledged their literary debts to George MacDonald.

2. Varieties of Children's Fantasy
In the wake of the great British creators of fantasy in the nineteenth century, a rich and various body of children's fantasy emerged. The following types of fantasy emerged by the end of the century and are still vital types today.
    a. Animal Stories
In his two *Jungle Books* (1894, 1895), Rudyard Kipling presented a young

child reared among animals in the jungle. He stresses Mowgli's fearless exuberance, his capacity to survive amid "Jungle Law," and his wisdom in learning from wise teachers. Kipling was perhaps influenced by stories of Peter the Wild Boy and traditional talking beast fables. His treatment, however, was entirely new.

The tradition of talking beast fables produced several other classics of children's literature early in the twentieth century. Kenneth Grahame's *The Wind in the Willows* (1908) created memorable animal characters which continue to be popular today. Later in the century children's writers produced classics that treat animal characters who sometimes interact with human beings: E.B. White's *Charlotte's Web* (1952), George Selden's *The Cricket in Times Square* (1960), Michael Bond's books about Paddington the Bear, and William Steig's *Dominic*.

While traditional talking beasts in fables illustrated moral principles, modern animal stories usually explore the human condition with humor and sympathy. E.B. White's clever intellectual spider Charlotte, for example, must use her wits and her blood-sucking talents to survive, yet she also reveals the highest and the best of humane values — friendship, loyalty, and artistic creation. As Wilbur lovingly remembers, Charlotte was both a true friend and a good writer.

b. Animated Toy Stories

A sturdy tradition of animated toy stories in children's literature was early established by such writers as Danish Hans Christian Andersen's "The Steadfast Tin Soldier" and German E.T.A. Hoffman's "The Nutcracker." Several booklength classics of this type remain popular with today's children. Written in 1880 by Carlo Lorenzini (pen name Collodi), *Pinocchio* was translated into English and published in the United States in 1892. The spirited and naughty puppet, carved by kindly old Geppetto, desperately desires to become a real boy. With the help of the Blue Fairy and Geppetto, Pinocchio at last overcomes his faults (symbolized by donkey ears and a long nose) to achieve his dream.

Other animated toy fantasies include A.A. Milne's *Winnie-the-Pooh* (1926) and *The House at Pooh Corner* (1928) with their memorable characters: the not-so-smart but amiable Pooh, the fidgety Tigger, the eternally pessimistic Eeyore the Donkey. One of the finest children's stories of this kind is Marjorie Williams Bianco's *The Velveteen Rabbit* (1922), which stresses the potent relationship between a child and a beloved toy. The velveteen rabbit clearly becomes real through the workings of the child's imagination.

One of the most complex and interesting children's books featuring animated toys is Russell Hoban's *The Mouse and His Child*, the intricate story of two wind-up toys' quest to become self-winding. Hoban's fantasy ultimately presents a utopian vision of a community in which fellowship, work, art, and technology function harmoniously.

c. Time Fantasy

E. Nesbit introduced time fantasy in children's fiction with *The Story of the Amulet*. In this work the child characters — Robert, Cyril, Anthea, and Jane — travel with the help of a magical amulet to ancient Egypt, ancient Babylon, Atlantis, and even into the future. Nesbit's time fantasies explore both past and future societies to reveal social folly in the present. At the same time she creates a sense of mystery of time and reflects her vivid awareness of the present-ness of the past in the experience of her child characters. In her beautifully crafted *Tom's Midnight Garden* (1959), British writer Phillipa Pearce explores the concept of "time no longer," when a young boy meets a young girl for midnight adventures. Pearce emphasizes the mutual emotional needs of her child characters, while Nesbit stresses social needs in her time fantasies.

Lucy Boston's popular *Green Knowe* books and Eleanor Cameron's *The Court of the Stone Children* blend elements of the ghost story, historical fiction, and time fantasy to reveal the imaginative engagement of a sensitive child character with the past.

d. Whimsical Fantasy

Mary Norton brilliantly combines realistic details and fantasy in her children's book *The Borrowers* (1953), in which a family of tiny people, Pod, Homily, and Arrietty live in a tiny world within a house. When Arrietty's youthful curiosity leads her to adventurous explorations, she becomes friends with the boy of the house. This situation eventually forces the Borrowers to leave the house. Memorable for its inventive detail, the book describes how the Borrowers use tiny artifacts to furnish their home, a feature of the book likely to appeal to the child's sense of pretend and play. Another strength of the book is its strong characterizations. Norton presents other adventures of these appealing little people in *The Borrowers Afield, The Borrowers Afloat,* and *The Borrowers Aloft*.

P.L. Travers' stern but magical *Mary Poppins* (1934) continues to delight young readers. Mary Poppins transforms ordinary life into an enchantment with her magical bag. In the same tradition, British fantasy writer Joan Aiken draws upon the tall-tale tradition, gothic romance, and ghost stories to create such witty and sophisticated fantasies as the humorous *The Wolves of Willoughby Chase* and *Black Hearts in Battersea*.

Few schemes for classifying fantasy are comprehensive enough to include all the fine works of fantasy which have appeared in recent years. One of the most notable, Natalie Babbitt's *Tuck Everlasting* (1975), truly defies classification. Because it draws so powerfully upon the myth of the Golden Age, it has been listed in the bibliography of the Literary Myth section in this anthology; the fantasy also draws upon several other literary traditions as well. In this complex fantasy, Babbitt explores matters of death and immortality. Ten-year-old Winnie

Foster becomes restless in her constrained home and decides to run away. In a nearby wood she meets Mae and Jessie Tuck, who tell her the strange story of a spring from which they had unwittingly drunk many years earlier. This spring had stopped the Tucks from aging; the Tuck family would never die and never change. Winnie's strange journey brings her a vivid awareness of the reality of death. In the end she makes a significant choice. Like many other romances, *Tuck Everlasting* features a circular journey in which the hero or heroine is tested. Winnie passes her tests and behaves heroically; her reward, however, is not what young readers may expect.

D. THE SCHOOL STORY

The school story has quite a long history in British children's fiction. The first novel for children, predating *The History of Little Goody Two Shoes*, was Sarah Fielding's *The Governess or, The Little Female Academy* (2nd ed., 1749), a collection of little stories told to or by the girls in the formidable Mrs. Teachum's school. Though the novel was sternly didactic, it did contain two fairy tales and hence later inspired the wrath of Mrs. Trimmer and Mrs. Sherwood.

The two writers who essentially established school story conventions were Thomas Hughes and Frederic Farrar. Hughes' famous school novel, *Tom Brown's School Days* (1856), reflects the author's memories of his days at Rugby. The book glorified the manly virtues of courage, good sportsmanship, and friendship. It clearly idealized the English public school experience. Farrar's *Eric, or Little by Little*: *A Tale of Roslyn School* sentimentalized the public school boy. Critics have derided the pious moral tone of the narrator and the stereotyped characters of the novel, as well as its blatant didacticism. However, both books inspired countless imitations. The boarding school became a place to nurture the highest values and the manliest virtues in society. On the playing field and in the classroom a young man proved himself worthy to become a gentleman.

In 1899 Rudyard Kipling published his well-known and popular *Stalky and Co.*, a novel which overturned many of the standard features of the school story by presenting the public school experience much more realistically. In the twentieth century some school stories have transcended conventional formulas to explore genuinely complex themes and characters as M.E. Kerr's *Is That You, Miss Blue?*

In general the school story takes place within one school term in a boarding school set in the country. Though teachers and school officials may play some role in the stories, much power is placed in the hands of the adolescent characters. Consequently school stories reflect the structure of society. In the nineteenth century the social organization of the adolescents turned on a well-defined system of prefects and fags. Less socially stratified than the nineteenth century, the twentieth century has produced school novels which provide more flexibility for the author. John Knowles explores the nature of friendship, leadership, the function of games, and the corrosive effect of war upon a group of adolescents in *A Separate Peace*. Similarly, Robert Cormier reveals abusive power and its tragic effects in his controversial novel *The Chocolate War* (1974).

Recent works of children's school novels have departed from previous conventional patterns and assumed a new set of formulas. The more recently published works present a harsher vision of school life than the earlier ones. The action occurs in a day school rather than in a boarding school. The plot usually centers upon an introverted protagonist who must contend with bullies, gangs, unsympathetic or corrupt teachers, and obtuse administrators. Such novels as Judy Blume's *Blubber* (1976), Betsy Byars' *The Eighteenth Emergency* (1973), and Nat Hentoff's *This School Is Driving Me Crazy* (1976) exemplify many of the recent changes in the school story formula.

E. HISTORICAL FICTION

Writers of historical fiction have an awesome responsibility. They must not only research the historical period accurately but must also make it exciting and accessible to young readers. Details of ordinary life as well as outstanding historical events must be presented dramatically and organically within the narrative. At the same time the writer of historical fiction must imagine what it was to be conscious in an earlier age. Characterization and conflict must emerge credibly from the historical milieu.

One of the earliest writers of historical fiction was Sir Walter Scott (1771-1832). With such novels as *Ivanhoe* (1819), *Waverley* (1814), *The Heart of Midlothian* (1818), and others, Scott pleased generations of young Victorian readers. He invested history with romance and inspired other writers of historical fiction. One of these was Charlotte Yonge (1823-1901), who read Scott's historical novels in the 1830s. In 1844 she created *Abbeychurch*, a blend of the domestic novel and historical fiction. In over one hundred books Yonge recreated life in many different countries and centuries.

Like those of Sir Walter Scott, such works as Captain Frederick Marryat's *Children of the New Forest* (1847) incorporated features of the hero tale and accurate historical detail. Marryat's rather pious work centers upon the adventures of Edward, Humphrey, Alice, and Edith, who live with their kindly servant, Jacob, in the New Forest. The novel reprehends Oliver Cromwell, espouses the Royalist cause, and celebrates the advent of King Charles II. Similarly, Charles Kingsley exhibits his patriotism, his protestantism, and his social view in *Hereward the Wake* (1865) and *Westward, Ho!* (1855). *Hereward the Wake* treats an early period of British history, while *Westward, Ho!* recounts the exploits of Sir Francis Drake and the glorious defeat of the Spanish Armada.

In America Howard Pyle immersed himself in medieval customs, legends, and literature and created memorable works of children's fiction about the period. In *Otto of the Silver Hand* (1888), Pyle creates a vivid and violent tale of Germany's robber barons. His *Men of Iron* (1892) centers upon the adventures of a young squire, Myles Falworth, as he undergoes the rigorous education and tests of character needed to become a knight. Myles must contend with external foes and his own character flaws to achieve his goal.

The twentieth century has also produced some exemplary historical novels for young readers. Esther Forbes' Newbery award-winning novel *Johnny Tremain* (1944) recounts the conflicts of a silversmith's apprentice, Johnny, who goes through a difficult ordeal near the beginning of the American Revolution. Forbes deals effectively not only with her character's conflicting emotions; she also vividly reveals the Revolutionary period of American history with insight and humanity. Likewise, Elizabeth George Speare illuminates the society of early American Puritans in *The Witch of Blackbird Pond*, Newbery winner of 1959. The story dramatizes the conflicts of a lovely young girl, Kit, who has been reared in the relaxed atmosphere of Barbados. She experiences intense culture shock when she comes to New England to live with Puritan relatives in the 1600s. Other first-rate writers of historical fiction who continue to produce excellent works for young readers include Scott O'Dell, Hester Burton, Rosemary Sutcliff, Erik Haugaard, and Paula Fox.

Notes

1 See Francelia Butler, Introduction, *Masterworks of Children's Literature, 1550-1739*, Vol. 1 (New York: The Stonehill Publishing Company, 1983), p. xxi. See also F.J. Harvey Darton, *Children's Books in England: Five Centuries of Social Life* (Cambridge: the University Press, 1932) from which much historical information included in this introduction was taken.

2 See Alison White, "*Pilgrim's Progress* as Fairy Tale," *Children's Literature*, I (1972), for a thorough discussion of Bunyan's work as fairy tale and as an influence upon children's literature.

3 See Robert Bator, Introduction to *Masterworks of Children's Literature*, Vol. 3, p. xxiii.

4 Maria Edgeworth, Preface to *The Parent's Assistant* (Rpt. London: Macmillan, 1897), p. 4.

5 See Peter Coveney, *Image of Childhood: The Individual and Society, A Study of the Theme in English Literature* (Santa Fe: Gannon Press, 1957), p.4. Coveney discusses the treatment of the child and imagination in the poetry of Wordsworth and Coleridge and traces the use of the child figure in ninteenth-century British literature. He argues that the Romantic child loses much of its vitality as a symbol in such late-century works as James Barrie's *Peter Pan*.

6 See Phyllis Bixler Koppes, "The Child in Pastoral Myth: A Study in Rousseau and Wordsworth, Children's Literature, and Literary Fantasy," Diss., University of Kansas, 1977, for a thorough discussion of "bucolic" and "Georgian" pastoral traditions and their effect on children's literature.

7 Darton, p. 115.

8 Cited in Darton, p. 276.

9 For a thorough discussion of this controversy and its impact upon children's literature, see Felicity A. Hughes, "Children's Literature: Theory and Practice," *ELH*, 45 (Fall 1978), p. 548.

In the following discussions of children's novels, an attempt has been made to select both classics and examples of excellent contemporary novels. This effort also extends to different types of children's novels. For example, included are examples of family stories (*The Story of the Treasure Seekers, M.C. Higgins the Great*, and *The Great Gilly Hopkins*); heroic romances or literary hero tales (*The Princess and the Goblin* and *The Hobbit*); adventure novels (*Treasure Island*); animal fantasy (*The Wind in the Willows* and *Charlotte's Web*); science fiction and ethical fantasy (*A Wrinkle in Time*); and hisorical fiction (*The Slave Dancer*). Space does not permit, however, the inclusion of examples of all types of novels discussed in section II of this appendix. Included also are both British and North American novels for children, including books by Canadian and Afro-American authors.

Alice's Adventures in Wonderland

by Lewis Carroll (Pseud. of Charles Lutwidge Dodgson) (1865)

Alice's Adventures in Wonderland is one of the richest and most complex children's books ever written. In depicting the child character as an assertive and aggressive female, in subverting adult authority, in revealing the internal psychological world of the child, and in satirizing didactic children's literature and school lessons, Lewis Carroll has created a truly revolutionary fantasy which continues to be popular with both child and adult readers, to command the serious attention of critics and scholars, and to influence other children's writers.

In the opening scene of the fantasy Alice suggests that her author is aware of writing a new kind of children's book when she asks, "What is the use of the book . . . without pictures or conversations?" Carroll depicts Alice herself as the product of an educational system which crams children's heads with worthless and irrelevant facts. As Alice falls down the rabbit hole, she wonders what latitude or longitude she has reached, though she has no idea what these words mean. Throughout the fantasy, Carroll makes fun of Alice's pretensions to learning and at didactic children's literature. For example, Alice checks the little bottle before drinking the liquid inside to make sure it is not poison, because "she had read several nice little stories about children who had got burnt, and eaten up by wild beasts, and other unpleasant things, all because they *would*

not remember the simple rules their friends had taught them". Carroll also directly parodies didactic verses and stories, such as Ann Taylor's "Twinkle, twinkle, Little Star," which becomes "Twinkle, twinkle, Little Bat."

Alice's Adventures in Wonderland is more however, than an adroitly constructed pastiche of parody, pantomime, nursery rhyme, and bits of fairy tale, which afford children a holiday from the lessons and demands of the ordinary world. The two *Alice* books offer a completed quest in which Alice does not grow to a conventional moral state but rather confronts and conquers some of her deepest fears, enacts some of her most subversive wishes against the tyranny of adults, and ultimately makes progress in both mental and physical growth.

Alice's growth and her quest for identity are in fact major themes in both *Alice* books. Her encounters with the creatures of Wonderland most often show her struggling against adult authority and constraint. She finds herself thrust into the role of mother too soon in the Pool of Tears scene, when the creatures demand prizes of her. She alternately finds herself too small and vulnerable to make progress, or too large to fit into the constrained houses of such childish adults as the White Rabbit. At times she worries about losing her identity altogether: images of extinction, annihilation, and her death recur throughout the fantasy.

In some important respects Carroll's fantasy questions the nature of the quest and of growth, at least as the archetypal pattern has been presented in literature. The basic literary form of the fantasy is that of a dream vision. In early dream visions, such as the medieval "The Pearl," characters experienced a dream which appeared to be designed to improve the dreamer morally and spiritually. Alice's dream, however, resembles the chaotic quality of nightmare with its bizarre and humorous transformations, not the orderly sequences of a *Divine Comedy*. Carroll thus suggests that the quest for growth is not as simple as becoming a better person; rather the child must use all of her capacities to shape and to order experience to survive the chaotic and complex process of growing.

Early in the fantasy, for example, Alice identifies a lovely garden as her goal. Traditionally the garden is the orderly place where plants and people grow, mature, and enter experienced emotional and psychological states. Once Alice enters the garden, however, she experiences just as much chaos as before. This garden appears to represent a telling vision of a child's coming to terms with the adult world; when Alice finds herself joining the adult game, she is just as muddled as everyone else. Rather than neatly completing quests, Carroll suggests that human beings remain confused children looking for the right rules in an ever-shifting and unmanageable reality. If Alice does not complete her quest in the garden as she had hoped, she does appear at the end of the fantasy to be sure of her identity and to see the true nature of her own dream: "My name is Alice, so pleasure Majesty. . . . Why they're only a pack of cards after all. I needn't be afraid of them".

In *The Adventures of Alice in Wonderland*, then, Carroll delineates several highly original functions of fantasy. First, through the parody of the didactic tradition, he suggests that fantasy frees children by allowing them to mock the conventional world of adults, while at the same time coming to recognize and to master their own anxieties and fears, a significant dimension of traditional folk tales which Carroll unconsciously appropriates. Children thus grow toward emotional maturity rather than

spiritual purity. Imagination and intelligence, Carroll suggests, and fantasy itself provide children with the means of asserting their own identities, of separating sense and nonsense, fantasy and reality.

Alice's quest, then, resembles the circular structure of romance, but her journey is an internal and symbolic one; the stakes are psychological and emotional rather than physical. This serious purpose, however, is embedded in the delightful nonsense of the fantasy with its strange and appealing characters: the grinning Cheshire Cat, the Mad Hatter, the treacle-loving Dormouse, the shy White Rabbit, the archly superior caterpillar, and the lugubrious Mock Turtle. Carroll's outrageous punning and his inventive use of language, his obsession with riddles and games, and his innovative uses of words all suggest that play is one important way that human beings endure the chaos of experience and even have fun doing it.

The Princess and the Goblin

by George MacDonald (1872).

Regarded today as a classic of children's literature, *The Princess and the Goblin* represents a significant development in the history of children's literature. Historians of children's literature have noted that George MacDonald and Lewis Carroll essentially established the traditions of modern fantasy. MacDonald had read much English and German Romantic literature. He had also read the dream-vision literature of earlier English writers, and had adapted the conventions of quest romance and fairy tales in writing his book-length fantasies for children. Heavily allegorical, *The Princess and the Goblin* reflects MacDonald's Romantic conceptions of nature and the child. The book also reveals aspects of MacDonald's religious and spiritual convictions.

The central character of the fantasy, Princess Irene, lives "in a large house, half castle, half-farmhouse, on the side of another mountain, about half-way between its base and its peak." Most of the time Irene is in the care of her rather childish and simpleminded nurse, Lootie. Once, as Irene explores the stairways of the house, she finds herself lost. At last she discovers a stairway, ascends it, and like Sleeping Beauty, encounters a lovely old lady in the attic spinning.

MacDonald's old lady, however, is there to bless and to protect Princess Irene. Though extremely old, the lady looks beautiful, wise, and kind. She is also rather majestic and awesome. This goddess-like maternal figure apparently represents a natural divine order, as she is closely associated with a luminous moon and with snowy-white pigeons. The silky invisible thread which she spins appears to represent faith. Eventually Irene must follow this fine thread deep within the mines near the castle to rescue her friend, the miner boy Curdie Peterson.

The house itself is deeply symbolic of the self; critics have interpreted it in both spiritual and psychological terms. At the top of the house one finds the most highly evolved spiritual being in the person of the great-grandmother. Hideous goblins, spiritually and physically "devolved" creatures, hide deep within the caves and undermine the foundations of the house. Princess Irene ascends to the heights and to the depths of the castle. She explores all aspects of the self. She can explore the evil depths safely, for she remains connected to the divine source in the attic.

The miner boy, Curdie, reflects some of MacDonald's radical ideas on social class. Both the Princess Irene and Curdie are in some respects Romantic idealizations of the child. Both characters are innocent and closely connected to the natural world. Together, they rid the castle of the goblins. Though Curdie possesses imagination, bravery, and resourcefulness, he has not grown spiritually to the point that he may perceive the old lady spinning in the attic. As a result of his experiences with the Princess Irene, however, Curdie grows in faith.

The Princess and the Goblin resembles a traditional romance in several respects. The hero and heroine endure severe tests of character and courage and eventually prevail against the comic but insidious goblins. Archetypal helping characters such as the Wise Old Woman come to the aid of the heroine. A symbolic flood at the end heralds a renewed creation, the end of a corrupt order, and the

promise of a renewed and redeemed society. The journeys of Irene and Curdie to the heights and depths indicate their internal quest for self-discovery, as well as the external quest to rid the kingdom of the goblins.

The novel also exhibits an intriguing structure of oppositions: attic with caverns and dungeons, the wise goddess-like figure with the ridiculous goblin queen; the grandmother's opal-encrusted shoes with the goblin queen's ugly stone ones. Most memorable are the passages of visionary description of the grandmother and the radiance surrounding her.

The Adventures of Tom Sawyer

by Samuel Clemens (1876).

In 1870, Samuel Clemens wrote a piece on the childhood love of a boy and girl. Two years later in London, he told friends the story of a boy who, required to whitewash a fence, tricks his friends into doing the job. In 1875, *The Atlantic Monthly* published the recollections of his youth and early manhood along the Mississippi. These three works served as the basis for his first boy's book and one of his best-known novels, *The Adventures of Tom Sawyer* (1876).

The novel describes a spring and summer in the life of the title hero, a boy living in the 1840s in Missouri, on the banks of the Mississippi River. Many of the chapters relate typical episodes in the life of an adventurous and mischievous child. Often the events happen at random, as the occasion arises and the mood hits Tom. However, there are two more serious and interrelated narrative threads running through the book: Tom's love of Becky Thatcher, and the consequences of having witnessed, along with his friend Huckleberrry Finn, Indian Joe's graveyard murder of Dr. Robinson.

When he was writing the book, Clemens told a friend: "It is *not* a boy's book at all. It will only be read by adults." However, in the preface to the novel, he speaks of two audiences: "Although my book is intended mainly for the entertainment of boys and girls, I hope it will not be shunned by men and women on that account, for part of my plan has been to try to pleasantly remind adults of what they once were themselves." In fact, *The Adventures of Tom Sawyer* has a double perspective: that of the child experiencing his world immediately, and that of the adult reflecting nostalgically on the happier moments of youth.

The element of the book which best approximates the child's point of view is the sense of time. The story encompasses only a few summer months of "real" time, yet during this period the children experience a variety of adventures which seem to span a much greater interval. Moreover, all of the events seem to be of equal importance to the children: even while they carry their fearful knowledge of the murder, Tom and Huck play pirates energetically.

Clemens is particularly skillful in depicting the intensity of fear in children's lives, as in the reaction of Huck and Tom at the graveyard, or Tom and Becky lost in the cave. However, when he is narrating the early days of Tom's courtship with Becky, or Tom's learning to smoke, he is the amused adult remembering his childhood. His tone here is similar to that used by the narrator in Kenneth Grahame's *The Golden Age*.

In his preface, Clemens also writes, "most of the adventures in this book really occurred; one or two were experiences of my own, the rest those of boys who were schoolmates of mine." However, even though he drew heavily on autobiographical materials, he changed these for the purpose of the story. His shaping of the materials was influenced by literary fashions of the time. Clemens was aware of the humorous exaggeration used in the tall-tale, and of the moralistic Sunday School paper type of story widely read by children of his time. Tom Sawyer was a bad boy similar to those found in these papers; but he did not go to Hell; instead, he became a hero and ended up rich. Clemens also satirized the popular boys' adventure stories of the period. Tom enjoys playing at pirates and Indians and devises elaborate rules for his games because, he says, "It's so in all the books." Yet the violent incidents which happen around St. Petersburg are more dangerous, and require greater courage to confront, than those in the story books Tom often reads.

In addition to the humor and adventure,

The Adventures of Tom Sawyer explores several serious themes. Most important of these is the moral development of Tom himself. At the beginning he is an imaginative, self-centered, thoughtless boy. He is unconcerned that his episodes cause real anxiety for Aunt Polly, and when things do not go his way, he wishes he were dead so that those who treated him unjustly would suffer. However, when he sees Muff Potter unjustly framed for murder, Tom's conscience begins to bother him and he sneaks tobacco to the prisoner and later courageously decides to take the witness stand on behalf of the town drunk. In the cave, lost with Becky, the death Tom had often imagined becomes a real possibility and he acts clearly and courageously to save himself and Becky. He becomes a true hero.

Treasure Island

by Robert Louis Stevenson (1882).

Scottish writer Robert Louis Stevenson began creating *Treasure Island* by drawing a map of an island for the amusement of his stepson. As the chapters of the adventure novel were written, Stevenson read them aloud to both his father and his stepson, who both responded enthusiastically. Today the book is regarded as a classic of children's literature; many readers believe that it is one of the best adventure stories ever written.

Robinson Crusoe, as we have noted previously, established the basic pattern for the adventure story. A civilized character finds himself stranded on a desert island and must use all of his physical and mental resourcefulness to survive. In Crusoe's case and in many other *Robinsonades* besides, the central character subdues nature and civilizes the island. The virtues and values which enable the character to survive on the island also enable him to rejoin middle class society. Though *Treasure Island* resembles this basic structure, the book introduces significant ambiguities to the well-established conventions of the adventure story. Jim Hawkins' father is an innkeeper of the Admiral Benbow at the time when a fierce old seaman, Billy Bones, comes to the inn for lodging. Bones drinks, sings songs, and tells wild stories about his adventures. The tough old reprobate both terrifies and fascinates the fourteen-year-old Jim.

After some time has passed, Billy Bones is assailed by old comrades, who wish to steal his map which shows the location of an enormously valuable treasure. After an encounter with the villainous Black Dog, Bones has a stroke and confides the secret of his treasure to Jim Hawkins. Meanwhile Jim's father has become ill and has died. The adventures begin in earnest when another stroke kills Billy Bones.

Jim and his mother barely escape a gang of buccaneers who come to the Admiral Benbow to find Billy Bones' treasure map and money. Jim takes the map and confides in his adult friends, Dr. Livesay and Squire Trelawney. Captivated by the map and Jim's vivid tale, the squire immediately drops his other duties, outfits a ship, hires a captain and crew, takes on Dr. Livesay as ship's doctor and Jim as cabin boy, and departs for Treasure Island. One of the most colorful characters on board is the one-legged Long John Silver, who carries a parrot on his shoulder and serves as the ship's cook.

When the ship has almost reached Treasure Island, Jim, hiding in an apple barrel, learns that Long John Silver and many of the crew members are former mates of Billy Bones. With Silver as the leader, the group plans a mutiny as soon as the treasure has been found.

Once on the island, Jim Hawkins meets Ben Gunn, a former member of Captain Flint's crew, the same one in which Billy Bones had served. Ben Gunn has been marooned on the island for three years and is eager to assist Jim, the squire, and Dr. Livesay in defeating the mutineers. Jim Hawkins deserts his post and boards the *Hispaniola*, where he is forced to kill Israel Hands; he then hides the ship and returns to the island. After desperate and hairraising battles in which many men on both sides are killed, Trelawney, Livesay, Jim, and Ben Gunn load the treasure on the ship and depart with Long John Silver, who has joined the squire's side, having realized that his own cause is hopeless. At the first port, however, Silver escapes with some of the money, never to be heard from again.

Treasure Island exhibits several characteristic features of the romance: the young hero departs on a voyage, proves himself a hero in daring struggles, and returns home in triumph. At the same time Stevenson not only stresses the growth of Jim into manhood; he also stresses the retreat of the men into boyhood. Squire Trelawney and Dr. Livesay become like boys as they drop all of their responsibilities to embark upon the voyage in search of treasure. Once they have left their customary roles, they both prove to be highly ineffectual at sea and on the island. They must rely upon a boy and the childlike Ben Gunn to survive.

Stevenson also introduces considerable moral ambiguity in the compelling character of Long John Silver, who appears at first to be merely a stereotyped caricature of a fierce old seaman. The reader and Jim Hawkins actually see Silver murder a good man by stabbing him in the back. Yet "Barbecue," as the buccaneers nickname him, also saves Jim's life. Somehow the reader is glad along with Jim, the squire, and Dr. Livesay when Long John Silver escapes hanging and even steals part of the treasure.

Jim himself undergoes a change not altogether heroic. He also has to kill a man and see the corpse sink into the sea. In proving himself to be a man, Jim moves from innocence to painful experience; this initiation exacts an emotional penalty. William Blackburn has shown that Jim's three visions of the island — from pleasant daydream, to the frightful actual landscape, to the retrospective nightmare — essentially shape the structure of the novel and the pattern of Jim's adventure.[1] Unlike Robinson Crusoe's experience on an island, which reinforced the values needed to live successfully in British society, Jim's experience has demonstrated the ambiguous nature of moral codes. Jim succeeds because he breaks rules — he deserts his post and kills a man.

In other respects, too, Stevenson reshapes and reinterprets literary conventions. Having

1 William Blackburn, "Mirror in the Sea: *Treasure Island* and the Internalization of Juvenile Romance," *Children's Literature Association Quarterly*, 8 (Fall 1983), 10. See also Kathleen Blake, "The Sea-Dream: *Peter Pan* and *Treasure Island*," *Children's Literature*, 6 (1977), 165-81.

lost his own father, who appeared to be a weak and passive person at best, Jim clearly searches for a father in the wise old men, Squire Trelawney and Dr. Livesay, both of whom embody middle class virtues. But Jim discovers that the supposed wisdom of these men is utterly useless on the island. Instead, Long John Silver, the lovable scoundrel or rogue, offers his own kind of wisdom and practical knowledge. Likewise, Ben Gunn, who appears to be a parody of Robinson Crusoe, emerges as the archetype of the Holy Fool, the innocent and naive character who unexpectedly prevails against the much shrewder and more worldly-wise Long John Silver. Ben Gunn manages this feat by playing upon the superstitions of the seamen; thus Ben's intuitive, folk ways of knowing triumph over the rational ways of knowing represented by Dr. Livesay and Squire Trelawney. Jim Hawkins undergoes a sea change, but it is not an entirely happy one. Like Coleridge's Ancient Mariner, Jim returns wiser but sadder.

The Story of the Treasure Seekers

by E. Nesbit (1899).

Beginning in 1896, E. Nesbit, who had been publishing verse, gothic thrillers, and sentimental novels for many years began writing a series of articles entitled "My Schooldays," for *The Girl's Own Paper*, a children's magazine. Reaching back into her own childhood, Nesbit discovered the mode, audience, and style which were to make her a great children's writer. Soon thereafter Nesbit began to write a series of stories called *The Story of the Treasure Seekers* and to publish them throughout 1898 in the *Pall Mall* and the *Windsor* magazines. In 1899, the stories were collected and published as the first volume of the "Bastable" stories. *The Story of the Treasure Seekers* was followed by *The Wouldbegoods* (1901), and *The New Treasure Seekers* (1904). *Oswald Bastable and Others* (1905) also included a few Bastable adventures.

In *The Story of the Treasure Seekers* E. Nesbit establishes some important conventions to modern children's fiction. First, she depicts a group of children enjoying imaginative and exciting adventures on their own, apart from the supervision of adults. Critic Marcus Crouch calls this strategy "the Nesbit tradition," although other writers had provided Nesbit with the idea. Harry and Laura Graham of Catherine Sinclair's *Holiday House* (1839) also participate in rather abandoned excursions on their own. Similarly Mark Twain's Tom Sawyer enjoys his adventures with Joe Harper and Huck Finn on Cardiff Hill and Jackson's Island. Still, Nesbit's novel is the first to employ a child narrator for recounting these adventures. In adopting the device of the child narrator and addressing the child audience in a colloquial idiom, Nesbit comes much closer to capturing an authentic sense of the child's voice.

In *The Story of the Treasure Seekers* Nesbit also fuses the structure of the fairy tale with the texture of realistic stories, a strategy which she may have appropriated from nineteenth-century novelist Charles Dickens.

The Story of the Treasure Seekers concerns the attempts of the six Bastable children — Dora, Oswald, Dicky, Alice, Noel, and H.O. (Horace Octavius) — "to restore the fallen fortunes" of their family. The Bastables' mother has died, and their father has problems with his business. In the episodes of the novel, the children attempt in one way or another to earn money to solve the family's financial problems. These money-making schemes include digging for treasure, being detectives, bandits, and editors, selling a foul-tasting sherry, and using a divining rod to locate treasure. Most of these schemes end in comic chaos. Noel, the poet, however, does succeed in selling his poetry to an editor, but the Bastables' financial problems are finally solved when a wealthy maternal uncle comes to the rescue. The final scene in the novel occurs in the uncle's mansion, as the family enjoys a bounteous Christmas dinner. Oswald, the narrator, defends this ending, while admitting that it does resemble a fairy tale or a Dickens novel.

One of the most interesting features of the novel is its child narrator, who pretends to hide his identity. Before long, however, the reader realizes that the narrator is Oswald. Rather conceited accounts of Oswald's deeds, as well as the narrator's habit of lapsing into first person when recounting Oswald's experiences quickly give the secret away. Throughout the novel Nesbit dramatizes Oswald as a child author in the process of discovering his craft. He makes the reader conscious of his narrative choices —selection of incident, choices of diction, aspects of description, etc. In introducing the process of writing the novel as a major theme, Nesbit produces one of the few examples of *metafiction* in children's literature; that is, a novel about the writing of a novel. Her purpose in this strategy may be to define herself as a new and modern kind of children's writer.

Another significant theme of *The Story of the Treasure Seekers* is its emphasis upon the child's reading. Books become a major way whereby Nesbit's child characters order their games and experience. Many of the chapter titles are actually taken from children's books. Nesbit underscores the importance of reading in the child's ability to function socially. For example, the Bastables' friend, Albert-next-door, does not know how to play because he has not read many books.

The reader of Nesbit's classic acquires a vivid sense of setting and of characters. The children live in a shabbily comfortable, semi-detached house in Lewisham. Oswald is not always fair, however, when delineating the characters of his brothers and sisters. His elder sister, Dora, for example, is apt to talk like the "good elder sister in books." The reader, though, comes to know the characters better than Oswald does. In this way Nesbit directs irony at her child narrator; the author, Nesbit, thus makes her presence felt in the tension between the narrator and the tale that he narrates. Oswald (according to his own account) is brave, fearless, inventive, forthright, and resourceful. He makes every attempt to be fair; vanity is his greatest flaw. Dicky is the most practical-minded of the children, while Noel emerges as the poet and dreamer who occupies his own sphere. Alice, however, is perhaps the most vibrant character in all of Nesbit's fiction. Even Oswald admits that she is a "brick," that she never minds playing boys' parts and never sneaks. H.O., the youngest, does not figure prominently in the first Bastable volume

but becomes more important in the later volumes.

The children's father is not an unsympathetic character, but he is preoccupied with business and rarely sees his children. The most sympathetic adults are Mrs. Leslie, the poet who is clearly modeled on Nesbit herself, and Albert's uncle, a writer who gives Oswald advice and talks "like a book."

Anne of Green Gables

by L.M. Montgomery (1908).

The best-known fictional heroine in Canadian Children's Literature is a skinny, freckle-faced orphan who possesses a very active imagination, a fiery temper, a big heart, and not a little insecurity. She is Anne Shirley, the central figure of *Anne of Green Gables*, the creation of L.M. Montgomery, a native of Prince Edward Island, and at the time, a fairly successful writer of short stories, poems, and other magazine pieces. The idea for the novel came when Montgomery noticed an old jotting in her journal: "Elderly couple apply to orphan asylum for a boy. By mistake a girl is sent them." She wrote the book in 1904 and 1905, and sent it to four publishers, all of whom rejected it. She revised it two years later, submitted it to the Boston firm of L. C. Page, and in 1908, it was published. The book was an immediate success and has been popular ever since.

The opening sentence of *Anne of Green Gables* symbolizes the life of the young heroine: "Mrs. Rachel Lynde lived just where Avonlea main road dipped down into a little hollow, fringed with alders and ladies' eardrops and traversed by a brook that had its source way back in the woods of the old Cuthbert place; it was reputed to be an intricate, head-long brook in its course through these woods, with dark secrets of pool and cascade; but by the time it reached Lynde's Hollow, it was a quiet, well conducted little stream, for not even a brook could run past Mrs. Lynde's door without due regard for decency and decorum . . ." Anne is somewhat impulsive and rash at the book's beginning; at the end, she has matured, and comes to accept and adapt to her social role. She has found the place where she belongs. No longer is she Anne Shirley, the orphan; she is Anne of Green Gables. The various incidents in the novel indicate the stages of her growth.

Anne's compulsive chatter to Matthew Cuthbert as they ride back from the train station reveals her insecurities; her renaming of the areas they travel through reveals her rich imaginative powers; and her outburst against Mrs. Lynde betrays her temper. However, when Marilla tells her that she can stay at Green Gables, the first phase of her socialization is complete. As she gratefully exclaims: "It's a million times nicer to be Anne of Green Gables than to be Anne of nowhere in particular."

She soon meets friends, or "kindred spirits" as she calls them, but she experiences difficulties, many of them humorous. As she tells her best friend Diana Berry: "There's such a lot of different Anne's in me. I sometimes think that is why I'm such a troublesome person. If I was just the one Anne it would be so much more comfortable, but then it wouldn't be half so interesting." Angry, she breaks her slate over Gilbert Blythe's head when he teases her about the color of her hair; over-imaginative, she frightens herself walking through what she calls the "Haunted Wood"; and vain, she mistakenly dyes her hair green.

But Anne is not always making mistakes; she is good, honest, and responsible. Although Mrs. Barry, because Anne inadvertently gets her daughter drunk, has refused to allow the two girls to see each other, Anne holds no grudges, and heroically saves one of the Barry children from a near fatal attack of croup. Her most responsible act takes place after Matthew has died and Marilla considers selling Green Gables. Anne unhesitatingly gives up the college scholarship she has won and takes a local teaching job so that Marilla can keep her home.

One of Anne's greatest achievements is her ability to influence the older people who surround her. Not long after the girl's arrival at Green Gables, Marilla notes, "I can't imagine the place without her." Anne not only wins her way into the hearts of the lonely Marilla and Matthew, she also gains the approval of Rachel Lynde and makes a friend of Diana's fiesty Aunt Josephine.

The continued popularity of *Anne of Green Gables* can be attributed to four aspects of the novel. Most important is the character of Anne herself: she is a fresh, original creation who does not fit the conventional mold of the girl heroine of late nineteenth century fiction. Second, she is surrounded by a memorable cast of characters, particularly the adults. Third, she is placed in a setting which comes to life because the author has wisely allowed the reader to see it through the wondering, imaginative eyes of the young heroine. Finally, Montgomery has taken these elements and unobtrusively shaped them into a classic fairy tale pattern: the story of the lonely, unwanted orphan who finds happiness and security in a new home.

The Wind in the Willows
by Kenneth Grahame (1908).

The Wind in the Willows grew out of a series of bedtime stories which Grahame invented for his four-year-old son, Alistair. Although this animal fantasy was not nearly as widely acclaimed as Grahame's previously published books about childhood, *The Golden Age* (1895) and *Dream Days* (1898), had been, the book eventually became a classic that remains popular, the novel having gone through over one hundred editions. Such artists as Ernest Shepard, Arthur Rackham, Tasha Tudor, and, most recently, Michael Hague, have been inspired to illustrate the book.

The story really focuses upon two young heroes and their development. Mole leaves his underground home for a more adventurous life in the upper world one spring day. Toad, the conceited and immature heir to the ancestral Toad Hall, pursues a yet more wildly adventurous life in the "wide world" in his mad obsession for "poop-pooping" motor cars. When he finally steals a car, Toad finds himself locked in a sturdy jail with only the jailor's daughter to befriend him.

The settings of *The Wind in the Willows* are centrally important. First, Grahame presents an orderly pastoral world in the River Bank, the home of Mole's beloved friend, Ratty. Animals live peacefully in this area, basking in the beauties of nature and the river. Near the placid order of the River Bank is the wild wood, a place where the animals and nature appear far more threatening. The animals are disorderly and lawless. Ratty warns Mole that the ferrets and stoats cannot be trusted. Square in the center of the wild wood lives the gruff but fatherly Badger safe in his undergound home with its stores of food. Badger's home has tunnels connecting it to the Wide World, the River Bank, and Toad Hall. Each of the animals knows and accepts his place. Toad, however, lacks the maturity to recognize his true home; he is drawn into dangerous adventures in the Wide World.

One of the most prominent features of the novel is the exquisite tension the characters feel between a love of home with its familiar pleasure and the urgent need to adventure in exotic spots far from home. Mole and Rat both experience this conflict. Mole's determination to embark upon a new way of life receives much attention in the novel. Eventually Mole synthesizes what he learns from Ratty and Badger and becomes a true hero when he saves Toad Hall from the ferrets and weasels. Mole thus appropriates the best of pastoral and romantic values and is the foil of Toad's uncontrolled and obsessive fantasies. At its several significant levels of meaning, *The Wind in the Willows* investigates the uses of romance, imagination, play, and escape.

Some critics have complained that Grahame's animal fantasy is structurally divided between the adventures of Rat and Mole on one hand and those of Toad on the other. They also note that the woodland scene of Pan is unrelated to other scenes in the book. In this scene, near the center of the book, Mole and Rat participate in a visionary experience when they hear the sweet notes of Pan's pipes and catch a fleeting glimpse of the kind woodland deity cradling the baby otter in his feet. The scene seems to celebrate not a transcendent vision but a joyous acceptance of nature itself. Grahame's mystical hymn to Pan informs both Rat's need for pastoral tranquillity and Toad's need for adventure. Because this vision informs Rat and Mole's way of life, they are able to enjoy life as it is and to imagine life as it might be lived. The result is a balance between the absolute and timeless stasis of Pan's power and the chaotic movement in the Wide World, a felicitous blend of reality and romance.

One important way that Grahame contrasts the two ways of life represented by the Rat-Mole episodes and the Toad adventures is through his use of language. The language used to describe the experiences of Rat and Mole is lyrical, while that recounting Toad's mad adventures is self-consciously literary and mock-heroic. Toad is presented as an actor. Since he is a child, he must practice various fantasy identities until he finally learns to submerge his need for adventure and to express it in the secrecy of his bedroom where he composes little verses in his own honor. Some readers remain unconvinced that Toad is truly reformed. He may well be practicing one more disguise, Toad the Respectable Gentleman of Property.

The Wind in the Willows, then, attests to an elusive desire in the human spirit that keeps it forever yearning — a vague but sweetly beautiful note, half-heard in the wind among the reeds. (This quality of the book places it squarely in the company of other British literature of the period; William Butler Yeat's *The Wind Among the Reeds* expresses similar longings.) Toad represents romance gone wrong and out of control. Mr. Badger in his formidable underground fortress clearly cuts himself off from romance. In between strict confinement and reckless adventure are Ratty and Toad.

The Secret Garden

by Frances Hodgson Burnett (1911).

The Secret Garden remains a popular realist work for children which incorporates elements of the moral tale, folktale, and the pastoral,[1] to reveal Mary Lennox's growth from a sour, unhealthy, and introverted girl to an independent healthy child capable of helping her in-

1 See Phyllis Bixler Koppes, "Tradition and the Individual Talent of Frances Hodgson Burnett's *The Secret Garden*," *Children's Literature*, 7 (1970), 191-207. Koppes explores these forms thoroughly in several of Burnett's children's stories.

valid cousin to overcome physical handicaps and self-pity.

In the opening scene of the novel, the reader learns that Mary Lennox is the daughter of a British Army captain stationed in India. Mary's vain mother cares little for her unattractive child and has turned Mary over to Indian servants. Mary's "ayah" has spoiled her until she is disliked by everyone. Mary shows little interest in anything outside herself, other than gardens and story books. Frequently incidents remind the child of fairy tales she has read.

A crisis descends upon Mary's home with an outbreak of cholera. Neglected by the panicky servants and forgotten by everyone, Mary plays in a little plot of earth, where she tries to make a garden by sticking scarlet blossoms into the soil. This provocative scene introduces Burnett's complex symbolic use of the garden as a unifying device of the novel. At this point in Mary's development, her experience has provided her with no "roots" from which she may grow. Her little play garden is doomed to wilt and to die; unless conditions in her life change, Mary is unlikely to bud or to blossom at all.

Mary sleeps through the terrible mass death resulting from the outbreak of cholera. Army officers find her after her parents and the servants have died; she is alone in this house of death, except for a little snake with "jewellike" eyes. Although critics have interpreted this snake as analogous to the serpent in the garden of Eden, it may have richer and more suggestive meanings. In India snakes are sacred; more important, they are often kept in bedrooms to keep the rats away. Thus, rather than representing evil, the snake may well represent the potential of the natural world for good or evil. It also represents survival, since rats often carry disease. In the course of the book nature turns out to be the agent of magic. In this first chapter Mary's connection with this creature of nature may well have saved her from death.

Mary, unhappy and orphaned, stays with a British clergyman's family for a short while before she departs for England. Unable to get on with the clergyman's children, she continues to play at making gardens. Because she is so unpleasant and unfriendly, the children tease her with the nursery rhyme chant, "Mistress Mary, Quite Contrary, How does your garden grow?" These early appearances of the garden foreshadow the role that the secret garden is to play in healing both Mary and her cousin Colin.

At last Mary arrives in England, where she is met by the stern housekeeper of Misselthwaite Manor, Mrs. Medlock. As Mary travels by train to her uncle's Yorkshire estate, Mrs. Medlock tells her that her hunchbacked uncle had married a lovely young woman but that he had secluded himself in his grief since the wife's death. The story reminds Mary of a fairy tale she has heard, Perrault's "Riquet a la Houppe," the tale about a hunchback married to a lovely princess, who is transformed into a handsome prince by the love of his wife. This allusion foreshadows the fairy-tale like transformation of Mary's invalid cousin Colin.

Once established at Misselthwaite Manor, Mary's growth begins in earnest. The friendly Yorkshire maid, Martha Sowerby, refuses to spoil Mary and insists that she dress herself, eat heartily, and play vigorously outdoors. Martha further enchants Mary with stories about the Sowerby family. The child is particularly intrigued by what she hears of Martha's twelve-year-old Dickon. Martha arouses Mary's curiosity even more about the tragic story of Mrs. Craven's death in the secret garden. Mary is intrigued to learn that the garden has been closed since the death and the key buried.

In the gardens of Misselthwaite Manor Mary meets the crusty gardener Ben Weatherstaff and a friendly robin, who lives in the secret garden. Ben is outwardly crusty but inwardly kind. A "Wise Old Man," Ben possesses the wisdom and knowledge of the folk and of nature. He is highly reminiscent of the crotchety, complaining servant Joseph in Emily Bronte's *Wuthering Heights*; his comic, gruff manners and use of dialect are qualities Ben shares with Joseph. Similarly Dickon and Mother Sowerby are close to the earth. Dickon plays his pipes and engages with Mary in the secret gardening necessary to bring the place back to life; he has been compared by critics to both Pan and to Hermes.[2] Like Pan, Dickon is close to nature; wild things respond to him and trust him. Like Hermes, he is full of tricks and also serves as a messenger.

Eventually the friendly robin helps Mary to find the key to the secret garden. The suspense which Burnett creates before Mary actually discovers the garden is a strong narrative feature which most child readers find memorable. With Dickon's help, she brings the dead garden back to life, just as the garden brings her to life. Like Sleeping Beauty, she is awakened, but Nature, not the prince, brings her to life.[3] Also Mary eventually brings the prince to life within the garden.

Critics have remarked that *The Secret Garden* contains some elements of the gothic romance and have compared it in particular to *Wuthering Heights* and *Jane Eyre*. One feature reminiscent of *Wuthering Heights* is the mysterious human cry which echoes pathetically in the corridors of Misselthwaite and causes the servants to look uncomfortable when Mary questions them about it. Once the suspense regarding the entry into the secret garden has been satisfied, the mystery of the cry remains to be disclosed. Mary discovers her hunchbacked invalid cousin Colin, who is just as spoiled and unpleasant as she had been when she arrived at Misselthwaite Manor. Colin also experiences the natural "magic" of the garden. In the final scene Colin has become the handsome young prince able to run to meet his father — his father has returned to England after dreaming that his dead wife was calling him back. This detail is reminiscent of both the fairy tale "Beauty and the Beast," when a dream warns Beauty to return to her dying beast, and of the function of dreams in *Jane Eyre*.

In her article "Quite Contrary: Frances Hodgson Burnett's *The Secret Garden*," Elizabeth Keyser argues that "As Mary becomes less disagreeable, she becomes, after a certain point,

less interesting. And Colin, as he becomes more agreeable in some ways, becomes something of a prig and a bore."[4] As Colin "grows up," Keyser suggests, Mary "grows down." The novel at least to some extent affirms patriarchal power; Colin eventually wins a foot race with Mary. In the final scene Mary is missing altogether. Inevitably, the orphaned Mary must assume second place to the heir of Misselthwaite Manor.

Structurally the novel resembles a romantic comedy. Like many fairy tales, the book ends on a note of rebirth and renewal within a natural green, sheltered setting. With both Mary and Colin having regained their health, the future of Misselthwaite Manor no longer belongs to the rather sinister Mrs. Medlock and Colin's dour physician. Youth, health, and nature (along with patriarchal power) prevail, even though Burnett does appear to turn the book over to Colin.[5]

4 *Ibid.*, 3.

5 See Phyllis Bixler, *Frances Hodgson Burnett* (Boston: Twayne Publishers, 1984) for further study.

The Hobbit

by J.R.R. Tolkien (1937).

During the 1930s, J.R.R. Tolkien, a respected professor of English at Oxford University, often marked school examination papers to provide money for his growing family. Later he recalled an experience which occurred while he was marking: "One of the candidates had mercifully left one of the pages with no writing on it . . . and I wrote on it: *In a hole in the ground there lived a hobbit*. Names always generate a story in my mind. Eventually I thought I'd better find out what hobbits were like. But that's only the beginning." That sentence became the first sentence in Tolkien's children's classic *The Hobbit*.

Published in 1937, the book embodied many of Tolkien's interests: his life-long fascination with languages, his knowledge of the literatures of medieval England and northern Europe, his hobby of inventing languages and creating mythologies to accompany them, and his habit of writing stories to be read to his

2 I am indebted to Roderick McGillis's article on *The Secret Garden*, published in *Studies of the Literary Imagination*, Fall, 1985. McGillis interprets the presence of the snake differently, however. I am also indebted to Professor McGillis for the comparison of Dickon to Hermes. Koppes compares Dickon to Pan in her article.

3 Elizabeth Keyser, "Quite Contrary: Frances Hodgson Burnett's *The Secret Garden*," *Children's Literature*, 11 (1983), 1-13.

children and such university colleagues as C.S. Lewis.

The hero of *The Hobbit* is Bilbo Baggins, a middle aged, comfortable, and relatively ordinary individual who is shaken from his lethargy when the wizard Gandalf virtually forces him to join a band of dwarves who wish to reclaim a treasure held by the dragon Smaug. The story describes not only Bilbo's adventures, but also his inner growth. At the beginning of his travels, he is bumbling and insecure and often wishes that he were in the secure confines of his hobbit-hole. However, when he is separated from his companions deep within a cavern, he discovers a ring: "It was a turning point in his career, but he did not know it." It is a ring of invisibility and with it he escapes from Gollum, a cannibalistic subterranean creature for whom Bilbo feels both fear and pity

Bilbo, who had not really been accepted by the dwarves, earns their respect when he helps them escape from enormous and venomous spiders: "They saw that he had some wits, as well as luck and a magic ring—and all three were useful possessions." He later frees the dwarves from the prison of the wood-elves, and, when, at last, they discover the lair of the dragon, he is the one who ventures forward to confront it: "Going on from there was the bravest thing he ever did . . . He fought the real battle in that tunnel alone, before he ever saw the vast danger that lay in wait."

Although Bilbo is knocked unconscious during the great battle in which the evil goblins and wolves confront the elves, men, and dwarves, he is instrumental in creating unity among the latter groups. In the dragon's cave he had taken the Arkenstone coveted by the dwarves; now he offers it to the wood-elves as a means of buying harmony between them and the dwarves.

Throughout his experiences, Bilbo is what critic Diana Waggoner has called a "low-mimetic hero," an ordinary person who rises to the occasion when necessary. Tolkien's biographer, Humphrey Carpenter, has said that the hobbits, especially Bilbo, represent what the author most admired about the English: their ability to shake themselves from their average life when they must. However, at the end of the novel, when Bilbo has returned to his home, the Wizard Gandalf does not allow him to become too proud: "You are only quite a little fellow in a wide world after all."

Although *The Hobbit* is told for children, it has serious undertones. Tolkien himself remarked: "Mr. Baggins began as a comic tale among conventional and inconsistent Grimms fairy-tale dwarves, and got drawn into the edge of it—so that even Sauron the terrible [the evil figure of *Lord of the Rings*] peeped over the edge. And what more can hobbits do? They can be comic, but their comedy is suburban unless it is set against things more elemental." The power of *The Hobbit* arises from the implied seriousness. An ordinary individual is placed in situations in which he must rise above his normal life and must prove his courage, not only to insure his own survival, but also the survival of all of his friends. This survival involves confronting evil forces such as Smaug the dragon, a creature whom those with less inner potential than Bilbo possesses would flee from in terror.

Charlotte's Web

by E.B. White (1952).

The story of the pig Wilbur and his spider friend Charlotte, *Charlotte's Web*, has been acclaimed for E.B. White's subtle blending of realistic description and imaginary adventures, and for his balance of a wide variety of moods from humor to pathos.

Although White wrote *Charlotte's Web* over a three-year period preceding 1952, the roots of the story go back to 1938 when he purchased a farm in Maine. Over the years he observed the barnyard animals carefully and reports that, while carrying slops to a pig one day, he realized he was making the animal healthy only to slaughter it in the fall. Feeling guilty, he determined to write a tale in which a pig would be saved. In 1948, he published in *Atlantic Monthly* a touching essay entitled "Death of a Pig," in which he described how moved he was by the illness and subsequent death of a barnyard animal. On his farm, White carefully observed the web weaving and egg laying of an Arenea Cavatica spider. He now had the ingredients for what he has called his "story of friendship and salvation on a farm." Realistic observation and imaginative narrative were blended; as White remarked: "*Charlotte's Web* . . . is, of course, a web of fantasy, but the web itself is structurally accurate."

About the novel, White also wrote, "*Charlotte's Web* is a tale of the animals in my barn, not of the people in my life. When you read it just relax." The book reflects the author's joy in his farm, contains many simply expressed emotions, and much of its success arises from the implicit aspects of characterization and theme. Charlotte and Wilbur, the central figures, are fully developed characters. The spider does not change, but, as the story develops, Wilbur, and along with him the reader, learns about the amazing depths of her personality. On first meeting her, Wilbur is somewhat revolted by her method of gathering food, but he comes to appreciate her patience, wisdom, cleverness, and pragmatic nature. Most of all, he learns that she is a totally unselfish friend. She was, Wilbur says, "brilliant, beautiful, and loyal to the end." Her web is a symbol of herself: spun from within, it is both beautiful and useful; glistening in the morning dew, it catches the flies she needs and contains the words she has woven to save Wilbur's life. White refers to the "miracle of the web." It is a double miracle, representing the wonders of both nature and loyal friendship.

Wilbur matures greatly. Early in the story, he is bored, lonely, and terrified of his mortality; he is a self-centered child. However, Charlotte's faith in him brings out his better qualities and, like the words in the web, he progressively becomes some pig, terrific, radiant, and, most important, humble, recognizing the great role played by Charlotte in his life. He too understands the meaning of friendship, taking Charlotte's 514 eggs back to the barn and revering her memory in the years that follow.

The barnyard is the novel's central setting. Not only is it realistically described, but also, as in George Orwell's *Animal Farm* and Roger Duvoisin's Petunia books, it is presented as a miniature world. There is a cross-section of character types ranging from Templeton the rat, who is completely self-centered, to Charlotte, who is completely selfless. Mr. Zuckerman and the other human adults are totally ethnocentric. Young Fern is the only child who is sensitive to the world of the animals, listening quietly, but never entering into their conversations. However, this relationship does not last, for as the summer wanes, she transfers her interests to Henry Fussy, and by midwinter, she seems to have forgotten the miracle she witnessed.

The book treats many themes, including the vanity of self-centeredness, the nature of true and false pride, and the quality of friendship. The most significant theme considers the inevitability of change and the reality of death in the ongoing cycle of the seasons. The book begins and ends with spring and, at various intervals, lyrical passages describe the movement toward fall and the changes this movement brings. During this time, Wilbur and Fern mature, and Charlotte moves closer to her death. However, unlike the prospect of Wilbur's possible slaughter, which Fern called "the most terrible case of unjustice I ever heard of", and Charlotte, "the dirtiest trick I ever heard of," Charlotte's death is part of the natural cycle and must be accepted. Wilbur learns to accept change, but equally important, he learns to reverse the memory of the greatest moments of his past, his times with Charlotte. He keeps these eternal amidst change.

A Wrinkle in Time

by Madeleine L'Engle (1962).

At the time she was writing her Newbery Medal-winning novel *A Wrinkle in Time*, Madeleine L'Engle reported that she was "trying to discover a theology by which I could live, because I *had* learned that I cannot live in a universe where there is no hope." In her earlier novels, she wrote, she had considered "the child in everybody, that part of us that is aware and open and courageous. It's also a part of us that isn't afraid to explore the mythical depth, that vast part of ourselves we know little about, and which we often fear because we do not know how to manipulate or control it." *A Wrinkle in Time* embodies both of these beliefs. In it, a young girl travels through the universe to rescue her father from great evil forces and, in the process, develops self-worth and self-knowledge.

The moral and psychological elements of the story are presented using symbols from folktales, mythology, and science fiction. For example, the three old ladies, Mrs. Who, Mrs, Which, and Mrs. Whatsit, are like fairy godmothers, giving magical gifts to Meg Murry, her brother Charles Wallace, and her friend, Calvin. They are also beings of great spiritual powers, using the powers of goodness and light in their struggles against those of evil and darkness. They are like gods or guardian angels. Finally, like many characters of science fiction, they are beings of vastly superior mental ability, able to understand theoretical problems incomprehensible to their earthly friends.

Meg's quest has affinities to themes found in hero tales and myths from around the world. Like Telemachus in the *Odyssey* or the Boy in Gerald McDermott's *Arrow to the Sun*, she is searching for her father. Like them, she is also searching for a sense of self-respect and self-worth. Although she is supported by the three old ladies and accompanied by her brother and friend, she must face the greatest challenges and dangers alone.

At the opening of *A Wrinkle in Time*, Meg is dissatisfied with her life. She has a genius five-year-old brother and two disgustingly average and efficient eleven-year-old brothers. She is doing poorly at school and gets into fights. Because she wears glasses and braces and has unmanageable hair, she feels hopelessly drab next to her beautiful scientist mother. And worst of all, her father, a famous scientist at work on a secret government project, has suddenly disappeared. The first stage of Meg's development occurs when the three old ladies take her, her brother, and Calvin, through the galaxy in search of her father. Before they arrive at Camazotz, the evil planet on which he is imprisoned, they learn that a dark cloud is invading the galaxy and threatens Earth. She must be one of a long line of individuals who have courageously fought against its evil.

On Camazotz, Meg discovers the nature of the evil: the planet has been transformed into a place of mindless conformity by a large, dis-

embodied brain called IT. L'Engle has written that "the brain tends to be vicious when not informed by the heart." Such is the case here; deviant behavior is swiftly corrected through painful reconditioning. After Charles Wallace's mind has been possessed by IT, Meg discovers her father, and, in a scene not unlike that in which Julie meets her father in *Julie of the Wolves*, learns that he is helpless to solve her problems.

It is appropriate that the title of the chapter following this revelation should be entitled "Absolute Zero." Taken to the planet Ixchel, Meg lies in a semi-coma, filled with bitterness, anger, and impatience toward her father, who, she feels, has failed her. She has reached her lowest emotional state in the novel. Now, the process of her real education begins. She must look inward to exorcise her faults and rediscover the love she possesses in her soul. Only now is she able to return to Camazotz to rescue her brother.

She must make the trip alone, without Mrs. Which to hold her hand, but with three gifts: Mrs. Whatsit's love, Mrs. Who's words about God's faith in the courage of the apparently weak of the world, and Mrs. Which's promise that Meg will find an inner strength that IT does not possess. What she discovers is the ability to love. And with this recognition, she is able to rescue Charles Wallace and complete her circular journey. At the end of the novel, reunited at home with her family, she has become stronger and more accepting of herself.

Julie of the Wolves

by Jean Craighead George (1972).

While researching an article on Arctic wolves, Jean Craighead George, a respected writer of nature books for children, saw a young Eskimo girl walking alone in the streets of Barrow, Alaska. George began thinking of the girl's life, imagining the conflicts she might have felt between traditional and modern life styles. These thoughts were combined with her studies of wolves in *Julie of the Wolves*, the story of a girl who is lost on the tundra and befriends a pack of wolves that help her to survive the winter.

In addition to being an accurate picture of the lives of Arctic wolves and a moving portrayal of the social problems experienced by many Native North Americans, *Julie of the Wolves* embodies two widely used literary traditions: the survival story and the pastoral lament for the passing of a simpler, purer way of life. Since the time of Daniel Defoe's *Robinson Crusoe*, novels depicting an isolated individual's efforts to survive in hostile, unfamiliar environments have been a staple of children's literature. With few material resources, the heroes of these books use ingenuity and great courage to produce the necessities of food, shelter, and clothing, and are finally reunited with their own people. In addition, they display great psychological strength to combat loneliness and fear. By remembering the lessons taught her by her father, a man wise in the old Eskimo ways, Julie survives physically and psychologically.

Pastoral literature is based on contrasts. On one side is a sullied, artificial, complex, urban world characterized by progress, greed, anxiety, and tension. On the other side is a natural, pure, and calm rural world marked by truth, tranquility, contentment, and innocence. The central action involves the withdrawal of a character from the urban to the rural world, and the inevitable return to the urban one. The departure is caused by dissatisfaction with the urban world. However, just when happiness seems to have been achieved, the urban, modern world breaks in, destroying the sense of peace and fulfillment. Progress cannot be avoided; to attempt to escape permanently would be an unhealthy refusal to accept reality. The return is marked by sadness, but also wisdom.

In *Julie of the Wolves*, the opposites are the gussak, or twentieth century civilized world, and the ages old, but fast disappearing Eskimo world. The civilized world is represented by the town of Barrow. Just as the physical influence of civilization on the Arctic cannot be destroyed, so too the psychological marks it makes on Eskimo society cannot be changed. TV dinners and drunkenness, quonset huts and electric stoves have replaced a life lived according to the rhythms of the land. The

novel focusses on the growth of Julie's character as she reacts to the two different worlds.

The golden age of the heroine's childhood was spent at the Nunivak Island seal camp, where her father hunted in the old ways, and she participated in the traditional ceremonies. However, after she is forced to move to Barrow to attend a government school, Julie becomes ashamed of her heritage and decides to run away to San Francisco, home of her pen pal and symbol of everything she feels is wonderful about civilization.

As she crosses the tundra in an attempt to reach Point Hope to catch a ship to San Francisco, her attitudes to the old and new ways gradually change. These changes are reflected in her thoughts about the wolves she encounters and eventually lives with. She constantly compares the leader of the pack to her father, and she understands that, like the old Eskimoes, the wolves live in harmony with the land. She reaches a point where she sees the landscape across which she is traveling as ideal, spiritually and physically. She has entered the pastoral world. However, this world cannot last in this life, and, even as Julie achieves it, it begins to fade. The civilized world breaks into the tundra; an airplane flies over the pack, its occupants shoot wantonly, killing the leader, Amaroq.

There is a brief period of false hope and happiness for Julie. Later in the winter, she discovers that her father, whom she had believed dead, is alive. She decides to join him and relive the old days of the seal camp. She will teach the children of his village the values of the old ways and will work with him to save the wolves. Entering his house, she experiences her final and greatest disappointment. Her father has married a white woman, his house is completely modernized, and he takes tourists bounty hunting in his plane. Civilization has destroyed him and he is now destroying the natural world. The victory of the forces of progress is complete. Julie now realizes that she cannot escape these forces and faces the grim future of life in civilization with her father.

The pastoral tradition is an appropriate one for the type of novel Jean George writes. Creating a juvenile book, she has examined the difficult and painful transition from the golden age of childhood to the fallen and complex world of adulthood. Such a passage is disillusioning and there are many ironies; such is the nature of adolescence. The past cannot be recaptured, as pastoral literature makes very clear. The greatest courage is found in the character's ability to learn from the past and to accept the reality of the present, unpleasant though it may be.

The Slave Dancer

by Paula Fox (1973).

Paula Fox's superbly crafted *The Slave Dancer*, winner of the Newbery Medal for 1974, is an historical novel set in 1840. The young protagonist, Jessie Bollier, is kidnapped from his home in New Orleans, where he lives with his mother and sister, and placed aboard *The Moonlight*, a slave ship commanded by the slightly mad Captain Cawthorne. Once aboard the slaver, Jessie is initiated into an awareness of evil. As most young heroes in literature are tested, so Jessie undergoes a moral test. Forced to play his fife while captured Africans shuffle in a pathetic and grotesque dance, Jessie comes close to hating them. In an intense moment of recognition, Jessie realizes his kinship with the slaves, especially with the African boy, Ras.

When the ship is wrecked in the Gulf of Mexico, only Jessie and Ras survive. Crouched in the dark hold of the ship, the boys are at last cast up on a Mississippi beach, where they are helped by a wise old man, Daniel. This wise fatherly figure sends Ras north to freedom and Jessie home to New Orleans. Ironically, Daniel cannot see beyond Jessie's white skin. Though Daniel helps Jessie, he cannot give him the affection which he directs towards Ras.

Once home, Jessie realizes that he cannot come to terms with his experience. After the encounter with the evil of slavery, Jessie finds himself alienated from home, even from the music which he had loved.

Fox's novel represents historical fiction at its best. All of the historical and nautical details are meticulously researched. But more important, Fox communicates intensely and powerfully what it was to be conscious in this dark era of American history. Through an exploration of character, she dramatically demonstrates the motives of greed and power that made slavery possible. Part of the novel's effect upon the reader is achieved because the author sets up expectations and reverses them drastically. A circular journey featuring a young hero leads the reader to expect that the young man will grow from his experiences, that he will return home more mature and confident in every way. Jessie, however, encounters what Joseph Conrad called "the heart of darkness," the incomprehensible evil at the core of humanity in which all human beings participate. Though Jessie refuses to say Yes to slavery, as every other crew member on *The Moonlight* has done, he is in many respects broken, disillusioned, and embittered by his quest.

In his experiences on board *The Moonlight*, Jessie encounters several manifestations of evil in the characters of the crew. Clay Purvis, the rough Irishman, treats Jessie with gruff kindness, yet he has justified slavery with a process of rationalization. Since Irish immigrants have had to suffer, Purvis somehow believes that the sufferings of the Africans are justified. Captain Cawthorne's motives appear to be based upon his enormous greed for material wealth. The most terrifying character on board the ship is Ben Stout, who announces the theme of the book early in the novel when he tells Jessie, "You'll see some bad things, but if you didn't see them, they'd still be happening so you might as well."

Fox's novel reveals the emotional needs of its young narrator with psychological insight. In the opening chapter the reader learns that Jessie's father had drowned when the boy was only four. Years later, Jessie still imagines his father's drowning and wishes fervently that he could somehow save the lost parent. Confined in a female world of sewing, Jessie visits the slave market against his mother's warning. A central dimension of Jessie's quest, his motive for prowling these forbidden streets is the archetypal search for the father. One of the reasons for Jessie's disillusionments is his failure to find a satisfactory father. All of the adult characters Jessie meets prove to be false fathers, even the wise and kindly Daniel.

Paula Fox's ability to capture so vividly the ambience of life aboard a slave ship, her concentrated and highly poetic language, and her capacity to render her story with both historical accuracy and emotional power contribute to the literary excellence of *The Slave Dancer*, a courageous book for the young which defies the strong convention of the happy ending in a children's book.

M.C. Higgins the Great

by Virginia Hamilton (1974).

Virginia Hamilton's most critically acclaimed novel, *M.C. Higgins the Great* explores its central character's attempts to come to terms with his past and to deal with terrifying and confusing aspects of the present. Winner of the Newbery Medal, the National Book Award, and the *Boston-Globe Horn Book* Award, the novel examines the complex relationship between M.C. and his father, a proud and sometimes overbearing patriarch, who nevertheless finds himself unable to protect his home and family from an enormous spoil heap, the result of strip-mining operations on Sarah's Mountain. Ultimately Jones acquires enough maturity to learn from his son. The final scene celebrates the cooperation of father, son, and neighbor to protect their home from destruction.

In Hamilton's complex and densely textured novel, plot is subordinated to intense character analysis, and the novel's structure essentially depends upon Hamilton's skillful handling of oppositions. M.C. loves his home on Sarah's Mountain. The past seems almost more alive to him than the present. In his mind's eye, he can vividly picture his ancestor, Sarah, moving in and out of the mist with a baby in her arms. This presence sometimes seems so vivid to him that he feels as if Sarah is alive and that he, M.C., is the ghost.

M.C. realizes the danger of the spoil heap and knows that it is slipping gradually toward his home. In his cave-like bedroom he has nightmares of suffocation. He creates fantasies of escape. He has heard of a "dude," who wishes to tape record Banina Higgins's singing. M.C. imagines that his mother will thus become famous and take him away from the danger-ous spoil heap along with his brothers and sisters. (Hamilton hints at an Oedipal conflict here, for M.C. does not imagine that his father will accompany the family.)

As he dreams of this glamorous future, M.C. experiences a sense of power and dominion over the landscape as he sits on a bicycle seat high atop a forty-foot pole. The pole had been a prize from his father when M.C. had swum successfully across the Ohio River. The pole not only symbolizes the macho feelings of M.C. as he rides high and thinks of himself as a hero, "M.C. Higgins the Great;" it also represents the patriarchal values of the Jones family. Both M.C. and his father are aggressively masculine; they are hunters. They know how to subdue the wilderness. While Banina works as a domestic servant, M.C. and his father hunt for small game to supplement the family's food supply. Ironically, they must also do domestic chores; this situation has clearly injured Jones's masculine pride. Because he is not allowed to belong to the white union, he cannot adequately provide for his family. Also the strip-mining and its devastating effects upon the environment are interfering with the Higgins's hunting and trapping activities and hence also threaten the family's food supplies. Another irony is that the patriarchal need to dominate and to conquer the natural world is taken to the extreme in the strip-mining.

One significant way that Jones attempts to control his son is to forbid him to play with the neighbor, Ben Killburn. The Killburns, red-haired albino Afro-Americans with six-fingered hands, are superstitiously known as "witchy" people. Killburn Mound, with its many children, its vegetable garden, its web woven of vines that the Killburns call the "eye to heaven," clearly represents a matriarchal society. The Killburn grandmother sits amid cabbages in a damp, fecund house. Ben explains that this grandmother "has always been there." Mr. Killburn sees the mountain as alive, as "body," and he tries to heal its gashes with his healing hands. Strip-mining is also destroying the Killburn way of life; the vegetables are not producing. Vegetation is wilting and dying from exposure to the pollution caused by the mining. Neither Jones Higgins nor Mr. Killburn can cope with the enormity of the spoil heap and the dangers it poses to their communities.

M.C.'s conflicts are brought to the surface when he meets Lurhetta Outlaw, a liberated young woman who walks around the mountain on her own with a knife dangling from her belt. M.C. is amazed to learn that she has a car bought with money she has earned. He thinks that the young woman must be tracked and conquered, just as the animals are. Encountering Lurhetta for the first time, M.C. actually restrains her with physical force. Lurhetta, however, does not respond to his assertive masculine behavior. In the presence of the powerfully male Jones, she bristles with hostility. In the presence of the Killburns, however, Lurhetta instantly softens. The nurturing, accepting qualities of the Killburns clearly remind Lurhetta of her own female nature, an essential part of her which she has tried to deny. In a telling scene Lurhetta leaves her knife for M.C. with a goodbye note.

For his part, M.C. comes to accept that Sarah's mountain with all its dangers is his home and that he can neither run away nor escape. At the end of the novel M.C. has taught his father to put dead ancestors in their place (their headstones help to build a wall to protect the home); he also insists upon choosing his own friends rather than accepting Jones's prejudice against the Killburns. Though the ending of the novel is not unequivocally happy, it reveals the extent to which M.C. has moved toward maturity. The novel shows, too, that Jones has matured, since he can learn from his son instead of competing with him.

The Great Gilly Hopkins

by Katherine Paterson (1978).

One of the most highly acclaimed realistic novelists for children in the past decade is American Katherine Paterson. In *The Great Gilly Hopkins* Paterson creates an unusual family story which features as its protagonist a tough foster child who wins a real family at last, only to lose it.

Like characters in many folktales, Gilly Hopkins had been abandoned as a baby by her mother Courtney Hopkins. All that she has of

her mother is a picture of a lovely young woman with long shining hair. Around this photograph Gilly has erected a fairy tale: some day her beautiful mother will find her, rescue her from the foster homes where she is not loved, and take her to a new and glorious home in California where she will live happily ever after. Holding on to this fantasy has enabled Gilly to survive the emotional chaos of her life, but it has also prevented her from accepting the actual conditions of her existence.

In her most recent foster home Gilly meets an overweight religious fanatic, Maime Trotter; a little boy, William Ernest; and a blind black man, Mr. Randolph, who comes to dinner each day. Gilly feels superior to people she considers beneath her. She objects to Trotter's religious views and to her weight; she considers that William Ernest is mentally retarded; and she is plainly racist in her attitude toward Mr. Randolph. To escape the situation, Gilly writes her mother, explaining that she finds her new foster home unbearable. Eventually this letter causes Gilly to lose the only real family that she has ever known.

The members of Gilly's family surprise her. They are not the stereotypes which Gilly has unkindly imagined. Trotter is not only an overweight "religious fanatic," she is also a true earth mother, who nourishes children with both superb fried chicken and abundant love. Full of humanity, Trotter accepts people as they are. When Gilly steals money and runs away to the bus station, Trotter loyally defends her and welcomes her home. When Gilly finds that she must leave her newly found home to live with her maternal grandmother, Trotter helps her to accept the situation, explaining that "all that stuff about happy endings is lies."

Mr. Randolph similarly overturns Gilly's stereotyped preconceptions. He is truly a wise old man; though he is physically blind, he possesses inner vision and teaches Gilly Wordsworth's poetry. By example, he shows Gilly that she need not succumb to her emotional handicap, as he does not surrender to his physical one. When Gilly steals from him, Mr. Randolph gracefully forgives her and behaves as if the theft had never happened.

William Ernest also surprises Gilly. He is

smart, but terribly shy and insecure. Gilly teaches him to be independent and tough. She becomes more humane through loving and teaching William Ernest. In an important recognition scene Gilly tells her friend Agnes that she has been out of school caring for her family — her mother, her uncle, and her brother.

Gilly Hopkins thus enacts a linear quest for identity and for a family. She must revise the story of her life to suit the actual harsh conditions she must confront. Although Gilly would prefer a different ending, she must accept both loss and disillusionment. She loses Trotter, William Ernest, and Mr. Randolph; when she at last meets her mother, Gilly finds not a fairy princess but "a flower child gone to seed." At the end the reader believes that Gilly will have the strength of character to endure her losses and to help her grandmother make a home and restore the broken Hopkins family.

Appendix C: Teaching Interpretive Skills to Children

An Introduction

Although the love of and need for stories is probably an inborn human characteristic, the ability to understand stories is learned. That is because creators of stories use language (and pictures) in a highly specialized way. It is insufficient for readers merely to know the language in which a work is told; they must also possess the special code of that language used to tell stories. Two years ago, a young teacher reported on her experiences in a remote Alaskan Eskimo community. Every Friday afternoon, one of the village elders would come to tell the children traditional stories. Although he spoke in English, the teacher could understand neither the stories nor the children's obvious delight in them. By the end of the school year, she found herself looking forward to the Friday visits and enjoying the stories as much as her students did. Quite simply, she had developed the skills necessary to understand the Eskimo stories; she had mastered a special code. The stories had not changed, but she was able to bring more to them. Through the intereaction between the reader/listener and the text, narrative meaning had been created.

One of the reasons many people, especially children, have difficulty in fully comprehending a story is that they lack both literary skills and literary experiences, or backgrounds, necessary to approach it. Authors have a right to expect, to a certain degree, that readers should possess these skills and backgrounds. In fact, authors do not explicitly present an entire story. They present details and arrange these implicitly, demanding (and hoping) that the readers will intuit the significance of details and perceive relationships between them. Readers are asked to be partners in making a story meaningful; they are asked to participate actively in the reading of the text.

There are actually many reasons why readers, especially children, have difficulties in assuming their roles in the partnership, why they are unskilled readers of stories. For our purposes, the most important of these is the fact that they have not been systematically trained; they have not been helped to acquire the necessary skills and experiences. Most adults will remember how, in late junior high school or early high school, they were suddenly introduced to literary analysis. They felt they were being asked to tear a story apart or to "read between the lines." Not having had adequate training, many students floundered and developed an aversion to the study of literature.

Perhaps with a stronger foundation in reading literature, with practice in elementary schools, we might have been able to avoid the confusion and fear and become good and enthusiastic readers of stories. In this section, how these literary skills and experiences can be introduced in elementary grades will be suggested. First, we shall examine recent investigations into the ways in which children respond to literature, and studies of children's reading preferences. Then suggestions of effective ways of introducing literary skills, and methods of developing literature curricula for elementary and lower junior high school grades, will be offered.

The Reader's Response to Literature

Traditionally teachers of literature have emphasized the role of the author in creating a work of literature, the literary qualities of the work itself, and perhaps also the social and historical conditions which produced or influenced the work. In elementary schools in which many teachers have lacked literary training, stories have more often offered opportunities for practice in reading skills. Often literary aspects of stories are ignored, while the teacher concentrates upon questions regarding content, definitions, or matters concerning other disciplines altogether.

While such approaches are valuable, they do not teach children to become more critical readers, nor do they promote understanding or appreciation of literature. Perhaps a more useful way for the elementary teacher to develop a curriculum in literature is to begin by considering the role of both the reader and the text in the literary experience.

Emerson's notion that " 'tis the good reader that makes the good book" is to the point in this matter. Such literary theorists as D.W. Harding, Louise Rosenblatt, and others have noted that teachers of literature must attend to the reader's response to the literary work as well as to the literature itself. Margaret Early's 1960 study in the stages of literary appreciation underscores the importance of the reader-text relationship in promoting more sophisticated levels of critical reading. According to Early these three stages are as follows:[1]

1. *Unconscious Enjoyment* — At this level of reading readers know what they like to read, but they are unable to explain why.
2. *Conscious Enjoyment* — Readers continue to enjoy literature just as they do in the first stage. However, they begin to look for logical development in characters. No longer satisfied with stereotyped characters, readers begin to ask why characters behave as they do. Readers may also note at this stage that stories often reflect their own actual and literary experiences, that stories resemble other stories. Hence readers may notice that literature has a larger meaning or theme. The reader's response at this stage, then, is essentially social and psychological.
3. *Aesthetic Stage* — At the highest level of literary appreciation readers not only know what they like to read, but they can also explain why. At this stage readers move beyond purely personal responses. They can comment not only upon ways that a literary work connects with their personal experiences but they can also explain how the author uses literary strategies to achieve certain effects. Readers can analyze how elements of a work function together in creating a whole. The reader's response includes not only psycho-social dimensions but also aesthetic ones.

In their book *Literature for Adolescents: Teaching Poems, Stories, Novels, and Plays*, Stephen Dunning and Alan B. Howes present a different scheme for describing the levels of literary appreciation. The most basic level is the *literal level*, in which readers can identify the *who, what,* and *when* of narrative and can follow a sequence of events in the story. This first stage is, of course, an essential part of the reading experience, since more sophisticated reading levels can scarcely be attained without it. This stage corresponds roughly to Early's "unconscious enjoyment" stage, except that it stresses cognitive skill rather than emotional response.

Some students may possess the skill to move to higher levels of appreciation and to perceive the *structural* dimensions of literature, a term which incorporates not only plot but also the author's use of such techniques as *foreshadowing* and *flashback*. Events or images in a story function as foreshadowing when they provide the reader with hints of events and incidents to come. Flashbacks break the chronological sequence of a story to present some past event.

Much more sophisticated readers may perceive the *rhetorical, symbolic*, and *contextual* levels of a narrative. The rhetorical level includes such matters as the function of *point-of-view*. That is, point-of-view refers to the character through whose eyes the author views action. The type of fictional narrator (first person, third person, omniscient narrator, etc.), the treatment of character and tone, as well as the author's use of figurative language, diction, and sentence structure, are matters[2] concerning the rhetorical aspects of the work.[2] The symbolic implications of a work concern the larger meaning which images or objects in the work may assume. The contextual level of a work refers to how the work may be viewed within some larger framework. Discussions of the context of a work would include how the story fits into the body of a writer's works, how it reflects literary trends or social-historical events of its period, and how it compares with other works similar either thematically or generically.

Students may respond emotionally to a given story because of their own emotional needs or because of their particular personal interests. To achieve mastery of the structural, rhetorical, symbolic, and contextual aspects of a text, however, readers must be trained in the critical approaches to literature. These aspects of literature are aspects of the *public* experience of literature. That is, sophisticated ways to read and respond to literature rely upon the practices of a reading community. In North America, for example, one literary approach, the formalist or New Critical approach, which stresses a close reading of the work itself, has become institutionalized. Teachers of literature, then, must take into account both private and personal responses of readers, as well as public institutionalized ways of reading. Ideally a reader should eventually integrate these two types of reading for the fullest understanding and appreciation of literature. The purpose of instructing students in critical approaches to literature is to give them the means for moving from naive emotional responses to mature and complex responses which incorporate emotional, cognitive, and aesthetic dimensions.

Psychologists and educators often use child development theory to decide what literature children may respond to. Tests of "readability" are applied to texts to determine whether or not children are capable of reading a given text. While not all children are ready to read or to understand literature at the same time, the editors have discovered that most elementary children can understand literary concepts quite well if they are presented without undue jargon. The tendency among most teachers and educators is to underestimate the capacities of child readers to comprehend significant literary dimensions of stories. The teacher should thus value the personal response and promote the more public critical response in designing a literature curriculum.

In considering children's responses to literature, teachers may learn much from recent work in reader-response theory. Two pioneering thinkers in this area are D.W. Harding and Louise Rosenblatt. Harding explored the complex relationship between text and reader in his 1962 essay "Psychological Processes in the Reading of Fiction."[3] In this essay Harding discards the much-discussed explanations of the reader's engagement with fiction, identification and vicarious satisfaction. Harding denies that the intensity of a reader's engagement with a text can be explained sufficiently by these two notions. On the contrary, Harding argues, the reader's relationship to the text is as a "non-participant" who assumes an evaluative attitude toward events presented in a text. As a non-participant, however, the reader may experience emotions much sharper in focus and intensity than an actual participant could. The more naive and inexperienced the reader is, the less distinction he or she can make between true narrative and fiction. Naive readers fail to recognize, according to Harding, that fiction is a convention for narrating imagined events. Rather than providing readers with vicarious experiences, Harding maintains, "It seems nearer the truth . . . to say that fictions contribute to defining the reader's or spectator's values, and perhaps to stimulating his desires."[4] More sophisticated readers realize that they are engaging in a special relationship with the author and he realizes "that the represented participants are only part of a convention by which the author discusses and proposes an evaluation of possible human experience."[5] The importance of Harding's ideas is that the emotional effects of literary texts and the reader's sophistication or lack of it are both significant components of the literary experience. Acquiring the conventions of literature that enable the reader to understand and appreciate fiction is also to experience the fullest and richest emotional response.

While some reader-response theorists stress the role of the reader exclusively and thus by implication eliminate the need for literature at all, Louise Rosenblatt has stressed the dynamic interaction of text and reader. In her now classic critical work *Literature as Exploration* (1938), Rosenblatt describes reading as a "performing" art; readers learn from experience with literary texts to "perform" and to create interpretations for themselves. In her more recently published *The Reader, the Text, and the Poem* (1978), Rosenblatt elaborates on her reading theory and insists that literary experience is a transaction between the reader and the text. Readers bring previous experiences, both actual and literary, to a story. These experiences in turn shape the reader's responses to a specific work and help the reader to make sense of works encountered in the future. As Rosenblatt explains this transaction: "The reading of a text is an event occurring at a particular time in a particular moment in the life history of the reader. The transaction will involve not only the past experience but also the present state and present interests or preoccupations of the reader."[6]

Still more recently Hugh and Maureen Crago have presented a massive study of their daughter's responses to children's stories. Their findings suggest, as do Rosenblatt's, that the relationship between the text and the reader is reciprocal, that children use texts to make sense of other literary and life experiences, and that children's books influence and shape children's tastes, language, and play.[7]

The findings of such reader-response critics as Harding, Rosenblatt, and the Cragos provide powerful evidence that the personal responses of readers must never be overlooked or undervalued. Teachers at all levels — kindergarten through graduate classes — need to provide opportunities for free responses to literature. Such activities may, indeed, be designed for the youngest reader. Children may be asked to draw a picture to express their feelings about a story and then to explain the picture. They may enact their favorite scenes from a book. Older students may respond freely in writing. Although a teacher's questions implicitly shape students' responses, open-ended, free-response questions may be devised. Some of the following may be useful.

1. What characters, scenes, or details do you remember most vividly from the story? (Students should write as fast as possible for a given length of time. The teacher can use these responses to introduce topics for further discussion.)
2. What was the funniest part of the story?
3. What was the saddest part of the story?

Teachers usually find that student's responses suggest potent ideas about both the reader and the text which would otherwise remain undisclosed. Also, many of the responses suggest literary elements which the teacher may explain.

While the personal response to literature should be valued and used to introduce literature, the teacher also has the obligation to offer child readers opportunities for understanding the more sophisticated levels of literary texts. As readers encounter stories, they gradually internalize literary conventions which enable them to perceive such literary qualities as theme, tone, conflict, symbol, and sophisticated uses of language, to practice such reading skills as classification and recognition of sequential events, and to predict outcome.

Recent findings in reading research indicate that just as speakers of a language assimilate a complex grammar enabling them to read a series of sounds as a sentence, so readers of literature acquire through their encounters with stories the mastery of various literary conventions which allow them to recognize the structural principles of literature and to endow these structures with meaning. Alan Purvis emphasizes this notion: "How well students read might be better described as how well students have learned the conventions."[8]

Included in the next section is a suggested method for designing and implementing a literature curriculum that will provide the child reader with a fundamental understanding of literary conventions needed to appreciate more complex forms of literature.

Some Practical Applications

We may say that the reading of a story has been completed when, on one level at least, the reader has created a meaning for the story which takes into account all of the words (or pictures). The more levels of meaning the reader creates the fuller or richer his reading will be.

In order to create meaning, readers must exercise three skills: they must notice the existence of the details of the story: the characters, the settings, and the actions. If they do not notice that these are present, they will not be able to exercise the second skill: the recognition of the importance of the details in the story. The third act requires that they remember the order in which the details are presented and perceive the significance of that order. In other words, they must notice the importance of the relationship between details. The performance of these acts is not easy, and it is not generally achieved during the first reading of a story. As critic Northrop Frye has noted, "The critical [that is the interpretive] operation begins with reading a work straight through, as many times as may be necessary to possess it in totality. At this point the critic can begin to formulate a conceptual unity corresponding to the imaginative unity of his text."[9] In other words, rereading will enable readers to remember better the details and their interrelationships and then to discover the significances of these.

How can teachers facilitate the development of these reading skills in children? We shall suggest answers by examining three steps in studying a story in the elementary classroom: preparation, presentation, and follow-up. Preparation involves taking into account the children's emotional, psychological, and intellectual stages of development, their factual knowledge, and their literary background. In bringing a child and a story together, the adult must consider whether or not the child can comprehend the significances of the experiences presented. A five year old will probably have little difficulty relating to the sense of inadequacy experienced by Peter in Ezra Jack Keats's *Whistle for Willie*. However, the same child would not relate to the conflict between opposing cultural systems presented in Jean Craighead George's *Julie of the Wolves*. Moreover, the language and sentence structure of George's novel would be too difficult for a five-year-old; those in *Whistle for Willie* would not.

Preparing children for reading a specific story involves helping them to understand unfamiliar words or objects in a story. A reader who has never heard of an elephant will have difficulty responding to the humor of Kipling's "The Elephant's Child." Greater familiarity with the geography and customs of traditional South Sea Islanders will enhance understanding of Armstrong Sperry's *Call It Courage*. Students should also be aware of the specific characteristics of supernatural beings found in folktales. The Baba-Yaga of Russia, the Trolls of Norway, and the Dragons of England all had definite characteristics, knowledge of which will make the stories in which they appear more meaningful. In studying stories dealing with cultural groups or historical periods different from those of modern readers, teachers should definitely supply background information because not to do so may result in children assuming that all times and people are the same as their own. Such assumptions could cause serious misreading of the implicit meanings of the stories in question.

Children should be gradually prepared for the reading of a story; to overload them with vocabulary and factual information immediately before the reading will usually not achieve the desired result of making them more skilled readers. Key words — only those absolutely necessary for comprehension — should be identified some time before the children hear or read the story and should be introduced over a period of a few days before consideration of the story. Similarly, unfamiliar customs, objects, and landscapes can be presented over a longer period. Pictures, short documentary films, and nonfictional books can be used. The key point is that children should be in possession of the necessary background before the story is considered.

The most important element of preparation is literary. Stories imitate other stories, and the ability to understand one story is enhanced by the reader's understanding of stories read before. After one has heard or read one story, one has background literary experience to help with the next story. As the poet Robert Frost remarked: "A poem is best read in the light of all the other poems ever written. We read A the better to read B (we have to start somewhere, we may get very little out of A). We read B the better to read C, C the better to read D, D the better to go back and get something more out of A." The teacher should thus present stories in relation to each other, ideally making each story a preparation for all stories to follow and making the understanding of each story draw in part from the reader's understanding of all the stories read before. In other words, to enhance literary understanding, it is necessary to develop a literature curriculum in which the books selected and the sequence of those books increases the development of the skills of literary interpretation.

A student in Grade Two who has examined the character changes which have taken place during the circular journeys of the title heroes of *Chanticleer and the Fox* (Barbara Cooney), *The Story About Ping* (Marjorie Flack), and *The Tale of Peter Rabbit* (Beatrix Potter), will better be able to study a similar pattern in *Jacob Two-Two Meets the Hooded Fang* (Mordecai Richler). Having recognized irony in "Hansel and Gretel," "Cinderella," "The Fisherman and his Wife," and "Little Red Ridinghood," Grade Three or Four students can consider in depth the many ironies of *The Lion, The Witch, and the Wardrobe* (C. S. Lewis). Upper elementary children who have traced the solitary journeys of initiation undertaken in "The Errand," (Harry Behn), *Arrow to the Sun*, (McDermott), and "Scarface" (George Bird Grinnell), are ready to apply the pattern to Meg Murry's travels in Madeleine L'Engle's *A Wrinkle in Time*.

In presenting a specific story, the teacher must ask him or herself, "What are the objectives for teaching this story and, Why am I teaching it at this particular point in time?" As we have seen, the goal of teaching any story is to assist the reader in developing the ability to perceive details, their organization, and the significances of these. We shall now trace in detail methods we have used in presenting a picture book, a short story, and a novel.

Arrow to the Sun is one of the most important works the editors have presented in Grade Two. It combines many of the visual and verbal aspects of texts already studied and so provides a review or recapitulation of concepts already introduced. Students can apply acquired skills to help them create meaning for a fairly complex work. The works studied previously have embodied such visual elements as location and size of characters on the page (Lionni's *Frederick* and Yashima's *Crow Boy*) as an indication of their peer group status, and the use of changing colors to indicate changing emotions or mood (Elizabeth Cleaver's *The Mountain Goats of Temlaham*). Character types such as the unlikely hero (*Crow Boy*, and Maria Campbell's *Little Badger and the Fire Spirit*), the helper (Andersen's "Inchelina"), and the tested hero (Gail Haley's *A Story, a Story*), have also been examined. Nearly all of the stories have involved meaningful journeys and significant character development.

By way of preparation, students are shown slides of the southwest desert and traditional Pueblo dwellings, and they are made familiar with the words *kiva* and *pueblo*. After a brief review of skills developed in studying the first six books in the sequence, they are ready for a first reading of *Arrow to the Sun*. Aspects of the introductory material (cover, endpapers, title and dedication pages) are shown to the children, who are told that after a first reading, they will be asked to reconsider these, noting their importance for the story itself. During the initial reading, few pauses are made, the objective being to familiarize readers with the plot. The Boy's logo is pointed out, as is the fact that Arrow Maker's eyes are open while those of Corn Planter and Pot Maker are not. Children are also asked to notice the effects the Boy has on the occupants of the first three Kivas. After the first reading, the introductory material is studied, with children noticing the appropriateness of the orange color (for sun and desert) and the logo design of the cover; the star, cloud, and step patterns of the end papers; the three arrows (indicative of three flights) of the title page; and the rainbow ribbon which crosses all the pages of the story and turns into a rainbow after the Boy emerges from the Kiva of Lightning. The initial presentation of the story, along with the follow-up examination of the preliminary materials, can easily be covered during a half-hour class.

During the second half-hour class, the teacher can lead the children in an in-depth analysis of the details, the structure, and the significances of the story. The goal here is to have the children notice specific aspects of the Boy's character development. Like many unlikely heroes, he begins lonely and rejected and ends happy and accepted. What, in this story, does the Boy do that makes him feel better and makes him a hero to those who had once rejected him? One way of helping students trace developing patterns is to have them see the entire story laid out on a storyboard. Two paperback copies of the work can be cut up and the pictures spread sequentially across the large sheets of black cardboard. Children can then view the story presented in a manner similar to that of a Sunday comic strip, and they can move back and forth between pictures, noticing similarities and interreplationships.

The first step in helping the children create a structural unity of the story involves having them compare the early picture in which the Boy, rejected by his peers, stands unhappily with his mother, and the final illustration, in which he leads his people in the Dance of Life. Size, facial expressions, head dress, clothing, and position on the page can be contrasted. It can be shown that all the details of the first picture communicate the Boy's unhappiness, and all those of the latter his new found fulfillment. With these two extremes in mind, the children can then examine key stages in the Boy's progression from one to the other, noticing how the illustrations help to communicate these. After this discussion, *Arrow to the Sun* can be placed within the context of stories already studied, with the children noticing similarities between the Boy and the heroes of earlier works.

Specific follow-up to *Arrow to the Sun* can include having the children view McDermott's animated film of the story, creating illustrations depicting important events of the narrative, and comparing this book with such other McDermott books as *Anansi the Spider*. Each of these activities is designed to reinforce the literary skills developed. The film-book comparison invites children to notice variations in the visual methods of presentation and their significance; the art work invites them to use color, size, and details in a purposeful manner as McDermott has; and the viewing of other of the author's books encourages them to recognize similar artistic techniques used in different stories.

In the middle elementary grades, students are capable of understanding, at a simple level, basic elements of irony and how these are embodied in specific stories. Irony, the children are initially told, occurs in a story where what happens is not what you (the reader or the characters) expect. Ironic aspects found in narrative reversals, tricks, willful deceptions, and lack of self-knowledge are all considered. Children are able not only to recognize the presence of irony in a story, but also to see how irony relates to character. Why is it that some characters are better able to deceive than others? Why do some characters always seem to be surprised? Children also notice that there are both positive and negative ironies, or as we call them in the elementary grades, good and bad irony. A story which contains many of these elements of irony is "Hansel and Gretel."

Before reading "Hansel and Gretel", in, for example, third grade, children should have been introduced to the idea of irony and to a number of stories containing irony and using the forest as a major setting. Lynd Ward's *The Biggest Bear*, Robert McCloskey's *Blueberries for Sal*, Brinton Turkle's *Deep in the Forest*, and Laura Ingalls Wilder's "Two Bears" from *Little House in the Big Woods* humorously present ironic meetings between bears and people. The last two also use the forest setting in the creation of ironies. In "The Wild Wood," from Kenneth Grahame's *The Wind in the Willows*, irony and the forest setting are linked. What the innocent Mole finds in the Wild Wood is not what he expected.

In a first reading of the Wanda Gág version of "Hansel and Gretel," children are merely asked to notice the ironies as they occur. As they bring them to the teacher's attention, the ironies can be listed on the board or a chart. After the story has been read, the teacher can suggest that there is both good and bad irony. Good irony results from positive motivations and/or produces positive results. Bad irony is motivated by evil and the results are extremely unpleasant. After looking at two or three examples of irony from "Hansel and Gretel" and explaining why these could be considered either good or bad irony, the teacher can invite members of the class to categorize the other ironies of the story as either good or bad. They should be encouraged to explain why they have categorized the examples the way they have. This activity can extend beyond the first half-hour period into a second.

During a second class, the students can be shown the relationship between setting and the ironies of the story. After a brief review of forests and homes in "Two Bears" and "The Wild Wood," students can be told that these are usually contrasting settings: forests usually represent fear, insecurity, and loneliness, while homes usually represent happiness, security, and integration. The teacher can now introduce a large map indicating the major settings of the story: the family cottage, the forest, the witch's cottage, and the cage behind it. "What kind of place," the children can be asked, "do you expect a home to be in a story? Is Hansel and Gretel's home what you expect? Why not?" One should notice not only the conditions in the house, but the ways in which the step–mother deliberately deceives, makes "bad ironies," which insure that this house is not a home. When the children are first abandonned in the woods, the step–mother expects that the place will be one from which they cannot return; when they are abandonned the second time, Hansel expects it to be a place from which they can easily return to the house. The witch's cottage is doubly ironic: Hansel and Gretel had expected to find neither so hospitable nor tasty a place in the dark forest; but, as we see, neither the house nor the owner turn out to be what we expected. The old lady is a witch and behind the candy cottage is the cage. By noting the ironies on the map, children are better able to perceive the relationships between setting and irony.

As a follow-up activity, children can compare different illustrated versions of "Hansel and Gretel," noticing which illustrations best reflect the ironies in the story.

Of course, as students gain a fuller grasp of the basic elements of simple irony, they can be introduced to stories in which the ironies are more complex and profound and can attempt to create a more precise definition of irony and the ways in which it works in specific stories.

Although novels can be read to children in the early elementary grades, detailed study of them is best begun in the upper elementary grades. The act of reading a novel is similar to that of reading picture books or shorter stories — noticing details and structure and their significances. However, there is a major difference: novels are much longer, and thus remembering details and the patterns they form is much more difficult. Yet the length of a novel is also one of its great strengths: it allows for fuller developments of conflicts, characters, and themes than is possible in shorter works. The challenge for the teacher is to find methods of presentation which help students to overcome the difficulties created by the length of a novel while at the same time assisting them in understanding the richness and the depth of meaning made possible by that length. Using *The Hobbit*, a challenging but not impossible read for sixth or seventh grade students, as an example, we will offer suggestions of ways to help students create a unified reading of a novel.

Our first step is to formulate a learning objective for teaching *The Hobbit*. Early in Chapter 1, Gandalf says about Bilbo: "There is a lot more in him than you guess, and a deal more than he has any idea of himself." Using this statement as our guide, we will trace the stages of Bilbo's character development during his circular journey. Before studying the novel, we shall engage in three preliminary activities which will assist us in the achievement of our goal.

First, we will read a number of shorter works which will introduce students to characters, settings, themes, and story structures similar to those found in *The Hobbit*. These stories will serve as "overtures" to the novel. *Arrow to the Sun* (McDermott) and *The Snow Queen* (Hans Christian Andersen, adapted by Naomi Lewis and illustrated by Errol LeCain) present unlikely heroes who perform valiant deeds during their circular journeys. "Beauty and the Beast" (Lang's version in *The Blue Fairy Book*), like *The Snow Queen*, uses changes in weather and the seasons to reflect changing emotions and presents symbolic landscapes. In addition, the idea of the beast-prince introduces the concept of an individual who has two sides. (In *The Hobbit*, Bilbo has Baggins and Tooke personality strains and Beorn is a shape-shifter.) The Greek myth of Prometheus and the account of the death of Beowulf in Rosemary Sutcliff's *Dragon Slayer* present the theme of courage, social responsibility, and self-sacrifice. The dragon-slaying episode also provides a good opportunity for children to discuss elements of dragon lore.

Second, we will read the novel in its entirety aloud to the students. Older children enjoy being read to as much as younger ones do. Also, this reading enables them to acquire an overview of the novel, a framework for their later detailed study. Moreover, by hearing the novel read by an accomplished reader, one whose voice emphasis helps to communicate nuances of tone and character, listeners, particularly those who have some difficulty in reading themselves, will not only enjoy experiencing the story, but also will be better able to understand it, at least on the level of plot and characterization. During this reading, a large map of *The Hobbit* can be placed on the wall. The location of individual episodes can be marked on the map as they occur.

We are now ready to begin our detailed study. At this point each student can be given a copy of the novel and the overall objective of the study, tracing the stages of Bilbo's character development, can be introduced. During the second reading, the students are encouraged to notice how carefully and deftly the author builds the story, weaving patterns, foreshadowing, building toward pivotal events. In a sense, they are invited to be detectives, looking for significant clues they might have missed the first time around. In fact, they are, with the teacher's guidance, engaging in the act of creating meaning through inter-acting with the text. Only through a second reading can the children really develop an analytical, critical understanding, which, along with simple enjoyment, is a vital result of the act of reading.

The first activity involves having the students notice the difference between Bilbo's character before he begins and after he completes his journey. The differences can be listed side by side on a chart and the chart can be placed beside the map on the wall. At various points in the study, students can be asked to refer to the chart, noticing how much Bilbo's character has changed since the first chapter.

Before students are asked to read individual chapters, they should be instructed to look for key points. What are the most important events which take place in a specific chapter, and what do they reveal about Bilbo's character development? In Chapter 2, "Roast Mutton," Bilbo burgles from the trolls. Students should notice that he performs this action alone, that he is not too skillful, but that the end results are not worthless. In reading Chapter 8, "Flies and Spiders," they should consider the significance of the fact that Gandalf has left the adventurers on their own, and they can compare Bilbo's actions with those of the dwarves. Individual passages can be carefully examined. Why, for example, does Tolkien make the following observation in Chapter 12, at the point where Bilbo prepares to descend into Smaug's cave? "It was at this point that Bilbo stopped. Going on from there was the bravest thing he ever did. The tremendous things that happened afterwards were as nothing compared to it. He fought the real battle in that tunnel alone, before he ever saw the vast danger that lay in wait."

As do most novels, *The Hobbit* contains a number of recurrent elements, patterns of similar events or settings which link chapters together into meaningful sequences. In Chapter 5, "Riddles in the Dark," Bilbo confronts a dangerous enemy, engages in a riddle contest, and wears his ring of invisibility. Chapter 12, "Inside Information," presents a similar situation, as Bilbo confronts the dragon Smaug. The reader is expected to make explicit the implicit connections between the chapters and to notice the character growth in Bilbo.

One way to assist students in seeing patterns in the novel is to create a series of charts, each one dealing with a specific pattern. For example, after Bilbo has completed his adventure with the trolls, a chart entitled "Folklore Creatures" can be introduced. In one column can be listed the names or types of characters Bilbo meets, in another the ways in which he reacts to them. Other charts could list such patterns as Bilbo's uses of his ring of invisibility, his stay at resting places, or his entry into and emergence from subterranean areas. The completed charts can be used as the basis for discussions of Bilbo's character development.

After their detailed study of the novel, students can engage in a number of follow-up activities. Reports or essays can be written on such subjects as "The Importance of the Folklore Creatures Bilbo Meets," "Is Bilbo Baggins a Hero?", or "The Importance of Dwelling Places in *The Hobbit*." Illustrations for *The Hobbit* created by Tolkien, Michael Hague, and the animated television special can be compared and evaluated. Students can view the 1977 television special and then discuss its relationships with and departures from the novel.

There are many ways of interpreting a story and there are many ways of assisting children to become fuller interpreters of stories. The methods presented in this appendix have been developed working in over sixty classrooms in Alberta, Michigan, Florida, and North Carolina. Not only the editors, but also numerous teachers to whom they have presented workshops have been extremely pleased with how students from a great variety of economic and cultural backgrounds have responded to the methods and become more careful and, most important, more enthusiastic readers of stories. And that, after all, should be the goal of any literature program.

Notes

1 Margaret Early, "Stages of Growth in Literary Appreciation," *English Journal*, 49 (March 1960), 163-166.

2 See Stephen Dunning and Alan B. Howes, *Literature for Adolescents* (Glenview, Illinois: Scott, Foresman, 1975), p. 103.

3 D.W. Harding, "Psychological Processess in the Reading of Fiction," *British Journal of Aesthetics*, Vol 2, 1962); Rpt. in *The Cool Web: The Pattern of Children's Reading*, ed. by Margaret Meek, Aidan Warlow, and Griselda Barton (New York: Atheneum, 1976), pp. 58-72.

4 Harding, p. 69.

5 Harding, p. 72.

6 Louise Rosenblatt, *The Reader, the Text, and the Poem* (Carbondale: Southern Illinois University Press, 1978).

7 Hugh and Maureen Crago, *Preludes to Literacy* (Carbondale; Southern Illinois University Press, 1978).

8 Alan Purvis, "The State of Research in Teaching Literature," *English Journal*, 70 (March 1981).

9 Northrop Frye, *The Great Code: the Bible and Literature* (Toronto: Academic Press Canada, 1982), p. xii.

Bibliographies

Critical and Scholarly Books

Bator, Robert. *Signposts to Criticism of Children's Literature*. American Library Association, 1983.
—An anthology of critical essays treating the major genres of children's literature; the book seeks to define the nature of children's literature, to examine perceptions about it, and to suggest possible critical approaches.

Blount, Margaret. *Animal Land: The Creatures of Children's Fiction*. Morrow, 1975.
—Discusses literary treatments and symbolic uses of animal characters in a wide range of children's literature.

Bratton, J.S. *The Impact of Victorian Children's Fiction*. Barnes and Noble, 1981.
—Brattton describes and evaluates the function of didactic Victorian children's literature.

Butler, Francelia and Richard W. Rotert, Eds. *Reflections on Literature for Children: Selected from the Annual, Children's Literature*, Shoe String Press, 1984.
—A selection of outstanding essays published in the first ten years of the Annual's history.

Butler, Francelia. *Sharing Literature with Children: A Thematic Anthology*. McKay, 1977.
—A selection of various genres of children's literature, arranged thematically, with critical essays on each theme.

Carpenter, Humphrey, and Mari Prichard. *The Oxford Companion to Children's Literature*. Oxford University Press, 1984.
—Nearly two thousand entries on authors, genres, titles, and historical periods. A worthy addition to a distinguished series.

Carr, Jo, Ed., *Beyond Fact: Nonfiction for Children and Young People*. American Library Association, 1982.
—A selection of essays on children's nonfiction, organized by theme and genre.

Chambers, Nancy. Ed. *The Signal Approach to Children's Books, A Collection*. Metuchen/Scarecrow, 1980.
—A selection of representative essays from the journal's first ten years of publication; the volume includes essays by Elaine Moss, Peter Hunt, and Charles Sarlord and exhibits various critical approaches to children's literature.

Children's Periodicals in the United States. R. Gordon Kelly, Ed. Historical Guides to the World's Periodicals and Newspapers.
—Lists 423 magazines for American children, beginning in 1789, and describes over 100 magazines thoroughly; contains a bibliography of sources, an index, library locations, and publishing details.

Crouch, Marcus. *The Nesbit Tradition: The Children's Novel in England*, 1945-1970. Ernest Benn, 1972.
—Author argues that E. Nesbit established and popularized many conventions of the modern children's novel; he discusses these features as reflected in specific children's novels published during the mid-twentieth century.

Crouch, Marcus. *Treasure Seekers and Borrowers: Children's Books in Britain*, 1900-1960. Library Association (London), 1970.
—Author presents critical assessments of twentieth-century children's books.

Dizer, John T. *Tom Swift and Company: "Boys' Books" by Stratemeyer and Others*. McFarland, 1982.
—Author discusses the impact of popular literature on children, identifies characteristic formulas for adventure and action, and provides historical information about the Stratemeyer syndicate.

Egoff, Sheila, et al, eds. *Only Connect: Readings on Children's Literature*. 2nd ed. Oxford University Press, 1980.
—A collection of critical essays featuring historical, social, and generic approaches. The volume includes articles by such major children's writers as C.S. Lewis, P.L. Travers, and Tolkien and by such eminent scholars as Roger Lancelyn Green and John Rowe Townsend.

Egoff, Sheila. *The Republic of Childhood: A Critical Guide to Canadian Children's Literature in English*. 2nd edition, Oxford University Press, 1975.
—Author analyzes and evaluates contemporary Canadian children's books from 1950-1974.

Fenwick, Sara I, ed. *Critical Approach to Children's Literature*. University of Chicago Press, 1976.
—A collection of critical essays by different authors, on such topics as social values in children's literature, children's book reviewing practices, and children's responses to literature.

Field, Elinor W., ed. *Hornbook Reflections on Children's Books and Reading*. Horn Book,1969
—Editor has selected outstanding and representative essays published in *The Horn Book Magazine* from 1949-66; volume includes articles on literary inspiration

of authors, illustration, historical fiction, poetry, fantasy, and story telling.

Fisher, Margery. *Intent Upon Reading*. 2nd. ed, rev. and enl. Brockhampton Press, 1964.

—Critical assessments of numerous English children's books.

Fisher, Margery. *Who's Who in Children's Books: A Treasury of the Familiar Characters of Childhood*. Holt, Rinehart and Winston, 1975.

—Affectionate descriptions of famous characters in children's literature.

Fox, Geoff et al, eds. *Writers, Critics, and Children. Articles from Children's Literature in Education*. Agathon Heinemann Educational Books, 1976.

—Editors have selected outstanding essays from the first six years of the journal's publication.

Haviland, Virginia. *Children and Literature: Views and Reviews*. Lothrop, 1973.

—Selected essays on several important topics: history of children's literature, the classics, children's reading interests, the creative process, illustration, folk tales, poetry, realistic fiction, internationalism in children's literature, and the nature of the criticism of children's books. Essays are written by outstanding writers and critics.

Heins, Paul, ed. *Crosscurrents of Criticism: Horn Book Essays 1968-77*. Horn Book Inc., 1977.

—Collection of essays from *The Horn Book Magazine*, focusing upon issues in the criticism of children's literature and suggesting possible future directions.

Hearne, Betsy and Marilyn Kaye, eds. *Celebrating Children's Books: Essays in Honor of Zena Sutherland*. Lothrop, 1981.

—Twenty-three prominent figures in the world of children's literature discuss aspects of their work: their childhood reading, aspects of their writing practices, and frustrations.

Inglis, Fred. *The Promise of Happiness: Value and Meaning in Children's Fiction*. Cambridge University Press, 1982.

Kamenetsky, Christa. *Children's Literature in Hitler's Germany: the Cultural Policy of National Socialism*. Ohio University Press, 1984.

—Author traces roots of Nazi policy regarding books for the young in nineteenth-century controversies in children's literature. Nazis wanted children's books to promote chauvinistic ideals of the German race — preferably historical novels and folktales. Other literature was severely censored. The author notes that children found ways to read what they desired despite the severe restrictions.

Karl, Jean. *From Childhood to Childhood: Children's Books and Their Creators*. Day, 1970.

—A distinguished editor discusses the world of children's literature publishing.

Kingston, Carolyn T. *The Tragic Mode in Children's Literature*. Teachers College Press, 1974.

—Author defines "tragic" broadly and discusses tragic moments in children's literature — rejection, entrapment, war, and loss.

Lanes, Selma. *Down the Rabbit Hole: Adventures and Misadventures in the Realm of Children's Literature*. Atheneum, 1976.

—Discusses several topics and figures in children's literature; method of approach is appreciative and evaluative.

Lukens, Rebecca. *A Critical Handbook of Children's Literature*. 2nd ed. Scott Foresman, 1981.

—Author discusses the elements of fiction — character, plot, setting, theme, point of view — with reference to children's literature and suggests ways that readers may evaluate these in children's books.

May, Jill, ed. *Children and Their Literature: A Readings Book*. ChLA Publications.

—A collection of critical essays on fairy tales, fantasy, films, picture books and illustration, poetry and literary criticism.

Meek, Margaret, et al, eds. *The Cool Web: The Pattern of Children's Reading*. Atheneum, 1978.

—A collection of essays which explore in various ways the role of the child reader in literary experience and the nature of narrative.

Miller, Bertha Mahony, and Elinor Whitney Field, eds. *Caldecott Medal Books, 1938-1957, with the Artists' Acceptance Papers and Related Material Chiefly from The Horn Book Magazine*. Horn book, 1957.

—Includes excellent information on illustration of children's books: an article on the illustration of Randolph Caldecott, biographies of each artist represented, and a critical essay, "What is a Picture Book?" by Esther Averill.

Moore, Anne C. *New Roads to Childhood*. Rpt. 1923 ed, Arden Library.

—Critical reviews and guides to children's books.

Morton, Miriam, ed. *A Harvest of Russian Children's Literature*. Introduction and commentary by Miriam Morton; foreward by Ruth Hill Viguers. Univ. of California Press, 1967.

Nodelman, Perry and Jill May, eds. *Festschrift: A Ten-Year Retrospective*. ChLA Publications, 1983.

—Publication contains selected articles from the first ten years of the *Children's Literature Association Quarterly*, including essays on such genres as teen romances, fairy tales, critical theory, ideas on canon formation, and such issues as censorship.

Paterson, Katherine. *Gates of Excellence: On Reading and Writing Books for Children*. Nelson Books, 1981.

—A highly acclaimed children's novelist discusses her practices as a writer and presents critical reviews of several children's books; the author's Newbery Medal acceptance speeches are also included.

Rudman, Masha K. *Children's Literature: An Issues Approach*. 2nd ed. Longman, Inc., 1984.

—A social approach to children's literature; the volume considers such issues as divorce, death, sexuality, sibling rivalry, presentation of minorities, and the handicapped, using psycho-social and political values as the bases for evaluating the books.

Sale, Roger. *Fairy Tales and After: From Snow White to E.B. White*. Harvard University Press, 1978.

—Author distinguishes between "man" reading and "child" reading and discusses the nature and function of folktales; he also presents critical analyses of several classics of children's literature, such as *Alice's Adventures in Wonderland, Wind in the Willows,* and *Charlotte's Web*.

Smith, James Steel, *A Critical Approach to Children's Literature*. McGraw Hill, 1967.

—Author analyzes various works of children's literature to assess their literary value; author argues that the same literary standards should apply to both children's literature and literature in general.

Smith, Lillian H. *The Unreluctant Years*. The Viking Press, 1953.

—Author presents a critical approach for evaluating the quality of children's literature and applies it to fairy tales, epics, romance, poetry, picture books, fantasy, and historical fiction.

Stewig, John W. *Children and Literature*. Houghton Mifflin, 1980.

—Designed as a text for college classes in children's literature, the book contains discussions of various types of children's literature and suggestions for classroom use.

Stott, Jon. *Children's Literature from A to Z: A Guide for Parents and Teachers*. McGraw Hill, 1984.

—Volume contains succinct descriptive and critical entries on major writers for children, past and present, as well as entries on types on genres, such as "ABC Books," folk tales, poetry, picture books, etc. Arranged alphabetically, the work also includes "Tips for Parents and Teachers" at the end of each entry.

Street, Douglas, ed. *Children's Novels and the Movies*. Frederick Ungar, 1983.

—Volume includes critical and analytical discussions of such major children's novels as *Tom Brown's School Days, Little Women, Alice's Adventures in Wonderland*, and discusses the films which have been made of these classics.

Sutherland, Zena, ed. *The Arbuthnot Lectures 1970-79*. American Library Association, 1980.

—Contains the text of lectures by major children's writers and critics.

Sutherland, Zena. *Children and Books*. 6th ed. Scott Foresman, 1981.

—This major reference book is often used as a text; it includes discussions of major genres of children's literature, using literature with children, and offers extensive bibliographies.

Tucker, Nicholas, ed. *Suitable for Children? Controversies in Children's Literature*. University of California Press, 1976.

—Author has collected articles dealing with various controversies in children's literature beginning with Mrs. Trimmer's 1803 attack on fairy tales; controversies included are fairy tales, comics, fear, and the function of children's literature.

Criticism: Folktales, Hero Tales, and Myths

Bettelheim, Bruno. *The Uses of Enchantment: The Meaning and Importance of Fairy Tales*. Alfred A. Knopf, 1976.

—An eminent scholar discusses the significance of fairy tales in addressing the urgent emotional needs of children.

Bloomfield, Morton W., ed. *Allegory, Myth, and Symbol*. Harvard University Press, 1982.

—Eminent scholars discuss literary functions and definitions of allegory, myth, and symbol.

Brombert, Victor, ed. *The Hero in Literature*. Fawcett Books, 1969.

—A collection of essays on the nature of the hero by eminent literary scholars. C.M. Bowra distinguishes between heroes of romance and epic, and Thomas Greene discusses the nature of the epic.

Brewer, Derek, *Symbolic Stories: Traditional Narratives of the Family Drama in English Literature*. Brewer, Rowman, and Littlefield, 1980.

—Author analyzes the fairy tale as a magical game in which characters exist to perform functions.

Briggs, K.M. *The Anatomy of Puck*. Rpt. Arno Press, 1977.

—Author examines superstitions, tales, and beliefs about fairies among Shakespeare's contemporaries and successors.

Briggs, K.M. *The Fairies in Tradition and Literature*. Routledge and Kegan Paul, 1967.

Briggs, K.M. Ill. by Mary I. French. *The Vanishing People: Fairy Lore and Legends*. Pantheon, 1978.

—Briggs discusses the traditional fairy lore of Great Britain and Ireland.

Burns, Norman T. and Christopher J. Reagan. *Concepts of the Hero in the Middle Ages and the Renaissance*. State University of New York Press, 1975.

—Volume contains eleven critical essays on the nature of the hero.

Campbell, Joseph. *The Flight of the Wild Gander*. Regnery-Gateway, 1972.

—An eminent anthropologist interprets many well-known stories.

Campbell, Joseph, *The Hero with a Thousand Faces*. Princeton University Press, 1968.

—Author begins with a description of the "mono-myth" and develops chapters on each stage of the hero's development.

Campbell, Joseph. *The Masks of God: Creative Mythology*. Penguin, 1983.

—A major interpretative study of myth.

Chant, Joy *The High Kings: Arthur's Celtic Ancestors*. Ill. by George Sharp. Bantam Books, 1983.

Clarke, Howard W. *The Art of the Odyssey*. Prentice-Hall, 1967.

—Succinct critical analysis of Homer's classic with useful discussion of the epic hero.

Cook, Elizabeth. *The Ordinary and the Fabulous: An Introduction to Myths, Legends, and Fairy Tales for Teachers and Storytellers*. Cambridge University Press., 1969.

—Author explores the nature of myths, legends, and folktales; she discusses the suitability of each form for children and examines the language and temper of several retellings of myths for children.

Cox, George W. *Creation Myths: Man's Introduction to the World*. Thomas Hudson, 1977.

—Author discusses the significant aspects of creation myths from many cultures.

Day, Martin S. *The Many Meanings of Myth*. University Press of America, 1984.

—Author offers interpretative strategies for the study of myth.

Downing, Christine. *The Goddess: Mythical Images of the Feminine*. Crossroad, 1981.

—Author compares pre-Hellenic versions of myths about goddesses with revised patriarchal versions, noting that the nature and power of the older goddesses had been radically altered; presents excellent discussions of Demeter, Hera, Pandora, Ariadne, and other goddesses.

Dundes, Alan, ed. *Cinderella: A Casebook*. Garland Publications, 1982.

—A collection of twenty-one essays on "Cinderella;" various approaches and interpretations of this most universal of fairy tales are represented along with thorough notes and introductions.

Dundes, Alan. *Interpreting Folklore*. Indiana University Press, 1980.

—Work presents a variety of approaches to the interpretation of folklore—structuralist to the psychological.

Eliade, Mircea. *Images and Symbols*. Sheed and Ward, 1952.

—Author explores the symbolic significance of "the Centre," time, knots, shells, baptism, and floods with reference to the myths of many cultures.

Ellis, John M. *One Fairy Story Too Many: The Brothers Grimm and Their Tales*. Uniiversity of Chicago Press, 1983.

—Ellis discusses the fact that the Grimms' fairy tales underwent much alteration and revision and makes the case that these popular tales are by no means "pure" expressions of the folk.

"Fairy Tales: Their Staying Power,"Ed. Christina Moustakis, special section of the *Children's Literature Association Quarterly*, Vol. 7 (Summer 1982).

—Special issue includes essays on the criticism of folk tales, nineteenth-century English fairy tales, discussions of approaches to folk tales, and reviews of scholarship.

Fromm, Erich. *The Forgotten Language: An Introduction to the Understanding of Dreams, Fairy Tales, and Myths*. Holt, Rinehart, and Winston, 1951.

—Fromm argues that dreams, myths, and fairy tales comprise a "symbolic language," which reveals the unconscious emotional lives of human beings; he discusses several myths, fairy tales, and novels from this perspective.

German Literary Fairy Tales. Ed. Frank G. Ryder and Robert M. Browning. Introduction by Gordon Birrell. Crossroads, 1983.

—Presents an excellent introduction and background of German Romantics; anthology includes tales of Goethe, Novalis, Tieck, and Kafka.

Graves, Robert. *The White Goddess: A Historical Grammar of Poetic Myth*. Rev. and enl. ed. Peter Smith, 1983.

—A massive and rich study of the white goddess as she appears in myth and literature — full of information and interpretative insight.

Hartland, E.S. *The Science of Fairy Tales*. 1891; Rpt. Singing Tree Press, 1968.

—An early attempt to classify and describe the function of fairytales; author considers characters, the concept of time in fairy tales, "savage ideas," births in fairyland, and variants of tales; author's style is quaintly old-fashioned but interesting and informative.

Kerenyi, Karl. *Goddesses of Sun and Moon*. Trans. Murray Stein. Spring Publications, 1979.

—One of the world's major scholars in mythology discusses four goddesses — Circe, Aphrodite, Medea, and Niobe.

Kirk, G.S. *Myth: Its Meaning and Functions in Ancient and Other Cultures*.

—Author explains the structuralist approach and surveys other possible approaches to the study of myth; he applies the structuralist method to myths of many cultures.

Leeming, David. *Mythology*. Pictorial narrative by Edwin Bayrd. Newsweek Books, 1976.

—Handsome volume includes chapters on the cultural evolution of myth, the relationship between myth and history, the psychological basis of mythmaking, and the role of the mythic hero; also explores the function of myth in modern society.

Lord, George de Forest. *Trials of the Self: Heroic Ordeals in the Epic Tradition*. Archon Books, 1983.
—Introduction includes interpretative discussion of various Greek heroes; author presents an especially excellent discussion of Homer's *The Odyssey*.

Luthi, Max. *The Fairytale as Art Form and Portrait of Man*. Trans. by Jan Erickson. Indiana Univ. Press, 1984.
—Luthi discusses the literary dimensions of many well-known fairy tales.

Luthi, Max. *Once Upon a Time: On the Nature of Fairy Tales*. Indiana University Press, 1976. Trans. Lee Chadeayne and Paul Gottwald.
—An eminent German scholar discusses structure, meaning and function of popular Grimm's fairy tales; though the author is a structuralist, he also possesses a sure sense of the poetic mysteries of the tales.

McGillis, Roderick. "Criticism in the Woods: Fairy Tales as Poetry," *Festschrift: A Ten-Year Retrospective*, ed. Jill May and Perry Nodelman. ChLA Publications, 1983.
—Author surveys psychological, social, and structural approaches to the criticism of fairy tales but argues finally for the form's integrity as rich and complex literature with the potential for many meanings.

Mallet, Carl-Heinz. *Fairy Tales and Children: The Psychology of Children Revealed through Four Grimm's Fairy Tales*. Schocken, 1984.
—An intensive psychological interpretation of the tales.

Metzger, Michael M, ed. *Fairy Tales as Ways of Knowing*. P. Lang Publishers, 1981.
—Ten essays compiled from papers presented at the 1979 meeting of the Modern Language Association; the essays deal exclusively with German folktales. Metzger argues that the fairy tale provides knowledge about self and the world unavailable any other way.

Propp. V. *Morphology of the Folktale*. Trans. Laurence Scott. Intro. by Svatava Pirkova-Jakobson. 2nd ed. rev. and ed. with preface by Louis A. Wagner. New introd. by Alan Dundes. University of Texas Press, 1977.
—Propp's seminal 1928 study examines the sequential structure of Russian folktales. The study exemplifies Russian formalist strategies for analyzing literary structures; he defines folk motifs in terms of their functions.

Rank, Otto. *Myth of the Birth of the Hero and Other Essays*. Random House, 1959.
—Examines the hero's development in many myths of the world.

Smith, Ron. *Mythologies of the World: A Guide to Sources*. National Council for Teachers of English, 1981.

Thompson, Stith. *The Folktale*. University of California, 1977.
—A definitive discussion of the forms, functions, and types of folktales. This eminent folklorist also includes a valuable chapter on the theories of folktales.

Von Franz, Marie-Louise. *Individuation in Fairy Tales*. Spring Publications, 1977.
—How fairy tales express the human need to integrate the conscious and unconscious forces of the psyche.

Von Franz, Marie-Louise. *An Introduction to the Interpretation of Fairy Tales*. Spring Publications, 1970.
—Author explains Jungian approach to the symbolic interpretation of the fairy tales.

Von Franz, Marie-Louise. *Problems of the Feminine in Fairy Tales*. Spring, 1972.
—Uses a Jungian approach to present an analysis of images of the female in fairy tales.

Waelti-Walters, Jennifer. *Fairy Tales and the Female Imagination*. Eden Press, 1982.
—Author analyzes fairy tales from a feminist perspective, especially concentrating on "Cinderella," "Snow White," "Sleeping Beauty," and "Beauty and the Beast;" author argues that these pervasively popular stories promote passive acceptance of patriarchal power in little girls, not autonomy and initiative.

Wilson, Anne Deirdre. *Traditional Romance and Tale: How Stories Mean*. Brewer, Rowman, and Littlefield, 1976.
—Author discusses traditional fairy tales in terms of dreams and argues for the intense identification between listener or reader and the tale's protagonist. She attempts to analyze this "magical" way of thinking and knowing as the situation appears in many tales.

Zipes, Jack. *Fairy Tales and the Art of Subversion: the Classical Genre for Children and the Process of Civilization*. Wildman Press, 1983.
—Author presents a social history of the fairy tale from the seventeenth century to the present, stressing the unconscious efforts of writers to revise early tales in light of their own social and political purposes and thereby to indoctrinate the young with established cultural bourgeois values. Book includes discussions of the fairy tales of Charles Perrault, the Brothers Grimm, Hans Christian Andersen, George Macdonald, Oscar Wilde, and L. Frank Baum.

Zipes, Jack. *Breaking the Magic Spell: Radical Theories of Folk and Fairy Tales*. University of Texas Press, 1979.
—Author examines socio-historical forces which transformed medieval folk tales into instruments of bourgeois "colonization" of young minds; he argues that these developments eventually corrupted the tales, which have lost their original "liberating potential."

Zipes, Jack. *The Trials and Tribulations of Little Red Riding Hood*. Bergin and Garvey Publishers, 1983.
—Author introduces over thirty of the most well-known versions of "Little Red Riding Hood" and provides detailed discussions of each. He demonstrates that various versions reflect prevailing social values and suggests that the earliest versions of the tale encourage female initiative, while later ones reflected the patriarchal need to keep women in the home under the protection of males.

Criticism: Literary Folktales, Hero Tales, and Myths

Alexander, Lloyd. "High Fantasy and Heroic Romance," in *Cross-currents of Criticism: Horn Book Essays 1968-1977*, ed. Paul Heins. Horn Book, 1977.
—Author of the "Chronicles of Prydain" describes his use of traditional materials.

Burrows, David J.; Lapides, Frederick R. and Shawcross, John T., eds. *Myths and Motifs in Literature*. Free Press, 1973.
—An anthology of archetypal themes and characters as found in traditional and modern adult literature, along with six critical essays.

DeGraff, Amy. *The Tower and the Well: a Psychological Interpretation of the Fairy Tales of Madame d'Aulnoy*. Summer.
—Psychoanalytical discussions of several of the literary fairy tales of the eighteenth-century French author.

Egoff, Sheila A. "Epic and Heroic Fantasy" in *Thursday's Child: Trends and Patterns in Contemporary Children's Literature*. American Library Association, 1981.
—A survey of trends of the past two decades.

Frye, Northrop. "Myth, Fiction, and Displacement" in *Fables of Identity: Studies in Poetic Mythology*. New York, 1963.
—A succinct statement of Frye's theory of how mythological patterns provide the underlying framework of modern literature.

Gould, Eric. *Mythical Intentions in Modern Literature*. Princeton University Press, 1981.
—Surveys definitions of myth and suggests mythic functions in literature. Although children's literature is not discussed the volume provides useful models for mythic approaches.

Hooper, Walter. *Past Watchful Dragons: The Narnian Chronicles of C.S. Lewis*. Collier, 1971.
—A discussion of backgrounds with a guide to interpretation.

LeGuin, Ursula K. *The Language of the Night: Essays on Fantasy and Science Fiction*, ed. by Susan Wood. Putnam's, 1979.
—The creator of the "Earthsea Trilogy" discusses such topics as "Dreams Must Explain Themselves" and "Myth and Archetype in Science Fiction."

Lewis, C.S. "On Three Ways of Writing for Children," in *Children and Their Literature: Views and Reviews*, ed. by Virgina Haviland. Scott, Foresman, 1972.
—The author discusses the nature of fantasy as it is revealed in his "Chronicles of Narnia."

Lochhead, Marion. *The Renaissance of Wonder in Children's Literature*, Canongate, 1977.
—A survey of fantasy since the middle of the nineteenth century, with emphasis on such writers as George Macdonald, C.S. Lewis, and J.R.R. Tolkien.

Moorman, Charles. *Arthurian Triptych: Mythic Materials in Charles Williams, C.S. Lewis, and T.S. Eliot*. University of California Press, 1960.
—Useful to children's literature students because the book provides a model for discussing uses of Arthurian legend in modern works. Many modern children's writers also use these materials in their works.

Noel, Ruth S. *The Mythology of Middle-Earth*. Houghton, Mifflin, 1978.
—Tolkien's fantasies are discussed under such topics as themes, places, beings, and things.

Scholes, Robert and Robert Kellogg. *The Nature of Narrative*. Oxford University Press, 1966.
—Although not about children's literature, the book contains two chapters of interest: "The Oral Heritage of Written Narrative" and "The Classical Heritage of Modern Narrative."

Thalmann, Marianne. *The Romantic Fairy Tale*, tr. by Mary B. Corcoran. University of Michigan Press, 1964.
—Thorough discussion of the background and social conditions which produced the German literary Fairy Tales of Tieck, Hoffman, Brentano, Novalis, and others.

Tolkien, J.R.R. "On Fairy-Stories," in *Tree and Leaf*. George Allen and Unwin, 1964.
—A classic essay explaining the nature of fairy-stories and outlining Tolkien's debt to the "Cauldron of Story."

Vickory, John B. *Myths and Texts: Strategies of Incorporation and Displacement*. Louisiana State University Press, 1983.
—Provides excellent models for discussing the relationship between myth and literature, although the author is not discussing children's literature.

Waggoner, Diana. *The Hills of Faraway: a Guide to Fantasy*. New York, 1978.
—Includes discussions of mythopoeic and heroic fantasy and detailed bibliographies of major and minor authors.

Yolen, Jane. *Touch Magic: Fantasy, Faerie and Folklore in the Literature of Childhood*. Philomel, 1981.
—A major writer of literary folktales discusses the enduring power of traditional motifs.

Criticism: Modern Stories
General Books

Blishen, Edward, ed. *The Thorny Paradise*. Kestrel, 1976.
—A selection of essays by twenty-one children's writers, who describe their creative processes and writing practices.

Broderick, Dorothy M. *Image of the Black in Children's Fiction*. Bowker, 1973.
—A thorough survey of the topic, examining social and cultural implications.

Cech, John, ed. *American Writers for Children, Nineteen Hundred to Nineteen Sixty*. Gale Research Co., 1983

—Essays by specialists on 43 major authors of twentieth-century children's literature. The emphasis is bio-critical.

Cott, Jonathan. *Pipers at the Gates of Dawn: the Wisdom of Children's Literature*. Random House, 1983; McGraw-Hill, 1984 (paper).

—The author discusses the salient features of the works of several important children's writers and illustrators; the method is often appreciative rather than critical.

Egoff, Sheila. *Thursday's Child: Trends and Patterns in Contemporary Children's Literature*. American Library Association, 1981.

—A discussion of the major trends and characteristic features of the children's literature of the past two decades; chapters are arranged chronologically and generically.

Haviland, Virginia, ed. *The Openhearted Audience: Ten Authors Talk About Writing for Children*. Library of Congress, 1980.

—Several children's writers discuss the creation of their major works — their inspirations, writing practices, and frustrations.

Kingman, Lee, ed. *Newbery and Caldecott Medal Books: 1956-1965, with Acceptance Papers, Biographies of the Award Winners, and Evaluating Articles*. Horn Book, 1965.

Kingman, Lee, ed. *Newbery and Caldecott Medal Books: 1966-1975, With Acceptance Papers, Biographies of the Award Winners, and Evaluating Articles*. Horn Book, 1976.

Kirkpatrick, Daniel, ed. *Twentieth Century Children's Writers*. 2nd edition. St. Martin's, 1984.

—Includes over 600 entries on late nineteenth-century and twentieth-century children's writers; includes biographical facts, brief descriptive and critical essays, and bibliographical information.

Novels and Novelists

Ellis, Anne W. *The Family Story in the Nineteen Sixties*. Shoe String, 1970.

—Discusses the prevailing themes, characteristics, and formulae of the contemporary family story.

Hunter, Mollie. *Talent is Not Enough*. Harper and Row, 1976.

—A contemporary Scottish novelist discusses her own writing and her theories of children's fiction.

Miller, Bertha and Elinor Field, eds. *Newbery Medal Books, 1922-1955*. Horn Book, 1955.

—Includes biographies, authors' acceptance speeches, and evaluative essays.

Paterson, Katherine. *Gates of Excellence: on Reading and Writing Books for Children*. Nelson, 1981.

—A highly acclaimed children's novelist discusses her practices as a writer and presents critical reviews of several children's books.

Rees, David. *The Marble in the Water: Essays on Contemporary Writers of Fiction for Children and Young Adults*. Horn Book, 1980.

—Critical essays on the work of several British and North American children's writers.

Rees, David. *Painted Desert, Green Shade*. Horn Book, 1984.

—Evaluative, appreciative essays on the works of twelve major contemporary British and North American children's writers.

Sims, Rudine. *Shadow and Substance: Afro-American Experience in Contemporary Children's Fiction*. National Council of Teachers of English, 1982.

—Evaluates the delineation of Afro-American experience in children's fiction published since 1965. Author discusses the implied audience, the implied interpretation of "Afro-American experience," which appears in these books, using cultural perspectives to evaluate them.

Southall, Ivan. *A Journey of Discovery: on Writing for Children*. Macmillan, 1975.

—Australia's foremost children's novelist discusses his own writings as well as themes and controversial issues in children's literature.

Townsend, John Rowe. *A Sense of Story: Essays on Contemporary Writers for Children*. Horn Book, 1973.

—Essays on selected British and North American authors; volume includes biographical information, bibliographies, and statements by the authors. This book has been revised and new essays included, as *A Sounding of Storytellers* (Lippincott, 1979).

Criticism: Picture Books and Illustration

Bader, Barbara. *American Picturebooks from Noah's Ark to the Beast Within*. Illus. with reproductions. Macmillan, 1976.

—Presents social and historical background for the rise of the modern American picture book and discusses the techniques, themes, media, and art styles of several major illustrators. The author explores different artistic treatments and interpretations of one subject by different illustrators, such as the depiction of the American Indian or the Afro-American.

Barr, Beryl. *Wonders, Warriors, and Beasts Abounding: How the Artist Sees His World*. Foreword by Thomas P.F. Hoving. Director of the Metropolitan Museum of Art. Doubleday, 1967.

—How illustrators and artists view their own creative processes and what vision they try to project through their art.

Bland, David. *A History of Book Illustration: The Illuminated Manuscript and the Printed Book.* World, 1958.
—Includes chapters on significant children's illustrators and places them in the history of illustration.

Cianciolo, Patricia. *Illustrations in Children's Books.* 2nd ed. W.C. Brown, 1976.
—Author discusses artistic techniques, art styles, media, and visual elements in picture books and includes suggestions for classroom use; volume includes annotated bibliographies and discusses standards of evaluation.

Cianciolo, Patricia. *Picture Books for Children.* 2nd ed. American Library Association, 1981.
—Includes a selective, annotated bibliography of significant picture book titles.

Engen, Rodney. *Randolph Caldecott: Lord of the Nursery.* Warne, 1977.
—Volume includes biographical and critical information and reproduces substantial portions of Caldecott's illustrations.

Ernest, Edward, comp. Assisted by Patricia Tracy Lowe. *The Kate Greenaway Treasury: An Anthology of the Illustrations and Writings.* World, 1967.
—Thorough and perceptive examination of the life and work of Kate Greenaway.

Feaver, William. *When We Were Young: Two Centuries of Children's Book Illustration.* Holt, Rinehart, and Winston, 1977.
—Reproduces a significant representative portion of children's book illustration from the last two centuries with critical notes and explanations.

Herdeg, Walter, ed. *An International Survey of Children's Book Illustration.* Publication no. 125. The Graphis Press, 1971.
—Articles in French, English and German on the publishing of contemporary picture books in several countries; volume contains superb reproductions of illustrations.

Hudson, Derek. *Arthur Rackham: His Life and Work.* Scribner's, 1961.
—Critical treatment of Rackham's life and work.

Hurlimann, Bettina, *Picture-Book World.* Trans. and Ed. Brian W. Alderson. World, 1969.
—A study of subjects and types of picture books from many countries.

Jacques, Robin, *Illustrators at Work.* Studio Books, 1963.
—Includes information on history of illustration, processes of reproduction, and guidelines for new illustrators.

James, Philip B. *English Book Illustration: 1800-1900.* Penguin, 1947.
—Reproduces examples of Blake, Cruikshank, Doyle, Tenniel, and many others.

Klemin, Diana. *The Art of Art for Children's Books: A Contemporary Survey.* Clarkson N. Potter, Inc., 1966.
—Includes discussions of characteristic themes, uses of visual elements, and art styles in the illustrated work of more than thirty major illustrators of children's books.

Lane, Margaret. *The Magic Years of Beatrix Potter.* Warne, 1978.
—An intense examination of Potter's most artistically productive period.

Larkin, David, ed. *The Art of Nancy Eckholm Burkert.* Intro. Michael Danoff. Harper, 1977.
—Introductory essay explores development of themes, art style, and technique of a gifted illustrator; many excellent full-color reproductions are included as well.

Lanes, Selma. *The Art of Maurice Sendak.* Abrams, 1980.
—Author discusses biography and the development of Sendak's art. The volume is lavishly illustrated with many full-color reproductions.

MacCann, Donnarae, and Olga Richard. *The Child's First Books: A Critical Study of Pictures and Texts.* Wilson, 1973.
—Discusses the art of picture books, emphasizing relationship between text and illustration.

Neumeyer, Peter and Harold Darling, ed. *Image and Maker.* Green Tiger Press, 1984.
—Contains critical essays assessing major picture books for children.

Pitz, Henry C. *Howard Pyle: Writer, Illustrator, Founder of the Brandywine School.* Potter, 1975.
—Discussion of the life and art of Howard Pyle, including excellent reproductions.

Pitz, Henry C. *Illustrating Children's Books: History-Technique-Production.* Watson-Guptill, 1964.
—A survey of the history of children's book illustration from the illustrator's perspective.

Poltarnees, Welleran. *All Mirrors Are Magic Mirrors.* Green Tiger Press, 1972.
—A consideration of the relation between the life and the work of several major illustrators.

Preiss, Byron, ed. *The Art of Leo and Diane Dillon.* Ballantine, 1981.
—An analytical discussion of the chronological development of the Dillons' art with beautifully reproduced plates.

Read, Herbert. *The Meaning of Art.* Penguin, 1949.
—Author introduces the understanding and appreciation of art.

Schwarcz, Joseph H. *Ways of the Illustrator: Visual Communication in Children's Literature.* American Library Association, 1982.
—Author studies children's illustration and book design in relation to visual perception and investigates the relationship between text and illustration.

Ward, Martha E. and Dorothy Marquardt. *Illustrators of*

Books for Young People. 2nd ed. Scarecrow, 1975.
　　—Includes biographical sketches of children's illustrators.

Whalley, Joyce Irene. *Cobwebs to Catch Flies: Illustrated Books for the Nursery and Schoolroom 1700-1900*. University of California Press, 1975.
　　—Volume discusses books published for children in England, the United States, France, and Germany over two centuries. The volume includes many reproduced illustrations, extensive bibliography, and an index of publishers.

White, Gleeson. *Children's Books and their Illustrators*. Gordon Press, 1984.
　　—Succinct descriptions of technique, art styles, and themes of many illustrators.

History of Children's Literature

Andrews, Siri, ed. *The Hewins Lectures, 1947-1962*. Intro. by Frederic O. Melcher. Boston: Horn Book, 1963.
　　—Volume includes fifteen lectures presented at New England Library Association meetings on publishing and writing for children. The series of lectures was named for Caroline M. Hewins, an outstanding librarian at the Public Library, Hartford, Connecticut.

Ashton, John, *Chap-Books of the Eighteenth Century*. London: Chatto and Windus, 1882.
　　—Texts, illustrations, title pages of 103 chapbooks at the British Library are printed in facsimile, along with discussion and descriptions of each.

Avery, Gillian. *Childhood's Pattern: A Study of the Heroes and Heroines of Children's Fiction, 1770-1950*. London: Hodder and Stoughton, 1975.
　　—Examines images of childhood in moral tales, matter-of-fact tales, school stories, etc. from 1770-1950; contains descriptive discussions of many early children's books.

———, with Angela Bull. *Nineenth Century Children: Heroes and Heroines in English Children's Stories 1780-1900*. London: Hodder and Stoughton, 1965.
　　—Analyzes social and cultural values implicit in children's fiction in nineteenth-century England; Angela Bull includes an excellent account of the development of Victorian literary fairy tales and fantasy.

Bingham, Jane, and Grayce Scholt. *Fifteen Centuries of Children's Literature: An Annotated Chronology of British and American Works in Historical Context*. Greenwood: 1980.
　　—Authors' present a chronological list of significant titles and provide historical and bibliographical information.

Blanck, Jacob. *Peter Parley to Penrod: A Bibliographical Description of the Best-Loved American Juvenile Books*. New York: Bowker, 1956.
　　—A list of outstanding children's books which have weathered changes in social values and literary taste.

Carpenter, Humphrey. *Secret Gardens: The Golden Ages of Children's Literature from Alice in Wonderland to Winnie the Pooh*. Houghton Mifflin, 1985.
　　—descriptive and critical essays on major authors.

Coveney, Peter. *Image of Childhood: The Individual and Society*. Sante Fe: William Gannon, 1957.
　　—Traces the changing image of childhood from the poetry of Wordsworth and Blake to the regressive and escapist presentation of the child in James Barrie's *Peter Pan*.

Darling, Richard L. *The Rise of Children's Book Reviewing in America*, 1865-1881. New York: Bowker, 1968.
　　—A meticulous study of the development of reviewing and criticism of American children's books; the author shows that this kind of publishing had reached a high level of sophistication by 1881.

Darton, Frederick Joseph Harvey. *Children's Books in England: Five Centuries of Social Life*. Rev. Brian Alderson. 3rd ed. Cambridge: University Press, 1982.
　　—A thorough social history of children's literature in England from the Middle Ages through the early twentieth century. The author examines social, religious, and political theories which influenced children's literature and discusses hundreds of children's books. The revised edition corrects errors, expands the bibliographies, and generally strengthens this important history of British children's books.

Egoff, Sheila. *Notable Canadian Children's Books: Un choix de livres canadiens pour la jeunesse*. Prepared by Sheila Egoff and Alvine Belisle, rev. Irene E. Aubrey. National Library of Canada, 1976.
　　—Arranged chronologically from the eighteenth century to the present, this catalogue presents historical and bibliographical information on French and English books for children in Canada.

Field, Mrs. E.M. *The Child and His Book*, 2nd ed. London: Darton, 1895.
　　—An early history of children's literature in England.

Ford, Paul Leicester, ed. *The New England Primer: A History of the Origin and Development*. Dodd, Mcad, 1897.
　　—Discusses background of this famous educational tool and a reprint of the earliest known copy of the work.

Gottlieb, Robin. *Publishing Children's Books in America, 1919-1976: An Annotated Bibliography*. Children's Book Council, 1978.
　　—The bibliography includes seven hundred and nine entries; includes an account of Macmillan's forming a specialized children's book department.

Goldstone, Bette P. *Lessons to be Learned: A Study of Late Eighteenth Century English Didactic Children's Literature*. American University Studies XIV. P. Lang Publishers, 1984.
　　—An intensive study of a specific period in children's literature with emphasis upon the implied func-

tion of children's books, images of the child, and social values.

Green, Roger Lancelyn. *Tellers of Tales*. Rev. ed. F. Watts, 1965.
—Author surveys British authors from 1839 to the twentieth century, arranging chapters chronologically and generically.

Halsey, R.V. *Forgotten Books of the American Nursery*. Goodspeed, 1911.
—Discusses the early development of American children's books from 1641-1840.

Haviland, Virginia. *Children's Literature: A Guide to Reference Sources*. Library of Congress, 1966. First Supplement, 1972; second supplement, 1977.
—Lists and annotates books, articles, and pamphlets useful to students and teachers of children's literature.

Hazard, Paul. *Books, Children and Men*. Trans. Marguerite Mitchell; intro. Sheila Egoff. 5th ed. Horn Book, 1983.
—A succinct and lively history of children's literature with emphasis upon developments in France and England.

Hoyle, Karen Nelson. *Danish Children's Literature in English: A Bibliography*, excluding H.C. Andersen. University of Minnesota Center for Northwest European Language and Area Studies, 1982.
—Lists Danish works which have been translated into English.

Hurlimann, Bettina. *Three Centuries of Children's Books in Europe*. Trans. and ed. Brian W. Alderson. World, 1968.
—A comprehensive reference source for European children's literature.

Jordan, Alice. *From Rollo to Tom Sawyer and Other Papers*. Decorations, Nora S. Unwin. Horn Book. 1948.
—Contains historical and critical discussions of the development of children's literature in America through the nineteenth century.

Kiefer, Monica. *American Children through Their Books, 1700-1835*. University of Pennsylvania, 1948.
—Assesses American children's books of the period from a socio-historical perspective.

Lystad, Mary H. *From Dr. Mather to Dr. Seuss: Two Hundred Years of American Books for Children*. Hall/Schenkman, 1980.
—A content analysis of a random sample of one thousand American children's books from the Rare Books Division of the Library of Congress; examines social values.

MacDonald, Ruth K. *Literature for Children in England and America from 1646 to 1774*. Whitson, 1982.
—Examines the social, historical, and religious forces surrounding the development of eighteenth-century children's literature.

MacLeod, Anne Scott. *A Moral Tale: Children's Fiction and American Culture*. Archon, 1975
—Discusses the rapidly changing values of developing American culture as reflected in children's books.

Meigs, Cornelia et al. *A Critical History of Children's Literature: A Survey of Children's Books in English*. Decorations, Vera Bock. Rev. ed. Macmillan, 1969.
—Cornelia Meigs, Anne Thaxter Eaton, Elizabeth Nesbitt, and Ruth Hill Viguers discuss children's literature according to chronology and genre.

Muir, Percival H. *English Children's Books, 1600-1900*. 2nd ed. Batsford, 1979.
—Surveys three centuries of children's books and includes reproductions of many illustrations.

Opie, Iona and Peter Opie. *The Oxford Dictionary of Nursery Rhymes*. Walck, 1955.
—Includes illustrations from old chapbooks and excellent background information.

Pellowski, Anne. *The World of Children's Literature*. Bowker, 1968.
—Surveys developments in children's literature in 106 countries and six continents.

Pickering, Samuel F. *John Locke and Children's Books in Eighteenth Century England*. University of Tennessee Press, 1981.
—Analyzes eighteenth-century British children's books and demonstrates John Locke's pervasive influence upon them.

Pierpont Morgan Library. *Early Children's Books and Their Illustration*. Godine, 1975.
—Using the large collection of early children's books at the Morgan Library, the authors have discussed the history of children's literature over several centuries.

Quayle, Eric. *Early Children's Books: A Collector's Guide*. David and Charles/Barnes and Noble Imports, 1983.
—Using his own collection as a resource, the author provides an historical overview of children's books from the sixteenth to mid-eighteenth centuries.

Richardson, Selma K., ed. *Research about Nineteenth-Century Children and Books*: University of Illinois, Library Information Science, 1980.
—The publication presents proceedings on a symposium on the topic and includes papers on various major genres of nineteenth-century English and American children's literature, studies of children's magazines, etc.

Rosenbach, Abraham. *Early Children's Books with Bibliographical Descriptions of the Books in His Private Collection*. Foreword, A. Edward Newton. Southworth Press, 1953.
—Arranged chronologically from 1682-1836, this collection contains 816 items with bibliographical data; the volume also contains facsimiles of title pages, frontispieces, and other pages from these early items.

Salway, Lance, ed. *A Peculiar Gift: Nineteenth Century Writings on Books for Children*. Kestrel, 1976.
—Author has collected critical essays on books for children and arranged them thematically and generically.

Sloane, William. *Children's Books in England and America in the Seventeenth Century: A History and Checklist*. Columbia University Press, 1955.

—Provides historical background and critical perspectives for the books listed in the bibliography.

Smith, Dora V. *Fifty Years of Children's Books*. Intro. Muriel Crosby. National Council of Teachers of English, 1963.

—A pioneering university teacher of literature for children and young adults discusses a personal selection of books bought between 1910 and 1959.

Smith, Elva S. *The History of Children's Literature: A Syllabus with Selected Bibliographies*. Rev. Margaret Hodges and Susan Steinfirst. American Library Association, 1980.

—Contains outlines of major works and trends in children's literature with bibliographies of major figures in children's literature.

Townsend, John Rowe. *Written for Children: An Outline of English-Language Children's Literature*, 2nd rev. ed. Harper, 1983.

—Author presents a succinct and concise history of English children's fiction from its beginnings to contemporary children's books; revised edition also includes discussion of poetry and picture books.

Anthologies and Reprints of Early Children's Literature

Cott, Jonathan, General Editor, *Masterworks of Children's Literature*: Vols. 1,2, *The Early Years 1550-1739*, ed. Francelia Butler; Vols. 3 and 4, *The Middle Period* 1740-1836, ed. Robert Bator; Vol. 7. *Victorian Color Picture Books*, commentary by Maurice Sendak, and Vols. 5 and 6 forthcoming. The Stonehill Publishing Company, 1983.

—The impressive and ambitious series presents complete texts with many reproductions of pages and illustrations of early children's literature. Editors provide thorough introductions and notes.

Demers, Patricia, and Gordon Moyles. *From Instruction to Delight: An Anthology of Children's Literature to 1850*. Oxford University Press, 1982.

—An anthology of primary sources of early children's literature. Editors have arranged the selections chronologically and generically; volume contains useful introductions, notes, and bibliographies.

Demers, Patricia, ed. *A Garland from the Golden Age: An Anthology of Children's Literature from 1850 to 1900*. Toronto: Oxford University Press, 1983.

—This useful anthology contains examples of literary fairy tales, allegorical fantasies, moral tales, domestic fiction, school stories, animal stories, and other types of children's literature, along with introduction, notes, and bibliographies.

De Vries, Leonard. *Little Wide-Awake: An Anthology of Children's Books and Periodicals*. World, 1967.

—Contains representative examples of nineteenth-century poems, stories, and many black-and-white pictures.

Facsimile Editions from the Osborne Collection of Early Children's Books. Bodley Head, 1982.

—Thirty-five titles from the Osborne Collection represent different stages in the history of children's literature.

Haviland, Virginia, and Margaret Coughlin, comp. *Yankee Doodle's Literary Sampler of Prose, Poetry, and Pictures*. Cromwell, 1974.

—An anthology with selections from the colonial period to the present in American children's literature from the collection of early children's books, Library of Congress, reproduced in facsimile.

Lurie, Alison, and Justin G. Schiller, eds. *Classics of Children's Literature 1621-1932*. Garland, 1976-79.

—Series includes 117 titles in 73 volumes. Each selection contains a preface written by a scholar in children's literature and bibliographies.

A St. Nicholas Anthology: The Early Years, ed. Burton C. Frye; foreword by Richard L. Darling, Meredith, 1969.

—A representative selection of stories, poems, and articles which appeared in one of America's most famous and popular children's magazines from 1870 to 1905.

Books on Teaching

Applebee, Arthur N. *The Child's Concept of Story Ages Two to Seventeen*. University of Chicago Press, 1978.

—Examines the potent relationship between stories and the language development of children; uses James Britton's description of the "spectator" role to discuss the child's relationship to story at certain ages.

Arbuthnot, May Hill. *Children's Reading in the Home*. Scott, Foresman, 1969.

—Suggestions for parents and teachers to help encourage the child's interest in reading and ideas to help adults guide the literary tastes of children.

Arnstein, Flora I. *Poetry and the Child*. Dover Publications, 1970.

—Practical advice on introducing poetry as an integral part of the classroom experience.

Briggs, Nancy E. and Joseph A. Wagner. *Children's Literature Through Story Telling and Drama*. 2nd ed. William C. Brown.

—Provides practical ideas for presenting children's literature and recommends specific children's books easily adapted to these activities.

Butler, Dorothy. *Babies Need Books*. Atheneum, 1980.

—Author presents a guide for parents in selecting books for children from the earliest months; she stresses the emotional and cognitive significance of the interaction involving parents, children, and books.

Butler, Dorothy. *Cushla and Her Books*. Horn Book, 1980.

—A parent's account of a severely handicapped

child's intense response to literature from the earliest months of life; Cushla's engagement with books, her parents believe, has helped her to achieve a more nearly normal life.

Chambers, Aidan. *Introducing Books to Children*. 2nd ed. Horn Book, 1983.
—Volume includes excellent approaches and ideas for parents and teachers in presenting literature to children; author includes information on the criticism of children's literature and children's responses.

Chambers, Dewey. *Children's Literature in the Curriculum*. Rand McNally, 1971.
—Author suggests possible uses of children's literature in teaching reading, social studies, science, and art.

Chukovsky, Kornei. *From Two to Five*. Trans and ed. Miriam Morton; foreword Frances Clark Sayers. University of California Press, 1968.
—A Soviet poet discusses the importance of imaginative literature in the emotional lives of young children.

Coody, Betty. *Using Literature with Young Children*. William C. Brown, 1983.
—Book includes many practical suggestions for using literature in elementary classes: reading aloud, book discussions, questioning and group work strategies, and other useful techniques.

Crago, Hugh and Maureen Crago. *Prelude to Literacy: A Preschool Child's Encounter with Picture and Story*. Southern Illinois University Press, 1983.
—An in-depth study of the authors' daughter's responses to literature from the earliest months; the researchers demonstrate that their child's early experience with literature has shaped her cognitive perceptions of heroes and villains, her tastes in color, art, and story.

Cullinan, Bernice E. *Literature and the Child*. Harcourt Brace, 1981.
—Author relates children's literature to child development and to the development of language arts skills.

Dunning, Stephen and Alan B. Howes. *Literature for Adolescents: Teaching Poems, Stories, Novels, and Plays*. Scott Foresman, 1975.
—Authors discuss types of young adult literature and present suggestions for classroom presentation and design of a literature curriculum. They also discuss useful critical approaches, levels of reading appreciation, and provide extensive bibliographies.

Frye, Northrop. *The Educated Imagination*. Indiana University Press, 1964.
—In a series of radio broadcasts for the Canadian Broadcasting Corporation, Frye presents a rationale for teaching literary criticism, beginning in the early grades, to develop an "educated imagination."

Glazer, Joan. *Literature for Young Children*. Charles E. Merrill, 1981.
—Volume includes chapters on selecting literature for children, presenting it through reading aloud, story-telling, and audio-visuals; author also discusses ways to integrate children's literature and the teaching of language-arts skills.

Glazer, Joan and Gurney Williams. *Introduction to Children's Literature*. McGraw-Hill, 1979.
—Authors discuss the major types of children's literature and suggest classroom uses.

Huck, Charlotte. S. *Children's Literature in the Elementary School*. 4th rev. ed. Holt, Rinehart, and Winston, 1985.
—A discussion of major types of children's literature. Volume emphasizes methods of children's literature and includes extensive bibliographies.

Jacobs, Leland B. ed. *Using Literature with Young Children*. Teachers College Press, 1965.
—Contains articles by different authors on selecting literature for children, reading aloud programs, story-telling, creative dramatics, choral speaking, and other strategies for classroom presentation of literature.

Kimmel, Margaret M. and Elizabeth Segal. *A Guide to Sharing Books with Children*. Dell, n.d. (paper) Delacorte, 1983.
—Authors stress the importance of reading aloud to elementary children and children in the middle grades as well. They recommend over 140 titles.

Larrick, Nancy. *A Parents' Guide to Children's Reading*. 5th ed. Westminster, 1983.
—Discusses ways of introducing books to infants and toddlers and includes annotated bibliographies.

Meek, Margaret. *Learning to Read*. Bodley Head, 1982.
—Author discusses the stages of development in the child's reading.

Paulin, Mary Ann. *Uses of Children's Literature*. Shoe String, 1982.
—Contains ideas for introducing children's books into every phase of the child's life — classroom, playground, and home; author includes chapters on using specific types of literature with children. The impressive bibliography includes 5,045 items.

Purves, Alan C. and Dianne L. Monson. *Experiencing Children's Literature*. Scott Foresman, 1984.
—Based upon Louise Rosenblatt's theory that literary experience is comprised of a transaction between reader and text, the book discusses children's responses to various types of children's literature.

Probst, Robert E. *Adolescent Literature: Response and Analysis*. Charles E. Merrill, 1984.
—Includes an explanation of the transactional theory of reading based upon the theoretical work of Louise Rosenblatt and suggests ways to implement it in the classroom. The author also considers literary genres and issues in young adult literature, and offers ways to design literature curricula.

Sloan, Glenna Davis. *The Child as Critic: Teaching Literature in the Elementary School*. Teachers College Press, 1975.

—The author summarizes the literary theories of Northrop Frye concerning the structural principles of literature and shows how teachers may implement these theories in teaching literature in elementary classes.

Stewig, John W. *Read to Write: Using Children's Literature as a Springboard for Teaching Writing*. Holt, Rinehart and Winston, 1980.

—Author demonstrates that children's literature can inspire good writing; offers practical suggestions for using children's literature as an important dimension of the writing class.

Tiedt, Iris M. *Exploring Books with Children*. Houghton Mifflin, 1979.

—Discusses methods of presenting literature in elementary classes.

Tucker, Nicholas. *The Child and the Book: A Psychological and Literary Exploration*. Cambridge University Press, 1981.

—Author discusses how the genres of children's literature meet the emotional and cognitive needs of children at various stages of development.

Vandergrift, Kay E. *Child and Story: The Literary Connection*. Neal-Schuman Publishers, 1981.

—Author summarizes critical theory, reading theory, and cognitive skills of children to discuss how to design and to present a literature curriculum.

White, Dorothy Neal. *Books before Five*. Oxford University Press, 1974.

—A mother keeps a daily record of her daughter's responses to books and draws some conclusions about the literary experience of young children.

Journals and Periodicals

The Advocate, ed. Joel Taxel, Center for the Study of Literature for young People, 125 Aderhold Hall, Education Department, University of Georgia, Athens, Georgia 30602.

—Established in 1982, published three times a year by the Southeastern Advocates for Literature for Young People, the journal includes articles by critics and children's authors, as well as practicing teachers, on a wide variety of topics; also reviews children's books and contains news about the activities of the sponsoring organization.

The ALAN Review, ed. W. Geiger Ellis, 125 Aderhold Hall, College of Education, University of Georgia, Athens, Georgia 30602.

—Sponsored by the Assembly on Literature for Adolescents of NCTE, this journal, published three times a year, features articles by and about young-adult writers, interviews with authors, ideas on teaching YA literature, and handy "clip and file" reviews.

The Baum Bugle: A Journal of Oz. The International Wizard of Oz Club, Inc., P.O. Box 95, Kinderhook, IL 62345.

—Established in 1957 as a "fanzine," the journal now carries articles about the OZ books, reviews of books on Baum, news of the organization's activities; in sum, the periodical has become increasingly scholarly.

Bookbird. International Board on Books for Young People and the International Institute for Children's Literature and Reading Research. Fuhrannsgasse 18a, Vienna.

—Published since 1963 quarterly, the publication contains publishing news on children's books from many different countries, articles featuring generic and historical approaches, news about IBBY, and information on librarianship.

Bulletin of the Center for Children's Books. Ed. Zena Sutherland, University of Chicago Press, Journals Division, P.O. Box 37005, Chicago, Illinois 60637.

—Presents succinct reviews of recently published children's books; an indispensable aid to book selection for librarians and teachers.

The Bulletin. Ed., Susan Hepler, 234 High Path Road, Windsor, CT 06095.

—Established by the Children's Literature Assembly of NCTE, this journal features short articles, reviews of children's books, review essays, and news of activities of sponsoring organizations.

Canadian Children's Literature: A Journal of Criticism and Review. Canadian Children's Press in cooperation with the Canadian Children's Literature Association, Box 335, Guelph, Ontario, Canada N1H 6K5.

—Focuses upon the critical assessment of Canadian literature for children and Young Adults; also features articles examining history of Canadian children's literature, reviews of recently published works, interviews with Canadian authors, and provides useful bibliographies.

Children's Literature. Eds., Francelia Butler and Ann Higanet. Annual of the The Modern Language Association Group on Children's Literature and The Children's Literature Association. (Previously titled *Children's Literature: the Great Excluded*.) Yale University Press, New Haven, CT.

—Since 1972, this annual has published scholarly and critical articles of high quality which exhibit a wide variety of approaches to children's literature. Review essays of scholarly and critical works on children's literature are included, as well as lists of notable dissertations in the field.

Children's Literature Association Quarterly. Ed, Perry Nodelman; Assoc. Ed., Jill May, Education Department, Purdue University, West Lafayette, Indiana 47907.

—Published quarterly since 1976, this journal includes critical articles, research information, reviews of critical, scholarly, and bibliographical works, and discussions of issues in children's literature. Regular columns on Young Adult literature, censorship, poetry, and Canadian children's literature are included.

Children's Literature in Education, 49 Sheridan Avenue, Albany, New York 12210. North American Ed., Anita Moss, University of North Carolina at Charlotte; Secretary of United Kingdom Editorial Committee, Geoff Fox, Exeter University.

—Founded in 1969 by the late Sidney Robbins of St. Luke's College, Exeter, *Children's Literature in Education* publishes articles on children's literature from North America and the United Kingdom. Critical approaches to children's literature, as well as ideas on teaching and presenting literature to children, are included.

The Horn Book Magazine. The Horn Book, Inc., Park Square Building, 31 St. James Avenue, Boston MA 02116.

—Founded in 1924, *The Horn Book* includes detailed essays by writers and critics, discussions of trends and issues, and succinct reviews of recently published children's books; journal is published monthly except for July and August.

Jabberwocky. The Lewis Carroll Society. 36 Bradgers Hill Road, Luton, Bedfordshire, England.

—Published quarterly since 1969, this publication includes news of its sponsoring organization and critical essays on the life and works of Lewis Carroll.

Language Arts. National Council of Teachers of English. Ed., David Dillon, Education Department, University of Alberta, Edmonton, Canada.

—Appears monthly and features ''Profiles'' on children's writers and reviews of children's books; the April issue is devoted to in-depth articles on aspects of children's literature and its relationship to the teaching of language arts.

The Lion and the Unicorn: A Critical Journal of Children's Literature. Eds., Roni Natov and Geraldine De Luca, Department of English, Brooklyn College, Brooklyn, New York 11210.

—Established in 1977, the journal began as a quarterly but now appears annually. Each issue is devoted to a topic or theme. Previous issues have dealt with fantasy, poetry, creativity, humor, social issues in children's literature, young adult literature, and adult writers who have also written for children; the editors tend to stress books still read by modern children.

Multi-Cultural Children's Literature. Ed., K.K. Roy, 55 Gariahat Road, P.O. Box 10210, Calcutta, India 700019.

—This journal publishes articles and reports designed to promote international understanding of children and their literature.

Mythlore: A Journal of J.R.R. Tolkien, C.S. Lewis, Charles Williams, General Fantasy, and Mythic Studies. Ed., Glen Goodknight.

—Although this periodical began as a ''fanzine'' of The Mythopoeic Society, it has become increasingly scholarly and includes scholarly and critical articles on children's fantasy and book reviews of recently published books on fantasy.

Phaedrus: An International Annual of Children's Litera-ture Research. Ed., James Fraser. Columbia University School of Library Service, Columbia University, 516 Butler Library, New York, New York 10027.

—Published annually since 1973, this publication features articles on children's literature from various countries, descriptive articles on special collections and on booksellers of children's books, annotated lists of dissertations, and reviews of recently published scholarship in the field.

The Quarterly Journal of the Library of Congress. Ed., Sarah L. Wallace. Vol. 30. April 1973.

—Features articles on books in the Library of Congress.

Signal: Approaches to Children's Books. Ed., Nancy Chambers. The Thimble Press, Lockwood, Station Road, South Woodchester, Stroud, Glos., England, GL5 5EQ.

—Published three times a year since 1970, this British periodical includes critical essays on a wide variety of topics relating to children's literature, interviews with authors, reprints of excellent articles on children's literature from the past, and reviews of children's books and studies of children's literature.

The Top of the News. Ed., Marilyn Kaye. Association for Library Services to Children and Young Adults Division of American Library Association.

—This timely journal publishes articles by critics, children's authors, issues and problems in the field of children's literature, library programs for children, as well as announcements and reviews.

Wilson Library Bulletin. Ed., Milo Nelson. H.W. Wilson Company, 950 University Avenue, Bronx, New York 10452.

—Published monthly except for July and August, this periodical contains general articles on library issues but also features regularly articles and reviews of children's literature.

Index

The page numbers that appear in *italics* in this index refer to selections contained in this anthology.

Illustration Credits

Acknowledgements

Atheneum Publishers, Inc.: "The Night of the Leonids," by E.L. Konigsburg, from *Altogether, One at a Time*, Copyright © 1971 E.L. Konigsburg. Reprinted by permission of Atheneum Publishers, Inc.

Richard W. Baron Publishing Co. Inc.: "People Who Could Fly," by Julius Lester, from *Black Folk Tales*, reprinted by permission of Richard W. Baron Publishing Co., Inc.

Beacon Press: "Demeter and Persephone" from *The Lost Goddesses of Early Greece* by Charlene Spretnak, Copyright ©1978, reprinted by permission of Beacon Press.

Behrman House Inc.: "Mayor Gimpel's Golden Shoes" from *More Wise Men of Helm and Their Merry Tales*, ed. by Hannah Goodman. Reprinted by permission of Behrman House Inc.

The Bodley Head Ltd.: "The Shrove Tuesday Visitor" from *Canadian Wonder Tales* by Cyrus Macmillan. Reprinted by permission of The Bodley Head Ltd; "The Death of Beowulf" from *Beowulf*, by Rosemary Sutcliff, reprinted by permission; Extract from *The Last Bottle* by C.S. Lewis, reprinted by permission of The Bodley Head, Ltd.

Curtis Brown Ltd.: "Tricksy Rabbit" from *Tales from the Story Hat*, by Verna Aardema. Copyright © 1980 by Coward-McCann, Inc. Reprinted by permission of Curtis Brown Ltd.

Caxton Printers Ltd.: "The Last Camp of Paul Bunyan" from *Paul Bunyan Swings His Axe*, by Dell McCormick. Reprinted by permission of The Caxton Printers, Ltd.

University of Chicago Press: "The Poor Woodcutter" and "The Little Guava" from *Folktales of Mexico*, trans. by Americo Paredes, Copyright © 1970, The University of Chicago Press.

Coward-McCann: "Hansel and Gretel" from *Tales From Grimm*, trans. by Wanda Gag, Copyright 1936 by Wanda Gag, renewed © 1964 by Robert Janssen.

Crown Publishing Group: excerpt from *The Annotated Casey at the Bat* by Martin Gardner, Copyright © 1967 by Martin Gardner, reprinted by permission of Clarkson N. Potter Inc.

E.P. Dutton: Excerpt from *Granny's Wonderful Chair* by Frances Brown, published by E.P. Dutton.

Doubleday and Co., Inc.: "The Fortune Hunt" by Uche Okeke, Copyright © 1971 by Uche Okeke; "The Emperor's New Clothes," "The Little Match Girl," and "The Ugly Duckling," from *Hans Christian Andersen: The Complete Fairy Tales and Stories*, by Erik Hauguard, Copyright © 1974 by Erik C. Hauguard. All reprinted by permission of Doubleday and Co., Inc.

Dover Publications, Inc.: "The Three Billy Goats Gruff," and "East o' the Sun and West o' the Moon" by George Webbe Dasent, Copyright © 1888 David Douglas; reprinted by permission of Dover Publications, Inc.

William B. Eerdmans Co.: "Little Daylight" from *The Gifts of the Child Christ*, ed. by George MacDonald. Used by permission of William B. Eerdmans Co.

Farrar, Straus & Giroux, Inc.: "Snow White and the Seven Dwarfs," from *The Juniper Tree and Other Tales From Grimm*, by Randall Jarrell, Copyright © 1973 by Lore Segal. Reprinted by permission of Farrar, Straus & Giroux, Inc., Excerpt from *The Search for Delicious*, By Natalie Babbitt, Copyright © 1969 by author. Reprinted by permission.

Victor Gallancz Ltd.: "Little Red Riding Hood" from *The Fairy Tales of Charles Perrault*, trans. by Angela Carter, Copyright © 1977 by Angela Carter. Reprinted by permission of Victor Gallancz, Ltd.

Harper and Row Publishers, Inc.: "The Dawn of the World," from *ANPAO* by Jamake Highwater, Copyright © 1977 by Jamake Highwater; "The Moon Ribbon" from *The Moon Ribbon and Other Tales*, by Jan Yolen, Copyright © 1976 by Jane Yolen; "From Tiger to Anansi" from *Anansi* by Philip M. Sherlock, Copyright © 1954 by Philip M. Sherlock; "Kate Crackernuts" from *Clever Gretchen*, by Alison Lurie, Copyright © 1980 by Alison Lurie; "The Ghost Owl" from *Plains Mythology* by Alice Marriot and Carol K. Rachlin, Copyright © 1975 by Alice Marriot and Carol K. Rachlin; "The Wolf Pack" from *Little House on the Prairie* by Laura Ingalls Wilder, Copyright © 1935 by Laura Ingalls Wilder, renewed 1963 by Roger L. McBride. From "The Great Above to the Great Below" from *Inanna* by Diane Wolkstein and Samuel Noah Kramer, Copyright © 1983 by Diane Walkstein and Samuel Noah; All reprinted with permission by Harper and Row, Publishers, Inc.

David Higham Associates Ltd.: excerpt from the *Sword and the Stone*, by T.H. White. Reprinted by permission.

Holt, Rinehart and Winston, Inc.: "Coyote Loses His Dinner", from *Coyote Tales*, Dorothy Hosford; "Stopping by Woods on a Snowy Evening," from *The Poetry of Robert Frost*, Copyright 1923, © 1969 by Holt, Rinehart and Winston, Copyright 1951 by Robert Frost. Reprinted by permission of Holt, Rinehart and Winston, Publishers.

Hurtig Publishers, Ltd.: "The Blind Boy and the Loon," from *Tales From the Igloo*, trans. by Maurice Metayer. Reprinted by permission of Hurtig Publishers Ltd.

JCA Literary Agency, Inc.: "A Legend of Knockmany" from *Celtic and Fairy Tales* by Nancy and Eric Potter, Copyright © 1966, reprinted by permission of JCA Literary Agency, Inc.

Little, Brown and Co.: "Cupid and Psyche," from *Mythology* by Dorian Fielding Reid and Doris Fielding Reid; "The Adventures of Isabel" from *Custard and Company* by Ogden Nash, Copyright © 1936 by Ogden Nash. Both are reprinted by permission of Little, Brown and Co., Inc.

Liveright Publishing Co. Inc.: "The Boy Who Drew Cats," from *Japanese Fairy Tales* by Lafcadio Hearn and others. Copyright © 1953 by Liveright Publishing Corporation, reprinted by their permission.

MacDonald and Company, Ltd.: *The Last of The Dragons* by E. Nesbit, reprinted by permission of MacDonald and Co. Ltd.

Macmillan of Canada, Ltd.: "Nicholas Knock", from *Nicholas Knock and Other People*, by Dennis Lee. Reprinted by permission of Macmillan of Canada Ltd., A division of Canada Publishing Corporation.

Macmillan Publishing Co.: "The Death of Baldur," by A. and G. Kedry; "Tattercoats," and "The Story of the Three Bears," from *English Fairy Tales*, by Flora Annie Steel, Copyright © 1918 by Macmillan Publishing, renewed © 1946 by Mabel H. Webster; "Odin Goes to Mimir's Well", from *The Children of Odin*, by Padraic Colum Copyright © 1948 by Padraic Colum; "The Story of the Blessing of El-ahrairah," from *Watership Down*, by Richard Adams, Copyright © 1972 by Richard Adams; "The White Cat" from *The White Cat and Other French Fairy Tales*, by Mme la Contesse d'Aulnoy, ed. by Rachel Field, Copyright © 1928 by Macmillan Publishing Co., Inc. All reprinted by permission of Macmillan Co., Inc.

Houghton Mifflin Company: "Jack in the Giant's Newground," from *The Jack Tales*, by Richard Chase Copyright © 1943 and renewed 1971 by Richard Chase; "Get Up and Bar the Door," "Robin Hood and Little John," and "Sir Patrick Spens," are all from *The English and Scottish Popular Ballads, Student's Cambridge Edition*. All reprinted by permission of Houghton Mifflin Co.

Modern Curriculum Press, Inc.: "The Tar Baby Tricks Brer Rabbit," from *The Days When Animals Talked*, by William J. Faulkner. Reprinted by permission.

William Morrow & Co., Inc.: "Pay Day" from *Ramona and Her Father*, by Beverly Cleary, Copyright © 1975, 1977 by Beverly Cleary, reprinted by permission of William Morrow & Co.

University of Nebraska Press: "Scarface" from *Blackfoot Lodge Tales* by George B. Grinnell, reprinted by permission of University of Nebraska Press, Lincoln, 1962.

University of New Mexico Press: "Guashi and the Bears" from *Hispano Folklife of New Mexico: The Lorin W. Brown Federal Writer's Manuscripts*, by Lorin W. Brown and others, Copyright © The University of New Mexico Press, reprinted by their permission.

Oxford University Press: "Jacques the Woodcutter," from *The Golden Phoenix and other French-Canadian Fairy Tales*, by Maurius Barbeau, by permission of Oxford University Press of Canada; selections from *The Oxford Dictionary of Nursery Rhymes*, ed. by Jona and Peter Opie, Copyright 1951 by Clarendon-Oxford Press. All reprinted by permission of Oxford University Press.

Pagurian Press, Ltd.: Excerpt from *Hockey in My Blood*, by Johnny Bucyk with Russ Conway. Reprinted by permission of and copyright by Pagurian Press.

Penelope Proddow: *Demeter and Persephone, Homeric Hymn Number Two*, trans. and adapted by Penelope Proddow. Reprinted by permission of the author.

Penguin Books Ltd.; "Beauty and the Beast," from the *Blue Fairy Book*, by Andrew Lang, Copyright © 1975 by Penguin Books Ltd; "Tottie Meets the Queen," from *The Dolls' House* by Rumer Godden, Copyright © 1975 by Rumer Godden; "Pippie Goes to the Circus," from *Pippi Longstocking* by Astrid Lindgren, Copyright © 1978 by Astrid Lindgren; "Nothing New Under the Sun (Hardly)," from *Homer Price*, by Robert McCloskey, Copyright © 1971 Robert McCloskey: *The Hundred Penny Box*, by Sharon Bell Mathis, Copyright © 1975 by the author. All selections reprinted by permission of Penguin Books Ltd.

Random House, Inc.: : "The Magic Orange Tree," from *The Magic Orange Tree and Other Haitian Folktales*, by Diane Wolkstein, reprinted by permission of Random House, Inc. "The Death of John Henry," from *John Henry and His Hammer*, by Harold W. Felton; "Cinderella," "Rapunzel," "Little Briar-Rose," "Little Red Cap," and "The Fisherman and His Wife," from *The Complete Grimm's Fairy Tales*, by Jakob Grimm and Wilhelm Grimm, all reprinted by permission of Pantheon Books, a division of Random House, Inc. "Gudgekin and the Thistle Girl," by John Gardner, Copyright © 1976 by Boskydell Artists, Ltd. Reprinted by permission of Alfred A. Knopf, Inc.

Scholastic, Inc.: "The Practical Princess" from *The Practical Princess and other Liberating Fairy Tales* by Jay Williams Copyright © 1978 by Jay Williams, reprinted by permission of Scholastic, Inc.

Scribner Book Co., Inc.: "The River Bank," from *The Wind in the Willows*, by Kenneth Grahame, Copyright © 1954, Charles Scribner's Sons, renewed 1981 Mary Eleanor Jessie Knox, Reprinted by permission of Charles Scribner's Sons, a division of Scribner Book Companies, Inc.

The Society of Authors: "Goliath," and "The Garden of Eden," from *Stories from the Bible*, by Walter de la Mare, reprinted by permission of the Literary Trustees of Walter de la Mare and The Society of Authors.

Jon C. Stott: *Sedna*, adapted from original sources, by John C. Stott. Reprinted by permission.

Tundra Books Ltd.: Excerpt from *A Child in Prison Camp*, by Shizuye Takashima, Copyright © 1971 Shizuye Takashima, reprinted by permission of Tundra Books Inc.

Viking Penguin Inc.: "Fire," and "An Ordinary Woman," from *The God Beneath the Sea*, by L. Garfield and E. Blishen, Copyright © 1970 by the authors; "Meleager and Atlanta," from *Tales of the Greek Heroes*, by Roger L. Green, Copyright © 1958 by the author; "La Belle au Bois Dormant," from *Fairy Tales* by Charles Perrault, trans. by Geoffrey Brereton, Copyright © 1957 by Geoffrey Brereton; all reprinted by permission of Penguin Books, a division of Viking Penguin, Inc.; "Cinderella," from *Tales From Times Past*, ed. by Bryan Holme, Copyright © 1977 by Viking Penguin Inc.

A.P. Watt, Ltd.: "The Elephant Child" from *Just So Stories* by Rudyard Kipling, reprinted by permission of The National Trust for Places of Historic Interest or Natural Beauty, Macmillan Ltd. and A.P. Watt Ltd.